Handbook of Interpersonal Communication

Edited by
Mark L. Knapp
Gerald R. Miller

SAGE PUBLICATIONS
Beverly Hills   London   New Delhi

For information address:

SAGE Publications, Inc.
275 South Beverly Drive
Beverly Hills, California 90212

SAGE Publications India Pvt. Ltd.
M-32 Market
Greater Kailash I
New Delhi 110 048 India

SAGE Publications Ltd
28 Banner Street
London EC1Y 8QE
England

Printed in the United States of America

Library of Congress Cataloging in Publication Data

Main entry under title:

Handbook of interpersonal communication.

 Includes bibliographies and indexes.
 1. Interpersonal communication.   I. Knapp, Mark L.
II. Miller, Gerald R.
BF637.C45H287   1985   153.6   85-1869
ISBN 0-8039-2120-9

FIRST PRINTING

CONTENTS

ACKNOWLEDGMENTS

Several people, who would otherwise go unrecognized, have made special contributions to this volume.

Ann Wooten and Debra Tigner never tired (or at least never complained) of doing detective work in the MSU library, calling contributors for various bits of information, and scanning galleys and pages for minor inconsistencies. Their assistance added appreciably to the quality of this volume.

Despite a more-than-full schedule of graduate student and faculty responsibilities, Carra Sleight labored countless hours over the index for minuscule monetary returns. Only her interest in the project and her intellectual curiosity can explain this kind of apparently masochistic behavior. Editors, contributors, and readers alike owe her a huge debt of gratitude.

The editorial and interpersonal moxie of Lisa Freeman-Miller of Sage Publications remains unrivaled in our publishing experiences.

The first editor recognizes that it is Lillian Davis's unswerving inclination toward, and preference for, sunshine that provides the correct dosage of personal motivation necessary to complete projects of this nature. The second editor thanks Pearl Ann, Patricia Anne, Greg, Caleb, Louie, and Betty for constantly reminding him of his strengths and shortcomings as an interpersonal communicator and dragging him off to the movies or the track at the slightest opportunity, thus spacing out his editorial tasks in a more leisurely pattern.

And finally, we would like to thank the community of scholars whose collective efforts to understand interpersonal transactions have made this volume possible.

INTRODUCTION: BACKGROUND AND
CURRENT TRENDS IN THE STUDY
OF INTERPERSONAL COMMUNICATION

C RAFTING a multiple-authored volume often proves comparatively simple and inordinately rewarding for the editors. They have but to conjure a list of representative topics or problem areas, identify a band of colleagues who can write insightfully, informatively, lucidly, and promptly about the topics, persuade these colleagues to participate, and sit back and enjoy the results. A fellow editor has likened the process to savoring a gourmet meal in a fine restaurant, rather than enduring the drudgery of preparing it in one's own kitchen—and even this analogy rests on the perhaps unwarranted assumption that the gourmand could have prepared a meal of equal sumptuousness if she or he had been willing to suffer the culinary toil of preparing it.

Our experience with this *Handbook* has conformed closely to the pleasant situation described above. As the chapters have reached our desks, we invariably have been pleased with their comprehensiveness, cogency, and clarity. Thus we have been reduced to suggesting the occasional expansion of an idea, polishing an infrequent errant phrase, blue penciling a typographical slip, and striving for consistency of format among the chapters. Indeed, our labors could have been confined to these areas with little or no injury to the volume's quality.

Nevertheless, three considerations have motivated us to prepare a brief introductory chapter for the *Handbook*. In ascending order of importance, they are as follows: First, handbooks and other edited collaborative volumes traditionally contain such a chapter; second, had we shirked this duty, our comparatively simple editorial task might have appeared *too* simple; third and most important, we felt that some readers would benefit from a short historical sketch of the project's background and from identification of some of the key recurring themes in the *Handbook*'s chapters. The historical sketch is just that, a sketch, and the themes discussed are neither exhaustive in scope nor treated comprehensively; to return to the analogy invoked earlier, our introductory comments are at best an appetizer preceding a full-course dinner.

A BIT OF HISTORY

Concerted interest in the study of interpersonal communication processes and outcomes is of relatively recent origin. Twenty years ago this *Handbook*, had it even been deemed worthy of preparation, would have possessed a narrow spine. To be sure, sociologists such as Erving Goffman, social psychologists such as Michael Argyle, and anthropologists such as Gregory Bateson were providing illuminating and provocative insights about interpersonal communication; for that matter, the venerable insights of writers such as Mead and Simmel predate this period. Notwithstanding this fact, few scholars of that era espoused a predominant interest in interpersonal communication. Meanwhile, the fledgling field of speech communication directed its energies primarily at understanding oral symbolizing as a platform activity, while most members of emerging departments of mass communication and communication continued their scholarly love affairs with persuasion as practiced in mass audience settings. Treatments of interpersonal communication usually centered on its role in other contexts, such as the organizational setting.

Thus the study of interpersonal communication did not commence to bloom profusely until the 1960s. As is frequently the case, the blossoms sprang primarily from pragmatic and societal roots, not from any purposeful consensual planting by communication theorists and researchers. The social turmoil accompanying the civil rights movement and our subsequent involvement in Vietnam triggered in many citizens, particularly the young and idealistic, a deep-seated aversion to the manipulative and deceitful aspects of many mass media messages. An emerging concern for self-development and personal awareness gave rise to such face-to-face communicative activities as sensitivity training and consciousness-raising groups. Attacks on the traditional public and mass communication orientations of most communication scholars emphasized the importance of interpersonal communication to personal authentication. The integrity of our personal relationships, proclaimed the critics, rather than the persuasive wiles of media messages crafted by Madison Avenue hucksters and political consultants, shapes the daily quality of our lives. Given the prevailing climate, it is hardly surprising that a book such as *Pragmatics of Human Communication* (Watzlawick, Beavin, & Jackson, 1967), which exerted a profound effect on the subsequent study of interpersonal communication, had nothing to say about the ways communication can be used to extract money or concessions from others but offered considerable advice about the ways people can think about and perform their communicative activities so as to improve their personal relationships with marital partners and close friends. In a similar vein, Barnlund's (1968) anthology of theoretical and empirical papers, which stimulated interest in interpersonal communication among persons in speech communication and communication departments, focused on factors influencing the origination, development, and maintenance of interpersonal relationships.

Other manifestations of this heightened interest in interpersonal communication are readily identifiable. The burgeoning number of college and university courses covering aspects of interpersonal communication and interpersonal relations was accompanied by a spate of textbooks dealing with these topics, for example, Giffin and Patton (1971), Keltner (1970), and McCroskey, Larson, and Knapp (1971). Formal establishment of areas of emphasis in scholarly and professional associations of the communication disciplines, such as the Interpersonal and Small Group Interaction Interest Group of the Speech Communication Association and the Interpersonal Communication Division of the International Communication Association, signalled accelerating interest in the teaching and study of interpersonal communication processes. Convention programs dealing with aspects of interpersonal communication became the rule rather than the exception; and one of these programs, held at the 1976 meeting of the International Communication Association in West Berlin, Germany, spawned two state-of-the art papers later published in the Association's major journal (Bochner, 1978; Miller, 1978). Evidence that interpersonal communication had become an important dimension of graduate education was provided by the convening of two national Doctoral Honors Seminars sponsored by the Speech Communication Association, one at Michigan State University and the other at Northwestern University.

The 1970s also witnessed the stirrings of some original theorizing about interpersonal communication among members of the communication and speech communication disciplines. Researchers in those fields, reluctant to heed the first half of the Bard's injunction, "Neither a borrower nor a lender be," had relied heavily on theories developed by scholars in other disciplines. Berger and Calabrese's (1975) publication of a developmental theory of initial interaction marked a departure from this practice; and a text authored by Miller and Steinberg (1975), though not presenting a full-blown theory, was founded on a developmental conception of interpersonal communication that assumed the degree of "interpersonalness" in a relationship is determined by the kind of information participants use to make predictions about message exchanges. During roughly the same time period, Barnett Pearce and his colleagues were working on a rules-oriented theory grounded in the coordinated management of meaning, with the most complete exposition of their position provided in a volume published at the turn of the decade (Pearce & Cronen, 1980). Though theoretical forays into other disciplines were still frequent occurrences, communication and speech communication researchers interested in interpersonal communication obviously had begun to heed the call to raise their fields above the status of purely derivative disciplines.

Throughout the scholarly sound and fury of the 1960s and 1970s, and for that matter, at the time of this writing, theoretical and empirical work in interpersonal communication has been characterized by several widely different conceptual, epistemological, and metatheoretical assumptions about the nature of the phenomena under investigation (see Chapter 1 for a more comprehensive discussion of some of the issues mentioned below). Much of the groundbreaking research relied heavily on a situational conception of interpersonal communication. Interpersonal communication was defined by the situational context in which it occurred, a setting consisting of a relatively small number of communicators (most frequently, two persons), face-to-face contact, potential availability of a maximum number of sensory channels, and opportunities for immediate feedback (Miller, 1978). As work has progressed, this conceptualization has been buttressed and extended by a greater concern for the qualitative characteristics of the communication relationship. This developmental perspective holds that, in a sense, interpersonal communication *emerges*—or at least, has the *potential to emerge*—as relationships progress through time and changes occur in the ways participants perceive each other and define the rules governing their relationship. In general, the qualitative changes focused upon are taken to signal increasing differentiation and individuation in the relationship, that is, participants begin to see each other as persons rather than as relatively undifferentiated cultural entities or role occupants, and they commence to define and to negotiate their own relational rules instead of being guided entirely by externally imposed societal prescriptions.

Reference to the term "rule" underscores a second major metatheoretical issue that continues to divide interpersonal communication researchers: Should attempts to understand interpersonal communication center on the quest for laws or rules? (See Chapters 1 and 3 for illustrations of how differences of opinion on this issue influence theorizing and research strategies.) Those opting for a more traditional, law-governed perspective emphasize causal environmental forces impinging upon communicators, or actors; advocates of this view argue that the explanatory mechanisms of interpersonal communication are, at a minimum, softly deterministic. By contrast, supporters of the rule-following perspective stress the role of communicators in defining their communicative activities. Proponents of this position hold that our understanding of interpersonal communication can best be enhanced by examining the choices people make about the rules governing their communicative transactions.

This *Handbook* goes to press without resolution of these conceptual, metatheoretical, and epistemological controversies. Furthermore, a case can be made for the scholarly desirability of this lack of closure. As our brief historical sketch suggests, the study of interpersonal communication has thus far progressed from infancy to adolescence. Perhaps a mature science of interpersonal communication will be guided by some reigning paradigm, though even this possibility remains open to question. For the moment, multiple perspectives seem to offer the best insurance of a rich, potentially heuristic scholarly enterprise. Moreover, to grant outstanding differences of opinion does not imply complete lack of agreement on theoretical and investigational priorities. Indeed, common themes emerge in many of the chapters that follow, and we next seek to identify some of the more persistent and important of these themes.

THEME #1: A FOCUS ON BEHAVIOR

A strong and persistent theme throughout this volume concerns the value of describing and analyzing naturally occurring overt verbal and nonverbal behavior. Surprisingly, this widespread concern for studying behavior manifested in interpersonal transactions is of relatively recent origin. It seems to have emerged as we realized the limitations of our earlier approaches for fully explaining interpersonal phenomena. These limitations included the need to supplement self-report data, the need to supplement verbal data, the need to develop a richer foundation for laboratory studies, and the need to focus on message components.

The Need to Supplement Self-Report Data

Probably the first explorations of the nature of interpersonal communication were based on observation of interactants' behavior. Indeed, the slow, painstaking work of systematically observing and recording microscopic and macroscopic patterns of interpersonal behavior has a rich tradition—represented by scholars such as Birdwhistell, Goffman, Scheflen, and Ruesch and Bateson. Until recently, however, this approach has been carried on by a fairly small group. From the mid-1960s to the mid-1970s, the predominant method for gathering data about interpersonal communication was the self-report questionnaire and/or scale. These inventories were easily administered to large numbers of respondents and were intended to provide a foundation for broad-based generalizations about interpersonal communication.

Although some research programs continue to rely heavily on self-report data (see the discussion of compliance-gaining strategies in Chapter 12 as one example), more and more researchers are questioning the adequacy of knowledge about communication behavior based solely on self-report data. Can people accurately recall or predict some aspects of their interpersonal communication behavior, for example, their touching behavior? Have we developed a body of knowledge that is limited to what people *think* they would do? Isn't there a need to supplement or seek validation of self-reports with observations of actual interaction behavior? Is it enough to know the attitudes, opinions, and perceptions of *one* interaction partner—often removed from any interaction context? How will the preferences expressed on the questionnaire manifest themselves in the presence of another person or persons governed by various situational constraints?

In order to address such questions, an expanding cadre of communication scholars has chosen to focus on manifest behavior. Interestingly, these efforts have provided both an important supplement to our understanding of interpersonal communication and have pointed out some inadequacies when we focus *exclusively* on overt behavior. Even though we still have much to learn from the study of overt behavior, it is already clear that, first, what transpires during interpersonal transactions is more than mere responses to manifest signals. Communicator expectations, fantasies, plans, and the like may provide the basis for response; behaviors *not* shown by the interaction partner may provide the basis for response; behaviors shown in previous interactions (with and not with the current partner) may guide and direct subsequent reactions. Ironically, then, our examination of overt behavior has shown us the necessity of obtaining self-report data. Unlike many past efforts, however, these self-descriptions are much more likely to be anchored by a specific context. In like manner, the study of behavior within the confines of a two-person transaction has made it clear that in order to understand dyadic behavior, we need to extend our analyses beyond the dyad. Interpersonal behavior will be more fully understood as we extend the boundaries of analysis to include the social networks impinging on the two communicators, the rules and constraints imposed by social and institutional cultures, interaction history, and so forth. Second, what transpires behaviorally during interpersonal transactions is often extremely subtle and complex—involving behavioral configurations amenable to multiple interpretations, multiple intensities, and multiple degrees of consistency.

The Need to Supplement Verbal Data

Even though interpersonal communication scholars probably recognized the vital contributions of proxemic, kinesic, olfactory, vocal, and verbal signals for understanding interpersonal behavior, the first wave of research focused on reports of verbal behavior almost exclusively. Interest in providing systematic accounts of nonverbal signals in communication research did not gain widespread acceptance until the early 1970s. And because many of these nonverbal signals were thought to be performed with little awareness by the participants, observing overt behavior became the predominant method of data collection (see Chapter 8). In subsequent years, a concern for dissecting interpersonal verbalizations with the same kind of close attention to detail required by nonverbal analyses developed (see Chapter 7).

Presently, the study of nonverbal behavior and verbal behavior often appear to be independent areas of study. Researchers who study facial expressions, eye gaze, or proxemics commonly do not spend much time analyzing co-occurring verbal behavior, and researchers who describe themselves as discourse or conversation analysts commonly do not claim expertise with nonverbal phenomena. We can learn much by tapping the depths of verbal and nonverbal behaviors separately, but we will learn more about interpersonal communication when the interaction of both systems forms the basis for analysis—as is the case with some analyses of turn-taking and lying behavior.

As we learn more about analyzing verbal and nonverbal signals, there will probably be fewer studies that simply sum the frequency of several behaviors and more that address the interdependence and coordination of behavior. When we have reached that point, our current preoccupation with the question of whether verbal or nonverbal behavior is more important should be moot. Studying the interrelationships of verbal and nonverbal behavior in social interaction will also demand more attention to how these signals are perceived. We do not observe all those signals made available to us, nor do we process all that we do perceive in the same way. Some of these questions about the perception of signals require an understanding of the perceiver and the signal interpretation process, but describing the nature of the signals themselves is also an integral part of understanding the process. There is much to learn about the impact of signals and combinations of signals that is related to their intensity, relevance, and location.

The Need to Develop a Richer Foundation
for Laboratory Studies

Once more popular than today, the study of communicative behavior in controlled laboratory settings attempted to discover the bases for predicting interpersonal behavior. Although behavior was the focus in the early experimental studies, the validity of the findings for naturally occurring interactive events was often challenged. For instance, some charged that we did not have enough descriptive information about how normal interaction proceeded to manipulate it realistically. As a result, it was argued, research participants were asked to react to unusual and sometimes extreme stimuli. Further, critics believed that a person's responses to an interaction partner who was unable to respond (presented in slides or on audio tape), unwilling to respond (a "neutral" confederate), or who inflexibly responded (programmed to respond only in certain ways) did not elicit typical interaction behavior from the research participants. Even a fundamental tenet of experimental research requiring some components of the interaction situation to be "kept constant" while others are manipulated seemed to run counter to the prevailing theoretical belief that constancy is not characteristic of ongoing interaction. As a result of these and other challenges, it became increasingly apparent that it was necessary to find out more about the structure and operation of interpersonal behavior in naturally occurring situations in order to construct more realistic laboratory situations.

The observation of behavior outside the laboratory context seems to have underlined the importance of the impact of context on behavior and to have given us a renewed appreciation for the difficulty in predicting behavior across different contexts. We also seem more aware of the need to measure the sequencing and quality of responses as well as the quantity. Some aspects of our research strategies remain the same, however. We still tend to build knowledge based on interaction between two people in nonintimate contexts with both expected to make about the same contribution to an interaction that is cooperative, informal, or social. The environmental, psychological, and behavioral context is a complex and changing perception that we are just now gaining momentum to understand.

The Need to Focus on
Message Components

Many of the early efforts to study interpersonal communication did not deal with the message itself but with more general types of action patterns, reactions, or anticipated reactions. It was not clear what distinguished communication studies from other social science investigations. The attempt to assert a distinguishing identity for communication studies by focusing specifically on the analysis of message components was probably another important force behind the evolved emphasis on studying overt behavior.

THEME #2: A FOCUS ON TIME

Most students of interpersonal communication believe it is most accurately thought of as a process—an ongoing, ever-changing event. Understanding the communication process, then, is largely a matter of understanding what happens over a given period of time. To understand the process of mutual adaptation in interpersonal communication, it is necessary to focus on moment-to-moment changes during interactive events. Of course, some communicative events depend less on their sequential placement for understanding and impact than others, but our knowledge of events in sequence is quite limited at present.

Despite the belief that interpersonal communication is best studied as a process, most of the pre-1980 work could be characterized as interaction snapshots rather than films; as static representations rather than ongoing ones; as observations at a single point in time rather than multiple observations over a given time span. Our measures of interpersonal attraction, conflict styles, persuasive strategies, and so forth were not always examined in the context of interactive events, but when they were, the variables measured were often isolated from the simultaneously and sequentially occurring events surrounding them. Sometimes measures were taken at time one and at time two, but as Duck points out in Chapter 14, we know very little about the pattern of ebb and/or flow taking place between these two points in time. Similarly, Seibold, Cantrill, and Meyers (Chapter 12) point to the importance of studying interpersonal persuasion as a series of events as well as a one-time effort.

As never before, the study of communication as a process is within our grasp. The availability of statistical methods, high-capacity data-processing equipment, and sophisticated measurement devices should increase our focus on time and timing in future studies of interpersonal communication behavior—as some noteworthy scholars have already done. Cappella and Planalp (1981), for example, analyzed a continuous audio record of informal conversation for moment-to-moment changes in vocalizations and pauses produced by both interactants; Kendon (1970), using a filmed record, described moment-to-moment changes in movement, eye gaze, and speech during the flow of interaction; and Gottman (1979) made some important discoveries about marital interaction from analyses of sequential exchanges between happy and unhappy couples (see Chapter 15).

Our studies of time, as Werner and Haggard point out in Chapter 2, will have to account for a variety of temporal characteristics. From both speaker and listener perspectives, it will be important to know how often a behavior occurs during a given period of time, what order or sequence characterizes the behavior under study, how long the behavior lasts when it occurs, and the rhythm, pacing, or "timing" of the behavior relative to co-occurring behaviors. Each of these temporal qualities occurs and can be analyzed at four levels: First, a specific utterance; second, a specific conversation (see Chapter 7); third, during the course of a relationship (see Chapter 14); or fourth, during the course of a lifetime (see Chapter 13). The study of time and timing in interpersonal transactions should also provide us with a much better understanding of how to behaviorally distinguish developmental phases common to many experiences, for example, accomplishing a goal for the first time, reestablishing the goal state, maintaining the goal state in the absence of threat, or maintaining the goal state in the presence of threat.

THEME #3: A FOCUS ON
SOCIAL COGNITION

In one way or another, each chapter in this book addresses the role of human thought processes as they interface with interpersonal transactions. The study of interpersonal communication has, from the beginning, recognized the important reciprocal relationship between thought and overt behavior; but in recent years we have greatly advanced our understanding of this area—largely because some scholars in communication and social psychology have made this their sole focus of investigation. The work in this area can be subdivided into two nonexclusive categories: Understanding the interrelationships of social cognition and social behavior and understanding the formation and organization of social cognition.

Understanding the Interrelationships of Social Cognition and Social Behavior

Virtually any thought about any aspect of our experience has the potential to affect behavior in any given encounter. However, the thoughts that are likely to have the most relevance for communicative events are thoughts about the nature of human interaction itself. Usually the thoughts about self, other, and situation are the designated units for investigation. Information representing thoughts is usually gathered before and/or after encounters, rarely during them. In the past, some researchers ignored perceptual information from actual interactants, relying instead on the reactions of large groups of uninvolved observers as a basis for understanding the overt and covert behavior of interactants.

Thoughts that influence behavior may be relatively abstract ("Friends are people who stick by you when the going gets tough") or concrete ("My friend, Mary, is a person who would probably turn me in at the first sign of trouble"). Similarly, more abstract thoughts of what kind of person we are and more concrete thoughts about what kind of person we are as a communicator or as a communicator with *this* person in *this* situation may influence the manifested behavior. Situations, too, are thought of in general ways and as a specific communication context. Researchers often focus on a single unit of analysis—for example, studies of others include impression formation, attribution theory or perspective-taking; studies of communicator cognition include work on self-consciousness, self-awareness, self-monitoring, and communicative apprehension; situational cognitions are fully reviewed in Chapter 6. We are just beginning to undertake the more complex job of studying the influence of combined self/other/situation thoughts on behavior. If it were merely a matter of determining how thoughts influence behavior, the task would be easier but less representative of what seems to actually happen. Thoughts affect behavior, and behavior, in turn, reshapes the memory of the original thought as well as ensuing thoughts. If the process of gathering information for research purposes is thought of as a communicative process, our understanding of social cognition will continue to affect our methods of research too—as it already has (see Chapter 3).

Understanding the Formation and Organization
of Social Cognition

As part of the effort to understand how social thoughts and social
behavior were interrelated, it became clear that we needed to know
more about how people form, organize, and interpret information
germane to human interaction. These processes are discussed
throughout this volume as attitudes, expectations, inferences, scripts,
schemas, fantasies, rules, and wishful thinking. The study of how we
form and organize our social thoughts has reemphasized the multilevel
process involved in interpreting and/or assigning meaning to behavioral
signals. Any given signal or sequence of signals may be taken at any one
or combination of at least five levels: (1) the literal message content, (2)
a response to how the partner's preceding response was interpreted, (3)
an indicator of how the partner should respond to a message, (4) an
indicator of how we feel about ourself or partner as a person, and/or (5)
whether further interaction (now or later) is desired.

The study of cognitive structures has also focused on communicator
behavior as well as that of the receiver. Interpersonal scholars no longer
think of communicator intent as something that is either present or
absent. There seem to be various degrees of conscious intent or
mindfulness prior to message delivery, which may change after the
message is performed. Similarly, it seems we often have multiple
objectives or intentions—some of which we are more aware of than
others. Sometimes behavior that is normally intentionally performed
may be performed with little consciousness, and the reverse may also
occur. In view of these and many other nuances associated with
understanding communicator plans, another popular perspective
currently employed is to assume that the only practical and important
perception of communicator intent in interpersonal transactions is that
of the receiver.

THEME #4: A CONCERN WITH
VARIOUS ASPECTS OF CONTROL

For students of communication, control in some form or another has
been a staple interest since antiquity. Aristotle conceived of rhetoric as
the ability to discover the available means of persuasion; while Plato,
like the critics of the 1960s and 1970s, warned citizens of Athens of the
manipulative powers and persuasive wiles of the Sophists. Attention to
the practice and the ethical merits of symbolic influence is manifest in

writings of the next 2000 years. And as noted earlier, the lion's share of pioneering social scientific research on communication was directed at identifying factors influencing the impact of persuasive blandishments directed at large audiences.

We have already noted that the ideological underpinnings of the interpersonal communication movement reflected a repugnance for the Machiavellian, manipulative dimensions of many control-oriented messages; terms such as "control," "persuasion," "social influence," and "compliance gaining" were an anathema to many of those championing the virtues of interpersonal communication in post-1950 American society. Notwithstanding their legitimate concerns, control is such a pervasive aspect of human symbolic activities that it is impossible to divorce its implications from the study of interpersonal communication.

In varying degrees, every chapter of this *Handbook* deals with some species of control as it impinges on and affects the study and practice of interpersonal communication. Traditional views of control as the end of persuasive discourse emerge sharply in Seibold, Cantrill, and Meyers's analysis of communication and interpersonal influence (Chapter 12) and in Berger's treatment of the role of social power in interpersonal settings (Chapter 10). Recent interest in the study of compliance-gaining message strategies is also reflected in Cody and McLaughlin's discussion of the importance of situational variables in interpersonal transactions (Chapter 6) and Burgoon's analysis of the relevance of these strategies to the study of nonverbal signals (Chapter 8). Bowers, Metts, and Duncanson (Chapter 11) consider how differing emotional states may influence people's susceptibility to control-seeking messages, while Giles and Street (Chapter 5) explore the role of numerous communicator variables in shaping perceptions of credibility— credibility, of course, being viewed as a necessary antecedent for control in both interpersonal and noninterpersonal transactions.

Not only is control treated in the traditional sense of persuasive end-product, it is also viewed as an essential ingredient of communicative competence (Chapter 4). If communicators lack the cognitive and behavioral skills needed to elicit desired responses, their competence is sure to be called to question, both by others and by themselves. To grant this commonsense fact is not to deny the wisdom of imposing a value dimension on assessments of competence. Interpersonal communicative competence, in its richest sense, involves the ability to purposefully affect the behaviors of others, the quest for ethically defensible communicative ends, and a decent communicative concern for others' feelings. Nevertheless, laudatory ends and humane attitudes are insufficient to achieve competence if their possessor is incapable of exercising a modicum of control.

From its infancy during the 1960s, the study of relational communication has evinced a hearty interest in the control dimension of relationships. Complementary relationships are typically conceptualized as reflecting varying possibilities for control on the part of participants, who either occupy a dominant, "one-up" position or a submissive, "one-down" role. Granted, this assumed disparity in control poses a problem when events are analyzed at the relational level because from this more macroscopic vantage point, control is best thought of as reciprocal or nonrecursive. Both the dominant and submissive partner have the means to encourage or to thwart the other's attempts at control. But to argue this way suggests the possible need for reconceptualization of the control construct, rather than implying its superfluousness or its irrelevancy. Indeed, the chapters by Duck (Chapter 14) and by Fitzpatrick and Badzinski (Chapter 15), to mention but two, underscore the significance of control for our overall understanding of the development of social, friendship, and kin relationships.

Even the most basic units of interpersonal communication, the verbal and nonverbal codes comprising message exchanges, are inextricably linked to the notion of control. It has become commonplace to assert that all language has a persuasive dimension, and several of the crucial implications of this assertion can be readily identified in Chapter 7 by Jacobs. Similarly, Burgoon (Chapter 8) emphasizes the role of nonverbal behavior as a critical element of relational control, negotiation, and persuasion strategies—these three areas, of course, representing instances of control-oriented message transactions.

Earlier we stressed that communicative behaviors probably run the gamut from mindfulness to mindlessness, that some actions are performed with a great deal of cognitive awareness while others occur almost unconsciously. This same range of awareness doubtless exists within the arena of control. Some issues raised in these chapters assume communicators who are keenly aware of their efforts at control, for example, most discussions of compliance-gaining message strategies rest on the belief that communicators can identify their persuasive goals, accurately analyze the other communicator or communicators involved in the transaction, and select strategies calculated to maximize persuasive outcomes. In contrast, it is doubtful that many of the subtle interaction moves and countermoves described by Cappella (Chapter 9) occur at a high level of awareness—even though failure to manage conversations effectively may indeed detract from a communicator's credibility. Similarly, the synchronized rhythms of control observed in many interpersonal relationships are probably orchestrated at relatively low levels of awareness. Dominant and submissive partners often fall into habitual patterns of message exchange, with neither of them very conscious of the influence patterns weaved by their messages.

A final word on the theme of control: In interpersonal relationships, potential controllers must not only evaluate the probable persuasive effectiveness of a particular strategy, they must also weigh the possible consequences of its use on the relationship itself. For better or worse, such constraints are often viewed as inconsequential or even irrelevant in communicative exchanges between strangers or casual acquaintances—clinching the sale or securing immediate political support is paramount, with minimal concern evinced for the eventual relational consequences of a particular strategy. Because interpersonal relationships are usually deemed important and involve substantial psychological investments, participants cannot ignore the potential damaging relational impact of strategies such as coercion or lying. This point is important to students of social influence in interpersonal settings, for it suggests that the paradigms typically used to study mass persuasion are often conceptually inadequate and operationally myopic when applied to processes of interpersonal influence.

THEME #5: A CONCERN WITH INDIVIDUAL DIFFERENCES

Contemporary students of communication differ on the explanatory value of individual difference variables. Whereas some researchers believe these variables contribute vitally to our understanding of communication processes, others view their contribution as relatively trivial. Despite this lack of consensus, individual difference variables continue to influence strongly our thinking about interpersonal communication, as these *Handbook* chapters amply illustrate.

Particularly appealing are those individual difference variables that seem to be logically yoked to a specific conception of interpersonal communication or to a set of theoretical propositions about interpersonal communication processes. To illustrate, consider the personality or trait characteristic of *self-monitoring* (Snyder, 1974, 1979). High and low self-monitors differ in their sensitivity to social cues as well as their ability to adjust their behaviors to conform with situational exigencies and expectations. More specifically, high self-monitors are sensitive to variations in situations and adjust their behavior accordingly. Conversely, low self-monitors approach situations consistently and project a relatively consistent "self" from one situation to the next. Thus, Elliott (1979) found that high self-monitors were more highly motivated to obtain information that might aid them in communicating effectively with another. In addition, when compared with their low self-monitoring counterparts, high self-monitors were more successful in convincing others that they subscribed to a particular attitudinal position, whether or not their espoused attitudes accurately mirrored their actual ones. Stated differently, high self-monitors both told the truth and deceived more persuasively than did low self-monitors.

Clearly, these differences are relevant to many of the issues examined in the following chapters. Cody and McLaughlin (Chapter 6) consider how self-monitoring influences situational preferences, citing research that demonstrates sharply varying views concerning desirable situational characteristics. Given their sensitivity to cues, high self-monitors would be expected to excel at selecting appropriate control strategies and at communicating control-oriented messages effectively (Chapter 12), an expectation confirmed by the Elliott study cited above. Finally, though not explored extensively by Parks (Chapter 4), relationships between level of self-monitoring and the conception of communicative competence developed in Chapter 4 are readily apparent.

Similar analyses can be offered for such personality variables as *communication apprehension* (Daly & McCroskey, 1984) and *Machiavellianism* (Christie & Geis, 1970). Parks devotes considerable attention to the theoretical and empirical links between communication apprehension, learned helplessness, and perceptions of interpersonal competence. Machiavellianism is particularly relevant to issues of interpersonal control because high Machiavellians are prone to treat people as objects and are likely to see successful control as an end in itself. They are relatively unconstrained in their selection of control strategies (Chapter 12). By contrast, low Machiavellians would be expected to be more sensitive to the ethical implications of using antisocial or deceptive strategies.

The three traits we have alluded to thus far are best thought of as organismic variables, that is, they signify dispositional states existing (or at least, postulated as existing) within communicators and *mediating* symbolic and nonsymbolic responses to symbolic and nonsymbolic stimuli. In addition, individual behavioral differences exert an impact on many of the interpersonal processes discussed in these chapters. To mention but one example, Giles and Street (Chapter 5) detail numerous speech behaviors, such as dialect, rate, and fluency, that influence perceptions of such communicator characteristics as competence and sociability. Although most of the research dealing with these communicative behaviors has involved judgments of relative strangers, the findings have the potential to contribute to our understanding of the development of interpersonal relationships.

We conclude our discussion of this theme by reemphasizing the fact that most individual difference variables discussed in these chapters are linked logically to other constructs and propositions of interest to the authors. In general, indiscriminate correlation of large batteries of individual difference measures with other communication variables, without reasonable a priori grounds for anticipating particular relationships, has proved to be a scientific dead-end. Students of interpersonal communication can probably employ individual difference variables to increase explanatory and predictive power, but only if such variables fit conceptually into a broader theoretical context.

A FINAL WORD

At the outset of this introductory chapter, we readily granted that our remarks about recurrent themes would be neither detailed nor exhaustive. Though we have alluded to additional themes, such as the theoretical and methodological diversity marking the various chapters, we leave it in the hands of our readers to identify other recurrent themes of particular interest, as well as to flesh out the themes we have briefly explored above. We promised but an appetizer; that course is now completed and it is time to progress to the heartier fare of the various chapters.

—Gerald R. Miller
Michigan State University
—Mark L. Knapp
University of Texas

REFERENCES

Barnlund, D. C. (1968). *Interpersonal communication: Survey and studies.* Boston: Houghton Mifflin.

Berger, C. R., & Calabrese, R. (1975). Some explorations in initial interaction and beyond: Toward a developmental theory of interpersonal communication. *Human Communication Research, 1,* 99-112.

Bochner, A. (1978). On taking ourselves seriously: An analysis of some persistent problems and promising directions in interpersonal research. *Human Communication Research, 4,* 179-191.

Cappella, J. N., & Planalp, S. (1981). Talk and silence sequences in informal conversations III: Interspeaker influence. *Human Communication Research, 7,* 117-132.

Christie, R., & Geis, F. L. (1970). *Studies in Machiavellianism.* New York: Academic Press.

Daly, J. A., & McCroskey, J. C. (Eds.). (1984). *Avoiding communication: Shyness, reticence and communication apprehension.* Beverly Hills, CA: Sage.

Elliott, G. C. (1979). Some effects of deception and level of self-monitoring on planning and reaction to a self-presentation. *Journal of Personality and Social Psychology, 37,* 1282-1292.

Giffin, K., & Patton, B. R. (1971). *Fundamentals of interpersonal communication.* New York: Harper & Row.

Gottman, J. M. (1979). *Marital interaction: Experimental investigations.* New York: Academic Press.

Keltner, J. W. (1970). *Interpersonal speech-communication: Elements and structures.* Belmont, CA: Wadsworth.

Kendon, A. (1970). Movement coordination in social interaction: Some examples described. *Acta Psychologia, 32,* 100-125.

McCroskey, J. C., Larson, C., & Knapp, M. L. (1971). *An introduction to interpersonal communication.* Englewood Cliffs, NJ: Prentice-Hall.

Miller, G. R. (1978). The current status of theory and research in interpersonal communication. *Human Communication Research, 4,* 164-178.

Miller, G. R., & Steinberg, M. (1975). *Between people: A new analysis of interpersonal communication.* Chicago: Science Research Associates.

Pearce, W. B., & Cronen, V. E. (1980). *Communication, action, and meaning: The creation of social realities.* New York: Praeger.

Snyder, M. (1974). Self-monitoring of expressive behavior. *Journal of Personality and Social Psychology, 30,* 526-537.

Snyder, M. (1979). Self-monitoring processes. In L. Berkowitz (Ed.), *Advances in experimental social psychology* (Vol. 12, pp. 85-128). New York: Academic Press.

Watzlawick, P., Beavin, J. H., & Jackson, D. D. (1967). *Pragmatics of human communication.* New York: Norton.

I BASIC POSITIONS
AND ISSUES

1 Perspectives on Inquiry: Representation, Conversation, and Reflection

ARTHUR P. BOCHNER

University of South Florida

I NTERPERSONAL communication is a vague, fragmented, and loosely defined subject that intersects all the behavioral, social, and cultural sciences. There are no rigorous definitions that limit the scope of the field, no texts that comprehensively state its foundations, and little agreement among practitioners about which frameworks or methods offer the most promise for unifying the field. It has become fashionable to view this state of affairs as an illness that can be remedied by identifying a global "perspective" capable of making the subject coherent (Cushman, 1977; Delia, 1977; Delia, O'Keefe, & O'Keefe, 1982; Pearce, 1977; Pearce & Cronen, 1980). But the "paradigms" that have been prescribed have not cured the patient because the diagnosis is incorrect (Miller, 1983). Interpersonal communication cannot be sensibly limited to the narrow range of problems and methods that would permit the unrestrained application of a single perspective to all conceivable inquiries. As Koch (1976) points out, "it is impossible to render an unspecified universe into a universe of discourse" (p. 476).

In this chapter interpersonal communication shall be viewed as a subject that can be legitimately approached in several different ways, described in several different vocabularies, and studied with several different purposes in mind. It is my view, as it was Bateson's (1972, 1979), that a uniquely correct scientific perspective does not exist because "natural events and processes always lend themselves to a variety and multiplicity of descriptions, depending on one's point of view" (Toulmin, 1981, p. 368). Accordingly, this chapter examines three modes of description on which scientific inquiry on interpersonal communication may be based.

It is not my intention to focus on specific theories of interpersonal communication. Many of the chapters of this book are charged with that responsibility, and space limitations make it difficult to provide the kind of analysis and criticism that would be useful to practitioners and students of the field. My purpose is to take stock of the different perspectives on scientific inquiry that may govern theory and research on interpersonal communication and related subjects. My assessment of these perspectives will be argumentative. I have a preference for the pragmatist view of inquiry and I will offer reasons for believing it is a useful way to approach studies of social life. I will proceed as follows: First, I will examine the origins and outcomes of the perceived "crisis of confidence" in social science. This issue is important because, in the absence of a sense of crisis, there would be no controversy over how to practice scientific inquiry of the social world. Second, I will assess several responses to this perceived crisis. This section will emphasize the contrasting responses of paradigm-promoters and pragmatists. Third, I will outline three different goals of scientific inquiry and describe the terminology suited to each goal. In the final section, I will consider the consequences of accepting the pragmatist conception of scientific inquiry.

CRISIS OF CONFIDENCE

I will begin by examining the scientific tradition within which interpersonal communication arose as a subject for inquiry. In the years following World War II, social psychology achieved unprecedented success by applying experimental methods to problems of persuasion, propaganda, opinion formation, and leadership (McGuire, 1969). The logical empiricist premises underlying this research were extended to the study of interpersonal relations in the late 1950s by Heider (1958) and Thibaut and Kelley (1959). By the time Barnlund published the first comprehensive synthesis of research on interpersonal communication in 1968, the hegemony of the "received view" of inquiry was so firmly entrenched that O'Keefe (1975, p. 169) could assume, only a few years later, that "the logical empiricist conception of the research enterprise has long dominated communication theory and research."

Because the premises and goals of the "received view" have been thoroughly described in numerous works (for example, Braithwaite, 1953; Hempel, 1966; Nagel, 1961; Popper, 1968; Rudner, 1966; Schlenker, 1974), I shall only sketch the main characteristics of this orientation to inquiry. First, *the goal of science is to represent reality.* Science seeks "to mirror nature," to construct an accurate representation of reality, a description that corresponds to the way nature would describe itself if it could talk (Rorty, 1979, 1982). By equating knowledge with representation, the received view makes truth dependent on method. The scientific discovery of truth thus requires an *objective* method by which the mind can construct accurate representations of nature; in short, "truth through method is the goal."

Second, *science seeks general laws that "cover" or "explain" the relations among observables.* To achieve this goal, it is necessary to divide inquiry into facts and theories. Facts are represented by the "observation language," which is neutral with respect to theories and uninfluenced by any theoretical preconceptions. Theories deal principally with the statements that are to be subjected to empirical evaluation. Observational statements are tied to theoretical propositions through operational definitions that are assumed "to exhaust the meanings of theoretical terms" (O'Keefe, 1975, p. 173). To guarantee objectivity, theoretical terms have to be unambiguously tied to observations. Without an unequivocal observation base, it is impossible to arbitrate disputes among competing theoretical accounts.

Third, *science focuses on stable and recurring relationships among observables*. Scientific theory and scientific method are both grounded on the assumption of stability. Most theories of social behavior assume that human nature is fixed; thus, as Skinner (1971, p. 210) states, "no theory changes what the theory is about." Scientific method is also premised on stability, for as Popper (1968, p. 95) observes: "Only when certain events recur in accordance with rules or regularities, as is the case with repeatable experiments, can our observations be tested in principle."

Fourth, *scientific progress is linear and cumulative*. Gergen refers to this assumption as "fundamental to the *hypothetico-deductive* conception of science" (1982, pp. 8-9). Progress involves the step-by-step accumulation of facts against which the truth claims of theoretical propositions are tested. As evidence supportive of a theory's predictions mounts, one gains confidence in the validity of the theory. This positive evidence, however, is never sufficient to validate a theory conclusively because inductions from particular observations to general propositions depend on inferential principles that are not logically justifiable (Popper, 1968). Thus scientists must rely on *negative* evidence or falsification principles (Popper, 1957, 1968), on the basis of which they can discard, abandon, and replace false theories. Because only theories that resist falsification are acceptable, it is incumbent on scientists to reach agreement on what will count as disconfirming evidence and on an algorithm for choosing which is the better theory, when theories addressing the same facts compete.

In the 1970s, these premises were undermined by numerous critics (for example, Gergen, 1976; O'Keefe, 1975; Rorty, 1979). Unimpressed by the achievements of experimental social psychology, proponents of "new paradigms" began to speak of "a crisis of confidence" in social science (Elms, 1975) and to call for radical transformations in the goals and aspirations of social science (Coser, 1975; Cronbach, 1975; Gergen, 1976; 1978; 1980; Israel & Tajfel, 1972). They expressed misgivings about experimental manipulation and deception (Harré & Secord, 1972; Kelman, 1972; McGuire, 1967, 1973; Ring, 1967; Tajfel, 1972), questioned the social relevance of laboratory fact-finding (Helmreich, 1975), doubted the possibility of establishing a cumulative social science (Cartwright, 1979; Gergen, 1978; Smith, 1972), rejected the premise of transhistorical prediction (Gergen, 1976), and found fault with the image of "man" underlying empiricism (Harré & Secord, 1972; Hollis, 1977;

Shotter, 1975), and deconstructed the representational theory of knowledge on which logical empiricism is based (Rorty, 1979).

This is not the place to dwell on these criticisms (see Gergen, 1982; Koch, 1976, 1981; O'Keefe, 1975; Schlenker, 1974; 1976), but I do want to underscore certain points. First, *transhistorical laws of social interaction have not been discovered*. Even Miller (1978, p. 171), a resolute defender of the empiricist orientation, had to admit that "if one wishes to hew religiously to the necessity implied by the idea of *constant, invariant conjunction*, the set of *interpersonal communiation laws* is an empty one." Although the failure to find a single law of social interaction does not, in principle, rule out the possibility that such laws still can be discovered, Miller (1978) found it necessary to reframe the concept of law in a manner that would free researchers from the bondage of transhistoricality. In his benevolent effort to rescue the concept of law, however, Miller (1978) arrived at a definition of law that he cautiously acknowledged has little utility unless it can cope with change.

Gergen (1976) identified two reasons to doubt whether such laws of social interaction can be found. The first is the communication system of science. Dissemination of research on social behavior produces a feedback loop that can alter the interactional patterns to which social laws are meant to apply. The second is the force of concrete social events. The effects of war, unemployment, inflation, and other social conditions can alter the dispositions of individuals on which social theories are premised. Because the events social science seeks to explain are not stable across time, Gergen concluded that investigation of social behavior is a historical, not a scientific, endeavor. The facts of social life are historical facts, not timeless ones (Cronbach, 1975).

Second, *theoretical terms are not unambiguously tied to observations*. The inherent versatility and ambiguity of language makes it untenable to assume that operational definitions can exhaust the meaning of theoretical concepts. In research on social interaction when investigators must classify the "meanings" of social actions, or at least apply labels to describe behaviors, there are enormous difficulties involved in delineating an observation base capable of providing meaningful and unequivocal discriminations for theoretical terms. Commenting on the loose connection between theoretical terms and empirical referents, Gergen (1978, p. 1351) observed:

> Any given behavior or concrete action may be defined in numerous ways, depending on its function within a given social context. Thus, there is no one transcontextual operation in which the investigator can afford to tie a theoretical term. The pointing of a finger, for example, may signal aggression in certain contexts, but in others may be used as altruistic giving of information, a positive or negative attitude, egocentrism, or high achievement motivation. In short, any behavior might, on any given occasion, serve as an operational definition for virtually any given term.

If the meaning of concepts is not unambiguously anchored in an observation base, then the possibility of subjecting theoretical propositions to objective testing is seriously jeopardized. In the absence of concrete empirical benchmarks for classifying behavior, a subject's responses are opened to multiple and varied interpretations. Hypotheses are able to be sustained, then, not because they resist falsification, but because the community of social scientists agrees *not* to challenge conventionalized experimental manipulations (Gergen, 1980).

Third, *no objective method has been found for resolving theoretical clashes.* This brings us to the vexing hypothesis of incommensurability so persuasively advanced by Kuhn (1962). Looking over the history of science, Kuhn concluded that there was no algorithm that had been or could be generally applied to arbitrate theoretical conflicts. When theories compete, according to Kuhn, a choice is made on the basis of criteria that "function not as rules which determine choice but as values that influence it" (Kuhn, 1977, p. 331). Whereas logical empiricists had looked upon "neutral observation language" as a solution to the problem of theory choice, Kuhn convincingly argued that the application of such an amorphous language was incapable of providing "objective" decision rules for settling theoretical controveries. This conclusion emasculated logical empiricism as "a method for finding truth" and transformed the definition of science from investigation aimed at truth to investigation aimed at *agreement.* As Rorty (1979, pp. 332-333) points out:

> Logical-empiricist philosophy of science, and the whole epistemological tradition since Descartes, has wanted to say that the procedure for attaining accurate representations in the Mirror of Nature differs in certain deep ways from the procedure for attaining agreement about "practical" or "aesthetic" matters. Kuhn gives us reason to say there are no deeper differences than between what happens in "normal" and "abnormal" discourse. That distinction cuts across the distinction between science and non-science.

The cornerstones of science—objectivity, falsification, separation of fact from theory, and linear progress—were badly damaged by the analyses of Kuhn and his contemporaries (see, for example, Feyerabend, 1976; Polanyi, 1962, 1966). Following their critiques, it no longer seemed reasonable to insist on a sharp distinction between a "context of discovery" and a "context of justification." If truth was always relative to a scheme (Davidson, 1973-1974), then all scientific observations were inextricably knotted to the world views of observers. Indeed, no scientific conclusions could possibly be reached without the intrusion of human judgment, for as Koch (1976, p. 556) observed:

> Even the most rigorous methods of science *enforce* no verdicts; verificational methodology *suggests*, gives us *clues* . . . but the conclusion, the *appraisal* is a *decision* [emphasis in original] which must disembed an underlying pattern in an intricate "environment" of meanings, only one strand of which is the naked empirical finding or distribution of such, however well verified.

THE PRAGMATIST RESPONSE

These serious objections to the covering premises of empiricist metatheory left social scientists in the 1970s with the heavy burden of a "crisis in confidence." If scientific inquiry could not be set apart on the basis of such principles as falsification, objectivity, moral neutrality, and linear development, then what were its special attributes? Kuhn seemed to be saying that it was consensus that made science special, and his work invited the interpretation that a scientific field is normally characterized by agreement. Although Kuhn (1970) later said it was wrong to assume that the scientific status of a field can be upgraded by legislating agreement on fundamentals, many social scientists undoubtedly reached exactly that conclusion (Koch, 1976). They read Kuhn's description of paradigms as an endorsement for the view that scientific status is achieved when a single vocabularly—paradigm, perspective, or framework—is accepted by a significant segment of the community of scholars, an outcome produced not so much by proof (the accumulation of facts) as by persuasion (the rhetorical defense of a theoretical perspective).

There are two problems with this interpretation of Kuhn's argument. First, it tends to encourage theorists to look for perspectives that have universal applicability. This "itch for the universal" (Miller, 1983) or "thirst for generality" (Koch, 1976) often results in polemical research. The goal of inquiry becomes finding the one perspective that "holds sway" as O'Keefe (1975) put it, and thereby unifies the field. Writers like O'Keefe mistakenly construe the proliferation of multiple perspectives as a problem to be overcome by acquiring "widespread allegiance [to] a more or less unitary viewpoint" (O'Keefe, 1975, p. 182). Currently, there is no sound reason to believe that the domain of communication research to which such a perspective would be universally applicable can be specified in a sufficiently concrete manner to make the goal of unification or integration accessible (Bochner & Eisenberg, in press).

Even if such a domain could be specified, the triumph of one theoretical perspective over others still would have to assume commensurability among competing viewpoints, and the main lesson to be learned from Kuhn is that no such common ground for theory choice has ever existed in the history of science. The proponents of universalized perspectives offer the customary list of criteria: consistency, coherence, noncontradiction, clarity, and so forth, but the human judgments necessitated by applying these "scientific values" give license to endless argument instead of indubious choice (see Rorty, 1979). This may explain why Stroebe (1980) found that in social psychology when theories compete directly, "crucial experiments . . . never seem to be very crucial" (p. 182). Stroebe (1980) discusses the interesting example of the strife between supporters of Festinger's cognitive dissonance theory (1957) and Bem's self-perception theory (1972), which lasted more than a decade. Finally, in 1970, Bem and McConnell threw in the towel, concluding:

> If the past history of controversies like this is any guide, it seems unlikely that a "crucial" experiment for discriminating between (dissonance and self-perception theory) will ever be executed. At this juncture each theory appears capable of claiming some territory not claimed by the other and one's choice of theory in areas of overlap is diminishing to a matter of loyalty or aesthetics. (p. 182)

Second, the goal of achieving consensus on a "unitary perspective" tends to overshadow other important questions about science raised by critics of the received view. Logical empiricists assumed that science led to truth through method. They thought there was a way to get in touch with "absolute reality" and to describe it in terms that would be absolutely independent of the subjective meanings reality can have for human perceivers. The rules of the game were objectivity, rigor, and replicability. By the empiricists' account, truth could be reached *only* if theory were disengaged from observation, scheme from reality, and interpretation from data. When these necessary conditions were blurred by the criticism of mid-twentieth century analytical and Continental philosophers, the premises of logical empiricism gradually became pragmatized (Rorty, 1982).

Kuhn's most telling observation was that the success of Galilean science *could not be attributed to its method* because what we assume to be the method of the natural sciences is nothing more than the moral imperatives dictated by the disciplinary matrices within which natural scientists function. Natural science did not become successful because Galileo found the right method for experiencing reality and describing nature "as it wants to be described," but because he devised "the right jargon in which to frame hypotheses in the first place" (Rorty, 1982, p. 193). According to Rorty (1982), since the seventeenth century we have mistakenly assumed that the mechanistic, morally neutral language that Galileo employed really captured what nature was like; and that this vocabulary, the language of prediction and control, defined once and for all what it meant to be "scientific." What we have learned more recently is that the achievements of natural science may be due *not* so much to a method that makes science "objective" as to a language that makes it "useful." This is the "pragmatist" viewpoint advanced by Rorty (1982) who reaches the conclusion that it is time "we give up the notion of science traveling toward an end called 'correspondence with reality' and instead say *merely* that a given vocabulary works better than another for a given purpose" (Rorty, 1982, p. 183). The pragmatist perspective offers a unique response to the criticisms of logical empiricism. For most social scientists, the crucial issue has been whether there is a unity to science that allows the method of natural science to be applied to the problems of social science. When faith in the premises of logical empiricism began to decline, critics of the received view became increasingly inclined to accept the split between the *Natur-* and the *Geisteswissenschaften* that Dilthey introduced in the late nineteenth century (Rickman, 1961). These writers took the position that the method of natural science, deductive-nomological theory, cannot be applied to *Geisteswissenschaften* because in the sciences of man the object is a subject. The special qualities of the human sciences, they proposed, require a special method of study (interpretive understanding and intersubjectivity) that is distinct from the method of natural science (prediction and control; see Taylor, 1980).

This division between nature and human beings is taken as the warrant for many of the "new" metatheories assumed to be applicable to the study of interpersonal communication. Among the numerous examples that could be mentioned are Pearce's (1976) distinction between influenced actions guided by rules and controlled behavior covered by laws; Mischel's (1969) division of responses to physical stimuli from responses to the meanings of situations for respondents; Taylor's (1980) separation of object-related from subject-dependent descriptions; Harré and Secord's (1972) differentiation of persons treated as objects and persons acting as agents; and Geertz's (1973) preference for thick, interpretive descriptions over brute, behavioral reductions. These writers represent an increasingly popular school of thought that characterizes the "human sciences" as *essentially* "interpretive." In opposition to the logical empiricists, who thought science had to proceed in the same way and according to the same ground rules regardless of the object being studied, the interpretivists begin by considering the nature of the object and the different constraints imposed on inquiry by different objects. They believe that progress in social science has been stifled by the assumption of a universal scientific method. In place of the unity of science, they substitute a duality based on the special nature of the human sciences and characterized by dichotomies such as persons/things, action/movements, and rule-governed/law-governed explanations. These polarizing distinctions are rooted in the interpretivists' axiom "that the web of meaning constitutes human existence" (Rabinow & Sullivan, 1979 p. 5) or that the essence of human behavior involves a certain notion of meaning (Taylor, 1977, 1980).

Rorty (1980, 1982) rejects the interpretivists' claim that there is a method of the human sciences that stands in opposition to the method of the natural sciences. First, "the method of the natural sciences" may have been a useful fiction but, as was noted above, Kuhn's evidence showed that it never amounted to much more than the moral dictates facilitated by disciplinary networks. Second, a clash over method ordinarily involves a common goal but disagreement over how to reach it. Those who contrast interpretation with empiricism, however, rarely agree on the goal. The quarrel is not over how to achieve prediction and control, but over whether such a goal is possible or desirable. Third, Rorty thinks the issue hinges on whether we want to hold on to the notion of truth as correspondence to reality. Interpretivists contend that the essence of man cannot be discovered by applying the method of natural science because man's essence is grounded on certain qualities—language, culture, intentionality, speech acts, and so forth—that are inaccessible to such methods. Because they continue to think of knowledge as representing reality, defenders of interpretation view the split between spirit and nature as a principled distinction based on "real" qualities that separate human beings from nature. Pragmatists, on the other hand, think that the spirit/nature distinction confuses ontology with morals by reintroducing "the bad old metaphysical notion that the universe is made up of two kinds of things" (Rorty, 1979, p. 351). It is a mistake, says Rorty, to assume that we know a priori that man and nature are distinct sorts of objects and that one set of terms can describe human beings more objectively or more like they really are than some other set of terms. What the interpretive view gives us, he claims, is not an ontological difference but a moral preference expressed in a particular jargon. Their descriptions are not more grounded in what human beings are "*in themselves*" (Rorty, 1980, p. 44). Their terms merely express a preference for doing certain things with persons, for example, understanding them, rather than other things, for example, predicting and controlling their behavior. Thus, the hermeneutic or interpretive jargon is not viewed by pragmatists as a distinct method of inquiry (understanding) that competes against the empiricist method (explanation). It merely provides a different vocabulary that introduces a certain point of view about human experience and aims to cope with it.

I have been emphasizing the counterpoints offered by pragmatists, like Rorty, because I believe this perspective can liberate social and behavioral science from the bondage of polarizing dichotomies that pit laws against rules, explanation against understanding, movements against actions, and quantities against qualities. Pragmatists see a unity to science but it is not the same unity to which the logical empiricists pledged their loyalty. The unity is hermeneutical, not methodological. Whether one seeks guidance about how to conduct inquiry by examining the work of such "hard" scientists as Galileo, Darwin, or Skinner on the one hand, or such "soft" scientists as Goffman, Garfinkel, or Bateson on the other hand, one finds the same point of departure: the need to find a vocabulary that can make the unfamiliar intelligible. What made Galileo's inquiry hermeneutical was his search for a set of terms that would work; and the mathematical jargon that he settled upon satisfied that goal. The reason that Galileo's vocabulary has not produced the same sort of progress in the behavioral and social sciences is not because it is the wrong method, but because the value-neutral, purely descriptive terms in which it frames hypotheses are not as helpful when one wants to decide what to do or how to act; that is, "it is not a good vocabulary for moral reflection" (Rorty, 1982, p. 198). This may be why Skinner's conception of an ideal world (Skinner, 1971) is often responded to so harshly. We frown at the terms he offers for predicting and controlling human behavior not because we are certain he is wrong, but because we do not like to think he could be right (Rorty, 1982).

Rorty (1982) argues that as long as we conceive of knowledge as representing reality, we will continue to engage in endless quibbling over "essences" and the associated problems of method. If we give up the notion of knowledge as representation, however, we will be free to see our task not as the discovery of essences but as the search for vocabularies that are suitable for particular purposes. The pragmatist point is that the terms that will prove most useful depend upon the purposes to which inquiry is directed. Because there are a number of legitimate goals that social scientists may seek to achieve, there are a number of different vocabularies that may be applied to these goals with varying degrees of success. Pragmatists do not ask "What is the right method?" or "What style of inquiry conforms to the essential qualities of human beings?" Rather, they try to determine which vocabularies are useful for which particular purposes.

To summarize, until the mid-1970s the "received view" of science maintained jurisdiction over most investigations of social behavior. The philosophical underpinnings of this "view" involved a commitment to the realist conception of truth and the representational theory of knowledge. In the 1960s and 1970s this tradition was attacked from all sides: by historians of science (Kuhn, 1970); philosophers of science (Davidson, 1973-1974; Feyerabend, 1976; Heidegger, 1971; Hesse, 1966; Polanyi, 1966; Rorty, 1982; Wittgenstein, 1953); prolific empirical researchers (Cronbach, 1975; Gergen, 1976); and social scientists of many different persuasions (Elms, 1975; Harré & Secord, 1972; Israel, 1972; Koch, 1976; Moscovici, 1972; O'Keefe, 1975; Sampson, 1977, 1978; Tajfel, 1972). The criticism reached crisis proportions by the late 1970s.

Reactions to this criticism took several different forms. First, there were those who saw these difficulties as signs of an immature but not an inadequate science (Greenwald, 1976; Miller, 1978; Schlenker, 1974, 1976). These orthodox defenders of traditional science refused to rule out the possibility that the study of social interaction could conform successfully to the premises of empiricism, at least in principle. Second, there were a few who thought that research on social behavior never adhered strictly to the premises of empiricism anyway (Miller & Berger, 1978). It was the *philosophy* not the *method* associated with empiricism that they saw as crucial, and they could not imagine any practical alternative to this "philosophical behaviorism" as they called it. Third, and by far most influential, were those who completely rejected the authority of the "received view." They thought the method of the natural sciences was at the root of the crisis and called for a new method, a method of the human sciences, which would conform to the essential characteristics of human beings (Harré & Secord, 1972; Taylor, 1977, 1980;

Winch, 1958). A host of "new" paradigms, perspectives, metatheories, and conceptual frameworks were proposed by those championing this cause (for example, Cushman & Whiting, 1972; Geertz, 1980; Pearce, 1976). Most of these "new" views shared the crucial premise that the human sciences require a different way of knowing than the natural sciences.

A fourth, and quite distinct response, has been termed here the pragmatist view. Finding its most articulate expression in the recent writings of Rorty (1979, 1980, 1982), the pragmatist position interprets the attacks on logical empiricism as having successfully undermined the theory of representation that has been foundational to all previous conceptions of science. Pragmatists are unsympathetic to the idea of splitting the human sciences from the natural sciences because they do not see "method" as the defining condition of science. After the critiques of rationality advanced by Kuhn, Heese, Wittgenstein, Polanyi, and others, pragmatists are convinced we must revise our conception of truth. The "realist" account of inquiry is rooted in the metaphor of *objectivity*. It assumes "there are procedures of justification of belief which are natural and not just merely local . . . a kind of justification which is not merely social but natural . . . procedures of justification [which] must lead to the truth, to correspondence to reality, to the intrinsic nature of things" (Rorty, 1984, pp. 3-4). Pragmatists, on the other hand, do not believe that truth can be separated from the familiar modes of justification adopted by a given community of scholars. The critical distinction is between construing truth as correspondence to reality and seeing it as well-justified beliefs (Rorty, 1984). The pragmatists believe that knowledge is conditioned by *solidarity* rather than *objectivity*, because all knowledge is subject to the same insurmountable and uncompromising barrier to representation: language. In this respect, science is in the same predicament as the arts and humanities. Indeed, all claims to truth share a dependence on what can be agreed upon by the scholarly community and on normative canons of argument. Thus, Rorty (1979) concludes that investigation should not seek to mirror reality but rather to carry on a "conversation." In the same spirit, he proposes that instead of offering another way of knowing, alternative conceptions of science, such as hermeneutics, actually provide "another way of coping."

Pragmatism offers a way to transcend the stifling conflict of dualities that has plagued communication research over the past decade (Bochner & Krueger, 1979). Instead of viewing motion as the opponent of action, or causes in conflict with reasons, the pragmatist option is to see each as "the other described in an alternative jargon" (Rorty, 1982, p. 200). Accordingly, predictive and interpretive approaches would not be construed as opposed methods of doing scientific research but as different vocabularies that may be more or less useful depending on the objectives to which they are directed. This conclusion assumes that some agreement can be reached about the objectives to which inquiry on social interaction can be legitimately directed.

In the next section, I will describe three distinct objectives of social science and briefly consider the terms that may be useful for coping with these objectives.

GOALS OF INQUIRY

My intention here to focus on the vocabularies of the social sciences. In applying the pragmatist line of thinking, I will seek to identify several legitimate goals to which inquiry on interpersonal communication can be directed. As I shall be assuming that certain descriptions are more suitable for coping with certain goals, I will briefly discuss the requirements imposed on description by different goals of inquiry.

Most previous attempts to differentiate research objectives or paradigms of inquiry have dichotomized studies along the lines of the natural sciences/social sciences distinction discussed above. This "methodological" distinction has been represented in three different ways. First, some writers have distinguished between a *generalizing* and a *particularizing* science. Allport (1937) introduced this distinction to psychologists by distinguishing between nomothetic sciences that seek general laws of behavior and idiographic sciences that investigate particular events. A similar distinction has been made by Geertz (1973), who differentiates operational sciences that attempt to generalize across cases from ethnographic sciences that attempt to generalize within cases. Second, some writers have separated *ahistorical* from *historical* inquiries. This distinction is central to Sampson's (1978) comparison of the natural science and historical science paradigms, and it also has been emphasized by Buss (1975), Levine (1976), and Rychlak (1968). Similarly, Harré (1977) has compared parametric studies in which the variables observed are context-free to structural studies in which the variables are context-dependent. Third, several writers have distinguished between *value-free* and *action-oriented* inquiry. This difference is reflected in Hanna's (1982) discussion of the extensional ideal, which promotes value-free science and in which the scientist acts like a spectator, and the intensional ideal, which is inherently political and value-laden and in which the researcher actively participates in the culture under investigation. Rorty (1982) also viewed the value dimension as the central criterion for differentiating the goal of prediction and control from the goal of policymaking. Roughly the same distinction is applied by Gergen (1978, 1982), who compared positivist/empiricist theories to rationalist/generative theories, and by Carey (1982), who contrasted a reference-oriented to an action-oriented approach.

Rather than thinking of these dualities as conflicting approaches to scientific inquiry, I will construe them as points of view that orient inquiry toward different ends. Empiricist and interpretivist inquiries, then, do not constitute *competing* modes of conducting research. They are merely dif-

TABLE 1.1
Summary of Three Aims of Science

Perspective	*Goals*	*View of Phenomena*	*Functions*	*How "Knowledge" Is Produced*	*How Truth Claims Are Judged*
Empiricism	Prediction and control	Facts (ahistorical)	Put under a covering law	By objectifying (mirroring)	Falsification (Popper)
Hermeneutics	Interpretation and understanding	Meanings (contextual)	Place in an intelligible frame	By edifying (conversing)	Juridicial validation (Ricoeur)
Critical theory	Criticism and social change	Values (historical)	Enlighten and emancipate	By reflecting (criticizing)	Free consensus (Habermas)

ferent points of view, characterized by different descriptions, and oriented toward different goals. The distinctions reviewed above point to three distinguishable, though not necessarily independent, goals of inquiry. The first is inquiry directed toward prediction and control; the second is inquiry targeted at interpretation and intelligibility; and the third is inquiry aimed at criticism and social action. These three goals correspond more or less to the categories of empiricist, hermeneutic, and critical inquiry, and to the "social media" of work, language, and social power discussed by Habermas (1971). Let us now examine the modes of description—forms of theory, criteria for justification, and research practices—that seem helpful in facilitating these goals.

Prediction and Control

The goal of prediction and control reflects the world view of logical empiricism. This world view exemplifies many of the characteristics of Hanna's (1982) extensional ideal and the exogenic theory of knowledge discussed by Gergen (1982). It emphasizes objectivity, value-neutrality, intersubjective verifiability, and either environmental determinism, as in behaviorist thought, or mental determinism, as in cognitive thought. These terms impose certain constraints on inquiry. First, reality is assumed to be independent of the observer and accessible to observation. The objects of observation, therefore, must be treated as things that stand apart from the observer, real things that are likely to remain stable and invariant. Because the aim is prediction and control, preference is given to stability over change, unless of course the change in question is predictable.

Second, facts are presumed to be separable from values. Because theories are supposed to be "data-driven," a high priority is assigned to the task of obtaining unbiased and verifiable facts. The objective is to secure "pure" facts. Theory is supposed to mirror or reflect facts, so there must be some assurance that facts have not been prejudiced by the investigator's beliefs or values. This is why so much importance is attributed to methods of measurement, operational definitions, experimental control, and assessment.

Third, claims to knowledge are judged by public deliberation; "because there are objectively correct and incorrect answers about the world, people of sound mind should reach common agreement. Science should thus ideally strive for consensus among practitioners" (Gergen, 1982, p. 176). Rationality holds the key to truth. What counts as knowledge is publically decidable. Thus replicability of results is regarded as a prime virtue (Miller, 1983).

In contrast to this egalitarian and antidogmatic view of knowledge, however, the search for prediction and control can lead to conservatism. By establishing rational criteria by which equal observers can reach agreement, empiricism takes the "world-order" as given (Cohen, 1963). The pursuit of "pure" facts encourages "the absorption of thought by the given," as Rossides (1968, p. 251) states it. Investigation is normally restricted to what Von Wright (1968) calls "positive facts," statements about the world "as it is now." The goal is to identify the characteristics of social events and experiences; to describe them, explaining why they occur; and to formulate generalizations and laws about their occurrence (Israel, 1972). This nonevaluative focus on what is, not what ought to be, tends to preserve the status quo by neglecting inquiry on change, by refraining from criticizing what is found, and by considering discussion of alternatives to the existing order out of place in science (Israel, 1972; Sampson, 1978). Thus, value-neutrality is not devoid of political consequences. Sampson (1978, p. 1337) believes that "value-free" science tends "primarily to solidify goals and values of vested interests." This alleged mystification of value-free social science is what led Gergen (1978, p. 1355) to warn that "the fruits of neutrality are passionate in their consequences." Ironically, the commitment to value-neutrality tends to make empiricism "largely dogmatic" (Israel, 1972, p. 207).

The pursuit of prediction and control usually involves two types of theoretical work. The first is the identification and analysis of important theoretical variables. Some writers refer to this research tradition as variable-analytic (Delia, 1977; Ellis, 1982). In this line of work, investigators isolate, measure, and/or manipulate variables that they consider to have a substantial impact on a limited range of social behavior. On the whole, variable-analytic research has conformed to the types of inquiry termed "taxonomic" and "differential" by Moscovici (1972). Taxonomic research seeks to identify and describe the different types of social stimuli, to classify the differences between them, and to determine the extent to which differences in these variables affect social processes. The classic example of the taxonomic mode of research is the Hovland group's studies of how communicator characteristics and message variations affect attitude formation and change (Hovland, Janis, & Kelley, 1953; McGuire, 1969; Miller & Burgoon, 1978). In the field of communication, recent research on compliance-gaining strategies (Cody & McLaughlin, 1980; McLaughlin, Cody, & Robey, 1980; Marwell & Schmitt, 1967; Miller, Boster, Roloff, & Seibold, 1977; Sillars, 1980); and on detecting deceptive communications (Bauchner, Kaplan, & Miller, 1980; Brandt, Miller, & Hocking, 1980; Hocking, Bauchner, Kaminski, & Miller, 1979; Knapp & Comadena, 1979) typify this approach. Differential research attempts to classify states or traits on which individuals differ and to assess the extent and range of experiences affected by such differences. McCroskey's (1977) formidable research program on communication apprehension, Rotter's (1955, 1975) on internal/external locus of control, and Snyder's (1979) on self-monitoring exemplify this orientation.

The second type of theoretical work associated with prediction and control is the development of deductive theories. Most empiricists "whole-heartedly endorse the position . . . that theory must be grounded in empirical data" (Blalock, 1969, p. 8; also see Glaser & Strauss, 1967). Theory is data-driven in two senses. First, theory arises from and is grounded in data. In this sense, theorizing is presumably an inductive effort. In Blalock's words: "One formulates the best theory he can in light of existing evidence" (1969, p. 8). Hall and Lindzey (1970, p. 13) also define one of the main functions of theory as *the incorporation of known empirical facts* within a logically consistent and reasonably simple framework." Second, theory facilitates further observation, that is, data collection. This is usually accomplished by using the hypothetico-deductive form of exposition (see Fisher, 1978, pp. 26-30). The theorist presents a set of interrelated hypotheses or propositions, delineating functional relationships among concepts and the range of events—the boundary conditions—under which these relationships are expected to hold. These propositions provide a benchmark against which new data can be checked. In this fashion, the theorist encourages the collection of new data concerning empirical relationships not previously observed. A theory, then, is both "a *tool* and an objective" (Marx, 1951, pp. 6-7). One examines data with the objective of building a theory to explain the functional relationships among the variables; and one expresses the proposi-tions of a theory formally to provide a tool for developing further tests of relationships. Many examples of this form of theorizing can be found in the literature of social psychology and in communication research (see Ajzen & Fishbein, 1972; Bandura, 1977; Berger & Calabrese, 1975; Burgoon, 1978; Burgoon, Jones, & Stewart, 1975; Festinger, 1950, 1957; Jones & Davis, 1965; Kelley, 1972; Walster, Walster, & Berscheid, 1978).

Interpretation and Intelligibility

The term "interpretive social science" encompasses an extremely broad range of philosophical, empirical, and methodological orientations. Because there are so many variations on the theme of interpretation, any attempt to characterize what is common to all interpretive approaches runs the risk of overstating similarities and neglecting important differences. Readers interested in a comprehensive treatment of different approaches to language and meaning should consult Grossberg (1979). Here I only wish to highlight, rather briefly, the philosophical roots of interpretive social science and the vocabulary that facilitates descriptions of human conduct in terms of interpretation and intelligibility.

The philosophical underpinnings of interpretive social science can be credited to several different sources. First, the emphasis on cyclical change and diachronic sequence dates back to the eighteenth century and the social thought of Vico, who focused on the idea of perpetual change and the recursive evolution of society (Rosnow, 1978; Vico, 1975). Second, the interest in rules-based explanations of social interaction (Cushman & Whiting, 1972; Harré & Secord, 1972; Pearce, 1976; Pearce & Cronen, 1980; Shimanoff, 1980; Sigman, 1980) is grounded largely in the "philosophical anthropology" of Kant (1909) who substituted "pragmatic explanations of conduct constructed from the 'standpoint' of agents" (Mischel, 1969, p. 19) for the Newtonian explanations of human behavior based on the causal model of mechanics. Kant rejected the Cartesian division of phenomenology and physiology in favor of a view in which intentional action, practical reason, and actions mediated by meanings were central. Third, Max Weber's (1949, 1968) conceptualization of sociology as a "cultural science" was inspired by Dilthey's historical studies and Heinrich Richert's formulation of cultural inquiry (Dallmayr & McCarthy, 1977). Although Weber tended to subordinate understanding to explanation, he did widen the scope of sociological inquiry to cover the value orientations of cultural events. Fourth, a turn toward discourse analysis was encouraged by the notions about language introduced in the later writings of Wittgenstein (1954) and extended by the theory of action (Care & Landsman, 1968) and the philosophy of speech acts (Austin, 1962; Searle, 1969). These writers blurred the distinctions between linguistic actions and behavior patterns by suggesting that the meaning of linguistic expressions is fixed by a larger constellation of nonlinguistic activities. Thus "questions about meaning lead one on to questions about linguistic routines; and these in turn to questions about how those linguistic routines are related to nonlinguistic attitudes and actions" (Toulmin, 1969, p. 75). Fifth, Weber's interest in the study of meaningful social action was extended by the phenomenologically informed writings of Alfred Schutz (1967, 1970), which emphasized the natural attitude of everyday life and the importance of describing how individuals establish and interpret meanings. This concern for interpretive practices is embodied in ethnomethodology (Garfinkel, 1967; Sacks, Jefferson, & Schegloff, 1974; Schegloff, 1972), a research program focusing on how the meanings of utterances are indexed by and for communicators and the ordering principles that enable interactants to display their meanings to each other. Sixth, there is the recent influence of "textualism." In contrast to the nineteenth-century idealists who took the position that "nothing exists but ideas," the textualists "start off from the claim that all problems, topics, and distinctions are language-relative—the results of our having chosen to use a certain vocabulary, to play a certain language game," and they end up saying things like, in Derrida's words, "there is nothing outside the text" (Rorty, 1982, p. 140). Merging the persuasive forces of poststructuralist thought (for example, Foucault & Derrida) and "new" literary criticism (for example, DeMan & Bloom), social scientists sympathetic to textualist thought (Rabinow & Sullivan, 1979) have taken the model of text-interpretation—hermeneutics—as a methodological paradigm for inquiry in the social sciences (Ricoeur, 1971; Taylor, 1977).

The goal of interpretation and intelligibility adopts the world view of hermeneutics. This world view embraces edification and thus moves away from epistemology (Rorty, 1979). It considers the quest for truth, associated with the pursuit of prediction and control as "just one among many ways in which we might be edified" (Rorty, 1979, p. 360). It does not renounce the search for knowledge, but it does take the position that "the way things are said is more important than the possession of truths" (Rorty, 1979, p. 359). Instead of "believing that we know ourselves by knowing a set of objective facts," (Rorty, 1979, p. 373) hermeneutics asserts that all of our knowledge about ourselves is conditioned by the terms of our descriptions. The goal, then, is not to collect facts that will produce objective truth, but to generate descriptions that will enable us to keep a conversation going (Rorty, 1979).

I have already suggested that interpretive social science is a generic term covering many different approaches to inquiry: the *verstehen* tradition of Dilthey, Richert, and Weber; the phenomenology of Husserl and Schutz transformed into enthnomethodology by Garfinkel, Sacks, and Schegloff; the symbolic interactionism of Mead, Cooley, Blumer, and Goffman among others; the followers of Ryle and the later Wittgenstein who emphasized ordinary language analysis, speech acts, accounts, and justifications; the ethogenics of Rom Harré; the dramatism of Kenneth Burke; the ethnographies of Clifford Geertz, and so on. Putting aside the differences that distinguish one interpretive approach from another, I want to concentrate on the terms shared by most of those assuming an interpretive stance.

First, the meaning of human actions figures prominently in most interpretive studies. Defining culture as webs of significance spun by man, Geertz (1973, p. 5) construed interpretive anthropology "not as an experimental science in search of law but an interpretive one in search of meaning." Rabinow and Sullivan (1979, pp. 4-5) observed that the interpretive approach turns "on the concrete varieties of cultural meaning . . . the circle of meaning within which we find ourselves and which we can never fully surpass." And Taylor (1977, p. 101) stipulated that interpretive sciences must deal "with one or another of the confusingly interrelated forms of meaning." The confusion to which Taylor refers has been noted by a number of investigators. There is considerable disagreement among advocates of interpretation about whether inquiry should focus on actors' accounts of their own meanings, theorists' readings of actors' meanings, theorists' interpretations of actors' accounts of their meanings, or what. Menzel (1978, p. 165) warned that the procedures for ascertaining subjects' meanings "require great efforts and long periods of time," and he is critical of how these difficulties are glossed over by investigators interested in studying meanings. Rommetveit (1980, p. 125) contended that Menzel (1978) understates these difficulties because "there is apparently no natural end, either in the form of literal meanings of expressions or ultimate knowledge of the world, to the explication of linguistically mediated meaning."

Second, interpretation focuses on symbol systems. Meanings are grasped by analyzing modes of expression: talk, discourse, symbolic action, social artifacts. The goal of inquiry is to retrieve meanings by placing structures of signification into an intelligible frame. By analyzing symbolic actions in terms of their meanings, the investigator hopes to gain access to the informal logic of social life. The strange and the familiar are both pertinent. The mysterious becomes sensible when it is cast in a luminous frame (for example, Bateson, Jackson, Haley, & Weakland, 1956). The commonplace becomes puzzling when its complexities are revealed (for example, Henry, 1971). Taylor (1977, p. 102) echoed these themes when he stipulated that "the object of a science of interpretation must be describable in terms of sense and nonsense, coherence and its absence; and must admit of a distinction between meaning and its expression."

Third, an interpretive stance admits to no sharp distinctions between fact and value or truth and belief. "Strictly speaking," says Schutz (1971, p. 228), "there are no such things as facts, pure and simple." In the pursuit of intelligibility, one is forced to relinquish the notion of "brute data" capable of being verified beyond interpretation. One must rely instead on interpretations for which there are no verification procedures to fall back on. The study of meaning leads the investigator toward topics on which it is relatively difficult to gain agreement, so it often seems that interpretive claims are "relativistic." But this charge only makes sense if one is looking at interpretation from a verificationist perspective that seeks truth through consensus. To take an interpretive posture, however, is to embrace "the burden of choice." If the aim is to keep the conversation going, then it makes sense to encourage optional descriptions and to continue to offer interpretations. Geertz (1973, p. 29) stressed this view when he argued that "to commit oneself to a semiotic concept of culture and an interpretive approach to the study of it is to commit oneself to a view of ethnographic assertion as . . . 'essentially contestable.' " Interpretive anthropology is a science whose progress is marked less by a perfection of consensus than by a refinement of debate. What gets better is the precision with which we vex each other."

This does not mean that all interpretations are equally valid. There may be a *"specific plurivocity* belonging to the meaning of human action," wrote Ricoeur (1971, p. 331), but

> human action too, is a limited field of possible constructions. . . . It is always possible to argue for or against an interpretation, to confront interpretations, to arbitrate between them and to seek for an agreement, even if this agreement remains beyond our reach. In the final analysis differences in interpretation can only be arbitrated by applying socially accepted modes of justification; i.e., what will count as a convincing argument.

Ricoeur (1971) reached the conclusion that the type of validation appropriate to interpretive claims is juridical, a form of reasoning associated with legal arguments in which the goal is to reach a verdict subject to appeal and to the power of public reaction.

Fourth, meaning is dependent on context. Thus the study of human actions must assign considerable importance to contextual determination. This makes interpretive inquiry historical, concrete, and particular, much like the conception of Paradigm II science discussed by Sampson (1978). The case studies and "thick descriptions" associated with interpretation have more in common with clinical inference than with nomothetic science.

Fifth, it is virtually impossible to formularize theoretical description. Much depends on the cases being analyzed. What one is after is a catalytic description, what I once called "a warm idea" (Bochner, 1981), and it is very difficult to state a formula for reaching this goal. Geertz (1973, pp. 24-27) indicated that interpretive theory should "stay rather closer to the ground" and not only fit past realities but also "survive—intellectually survive— realities to come." This survival is not dependent on predicting future outcomes but rather on how well the same conceptual framework applies to the interpretation of new instances. The double-bind theory (Bateson et al., 1956; Sluzki & Ransom, 1976; Wilder-Mott & Weakland, 1981) satisfies this criterion exceptionally well.

Criticism and Social Change

The term "critical theory" usually refers to a view about the nature of knowledge developed by a group of German philosophers known as the Frankfurt School (see Geuss, 1981; Held, 1980; Lanigan & Strobl, 1981; Rogers, 1982; Slack & Allor, 1983). Recent scholarship (for example, Habermas, 1971) has radically revised many of the ideas introduced by earlier members of Frankfurt's Institute of Social Research (for example, Hork- heimer, Adorno, & Marcuse). Nevertheless, critical theory is still considered by some writers (for example, Rogers, 1982) to embody a monolithic perspective on social theory that stands in opposition to the objectifying orientation of empiricism (Geuss, 1981; Lanigan & Strobl, 1981). Treated as a unified school of thought, critical theory presumes that reflection can produce knowledge, whereas empiricism finds no convincing justification for conceiving of a kind of knowledge that is nonobjective (Geuss, 1981). As a goal of social inquiry, however, criticism is not so much a rejection of empiricism as it is a repudiation of empiricist dogma about what counts as knowledge (Israel, 1972). From the pragmatist viewpoint, empiricism and criticism simply belong to two different universes of discourse. Empiricists seek prediction and control through objectifying methods. Critical theorists seek enlightenment and social change through reflective methods. They do not speak to the same issues.

The goal of criticism and social change is not restricted to the development of critical theories but rather includes all inquiry that calls attention to the prescientific conceptions associated with social research. Critical research refuses to ignore the extensive reflexivity involved in "man's study of man." The fact that we are inside what we study is not just another methodological obstacle to objectivity. It is a warrant to make social science more reflective.

From the critical perspective, two features of the relations between the practices of scientists and the functioning of society need to be highlighted. First, science is a social institution. This means that science is contextually embedded in a network of relations that serve the political, economic, and ethical interests of society. The dynamic relations among these institutions virtually guarantee that social theories will be influenced by cultural norms, traditions, and beliefs of the society that it seeks to describe. The danger is that social science will be corrupted by the institutions it serves, that it will do no more than reaffirm the values of the existing social order. Second, if it is true that theories may be prejudiced by social and cultural norms, it is also true that theories can potentially alter these norms. Empiricist theories tend to construct reality insofar as they determine which data are relevant and what these data can mean (Israel, 1972). According to Gergen (1978, pp. 1349-1350), "in the process of description and explanation, the scientist is inevitably engaged in the creation of social phenomena, both in the fashioning of the theoretical lenses through which social action is observed and in the reconstitution of the culture's system of meaning."

Critical research, then, assumes that science cannot exist without ideology. The aims of criticism are, first, to expose the values implicit in theories in order to enlighten social agents and, second, to offer alternatives that will emancipate the agents (Geuss, 1981). In assuming that social agents may not be able to "see what is there," or if they do "see what is there" they may want to change it, the critical school of thought fits squarely within the boundaries of what Sampson has called "Paradigm II—the historical model of science" (1978, p. 1333). Instead of regarding the "facts" produced by empirical research as a path leading to the accumulation of general, universal, and timeless knowledge, the historical model views such "facts" as contextually embedded truths that necessarily reflect the sociohistorical standpoint of a given culture (Sampson, 1978). Social facts thus become "relational facts" because such facts connect what is experienced to the specific, concrete, sociohistorical context in which experience occurs.

The premise that social facts are historically situated has been taken most seriously by Kenneth Gergen (1973, 1976, 1978), who considers social psychology to be primarily "the systematic study of contemporary history" (1973, p. 319). Gergen (1978) draws two implications from the evidence supporting historical contingency. First, if one can assume that most patterns of social behavior are temporary (not enduring), then the function of social theories need not be confined to describing existing circumstances. The purposes of social theory can be expanded to include a thorough consideration of alternatives to the contemporary situation. Second, if one grants the point that social theories not only describe but also shape social behavior, then the theorist can be seen as an agent of change. Theories have consequences, one of the most important of which is the potential to transform the present situation.

Gergen's view of theory focuses on the value commitments of theories. Behavioral description is not a "reflection" as much as it is an "expression" of events and experiences. The most important feature of a theory is the *language* it employs, and in this respect, like other "language games," theorizing involves social negotiation. "The chief question confronting the theorist," says Gergen, "is not 'how accurate is the description?', but rather 'what function is the selected theoretical language to play within the human arena?' " (1982, p. 98). Value investments are therefore inextricably connected to the construction of theories:

> The scientist's values are almost inevitably linked to the phenomena selected for study, the labels attached to those phenomena, the manner of interpreting new findings, the amount of confirming evidence required for a conclusion, and the manner of applying social theory. For present purposes, the most significant implication is that all such valuational influences serve as "ought expressions" for the recipient of knowledge. As such, they have the potential to shape the society; they may favor certain forms of social conduct at the expense of potential alternatives. As its implications and alternatives are borne out, every theory becomes an ethical or ideological advocate. (Gergen, 1978, p. 1354)

Gergen (1978) introduces the term "generative theory" to underscore the value commitments and transformative functions of critical theories: "When a theory is used generatively, it will challenge the commonly shared construction of the world; it will generate doubt in such constructions and thereby engender flexibility. When used generatively, theory may increase the adaptive potential of an individual or a culture" (Gergen, 1982, p. 168).

Israel (1972) shares Gergen's discontentment with the empiricists' claim to ethical neutrality. He argues that all empiricist theories of social behavior make tacit claims about the nature of man, the nature of society, and the relationship between man and society. The problem is that these "stipulations" are normative statements disguised as descriptive ones (Israel, 1972). As long as it is assumed that empirical statements only function descriptively, the values they imply remain concealed. The risk is that hidden stipulations can become self-fulfilling prophecies. Unexamined ideals can begin to regulate social behavior without any serious reflection by social agents about the relative advantages and disadvantages of alternative descriptions.

The critical attitude advocated by writers like Gergen, Israel, Moscovici, and Sampson has inspired a number of reflective studies of social behavior. For instance, Sampson (1975, 1977, 1978) has published several critical reviews focusing on the value interests of American social psychology. In these papers, Sampson argues that our notions about social psychology do not point to general, abstract, and universal principles of psychological functioning but rather reflect the cultural ethos of our historical situation. Drawing on the literature dealing with equity, androgeny, moral development, social cognition, mental health, encounter groups, and personality, Sampson (1977) showed that American social psychology implicitly endorses the value of "self-contained individualism." This is the idea that self-sufficiency is preferable to dependence on others, that the locus of causality in human relations is inside the person rather than between people, and that autonomy is a higher value than community (Sampson, 1977). Sampson did not take issue with the research "findings" in these areas. His grievance was over what these "findings" mean. Do these studies produce evidence of general and invariant principles of psychological functioning or do they merely reflect the cultural ethos of a particular moment in history? Sampson argued that none of this work establishes fundamental principles of psychological functioning. What these studies reveal, he claimed, is something about the psychological consequences of the socialization practices of American culture. If the social practices were changed, the psychological outcomes would change as well. Therefore, Sampson offered an interdependent alternative to the ideal of self-contained individualism. As a critical theorist, Sampson's position is that unless alternatives are critically examined, there can be no role for science to play in policymaking and social change because a science limited to describing "what is" can only affirm existing ideals and/or reproduce them. It cannot participate in changing them.

In addition to promoting individualism, American social psychology strongly endorses "rationalist models" of social behavior. Reviewing the research literature "in every conceivable domain, from motivational theory through attitude change to moral development," Hogan and Embler (1978, p. 522) found social psychologists "swamped by a tidal wave of enthusiasm for rationalist models" that attribute maximum importance to cognitive activity and underestimate or entirely ignore the role of experience and the influence of the community. This tacit ideological emphasis on individualism and rationalism has produced "one of the most remarkable features of current social psychology . . . [I]ts systematic denial of man's social nature" (Hogan & Embler, 1978, p. 487). The problem is not that social psychology has a distinctive ideological bias but rather that many social psychologists think their work can be free of values and ideals. Thus Hogan and Embler (1978, pp. 530-531) concluded that

> it is necessary to understand, once and for all, that every point of view in the social sciences, every theoretical model, every hypothesis, will have value implications—because that is the way nature is constructed and the human mind operates. Thus ultimately it is not a question of being careful, and using only operational definitions, of employing an objective data language. The problem of ideology is a problem from which there is no escape—in principle. . . . The best and perhaps the only protection social science can have against serious ideological distortion is to nurture a plurality of perspectives.

The ideological biases identified by Sampson and by Hogan and Embler have turned up repeatedly in reports examining other areas of research. For instance, Bochner (1984) found a decided rationalist emphasis in the literature on relational development; and Geller (1982) argued that the self-actualization theories of Rogers (1961) and Maslow (1968) fail to take into account the social foundations of the self.

Several other ideals have been scrutinized by writers taking a critical approach to theorizing. Emphasizing alternatives to the hegemony of dominant value orientations, Gergen (1977) compared the advantages of considering human development from the viewpoint of continuous change with the more common views of development as stability or orderly change; Bochner (1981) doubted the efficacy of highly disclosive communication in close relationships, suggesting that candor must be tempered by discretion because both trust and respect are necessary for the development of a satisfying interpersonal relationship; and Sampson (1975) tried to show that equality is a viable alternative to equity as a solution to the "distribution problem."

The issue of how to validate or falsify the claims of a critical theory is far from being settled. The matter seems to boil down to how one views "objectivity" and "rationality." On the one hand, Rorty (1982) and his fellow pragmatists think it is useless to pursue the traditional concepts of rationality and objectivity in order to arrive at some universal ethical principles. A good conversation, one that is "edifying," is the best we can hope for. All such conversations can lead to moral and ethical insight but none can establish "objective" and universal ethical standards.

Habermas (1971, 1976) and his followers, on the other hand, believe that objectivity can be redeemed through rational discourse aimed at consensus:

> If an unrestricted community of rational agents investigates a state of affairs under conditions of complete freedom and eventually reaches a stable consensus, the judgment which expresses that consensus is the "objective truth" about that state of affairs. (Geuss, 1981, p. 72)

Geuss (1981) refers to this account of objectivity as "the principle of internal criticism." According to this principle, the agents affected by an ethical standard must be the arbiters of truth. Thus the acceptability of a critical theory is subject to two tests: A test of empirical adequacy and a search for consensus among the agents to whom the theory is addressed. In order to produce such a consensus, agents must be presented with a theory that is expressed in terms they can understand. The theory must also "provide the criterion by which to evaluate whether or not the critical theory itself and the information it provides are acceptable" (Geuss, 1981, p. 79). These features of a critical theory distinguish it from other forms of theoretical work. Only in critical theory are the agents to whom the theory is addressed also the agents who judge its acceptability; and only in critical theory are the standards by which the theory is to be judged located within the theory itself.

The vocabulary of critical research emphasizes *moral reflection*. It is a vocabulary suited to coping with questions about what should be, thus the terms it applies focus attention on ethical standards, ideology, and social change. Grounded on the premises that social knowledge is historically situated and may be conditioned by the hegemony of vested interests, the critical approach seeks enlightenment and emancipation through the rational investigation of alternative descriptions of reality.

CONCLUSIONS

I want to close this chapter by restating the convictions and implications of the pragmatist thesis. My principal goal has been to undermine the venerable idea that either there is a universal *method* of science applicable both to nature and to man, or there are two different methods of science, one suited to the puzzles of nature, the other to the puzzles of man. Scholars of different persuasions have tried hard to sabotage one of these methods and promote the other.

Pragmatists reframe the controversy by focusing on aims and outcomes rather than on methods. They do not believe that any method is uniquely applicable to the study of human nature because human beings do not have "a nature." It is not necessary, therefore, to corrupt the virtue of empiricist method because the core of the problem has nothing to do with method. None of the critiques of the use of empiricism in social science has established that it is impossible to predict and control human behavior, nor has any shown that if your goal is to predict and control certain aspects of human behavior there is a better way to go about it than by rigorously applying the method of Gallilean science. According to pragmatists like Rorty, it is the theory of knowledge underlying empiricism, not its method, that is at issue. And here the battle lines are drawn quite clearly. Either we try to redeem the view of truth as correspondence with reality that has been emaciated by the criticisms of historians and philosophers of science or we replace it with the notion that the best we can do is cope with reality. We cannot represent its intrinsic nature (Rorty, 1982).

Pragmatism offers a conception of inquiry that focuses on the connection between purpose and mode of description. It starts with the question, "What do we want to do (with human beings)?" and then considers the modes of description that are useful for our particular purposes. In this chapter I have discussed three different goals to which studies of human behavior (or action) may legitimately be addressed and have introduced some of the terminology and modes of description that can be usefully applied to these goals. I have implied that we have good reasons to enlarge the scope of our inquiry so we may view our phenomena not just as "facts," but also as "meanings" *and* as "values." As the aims of our work shift, so does the language we apply. Thus the goals of prediction and control, interpretation and understanding, and criticism and social change are not construed as competing modes of conducting research that match laws against rules, quantitative against qualitative methods, objectivity against subjectivity, or rigor against imagination. They are merely preferences for taking certain points of view toward our subject matter. In Rorty's words, these different views are "not issue(s) to be resolved, only . . . difference(s) to be lived with" (1982, p. 197).

Several important consequences follow the acceptance of a pragmatist conception of inquiry. First, in the development and application of theories, the emphasis shifts from the objectifying to the discursive features of theorizing. Theoretical work is aimed at developing vocabularies that are useful for particular purposes, rather than descriptions that reveal the essence of things. The "facts" that we see are inextricably tied to our forms of expression. Toulmin (1969, p. 71) has suggested, following Lavosier, that "questions of terminology [have] turned out to be inseparable from questions of substance, and vice versa." Gergen (1982, p. 101) also showed a clear preference for the linguistic aspects of theorizing when he boldly declared that "the chief product of research is language."

Second, the pragmatist perspective provides an opportunity to escape from the bondage of a monolithic conception of science. If there is one thing communication scholars have learned from the seemingly endless controversy over whether covering-law theories or rules-based theories offer the greatest promise for advancing the study of interpersonal communication, it is that there is very little agreement on the matter. Why is there no general agreement on this issue? I have suggested it is because one side believes that human beings can be objectified for scientific purposes and treated as if they were no different than rocks, while the other side believes that there is an essential difference between them that must be granted. Unfortunately, there is no evidence that can possibly arbitrate this dispute, so each side continues to believe what they think it is better to believe—that the other side is wrong. Pragmatists view this as a disagreement over aims. Unless we can agree on a goal, we cannot agree on the terms by which we can judge how to achieve it. And law-seekers and rule-seekers cannot agree on a goal. By admitting that there are at least three legitimate goals to which our scientific work can be addressed, we are liberated from the obligation to find a universally accepted standard for judging which point of view about scientific inquiry is ultimately correct. Presently, the preference for one scientific approach over another is arbitrary, not rational (see Bartley, 1964).

Third, by extending the aims of science to include interpretation and criticism, the line separating scientific from humanistic modes of inquiry becomes quite indistinct. This "blurring of genres" (Geertz, 1980) frees investigators to apply terms that are suited to their objectives rather than forcing them to confine their inquiries to a narrow range of methodologies that may be scientifically acceptable but poorly suited to their objectives. Obviously, this has already started to happen. As Geertz (1980, p. 166-167) reports, "Freed from having to become taxonomically upstanding, because nobody else is, individuals thinking of themselves as social (or behavioral or human or cultural) scientists have become free to shape their work in terms of its necessities rather than received ideas as to what they ought or ought not to be doing."

Finally, there is the issue of whether to conceive of our work as "representational," "conversational," or "reflective." The hardest pill for empiricists to swallow is the notion that all truth claims rest on canons of argument rather than on methods and tests of inference. The implication is that apart from terminology the main difference among the objectives of prediction and control, interpretation and understanding, and criticism and social change is that it is easier to reach agreement about prediction and control than about anything else. It is, to use Rorty's (1984) terms, a matter of "solidarity," not "objectivity." Thus none of the "paradigms" of inquiry occupies a privileged position in the court of truth; all share the burden of justification.

REFERENCES

Ajzen, I., & Fishbein, M. (1972). Attitudes and normative beliefs as factors influencing behavioral intentions. *Journal of Personality and Social Psychology, 21*, 1-9.

Allport, G. W. (1937). *Personality: A psychological interpretation.* New York: Holt.

Austin, J. L. (1962). *How to do things with words.* New York: Oxford University Press.

Bandura, A. (1977). Self-efficacy: Toward a unifying theory of behavioral change. *Psychological Review, 84*, 191-215.

Barnlund, D. C. (1968). *Interpersonal communication: Survey and studies.* Boston: Houghton Mifflin.

Bartley, W. W. (1964). Rationality versus the theory of rationality. In M. Bunge (Ed.), *The critical approach to science and philosophy* (pp. 3-31). London: Collier-Macmillan.

Bateson, G. (1972). *Steps to an ecology of mind.* New York: Ballantine Books.

Bateson, G. (1979). *Mind and nature: A necessary unity.* New York: Dutton.

Bateson, G., Jackson, D. D., Haley, J., & Weakland, J. H. (1956). Toward a theory of schizophrenia. *Behavioral Science, 1*, 251-264.

Bauchner, J. E., Kaplan, E. P., & Miller, G. R. (1980). Detecting deception: The relationship of available information to judgmental accuracy in initial encounters. *Human Communication Research, 6*, 251-264.

Bem, D. J. (1972). Self-perception theory. In L. Berkowitz (Ed.), *Advances in experimental social psychology* (Vol. 6, pp. 1-62). New York: Academic Press.

Bem, D. J., & McConnell, H. K. (1970). Testing the self-perception explanation of dissonance phenomena: On the salience of premanipulation attitudes. *Journal of Personality and Social Psychology, 14*, 23-31.

Berger, C. R., & Calabrese, R. J. (1975). Some explorations in initial interaction and beyond: Toward a developmental theory of interpersonal communication. *Human Communication Research, 1*, 99-112.

Blalock, Jr., H. M. (1969). *Theory construction.* Englewood Cliffs, NJ: Prentice-Hall.

Bochner, A. P. (1981). Forming warm ideas. In C. Wilder-Mott & J. H. Weakland (Eds.), *Rigor and imagination: Essays from the legacy of Gregory Bateson* (pp. 65-81). New York: Praeger.

Bochner, A. P. (1984). The functions of human communication in interpersonal bonding. In C. C. Arnold & J. W. Bowers (Eds.), *Handbook of rhetorical and communication theory* (pp. 544-621). Boston: Allyn and Bacon.

Bochner, A. P., & Eisenberg, E. M. (in press). Legitimizing speech communication: An examination of coherence and cohesion in the development of the discipline. In T. W. Benson (Ed.), *Speech communication in the twentieth century.* Carbondale, IL: Southern Illinois University Press.

Bochner, A. P., & Krueger, D. (1979). Interpersonal communication theory and research: An overview. In D. Nimmo (Ed.), *Communication yearbook 3* (pp. 197-211). New Brunswick, NJ: Transaction Books.

Braithwaite, R. B. (1953). *Scientific explanation.* London: Cambridge University Press.

Brandt, D. R., Miller, G. R., & Hocking, J. E. (1980). The truth-deception attribution: Effects of familiarity on the ability of observers to detect deception. *Human Communication Research, 6*, 99-110.

Burgoon, J. K. (1978). A communication model of personal space violations: Explication and initial test. *Human Communication Research, 4*, 129-142.

Burgoon, M., Jones, S. B., & Stewart, D. (1975). Toward a message centered theory of persuasion: Three empirical investigations of language intensity. *Human Communication Research, 1*, 240-256.

Buss, A. R. (1975). The emerging field of the sociology of psychological knowledge. *American Psychologist, 30*, 988-1002.

Byrne, D. (1971). *The attraction paradigm.* New York: Academic Press.

Care, N. S., & Landesman, C. (Eds.). (1968). *Readings in the theory of action.* Bloomington: Indiana University Press.

Carey, J. W. (1982). The mass media and critical theory: An American view. In M. Burgoon (Ed.), *Communication yearbook 6* (pp. 18-33). Beverly Hills, CA: Sage.

Cartwright, D. (1979). Contemporary social psychology in historical perspective. *Social Psychology, 42,* 82-93.

Cody, M. J., & McLaughin, M. L. (1980). Perceptions of compliance-gaining situations: A dimensional analysis. *Communication Monographs, 47,* 132-148.

Cohen, R. S. (1963). Dialectical materialism and Carnap's logical empiricism. In P. A. Schilpp (Ed.), *The philosophy of Rudolph Carnap* (pp. 99-158). Chicago: Open Court.

Coser, L. A. (1975). Presidential address: Two methods in search of substance. *American Sociological Review, 40,* 691-699.

Cronbach, L. J. (1975). Beyond the two disciplines of scientific psychology. *American Psychologist, 30,* 116-127.

Cushman, D. (1977). The rules perspective as a theoretical basis for the study of human communication. *Communication Quarterly, 25,* 30-45.

Cushman, D., & Whiting, G. (1972). An approach to communication theory: Toward consensus on rules. *Journal of Communication, 22,* 219-238.

Dallmayr, F. R., & McCarthy, T. A. (Eds.). (1977). *Understanding and social inquiry.* Notre Dame, IN: University of Notre Dame Press.

Davidson, D. (1973-1974). On the very idea of a conceptual scheme. *Proceedings of the American Philosophical Association, 17*(11).

Delia, J. (1977). Constructivism and the study of human communication. *Quarterly Journal of Speech, 63,* 66-83.

Delia, J., O'Keefe, B., & O'Keefe, D. (1982). The constructivist approach to communication. In F. Dance (Ed.), *Human communication theory: Comparative essays* (pp. 147-191). New York: Harper & Row.

Ellis, D. G. (1982). Language and speech communication. In M. Burgoon (Ed.), *Communication yearbook 6* (pp. 34-62). Beverly Hills, CA: Sage.

Elms, A. (1975). The crisis in confidence in social psychology. *American Psycholgist, 30,* 967-976.

Festinger, L. (1950). Informal social communication. *Psychological Review, 57,* 271-282.

Festinger, L. (1957). *A theory of cognitive dissonance.* Palo Alto, CA: Stanford University Press.

Feyerabend, P. K. (1976). *Against method.* New York: Humanities Press.

Fisher, B. A. (1978). *Perspectives on human communication.* New York: Macmillan.

Garfinkel, H. (1967). *Studies in ethnomethodology.* Englewood Cliffs, NJ: Prentice-Hall.

Geertz, C. (1973). *The interpretation of cultures.* New York: Basic Books.

Geertz, C. (1980). Blurred genres: The refiguration of social thought. *The American Scholar, 49,* 165-182.

Geller, L. (1982). The failure of self-actualization theory: A Critique of Carl Rogers and Abraham Maslow. *Journal of Humanistic Pschology, 22,* 56-73.

Gergen, K. (1973). Social psychology as history. *Journal of Personality and Social Psychology, 26,* 309-320.

Gergen, K. (1976). Social psychology, science and history. *Personality and Social Psychology Bulletin, 2,* 373-383.

Gergen, K. (1977). Stability, change, and chance in understanding human development. In N. Datan & H. Reese (Eds.), *Life-span developmental psychology: Dialectical perspectives on experimental research* (pp. 135-158). New York: Academic Press.

Gergen, K. (1978). Toward generative theory. *Journal of Personality and Social Psychology, 36.*

Gergen, K. (1980). Toward intellectual audacity in social psychology. In R. Gilmour & S. Duck (Eds.), *The development of social psychology* (pp. 239-270). London: Academic Press.

Gergen, K. (1982). *Toward transformation in social knowledge.* New York: Springer-Verlag.

Geuss, R. (1981). *The idea of a critical theory.* Cambridge: Cambridge University Press.

Glaser, B. G., & Strauss, A. (1967). *The discovery of grounded theory.* Chicago: Aldine.

Greenwald, A. G. (1976). Transhistorical lawfulness of behavior: A comment on two papers. *Personality and Social Psychology Bulletin, 2,* 391.

Grossberg, L. (1979). Language and theorizing in the human sciences. In N. Denzin (Ed.), *Studies in symbolic interaction* (pp. 189-231). Greenwich, CT: Jai Press.

Habermas, J. (1971). *Knowledge and human interest.* Boston, MA: Beacon Press.

Habermas, J. (1976). *Communication and the evolution of society* (T. M. McCarthy, trans.). Boston: Beacon Press.

Hall, C. S., & Lindzey, G. (1970). *Theories of personality.* New York: John Wiley.

Hanna, J. (1982). Two ideals of scientific theorizing. In M. Burgoon (Ed.), *Communication yearbook 5* (pp. 29-47). New Brunswick, NJ: Transaction Books.

Harré, R. (1977). The ethogenic approach: Theory and practice. In L. Berkowitz (Ed.), *Advances in experimental social psychology* (Vol. 10, pp. 283-314). New York: Academic Press.

Harré, R., & Secord, P. F. (1972). *The explanation of social behavior.* Oxford: Blackwell.

Heidegger, M. (1971). *On the way to language* (P. D. Hertz & J. Stambaugh, Trans.). New York: Harper & Row.

Heider, F. (1958). *The psychology of interpersonal relations.* New York: John Wiley.

Held, D. (1980). *Introduction to critical theory.* Berkeley: University of California Press.

Helmreich, R. (1975). Applied social psychology: The unfulfilled promise. *Personality and Social Psychology Bulletin, 1,* 548-560.

Hempel, C. (1966). *Philosophy of natural science.* Englewood Cliffs, NJ: Prentice-Hall.

Henry, J. (1971). *Pathways to madness.* New York: Vintage Books.

Hesse, M. B. (1966). *Models and analogies in science.* Notre Dame, IN: University of Notre Dame Press.

Hocking, J. E., Bauchner, J. E., Kaminski, E. P., & Miller, G. R. (1979). Detecting deceptive communication from verbal, visual, and paralinguistic cues. *Human Communication Research, 6,* 33-46.

Hogan, R. T., & Embler, N. P. (1978). The biases in contemporary social psychology. *Social Research, 45,* 478-534.

Hollis, M. (1977). *Models of man.* London: Cambridge University Press.

Hovland, C. I., Janis, I. L., & Kelley, H. H. (1953). *Communication and persuasion.* New Haven, CT: Yale University Press.

Israel, J. (1972). Stipulations and construction in the social sciences. In J. Israel & H. Tajfel (Eds.), *The context of social psychology: A critical assessment* (pp. 123-211). New York: Academic Press.

Jones, E. E., & Davis, K. E. (1965). From acts to dispositions: The attribution process in person perception. In L. Berkowitz (Ed.), *Advances in experimental social psychology* (Vol. 2, pp. 219-266). New York: Academic Press.

Kant, I. (1909). Fundamental principles of the metaphysics of morals. In T. K. Abbott (trans.), *Critique of practical reason and other works* (pp. 1-84). New York: Longmans. Originally published in 1785.

Kelley, H. H. (1972). *Causal schemata and the attribution process.* Morristown, NJ: General Learning Press.

Kelman, H. C. (1972). The rights of the subject in social research: An analysis in terms of relative power and legitimacy. *American Psychologist, 27,* 989-1016.

Knapp, M. L., & Comadena, M. E. (1979). Telling it like it isn't: A review of theory and research on deceptive communications. *Human Communication Research , 5,* 270-285.

Koch, S. (1976). Language communities, search cells, and the psychological studies. In W. J. Arnold (Ed.), *Nebraska symposium on motivation 1975* (pp. 477-559). Lincoln: University of Nebraska Press.

Koch, S. (1981). The nature and limits of psychological knowledge: Lessons of a century qua "science." *American Psychologist, 36,* 257-269.

Kuhn, T. S. (1962). *The structure of scientific revolutions.* Chicago: University of Chicago Press.

Kuhn, T. S. (1970). Reflections on my critics. In I. Lakatos & A. Musgrave (Eds.), *Criticism and the growth of knowledge* (pp. 231-278). Cambridge, England: University Press.

Kuhn, T. S. (1977). *The essential tension: Selected studies in scientific tradition and change.* Chicago: University of Chicago Press.

Lanigan, R. L., & Strobl, R. L. (1981). A critical theory approach. In D. D. Nimmo & K. R. Sanders (Eds.), *Handbook of political communication* (pp. 141-167). Beverly Hills, CA: Sage.

Levine, N. (1976). On the metaphysics of social psychology: A critical view. *Human Relations, 29,* 385-400.

Marwell, G., & Schmitt, D. R. (1967). Dimensions of compliance-gaining behaviors: An empirical analysis. *Sociometry, 30,* 350-364.

Marx, M. H. (Ed.). (1951). *Psychological theory: Contemporary readings.* New York: Macmillan.

Maslow, A. (1968). *Toward a psychology of being.* New York: Van Nostrand.

McCroskey, J. C. (1977). Oral communication apprehension: A summary of recent theory and research. *Human Communication Research, 4*, 78-96.

McGuire, W. J. (1967). Some impending reorientations in social psychology: Some thoughts provoked by Kenneth Ring. *Journal of Experimental Social Psychology, 3*, 124-139.

McGuire, W. J. (1969). The nature of attitudes and attitude change. In G. Lindsey & E. Aronson (Eds.), *Handbook of social psychology* (Vol. 3, pp. 136-314). Reading, MA: Addison-Wesley.

McGuire, W. J. (1973). The yin and yang of progress in social psychology: Seven Koans. *Journal of Personality and Social Psychology, 26*, 446-456.

McLaughlin, M. L., Cody, M. J., & Robey, C. (1980). Situational influences on the selection of strategies to resist compliance-gaining attempts. *Human Communication Research, 7*, 14-36.

Menzel, H. (1978). Meaning—Who needs it? In M. Brenner, P. Marsh, & M. Brenner (Eds.), *The social contexts of method* (pp. 140-171). New York: St. Martin's Press.

Miller, G. R. (1978). The current status of theory and research in interpersonal communication. *Human Communication Research, 4*, 164-178.

Miller, G. R. (1983). Taking stock of a discipline. *Journal of Communication, 33*, 31-41.

Miller, G. R., & Berger, C. R. (1978). On keeping the faith in matters scientific. *Western Journal of Speech Communication, 42*, 44-57.

Miller, G. R., Boster, F., Roloff, M., & Seibold, D. (1977). Compliance-gaining message strategies: A typology and some findings concerning effects of situational differences. *Communication Monographs, 44*, 37-51.

Miller, G. R., & Burgoon, M. (1978). Persuasion research: Review and commentary. In B. D. Ruben (Ed.), *Communication yearbook 2* (pp. 29-47). New Brunswick, NJ: Transaction.

Mischel, T. (1969). Scientific and philosophical psychology: A historical introduction. In T. Mischel (Ed.), *Human action* (pp. 1-40). New York: Academic Press.

Moscovici, S. (1972). Society and theory in social psychology. In J. Israel & H. Tajfel (Eds.), *The context of social psychology: A critical assessment* (pp. 17-68). New York: Academic Press.

Nagel, E. (1961). *The structure of science*. New York: Harcourt Brace Jovanovich.

O'Keefe, D. J. (1975). Logical empiricism and the study of human communication. *Speech Monographs, 42*, 169-183.

Pearce, W. B. (1976). The coordinated management of meaning: A rules-based theory of interpersonal communication. In G. R. Miller (Ed.), *Explorations in interpersonal communication* (pp. 17-35). Beverly Hills, CA: Sage.

Pearce, W. B. (1977). Metatheoretical concerns in communication. *Communication Quarterly, 25*, 3-6.

Pearce, W. B., & Cronen, V. (1980). *Communication, action, and meaning*. New York: Praeger.

Polanyi, M. (1962). Tacit knowing and its bearing on some problems of philosophy. *Review of Modern Physics, 34*, 601-616.

Polanyi, M. (1966). *The tacit dimension*. Garden City, NY: Doubleday.

Popper, K. R. (1957). *The poverty of historicism*. London: Routledge and Kegan Paul.

Popper, K. R. (1968). *The logic of scientific discovery*. New York: Harper & Row.

Rabinow, P., & Sullivan, W. M. (Eds.). (1979). *Interpretive social science*. Berkeley: University of California Press.

Rickman, H. P. (Ed.). (1961). *Meaning in history: W. Dilthey's thoughts on history*. London: George Allen and Unwin.

Ricoeur, P. (1971). The model of the text. *Social Research, 38*, 529-555.

Ring, K. (1967). Some sober questions about frivolous values. *Journal of Experimental Social Psychology, 3*, 113-123.

Rogers, C. (1961). *On becoming a person*. Boston: Houghton Mifflin.

Rogers, E. M. (1982). The empirical and the critical schools of communication research. In M. Burgoon (Ed.), *Communication yearbook 5* (pp. 125-144). New Brunswick, NJ: Transaction Books.

Rommetveit, R. (1980). On "meanings" of acts and what is meant and made known by what is said in a pluralistic social world. In M. Brenner (Ed.), *The structure of action* (pp. 108-149). New York: St. Martin's Press.

Rorty, R. (1979). *Philosophy and the mirror of nature*. Princeton, NJ: Princeton University Press.

Rorty, R. (1980). A reply to Dreyfus and Taylor. *Review of Metaphysics, 34*, 47-55.

Rorty, R. (1982). *Consequences of pragmatism (Essays: 1972-1980)*. Minneapolis: University of Minnesota Press.

Rorty, R. (1984). *Solidarity or objectivity*. Paper presented at the University of Iowa Symposium on the rhetoric of the human sciences, Iowa City, Iowa.

Rosnow, R. L. (1978). The prophetic vision of Giambattista Vico: Implications for the state of social psychological theory. *Journal of Personality and Social Psychology, 36*, 1322-1331.

Rossides, D. W. (1968). *The history and nature of sociological theory*. Boston: Houghton Mifflin.

Rotter, J. B. (1955). The role of the psychological situation in determining the direction of human behavior. In M. R. Jones (Ed.), *Nebraska symposium on motivation* (Vol. 3, pp. 245-268). Lincoln: University of Nebraska.

Rotter, J. B. (1975). Some problems and misconceptions related to the construct of internal versus external control of reinforcement. *Journal of Consulting and Clinical Psychology, 43*, 56-67.

Rudner, R. (1966). *Philosophy of social science*. Englewood Cliffs, NJ: Prentice-Hall.

Rychlak, J. F. (1968). *A philosophy of science for personality theory*. Boston: Houghton Mifflin.

Sacks, H., Jefferson, G., & Schegloff, E. A. (1974). A simplest systematics for the organization of turn-taking for conversation. *Language, 50*, 696-735.

Sampson, E. E. (1975). On justice as equality. *Journal of Social Issues, 31*, 45-64.

Sampson, E. E. (1977). Psychology and the American ideal. *Journal of Personality and Social Psychology, 35*, 767-782.

Sampson, E. E. (1978). Scientific paradigms and social values: Wanted—a scientific revolution. *Journal of Personality and Social Psychology, 36*, 1332-1343.

Schegloff, E. A. (1972). Notes on a conversational practice: Formulating place. In D. N. Sudnow (Ed.), *Studies in social interaction*. New York: Free Press.

Schlenker, B. R. (1974). Social psychology and science. *Journal of Personality and Social Psychology, 29*, 1-15.

Schlenker, B. R. (1976). Social psychology and science: Another look. *Personality and Social Psychology Bulletin, 2*, 418-420.

Schutz, A. (1967). Concept and theory formation in the social sciences. In M. Natanson (Ed.), *Collected papers of Alfred Schutz* (pp. 48-66). The Hague: Martinus Nijhoff.

Schutz, A. (1970). *On phenomenology and social relations* (H. R. Wagner, Ed.). Chicago: University of Chicago Press.

Schutz, A. (1971). Collected papers: Volume I: The problems of social reality (M. Natanson, Ed.). The Hague: Matinus Nijoff.

Searle, J. R. (1969). *Speech acts: An essay in the philosophy of language*. London: Cambridge University Press.

Shimanoff, S. B. (1980). *Communication rules: Theory and research*. Beverly Hills, CA: Sage.

Shotter, J. (1975). *Images of man in psychological research*. London: Methuen.

Sigman, S. J. (1980). On communication rules from a social perspective. *Human Communication Research, 7*, 37-51.

Sillars, A. L. (1980). Stranger and spouse as target persons for compliance-gaining strategies. *Human Communication Research, 6*, 265-279.

Skinner, B. F. (1971). *Beyond freedom and dignity*. New York: Random House.

Slack, J. D., & Allor M. (1983). The political and epistemological constituents of critical communication research. *Journal of Communication, 33*, 208-218.

Sluzki, C., & Ransom, D. C. (Eds.). (1976). *Double bind: The foundation of the communicational approach to the family*. New York: Grune and Stratton.

Smith, M. B. (1972). Is experimental social psychology advancing? *Journal of Experimental Social Psychology, 8*, 86-96.

Snyder, M. (1979). Self-monitoring processes. In L. Berkowitz (Ed.), *Advances in experimental social psychology* (Vol. 12, pp. 85-128). New York: Academic Press.

Stroebe, W. (1980). Process loss in social psychology: Failure to exploit? In R. Gilmour & S. Duck (Eds.), *The development of social psychology* (pp. 181-205). New York: Academic Press.

Tajfel, H. (1972). Experiments in a vacuum. In J. Israel & H. Tajfel (Eds.), *The context of social psychology* (pp. 69-119). New York: Academic Press.

Taylor, C. (1977). Interpretation and the sciences of man. In F. R. Dallmayr & T. A. McCarthy (Eds.), *Understanding and social inquiry* (pp. 101-131). Notre Dame, IN: University of Notre Dame Press.

Taylor, C. (1980). Understanding in human science. *Review of Metaphysics, 34,* 3-23.

Thibaut, J. W., & Kelley, H. H. (1959). *The social psychology of groups.* New York: John Wiley.

Toulmin, S. (1969). Concepts and the explanation of human behavior. In T. Mischel (Ed.), *Human action* (pp. 71-104). New York: Academic Press.

Toulmin, S. (1981). The charm of the scout. In C. Wilder-Mott & J. Weakland (Eds.), *Rigor and imagination: Essays from the legacy of Gregory Bateson* (pp. 357-368). New York: Praeger.

Vico, G. (1975). *The life of Giambattista Vico: Written by himself* (M. H. Fisch & T. G. Bergen, Eds. and Trans.). Ithaca, NY: Cornell University Press. Orginally published in 1725.

Walster, E., Walster, G. W., & Berscheid, E. (1978). *Equity: Theory and research.* Boston, MA: Allyn and Bacon.

Weber, M. (1949). "Objectivity" in social science and social policy. In E. A. Shils & H. A. Finch (Eds.), *The methodology of the social sciences* (pp. 72-111). New York: Macmillan.

Weber, M. (1968). Basic sociological terms. In G. Roth & C. Wittich (Eds.), *Economy and society* (pp. 4-26). New York: Bedminster Press.

Wilder-Mott, C., & Weakland, J. H. (Eds.). (1981). *Rigor and imagination: Essays from the legacy of Gregory Bateson.* New York: Praeger.

Winch, P. (1958). *The idea of a social science and its relation to philosophy.* London: Routledge and Kegan Paul.

Wittgenstein, L. (1953). *Philosophical investigations* (G. Anscombe, Trans.). New York: Macmillan.

Von Wright, G. W. (1968). An essay in deotic logic and the general theory of action. *Acta Philosophica Fennica, 21,* 11-107.

2 Temporal Qualities of Interpersonal Relationships

CAROL M. WERNER
LOIS M. HAGGARD

University of Utah

I T is a common experience that time is an integral aspect of interpersonal relationships. Relationships grow and change, continue, develop, and even disintegrate over time. Although theorizing has often addressed these dynamic qualities, research on relationships is often criticized for its static approach (for example, emphasis on brief interactions between strangers; absence of longitudinal research), and there have been exhortations to treat relationships from a more dynamic perspective (for example, Burgess & Huston, 1979; Rogers & Kincaid, 1981; Wiggins, 1979). The purpose of the present chapter is to provide a framework and an expanded vocabulary for identifying a variety of temporal aspects of interpersonal relationships, especially aspects pertaining to communication processes between individuals. Our goal is to begin to understand time in relation to and as an integral aspect of communication and relationships.

A number of authors have examined various psychological qualities of time, and we will draw heavily on their analyses in the present overview (Gibson, 1975; Hoornaert, 1973; Lynch, 1972; McGrath & Rotchford, 1983; Rakowski, 1979; Werner, Altman, & Oxley, in press). To begin, we will develop a framework based on one originally used for examining homes as transactional unities (Werner et al., in press) but that can fruitfully be applied to communication in interpersonal relationships. We will show how temporal qualities contribute in important ways to defining, developing, and maintaining relationships. In this review, we will focus on communication broadly defined and at many levels of analysis, that is, things that people do to and for each other that define their relationship, ranging from micro-level (for example, communication patterns, exchange processes) to macro-level analyses (for example, friendship stages, social networks) and including such topics as communication processes, social exchange, social penetration and self-disclosure, network analysis, interpersonal responsivity, and interpersonal attraction. In all of this, we will endeavor to show how an understanding of

AUTHORS' NOTE: We would like to thank Irwin Altman for helpful comments on an earlier draft of this chapter.

time will enhance our understanding of interpersonal relationships, as an understanding of relationships will enhance our understanding of time.

In their excellent review, McGrath and Rotchford (1983) summarized several questions about time that—despite considerable debate and attention —have remained unresolved for centuries. McGrath and Rotchford suggested that the questions actually are not resolvable, but that cultures develop ways of viewing time that represent a particular orientation to the issues (see also Hall, 1983). One of their central questions is whether time is linear or cyclical, and another is whether it is integral to events or separate from them. McGrath and Rotchford suggested that psychologists have adopted both views on both issues, and we will do the same. Our intention is to explore the heuristic utility and implications of these constructs rather than arbitrarily choose between them at the outset.

The proposed model is composed of the two overarching dimensions of linear and cyclical time, and the four subordinate qualities of temporal salience, sequencing, scale, and pace/rhythm. Thus we retain the traditional distinction between linear and cyclical time and will examine how the two might operate in interpersonal relationships. As we shall see, each quality contributes somewhat differently to development, maintenance, stability, and dissolution.

LINEAR AND CYCLICAL TIME

Linear time and its familiar continuum of past/present/future contains two important qualities: First is the dynamic, flowing, changing, and ongoing aspect of events; and second is continuity. Dynamic linear time can be seen readily in work on initiating and ending encounters (for example, Albert & Kessler, 1976, 1978; Berscheid & Graziano, 1979) and the development and dissolution of relationships (for example, Altman & Taylor, 1973; Braiker & Kelley, 1979; Levinger, 1976, 1979; Hill, Rubin, & Peplau, 1976). All of this work focuses on understanding how behaviors and relationships change over time. Dynamic qualities can also be seen in work that examines micro aspects of relationships, that is, specific things that people do to and for each other that maintain or otherwise affect the quality of their relationship, such as theory and research on self-fulfilling prophecy (Darley & Fazio, 1980; Snyder, Tanke, & Berscheid, 1977), behavioral exchange and interdependence (Gergen, 1969; Kelley & Thibaut, 1978; Thibaut & Kelley, 1959), and interpersonal responsivity (Davis, Rainey, & Brock, 1976; Rosenfeld, 1966a, 1966b; Werner & Latané, 1974).

The second quality, continuity, indicates that aspects of the past are carried into the present and projected into the future. It can be seen in work that examines the history of relationships and the role of history in the quality and future of relationships (Altman & Taylor, 1973; Levinger & Huesmann, 1980; Kelley & Thibaut, 1978), as well as studies of how friendship networks remain stable over time.

Although continuity and change can be defined independently, they generally coexist and complement one another. As we shall see below, a number of models of friendship formation address the issue of how continuity (history of the relationship) and change (increasing range of communication or information exchange, affect, and activities) fit together to define the nature of a relationship. Continuity and change have also been studied in social networks in which continuity usually refers to long-term relations and change refers to the incorporation of new members or the loss of old members (Mitchell, 1969; Wellman, 1979; Wellman & Leighton, 1979). Traditionally, researchers studied social structure and composition and were only interested in enduring relationships; they considered the loss of a group member or the inclusion of a new member to be nuisances because such changes reduced statistical reliability and therefore the researcher's ability to demonstrate that the structure was genuine (Nadel, 1958). More recently, with the advent of network concepts, both continuity and change in network membership have become topics of interest (Rogers & Kincaid, 1981; Whitten & Wolfe, 1973). For example, Rogers and Kincaid (1981) suggested that changes in network members would be likely unless (1) members were in close spatial proximity; (2) members had made reciprocal choices; (3) the links were homophilous (based on attitudinal similarity); and (4) the links were ascribed (for example, based on kinship) rather than achieved.

A number of studies demonstrate the utility of examining networks for continuity and change, and the mechanisms that contribute to each. In a study of grade-school children's networks, Hallinan (1978) found that (1) symmetric dyads (dyads involving mutual choice of partners or mutual liking) were more stable over six-week intervals than asymmetric dyads and (2) asymmetric dyads were more likely to change to null dyads than to become symmetrical. The children seemed to have stable friendships, and the inclusion of a new member (mutual choice following asymmetric choice) was the exception rather than the rule. In a study of adults' networks, Hammer (1980) found that the best predictor of whether individuals would be included in each others' networks over time was network density (the proportion of mutual acquaintances when interviewed one, two, or six months previously). Hammer concluded that in densely connected networks, there was pressure toward completing the missing connections, that is, friends introduced their friends to each other. However, in relatively loosely connected networks, there was little pressure for maintenance, and the connections tended to be broken off. However, Hammer cautioned that other pressures may operate, and continuity should not be assumed in either the loose or dense situation because networks are fluid and changing entities: To Hammer, change, not continuity, should be assumed.

The second overarching dimension that we will consider refers to cyclical properties of relationships, that is, repetitive and recurring activities, patterns of activity, and psychological experiences between people. A precise definition of cyclical time denotes identical repetitions, time after time. However, Werner et al. (in press) noted that in Western culture, cyclical time contains a linear underlining, such that what occurred once may recur in similar but not identical form. They proposed the term "spiralling time" to capture this notion that repeated activities can contain both continuity and change.

Phenomenologically oriented writers have been most sensitive to cyclical or regular patterns of behavior (Bachelard, 1964; Eliade, 1959; Korosec-Serfaty, in press; Saile, in press; Seamon, 1979, 1982), suggesting that cyclical patterns are comfortable and predictable, and promote stronger bonds between interactants and greater satisfaction with relationships. However, it is also possible that familiar routines can become stultifying and boring (Rodin, 1982), and the idea of spiralling time suggests a need for a balance between regularity and change. Indeed, Werner and Latané (1974) argued that an important basis for conspecific attraction is an optimum degree of novelty and unpredictability. Similarly, Kelvin (1977), citing Helson's adaptation-level theory, suggested the need for "optimal" levels of predictability in relationships.

A number of authors have used the terms cycle, cycling, or cyclicity in theories about relationship development, maintenance, and change. For example, exchange theorists often articulate the exchange process as one involving cycles of interaction followed by reward/cost evaluations; marriage and family counselors suggest that aversive cyclical events often underlie spousal problems and other aspects of troubled families (Patterson & Cobb, 1973; Stuart, Broderick, & Gurman, 1982; Turner & Dodd, 1979); similarly, cyclical processes have been used to explain self-fulfilling prophecy (Darley & Fazio, 1980), comprehensibility of conversations (Argyle, 1978; Riegel & Meacham, 1978); mutual influence in expressive behavior (Cappella, 1981), and other micro-level interpersonal behaviors. At a somewhat broader level of analysis is Rodin's (1982) hypothesis that in friendship formation, people take into consideration the "implicit reciprocation cycle" (p. 41) and gauge their interactions so as to pace the implicit degree of commitment and obligatory future interaction. Altman, Vinsel, and Brown (1981) discussed the various ways in which friends cycle back and forth between periods of openness and closedness, intimacy and nonintimacy, and how the cycles might change over the course of a relationship.

As we shall see, it is sometimes difficult to distinguish cyclical from linear patterns, especially when continuity and change are incorporated into cyclical/spiralling time. For heuristic purposes, we will keep distinct linear from cyclical by stressing that linearity refers to constancy and accumulation, overlaid with change and growth, whereas cyclicity refers to the cessation and recurrence of similar activities and feelings, or, in other cases, to a cycle in which behavior progresses repeatedly from a point of origin, through a pattern, and back to the same or very similar point of origin.

An interesting aspect of cyclical time is synchrony (Lynch, 1972) or entrainment (McGrath & Rotchford, 1983; McGrath, Kelly, & Matchatka, 1984), in which one cycle is adapted to or coordinated with another. Riegel and Meacham (1978) described conversation, or the dialogue process, as a series of cycling exchanges that must be coordinated if a conversation is to progress smoothly. As an example, they stressed that one of the critical aspects of language development resides in the mother's and child's ability to coordinate or synchronize the pace and complexity of their communication. In a similar vein, Thibaut and Kelley (1959) and Gergen (1969) suggested that people are able to develop satisfying exchanges to the extent that they can accommodate their reward/cost patterns to their partner's. Thibaut and Kelley suggested that synchronization of rewards was most likely to occur when both partners were responding to the same external cue, were in roles that fit together well, or one partner was highly accomodating to the other; however, they did not provide evidence to support these ideas.

Entrainment also occurs at more general levels of behavior: Couples adapt their day to one or both partners' work schedules; married couples live apart (Pepitone-Rockwell, 1980); and shift-workers and their families (McGrath et al., 1984) must make extensive adjustments to see each other. Often the inability to entrain can be disruptive to the relationship. Altman, Taylor, and Wheeler (1971) suggested that two strangers could tolerate isolation together if they were able to mesh or synchronize their activity patterns early in the isolation period. Hill et al. (1976), in a two-year longitudinal study, found that dating couples tended to be more likely to break up during "key turning points of the school year" (p. 156), such as between school terms and during vacations. One of Hill et al.'s explanations for this phenomenon was that changes in course schedule or other activities made it difficult for students to maintain their previous routine of interaction. Hill et al. speculated that this disruption could also interact with internal factors by providing a convenient excuse for the breakup. Thus entrainment can play a potentially important pragmatic and psychological role in relationship formation and maintenance.

The concepts of linear and cyclical time are overarching features of the proposed framework. As noted above, they are not wholly separable; nevertheless, for our purposes, it is heuristically useful to distinguish between them. Linear and cyclical time can be described in terms of a variety of other qualities, four of which will be detailed below. These are the qualities of *temporal salience, sequencing, scale, and pace/rhythm*. The choice of three of these qualities (salience, scale, and pace/rhythm) was based on the framework proposed by Werner et al. (in press), and all four have been included because of the ready availability of examples in the interpersonal relations literature.

Salience

Linear Salience

The first quality is temporal salience, or time orientation (Hoornaert, 1973; Rakowski, 1979), which refers to the extent to which one's thoughts are relatively past-, present-, or future-oriented. Linear salience could refer to a single relationship or many and would indicate that one's thoughts about the friends were focused primarily on one time period, or a comparison of one time period to another. It could also refer to a comparison between friends, such as when one compares a current partner with a former one (for example, Newman, 1982). Linear salience is a central notion of many theories of interpersonal attraction and friendship. Three areas in which linear salience was found to play an important role were (1) possessions, (2) self-presentation, and (3) evaluation.

Possessions and Places. In their extensive interviews with people about the meanings of personal possessions, Csikszentmihalyi and Rochberg-Halton (1981) found that for many people, things had meaning because of their association with family and friends. Salience in this context refers to whether the object triggered memories of the past (for example, a family vacation), experiences of the general present (for example, ongoing family activities), or plans for the future (for example, an intended heirloom). Korosec-Serfaty (in press) also found that people kept things in their attics and cellars because they provided continuity, both within a respondent's own lifetime (for example, reminding him of people from the past) and across the generations (for example, family heirlooms, even those contributed by the current resident as a way of inserting himself into the generational flow). Werner et al. (in press) noted that objects could have more than one temporal locus, even being simultaneously past, present, and future salient, depending upon the memories that were elicited at any particular time.

Both Furby (1978) and Howell (1980) have suggested that objects can represent relationships and that people would keep even nonutilitarian possessions because of the memories that they contained. In particular, they pointed to people living in small apartments or retirement homes who lived crowded by furniture and memorabilia from their homes rather than lose their pasts. Furby's and Howell's work would suggest that one could use attachment to possessions as an index of the quality of a relationship, however, others (Csikszentmihalyi & Rochberg-Halton, 1981; Rakowski, 1979; Tognoli, 1980) argued that there are large individual differences in the extent to which this is true. Furthermore, Lynch (1972) noted that people are selective in what artifacts are retained as present representations of the past and generally only retain things congruent with a desired image.

With respect to possessions, the concept of salience suggests that people can communicate through what they give to each other, what they choose to display or hide, keep or discard, and—especially—through what temporal qualities are evident in what they say about their possessions.

Self-Presentation. Some of the most striking effects of temporal salience occur when experimental subjects expect to interact with an alleged partner. Sometimes subjects are led to anticipate interaction simply to induce honest responding (for example, Derlega, Harris, & Chaikin, 1973). However, in many studies, the impact of expected interaction has been the researcher's focus. In general, people are much nicer to each other when they expect to meet. For example, Darley and Berscheid (1967) and Sutherland and Insko (1979) found that subjects thought they were more similar to a person they expected to meet than one they did not expect to meet. And, using the Prisoner's Dilemma paradigm, Shure and Meeker (1968), Marlowe, Gergen, and Doob (1966), and Bond and Dutton (1975) found more cooperative than competitive choices when future interaction was anticipated.

Davis et al. (1976) conducted a series of studies in which subjects were instructed to give pleasurable vibrations to an unknown partner when the partner (actually a confederate of the experimenter) performed a task correctly. In one version of the experiment, subjects anticipated future interaction with the confederate. The results are very complex, especially because of the sexual connotations of the pleasuring. However, when sexual connotations were reduced, Davis et al. found that subjects administered more pleasure when they anticipated future interaction than when they did not.

These studies suggest that merely expecting to meet someone induces positive behaviors, and because each study focused on a different underlying motive for the behavior (for example, fear of retaliation, desire for a positive interaction, wanting to be liked), a future orientation seems to have broad impact.

Anticipation of a partner's future *behaviors* can also influence current behaviors toward the partner (Altman & Taylor, 1973; Davis, 1962; Kelley & Thibaut, 1978; Levinger & Huesmann, 1980). Davis (1962) conducted a study in which women expected to interact with either a dominating or a passive partner. When the situation favored cooperation, those who expected a passive partner were themselves more dominating, presumably in order to offset the partner's anticipated passivity; those who expected a dominant partner were more passive, as though waiting for the other to take control. Similarly, in the Marlowe et al. (1966) study mentioned above, some subjects expected to interact with a humble, self-effacing person and others expected to interact with an egotistical, self-centered person. Cooperation was greater in anticipation of a humble partner, and competition was greater in anticipation of an egotistical partner. These various studies indicate that a future orientation can be an important determinant of behavior and that subjects tend to be positive unless the partner's anticipated behavior contraindicates that approach.

Evaluation. The roles of past, present, and future salience have been considered much more systematically in several "exchange theories" of interpersonal behavior. The concept of salience is a familiar part of Thibaut and Kelley's (1959) interdependence theory and Rusbult's recent extensions of it (Rusbult, 1980, 1983; Rusbult, Zembrodt, & Gunn, 1982). In the original formulation, Thibaut and Kelley proposed that people develop friendships with others that maximize their perceived rewards while minimizing their perceived costs. Judgments of a relationship's quality are not absolute, but are made relative to a person's internal standard, or comparison level (CL). The comparison level represents the cumulation of past experiences, reward/cost comparisons, and satisfactions with other partners, and is based only on information that is salient at the time of evaluation.

The concept of salience also fits in a similar way into Thibaut and Kelley's second comparison standard: The comparison level for alternatives (CL-alt). According to Thibaut and Kelley (1959), the CL-alt is used to decide whether the relationship being evaluated is better than others currently available; one might stay in a relationship that is less satisfying than one's typical relationship (the CL) simply because nothing more favorable can be found. Thus if a person forgets about a more attractive partner (that is, assigns that partner zero weight in the CL-alt calculation) or doesn't expect the other relationship to flourish (assigns low weight), the current partner will be more attractive than the CL-alt, and future interaction with him or her will be anticipated.

The two comparison standards can contain information from the past and present, and therefore can be past- or present-salient. To the extent that they determine future interaction, they are also future-salient. Thibaut and Kelley said that the two standards could be highly variable because of the variable salience of information in memory. They suggested that salience could be influenced by differential importance and validity of information, as well as inaccuracy of memory as affected by recency of interaction, environmental stimuli that triggered memories, the locus of behavior, optimism, and other such factors. For example, if most of one's relationships have been going well recently, that is given more weight than past unpleasantness and the CL will rise; similarly, if one expects to obtain high rewards from an interaction sometime in the near future, the CL will also rise. In this theory, temporal salience is an inherently dynamic construct and an important aspect of satisfaction with and commitment to a relationship.

In their second examination of interdependence, Kelley & Thibaut (1978) described how temporal salience could affect one's evaluation of a partner even without comparing him or her to other relationships. As partners interact, they develop probability estimates of each other's future behaviors and use those forecasts to decide whether to make a deeper commitment to the relationship. "The individual's decision to move further into the relationship is made on the basis of some increase in certainty that (a) the relationship will be rewarding (and low in cost) and (b) he [sic] will not be exploited or abruptly abandoned" (p. 232). Kelley and Thibaut's discussion of this process is primarily present- and future-oriented, however, presumably past experiences with the partner enter into the probability estimates, thereby making the evaluation of the partner a mix of past-, present-, and future-salient.

Levinger and Huesmann's (Huesmann & Levinger, 1976; Levinger & Huesmann, 1980) "incremental exchange theory" is similarly past-, present-, and future-salient. They proposed that two people could be in a variety of states of involvement (that is, degrees of friendship) in a relationship and that each partner would have a set of possible behaviors appropriate to each state, as well as holding a probability estimate for predicting each behavior that his or her partner could do. Each partner would also know the costs of each behavior in his or her repertoire, though the costs/rewards of identical behaviors would be different for different states of the relationship. In addition, Levinger and Huesmann proposed that each person would be aware of the payoff matrix, or outcomes for each partner after the pair interacted. The person's decision of how to act would be based on a complex assessment of these past- and future-oriented considerations. Levinger and Huesmann were not specific about how information would be weighted and combined to make these estimates.

There are two additional future-oriented features to their model: "depth of search" and "reward slope." Levinger and Huesmann proposed that people anticipate future interactions and their outcomes before deciding on a current behavior. People could look ahead to one exchange, a chain of exchanges, or a variety of chains of exchanges. The "depth of search" refers to the number of future exchanges that would be included in this look-ahead period. The "reward slope" refers to the idea that reward values might change over time, and one might stay in a costly relationship now in anticipation of large rewards in the future. Levinger and Huesmann proposed that during the period of looking toward the future, and prior to deciding how to act, the partner would consider all possible behavior combinations and their outcomes, as well as the state or stage of relationship that they implied. These authors proposed that differential weights could be assigned to expected behaviors at each future step, but that on the whole, the current behavior would be chosen so as to maximize the payoffs over the anticipated series of behaviors. Their model is extremely complex and assumes that people combine information from different temporal periods in deciding on behavior. In this model, future orientation is stressed, however, it is implicit that the future is based in part on the past, and, furthermore, in allowing for differential weighting, it permits the past to play a relatively strong or weak role in determining behavior.

Temporal salience also fits prominently into Altman and Taylor's (1973) Social Penetration Theory. They, too, proposed that partners evaluate and compare their current relationship's quality to an internal subjective standard based on prior experiences (that is, the past-salient "central memory"). In addition, Altman and Taylor proposed a forecasting process in which partners attempted to predict what the future rewards and costs of interaction would be and tried to develop a general picture of the other person. Similar to Thibaut and Kelley's CL-alt, these forecasts fit into the decisions to remain in the relationship.

A more critical and unique feature of the proposed forecast process was that it was instrumental in moving the relationship into deeper intimacy. That is, partners would imagine interactions of a more intimate nature and visualize the costs and rewards of intimacy; if the forecast was positive, then the individual would anticipate a closer friendship, otherwise the relationship would continue at the same intimacy level. Altman and Taylor argued that without this forecast mechanism, no relationship would grow or become intimate; people would only participate in exchanges of known cost/reward ratios. In their view, then, future salience is what determines the future growth of the relationship.

In this brief review, we have shown how past, present, and future salience have been included in several models that stress behavioral exchange as a basis for relationship development. In each of them, current behavior can be influenced by memories of past experiences in the current relationship, memories of past experiences in other relationships, evaluations of present alternatives, and predictions and expectations for the current as well as alternative relationships. Each model emphasizes the temporal aspects a little differently and fits them into behavior somewhat differently. For example, in Altman and Taylor's work, as well as in Levinger and Huesmann's, the forecast mechanism is what moves the relationship into deeper and more intimate levels; Kelley and Thibaut do not consider intimacy per se in their description of forecasting, but simply say that there is a greater commitment to the relationship if prospects for continued low-cost rewards are high.

There is a need for greater precision in all of these models with respect to temporal salience. Only Levinger and Huesmann are very specific about how far the future extends in the "look-ahead" process, whereas Altman and Taylor and Kelley and Thibaut refer to a vague and unspecified future. Furthermore, although all of them allowed for differential weighting of the past, present, and future, none provided details about the determinants of the weights. And although temporal salience was often implicit in discussions (for example, persons whose comparison levels were based on romanticized recollections of the past; Levinger's [1976] discussion of length of marriage as a "barrier" to its dissolution, and so forth), none explicitly considered the consequences of assigning greater weight to one temporal orientation or another.

And finally, although each model acknowledges that people evaluate their friends subjectively, the tone of all of these models is that once the information is in memory, the representation is accurate. There is little if any sensitivity to reconstructive memory processes, and how such processes might affect evaluations of the current or alternative relationships. People often reconstruct memories of events so that they "make sense" and in the process often distort memories to be consistent with original expectations or current needs (for example, Srull & Wyer, 1980; Wyer & Carlson, 1979; Wyer & Srull, 1980; see also Linton, 1975). For example, Matlin and Stang (1978) suggested that a "Pollyanna principle" guides memory, such that negative events are lost or modified and generally less available than are positive events. Linton (1983) suggested that negative information could be accessed, but that stronger cues were needed to elicit negative than positive information. In contrast, of course, are people who romanticize the past, falsely emphasizing the positive and deemphasizing the negative. Thus the memories on which individuals base their comparison levels (CL and CL-alt, Central Memory, and so forth) should not be assumed to be accurate and indeed may be more interesting for their subjectivity.

Cyclical Salience

In cyclical time, temporal salience refers to the time orientation of a recurrent activity. This could occur during a current enactment, when one recalls a previous similar event or projects to a future one. For example, during Christmas holiday celebrations in many families, it is customary to reminisce about previous Christmas celebrations, as well as to anticipate the next one. Or cyclical salience could refer to recollections and anticipations in the absence of a current enactment, such as when one discusses Christmas preparations or past Christmas activities during the summer. Although we have given the example of an important annual event, cyclical salience could refer to any kind of event, of any temporal scope.

As there is little systematic research on cyclicity, it is difficult to know what its role might be in interpersonal processes. Cyclical salience would likely parallel linear salience in terms of the three areas described above (possessions, self-presentation, and evaluation), but salience would only refer to recurrent activities or uses. Thus possessions would have meaning because of their recurrent use in family rituals; self presentation processes would intensify because of expected extended involvement; and evaluations (for example, the CL and CL-alt) would include recurrent activities between friends (for example, recollections of weekly tennis matches; anticipation of regular Sunday brunches, and so forth). An important question is whether recurrent experiences differ from linear ones only quantitatively, or if they also differ qualitatively; that is, is there something special about an event because it is part of a recurring cycle, and will recurrent events be given different salience or weight in memory than single incidents?

One possible additional contribution of cyclical salience is suggested by anthropologists who have said that among traditional people, the primary function of particular annual ceremonies is to bind the people together (Blundell, 1980; Hoebel, 1960). Ceremonies help to bind people into a more cohesive living unit (present salient) and to bind them to their ancestors (past salient) and descendants (future salient). Therefore, cyclical events may contribute to friendship and familial bonds both by the specific events and by their cyclical pattern. The regularity with which one attends these events may contribute to attachment to the group, as well as reflecting such attachment.

In a detailed description, Jones (1980) showed how annual Southern homecoming ceremonies could serve a bonding function. She stressed that primary features of these very elaborate and ritualized events included descriptions of the extensive family tree and explanations of how each celebrant was connected to the family's progenitor and the others in attendance. The history of the family and of family homecomings was also discussed. Jones suggested that this ceremony served to unite the individuals with other family members and with the family's past, and to distinguish them from other familial groups in the local area. Although she could point to different features in the ceremonies that could serve these functions, her study was not designed in a way to show a causal link between participation and the development of family loyalty, nor between recurrent participation and family loyalty. She did show that participation *reflected* family loyalty and that nonparticipation in the ceremony was tantamount to withdrawing from the clan, but it was not clear how many ceremonies one had to miss for this symbolic withdrawal to occur.

Altman and his colleagues (Werner et al., 1983) conducted an intensive analysis of Christmas Street, a block of 30 homes that have participated in extensive decorations and communal Christmas activities for almost 40 years. Although cyclical salience was not the focus of Werner et al.'s investigation, they did obtain interview data in the summertime that are pertinent to this construct. Residents often spontaneously indicated that the block was "Christmas Street" and described the traditional recurrent activities (for example, the annual party, decorating the communal tree, and so forth). There was no relationship, however, between the richness of these past-salient cyclical recollections and liking for or participation in current Christmas activities, or attitudes toward the block and neighbors. Thus although cyclicity was salient to many residents, the cyclicity seemed unrelated to commitment to or involvement with people on the block.

These descriptive studies are tantalizing in that they suggest opportunities for studying cyclicity and cyclical salience. Although we can describe these and other activities having cyclical salience, we have been unable to locate research that relates cyclical activities and cyclical salience to relationship bonds. For example, although there are many opportunities for annual celebrations in United States culture (birthdays, Mother's and Father's Days, the Fourth of July, Christmas, Easter, and so forth), as well as many opportunities for daily or weekly interaction patterns, we don't know the role of their cyclicity in developing and maintaining familial and friendship ties. Similarly, Rodin (1982) implied that recurrent shared activities are more special because of the commitment that they connote (pp. 40, 41, 43), however, no data were provided. Naturally, more systematic evidence is needed that cyclical salience is an important aspect of relationships (for example, the extent of cyclical activities, how they differ from noncyclical activities, how they are described, and so forth).

Summary. The concept of linear salience had clear representations in research on possessions, self-presentation, and especially evaluation. In all of these research areas, the extent to which persons stressed the past, present, or future affected what they said, did, and felt. Cyclical salience was less apparent in research; however, this does not necessarily mean that cyclicity is not important, and indeed some would say that cyclical events are important *because* they are cyclical, that is, that even a trivial act becomes significant through repetition (for example, Korosec-Serfaty, in press).

Sequencing

The second subordinate quality to be considered is "sequencing," which refers to sequences of events or patterns of activities and communication between people. In linear time, the pattern or sequence involves changing and nonrecurrent activities, whereas in cyclical time, the focus is on recurrent patterns or sequences. As will be shown, these sequences can occur at micro- (for example, conversations) and macrolevels (long-term exchange processes) of interpersonal exchange, and often, a linear sequence can be transformed over time into a cyclical one.

Linear Sequences

Linear sequences have been discussed in two general ways: (1) As giving order, meaning, and predictability to interactions and (2) as demonstrating reinforcement contingencies between behaviors.

Order and Meaning. There is quite a bit of evidence that linear dynamic processes can function as normative or even scripted behaviors that define and give meaning to interactions (Bower, Black, & Turner, 1979; Schank & Abelson, 1977), and that disrupting the expected sequence of events can disrupt an ongoing interaction, as well as the development of a relationship if negative inferences are made about the disruption.

Argyle (1978) described several sequences of ritualized social events such as the "greeting," the patient-doctor exchange, teacher-student exchanges, and the "remedial sequence" (steps taken to correct a faux pas), implying that a failure to follow a particular appropriate pattern would disrupt the interaction either because interactants would not know how to interpret each other's behavior or because they would make unflattering interpretations about each other (for example, the person is socially inept, the person is deliberately rude, and so forth).

Interpretations that people make about sequences of positive or negative comments can also be important. Aronson and Linder (1965) studied the "gain" effect in interpersonal attraction, or the idea that we like a person whose initially negative evaluation of us turns positive more than we like a person whose evaluation is consistently positive. (The complementary prediction, the "loss" effect, has received little empirical support, see Clore,

1976.) Over the years, research has suggested that the "gain" effect can be due to a number of factors, including a contrast effect (the positive evaluation was perceived to be more positive in the context of the negative evaluation), an efficacy effect (winning over the initially negative evaluator made the person feel effective), or relief (it felt good to hear good comments after bad, see Clore, 1976; Clore, Wiggins, & Itkin 1975; Jones & Goethals, 1972), therefore this line of research indicates that the reward sequence is important. We would point in particular to the importance of the interpretation that the recipient makes of the sequence, that is, when the recipient believed that the changing evaluation reflected a real impact that he or she had made on the evaluator.

A number of researchers have considered the meaning and interpretation of intimate self-disclosure and indicate that its appropriateness is determined by how it fits into an ongoing sequence of events (for example, see Luft, 1969). Altman and Taylor (1973) hypothesized that relationships grow and change in systematic and predictable ways as people begin by learning superficial information about each other, and then begin to "penetrate" into deeper and more intimate layers of each other's personality. As they said, the "social penetration process is orderly and proceeds through stages over time. Specifically, it is hypothesized that interpersonal exchange gradually progresses from superficial, nonintimate areas to more intimate, deeper layers" (p. 6). Altman and Taylor reported several studies in which there was evidence that disclosure to a stranger was a gradual process, easily disrupted by moving to intimacies before neutral information had been exchanged.

Since then, other researchers have demonstrated that people are aware of norms regarding self-disclosure and that people who disclose out of sequence are considered to be odd or deviant (for example, see Derlega & Chaikin, 1976; Derlega et al., 1973) and often dislikable (Cozby, 1972; Cunningham, 1981). However, Derlega, Walmer, and Furman (1973) hypothesized that the interpretation the recipient made of the disclosure could affect reactions to an unexpected disclosure. In support of this, Archer, Berg, and Runge (1980) found that if the recipient believed that the disclosure was evidence that the discloser liked the recipient, then the discloser would not be considered deviant and would in fact be liked even more. It would seem that sequences of intimate disclosure are important, as are the interpretations made regarding disclosure.

Albert and Kessler (1976, 1978) have identified a sequence of five kinds of statements that people use to end encounters (for example, summaries, justification for ending the interaction). Albert and Kessler found that, although there was a predominant sequence, there was also variability: People used different sequences and emphases depending on their relationship and the nature of their interaction. Albert and Kessler hypothesized that a primary function of these patterns was to permit the interaction to end in a positive way, implying that a deviation from the pattern would be rude, connote dislike between the interactants, or otherwise have a disruptive impact on the relationship.

Knapp, Hart, Friedrich, and Shulman (1973) also stressed the importance of effective leave-taking and said explicitly that leave-taking served a number of normative functions, including assuring each other that the interaction might end but that the friendship would not. They also pointed to the importance of participants following the proper sequence if the interaction were to end smoothly, leaving participants feeling good about each other. Thus one interactant should not stand up too soon during the leave-taking process lest he or she be considered too eager to escape; but once standing had occurred, the other interactant's appropriate response would be to end the encounter.

Both Albert and Kessler and Knapp et al. were interested only in the endings of encounters, not the endings of relationships; however, their work has been complemented by work on friendship networks and how important friendships can be maintained by a careful step-by-step withdrawal process. For example, Milardo, Johnson, and Huston (1983) looked at the effects of forming a pair-bond over time on the individuals' other relationships in their intimate networks. In a longitudinal analysis, they found that "as couples become more involved with one another, their separate social networks shrink in size, and their mutual or joint networks grow" (p. 965). The shrinkage was a gradual process, and the couples first reduced the duration and frequency of interactions with others, indicating the onset of a period of "bowing out gracefully" from other friendships. Less intimate and more singular relationships went first, until, in later stages of the exclusive relationship, couples saw fewer people less often, and for shorter periods of time. Couples took more care with close friends than acquaintances in this bowing out process. Nonintimates and acquaintances simply dropped out of the network, but with intimates, a graceful, tactful, and slower process was undertaken. Hays and Oxley (1984) have also noted a gradual process in the transformation from an old to a new network. They studied the formation of social networks among college dormitory residents who had just moved from out-of-state and found that as new ties were formed, old home ties were used less frequently for both companionship and socioemotional support.

Both of these studies suggest that changes in network composition are undertaken carefully and gradually, possibly in order to assure that the original friends would still be available at a later time, for example, if/when the exclusive relationship dissolved or became less time-consuming, or when the college students returned to their former homes. Thus the gradual withdrawal process can be seen as promoting a hiatus, rather than an end to these relationships.

Work on the dissolution of relationships has focused not on the hiatus, but on the end of relationships (Duck, 1982; Levinger & Moles, 1979). Here, too, sequences have been thought to be important for successful functioning, especially for minimizing the stress of dissolution. For example, Miller and Parks (1982) pointed out that the dissolution of a relationship can be viewed as a type of persuasive encounter in which one member attempts to persuade the other to end the relationship. Miller and Parks hypothesized that individuals would use mild appeals and only progress to more hostile and acrimonious strategies as needed.

Hagestad and Smyer (1982) described the importance of timing and sequences in rites of passage and suggested that one of the reasons that divorce can be a crisis is that cultures have not yet developed transition rituals that signify and support the divorce process in the way that cultures have developed marriage and widowhood rituals. Hagestad and Smyer argued that when people could anticipate and control the divorce, and could prepare themselves for their new status, their adjustment was quicker and more satisfactory.

> We suggest that in an 'orderly' process the marital dissolution follows the sequence found in the process of becoming married. That is, the individual decathects from the partner and the role of spouse and leaves the routines of shared living prior to the legal status change. . . . A *disorderly* divorce process is one in which some or all of the relationship ceasings are left undone at the time of the divorce. (pp. 165-166)

Thus the desired sequence of events for an orderly divorce is that the person anticipates and expects divorce in the way he or she expected marriage and ceases to be attached to the partner, the role, and the lifestyle in the way he or she separated psychologically from singlehood; and the accomplishment of these two steps should precede or coincide with the legal state of divorce.

In this brief review, we have seen that sequences have been studied at many levels of behavior, in a variety of behavioral domains. Sequences give meaning and interpretive clarity to interpersonal exchanges, and they can also give a sense of order and control.

Behavioral Contingencies. We include in this section theory and research about a variety of dependencies between behaviors such as those that derive from reinforcement processes, comprehensibility, and the like. Note that behavioral contingencies usually (though not always) refer to the relationship or interaction as the unit of analysis, whereas in the previous section, the focus was generally on one individual in the interaction. Some of these contingencies have been treated as though independent of the interpretations that people make about the sequence. It does not mean that interpretations are not important in the following areas, but only that the researchers have not considered interpretation in their theorizing.

In his description of the role of social skills in effective interpersonal functioning, Argyle (1978) reported that verbal and nonverbal exchanges must follow certain sequences if the interaction is to go smoothly (for example, nonverbal behaviors fit together in comprehensible patterns; certain behaviors follow predictably from other behaviors; and so forth). Support for this view can be found in a variety of studies, such as one by Kraut, Lewis, and Swezey (1982) who found that disrupting the normal sequences in verbal exchange reduced the efficiency of communication.

In a more detailed analysis, Krain (1975) suggested that the kinds of responses partners made to each other would strengthen or weaken their relationship. He categorized sentences as one of three types—entropic communication (statements that weaken bonds between couples, that is, teasing, hostility), negentropic communication (statements that strengthen or contribute to such bonds, that is, sympathy, understanding), and potential communication (civil and polite conversation)—and then examined sentence-to-sentence sequences for their negentropy (second sentence negentropic), entropy (second sentence entropic), and potential. He argued that the negentropic communication patterns were necessary for a relationship to flourish and hypothesized that such patterns would be more typical of couples who described themselves as marriage-bound than those who described themselves as casual daters. His hypotheses were supported; however, he pointed out that because he used a cross-sectional design, it is not clear whether effective communication is a developing skill (that is, couples learn not to use an entropic style over time) or if the results represent a selection process (couples who use entropic styles eventually break up). Thus the contingencies that develop in conversation can affect relationship progress.

Several studies indicate that a lack of responsivity between interactants affects a number of qualities of the exchange, such as involvement, influence, and liking. For example, in a series of studies, Rosenfeld (1966a, 1966b) examined the behaviors chosen by people in an unstructured situation who had been instructed to get a partner to like or dislike them. Consistently, the approval-seeking participants indicated a responsivity to their partner by nodding their heads, smiling, and using appropriate verbal comments; in contrast, the approval-avoiding participants assiduously avoided these kinds of responsive behaviors. Importantly, these behaviors had the desired effects: Participants liked the responsive more than the nonresponsive partner.

Werner and Latané (1976) manipulated responsivity by asking subjects to interact with a partner through one of three communication media (videophone, audiophone, or letter); some of the subjects engaged in real conversations, but others were "yoked" to one member of an interacting pair. Relative to real partners, "yoked" subjects found their partners to be unresponsive, uninteresting, and unpersuasive. Even though the content and the interaction style were identical for the real and the yoked partners, the contingency was not, and this affected the yoked partner in a negative way. Although Rosenfeld's and Werner and Latané's work might suggest that recipients of nonresponsivity made negative interpretations about the speaker's intent (for example, she was being deliberately rude), data about interpretations were not provided. On the other hand, a later study suggests that negative interpretations are not necessary for a nonresponsive partner to be liked less.

Insko and Wilson (1977) controlled conversations so that group members could only speak to certain others in the group. The instructions prevented participants from attributing rudeness to partners who ignored them. The mutual evaluations of the interacting participants were significantly higher than those of the noninteracting participants. These evaluations differed even though all participants heard the same conversation. Insko and Wilson discussed this result in terms of the lower relevance of the conversation to the ignored member and to her lack of control over the topics and issues raised. Thus contingencies in communication have broad and substantial impacts, with participants feeling that the noninteracting partner had been deliberately rude to them.

Sequencing and contingencies between behaviors has been a primary component of the work on interpersonal exchange. Homans (1961), Thibaut and Kelley (1959), Kelley and Thibaut (1978), Foa and Foa (1976), Levinger and Huesmann (1980), and others have all specified explicit processes and sequential steps through which relationships progress. For example, Thibaut and Kelley (1959) described the "behavior sequence," or "specific motor and verbal acts that exhibit some degree of sequential organization directed toward the attainment of some immediate goal or end state" (p. 11). They suggested that people would evaluate their rewards and costs at each step in the sequence as well as at the end, and decide whether to stay in the relationship. Furthermore, they said that the reward/cost value of behavior might change with repetition. Satiation would occur with positive behaviors, so that they became less positive with repetition; and fatigue would occur with negative behaviors, so that they became even more costly with repetition.

Although acknowledging that satiation and fatigue would be important because they would encourage partners to try out different behavior patterns, Thibaut and Kelley said that it would be difficult to study them within their cost/reward matrix paradigm. However, Levinger and Huesmann (Huesmann & Levinger, 1976; Levinger & Huesmann, 1980) have revitalized the idea in their "incremental exchange theory," in which the costs and rewards of different behaviors are *expected* to change with each occurrence, and partners are expected to be aware of the changing values of their behaviors. The changing values do not necessarily connote a change in the nature of the relationship, but simply acknowledge the idea that (for example) a joke is usually only funny on the first telling.

Cyclical Sequencing

Sequences in cycling time refer to repeated sequences of the same or very similar behaviors. The repetitions should be part of a cycle, such that the sequences begin at a point of origin, proceed through certain steps, and return to the same or similar point of origin. The primary difference between linear and cyclical sequencing is recurrence; thus, a linear sequence can become cyclical if it is part of a repeated pattern of behavior. For example, Argyle's (1978) description of sequenced behaviors contained both linear and cyclical aspects. He described several patterns used in teacher-student exchanges (for example, teacher asks question, student answers) and said that the patterns would be repeated and combined during the class period. In Argyle's example, the series of steps in a discrete exchange would be the "linear sequence" and the patterns of movement from one kind of exchange to another would be the "cyclical sequence."

The process by which a linear pattern is transformed into a cyclical one has been described as a gradual one, and such things as how aware participants are of the transformation and at what point it is cyclical have not been discussed. However, once established, the patterns seem to function smoothly. As we shall see, these cycles are similar to linear sequences in that they define behavioral contingencies that enhance comprehensibility. Cyclical sequences also provide order and normative information, and a change in a sequence is noticed and interpreted. In addition, they are the foundations of relationships; they are the expected patterns of interaction that provide the rewards (and costs) that keep people interacting and that can give continuity to the relationship.

Behavioral Contingencies. Cyclical sequences have been described as fitting together in meaningful ways. For example, in presenting the example of instructor-student exchanges, Argyle said that a skilled instructor would know how to control the flow of the classroom by controlling the flow from one exchange sequence to another during a lesson. Cyclical sequencing also contributes to conversational flow, such as when redundancy is built into the exchange pattern, thereby providing repetition and a cumulation of information. For example, Riegel and Meacham (1978) have described the dialogue process in which "each successive statement reflects at least the two immediately preceding it, and has to be consistent with the speaker's own previously expressed views" (p. 32). They referred to this pattern as "reflective coordination" and argued that conversations would disintegrate without this form of redundancy and repetition. Moscovici (1967) described a similar function of redundancy and found that its use seemed to make conversations more efficient. Dyads who were pressed to reach a conclusion in a short amount of time used more redundant speech patterns than those who were not under pressure.

Order and Meaning/Continuity and Change. Thibaut and Kelley (1959) described how people developed familiar patterns of activities by trying out a variety of sequences until a comfortable cycle was achieved. Thus they described selectivity (p. 12) as a situation in which people would only engage in certain behaviors or patterns of exchange because they had learned that those produced the most rewards in the relationship. Ultimately, after much

experience with the contingencies and partners, an individual (and by implication, the couple) might engage in routines or automatic sequences without
constantly evaluating the rewards and costs or worrying about the routine's
impact on the partner. These routines would persist until the partner or some
external force changed the behavior-reward contingency. The change would
be disruptive if the partner could not accept or accommodate to the change,
or the change was accompanied by a change in reward contingencies. Cyclical sequences and patterned behaviors are an integral aspect of Thibaut and
Kelley's model; they provide continuity as well as opportunity for change, but
there are a variety of consequences for deviating from the expected pattern,
and not all changes are welcomed by the partner. Unfortunately, although
their description is rather detailed and makes intuitive sense, there are no
data from ongoing relationships to support them.

Whereas Thibaut and Kelley (1959) were primarily interested in routines
that maximized positive outcomes for interactants, cyclical routines are not
always positive. For example, Patterson and Cobb (1973) and Turner and
Dodd (1979) have discussed how sequences can become repeated aversive
events, such as when a child's fussing behavior precipitates increasingly
brutal abuse by the parent. Similarly, Lloyd and Cate (1984) have discussed
how disagreements between couples can become aversive if they occur time
after time without resolution. Lloyd and Cate suggested that disagreements
were healthy if they led to greater understanding between the couple, but
recurrent unresolved disagreements would lead to dissatisfaction with the
relationship. Clearly, these kinds of negative cyclical sequences would have a
different impact on a relationship than more positive ones.

Cyclical sequences of behaviors and feelings are also evident in Altman
and Taylor's (1973) social penetration process. The process of social penetration begins with strangers interacting briefly with each other, and then
evaluating the rewards and costs against their own personal subjective
standard, as well as against their other relationships and the anticipated
futures of those relationships. If the evaluations are positive, the individual(s)
will decide to pursue the relationship further. "Thereafter, a continuous
cycling occurs involving storage of outcomes in central memory, forecast
assessment, revised forecast, decision, and new interaction" (p. 38). Thus in
this model, sequences are an integral part of the friendship formation process. As we mentioned earlier, part of the function of this cycling is to assess
the state of the relationship and to determine whether the relationship will
stay at its present intimacy level or become more or less intimate. Unfortunately, although the theory is intriguing, no data from ongoing relationships
are available to substantiate this cycling assessment process.

In this brief summary, we have described the role of sequences and
patterns of behavior in interpersonal functioning. Sequences are ordered
events; they comprise expected patterns of behavior, and different patterns
have different meanings. Thus sequences facilitate interaction by providing

order, continuity, an interpretive framework, and predictability. Cyclical sequences may serve the additional functions of providing deliberate redundancy, providing automaticity and routine in relationships, as well as providing a continuous assessment of the state of a relationship.

Scale

Linear Scale

The third temporal quality in the proposed framework is scale, which Werner et al. (in press) referred to as the temporal scope or duration of events and relationships. In simple terms, scale defines how long a behavior, experience, or relationship lasts. Brief or small-scale events can be termed incidents and might include chance encounters, a date, and so forth. Lengthy or large-scale events can be termed stages and might include an entire friendship, a holiday season, or an entire era, such as one's college days.

Two questions or themes that scale addresses are (1) whether duration and significance are correlated, that is, are long-duration experiences more significant than short ones and (2) is time integral to or outside of events, that is, do the events determine their own duration or does an external clock determine the events, and in what respect can events and scale be mutually defining? These are complex questions and we can only begin to discuss them in the present review; indeed, we will not try to answer them, but will instead illustrate how they have been addressed in theory and research. Furthermore, the questions are substantially interrelated, and we will address them simultaneously.

There are instances in which time has been treated simultaneously as being outside of events and as an index of their significance. For example, time is often used as an indicator of attraction or caring, such as when one asks how much time partners and friends spend with each other (Ridley & Avery, 1979), how much time parents spend with their children (Foa & Foa, 1976), or how long people have been friends. On the other hand, time per se is often not a sufficient index, and the trend is to consider both duration and subjective quality of events (for example, see Foa & Foa, 1976), suggesting that duration itself has meaning—it tells us something about caring, attraction, enduringness, and so forth—but that additional complementary information is also needed if we are to understand the event or relationship.

Although it is possible to measure interactions or entire relationships according to a clock or calendar, most researchers have opted to use a temporal measure internal to the event and to let the events, not the calendar, define significance. For example, Linton (1983), in her examinations of everyday memory, distinguished between small-scale experiences, which she refers to as events or episodes, and large-scale experiences, which she termed extendures. Her memories were constructed around the natural starting and ending points of episodes and extendures, rather than around a clock or calendar. Furthermore, she found that the natural starting and endpoints were often discerned not at the time of occurrence, but in retrospect, when the event was fit together with succeeding events into a coherent unity. Similarly, the significance of events was rarely related to their duration and was often inferred retrospectively, when fit into succeeding events. As an example, she noted that one cannot know when one is being introduced to a future spouse, yet although one forgets many first encounters, the first meeting with the spouse takes on special significance and is usually easily recalled.

Albert and Kessler (1978) did not discuss the relationship between duration and significance; however, they did consider the question of whether time was internal or external to interactions. They said that one could not tell in advance when an encounter would end, and that even during observation, it was difficult to tell exactly when the final stages of the encounter began to emerge. The encounter would end when the business had been accomplished or one of the interactants could justify leaving, and the natural ending would occur independently of an external clock. Indeed, when they gave participants in a study an unstructured amount of time to talk, the range of conversation lengths was from two minutes to over an hour, and the durations of the ending process were also variable.

Other research suggests that scale or duration can have normative properties, and researchers in this area also treat temporal scale as an inherent part of the events. For example, in verbal exchange, there are norms for the appropriate lengths of utterances. Interactants are expected to speak for a particular (though not rigidly fixed) length of time and to permit the other to speak. Although there are temporal boundaries that define appropriateness, these rules can be overturned easily by the use of vocal inflexions, nonverbal signals, or if the interactants are in a situation in which it is appropriate for one person to dominate the conversation (Argyle, 1978). Thus the scale of the events is defined by the context rather than being imposed externally. Unfortunately, the relationship between scale and significance was not considered by Argyle, but one can easily think of examples of events in which duration and significance are independent, for example, a lengthy exchange of platitudes. On the other hand, deferring greater speaking time to someone implies that his or her comments are more significant, suggesting that duration and significance have at least a symbolic relationship.

At a broader level of analysis, temporal scale can also refer to discrete, measurable, and temporally and psychologically bound stages, such as the stage of a relationship, the stage of life, or the stage of marriage. Each of these stages has been defined by social-psychological qualities rather than time per se. So the stage of a relationship refers to the degree of intimacy that has been achieved by people, and the terms "acquaintance," "friend," and "close friend" have psychological meaning beyond the mere length of time of friendship (Altman & Taylor, 1973; Levinger & Huesmann, 1980; McCarthy &

Duck, 1976). Dating couples can define themselves as "casual," "serious," and "marriage-bound," and this is somewhat, though not completely, independent of the length of their friendship (Krain, 1975). Stage of life does not refer to one's age, but to how one fits into the larger social structure, for example, single young adult, elderly retired, and so forth (Shulman, 1975). And the stage of marriage or family life cycle refers not only to length of marriage, but to one's status with respect to childbearing, for example, beginning family, childbearing years, and so forth. There is a great diversity of family styles (especially with the recent emergence of child-free marriages and delayed childbearing), and researchers have used different criteria for these stages, so even these stages are not rigidly defined (Spanier, Lewis, & Cole, 1975).

In these descriptions, time appears as both an external and an internal characteristic. That is, time is external in that it sets some boundaries: It takes time for a couple to become intimate, or for a family to mature to the empty nest stage. Simultaneously, time is internal in that, as stressed above, time alone does not define the stage that the relationship or family has achieved. Indeed, many researchers acknowledge this interplay between time as external clock and time as internal state when they invite research participation from couples who must qualify on both dimensions to be included in the research (for example, see McCarthy & Duck, 1976). This strategy suggests that researchers believe that there is a difference between a couple that defines itself as "casual" after six months and one that defines itself as "casual" after 16 months of dating, that is, there is some suspicion that the lengthier relationship will not get more intimate, but the less lengthy one might.

In a somewhat different way, time is both internal and external to stages because the scale or stage defines and is defined by events and activities, thus one can infer the relationship between people from their behaviors, and the relationship between people often defines the range of acceptable behaviors. For example, there is general consensus that relationship stage and intimacy of self-disclosure are mutually defining; that is, relationship stage determines the degree of intimacy exchange between partners, and the degree of intimacy is an index of the stage of a relationship. A number of self-report studies indicate that people say they have discussed more intimate information with family members and close friends than with acquaintances (for reviews, see Chaiken & Derlega, 1976; Cozby, 1972; Jourard, 1971); there is some evidence that people actually disclose more to a friend than a stranger (for example, see Broder, 1982; Gaebelein, 1976; Morton, 1978). Complementary research indicates that naive observers attribute greater friendship and liking between people who disclose intimacies (for example, see Derlega & Chaikin, 1976).

A number of studies indicate that other aspects of interpersonal distancing are also affected by friendship stage. For example, friends stand closer together than strangers (for example, see Altman, 1975; Beier, 1975; Willis, 1966); when working together on a project, intimate couples are more likely than strangers to touch, share materials, and move in and out of each other's work space (Levinger, 1980). Working within Altman's (1975) territoriality theory, Parmelee, Werner, and Diefenderfer (1979) proposed that the perceived intrusiveness of a behavior depended both on the behavior and the relationship between interactants. Strangers were permitted much less access to places, objects, and personal ideas than were friends and roommates. There was also some evidence that friends were *expected* to intrude, for example, drop by unexpectedly, call when they needed help, and so forth. And finally, Levinger and Huesmann (1980) used the term "state" to refer to the degree of friendship and proposed that a variety of behaviors in addition to intimacy of self-disclosure (for example, altruism) could be influenced by partners' self-defined present and expected relationship state. Anticipating a stronger bond was conducive to more positive interactions.

In summary, the scale of events can be treated as both an internal and an external quality; events can be measured by clocks and calendars, but they can also be measured according to psychological qualities, such as how people describe their relationship and the kinds of behaviors in which they engage. Furthermore, relationships and behaviors are often mutually defining, and in a number of behavioral domains, it appeared that the stage of relationship determined behaviors and behaviors led to inferences about the stage of the relationship. Although the trend was for researchers to treat time as an integral part of the relationship, we noted other cases in which scale as an external constraint could influence behavior. Therefore it seems appropriate to be aware that this internal/external distinction can be made and to understand how time operates in each perspective, rather than to exclude one viewpoint from consideration. And finally, there is little research about the relationship between duration and significance. Brief events can be significant, especially in retrospect; however, time can be thought of as a commodity, and long duration events can often connote a special sense because of their length. Tuan (1977) observed that there was no implication that the length of an experience was directly correlated with significance or intensity of meaning, but our impression is that this remains unresolved.

Cyclical Scale. The concept of scale in cyclical time refers to the length of the cycle, or the time it takes to originate, complete, and return to a recurrent event. Cycles are often illustrated with a sine wave, which rises and falls around a base or center line, and in which the scale is defined as the "period" or the time to complete one cycle (Orme, 1969). Werner et al. (in press) found it useful to identify two aspects of scale: the duration of the event or experience and the length of the interval between recurrences. Events could be of variable duration (for example, short, intermediate, long), as could the interval between recurrences. Furthermore, the same events could have variable durations and intervals and, in spite of this erratic pattern, could still be considered part of an ongoing pattern of cyclical activities. Given this variability, a sine wave, with its smooth and regular shape, does not seem appropriate for depicting interpersonal activities. We will return to this point in our discussion of cyclical rhythm.

Scale as Internal/External to Events. A discussion of scale as internal or external to cyclical events and the significance of scale in cyclical events would likely parallel our previous discussion of linear scale. However, because we have not found a database, we will forego such a discussion until one is available and turn instead to two issues that have emerged.

Determinants and Consequences of Cyclical Scale. Two issues that emerge in descriptions of cyclical events are (1) what are the determinants of scale (that is, what determines the frequency and duration of recurrent events) and (2) what, if any, are the consequences of scale (for example, how are scale and cyclicity perceived; do frequency and duration affect relationships; and so forth)? There have been descriptions of recurrent events that provide information about and give examples of cyclical scale, and in general it is clear that people vary in how much time they devote to recurrent activities and how regularly they are scheduled. For example, Christmas is an annual event scheduled for the same date, which is celebrated for varying periods, from a day, a few days, to an entire month in some situations (Werner et al., 1983). Jones (1980) described annual homecoming events that were celebrated by some but not all groups on precisely the same date, but the length of the celebration would vary depending on the number of people and the particular events for that year (for example, the lengths of speeches, how many letters of support were read). Similarly, Rowles (1981) described daily patterns of social activities among elderly house-bound individuals, but there were substantial differences in how much time was devoted to them and how regular people were in their participation. Sometimes variability was determined by illness and other unusual events, and sometimes by variations in the friends' behaviors (for example, neighbors who were only home on weekends). These descriptions indicate that there is variability between individuals, as well as from one time to another in both event and interval durations, and that scale can be determined by a calendar, individual preferences, the need to coordinate with others, and the like.

The view that interpersonal contacts can ebb and flow in regular or somewhat regular patterns is akin to Altman and his colleagues' (Altman, 1975; Altman et al., 1981) descriptions of privacy regulation as a dialectic process. In their view, privacy is a boundary regulation process in which people sometimes seek and sometimes avoid contact with others. Privacy can operate at physical (for example, proximity, interaction) and psychological levels (for example, topic intimacy) so people could be variably open and closed at several levels. Altman (1975) explicitly argued that the regulation process would not necessarily fit a regular pattern and that the pattern could be influenced by either internal or external forces: "The desire for social interaction or noninteraction changes over time and with different circumstances. The idea of privacy as a dialectic process, therefore, means that there is a balancing of opposing forces—to be open and accessible to others and to be shut off or closed to others—and that the net strength of these competing forces changes over time" (p. 23). To illustrate this point, Altman pointed to married couples who arranged to be apart on a regular or somewhat regular basis, either daily or on a longer period, and cited his work with military personnel (Altman et al., 1971), who, when isolated with another person, had variable interaction and noninteraction times.

It was apparent from Altman's (1975) description that any number of factors might influence scale in privacy regulation (for example, individual differences, anticipated length of forced isolation, complementarity and liking between interactants, and so forth), however, he did not discuss these in detail. He did describe serious consequences of inadequately regulated privacy, such as social-psychological distress, poor task performance, disruption of a developing relationship, and other such problems; so in Altman's view, an ability to control the scale of interaction cycles has important consequences.

Additional support for this view can be found in Rowles's descriptions of daily activity patterns among the elderly. Rowles (1980, 1981) found that recurrent patterns were frequently used to develop and maintain contacts between neighbors. Many individuals would arise at a particular time, raise their window shades to wave to neighbors and other regular passersbys, or telephone friends at a particular time. Although the routines might have been variable, they were described by Rowles and his participants as being regular patterns of activity that gave a sense of order, predictability, and continuity. Furthermore, the elderly reported that they would become disconcerted by a change in the routine. The routines also connoted safety because neighbors expected to see each other at these times and would check up on each other if the routines were missed. Rowles's interviews suggest that daily patterns became an integral aspect of friendships, and that they served both psychological and pragmatic functions.

In a more systematic study of interaction routines, Schulz (1976) studied the impact of regular and irregular visits to nursing home residents. Because his primary interest was in the perceived controllability of the visits, he did not manipulate cyclicity directly, nor did he report the regularity with which visits were made. Schulz arranged to have undergraduate students visit a number of nursing home residents over a two-month period. The visits were arranged so that one-third of the subjects were able to control the time and duration of visits, one-third were notified in advance so that they could predict the time and duration of an impending visit, and one-third were visited on a random schedule and given no advance notice. By yoking subjects together in sets of three, he was able to equate frequency and duration of the visits across the three treatment conditions. A fourth group was not visited, but completed the questionnaires containing the dependent variables, thereby providing a baseline comparison group.

Schulz found no differences in physical or psychological well-being between subjects who controlled the visits and those who were able to predict them; however, both of these groups were significantly better off than the random-visit and no-visit groups. Schulz concluded that the social visits had been positive reinforcers and that controlling or being able to predict the visits were equivalent at enhancing the residents' self-efficacy. This set of results suggests that cyclical patterns are important to both psychological and physical health, and that the pattern can be irregular as long as it is fairly predictable.

In terms of satisfaction with the interactions, the results are even more intriguing. Schulz reported that the three treatment groups did not differ in rated enjoyment of the visits, so apparently even surprise visits were pleasurable. A number of interpretations could be made as to why predictability was important for health, but not for pleasure, and only additional research will distinguish among them (for example, ratings were made after the two-month visiting period, at a time when randomly visited residents could perceive, in retrospect, that the visits had been fairly regular. If these perceptions were equal for the groups, it is not surprising that their evaluations of the visits were equal). The critical issue is that Schulz has begun to examine some important questions regarding cyclicity and friendship formation that could be pursued in future research.

For example, Schulz reported that people who controlled the frequency and duration of visits requested, on average, one-hour visits, approximately once per week. It would be interesting to know the degree of variability of requests, both within and between people, and what factors determined these choices. Also of interest would be the reactions and experiences of yoked subjects, whose visits came on somebody else's preferred schedule. Based on Altman et al.'s (1981) discussion of privacy regulation, we suspect that there is some normative range as to what durations and intervals would be acceptable to most residents (for example, in Schulz's study, approximately one-hour per week), and that only noticeable deviations from that expectation, or transitory changes in mood or health, would affect satisfaction.

The use of one's social network to provide social support has also been described as a cyclical process with variable intervals between and variable durations of the events, and as having serious consequences for the individual. Usually, some event outside of the individual, such as unexpected and uncontrollable environmental stressors, would lead the individual to contact members of the social support system. The extent to which network members were able to ameliorate the stress would determine how many members would be contacted and how long the stress experience would last (Hirsch, 1980; Selye, 1973).

Both Harries-Jones (1969) and Kapferer (1969) described social support-seeking as a cyclical process, as the stressed individual would contact first one, then another friend until relief was achieved. Harries-Jones (1969) referred to an "action-set" as a short-term response to a specific crisis event: "A series of links within a personal network which described ego's communication for a specific purpose . . . over a short period of time" (p. 301). Kapferer (1969) described the mobilization of an action-set as a cycling process. A person under stress would attempt to recruit other individuals to support his or her cause, and if relief was not achieved, would reenter the cycle and again attempt to recruit support from individuals in the network. Once relief was achieved, the person would not call on network members until another environmental stimulus was perceived as threatening, but would then begin the cyclical coping process once again.

Kapferer (1969) also discussed a variety of the consequences of drawing on the social support network in this fashion. Relationships with the network members may be redefined, and some weak relationships may deteriorate, whereas others may strengthen to meet the occasion. Relationships that may have previously become inactive may be reactivated, and new relationships may also be formed.

For example, Lee (1969) studied the use of social networks among women seeking an abortion and found that women reported that they often had to contact a number of people in order to gain adequate support. Many never succeeded, and others found that they would lose friends who disapproved of abortion. In addition, the abortion experience often changed their relationships with network members, especially the male partner. Many women reported that their relationship with their partner worsened, whereas for others, it stayed the same or actually improved, depending on how the partner had behaved during the crisis period. After the abortion, some women actually broke off relationships with the very people who had provided support during the experience, whereas others strengthened their ties with these supportive individuals. Some of the women formed new friendships when they joined lobbying organizations, expanding their social networks to include individuals who could validate their decision after-the-fact and themselves becoming part of a behind-the-scenes action-set for other women seeking abortions. Thus, using the social support network was precipitated by a crisis situation; many women cycled through a variety of friends prior to locating support; and the experience with the support group had major implications for the women's lives and their friendships.

Cyclical scale refers both to the duration of events and the duration of the interval between events. Research and descriptions of cyclical activities between friends indicate that both events and intervals can be of variable duration and that the variability can derive from a variety of sources, both inside and outside of the individual. There is some evidence that privacy regulation, or a pattern of contact and noncontact, is important for psychological functioning (for example, control over visitors, access to needed social support); however, it also appears that there is tolerance for a range of scales and the pattern of regulation can vary somewhat without negative consequences (for example, being visited on a schedule determined by someone else had no impact on health or satisfaction with the visit). On the other hand, there is still a need to determine what this range of tolerance is and how regularity and predictability fit together in this process.

Pace and Rhythm

Linear Pace

Pace refers to the speed or rapidity with which events pass. There are two ways of looking at pace, one in which time is internal, and the other in which it is external to events. Pace can refer to activity density, or how rapidly events occur per some external unit of time, or it can refer to one's psychological experience of pace, that is, how rapidly events and activities are perceived to pass without regard to an external clock. Both conceptualizations have emerged in the literature on interpersonal relationships. Activity density is a familiar idea, so it will not be elaborated here; however, the psychological experience of pace warrants explanation. It has been argued (Gibson, 1975; Hartocollis, 1983) that time per se is not experienced; rather the experience of time passing results from the simultaneous perception of change and stability. "That is to say, the observer perceives both what is altered and what remains unaltered in the environment" (Gibson, 1975, p. 298). Without change, there is no sense of time passing, but the more rapid the change, the more rapidly time seems to flow. This view gives special meaning to the adage that "time stood still"; time appears to stand still when one's attention is riveted on a single aspect of the environment. Without external events intruding into one's consciousness, there is no change and therefore no sense of time's passage.

Pace in interactions has been discussed in two general ways, one of which involves similarity of pacing between interactants, and another that involves the pace with which people penetrate to more intimate aspects of each other's personalities, that is, the self-disclosure process.

Pace Similarity and Liking. There has been some research on the psychological experience of pace that seems to combine both the time-internal and time-external views. McGrath and Rotchford (1983) found a variety of studies that indicated that the psychological experience of time depends more on the events involved than on the actual amount of chronological time that passes, and on whether the event is current or being recollected. An hour of time seems brief when filled with activities, and long when filled with emptiness. However, that same hour when remembered seems longer when filled with activities and shorter when empty of activities. As McGrath and Rotchford (1983) stated, we seem to assume some normal activity-to-time ratio, and variations around that expectation or standard affect our psychological experience and recollection of time. This research has been based on task performance rates, and it should be noted that the standard may differ for more friendly exchanges. Nonetheless, one should find that the pace of an interaction should correspond to its psychological quality and that boring (slow-paced) interactions should differ from stimulating (slightly faster than normal) and exhausting (fast-paced) interactions in their experience and recollection. Furthermore, one should find the experiences and recollections of each pace to be represented differently in the subjective memories (for example, CL) and expectations (for example, CL-alt) of participants.

The question of how interaction pace might influence human interaction has received little attention; however, there is some evidence that desirable paces for activities vary with the activity. For example, Foa and Foa (1976) reported a study by Teichman that suggested that affectional exchanges were expected to last longer than more functional exchanges. Although participants were equally satisfied to exchange money in a short or long amount of time, they were unhappy at having to exchange affectionate notes quickly. Foa and Foa reported that the content of notes was the same in short and long periods, and argued that satisfaction with the greater amount of time indicated that affectionate information simply took a longer amount of time to process. It is also possible that individuals differ in their preferred amount of time for processing affectionate information and that similarity between couples in this regard is important; however, Foa and Foa did not discuss this possibility.

Latané and his colleagues (see Latané & Hothersall, 1972, for review) have observed that animals are attracted to partners whose activity rates match their own. This suggests that people, too, may prefer others of similar paces. There is some evidence that speech comprehension can be facilitated by modest increases in speech rate, especially when the speech is compressed rather than simply accelerated (Bancroft & Bendinelli, 1982; de Haan, 1982); however, too great an increase reduces comprehension (see Foulke, 1971; Foulke & Sticht, 1969). For the most part, the focus has been on comprehension rather than the relationship between pace and liking. Street and Brady (1982) proposed that speech rate could affect evaluations of the speaker, especially when the listener's and speaker's rates were similar. They found that listeners attributed greater social competency to and liked better speakers who spoke at a faster rate than others. There was some tendency for listeners also to like a speaker whose speech rate matched their own, but this seemed to be overridden by a greater tolerance for different speech rates by persons whose own speech rate was rather slow. Smith, Brown, Strong, and Reucher (1975) replicated the pace and perceived competency effect, but also found that a slower pace made the speaker appear more benevolent, so speech rate may affect a variety of inferences made about a speaker. Smith et al. did not evaluate the impact of similarity on person perception, so more work is needed in this area.

Interaction pace has also been noted as part of the physiological basis for introversion/extroversion (Eysenck, 1967). Extroverts have higher activity levels and prefer more stimulation than introverts, and research indicates that relative to introverts, extroverts participate spontaneously in and are more satisfied with situations with higher activity levels (Campbell & Hawley, 1982; Quottrochi-Tubin & Jason, 1983). However, the research often confounds social contact with activity level, so this line of research does not show clearly that people are drawn to others with similar activity levels.

There is quite a bit of evidence that activity similarity or "companionship" is an important basis of marital compatibility (Barnett & Nietzel, 1979; Birchler & Webb, 1977; Christensen & King, 1982; Jacobson, Waldron, & Moore, 1980; Levinger, Senn, & Jorgensen, 1970; Weiss & Isaac, 1976), especially when the activity requires interaction rather than coaction (Orthner, 1975). There is also some evidence that activity preferences are more similar than attitudes among same-sex college friends (Werner & Parmelee, 1979). These studies do not consider as a separate aspect the pace of the activities or the similarity of the participants' paces, so more work is also needed in this area.

Social Penetration. The clearest exposition of pace is in Social Penetration Theory (Altman & Taylor, 1973), which addresses questions of how early in a relationship people begin to share intimacies, how rapidly and frequently they do so, and the consequences of disclosing too rapidly or too slowly. Altman and Taylor (1973, p. 30) suggested that the rate of social penetration, or the rate at which people opened themselves up to each other, could vary from person to person, from topic to topic, and from interaction to interaction:

> We do not intend to suggest that both parties necessarily show equivalent changes on the social penetration dimensions. . . . Also, the process is not a mechanical one in which increases in interaction in one area of personality occur at all levels of depth until the area is exhausted or "worked dry." On the contrary, changes in interaction are viewed as happening in several areas simultaneously and at different rates. Furthermore, rate of exchange can shift over time within and between areas (for example, initially accelerated interaction in one area may later fall off and then pick up again).

The rate would depend on the many factors that have been discussed previously concerning the subjective evaluation of the relationship, comparison to other relationships, and the forecast process, in which the individual forms a subjective impression of the consequences of disclosing an intimacy.

Theorizing about pace has not been matched by equally sophisticated data-collection techniques. Researchers have rarely conducted longitudinal studies of self-disclosure in friendship formation or in stable relationships

(Altman, 1975; Levinger, 1980; Rubin, 1975), and even when they do, they tend not to report changes in the degree of intimacy (for example, see Broder, 1982) or how fast those changes occurred.

Other researchers have not studied pace explicitly, but have studied some determinants of self-disclosure that bear on the issue of pace. Most research examines the "dyadic effect" or the finding that people will reciprocate a (usually unknown) partner's intimate disclosure by themselves being more intimate, though they do not match the partner in rated degree of intimacy. The mechanisms that seem to influence reciprocity of disclosure are trust, liking, and a sense of obligation to reciprocate intimacy with intimacy (ano-nymity will also increase reciprocity, however, anonymity does not seem relevant to relationship exchange). Reciprocity in the dyadic effect seems to be a short-term phenomenon, and it is generally acknowledged that reciproc-ity takes place over a much broader time period in established rather than establishing relationships (Altman & Taylor, 1973; Levinger, 1979; Morton, 1978), hence self-disclosure based on a reciprocity norm would have a more rapid pace. However, because both liking and trust take some time to develop, one would expect self-disclosure based on these processes to be slower paced.

Trust has been stressed as a precondition to self-disclosure by several authors (for example, Altman, 1973; Jourard, 1971; Rubin, 1975). Jourard (1971) said that before a recipient would return intimacy with intimacy, the recipient must trust the partner, that is, the recipient must be certain that (1) the partner would not disclose the confidence to anyone else and (2) the partner would not punish the recipient for the contents of the disclosure. Both of these have received some support in research. Wheeless and Grotz (1977) have developed measures of trust and interpersonal solidarity. Sub-jects described themselves as feeling more trust and solidarity with people whom they had known longer and were also more likely to disclose to them, supporting the idea that trust mediated subjects' self-reported self-disclosure. Wheeless concluded that trust was a necessary but not a sufficient basis for the disclosure of intimacies. Barrell and Jourard (1976) found in a self-report study that participants said they would not reveal a confidence to another if they expected the confidence to destroy the relationship. These studies support Jourard's idea that the discloser must anticipate confidentiality and acceptance before disclosure will occur.

Beliefs that one can trust one's partner take some time to develop, hence the pace with which a relationship can develop along these lines will be bounded by the time required for the establishment of trust. However, we suspect that the temporal pace varies for belief in confidentiality and belief in acceptance. Confidentiality can be inferred over time from how the partner treats other persons' confidences; if the partner gossips about somebody else, one will probably assume that the partner cannot be trusted with intimate information. If the partner passes this test, one might disclose, but will probably wait some time to see whether the information "comes back" through another person—that is, did the partner keep this particular information confidential. Thus there would be two waiting periods involved in assessing the partner's trustworthiness with confidential information; however, if the partner proves trustworthy after these waiting periods, confidentiality is no longer an issue and would not slow the pace of future disclosures. On the other hand, trust in the partner not to ridicule one for one's foibles might require a series of waiting periods, as one tests reaction to a variety of behaviors in a variety of psychological domains.

Linear pace has not been well-represented in the literature on friendship formation. There is some evidence that similarity of pace might be an important basis of attraction; however, direct evidence to support this notion was not presented, and only indirect evidence, such as evaluations of speakers and the role of activity similarity in relationships, could be found. Evidence for a need for appropriate pacing in self-disclosure intimacy and social penetration was stronger, but more research is needed to support this view as well.

Cyclical Pace/Rhythm

Cyclical or recurrent events can also vary in their pace, either when the event itself is paced differently or when the interval between recurrences changes. Although we might speculate as to how such changes might affect satisfaction with events or relationships, we have no empirical studies that address this issue. McGrath et al.'s (1984) work suggests that it is difficult for people to adjust their established cyclical work pace to changing time pressures, but this finding may not generalize to the interpersonal domain. Indeed, a number of authors would suggest that variably paced activities are more appealing to partners than similarly paced ones (for example, Altman, 1975; Werner & Latané, 1974).

Rhythm has been similarly ignored as a component of friendship patterns. Rhythm is by definition an aspect of cyclicity because it involves repetition, namely, "the recurrence or repetition of stress, beat, sound, accent, motion, etc., usually occurring in a regular or harmonious pattern or manner" (Standard College Dictionary, 1968). This definition provides an important distinction between cyclical scale and cyclical rhythm. In cyclical scale, the durations and intervals can vary somewhat, and the pattern will still be perceived as cyclical. In rhythm, the scale or pattern of the cycle must be regular to be perceived as rhythmic. Thus Altman's (1975) concept of privacy regulation as a dialectic process explicitly eschews a regular rhythmic pattern, whereas Latané & Werner's (1978) concept of a "sociostat" implies more regularity and therefore a more rhythmic quality to interaction.

Phenomenologically oriented writers have been most sensitive to the idea that interpersonal behavior can have a rhythmic quality. For example, Seamon (1979) described routine patterns of activities that, for some people, facilitated social contact and friendship formation. Being in the same place at the same time on a regular basis gave a rhythm to people's lives and also put them in contact with other people whose routines similarly brought them to that place at that time. Such synchrony Seamon referred to as "place ballet" (p. 56): "The regularity is unintentional, arising slowly over time as the result of many repeated 'accidental' meetings. People who otherwise might not know each other become acquainted—even friends. At a minimum, there is recognition. Participants generally appreciate the climate of familiarity which grows and to which they become attached" (p. 57). Thus the rhythm of a place ballet contains two features: People enjoy the rhythmic pattern, and with synchronization or entrainment, the rhythm facilitates acquaintanceship and friendship formation.

As with most of the work on cyclical patterns, research on rhythm and friendship processes is primarily descriptive. Seamon's (1979) inferences about rhythm were based on open-ended interviews, and no systematic data were presented. Because he described the patterns as rhythmic, his work has been included as an example of rhythm. On the other hand, Rowles's (1980, 1981) interviews with elderly house-bound individuals were not designed to distinguish between irregular and regular (that is, rhythmic) patterns. We included Rowles's descriptions as irregularly patterned activities when they might have been more regular, and hence rhythmic. Furthermore, neither Seamon nor Rowles attempted to evaluate the generality of the rhythmic patterns that they described, but were primarily interested in drawing attention to these regular patterns of contact. Unfortunately, without systematic samples and interviews, it is impossible to tell whether rhythmic patterns are typical of many, or only a few poetic respondents.

Cyclical pace and cyclical rhythm are provocative areas for additional research and have been included in the framework because of their potential as heuristic devices rather than on the basis of substantial support in the literature. The idea that daily, weekly, or longer rhythms might provide continuity, flow, or some other quality has been evident in phenomenological writings and research, but has been missing from more systematic analyses. Anecdotal evidence, intuition, and descriptions suggest that these are characteristics of people and relationships that warrant additional attention.

SUMMARY AND DISCUSSION

In this chapter, we have presented a framework of temporal qualities intended to illuminate some of the heretofore hidden qualities that make communication and interpersonal relationships dynamic. We selected four aspects of time (salience, sequencing, scale, and pace/rhythm), showed how they had been used or treated in theory and research, and discussed how each contributed in a somewhat different way to the communication and exchange involved in friendship development, maintenance, continuity, and/or change. Some of the dynamic characteristics contributed to stability, others lent variety, and still others represented changes in the individual or the relationship. In this perspective, time connotes more than change, and relationships deserve to be studied for their dynamic stabilizing and revitalizing qualities as well as for their dynamic changing qualities.

To enhance clarity and to permit detailed examinations of the qualities, each was presented and explored separately. However, in actuality they occur in combination and therefore should be considered holistically rather than separately. For example, a recurrent argument that escalates with each repetition would be a fast-paced, past-salient, short-interval, short-duration, cyclical sequence, which probably differs in important ways from an argument that fits a different combination of characteristics (for example, the same pattern but with a long interval between recurrences would probably be less damaging to the relationship). This does not mean that all examinations of relationships must include all factors, but it does mean that this level of complexity should be kept in mind.

A few comments about these variables is also in order. As was mentioned earlier, the four qualities were chosen primarily because they are common temporal qualities and have been represented in the relevant literature. Other qualities were not included (for example, the amplitude of cycles; time perspective) primarily because it was not immediately apparent how they were relevant. Further examination of the literature may reveal that these additional qualities can also enhance our understanding of interpersonal relationships. Psychological intensity, or the amplitude of cycles, should certainly be considered, especially if included in both linear and cyclical domains.

It was disappointing to find so little information about cyclical or rhythmic aspects of relationships. To a certain extent, this likely represents Western scientists' preferences for thinking of time as a linear quality, but it probably also represents the difficulty of studying ongoing cyclical events and the problem of deciding whether a linear phenomenon is being or has been transformed into a cyclical one.

And finally, the model and its four variables were supported by evidence from diverse literatures, representing many levels of analysis and approaches to interpersonal phenomena. We drew general conclusions about the roles of each quality from this broad sample; however, it may be that their roles will differ depending on the particular aspect of behavior that is being considered.

Although there may be weaknesses with this model and its four main categories, on balance they have served their purposes well. They have united some very diverse literatures, illuminated several dynamic characteristics of relationships, and pointed to areas of needed research and theorizing. We found that people have been thinking about relationships as dynamic entities, but that more research and more integration are needed.

REFERENCES

Albert, S., & Kessler, S. (1976). Processes for ending social encounters: The conceptual archaeology of a temporal place. *Journal for the Theory of Social Behavior, 6,* 147-170.

Albert, S., & Kessler, S. (1978). Ending social encounters. *Journal of Experimental Social Psychology, 14,* 541-553.

Altman, I. (1973). Reciprocity of social exchange. *Journal for the Theory of Social Behavior, 3,* 249-261.

Altman, I. (1975). *The environment and social behavior: Privacy, personal space, territory, crowding.* Monterey, CA: Brooks/Cole.

Altman, I., & Taylor, D. A. (1973). *Social penetration: The development of interpersonal relationships.* New York: Holt, Rinehart & Winston.

Altman, I., Taylor, D. A., & Wheeler, L. (1971). Ecological aspects of group behavior in social isolation. *Journal of Applied Social Psychology, 1,* 76-100.

Altman, I., Vinsel, A., & Brown, B. B. (1981). Dialectic conceptions in social psychology: An application to social penetration and privacy regulation. In L. Berkowitz (Ed.), *Advances in experimental social psychology* (Vol. 14, pp. 107-160). New York: Academic Press.

Archer, R. L., Berg, J. H., & Runge, T. E. (1980). Active and passive observer's attraction to a self-disclosing other. *Journal of Experimental Social Psychology, 16,* 130-145.

Argyle, M. (1978). *The psychology of interpersonal behaviour.* Middlesex, England: Penguin.

Aronson, E., & Linder, D. (1965). Gain and loss of self-esteem as determinants of interpersonal attractiveness. *Journal of Experimental Social Psychology, 1,* 156-171.

Bachelard, G. (1964). *The poetics of space.* New York: Orion.

Bancroft, N., & Bendinelli, L. (1982). Listening comprehension of compressed, accelerated and normal speech by the visually handicapped. *Journal of Visual Impairment and Blindness, 76,* 235-237.

Barnett, L. R., & Nietzel, M. T. (1979). Relationship of instrumental and affectional behaviors and self-esteem to marital satisfaction in distressed and nondistressed couples. *Journal of Consulting and Clinical Psychology, 47,* 946-957.

Barrell, J., & Jourard, S. (1976). Being honest with persons we like. *Journal of Individual Psychology, 32,* 185-193.

Beier, E. (1975). *People reading.* New York: Stein and Day.

Berscheid, E., & Graziano, W. (1979). The initiation of social relationships and interpersonal attraction. In R. L. Burgess & T. L. Huston (Eds.), *Social exchange in developing relationships* (pp. 31-60). New York: Academic Press.

Birchler, G. R., & Webb, L. J. (1977). Discriminating interaction behaviors in happy and unhappy marriages. *Journal of Consulting and Clinical Psychology, 45,* 494-495.

Blundell, V. (1980). Hunter-gatherer territoriality: Ideology and behavior in Northwest Australia. *Ethnohistory, 27,* 103-117.

Bond, M. H., & Dutton, D. G. (1975). The effect of interaction anticipation and experience as a victim on aggressive behavior. *Journal of Personality, 43,* 515-527.

Bower, G. H., Black, J. B., & Turner, T. J. (1979). Scripts in memory for text. *Cognitive Psychology, 11,* 177-200.

Braiker, H. B., & Kelley, H. H. (1979). Conflict in the development of close relationships. In R. L. Burgess & T. L. Huston (Eds.), *Social exchange in developing relationships* (pp. 135-168). New York: Academic Press.

Broder, S. N. (1982). Liking, own disclosure, and partner disclosure in female roommates. *Journal of Social Psychology, 117,* 303-304.

Burgess, R. L., & Huston, T. L. (Eds.). (1979). *Social exchange in developing relationships.* New York: Academic Press.

Campbell, J., & Hawley, C. W. (1982). Study habits and Eysenck's theory of extraversion-introversion. *Journal of Research in Personality, 16,* 139-146.

Cappella, J. N. (1981). Mutual influence in expressive behavior: Adult-adult and infant-adult dyadic interaction. *Psychological Bulletin, 89,* 101-132.

Chaikin, A. L., & Derlega, V. J. (1976). Self-disclosure. In J. W. Thibaut, J. T. Spence, & R. C. Carson (Eds.), *Contemporary topics in social psychology* (pp. 177-210). Morristown, NJ: General Learning Press.

Christensen, A., & King, C. E. (1982). Telephone survey of daily marital behavior. *Behavioral Assessment, 4,* 327-338.

Clore, G. (1976). Interpersonal attraction: An overview. In J. W. Thibaut, J. T. Spence, & R. C. Carson (Eds.), *Contemporary topics in social psychology* (pp. 135-175). Morristown, NJ: General Learning Press.

Clore, G., Wiggins, N., & Itkin, S. (1975). Gain and loss in attraction: Attributions from nonverbal behavior. *Journal of Personality and Social Psychology, 31,* 706-712.

Cozby, P. C. (1972). Self-disclosure, reciprocity and liking. *Sociometry, 35,* 151-160.

Csikszentmihalyi, M., & Rochberg-Halton, E. (1981). *The meaning of things: Domestic symbols and the self.* Cambridge, MA: Cambridge University Press.

Cunningham, J. (1981). *Effects of intimacy and sex-role congruency of self-disclosure.* Unpublished doctoral dissertation, University of Utah, Salt Lake City.

Darley, J. M., & Berscheid, E. (1967). Increased liking as a result of the anticipation of personal contact. *Human Relations, 20,* 29-40.

Darley, J. M., & Fazio, R. H. (1980). Expectancy confirmation processes arising in the social interaction sequence. *American Psychologist, 35,* 867-881.

Davis, D., Rainey, H. G., & Brock, T. C. (1976). Interpersonal physical pleasuring: Effects of sex combinations, recipient attributes, and anticipated future interaction. *Journal of Personality and Social Psychology, 33,* 89-106.

Davis, K. E. (1962). *Impressions of others and interaction context as determinants of social interaction and perception in two person discussion groups.* Unpublished doctoral dissertation, Duke University. (Described in E. E. Jones & H. B. Gerard (Eds.), *Foundations of social psychology.* New York: John Wiley, 1967.)

de Haan, H. J. (1982). The relationship of estimated comprehensibility to the rate of connected speech. *Perception and Psychophysics, 32,* 27-31.

Derlega, V. J., & Chaikin, A. L. (1976). Norms affecting self-disclosure in men and women. *Journal of Consulting and Clinical Psychology, 44,* 376-380.

Derlega, V. J., Harris, M. S., & Chaikin, A. L. (1973). Self-disclosure reciprocity, liking, and the deviant. *Journal of Experimental Social Psychology, 9,* 277-284.

Derlega, V. J., Walmer, J., & Furman, G. (1973). Mutual disclosure in social interactions. *Journal of Social Psychology, 90,* 159-160.

Duck, S. (1982). A topography of relationship disengagement and dissolution. In S. Duck (Ed.), *Personal relationships: Dissolving personal relationships* (Vol. 4, pp. 1-30). New York: Academic Press.

Eliade, M. (1959). *The sacred and the profane: The nature of religion.* New York: Harcourt Brace Jovanovich.

Eysenck, H. J. (1967). *The biological basis of personality.* Springfield, IL: Charles C Thomas.

Foa, E. B., & Foa, U. G. (1976). Resource theory of social exchange. In J. W. Thibaut, J. T. Spence, & R. C. Carson (Eds.), *Contemporary topics in social psychology* (pp. 99-131). Morristown, NJ: General Learning Press.

Foulke, E. (1971). The perception of time compressed speech. In D. L. Horton & J. J. Jenkins (Eds.), *Perception of language* (pp. 79-107). New York: Charles E Merrill.

Foulke, E., & Sticht, T. G. (1969). A review of research on time compressed speech. *Psychological Bulletin, 72,* 50-62.

Furby, L. (1978). Possessions: Toward a theory of their meaning and function throughout the life cycle. In P. B. Baltes (Ed.), *Life-span development and behavior* (Vol. 1, pp. 297-336). New York: Academic Press.

Gaebelein, J. W. (1976). Self-disclosure among friends, acquaintances and strangers. *Psychological Reports, 38,* 967-970.

Gergen, K. S. (1969). *The psychology of behavior change.* Reading, MA: Addison-Wesley.

Gibson, J. J. (1975). Events are perceivable, but time is not. In J. R. Fraser & N. Lawrence (Eds.), *The study of time: II. Proceedings of the second conference of the International Society for the Study of Time* (pp. 295-301). New York: Springer-Verlag.

Hagestad, G. O., & Smyer, M. A. (1982). Dissolving long-term relationships: Patterns of divorcing in middle age. In S. Duck (Ed.), *Personal relationships: Dissolving personal relationships* (Vol. 4, pp. 155-188). New York: Academic Press.

Hall, E. T. (1983). *The dance of life: The other dimension of time.* Garden City, NY: Anchor Press/Doubleday.

Hallinan, M. T. (1978). The process of friendship formation. *Social Networks, 1,* 193-210.

Hammer, M. (1980). Predictability of social connections over time. *Social Networks, 2,* 165-180.

Harries-Jones, P. (1969). "Home boy" ties and political organization in a copperbelt township. In J. C. Mitchell (Ed.), *Social networks in urban situations* (pp. 297-347). Manchester: Manchester University Press.

Hartocollis, P. (1983). *Time and timelessness.* New York: International Universities Press.

Hays, R., & Oxley, D. (1984). *Social networks among college students.* Unpublished manuscript, University of Texas at Austin, Department of Psychology.

Hill, C. T., Rubin, Z., & Peplau, L. A. (1976). Breakups before marriage: The end of 103 affairs. *Journal of Social Issues, 32,* 147-168.

Hirsch, B. J. (1980). Natural support systems and coping with major life changes. *American Journal of Community Psychology, 8,* 159-172.

Hoebel, E. A. (1960). *The Cheyennes: Indians of the great plains.* New York: Holt, Rinehart & Winston.

Homans, G. C. (1961). *Social behavior: Its elementary forms.* New York: Harcourt Brace Jovanovich.

Hoornaert, J. (1973). Time perspective: Theoretical and methodological considerations. *Psychologica Belgica, 13,* 265-294.

Howell, S. (1980). Environments as hypotheses in human aging research. In L. W. Poon (Ed.), *Aging in the 1980s: Psychological issues* (pp. 424-432). Washington, DC: American Psychological Association.

Huesmann, L. R., & Levinger, G. (1976). Incremental exchange theory: A formal model for progression in dyadic social interaction. In L. Berkowitz (Ed.), *Advances in experimental social psychology* (Vol. 9, pp. 191-229). New York: Academic Press.

Insko, C. A., & Wilson, M. (1977). Interpersonal attraction as a function of social interaction. *Journal of Personality and Social Psychology, 35,* 903-911.

Jacobson, N. S., Waldron, H., & Moore, D. (1980). Toward a behavioral profile of marital distress. *Journal of Consulting and Clinical Psychology, 48,* 696-703.

Jones, E. E., & Goethals, G. R. (1972). Order effects in impression formation: Attribution context and the nature of the entity. In E. E. Jones, D. E. Kanouse, H. H. Kelley, R. E. Nisbett, S. Valins, & B. Weiner (Eds.), *Attribution: Perceiving the causes of behavior* (pp. 27-46). Morristown, NJ: General Learning Press.

Jones, Y. V. (1980). Kinship affiliation through time: Black homecoming and family reunions in a North Carolina County. *Ethnohistory, 27,* 49-66.

Jourard, S. M. (1971). *The transparent self* (rev. ed.). New York: Van Nostrand.

Kapferer, B. (1969). Norms and the manipulation of relationships in a work context. In J. C. Mitchell (Ed.), *Social networks in urban situations* (pp. 181-245). Manchester: Manchester University Press.

Kelley, H. H., & Thibaut, J. W. (1978). *Interpersonal relations: A theory of interdependence.* New York: John Wiley.

Kelvin, P. (1977). Predictability, power, and vulnerability in interpersonal attraction. In S. Duck (Ed.), *Theory and practice in interpersonal attraction* (pp. 355-378). New York: Academic Press.

Knapp, M. L., Hart, R. P., Friedrich, G. W., & Shulman, G. M. (1973). The rhetoric of goodbye: Verbal and nonverbal correlates of human leavetaking. *Speech Monographs, 40,* 182-198.

Korosec-Serfaty, P. (in press). Attics and cellars. *Journal of Environmental Psychology.*

Krain, M. (1975). Communication among premarital couples at three stages of dating. *Journal of Marriage and the Family, 37,* 609-618.

Kraut, R. E., Lewis, S. H., & Swezey, L. W. (1982). Listener responsiveness and the coordination of conversation. *Journal of Personality and Social Psychology, 43,* 718-731.

Latané, B., & Hothersall, D. (1972). Social attraction in animals. In P. C. Dodwell (Ed.), *New horizons in psychology II* (pp. 259-275). Harmondsworth, England: Penguin.

Latané, B., & Werner C. M. (1978). Regulation of social contact in laboratory rats: Time, not distance. *Journal of Personality and Social Psychology, 36,* 1128-1137.

Lee, N. (1969). *The search for an abortionist.* Chicago: University of Chicago Press.

Levinger, G. (1976). A social psychological perspective on marital dissolution. *Journal of Social Issues, 32,* 21-48.

Levinger, G. (1979). A social exchange view on the dissolution of pair relationships. In R. L. Burgess & T. L. Huston (Eds.), *Social exchange in developing relationships* (pp. 169-193). New York: Academic Press.

Levinger, G. (1980). Toward the analysis of close relationships. *Journal of Experimental Social Psychology, 16,* 510-544.

Levinger, G., & Huesmann, L. R. (1980). An "incremental exchange" perspective on the pair: Interpersonal reward and level of involvement. In K. J. Gergen, M. S. Greenberg, & R. J. Willis (Eds.), *Social exchange: Advances in theory and research* (pp. 165-188). New York: Plenum.

Levinger, G., & Moles, O. C. (Eds.). (1979). *Divorce and separation: Context, causes and consequences.* New York: Basic Books.

Levinger, G., Senn, D. J., & Jorgensen, B. W. (1970). Progress towards permanence in courtship: A test of the Kerckhoff-Davis hypothesis. *Sociometry, 33,* 427-443.

Linton, M. (1975). Memory for real-world events. In D. A. Norman & D. E. Rumelhart (Eds.), *Explorations in cognition* (pp. 376-404). San Francisco: Freeman.

Linton, M. (1983, August). *Contents of memory: Methods and problems.* Paper presented at the International Society for the Study of Behavioral Development, Munich, Germany.

Lloyd, S., & Cate, R. (1984). *Developmental course of conflict in premarital relationship dissolution.* Unpublished manuscript, University of Utah, Department of Family and Consumer Studies.

Luft, J. (1969). *Of human interaction.* Palo Alto, CA: National Press Books.

Lynch, K. (1972). *What time is this place?* Cambridge, MA: MIT Press.

Marlowe, P., Gergen, K. J., & Doob, A. N. (1966). Opponent's personality, expectation of social interaction, and interpersonal bargaining. *Journal of Personality and Social Psychology, 3,* 206-213.

Matlin, M., & Stang, D. (1978). *The Pollyanna principle: Selectivity in language, memory and thought.* Cambridge, MA: Scheukman.

McCarthy, M. F., & Duck, S. W. (1976). Friendship duration and responses to attitudinal agreement-disagreement. *British Journal of Social Clinical Psychology, 15,* 377-386.

McGrath, J. E., Kelly, J. R., & Matchatka, D. E. (1984). The social psychology of organizations: Entrainment of behavior in social and organizational settings. In S. Oskamp (Ed.), *Applied social psychology annual: Applications in organizational settings* (Vol. 5, pp. 21-44). Beverly Hills, CA: Sage.

McGrath, J. E., & Rotchford, N. L. (1983). Coping with time: Time, stress, and coping in organizational settings. In B. Staw & L. Cummings (Eds.), *Research in organizational behavior* (Vol. 5, pp. 57-101). Greenwich, CT: JAI Press.

Milardo, R. M., Johnson, M. P., & Huston, T. L. (1983). Developing close relationships: Changing patterns of interaction between pair members and social networks. *Journal of Personality and Social Psychology, 44,* 964-976.

Miller, G. R., & Parks, M. R. (1982). Communication in dissolving relationships. In S. Duck (Ed.), *Personal relationships: Dissolving personal relationships* (Vol. 4, pp. 127-154). New York: Academic Press.

Mitchell, J. C. (1969). The concept and use of social networks. In J. C. Mitchell (Ed.), *Social networks in urban situations.* Manchester: Manchester University Press.

Morton, T. (1978). Intimacy and reciprocity of exchanges: A comparison of spouses and strangers. *Journal of Personality and Social Psychology, 36,* 72-81.

Moscovici, S. (1967). Communication processes and the properties of language. In L. Berkowitz (Ed.), *Advances in experimental social psychology* (Vol. 3, pp. 225-270). New York: Academic Press.

Nadel, S. F. (1958). *The theory of social structure.* Glencoe, IL: The Free Press.

Newman, H. M. (1982). Talk about a past relationship partner: Metacommunicative implications. *The American Journal of Family Therapy, 10,* 24-32.

Orme, J. E. (1969). *Time, experience and behavior.* London: Iliffe Books.

Orthner, D. K. (1975). Leisure activity patterns and marital satisfaction over the marital career. *Journal of Marriage and the Family. 37,* 91-104.

Parmelee, P., Werner, C. M., & Diefenderfer, J. (1979, April). *Subjective and territoriality of single and shared dwellers: It's who you are and what you do.* Paper presented at the meeting of the Western Psychological Association, San Diego, CA.

Patterson, G. R., & Cobb, J. A. (1973). Stimulus control for classes of noxious behaviors. In J. F. Knutson (Ed.), *The control of aggression* (pp. 145-199). Chicago: Aldine.

Pepitone-Rockwell, F. (Ed.). (1980). *Dual career couples.* Beverly Hills, CA: Sage.

Quottrochi-Tubin, S., & Jason, L. A. (1983). The influence of introversion-extraversion of activity choice and satisfaction among the elderly. *Personality and Individual Differences, 4,* 17-22.

Rakowski, W. (1979). Future time perspective in later adulthood: Review and research directions. *Experimental Aging Research, 5,* 43-88.

Ridley, C., & Avery, A. (1979). Influence of social network on dyadic interaction. In R. L. Burgess & T. L. Huston (Eds.), *Social exchange in developing relationships* (pp. 223-246). New York: Academic Press.

Riegel, K. F., & Meacham, J. A. (1978). Dialectics, transaction, and Piaget's theory. In L. A. Pervin & M. Lewis (Eds.), *Perspectives in interactional psychology* (pp. 23-47). New York: Plenum.

Rodin, M. J. (1982). Non-engagement, failure to engage, and disengagement. In S. Duck (Ed.), *Personal relationships: Dissolving personal relationships* (Vol. 4, pp. 31-49). New York: Academic Press.

Rogers, E., & Kincaid, D. L. (1981). *Communication networks: Toward a new paradigm for research.* New York: The Free Press.

Rosenfeld, H. M. (1966a). Approval-seeking and approval-inducing functions of verbal and non-verbal responses in the dyad. *Journal of Personality and Social Psychology, 4,* 597-605.

Rosenfeld, H. M. (1966b). Instrumental affiliative functions of facial and gestural expressions. *Journal of Personality and Social Psychology, 4,* 65-72.

Rowles, G. D. (1980). Growing old "inside": Aging and attachment to place in an Appalachian community. In D. Datan & N. Lohmann (Eds.), *Transitions of aging* (pp. 153-170). New York: Academic Press.

Rowles, G. D. (1981). The surveillance zone as meaningful space for the aged. *The Gerontologist, 21*(3), 304-311.

Rubin, Z. (1975). Disclosing oneself to a stranger: Reciprocity and its limits. *Journal of Experimental Social Psychology, 11,* 233-260.

Rusbult, C. E. (1980). Commitment and satisfaction in romantic associations: A test of the investment model. *Journal of Experimental Social Psychology, 16,* 172-186.

Rusbult, C. E. (1983). A longitudinal test of the investment model: The development (and deterioration) of satisfaction and commitment in heterosexual involvements. *Journal of Personality and Social Psychology, 45,* 101-117.

Rusbult, C. E., Zembrodt, I. M., & Gunn, L. K. (1982). Exit, voice, loyalty, and neglect: Responses to dissatisfaction in romantic involvements. *Journal of Personality and Social Psychology, 43,* 1230-1242.

Saile, D. (in press). The ritual establishment of home. In I. Altman & C. M. Werner (Eds.), *Human behavior and the environment: Current theory and research: Home environments* (Vol. 8). New York: Plenum.

Schank, R. C., & Abelson, R. P. (1977). *Script, plans, goals and understanding: An inquiry into human knowledge structures.* Hillsdale, NJ: Lawrence Erlbaum.

Schulz, R. (1976). Effects of control and predictability on the physical and psychological wellbeing of the institutionalized aged. *Journal of Personality and Social Psychology, 33,* 563-573.

Seamon, D. (1979). *A geography of the lifeworld: Movement, rest, and encounter.* New York: St. Martins Press.

Seamon, D. (1982). The phenomenological contribution to environmental psychology. *Journal of Environmental Psychology, 2,* 119-140.

Selye, H. (1973). The evolution of the stress concept. *American Scientist, 61,* 692-699.

Shulman, N. (1975). Life-cycle variations in patterns of close relationships. *Journal of Marriage and the Family, 37,* 813-822.

Shure, G. H., & Meeker, R. J. (1968). Empirical demonstration of normative behavior in the prisoner's dilemma. In *Proceedings of the 76th Annual Convention* (pp. 61-62). Washington, DC: American Psychological Association.

Smith, B. L., Brown, B. L., Strong, W. J., & Reucher, A. C. (1975). Effects of speech rate on personality perception. *Language and Speech, 18,* 145-152.

Snyder, M., Tanke, E. D., & Berscheid, E. (1977). Social perception and interpersonal behavior: On the self-fulfilling nature of social stereotypes. *Journal of Personality and Social Psychology, 35,* 656-666.

Spanier, G. B., Lewis, R. A., & Cole, C. L. (1975). Marital adjustment over the family life cycle: The issue of curvilinearity. *Journal of Marriage and the Family, 37,* 263-276.

Srull, T. K., & Wyer, R. S. (1980). Category accessibility and social perceptions: Some implications for the study of person memory and interpersonal judgments. *Journal of Personality and Social Psychology, 38,* 841-856.

Standard College Dictionary. (1968). New York: Funk & Wagnalls.
Street, R. L., & Brady, R. M. (1982). Speech rate acceptance ranges as a function of evaluative domain, listener speech rate and communication context. *Communication Monographs, 49,* 290-308.
Stuart, R. B., Broderick, C., & Gurman, A. S. (1982). *Helping couples change: A social learning approach to marital therapy.* New York: Guilford.
Sutherland, A. E., & Insko, C. (1979). Attraction and interestingness of future interaction. *Journal of Personality, 41,* 234-243.
Thibaut, J. W., & Kelley, H. H. (1959). *The social psychology of groups.* New York: John Wiley.
Tognoli, J. (1980). Male friendship and intimacy across the life span. *Family Relations, 29,* 273-279.
Tuan, Y. (1977). *Space and place: The perspective of experience.* Minneapolis: University of Minnesota Press.
Turner, C. W., & Dodd, D. K. (1979). The development of anti-social behaviors. In R. L. Ault (Ed.), *Selected readings in child development* (pp. 267-319). Santa Monica, CA: Goodyear.
Weiss, R. L., & Issac, J. (1976, April). *Behavioral vs. cognitive measures as predictors of marital satisfaction.* Paper presented at the meeting of the Western Psychological Association, Los Angeles, CA.
Wellman, B. (1979). The community question: The intimate networks of East Yorkers. *American Journal of Sociology, 84,* 1201-1231.
Wellman, B., & Leighton, B. (1979). Networks, neighborhoods and communities: Approaches to the study of the community question. *Urban Affairs Quarterly, 14,* 363-390.
Werner, C. M., Altman, I., & Oxley, D. (in press). Temporal aspects of homes: A transactional analysis. In I. Altman & C. M. Werner (Eds.), *Human behavior and the environment: Current theory and research: Home environments* (Vol. 8). New York: Plenum.
Werner, C. M., & Latané, B. (1974) Interaction motivates attraction: Rats are fond of fondling. *Journal of Personality and Social Psychology, 29,* 328-334.
Werner, C. M., & Latané, B. (1976). Responsiveness and communication medium in dyadic interactions. *Bulletin of the Psychonomic Society, 8,* 569-571.
Werner, C. M., Oxley, D., & Altman, I. (1983, April). *Christmas Street.* Paper presented at the Environmental Design Research Meetings, Lincoln, NE.
Werner, C., & Parmelee, P. (1979). Similarity of activity preferences among friends: Those who play together stay together. *Social Psychology Quarterly, 42,* 62-66.
Wheeless, L. R., & Grotz, J. (1977). The measurement of trust and its relationship to self-disclosure. *Human Communication Research, 3,* 250-257.
Whitten, N. E., Jr., & Wolfe, A. W. (1973). Network analysis. In J. J. Honigmann (Ed.), *Handbook of social and cultural anthropology* (pp. 717-746). Chicago: Rand McNally.
Wiggins, J. A. (1979). Dynamic theories of social relationships and resulting research strategies. In R. L. Burgess & T. L. Huston (Eds.), *Social exchange in developing relationships* (pp. 381-407). New York: Academic Press.
Willis, F. N. (1966). Initial speaking distance as a function of the speaker's relationship. *Psychonomic Science, 5,* 221-222.
Wyer, R. S., & Carlston, D. E. (1979). *Social cognition, inference, and attribution.* Hillsdale, NJ: Lawrence Erlbaum.
Wyer, R. S., & Srull, T. K. (1980). The processing of social stimulus information: A conceptual integration. In R. Hastie, T. M. Ostrom, E. B. Ebbesen, R. S. Wyer, D. L. Hamilton, & D. E. Carlston (Eds.), *Person memory: The cognitive basis of social perception* (pp. 227-300). Hillsdale, NJ: Lawrence Erlbaum.

3 Methodology in Interpersonal Communication Research

MARSHALL SCOTT POOLE

University of Illinois, Urbana-Champaign

ROBERT D. McPHEE

University of Wisconsin—Milwaukee

T
HE history of thought about social science is a history of metaphors. Social researchers have been likened to physicists, biologists, alchemists, high priests, and even laypersons. There is truth in most of these metaphors and even a degree of irony in some, but they miss something essential and intangible in the social scientist's condition. Most of all, we believe that social scientists resemble detectives in a murder mystery. Like a good detective, the researcher is confronted by a confusing pattern of clues that is meaningful in both an immediate and a deeper, sometimes hidden sense. To get at this deeper meaning and unravel the mystery, the detective (researcher) must probe and order this "reality," often relying on improvisation, inspiration, and luck. Once things fall into place there is the possibility of true understanding and insight, but there is also the danger of misinterpreting the multitude of available signs. Some things, such as motives, can never be determined with certainty. Just as it is often not clear whether a crime has been committed, so it is that many research problems are unclear or unformulated. As the detective deduces the crime, so must the researcher constitute and cast up the object of research. This requires a capacity to ask the right questions as well as a sense of what form the answer should take. Detective novels are replete with devices and strategies for attacking a mystery, and this is no less true of social scientific writing. Foremost among such devices is theory.

Theory, as Cappella (1977) has noted, is a "god-term" of social science. Theory is supposed to be a guiding light that orders observations and imposes pattern on an overwhelmingly complex world. Theory determines method: It indicates what data are appropriate and places limits on how these

AUTHORS' NOTE: We would like to thank Kathryn Dindia, Mary Anne Fitzpatrick, Joe Folger, Dean Hewes, Ed Mabry, Sally Planalp, and Kathy Zoppi for their suggestions and comments. We have persisted in our errors despite their sound advice.

data may best be obtained. On this view, an emphasis on method apart from theory is misguided and may be downright misleading.

Accordingly methods are condemned as mindless technicianship, the resort of tinkerers steeped in "dust-bowl empiricist" philosophy. Of course, there is much justice in this position. Cappella (1977) points out that researchers tend to obey the "law of the hammer" with respect to methods: Whatever methodologies are in vogue tend to be used over and over, even if they are ill-suited for the questions being asked. However, the sharp distinction between theory and method implied by many discussions is based on a vastly oversimplified picture of how research operates. While it is true that all observation is theory-laden, it is also true—as the pragmatist philosophers realized—that what we can know is determined by the available methods for knowing. Like Hercule Poirot, the social detective must have an effective method because method is one's point of contact with the world. The types of constructs and propositions in our theories, as well as the degree of certainty attached to them, are all dependent on our methodological repertoire. Rather than theory-types, it is more accurate to think of *theory-method complexes* as the driving force in the research enterprise.

Consider the example of interpersonal attraction theory. Those research programs employing laboratory methods, such as Byrne's (1969) and Anderson's (1981), tend to focus on variables conducive to experimental control—reinforcement schedules, uncertainty, and balance of positive and negative remarks. Other programs, like Altman and Taylor's (1973), began with a focus on development of relational attraction over fairly long periods of time and thus tended to focus more on field-centered methods, which in turn supported the dynamism and complexity of their model of shared experience during relational development. Theoretical choices and methodological choices determine each other in a dialectical manner. Methodological preferences shape the types of theory that evolve, just as theories shape methods.

No discussion of methods can be separated from a consideration of how theory and methodology articulate, and the key point of articulation is where method ties into the process of scientific reasoning. To understand this tie, it is useful to distinguish four elements: substantive theoretical assumptions, modes of explanation, modes of inquiry, and methodological technique. *Substantive theoretical assumptions* are those aspects of a theory's content that are particular to the phenomena the theory covers. Substantive assumptions may be quite specific (for example, a definition of self-disclosure) or general, but expressing some assumption about the way a phenomenon "is" (as, for example, the assumption that cognitive processes rather than social forces are the key to explaining self-disclosure). In addition to substantive assumptions, all theories take a characteristic approach to explaining or understanding phenomena, a characteristic *mode of explanation*. Some theories attempt to delineate causal forces determining a

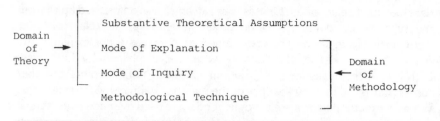

Figure 3.1   Four Elements of the Theory-Method Complex

phenomenon, whereas others explain them as a product of rule-governed action, and still others employ a complex of the two modes. *Mode of inquiry* refers to the strategy the researcher employs in studying a phenomenon. In particular it indexes the relationship between theory (or expectations) and observational practices: Does theory precede or follow from observation, or do the two develop simultaneously? Finally, *methodological technique* represents what have traditionally been referred to as "methods," pro- cedures of design, data collection, and analysis used to investigate inter- personal phenomena.

Substantive assumptions clearly belong to the realm of "theory" and techniques clearly belong to "methods." Modes of explanation and modes of inquiry are sometimes treated as part of theory and sometimes as part of methodology.: They constitute the linking-pin of the theory-method complex. Together substantive assumptions, modes of explanation, and modes of inquiry should dictate the range of appropriate techniques. In practice, choice of techniques is usually determined by the researcher's preferences in one of the three areas—for example, a commitment to grounded theory—but ideally all three elements should be considered. The relationship among substantive assumptions, modes of explanation, and modes of inquiry is complex. In combination a mode of inquiry and a mode of explanation form a *template* that determines the form substantive theory can take, in the fashion shown in the previous example. At the same time, the nature of the phenomenon under study (and hence of substantive assumptions) makes some templates more suitable than others. Clearly the researcher must strike a balance among substantive assumptions, mode of inquiry, and mode of explanation, trading off one against the others until a fruitful combination ensues.

Having said this, we hasten to add that explicit theories do not always precede and guide research. Sometimes researchers do not grapple with their implicit theories until data are gathered, and many good ideas emerge after a study is done, during periods of speculation and reinterpretation. However, establishing a clear sense of the relevant theory-method complex is also important in these cases. After-the-fact sense-making and reformulation are just as critical as a priori planning. Being clear on where one's post hoc theorizing stands makes extensions and future work more systematic and useful.

In this chapter we will define methodology in its broadest sense, encompassing modes of explanation, modes of inquiry, and techniques. The first section considers the modes of explanation and modes of inquiry applicable to the study of interpersonal communication. We will explore various templates implied by combinations of modes of inquiry and explanation, the techniques templates emphasize, and their untapped potential. The second and third sections are concerned with various techniques and how they relate to the theoretical templates. The second section covers data collection and measurement techniques, while the third discusses a broad spectrum of techniques for data analysis. In the conclusion we consider new moves and likely directions in interpersonal methodology.

The primary concern of this chapter is not on how to employ the techniques in question: Full discussions are available in primary sources and are not the concern of this review. Rather, we will focus on (1) what a given technique can do; (2) the crucial assumptions required to employ the technique properly; (3) the kinds of claims that can be made using the technique and which templates these apply to; and (4) common abuses and how they might be avoided. In short, this chapter is concerned with methods-in-use and their implications for theory development in interpersonal communication. It attempts to specify guidelines for technical choices that permit the most effective possible match between theory and technique. Hopefully it will equip the social sleuth with a "method" for detecting the patterns and determinations in the interpersonal communication.

MODES OF EXPLANATION, MODES OF INQUIRY, AND THEORETICAL TEMPLATES

In the introduction we defined modes of inquiry and modes of explanation in general terms. Here we will explore them in more detail, laying out three basic modes of explanation and three modes of inquiry. In combination the modes of explanation and inquiry form nine theoretical templates. These templates, discussed below and portrayed in Figure 3.2, determine the form an interpersonal theory can take. They constitute a terrain of possibilities for interpersonal communication research. The templates should be regarded as ideal types for research; although few studies exactly conform to the descriptions below, the templates constitute standards for selecting and planning research strategies and making technical choices. In order to understand them it is first necessary to consider the two sets of modes.

Mode of Inquiry

Hypothetico- Deductive	Modeling	Grounded	
1	2	3	Causal
4	5	6	Conventional
7	8	9	Dialectical

Mode of Explanation

Figure 3.2   Research Templates

Modes of Explanation

The goals of social science are explanation and understanding. However, the meaning of the two terms is elusive. There have been many attempts to define explanation and understanding in the abstract, but they are better understood by considering the operations they involve. We can distinguish three types of explanation and understanding (generally called explanation here), each involving different operations and assumptions and a different sense of what scientific inquiry is—causal explanation, conventional explanation, and dialectical explanation. Causal, conventional, and dialectical explanations can be distinguished in terms of (1) the assumptions they make about the researcher's relation to the object of study; (2) the forms of explanation they advance and the criteria by which these explanations are evaluated; and (3) their assumptions about the proper reference point for inquiry.

Causal explanations assume the researcher is an independent observer of the phenomenon under study. The object of research is taken to exist in a real, existent, objectifiable world that serves as the starting point of inquiry (even social phenomena are assumed to be objectifiable). Explanations consist of networks of propositions of the form "X causes Y, under conditions $C_1 \ldots C_n$," where X and Y are variables or constructs identified by the researcher and $C_1 \ldots C_n$ are statements of scope or qualifying conditions for the causal relation to hold. For example, Leary's (1957) "interpersonal reflex" can be explained by a law of the form : "Hostile (affiliative) behavior from one party causes the other to respond in like manner, when (1) the two parties have nearly equal power, (2) the parties belong to the same culture." The list of scope conditions would become unmanageably long if every possible qualifier were included, so most causal propositions include an "other things being equal" clause. The nature of causality is the subject of considerable debate, but there is general agreement that a valid causal law must (1) be general and (2) describe a necessary relationship between cause and effect (Achinstein, 1971). The causal linkage in the law may be strictly deterministic or it may state that effect follows cause only with a certain probability. Causal explanation grants the researcher a privileged position with respect to defining constructs, discerning causal linkages, and testing or verifying causal hypotheses. The researcher's perspective by itself is assumed to give an adequate depiction of the world, with no need for cross-checking or verification from the subjects of study. Evaluation of causal explanations thus turns on tests of the adequacy of the researcher's reasoning and procedures: The researcher's explication of constructs is checked for internal logic and richness (Hage, 1972); measures are checked for construct validity with reference to the researcher's theoretical network (Cronbach & Meehl, 1955); and causal linkages are tested using designs and statistical procedures that permit control of intrusive factors and errors not allowed for in the researcher's formulation (Argyris, 1968). In short, causal explanation privileges the researcher's perspective as an objective, legitimate viewpoint for scientific inquiry.

Like causal explanations, *conventional explanations* presume the independence of researcher and the subject of research. However, rather than assuming an objectifiable, natural world, conventional explanation assumes the world is a social product and takes the perspectives of subjects in that world as its starting point. Subjects are assumed to actively monitor and control their behavior with reference to conventions, variously conceived as rules, schemas, types, or structures, among other things. Conventional explanations consist in demonstrating how subjects—who could have done otherwise—acted or reacted in a fashion that is meaningful, understandable, or efficacious in the context of pertinent conventions. An adequate conventional explanation does not have to be necessary or general, nor does it have to show temporal ordering of cause to effect: A conventional explanation seeks to fit phenomena into a pattern meaningful to the active subject, and this pattern entails the possibility of events and the capability of actors rather than a necessary connection. For example, a conventional explanation of Leary's interpersonal reflexes might explore what behaviors counted as hostile or affiliative to subjects and account for matching behavior in light of subjects' adherence to the norm of reciprocity. This explanation would not rest its claim to validity on its generality or on showing a necessary linkage between behavior and norm, but rather on its ability to show how the norm makes matching behavior meaningful and sensible to subjects. In form, conventional explanations range from the rather loose interpretive account implied above to deductive models like the practical syllogism (Cushman & Pearce, 1977; Von Wright, 1971). Regardless of their level of formality, conventional explanations are grounded in the subjects' point of view: The researcher discovers conventions by probing the actor's phenomenology and culture, and conventional explanations attempt to account for action in a manner that reflects subjects' experience. The researcher's formulation of conventions and his or her explanations may differ from the actor's own statements (as do those of conversational analysts), but even these second-order formulations are presumed to be grounded in the actor's rules and meanings. Conventional schemes may be tested by assessing whether the behaviors or cognitions they entail are consistent with the actor's behaviors or cognitions (as is done with systems of linguistic rules), by determining whether the conventions enable an outsider to "pass" as a native, or by asking subjects directly whether the rules or schemes hold. Conventional explanation subordinates the researcher's point of view to the subject's, but leaves the researcher independent, as knower and cataloger of the subject's schemes.

Like conventional explanation, *dialectical explanation* assumes its objects of study are socially constituted. However, in contrast to causal or conventional types, dialectical explanations do not presume the independence of researcher and the subject of research. Instead, scientific inquiry is taken to consist of mediation between two perspectives—the researcher's and the subject's—and neither is privileged. Because of this, dialectical explanations combine aspects of causal and conventional explanations: They specify how causal forces condition action while actors influence the operation of these same forces. Causality plays an important role in dialectical explanation, but it moves along a complex path. People act, but not in circumstances of their own choosing. Forces beyond actors' control determine the available rules, schemes, and structures, and how they can be applied. Within this determination, actors' conventions form the grounds for the operation of causal forces and shape the impact of those forces in the situation. Moreover, systems of action are themselves involved in the generation and movement of causal forces. So action is conditioned by causal forces, which are themselves shaped by action, which is conditioned by causal forces, which are shaped by action, and so forth.

A dialectical explanation of Leary's interpersonal reflexes might emphasize a norm such as reciprocity, but it would also take into account the larger conventional and causal context that shapes how that norm operates in any specific instance. For instance, A's friendly gesture might be systematically misinterpreted (or strategically interpreted) as submissiveness in a situation where B thinks (or wants) status differences to be important and has (or wants) high status. If A anticipated this situation, A would have to be careful to design his or her gesture of simple friendliness to appear "friendly but not weak." The appropriateness of this strategy would depend on the larger conventional and causal context, and other conditions might render it ineffective: Such a gesture might be inappropriate in a more egalitarian situation; it might be impossible to avoid B's status consciousness; or showing friendliness might be possible only if causal factors like A's cultural experience and communicative competence permit. Unlike conventional explanations, whose only requirement is the explanation of action in terms of rules or schemes, dialectical explanations must also specify causal forces that determine the types of conventions available and how actors can use these conventions. Hence, the dialectical explanation must probe the nature of domination in our society and how this carries over into interpersonal relationships. The researcher cannot take rules as given (as a conventional explanation does) but must explore what gives the rules pattern and force. Historical evidence frequently plays an important role in this process because causes are embedded in previous, often long-established action systems. However, discovering causal forces does not complete a dialectical explanation. Causes operate through shaping the action system, and because of this the mediation of causal forces by action must be explored. In this case the impact of causal forces on matching behavior must be understood as actively "filtered" through schemes and structures associated with interpersonal relationships. This filtering does not represent "slippage" or "error" (as a purely causal explanation would assume), but rather is the mechanism through which the cause operates and is regarded as an integral aspect of any explanation. Causality does not entail a direct "X-Y" relationship, but rather something like "X influences conventions $Z_1 \ldots Z_n$, which lead to Y, in the context of the action system W." Causes and conventions interact in this explanation and the ratio of determinism to action varies from case to case. In some instances causal determination is so rigid subjects have little latitude (though in principle they always "could have done otherwise"), whereas in others, causal forces are largely attenuated by actors' control over conventions and contingencies.

This interpenetration of cause and action necessitates the double mediation of researcher's and subject's perspectives: The researcher is in a better position to identify causal forces, but can only understand how these forces operate and how significant they are by taking the active role of the subject and the channeling influence of society into account. Hence, evaluation of dialectical explanations is subject to two sets of criteria, those for causal explanations and those for conventions. Once the operation of causal forces has been established by statistical techniques, their impact on the action system must be spelled out. A successful dialectical explanation articulates causal forces and their impact on acting subjects.

Causal explanations emphasize objectifiable forces; conventional explanations focus on subjectivity (or intersubjectivity); and dialectical explanations emphasize conditioned subjectivity (or intersubjectivity). In drawing these distinctions, it is not necessary to argue that one mode of explanation is better than any other. Each mode has its advocates and each possesses strengths and weaknesses relative to the others. Judging by the programmatic statements of communication scholars, most researchers in our field would claim to be aiming at explanations that account for action in complex systems, that is, at dialectical explanations. However, in practice, the great majority of communication researchers employ either causal or conventional explanations and do not probe their interpenetration. The dialectical mode will not necessarily work better than the others, but it does seem to aim at many of the goals put forth by interpersonal researchers and therefore deserves more explicit attention than it has previously received.

Modes of Inquiry

Even when a researcher is clear on his or her substantive assumptions and mode of explanation, there is still the question of how theory and data are related during the process of inquiry. Three modes of inquiry can be distinguished.

In the *hypothetico-deductive* mode of inquiry, the researcher generates hypotheses from theory, develops operational definitions of theoretical constructs, and sets up a study (experimental, field, or survey) to test the hypotheses. Theory is prior to data collection and hypothesis testing and these steps are strictly separated. By far the majority of interpersonal communication studies operate in this mode.

A second mode of inquiry is *modeling*, in which theory, operationalization, and data patterns are treated simultaneously (see McPhee & Poole, 1981). A model is a representation of a situated theory. It gives a direct depiction of how the theory generates the observed data in a specific context. For example, Newton's mechanics presents a general theory of motion; a *model* of the solar system would consist of equations consistent with Newtonian principles, but representing the forces exerted on each specific planet by others and by the sun. The behavior of the data (in this case, the paths of planets around the sun) is directly described by the equations of the model, which represent a situated case of the general theory. Models often use mathematical representations (for example, Hunter, Levine, and Sayers's [1976] model of attitude change) but may also be cast in logical verbal or pictorial formalisms (for example, Pearce & Conklin's [1979] model of rule-following or Brown & Levinson's [1978] politeness hierarchy). Comparing model predictions with observed data enables the researcher not only to test the model, but also to pinpoint those aspects of the model that are problematic. Treating theory, operationalization, and data simultaneously is obviously more demanding and difficult than the traditional mode of inquiry, but it has the advantages of greater precision and of clarifying assumptions behind the theory (Cappella, 1977; McPhee & Poole, 1981).

The third mode of inquiry is the development of *grounded theory* (Glaser & Strauss, 1967). The researcher goes directly to the phenomenon itself and develops concepts, hypotheses, and theoretical propositions from direct experience with the data. Grounded theory takes a "bottom-up" approach, as opposed to the "top-down" move of the traditional mode: Theory emerges from observation, rather than being prior to it. Once hypotheses or generalizations have been developed, they may be "tested" in the situation or in another context, but this is by no means equivalent to hypothesis testing in the traditional mode. Advocates of grounded theory argue that it makes the researcher more sensitive to particular nuances of the phenomenon and removes "blinders" imposed on the researcher by an a priori theory. Opponents argue that the situated nature of grounded theory does not allow for generalization or for rigorous testing of its propositions.

In recent years there has been considerable roiling of waters concerning which mode of inquiry is best for the study of interpersonal communication. There have been militant advocates of grounded theory (Browning, 1978; Fisher & Hawes, 1971) and of modeling (Cappella, 1977), and equally militant defenders of traditional hypothesis testing (Berger, 1975; Miller & Berger, 1978). Taken together, these show there is a good case for the employment of each mode of inquiry as well as disadvantages or problems with the employment of any mode. Rather than correct or incorrect, we would submit that the three modes of inquiry are comparatively advantageous or disadvantageous, depending on the subject of study, and encourage flexibility in choosing a mode of inquiry.

Templates and Tools

When modes of explanation and modes of inquiry are crossed, nine templates result, each of which represents a different methodological strategy. These templates form the grounds for methodological choice and function on at least two levels.

First, the templates are *descriptions* of the range of options open to interpersonal communication research. In addition to the many efforts that fall clearly in a single template, there are numerous "borderline" or mixed studies that seem to combine aspects of several templates. Some of these are misconceived projects that should be organized by a single template, but are complicated by extraneous concerns or assumptions. Others are hybrids that employ different templates in different phases of research (for example, grounded inquiry at first, then modeling in later stages) or different templates side-by-side in parallel research efforts (for example, research into rules that poses some hypotheses, but also uses grounded inquiry to look for other rules). The scheme presented here is useful in both cases. For misconceived projects it can be used to clarify the researcher's planning and elucidate why dissonant premises "don't belong." For hybrid projects, the templates can be used as points of reference for the various thrusts, and the entire scheme can suggest how and to what extent combinations are feasible.

The templates also have a *normative* function. Each template embodies different assumptions and characteristic forms of inference and proof. Within these limits some techniques are more appropriate than others. The scheme can be used to guide selection of techniques and evaluation of previous technical choices. Further, the templates also suggest how the results of applying techniques should be interpreted. Most techniques can be used in several different templates. Because each template involves different types of claims and makes different assumptions about the nature of the phenomenon under study, the same technique can yield quite different evidence and conclusions under different templates. For example, a contingency table analysis of the distributions of dominant and submissive acts by sex in marital interaction might be adduced to support a "law" of male dominance for a study conducted in Cell 1, which aims for causal explanations and uses the hypothetico-deductive mode of inquiry. The same result might be interpreted as supporting a set of inductively derived rules of male-female interaction when employed in Cell 6, which uses conventional explanations and grounded techniques to derive rules; the contingency table analysis would be post hoc evidence verifying researcher intuitions. The various uses for techniques will become apparent as each cell in Figure 3.2 is discussed, along with its strengths, weaknesses, and technical affinities.

Cell 1: Causal Explanation, Hypothetico-Deductive Inquiry. Traditionally, this template has been regarded as the norm for empirical research in interpersonal communication. As its name implies, the researcher first specifies causal hypotheses, then sets up a research design to test the hypotheses, and rejects or fails to reject the hypotheses based on the data. Theory development precedes and is independent of data collection and analysis. Cell 1 is by far the most frequently employed strategy in interpersonal communication research; most attraction and self-disclosure research, for example, falls in Cell 1 (see, for example, Berger & Calabrese, 1974; Bradac, Hosman, & Tardy, 1978; Pearce, Wright, Sharp, & Slaura, 1974; Sunnafrank & Miller, 1981). At present the techniques most commonly employed in this cell include experimental designs, statistical model-testing methods (such as path analysis), and those developmental techniques designed to establish causality.

Causal, hypothetico-deductive research has several advantages: (1) It yields general, necessary explanations; (2) cast correctly, its hypotheses are clearly falsifiable; and (3) it can result in extremely powerful theories that permit precise prediction and control. Along with these strengths come weaknesses and biases as well. Cell 1 research tends to gloss over unique, particular aspects of the phenomenon under study. It favors precise, tightly controlled conceptualization and measurement of constructs, and this can lead to reification of variables and ignore the subject's perspective when it should be taken into account (see section entitled "Critiquing Constructs and Measures"). Moreover, there are some cases in which causal, hypothetico-deductive explanation is not adequate, notably instances with recursive, layered effects and those in which phenomena are continually renegotiated and redefined by actors. Overemphasis on causal understanding can lead to distortion and oversimplification of cases in which determinations are not strong or play a secondary role. A new direction of particular interest is the role qualitative techniques could play in supporting claims of temporal ordering and causal influence. The discussion sections of Cell 1 studies often contain anecdotal reports of qualitative observations that support one or the other interpretation of results, and there is no reason why qualitatively based techniques could not be built into Cell 1 studies.

Cell 2: Causal Explanation, Modeling Inquiry. Cappella (1977) strongly advocates this approach to communication research, which has been used increasingly in recent years. In this template a causal theory is represented as a model directly depicting the pattern or "behavior" of data. For example, if disclosure of similarities is assumed to lead to liking, the amount of self-disclosure can be related to liking in a mathematical equation linking the two variables (for example $Y_1 + \alpha \sum_{i=1}^{n} V_i = Y_2$ where Y_1 is the initial attraction level to the other, V_1 is the valence of the ith message received about the other, α is an "effect strength" constant for the sum of n messages received between times 1 and 2, and Y_2 is the resulting attraction level). This equation directly links theory and observables and can be tested by comparing its predictions against actual observations. Cappella has used this approach to study talk-silence sequences in conversations (Cappella, 1979, 1980; Cappella & Planalp, 1981), and McLaughlin and Cody (1982) used it to study awkward silences in conversation (see also Hunter et al., 1976; McLaughlin & Jordan, 1975). This approach should not be confused with path analysis and structural equation modeling techniques, which are often termed "causal modeling." These two are statistical techniques rather than research strategies and can be used with any cell based on causal or dialectical explanation forms.

The advantages of the causal, modeling template include: (1) it yields general, necessary explanations; (2) it yields falsifiable predictions; (3) models can be quite powerful; and (4) it forces the researcher to specify precisely and completely the theoretical assumptions, constructs, and connections between variables (see Cappella, 1977). One particularly interesting feature of this and the other modeling cells is that the researcher often learns more when the model fails than when it succeeds. Tracing a failure can make us aware of previously unnoticed aspects of the phenomenon and permits modification of basic theoretical assumptions (McPhee & Poole, 1981). The methods generally used to test causally-based models include statistical model-testing methods, techniques for evaluating descriptive models, time-series techniques, and developmental techniques.

There are several shortcomings of this template. Causal theories based on models are often less generalizable than Cell 1 theories because models are tied to particular cases and particular instantiations of variables. Then, too, some theoretical statements cannot be represented in a model (especially a mathematical model) without distorting or impoverishing them (see McPhee

& Poole, 1981, for examples). Finally, data are often so unreliable and "fuzzy" that they do not permit us to select among competing models. With subjective expected utility models, for example, a model with multiplicative combinations of attributes cannot be distinguished empirically from an additive model (Behling & Dillard, 1984). Hence the precision of causally based models often goes for naught. Notwithstanding these problems, its precision makes Cell 2 research valuable and it is certainly an underutilized resource in interpersonal research.

Cell 3: Causal Explanation, Grounded Theory. The grounded theory approach modifies the causal explanatory pattern considerably. In Cell 3 the researcher looks for causal linkages embedded *in a particular situation.* These may be generalized to other situations but they do not have to be; grounded theories may cover only a single case. Because Cell 3 research is tied to a particular context and because it does not employ classical hypothesis testing, it is not possible to determine wth certainty what feature of an action or context is responsible for an effect, though certain possibilities can be excluded by the nature of the situational description (Menzies, 1982). Causal linkages in Cell 3 do not have the abstract, necessary entailments implied in Cells 1 and 2, though they can claim sufficiency. For example, Izraeli (1977, example from Menzies, 1982) mentions a manager promoting a deputy to gain a supporter. That this is causally effective depends on the unspecified context: The character of the deputy, norms in the plant, the plant's institutional arrangements and so forth—all things that are not controlled to see if the obtained effects are the direct result of the action. Instead the researcher relies on common sense and his or her knowledge of the social world to deduce causality. To generate causal, grounded theory the researcher engages the phenomenon, derives sensitizing concepts and key linkages, and uses these to put together an account of causal determinations in the situation. Although most studies employing ethnographic and symbolic interactionist approaches make causal claims, we have found no inter-personal communication studies that use this approach self-consciously. A good example relevant to interpersonal communication is Bott's (1971) book, *Family and Social Network,* which induces from interviews of 20 families a set of variables and a causal hypothesis that it uses to explain differences in conjugal relations.

Compared to Cells 1 and 2, Cell 3 has the disadvantages of being less general and having weaker necessity. Further, although Cell 1 and Cell 2 hypotheses are falsifiable if set up properly, the situation is more ambiguous for Cell 3 propositions. Because they are derived by grounded methods, no a priori test of Cell 3 propositions is possible; however, once a causal linkage has been isolated, it is possible to test it in other contexts. The advantages of Cell 3 vis-à-vis Cells 1 and 2 include its ability to generate a much more detailed account of causality than a general theory allows and much greater sensitivity to particular features of the phenomenon. Vis-à-vis templates based on conventional explanation (which it is commonly combined with), Cell 3 has two advantages: (1) It provides an account that orders determinants and consequences, rather than simply fitting things into a pattern; and (2) it permits the researcher to focus on causality, a crucial part of subjects' interpretive schemes and, arguably, the key scheme employed by acting subjects.

Cell 3 is underutilized in interpersonal communication research. Probably the reason for this is the long-standing suspicion of causal researchers toward any particularized inquiry and the equally well-established leariness of conventionalists toward causal-based accounts. Certainly most "qualitative" research reports contain causal reasoning. There is no reason this could not benefit from greater formalization. Nor is there any reason techniques commonly used in Cells 1 and 2 cannot be used to test grounded propositions in context or to aid in deriving them.

Cell 4: Conventional Explanation, Hypothetico-Deductive Inquiry. Most conventionalist research employs the grounded mode of inquiry, but in this template a set of rules or interpretive scheme is specified and then tested empirically. The rules or schemes serve as a hypothesis that is tested by comparing subjects' behavior in a particular situation to patterns that would be expected if the rules held. Interpersonal communication studies employing this template include Planalp and Tracy's (1980) research on rules governing topic changes and Cushman and Nishida's (1983) study on mate selection.

The advantages of this cell include those of conventionalist inquiry in general: It is sensitive to the active role of subjects and does not require strict assumptions about cause and effect (which may not reflect the nature of human action), but allows for loose, multiple linkages between "inputs" and action. Vis-à-vis Cell 6—grounded explanation, conventional inquiry—it has the advantage of systematically testing for whether rules hold rather than allowing the validity of rules to rest wholly on the researcher's "discovery techniques." The disadvantages of this template include (1) weaker generality than the causal cells; (2) its explanations are not necessary in the way causal explanations are (Cushman & Pearce, 1977, have argued that conventional explanations possess a form of necessity based on normative force, that is, *practical necessity*); (3) due to its emphasis on the testing of conventions, Cell 4 can lead to neglect of the discovery process, which is an essential preliminary to the testing process; and (4) emphasis on testing can also create a tendency to stress the researcher's perspective over the subject's, thus violating a basic premise of conventionalist inquiry. The techniques normally used in Cell 4 research are experimental design and statistical model-testing techniques, although in principle descriptive quantitative techniques, developmental techniques, and some qualitative techniques could also be applied (see below).

Cell 5: Conventional Explanation, Modeling Inquiry. This template is similar to Cell 4, but rather than a convention or set of conventions, the researcher posits a model of convention-use or a hierarchical model of conventions. In Cell 5 the researcher is explicit about the process by which conventions enter into behavior and the relationships among conventions. Unlike models in Cell 2, Cell 5 models are usually verbal or logical in form. Once a model is developed, it is tested against actual behavior, as in Cell 4. Further, as in Cell 4, the test should involve checking to see whether subjects actually hold the conventions in question. Examples of Cell 5 research include Pearce and Conklin's (1979) hierarchical model of conversational interpretation, Sacks, Schegloff, and Jefferson's (1974) model of turn-taking in conversation, and Donohue's (1981) model of negotiation rules (see Vroom & Jago's 1974 model of leadership behavior for a classic, paradigmatic example of rule modeling).

The advantages of Cell 5 include all those for Cell 4, plus the benefits of modeling over hypothetico-deductive inquiry discussed under Cell 2. Like other modeling templates, this one may require more precision than the phenomenon allows. Moreover, a large number of models involving different conventions may fit a single phenomenon and it may be impossible to determine which model works the best. The techniques commonly used in this cell include experimental designs, statistical model-testing, and quantitative descriptive techniques such as Markov modeling. Both Cells 4 and 5 are used too seldom. They provide the critical step of falsification or verification needed to supplement the discovery stage, which represents the extent of most conventionalist research (see Tudor, 1976, for a critique of classic conventionalist positions).

Cell 6: Conventional Explanations, Grounded Theory. Studies falling in this cell are by far the most common among conventionalist research in interpersonal communication. Indeed, for many, conventionalist research and grounded theory are synonymous. In Cell 6 research, the investigator uses qualitative techniques of discovery and analysis to uncover conventions and how they are used (see below). Although there is room for informal testing of conventions by cross-checking and testing expectations in the situation, the burden of validity rests primarily on the strength of the researcher's insight and his or her discovery techniques. There is no hypothesis testing. Examples of research in this template include Philipsen's (1975) study, "Speaking Like A Man In Teamsterville," and Nofsinger's (1975) study of the "demand ticket."

The advantages of this template compared to Cells 1 through 3 have been covered in the discussions of Cells 4 and 5. Compared to these cells, the conventional, grounded theory template has the advantage of emphasizing discovery procedures, thereby sensitizing the researcher to particularities of the phenomenon. Indeed, of all the templates, Cell 6 brings the researcher into the most intimate contact with his or her subject. It is certainly the template with the least systematic approach and therefore is not as likely to impose formalisms that disguise or distort a subject. In terms of disadvantages, its general lack of systematic evaluation can reduce confidence in the representativeness and generality of Cell 6 findings. In particular, there is no test of a basic assumption of conventionalist explanation—that the conventions reflect subjects' rules or schemes accurately. Rather, the researcher's techniques of contact, observation, and analysis are supposed to guarantee adequate penetration of the subjects' perspective. No doubt this is usually the case; however, there is often no way of determining whether it is or not. Some means of avoiding this and other problems with Cell 6 research are considered below.

Cell 7: Dialectical Explanation, Hypothetico-Deductive Inquiry. As noted above, dialectical cells are seldom represented in interpersonal communication research. Of the three dialectical templates this one is the most common. It requires the researcher to hypothesize how conventions and the causal factors that give them form and force will function in action. This requires multiple layers of observation and multiple hypothesis-testing procedures. The researcher must test hypotheses about how the subject behaves in the given action system as well as several hypotheses about the action system itself. These system tests include (1) whether the hypothesized conventions are held and used by subjects; (2) whether causal factors hold and operate as hypothesized; and (3) whether subjects are conscious of the causal factors or not and, if so, how this consciousness shapes the system. Generation of the insights needed to produce a dialectical theory suggests the need for powerful discovery techniques, which are then complemented by hypothesis-testing techniques. In our review of the literature we found no interpersonal communication studies employing Cell 7. Poole, Seibold, and McPhee (1982; see also Poole, 1983) report a research program on small group decision making that uses this template. An example of organizational communication research in this cell is Laird, Johnson, and Downs's (1982) research on differences in rule use in different parts of an organization.

Cell 7 studies combine many of the advantages of Cells 1 and 4. They have a degree of sensitivity to the phenomenon characteristic of conventional studies, but also incorporate strong tests in the tradition of causal, hypothetico-deductive studies. Moreover, dialectical studies are more powerful than conventional research because they penetrate beneath conventions to the forces that shape them and condition their operation. However, the same features that give Cell 7 studies their unique advantages can also generate problems. For one thing, Cell 7 studies are quite complex and require considerable time and resources; the payoff in terms of insight may not justify the investment for many projects. Compared to the straightforward, powerful accounts provided by the causal cells, dialectical theories may sometimes seem overly complex and convoluted. Second, because dialectical theories posit a recursive spiral of dependencies among causal and conventional features, their constructs may sometimes lack integrity. It is all well and good to argue, as we did above, that matching in interpersonal systems is based on interpretations shaped by systems of domination in our culture, which are themselves shaped by interpretations and actions within the systems of domination and so forth. In this argument the interpretive scheme is conditioned by causal forces that are themselves dependent on action, which is further conditioned and so forth—all of which makes the stability, and therefore the scientific usefulness, of explanatory constructs problematic. Unless these interweaving influences are carefully specified and traced out, the resulting account may be too fluid to be useful. Although Cell 7 assumptions may offer an appealing match to many theories of social life, research in this and other dialectical templates is difficult and demanding.

   Cell 8: Dialectical Explanation, Modeling Inquiry. Studies in Cell 8 bear the same relation to those in Cell 7 as do Cell 2 studies to those in Cell 1. Much the same reasoning and relations are involved in Cell 7 and Cell 8, but instead of hypotheses and corresponding observables, the researcher posits a model that directly depicts the pattern of observable behavior in the system. The model—which may be mathematical, logical, or verbal—specifies the causal forces and conventions operating in the system and uses these to derive predicted behavioral patterns. These are then compared to observed patterns to test the model. In addition, independent tests for the existence of causal forces and conventions must also be conducted. Once again, evidence for the model is accumulated through multiple, layered studies and tests. We could find no examples of such models in the interpersonal literature, though the Pearce and Conklin (1979) model discussed under Cell 5 could be a Cell 8 model if it were supplemented by an analysis of causal forces conditioning their rules and the rule-following process and of how the operation of causal forces depended on actors' use of conventions.

   The advantages and disadvantages of Cell 8 compared with Cells 1 through 6 were discussed under Cell 7. Vis-à-vis Cell 7, Cell 8 studies have the advantages and disadvantages of modeling vis-à-vis hypothetico-deductive inquiry, as discussed under Cell 2.

   Cell 9: Dialectical Explanation, Grounded Inquiry. In this template the researcher develops a dialectical account through immediate observation and grounded induction. Theories in this template are similar to those in Cells 7 and 8, except for their notion of causality, which is the embedded causality discussed under Cell 3 above. As with the other dialectical templates, multiple studies are usually required to pin down the different aspects of the theory, and both immediate and historical data are used. In common with all grounded theories, Cell 9 research is tied to the limited context of its induction. R. D. Laing's (1962) theories in *Self and Others* are examples of Cell 9 research in interpersonal communication. Burawoy (1979) provides an excellent example of Cell 9 work in an industrial setting.

Advantages and disadvantages of Cell 9 versus the first six cells have been discussed under Cell 7. In comparison with Cells 7 and 8, Cell 9 has the advantages and disadvantages of grounded theories mentioned under Cells 3 and 6. A particular problem with Cell 9 is the difficulty of developing embedded causal claims. A key move in dialectical explanation is to explore historical connections in the larger society. It is difficult to do this in a purely grounded theory because such connections involve that general causes and a priori assumptions be brought to bear. Any theory that does this has a tendency to become a hybrid of Cells 7 or 8 and Cell 9. Notwithstanding, its capacity to incorporate both causal and conventional features in grounded theory makes this template an unexploited resource for interpersonal communication research.

Summary. Certainly much of the terrain marked out by the templates has yet to be explored. Social science is ideological, and arguments about the "right" way to conduct inquiry tend to create the assumption that only certain templates are valid. For example, causal explanation is generally associated with the traditional hypothetico-deductive mode of inquiry and conventional explanation with development of grounded theory. There is no reason why either causal or conventional explanations cannot be associated with another mode of inquiry, but their uses with the other templates are not widely advertised. Arguments in favor of particular templates are often cast as critiques of other positions, and, unfortunately, defending a particular mode of inquiry or explanation sometimes assumes more importance than addressing substantive questions. We would suggest that although debate is valuable, generalized attacks often hide other possibilities and blind us to the fact that all research involves choice from a range of potential approaches, each of which should be considered on its own merits for the question at hand. Advocacy of one "correct" template flies in the face of effective, creative research. But beyond innovation, effective research is grounded in the capacity to match investigative strategies to the object of research. The matching process not only creates a happy marriage of theory and technique, but also serves as an important means of exploring the nature of the phenomenon by finding out how it can be conceptualized, measured, and analyzed.

The template adopted by a researcher influences his or her technical choices, as well as how a chosen technique is employed. It is, however, important to reemphasize that the templates are not the only consideration in choosing methods. Selection of techniques depends just as much on the substantive nature of the phenomenon and the researcher's substantive theoretical assumptions. Only through a complicated process of practical reasoning can the researcher arrive at the proper combination of substantive premises, template, and technique that gives a project coherence and power. There are many ways of doing this, and the process defies codification into a set of rules and guidelines that state in definitive terms the connection between templates and techniques. There is no one-to-one correspondence between templates and techniques. Each template places different demands on the researcher and thereby creates certain technical preferences and affinities, but many of the techniques discussed below can be applied to numerous templates in one form or another.

The matrix of templates is designed to serve as a unifying scheme for practical choice, to indicate how the techniques in the next two sections could be used, and to suggest the various sorts of claims that could be made with them. Although it is not always explicitly present, this scheme forms the backdrop for the discussion to follow.

DATA GATHERING AND MEASUREMENT TECHNIQUES

Interpersonal communication research has always been eclectic in its choice of observational methods. They span the entire range, from psychometric instruments to participant observation, with considerable distance covered in between. This section considers key issues relevant to these methods, in particular problems of validity and reliability in measurement and observation. Validity is the most important issue in any consideration of data collection procedures. Research is fruitless without valid data, and it is not sufficient simply to assume our data are good. In the case of quantitative instruments we must ask whether our measures do indeed tap the variables or constructs they are designed to assess. With direct observational methods we must inquire whether our observational strategies contaminate the phenomenon and whether the interpretations and inferences drawn from observations are sound or biased. Reliability is a necessary condition for validity. In its technical sense it is defined only for quantitative measures; but in its broader sense, as an assessment of how much error is in an observation or measurement, reliability is also meaningful for qualitative techniques.

This section is divided into four parts. First we will consider the construction and validation of tests and questionnaire instruments, the most commonly employed quantitative tools in interpersonal communication research. The second part concerns direct observational techniques, including interaction analysis, stimulated recall, and ethnographic observation. Third, we consider the measurement of change and its attendant problems. Finally, we elaborate common places for critiquing and reformulating constructs and variables.

Tests and Questionnaire Instruments

A substantial proportion of interpersonal communication research depends on the use of questionnaires, interviews, and similar techniques for eliciting subjects' descriptions of various objects of interests—attitudes and beliefs, expressible patterns of reasoning or memory, reports of their own behavior, attributes, and communication, reports of their knowledge of others' behavior, and so forth. Social science methodology related to such instruments is quite sophisticated and has undergone a number of recent developments. We will start by reviewing some of these and describing an "ideal" process of instrument construction. Then we will discuss some of the problems in current interpersonal communication research and suggest how they might be ameliorated. The process of instrument construction can be broken into five stages: (1) conceptual development, (2) preliminary construction of a universe of items, (3) measure design, (4) empirical evaluation of measure properties and redesign, and (5) evaluation in research practice, with adaptation or redesign. The first stage, conceptual development is necessarily part of theory-building, but experience shows that it must also be repeated just before writing a questionnaire. Communication journals are full of debate about *instruments* that have been written, empirically evaluated, and used many times, centering on issues such as, Is the variable measured a state or a trait, an externally verifiable report or a description of a private subjective state, a uni- or multidimensional construct? This debate reflects slippage between conception and questionnaire execution that might be reduced if researchers recognized that measures are continually being reconceptualized as they are formulated and used.

Ideally, the conceptual analysis directly guides the generation of items or questions. In the optimal case it will specify *facets*, a set of independent item properties that stakes out the universe of possible items that could be included in the measure (Borg, 1979; Foa, 1965; Guttman, 1947). Some facets are allowed to vary between items, but others represent properties that must be present for item validity. For instance, a network-related question about amount of communication might be, "How often per week do you talk with your best friend _____ (name previously supplied)?" Facets characterizing such an item might include (1) focus—own communication behavior; (2) object—own best friend; (3) behavior specification—"talk with"; (4) time period—week; and so on. Some of those facets might be varied to generate items (for example, "talk with" might be changed to "influence" to generate another item), whereas others would remain stable. There will always be minor variations not worth specifying, but ideally the facet list makes us specify the *universe* of possible items fairly exactly, by stating which facets are important.

Measure design then becomes at least partly a matter of sampling from the universe of possible (and the range of actually constructed) items, in order to meet certain specifications. Some specifications refer to practical limitations, such as the number and length of items. Others are methodological in that items must be designed to "fit" the researcher's method of analysis. Loevinger (1957) has also emphasized the importance of *substantive* requirements, those related directly to content. She argues that items should "span the range" of conceptual content, covering content areas most relevant to theory (facet analysis can aid in the identification of these areas). Ideally, items should also go beyond the bounds set by the conceptual analysis to allow empirical examination of those bounds. In addition, items should vary in format to allow study of possible item-format interaction.

A second source of guidance for measure design is the rapidly growing empirical base of knowledge about instrumentation effects. The database goes beyond matters of question design to include questionnaire package design and interviewer conduct. Some representative reviews include Dillman (1978), Dijkstra and Van der Zouwen (1982), Sudman and Bradburn (1983), and Rossi, Wright, and Anderson (1983).

In test design and evaluation it is important to remember that all tests refer to a model of the relationship between responses and the underlying attribute, trait, or construct. The most common and robust model is *classical true-score theory* (Allen & Yen, 1979; Lord & Novick, 1968). This model assumes responses are distributed normally about the value of the measured trait or construct. The use of factor analysis to construct and evaluate tests assumes the classical true-score model. A second family of models, *latent trait models,* has enjoyed increasing popularity in recent years (Hambleton, Swaminathan, Cook, Eignor & Gifford, 1978; Lord & Novick, 1968). Latent trait models with logistic, Poisson, and normal-ogive trait-response distributions have been developed. Although these models require more restrictive assumptions than classical test theory, tests that fit latent trait model assumptions have certain advantages, including (1) a latent trait model enables precise estimation of the examinee's latent trait value from any subset of items that fits the model, thus reducing testing time; and (2) latent trait models also allow precise determination of item difficulty and discrimination power, which facilitates questionnaire composition and evaluation of subgroup response differences. In a third development, Coombs presents a still more comprehensive range of data models in his *Theory of Data* (1976). These models elaborate a number of scaling strategies employing unidimensional and multidimensional scaling techniques (see Lingoes, Roskam, & Borg, 1979).

In general, interpersonal communication research has paid too little attention to test and scaling models. Alternatives to the classical model are rarely considered and there has been less rigor in scale design than would be ideal (for an exception see Woelfel & Fink, 1980).

Empirical analysis of a test should follow test design. Logically, such analysis breaks down into what Loevinger (1947) calls *structural* (interitem relation) and *external* issues. A preliminary study is usually conducted to determine a questionnaire's structural and external properties. Loevinger points out that the usual structural requirement of high internal homogeneity must be subordinated to a broader requirement that she calls "structural fidelity"—correspondence of item behavior to predictions of a theoretically derived measurement model. For instance, items low and high in difficulty on a Guttman scale do not correlate very highly, by definition, so using coefficient alpha to evaluate the internal consistency reliability of such a set of items is senseless. Another more interesting example, common in our literature, is what Fornell and Bookstein (1982) call a "formative" construct— one in which items "add up" to the variable of interest. Thus anxiety or satisfaction may have a number of sources (Honeycutt, 1984), and overall anxiety or satisfaction may be the sum of components from these various sources. The various sources may not correlate and a factor analysis would show them to be unrelated. However, as Fornell shows, the summed score is unidimensional and may be perfectly reliable. Any evaluation of a test and its internal consistency should be generated with reference to a measurement model.

Once a proper criterion of internal consistency has been met, the state-of-the-art approach is in terms of *generalizability* (Cronbach, Gleser, Nanda, & Rajaratnam, 1972), which combines aspects of reliability and validity. The theory of generalizability posits that a measure is useful insofar as its findings generalize, that is, insofar as this observation is related to another class of observations. For instance, from this observation we might wish to generalize to observations made using other tests constructed in an identical way (the idea behind internal-consistency reliability), observations made at a later time (time one-time two reliability or stability), observations by other raters (inter-rater reliability) or observations using different but valid measures of the same construct (convergent validity). Two important consequences follow from the generalizability notion. First, the term "reliability" is very vague: To be correct, we must specify a universe of observations to which we wish our test results to generalize. Second, to evaluate "reliability," we must study it over precisely that universe, doing what is called a "generalizability study," described in detail by Cronbach et al. (1972).

Loevinger's external requirements have to do with validity as classically conceived, in particular with convergent and discriminant validity (Allen & Yen, 1979; Nunnally, 1967). In the past, a valid test exhibited high raw correlations with theoretically related measures and low correlations with theoretically unrelated measures. More powerful statistical procedures like causal modeling (to be discussed below) have transformed this requirement: Models can be fitted that isolate and evaluate even relatively small valid components in the variance of tests so that we can identify valid components (Kenny, 1979, p. 250ff.).

Embretson (1983) has recently advanced important revisions in the theory of construct validity. Rather than viewing constructs as isolated qualities or attributes, as does classical construct validity theory, she proposes that constructs must be viewed as components of information processing systems. This reformulation permits two types of validity issues to be distinguished. *Construct representation* is concerned with identifying the theoretical mechanisms that underlie item responses, such as information processes, strategies, and knowledge stores. *Nomothetic span* is concerned with the network of relationships of the test score with other variables. Hence, in addition to Cronbach and Meehl's (1955) concern with the construct as a part of a "nomological net," Embretson argues that researchers should also be concerned with the components underlying the test score. She details methods for validating construct representation and nomothetic span. The resulting theory seems to be better specified and more inclusive than previous theories of construct validation.

Ideally, we should not stop once this is done: Evaluation of a measurement instrument should continue during its use in research. In particular, it is often wise to dry-run several subjects through the whole study procedure, then interview them about their understanding of and reasons for responses to the measurement instrument to make sure the research context does not invalidate it. Also, during the process of data analysis a number of statistical techniques allow us to identify and adjust for discrepancies in measurement instruments that do not perform as intended (see McPhee & Babrow, in press).

It is rare that any social scientific study follows this ideal procedure, but two departures from the ideal are cause for particular concern. First, communication researchers seem to rely far too often on the factor analytic model as a basis for understanding and evaluating questionnaire instruments. Exploratory factor analysis is very broad, flexible, and complex, but the information it gives about a test is also complex. Any simple approach to test evaluation using factor-analytic results is likely to be either misleading or inappropriate because the factor analytic model is simply not designed to supply all the information needed to validate instruments. The methods and findings mentioned above are more powerful and comprehensive (see also the discussion of factor analysis below). Nonetheless, several recent factor-analytic studies in our field have delivered useful information about questionnaire methods. Cronkhite (1976) reports useful confirming but also descriptive information about interaction effects of rater, concept rated, and scale identity on the factor structure of responses elicited using multiitem evaluative semantic differential scales. Porter (1981) combines factor analysis with other techniques to demonstrate nonhomogeneity of the communication apprehension measure PRCA-25, which might have serious consequences for its use to study interpersonal communication anxiety.

A second common failing of communication test development procedures is that too often important properties of the measure, or the concept being measured, are not adequately articulated and evaluated. Hewes and Haight (1979) examined the "cross-situational consistency" of several supposed communication "traits" that were thought to characterize subjects. The relatively low correlations they found seem to indicate that the behaviors being measured actually display much less consistency than the term "trait" suggests. (See Hewes & Haight, 1980; Jaccard & Daly, 1980, for discussion of the specific application of this problem to questionnaire measures.)

The ideal process described above seems to be associated most strongly with the traditional-causal template described above, but it is also consistent with modeling and grounded theory development. There is no way to avoid consideration of an underlying data model in the valid development of a test; indeed, measure development is one of the areas in which traditional theory development is traditionally closest to modeling. And grounded investigation is a frequent and often necessary prelude to sound concept development and item universe specification.

Grounded theory itself tends to avoid standardized tests, perhaps because of the element of "apriorism" such tests naturally involve. However, full-blown test development would seem to be useful in later stages of grounded inquiry because of the extra insights it provides into the nature of concepts induced earlier.

Questionnaires and other tests are also useful in studying phenomena that call for conventional or dialectical explanation, if item generation and test design and validation can be shown to reflect subject understandings and concepts. A measurement model must be discovered, not imposed a priori, probably through an initial phase of grounded research, and the final test should possess representational validity (discussed in the next section).

Observational Techniques of Data Collection

Measurement techniques based on direct observation of behavior have a long history in interpersonal communication research. Here we will discuss three major types of observational techniques: interaction analysis, reviewing methods, and ethnographic observation. These run the gamut of researcher-subject relationships, from relatively distant interaction coding procedures to the immediacy of participant observation.

In this discussion we have avoided giving detailed "how to" descriptions of the methods; these are available in other works listed in the references. Instead, we have chosen to focus on the interlocking problems of validity and proof in observational research because skepticism of the knowledge claims based on observational methods is the main obstacle to their acceptance in communication research. Unfortunately, the skepticism many "traditional" researchers accord to qualitative research is well-founded: Many current studies seem impressionistic and shallow. It is by working out routines for validating and supporting observational conclusions that these problems can be remedied.

One initial distinction important for direct observational techniques (as well as for related techniques like open-ended interviewing) involves the phenomenon observed, the observational record, and the derived "data."

For instance, a *phenomenon* like group discussion may be videotaped (a first *record*); then that videotape is transcribed (producing a transcript—a second record); then "acts" in the transcript are coded, with the sequence of codes analyzed as *data*. Scientists inevitably study records (whether they are fieldnotes, transcripts, tapes, pencil marks on a questionnaire), but we should not be deluded into thinking that such records are *what* we are studying or are above critical reproach. For instance, videotaping methods are not "transparent" records of events, but introduce many sorts of bias (Weimann, 1981). Especially interesting is Labov and Fanshel's (1977) "paradox of microanalysis," that minute analysis and repetitive observation allowed by tapes "magnifies the aggressive mechanisms of conversation and effectively cancels the work done by the mitigating devices" (see also Grimshaw, 1982). The same kind of biases are possible in even the most accurate transcript: Transcription conventions can highlight the control or coherence of one speaker at the expense of another (Ochs, 1979) or alter our understanding of phenomena like "having the floor" in a conversation (Edelsky, 1982). These theory-relevant biases are joined by possible failures of reliability and it is important to take them into account.

(1) Interaction Analysis. This rubric includes any systematic method of classifying verbal and nonverbal behavior, ranging from formal category systems such as Bales's (1970) IPA and Fisher's (1970) Decision Proposal Coding System, to systems for classifying speech acts (Searle, 1976; Vendler, 1972), to discourse analytic methods such as the identification of adjacency pairs (Jackson & Jacobs, 1980). These methods have in common the interpretation of utterances according to a (relatively) standard set of rules developed by the researchers. Four key issues facing interaction analysis are category construction, category reliability, validity, and the adaptation of coding systems to different contexts.

There are several good discussions of how interaction analysis systems can be constructed (Folger, Hewes, & Poole, 1984; Lazarsfeld & Barton, 1969). The construction of systems can follow two paths. In one, a logically complete system is elucidated. The internal logic of such a system yields an exhaustive classification of acts, usually according to a logical choice tree that rigidly specifies coding choices (see, for example, Anderson, 1983). Such an approach makes classification straightforward, as long as it does not do so at the expense of distorting the natural meaning of the discourse. The second, more common approach involves compiling categories indexing relevant functions in the discourse being studied. These functions are often specified by the researcher's theory, as in the case of the Rogers-Farace (1975) relational coding system; and they may also have considerable internal structure, as does Bales's IPA system. Alternatively, the system may be developed with a grounded approach to reflect the functions the observer sees in the situation. Jefferson's (Sacks et al., 1974) transcription rules and Hawes's (1972) interview coding system seem to reflect this approach. As opposed to the logically complete approach, this second strategy relies more on the observer's natural interpretive abilities to determine classifications. The second means of designing classificatory systems is advantageous because it is more responsive to the particular nature of the discourse than the first, but it is correspondingly less "clean" and its rules harder to apply consistently. Regardless of how the system is designed, researchers also face other crucial choices, as outlined in an excellent article by Hewes (1979).

Reliability is a necessary condition for classificatory validity. Although it is generally accepted that formal interaction coding systems need to establish reliability, communication researchers employing other interaction analysis techniques such as conversational analysis do not usually report reliability assessments. Notwithstanding, these informal schemes should also be subjected to reliability analysis because they specify standard rules for displaying or classifying data, rules that could be ambiguous or flawed (see, for example, Edelsky's 1982 discussion of problems using Jefferson's conversational transcription rules).

Coding reliability can be separated into two components: *unitizing* reliability, which refers to the coder's ability to agree on how the discourse should be parsed into units, and *classificatory* reliability, which refers to the level of agreement on how units should be classified. Folger et al. (1984) provide an extensive discussion of different means of assessing reliability and of special cases in which reliability is particularly critical. One especially worth mentioning here is the problem of "coder drift" (Fisher, 1977). Even with high reliability during training periods, over time coders may gradually shift their judgments out of line, resulting in a significant reduction of reliability. Reassessments of reliability during coding and corrective retraining are critical.

In abstract terms the validity of interaction analysis systems is the degree to which they actually yield the types of information they are designed to obtain. Exactly what constitutes validity and how validity is assessed depends on what types of claims the researcher is attempting to make about interaction (Folger et al., 1984; Poole & Folger, 1981b). At least three types of claims might be made about observations of interaction. First, a researcher may only want to identify acts theoretically interesting to him or her, regardless of how the actors themselves interpret the acts. In this mode of observation, which Poole and Folger (1981b) term the *experienced* mode, the researcher aspires to explain interaction from the outside, without reference to subjects' perspectives. Much research with interaction analysis, particularly in the causal templates, works under this assumption. But a reasearcher may also want to use a coding system to identify how *subjects* interpret interaction. The researcher may seek to develop categories that identify the shared meanings utterances have for members of a culture. This observational mode, the *experiencing* mode, is the aspiration of many coding systems, including those based on the identification of speech acts. But the researcher may try to go even further and use a coding system to identify the idiosyncratic meanings of utterances for people in a particular relationship. Labov and Fanshel (1977) use this *experiencer* mode of observation in their book *Therapeutic Discourse*.

It is easy to aspire to one of the three modes of observation, but the researcher's claims about his or her classifications must be backed up by evidence for their validity. Each mode of observation requires different types of evidence. For experienced systems, which only code according to the researcher's point of view, the classic techniques of assessing construct validity (Allen & Yen, 1979; Cronbach & Meehl, 1955) are sufficient. However, for experiencing and experiencer systems, which attempt to get at subjects' meanings, the researcher also must provide evidence that they actually represent subjects' interpretations. Several methods for assessing the representational validity of coding systems have been developed (see Folger et al., 1984, for a review of these methods; see also Folger & Sillars, 1980; Poole & Folger, 1981a).

Establishing the validity of coding systems is very important because researchers may be mistaken about whether they are measuring the constructs they are attempting to measure or tapping subjects' perspectives. Face validity, the traditional resort of interaction analysts, is not sufficient. This is clearly illustrated by O'Donnell-Trujillo's (1982) recent comparison of two relational coding systems that purported to code the same constructs. He found a very low degree of overlap in codings, suggesting that one or both were "off base." But which one is? Without validity assessment it is impossible to establish.

Finally, even systems designed for general use must be adapted to specific cases. This generally involves making special assumptions about what rules mean and how they are applied. Cicourel (1980) has argued that these adaptations should be reported in a methodological appendix, along with more detail on coder background and training than is normally supplied.

(2) Stimulated Recall. This introduces the subject into the interpretive process. Subjects are asked to review a video- or audiotape of their interaction and comment on it. Some researchers structure the form of these comments. Gottman (1981), for example, has his subjects rate their marital interaction on an affect scale. However, generally subjects are asked to simply stop the tape and comment whenever a thought hits them (Frankel & Beckman, 1982; Hawes, 1972).

Stimulated recall yields several important benefits. Most obvious, it goes directly to the subject for interpretations and can therefore help eliminate or rule out researchers' misinterpretations and biases. Subjects can report the particular cues they attend to, which gives researchers a means for sorting out "important" from "unimportant" information.

However, several caveats must be considered in using stimulated recall. First, because it is after-the-fact, stimulated recall may suffer from distortions in subjects' reconstructions of their feelings, thoughts, and emotions. The recent debate over the adequacy of subjects' self-reports between Nisbett and Wilson (1977), Ericsson and Simon (1980), and others seems to suggest that at least certain types of information cannot be reported accurately by subjects. And, even if subjects do recall accurately, they may misunderstand themselves or be wary of reporting important feelings. For example, the husband who believes married couples should always present an outward show of harmony may not report disagreement or anger when reviewing a tape of a discussion with his wife.

(3) Ethnographic Observation. This technique is underutilized in interpersonal communication research. Recent studies of comunication have focused on close analysis of discourse or on theories based on the reading of participant observers from other fields (for example, Stanback & Pearce, 1981). Moreover, the participant observation studies in communication are generally quite diverse in their approach and fairly unreflective about their assumptions (for an exception to this, see Philipsen, 1975). Notwithstanding, participant observation has extremely great potential because it gives the researcher detailed knowledge of communication processes in context. It can also give the researcher something laboratory studies can never yield, namely, some determination of whether the factor or process under study really is important in the social world, or whether instead it "washes out" in the context of other more important forces.

The best treatments of participant observation (Becker, 1958; Cicourel, 1964, Chaps. 2, 3, 8, & 9; Dalton, 1959, appendix; Denzin, 1970; Schwartz & Jacobs, 1979, Chaps. 3, 4, 9, 11) give extensive suggestions on the "how tos" and suggest certain general points related to validity of accounts.

It is commonplace in this literature that the participant observer can take a number of different roles, which differ in terms of "distance" from the subject of study. Gold (1958) distinguishes four roles: the complete observer, the observer-as-participant, the participant-as-observer, and the complete participant. This considerable range of roles carries with it an easily neglected feature: They all assume that the researcher has a definite theoretical model that guides the selection of the role and how the role is put into action in the research situation.

This observation seems to go against the common notion of participant-observation, namely, that the research is open or dedicated to the development of "grounded" theory. However, although it is true that the particular explanatory concepts or mechanisms are drawn out "inductively" or "retroductively" or by means of "situationally guided hypotheses," the *types* and *forms* of these concepts or mechanisms are limited by the researcher's theory of what it is important to look for in the situation. Consider, for example, Philipsen's (1975) study of the ethnography of communication in "Teamsterville." Philipsen took the role of participant-as-observer and found a set of communicative rules because these are the things his ethnographic perspective sensitized him to look for. Had Philipsen been operating from Garfinkel's or Cicourel's ethnomethodologies, he would have focused on practical reasoning and accounting behaviors. Had he been using Goffman's frame he would likely have found self-presentation and strategic behavior to play a critical role in being a "Man" in "Teamsterville." Each perspective sensitizes the researcher to some concepts or phenomena and deemphasizes others, determining what can be discovered and the form the findings can take. In addition, the researcher's perspective may also favor or rule out certain participant-observer roles. For example, a thoroughgoing enthographer is unlikely to favor the pure observer role.

These considerations underscore the need for the researcher to have worked out his or her theoretical approach prior to entering the field (Cicourel, 1964). It is certainly a mistake to go in with strong hypotheses about the content of what will be found; they too easily turn into self-fulfilling prophecies. However, it is equally a mistake to go in without clear ideas on the form and types of concepts that we are looking for; without these it is difficult, if not impossible, to integrate findings and carry out a meaningful observation.

A second theme runs through the literature on participant observation. What the participant-observer finds out is, in a very real sense, dependent on how he or she interacts with subjects and enters in or is exposed to their practices. The observer can only observe and perhaps ask questions; he or she cannot experience practices firsthand. The participant-as-observer experiences them firsthand, but his or her experience is conditioned and limited by the degree of access gained to the practices under study. If the participant-as-observer never advances beyond novitiate training in a religion, he or she cannot know what the "inner" workings of the religion are to those who are full-fledged members. For this reason, the way in which the participant-observer gains access to the field setting, the problems and refusals encountered there, the shifts in his or her interpretations as time goes by and he or she becomes more "experienced"—all are important to understanding the researcher's account. They specify the relationships that underlie and "contextualize" the researcher's findings.

Several strategies are available for dealing with this issue and for enhancing the validity of participant-observer accounts in general. Becker (1958) suggests that research reports should be written as "natural histories" that recount the entire research process from beginning to end, emphasizing the researcher's interpretations (and changes in them) at each point along the way. Such an account enables the reader to identify shifts in the researcher's attitude and interpretations as the project unfolded and gives the reader hints about mistakes or narrowness in the researcher's interpretations. Second, Cicourel (1964) suggests that details such as making contacts and problems with interviews or encounters should be reported alongside relevant findings to give them perspective. Alternatively, he suggests a methodological appendix for reporting these details. Third, participant-observers should pay more attention to the practical reasoning behind their interpretations. Just like quantitative researchers, they should consider likely alternative interpretations and adduce evidence in their reports to rule these out. By exhausting at least the most plausible alternatives, they can pin down their points more definitely and tighten them considerably.

Measuring Change

An important specific measurement topic is the measurement of *change* in some specific variable. Simple change is clearly an important component or result of phenomena like process and growth; it is a basic result of attempted experimental manipulations; it is an obvious goal of practical innovations, and the amount of change produced might be used to evaluate such programs. Moreover, several of the points to be made about change generalize to differences along other dimensions than time—differences between people, cultures, and so forth. Although change or difference measures have been used mainly in coorientation studies of interpersonal communication (cf. Pavitt & Cappella, 1979), they may become more common with the trend toward studying process and development using data sets over time.

Although calculating change scores may seem to be a simple matter of subtraction, such scores introduce numerous methodological problems. These problems, well-elucidated in psychometric articles by Bereiter (1963) and Cronbach and Furby (1970), include:

(1) Low reliability, due to measurement error from Time 1 and Time 2 scores, and often low true change and low true variance of change as well. Such low reliabilities often conceal the true precision and worth of the scores, yet it is often dangerous to attempt to correct for attenuation or otherwise remedy the situation.
(2) Apparent "regression toward the mean" and a related artifactual negative correlation between change and Time 1 scores.
(3) A tendency for measures to change in theoretical meaning over time, so that change scores compare apples to oranges.
(4) A variety of statistical ways to treat change, many of which are appropriate only for specific uses of change scores.

Given these problems, there are a few things that can be recommended to interpersonal communication researchers regarding the measurement of change. Among the general maxims are:

(1) Simple change scores rarely should be used. Maxwell and Howard (1981) suggest several very limited uses, making special mention of "retrospective change scores," calculated using a retrospective pretest score elicited at the time of the posttest, which eliminate biases due to transformation of scale meaning over time.
(2) If a measure of change is desired, Cronbach and Furby (1970) suggest a

difference score between regression-based estimates of true Time 1 and Time 2 values, with each estimate based on both values as well as any available and relevant outside variables (pp. 72-74).

(3) If change is to be used as a variable in analysis, statistical procedures not based on change scores at all are usually recommended. If change is the criterion in an experiment, an analysis of covariance with Time 1 score as the covariate is usually recommended if its assumptions are met (Linn & Slinde, 1977; Reichardt, 1979). If a correlational study is intended, Cronbach and Furby (1970) recommend operations using the original Time 1 and Time 2 scores rather than the difference score.

Critiquing Constructs and Measures

In previous sections variables were treated as nonproblematic. However, there has been heated debate over whether quantitative variables are meaningful, and this debate provides formidable resources for critiquing and improving our measures and observational techniques. Numerous thinkers, among them Blumer (1956), Schutz (1964), Garfinkel (1967), Cicourel (1964), and Churchill (1963), have raised powerful objections to quantitative measurement as traditionally practiced.

Once a variable or construct is defined it often becomes a taken-for-granted feature of the world. For researchers, constructs like attitude, norm, or attraction are second nature, and it is easy to confuse the construct measured by a set of technical rules with the phenomenon itself. Several writers have commented on this tendency to reify variables and its attendant dangers. One problem with this interpretation of variables is that it may "freeze" or present too static a picture of a construct that is negotiated or "in process." In a famous analysis of role and status, Cicourel (1972) demonstrates that these constructs are active accomplishments of members, continuously negotiated and subject to reinterpretation in different situations. To turn such a phenomenon into a more or less static variable runs a severe risk of distortion and oversimplification.

Related to this is Schutz's dictum that scientific constructs should be rooted in actors' meanings. This concern seems particularly appropriate for interpersonal communication research because many theories explicitly attempt to explain interpersonal behavior from the subjects' point of view. Despite this goal, it is easy for researchers to impose their own constructs and models on subjects, substituting observers' insights for actors' processes and understandings. This substitution often occurs unaware, because researchers take social scientific constructs for granted and do not consider that they may only reflect professional discourse and not the reality of subjects. Taking this point of view seriously means that researchers should ask hard questions about their constructs: For example, is the way we conceptualize relational control consistent with how subjects see control issues? Are the statements we call dominant actually seen as such by subjects? Are subjects even concerned with control in day-to-day interaction? At least for those theories that purport to capture subjects' perspectives (to use the terms mentioned above, those working in the experiencing and experiencer perspectives), continuous attention to the representativeness of their constructs and measures is the price of their greater immediacy.

These are the two most obvious lessons to be learned from the interpretive critique of social science. However, there is a further, more complex issue that stems from the fact that all variables or constructs are derived from and embedded in a theoretical framework (however vague and unarticulated). The danger here is that variables or constructs will be chosen to fit theoretical needs, without regard for their relevance and realism. In an insightful critique of mathematical modeling, Churchill (1963) gives several excellent examples of this. For a variable to be useful in a mathematical equation it must be possible to assign a numerical scale value to it. If we are interested in building a mathematical model, there is therefore pressure to conceptualize phenomena in terms of numerical variables. If we are modeling attraction, for example, we might assume attraction varies along a scale from 1, "very attracted," to 7, "not at all attracted." However, in doing this we are assuming attraction is unidimensional and varies directly in intensity. This would lead to severe distortions if attraction is complex (for example, if people feel ambivalent—both attracted and repulsed simultaneously) or if it is a phenomenon that simply does not lend itself to intensity scaling. Whether or not these caveats are correct, a strong temptation to avoid considering them as implicit is in the rationalization, "It will fit better into the model if we can scale it." Taylor (1971) makes a similar argument with respect to the construct attitude. It is, he contends, a violation of the nature of the term "attitude" to assess public attitudes by averaging responses to attitude surveys. Rather, Taylor maintains, public attitudes are best regarded as collective properties, features of an entire culture at a particular point in time. On this view, numerical methods are an inappropriate, or at least inferior, means of getting at attitudes.

These arguments by advocates of interpretive approaches can be taken as indictments of quantitative research. However, we believe it is more profitable to consider them as *topoi* for critiquing and gaining insight into our constructs and measures. Raising these questions does take considerable time and could throw a monkey wrench into fast-burgeoning theoretical machinery, but the increased sensitivity this endeavor lends to our constructs will more than repay the effort. Studies like Rawlins's (1983) research on openness clearly illustrate the power of scrutinizing traditional concepts.

Figure 3.3 presents a summary of some measurement and observational techniques discussed in this section and their relationship to the templates. The upper triangle of each box represents the degree to which the technique is currently used by interpersonal communication researchers working in the various templates. The lower triangle represents our judgment of the potential usefulness of the technique in each template. Although somewhat impressionistic, this figure illustrates current practice and promising applications of these techniques.

ANALYTICAL TECHNIQUES

This section focuses on patterns of analytical reasoning inherent in statistical techniques and qualitative analysis. Patterns of reasoning are the most important aspect of analysis, though more attention is often devoted to technical aspects and details of application. Although the patterns discussed here are usually associated with either quantitative or qualitative techniques, most can be employed in both areas. Despite the supposed rift between quantitative and qualitative methods, both are subject to the same requirements of inference and proof, and both can employ similar canons of reasoning.

We have grouped analytical techniques into six families: Experimental design, statistical model testing, descriptive techniques, time-series techniques, developmental techniques, and qualitative techniques. For each family we discuss their assumptions and range of applications, available techniques, their affinities to the templates, their strengths and weaknesses, and new methodological opportunities.

Experimental Design

When social scientists discuss methods, their most general concerns are with matters of measurement, design, and analysis. The middle term, design of research procedures, is at least as broad as the other two, yet we will give relatively very little space to it, in part because it is the area in which the least fundamental change and debate has occurred, and in part because it has been covered in the discussion of the nine templates (see Keppel, 1973; Kirk, 1968; Myers, 1972; Winer, 1978, for extensive treatments of experimental design).

The design of studies is generally concerned with three goals: uncovering or bringing into focus the effects of interest, avoiding or controlling threats to the validity of inferences, and building a justification for generalizing the conclusions to some universe of interest. Influenced by critiques of positivism to disregard the natural science model, social science researchers sometimes underemphasize the ingenuity required to strip away distracting or deceptive matters to isolate and analyze the effects of interest. Yet classic work in social science seems to have been characterized by this quality above all, and it is this capacity that makes choosing the appropriate design important. Overall, interpersonal communication researchers have tended to use simple, traditional designs (for example, two- and three-way ANOVAs or analysis of covariance). More complex and "exotic" designs, such as Latin square or

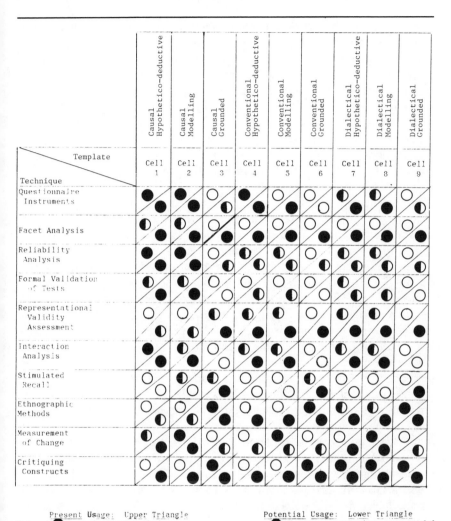

Figure 3.3 Selected Measurement and Observational Techniques and Their Actual and Potential Use in the Templates

blocked designs, have advantages over the simple designs in terms of efficiency (fewer subjects needed for the analysis) and power. Hewes, Graham, Doelger, and Pavitt (1984) provide a good example of this.

The second goal, that of dealing with validity threats, has been articulated by Campbell and Stanley (1966). In their extension of this theme, Cook and Campbell (1979) note four major sorts of validity: the construct validity of causes and effects, statistical conclusion validity, internal validity, and external validity. These refer to our confidence in our ability to answer four questions about a study: (1) Do the manipulations and measurements correspond to the variables we intend to study? (2) Do the data indicate a relationship between these variables? (3) Given the relationship, is it causal or "forcing" in this study? (4) Can we generalize the presence of causation to a wider context than this sample? Cook and Campbell argue that internal validity is primary, although they note disagreements and strong necessary qualifications on this primacy (pp. 83-91). Therefore much of their analysis is concentrated on set-ups that can remove the threats to internal validity.

Randomization and controlled manipulation are important means of guarding against validity threats. The classic experimental design with random assignment to treatments and controlled manipulation is the most rigorous protection. It enables unambiguous identification of causal effects and partitioning of variance among effects. Neither nonexperimental designs, which do not control manipulations, nor quasi-experimental designs, which do not have random assignment, permit this degree of protection or inferential rigor. Numerous analytical adjustments are available for improving the rigor of these designs. Campbell and Stanley (1966) lay out a number of quasi-experimental designs, some of which are tailored to solve troublesome inferential problems. Path analytic and structural equation modeling (see below) permit causal analysis in nonexperimental designs. There are also methods for achieving approximate variance partitions for factors in nonexperimental designs (McPhee & Seibold, 1979). Experimental designs are the surest guarantee of validity, but other designs can be made strong as well.

Our third goal, generalization of conclusions to a broader context, is the one on which most controversy in interpersonal communication has centered. Interest in this issue has been raised by Jackson and Jacobs's (1980) article on messages as variables (Hewes & Haight, 1979, also raise this issue). Jackson and Jacobs note that studies often use a single message to represent a communication variable category or level. And when multiple messages are employed, an incorrect statistical tool (fixed-effects rather than random-effects ANOVA) is almost always used. Neither procedure supports conclusions that generalize to messages in general, and Jackson and Jacobs show that general conclusions drawn in the past are subject to error. They recommend sampling multiple messages, despite the difficulty of that enterprise, and the use of random-effects ANOVA procedures.

Jackson and Jacobs's argument, and our observation of trends in interpersonal communication research, suggest that generalization concerns have received too little emphasis in our field. We would argue, first, that the vocabulary of research validity is misconceived because no study results ever "logically, validly imply" the conclusions we draw with the rigor that phrase connotes (Popper, 1959). Rather we end up with strong or weak evidence along the several dimensions Cook and Campbell distinguish.

Second, studies can be divided into two types, which McPhee (1982) calls "can-cause" and "does-cause" studies. Given the complexity of determination of any human phenomenon, any "cause" likely operates only under certain conditions, with other variables lying within limited ranges. So a study can give evidence that, for *some* possible set of conditions (often ideally contrived or "staged-managed," see McGuire, 1973), a causal variable *can* produce an effect. Or it can show that a causal variable *does* have a meaningful effect in conditions that obtain in natural circumstances. For example, in a "can-cause" study Sillars (1980) studied the effects of subjective expected utility (SEU) and situation type (interpersonal versus noninterpersonal) on choice of compliance-gaining strategy. His study is effective in showing that SEU variation can explain differences in strategy choice, but his conclusion that situation type cannot cause choice differences is weakened by several factors. For instance, the two role-played situations involve an imagined spouse and an imagined new neighbor: These objects of persuasion may be too similar on general "interpersonalness" and provide too little concrete information about the other (the variable underlying the predicted situational difference) to generate observable differences in strategy choice. Although the situation manipulation does not seem to have been "stage-managed" to maximize the study's power, the study is not a "does-cause" study, as Sillars agrees (p. 277). A does-cause study of compliance-gaining would have to allow such factors as habit, communicative inflexibility, and interactive moves by the other to vary as they do in real life, so that we could assess how much of a difference SEU and situation type actually *do* make. This may require that the study be conducted in a natural setting, though it does not have to as long as ecological validity is maximized.

A typical study in our field is a "can-cause" study, perhaps with limited attempts to increase external validity, which draws "does-cause" conclusions. A clearer separation of the goals and designs of these types of study, with acknowledgement of the value of each, might reduce the frequency of these ambiguous mixtures. And our discipline would benefit from more well-designed studies with a primarily "does-cause," representative, or topological mission, letting us know the real current range and distribution of communication phenomena and effects despite possible weaknesses of internal validity.

Statistical Model-Testing Techniques

Many approaches to statistical analysis of data retain the emphasis on finding causal/productive relationships between variables stressed by traditional approaches to design. The mainstream of statistical analysis in social science involves (1) developing a hypothesis that one or more (independent) variables are unidirectionally related to another (dependent) variable, (2) working out a statistical model that reflects this hypothesis, (3) using statistical methods to decide whether the data conform to this model to an extent greater than chance would predict. This approach is consistent with the hypothetico-deductive mode of inquiry. Such a statistical model is clearly subordinate and subsequent to the conceptual hypothesis, and thus is not related to the modeling mode of inquiry. The decision about data-model conformity can be highly complex and often proceeds in accord with formal decision theory. However, usually it simply consists of rejecting a general null hypothesis of no relationship between dependent and independent variables in favor of the hypothesis of relationship. Also typically, the statistical models involved here are special versions of the "General Linear Model," a relatively simple and flexible functional form that is very well understood by statisticians and is easy to use in most cases of interest to social scientists (Searle, 1971).

The array of techniques for statistical hypothesis testing include correlation, ANOVA, regression, multivariate analysis of variance (MANOVA), canonical correlation, path analysis, structural equation modeling, and multivariate categorical analysis (log-linear analysis, logit analysis, and so forth). This literature is so large that it is impractical to attempt a summary. Instead we will focus on developing trends and problems in our field. Particularly good sources include (listed in descending order of readability): Draper and Smith (1966), Pedhazur (1982), and Cohen and Cohen (1975) for regression and its variants; Van de Geer (1971), Harris (1975), and Morrison (1976) for multivariate techniques in general; Cappella (1975), McPhee and Babrow (in press), Duncan (1975), and Blalock (1971) for path analysis; Wonnacott and Wonnacott (1979) and Kmenta (1971) for structural equation modeling and regression; and Feinberg (1977), Everitt (1977), and Bishop, Holland, and Feinberg (1975) for multivariate categorical analysis.

Perhaps the major trend in interpersonal communication research is a move toward "multivariate" analyses, in which that term connotes, especially, multiple *dependent* variables (see, for example, Bradac et al., 1978). Specific techniques include canonical correlation, multivariate analysis of variance and covariance, and tests of equality of vectors of means or covariance matrices, as well as the more traditional factor analysis and causal modeling techniques (both dealt with below). These techniques are described in numerous sources (for example, Monge & Cappella, 1980; Morrison, 1976). An important point about these techniques deserves mention. Often researchers resort to multivariate analyses when they believe that some independent variable affects *each* of a series of dependent variables. There is some sense in this move—the test seems to be more powerful and problems with hypothesis-testing probability levels due to multiple statistical tests are avoided. But there is also a catch: A multivariate statistical test is generally directed to hypotheses involving a *linear combination*—

a weighted sum—not a set of discrete variables. If one is really interested in variables on their own, not their weighted sums, then the gains in power are sometimes illusory (Morrison, 1976).

Path analysis or causal modeling methods are also commonly used in communication research (Cappella, 1975; Fink, 1980; McPhee & Babrow, in press). Causal modeling methods give unusual power to the researcher to deal with cases in which there are multiple dependent variables that cause one another (even if two variables cause each other in a two-way process), relations among variables are partly due to some factor that has not or cannot be measured, and multiple indicators of conceptual variables are present and should not be combined by summing or equal weighting. Such methods also have great flexibility and suggestiveness. However, they are also prone to misuse. McPhee and Babrow (in press) surveyed six years of communication research and found that in literally hundreds of studies, certain method-ological errors could have been avoided if causal modeling methods had been used; but in research using causal modeling, it was nearly always misused and misreported, often grievously so. They list standards for use and reporting of this clearly valuable technique.

A third trend in interpersonal research is toward the use of a half-relative of causal modeling: Log-linear analysis (Feinberg, 1977; Goodman, 1978). This statistical technique is specifically designed for the analysis of contingency tables involving multiple categorical variables. Goodman has developed a way of modeling those tables that expresses relations between the variables in a simple, elegant way. The models are related to a common statistical technique, analysis of variance, and thus are easily understood. This technique has begun to receive widespread use in our field (McPhee, Poole, & Seibold, 1981; Planalp & Tracy, 1980; Poole, McPhee, & Seibold, 1982), yet it too has its potential dangers. Although the models employed seem simple, a hypothesis of interest must often employ a complex model that is hard to interpret relative to other available techniques. Moreover, finding an adequate model requires extensive reliance on statistical tests that are perhaps overly sensitive to sample size, as available measures of "effect size" are open to serious question (Rosenthal, 1980).

Although not currently used by interpersonal researchers, a promising development is a set of methods designed to distinguish effects due to individuals from effects due to *relations* between those individuals, collectively termed the "social relations model" (Kenny & La Voie, 1984; cf Warner, Kenny, & Stoto, 1979). This approach (basically a variant of ANOVA) uses data from cases in which each person in a group interacts with everyone else to isolate effects on each person's behavior due to (1) the person's own general tendencies, (2) the general tendencies of the other with whom he or she is interacting, (3) the specific relationship of the two, and (4) occasion-specific error variance. The method also allows us to determine the two critical correlations among these effects. First, an "actor-partner correlation" tells us the extent to which a person's effect on his or her own behavior is like the person's impact on other's behavior: "Do persons who smile, make others smile?" Second, a "relationship correlation" lets us explore a similar pattern of coordination that might exist inside specific relationships: "If A is extra-dominant in our relationship, does that imply that B is likely to be extra-submissive in that relationship?" However, the social relations model suffers from an important drawback as well: It only allows for dyadic influence and omits triadic, tetradic, and higher-order influences. Thus it has severe limitations as a general model of "group effects."

These trends primarily involve special adaptations or forms of the traditional general linear model approach. Two broader developments are worthy of mention: First, statistics have recently focused attention on "robust" procedures for estimation and analysis (Wainer & Thissen, 1976; Winer, 1978b). The general linear model depends on fairly restrictive assumptions that may often be violated in actual research situations; these robust procedures are less likely to be "thrown off" by violations of assumptions. An especially interesting pair of approaches to statistical testing of unusual indices under unusual circumstances are called the "jackknife" and the "bootstrap" (Efron & Gong, 1983). Both these techniques involve subsampling from an original sample, then using the subsample to generate lots of estimates of the index of interest. The distribution of these estimates is used to allow the researcher to compute data-based, robust estimates of the standard errors of estimate and statistical confidence intervals for a wide variety of indices. Second, there has also been increasing attention to "exploratory data analysis" (Tukey, 1969, 1977). Rather than simply apply a prefabricated model to data and interpret prefabricated results, techniques have been developed to look "inside" data-sets, discovering relationships as well as testing them. Here the researcher becomes more of a "detective" and less of a "sanctifier" (Tukey, 1969).

An important concern applies to all procedures employing statistical tests in this and other sections—statistical power. The assessment of power is important because it permits researchers to calculate sample sizes and alpha levels needed to avoid Type II errors. Although it is generally recommended that estimates of power of statistical tests be reported, this is seldom done in practice. In a review of communication studies, Chase and Tucker (1975) found that few assessed power and that actual power was low for small- or medium-effect sizes and interaction effects, making Type II errors extremely likely. Cohen's (1977) well-known book gives power levels for many statistics. Walster and Cleary (1970) report a method of jointly setting power and alpha level for a given sample size so as to minimize both Type I and Type II errors.

Descriptive Techniques

In addition to methods designed to test statistical hypotheses, a number of techniques have been developed to simply describe or dimensionalize data. This review will consider two genres of such techniques: (1) techniques for clustering or dimensionalizing items or persons, including factor analysis, multidimensional scaling (MDS), and cluster analysis; and (2) techniques for displaying dependencies among observations, notably Markov modeling.

(1) Clustering Techniques. Factor analysis, MDS, and cluster analysis are similar in many respects, but there are critical differences. All three methods permit the researcher to identify clusters of items or persons. However, factor analysis and MDS are more complex than cluster analysis because they also identify dimensions along which items or persons vary. In turn, factor analysis is more complex than MDS procedures because it assumes that the dimensions reflect variables or constructs underlying the items or persons, whereas MDS makes no such assumption. This discussion will focus not so much on full discussions of the three techniques as on strengths and weaknesses of the various techniques and on problems in their use and possible solutions.

Factor analysis is by far the most common clustering technique in interpersonal communication research (for example, Marr, 1973; McCroskey, 1978; McCroskey & McCain, 1974; Norton & Pettigrew, 1979). As noted above, the factor analytic model posits one or more factors underlying a set of items. The factors may be a personality variable, such as communication apprehension, or variables that allow discrimination among or ordering of a number of stimuli, such as the compliance-gaining situations studied by Cody and McLaughlin (1980). In each case, subjects respond to a number of items designed to be representative of the underlying constructs and the analysis derives the factors basic to the items. Compared to the other two clustering methods, factor analysis is advantageous because it attempts to allow for measurement error through the use of communalities. It also permits a clear determination of the amount of variance in the items accounted for by the factor solution.

Among the problems in using factor analysis is that the solution is not unique with respect to rotation. The dimensions can be rotated to numerous different orientations that fit equally well, and many of the orientations will yield very different substantive interpretations of the dimensions. Hence, interpretation of factors has a large subjective component and is influenced by the researcher's theories or preconceptions. This can be problematic because researchers often label factors with names drawn from previous factor analyses, even though they may load quite different items (see Cronkhite & Liska, 1976). This has the advantage of maintaining continuity, but may delete or distort real differences. Second, as Cronkhite and Liska (1976) note, a factor analysis is only as good as the item pool. They recommend having subjects generate items to replace the common practice of using researcher-generated items, which may artificially restrict the scope of the analysis. Cronkhite (1976) also found instability in evaluative-factor solutions based on rater-concept-scale interactions, suggesting that much more care must be taken with factor analytic designs than is often recognized; he offers several suggestions.

There are at least four problems with current uses of factor analysis in interpersonal communication research. First, once a set of items representative of a factor has been identified, subject scores on the dimension are often obtained by simply summing their response values on the item. Instead, the classical procedure is to use factor loadings and subject responses to calculate subjects' factor scores on the dimension (see Gorsuch, 1974; Nunnally, 1967, for procedures). If this is not done, item-weighting information provided by the factor analysis may be discarded.

Second, it has been common to employ the classic "60-40" rule to determine whether an item should be used to represent a factor. According to this rule, an item should only be used as an indicator of a factor if its loading is greater than .60 on the factor and less than .40 on other factors. The problem with this practice is that it often causes researchers to discard high-loading items because they are "contaminated" by other factors. There is no reason to reject these items if factor scores are computed because factor score computations allow for multifactor loadings.

Third, interpersonal communication research has placed too much emphasis on orthogonal factor rotations. Although orthogonality guarantees that dimensions are independent, it is unclear why this is always a desirable property. Often subjects' judgmental criteria are correlated (for example, Hayes & Sievers, 1972), and forcing a solution into orthogonality may distort the representation. Using an oblique rotation may better represent underlying dimensions and certainly facilitates identification of clusters of variables.

A fourth misuse of classic factor analytic procedures in interpersonal communication is to try to use them to show the internal consistency of a scale or set of items being used in a study. Factor analysis is not as good a method of showing consistency as the scale analysis techniques referenced above. Moreover, if the researcher is attempting to test a hypothesis related to the dimensionality of a set of items, confirmatory factor analysis is to be preferred (for example, Jöreskog, 1969). In this technique a hypothesized factor structure is tested against the data (see Cody & McLaughlin, 1980; Seibold & McPhee, 1980, for examples of confirmatory procedures).

MDS derives a multidimensional representation of a set of items (persons) based on a measure of distance between each pair of items (see Green & Wind, 1973; Lingoes et al., 1979; Shepard, 1974). The nature of this measure can vary widely, from correlations (smaller correlations signaling greater distances) to subjects' judgments of similarity of each pair of items (see Shepard, 1974, for a comparison of measures). Varieties of MDS can be distinguished along two dimensions. First, we can distinguish metric procedures, which assume distance measures are continuous, from nonmetric procedures, which assume only that distance measures reflect a rank order of distances among points (see Cody & McLaughlin, 1980; Norton, 1978, for examples of nonmetric MDS; Poole & Folger, 1981a; Woelfel & Fink, 1980, for metric MDS applications; and Craig, 1983, for a critique of metric methods). Nonmetric MDS techniques obviously make less rigorous demands on the data than metric methods, but they do not yield unique solutions, whereas most metric techniques do. This latter property represents a clear advantage of metric techniques over factor analysis. A disadvantage of nonmetric techniques lies in the difficulty of determining the correct dimensionality of the solutions, which is normally done by comparing a stress (or alienation) coefficient for various solutions. Distributions of stress values derived via Monte Carlo techniques make this judgment somewhat easier (Spence & Ogilvie, 1973). In addition, nonmetric methods are also problematic when there are clusters of items such that within-cluster distances are all smaller than between-cluster distances. In this case, nonmetric MDS leads to degenerate solutions (Shepard, 1974). Metric MDS does not have this problem. Weeks and Bentler (1979) compared metric and nonmetric techniques and found that metric methods gave better results than nonmetric techniques, even with rank distance data.

Second, MDS procedures that collapse individual responses can be distinguished from those that do not. Most traditional MDS models take averages or weighted averages of distances across subjects as their distance measures. This makes it impossible to determine whether there are differences among respondents or whether the representation maps common perceptions. However, determining whether a representation is common is an important problem for several areas of interpersonal communication research. For researchers interested in rules or interpretive schemes, testing for a common representation is one way of establishing whether rules or schemes are shared or whether there are interpretive subcommunities. For researchers interested in communication-related traits, it is a way to identify subgroups with different reactions to messages. At least three types of MDS methods can take intersubject differences into account. Unfolding analysis, developed by Guttman and Lingoes (Lingoes et al., 1979), scales subjects and items simultaneously, allowing determination of subgroups of subjects, among other things. The most famous individual difference model, INDSCAL (Carroll & Chang, 1970), finds a common space and determines the weights subjects attach to different dimensions. Although this model permits identification of subsets of subjects, there is some question as to whether these weights really improve fit over a common solution. The third method, PINDIS, allows this to be determined (Lingoes & Borg, 1978). PINDIS fits a common solution and then several solutions with additional constraints, including (1) individual weights for dimensions, like INDSCAL, (2) unique perspectives (origins) for each subject, and (3) shifts in certain items for subsets of subjects. Each of these solutions has a unique psychological interpretation, and PINDIS estimates the amount of variance accounted for by each, permitting determination of which solution, if any, is better than a common solution for all subjects. Three-mode factor analysis (Tucker, 1972) can allow determination of individual differences.

Cluster analysis groups items on the basis of some measure of association (see Cormack, 1971, for an excellent review). These techniques operate through iteratively combining (or dividing) items and clusters one pair at a time. Four major types of cluster analysis can be identified: (1) single linkage, which combines at each step whichever pair of items or clusters are "nearest neighbors"; (2) complete linkage, which combines items into a cluster only if they are all closer to each other than some minimum distance (specified by the researcher); (3) group average methods, which combine an item with a cluster only if it is closer to the average item in the cluster than some minimum distance; and (4) centroid sorting, which combines points into clusters that minimize the distance from or variance about the center of the cluster. Of the four methods, single linkage is the most problematic because it tends to lead to a single giant cluster and to combine items from distant quadrants of the item-space. Several comparative studies have been conducted, and they fairly consistently find centroid methods to be superior to the other techniques (for example, see Cormack, 1971; Morey, Blashfield, & Skinner, 1983; Tainter, 1975). A related problem is the lack of a test of "fit' to help determine which of the iteratively produced sets of clusters gives the best representation. Hubert and Baker (1976) have developed a procedure for testing the fit of single and complete link solutions that could probably be extended to other types (tests for a few procedures are reported in Cormack, 1971).

All three methods just discussed describe items or persons by assigning them values on dimensions or clustering them into groups that are interpreted ex post facto by the researcher. However, it is also possible to group subjects on predetermined grounds into theoretically determined types. The most common means of doing this is to measure a number of variables and group subjects on the basis of similar score profiles across the variables. Fitzpatrick and Best (1979), for example, measured a number of dimensions of relational life and used discriminant analysis to isolate three groups of individuals with different approaches to intimate relationships. Norton and Pettigrew (1979) employ facet analysis to explicate the attentiveness style construct and develop a measure to group items measuring various levels of attentiveness. Obviously, several of the clustering techniques described above could also be employed in the development of typologies.

Markov Analysis. Markov analysis could also be discussed under time-series methods, but its use as a method for display and analysis of sequential data is well-known in our field (see Hewes, 1975, 1979, for a good introduction to sequential analysis; examples of Markov analyses include Ellis & Fisher, 1975; Hawes & Foley, 1973).

Basically, Markov analysis tests how well we can predict acts on the basis of preceding acts. A first-order Markov process would predict the occurrence of acts from the immediately preceding act, a second-order process from the two immediately preceding acts, a third-order process from three, and so on. The core of the model is a transition matrix displaying the probability that an act (or two acts, or three acts, and so forth) will be followed by various other acts. In employing this technique communication researchers typically (1) measure or observe a sequence of responses; (2) use them to calculate transition matrices; (3) test these matrices for order, stationarity (whether the same matrix holds for the entire series of acts), and homogeneity (whether the same matrix holds for all subjects); and (4) once an appropriate matrix has been identified, interpret it for ideas about the sequential structure in the observed interaction. For example, Ellis and Fisher (1975) found three distinct phases in dyadic conflicts, each of which had a different constellation of act-to-act sequences.

The use of Markov analysis to describe sequential structure can be justified on two grounds. For one thing, interaction is responsive, and the Markov model describes this responsiveness very powerfully. Second, researchers have had considerable success with such models; they fit well and have generated insights. However, several critiques suggest that these reasons may be contestable (Hewes, 1979; McPhee & Poole, 1981; O'Keefe, Delia, & O'Keefe, 1980). At base, the use of Markov models as descriptions assumes interaction unfolds in an orderly, sequential manner and can be described in terms of categorical state changes. O'Keefe, Delia, and O'Keefe (1980) note that interaction is seldom this orderly, with responses often coming several statements after an act. Second, as McPhee and Poole (1981) observe, merely establishing that certain order, stationarity, and homogeneity conditions hold does not necessarily yield meaningful information; only in the context of theoretical assumptions not implicit in descriptive attempts are these conditions interpretable. Hewes (1979) discusses several techniques that incorporate theoretical assumptions into Markov models. A particularly interesting move takes the values in the Markov transition matrix as dependent variables in a causal model specifying factors that determine transition probabilities. This approach, employed by Cappella (1979, 1980) permits direct inclusion of theoretical factors in the model. For other examples of theoretical uses of Markov models, see Hewes (1980) and McLaughlin and Cody (1983). A variant of Markov analysis with theory-building potential is lag-sequential analysis (Sackett, 1977; cf McLaughlin & Cody, 1982). This form of analysis focuses on prespecified or especially strong links from particular Time 1 and particular Time 2 (or later) categories. It has allowed researchers to characterize frequently occurring act sequences, for instance, chains of interaction leading to or following some criterial event. Some controversy still exists about proper preconditions and testing procedures for this sort of analysis (Allison & Liker, 1982).

In general, the techniques discussed in this section have been employed by researchers using hypothetico-deductive templates (Cells 1, 4, and 7). Markov analysis and confirmatory clustering techniques have also been used by those working in the modeling templates. These techniques, particularly clustering and typological methods, represent an untapped resource for grounded theory research. For example, once a Markov transition matrix is computed, the grounded researcher might look at examples of both frequent and rare interacts to see if the interact categories have a homogeneous meaning that goes beyond the act category definitions or that might be correlated with some contextual or other variable (see Ellis & Fisher, 1975). Clustering and typological methods could be employed by grounded theory research to identify groups of similar subjects; once groups have been isolated, researchers could use grounded strategies to identify features or processes that account for this differentiation. Factor analytic and MDS methods can also be employed to map a subject's interpretive schemes (for example, Cody & McLaughlin, 1980; Poole & Folger, 1981a). This is not only useful for grounded research, but also for conventional and dialectical approaches.

Time-Series Analysis

Interest in time-series analysis is spreading among students of interpersonal and related fields, as attempts to study "process" increase (Monge, Farace, Eisenberg, Miller, & White, 1984) and as data-sets appropriate to such forms of analysis become increasingly available. A number of texts outlining the statistics and procedures for social scientists are available (Chatfield, 1975; Gottman, 1981; Gregson, 1983; McCleary & Hay, 1980; for experiment-related time-series, see Cook & Campbell, 1979; two good article-length summaries of current practice are given in Catalano, Dooley, & Jackson, 1983; Frederiksen & Rotondo, 1979). Time-series methods have seldom been used to study interpersonal communication; Gottman (1981) describes one example, and some other relevant studies are mentioned by Rogosa (1979).

Time-series analysis assumes a two-dimensional database: Rather than looking at simple responses by N individuals, it looks at responses or behavior by N individuals (or groups, or other units of analysis) over a time interval of T units—an $N \times T$ "data rectangle" for each variable to be analyzed. Of course, such a database can take many forms. For instance, one may have data for only one subject over time, that is, $N = 1$. Time-series analysis allows us to make statistically based statements about the form of that individual's change over time. These may be generalized if we know that individual is representative of others: Indeed, time-series methods have been developed primarily within economics, an advanced science based overwhelmingly on single unit-of-analysis study.

There is a wide range for variation in how time is represented in the data set. Data may be collected at regular or irregular discrete intervals, or continuously throughout time; the usual assumption is of regular discrete intervals. Arundale (1977, 1980) provides detailed information on the importance of the length of the interval between data points. Time-series variables may be continuous or discrete and categorical—the latter sort of data are usually analyzed with the Markov models discussed earlier. So time-series analysis usually involves one or more continuous variables, measured for one or more "subjects," at several regularly spaced points in time ($T > 29$ is a traditional cutoff for proper time-series analysis).

Such a data set allows a complex range of possibilities—so complex that cautious authors emphasize that current approaches are fallible and known to be provisional (Catalano et al., 1983; McCleary & Hays, 1980). One approach is to conduct an analysis that is basically "outside time" (Gregson, 1983). This approach assumes that temporal dependency is relatively simple and easily removed, and constructs a primary statistical model that describes temporal effects as time-varying coefficients or residuals (Dielman, 1983). The other extreme is to construct a model in which time as process is represented in the mathematical operators of the model: for instance, a differential-integral equation (see McPhee & Poole, 1981, for some simple examples). Both these "extremes" overlap with what we will describe as the standard approach in very complex ways.

In the "standard approach," the initial interest is to distinguish six aspects of temporal phenomena. The first two phenomena are *trend* (for example, constant growth) and *periodicity* (for example, yearly or other regular cycles). The first thing one learns when studying time-series analysis is that these phenomena look just like a third random phenomenon called ("integrated") *drift*, which can completely fool our intuitions as well as standard statistical techniques (such as regression with time as an independent variable). A fourth phenomenon, common in series that approach a floor or ceiling, is *nonstationarity of variance*. What remains are two phenomena describing the temporal interdependence of observations: *autoregression* (dependence of each observation on past observations) and *moving average processes* (dependence of each observation on some of the "shocks" that caused change in past observations). These two sorts of temporal interdependence are the heart of standard time-series analysis. Simple time-series analysis supplies means of describing these processes and telling them apart. In more complex cases (analogues of which Markov modelers find with depressing regularity in interaction data), these methods are liable to fail or mislead (McCleary & Hays, 1980).

Our bias is that time-series methods should be studied more by social scientists, but should only be used rarely. Such methods provide three valuable resources for research on "process." First, they provide rigorous descriptions of the nature and constitution of temporal processes, along with clear accounts of the complexities of temporal data. Second, where theory or quasi-experimental controls are available, time-series methods enable us to disentangle effects of interest (Catalano et al., 1983, list a hierarchy of strategies). Thus such methods are most valid within the traditional, causal template we have described; in modeling or grounded inquiry they must be used with care and critically. Third, knowledge of time-series methods aids one in recognizing, describing, and analyzing rather unique effects, such as hysteresis—a series that follows two different paths depending on whether it runs forward or backward (Gregson, 1983).

Techniques for the Analysis of Development

The use of a developmental framework is important because it allows for the effects of previous experience and of progress or decay on interpersonal communication. Areas to which developmental perspectives have been applied include interpersonal communication among children (for example, Clark & Delia, 1976; Delia, Kline, & Burleson, 1979), relationship development (for example, Huston, Surra, Fitzgerald, & Cate, 1981), and interpersonal conflict (Ellis & Fisher, 1975). The study of development requires research strategies and techniques different from those discussed up to now.

First, development should be distinguished from both change and growth. By definition, development involves more than simple change. It implies continuous and patterned change, with a clear sense of directionality, either progress or decay. Development also implies more than simple growth because it involves the interrelationship of several variables over time, whereas growth can refer simply to increase in a single variable. Nagel (1957) provides a good definition of development:

> [Development involves] the notion of a system possessing a definite structure and a definite set of preexisting capacities; and the notion of a sequential set of changes in the system, yielding relatively permanent, but novel increments not only in its structure, but in its modes of operation as well.

The study of development is generally presumed to require longitudinal data from the same subjects, though cross-sectional designs have also been used (for example, a cross-sectional study of relational development might sample couples who have been together for one, three, and six months in a single administration, as opposed to a longitudinal study tracking the couples through six months).

Schaie (1965, 1970; Schaie & Baltes, 1975) has developed a comprehensive analysis of the components underlying developmental change. According to Schaie, three classes of independent variables can account for developmental changes:

(1) *Age:* Variables associated with the aging process in the subject at the time of measurement. This component indexes effects tied to "purely" developmental processes.
(2) *Cohort:* Variables that influence all subjects born or initiated at the same time. This class includes general environmental and historical effects that the set of subjects of a given age or length of participation may have experienced in common. For example, in a study conducted in 1984, middle-class couples who have been together two years would have gone through a recession together,

whereas couples together three months would likely have a relationship not touched by serious economic fears.

(3) *Time of measurement:* Variables affecting subjects at the time they are measured, but which are noncumulative. These have only an immediate or transient effect, though their effects may be important.

Schaie and his colleagues lay out several designs for sorting out which of the three effects is responsible for observed developmental changes. Clearly, only *age* effects index developmental influences in the "pure," internally driven sense. *Cohort* effects index the influence of exogeneous forces on development and are therefore also important. *Time of measurement* effects are accidental and do not index developmental processes.

Schaie's model has provoked considerable critical debate (Adam, 1978; Baltes, 1968), but his distinctions seem to be quite useful. They point out possible problems with cross-national data: In particular, it is difficult to separate time and cohort effects from age effects (for example, see Rubin and Loevinger's [1974] critique of Murstein's [1970] Stimulus-Value-Role Theory of mate selection). Schaie's model also indicates the different classes of determinants that could be operating in developmental data. Researchers interested in establishing a true developmental effect should show that observed effects are not the result of accidental factors, something few interpersonal researchers interested in development have done. Greater attention to Schaie's components and their interrelations would pay off in enhanced understanding of interpersonal processes and greater confidence in the reliability of research results.

Within this theoretical frame, two classes of techniques for studying development can be distinguished: Techniques for describing and testing whether a given developmental pattern occurs and techniques for assessing correlational or causal relationships among developmental variables (Wohlwill [1973] presents an excellent introduction to developmental methods).

Establishing Developmental Patterns. Techniques for describing and testing developmental patterns can use either nominal or continuous data. Nominal data generally consist of a series of longitudinal observations indicating whether or not a particular stage or indicator of stage is present at each point in time. In this case, a developmental description can best be derived and tested through the analysis of the observed pattern as a Guttman scale or some variation thereof. Basically a Guttman scale is an ordered set of items such that each indicates a certain progression along the scale; choosing any item further up on the scale implies choice of all previous items as well. Assume, for example, that we have a four-stage sequential model of relational development with clear indicators of each stage ("0" if the stage has not been entered; "1" if it has). Going through the first stage implies that no other

		a	b	c	d	e
	1	1	0	0	0	0
Time	2	1	1	0	0	0
Periods	3	1	1	1	0	0
	4	1	1	1	1	0
	5	1	1	1	1	1

(a) Cumulative Development

	a	b	c	d	e
1	1	0	0	0	0
2	1	1	0	0	0
3	0	1	1	1	0
4	0	0	1	1	0
5	0	0	0	1	1

(b) Decalage, Persistent Development

	a	b	c	d	e
1	1	1	0	0	0
2	0	1	1	0	0
3	0	0	1	1	0
4	0	1	1	0	0
5	0	0	0	1	1

(c) Decalage, Bidirectional Development

Figure 3.4   Matrices of Phasic Development Indicating Time of Appearance of Characteristic

stages have been entered (giving a pattern of 1000); being in the second stage implies having come through the first (1100); being in the third implies having been through the first two (1110); and being in the fourth means having come through the first three (1111). If these particular patterns of phasic occurrence are all that are found, we have evidence of a Guttman Scale indicating a sequential phasic progression; to the extent that data depart from this pattern, the assumption of a phasic sequence is not upheld. There are also variations on this pattern that can be employed to test other developmental hypotheses. Figure 3.4 shows several matrices showing phasic patterns over time: (a) represents the case discussed above, in which attainments in each previous phase are retained in the next; (b) represents a progression in which several stages can occur simultaneously, but earlier attainments are obscured by later developments; and (c) represents the case in which development is not unidirectional, but may decay to earlier states; other matrix patterns are also possible.

Several methods are available for testing these patterns. Simplest is clustering the nonzero elements together to show what patterns hold. For patterns that do not differ too much from the Guttman simplex, several tests of a scalability are available (Green, 1956; Guttman, 1947; Loevinger, 1947; Ten-Houten, 1969). The existence of more complex patterns can be tested by comparing a hypothesized pattern matrix to the observed matrix; Leik and Matthews (1968), Wohlwill (1973), and Hubert and Schultz (1976) report tests for this. Bart and Airasian (1974) report a particularly interesting method of ordering stages or variables to determine whether various hierarchical patterns occur.

Several methods are also available for describing and testing hypotheses about developmental curves based on continuous measures. The most well known is trend analysis, which permits tests for nonlinear components of curves (quadratic, cubic, quartic, and so forth, see Grant, 1956; Myers, 1972;

Wohlwill, 1973). In addition, a number of mathematical programs permit the fitting of an equation to a curve, revealing its essential properties and relation to time or other variables (see, for eample, STEPIT, by Chandler, 1969). Finally, Tucker (1966) has developed a procedure that takes a set of curves for a sample of subjects and groups the subjects together based on similarity in development. Huston et al. (1981) have used this procedure to identify distinct types of relational development patterns during courtship.

Relationships Among Variables. Two sorts of relationships among variables can be considered in developmental studies. First, researchers may be interested in whether two or more ordered variables are linked together in developmental processes, that is, whether they codevelop or one leads another. For example, this issue is very important in studies of the development of communicative skills. Are certain skills correlated and therefore related to an underlying developmental process or does one skill presuppose (or prefigure) another? It is also important for phenomena that involve parallel development on two or more variables; for example, relational development might involve parallel evolution of intimacy and life aspirations, and it would be useful to know if these progress through the same stages. Wohlwill (1973) discusses several ways of teasing out codeveloping relationships with contingency tables. It is also possible to use factor analysis to probe developmental associations (Bentler, 1973). Factor analysis can be used to determine whether a single dimension underlies diverse developmental phenomena. For example, Rubin (1973) factored measures of four types of egocentrism—communicative egocentrism, cognitive egocentrism, spatial egocentrism, and role-taking egocentrism—for children from ages two to eight. He found all measures loaded on a single factor and argued all four measures were manifestations of a unitary construct. Factor analysis can also be used to find changes in the factor structure through the course of development.

Researchers may also be interested in causal relationships among developmental variables. Most often, this refers to linear causality, which can be assessed via panel designs and structural equation modeling discussed above. However, as Overton and Reese (1973) note, linear causality may hold unambiguously only for mechanistic developmental models. A whole other class of models, organismic models, posit reciprocal and dialectical causation, governed by a teleological relationship implicit in the evolving whole (Werner's theory of development is one example of an organismic model). Because it is difficult to sort out reciprocal causation (particularly in cases with uneven development), codevelopment may be the only relationship researchers can establish for many organismic models.

Our review of interpersonal communication research shows remarkably little attention to the issues raised in this section. Most research concerned with development simply compares correlations for different ages or cohorts or simply uses ANOVA designs, without regard to possible confounding factors or problems of proof. Greater attention to these issues will undoubtedly increase the confidence we can place in studies of interpersonal development. The methods considered here are clearly applicable to hypothetico-deductive and modeling modes of inquiry. The mechanistic model is appropriate for causal research, whereas the organismic model may be more useful for conventional or dialectical modes of explanation.

Qualitative Techniques

Because quantitative studies are numerically-based, they generally rest on assumptions of comparability and homogeneity of units of analysis. Qualitative studies need not involve such assumptions and therefore are likely to be relatively diverse. Databases for qualitative studies range from direct observations by participants or nonparticipants, through video- or audio-tapes of interaction, informant reports, more or less open-ended interviews, official or subjective report documents, to segments of interaction reconstructed or created by the researcher. Researchers work from these bases using general methods such as inductive concept formation, interpretative reconstruction, and critical analysis of implicit "native" grounds and assumptions, as well as contradictions and problems in the data and "loading" (Meehan, 1968) or critique of "given" theoretical concepts. Moves like these are often made in the course of an ongoing dialogue with the "subjects" of the inquiry. And both inference and reporting are often guided by models drawn from disciplines like literary criticism, history and biography, philosophy, and psychoanalysis.

Qualitative studies are most often carried out in the grounded mode of inquiry (although features of modeling are sometimes present), and qualitative researchers generally assume that conventional or dialectical explanatory postures are required by their subject matters. It was not always so: Qualitative methods developed early in sociology and anthropology, and many early theorists emphasized their compatibility with traditional modes of inquiry and explanation. Communication researchers have explicitly claimed the advantages of such methods: They seem to treat directly the meaningful "stuff" of communication and pay attention to history and context, matters that clearly influence interaction, yet are neglected in the typical quantitative analysis. Seeking these advantages, social scientists from a number of schools have argued that qualitative research has greater validity than quantitative research and that qualitative methods need to be used to critique, validate, and explicate quantitative studies (Cicourel, 1981; McPhee & Poole, 1980; O'Keefe et al., 1980).

However, with the increasing stature of qualitative work has come an increasing awareness of its vulnerabilities. Like quantitative methods, qualitative methods can and often do fail to meet standards of scientific adequacy. A good review of methodological pitfalls for qualitative methods is provided by LeCompte and Goetz (1982), who advance standards for reliability and validity of ethnographic research. Before we analyze their standards more closely, though, it should be noted that influential theorists of qualitative analysis procedures have questioned the applicability of any standards at all to social research. Two main qualities claimed for social data are historicality and historicity (Bleicher, 1980). Social texts, and other meaningful products of action, are *historical* in two senses: First, they can be understood only in the process of developing experience that takes place in time, that is, social phenomena are intrinsically *dynamic*. Second, historicality denotes that social texts are separate from us due to discontinuities or gaps in time, culture, and circumstance. Therefore, their interpretation is problematic. But beyond that, social phenomena are generally *historic*—they are important to us, part of our tradition, and have helped make us what we are. To treat such phenomena using methods that reduce them to static, objective data is to mistreat them, to strip them of their essential qualities. Therefore, it is claimed, standards of social scientific method (and perhaps method-bound approaches in general) are inappropriate for the study of social phenomena (Gadamer, 1975).

However, although social scientific standards and methods may distort social phenomena, they embody a skepticism of the validity of research results that is important. LeCompte and Goetz (1982) make two general points about the reliability and validity of qualitative data. First, because qualitative inquiry is generally grounded and processual, the qualities of reliability and validity, and factors that affect these properties, are transmogrified. For instance, in quantitative contexts reliability means that another researcher studying the same phenomena will come to the same or parallel descriptive results. But in grounded inquiry, the cultural description will rest in large part on the process of concept formation and linkage, that is, on pattern recognition and creative but theoretically guided inference by the researcher. So differences in theoretical position or inference style may be considered as reliability threats, just like differences in coder interpretation of categories. And, more importantly, reliability on this interpretation is related not just to particular variables but to the whole conceptual frame resulting from research.

Another interesting reliability threat is the social structural position of researcher and informants or interviewees. LeCompte and Goetz mention several cases in which researchers have offered very different descriptions of the same culture or interaction system because they and their informants have different social roles within the research site. Related to this is the problem of bias in informant selection—the subjects who are willing and able to talk to an outside researcher may be systematically different from other "natives," especially in their attitude toward and access to the researcher's perspective.

A third important reliability/validity issue has been raised in discussions of qualitative microanalyses. Grimshaw (1982) has emphasized the "paradox of microanalysis," also discussed by Labov and Fanshel (1977) and Pittenger, Hockett, and Daheny (1960). Minute and repeated analysis of recordings and transcripts may expose and highlight features that are not important in practice. For example, microanalysis may find incoherence or conflict in interaction without equally exposing the inattention and work that neutralize such disharmony in practice. "Lengthy concentration of attention on the one event can easily blow up its significance far out of proportion to its original duration and its actual setting. One must not mistake the five-inch scale model for the fly itself" (Pittenger, Hockett, & Daheny, 1960, cited in Labov & Fanshel, 1977, p. 22).

These factors, and others, have awakened researchers from the dream of direct contact with reality that the density and meaningfulness of qualitative data sometimes arouses; recent work has explicitly emphasized some of the resources by which qualitative method can guard against threats to reliability and validity. One such resource is replication. Research involving inference from a number of qualitative case studies is becoming more common. Jules Henry (1975) and Ralph Larossa (1977) have reported in-depth analyses of interaction patterns of a number of families to support general conclusions. Another resource is triangulation—reliance on data from a number of sources and observers, often with the capacity to ask for further information or explanations to resolve inconsistencies or unclarities.

A third resource for research with large-scale focus is supplemental microanalysis (provided the paradox of microanalysis can be counteracted). Agar and Hobbs (1982), for instance, use knowledge of coherence strategies drawn from discourse analysis and artificial intelligence work to separate and identify themes and norms of a drug user's subculture from communicative adaptations by the user to interviewers. A fourth resource is the extensive body of work on reasoning in qualitative research. Denzin (1970) provides an excellent discussion of techniques for insuring that conclusions drawn from qualitative data are valid. Some of these, such as the importance of ruling out competing interpretations, are adapted from quantitative research systems.

There have also been advances in techniques for working through the huge masses of data typical of qualitative research. It is not uncommon for an ethnographic study to run for months and generate hundreds of pages of fieldnotes. Close analysis of interaction often involves reconciling thousands of data specimens at different levels of abstraction (see, for example, Labov & Fanshell, 1977). This problem is compounded for studies involving multiple sites and longitudinal data collection. With large data sets it is often difficult for the research to maintain consistent standards of classification and evaluation; standards used on one day may shift the next, and human fatigue makes mistakes likely, if not unavoidable. Indeed, quantitative techniques are often advocated over qualitative methods because computers and numerical coding of data maintain a consistency that qualitative judgments do not allow. For qualitative analysts the problem is to achieve consistency, but at the same time to preserve closeness to phenomena and fine judgmental capacities.

Huberman and Miles (1983; Miles, 1979) discuss several methods for display and reduction of qualitative data to ease the task of managing large databases but to preserve qualitative strengths. They argue that one key to qualitative analysis lies in methods of displaying data in graphic or matrix forms. These displays help researchers make sense of large data sets, which may be spread over hundreds of pages. These also can do the basic work of laying out main findings for the reader, leaving the text to provide illustrations and qualifications. Huberman and Miles (1983) discuss several varieties of displays, including checklist matrices, progressive matrices, causal matrices, predictor-outcomes matrices, event networks, and causal networks, as well as principles for coding and classifying qualitative data. These displays aid the researcher in moving from the identification of key constructs to specification of influences in the system. These developments are very important. For too long qualitative research in interpersonal communication has relied on inspiration and a seat-of-the-pants approach. Systematic aids to reasoning enable researchers to work out their decision rules and logic of analysis publicly. They bring some force of help to fuse the strengths of quantitative analysis with the strengths of qualitative approaches.

These resources are formidable. However, they do not overcome the fact that, despite the narrative realism or qualitative presentations, such analyses are liable to be *subjective*—informed by the values, perspective, and choices of the researcher. They are also *limited*—by matters as practical as static on tapes and as abstract as the bounded contextual and process knowledge of the researcher. Qualitative researchers increasingly recognize these problems and consequently resort to more philosophically grounded approaches in two directions.

The first is the continued rise of formal models derived to "explain" qualitative findings. Well-known examples are the structuralism of Piaget, Levi-Strauss, and Chomsky, and the systems of rules offered by Searle (1976), Sacks et al. (1974), and by Brown and Levinson (1978). In communication, examples include the rules approaches offered by Cushman (1977; Cushman & Cahn, 1984) and Pearce and Cronen (1980), and the language-action hierarchy of Frentz and Farrell (1976). Research related to this formal modeling approach has had either (or both) of two goals: Either to support some specific formal model underlying interaction or to explain more abstract properties of the model (for instance, differentiation, see McPhee, 1978). The latter aim is often adopted because of presumed individual differences, instability, or cross-model consistency in properties.

When specific formal models are being developed, theorists have articulated sets of standards for model validation; such standards affect both the type of models developed and the procedures and data that must be used in validation. For instance, Pearce and Cushman (n.d.) suggest three standards for studies of communication rules based on practical force: (1) A task that is the generative mechanism for the rules must be located; (2) episodic sequences stipulated by the rules must be described and assessed for generality and necessity; and (3) the structure of rule-based inference leading to action must be stipulated. Pearce and Cushman argue that each of these three claims needs empirical support and develop this argument in a critique of four putative rules studies. Another set of standards has been articulated by Chomsky (1957): (1) Observational adequacy (the rules generate all and only the appropriate behaviors), (2) descriptive adequacy (the rules assign correct "structural descriptions" to behaviors which indicate the similarities and differences among the meanings of different behaviors), and (3) explanatory adequacy (underlying the rules is a conception of behavior that shows how that set of rules comes to be learned or developed). Later writers (for example, Cicourel, 1972) have argued that this set of standards must be supplemented with two additional standards: (1) An adequate rules theory must explain the meaningful relations of rule violations to rule-consistent behavior; and (2) it must explain process (for example, the cognitive operations involved in generating the behavior) as well as outcome facts. These standards are reflected in the range of data that might be required to adequately support a rules theory: data about the behaviors generated by the rules, data about how those behaviors are different or similar to one another in meaning and structure, data about the process of learning to perform the behaviors, data about the cognitive operations involved in behaving, and data about the relations of rule-governed behaviors to rule-violating behaviors.

Heightened awareness of the difficulty of adequately supporting a formal model with data has led to some demanding standards for datasets. An example is the set of criteria outlined by Grimshaw (1982) for conversational studies: more than two participants, with varying power, all *involved* in the interchange; a *full* (audio plus visual) recording, supplemented by extensive knowledge of historical and factual context; and rights to publish data and analysis. Even such a dataset could not meet all the standards suggested by Chomsky above.

Another direction for qualitative analysis, away from a naive depictive stance, is toward a more critical, redescriptive focus. Examples here include Henry's (1963) examination of culture against man and Katriel and Philipsen's (1981) examination of "communication" as an American cultural category. Such studies rest on qualitative analyses and draw on the resources listed above. Both studies just referred to, for instance, use information from multiple sources and about multiple cases. These studies reflect a relative awareness of their limits and use their data and analysis not as verification of general patterns or hypotheses, but as evidence drawn on to develop as well as to support an argument. The argument itself in such studies tends to be either critical—oriented to expose an underlying structure of social phenomena in conflict with general values (for example, see Fletcher, 1974)—or dialectical, in the sense of Wittgenstein's *Tractatus* or Stanley Fish's *Self-Consuming Artifacts*—oriented to "raise" our consciousness using ethnographic evidence in a way that carries us beyond the evidence itself.

New Directions

A review of methods for studying interpersonal communication cannot end without mentioning methods and information sources which have been neglected by students of interpersonal communication.

Network Theory. One approach which seems especially promising is the use of network methods and conceptions. Network research on interpersonal relations and social-personality tendencies of individuals is not uncommon (Boissevain, 1974; Bott, 1971; Feld, 1981; Feld & Elmore, 1982; Fischer, 1982; Fischer, Jackson, Stueve, Gerson, & Jones, 1977; Huckfeldt, 1983; Newcomb, 1961; Salzinger, 1982) and has demonstrated that interpersonal relationships and behavior can be affected significantly by the network context in which they are embedded, yet the network-based study of interpersonal communication per se has been limited to Parks, Stan, and Eggert (1983). Because network technology is well-known and developed in the study of communication (Rogers & Kincaid, 1982), it is unfortunate that the study of interpersonal communication has not drawn on this general resource more extensively.

Historical-Critical Research. Another promising resource is the historical-critical study of interpersonal interaction patterns. Typically, the results of empirical studies are treated as laws or regularities with unbounded general implications, and concerns about external validity are approached by discussing the need to sample various available subpopulations. All the relevant information indicates that this approach is completely inadequate. Visible patterns of interpersonal communication are constituted in a social, economic, and cultural context that is unique and in transition: Interpersonal communication is different now than it was and will be different still in the future. For instance, Poster (1980) and Zaretsky (1976) discuss family relationships; Sennett (1974) describes self presentation and role development; and Willis (1977) analyzes adolescent relationships, as overwhelmingly transformed and twisted by the sociopolitical and economic context of capitalism. Our studies of interpersonal communication need to, but rarely do, take cognizance of these contextual effects. This would require them to use analytic methods and information sources that allow separation of context effects from cross-context regularities. One research current that displays historical-critical awareness is the feminist approach to interaction style (for an overview, see Kramarae, 1980). Historical-critical methods clearly are related to more traditional qualitative methods and to the conception of "does-cause" studies mentioned above.

Meta-analysis. Articles reviewing and synthesizing literature have been criticized on grounds that they are overly impressionistic, have no trustworthy means of assessing consistency of results across studies, and are often selective in their use of evidence. Meta-analysis (Glass, McGaw, & Smith, 1981; Hunter, Schmidt, & Jackson, 1982) is an empirical technique that attempts to correct for these problems while still maintaining the vital synthesis function of a good review. Meta-analysis uses statistical techniques to integrate findings from a number of studies concerned with a single problem. It permits the researcher to test for the size of an effect across all studies and to sort out variables that moderate the effect. Correctly done, it can also permit evaluation of competing explanations (for example, Dillard, Hunter, & Burgoon, 1984). Meta-analysis has two advantages over traditional approaches to research synthesis: (1) It spells out systematic rules for integrating findings that eliminate the unreliable and uneven application of judgmental criteria; and (2) it permits statistical reasoning about these results.

Hunter et al. (1982) provide the most rigorous procedure for meta-analysis and recommend the following steps:

(1) Accumulate as nearly as possible the entire corpus of studies on an issue. This includes searching computer databases for publications in a wide range of fields, locating dissertations, theses, and government reports, and including unpublished studies as well. These latter two sources are important because published work is likely to have the most significant and clearcut results and to omit null results.
(2) Calculate a mean effect size across studies.
(3) Test the hypothesis that there is no difference in effect sizes across studies. If this hypothesis cannot be rejected, the analysis stops here and the mean effect size is reported and explicated.
(4) If there is a difference in effect sizes across studies, the influence of various moderators on effect sizes can be tested. Only those moderator variables for which there is a substantive theoretical justification should be included. Hunter et al. explicitly recommend against coding every possible moderator regardless of level of justification because the resulting tests are difficult to interpret without theory.

Dillard et al. (1984) provide a good application of this method to studies on two compliance-gaining techniques.

Meta-analysis obviously has great promise. However, users must bear several issues in mind. First, meta-analyses are likely to overestimate effect size because most studies that show no effects end their lives in file drawers. Even with a determined search, many null results simply may not be available. Second, because research in most areas is not conducted under a unifying theoretical umbrella, many key moderator variables may not be measured or may only appear in one or two studies, and there may be many "garbage" variables. Anyone who has attempted to synthesize a large body of studies is familar with this problem: The variables measured by various researchers neither fit together nor cover the whole range of moderators. The aspiring meta-analyst is at the mercy of his or her predecessors, and lack of coverage may make it impossible to make sense of an analysis.

Third, there exists a controversy over whether studies judged to be methodologically defective should be omitted from meta-analyses. Some authors (Eysenck, 1978) argue that it is "mega-silliness" to include all studies, however flawed they may be. Others (Hunter et al., 1982) argue that flaws are in the eye of the beholder and may not turn out to be flaws at all in the larger scheme of things. They suggest empirical tests for determining whether possible flaws really distort meta-analysis results (Hunter et al., 1982, pp. 151-153). Finally, the use of statistical tests in meta-analysis may create a tendency to substitute statistics for substantive reasoning, a problem all too widespread already. There is simply no substitute for having clear ideas on what is going on in the studies one is reviewing. Given a good theory, meta-analysis has real potential to improve the conclusions we draw. Without a theory, it runs the risk of becoming another dust-bowl exercise that only sanctifies rootless conclusions with numbers.

Figure 3.5 presents a summary of selected techniques discussed in this section and their actual and potential use in interpersonal communication research.

CONCLUSION

This review has been guided by our conviction that interpersonal communication research should pay greater attention to the theory-technique linkage. The need for researchers to justify methodological choices in terms of their adequacy for answering research questions is one of the foundations of social science. Yet these justifications are too often missing or sorely inadequate in reports of interpersonal communication research (and social research in general). Our investigative reasoning needs to convey a greater sense of continuity between theory and technique. This requires increased precision in linking theory and method and a larger awareness of how theory, template, and technique mesh to create knowledge of inter-personal communication. It is especially important to notice how templates and techniques shape theory; this influence is often ignored and being aware of it enables us to make conscious choices regarding our modes of knowing. Cappella's (1977) review emphasized the need to spell out theory-method linkages and advocated modeling as the means of doing this. We would build

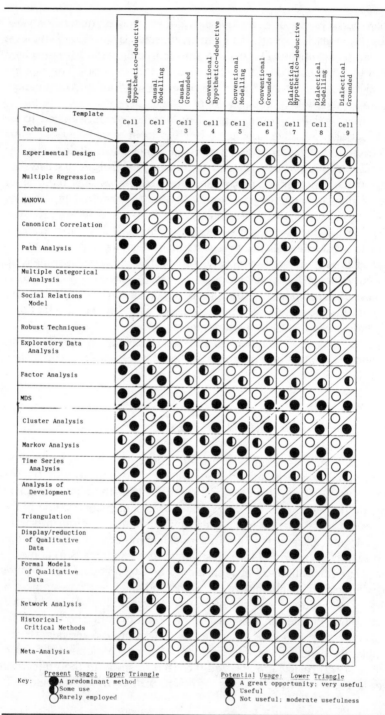

Figure 3.5   Selected Analytical Techniques and Their Actual and Potential Use in the Templates

on his insights by recognizing that modeling is not the only form of inquiry suited for this clarification. All nine templates can be used to bridge the gap between abstract theory and technique and each has its own strengths and weaknesses.

In the second and third sections we attempted to spell out some actual and possible links between templates and techniques, but the range of these relationships is so extensive that it defies full explication. Following the pattern set forth in those sections should enable the reader to generate many others. The key is to use the intersection of inquiry mode and explanation as a criterion for selecting or eliminating techniques. The selection process may also differ, depending on the stage of inquiry the research is in. For example, in the conventional, grounded template the use of clustering or hypothesis-testing techniques is not appropriate early on, when the researcher is searching for insights, but may be during later stages, after interesting constructs and relationships have been uncovered.

It is important to break the tyranny of certain theory-technique links, in particular the marriage of causal explanation to hypothetico-deductive inquiry and conventional explanation to grounded inquiry. These templates represent valuable approaches, but they often serve as norms that keep researchers from trying other approaches. Greater use of these templates could greatly enhance the power and sensitivity of communication research. Truly important and robust discoveries should hold across investigative domains, and exploring them with several distinct approaches should make their implications much clearer than does a one-sided strategy.

It is also important to bridge the greatly overestimated gap between "qualitative" and "quantitative" approaches. Close examination of the patterns of reasoning underlying the various techniques clearly shows affinities in both "camps." Canons of causal analysis such as the necessity to assess or control for competing causes, to establish necessary connections, to control for factors introducing errors, and to employ systematic sampling are also exhibited in qualitative reasoning. Conversely, premises of interpretive research—for example, going below surface phenomena to uncover underlying meanings, focusing on the significance or meaning of phenomena rather than objectifying them, and strategies for avoiding reification of the researcher's constructs—can be important correctives for quantitative investigations. Greater penetration of each domain by the other increases the validity of interpersonal communication research substantially.

Finally, there is a need to fight against the narcissism of technique. Communication research, and social science generally, has witnessed an ever-increasing emphasis on the importance of method. The huge market for texts on both quantitative and qualitative methodology attests to this trend. This is a healthy development in many respects because it contributes to more deliberate and discriminating technical choices. However, problems lurk beneath the shimmering surface of this technical emphasis. Researchers without extensive background in statistics and mathematics must take the operations of complex procedures on faith. Techniques such as time-series analysis, LISREL, and complex factor analytic or clustering procedures involve sophisticated algorithms and restrictive assumptions that can easily be misunderstood and misapplied by even the wariest investigator. The statistical properties of many procedures are not well-understood, and even their creators acknowledge ambiguous areas.

These considerations recommend great care in interpreting the results of these procedures; they are not fully understood and the path from raw data to output is often torturous and unclear. However, the ethos of technique can cause us to adopt an uncritical attitude and to assume that results from these methods are valid and meaningful, simply because they are on the cutting edge of the methodological advance and because we are accustomed to trusting statistics—we transfer our faith in means and variances to the parameters of a LISREL solution. This can lead to an unjustified overestimation of the validity and generalizability of our results. The only corrective is careful testing of assumptions underlying the methods and attention to features that might qualify results, such as standard errors of estimates, as well as a healthy dose of skepticism. Nor are qualitative methods immune from this problem. Qualitative discussions are filled with invocations of the magic term "triangulation," without much attention to the validity of data being triangulated and of how contradictory findings can be reconciled.

The narcissism of technique also supports another dangerous tendency: the substitution of method for thinking. In the introduction we argued that theory and method interpenetrate and advocated greater attention to their interrelationship. This was not meant to deny that insight and creativity are the wellsprings of good research. Without good, solid ideas the most sophisticated and careful research strategy is fruitless. The complexities of analytical reasoning encourage greater attention to method than to ideas, and this can result in sophisticated studies that advance the field a little. The social detective, like his or her novelistic counterpart, must constantly push toward a truer picture until all pieces of the mystery fall into place. Significant progress depends both on substance and on method, and neither can be slighted without harming the whole.

REFERENCES

Achinstein, P. (1971). *Laws and explanation.* Oxford: Oxford Press.

Adam, J. (1978). Sequential strategies and the separation of age, cohort, and time-of-measurement contributions to developmental data. *Psychological Bulletin, 85,* 1309-1316.

Agar, M., & Hobbs, J. R. (1982). Interpreting discourse: Coherence and the analysis of ethnographic interviews. *Discourse Processes, 5,* 1-32.

Allen, M., & Yen, W. (1979). *Introduction to measurement theory.* Monterey, CA: Brooks Cole.

Allison, P. D., & Liker, J. K. (1982). Analyzing sequential categorical data on dyadic interaction: A comment on Gottman. *Psychological Bulletin, 91,* 393-403.

Altman, I., & Taylor, D. A. (1973). *Social penetration.* New York: Holt, Rinehart & Winston.

Anderson, N. A.(1981). *Foundations of information integration theory.* New York: Academic Press.

Anderson, P. A. (1983). Decision making by objective and the Cuban missile crisis. *Administrative Science Quarterly, 28,* 201-222.

Argyris, C. (1968). Some unintended consequences of rigorous research. *Psychological Bulletin, 70,* 185-197.

Arundale, R. B. (1977). Sampling across time for communication research: A simulation. In P. M. Hirsch, P. V. Miller, & F. G. Kline (Eds.), *Strategies for communication research* (pp. 257-285). Beverly Hills, CA: Sage.

Arundale, R. B. (1980). Studying change over time: Criteria for sampling from continuous variables. *Communication Research, 7,* 227-263.

Bales, R. F. (1970). *Personality and interpersonal behavior.* New York: Holt, Rinehart & Winston.

Baltes, P. (1968). Longitudinal and cross-sectional sequences in the study of age and generation effects. *Human Development, 11,* 145-171.

Bart, W. H., & Airasian, P. W. (1974). Determination of the ordering among seven Piagetian tasks by an ordering-theoretic method. *Journal of Educational Psychology, 66,* 277-284.

Becker, H. S. (1958). Problems of inference and proof in participant observation. *American Sociological Review, 23.*

Behling, O., & Dillard, J. F. (1984). A problem in data analysis: Implications for organizational behavior research. *Academy of Management Review, 9,* 37-46.

Bentler, P. M. (1973). Assessment of developmental factor change at the individual and group level. In J. R. Nessleroade & H. W. Reese (Eds.), *Life-span developmental psychology: Methodological issues.* New York: Academic Press.

Bereiter, C. (1963). Some persisting dilemmas in the measurement of change. In C. W. Harris (Ed.), *Problems in measuring change* (pp. 3-20). Madison, WI: University of Wisconsin Press.

Berger, C. R. (1975). The covering law perspective as a basis for the study of human communication. *Communication Quarterly, 25,* 7-18.

Berger, C. R., & Calabrese, R. J. (1974). Some explorations in initial interaction and beyond: Toward a developmental theory of interpersonal communication. *Human Communication Research, 1,* 99-112.

Bishop, Y. M., Feinberg, S., & Holland, P. W. (1975). *Discrete multivariate analysis: Theory and practice.* Cambridge, MA: MIT Press.

Blalock, H. H. (Ed.). (1971). *Causal models in the social sciences.* Chicago: Aldine.

Bleicher, J. (1980). *Contemporary hermeneutics.* London: Routledge & Kegan Paul.

Blumer, H. (1956). Sociological analysis and the "variable." *American Sociological Review, 21,* 683-690.

Boissevain, J. (1974) *Friends of friends.* New York: St. Martin's Press.

Borg, I. (1979). Some basic concepts of facet theory. In J. C. Lingoes, E. E. Roskam, & I. Borg (Eds.), *Geometric representations of relational data: Reading in multidimensional scaling* (pp. 65-102). Ann Arbor, MI: Mathesis Press.

Borg, I., & Lingoes, J. C. (1978). What weight should weights have in individual differences scaling? *Quality and Quantity, 12,* 223-237.

Bott, E. (1971). *Family and social network.* New York: Free Press.

Bradac, J. J., Hosman, L. A., & Tardy, C. A. (1978). Reciprocal disclosures and language intensity: Attributional consequences. *Communication Monographs, 45,* 1-17.

Brown, P., & Levinson, S. (1978). Universals in language usage: Politeness phenomena. In E. N. Goody (Ed.), *Questions and politeness: Strategies in social interaction* (pp. 56-289). Cambridge: Cambridge University Press.

Browning, L. D. (1978). A grounded organizational communication theory derived from qualitative data. *Communication Monographs, 45,* 93-109.

Byrne, D. (1969). Attitudes and attraction. In L. Berkowitz (Ed.), *Advances in experimental social psychology* (Vol. 4, pp. 35-89). New York: Academic Press.

Burawoy, M. (1979). *Manufacturing consent.* Chicago: University of Chicago Press.

Campbell, D. T., & Stanley J. C. (1966). *Experimental and quasi-experimental designs for research*. Skokie, IL: Rand McNally.

Cappella, J. N. (1975). An introduction to the literature of causal modeling. *Human Communication Research, 1*, 362-377.

Cappella, J. N. (1977). Research methodology in communication: Review and commentary. In B. D. Ruben (Ed.), *Communication yearbook 1* (pp. 37-53). New Brunswick, NJ: Transaction Books.

Cappella, J. N. (1979). Talk-silence sequences in informal conversations 1. *Human Communication Research, 6*, 3-17.

Cappella, J. N. (1980). Talk and silence sequences in informal conversations II. *Human Communication Research, 6*, 130-145.

Cappella, J. N., & Planalp, S. (1981). Talk and silence sequences in informal conversations III. Interspeaker influence. *Human Communication Research, 7*, 117-132.

Carroll, J. D., & Chang, J. J. (1970). Analysis of individual differences in multidimensional scaling via an N-way generalization of "Eckart-Young decomposition. *Psychometrika, 35*, 283-320.

Catalano, R. A., Dooley, D., & Jackson, R. (1983). Selecting a time-series strategy. *Psychological Bulletin, 94*, 506-523.

Chandler, J. P. (1969). STEPIT—Find local minima of a smooth function of several parameters. *Behavioral Science, 14*, 81-82.

Chase, L. J., & Tucker, R. K. (1975). A power-analytic examination of contemporary communication research. *Communication Monographs, 42*, 29-41.

Chatfield, C. (1975). *The analysis of time-series: Theory and practice*. London: Chapman and Hill.

Chomsky, N. (1957). *Syntactic structure*. The Hague: Mouton.

Churchill, L. (1963). Types of formalization in small-group research. *Sociometry, 26*, 373-390.

Cicourel, A. V. (1964). *Method and measurement in sociology*. New York: Free Press.

Cicourel, A. V. (1972). Basic and normative rules in the negotiation of status and role. In D. Sudnow (Ed.), *Studies in social interaction* (pp. 229-258). New York: Free Press.

Cicourel, A. V. (1980). Three models of discourse analysis: The role of social structure. *Discourse Processes, 3*, 101-132.

Cicourel, A. V. (1981). The role of cognitive-linguistic concepts in understanding everyday social interactions. *Annual Review of Sociology, 7*, 87-106.

Clark, R. A., & Delia, J. G. (1976). The development of functional persuasive skills in childhood and early adolescence. *Child Development, 47*, 1008-1014.

Cody, M. J., & McLaughlin, M. L. (1980). Perceptions of compliance-gaining situations: A dimensional analysis. *Communication Monographs, 47*, 132-148.

Cody, M. J., Woelfel, M. L., & Jordan, W. J. (1983). Dimensions of compliance-gaining situations. *Human Communication Research, 9*, 99-113.

Cohen, J. (1977). *Statistical power analysis for the behavioral sciences*. London: Academic Press.

Cohen, J., & Cohen, P. (1975). *Applied multiple regression/correlation analysis for the behavioral sciences*. Hillsdale, NJ: Lawrence Erlbaum.

Cook, T. D., & Campbell, D. T. (1979). *Quasi-experimentation: Design and analysis issues for field settings*. Chicago: Rand McNally.

Coombs, C. (1976). *A theory of data*. Ann Arbor, MI: Mathesis Press.

Cormak, R. M. (1971). A review of classification. *Journal of the Royal Statistical Society, 143*, 321-367.

Craig, R. T. (1983). Galilean rhetoric and practical theory. *Communication Monographs, 1983*, 395-412.

Cronbach, L., & Furby, L. (1970). How should we measure "change"—or should we? *Psychological Bulletin, 74*, 68-80.

Cronbach, L. J., Gleser, G. C., Nanda, H., & Rajaratnam, N. (1972). *The dependability of behavioral measurements: Theory of generalizability for scores and profiles*. New York: John Wiley.

Cronbach, L. J., & Meehl, P. E. (1955). Construct validity in psychological tests. *Psychological Bulletin, 52*, 281-302.

Cronkhite, G. (1976). Effects of rater-concept-scale interactions and use of different factoring procedures upon evaluative factor structure *Human Communication Research, 2*, 316-329.

Cronkhite, G., & Liska, J. (1976). Critique of factor analytic approaches to the study of credibility. *Communication Monographs, 43,* 91-107.

Cushman, D. P. (1977). The rules perspective as a theoretical basis for the study of human communication. *Communication Quarterly, 25,* 30-45.

Cushman, D. P., & Cahn, D. (1984). *Communication in interpersonal relationships.* Albany, NY: SUNY Press.

Cushman, D. P., & Nishida, T. (1983). *Mate selection in the United States and Japan.* Unpublished manuscript, SUNY at Albany, Department of Communication.

Cushman, D. P., & Pearce, W. B. (1977). Generality and necessity in three types of human communication theory with special attention to rules theory. *Human Communication Research 3,* 344-353.

Dalton, M. (1959). *Men who manage.* New York: John Wiley.

Dean, J. P. (1954). Participant observation and interviewing. In J. T. Doby (Ed.), *Introduction to social research* (pp. 52-75). Harrisburg, PA: Stackpole.

Delia, J. G., Kline, S. K., & Burleson, B. R. (1979). The development of persuasive communication strategies in kindergartners through twelfth-graders. *Communication Monographs, 46,* 241-256.

Denzin, N. K. (1970). *The research act.* Chicago: Aldine.

Dielman, T. E. (1983). Pooled cross-sectional and time series data: A survey of current statistical methodology, *American Statistician, 37* 111-122.

Dijkstra, W., & Van der Zouwen, J. (Eds.). (1982). *Response behavior in the survey-interview.* New York: Academic Press.

Dillard, J. P., Hunter, J. E., & Burgoon, M. (1984). Sequential-request persuasive strategies: Meta-analysis of foot-in-the-door and door-in-the-face. *Human Communication Research 10,* 461-488.

Dillman, D. A. (1978). *Mail and telephone surveys: The total design method.* New York: John Wiley.

Donohue, W. A. (1981). Development of a model of rule use in negotiation interaction. *Communication Monographs, 48,* 106-120.

Draper, N. R., & Smith, H. (1966). *Applied regression analysis.* New York: John Wiley.

Duncan, O. D. (1975). *Introduction to structural equation models.* New York: Academic Press.

Edelsky, C. (1982). Who's got the floor? *Language in Society, 10,* 383-421.

Efron, B., & Gong, G. (1983). A leisurely look at the bootstrap, the jacknife, and cross-validation. *The American Statistician, 371,* 36-48.

Ellis, D., & Fisher, B. A. (1975). Phases of conflict in small group development: A Markov analysis. *Human Communication Research, 1,* 195-212.

Embretson, S. (1983). Construct validation: Construct representation versus nomothetic span. *Psychological Bulletin, 93,* 179-197.

Ericsson, K. A., & Simon, H. A. (1980). Verbal reports as data. *Psychological Review, 87,* 215-251.

Everitt, B. (1977). *The analysis of contingency tables.* New York: John Wiley.

Eysenck, H. J. (1978). An exercise in mega-silliness. *American Psychologist, 33,* 517-518.

Feinberg, S. (1977). *The analysis of cross-classified categorical data.* Cambridge, MA: MIT Press.

Feld, S. L. (1981). The focused organization of social ties. *American Journal of Sociology, 86,* 1015-1035.

Feld, S. L., & Elmore, R. (1982). Patterns of sociometric choices: Transitivity revisited. *Social Psychology Quarterly, 45,* 77-85.

Fink, E. L. (1980). Unobserved variables within structural equation models. In P. R. Monge & J. N. Cappella (Eds.), *Multivariate techniques in human communication research* (pp. 111-142). New York: Academic Press.

Fink, E. L., & Monge, P. R. (in press). An exploration of confirmatory factor analysis. In B. Dervin & M. Voigt (Eds.), *Progress in communication sciences* (Vol. 6). Norwood, NJ: Ablex.

Fischer, C. S. (1982). *To dwell among friends: Personal networks in town and city.* Chicago: University of Chicago Press.

Fischer, C. S., Jackson, R. M., Stueve, C. A., Gerson, K., & Jones, L. M., with Baldassare, M. (1977). *Networks and places: Social relations in the urban setting.* New York: Free Press.

Fisher, B. A. (1970). Decision emergence: Phases in group decision making. *Speech Monographs, 37,* 53-66.

Fisher, B. A. (1970). *Functions of category systems in interaction analysis.* Paper presented at the annual meeting of the Speech Communication Association, Washington, DC.

Fisher, B. A., & Hawes, L. C. (1971). An interact system model. Generating a grounded theory of small groups. *Quarterly Journal of Speech, 57,* 444-453.

Fitzpatrick, M. A., & Best, P. (1979). Dyadic adjustment in relational types: Consensus, cohesion, affectional expression, and satisfaction in enduring relationships. *Communication Monographs, 46,* 167-178.

Fletcher, C. (1974). *Beneath the surface.* London: Routledge & Kegan Paul.

Foa, U. G. (1965). New developments in facet design and analysis. *Psychological Review, 72,* 262-274.

Folger, J. P., Hewes, D., & Poole, M. S. (1984). Coding social interaction. In B. Dervin & M. Voight (Eds.), *Progress in the communication sciences* (pp. 115-161). New York: Ablex.

Folger, J. P., & Sillars, A. (1980). Relational coding and perceptions of dominance. In B. Morse & L. Phelps (Eds.), *Interpersonal communication: A relational perspective* (pp. 322-333). Minneapolis: Burgess.

Fornell, C., & Bookstein, F. L. (1982). Two structural equation models: LISREL and PLS applied to consumer exit-voice theory. *Journal of Marketing Research, 19,* 440-452.

Frankel, R. M., & Beckman, H. B. (1982). Impact: An interaction-based method for preserving and analyzing clinical interactions. In L. S. Pettegrew, P. Arnston, D. Bush, & K. Zoppi (Eds.), *Explorations in provider and patient interaction* (pp. 71-86). Nashville: Humana.

Frederiksen, C. H., & Rotondo, J. A. (1979). Time-series models and the study of longitudinal change. In J. R. Nesselroade & P. B. Baltes (Eds.), *Longitudinal research in the study of behavior and development* (pp. 111-154). New York: Academic Press.

Frentz, T. A., & Farrell, T. B. (1976). Language-action: A paradigm for communication. *Quarterly Journal of Speech, 62,* 333-349.

Gadamer, H. G. (1975). *Truth and method.* New York: Crossroad.

Garfinkel, H. (1967). *Studies in ethnomethodology.* Englewood Cliffs, NJ: Prentice-Hall.

Glaser, B. G., & Strauss, A. (1967). *The discovery of grounded theory: Strategies for qualitative research.* Chicago: Aldine.

Glass, G. V., McGaw, B., & Smith, M. L. (1981). *Meta-analysis in social research.* Beverly Hills, CA: Sage.

Goersuch, R. L. (1974). *Factor analysis.* Philadelphia: W. B. Saunders.

Gold, R. L. (1958). Roles in sociological field observations. *Social Forces, 36,* 217-223.

Goodman, L. A. (1978). *Analyzing qualitative/categorical data: Log-linear models and latent structure analysis.* Cambridge, MA: Abt Books.

Gottman, J. M. (1981). *Time-series analysis: A comprehensive introduction for social scientists.* New York: Cambridge University Press.

Grant, D. A. (1956). Analysis of variance tests in the analysis and comparison of curves. *Psychological Bulletin, 53,* 141-154.

Green, B. (1956). A method of scalogram analysis using summary statistics. *Psychometrika, 21,* 79-88.

Green, P. E., & Wind, Y. (1973). *Multiattribute decisions in marketing: A measurement approach.* Hinsdale, IL: Dryden.

Gregson, R.A.M. (1983). *Time-series in psychology.* Hillsdale, NJ: Lawrence Erlbaum.

Grimshaw, A. (1982). Comprehensive discourse analysis: An instance of professional peer interaction. *Language in Society, 11,* 15-47.

Guttman, L. (1947). The Cornell technique for scale and intensity analysis. *Educational and Psychological Measurment, 7,* 247-279.

Hage, J. (1972). *Techniques and problems of theory construction in sociology.* New York: John Wiley.

Hambleton, R., Swaminathan, H., Cook, L., Eignor, D., & Gifford, J. (1978). Developments in latent trait theory: Models, technical issues, and applications. *Review of Educational Research, 48,* 467-510.

Harris, R. J. (1975). *A primer of multivariate statistics.* New York: Academic Press.

Hawes, L. (1972). Development and application of an interview coding system. *Central States Speech Journal, 23,* 92-99.

Hawes, L. C. (1976). How writing is used in talk: A study of communicative logic-in-use. *Quarterly Journal of Speech, 62,* 350-360.

Hawes, L. C., & Foley, J. (1973). A Markov analysis of interview communication. *Communication Monographs, 40,* 208-219.

Hayes, D., & Sievers, S. (1972). A sociolinguistic investigation of the "dimensions" of interpersonal behavior. *Journal of Personality and Social Psychology, 24,*254-261.

Henry, J. (1963). *Culture against man.* New York: Vintage.

Henry, J. (1975). *Pathways to madness.* New York: Vintage.

Hewes, D. E. (1975). Finite stochastic modelling of communication processes. *Human Communication Research, 1,* 217-283.

Hewes, D. E. (1979). The sequential analysis of social interaction. *Quarterly Journal of Speech, 65,* 56-73.

Hewes, D. E. (1980). An axiomatized stochastic process theory of the relationships among messages, mediating variables, and behaviors. In D. P. Cushman & R. D. McPhee (Eds.), *The message-attitude-behavior relationship* (pp. 43-88). New York: Academic Press.

Hewes, D. E., Graham, M. L., Doelger, J., & Pavitt, C. (1984). *"Second guessing": Message interpretation in social networks.* Paper presented at International Communication Association Convention, San Francisco, CA.

Hewes, D. E., & Haight, L. R. (1979). The cross-situational consistency of communication behaviors: A preliminary investigation. *Communication Research, 6,* 243-270.

Hewes, D. E., & Haight, L. R. (1980). Multiple-act criteria in the validation of communication traits: What do we gain and what do we lose? *Human Communication Research, 6,* 354-366.

Honeycutt, J. N. (1984, May). *A structural equation model of marital functioning using attraction paradigm and social penetration dimensions.* Paper presented at the annual convention of the International Communication Convention, San Francisco, CA.

Huberman, A. M., & Miles, M. (1983). Drawing valid meaning from qualitative data: Some techniques of data reduction and display. *Quality and Quantity, 17,* 281-339.

Hubert, L., & Baker, F. (1976). Data analysis by single-link and complete-link hierarchical clustering. *Journal of Educational Statistics, 1,* 87-111.

Hubert, L., & Schultz, J. (1976). Quadratic assignment as a general data analysis strategy. *British Journal of Mathematical and Statistical Psychology, 29, 190-241.*

Huckfeldt, R. R. (1983). Social contexts, social networks, and urban neighborhoods: Environmental constraints on friendship choice. *American Journal of Sociology, 89,* 651-669.

Hunter, J. E., Levine, R. L., & Sayers, S. E. (1976). Attitude change in hierarchical belief systems and its relationship to persuasibility, dogmatism, and rigidity. *Human Communication Research, 3,* 3-28.

Hunter, J. E., Schmidt, F. L., & Jackson, G. B. (1982). *Meta-analysis: Cumulating research findings across studies.* Beverly Hills, CA: Sage.

Huston, T. L., Surra, C., Fitzgerald, N., & Cate, R. (1981). From courtship to marriage: Mate selection as an interpersonal process. In S. Duck & R. Gilmour (Eds.), *Personal relationships 2: Developing personal relationships* (pp. 53-90). New York: Academic Press.

Izraeli, D. (1977). Settling in: An interactionist perspective on the entry of a new manager. *Pacific Sociological Review, 20,* 135-160.

Jaccard, J., & Daly, J. (1980). Personality traits and multiple-act criteria. *Human Communication Research, 6(4),* 367-377.

Jackson, S., & Jacobs, S. (1980). Structure of conversational argument: Pragmatic bases for the enthymeme. *Quarterly Journal of Speech, 66,* 251-265.

Jöreskog, K. G. (1969). A general approach to confirmatory maximum likelihood factor analysis. *Psychometrika, 34,* 183-202.

Katriel, T., & Philipsen, J. (1981). "What we need is communication:" "Communication" as a cultural category in some American Speech. *Communication Monographs, 48,* 301-317.

Kenny, D. A., (1979). *Correlation and causation.* New York: Wiley-Interscience.

Kenny, D. A., & La Voie, L. (1984). The social relations model. In L. Berkowitz (Ed.), *Advances in experimental social psychology* (Vol. 18, pp. 141-182). New York: Academic Press.

Keppel, G. (1973). *Design and analysis: A researcher's handbook*. Englewood Cliffs, NJ: Prentice-Hall.

Kirk, R. E. (1968). *Experimental design: Procedures for the behavioral sciences*. Belmont, CA: Brooks/Cole.

Kmenta, J. (1971). *Elements of econometrics*. New York: Macmillan.

Labov, W., & Fanshel, D. (1977). *Therapeutic discourse: Psychotherapy as conversation*. New York: Academic Press.

Laing, R. D. (1962). *The self and others*. Chicago: Quadrangle Press.

Laird, A., Johnson, K., & Downs, C. (1982, May). *Communication productivity: From structure to structuration*. Paper presented at the annual meeting of the International Communication Association, Boston, MA.

LaRossa, R. (1977). *Conflict and power in marriage*. Beverly Hills, CA: Sage.

Lazarsfeld, P., & Barton, A. (1969). Qualitative measurement: A codification of techniques for the social sciences. In L. Krimmerman (Ed.), *The nature and scope of the social sciences* (pp. 514-539). Englewood Cliffs, NJ: Prentice-Hall.

Leary, T. (1957). *Interpersonal diagnosis of personality*. New York: Ronald.

LeCompte, M. D., & Goetz, J. P. (1982). Problems of reliability and validity in ethnographic research. *Review of Educational Research, 52*, 31-60.

Leik, R., & Matthews, M. (1968). A scale for developmental processes. *American Sociological Review, 33*, 62-75.

Lingoes, J. C., & Borg, I. (1978). A direct approach to individual differences scaling using increasingly complex transformations. *Psychometrika, 43*, 491-519.

Lingoes, J. C., Roskam, E. E., & Borg, I. (Eds.). (1979). *Geometric representations of relational data: Readings in multidimensional scaling*. Ann Arbor, MI: Mathesis.

Linn, R. L., & Slinde, J. A. (1977). The determination of the significance of change between pre- and posttesting periods. *Review of Educational Research, 47*, 121-150.

Loevinger, J. (1947). A systematic approach to the construction and evaluation of tests of ability. *Psychological Monographs, 61*, (Whole No. 4).

Loevinger, J. (1957). Objective tests as instruments of psychological theory. *Psychological Reports, 3(9)*, 635-694.

Lord, F. M., & Novick, M. R. (1968). *Statistical theories of mental test scores*. Reading, MA: Addison-Wesley.

Marr, T. J. (1973). Q and R analyses of panel data on a political candidate image and voter communication. *Speech Monographs, 40*, 56-65.

Maxwell, S. E., & Howard, G. S. (1981). Change scores—necessarily anathema? *Educational and Psychological Measurement, 41*, 747-756.

McCleary, R., & Hays, R. L. (1980). *Applied time series analysis for the social sciences*. Beverly Hills, CA: Sage.

McCroskey, J. C. (1978). Validity of the PRCA as an index of oral communication apprehension. *Communication Monographs, 45*, 192-203.

McCroskey, J. C., & McCain, T. A. (1974). The measurement of interpersonal attraction. *Speech Monographs, 41*, 261-266.

McGuire, W. J. (1973). The yin and yang of progress in social psychology: Seven koan. *Journal of Personality and Social Psychology, 26*, 446-456.

McLaughlin, M., & Cody, M. (1982). Awkward silences: Behavioral antecedents and consequences of the conversational lapse. *Human Communication Research, 8*, 299-316.

McLaughlin, M., & Jordan, W. J. (1975). Impression formation in triads. *Communication Monographs, 42*, 47-55.

McPhee, R. D. (1978). *A rules theory of organizational communication*. Unpublished Ph.D. dissertation, Michigan State University.

McPhee, R. D. (1982, November). *Can-cause or does-cause: The research dichotomy*. Paper presented at the annual meeting of the Speech Communication Association, Louisville, KY.

McPhee, R. D., & Babrow, A. S. (in press). Causal modeling in speech communication research: Use, disuse and misuse. *Communication Monographs*.

McPhee, R. D., & Poole, M. S. (1981). Mathematical modeling in communication research: An overview. In M. Burgoon (Ed.), *Communication yearbook 5* (pp. 159-161). New Brunswick, NJ: Transaction.

McPhee, R. D., Poole, M. S., & Seibold, D. R. (1981). The valence model unveiled: A critique and reformulation. In M. Burgoon (Ed.), *Communication yearbook 5* (pp. 159-177). New Brunswick, NJ: Transaction.

McPhee, R. D., & Seibold, D. R. (1979). Rationale, procedures, and applications for decomposition of explained variance in multiple regression analysis. *Communication Research, 6,* 345-384.

Meehan, E. (1968). *Explanation in the social sciences: A system paradigm.* Homewood, IL: Dorsey.

Menzies, K. (1982). *Sociological theory in use.* London: Routledge & Kegan Paul.

Miles, M. B. (1979). Qualitative data as an attractive nuisance: The problem of analysis. *Administrative Science Quarterly, 24,* 590-601.

Miller, G. R., & Berger, C. (1978). On keeping the faith in matters scientific. *Western Journal of Speech Communication, 42,* 44-57.

Monge, P. R., & Cappella, J. N. (Eds.). (1980). *Multivariate techniques in human communication research.* New York: Academic Press.

Monge, P. R., & Day, P. D. (1976). Multivariate analysis in communication research. *Human Communication Research, 1976, 2,* 207-220.

Monge, P. R., Farace, R. V., Eisenberg, E. M., Miller, K. I., & White, L. L. (1984). The process of studying process in organizational communication. *Journal of Communication, 34,* 22-43.

Morey, L. C., Blashfield,, R. K., & Skinner, H. A. (1983). A comparison of cluster analysis techniques within a sequential validation framework. *Multivariate Behavioral Research, 18,* 309-329.

Morrison, D. F. (1976). *Multivariate statistical methods.* New York: McGraw-Hill.

Murstein, B. I. (1970). Stimulus-value-role: A theory of marital choice. *Journal of Marriage and the Family, 32,* 465-481.

Myers, J. L. (1972). *Fundamentals of experimental design.* Boston: Allyn & Bacon.

Nagel, E. (1957). *Logic without metaphysics.* New York: Free Press.

Newcomb, T. (1961). *The acquaintance process.* New York: Holt, Rinehart & Winston.

Nisbett, R. E., & Wilson, T. D. (1977). Telling more than we can know: Verbal reports on mental processes. *Psychological Review, 84,* 231-259.

Nofsinger, R. E. (1975). The demand ticket: A conversational device for getting the floor. *Communiction Monographs, 42,* 1-9.

Norton, R. W. (1978). Foundation of a communicator style construct. *Human Communication Research, 4,* 99-112.

Norton, R. W., & Pettigrew, L. (1979). Attentiveness as a style of communication: A structural analysis. *Communication Monographs, 46,* 13-26.

Nunnally, C. J. (1967). *Psychometric theory.* New York: McGraw-Hill.

Ochs, E. (1979). Transcription as theory. In E. Ochs & B. Schieffelin (Eds.), *Developmental pragmatics* (pp. 43-72). New York: Academic Press.

O'Donnell-Trujillo, N. (1982). Relational communication: A comparison of coding systems. *Communication Monographs, 48,* 91-105.

O'Keefe, B., Delia, J., & O'Keefe, D. (1980). Interaction analysis and the analysis of interactional organization. In N. K. Denzin (Ed.), *Studies in symbolic interactionism* (Vol. 3, pp. 25-57). Greenwich, CT: JAI Press.

Overton, W. F., & Reese, H. W. (1973). Models of development: Methodological implications. In J. R. Nesslroade & H. W. Reese (Eds.), *Life span developmental psychology: Methodological issues* (pp. 65-86). New York: Academic Press.

Parks, M. R., Stan, C. M., & Eggert, L. L. (1983). Romantic involvement and social network involvement. *Social Psychology Quarterly, 46,* 116-131.

Pavitt, C., & Cappella, J. N. (1979). Coorientation accuracy in interpersonal and small group discussions: A literature review, model, and simulation. In D. Nimmo (Ed.), *Communication yearbook 3* (pp. 123-156). New Brunswick, NJ: Transaction.

Pearce, W. B., & Conklin, F. (1979). A model of hierarchical meaning in coherent conversation and a study of indirect responses. *Communication Monographs, 46,* 75-87.

Pearce, W. B., & Cronen, V. E. (1980). *Communication, action and meaning.* New York: Praeger.

Pearce, W. B., & Cushman, D. P. (n.d.). Research about communication rules: A critique and reappraisal. Unpublished manuscript, University of Massachusetts, Department of Speech Communication.

Pearce, W. B., Wright, P. H., Sharp, S. M., & Slama, K. M. (1974). Affection and reciprocity in self-disclosing communication. *Human Communication Research, 1,* 5-14.

Pedhazur, E. J. (1982). *Multiple regression in behavioral research: Explanation and prediction.* New York: Holt, Rinehart & Winston.

Philipsen, G. (1975). Speaking "like a man" in Teamsterville: Cultural patterns of role enactment in an urban neighborhood. *Quarterly Journal of Speech, 61,* 13-22.

Philipsen, G. (1977). Linearity of research design in ethnographic studies of speaking. *Communication Quarterly, 25,* 42-50.

Pittenger, R. E., Hockett, C. F., & Daheny, J. J. (1960). *The first five minutes.* Ithaca, NY: Paul Martineau.

Planalp, S., & Tracy, K. (1980). Not to change the topic but . . . : A cognitive approach to the management of conversation. In D. Nimmo (Ed.), *Communication yearbook 4* (pp. 237-258). New Brunswick, NJ: Transaction.

Poole, M. S. (1983). Structural paradigms and the study of group communication. In M. Mander (Ed.), *Communications in transition* (pp. 186-205). New York: Praeger.

Poole, M. S., & Folger, J. P. (1981a). A method for establishing the representational validity of interaction coding systems: Do we see what they see? *Human Communication Research, 8,* 26-42.

Poole, M. S., & Folger, J. P. (1981b). Overture to interaction research: Modes of observation and the validity of interaction coding systems. *Small Group Research, 17,* 477-494.

Poole, M. S., McPhee, R. D., & Seibold, D. R. (1982). A comparison of normative and interactional explanations of group decision-making: Social decision schemes versus valence distributions. *Communication Monographs, 49,* 1-19.

Poole, M. S., Seibold, D. R., & McPhee, R. D. (1982). *A structurational theory of group decision making.* Paper presented at Pennsylvania State University Conference on Small Group Communication Research, College Park, PA.

Popper, K. (1959). *The logic of scientific discovery.* New York: Basic Books.

Porter, D. T. (1981). An empirical appraisal of the PRCA for measuring oral communication apprehension. *Human Communication Research, 8*(1), 58-71.

Poster, M. (1980). *Critical theory of the family.* New York: Seabury.

Rawlins, W. K. (1983). Openness as problematic in ongoing friendships: Two conversational dilemmas. *Communication Monographs, 50,* 1-13.

Reichardt, C. S. (1979). The statistical analysis of data from nonequivalent group designs. In T. D. Cook & D. T. Campbell (Eds.), *Quasi-experimentation: Design and analysis issues for field settings* (pp. 147-206). Chicago: Rand McNally.

Rogers, E., & Farace, R. (1975). Analysis of relational communication in dyads: New measurement procedures. *Human Communication Research, 1,* 222-239.

Rogers, E., & Kincaid, L. (1982). *Communication networks.* New York: Basic Books.

Rogosa, D. (1979). Causal models in longitudinal research: Rationale, formulation, and interpretation. In J. R. Nesselroade & P. B. Baltes (Eds.), *Longitudinal research in the study of behavior and development* (pp. 263-302). New York: Academic Press.

Rosenthal, H. (1980). Review of L. A. Goodman's *Analyzing qualitative/categorical data: Log-linear models and latent structure analysis. Contemporary Sociology, 9,* 207-211.

Rossi, P. H., Wright, J. D., & Anderson, A. B. (Eds.). (1983). *Handbook of survey research.* New York: Academic Press.

Rubin, K. H. (1973). Egocentrism in childhood: A unitary construct. *Child Development, 14,* 102-110.

Rubin, Z., & Levinger, G. (1974). Theory and data badly mated: A critique of Murstein's SVR and Lewis's POF models of mate selection. *Journal of Marriage and the Family, 36,* 226-231.

Sackett, G. P. (1977). The lag sequential analysis of contingency and cyclicity in behavioral interaction research. In J. Osfsky (Ed.), *Handbook of infant development* (pp. 300-340). New York: John Wiley.

Sacks, H., Schegloff, E. A., & Jefferson, G. (1974). A simplest systematics for the organization of turn-taking in conversation. *Language, 50,* 696-735.

Salzinger, L. L. (1982). The ties that bind: The effects of clustering in dyadic relationships. *Social Networks, 4,* 117-145.

Schaie, K. W. (1965). A general model for the study of developmental problems. *Psychological Bulletin, 64,* 92-107.

Schaie, K. W. (1970). A reinterpretation of age-related changes in cognitive structure and functioning. In L. R. Goulet & P. B. Baltes (Eds.), *Life-span developmental psychology: Research and theory* (pp. 485-507). New York: Academic Press.

Schaie, K. W., & Baltes, P. B. (1975). On sequential strategies in developmental research: Description or explanation. *Human Development, 18,* 384-390.

Schutz, A. (1954). Concept and theory formation in the social sciences. *Journal of Philosophy, 11.*

Schutz, A. (1964). *Collected papers II: Studies in social theory.* The Hague: Martinus Nijhoff.

Schwartz, H., & Jacobs, J. (1979). *Qualitative sociology: A method to the madness.* New York: Free Press.

Searle, J. R. (1976). A classification of illocutionary acts. *Language in Society, 5,* 1-23.

Searle, S. R. (1971). *Linear models.* New York: John Wiley.

Seibold, D. R., & McPhee, R. D. (1980). A new analysis of Daly's "assessment of social-communicative anxiety via self-reports: A comparison of measures." *Communication Monographs, 47,* 149-152.

Sennett, R. (1974). *The fall of public man.* New York: Random House.

Shepard, R. N. (1974). Representation of structure in similarity data: Problems and prospects. *Psychometrika, 39,* 373-421.

Sillars, A. L. (1980). The stranger and the spouse as target persons for compliance-gaining strategies: A subjective expected utility model. *Human Communication Research, 6,* 265-279.

Spence, I., & Ogilvie, J. (1973). A table of expected stress values for random rankings in nonmetric multidimensional scaling. *Multivariate Behavioral Research, 8,* 511-517.

Stanback, M., & Pearce, W. B. (1981). Talking to "The Man": Some communication strategies used by members of "subordinate" social groups. *Quarterly Journal of Speech, 67,* 21-30.

Sudman, S., & Bradburn, N. M. (1983). *Asking questions: A practical guide to questionnaire design.* San Francisco: Jossey-Bass.

Sunnafrank, M. J., & Miller, G. R. (1981). The role of initial conversations in determining attraction to similar and dissimilar strangers. *Human Communication Research, 8,* 16-25.

Tainter, J. A. (1975). Social inference and mortuary practices: An experiment in numerical classification. *World Archeology, 7,* 1-15.

Taylor, C. (1971). Interpretation and the sciences of man. *Review of Metaphysics, 25,* 1-45.

TenHouten, W. (1969). Scale gradient analysis. *Sociometry, 32,* 80-98.

Tucker, L. R. (1966). Learning theory and multivariate experiment: Illustration by determination of generalized learning curves. In R. B. Cattell (Ed.), *Handbook of multivariate experimental psychology* (pp. 476-501). Chicago: Rand McNally.

Tucker, L. R. (1972). Relations between multidimensional scaling and three-mode factor analysis. *Psychometrika, 37,* 3-27.

Tudor, A. (1976). Misunderstanding everyday life. *Sociological Review, 24,* 479-503.

Tukey, J. W. (1969). Analyzing data: Sanctification or detective work. *American Psychologist, 24,* 83-91.

Tukey, J. W. (1977). *Exploratory data analysis.* Reading, MA: Addison-Wesley.

Van de Geer, J. P. (1971). *Introduction to multivariate analysis for the social sciences.* San Francisco: Freeman.

Vendler, Z. (1972). *Res cogitans: An essay in rational psychology.* Ithaca, NY: Cornell University Press.

Von Wright, G. H. (1971). *Explanation and understanding.* Ithaca, NY: Cornell University Press.

Vroom, V., & Jago, A. (1974). Decision making as a social process: Normative and descriptive models of leader behavior. *Decision Sciences, 5,* 160-186.

Wainer, H., & Thissen, D. (1976). Three steps toward robust aggression. *Psychometrika, 41*(1), 9-34.

Walster, G. W., & Cleary, T. A. (1970). Statistical significance as a decision rule. In E. F. Borgatta & G. W. Bohrnstedt (Eds.), *Sociological methodology, 1970* (pp. 246-256). San Francisco: Jossey-Bass.

Warner, R. M., Kenny, D. A., & Stoto, M. (1979). A new round robin analysis of variance for social interaction data. *Journal of Personality and Social Psychology, 37,* 1742-1757.

Weeks, D. B., & Bentler, P. M. (1979). A comparison of linear and monotone multidimensional scaling models. *Psychological Bulletin, 8,* 349-354.

Weimann, J. M. (1981). Effects of laboratory videotaping procedures on selected conversational behaviors. *Human Communication Research, 7,* 302-311.

Willis, P. (1977). *Learning to labor.* New York: Columbia University Press.

Winer, B. J. (1978a). Statistics and data analysis: Trading bias for reduced mean squared error. *Annual Review of Psychology, 29,* 647-681.

Winer, B. J. (1978b). *Statistical principles in experimental design.* New York: McGraw-Hill.

Woefel, J., & Fink, E. L. (1980). *The measurement of communication processes: Galileo theory and method.* New York: Academic Press.

Wohlwill, J. (1973). *The study of behavior development.* New York: Academic Press.

Wonnacott, R. J., & Wonnacott, T. H. (1979) *Econometrics.* New York: John Wiley.

Zaretsky, E. (1976). *Capitalism, the family, and social life.* New York: Harper & Row.

4 Interpersonal Communication and the Quest for Personal Competence

MALCOLM R. PARKS

University of Washington

A six-month-old infant moves her mouth toward the spoon held by her father. She takes the food into her mouth, but quickly spits it out. The father gives her another spoonful of food. Now she spits it out with a shake of the head and a screech. Her father gets up and returns a moment later with different food. This time she hesitantly accepts it and then swallows with a smile.

This chapter is about what that little girl just did and what each of us tries to do every day. Her communicative competence, like ours, stems from a continual struggle to survive and, when possible, to obtain and maintain satisfactory conditions. In the first section I will define communicative competence in terms of the personal control process. Communicative competence is, of course, an extremely broad theoretic construct. So in the second section I will integrate literature from several different perspectives in order to identify some of the more specific behavioral and cognitive processes by which competency occurs. Communicative competence is also, as Phillips (1984) emphasizes, an evaluation, a criticism of behavior rather than behavior itself. Although there are obviously many relevant critical perspectives, there is also a great deal of consensus. We can agree that it is undesirable to communicate in ways that result in generalized damage to one's self-esteem, in an inability to accomplish even simple social tasks, and in damage to one's physical health. We can also agree that socially inappropriate and violent behavior is usually undesirable. For some, like Phillips, the critical nature of competence judgments implies that scientific research is largely tangential. In the last two parts of this chapter I will argue that failures of personal control result in just such undesirable consequences. Scientific research can inform our larger critical consensus because it can reliably identify the ways in which competence and incompetence occur. Therefore, I will summarize the research on learned helplessness and a number of related concepts in the third section of the chapter and, in the final section, examine how the quest for personal control ultimately promotes socially appropriate behavior.

COMMUNICATIVE COMPETENCE DEFINED

Attempts to summarize the literature on communication competence inevitably encounter widely varying definitions, disagreements concerning the way in which people "possess" competence, and inconsistent explications of the various components or attributes of competence (Wiemann & Backlund, 1980). As Phillips (1984, p. 24) observed, "Defining competence is like trying to climb a greased pole."

Competence as Control

Competence is a slippery concept partly because it is fundamental in such a wide variety of perspectives and disciplines. If we look closely, however, we find broad agreement beneath the differences. Many investigators agree that human action is directed toward influencing the environment and that it is useful to conceptualize this influence as an effort to satisfy goals. For example, psychological concepts such as optimal stimulation (Hebb & Thompson, 1954; Leuba, 1955) and exploratory behavior (White, 1959; Woodworth, 1958) implicitly presume that individuals are active participants in environmental events and that they seek to influence their surroundings in specific ways. In his theory of personal causation deCharms (1968) argued that people need to feel a sense of effectance toward the environment and that a lack of control may lead to feelings of incompetence.

Theories of social exchange also reflect the control orientation. Exchange theorists assume that participants have goals and seek to attain them through the exchange process. Thus it is presumed that interpersonal behavior is essentially control-oriented and manipulative (Wood, Weinstein, & Parker, 1967).

Even more obvious examples of the control orientation can be found in the literature on persuasion and attitude change (see Chapter 12 in this volume). Typologies of power and social influence testify to the richness and variety of interpersonal control strategies (for example, Etzioni, 1961; French & Raven, 1960; Kelman, 1961; Marwell & Schmitt, 1969). So, too, does the more dyadically oriented literature on relational control strategies (for example, see Parks, 1977).

Goffman (1959, 1967) and others working from a dramaturgical perspective recognize the centrality of personal control in everyday life. When we view social interaction as theater, with actors playing roles and improvising performances, we should not assume that the "cast" works for nothing. Rather, these intricate performances are orchestrated for the fulfillment of personal goals and needs. Control over the situation will be the primary motive for the actor (Goffman, 1959).

In recent years communication and personality theorists have placed great importance on the attributional and social cognitive processes through which social knowledge is constructed (for example, Athay & Darley, 1981; Berger & Bradac, 1982; Delia, O'Keefe, & O'Keefe, 1982; Roloff & Berger, 1982a; see also Chapter 10 in this volume). Although these researchers emphasize cognitive activities, none of them presume that social knowledge is developed merely to add another volume to some cognitive library. Instead, social knowledge serves the larger control process (Hewes & Planalp, 1982; O'Keefe & Delia, 1982). Kelley (1971, p. 220) is most explicit about the ultimate purpose of causal analysis in attribution theory:

> The purpose of causal analysis—the function that it serves—is effective control. The attributor is not simply an attributor, a seeker of knowledge. His latent goal in gaining knowledge is that of effective management of himself and his environment.

Although the various principles and perspectives discussed above obviously differ from one another in important ways, they converge in a common view of human action. Each portrays people in active rather than passive terms. Each presumes, although in somewhat different terms, that people have a basic need or desire to affect their environment—often beyond the fulfillment of basic survival needs (White, 1959). Finally, each assumes that control or goal-seeking is a major organizing theme in human behavior. Although coordinated social action, understanding, and culture are important topics for communication scholars, we should recognize that they are created and sustained by the control activities of individuals. The basic function of communication is control over the physical and social environment (Miller & Steinberg, 1975).

The concept of effectance or control is also at the intellectual core of almost all conceptualizations of communicative competence. Although the definitions presented in Table 4.1 contain a certain variety, the theme of effectiveness and goal attainment runs through nearly all of them. Wiemann (1977) identified three major traditions in the study of communicative competence: (1) the human relations or T-group tradition, (2) the social skills tradition, and (3) the self-presentation tradition. He concluded that all three of these traditions share a belief in personal effectiveness as a defining characteristic of communicative competence.

Competence as Both Cognition and Behavior

Thinking about communicative competence has frequently suffered from a rather schizophrenic approach to terminology. Many writers reserve the term "competence" for the cognitive aspects of action. For them competence refers to the individual's ability to understand or report knowledge of how goals can be satisfied (for example, Chomsky, 1965; McCroskey, 1982a; Phillips, 1984; Pylyshyn, 1973). These writers use terms like "performance" or "skill" to describe the process by which actual behavior occurs. Other writers

TABLE 4.1
Representative Definitions of Communicative Competence

"The ability of an interactant to choose among available communicative behaviors in order that he may successfully accomplish his own interpersonal goals during an encounter while maintaining the face and line of his fellow interactants within the constraints of the situation" (Wiemann, 1977, p. 195).

"The ability of an individual to demonstrate knowledge of the appropriate communicative behavior in a given situation" (Larson, Backlund, Redmond, & Barbour, 1978, p. 21).

"The fitness or ability to carry on those transactions with the environment which result in [an organism] maintaining itself, growing, and flourishing" (Argyris, 1965, p. 59).

"The ability to formulate and achieve objectives, to collaborate effectively with others, to be interdependent; and the ability to adapt appropriately to situational and environmental variation" (Bochner & Kelly, 1974, p. 288).

"An organism's capacity to interact effectively with its environment" (White, 1959, p. 297).

"A synonym for ability. It means a satisfactory degree of ability for performing certain implied kinds of tasks. . . . our main strategy of definition will be analytical, to name its parts, as manifested in observable behavior. These we take to be: (1) health, (2) intelligence, (3) empathy, (4) autonomy, (5) judgment, and (6) creativity" (Foote & Cottrell, 1955, pp. 36 & 41).

"The ability to accomplish interpersonal tasks. . . . interpersonal competence boils down to the ability to manipulate others' responses" (Weinstein, 1969, p. 755).

"The ability to attain relevant interactive goals in specified social contexts using socially appropriate means and ways of speaking that result in positive outcomes with significant others" (Stohl, 1983, p. 688; see also Ford, 1982).

reject the bifurcation of cognition and behavior by suggesting that competence is a higher-order term having both cognitive and behavioral dimensions (for example, Allen & Brown, 1976; Hymes, 1974; Wiemann, 1977; Wiemann & Backlund, 1980).

It is wise to remember that the difference between behavior and cognition is only skin deep. Although conceptualizing competence in the pure cognitive sense may have some value to a theoretical linguist, it is useless to the communication scholar who by definition must examine the world of action. I stand solidly with the unified view of competence. Action occurs on both sides of the skin. Cognition and overt behavior are merely different aspects of the same larger process. To be competent, therefore, we must not only "know" and "know how," we must also "do" and "know that we did."

Competence as Both Specific and General

A final source of conceptual slippage is the confusion surrounding the generality of the concept of communicative competence. Some writers view competence as a highly generalized, enduring, trait-like concept (for example, Foot & Cottrell, 1955; McCroskey, 1982a). Other writers define and measure competence as something that occurs in a specific context and with a particular audience (for example, Wiemann, 1977). Some suggest that it has both trait and state dimensions (for example, Cupach & Spitzberg, 1983; Spitzberg & Cupach, 1984).

I take the view that whether competence is general or specific depends largely on the type of assessment one wishes to make and on the degree of generality exhibited in an individual's action. We may assess one or more specific components of the process by which competency occurs or we may assess some indicator of the overall process. It should be clear, however, that competency is not a fixed quality that we "carry" around with us. Instead, it is a quality of the process by which we interact with others. The question of whether a given person's competence is generalized or limited to specific situations or audiences is an empirical one.

A Working Definition

The considerations outlined above lead me to conceptualize communicative competence in the following way:

> Communicative competence represents the degree to which individuals perceive they have satisfied their goals in a given social situation without jeopardizing their ability or opportunity to pursue their other subjectively more important goals.

This definition clearly locates communicative competence judgments in the cognitive and behavioral activities associated with personal control. Successful personal control does not necessarily imply that people have to maximize their outcomes. Success is a continuum, and, as Simon (1979) points out, we are often satisfied by an outcome that is merely adequate rather than maximal. In the next section we will examine the more specific behavioral and cognitive activities by which personal control is actualized. However, this definition does not simplistically equate competence with goal satisfaction. There is a difference between competence and good fortune. Competence in my definition occurs only when the person feels responsible for satisfying goals. This in turn implies that assessment techniques based on how others evaluate the individual's competence (for example, Rubin, 1982; Stohl, 1983; Wiemann, 1977) will be incomplete because they do not tap the individual's own assessments. The way in which individuals make their own competency assessments is previewed at the end of the next section and examined in more detail in the section after that. Finally, by this definition, competent communicators act with foresight. Although no one can fully predict the consequences of his or her actions as they ripple out into a social system and back again, the ability to recognize how attempts to satisfy one goal might influence the chance to satisfy other goals is a mark of competence. The implications of personal control for individuals embedded in larger social systems are explored in the fourth section.

HOW COMMUNICATIVE COMPETENCE OCCURS

Consider the case of Jill who has just approached her friend Tom. As she comes nearer, her face brightens as she smiles and says, "Tom, it's so good to see you." Tom returns her greetings and asks her how things have been going. Jill sighs and says, "OK, I guess, but I'm having a hard time getting the fifteen dollars I need for the concert ticket." Tom responds, "I'd like to help you but I'm nearly broke, too." "That's too bad," Jill says, "I was hoping you'd lend it to me, but you're a friend and I'd never want to put you in a bad spot." She pauses and then adds, "Even five dollars would really help." Tom pauses for a moment, but then agrees to loan her five dollars. Jill thanks him profusely and, as she prepares to leave, adds "Remember you can always count on me when things are the other way around."

Even apparently simple human encounters like this one stimulate widely ranging assessments of communicative competence. As Pearce, Cronen, and Conklin (1979) note, we may analyze such encounters at many different levels. We might evaluate this encounter in terms of the precision with which specific muscle movements produce phonemes or facial expressions. Or we could consider if the speakers' morphemes are appropriate for a given speech community, dialect, or language. We could also judge the application of transformational rules to grammar, the use of speech acts, the application of personal constructs or scripts, or the use of particular compliance-gaining strategies. Another analysis might examine the sequential development of the episode as it progresses from greeting to leave-taking. Still another analysis might examine how this particular episode reflects on the unfolding relationship between Tom and Jill.

Many of these analytic perspectives, as I have already noted, share the assumption that human action is control-oriented. Even so, the various perspectives differ widely in abstraction. In addition we must recognize the fact that communicators are often pursuing more than one goal at a time (O'Keefe & Delia, 1982). In my story, for example, Jill appears to desire both money and a continued relationship with Tom. Finally, attempts to explicate the control process must allow for the fact that a given act may realize a goal by itself or only be one of many acts making up some higher-order goal. In Jill's case, the encounter with Tom may be part of some larger plan for getting to the concert.

One way to begin accounting for this complexity is to conceptualize the control process in terms of hierarchy of actions ranging from raw sensory input and output to higher-order cognitive processes. The hierarchical approach interrelates widely varying levels of analysis under a single theoretic umbrella (Carver & Scheier, 1982). The usefulness of a hierarchical approach to communication competence has already been recognized. Allen and Brown (1976), for instance, view competence as a process in which the communicator first chooses a communication strategy consistent with his or her desires, implements the strategy, and then evaluates the results of his or her communication. Hierarchical conceptualizations also appear in several areas directly relevant for the study of communication competence, including rules theory perspectives on the management of meaning (for example, Pearce et al., 1979), constructivist perspectives on the impression formation process (for example, Delia, 1976), and social learning perspectives on human interaction (for example, Mischel, 1973).

One of the most explicit and fruitful hierarchical models comes from Powers's (1973) control theory, particularly as it has been applied and extended by Carver and Scheier (1982). These investigators conceptualize the control process in terms of a series of nine cybernetically interconnected and hierarchically organized levels. In ascending order these levels are (1) intensity control, (2) sensation control, (3) configuration control, (4) transition control, (5) sequence control, (6) relationship control, (7) program control, (8) principle control, and (9) system concept control.

Each of these levels is linked to the ones immediately above and below it by means of a negative feedback loop (Carver & Scheier, 1982; Powers, 1973). That is, each level operates by sensing the present condition in the level below it, comparing that condition to a reference value from the level above it, and then acting so as to reduce the discrepancy between the present state of affairs and the standards implied by the level above it. Carver and Scheier (1982, p. 113) point out that the primary function of each of these cybernetic loops "is to create and maintain the perception of a specific desired condition."

The reference values constitute the "goals" of the system. Although the goal at each level would be described in different terms, all of the goals function together to produce and direct behavior. The goals implied by the reference values are not static, but rather change as one's own behavior and the behavior of others alter the physical and social environment and as emerging higher-order understandings create new aspirations and modify old ones. If the probability of satisfying the reference value becomes too low, the individual may attempt to withdraw (Carver & Scheier, 1982). Except in extreme cases of helplessness, however, the withdrawal from one situation leads to engagement in another and the cycle of attempted control continues.

Competence in this hierarchical conceptualization is gauged generally by the extent to which the individual's communicative behavior is able to satisfy that person's reference values across the hierarchy. In order to outline some of the more specific ways in which competence occurs, I will devote the remainder of this section to discussing each of the nine levels in the control hierarchy.

Level 1 Competency: Intensity Control

This level occupies the world just inside the skin; the world of "raw" sensory contact with the outside environment, muscle movements, and basic spinal activities (Powers, 1973). Here we control the motions of specific muscles by which all larger behaviors, including speech, are produced. As we move, sensory receptors monitor our movement in terms of the ever-changing perceptual field we impose on the environment. This level contains only the most rudimentary information. It is just about the intensity of a sensation or muscle movement and does not contain labels for what is occurring. Those come from higher levels. However, this does not mean that information is passed along without revision. As a given piece of information is passed toward the brain it mixes with others and is thereby transformed (Powers, 1973).

Even though scholars and practitioners have rarely considered it, competence at the level of intensity control has implications for evaluating communicative competence in the larger social sense. For example, damage to specific muscles or to sensory receptors may have far-reaching consequences for the individual. Harless and McConnell (1982) found that hearing loss was associated with reductions in self-esteem among the elderly and that self-esteem was higher among those who compensated for their hearing loss with hearing aids. Practitioners interested in the treatment of competency problems are urged to begin with an assessment of the physical aspects of hearing, seeing, and speaking. There is little point treating higher-order problems like an inability to take the role of the other without first determining if the basic physiological equipment is impaired.

Level 2 Competency: Sensation Control

Neither our overt behaviors nor our sensation of events in the environment occurs as isolated bits and pieces. The diverse and concrete activities of the lower level are gathered and directed by a higher-order process that Powers (1973) calls sensation or vector control. He locates this function in sensory nuclei found in the upper spine and brain stem. These nuclei bring together strands of sensory information. They creatively organize strands of sensory information into "packages." Comparisons to higher-order standards direct the pattern of discrete muscle actions that make up a larger motion such as tilting one's head upward.

As Pearce et al. (1979) emphasize, these lower levels in the hierarchy are critical because even the most subtle insight or eloquently expressed idea must pass through them. Competence in these lower levels consists of the individual's ability to accurately sense information and faithfully execute the specific muscle actions required by higher levels in the hierarchy.

Level 3 Competency: Configuration Control

The still relatively small packages of sensory information and muscle movements at the previous level are themselves organized into somewhat broader configurations at the next higher level. According to Powers (1973), these broader configurations control things like overall body position, movement of limbs, perception of visual forms, and speech at the phonemic level.

Once we reach the level of bodily movement and speech sounds, the discussion of the control hierarchy will become increasingly familiar to those interested in communicative competence. However, the increasing familiarity of the terminology should not mislead the reader into assuming that communicators are routinely conscious of their activities at these lower levels. Powers (1973, p. 115) argues that configuration control usually occurs "without the need of, or apparently the possibility of, conscious awareness."

Level 4 Competency: Transition Control

Transition control is what allows us to execute an organized movement such as nodding the head, changing the tone of the voice, or pronouncing a word. It is also what allows us to recognize those same actions in others. Transition control summarizes and directs the more microscopic changes in lower-order configurations, sensations, and intensities. Even so, this level of control does not determine what movements should occur, their combination, or their timing (Powers, 1973).

Level 5 Competency: Sequence Control

Much of what we do and interpret is based on relatively unitary blocks or sequences of action. Sequence control is what allows us to place widely varying concrete behaviors into some sequence. For example, sequence control allows us to put words together to form phrases (Powers, 1973). Through sequence control we also create perceptions regarding the order and pattern in information from lower levels, and ultimately from the environment and behavior of others themselves.

Communicative competence at this level generally consists of the ability to organize perception and action in ways that serve higher-order goals. To do so, the communicator must have a rather highly developed skill in discriminating between the various blocks and sequences of perception and behavior (cf Athay & Darley, 1981). This discriminative ability will depend in part on more specific factors like the individual's ability to accurately decode nonverbal cues (for example, Gottman & Porterfield, 1981) and to recognize when others' verbal messages are garbled or incomplete (for example, Beal & Flavell, 1982; Flavell, Speer, & Green, 1981). These discriminations will, of course, only be as sensitive as the output of lower levels allows and the goals of higher levels require. Another specific competency at this level deals with one's skill in timing and placing one's behaviors into the steam of interaction. In one study, for example, researchers found that even when women who were socially incompetent in dating situations knew how to convey understanding and rapport, they often failed because they had difficulty synchronizing their comments with the comments of their partner (Peterson, Fischetti, Curran, & Arland, 1981).

Level 6 Competency: Relationship Control

If the primary activity of the previous level was to detect and direct sequences of behavior, the primary activity of the next level is to detect and behaviorally express the larger relationships among the communicator's actions, the actions of others, and events in the environment. These relationships may be of many types: cause-effect, exclusive-inclusive, statistical, space-time, association, and implication (Powers, 1973).

We have now reached a level in the hierarchy that is sufficiently abstract to encompass a broad range of theoretical perspectives. Cognitive social learning theorists (for example, Cantor & Mischel, 1977; Mischel, 1973) talk about the processes in which people categorize behavior and develop expectancies for events. Rules theorists (for example, Pearce et al., 1979) and speech act theorists (for example, Searle, 1969) emphasize the importance of "constitutive" rules—rules by which lower-order behaviors are labeled as instances of higher-order cognitive categories. My approach to relationship control focuses on the concept of personal constructs (Kelly, 1955) and on the nature of the causal attribution process because these factors cut across a variety of other theoretic perspectives.

Although published nearly 30 years ago, Kelly's (1955) personal construct theory set the stage for a great deal of the recent work on social cognition (Mischel, 1981). Kelly focused on the process by which people construed the actions of themselves and others into catergories or constructs. As social beings, the content of our personal constructs is dominated by perceptions of how communicators relate to each other and to their environment. Categorizing a person as "cold" or "outgoing," for instance, implies something about that person's relationship to others. Personal constructs therefore pertain to the relationship control level of the overall hierarchy.

The constructivist tradition spawned by Kelly emphasizes that control at the relationship level occurs in terms of a system of personalized interpretations or constructs that summarize and direct action. This system can be described not only in terms of its contents, but also in terms of its organization. Delia and his associates, for example, have repeatedly demonstrated that the degree of differentiation and abstraction in subjects' personal construct systems is positively related to the effectiveness and adaptiveness of their persuasive messages (for example, Delia et al., 1982; O'Keefe & Delia, 1982). That is, people create more effective messages when they are able to construe others from a variety of perspectives and when they can construe others in abstract rather than surface-level terms. These abilities probably represent specific competencies at the relationship control level, although differentiation and abstraction in one's construct system contribute to one's overall level of competence only insofar as they are required to satisfy higher-order goals.

The importance of differentiation and abstraction in construal systems is underscored by research quite removed from the constructivist tradition. Studies on the difference between good and poor problem solvers, for example, have consistently shown that good problem solvers were more skilled at applying information from one context to another and at conceptualizing problems in abstract, rather than concrete, terms (Hunt, 1983).

Another basic competency might involve the ability to reorder or revise constructs and problem representations according to situational demands. Mischel (1973), for instance, found that self-control in children varied with the way in which a desirable reward (pretzels or marshmallows) was construed. Children who had conceptualized the food in terms of the pleasure of eating it were not able to obey instructions to resist it as well as children who had been encouraged to conceptualize the pretzels as logs and the marshmallows as clouds.

Our understanding of social cognitive processes has also been enriched by attribution theories. Heider (1958) noted that people very rapidly attribute causes to others' behavior. In fact the attribution process is so pervasive that people may have difficulty remembering specific behaviors and instead operate according to the broader labels or traits they have attributed to others' behavior (for example, Kelley, 1979). Although even a brief summary of the various attribution theories is beyond the scope of this chapter (for such summaries, see Berger & Bradac, 1982; Sillars, 1982), these theories are rich in implications for the study of communicative competence.

One area of special relevance to the study of communication competence is the research focusing on errors in the attribution process. The typical person's approach to attribution seems riddled with shortcomings when judged against rigorous logical standards (for example, Major, 1980; Mischel, 1968, 1969, 1973; Nisbett & Ross, 1980; Snyder & Swann, 1978a, 1978b; Tversky & Kahneman, 1971). Among the biases we routinely bring to the attribution process are tendencies to give more weight to information that is vivid, concrete, or readily available; to treat a very small amount of information as if it were highly representative; to search only for information that confirms our preconceptions; to distort or ignore information that violates our expectations; and to overestimate the consistency and constancy of others' behavior. Our efforts to understand behavior are also biased by tendencies to rely on a priori ideas of what types of causes ought to go with certain types of effects, to prefer simple explanations over complex ones, to prefer explanations that easily present themselves, to underestimate situational influences on others' behavior and to prefer instead internal or dispositional causes for their behavior, to undervalue information about how a person's behavior compares to others' behavior in the same situation, and to treat genuinely irrelevant information as if it were relevant.

These findings probably paint an overly dismal picture of our capacities to exert relationship control. Nonetheless, awareness of these biases and the ability to correct for them represent basic competencies at this level of the overall control hierarchy. Although some of these biases may be deeply embedded, the literature on human inference is rich in ideas for improving the way we judge relationships among our own actions, the actions of others, and events in the environment (for example, Nisbett & Ross, 1980).

Level 7 Competency: Program Control

Programs represent comparatively broad and structured sequences of action. They go beyond simple lists of acts to specify a coherent structure, a series of decision rules for determining how to act at any given point, and may themselves be hierarchically organized (Carver & Scheier, 1982; Powers, 1973). The ability to cognitively organize the welter of constructs and attributions into a coherent framework must count as a fundamental communicative competence. Programs not only direct our behavior in a given situation, but also provide predictions and explanations for behavior, thereby helping us reduce uncertainty (Berger & Bradac, 1982).

The concept of a program goes by many names. Some researchers speak of "cognitive schemata" (for example, Cohen, 1981; Crockett, 1977; O'Keefe & Delia, 1982), whereas others speak of "scripts" (for example, Abelson, 1976; Berger & Bradac, 1982; Schank & Abelson, 1977). Some describe programs in terms of "regulative rules" and "episodes" (for example, Gumperz, 1972; Harré & Secord, 1973; Pearce et al., 1979; Searle, 1969), while still others refer to "self-regulatory plans" (for example, Mischel, 1973). A common theme running through each of these perspectives is that people punctuate the stream of interaction into relatively coherent "chunks" that represent general plans for action and evaluation.

Individuals probably have thousands of program-like representations by the time they reach adulthood (Abelson, 1976; Schank & Abelson, 1977). Some may represent information in verbal form, whereas others may represent it in nonverbal forms (Roloff & Berger, 1982b). Whatever their number or form, however, all programs are goal-oriented. They impose, organize, and direct lower-order perceptions and behaviors according to some scenario that is itself subordinate to some higher perception of the way things ought to be.

Scholars of communicative competence often assert that one's competence depends partly upon having a large repertoire of behavioral strategies (for example, Allen & Brown, 1976; Steffen & Redden, 1977; Weinstein, 1969). That is, one ought to have a large number of programs and the lower-order behaviors to go with them. I believe that competence depends not so much on the sheer size of the repertoire per se as on the adequacy of the repertoire. Strictly speaking one's "programming" need only be as extensive as the activities one must pursue.

Scholars of communicative competence have also devoted a great deal of attention to the specific contents or components of programs. Allen and Brown (1976), for example, suggest that to be competent people must possess programs to persuade others, to seek or give information, to express feelings, and to engage in culturally determined rituals such as greetings or verbal games. A number of investigators argue that programs should always contain components that function to maintain and support the identities of other communicators (for example, Weinstein, 1969; Wiemann, 1977). Educators have devised long lists of ideal speaking and listening skills. Some of the more common entries include abilities to use language in emergency situations, to question others' viewpoints, to organize messages, to use appropriate facial expressions and paralanguage, to distinguish facts from opinions, and to seek or give directions (for example, Allen & Brown, 1976; Backlund, Brown, Gurry, & Jandt, 1982; Rubin, 1982).

Although efforts to conceptualize competence in terms of a list of program contents are extremely useful to communication educators and other practitioners, they can not tell the whole story. The various skills and abilities noted above are only useful to the extent that they serve the more general goal orientation of the individual. Moreover, a given behavior may be either an asset or a liability depending on the goal or the situation. Finally, programs are more than lists of specific behaviors. They are also decision-making mechanisms. If one condition occurs at a choice point in the program, a particular response is given; but if a different condition occurs, then a different response will be given (Carver & Scheier, 1982). How the individual makes these decisions about perception and action is at least as important as what the specific perceptions and actions are.

Our awareness of making the myriad decisions involved at the level of program control may vary quite widely. We are most aware of our progress through episodes when uncertainty is aroused by novel conditions or violated expectations. However, most of our social interactions are so routine that they become highly scripted and are enacted with relatively little conscious awareness. They are performed "mindlessly" (Langer, 1978).

In some cases mindlessness may be an asset to the individual. It can contribute to action in contexts far removed from the present one by freeing the conscious to focus elsewhere. It frees the individual to devote conscious attention to other domains and to engage in more than one activity at a time. It allows the person to conserve energy and respond more rapidly and effectively. Highly routine social behaviors, for example, tend to be performed more effectively in a relatively mindless state (Langer & Weinman, 1981).

Persistent or extreme mindlessness, however, creates several problems for the individual. Mindlessness may cause the individual to ignore or fail to collect information that is sufficiently detailed to warn of potential opportunities or dangers in the environment (cf Carver & Scheier, 1982). For example, the person who is mindlessly performing the "drive to work" program may not notice the brake lights of the car in front in time to prevent a collision. More generally, persistent mindlessness can rob the individual of the experience of having exerted control. Persistent mindlessness can contribute to the belief that one lacks control, and such a belief can impair future performances, reduce self-esteem, and may even be associated with the physical deterioration and death of the individual (for example, Langer & Rodin, 1976).

It is not so much the degree of conscious awareness of programs that influences communicative competence as the degree to which the level of awareness is commensurate to the level of novelty and change in the social and physical context. Chronic or extreme mindlessness is undoubtedly dangerous, but there are many routine social situations in which a low level of awareness is acceptable, perhaps even desirable. These situations lack enough change and variety to make extensive conscious monitoring unnecessary. Although many introductory discussions take the position that communicative competence requires a constant and high degree of conscious awareness, I take the view that competence requires the ability to shift the focus of conscious awareness in accordance with situational demands.

Level 8 Competency: Principle Control

Communicative competence, of course, requires much more than merely executing the accumulated software of socialization. As we move from program control to still higher levels in the control hierarchy, we encounter a series of general principles that function to decide which programs will be executed, to create new programs, to monitor the degree to which lower order operations require conscious attention, and to evaluate the successfulness of programs in achieving one's goals (Carver & Scheier, 1982; Newell, Shaw, & Simon, 1963; Powers, 1973).

Principles are very similar to what we often describe as the communicator's abstract goals in a given situation. Carver and Scheier (1982) provide an extended example about a person whose goal or principle is to "follow through on commitments" with respect to the return of some borrowed class notes to a friend. Adherence to this principle sets in action a program to "drive over and return the notes," which in turn triggers and directs a sequence of actions that ripple down through the hierarchy to generate overt behavior. In many situations, of course, we will attempt to adhere to more than one principle. In a chess game, for instance, the principle that one should "develop strength at the center of the board" might be only one of a series of principles used to achieve the overall goal of winning (Newell et al., 1963).

Principles operate to make choices about which programs to enter. Of course, a given principle may be satisfied by more than one program. There are, to return to my examples above, several ways one might follow through on commitments or claim the center of a chessboard.

Communicative competence at the level of principle control rests on the ability to select or create programs that achieve the goals inherent in the principles. Maladaptive, unsuccessful behavior often occurs because individuals lack the necessary programming to actualize their principles (Carver & Scheier, 1982). They may, for example, have the goal of being liked by others, but have no idea of specific ways to achieve that goal. Or they may think they know how to be liked, but discover that their behavior fails to elicit liking from others. The fact that programming may be absent or inadequate to achieve goals underscores the importance of the creative aspects of competence. Indeed the ability to creatively pursue goals under novel circumstances or in the face of disruptions in interaction is a fundamental competency (cf Mischel, 1973; Reardon, 1982).

One way to approach the creative aspects of principle control is to consider the types of information individuals might use to revise or create general courses of action. A major input is information about the adequacy of the programs currently being employed. This information, in turn, depends on the input from relationship control operations, the next lower level in the hierarchy. I have already noted that creativity can arise at the level of relationship control as communicators revise and reorder their construals of the situation. As these creative reconstruals are abstracted upward through the program control level to the principle control level, creative options may be presented.

Another source of information for program revision is the individual's memory of past programs. Cognitive research shows that we do not so much retrieve memories as recreate them afresh (for example, Kihlstrom, 1981; Neisser, 1976). As memories are recreated they will be creatively recontextualized according to the principles of the moment. Communicative competence at this level will depend on the ability to recontextualize memories, that is, to adapt information from different domains and apply it to present problems. Such an ability is closely related to cognitive complexity, and there is some research (for example, Reardon, 1982) to support the belief that cognitively complex individuals should be able to perform more competently in situations in which existing programs have been disrupted.

Level 9 Competency: System Concept Control

At last we have reached the highest level of the control hierarchy. Although previous writers admit they are speculating, most appear to agree that this level involves a system of idealized self-concepts (for example, Carver & Scheier, 1982; Markus & Smith, 1981; Powers, 1973). These idealized self-concepts represent the richest and most enduring reference points for our communication (Keenan & Baillet, 1980; Rogers, 1981). More specifically, they function to provide a set of principles or goals, which in turn, as we have already observed, direct and decipher our social encounters. Thus a person whose idealized self-concept contained the system concept "be a responsible person" might attempt to realize it by drawing on the principle "follow through on commitments" (Carver & Scheier, 1982).

One obvious competency at the level of system concept control is the person's ability to translate idealized self-concepts into guiding principles. A person may believe in being a responsible person, but behave incompetently because he or she lacks ideas about how to behave as a responsible person.

System concept control also involves our most generalized self-esteem evaluations. Writers from William James (1890) onward have conceptualized self-esteem as our evaluation of our ability to successfully control, that is, to satisfy the goals selected by our idealized self-concepts. Thus, the highest level of the control hierarchy contains its own mechanisms for evaluating communicative competence. Any of a wide variety of measures that tap the individual's evaluation of his or her ability to exert control (for example, self-esteem, communication apprehension, perceived control, satisfaction, helplessness) should also measure communicative competence at least to some degree.

Although system concepts do change over time, they change gradually. At any one point, they may be comparatively fixed, and the individual will act so as to maintain them. The simplest way to do this, of course, is to invoke principles, programs, and lower-order operations in ways that reinforce the system concepts. Yet failures do occur, and when behavioral strategies fail to satisfy our goals, we may need to turn to cognitive strategies for maintaining system concepts and the perception of competence (cf Thompson, 1981). Or we may use what Berglas and Jones have called "self-handicapping" strategies to maintain our perception of competence when we expect to fail. These researchers found, for example, that students who expected they would fail on a problem-solving task drank more alcohol prior to the task than those who expected to succeed. If the drunken student then failed, he or she could claim that the failure was really caused by the alcohol and thereby minimize the effect on the perception of competence. If the drunken student managed to succeed, competence evaluations would be enhanced because the student could claim success in spite of the handicap (Berglas & Jones, 1978; Jones & Berglas, 1978).

The Control Hierarchy in Perspective

The control hierarchy articulated in the last several pages seems ideally suited to the study of communicative competence. Competence is an extremely broad concept. The hierarchical approach acknowledges this by presenting a framework in which extremely diverse activities (for example, specific muscle movements and impression formation) can be analyzed together.

The fact that we are both sources and receivers is also incorporated in the hierarchical approach. From a source-oriented or top-driven perspective, the individual's idealized self-conceptions are realized by forming goals that are satisfied by programs, which in turn create successively more detailed instructions for overt behavior. From a receiver-oriented or bottom-driven perspective, raw sensory input is transformed into progressively larger and more abstract perceptions that allow us to understand larger and larger sequences of interaction and from which we identify our goals and discover both what we are and want to be. Both of these perspectives are easily accommodated in the hierarchical approach. In fact they are united because action at any given level is simultaneously a product of both higher-order standards and lower-order contingencies.

Finally, the hierarchical approach to control allows us to evaluate either specific competencies or competency in general. Throughout this section I have endeavored to identify specific competencies. About 20 of these have been summarized in Table 4.2. Although my discussion is admittedly incomplete, it does provide a basis for assessing a wide range of specific skills. I have also suggested that people make their own competency assessments at the highest level of the hierarchy. A person's own sense of competence is determined by the ability to satisfy goals and to take responsibility for satisfying them, and by the ability to react to failure in a way that promotes satisfaction in the future. Thus we can evaluate competency in general by tapping the individual's own competency judgments. Because these personal competency judgments have far-reaching consequences for the individual, I will explore them in greater detail in the next section.

COMPETENCE AND HELPLESSNESS

Although many lines of research are relevant to the conceptualization of personal competence judgments, I have chosen to organize my comments around the concept of learned helplessness (cf Seligman, 1974, 1975). Early research on learned helplessness examined the behavior of animals who had been exposed to uncontrollable aversive stimuli. Later reconceptualizations of the construct recognized important cognitive components and extended its application to a wide range of human social phenomena (Abramson, Seligman, & Teasdale, 1978; Miller & Norman, 1979).

Components of Helplessness

The development of learned helplessness begins with some failure of control. Researchers usually describe this failure in terms of some behavioral noncontingency that produces negative results for the actor (Abramson et al., 1978; Miller & Norman, 1979). That is, the actor finds that his or her actions are incapable of altering the undesirable outcomes. The perception of failure can take two forms (Bandura, 1977). It may be based on the assumption that although there is a response that would produce preferred

TABLE 4.2
Summary of Specific Communicative Competencies

Level in Control Hierarchy	Competency
System concept control	Ability to satisfy personal goals in a given context without jeopardizing more important goals in other contexts. Ability to translate idealized self-concepts into principles of social action. Ability to use cognitive strategies to preserve the perception of competence when failure occurs.
Principle control	Ability to improvise plans of action when interaction is disrupted. Ability to translate principles of action into specific programs of action. Ability to recontextualize information across situational domains. Ability to monitor awareness levels and adjust them to the degree of change in the situation.
Program control	Ability to organize diverse constructs and attributions into a coherent plan of action. Ability to draw on a repertoire of programs sufficiently large to address situational needs. Ability to predict and explain another's behavior, to empathize or role-take to the degree required to satisfy one's personal goals.
Relationship control	Ability to construe one's own actions and the actions of others from a variety of perspectives. Ability to revise construals of events and people in accordance with one's goals and changing situational demands. Ability to recognize and adjust to common attributional biases.
Sequence control	Ability to decode verbal and nonverbal cues accurately enough to pursue one's personal goals. Ability to produce verbal and nonverbal codes in coherent sequences or "chunks."
Transition control Configuration control	Ability to organize muscle movements into decodable nonverbal cues and words. Ability to decode sensations into nonverbal cues and words.
Sensation control Intensity control	Ability to organize specific muscle movements into discrete pieces of verbal and nonverbal cues. Ability to faithfully code and decode sensory information.

outcomes, one lacks the ability or skill to make it. Or it may be based on the assumption that there is simply no response that could influence the environment in positive ways.

Failure, however, is not a sufficient condition for the development of learned helplessness. Failure may lead to either helplessness or renewed efforts to achieve positive outcomes depending on the causal attribution the actor makes for his or her failure. In commonsense terms, what we make of our failures may determine our ultimate degree of success. When failure can be attributed to external or transitory causes (for example, task difficulty, lack of effort), helplessness is reduced and future performance may be less affected or even improved. However, when failure is attributed to internal causes (for example, personality faults, lack of ability), a feeling of helplessness occurs and future performance suffers (Abramson et al., 1978; Miller & Norman, 1979). Deficits in future performance, in turn, reinforce the internal attribution and the accompanying expectation of failure.

These findings support the belief that training aimed at cognitively restructuring the attribution process can alleviate the effects of learned helplessness and its conceptual relatives. Dweck (1975) demonstrated that teaching children to reattribute the causes of certain types of problems to external or transitory causes rather than internal causes could alleviate their helplessness. Research with depressed adults shows that similar cognitive therapies are often more effective than therapies involving antidepressive drugs or behavioral skills training (for example, Rush, Beck, Kovacs, & Hollon, 1977; Shaw, 1977). Even cognitive interventions as simple as having subjects read a series of positive statements about themselves can temporarily alleviate the effects of helplessness (Raps, Reinhard, & Seligman, 1980). Together, these findings imply that cognitive restructuring that focuses on reattribution training should be used more widely in treatment programs. Only about half of the communication apprehension and reticence treatment programs in the United States, for example, appear to use such procedures (Hoffman & Sprague, 1982).

Before going on, it is worth briefly considering the similarities between learned helplessness and a series of concepts more familar to communication scholars. These include communication apprehension (McCroskey, 1977, 1982b), reticence (Phillips, 1968, 1980), stage fright (Clevenger, 1959), shyness (Zimbardo, 1977), the unwillingness to communicate (Burgoon, 1976), and predispositions toward verbal behavior (Mortensen, Arntson, & Lustig, 1977).

Fine-grained analysis reveals a number of important conceptual distinctions among these concepts (cf Leary, 1984; McCroskey, 1982b). Some focus primarily on behaviors, whereas others focus primarily on emotional responses like anxiety. Some apply to a narrow range of communication contexts, whereas others apply more generally. Yet noting these and other fine-grained distinctions should not blind us to molar similarities. In one way or another all of these constructs deal with the actual and anticipated failure to produce predictable, positive outcomes in communicative settings (cf Greene & Sparks, 1983; Kelly, 1982). Each can be thought of in terms of the more general construct of learned helplessness. Recent research on communication apprehension (for example, Greene & Sparks, 1983) has begun to explicate the cognitive domain, which, as I noted above, is an important part of helplessness. At least one researcher (McCroskey, 1982b) has explicitly acknowledged the parallel between communication apprehension and at least the early conceptualizations of learned helplessness.

Consequences of Helplessness

Learned helplessness is generally believed to create disruptions in the motivation to perform and in actual performance, to result in negative emotional responses, and to result ultimately in certain forms of clinical depression and physical illness (Abramson et al., 1978; Miller & Norman, 1979).

The first recourse of the helpless individual is simply to avoid those situations in which failure is expected. For example, Mischel and Staub (1965) found that subjects tended to avoid situations similar to one in which they had just failed even when there was a substantial reward for successful performance. A large number of studies on learned helplessness (for example, Diener & Dweck, 1978), communication apprehension (for example, McCroskey, 1977), and shyness (for example, Zimbardo, 1977) point to the tendency for those who expect impaired performance to avoid or withdraw from social settings.

People typically experience anxiety when they find themselves confronted with tasks or situations in which they lack control or expect to fail (Thompson, 1981). Research on communication apprehension and shyness (for example, McCroskey, 1977; Zimbardo, 1977) demonstrates that anxiety is a common response to situations in which individuals doubt their ability to produce positive outcomes.

Once involved in a task, helpless individuals tend to perform poorly, and this in turn reinforces their sense of helplessness and anxiety. Performance difficulties have been widely documented in the literature on learned helplessness (Miller & Norman, 1979), communication apprehension (McCroskey, 1977), and shyness (Zimbardo, 1977). Furthermore, the belief that one has been unable to control a past unpleasant event complicates and prolongs the recovery period (Bulman & Wortman, 1977; Thompson, 1981).

In addition to deficits in actual performance, helpless individuals experience a number of of cognitive deficits that ultimately impair future performance and reinforce the expectation of failure. For example, Diener and Dweck (1978) found that helpless subjects were less likely to engage in "self-instruction" (for example, reminding themselves to concentrate) and "self-monitoring" (for example, checking to make sure that their behaviors would facilitate performance). Helpless individuals tend to underestimate their number of successes and overestimate their number of failures (Diener & Dweck, 1980). Moreover, helpless individuals do not allow their successes to alter their expectation of future failure (Abramson et al., 1978).

Learned helplessness has also been associated with a large number of negative emotional responses including anger, hostility, fatigue, stress, and frustration (Miller & Norman, 1979). Many of these negative responses are directed at the self. Feelings of incompetence, guilt, self-blame, self-criticism, and lowered self-esteem have all been associated with learned helplessness

(Abramson et al., 1978; Miller & Norman, 1979). Finally, learned helplessness has frequently been linked to clinical depression. In fact some researchers equate severe helplessness and reactive depression (for example, Abramson et al., 1978; Miller & Norman, 1979; Seligman, 1974, 1975).

In extreme circumstances the inability to exert control may be fatal. Aside from the obvious cases in which a person fails to deal successfully with some dire threat, there may also be life-threatening consequences when people are deprived of control over the routine aspects of their daily lives. Langer and Rodin, for example, tracked nursing home residents who varied in their degree of control over their daily routine for an 18-month period. Those who had low levels of control tended to be less happy, to participate in fewer activities, and to be more likely to die over the 18-month period (Langer & Rodin, 1976; Rodin & Langer, 1977).

Obviously people do differ in the intensity of their response to the inability to control. Not all helpless individuals are clinically depressed. Two factors appear to mediate the experience of learned helplessness. One is the subjective importance of the situation in which the lack of control occurs. The more important a task or situation is to a person, the more intense the feeling of helplessness that results from failure (Abramson et al., 1978; Miller & Norman, 1979). The other factor involves the individual's ability to predict that an event will be uncontrollable or stressful. Information can help reduce feelings of stress and helplessness by allowing the person to better predict the nature and duration of the stressful event (Miller, 1979; Swann, Stephenson, & Pittman, 1981; Thompson, 1981).

Generalization of Helplessness

Communication researchers have long recognized that avoidance, anxiety, and withdrawal occur with varying degrees of generalization. Several of the more recent approaches to communication competence have also recognized differences in generalization (for example, Cupach & Spitzberg, 1983; Spitzberg & Cupach, 1984). These differences have usually been described in terms of some sort of trait-state distinction. Trait anxiety, for example, is thought to be highly generalized, occurring over time and across a wide range of situations. State anxiety, on the other hand, is more specific, occurring only in a specific type of situation. Recent conceptualizations of communication apprehension include even more levels of generalization. McCroskey (1982b), for example, describes four levels of generalization: (1) trait-like apprehension, which occurs across a wide variety of contexts; (2) generalized-context apprehension, which occurs in a given type of context such as public speaking; (3) person-group apprehension, which occurs with a particular person or group; and (4) situational apprehension, which occurs with a particular person or group on a particular occasion.

Although research on communication apprehension and its conceptual cousins is useful for identifying degrees of generalization, it has less to say about the causes of generalization. The reconceptualizations of learned helplessness are much more informative in this respect (for example, Abramson et al., 1978; Miller & Norman, 1979). From the perspective of learned helplessness research, the degree of generalization depends on the nature of the causal attribution for failure.

Three specific attributional factors ought to influence the degree of generalization across time, contexts, and audiences (Abramson et al., 1978; Miller & Norman, 1979). First, generalization ought to be greater when failure is attributed to internal rather than external causes. One is more likely to generalize an internal cause for failure (for example, a low level of interpersonal sensitivity) because it can be applied to more settings than a given external cause for failure (for example, the other person did not give clear instructions). Second, generalization ought to be greater when failure is attributed to stable causes rather than transitory causes. For example, Diener and Dweck (1978) found that helpless subjects tended to attribute their failures to a permanent loss of ability, whereas mastery-oriented subjects tended to attribute their failures to "mistakes" and were thus able to maintain the belief that they would soon be successful. Finally, generalization ought to be greater when failure is attributed to global rather than specific causes. For instance, helplessness should generalize more when one attributes failure to persuade someone to an inability to use *any* persuasive strategy effectively than when one attributes failure to an inability to use one particular type of persuasive strategy successfully.

Thus the learned helplessness literature is at once more specific and parsimonious than the communication apprehension literature. Instead of providing a proliferation of traits and states, the learned helplessness perspective places the generalization process on a single, unified continuum and identifies specific factors that promote generalization of helplessness across time, contexts, and audiences.

Finally, it is worth noting that the generalization of learned helplessness (or, for that matter, "learned successfulness") has a self-reinforcing quality. Once expectations of success or failure begin to generalize, there will be a tendency toward further generalization because outcomes that are consistent with expectations are more likely to be attributed to internal causes than outcomes that are inconsistent with expectations (Feather, 1969; Feather & Simon, 1971a, 1971b; Gilmor & Minton, 1974).

PERSONAL CONTROL IN SOCIAL CONTEXT

I have chosen to define communicative competence in terms of the process by which the individual satisfies his or her goals. The literature on learned helplessness and its conceptual relatives helps justify this perspective by pointing to the negative consequences of an inability to satisfy personal goals. Helpless people tend to experience difficulties with tasks, develop negative self-images, and are more likely to develop mental and physical illnesses.

In spite of the obvious value of personal control, many writers question the wisdom of defining communicative competence purely in terms of personal control. In fact personal control has something of a bad name. It connotes social irresponsibility. For many it conjures up images of ruthless Machiavellians. Its bad reputation is further reinforced by the preoccupation of Goffman and others with the control strategies used by a rather unsavory cast of con men, impersonators, and spies, and by ideologies that view interpersonal communication as a quest for unbounded intimacy and warmth (Athay & Darley, 1981; Parks, 1982).

It is not surprising, therefore, to find that most writers endorse limits on the pursuit of person control (see Table 4.1). The most frequently advocated limit is social appropriateness. That is, communicators' control activities are competent only so long as they are confined to what others judge to be socially appropriate (for example, Allen & Brown, 1976; Larson et al., 1978; Stohl, 1983; Wiemann & Backlund, 1980; Wood, 1975). Competent people pursue their goals up to the point at which it becomes socially inappropriate to continue. The appropriateness criterion is particularly evident in measurement strategies that ignore the individual's own sense of competence and focus instead on how other participants or observers judge the individual's communicative behavior (cf Wiemann & Backlund, 1980). The concern with appropriateness has led some writers to argue that one is competent only to the degree that he or she fosters more lasting relationships with other participants by supporting their identities (for example, Wiemann, 1977; Weinstein, 1969).

Although I am also concerned with appropriate behavior, I believe many perspectives on communicative competence oversimplify the relationship between personal control and social propriety. Codes of appropriateness are not merely constraints on the pursuit of personal control. They are also both a means of achieving personal control and a product of personal control.

Competent communication is based on foresight. The ability to recognize when a given course of action is likely to result in punishment by others or in the frustration of one's more important goals is a basic characteristic of communicative competence as I conceptualize it. Thus the salesperson who makes a sale by treating the customer in socially inappropriate, yet effective, ways is judged to be comparatively incompetent because in the long run he or she will get more complaints, fewer repeat customers, and fewer new customers by referral. More generally, the pursuit of personal control will often be dependent on the responses of others. Appropriate behavior is prompted by the fact that we will often have to help others satisfy their goals in order to get them to help satisfy our goals. As Athay and Darley (1981) point out, the ability to make and honor social contracts is another basic characteristic of competence. Put another way, people subscribe to codes of appropriateness because more often than not adherence to those codes helps them satisfy their personal goals.

Socially approved or prosocial behavior is also the product of successful goal satisfaction. People who consistently fail to satisfy their goals are likely to display more anger, to be more exploitive, less generous, and less cooperative (Forsyth & McMillan, 1981; Hokanson, Sacco, Blumberg, & Landrum, 1980; Isen, Horn, & Rosenhan, 1973; Taylor, 1979). Their helplessness may erupt in hostility and violence (Miller & Norman, 1979; Zimbardo, 1977). Consequently it will usually be in the larger social interest if codes of conduct allow individuals to satisfy their goals.

In short, the image of the controller as interpersonal terrorist, so prevalent in the literature on communicative competence, is misleading. It is certainly true that some types of control activities should be thwarted, but it is also true that the justification for thwarting antisocial behavior is that such behavior threatens the freedom of others to pursue their personal goals. Rules of social conduct are the mechanism by which people protect their ability to pursue their desires. In the vast majority of cases the pursuit of our own personal satisfactions requires at least some accommodation to the desires of others and thus to broader codes of social propriety. Moreover, antisocial behavior probably results more often from the inability of individuals to satisfy personal goals than from overzealous and unprincipled control attempts. Finally, we should remember that goals can be personal and shared at the same time. My goals may be the same as yours. Or satisfying my desires may require that I help you satisfy your desires. In this sense, control-oriented behavior is not just something we do *to* others; it is also something we do *for* and *with* others.

SUMMARY

In many ways the study of communicative competence represents a set of skills in search of a theory, a set of definitions in search of substance, and a set of theories in search of a uniting metatheoretic construct. The theoretician's challenge is all the more frustrating because the concept of competence touches nearly every corner of the study of human communication. It is as traditional as classical rhetoric and as new as modern communication science. It is at once critical and empirical, general and specific, cognitive and behavioral, theoretic and applied. It is tempting to simply walk away from this theoretic morass and concentrate instead on less global constructs. Unfortunately this is a luxury we can not afford. If our own curiosity is not sufficient to prompt a more general consideration of competence, recent legislative and educational agendas oblige it.

I have defined communicative competence as follows:

Communicative competence represents the degree to which individuals perceive they have satisfied their goals in a given social situation without jeopardizing their ability or opportunity to pursue their other subjectively more important goals.

This definition emphasizes three interdependent themes that I feel are essential to any discussion of communicative competence: *control, responsibility,* and *foresight.*

The concept of personal control or effectiveness is at the heart of almost all definitions of communicative competence. It is also a uniting metatheoretic construct implicit in many contemporary and traditional research perspectives. The notion of control simply implies that people find some consequences of their communication to be more desirable than others and therefore communicate so as to obtain the more desirable ones (Miller & Steinberg, 1975). This does not mean that people are relentless profit maximizers. We usually move on to other tasks as soon as an adequate solution is found. We satisfy rather than maximize (Simon, 1979).

As a theoretic orientation, the competence-as-control perspective presumes that almost all of our cognitive and behavioral activities are subordinate to our broader pursuit of goal satisfaction. It therefore transcends the unfortunate bifurcation of cognition and behavior and instead portrays each as part of the same larger control process. In order to describe this larger process I have drawn extensively on control theory (Carver & Scheier, 1982; Powers, 1973). Control theorists conceptualize personal action in terms of nine hierarchically organized and cybernetically interconnected levels of activity. These levels range from lower-order phenomena such as raw sensory input and muscle action to higher-order phenomena such as creativity and self-concept maintenance. All are integrated by negative feedback loops. That is, each level functions to reduce the discrepancy between the state of affairs at the next lower level and the standards imposed by the next higher level.

I believe that control theory has two advantages over more traditional approaches to communicative competence. First, it is capable of describing an incredibly diverse range of activities within a single metatheoretic format. Second, it allows investigators to identify and interrelate a much more comprehensive set of specific competencies. Many of these specific communicative competences were summarized in Table 4.2. The heuristic value of the control theory approach to communicative competence is underscored by the fact that many of the entries in Table 4.2 have not emerged in previous discussions. Of course, many of the specific competencies have a familiar ring. Like many other writers, I believe that one's communicative competence depends in part on processes like uncertainty reduction, role-or perspective-taking, empathy, accuracy, and cognitive complexity. Unlike many previous writers, however, I do not uncritically endorse these constructs. These abilities contribute to competence only to the degree that they facilitate the overall control process. Thus we do not require unbounded empathy or accuracy to be competent. We only require enough empathy or accuracy to pursue our goals. In many cases we will be able to pursue our goals effectively with far less than maximal accuracy and empathy (Parks, 1982). The need for cognitive complexity is similarly bounded by the complexity of the goals being pursued.

People make their own competency judgments at the very highest levels of the control hierarchy. These judgments, and the feeling of self-esteem that follows from them, appear to depend on two factors. One is simple goal satisfaction and the other is a sense of responsibility. To be competent, the communicator must feel responsible for the satisfaction of his or her goals (Miller & Steinberg, 1975). If one does not feel responsible for producing positive consequences, then he or she will not usually feel competent. More specifically, if one believes that his or her actions produce only negative consequences or that his or her actions are unconnected to consequences, then a sense of helplessness sets in.

Researchers examining learned helplessness and its conceptual relatives like reticence, communication apprehension, and shyness have underscored the importance of control and responsibility. Learned helplessness has been associated with a loss of motivation to perform, deficits in actual performance, social withdrawal and anxiety, negative self-evaluations, depression, and physical illness. Moreover, helpless individuals tend to treat others poorly, sometimes reacting with hostility and violence. Therefore a sense of control and responsibility is not only essential for the individual's own well-being but is also crucial for prosocial behavior toward others.

The fact that we require both control and responsibility raises the potential for something we might call "false competence." That is, there may be cases in which individuals take responsibility for positive consequences even when their actions did not really produce them. Miller and Steinberg (1975) refer to these cases as examples of "fairyland" control strategies. Although "true competence" requires both active control and actual responsibility, the use of fairyland strategies is not automatically a sign of incompetence. These delusions may sometimes help the individual preserve self-esteem and the motivation to try again in the face of failure (Thompson, 1981). Nonetheless, the feeling of responsibility will generally be more enduring and motivating when it is based on relatively more objective external feedback.

The fact that we require both control and responsibility also creates the possibility for something we might call "ignorant competence." That is, there may be situations in which the individual controls successfully, but fails to take responsibility for it. One factor contributing to this problem, as we have already noted, is chronic or extreme mindlessness. Those who communicate with a chronic or extreme lack of awareness are robbed of the sense of competence even when they are successful.

The final characteristic of communicative competence as I have defined it is foresight. Communicative controllers are sometimes portrayed as interpersonal profiteers and terrorists. Nothing could be further from what I have in mind. Competent communicators have the foresight to recognize two essential qualities of social life. First, they recognize that their goals are interdependent. The pursuit of any one goal may influence the opportunity to pursue other goals. Success at all costs is a mark of incompetence because it usually results in the frustration of the individual's other goals. Second, competent communicators have a vested interest in maintaining the rules of social conduct because they realize, however dimly, that their ability to pursue their own goals depends on the freedom of others to pursue their goals. Personal control, then, is more often an ally of social appropriateness than its enemy.

REFERENCES

Abelson, R. P. (1976). Script processing in attitude formation and decision-making. In J. S. Carroll & J. W. Payne (Eds.), *Cognition and social behavior* (pp. 33-45). Hillsdale, NJ: Lawrence Erlbaum.

Abramson, L. Y., Seligman, M.E.P., & Teasdale, J. D. (1978). Learned helplessness in humans: Critique and reformulation. *Journal of Abnormal Psychology 87*, 49-74.

Allen, R. R., & Brown, K. L. (Eds.). (1976). *Developing communication competence in children.* Skokie, IL: National Textbook.

Athay, M., & Darley, J. M. (1981). Toward an interaction-centered theory of personality. In N. Cantor & J. F. Kihlstrom (Eds.), *Personality, cognition, and social interaction* (pp. 281-308). Hillsdale, NJ: Lawrence Erlbaum.

Backlund, P. M., Brown, K. L., Gurry, J., & Jandt, F. (1982). Recommendations for assessing speaking and listening skills. *Communication Education, 31,* 9-17.

Bandura, A. (1977) Self-efficacy: Toward a unifying theory of behavioral change. *Psychological Review, 84,* 191-215.

Beal, C. R., & Flavell, J. H. (1982). Effect of increasing the salience of message ambiguities on kindergartners' evaluations of communicative success and message adequacy. *Developmental Psychology, 18,* 43-48.

Berger, C. R., & Bradac, J. J. (1982). *Language and social knowledge.* London: Edward Arnold.

Berglas, S., & Jones, E. E. (1978). Drug choice as an externalization strategy in response to noncontingent success. *Journal of Personality and Social Psychology, 36,* 405-417.

Bulman, R. J., & Wortman, C. B. (1977). Attributions of blame and coping in the "real world." Severe accident victims react to their lot. *Journal of Personality and Social Psychology, 35,* 351-363.

Burgoon, J. K. (1976). The unwillingness-to-communicate scale: Development and validation. *Communication Monographs, 43,* 60-69.

Cantor, N., & Mischel, W. (1977). Traits as prototypes: Effects on recognition memory. *Journal of Personality and Social Psychology, 35,* 38-48.

Carver, C. S., & Scheier, M. F. (1982). Control theory: A useful conceptual framework for personality-social, clinical, and health psychology. *Psychological Bulletin, 92,* 111-135.

Chomsky, N. (1965). *Aspects of a theory of syntax.* Cambridge, MA: MIT Press.

Clevenger, T. (1959). A synthesis of experimental research in stage fright. *Quarterly Journal of Speech, 45,* 134-145.

Cohen, C. E. (1981). Goals and schemata in person perception: Making sense from the stream of behavior. In N. Cantor & J. F. Kihlstrom (Eds.), *Personality, cognition, and social interaction.* Hillsdale, NJ: Lawrence Erlbaum.

Crockett, W. H. (1977). *Impressions and attributions: Nature, organization, and implications for action.* Paper presented at the annual convention of the American Psychological Association, Washington, DC.

Cupach, W. R., & Spitzberg, B. H. (1983). Trait versus state: A comparison of dispositional and situational measures of interpersonal communication competence. *Western Journal of Speech Communication, 47,* 364-379.

deCharms, R. (1968). *Personal causation: The internal affective determinants of behavior.* New York: Academic Press.

Delia, J. G. (1976). Change of meaning processes in impression formation. *Communication Monographs, 43,* 143-157.

Delia, J. G., O'Keefe, B. J., & O'Keefe, D. J. (1982). The constructivist approach to communication. In F.E.X. Dance (Ed.), *Human communication theory: Comparative essays* (pp. 147-191). New York: Harper & Row.

Diener, C. I., & Dweck, C. S. (1978). An analysis of learned helplessness: Continuous changes in performance, strategy, and achievement cognitions following failure. *Journal of Personality and Social Psychology, 36,* 451-462.

Diener, C. I., & Dweck, C. S. (1980). An analysis of learned helplessness: II. The processing of success. *Journal of Personality and Social Psychology, 39,* 940-952.

Dweck, C. S. (1975). The role of expectations and attributions in the alleviation of learned helplessness. *Journal of Personality and Social Psychology, 31,* 674-685.

Etzioni, A. (1961). *A comparative analysis of complex organizations.* New York: Free Press.

Feather, N. T. (1969). Attribution of responsibility and valence of success and failure in relation to initial confidence and task performance. *Journal of Personality and Social Psychology, 13,* 129-144.

Feather, N. T., & Simon, J. G. (1971a). Attribution of responsibility and valence of outcome in relation to initial confidence and success and failure of self and other. *Journal of Personality and Social Psychology, 18,* 173-188.

Feather, N. T., & Simon, J. G. (1971b). Causal attributions for success and failure in relation to expectations of success based on selective or manipulated control. *Journal of Personality, 39,* 522-541.

Flavell, J. H., Speer, J. R., & Green, F. L. (1981). The development of comprehension monitoring and knowledge about communication. *Monographs for the Society for Research in Child Development, 46,* 1-65.

Foote, N. N., & Cottrell, L. S. (1955). *Identity and interpersonal competence.* Chicago: University of Chicago Press.

Forsyth, D. R., & McMillan, J. H. (1981). Attributions, affect, and expectations: A test of Weiner's three-dimensional model. *Journal of Educational Psychology, 73,* 393-403.

French, R. P., & Raven, B. (1960). The bases of social power. In D. Cartwright & A. Zander (Eds.), *Group dynamics* (pp. 607-623). Evanston, IL: Row, Peterson.

Gilmor, T. M., & Minton, H. L. (1974). Internal versus external attribution of task performance as a function of locus of control, initial confidence, and success-failure outcome. *Journal of Personality, 42,* 159-174.

Goffman, E. (1959). *The presentation of self in everyday life..* Garden City, NY: Doubleday/Anchor.

Goffman, E. (1967). *Interaction ritual.* Garden City, NY: Doubleday/Anchor.

Gottman, J. M., & Porterfield, A. L. (1981). Communicative competence in the nonverbal behavior of married couples. *Journal of Marriage and the Family, 43,* 817-824.

Greene, J. O., & Sparks, G. G. (1983). Explication and test of a cognitive model of communication apprehension: A new look at an old construct. *Human Communication Research, 9,* 349-366.

Gumperz, J. J. (1972). Introduction. In J. J. Gumperz & D. Hymes (Eds.), *Directions in sociolinguistics* (pp. 1-25). New York: Holt, Rinehart & Winston.

Harless, E. L., & McConnell, F. (1982). Effects of hearing aid use on a self concept in older persons. *Journal of Speech and Hearing Disorders, 47,* 305-309.

Harré, R., & Secord, P. F. (1973). *The explanation of social behavior.* Totowa, NJ: Littlefield, Adams.

Hebb, D. O., & Thompson, W. R. (1954). The social significance of animal studies. In G. Lindzey (Ed.), *Handbook of social psychology* (Vol. 1, pp. 532-561). Cambridge, MA: Addison-Wesley.

Heider, F. (1958). *The psychology of interpersonal relations.* New York: John Wiley.

Hewes, D. E., & Planalp, S. (1982). There is nothing as useful as a good theory. . . . The influence of social knowledge on interpersonal communication. In M. E. Roloff & C. R. Berger (Eds.), *Social cognition and communication* (pp. 107-150). Beverly Hills, CA: Sage.

Hoffman, J., & Sprague, J. (1982). A survey of reticence and communication apprehension treatment programs at U.S. colleges and universities. *Communication Education, 31,* 185-193.

Hokanson, J. E., Sacco, W. P., Blumberg, S. R., & Landrum, G. C. (1980). Interpersonal behavior of depressive individuals in a mixed-motive game. *Journal of Abnormal Psychology, 89,* 320-332.

Hunt, E. (1983). On the nature of intelligence. *Science, 219,* 141-146.

Hymes, D. (1974). *Foundations in sociolinguistics.* Philadelphia: University of Pennsylvania Press.

Isen, A., Horn, N., & Rosenhan, D. (1973). Effects of success and failure on children's generosity. *Journal of Personality and Social Psychology, 27,* 239-247.

James, W. (1890). *The principles of psychology.* New York: Holt, Rinehart & Winston.

Jones, E. E., & Berglas, S. (1978). Control of attributions about the self through self-handicapping strategies: The appeal of alcohol and the role of underachievement. *Personality and Social Psychology Bulletin, 4,* 200-206.

Keenan, J. M., & Baillet, S. D. (1980). Memory for personally and socially significant events. In R. S. Nickerson (Ed.), *Attention and performance, VIII* (pp. 651-669). Hillsdale, NJ: Lawrence Erlbaum.

Kelley, H. H. (1971). Attribution theory in social interaction. In E. E. Jones et al. (Eds.), *Attribution: Perceiving the causes of behavior* (pp. 1-26). Morristown, NJ: General Learning Press.

Kelley, H. H (1979). *Personal relationships: Their structures and processes.* Hillsdale NJ: Lawrence Erlbaum.

Kelly, G. A. (1955). *The psychology of personal constructs* (Vols. 1 & 2). New York: Norton.

Kelly, L. (1982). A rose by any other name is still a rose: A comparative analysis of reticence, communication apprehension, unwillingness to communicate, and shyness. *Human Communication Research, 8,* 99-113.

Kelman, H. C. (1961). Processes of opinion change. *Public Opinion Quarterly, 25,* 57-78.

Kihlstrom, J. F. (1981). On personality and memory. In N. Cantor & J. F. Kihlstrom (Eds.), *Personality, cognition and social interaction* (pp. 123-149). Hillsdale, NJ: Lawrence Erlbaum.

Langer, E. J. (1978). Rethinking the role of thought in social interaction. In J. H. Harvey, W. J. Ickes, & R. F. Kidd (Eds.), *New directions in attribution research: Volume 2* (pp. 35-58). Hillsdale, NJ: Lawrence Erlbaum.

Langer, E. J., & Rodin, J. (1976). The effects of choice and enhanced personal responsibility for the aged: A field experiment in an institutional setting. *Journal of Personality and Social Psychology, 34,* 191-198.

Langer, E. J., & Weinman, C. (1981). When thinking disrupts performance: Mindfulness on an overlearned task. *Personality and Social Psychology Bulletin, 7,* 240-243.

Larson, C., Backlund, P., Redmond, M., & Barbour, A. (1978) *Assessing functional communication.* Falls Church, VA: Speech Communication Association and ERIC.

Leary, M. R. (1984). The conceptual distinctions are important: Another look at communication apprehension and related constructs. *Human Communication Research, 10,* 305-312.

Leuba, C. (1955). Toward some integration of learning theories: The concept of optimal stimulation. *Psychological Reports, 1,* 27-33.

Major, B. (1980). Information acquisition and attribution processes. *Journal of Personality and Social Psychology, 39,* 1010-1023.

Markus, H., & Smith, J. (1981). The influence of self-schema on the perception of others. In N. Cantor & J. F. Kihlstrom (Eds.), *Personality, cognition, and social interaction* (pp. 233-262). Hillsdale, NJ: Lawrence Erlbaum.

Marwell, G., & Schmitt, D. (1969). Dimensions of compliance-gaining behavior: An empirical analysis. *Sociometry, 30,* 350-364.

McCroskey, J. C. (1977). Oral communication apprehension: A summary of recent theory and research. *Human Communication Research, 4,* 78-96.

McCroskey, J. C. (1982a). Communication competence and performance: A research and pedagogical perspective. *Communication Education, 31,* 1-7.

McCroskey, J. C. (1982b). Oral communication apprehension: A reconceptualization. In M. Burgoon (Ed.), *Communication yearbook 6* (pp. 136-170). Beverly Hills, CA: Sage.

Miller, G. R., & Steinberg, M. (1975). *Between people: A new analysis of interpersonal communication.* Chicago: Science Research Associates.

Miller, I. W., & Norman, W. H. (1979). Learned helplessness in humans: A review and attribution-theory model. *Psychological Bulletin, 86,* 93-118.

Miller, S. M. (1979). Controllability and human stress: Method, evidence and theory. *Behaviour Research and Therapy, 17,* 287-304.

Mischel, W. (1968). *Personality and assessment.* New York: John Wiley.

Mischel, W. (1969). Continuity and change in personality. *American Psychologist, 24,* 1012-1018.

Mischel, W. (1973). Toward a cognitive social learning reconceptualization of personality. *Psychological Review, 80,* 252-283.

Mischel, W. (1981). Personality and cognition: Something borrowed, something new. In N. Cantor & J. F. Kihlstrom (Eds.), *Personality, cognition, and social interaction* (pp. 3-19). Hillsdale, NJ: Lawrence Erlbaum.

Mischel, W., & Staub, E. (1965). Effects of expectancy on working and waiting for larger rewards. *Journal of Personality and Social Psychology, 2,* 625-633.

Mortensen, C. D., Arntson, P. H., & Lustig, M. (1977). The measurement of verbal predispositions: Scale development and application. *Human Communication Research, 3,* 146-158.

Neisser, U. (1976). *Cognition and reality.* San Francisco: Freeman.

Newell, A., Shaw, J., & Simon, H. A. (1963). Chess-playing programs and the problem of complexity. In E. Feigenbaum & J. Feldman (Eds.), *Computers and thought* (pp. 39-70). New York: McGraw-Hill.

Nisbett, R., & Ross, L. (1980). *Human inference: Strategies and shortcomings of social judgment.* Englewood Cliffs, NJ: Prentice-Hall.

O'Keefe, B. J., & Delia, J. G. (1982). Impression formation and message production. In M. E. Roloff & C. R. Berger (Eds.), *Social cognition and communication* (pp. 33-72). Beverly Hills, CA: Sage.

Parks, M. R. (1977). Relational communication: Theory and research. *Human Communication Research, 3,* 372-381.

Parks, M. R. (1982). Ideology in interpersonal communication: Off the couch and into the world. In M. Burgoon (Ed.), *Communication yearbook 5* (pp. 79-107). New Brunswick, NJ: Transaction Books.

Pearce, W. B., Cronen, V. E., & Conklin, F. (1979). On what to look at when analyzing communication: A hierarchical model of actors' meanings. *Communication, 4,* 195-220.

Peterson, J., Fischetti, M., Curran, J. P., & Arland, S. (1981). Sense of timing: A skill deficit in heterosocially anxious women. *Behavior Therapy, 12,* 195-201.

Phillips, G. M. (1968). Reticence: Pathology of the normal speaker. *Speech Monographs, 35,* 39-49.

Phillips, G. M. (1980). On apples and onions: A reply to Page. *Communication Education, 29,* 105-108.

Phillips, G. M. (1984). A competent view of "competence." *Communication Education, 33,* 24-36.

Powers, W. T. (1973). *Behavior: The control of perception.* Chicago: Aldine.

Pylyshyn, Z. W. (1973). The role of competence theories in cognitive psychology. *Journal of Psycholinguistic Research, 2,* 21-50.

Raps, C. S., Reinhard, K. E., & Seligman, M.E.P. (1980). Reversal of cognitive and affective deficits associated with depression and learned helplessness by mood elevation in patients. *Journal of Abnormal Psychology, 89,* 342-349.

Reardon, K. K. (1982). Conversational deviance: A structural model. *Human Communication Research, 9,* 59-74.

Rodin, J., & Langer, E. J. (1977). Long-term effects of control-relevant intervention with the institutionalized aged. *Journal of Personality and Social Psychology, 35,* 897-902.

Rogers, T. B. (1981). A model of the self as an aspect of the human information processing system. In N. Cantor & J. F. Kihlstrom (Eds.), *Personality, cognition, and social interaction* (pp. 193-214). Hillsdale, NJ: Lawrence Erlbaum.

Roloff, M. E., & Berger, C. R. (Eds.). (1982a). *Social cognition and communication.* Beverly Hills, CA: Sage.

Roloff, M. E., & Berger, C. R. (1982b). Social cognition and communication: An introduction. In M. E. Roloff & C. R. Berger (Eds.), *Social cognition and communication* (pp. 9-32). Beverly Hills, CA: Sage.

Rubin, R. B. (1982). Assessing speaking and listening competence at the college level: The communication competency assessment instrument. *Communication Education, 31,* 19-32.

Rush, A. J., Beck, A. T., Kovacs, M., & Hollon, S. (1977). Comparative efficacy of cognitive therapy and pharmacotherapy in the treatment of depressed out-patients. *Cognitive Therapy and Research, 1,* 17-37.

Schank, R. C., & Abelson, R. P. (1977). *Scripts, plans, goals, and understanding.* Hillsdale, NJ: Lawrence Erlbaum.

Searle, J. (1969). *Speech acts.* London: Cambridge University Press.

Seligman, M.E.P. (1974). Depression and learned helplessness. In R. J. Friedman & M. M. Katz (Eds.), *The psychology of depression: Contemporary theory and research* (pp. 83-125). New York: John Wiley.

Seligman, M.E.P. (1975). *Helplessness: On depression, development, and death.* San Francisco: Freeman.

Shaw, B. F. (1977). Comparison of cognitive therapy and behavior therapy in the treatment of depression. *Journal of Consulting and Clinical Psychology, 45,* 543-551.

Sillars, A. L. (1982). Attribution and communication: Are people "naive scientists" or just naive? In M. E. Roloff & C. R. Berger (Eds.), *Social cognition and communication* (pp. 73-106). Beverly Hills, CA: Sage.

Simon, H. A. (1979). *Models of thought.* New Haven: Yale University Press.

Snyder, M., & Swann, W. B. (1978a). Behavioral confirmation in social interaction: From social perception to social reality. *Journal of Experimental Social Psychology, 14,* 148-162.

Snyder, M., & Swann, W. B. (1978b). Hypothesis-testing processes in social interaction. *Journal of Personality and Social Psychology, 36,* 1202-1212.

Spitzberg, B., & Cupach, W. (1984). *Interpersonal communication competence.* Beverly Hills, CA: Sage.

Steffen, J. J., & Redden, J. (1977). Assessment of social competence in an evaluation-interaction analogue. *Human Communication Research, 4,* 31-37.

Stohl, C. (1983). Developing a communicative competence scale. In R. N. Bostrom (Ed.), *Communication yearbook 7* (pp. 685-716). Beverly Hills, CA: Sage.

Swann, W. B., Stephenson, B., & Pittman, T. S. (1981). Curiosity and control: On the determinants of the search for social knowledge: *Journal of Personality and Social Psychology, 40,* 635-642.

Taylor, S. E. (1979). Hospital patient behavior: Reactance, helplessness or control? *Journal of Social Issues, 35,* 156-184.

Thompson, S. C. (1981). Will it hurt less if I can control it? A complex answer to a simple question. *Psychological Bulletin, 90,* 89-101.

Tversky, A., & Kahneman, D. (1971). Belief in the law of small numbers. *Psychological Bulletin, 76,* 105-110.

Weinstein, E. A. (1969). The development of interpersonal competence. In D. A. Goslin (Ed.), *Handbook of socialization theory and research.* Chicago: Rand McNally.

White, R. W. (1959). Motivation considered: The concept of competence. *Psychological Review, 66,* 297-333.

Wiemann, J. M. (1977). Explication and test of a model of communicative competence. *Human Communication Research, 3,* 195-213.

Wiemann, J. M., & Backlund, P. (1980). Current theory and research in communicative competence. *Review of Educational Research, 50,* 185-199.

Wood, B. S. (1975). *Children and communication.* Englewood Cliffs, NJ: Prentice-Hall.

Wood, R., Weinstein, E. A., & Parker, T. B. (1967). Children's interpersonal tactics. *Sociological Inquiry, 37,* 129-138.

Woodworth, R. S. (1958). *Dynamics of behavior.* New York: Holt, Rinehart & Winston.

Zimbardo, P. (1977). *Shyness: What it is, what to do about it.* Reading, MA: Addison-Wesley.

II FUNDAMENTAL UNITS

5 Communicator Characteristics and Behavior

HOWARD GILES

University of Bristol

RICHARD L. STREET, Jr.

Texas Tech University

R ESEARCHERS exploring the role of communicator characteristics have usually fallen into one of two broad categories. First, investigators have examined how individual differences—such as personality, psychological, and sociodemographic variables—associated with the communicator have been marked in verbal and nonverbal behavior. Second, researchers in the language attitude and speech style evaluation domain have been concerned with mapping receivers' beliefs toward communicators possessing different linguistic and paralinguistic attributes. Our review of this research in Part I, although not exhaustive, is comprehensive and representative. The first two sections consider research focusing on psychological and sociodemographic variables and the third entails the speech style evaluation literature. In Part II of this chapter, we shall attempt to propose ways in which the traditional paradigms of communicator characteristics can be enriched. The first section outlines some of the limitations of previous approaches. The second focuses upon research and theory into involvement behaviors and impression management, which constitute the underpinnings to generalizations pertaining to, and a complex speculative model of, *cognitive characteristics of communicators* in the third section. This latter approach is proffered as a complement to the traditional paradigms reviewed in Part I and the two generalizations considered arising from it. It is our belief that such a perspective is a priority and necessary precursor to theoretically substantive and pragmatically relevant advances being made in the communicator characteristics domain of interpersonal communication.

AUTHORS' NOTE: We are grateful to colleagues in Communication Arts, University of Wisconsin—Madison for their constructive comments on an earlier draft of this chapter, and in particular to Joseph Cappella and Mark Palmer.

PART I: TRADITIONAL PARADIGMS OF EMPIRICAL RESEARCH

1. Psychological Variables

Self-Monitoring

According to Snyder (1974, 1979), the high self-monitor (HSM) is sensitive to self-presentation and expression to relevant others due to a concern of appropriateness of his or her social behavior. Thus, HSM individuals carefully monitor their verbal and nonverbal behavior. The low self-monitor (LSM) is not so concerned about appropriate self-presentation, nor does he or she have a well-developed repertoire of social behavior skills. Research has indicated that HSMs are better able to express emotional states through facial and vocal channels (Snyder, 1974), have shorter turns and more interruptive simultaneous speech (Dabbs, Evans, Hopper, & Purvis, 1980), and are more likely to initiate conversations (Ickes & Barnes, 1977) than LSMs. However, Dabbs et al. (1980) observed no differences between HSMs and LSMs regarding gaze patterns and matching of pause and turn length duration. Finally, HSMs are more likely to reciprocate the intimacy, emotionality, and descriptive content of a partner's self disclosure than LSMs (Shaffer, Smith, & Tomarelli, 1982).

Extraversion-Introversion

Relative to introverts, extraverts spend less time pausing prior to assuming a speaking turn (Ramsay, 1966; Siegman & Pope, 1965). However, in his study of American and German jurors, Scherer (1979a) reported that extraversion was negatively related to the *number* of silent periods but not their *duration*. Siegman (1978) suggested that the greater amount of pausing among introverts results from higher cognitive activity and less impulsivity relative to extraverts. On other speech dimensions, differences between extraverts and introverts are equivocal. Markel, Phillis, Vargas, and Harvard (1972) reported that fast speakers were more extraverted than slow speakers, but Steer (1974) observed no differences in speech rate of extraverts and introverts when expressing emotions (see also Ramsay, 1968). Mallory and Miller (1958) reported a low positive correlation between extraversion and vocal intensity, whereas Trimboli's (1973) correlation was higher and significant. Finally, several studies have indicated that extraverts speak a greater proportion of the time than introverts (Scherer, 1979a), but extraverts appear not to self-disclose significantly more (Morris, 1979).

Within the nonverbal domain, Morris (1979) reported that extraverts are more accurate than introverts in sending emotions, concluding that extraverts use the nonverbal domain more than introverts. Exline and Fehr (1978) suggested that extraverts may be more visually active and look at partners more than do introverts (see, for example, Mobbs, 1968), but only regarding frequency of and not duration of looks (see, for example, Rutter, Morley, & Graham, 1972). The relationship between extraversion and interaction distance remains unclear. Some research has revealed that extraverts prefer closer interaction distances than introverts (Cook, 1970; Pedersen, 1973; Williams, 1976), whereas other studies report no differences between the two groups (Patterson, 1973; Patterson & Holmes, 1966; Tolor, 1975). Knapp (1978) speculated that the conflicting findings may be due to the intimacy of the encounter. In intimate settings, introverts may prefer more space between interactants. In less intimate settings, interaction distance preferences may not discriminate between extraverts and introverts.

Dominance-Submissiveness

Individuals having dominant personalities seem to employ a confident and assertive interaction style. Relative to their submissive counterparts, dominant communicators have been reported to hold the floor more, interrupt more (Martindale, 1971; Rogers & Jones, 1975; Scherer, 1979b), participate more actively in groups (Weinstein & Hanson, 1975), use fewer silent pauses (Scherer, 1979b), have more resonant voices (Mallory & Miller, 1958; Weaver & Anderson, 1973), and use more certainty words (for example, "obviously," "without any doubt"; see Scherer, 1979a). However, in Scherer's (1979a) study, the positive relationship between a certainty/uncertainty ratio and dominance was observed for American jurors and not German jurors.

For other speech behaviors, the findings are less clear. Some research has indicated that dominance is positively related to vocal intensity (Mallory & Miller, 1958; Weaver & Anderson, 1973), whereas others found no relationship (Scherer, 1979a). The relationship between pitch and dominance is more confusing as dominance has been associated with high pitch (Scherer, 1979a), low pitch (Weaver & Anderson, 1973), and pitch range (Scherer, 1979b). The speech behavior of dominant personalities has been attributed to habitually elevated arousal levels (Scherer, 1979a) and to amount of muscle tension throughout the vocal system (Laver, 1975).

Machiavellianism

The high Machiavellian (Mach) individual manipulates others for personal objectives more than does the low Mach. The limited amount of research on Machiavellianism and communication has primarily focused on nonverbal behavior. During social interaction, high Machs tend to look at partners more than do low Machs (Knapp, 1978). For example, one study reported that, after being accused of cheating, high Machs gazed at the accuser to present an appearance of innocence whereas low Machs looked away (Exline, Thibaut, Hickey, & Gumpert, 1970). Geis and Moon (1981) observed that lying high Machs were more believable than were lying low Machs, although

O'Hair, Cody, and McLaughlin (1981) could not distinguish between high and low Machs in terms of leakage of nonverbal cues of deception. Knapp, Hart, and Dennis (1974) reported minimal behavioral differences among deceivers and nondeceivers as a function of Machiavellianism.

Reticence/Communication and Apprehension/Anxiety

Under this general rubric, we consider research related to reticence (Phillips, 1968), communication apprehension (McCroskey, 1977), predisposition toward verbal behaviors (Mortensen & Arntson, 1974), and social anxiety. These constructs in some fashion tap into an individual's predilection to engage in communication or social activity with others. Although much research has been conducted with these variables, surprisingly little has focused on actual communication behaviors (a notable exception is Burgoon & Koper, 1984).

Phillips (1968) reported that reticent speakers produced more hesitancies in speech than nonreticent speakers. McKinney (1982) observed that group interaction processes were not impeded by reticent group members but these individuals were less effective participants due to limited vocal activity and were less likely to emerge as leaders. Van Kleeck and Street's (1982) study of adult interaction with talkative and reticent 3-year-olds indicated that not only did the reticent children talk less, but their speech was characterized by lower mean length of utterance (MLU), less lexical diversity, a smaller proportion of complex sentences, a higher proportion of assertive statements, and a lower proportion of requestive remarks.

Regarding communication apprehension, McCroskey (1977) has reviewed research suggesting that high communication apprehensives talk and disclose less than low apprehensives. On the other hand, Burgoon and Hale (1983) reported that, on essay tasks and prepared messages in which subjects filled in the blanks, high oral communication apprehensives displayed greater productivity, less intense language, more varied vocabulary, more complex language, and less comprehensible vocalizations. Jordan and Powers (1978) reported verbal behavior differences between the two groups but only as a function of context. In personal, informal settings, high communication apprehensives used shorter words, more adjectives and adverbs, and more phrase repetitions than low apprehensives. However, there were no differences between the two groups in a social, formal context. Powers (1977) reported that communication apprehension leads to increased rhetorical interrogative (for example, "You know?" "Okay?") ratios but only as a function of high apprehensives talking less than lows. However, Street and Jordan (1981) reported no significant differences between high and low apprehensives regarding lexical diversity or rhetorical interrogative usage.

Research regarding predisposition toward verbal behavior (PVB) and communication have been mixed. Arntson, Mortensen, and Lustig (1980) observed high PVB subjects talking longer, interrupting less, and initiating more ideas than their low PVB counterparts. However, in a highly structured interview setting, no differences between high and low PVB persons were found for response durations (Arntson & Mortensen, 1976; Mortensen & Arntson, 1974).

Recently Hewes and his colleagues (Hewes & Haight, 1979, 1980; Hewes, Haight, Szalay, & Evans, 1977) have criticized the cross-situational validity of related measures of communication avoidance such as reticence and PVB. Using a composite index of six situational behaviors (duration of an impromptu speech, duration of interaction in a small group, duration of responses in an interview, latency of responses, number of persons contacted, and choice of written versus oral assignments), Hewes and Haight (1979, 1980) found no support for the proposition that reticence and PVB influence these behaviors across situations. However, within specific domains, Hewes and Haight (1979) reported significant negative correlations between PVB and response durations in a free association task and in duration of interaction in small groups. However, in two studies, Burgoon and Koper (1984) found consistent behavioral patterns associated with communication reticence (as measured in the PRCA and UCS scales). As reticence increased, subjects nodded less, showed less facial pleasantness and animation, displayed more anxiety and tension, leaned away more, and communicated greater disinterest.

There appear to be curvilinear relationships between anxiety and speech tempo and productivity measures. Siegman (1978) has proposed that mild and moderate levels of anxiety tend to accelerate speech (faster rates and fewer pauses), whereas very low and very high anxiety levels produce slower speech and longer pauses. However, nature of the task and differences between state and trait anxiety may confound this relationship. For example, Helfrich and Dahme (1974, cited in Scherer, 1979a) showed that, relative to low anxious subjects, highly anxious individuals increased their number of pauses but only in threatening situations. No differences were observed between the two groups in positively valued situations. Also, anxiety arousal appears to facilitate performance of simple and familiar tasks (that is, tasks requiring minimal cognitive activity and habituated speech sequences) but interfere with complex and unfamiliar tasks. Following a comprehensive literature review, Murray (1971) concluded that verbal quantity (that is, amount or time of talk) was positively related to trait anxiety but negatively associated with situational anxiety. However, silence was negatively associated with trait anxiety but positively correlated with situational anxiety. Similarly, increases in situational anxiety appear to increase speech disturbances (for example, false starts, incomplete phrases, and so forth), though no relationship appears between trait anxiety and speech disturbances (Siegman, 1978).

Cognitive stress (operationalizations range from anticipated audience disagreement to anticipated suicide; see Bradac, Bowers, & Courtright, 1979) conceivably represents a form of anxiety. Bradac et al's (1979) review proposed that cognitive stress was inversely related to verbal immediacy (that is, the degree to which a subject's language reflects avoidance or approach toward a person or topic), language intensity, and lexical diversity. Finally, anxiety-prone individuals maintain greater distances than those not anxiety prone (Knapp, 1978; Patterson, 1982a). Patterson (1982a) reported that increases in social anxiety have been marginally related to decreased gaze, though Hobson, Strongman, Bull, and Craig (1973) claimed that anxiety appears unrelated to visual behavior.

In sum, there is no clear picture regarding the relationship between anxiety and communication behavior. This relationship appears to be mediated by a host of influences including situation, state versus trait anxiety, operationalization of anxiety, and nature of the task (Scherer, 1979a; Siegman, 1978).

Cognitive Complexity

Much of the research on cognitive complexity (that is, the extent of differentiation and/or abstractness of one's construct system for perceiving others) and communication has focused on the ability of communicators to adapt messages (given listener characteristics) to meet persuasive or other interpersonal needs. D. O'Keefe and Sypher (1981) concluded that there is considerable evidence that positive relationships exist between cognitive complexity and indices of sophisticated communication such as the degree of listener-adaptedness among children's persuasive messages (Clark & Delia, 1977; however, null results were reported by Ritter, 1979), children's ability to adapt to conversational deviance (Reardon, 1982), adults' ability to modify the number and quality of persuasive messages toward targets (Applegate, 1982; B. O'Keefe & Delia, 1979), communication effectiveness in a password game and tinker-toy building tasks (Hale, 1980), and the development of person-centered regulative strategies (Applegate & Delia, 1980). Also, during informal conversation high cognitively complex participants spent more time talking about themselves, whereas low cognitively complex individuals spent more time talking about external topics (Delia, Kline, & Burleson, 1979).

Although cognitive complexity appears positively related to sophisticated communication, the nature of "complexity" in this relationship changes with age. Communication effectiveness in childhood is related to construct differentiation (that is, the number of constructs). However, into adolescence and adulthood, communication effectiveness becomes a function of construct abstractness (that is, interrelationships among constructs; see Delia et al., 1979; D. O'Keefe & Sypher, 1981).

Field Dependence/Independence

Field dependence refers to differential responsiveness of individuals to external and internal cues (Feldstein & Welkowitz, 1978). Field dependent persons are more responsive to external cues whereas field independent persons are responsive to internal cues. Doob (1958) observed no significant relationship between field independence (or psychological differentiation) and number of adverbs, noun qualifiers, pronouns, and action verbs in essays. However, Steingart, Freedman, Grand, and Buchwald (1975) reported that for female subjects field independence was positively related to amount of talk but negatively correlated with words per sentence. Sousa-Poza and Rohrberg (1977) found field dependents to produce more continuous body touching movements than field independents. Finally, relative to more differentiated (field independent) persons, individuals with less psychological differentiation (these persons are also more sensitive to interpersonal cues) matched partners' switching pauses to a greater extent (Feldstein & Welkowitz, 1978). Findings regarding field dependence/independence and gaze have been mixed (Patterson, 1982a).

Need for Affiliation and Approval

Those that have a high need for affiliation tend to prefer closer distances and glance at partners more than those with lower affiliation needs (Knapp, 1978; Patterson, 1978). Duncan and Fiske (1977) reported no stable patterns among inclusion needs and turn length, number of turns, and turn time.

Those that have a high need for approval matched partners' vocal intensity (Natalé, 1975a) and pause durations (Natalé, 1975b) more than did individuals with low approval needs. The proposition that persons with high approval needs look at interaction partners more has received mixed support (Efran, 1968).

Miscellanea

Relative to their normal counterparts, schizophrenics maintain greater interpersonal distances (Patterson, 1978), are less visually attentive (Exline & Fehr, 1978), and speak with lower pitched (females) or harsher (males) voices (Weaver & Anderson, 1973). Research has indicated closer interaction distances are preferred by persons with high self-esteem (Frankel & Barrett, 1971; Knapp, 1978; Stratton, Tekippl, & Flick, 1973), emotional stability (Kendall, Deardoff, Finch, & Graham, 1976), low authoritarianism (Frankel & Barrett, 1971; Knapp, 1978), and high exhibitionism and impulsivity (Sewell & Heisler, 1973). Although Kendall et al. (1976) found boys with an external locus of control required more space than those with an internal locus of control, Duke and Nowicki (1972) argued this proposition is mediated by the relationship among participants. In the Duke and Nowicki study, internals approached strangers more closely, but no distance differences were observed between externals and internals among friends and relatives. Also, internals have been shown to talk less, gaze less, and to be more vocally assertive but less verbally assertive than their external counterparts (Patterson, 1982).

Depression has been associated with more frequent and longer pauses (Fieldstein, 1964; Pope, Blass, Siegman, & Raher, 1970), slower rates, and reduced productivity (Aronson & Weintraub, 1972; Siegman, 1978). However, Weaver and Anderson (1973) reported that vocal correlates of depression varied as a function of sex. The depressed female had varied speech rate but little vocal force, whereas the depressed male had a rapid rate and varied pitch levels.

2. Sociodemographic Variables

Sex

Of all communication individual difference variables, sex appears the most predominantly studied. We discuss sex effects under headings of noncontent speech, verbal, and nonverbal behavior.

Noncontent Speech. The speech of men and women differ most regarding vocal pitch. Adult women have higher pitch levels and greater pitch variability than do adult men because of the male's thicker vocal folds (Smith, 1979). Other sex differences in speech appear due to socialization processes as opposed to biological factors.

Across many cultures, men and women sometimes have discriminating pronunciation patterns (Smith, 1979). For example, in Montreal, females tend to pronounce the liquid "l" more often (Sankoff & Cedergren, 1971). In Scotland, Romaine and Reid (1976) observed girls articulating the dental "t" (for example, *water, got*) more often than boys. In the United States, a few studies have indicated that females pronounce postvocalic "r" and "ing" verb endings (as opposed to "in") more than males (see Smith, 1979, for review). Such differences led Lakoff (1975) and Kramarae (1982) to conclude that women use more standard and hypercorrect speech forms than men. However, several comprehensive reviews (Fisher, 1983; Hass, 1979; Smith, 1984) have demonstrated conflicting findings and give little credence to this proposition.

Males have been shown to speak louder than women but only in same-sex dyads. Both men and women increased vocal intensity with opposite sex partners (Markel, Prebor, & Brandt, 1972). On the other hand, Kimble, Yashikawa, and Zehr (1981) reported women spoke louder to women than to men, whereas men did not vary vocal intensity as a function of partner sex. During interaction, women may compensate for external noise more than men by adjusting vocal intensity (Von Raffler-Engle & Buckner, 1976), which supports the claim that women may be more sensitive to interpersonal cues than men. Finally, research on sex and speaking time has generated mixed results. In mixed-sex dyads, men have talked longer (Argyle, Lalljee, & Cook, 1968; Hilpert, Kramer, & Clark, 1975; Wood, 1966); in same-sex dyads, women had longer vocalization durations (Ickes & Barnes, 1977; Markel, Lang, & Saine, 1976); in groups, men talked more (Eakins & Eakins, 1976; Strodtbeck & Mann, 1956); in groups, a responsive group leader received more responses from men, whereas an unresponsive group member received more talk from females (Wright, 1976); during picture description tasks, men spoke longer (Swacker, 1975); and among couples, feminist wives spoke for longer periods than their husbands, with the opposite being true for couples having a nonfeminist wife (Hershey & Werner, 1975).

Verbal Behavior. No consistent relationship emerges regarding sex and conversational dominance. Two studies (Eakins & Eakins, 1976; Zimmerman & West, 1975) indicated that men interrupt more than do women, especially in mixed sex interactions. However, Rogers and Jones (1975) found no sex effects for interruption and floor time. Kimble et al. (1981) reported no clear pattern regarding verbal and vocal assertiveness among men and women in same and mixed-sex dyads. Similarly, regardless of sexual composition of groups, Fisher (1983) observed no significant sex effects on patterns of cooperativeness and competitiveness.

Women have self-reported more self-disclosure than men (Rosenfeld, 1979), although Morgan's (1976) study revealed greater disclosure by females for intimate and not for nonintimate topics. Regarding other conversational features, women have used more questions (Fishman, 1980), talked less about money, sex, sports, and news (Hass & Sherman, 1982), and used fewer obscene and profane expletives (Bailey & Timm, 1976) than did men. When storytelling, McLaughlin, Cody, Kane, and Robey (1981) reported that women make greater use of story sequencing services, suggesting that women were more likely to provide a warrant for introducing a story into ongoing talk. Finally, Garai and Scheinfeld (1968) indicated that women were more fluent than men, though other studies failed to substantiate this finding (Cherry, 1975; Silverman & Zimmer, 1976; Smith, 1979).

For some verbal behaviors, sex differences appear to be a function of the sex of the interaction partners. Piliavin and Martin (1978) concluded that, in general, men tend to use more task-oriented remarks and women more socioemotional statements (using Bales's content categories). However, in mixed-sex groups, women became more task-oriented and less socioemotional. Martin and Craig's (1983) findings included the following: (1) unacquainted males and females produced about the same number of qualifying words (for example, "maybe," "sort of") when talking to males, but males produced more and females less when talking to females; (2) both men and women produced more false starts when speaking to someone of their own rather than opposite sex; and (3) inequality between dyad members in number of words spoken was greater in female than in male and mixed-sex dyads. Martin and Craig concluded that these results suggest a more relaxed pattern of talk within same-sex dyads, especially for women.

Aries (1967) reported that in same-sex groups a few men did most of the talking, and themes included competition, sports, and physical aggression. Women, however, directed comments to the entire group and discussed home, family, feelings, and self. In mixed-sex groups, men initiated and received more talk. Also, men spoke less of aggression and competition and women talked less of home and family. Shimanoff (1983) observed men and women talking relatively equally about emotions. Women did not seem to vary emotional expressions as a function of partner's sex, but men used more affect words and talked more about emotions with women.

Sex differences among verbal behaviors are also influenced by age. Girls apparently develop more mature conversational styles earlier than boys such as fewer interruptions and talk-overs (Smith, 1977), more adaptive and complex conversational strategies (Haslett, 1983a, 1983b), and more efficient communication during cooperative tasks (Stipek & Nelson, 1980). Staley (1982) reported that 4-year-old boys talked twice as much as girls, and Brounell and Smith (1973) observed the opposite in dyads and groups. Staley (1982) also found sex differences in the use of interpretive, reflexive, and descriptive language to diminish between the ages of 4 to 16.

In short, few robust generalizations can be made regarding verbal behavior differences between men and women. Smith (1979) has posited that what differences do exist likely reflect sex *preferential* tendencies rather than sex *exclusive* tendencies. In a similar vein, Brown and Levinson (1979; see also Kramarae, 1982) concluded that most sex speech markers result from the hierarchical status relationship between men and women or from divergent social networks. An additional factor may be that, though sex differences exist in language use, researchers have not identified them. For example, Mulac and his associates (Mulac & Lundell, 1980; Mulac & Rudd, 1977) found subjects rated transcripts of female talk higher on aesthetic quality, whereas male talk was viewed as more dynamic, aggressive, and strong. Shaw (1977, cited in Martin & Craig, 1983) reported the verbal behavior of male job applicants was rated more fluent, active, confident, and effective than female applicants. In all three studies, the speech was presented in transcripts and all obvious cues of gender deleted. Thus these findings must represent actual differences, though the authors could not identify them (Martin & Craig, 1983).

Nonverbal Behaviors. Interaction distance preferences between men and women are influenced by sex of partner, the relationship between interactants, and other situational factors. In same-sex dyads and groups, females interact more closely than males (Patterson, 1978; Willis, 1966). In mixed-sex dyads, women's approaches toward men reflect greater distance than toward women, but men approach either sex at similar distances (Knapp, 1978; Patterson, 1978; Willis, 1966). White (1975) reported that subjects sat farther from a high-status female confederate than from an equal status female, but sat closer to a high-status rather than low-status male. Finally, Marshall and Heslin (1975) observed that, under crowded conditions, women reacted more positively than men with same-sex others. However, if the task was long, men responded more favorably under the crowded conditions.

Several studies have indicated that women gaze more at cointeractants regardless of sex than do men (Dabbs et al., 1980; Duncan, 1983; Exline,

1963; Exline, Gray, & Schuette, 1965; Henley, 1977; Knapp, 1978). However, two studies found no sex effects for gaze (Coutts & Schneider, 1975; La-France & Mayo, 1976). However, in the Coutts and Schneider study, the persons present were not allowed to talk during an audio-discrimination task. Women have nonverbally demonstrated more interaction involvement and affiliation than men (Ickes & Barnes, 1977). On the other hand, Cegala, Savage, Brunner, and Conrad (1982) have proposed that interaction involvement is differentially manifested for men and women. For males, high interaction involvement is indexed by less body movement and more eye gaze during speaking. For females, high involvement is represented by object-focused gesturing and discrete movements during speaking. Women also have used fewer gestures than men (Ekman & Friesen, 1972). In interactions with disliked others, males have exhibited less sideway-leans (for male partners only), whereas females exhibited more sideway-leans (Mehrabian, 1969). Finally, some studies have indicated females display emotions better than do males (Buck, Miller, & Caul, 1974; Zaidel & Mehrabian, 1969; Zuckerman, Hall, DeFrank, & Rosenthal, 1977), but other investigations have reported null results (Buck, 1975; Dunhame & Herman, 1975).

In summary, identification of communication behavior differences solely as a function of sex has been confounded by the use of perceptual measures, observing isolated behaviors, sexual composition of interaction partners, and changes in men's and women's societal roles. As mentioned earlier, perhaps scholars should examine sex effects in communication as sex preferential rather than sex exclusive (Smith, 1979).

Age

Obviously children's communication skills improve and expand rapidly into adolescence as their speech becomes more phonologically, grammatically, and semantically complex (for reviews, see Foss & Hakes, 1978; Helfrich, 1979). Although little is known about such changes from young adulthood to middle age, old age is often characterized by decrements in cognitive, linguistic, and vocal prowess.

Regarding verbal behavior, initially 2- and 3-year-olds verbally master information about the environment (interpretation) and use speech to express needs and ideas (expressive and relational functions). However, conflict episodes with peers are still characterized by physical force and nonword vocal signals. From 4 to 5 years of age, a projective function emerges (messages concerned with exploring situations through imagination and past experiences). Also, 5 year-olds begin to manage conflict episodes by using adaptive strategies with sustained discourse focusing on triggering events (Haslett, 1983a, 1983b). Whereas syntax development progresses dramatically through the first six years (for example, increases in differentiated structure and embeddedness; see Hass & Wepman, 1974), syntactic differences between adults and children after age 6 are not obvious (Helfrich, 1979). We should note, however, that age alone is not a good predictor of syntactic development because of strong individual differences in the rate of development (Helfrich, 1979).

As age increases from 3 to 7, there are accompanying increases in children's abilities to match the switching pause duration, turn length, utterance number, and speech rate of interactant partners (Garvey & BenDebba, 1974; Street, 1983; Street, Street, & Van Kleeck, 1983; Welkowitz, Cariffe, & Feldstein, 1976). Finally, younger children (3-year-olds) observe closer interaction distances than older children (7-year-olds; see Knapp, 1978).

The ability to adapt persuasive and other messages toward characteristics of targets progresses in a roughly linear fashion between the ages of 6 to 18 (Clark & Delia, 1976; Delia & Clark, 1977; Delia et al., 1979; Ritter, 1979). Dittmann (1972) reported that children in first through fifth grades used virtually no back-channel reinforcing remarks such as "yeah," "I see," and "mm-hmm." By the eighth grade, Dittmann observed a dramatic increase in these responses. Willis and his associates (Willis & Hoffman, 1975; Willis & Reeves, 1976) reported that between kindergarten and adulthood, touching readily declines.

A few studies have examined speech development across the entire life span. From childhood into adulthood, pitch decreases, pitch range increases, speech rate increases, and number and duration of pauses decreases. Into middle and old age, these trends reverse themselves (Helfrich, 1979; Kowal, O'Connell, & Sabin, 1975; Mysak, 1959; Sabin, Clemmer, O'Connell, & Kowal, 1979; Yairi & Clifton, 1972). These dramatic changes in childhood and in old age are attributed to vocal and cognitive maturation and deterioration, respectively (Helfrich, 1979). The increase in pause behavior and slower speech rates in middle-aged relative to young adults may be due to more reflective speech of the former (Sabin et al., 1979).

Finally, research on the interaction styles of the elderly is quite limited. One study examined crowding, task performance, and interactions of young (college) and old (over 60) females. Smith, Reinheimer, and Gabbard-Alley, (1981) observed older women exhibiting positive communication behavior in response to close distances in a small room, whereas the younger women responded more negatively in the same condition. Clearly, justification exists for more research on variables influencing the behaviors and consequences of the social interaction of middle-aged and elderly adults. Encouragingly, an upsurge of research interest in talk from and talk to the elderly appears to be underway (for example, Caporael, Lukaszewski, & Culbertson, 1983; Giles & Ryan, 1982).

SES

Basil Bernstein (1962, 1964, 1972) was primarily responsible for the recent interest in communication differences among socioeconomic classes. Bernstein proposed that the middle- and upper-classes used "elaborated codes," speech characterized by verbal elaboration of meaning and the articulation of a speaker's intent through explicit verbal forms. The lower classes used a "restricted code," characterized by limited lexical and syntactic choices and thus highly predictable speech (Siegman, 1978). Relative to middle and high SES speakers in England and the United States, low SES communicators have been reported to be more likely to increase the proportion of high-status phonological variants as situations become more formal (Labov, 1966; Trudgill, 1974), maintain greater conversational distance (Scherer, 1974), talk less (Jones & McMillan, 1973; Lawton, 1968), use less complex syntax, exhibit less lexical diversity of nouns, verbs, adjectives, and adverbs (Robinson, 1979), and communicate fewer descriptive attributions of stimulus pictures (Baldwin, McFarlane, & Garvey, 1971) or game rules (Pozner & Saltz, 1974). In addition, several studies have indicated that naive listeners are generally able to identify a speaker's social class given only vocal cues (Harms, 1963; Moe, 1972; Putman & O'Hern, 1955).

However, Bernstein's hypothesis has been widely criticized (see, for example, Arntson, 1982; Houston, 1970; Robinson, 1979; Stipek & Nelson, 1980; Taylor & Clément, 1974). First, contradictory findings are evident. Bernstein (1962) reported that a lower-class group of 16-year-olds spent less time pausing than a middle-class group. Siegman and Pope (1965a) found that, among female nursing students, lower-class students used more pauses on topics when an interviewer focused on family topics. No significant relationship emerged between social class and pause behavior on topics of school experiences. Robinson (1979) concluded that lower SES children and adults are less effective communicators of referential information. However, Stipek and Nelson (1980) observed no communication effectiveness differences between high and low SES children.

Second, many studies of SES and speech are questionable on methodological grounds (Robinson, 1979). When one considers evidence across an array of speech measures, Arnston (1982) concludes that there is little support for elaborated and restricted codes.

Status/Power Relationship

In high-and low-power dyads, low-power participants have directed more eye contact toward high-power partners when listening than when speaking (Efran, 1968). However, high-power participants tended to look more when speaking than when listening (Exline, Ellyson, & Long, 1975). Knapp (1978) summarized findings suggesting that gazing is moderate toward very high-status addressees, high toward moderately high-status addressees, and minimal toward low-status partners.

Regarding body orientation, shoulder orientation was reported more direct (when standing) with a high-status rather than a low-status listener (Mehrabian, 1969), superior position persons kept heads raised more

(Knapp, 1978), and, in psychiatric sessions, psychiatrists (high status) usually held relaxed postures, whereas clients (low status) were more rigid and formal (Goffman, 1961). Finally, high-status persons seemed to initiate more touch than low-status counterparts (Knapp, 1978).

Within the speech domain, Giles and Powesland (1975) have suggested that low-status/power participants should converge more toward high-status/power partners than vice versa because of the former's greater need for the latter's approval (for example, an employment interview). However, Thakerar, Giles, and Cheshire (1982), after observing high-low status dyads of staff nurses and nursing students, reported mutual speech rate and accent convergence. Presumably, the high-status party converged to foster communicative effectiveness; the low-status party converged to earn approval.

Race/Culture

Obviously, members of various races and cultures have developed dialects differing on phonological, syntactic, and lexical levels. Ethnic speech markers are usually attenuated when an ethnic group (usually subordinate) has a desire to assimilate into a dominant culture. However, if the groups strive for psycholinguistic distinctiveness, ethnic markers are likely to be emphasized (Giles, 1979).

Blacks in conversations have been reported to gaze more as speakers and less as auditors, whereas whites exhibited the opposite patterns (LaFrance & Mayo, 1976). Similarly, whites have looked more at authority figures when the figure was talking (Exline et al., 1975), but blacks usually did not look the speaking authority figure in the eye (Johnson, 1972).

Some have proposed that "high contact" cultures such as in Latin America, Italy, and the Middle East prefer closer interaction distances than "low contact" cultures such as in the United States and Northern Europe (see Patterson, 1978, for review). Watson and Graves (1966) reported that Italians and Arabs touch more and stand closer together than do Americans. However, one study observed no significant distance differences between Latin American students and American students (Forston & Larson, 1968). Bauer's (1973) study revealed that, among college students, blacks made closer approaches than whites. However, Aiello and Jones (1971; Jones & Aiello, 1973) reported that black children in the first and second grades interacted more closely than whites of the same age, but these differences began to reverse themselves by the time children were in the fifth grade. Comparing the conversational distance preferences of Japanese, Venezuelans, and Americans, Sussman and Rosenfeld (1982) found that preferred distance was a function of race and the language used in the interaction. When using their native languages, Japanese sat farther apart than did Americans, who in turn sat farther apart than did the Venezuelans. However, when speaking English, the Japanese and Venezuelans more closely approximated American conversational distance.

As Knapp (1978) has observed, much of the research on culture and distance is conflicting. One confounding variable in these studies appears to be SES (Patterson, 1978; Scherer, 1974). One study that controlled for SES reported no distance differences among black, Puerto Rican, Italian, and Chinese adults (Jones, 1971).

Physical Handicaps

Thompson (1981, 1982a) has found that, relative to their nonhandicapped counterparts, physically handicapped children were less able to adapt persuasive messages to various situations. Thompson (1982b) also observed both handicapped and nonhandicapped children had difficulty communicating to handicapped peers. Thompson concluded that mainstreaming helped children overcome these deficiencies.

3. Speech Evaluation and Language Attitudes

In this section, we consider listeners' evaluative and personality judgments of speech style. We purposely excluded literature on nonverbal decoding studies because of space limitations and because other reviews of this literature were available (see Cappella, in press). We initially focus on single behavior channels, followed by examination of multiple behaviors and perceptual/evaluative biases influencing speech judgments.

Dialect/Accent/Language

Following extensive literature reviews, Giles (1979), Ryan (1979), and Street and Hopper (1982) similarly concluded that receivers generally upgrade dominant or prestigious group accents and dialects on dimensions of perceived competence, status, intelligence, and success. These standard or dominant group speech varieties are usually preferred in formal contexts such as at businesses and schools. Regional or inferior group speech variants are usually perceived trustworthy and likable and are preferred by ingroup members in informal contexts such as at bars and at home. Support for these claims have been found in the United States (Bradford, Ferror, & Bradford, 1974; Buck, 1968; de la Zerda & Hopper, 1979; Hopper, 1977), the United Kingdom (Cheyne, 1970; Elyan, Smith, Giles, & Bourhis, 1978; Giles, 1971a, 1971b; Giles & Powesland, 1975; Strongman & Woosley, 1967), Canada (Lambert, 1967; Lambert, Hodgson, Gardner, & Eillenbaum, 1960; Miller, 1975; Taylor & Clément, 1974), and Peru (Wölck, 1973).

The consequences of these speech preferences are apparent in various contexts. In the United States, standard speech is favored for white-collar and supervisory positions, whereas nonstandard speech (black or Spanish accented) is appropriate for manual labor positions (Hopper, 1977; Hopper & Williams, 1973). In educational contexts, teachers' evaluations of students' language are good predictors of teachers' expectancies for performance

(Williams, 1976). Students with standard or middle-class speech are likely to be perceived as more intelligent and ambitious as well as receive better grades in the United States (Hewett, 1971; Williams, 1976), Ireland (Edwards, 1979a, 1979b), and Canada (Frender, Brown, & Lambert, 1970). Persuasion studies in England have produced mixed results. Powesland and Giles (1975) reported a nonsignificant trend for the prestigious Received-Pronunciation accent (R-P) to elicit more attitude change than the Bristol variant. However, Giles (1973) reported that although the more prestigious accents generated perceptions of better quality arguments, more nonstandard speech forms were more persuasive. Finally, prospective doctors tended to diagnose R-P accented symptoms as psychosomatic-related and the same symptoms in a regional guise as physically related (Fielding & Evered, 1980).

The dialect/accent evaluation process is also mediated by speaker-listener similarity, contextual information, and message content. Both dominant and subordinate group members have upgraded standard speech on competence dimensions. However, ingroup members have preferred their own speech in informal contexts, and have evaluated it as more sociable and trustworthy than the speech of outgroup members, especially if ingroup members value their ethnic speech. Support for this claim has come from Wales (Bourhis & Giles, 1977), Mexican-Americans in the United States (Carranza & Ryan, 1975; Flores & Hopper, 1975), England (Giles, 1971a, 1971b), and southern whites and blacks in the United States (Tucker & Lambert, 1969). Likewise, some ethnic groups (for example, whites in the United States) have perceived some outgroup speech (for example, German-accented or black English) negatively on competence and sociability dimensions (Hewett, 1971; Naremore, 1971; Ryan & Bulik, 1982). Perceptions of accent similarity have led to beliefs of attitude similarity (Delia, 1972; Sebastian & Ryan, in press). Lastly, in bilingual contexts, interactants who used the dominant language of interlocutors are usually perceived more favorably than those who do not (Genesee & Bourhis, 1982; Giles, Taylor, & Bourhis, 1973; Simard, Taylor, & Giles, 1976).

Most dialect/accent evaluation studies probably reflect ethnic and speech stereotyping processes. However, stereotypic responses may be altered by other information contextualizing the speech stimulus (Delia, 1972). Aboud, Clément, and Taylor (1974) posited that persons with characteristics more socially desirable than expected (for example, standard speech forms) may overcome an initially negative cue (for example, race). Hopper (1977) reported that blacks using standard English received more positive evaluations than white standard speakers in job interview settings. Ryan and Sebastian (1980) noted that Spanish-accented speech was viewed more favorably when the speaker was middle status rather than low status (see also Dowd & Bengtson, 1978; Sebastian & Ryan, in press).

On the other hand, negative or neutral information can diminish initially favorable impressions. Delia (1972) revealed that the relatively positive evaluations of the General American dialect speakers (as opposed to Southern and New England dialects) were attenuated with the advent of neutral information. The impact of contextual information is likely to depend on the strength of the stereotype. For example, Williams, Whitehead, and Miller (1972) demonstrated that observers perceived black children's standard speech as more ethnic and nonstandard than the same speech from white children. Similarly, Giles and Sassoon (1983) reported that a middle-class social standing did not overcome the negative attributions given to a Cockney-accented speaker.

Message content can interact with vocal behavior to influence interpersonal judgments (Hart & Brown, 1974). Schenck-Hamlin (1978) reported the speech stereotyping process was most intense for listeners when Southern speakers spoke on an issue relevant to the stereotype (for example, desegregation) than when speaking on a less relevant issue (for example, grain reserves). Although finding an insignificant trend for R-P accents to be more persuasive, Powesland and Giles (1975) observed the greatest attitude change when the R-P accented speaker delivered a left-wing message against the Industrial Relations Act. Presumably, this message was incompatible with what one would expect of R-P accented speakers. Finally, Johnson and Buttny (1982) demonstrated that black speech was downgraded relative to white speech, but only when message content was abstract rather than experiential.

Speech Rate

Speech rate evaluation research has similarly focused on receivers' competence and sociability judgments of speakers. Brown's (1980, for review) and Street and Brady's (1982; Street et al., 1983) research has consistently revealed (1) denigration of slow speech on dimensions of competence and sociability and (2) linear relationships between rate and competence, with faster rates being judged most competent. Woodall and Burgoon (1983) did not find rate to be related to competence, but this study reported very low statistical power.

Using machine-manipulated speech, Brown (1980) has uniformly revealed a curvilinear relationship between rate and sociability (his measure was labeled "benevolence"). Street and Brady (1982; Street et al., 1983; Street, Brady, & Lee, 1984), however, have used speakers fluently and naturally manipulating rate and reported moderate to relatively faster rates to be most socially attractive. Similarly, Miller, Marayama, Beaber, and Valone (1976) observed that listeners perceived fast speech more trustworthy than moderate and slow rates. Siegman and Reynolds (1982) and Stewart and Ryan (1982) also reported favorable responses to fast speech. Street et al. (1983) concluded that relatively fast, fluent speech (197-324 syllables per minute) can also be considered socially attractive, but rates toward fast extremes (e.g., 376 syllables per minute) diminish in attractiveness.

These data suggest that receivers have speech rate stereotypes associating fast speech with competence and moderate to somewhat faster speech with sociability. Although such stereotypes appear to exist (Brown, 1980; Street et al.,1983), speech rate evaluation is mediated by additional factors such as speaker-listener rate similarity, communication context, speaker age and sex, persuasive objectives, and mode of presentation.

From the speech accommodation perspective (see Giles & Powesland, 1975; Street & Giles, 1982), Giles and Smith (1979) proposed and supported the claim that adjusting one's speech rate level to that rate level characteristic of one's listeners enhances communicative effectiveness and favorable impression formation. Street (1982) and Putnam and Street (1984) also provided support for this proposition. Street and Brady (1982) suggested that moderate rates were judged most sociable because most listeners typically spoke at moderate rate levels. Although speech rate stereotypes may govern competence judgments, rate similarity mediated social attractiveness judgments. In two tests of these claims, Street and Brady (1982, Street et al., 1983) found speaker rate level and rate similarity to significantly influence both competence and social attractiveness judgments. Street et al. (1983) concluded that interactants' speech rate preference regions encompass rates similar to somewhat faster than their own.

Communication context also influences speech rate judgments. Giles, Brown, and Thakerar (1981) reported that the detrimental effects of slow speech may be nullified if listeners can favorably account for the slow speech (for example, helping an audience understand an unfamiliar topic). Also, for intimate topics (for example, how one can tell if becoming sexually aroused), slow speech is tolerated, if not preferred (Siegman & Reynolds, 1982). For formal contexts requiring careful and deliberate formulation of responses (such as employment interviews), slower speech may be more acceptable than in informal settings (such as casual conversation; see Street et al., 1983). Siegman (1978) has reviewed similar findings regarding stressful topics.

Most speech rate evaluation studies have employed male voices and have generalized findings to the entire population (see, for example, Brown, 1980; Street & Brady, 1982). For women speakers, faster rates are also associated with competence and status (Aronovitch, 1976; Ball et al., 1982; Street et al., 1984; Thakerar et al., 1982). However, speech rate appears *unrelated* to the perceived social attractiveness of women speakers (Aronovitch, 1976; Crown, 1980; Siegman & Reynolds, 1982; Street et al., 1984).

Generally, young adults negatively respond to the speech of the elderly (Ryan & Capadano, 1978). However, when exhibiting positive speech features (such as relatively fast speech), elderly speakers are upgraded on competence dimensions. Similar to the effects of speaker sex, young adult listeners appear to have differing speech criteria for evaluating the social attractiveness of young and old male speakers. On impressions of benevolence, young males with slow rates were downgraded. Speech rate did not influence similar impressions of elderly male speakers. Thus it appears that speech rate affects the perceived attractiveness of young males but not of women and older males.

The relationship between speech rate and persuasive effectiveness remains unclear. Some have found persuasiveness to be enhanced by fast rates (Mehrabian & Williams, 1969; Miller et al., 1976) and moderate rates (Apple, Streeter, & Krauss, 1979). Woodall and Burgoon (1983) reported no significant relationship between rate and attitude change. It would appear that rate interacts with other features of the communication event in determining persuasiveness.

Finally, one study observed differential speech rate effects as a function of presentational mode (Woodall & Burgoon, 1983). Subjects hearing audio-only messages were more influenced by speaker rate than those receiving the same message audiovisually. Perhaps when listeners are able to process only the speech signal, vocal behaviors such as rate have greater impact upon perceptual judgments.

Pauses

Two types of pauses in discourse are internal pauses (pauses within a speaker's turn) and response latencies (pauses between speaker turns). Several studies have revealed inverse relationships between favorable speaker evaluations and length of internal pauses (Lay & Burron, 1968; Newman, 1982; Scherer, 1979a; Siegman & Reynolds, 1982), and of response latencies (Baskett & Freedle, 1974; Street, 1982). However, Baskett and Freedle found that short latencies (less than 1 second) were perceived as the most competent but moderate latencies (1-3 seconds) the most trustworthy. Consistent with these findings, Williams (1976) suggested that, relative to standard speech, black nonstandard speech contained more pauses. This may be one reason this speech style has been downgraded.

Two factors mediating these evaluative processes are speaker-listener pause duration similarity and context. Street (1982) reported that, in fact-finding interview settings, the interviewee was perceived as most socially attractive and confident when adjusting his original response latency (3 seconds) to that of the interviewer (1 second) than when maintaining the original latency or making it more dissimilar (5 seconds). Of course, it is uncertain whether this finding is due to *length* of latencies or latency *similarity*. However, Street (1984) found that during fact-finding interviews, response latency similarity was significantly related to the favorability of participants' evaluations of interlocutors. Regarding context, Newman (1982) reported that legitimized periods of silence (that is, participants were conversing while working on a sculpting assignment) did not elicit negative responses from observers.

Vocal Intensity

Up to a moderately high level, increments in perceived vocal intensity are positively related to impressions of extraversion, sociability, emotional stability, boldness, and dominance (Aronovitch, 1976; Scherer, 1979a). However, excess loudness may inhibit speakers' effectiveness in public communication contexts (Pearce & Brommel, 1971). Speakers' sex may influence listeners' perception of communicators having varying loudness levels. Although increases in vocal intensity enhanced perception of logical abilities for both male and female speakers, male voices were rated as less nervous and emotional than female voices of the same intonation and vocal intensity characteristics (Robinson & McArthur, 1982).

Vocal Pitch

Research on listeners' impressions of speakers' varying pitch levels is conflicting. Apple et al. (1979) reported negative attributions such as deceit and nervousness with increases in speaker pitch. However, Scherer (1978; Scherer, London, & Wolf, 1973) noted that higher vocal pitch fostered impressions of competence, dominance, and assertiveness. Aronovitch (1976) reported higher vocal pitch levels were characteristic of kind, humorous, emotional, and immature women but did not influence impressions of male speakers. Scherer (1979a) attributes these inconsistencies for male speakers to two factors. First, Apple et al. used machine-manipulated pitch, whereas Scherer employed voices naturally varying in pitch. Natural voices may be viewed more positively than synthetic speech. Second, Scherer proposes that, up to a certain threshold within the male pitch range (around 140 Hz), higher pitch is associated with extraversion, competence, confidence, and assertiveness. However, if male vocal pitch approaches the female pitch range, impressions quickly become unfavorable.

The findings on pitch variability are consistent. Greater pitch variability has been linked to perceived speaker dynamism, potency, extraversion, and benevolence (Scherer, 1979a).

Talk Duration

Amount of talk in group contexts has correlated significantly with impressions of dominance, likability, extraversion, and emotional stability (Scherer, 1979a). Interactants with long floor-holdings have scored highly on dimensions of emotional stability, conscientiousness (Scherer, 1979a), and competence (Hayes & Meltzer, 1972). However, Stang (1973) indicated that medium-length turns elicited higher attractiveness ratings. Finally, Street (1982) reported that interviewees who maintained a consistent turn duration throughout the interview or who modified turn length concordantly with the interviewer were viewed as more socially attractive than interviewees adjusting turn durations opposite the interviewer's.

Miscellaneous Vocal Behaviors

Breathiness has been associated with youth and artistic personality for male voices but with femininity and prettiness for female voices. Increased throatiness made men appear stable but women oafish. Orotundity has been perceptually linked to vitality and aggressiveness, nasality to perceived neurosis and unattractiveness, and flatness to sluggishness and immaturity (Addington, 1968). Disfluent speech appears to diminish perceived competence but may not lessen perceived trustworthiness (Miller & Hewgill, 1964; Sereno & Hawkins, 1967).

Whereas the above speech variables focused on vocalic and dialect behavior, the following concern verbal and linguistic dimensions of talk.

Self-Disclosure

Of the content dimensions of talk, self-disclosure has been most widely researched. Initially, researchers assumed that revealing intimate information about oneself was healthy, fostering favorable impressions and relationship development (see, for example, Jourard & Friedman, 1970; Worthy, Gary, & Kahn, 1969). Self-disclosures by one participant were likely to elicit disclosures of equal intimacy by that participant's partner (Cozby, 1972; Davis, 1977; Derlega, Harris, & Chaikin, 1973). Interactants not reciprocating partners' intimacy level of disclosures have been liked less than those matching disclosure levels (Chaikin & Derlega, 1974).

Recent investigations have questioned the generality of these phenomena. The dynamics of self-disclosure processes appear to be influenced by a host of factors including norms, valence, topic, relationship among interactants, setting, and other language variables (Bradac, Hosman, & Tardy, 1978; Gilbert, 1976; Tardy, Hosman, & Bradac, 1981). Disclosing intimate information to strangers can be deemed inappropriate (Berger, Gardner, Clatterbuck, & Schulman, 1976) or may be viewed more acceptable if the information is positive rather than negative (Gilbert, 1976). For very intimate relationships, Gilbert (1976) proposed that positive revelations about self may not foster relational growth as well as negative information. Socially deviant information appears inappropriate regardless of the intimacy level (Chaikin & Derlega, 1974). Yet, communication about a physical disability can make participants more comfortable and handicapped persons more acceptable as partners (Thompson, 1982a). Rosenfeld (1979) indicated that disclosure deemed appropriate can increase love, liking, attraction, trust, and mental health.

Language intensity mediates responses to violations of the self-disclosure reciprocity norm. Bradac et al. (1978) reported that listeners favorably evaluated interactants who reciprocated highly intense and highly intimate messages from partners. However, interactants were liked more when responding to a low intensity-low intimacy message with a high intimate-low intense message rather than a reciprocal one. Apparently the former response constitutes a move toward relationship escalation.

Although not dealing with evaluative processes per se, Dindia (1982, 1983, 1985) has reported little support for the reciprocity norm among strangers during their initial interaction, though their perceived disclosure rates were correlated. Dindia (1982) did indicate that second and third interactions among strangers were characterized by related amounts of disclosure but not on a reciprocal, act-by-act basis. Dindia (1983, 1985) posited that generalizing about reciprocal patterns of disclosure are hindered by inconsistencies between observational and experimental findings, incongruities between perceived versus actual disclosure, the questionable validity of self-reports, and the assumption that positively related disclosure is reciprocal.

Language Intensity

As previously defined, language intensity refers to the degree to which language deviates from affective neutrality. "Love" is more intense than "like"; "utterly devastated" is more intense than "disappointed." In their review, Bradac et al. (1979) concluded the following: (1) Language intensity enhances attitude reinforcement of attitudinally congruent messages but hinders attitude change and perceived competence when message content is discrepant to receivers' attitudes; and (2) obscenity (a form of intensity) is inversely related to attitude change and perceived competence.

Miscellaneous Verbal Behaviors

Powerless speech includes hedges, intensifiers, polite forms, and hesitations, whereas powerful speech omits these. In courtroom settings, powerful testimony was perceived as more competent, trustworthy, dynamic, and convincing than powerless testimony (Lind & O'Barr, 1979). However, Bradac, Hemphill, and Tardy's (1981) study indicated that subjects attributed greater fault to defendants and plaintiffs using high-power styles. In Study 2, though, subjects exposed to both styles did not differ between the two regarding fault ascription.

Cantor (1979) noted that polite imperatives (for example, "Please contribute to our fund" were persuasive in soliciting funds relative to other grammatical forms. However, Bradley (1981) posited that impact of grammatical forms may vary as a function of speakers' sex. In mixed-sex groups, females who used arguments with more qualifying phrases (for example, tag questions and disclaimers) exerted less influence and were perceived not as intelligent and knowledgeable as women not using qualifiers. Evaluations of men did not tend to vary in accordance with the presence or absence of qualifiers. Bradley suggested certain linguistic devices by women may be more readily devalued due to the lower status of the female source.

Verbal immediacy has been positively related to perceptions of "open communication" (Montgomery, 1981), competence, and character (Bradac et al., 1979). In their review, Bradac et al. (1979) proposed that lexical diversity is positively related to competence, socioeconomic status, message effectiveness, and similarity. Also, the effects of lexical diversity appear to be greater when the source is ascribed high status.

Speech evaluation research has primarily manipulated speech behaviors singularly (for example, speech rate or self-disclosure). Speech behavior, of course, is not produced singularly but concomitantly. Several speech behaviors can influence evaluative processes in a complex interactive fashion.

Multiple Speech Behaviors and Perceived Speech

Scherer (1979b) reported that influence among American jurors was related to utterance number, number of repetitions and interruptions, loudness, number of silent pauses, and pitch range contours. Pearce and Brommel (1972) noted that speakers using a "conversational style" (that is, lower pitch, less volume, less use of pause, less pitch variety) were rated as more credible than those using a "dynamic" style. This finding is inconsistent with other studies that have reported denigration of lower pitch and loudness levels (Aronovitch, 1976; Scherer, 1979a). Apparently, consideration of these multiple speech behaviors in this public speaking context affected the gestalt view of the communicative event such that the evaluations were not in line with previous research on these behaviors individually.

Although speech convergence usually facilitates favorable impressions, Giles and Smith (1979) observed that an English speaker was most positively evaluated by a Canadian audience when he converged speech rate and message content, but maintained his normal accent than when he converged all three behaviors. In a fact-finding interview setting, Street (1982) studied observers' reactions to an interviewee variously accommodating speech rate, response latency, and turn duration toward the interviewer. Two speech patterns emerged most favorably: (1) when the interviewee converged response latency and maintained a faster speech rate and longer turn duration and (2) when the interviewee converged speech rate and held the floor for a duration comparable to the interviewer's floor-holding. Street interpreted these results as observers' approval of two speech strategies. The second established a more egalitarian speech format to the interviewer and the first maintained optimal sociolinguistic distance given the interviewee-interviewer role differences.

Most speech evaluation research manipulates *actual* message features. Such an assumption may be suspect. Street and Hopper's (1982) review indicated that factors such as racial prejudices (Williams et al., 1972), prototypes (Cantor & Mischel, 1979; Scherer, 1979a), sex role expectations (Haas, 1979; Lowery, Snyder, & Denney, 1976), status (Ball et al., 1982;

Thakerar & Giles, 1981; Thakerar et al., 1982), and listeners' goals or motivations (Bourhis, Giles, Leyens, & Tajfel, 1979; Larsen, Martin, & Giles, 1977) can result in interactants' perceiving interlocutors' message characteristics that are not actually in the speech or in exaggerating the existence of certain speech features. Bond and Feldstein (1982) reported that perceived speech rate is positively related to vocal frequency and intensity. The authors proposed that these relationships are a function of repeated experience of almost always hearing such covariations in naturally occurring speech.

PART II: FUTURE DIRECTIONS

1. A Critical Appraisal of Traditional Paradigms Research

Although the foregoing has obviously provided us with an essential and valuable foundation to the study of communicator characteristics in interpersonal communication, the novice to this area may well have been "disappointed" by our literature review, particularly with respect to Sections 1 and 2 in Part I. After all, it is axiomatic that characteristics of the communicator will affect the nature of messages produced. Yet, the net result of Part I has been a noticeable empirical absence of substantive and main effect findings for communicator characteristics. Few personality dimensions afford us with interesting communicator profiles, and those that do, such as self-monitoring, extraversion, and dominance, hardly sparkle with emancipating insights. Oftentimes predicted differences were not forthcoming, and, as we have seen, *apparently* contradictory results are not that uncommon. One of the problems seems to be that personality dimensions in themselves are not sufficient to account for the variance in communicator behaviors. Many of them interact with sociodemographic variables (for example, sex and age) as well as features of the context—anxiety being an archetypal case. In the light of the psychological literature on the person × situation (Argyle, Furnham, & Graham, 1981) and attitude/behavior (Ajzen & Fishbein, 1980) debates, perhaps this is all none too surprising. Indeed, where main effects have been documented, undoubtedly many of these would likewise dissipate if potent situational and sociodemographic variables were introduced into our experimental designs. Although Section 2, Part I provides us with more concrete profiles regarding the communicator correlates of sociodemographic characteristics, here again few substantive main effects emerged. For instance, sex of communicator is heavily influenced by the sex of receiver, socioeconomic status grossly affected by contextual factors, race/ethnicity by the particular subgroups one is investigating, and even age by level of cognitive development and sex.

Rather than extol the virtues of traditional research on communicator characteristics, we feel it incumbent upon us to assess critically our cumulative knowledge in a constructive manner that can outline some priorities for future research directions. Part of the problem has been of course that research in this domain has not been sufficiently programmatic or systematic.

Different investigators have measured different communicative dependent measures according to their own predilections and intuitions, with a heterogeneity of interaction goals and situations reigning supreme. Indeed, and in line with much work in the social psychology of language (Giles, 1983), research in Sections 1 and 2, Part I can be characterized as

(1) being overly concerned with student populations and *un*familiar others;
(2) affording negligible attention to how communicators themselves construe their identity and the dimensions of the situations they are in (too often communicators and communicatees are allocated objectively to membership of large-scale, social categories and social situations according to external criteria decided upon by investigators themselves);
(3) studying communicative dependent measures largely in isolation from each other; that is, we look at speech rate, you examine fundamental frequency;
(4) being largely *either* encoder- or decoder-biased;
(5) giving negligible attention to the influence of extrasituational social forces such as the perceiver relevance of the social network to the interaction and the nature of the social structure;
(6) proliferating "in-out" studies in which people are studied on one (usually exceptionally brief) static occasion in which the focus has been on relegating language behaviors to the status of passive, dependent variables of social processes; and
(7) having little recourse to the functions of language or to the nature of the strategies employed.

The clearest-cut findings emerge from Section 3, Part I. There is some consensus about the social meanings of verbal and vocal (as well as visual and nonverbal; see Cappella, in press) behaviors. Use of a standard accent, high lexical diversity, fast speech rate, immediacy, certainty phrases, moderate loudness and talkativeness, and few pauses afford communicators attributions of high competence and assertiveness. Yet here again, cultural context, nature of setting, stage of relationship, topic, type of listener, interactive goals, and so forth can all interact to produce quite different and sometimes what might appear to be superficially, "contradictory" evaluative patterns; self-disclosure is a prime case. Nevertheless, main effects for the social meanings of language behaviors have been abundant and found to have profound consequences in many applied (albeit simulated) settings (Kalin, 1982). At the same time, and despite recent theoretical advances in the language attitudes domain with respect to interethnic relations (Ryan, Giles, & Sebastian, 1982; Ryan, Hewstone, & Giles, 1984), studies in this genre have also not passed by uncriticized. Giles and Ryan (1982, p. 210) characterized deficiencies in this area to the extent that

> independent speech variables are concocted in a social, psychological and linguistic vacuum; listener-judges are featured almost as cognitive nonentities; aspects of context are socially and subjectively sterile; and dependent variables

are devised without recourse to their situational, functional and behavioral implications.

A number of plausible alternatives for the future might emerge on the basis of our discussion. The first might be to expend energy in the pursuit of systematic, programmatic research aimed at investigating communicative behaviors at multiple levels of analysis as advocated by Street and Cappella (1985) while controlling for so-called, "extraneous" interacting variables. In other words, we need to extend our methodologies and analytical procedures. Such an approach will inevitably lead to important amplifications of two generalizations that emerge from Part I of this chapter, namely:

GENERALIZATION I: Communicative behavior can be a function of the personality, sociodemographic, and physical characteristics of the interactants involved.

GENERALIZATION II: Trait attributions afforded communicators can be a function of their vocal characteristics.

A second alternative might be, and ironically so in the context of *this* Handbook chapter, to *abandon* henceforth any exclusive attention to studying the effects of communicator characteristics on message variables and to invest our efforts more eclectically at focusing upon the vast array of interactions between communicator variables, context, and communicatee attributes. A third possibility is an extended amalgamation of these approaches. We would wish to *complement* research attention of the "old" paradigm type (Sections 1 and 2, Part I) of manipulating objective communicator states or social category memberships by seeking out the more subjective *cognitive characteristics* of our communicators and to do so on the basis of a solid conceptual formulation. Needless to say, we would not wish to undermine the value of so-called old paradigm studies. However, the aim of the rest of this chapter is to argue for a *complementary* framework of cognitive characteristics of communicators that can guide our future work in a manner that not only extends the types of variables examined in Sections 1 and 2 of Part I, but also *integrates* language attitudes research of Section 3 as well.

2. Influential Frameworks

The development of our own thinking has been influenced heavily by two recent perspectives, namely, Patterson's (1982a, 1982b, 1983) sequential model of nonverbal exchange and social psychological research into impression management (Arkin, 1981; Tedeschi, 1981; Tedeschi & Norman, in press; Weary & Arkin, 1981), the nature of both of which can of course only be sketchily drawn in this context. As will become evident later, these ideas underscore the guiding principles (or generalizations) of our own approach. Let us overview briefly Patterson's model first.

Patterson's Model and a Critique

Although Patterson's behavioral focus is on involvement, the author does make claims as to its utility for interactive behavior in general. Moreover, it is arguably one of, if not *the* most comprehensive conceptual formulations in interpersonal communication to date. Among its attractive features, and ones that counter some of the deficiencies in the area outlined above, are that it attends explicitly to interactional functions, the sequential nature of cognitive processes, and addresses (as do Cappella & Greene, 1982) the potential role of arousal, as well as highlights the salience of the other's behavior and subsequent behavioral adjustments to it. In overview, and largely in Patterson's own words, the model can be described as follows.

The sequential functional model assumes that each person brings to an interaction a specific set of personal characteristics (and these are articulated largely in such terms as personality traits and membership of large-scale social categories), past experiences, and relational-situational constraints. With respect to the last component, Patterson focuses mainly on an ecological psychological analysis of objective features of a situation, molding the behaviors appropriate to a given relationship. This group of so-called, "antecedent" factors exercises its influence covertly at the "preinteractional stage" by determining behavioral dispositions with which communicators are comfortable, precipitating a potential arousal change, and developing cognitive and affective expectancies. The joint effect of these three mediators shapes the perception of the interaction's function and limits the range of involvement behaviors displayed. The combined influence of each person's preferred involvement level and five functional cognitions (namely, information exchange, regulation, intimacy, social control, and service-task) in turn shapes expectancies about the other person's level of involvement. A stable exchange is defined as one in which the discrepancy between the expected and the actual involvement of the other person is minimal. When that discrepancy is large, instability results inducing cognitive-affective assessments of it. This can lead to either adjustments in nonverbal involvement (see Cappella & Greene, 1982), a reassessment of the interaction's function, or perhaps a combination of both. Successful involvement adjustments and a more complementary functional reassessment (relative to the other person's functional assessment) should facilitate a more stable exchange.

We see a number of problems with adopting Patterson's extremely useful and insightful model wholesale for our own communicator characteristics framework. Some of our concerns are perhaps minor; others more telling. First, the model is overly ambitious in assigning mechanisms for the *termination* of an interaction. Although instabilities of the type espoused by Patterson in terms of differential perceived functions and involvement levels could conceivably facilitate swifter termination, on many occasions interaction rules (see Higgins, 1980) are so potent as to temper these effects, and in any case other factors such as misattributions of intent, differential knowledge, threat to identity, interpersonal justice, and so forth might assume more importance (Blakar, in press; Dubé-Simard, 1983). A separate model for the determinants of communication termination in intergroup and interpersonal encounters is really required here.

Second, there is some lack of conceptual clarity in the model. For instance, the distinctions between antecedents, preinteractional, and interactional phases are difficult to conceptualize differentially, let alone operationalize. One wonders why the situational-relational component is an antecedent, whereas the functional component appears to have some autonomous influence much later sequentially in the so-called, interactional phase. Function is accorded an extremely important explanatory role in this model that may well be unwarranted. In any case, *how* the functional analysis defines level of involvement enacted is left rather vague. The role of "expectancies" is also rather confusing; sometimes it is articulated as being activated at the antecedent phase of relational-situational variables, other times in the preinteractional phase of cognitive assessment, and then also at the interactional phase itself. Finally, the "cognitive-affective" component appears as an unconvincing potpourri of "any kind of evaluative response. . . to more complex patterns of cognition" (Patterson, 1983, p. 24). In other words, here sit smoldering, preferences, automatic scripts, and complex decision-making mechanisms.

Third, the antecedent factors appear too *simplistic* and *asocial* for our tastes. As mentioned previously, personal factors are defined almost exclusively in objective terms. The important role of the communicator's subjective definition of personal and social identity is afforded no central role here. Work along the traditional lines of Tajfel (Tajfel, 1982; Turner & Giles, 1981) has pointed to the fact that defining an interaction, albeit a dyadic encounter, can have a profound effect on encoding *and* decoding communicative behaviors as can one's cognitive representations of sociostructural forces (Bourhis & Giles, 1977; Johnson, Giles, & Bourhis, 1983). Similarly, and in the light of, the burgeoning of interest in construals of the situation by Forgas (1981), Wish (1978), and Cody and McLaughlin (1980), on the one hand, and work on the development and dissolution of relationships by Duck (1982), Berger and Bradac (1982), Fitzpatrick (1984), and Gottman (1982), to name a few on the other, suggests not only a simplistic, underworked "relational-situational component" but that there is much heavy-duty cognitive processing of situations and relationships operating *potentially* in different interactions. Thus how individuals define a situation in terms of Wish's dimensions, construe its specific goals (Argyle et al., 1981), perceive its macrosituational norms in terms of modesty, fairness, competitiveness, and so forth (Weary & Arkin, 1981), and define the components of the specific norms (McKirnan & Hamayan, 1980) and communication rules operating influence the nature of message output. Also, how individuals define their relationships in terms of uncertainty levels (Berger & Bradac, 1982) and their perceived rules and norms, ideologize their relationships (Fitzpatrick, 1984), and cognize the importance of others present or even absent in the network (Milardo, 1982) have other important influences. As an illustrative example of the importance of just a few of the foregoing, Giles and Hewstone (1982, p. 198) proposed that

> objectively describing a social situation *as* a formal interview on a serious topic with a 90-year-old Black woman may have little predictive value concerning her likely speech patterns if she herself defines the interview informally, considers the subject matter irrelevant and trivial and feels "White" and 50 years of age.

Fourth, and relatedly, Patterson's model focuses upon *sequential* processing among the model's components, although no such evidence exists clearly for it, let alone the precise nature of it. At the present time, we would prefer to consider the possibility of *parallel* processing of many of the cognitive elements until such a time as convincing arguments and data afford us reasonable levels of certainty as to how it operates (cf Bock, 1982; Johnson-Laird, 1983). Interestingly, however, Patterson (1983) does afford some credence to the notion of *multiple* functions being involved in an interaction at any one time, although no schematic status is afforded it in his model. Fifth, in Patterson's model and in others, there are presumed isomorphisms between actual own and actual other's message variables on the one hand and one's perceptions of these on the other (see Weary & Arkin, 1981). Street and Hopper (1982) reviewed the literature showing that one's identities, goals, and aspirations can dictate one's perceptions, evaluations of, and attributions about a message that can in no way correspond to the *actual* objective qualities of the message produced in some situations. This, together with the lack of explicit attention to actual versus perceived arousal, is a distinction that needs to be drawn theoretically in any further robust formulation; this is a cognitive issue much akin to the brunt of our argument in our third bone of contention above. Sixth, and finally, there is little social motivational force guiding individuals A and B in Patterson's model; one has the impression of the individual as a cognitive-physiological automaton. Although Patterson does have recourse to highlighting the importance of impression management and self-presentation in the context of his "social control" function, no attention is afforded the important work of James Tedeschi, Robert Arkin, and others (see below), which we believe to be fundamental in pointing to crucial social needs of interactants and the verbal strategies they use in this regard. As their analyses help provide a succinct motivational basis for our own approach, it is to this area of inquiry we now turn. At the same time, it is not our intent to belittle Patterson's *important* work and contribution to this area. It is possible that a number of the foregoing issues, with flexibility, could be implicated in the model as it stands or at least in a revision of it. As will be seen, we owe much to Patterson's initiative and advances. Our own contribution to communicator characteristics is proferred later as a modest elaboration of some of the variables, mechanisms, and processes perhaps underdeveloped in the context of a broader view of communicational features beyond involvement behaviors.

The Social Psychology of Impression Management

Tedeschi and Reiss (1981a) rightly point to the fact that current research in impression management obviously had its impetus from outside social psychology, including the dramaturgical perspective of Goffman (1959). They claim that it is likely to be a zeitgeist of the 1980s in social psychology owing to its avowed explanatory potential for dealing with a wide range of social psychological phenomena (Baumeister, 1982; Tedeschi, 1981). As social psychologists of language, we are excited by this prospect. Not only does it sidestep some of the dangers inherent in much, although obviously not in all (Higgins & McCann, 1984), current social cognition, but it also resurrects the study of verbal activity as a valued resource of social behavior to its rightful status as a core interest of social psychologists (Farr, 1980). Furthermore, Baumeister (1982) points to humans not only needing to cognitively process informational input, but also to their needing to *communicate* with their social environment in order to organize, simplify, and control it.

As Tedeschi and Norman (in press) state:

> People have few goals which do not require the aid or mediation of others. . . . If people want love, respect, status or esteem, they must do something to get others to react to them in these ways. . . . Since these others are not simply waiting to provide what we want, it is necessary to assert ourselves and try to be effective in influencing others to do what we need them to do, so we can have what we want. If actors have those characteristics, attributes, or identities that facilitate various forms of influence, they should experience greater success and obtain more rewards than people who do not possess them.

In this vein, Tedeschi and his colleagues, since the early 1970s (Tedeschi, 1972, 1974), have characterized individuals as possessing a primary motive of wishing to proliferate their sphere of social influence and power. Tedeschi and Reiss (1981a) argue that it is little wonder people try to achieve the power resource of inducing others to like them as this increases the probabilities that the target will (1) trust them more; (2) accept and believe more readily their accounts, communications, and claims; (3) harm them less; and (4) reward them more.

In a recent chapter, Tedeschi and Norman (in press) speculate on the relationship between self-esteem and social influence. The idea here is, as elsewhere, that individuals possess more self-esteem the more they believe their real self corresponds to their *ideal* self. The latter is envisaged as that cognitive construction that has been provided us by those whom we value positively and model as being socially influential. Many of our self-presentations are, therefore, aimed at instilling in others feelings and attributions that accept us as being akin to our own particular, ideal identities. From social comparison (Festinger, 1954) and symbolic interactionist (Mead, 1934) traditions, it is argued that much of our self-perception is molded by our views of how others construe us. It follows, therefore, as Weary and Arkin's (1981) model of attributional self-presentation highlights, that we monitor very carefully our own impression management behaviors and significant others' reactions to them not infrequently. (This is not, however, to suggest that such self-presentations are always, or even usually, deliberate and at the level of conscious awareness; oftentimes, they could be conceived in terms of scripts; see Abelson, 1981; Patterson, 1983.) In this vein, then, increases in self-esteem are barometers of how much social influence we are enjoying. The more discrepancy that is perceived to exist between our real and ideal selves, the more negative self-esteem we feel, and by implication, the less social influence we feel we can espouse. Situations, or predicaments that provide us with so-called "spoiled identities," require us to initiate "defensive" impression management behaviors so as to "save face" (Goffman, 1959), eliminate our loss of self-esteem, and restore our own sphere of social influence (Schlenker, 1980). Arkin (1981) introduces a particular form of this mechanism in terms of "protective" self-presentation. This author argues that such behaviors are enacted when the individual construes a high subjective probability of a particular assertive presentation *failing*. This is likely, particularly when (1) the other is capricious or ambiguous in terms of beliefs, qualifications, and so forth (cf Berger & Bradac, 1982); (2) significant others are likely suddenly to present themselves; (3) the relationship is likely to be a lasting one, socially, occupationally, and so forth; and (4) the speaker may not be able to enact or monitor influence behaviors effectively. In such situations, individuals might manifest protective presentations by adopting an innocuous or attentive communication style (Norton, 1983) aimed at avoiding social disapproval until such a time as cognitive uncertainty about the other(s) and the situation are decreased or the opportunity for adopting appropriate assertive presentational behaviors occurs.

Recently, Tedeschi and associates (Tedeschi & Melburg, in press) proffered a distinction between assertive and defensive tactical and strategic self-presentations. Assertive tactics (e.g., ingratiation, self-promotion, enhancements) are undertaken from moment-to-moment in order to achieve short-term goals of asserting one's social power given expediencies of the immediate situation. Assertive strategies, on the other hand, are those longer-term, transsituational presentations (e.g., credibility, status, esteem) that are aimed at fostering a reputation for oneself as close to the ideal self as possible. Baumeister (1982) terms these "self-constructive" presentations. After all, it is rare that individuals will accrue enduring reputational benefit from single, isolated tactics. If, however, a person has had a history of needing perpetually to activate defensive *tactics* (e.g., accounts, disclaimers, restitution, prosocial behavior), it is possible that such adaptive presentations will habituate into a defensive *strategy* (e.g., phobias, learned helplessness, drug abuse). As Tedeschi and Norman (in press) claim, these "behaviors tend to lock the person into a life style characterized by defensive, avoidance and escape reactions at the expense of assertive, approach, and acquisitive patterns of behavior." In this light, self-presentation theorists have begun to explore the ramifications of their analysis for understanding individual differences in personality (Arkin, 1981; Tedeschi & Norman, in press; Weary & Arkin, 1981). Although these ideas are as yet admittedly embryonic, it does not seem unreasonable to conceive of self-monitoring, needs for approval and affiliation, extraversion, Machiavellianism, internal locus of control, and exhibitionism as specific strategies of assertive impression management, whereas those of reticence/apprehensiveness/social anxiety, submission, introversion, and external locus of control could be more defensive strategies. Such an approach, in and of itself, might imply a radical reappraisal of research orientations of the type depicted in Section 1, Part I of this chapter in terms of performance styles.

Research recently has been concerned with documenting and providing a taxonomy of the different forms of self-presentation that exist. Unfortunately, space precludes any actual description of these tactics and strategies (see, for example, Kolditz & Arkin, 1982; Jones & Wortman, 1973; Schlenker, 1980; Tedeschi & Reiss, 1981b), yet suffice to say that a mere superficial perusal of them suggests that the majority are manifest behaviorally by nonverbal, vocal, and linguistic means. Although self-presentation theorists have not yet had recourse to the relevant literatures in communication science, the social psychology of language, or sociolinguistics, it is obvious that a symbiotic relationship would prove theoretically important. For instance, tactics of speech convergence (Street & Giles, 1982) and compensatory warmth (Ickes, Patterson, Rajecki, & Tanford, 1982) can be understood as tactics of assertive self-presentation; accent and speech rate divergence might be profitably considered a defensive tactic; and the oft-quoted case of the "nonverbal" lower-class, ethnic minority child (Edwards, 1979a, 1979b) might on some occasions be construed as a protective, self-presentational tactic (Kochman, 1982). Currently, Cappella (1984) is investigating the role of communicator style as a mediator of interpersonal attraction with a view to determining whether a meshing of interpersonal styles (be it similarity or complementarity) is as good, if not better, an indicator of mutual liking than the ubiquitous, belief congruity construct (see also, Norton, 1983). If such a perspective is shown to have merit, it may well be that the other's actual and/or perceived style has such potency in different situations owing to its value in facilitating the actor's own self-constructive presentational tactics and hence social power. Furthermore, strategies of assertive impression management, be they in terms of reputational trustworthiness, attractiveness, or status, are all manifest importantly by nonverbal, vocal, and verbal behaviors and styles (see Section 3, Part I).

3. Cognitive Communicator Characteristics:
Generalizations and a Model

Having overviewed Patterson's model, highlighted some problems with it for developing our own communicator characteristics approach, and outlined self-presentation theory, let us now build on these foundations. The guiding principles forming the core of our complementary framework for future research into communicator characteristics are enumerated below. Although we have not highlighted all aspects of the approach, such as the roles of behavioral repertoire, measured arousal, scripts, and so forth, we feel the following encapsulates the essense of our position:

> GENERALIZATION III: Communicative behavior can be a function of the self-presentational tactics or strategies employed by interactants in asserting or defending their spheres of social influence.

> GENERALIZATION IV: Language attitudes can function as important mediators in shaping such self-presentations.

> GENERALIZATION V: Communicative behavior can be a function of inter-actants' changing cognitive representations of their (1) identities, (2) situational and relationship definitions and goals, and (3) levels of arousal.

> GENERALIZATION VI: Communicative behavior can be a function of (1) monitored own and partner's perceived behaviors, and (2) the evaluations and attributions accorded these.

With due regard to the valued law of parsimony in scientific inquiry, we could have concluded this chapter by means of an elaboration of these guiding principles. Instead, we have opted to formulate our discussion in terms of a highly speculative model that, although it can not be derived from current empirical research, attempts to generate some specific relationships between elements inherent in the generalizations. For some tastes, un-doubtedly the scheme will appear overly complex. Nevertheless, it is our belief that current models of interpersonal communication only scratch the surface of the cognitive variables, mechanisms, and processes involved. Although we are fully aware of the dangers inherent in proliferating models ad infinitum, we do see the necessity for a new, more complex heuristic to emerge of the type we are to espouse. Accordingly, the following has the aim of alleviating limitations in the sequential model of nonverbal exchange by highlighting the wealth of cognitive characteristics potentially available to communicators in such a way that is informed by self-presentation theory. Let us therefore briefly weave the gist of our Generalizations III to VI within the context of our model schematized as in Figure 5.1 below.

"Personal factors" in Figure 5.1 refer to those objective features of oneself and one's socialization, such as physical states and sociodemographic characteristics (for example, age, sex, SES, ethnicity) that affect "experiential knowledge" (memory) on the one hand and "behavioral repertoire" possi-bilities on the other. Our experiential knowledge component contains at least four important, interrelated elements: (1) the cultural content of appropriate

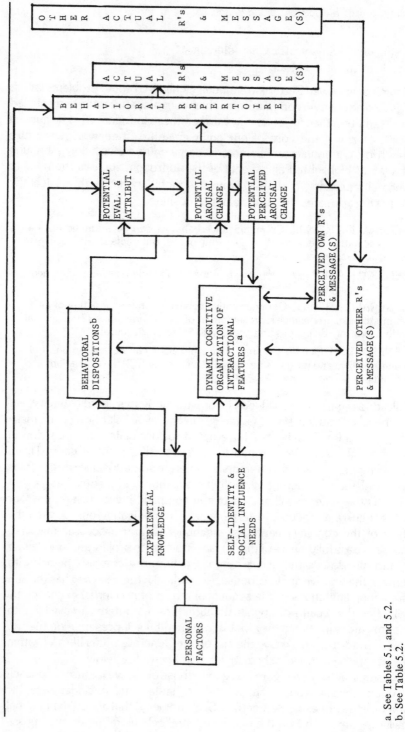

Figure 5.1 A Cognitive Communicator Characteristics Model

a. See Tables 5.1 and 5.2.
b. See Table 5.2.

behaviors suited to specific social contexts; (2) the content of our social stereotypes for various social groupings considered hierarchically in terms of superordinate categories (for example, the elderly) and basic categories (for example, senior citizen, grandmother) and their prototypes (Brewer, Dull, & Lui, 1981); (3) the content of our linguistic and communicative expectancies (Burgoon & Miller, in press; Kramer, 1977) of these social categories (this component allies well with Section 3, Part I of this chapter on language attitudes, albeit more or less detailed in specific ways depending upon our personal factors and self-concept); and (4) our knowledge about our own communicative capabilities and social skills, that is, our *subjective* behavior repertoire. This font of experiential knowledge, like the aforementioned behavioral repertoire, can be selected from according to our own functional needs (Tajfel, 1981) and mediates our self-presentational tactics and behavioral dispositions. This socially dynamic, experiential knowledge constantly shapes our real and ideal self-concepts that form the motivational driving force behind our needs for social power and influence (à la the self-presentationists). In Figure 5.1, the latter constitute our "self-identity and social influence needs" component.

Self-identity/needs and experiential knowledge influence our ongoing "cognitive organization of interactional features" (see Fig. 5.1). Table 5.1 presents an array of the cognitive representations that can be activated potentially in ongoing situations. We believe that Items 3 and 4 in Table 5.1 are activated perpetually at least at a minimal level. As with Lugarski's Law of Cybernetic Entomology, which claims there is always yet one more bug to discover (cf Boster, Stiff, & Reynolds, 1983), the list is historically representative, but not exhaustive. We also do not consider these cognitive representations to be mutually exclusive; many are interdependent. For instance, activation of Item 2 (Table 5.1) is likely to coactivate Item 6, or vice-versa; 9 is likely to coactivate 10, 12, 14, 22, and so forth. Indeed, it is just possible to provide a speculative, implicational analysis of such cognitive representational interdependences, although future empirical research along these lines would likely prove this exercise presently less than worthwhile. It should be noted that this scheme, unlike Patterson's model, affords no autonomous status to interactional function(s). The perspective at this stage of model-building is on the *parallel* processing of those cognitive presentations in Table 5.1 and relies upon the multilevel simultaneous capacity of the human mind (Bock, 1982; Johnson-Laird, 1983).

For the moment, let us take the very simplest of cases in which very little is activated in Table 5.1, just Item 4, a self-constructive, presentational goal. The actual content of this habitual goal—for example, to appear friendly and sociable—is not likely to induce arousal or evaluative changes in its own right (see latter components in Figure 5.1). The "behavioral disposition" in this case, perhaps a self-presentation strategy of an open and dramatic style (see Norton, 1983), also itself is not likely to cause arousal or affective changes

TABLE 5.1

Communicator Characteristics in Terms of Cognitive Representations

1. Personal Identity (Suls, 1982)
2. Social Identity (Giles & Johnson, 1981)
3. Self-Presentational Immediate Goals (Arkin, 1981)
4. Self-Constructive Presentational Goals (Baumeister, 1982)
5. Social Network (Milardo, 1982)
6. Sociostructural Forces (Johnson et al., 1983)
7. Prior Experiences
8. Temporal Constraints
9. Situational Construals (Forgas, 1983)
10. Situational Norms of Language (McKirnan & Hamayan, 1980)
11. Social Norms (Weary & Arkin, 1981)
12. Rules of Communication (Higgins, 1980)
13. Relational Identity (Fitzpatrick, 1984)
14. Relationship Rules/Norms (Rand & Levinger, 1979)
15. Relationship Construals (Forgas & Dubosz, 1980)
16. Relationship/Other Knowledge (Berger & Bradac, 1982)
17. Expectations about Other(s) (Caporael et al., 1983)
18. Anticipations of Other's Expectations about Self (Burgoon & Miller, in press)
19. Topic Construals (Maynard, 1980)
20. Information Exchange Function (Brown, 1977)
21. Interactional Regulation Function (Street et al., 1983)
22. Intimacy Function (Duck, 1982)
23. Service-Task Function (Abelson, 1981)
24. Control Function (Miller, 1983)
25. Mode (Rimé, 1983)
26. Cognitive Planning/Behavioral Rehearsal (Burgoon, 1983)
27. Role Requirements (Brown & Levinson, 1979)

(see Figure 5.1). It will simply be selected scriptually from the behavioral repertoire as it very often has been. In this instance, perceptions of one's own communication, the perception of the other's reactions to it, as well as perceptions of the other's message subsequently are probably going to be monitored by the communicator at a minimal level of awareness. This assumes, of course, that the self-presentation appears effective and the partner does not produce counterstereotypical or unexpected communicative patterns. We have thus moved through the model in Figure 5.1 rather swiftly when few cognitive representations of identity, situation, interactional goals, and the relationship are activated.

Probably the more general case is that in which a number of, and even many, cognitive representations assume subjective salience. Obviously, there is some processing limit to the number and type of cognitive representations possible at any given time (Norman, 1981). Future research might well be able to discover the manner in which different individuals and groups perhaps cognitively factor analyze the items in Table 5.1 into coherent, manageable proportions. Indeed, current models of speech perception and word processing may guide our research in this direction (for example, Morton, 1969; Repp, 1977). Our own preference (after Palmer, 1984) would be in exploring the valuable ideas of Oden and Massaro's

(1978) fuzzy logical model of sound perception for the identification of situational and identity patterns. This perspective could be extended to allow for communicators scanning and extracting features from the situation, self, and behavior of others, which are combined in a composite abstract pattern and then matched to prototypes stored in memory (our "experiential knowledge" component). In any case, the more cognitively complex and field independent the speaker, the more likely more cognitive representations and their resultant identification patterns will assume salience, and perhaps the more they will change from moment-to-moment as one's own output and one's partner's input are perceived and evaluated. Obviously, the specific contents of each of these representations are crucial. Separate illustrations of such cognitive representational contents are provided in a compact manner in the left-hand column of Table 5.2. Needless to say, the actual nature of these cognitive representational contents in any instance will be mediated by self-identity/needs and experiential knowledge. Cognitive contents can of course vary in their idealized specificity. For instance, sometimes we are not that certain about the precise norms of the situation we are in or the strength of the "grapevine" operating between our friends and acquaintances. Interestingly, on some occasions, the cognitive contents may be more a function of the influential people who are actually *not* there, but who will subsequently hear details about the encounter that will determine communicators' message output, than those who are physically present at the time. Given that cognitive representational contents influence our behavioral dispositions (see Figure 5.1), the less ambiguous they are, the stronger the tendency will be.

As the model suggests, the actual resultant behavioral dispositions are mediated by experiential knowledge, and this occurs on two important counts. First, our experiential knowledge—and particularly the language attitudes element of that—will shape the appropriate behavioral disposition. Based on findings from the sociolinguistics and communication literatures, the right-hand column of Table 5.2 provides examples of potential behavioral dispositions arising from the corresponding contents on the left-hand side of that table. For instance, in the case of Item 18, such a content will dictate the nature of the refinements and the metaphoric usage employed. In the case of Item 17 (Table 5.2), the contents define the communicative behaviors that correspond best to our stereotype of the elderly or some basic subcategory of it. Most certainly our experiential knowledge elements will define the nature of the ingratiation tactics employed as well as perhaps their sequential occurrence in Item 3 (Table 5.2). Second, however, experiential knowledge will render the behavioral dispositions more or less realistic for the actor. For instance, a presumed inability (be it correct or false, objectively) to tell jokes would eliminate such a behavioral disposition arising in the case of the cognitive representation Content 5. In other words, having the social knowledge and will is one thing; believing you have the necessary communicative

TABLE 5.2

Illustrative Contents of Cognitive Representations Having High Subjective Salience
and Their Exemplified Potential Behavioral Dispositions

Cognitive Representations	Contents	Behavioral Dispositions
1.	Self-focus	Self-referencing
2.	Ethnic and class identifications	(Downward) accent divergence
3.	Gain other's liking	Ingratiation, enhancements, blasting
4.	Appear friendly, intriguing, having sense of humor	Open, dramatic style, self-disclosures, jokes
5.	Partner likely to divulge to significant others	Avoid negative self-disclosures, jokes
6.	Highly inequitous institutional support for ingroup	Downward accent convergence
7.	Bad news	No pitch variety, slow rate
8.	Brief, once-only encounter, opportunity	Concise, precise language
9.	Cooperative, relaxed, equal	Informal, verbal style
10.	Wide range of informality felt appropriate	Use of slang, colloquialisms, obscenities
11.	Altruism	Attentive, other-focused, negotiative
12.	Take the role of the other	Speech rate and content convergences
13.	"Separate" ideology	Interpersonal distance, avoid conflict
14.	Affective interdependence	Agree, ingroup terms, looking
15.	Sexuality	Touching, taken-for-granteds
16.	Very uncertain about state relationship is in	Interrogation, knowledge-gaining tactics
17.	Aged, cold	Accommodate to aged stereotype, compensatory warmth
18.	Very British	Refined, metaphoric usage
19.	Important, expertise available	Talkative, assertive style, certainty phrases
20.	Providing instructions	Nominal style, gesture
21.	Maintain floor as long as possible	Few pauses, counter interruptions
22.	Become more friendly with	Involvement behaviors
23.	Delivering a colloquium	Technical language, nominal style
24.	Persuade person to donate money	Altruistic compliance-gaining strategy
25.	Unfamiliarity with television conferencing	Attentive to facial expressions, self-monitor
26.	Practiced one's testimony	Fluent, discourse sequenced
27.	Good interviewee	Deferent, polite

skills is another. The resultant dispositions will manifest only those behaviors considered feasible by self.

Both the cognitive representational contents *and* the ultimate behavioral dispositions are subject to *potential* evaluative and arousal analyses as depicted in Figure 5.1. For instance, activation of Contents 8, 17, 21, and 23 (see Table 5.2 again) *and or* dissatisfaction with one's behavioral dispositions (as in the case in which there is a perceived discrepancy between what is situationally appropriate and what is actually possible) could well lead to a *potential* negative affective state. This could induce increased arousal, which may or may not be perceived as such by the sender. If such an arousal change is perceived in this particular case, it could cause cognitive representational reactivation affecting self, other, and situational attributional processes, and perhaps accentuate the aforementioned negative feelings. Alternatively, other routings could take place (see Figure 5.1). The cognitive representational contents and behavioral dispositions could lead *directly* to arousal changes. These again may or may not (as in the case of a jogger who is still physiologically aroused unbeknown to himself or herself some time after apparent recovery) be perceived by the sender. If they are inwardly detected, they could (in line with Patterson's [1976] arousal-labeling model) stimulate cognitive representational reactivity and/or affective-attributional processing. Herein, potential negative feelings might then accompany this increased and felt arousal. In sum, then, whether or not the actual behavioral dispositions are isomorphic with actual message outcomes selected from the behavioral repertoire depends on evaluative/arousal processing, itself potentially mediated by cognitive representational reactivation (see Figure 5.1).

We are now in a position to propose some initial, and admittedly highly speculative, hypotheses about the nature of the sender's message outcome and its implications for self- and other-monitoring:

> HYPOTHESIS 1: Behavioral dispositions will be selected from the behavioral repertoire when (1) no or only moderate arousal change occurs, and the arousal is *not* perceived by the individual, and (2) moderate to high arousal is perceived and labeled positively (for example, happiness, pride).
>
> HYPOTHESIS 2: Behavioral dispositions will not be manifest in performance when (1) arousal change is not perceived by the sender, but is actually high, and (2) moderate to high arousal is perceived and labeled negatively (for example, anger, irritation, threat).

The performances subsequent to Hypothesis 2 above would be characterized by disruptions such as disfluencies, ill-conceived taken-for-granteds, redundancies, and overabstractions, among others. The extent of these disruptions would be a direct function of negative affect and/or arousal. In addition, we would propose that those high in social self-esteem would select self-*protective* presentational tactics from their behavioral repertoires until negative affect and or arousal had dissipated, whereas those low in social self-esteem would select self-defensive *strategic* scripts.

Following Weary and Arkin's (1981) attributional self-presentational model, we would propose that monitoring of own message, and others' feedback cues to it, is an important process in our model. Self-and situational-monitoring are crucial to guiding our self-identity needs for gaining and effecting social influence. However, following Street and Hopper's (1982) model of speech style evaluation, we would also wish to make a distinction (often not explicit in many other models) concerning actual versus *perceived* message outcomes from self and partner(s). After all, our self-identity and cognitive representational activity will influence, oftentimes dramatically, what we *think* we and others are doing as schematized in Figure 5.1. We propose further tentative hypotheses based mostly on *potential* attributional outcomes (cf Langer & Newman, 1979) of felt arousal:

> HYPOTHESIS 3: If no arousal is felt, then self- and other-monitoring will both be moderately high.
>
> HYPOTHESIS 4: Monitoring of *own* message will be especially high when felt arousal (positive or negative) is attributed to *own* dispositions and attributes. Under these conditions, blame for poor self-presentation can be laid at the door of the sender.
>
> HYPOTHESIS 5: Monitoring of *other's* reactions to own messages will be especially high when felt arousal (again positive or negative) is attributed to sources *external* to self (that is, formal situation, novel task, unexpected behaviors from other). Under these circumstances (see Roloff & Berger, 1982), the most important cues guiding social influence attempts are considered somewhat outside the self's control.

Obviously, perceived negative or ambiguous cues from either self or the other will reactivate perhaps different cognitive representational contents beyond but including those of interactional function mentioned by Patterson (for example, change in situational definition, perceived norms, relationship, identity of the other). This may cause a potential modification of behavioral dispositions (see Figure 5.1). These communicative tendencies are then potentially subject to evaluative-arousal analyses, which accordingly may determine the actual adjustments made. Positively perceived self-presentations and other's reactions to them are likely to bolster self-esteem (Weary & Arkin, 1981). Indeed, this is likely to influence the nature of further self-presentational tactics and especially self-constructive strategies. The perception of negative outcomes, on the other hand, has the potential for decreasing self-esteem and inculcating self-protective or defensive tactics. Following the work of Higgins and colleagues (see Higgins & McCann, 1984), the manner in which one accommodates a message according to the characteristics of the audience has a crucial impact on the ways in which the actual events and information one is transmitting to another are stored in memory or experiential knowledge; "saying is believing." All the previous feedback loops are depicted in Figure 5.1.

Naturally enough, the other's subsequent and reactive *message* (rather than listener cues) is a substantive component of this and other models (see Cappella & Greene, 1982; Patterson, 1982b). However, an important component lacking in many theoretical systems is the fact that individuals monitor not only their own *listening* reactions to others' messages, but the others' perceptions of those very same decoding reactions. In other words, self-presentation is affected potentially just as much by listening behaviors as by speaking. In any case, the self's perception of the other's message (again mediated by cognitive representational forces) acts as an *independent* variable (rather than the typical dependent status afforded it in studies), partly defining social reality for the self (Giles & Hewstone, 1982). For instance, a high status other's message may well provide us with the cognitive representational material we have been awaiting as lower-status persons ourselves in order to increase content specificity and guide our behavior effectively (cf Berger & Bradac, 1982). Also, and in line with discrepancy-arousal theory (Cappella & Greene, 1982), *un*expected involvement and perceived radicalism, modernism, and competence from an elderly other (see Item 17, Table 5.2) could lead directly to arousal, negative affect, and compensatory performance. However, it is our contention that other potential cognitive representational contents, coactivated together with their own behavioral dispositions and attending evaluative-attributional analyses, let alone self-identity, can be important mediating mechanisms determining the actual subsequent responses and messages from the self.

In a recent model of language attitudes in intergroup settings, Ryan et al. (1984) discussed the ways in which perceived sociohistorical relationships between groups affect perceptions of each other's language behaviors. Indeed, the precise nature of these cognitive representations is argued as influencing the nature of the evaluative traits brought into affective salience. Hence, it is likely that the evaluative component of our model is a bubbling reservoir of affective criteria brought to life (and perhaps having feedback potential) according to the dictates of cognitive representational contents. Such a perspective offers much hope for understanding the tremendous heterogeneity that underlies different language attitudes toward similar stimulus material depending on context, historical time, and subgroup involved (Ryan & Giles, 1982).

Finally, our model, like Patterson's, is a self-perpetuating one with cognitive representations being activated, eliminated, and reactivated in different combinations much like a departure board at a busy international airport with its flashing lights and destination signs. Although the aforementioned components and processes have their input in determining the termination of an encounter, we believe a further theoretical system is necessary as a heuristic to do justice to the many variables involved (Blakar, in press).

PART III: CONCLUSIONS

We have, then, a dynamic model that has some important advantages over its forefathers. Indeed, as we have seen, it has some modest predictive value and potential. It is truly cognitive in its effort after reflecting the enormous capacity we, as humans, have for processing, evaluating, and attributing cognitive representations. Perhaps its strongest feature, however, is its *social* character. This can be gleaned from the model's allusion to relational knowledge and the social network implications of the actual interaction in the context of the macrostructure, by focusing upon perceived output and input from a speaker-hearer perspective (cf McGregor, 1983) and by highlighting social influence needs allied to self-identity. Another important strength is its heuristic potential for being able to integrate conceptually (in ways space precluded) important features of other models such as communication-game (Higgins, 1980), cognitive-motor (Rimé, 1984), arousal-labeling and nonverbal functional exchange (Patterson, 1976, 1983), cognitive uncertainty (Berger & Bradac, 1982), arousal-discrepancy (Cappella & Greene, 1982), and language attitude (Ryan et al., 1984) theories. Presentation of this model does not mean we advocate all work at this global, heuristic level. Yet it does, in line with Table 5.2 and Street and Cappella's research (1985), suggest that we should pursue *multiple* levels of communicative analysis. Researchers obviously must pursue their own particular quirks and interests, but it seems eminently possible for us to look to ways in which we can all articulate our concerns in a macroconceptual scheme, be it this one or another. Models such as Patterson's and our cognitive communicator characteristics model allow us to fight our way out of a general theoretical vacuum and enable us to construct more specific, detailed models of behavioral sequencing, interpersonal relationship development, intergroup communication, and so forth. As importantly, our model stresses the need for self-presentation theory and the communication-game approach to consider more explicitly intergroup processes, rules, and strategies. It also nudges speech accommodation theory, on the one hand, to contemplate the value of arousal mechanisms and discrepancy-arousal and, on the other, to assess the value of self-identity processes.

Obviously, we would echo Patterson's sentiments regarding his own model in that the one we have presented herein will be replaced somewhat quickly. There are of course many fuzzy edges and enormous chasms as well as a dearth of empirical data, all of which could benefit from cognitive science and psychophysiological inputs. Among the most compelling of problems revolve around the manner in which communicators come to process the cognitive representations apparent in Table 5.1 and the implied sequential primacy of this over the evaluative and arousal components of the model. Nevertheless, the precise relationships in the model are to our mind ultimately less important than the components themselves as highlighted in

Generalizations III-VI. In other words, the sum of the parts is greater than the whole. But if we persist in following *only* the "old" paradigms of Part I of this chapter, which have led to Generalizations I and II, continue to measure social categories objectively and to analyze solely communication variables in isolation from each other, deny the importance of self-identity processes, and construct our studies in a social vacuum without due respect to theory-building, the empirical status of "communicator characteristics" research will suffer as a result. Indeed, until we investigate the ways in which interpersonal communication is influenced by, and itself shapes, the cognitive character-istics of interactants, many apparently contradictory findings will continue to emerge. Generalization III-VI suggest that interactants' cognitive character-istics of themselves, their relationships, situational definitions, and so forth mediate communicative behaviors in ways thus far unexplored empirically. Table 5.1, for example, affords us a concrete handle methodologically and theoretically on some of the literature sources that should prove helpful in that direction. As emphasized at the outset of Part II, we do not advocate the abandonment of studies allocating people to objective social categories or personality variables, yet we do recommend understanding fully the dynam-ics and processes of interpersonal communication. These are just a set of starting blocks available to us.

REFERENCES

Abelson, R. P., (1981). Psychological status of the script concept. *American Psychologist, 36,* 715-729.

Aboud, F. D., Clément, R., & Taylor, D. M. (1974). Evaluative reactions to discrepancies between social class and language. *Sociometry, 37,* 239-250.

Addington, D. W. (1968). The relationship between selected vocal characteristics to personality perception. *Speech Monographs, 35,* 492-503.

Aiello, J. R., & Jones, S. E. (1971). Field study of the proxemic behavior of young school children in three subcultural groups. *Journal of Personality and Social Psychology, 19,* 351-356.

Ajzen, I., & Fishbein, M. (1980). *Understanding attitudes and predicting social behavior.* Englewood Cliffs, NJ: Prentice-Hall.

Apple, W., Streeter, L. A., & Krauss, R. M. (1979). Effects of pitch and speech rate on personal attributions. *Journal of Personality and Social Psychology, 37,* 715-727.

Applegate, J. L. (1982). The impact of construct system development on communication and impression formation in persuasive context. *Communication Monographs, 49,* 277-289.

Applegate, J. L., & Delia, J. G. (1980). Person-centered speech, psychological development, and the contexts of language usage. In R. N. St. Clair & H. Giles (Eds.), *The social and psychological contexts of language* (pp. 245-282). Hillsdale, NJ: Lawrence Erlbaum.

Argyle, M., Furnham, A., & Graham, J. (1981). *Social situations.* Cambridge: Cambridge University Press.

Argyle, M., Lalljee, M., & Cook, M. (1968). The effects of visibility on interaction in a dyad. *Human Relations, 21,* 3-17.

Aries, E. (1967). Interaction patterns and themes of male, female, and mixed groups. *Small Group Behavior, 7,* 7-18.

Arkin, R. M. (1981). Self-presentation styles. In J. T. Tedeschi (Ed.), *Impression management theory and social psychological research* (pp. 311-333). New York: Academic Press.

Arntson, P. (1982). Testing Basil Bernstein's sociolinguistic theories. *Human Communication Research, 9,* 33-48.

Arntson, P., & Mortensen, C. D. (1976, December). *Predispositions toward verbal behavior: Replication and extension.* Presented at the Annual Meeting of the Speech Communication Association, San Francisco, CA.

Arntson, P., Mortensen, C. D., & Lustig, M. W. (1980). Predispositions toward verbal behavior in task-oriented interaction. *Human Communication Research, 6,* 239-252.

Aronovitch, C. D. (1976). The voice of personality: Stereotyped judgments and their relation to voice quality and sex of speaker. *Journal of Social Psychology, 99,* 255-270.

Aronson, E., & Weintraub, W. (1972). Personal adaptation as reflected in verbal behavior. In A. W. Siegman and B. Pope (Eds.), *Studies in dyadic communication* (pp. 265-280). New York: Pergamon.

Bailey, L. A., & Timm, L. A. (1976). More on women's- and men's-expletive. *Anthropological Linguistics, 18,* 438-449.

Baldwin, T. L., McFarlane, P. T., & Garvey, C. J. (1971). Children's communication accuracy related to race and socioeconomic status. *Child Development, 42,* 345-357.

Ball, P., Byrne, J., Giles, H., Berechree, P., Griffiths, J., MacDonald, H., & McKendrick, I. (1982). The retrospective speech halo effect: Some Australian data. *Language and Communication, 2,* 277-284.

Baskett, G. D., & Freedle, R. O. (1974). Aspects of language and the social perception of lying. *Journal of Psychololinguistic Research, 3,* 117-130.

Bauer, E. A. (1973). Personal space: A study of blacks and whites. *Sociometry, 36,* 402-408.

Baumeister R. F. (1982). A self-presentation view of social phenomena. *Psychological Bulletin, 91,* 3-26.

Berger, C. R., & Bradac, J. J. (1982). *Language and social knowledge.* London and Baltimore: Edward Arnold.

Berger, C. R., Gardner, R. R., Clatterbuck, G. W., and Schulman, L. S. (1976). Perceptions of information sequencing in relationship development. *Human Communication Research, 3,* 29-46.

Bernstein, B. (1962). Linguistic codes, hesitation phenomena, and intelligence. *Language and Speech, 5,* 31-46.

Bernstein, B. (1964). Elaborated and restricted codes: Their social origins and some consequences. *American Anthropologist, 66,* 55-64.

Bernstein, B. (1972). Social class, language, and socialization. In S. Moscovici (Ed.), *The psychology of language* (pp. 222-242). Chicago, IL: Markham.

Blakar, R. (in press). Towards a theory of communication in terms of preconditions: A conceptual framework and some empirical explorations. In H. Giles & R. St.Clair (Eds.), *Recent advances in language, communication and social psychology.* London: Lawrence Erlbaum.

Bock, J. K. (1982). Toward a cognitive psychology of syntax: Information processing contributions to sentence formulation. *Psychological Review, 89,* 1-47.

Bond, R. N., & Feldstein, S. (1982). Acoustical correlates of the perception of speech rate: An experimental investigation. *Journal of Psycholinguistic Research, 11,* 539-557.

Boster, F., Stiff, J. B., & Reynolds, R. A. (1983, May). *Do persons respond differently to inductively-derived lists of compliance-gaining messages?* Paper presented at the annual meeting of the International Communication Association, Dallas, TX.

Bourhis, R. Y., & Giles, H. (1977). The language of intergroup distinctiveness. In H. Giles (Ed.), *Language, ethnicity, and intergroup relations* (pp. 119-135). London: Academic Press.

Bourhis, R. Y., Giles, H., Leyens, J-P., & Tajfel, H. (1979). Psycholinguistic distinctiveness: Language divergence in Belgium. In H. Giles & R. St. Clair (Eds.), *Language and social psychology* (pp. 158-185). Oxford: Blackwell.

Bradac, J. J., Bowers, J. W., & Courtright, J. A. (1979). Three language variables in communication research: Intensity, immediacy, and diversity. *Human Communication Research, 5,* 257-269.

Bradac, J. J., Hemphill, M. R., & Tardy, C. H. (1981). Language style on trial: Effects of "powerful" and "powerless" speech upon judgments of victims and villains. *Western Journal of Speech Communication, 45,* 327-341.

Bradac, J. J., Hosman, L. A., & Tardy, C. H. (1978). Reciprocal disclosures and language intensity: Attributional consequences. *Communication Monographs, 45,* 1-17.

Bradford, A., Ferror, D., & Bradford, G. (1974). Evaluative reactions of college students to dialect differences in the English of Mexican-Americans. *Language and Speech, 17,* 255-270.

Bradley, P. H. (1981). The folk-linguistics of women's speech: An empirical examination. *Communication Monographs, 48,* 73-90.

Brewer, M. B., Dull, V., & Lui, L. (1981). Perceptions of the elderly: Stereotypes as prototypes. *Journal of Personality and Social Psychology, 41,* 656-670.

Brounell, W., & Smith, D. R. (1973). Communication patterns, sex, and length of verbalization in the speech of four-year-old children. *Speech Monographs, 40,* 310-316.

Brown, B. L. (1980). Effects of speech rate on personality attributions and competing ratings. In H. Giles, P. W. Robinson, & P. M. Smith (Eds.), *Language: Social psychological perspectives* (pp. 293-300). Oxford: Pergamon.

Brown, P., & Levinson, S. (1979). Social structure, groups, and interaction. In K. R. Scherer & H. Giles (Eds.), *Social markers in speech* (pp. 291-342). Cambridge: Cambridge University Press.

Brown, R. (1977). Introduction. In C. E. Ferguson & C. A. Ferguson (Eds.), *Talking to children: Language input and acquisition* (pp. 1-27). New York: Cambridge University Press.

Buck, J. (1968). The effects of Negro and White dialectical variations upon attitudes of college students. *Speech Monographs, 35,* 181-186.

Buck, R. (1975). Nonverbal communication of affect in children. *Journal of Personality and Social Psychology, 31,* 644-653.

Buck, R., Miller, R. E., & Caul, W. F. (1974). Sex, personality, and physiological variables in the communication of affect via facial expression. *Journal of Personality and Social Psychology, 30,* 587-596.

Burgoon, M. (1983). Argument from Aristotle to analysis of variance: A modest reinterpretation. *Journal of Language and Social Psychology, 2,* 105-121.

Burgoon, J. K., & Hale, J. L. (1983). Dimensions of communication reticence and their impact on verbal encoding. *Communication Quarterly, 31,* 302-312.

Burgoon, J. K., & Koper, R. J. (1984). Nonverbal and relational communication associated with reticence. *Human Communication Research, 10,* 601-626.

Burgoon, M., & Miller, G. R. (in press). An expectancy theory interpretation of language and persuasion. In H. Giles & R. N. St. Clair (Eds.), *Recent advances in language, communication and social psychology.* London: L E A.

Cantor, J. R. (1979). Grammatical variations in persuasion: Effectiveness of four forms of request in door-to-door solicitations for funds. *Communication Monographs, 46,* 296-305.

Cantor, N., & Mischel, W. (1979). Prototypes in person perception. In L. Berkowitz (Ed.), *Advances in experimental social psychology* (Vol. 12, pp. 1-52). New York: Academic Press.

Caporael, L. R., Lukaszewski, M. P., & Culbertson, G. H. (1983). Secondary baby talk: Judgments by institutionalized elderly and their care givers. *Journal of Personality and Social Psychology, 44,* 746-754.

Cappella, J. N. (1984). The relevance of the microstructure of interaction to relationship change. *Journal of Personal and Social Relationships, 1,* 239-264.

Cappella, J. N. (in press). Controlling the floor in conversation. In A. Siegman & S. Feldstein (Eds.), *Nonverbal communication.* Hillsdale, NJ: Lawrence Erlbaum.

Cappella, J. N., & Greene, J. (1982). A discrepancy-arousal explanation of mutual influence in expressive behavior for adult-adult and infant-adult interaction. *Communication Monographs, 49,* 89-114.

Carranza, M. A., & Ryan, E. B. (1975). Evaluative reactions of bilingual Anglo and Mexican-American adolescents toward speakers of English and Spanish. *International Journal of the Sociology of Language, 6,* 83-104.

Cegala, D. J., Savage, G. T., Brunner, C. C., & Conrad, A. B. (1982). An elaboration of the meaning of interaction involvement: Toward the development of a theoretical concept. *Communication Monographs, 49,* 229-248.

Chaikin, A. L., & Derlega, V. J. (1974). Liking for the norm-breaker in self-disclosure. *Journal of Personality, 42,* 117-129.

Cherry, L. (1975). Teacher-child verbal interaction: An approach to the study of sex differences. In B. Thorne & N. Henley (Eds.), *Language and sex: Difference and dominance* (pp. 172-183). Rowley, MA: Newbury House.

Cheyne, W. (1970). Stereotyped reactions to speakers with Scottish and English regional accents. *British Journal of Social and Clinical Psychology, 9,* 77-79.

Clark, R. A., & Delia, J. G. (1976). The development of functional persuasive skills in childhood and early adolescence. *Child Development, 47,* 1008-1014.

Clark, R. A., & Delia, J. G. (1977). Cognitive complexity, social perspective-taking and functional persuasive skills in second- to ninth-grade children. *Human Communication Research, 3,* 128-134.

Cody, M., & McLaughlin, M. L. (1980). Perceptions of compliance-gaining situations: A dimensional analysis. *Communication Monographs, 47,* 132-148.

Cook, M. (1970). Experiments on orientation and proxemics. *Human Relations, 23,* 61-76.

Coutts, L. M., & Schneider, F. W. (1975). Verbal behavior in an unfocused interaction as a function of sex and distance. *Journal of Experimental Social Psychology, 11,* 64-77.

Cozby, P. C. (1972). Self-disclosure, reciprocity, and liking. *Sociometry, 35,* 151-160.

Crown, C. L. (1980). Impression formation and the chronography of dyadic interactions. In M. Davis (Ed.,) *Interaction rhythms: Periodicity in communicative behavior* (pp. 225-248). New York: Human Sciences Press.

Dabbs, J. M., Evans, M. S., Hopper, C. H., & Purvis, J. A. (1980). Self-monitors in conversation: What do they monitor? *Journal of Personality and Social Psychology, 39,* 278-284.

Davis, J. (1977). Effects of communication about interpersonal process on the evolution of self-disclosure in dyads. *Journal of Personality and Social Psychology, 35,* 31-37.

de la Zerda, N., & Hopper, R. (1979). Employment interviewers' responses to Mexican-accented speech. *Communication Monographs, 46,* 126-134.

Delia, J. G. (1972). Dialects and the effects of stereotypes on interpersonal attraction and cognitive processes in impression formation. *Quarterly Journal of Speech, 58,* 285-297.

Delia, J. G., & Clark, R. A. (1977). Cognitive complexity, social perception, and the development of listener-adapted communication in six-, eight-, ten-, and twelve-year-old boys. *Communication Monographs, 44,* 326-345.

Delia, J. G., Kline, S. L., & Burleson, B. R. (1979). The development of persuasive communication strategies in kindergarteners through twelfth-graders. *Communication Monographs, 46,* 241-256.

Derlega, V. J., Harris, M. S., & Chaikin, A. L. (1973). Self-disclosure, reciprocity, liking, and the deviant. *Journal of Experimental Social Psychology, 9,* 277-284.

Dindia, K. (1982). Reciprocity in self-disclosure: A sequential analysis. In M. Burgoon (Ed.), *Communication yearbook 6* (pp. 506-528). Beverly Hills, CA: Sage.

Dindia, K. (1983, May). *Reciprocity of self-disclosure: Limitations and illusions.* Paper presented at the annual meeting of the International Communication Association, Dallas, TX.

Dindia, K. (1985). A functional approach to self-disclosure. In R. L. Street, Jr., & J. N. Cappella (Eds.), *Sequence and pattern in communicative behavior* (pp. 142-160). London: Edward Arnold.

Dittmann, A. T. (1972). Development factors in conversational behavior. *Journal of Communication, 22,* 404-423.

Doob, L. W. (1958). Behavior and grammatical style. *Journal of Abnormal and Social Psychology, 56,* 398-401.

Dowd, J. J., & Bengtson, V. L. (1978). Aging in minority population: An examination of the double jeopardy hypothesis. *Journal of Gerontology, 33,* 427-436.

Dubé-Simard, L. (1983). Genesis of social categorization, threat to identity and perception of social injustice: Their role in intergroup communication. *Journal of Language and Social Psychology, 2,* 183-205.

Duck, S. (1982). *Personal relationships 4: Dissolving personal relationships.* London: Academic Press.

Duke, M. P., & Nowicki, S. (1972). A new measure and social-learning model for interpersonal distance. *Journal of Experimental Research in Personality, 6,* 119-132.

Duncan, S. D., Jr. (1983). Speaking turns: Studies of structure and individual difference. In J. M. Wiemann & R. P. Harrison (Eds.), *Nonverbal interaction* (pp. 149-178). Beverly Hills, CA: Sage.

Duncan, S. D., Jr., & Fiske, D. W. (1977). *Face-to-face interaction: Research, methods, and theory.* Hillsdale, NJ: Lawrence Erlbaum.

Dunhame, R., & Herman, J. (1975). Development of a female faces scale for measuring job satisfaction. *Journal of Applied Psychology, 60,* 629-631.

Eakins, B. W., & Eakins, C. (1976). Verbal turn-taking and exchanges in faculty dialogue. In B. Dubois & I. Crouch (Eds.), *The sociology of the languages of American women* (pp. 53-62). San Antonio, TX: Trinity University Press.

Edward, S., Jr. (1979). Judgments and confidence in reaction to disadvantaged speech. In H. Dubois & I. Crouch (Eds.), *The sociology of the languages of American women* (pp. 53-62). San Antonio, TX: Trinity University Press.

Edward, J., Jr. (1979a). Judgments and confidence in reaction to disadvantaged speech. In H. Giles & R. St. Clair (Eds.), *Language and social psychology* (pp. 22-44). Oxford: Basil Blackwell.

Edward, J., Jr. (1979b). *Language and disadvantage.* London: Edward Arnold.

Efran, J. S. (1968). Looking for approval: Effect on visual behavior of approbation from persons differing in importance. *Journal of Personality and Social Psychology, 10,* 21-25.

Ekman, P., & Friesen, W. V. (1972). Hand movements. *Journal of Communication, 22,* 353-374.

Elyan, O., Smith, P. M., Giles, H., & Bourhis, R. Y. (1978). R-P female-accented speech: The voice of perceived androgyny? In P. Trudgill (Ed.), *Sociolinguistic patterns in British English* (pp. 122-130). London: Edward Arnold.

Exline, R. V. (1963). Explorations in the process of person perception: Visual interaction in relation to composition, sex, and need for affiliation. *Journal of Personality, 31,* 1-20.

Exline, R. V., Ellyson, S. L., & Long, B. (1975). Visual behavior as an aspect of power role relationships. In P. Pilner, L. Krames, & T. Holloway (Eds.), *Advances in the study of communication and affect* (Vol. 2, pp. 21-51). New York: Plenum.

Exline, R. V., & Fehr, B. J. (1978). Applications of semiosis to the study of visual interaction. In A. Siegman & S. Feldstein (Eds.), *Nonverbal behavior and communication* (pp. 117-158). Hillsdale, NJ: Lawrence Erlbaum.

Exline, R. V., Gray, D., & Schuette, D. (1965). Visual behavior in a dyad as affected by interview content and sex of respondent. *Journal of Personality and Social Psychology, 1,* 201-209.

Exline, R. V., Thibaut, J., Hickey, C. B., & Gumpert, P. (1970). Visual interaction in relation of Machiavellianism and an unethical act. In R. Christie & F. Geis (Eds.), *Studies in Machiavellianism* (pp. 53-75). New York: Academic Press.

Farr, R. M. (1980). Homo loquens in social psychological perspective. In H. Giles, W. R. Robinson, & P. M. Smith (Eds.), *Language: Social psychological perspectives* (pp. 409-413). Oxford: Pergamon.

Feldstein, S. (1964). Vocal patterning of emotional expression. In J. H. Masserman (Ed.), *Science and psychoanalysis* (Vol. 7, pp. 193-210). New York: Grune & Stratton.

Feldstein, S., & Welkowitz, J. (1978). Achronography of conversation: In defense of an objective approach. In A. Siegman & S. Feldstein (Eds.), *Nonverbal behavior and communication* (pp. 329-378). Hillsdale, NJ: Lawrence Erlbaum.

Festinger, L. (1954). A theory of social comparison processes. *Human Relations, 7,* 117-140.

Fielding, G., & Evered, C. (1980). The influence of patients' speech upon doctors: The diagnostic interview. In R. N. St. Clair & H. Giles (Eds.), *The social and psychological contexts of language* (pp. 51-72). Hillsdale, NJ: Lawrence Erlbaum.

Fisher, B. A. (1983). Differential effects of sexual composition and interactional context on interaction patterns in dyads. *Human Communication Research, 9,* 225-238.

Fishman, P. M. (1980). Conversational insecurity. In H. Giles, W. P. Robinson, & P. M. Smith (Eds.), *Language: Social psychological perspectives* (pp. 127-132). Oxford: Pergamon.

Fitzpatrick, M. A. (1984). A typological approach to marital interaction: Recent theory and research. In L. Berkowitz (Ed.), *Advances in experimental social psychology* (Vol. 18, pp. 1-47). New York: Academic Press.

Flores, N., & Hopper, R. (1975). Mexican-Americans' evaluations of spoken Spanish and English. *Speech Monographs, 42,* 91-98.

Forgas, J. (1981). *Social episodes: The study of interaction routines.* London: Academic Press.

Forgas, J., (1983). Language, goals, and situation. *Journal of Language and Social Psychology, 2,* 267-293.

Forgas, J., & Dubosz, B. (1980). Dimensions of romantic involvement: Towards a taxonomy of heterosexual relationships. *Social Psychology Quarterly, 43,* 290-300.

Forston, R. F., & Larson, C. U. (1968). The dynamics of space: An experimental study in proxemic behavior among Latin Americans and North Americans. *Journal of Communication, 18,* 109-116.

Foss, D. J., & Hakes, D. T. (1978). *Psycholinguistics.* Englewood Cliffs, NJ: Prentice-Hall.

Frankel, A. S., & Barrett, J. (1971). Variations in personal space as a function of authoritarianism, self-esteem, and racial characteristics of a stimulus situation. *Journal of Consulting and Clinical Psychology, 37,* 95-98.

Frender, R., Brown, B., & Lambert, W. E. (1970). The role of speech characteristics in scholastic success. *Canadian Journal of Behavioral Sciences, 2,* 299-306.

Garai, J. E., & Scheinfeld, A. (1968). Sex differences in mental and behavioral traits. *Genetic Psychology Monographs, 77,* 169-299.

Garvey, C., & BenDebba, M. (1974). Effects of age, sex, and partner on children's dyadic speech. *Child Development, 45,* 1159-1161.

Geis, F. L., & Moon, T. H. (1981). Machiavellianism and deception. *Journal of Personality and Social Psychology, 41,* 766-775.

Genesee, F., & Bourhis, R. Y. (1982). The social psychological significance of code switching in cross-cultural communication. *Journal of Language and Social Psychology, 1,* 1-28.

Gilbert, S. J. (1976). Empirical and theoretical extensions of self-disclosure. In G. R. Miller (Ed.), *Explorations in interpersonal communication* (pp. 197-216). Beverly Hills, CA: Sage.

Giles, H. (1971a). Ethnocentrism and evaluation of accented speech. *British Journal of Social and Clinical Psychology, 10,* 187-188.

Giles, H. (1971b). Patterns of evaluations to RP, South Welsh, and Somerset accented speech. *British Journal of Social and Clinical Psychology, 10,* 280-281.

Giles, H. (1973). Communicative effectiveness as a function of accented speech. *Speech Monographs, 40,* 330-331.

Giles, H. (1979). Ethnicity markers in speech. In K. R. Scherer & H. Giles (Eds.), *Social markers in speech* (pp. 251-290). Cambridge: Cambridge University Press.

Giles, H. (1983). The Second Bristol Conference: A personal assessment. *Journal of Language and Social Psychology, 2,* 301-314.

Giles, H., Brown, B. L., & Thakerar, J. N. (1981). *The effects of speech rate, accent, and context on the attribution of a speaker's personality characteristics.* Unpublished manuscript, University of Bristol.

Giles, H., & Hewstone, M. (1982). Cognitive structures, speech and social situations: Two integrative models. *Language Sciences, 4,* 188-219.

Giles, H., & Johnson, P. (1981). The role of language in ethnic group relations. In J. C. Turner & H. Giles (Eds.), *Intergroup behavior* (pp. 199-243). Oxford and Chicago: Blackwell and Chicago University Press.

Giles, H., & Powesland, P. F. (1975). *Speech style and social evaluation.* London: Academic Press.

Giles, H., & Ryan, E. B. (1982). Prolegomena for developing a social psychological theory of language attitudes. In E. B. Ryan & H. Giles (Eds.), *Attitudes towards language variation* (pp. 208-223). London and Baltimore: Edward Arnold.

Giles, H., & Sassoon, C. (1983). The effect of speaker's accent, social class background, and message style on British listeners' social judgments. *Language and Communication, 3,* 305-313.

Giles, H., & Smith, P. M. (1979). Accommodation theory: Optimal levels of convergence. In H. Giles & R. N. St. Clair (Eds.), *Language and social psychology* (pp. 45-65). Baltimore, MD: University Park Press.

Giles, H., Taylor, D. M., & Bourhis, R. Y. (1973). Towards a theory of interpersonal accommodation through language: Some Canadian data. *Language in Society, 2,* 177-192.

Goffman, E. (1959). *The presentation of self in everyday life.* New York: Doubleday.

Goffman, E. (1961). *Encounters: Two studies in the sociology of interaction.* Indianapolis, IN: Bobbs-Merrill.

Gottman, J. (1982). Emotional responsiveness in marital conversations. *Journal of Communication, 32,* 108-120.

Haas, A. (1979). Male and female spoken language differences: Stereotypes and evidence. *Psychological Bulletin, 86,* 616-626.

Haas, A., & Sherman, M. A. (1982). Reported topics of conversation among same-sex adults. *Communication Quarterly, 30,* 332-342.

Hale, C. L. (1980). Cognitive complexity as a determinant of communication effectiveness. *Communication Monographs, 47,* 304-311.

Harms, L. S. (1963). Status cues in speech: Extra-race and extra-region identification. *Lingua, 12,* 300-306.

Hart, R. J., & Brown, B. L. (1974). Interpersonal information conveyed by the content and vocal aspects of speech. *Speech Monographs, 41,* 371-380.

Haslett, B. J. (1983a). Communication functions and strategies in children's conversations. *Human Communication Research, 9,* 114-129.

Haslett, B. J. (1983b). Preschoolers' communicative strategies in gaining compliance from peers: A developmental study. *Quarterly Journal of Speech, 69,* 84-99.

Hass, W. A., & Wepman, J. M. (1974). Dimensions of individual difference in the spoken syntax of school children. *Journal of Speech and Hearing Research, 17,* 455-469.

Hayes, D. P., & Meltzer, L. (1972). Interpersonal factors based on talkativeness: Fact or artifact. *Sociometry, 35,* 538-561.

Helfrich, H. (1979). Age markers in speech. In K. R. Scherer & H. Giles (Eds.), *Social markers in speech* (pp. 63-107). Cambridge: Cambridge University Press.

Henley, N. (1977). *Body politics: Power, sex, and nonverbal communication.* Englewood Cliffs, NJ: Prentice-Hall.

Hershey, S., & Werner, E. (1975). Dominance in marital decision making in women's liberation and non-women's liberation families. *Family Process, 14,* 223-233.

Hewes, D. & Haight, L. (1979). The cross-situational consistency of communicative behaviors. *Communication Research, 6,* 243-270.

Hewes, D., & Haight, L. (1980). Multiple-act criteria in the validation of communication traits: What do we gain and what do we lose? *Human Communication Research, 6,* 352-366.

Hewes, D., Haight, L., Szalay, S., & Evans, D. E. (1977). *On predicting none of the people none of the time: A test of two alternative relationships between personality and communicative choice.* Paper presented at the annual meeting of the International Communication Association, Berlin, Germany.

Hewett, N. (1971). Reactions of prospective English teachers toward speakers of a nonstandard dialect. *Language Learning, 21,* 205-212.

Higgins, E. T. (1980). The "communication game": Implications for social cognition and persuasion. In E. T. Higgins, C. P. Herman, & M. P. Zanna (Eds.), *Social cognition: The Ontario symposium* (pp. 343-392). Hillsdale, NJ: Lawrence Erlbaum.

Higgins, E. T., & McCann, C. D. (1984). Social encoding and subsequent attitudes, impressions, and memory: "Context-driven" and motivational aspects of processing. *Journal of Personality and Social Psychology, 47,* 26-39.

Hilpert, F., Kramer, C., & Clark, R. A. (1975). Participants' perceptions of self and partner in mixed-sex dyads. *Central States Speech Journal, 26,* 52-56.

Hobson, G. N., Srongman, K. T., Bull, D., & Craig, G. (1973). Anxiety and gaze aversion in dyadic encounters. *British Journal of Social and Clinical Psychology, 12,* 122-129.

Hopper, R. (1977). Language attitudes in the employment interviews. *Communication Monographs, 44,* 346-351.

Hopper, R., & Williams, F. (1973). Speech characteristics and employability. *Speech Monographs, 40,* 296-302.

Houston, S. (1970). A re-examination of some assumptions about the language of the disadvantaged child. *Child Development, 41,* 947-962.

Ickes, W., & Barnes, R. D. (1977). The role of sex and self-monitoring in unstructured dyadic interactions. *Journal of Personality and Social Psychology, 35,* 315-330.

Ickes, W., Patterson, M. L., Rajecki, D. W., & Tanford, S. (1982). Behavioral and cognitive consequences of reciprocal versus compensatory responses to pre-interaction expectancies. *Social Cognition, 1,* 160-190.

Johnson, F. L., & Buttny, R. (1982). White listeners' responses to "sounding black" and "sounding white": The effect of message content on judgments about language. *Communication Monographs, 49,* 33-49.

Johnson, J., Giles, H., & Bourhis, R. Y. (1983). The viability of ethnolinguistic vitality: A reply to Husband and Khan. *Journal of Multilingual and Multicultural Development, 4,* 255-269.

Johnson, K. R. (1972). Black kinesics: Some nonverbal communication patterns in the black culture. In L. A. Samovar & R. E. Porter (Eds.), *Intercultural communication: A reader* (pp. 259-268). Belmont, CA: Wadsworth.

Johnson-Laird, P. N. (1983). *Mental models: Toward a cognitive science of language, inference, and consciousness.* Cambridge, MA: Harvard University Press.

Jones, A. J., & McMillan, W. B. (1973). Speech characteristics as a function of social class and situational factors. *Child Development, 44,* 117-121.

Jones, E. E., & Wortman, C. (1973). *Ingratiation: An attributional approach.* Morristown, NJ: General Learning Press.

Jones, S. E., & Aiello, J. R. (1973). Proxemic behavior of black and white first-, third-, and fifth-grade children. *Journal of Personality and Social Psychology, 25,* 21-27.

Jordan, W. J., & Powers, W. G. (1978). Verbal behavior as a function of apprehension and social context. *Human Communication Research, 4,* 294-300.

Jourard, S. M., & Friedman, R. (1970). Experimenter-subject "distance" and self-disclosure. *Journal of Personality and Social Psychology, 15,* 278-282.

Kalin, R. (1982). The social significance of speech in medical, legal and occupational settings. In E. B. Ryan & H. Giles (Eds.), *Attitudes towards language variation* (pp. 148-163). London and Baltimore: Edward Arnold.

Kendall, P. C., Deardorff, P. A., Finch, A. J., Jr., & Graham, L. (1976). Proxemics, locus of control, anxiety, and type of movement in emotionally disturbed and normal boys. *Journal of Abnormal Child Psychology, 4,* 9-16.

Kimble, C. E., Yoshikawa, J. C., & Zehr, H. D. (1981). Vocal and verbal assertiveness in same-sex and mixed-sex groups. *Journal of Personality and Social Psychology, 40,* 1047-1054.

Knapp, M. L. (1978). *Nonverbal communication in human interaction.* New York: Holt, Rinehart & Winston.

Knapp, M. L., Hart, R., & Dennis, H. (1974). An exploration of deception as a communication construct. *Human Communication Research, 1,* 15-29.

Kochman, T. (1982). *Black and white styles in conflict.* Chicago: University Press.

Kolditz, T. A., & Arkin, R. M. (1982). An impression management interpretation of the self-handicapping strategy. *Journal of Personality and Social Psychology, 43,* 492-502.

Kowal, S., O'Connell, D. C., & Sabin, E. J. (1975). Development of temporal patterning and vocal hesitations in spontaneous narratives. *Journal of Psycholinguistic Research, 4,* 195-207.

Kramarae, C. (1982). Gender: How she speaks. In E. B. Ryan & H. Giles (Eds.), *Attitudes towards language variation* (pp. 84-98). London: Edward Arnold.

Kramer, C. (1977). Perceptions of female and male speech. *Language and Speech, 20,* 151-161.

Labov, W. (1966). *The social stratification of English in New York City.* Washington, DC: Center for Applied Linguistics.

LaFrance, M., & Mayo, C. (1976). Racial differences in gaze behavior during conversations: Two systematic observational studies. *Journal of Personality and Social Psychology, 33,* 547-552.

Lakoff, R. (1975). *Language and woman's place.* New York: Harper & Row.

Lambert, W. E. (1967). A social psychology of bilingualism. *Journal of Social Issues, 23,* 91-109.

Lambert, W. E., Hodgson, R., Gardner, R.C., & Eillenbaum, S. (1960). Evaluation reactions to spoken languages. *Journal of Abnormal and Social Psychology, 60,* 44-51.

Langer, E., & Newman, H. (1979). The role of mindlessness in a typical social psychological experiment. *Personality and Social Psychology Bulletin, 5,* 295-298.

Larsen, K. S., Martin, H. J., & Giles, H. (1977). Anticipated social cost and interpersonal accommodation. *Human Communication Research, 3,* 303-308.

Laver, J.D.M. (1975). *Individual features in voice quality.* Unpublished doctoral dissertation, University of Edinburgh, Scotland.

Lawton, D. (1968). *Social class, language, and education.* Routledge & Kegan Paul.

Lay, C. H., & Burron, B. F. (1968). Perception of the personality of the hesitant speaker. *Perceptual and Motor Skills, 26,* 951-956.

Lind, E. A., & O'Barr, W. M. (1979). The social significance of speech in the courtroom. In H. Giles & R. N. St. Clair (Eds.), *Language and social psychology* (pp. 66-87). Baltimore, MD: University Park Press.

Lowery, C. R., Snyder, C. R., & Denney, N. W. (1976). Perceived aggression and predicted counteraggression as a function of sex of dyad participants: When males and females exchange verbal blows. *Sex Roles, 2,* 339-346.

Mallory, E., & Miller, V. A. (1958). A possible basis for the association of voice characteristics and personality traits. *Speech Monographs, 25,* 255-260.

Markel, N. N., Lang, J. F., & Saine, T. J. (1976). Sex effects in conversational interaction: Another look at male dominance. *Human Communication Research, 2,* 356-364.

Markel, N. N., Phillis, J. A., Vargas, R., & Harvard, K. (1972). Personality traits associated with voice types. *Journal of Psycholinguistic Research, 1,* 249-255.

Markel, N. N., Prebor, L. D., & Brandt, J. F. (1972). Biosocial factors in dyadic communication. *Journal of Personality and Social Psychology, 23,* 11-13.

Marshall, J. E., & Heslin, R. (1975). Boys and girls together: Sexual composition and effect of density and group size on cohesiveness. *Journal of Personality and Social Psychology, 31,* 952-961.

Martin, J. N., & Craig, R. T. (1983). Selected linguistic sex differences during initial social interactions of same-sex and mixed-sex student dyads. *Western Journal of Speech Communication, 47,* 16-28.

Martindale, D. A. (1971). *Effects of environmental context in negotiating situations: Territorial dominance behavior in dyadic interactions.* Unpublished doctoral dissertation, City University of New York.

Maynard, D. W. (1980). Placement of topic changes in conversation. *Semiotica, 30,* 263-290.

McCroskey, J. C. (1977). Oral communication apprehension: A summary of recent theory and research. *Human Communication Research, 4,* 78-98.

McGregor, G. (1983). Listener's comments on conversations. *Language and Communication, 3,* 271-304.

McKinney, B. C. (1982). The effects of reticence in group interaction. *Communication Quarterly, 30,* 124-128.

McKirnan, D., & Hamayan, E. (1980). Language norms and perceptions of ethnolinguistic group diversity. In H. Giles, P. W. Robinson, & P. M. Smith (Eds.), *Language: Social psychological perspectives* (pp. 161-170). Oxford: Pergamon.

McLaughlin, M. L., Cody, M. J., Kane, M. L., & Robey, C. S. (1981). Sex differences in story receipt and story sequencing variables. *Human Communication Research, 7,* 99-116.

Mead, G. H. (1934). *Mind, self and society.* Chicago: University of Chicago Press.

Mehrabian, A. (1969). Significance of posture and position in the communication of attitude and status relationships. *Psychological Bulletin, 71,* 359-373.

Mehrabian, A., & Williams, M. (1969). Nonverbal concomitants of perceived and intended persuasiveness. *Journal of Personality and Social Psychology, 13,* 37-58.

Milardo, R. M. (1982). Friendship networks in developing relationships: Converging and diverging social environments. *Social Psychology Quarterly, 45,* 162-172.

Miller, D. T. (1975). The effect of dialect and ethnicity on communicator effectiveness. *Speech Monographs, 42,* 69-74.

Miller, G. R. (1983). On various ways of skinning symbolic cats: Recent research on persuasive message strategies. *Journal of Language and Social Psychology, 2,* 123-140.

Miller, G. R., & Hewgill, M. A. (1964). The effect of variations in nonfluency on audience ratings of source credibility. *Quarterly Journal of Speech, 50,* 36-44.

Miller, N., Marayama, G., Beaber, R. J., & Valone, K. (1976). Speed of speech and persuasion. *Journal of Personality and Social Psychology, 34,* 615-624.

Mobbs, N. A. (1968). Eye contact in relation to social introversion-extraversion. *British Journal of Social and Clinical Psychology, 7,* 305-306.

Moe, J. D. (1972). Listener judgments of status cues in speech: A replication and extension. *Speech Monographs, 39,* 144-147.

Montgomery, B. M. (1981). Verbal immediacy as an indicator of open communication content. *Communication Quarterly, 30,* 24-34.

Morgan, B. S. (1976). Intimacy of disclosure topics and sex differences in self-disclosure. *Sex Roles, 2,* 161-166.

Morris, L. W. (1979). *Extraversion and introversion.* New York: John Wiley.

Mortensen, C. D., & Arntson, P. H. (1974). The effects of predispositions toward verbal behavior on interaction patterns in dyads. *Quarterly Journal of Speech, 61,* 421-430.

Morton, J. (1969). Interaction of information in word recognition. *Psychological Review, 76,* 165-178.

Mulac, A., & Lundell, T. L. (1980). Differences in perception created by syntactic-semantic productions of male and female speakers. *Communication Monographs, 47,* 111-118.

Mulac, A., & Rudd, M. J. (1977). Effects of selected American regional dialects upon regional audience members. *Communication Monographs, 44,* 185-195.

Murray, D. C. (1971). Talk, silence, and anxiety. *Psychological Bulletin, 75,* 224-260.

Mysak, E. D. (1959). Pitch and duration characteristics of older males. *Journal of Speech and Hearing Research, 2,* 46-54.

Naremore, R. C. (1971). Teachers' judgments of children's speech: A factor analytic study of attitudes. *Speech Monographs, 38,* 17-27.

Natalé, M. (1975a). Convergence of mean vocal intensity in dyadic communications as a function of social desirability. *Journal of Personality and Social Psychology, 32,* 790-804.

Natalé, M. (1975b). Social desirability as related to convergence of temporal speech patterns. *Perceptual and Motor Skills, 40,* 827-830.

Newman, H. M. (1982). The sounds of silence in communicative encounters. *Communication Quarterly, 30,* 142-149.

Norman, D. A. (1981). Categorization of action slips. *Psychological Review, 88,* 1-15.

Norton, R. (1983). *Communicator style.* Beverly Hills, CA: Sage.

Oden, G. C., & Massaro, D. W. (1978). Integration of featural information in speech perception. *Psychological Review, 85,* 172-191.

O'Hair, H. D., Cody, M. J., & McLaughlin, M. L. (1981). Prepared lies, spontaneous lies, Machiavellianism, and nonverbal communication. *Human Communication Research, 7,* 325-339.

O'Keefe, B. J., & Delia, J. G. (1979). Construct comprehensiveness and cognitive complexity as predictors of the number and strategic adaptation of arguments and appeals in a persuasive message. *Communication Monographs, 46,* 231-240.

O'Keefe, D. J., & Sypher, H. E. (1981). Cognitive complexity measures and the relationship of cognitive complexity to communication. *Human Communication Research, 7,* 72-92

Palmer, M. T. (1984). *A fuzzy approach to comprehending nonverbal communication.* Unpublished paper, University of Wisconsin-Madison.

Patterson, M. L. (1973). Compensation in nonverbal immediacy behaviors: A review. *Sociometry, 36,* 237-252.

Patterson, M. L. (1976). An arousal model of interpersonal intimacy. *Psychological Review, 83,* 235-245.

Patterson, M. L. (1978). The role of space in social interaction. In A. W. Siegman & S. Feldstein (Eds.), *Nonverbal behavior and communication* (pp. 265-290). Hillsdale, NJ: Lawrence Erlbaum.

Patterson, M. L. (1982a). Personality and nonverbal involvement: A functional analysis. In W. Ickes & E. S. Knowles (Eds.), *Personality, roles, and social behavior* (pp. 141-164). New York: Springer-Verlag.

Patterson, M. L. (1982b). A sequential functional model of nonverbal exchange. *Psychological Review, 89,* 231-249.

Patterson, M. L. (1983). *Nonverbal behavior: A functional perspective.* New York: Springer-Verlag.

Patterson, M. L., & Holmes, D. S. (1966). Social interaction correlates of the MPI extraversion-introversion scale. Paper presented at the annual meeting of the American Psychological Association, New York, NY.

Pearce, W. B., & Brommel, B. J. (1972). Vocalic communication in persuasion. *Quarterly Journal of Speech, 58,* 298-306.

Pedersen, D. M. (1973). Correlates of behavioral personal space. *Psychological Reports, 32,* 828-830.

Phillips, G. M. (1968). Reticence: Pathology of normal speakers. *Speech Monographs, 35,* 39-49.

Piliavin, J. A., & Martin, R. R. (1978). The effects of sex composition of groups on style of social interaction. *Sex Roles, 4,* 281-296.

Pope, B., Blass, T., Siegman, A. W., & Raher, J. (1970). Anxiety and depression in speech. *Journal of Consulting and Clinical Psychology, 35,* 128-133.

Powers, W. G. (1977). The rhetorical interrogative: Anxiety or control? *Human Communication Research, 4,* 44-47.

Powesland, P. F., & Giles, H. (1975). Persuasiveness and accent-message incompatibility. *Human Relations, 28,* 85-93.

Pozner, J., & Saltz, E. (1974). Social class, conditional communication, and egocentric speech. *Developmental Psychology, 10,* 764-771.

Price, R., & Boffard, D. L. (1974). Behavioral appropriateness and situational constraint as dimensions of social behavior. *Journal of Personality and Social Psychology, 30,* 579-586.

Putman, G. N., & O'Hern, E. (1955). The status significance of an isolated urban dialect. *Language, 31,* 1-32.

Putman, W., & Street, R. L., Jr. (1984). The conception and perception of noncontent speech performance: Implications for speech accommodation theory. *International Journal of the Sociology of Language, 46,* 97-114.

Ramsay, R. W. (1966). Personality and speech. *Journal of Personality and Social Psychology, 4,* 116-118.

Ramsay, R. W. (1968). Speech patterns and personality. *Language and Speech, 11,* 54-63.

Rand, M., & Levinger, G. (1979). Implicit theories of relationship: An intergenerational study. *Journal of Personality and Social Psychology, 37,* 645-661.

Reardon, K. K. (1982). Conversational deviance: A structural model. *Human Communication Research, 9,* 59-74.

Repp, B. H. (1977). Dichotic competition of speech sounds: The role of acoustic stimulus structure. *Journal of Experimental Psychology: Perception and Performance, 3,* 37-50.

Rimé, B., (1984). Nonverbal communication: A cognitive-motor theory. In W. Doise & S. Moscovici (Eds.), *Current issues in European psychology.* Cambridge: Cambridge University Press.

Ritter, E. M. (1979). Social perspective-taking ability, cognitive complexity, and listener-adapted communication in early and late adolescence. *Communication Monographs, 46*, 40-51.

Robinson, J., & McArthur, L. Z. (1982). Impact of salient vocal qualities on causal attributions for a speaker's behavior. *Journal of Personality and Social Psychology, 43*, 236-247.

Robinson, W. P. (1979). Speech markers and social class. In K. R. Scherer & H. Giles (Eds.), *Social markers in speech* (pp. 211-249). Cambridge: Cambridge University Press.

Rogers, W. T., & Jones, S. E. (1975). Effects of dominance tendencies on floor-holding and interruption behavior in dyadic interaction. *Human Communication Research, 1*, 113-122.

Romaine, S., & Reid, E. (1976). Glottal sloppiness? A sociolinguistic view of urban speech in Scotland. *CITE Journal "Teaching English," 9*, 12-16.

Rosenfeld, L. B. (1979). Self-disclosure avoidance: Why I am afraid to tell you who I am. *Communication Monographs, 46*, 63-74.

Rutter, D. R., Morley, I. E., & Graham, J. C. (1972). Visual interaction in a group of introverts and extroverts. *Journal of Social Psychology, 2*, 371-384.

Ryan, E. B. (1979). Why do low prestige language varieties persist? In H. Giles & R. N. St. Clair (Eds.), *Language and social psychology* (pp. 145-157). Baltimore, MD: University Park Press.

Ryan, E. B., & Bulik, C. M. (1982). Evaluations of middle-class and lower-class speakers of standard American and German-accented English. *Journal of Language and Social Psychology, 1*, 51-61.

Ryan, E. B., & Capadano, H. L. (1978). Age perceptions and evaluative reactions toward adult speakers. *Journal of Gerontology, 33*, 98-102.

Ryan, E. B., & Giles, H. (Eds.). (1982). *Attitudes towards language variation*. London and Baltimore: Edward Arnold.

Ryan, E. B., Giles, H., & Sebastian, R. J. (1982). An integrative perspective for the study of attitudes toward language variation. In E. B. Ryan & H. Giles (Eds.), *Attitudes towards language variation* (pp. 1-19). London: Edward Arnold.

Ryan, E. B., Hewstone, M., & Giles, H. (1984). Language and intergroup attitudes. In J. R. Eiser (Ed.), *Attitudinal judgment* (pp. 135-158). New York: Springer-Verlag.

Ryan, E. B., & Sebastian, R. (1980). The effects of speech style and social class background on social judgments of speakers. *British Journal of Social and Clinical Psychology, 19*, 229-233.

Sabin, E. J., Clemmer, E. J., O'Connell, D. C., & Kowal, S. (1979). A pausological approach to speech development. In A. W. Siegman & S. Feldstein (Eds.), *Of speech and time* (pp. 35-55). Hillsdale, NJ: Lawrence Erlbaum.

Sankoff, G., & Cedergren, H. (1971). Some results of a sociolinguistic study of Montreal French. In R. Darnell (Ed.), *Linguistic diversity in Canadian society* (pp. 61-87). Edmonton, Canada: Linguistic Research.

Schenk-Hamlin, W. J. (1978). The effects of dialectical similarity, stereotyping, and message agreement on interpersonal perception. *Human Communication Research, 5*, 15-26.

Scherer, K. R. (1974). Voice quality analysis of American and German speakers. *Journal of Psycholinguistic Research, 3*, 281-290.

Scherer, K. R. (1979a). Personality markers in speech. In K. R. Scherer & H. Giles (Eds.), *Social markers in speech* (pp. 147-209). Cambridge: Cambridge University Press.

Scherer, K. R. (1979b). Voice and speech correlates of perceived social influence in simulated juries. In H. Giles & R. St. Clair (Eds.), *Language and social psychology* (pp. 88-120). London: Basil Blackwell.

Scherer, K. R., London, H., & Wolf, J. J. (1973). The voice of confidence: Paralinguistic cues and audience evaluation. *Journal of Research in Personality, 7*, 31-44.

Schlenker, B. R. (1980). *Impression management: The self-concept, social identity and interpersonal relations*. Monterey, CA: Brooks/Cole.

Sebastian, R. J., & Ryan, E. B. (in press). Speech cues and social evaluation: Markers of ethnicity, social class, and age. In H. Giles & R. N. St. Clair (Eds.), *Recent advances in language, communication, and social psychology*. Hillsdale, NJ: Lawrence Erlbaum.

Sereno, K. K., & Hawkins, G. J. (1967). The effects of variations in speakers' nonfluency upon audience ratings of attitude toward the speech topic and speakers' credibility. *Speech Monographs, 34*, 58-64.

Sewell, A. F., & Heisler, J. T. (1973). Personality correlates of proximity preferences. *Journal of Psychology, 85*, 151-155.

Shaffer, D. R., Smith, J. E., & Tomarelli, M. (1982). Self-monitoring as a determinant of self-disclosure reciprocity during the acquaintance process. *Journal of Personality and Social Psychology, 43*, 163-175.

Shimanoff, S. B. (1983). The role of gender in linguistic references to emotive states. *Communication Quarterly, 30*, 174-179.

Siegman, A. W. (1978). The telltale voice: Nonverbal messages of verbal communication. In A. W. Siegman & S. Feldstein (Eds.), *Nonverbal behavior and communication* (pp. 183-244). Hillsdale, NJ: Lawrence Erlbaum.

Siegman, A. W., & Pope, B. (1965a). Effects of question specificity and anxiety producing messages on verbal fluency in the initial interview. *Journal of Personality and Social Psychology, 4*, 188-192.

Siegman, A. W., & Pope, B. (1965b). Personality variables associated with productivity and verbal fluency in the initial interview. *Proceedings of the 73rd Annual Convention of the American Psychological Association*, 273-274.

Siegman, A. W., & Reynolds, M. (1982). Interviewee-interviewer nonverbal communications: An interactional approach. In M. Davis (Ed.), *Interaction rhythms: Periodicity in communicative behavior* (pp. 249-276). New York: Human Sciences Press.

Silverman, E. M., & Zimmer, C. H. (1976). The fluency of women's speech. In B. Dubois & I. Crouch (Eds.), *The sociology of the languages of American women* (pp. 131-136). San Antonio, TX: Trinity University Press.

Simard, L., Taylor, D. M., & Giles, H. (1976). Attribution processes and interpersonal accommodation in a bilingual setting. *Language and Speech, 19*, 374-387.

Smith, H. (1977). Small group interaction at various ages: Simultaneous talking and interruption of others. *Small Group Behavior, 8*, 65-74.

Smith, M. J., Reinheimer, R. E., & Gabbard-Alley, A. (1981). Crowding, task performance, and communicative interaction in youth and old age. *Human Communication Research, 7*, 259-272.

Smith, P. M. (1979). Sex markers in speech. In K. R. Scherer & H. Giles (Eds.), *Social markers in speech* (pp. 109-146). Cambridge: Cambridge University Press.

Smith, P. M. (1984). *Language, the sexes, and society.* Oxford and New York: Blackwell.

Snyder, M. (1974). Self-monitoring of expressive behavior. *Journal of Personality and Social Psychology, 30*, 526-537.

Snyder, M. (1979). Self-monitoring processes. In L. Berkowitz (Ed.), *Advances in experimental social psychology* (Vol. 12, pp. 85-128). New York: Academic Press.

Sousa-Poza, J. F., & Rohrberg, R. (1977). Body movement in relation to type of information (person- and nonperson-oriented) and cognitive style (field dependence). *Human Communication Research, 4*, 19-29.

Staley, C. M. (1982). Sex-related differences in the style of children's language. *Journal of Psycholinguistic Research, 11*, 141-158.

Stang, D. J. (1973). Effect of interaction rate on ratings of leadership and liking. *Journal of Personality and Social Psychology, 27*, 405-408.

Steer, A. B. (1974). Sex differences, extraversion, and neuroticism in relation to speech rate during the expression of emotion. *Language and Speech, 17*, 80-86.

Steingart, I., Freedmann, N., Grand, S., & Buchwald, C. (1975). Personality organization and language behavior: The imprint of psychological differentiation on language behavior in varying communication conditions. *Journal of Psycholinguistic Research, 4*, 241-255.

Stewart, M. A., & Ryan, E. B. (1982). Attitudes toward younger and older adult speakers: Effects of varying speech rates. *Journal of Language and Social Psychology, 1*, 91-110.

Stipek, D., & Nelson, K. (1980). Communication efficiency in middle- and lower-SES dyads. *Human Communication Research, 6*, 168-177.

Stratton, L. O., Tekippl, D. J., & Flick, G. J. (1973). Personal space and self-concept. *Sociometry, 36*, 424-429.

Street, R. L., Jr. (1982). Evaluation of noncontent speech accommodation. *Language and Communication, 2*, 13-31.

Street, R. L., Jr. (1983). Noncontent speech convergence and divergence in adult-child interactions. In R. N. Bostrom (Ed.), *Communication yearbook 7* (pp. 369-395). Beverly Hills, CA: Sage.

Street, R. L., Jr. (1984). Speech convergence and speech evaluation in fact-finding interviews. *Human Communication Research, 11,* 139-169.

Street, R. L., Jr., & Brady, R. M. (1982). Speech rate acceptance ranges as a function of evaluative domain, listener speech rate, and communication context. *Communication Monographs, 49,* 290-308.

Street, R. L., Jr., Brady, R. M., & Lee, R. (1984). Evaluative responses to communicators: The effects of speech rate, sex, and interaction context. *Western Journal of Speech Communication, 48,* 14-27.

Street, R. L., Jr., Brady, R. M., & Putman, W. B. (1983). The influence of speech rate stereotypes and rate similarity on listeners' evaluations of speakers. *Journal of Language and Social Psychology, 2,* 37-56.

Street, R. L., Jr., & Cappella, J. N. (Eds.). (1985). *Sequence and pattern in communicative behavior.* London: Edward Arnold.

Street, R. L., & Giles, H. (1982). Speech accommodation theory: A social cognitive approach to language and speech behavior. In M. Roloff & C. Berger (Eds.), *Social cognition and communication.* Beverly Hills, CA: Sage.

Street, R. L., Jr., & Hopper, R. (1982). A model of speech style evaluation. In E. B. Ryan & H. Giles (Eds.), *Attitudes towards language variation* (pp. 175-188). London: Edward Arnold.

Street, R. L., Jr., & Jordan, W. J. (1981). Lexical diversity and rhetorical interrogatives as adaptations to communication environments. *Communication Quarterly, 29,* 276-282.

Street, R. L., Jr., Street, N. J., & Van Kleeck, A. (1983). Speech convergence among talkative and reticent three-year-olds. *Language Sciences, 5,* 79-96.

Strodtbeck, F. L., & Mann, R. D. (1956). Sex role differentiation in jury deliberations. *Sociometry, 19,* 3-11.

Strongman, K., & Woosley, J. (1967). Stereotyped reactions to regional accents. *British Journal of Social and Clinical Psychology, 6,* 154-162.

Suls, J. (1982). *Psychological perspectives on the self.* Hillsdale, NJ: Lawrence Erlbaum.

Sussman, N. M., & Rosenfeld, H. M. (1982). Influence of culture, language, and sex on conversational distance. *Journal of Personality and Social Psychology, 42,* 66-74.

Swacker, M. (1975). The sex of the speaker as a sociolinguistic variable. In B. Thorne & N. Henley (Eds.), *Language and sex: Difference and dominance* (pp. 76-83). Rowley, MA: Newbury House.

Tajfel, H. (1981). Social stereotypes and social groups. In J. C. Turner & H. Giles (Eds.), *Intergroup behavior* (pp. 144-167). Oxford and Chicago: Blackwell and Chicago University Press.

Tajfel, H. (1982). *Social identity and intergroup relations.* Cambridge: Cambridge University Press.

Tardy, C. H., Hosman, L. A., & Bradac, J. J. (1981). Disclosing self to friends and family: A re-examination of initial questions. *Communication Quarterly, 29,* 263-268.

Taylor, D. M., & Clément, R. (1974). Normative reactions to styles of Quebec French. *Anthropological Linguistic, 16,* 212-217.

Tedeschi, J. T. (Ed.). (1972). *Social influence processes.* Chicago: Aldine.

Tedeschi, J. T. (Ed.). (1974). *Perspectives on social power.* Chicago: Aldine.

Tedeschi, J. T. (Ed.). (1981). *Impression management theory and social psychological research.* New York: Academic Press.

Tedeschi, J. T., & Melburg, V. (in press). Impression management and influence in the organization. In S. B. Bacharach & E. J. Lawler (Eds.), *Perspectives in organizational psychology: Theory and research.* Greenwich, CT: JAI Press.

Tedeschi, J. T., & Norman, N. (in press). Social power, self-presentation and the self. In B. R. Schlenker (Ed.), *Self and identity.* New York: McGraw-Hill.

Tedeschi, J., & Reiss, M. (1981a). Identities, the phenomenal self, and laboratory research. In J. T. Tedeschi (Ed.), *Impression management theory and social psychological research* (pp. 3-22). New York: Academic Press.

Tedeschi, J. T., & Reiss, M. (1981b). Verbal tactics of impression management. In C. Antaki (Ed.), *Ordinary language explanations of social behavior* (pp. 271-309). London: Academic Press.

Thakerar, J. N., & Giles, H. (1981). They are—so they speak: Noncontent speech stereotypes. *Language and Communication, 1,* 251-256.

Thakerar, J. N., Giles, H., & Cheshire, J. (1982). Psychological and linguistic parameters of speech accommodation theory. In C. Fraser & K. R. Scherer (Eds.), *Advances in the social psychology of language* (pp. 205-255). Cambridge: Cambridge University Press.

Thompson, T. L. (1981). The development of communication skills in physically handicapped children. *Human Communication Research, 7,* 312-324.

Thompson, T. L. (1982a). "You can't play marbles—you have a wooden hand": Communication with the handicapped. *Communication Quarterly, 30,* 108-115.

Thompson, T. L. (1982b). The development of listener-adapted communication on physically handicapped children: A cross-situational study. *Western Journal of Speech Communication, 46,* 32-44.

Tolor, A. (1975). Effects of procedural variations in measuring interpersonal distance by means of representational space. *Psychological Reports, 36,* 475-491.

Trimboli, F. (1973). Changes in voice characteristics as a function of trait and state personality variables. *Dissertation Abstracts International, 33,* 3965.

Trudgill, P. (1974). *The social differentiation of English in Norwich.* London: Cambridge University Press.

Tucker, G. R., & Lambert, W. E. (1969). White and Negro listeners' reactions to various American-English dialects. *Social Forces, 47,* 463-468.

Turner, J., & Giles, H. (Eds.). (1981). *Intergroup behavior.* Oxford and Chicago: Blackwell and Chicago University Press.

Van Kleeck, A., & Street, R. L., Jr. (1982). Does reticence mean just talking less? Qualitative differences in the language of talkative and reticent preschoolers. *Journal of Psycholinguistic Research, 11,* 609-629.

Von Raffler-Engel, W., & Buckner, J. (1976). A difference beyond inherent pitch. In B. Dubois & I. Crouch (Eds.), *The sociology of the languages of American women* (pp. 115-118). San Antonio, TX: Trinity University Press.

Watson, O. M., & Graves, T. D. (1966). Quantitative research in proxemic behavior. *American Anthropologist, 68,* 971-985.

Weary, G., & Arkin, R. M. (1981). Attitudinal self-presentation. In J. H. Harvey, M. J. Ickes, & R. Kidd (Eds.), *New directions in attribution theory and research* (Vol. 3). Hillsdale, NJ: Lawrence Erlbaum.

Weaver, J. C., & Anderson, R. J. (1973). Voice and personality interrelationships. *Southern Speech Communication Journal, 38,* 262-278.

Weinstein, M., & Hanson, R. G. (1975). Personality trait correlates of verbal interaction levels in an encounter group context. *Canadian Journal of Behavioral Sciences, 7,* 192-200.

Welkowitz, J., Cariffe, G., & Feldstein, S. (1976). Conversational congruence as a criterion for socialization in children. *Child Development, 47,* 269-272.

White, M. J. (1975). Interpersonal distance as affected by room size, status, and sex. *Journal of Social Psychology, 95,* 241-249.

Williams, F. (1976). *Exploration of the linguistic attitudes of teachers.* Rowley, MA: Newbury.

Williams, F., Whitehead, J. L., & Miller, L. (1972). Relations between attitudes and teacher expectancy. *American Educational Research Journal, 9,* 263-277.

Willis, F. N. (1966). Initial speaking distance as a function of the speaker's relationship. *Psychonomic Science, 5,* 221-222.

Willis, F. N., & Hoffman, G. E. (1975). Development of tactile patterns in relation to age, sex, and race. *Developmental Psychology, 11,* 886.

Willis, F. N., & Reeves, D. L. (1976). Touch interactions in junior high students in relation to sex and race. *Developmental Psychology, 12,* 91-92.

Wish, M. (1978). Dimensions of dyadic communication. In S. Weitz (Ed.), *Nonverbal communication* (pp. 371-378). New York: Oxford University Press.

Wölck, W. (1973). Attitudes toward Spanish and Quechua in bilingual Peru. In R. W. Shay & R. W. Fasold (Eds.), *Language attitudes: Current trends and prospects* (pp. 148-173). Washington, DC: Georgetown University Press.

Wood, J. (1966). The influence of sex and knowledge of communication effectiveness on spontaneous speech. *Word, 22,* 112-137.

Woodall, G. W., & Burgoon, J. K. (1983). Talking fast and changing attitudes: A critique and clarification. *Journal of Nonverbal Behavior, 8,* 126-142.

Worthy, M. A., Gary, I., & Kahn, G. M. (1969). Self-disclosure as an exchange process. *Journal of Personality and Social Psychology, 13,* 59-63.

Wright, F. (1976). The effects of style and sex of consultants and sex of members in self-study groups. *Small Group Behavior, 7,* 433-456.

Yairi, E., & Clifton, N. F., Jr. (1972). Disfluent speech behavior of preschool children, high school seniors, and geriatric persons. *Journal of Speech and Hearing Research, 15,* 714-719.

Zaidel, S., & Mehrabian, A. (1969). The ability to communicate and infer positive and negative attitudes facially and vocally. *Journal of Experimental Research in Personality, 3,* 233-241.

Zimmerman, D. H., & West, C. (1975). Sex roles, interruptions, and silences in conversation. In B. Thorne & N. Henley (Eds.), *Language and sex: Difference and dominance* (pp. 105-129). Rowley, MA: Newbury House.

Zuckerman, M., Hall, J. A., DeFrank, R. S., & Rosenthal, R. (1977). Encoding and decoding of spontaneous and posed facial expressions. *Journal of Personality and Social Psychology, 34,* 966-977.

6 The Situation as a Construct in Interpersonal Communication Research

MICHAEL J. CODY
MARGARET L. McLAUGHLIN

University of Southern California

T HE emerging line of research on situation perception and categorization today is predicated on two related trends in theory and research. First, theorists have increasingly voiced dissatisfaction with oversimplistic and mechanistic models that have tried to link personality traits or attitudes to our behavior. In persuasion research, both Reardon (1981) and Smith (1982) argue that the lay person's perceptions of the relevant features of the context are intimately linked to the application of rules and to the configuration of "available action/consequence expectancies that govern people's persuasive behavior" (Smith, p. 342). In personality-social psychology, Mischel (1979, p. 740) has argued against models of behavior in which prediction is based on a "few behavioral signs" and has called attention to the necessity of studying the reciprocal interaction between person and context in fine-grained detail. Similarly, "interactionists" (Endler, 1982; Endler & Edwards, 1978) advocate that research focus on "modern interactionism," which holds that overt behavior is a function of the continuous feedback between the person and the situation, that the person is an intentional and active agent in the interaction process, that cognitive factors are the essential determinants of behavior, and that the psychological meaning assigned to the situation is a major determinant of behavior.

Second, the decline in interest in consistency theories, the rise in attribution theories and cognitive heuristics, and evidence that individuals view the world through cognitive filters have led scholars to borrow, increasingly since the mid-1970s, constructs and processes from cognitive psychology in the hope that the integration of cognition, memory, social learning, and person-variables would provide direction in the understanding of naturally occurring behavior (see Taylor, 1981). These trends have necessitated the rejection of the view of individuals as organisms that simply

AUTHORS' NOTE: We wish to thank John O. Greene for his helpful comments on an earlier draft of this chapter.

(or that only) react to external environmental cues and have raised the status of individuals to that of cognitive information processors who, in order to act effectively, "must define situations, perceive other people, plan strategically, construct performance patterns, satisfy role demands and enforce them on others, and so on" (Athay & Darley, 1981, p. 282).

As communication scholars our purpose is to advance an ecologically sound understanding and prediction of naturally occurring communicative behavior. To pursue such a lofty goal requires an integration of the various ways in which individuals interact with the external environment, how they attempt to achieve goals, and how they use rules for appropriate behavior. Consequently, we will first overview how individuals use situational knowledge both in the processing of information and in the regulation of behavior. Second, we propose a tentative model for the production of overt behavior as it is influenced by situational knowledge, interactional constraint,, and so forth, and as it is mediated by cognitive processes. Third, we will review literature on dimensional and prototypical analyses of situations and settings; and fourth, we will review existing literature linking situation perception to communicative behaviors. We will then discuss rules of appropriate behavior and make recommendations for future research. Our first task, however, is to define "situation."

DEFINITION OF SITUATION

As Argyle, Furnham, and Graham (1981, p. 2) note, there has been an "unprecedented abuse and overuse of the term 'situation'." Argyle et al. describe a situation as "the sum of features of the behavior system, for the duration of a social encounter" (p. 30). Goffman (1961, p. 144) uses the term social situation to "refer to the full spatial environment anywhere within which an entering person becomes a member of the gathering that is (or does then become) present. Situations begin when mutual monitoring occurs and lapse when the next to last person has left." Harré and Secord define an episode as "any part of human life, involving two or more people, in which some internal structure can be found" (1972, p. 153). Forgas (1979) discusses three aspects of episodes (p. 9): *episode expectation* (a set of cultural expectations of patterns of action appropriate for a given episode), *episode definition* (the cues that are made available for the individual to select or identify episode enactment), *and episode performance* (the actual sequence of behaviors that make up an interaction). Pervin (1978) notes that global-level situations can be differentiated on the basis of who is present, where they are, and what takes place.

We will use the term social situation to denote the case in which two or more individuals are interacting within a physical setting, in which the interaction has an observable beginning and ending (defining by mutual monitoring). The behavior that occurs during the interaction is the *situational performance* (overt behavior). Situational performance is assumed to be a function of how individuals process input stimuli and interact with the external environment via mental processes. Later, we will present a model of overt behavior that links situational performance to situational knowledge and other antecedents.

THE UTILITY OF
SITUATIONAL KNOWLEDGE

There are at least four major ways in which individuals use situational knowledge. The first two deal with information processing; the latter two deal with the regulation of behavior:

(1) People use knowledge of situations as a framework for evaluating others.
(2) People process information, as situations unfold, on the basis of their purposes for being in the situation.
(3) People elect to enter into, avoid, or change a situation according to their self-in-situation scenarios, self-knowledge, or perceived competencies.
(4) People use situational knowledge as a guideline for how to behave.

Each of these features is relevant to understanding how behavior unfolds in daily contexts; each represents part of the fine-grained analysis of the person-environment interface, and each necessarily implies that we study the operation of structures for perceiving others, the operation of structures for perceiving situations, and the way individuals view the external environment and economize on activity choices via self-perceptions (see, for instance, Athay & Darley, 1981).

First, because human information processors can not attend to or process all relevant information in the environment, they naturally develop schemes for perceiving individuals and situations. In the former, implicit theories of personality, person prototypes, stereotypes, and so forth provide the observer with an efficient means by which to organize perceptions of others, a framework for "filling in" missing data, and providing information that influences behavior directed toward the observed individual, either through behavioral confirmation of labeling or by adapting messages to the audience. Indeed, certain replicable factors in situation perception reviewed below specifically deal with the perceptions of the persons in the situations.

In the development of situation perception structures, the outcomes of their previous experiences, observations, modeling, and so forth allow individuals to come to know that one type of situation is different from another (Cody & McLaughlin, 1980; Reardon, 1981), to know cultural rules (Argyle et al., 1981; Forgas, 1982), to know what is "appropriate" (Price & Bouffard, 1974), to learn whether or not a specific event is an "exemplar" of a general type of situation (Cantor, Mischel, & Schwartz, 1982a, 1982b), and, generally, to store perceptions of situations (in abstract or summarized form) in long-term memory (often on the basis of affective features; see Forgas, 1982 and below). Bandura (1977, p. 192) suggests that even "transitory experiences leave lasting effects by being coded and retained in symbols for memory representation." Research has explored the memory representations of situations in one of two ways: dimensional and "categorical." In the dimensional approach, the theorist attempts to uncover the salient features naive observers use to differentiate one situation from another. In the categorical approach, research explores the internal structure of features and action sequences of such representations as schemata (see Hewes & Planalp, 1982; Taylor & Crocker, 1981), prototypes, and scripts (Abelson, 1976, 1981; Schank & Abelson, 1977). In either of the approaches, we will use the term *long-term situational knowledge* to denote, generally, any information the actor possesses in long-term memory regarding what is likely to occur in the situation and how people are likely to behave in the situation.

    The production of overt behavior is further assumed to be a product of both the perceived social environment and personality, in which increases in situational constraint (for example, being in church) decrease person influences, whereas decreases in constraint allow for individual differences to emerge. Communication scholars are well aware of the fact that trait measures (as behavioral predispositions) predict overt behavior within a limited range of events. Briefly summarizing this earlier work, we know that (1) some person characteristics (intelligence) achieve greater consistency than others (anxiety); (2) traits can predict to behavior over time (longitudinally) across similar situations; (3) traits predict behaviors when one averages over performances across a set of events that should allow for variation on the criterion variable; and (4) traits achieve moderate levels of predictive ability across "similar" contexts—in which similarity either means that the individuals being assessed agree with the experimenter's perception that the situation belongs to a "common equivalence class" and agree among themselves on how to scale the behaviors and situations, or, that "similarity" exists when one variable of group composition is altered, but not when two or more variables are altered (Bem & Allen, 1974; Block, 1971, 1977; Epstein, 1979, 1983; Endler, 1982; Endler & Edwards, 1978; Jaccard & Daly, 1980; Mischel, 1968; Mischel & Peake, 1982a, 1982b).

    However, the current work from the perspective that individuals are active information processors provides evidence that individuals attempt cognitive control over the external environment as well as behavioral control. Generally, due to the previous experiences that led to the development of person perception and situation perception structures, individuals also develop *self-schemas,* a perceived level of *self-efficacy* for behavioral change (Bandura, 1977, 1978), *self-perceived competencies* (Mischel, 1973, 1979, 1983), and *self-in-situation scenarios* (Snyder, 1979; Snyder & Cantor, 1980).

According to Markus (1977, 1983), the self-schema serves as a reference point or anchor for perceiving others and is linked to situation selection/avoidance and to situation performance by the need to confirm one's self-description (in situations in which information is relevant to the particular schemata and that allow for flexibility in constructing behavior; see Markus, 1983, p. 549). Similarly, trait orientations are increasingly viewed as associated with characteristic ways of viewing the external environment (see, for example, Mischel, 1983; Snyder, 1979, 1981, 1983; Snyder & Cantor, 1980; Snyder & Gangestad, 1982; Snyder, Gangestad, & Simpson, 1983; Snyder & Kendzierski, 1982).

Individuals use knowledge of situations as a framework for evaluating others. Specifically, individuals take into consideration both knowledge of what is normative for the observational context and the prototypicality (and frequency) of acts the actor engages in (Buss & Craik, 1983) when determining whether the individual is a "prototypical" extravert, "cultured person," and so forth (Cantor, 1981; Cantor et al., 1982a, 1982b). In Cantor's work, for example, an actor who was described as outgoing in three situations that typically elicit outgoing behavior (for example, a party) was rated *less* prototypical than an actor who performed the same behaviors in situations that do not tend to elicit outgoing behaviors (for example, a library). Observers, apparently, were willing to infer more cross-situational consistency in the latter case than in the former (Cantor, 1981). More recently, Schneider and Blankmeyer (1983) found that increasing the salience of a prototype increased the strength of implicature among behaviors relevant to the prototype domain. Obviously, the context-based perceptions of others influence how certain the observer is in inferring predispositions and, thus, should influence how observers interact with others.

Individuals also process information as a situation unfolds on the basis of their goals and purposes in the situation. Two tactics have been employed in this line of research. First, a number of studies attempt to understand how observers naturally go about processing information in the ongoing stream of behavior (Atkinson & Allen, 1983; Cohen & Ebbesen, 1979; Ebbesen, 1980) and investigate how observational goals given to the observers influence allocation of attention (Hoffman, Mischel, & Mazze, 1980; Jeffrey & Mischel, 1979; also see Cantor et al., 1982a). Second, research has focused on how individuals processing self-schemata or self-in-situation perceptions naturally attend to different situational features. For our purpose, the second issue deserves some attention.

Markus (1983, p. 548) succinctly summarizes the information-processing consequences of self-schemas:

With respect to the self, individuals with self-schemas in particular domains: (1) can process information about the self efficiently (make judgments with relative ease and certainty); (2) are consistent in their responses; (3) have relatively better recognition, memory, and recall for information relevant to this domain; (4) can predict future behavior in the domain; (5) can resist information that is counter to a prevailing schema; and (6) evaluate new information for its relevance to a given domain. With respect to processing information about others, these individuals: (1) make accurate discriminations in the domain in question; (2) categorize or chunk schemata-relevant information differentially; (3) are relatively more sensitive to variations in this domain; (4) select and prefer information that is relevant to this domain; (5) make confident attributions and inferences about behavior in this domain.

Individuals who possess self-schemas for particular domains selectively focus attention on the self-relevant features of the social situations and thus have different expectations for events, and interpret and draw inferences differently (Cacioppo, Petty, & Sidera, 1982; Fong & Markus, 1982). The work by Kuiper and Derry (1981), for instance, indicates that depressives not only have a negative view of self and of the world, but (presumably by focusing on negative aspects) secure lower evaluations from interactants than do nondepressives and also make their partners feel greater depression, anxiety, and hostility (see Coyne, 1976).

Individual Differences in Situational Analysis

A number of personality constructs are similarly related to cognitive views of the external environment and are thus related to one important feature in regulating behavior: selecting to enter into or to avoid situations. This line of research is important for a number of reasons. Most obviously, earlier work in attribution theory suggested that observers tended to see more consistency in behavior than what actually existed.

This observation, although still true, may be somewhat tempered by the fact that individuals actively select situations that foster and encourage the behavioral expression of their own characteristic dispositions, which consequently leads to the construction of qualitatively different social environments and facilitates our understanding of how individuals economize on behavioral choices. This latter point is important for the obvious reason that actors can not be assumed to be either motivated to construct or competent at constructing any behavioral response at any time and thus routinize much of their interactive behaviors (Athay & Darley, 1981). Examples of some personality constructs related to situation selection/avoidance discussed here include: self-monitoring, internal-external locus of control, competitive orientations, and loneliness/communication apprehension.

Self-Monitoring. Low self-monitoring individuals are highly skilled at constructing cognitive images involving their self-characteristics, whereas high self-monitoring individuals are skilled at constructing informative cognitive images involving other individuals who are prototypical examples of persons for a wide range of behavioral domains (Snyder, 1979; Snyder & Cantor, 1980). Snyder and Gangestad (1982) and Snyder and Kendzierski (1982) found that such cognitive images influence whether individuals wanted to enter a situation and the likelihood of their attempting to redefine the situation. High self-monitoring individuals preferred entering into situations that provided them with clearly defined cues as to how to behave, whereas low self-monitoring individuals preferred entering into situations in which they could exhibit their own underlying predispositions. Snyder et al. (1983) further provide evidence that high self-monitoring individuals preferred relatively partitioned and compartmentalized social environments in which they would engage in particular activities only with specific partners. However, low self-monitoring individuals preferred homogeneous and undifferentiated social environments in which they could spend time with friends who were globally similar to themselves (thus making it easier to behave in a manner characteristic to one's attitudes and so forth). Also, it is clear that actively choosing the social situation to enter enhances the relationship between dispositional measures and actual behavior (Monson, McDaniel, Menteer, & Williams, in press; Snyder, 1983).

Internal/External Locus of Control. Internal/external control is similarly related to cognitive processes and to behaviors congruent with self-perceptions (Rotter, 1966; Rotter & Mulry, 1965). Internals value positive reinforcement more highly when they think that reinforcement is conditional on their own actions rather than on the basis of luck or chance and thus feel a greater sense of motivation to achieve when they perceive task accomplishment is due to their own efforts. On the other hand, a salient consideration for externals is the basic question of whether or not they are lucky; consequently, they derive little value from being attentive in a "skills-determined" task "since success or failure cannot necessarily be attributed to luck in such a situation" (Brownell, 1982, p. 759). A number of studies have found that internals perform better in a "skills" type of task than in a "chance" type of task, whereas externals perform better in a "chance" task (Baron, Cowan, Ganz, & McDonald, 1974; Baron & Ganz, 1972; Houston, 1972). Kahle (1980) similarly found that externals seek out situations in which outcomes are determined by chance, whereas internals choose situations in which outcomes are determined by their skills. Further, despite receiving identical instructions concerning the tasks, some studies have found that internals are more likely to accept the "skills" induction (Lefcourt, 1972). Also, internals allocate more resources to scanning the environment than do externals, especially when pursuing a valued outcome and as a means by which to resolve unexpected occurrences (Lefcourt & Wine, 1969). Further, internals are more likely to make errors when preparing for a task described as "chance," whereas externals are more likely to make errors when preparing for a "skills" task (Lefcourt, 1972). Along with the findings that internals desire more control and autonomy, are resistant to influence and pressure, are more confident in their behavior, and are less likely to conform than externals, these observations indicate that internals have fixed expectations about their own competencies, select situations compatible with those competencies, occasionally distort the perceived task in ways consistent with those competencies, and are more highly motivated when there exists agreement between situational preferences tasks.

Competitive Orientations. Individuals with competitive conceptualizations of self believe that the world is populated homogeneously by competitive others, whereas those with cooperative concepts of self believe the world is populated by both competitive and cooperative people (Kelley & Stahelski, 1970). Consequently, if individuals with competitive orientations treat other individuals as if they were competitive and thereby elicit competitive responses from others, then individuals with such orientations may "not only provide behavioral confirmation of their stereotypical beliefs that all people are competitive, but also justify and maintain their own competitive dispositions" (Snyder, 1981, pp. 313-314). A variation on this approach is Toch's (1969) analysis of violent-prone men. In one of Toch's analyses, two of the most common categories of violent-prone individuals included the "self-image promoter" and the "self-image defender." The promoter type was found to focus attention on impressing his audience with the fact that he is manly, formidable, and fearless, and that the audience should keep this in mind in all future interactions. To do so, the promoter type may purposefully arrange "tests of manhood" in which he manufactures situations in which his status may be questioned. The self-image defender, however, was extremely sensitive to implications of other people's actions for his integrity, manliness, and so forth, and was particularly keen on scanning the environment for the purpose of finding offenses to his rights and self-perceptions, possibly exaggerating offenses when they emerged. Obviously, competitively oriented or violence-prone individuals have particular ways of viewing the self in the environment, attend to different features in the environment, and construct social situations that most readers of this chapter will not normally experience.

Other Dispositions. Lonely individuals who attribute their loneliness to personal shortcomings are less active in meeting other people (Peplau, Russell, & Heim, 1979). Further, the negative view of self, lack of social skills, and low trust in others appear to place lonely individuals in positions that perpetuate loneliness (Jones, Freeman, & Goswick, 1981; Solano, Batten, & Parish, 1982). *Communication apprehension, shyness,* and *unwillingness to communicate* are similarly related to avoidance of selected situations (Burgoon, 1976; McCroskey, 1982; Pilkonis, Heape, & Klein, 1980). *Extraverts,* as opposed to *introverts,* seek out more stimulating social situations that involve assertiveness, competitiveness, and intimacy (Furnham, 1981; Argyle et al., 1981). *Sensation seekers* seek out situations and activities that are highly stimulating and "risky" (Zuckerman, 1974). Similarly, *arousal seekers* approach more varied settings than low arousal seekers (Mehrabian, 1978; Mehrabian & Russell, 1974). *Authoritarians* enter into more authoritarian educational settings than low authoritarians (Stern, Stein, & Bloom, 1956). In passing, it is worth reminding the reader that when the "social science experiment" occurs in the college sophomore's environment, females and persons who are younger, more unconventional, less authoritarian, more sociable, more intellectual, and who score higher on need for approval are more likely to volunteer to participate than their counterparts (Rosenthal, 1965).

Possessing situational knowledge enables individuals selectively to enter into or to avoid situations. Yet the prediction of actual behavior within a situation is a more complicated task. At a general level, individuals may have expectations about how they will behave in a situation due to generalizations drawn from past experiences concerning the most "ideal" or efficacious behavior for the situation (that is, overcoming perceived resistance to persuasion requires the communicator to justify a request with the use of "supporting evidence"). In determining the efficacy of message strategies, individuals take into consideration the situationally induced variations in the risks/costs associated with implementing tactics (Fitzpatrick & Winke, 1979; McLaughlin, Cody, & Robey, 1980; Sillars, 1980b), the "ethical threshold" of tactics (Hunter & Boster, 1979, 1984), and the situationally defined rules for appropriate conduct (Argyle, 1980; Argyle et al., 1981; McLaughlin, 1984). For instance, even at a young age individuals know that if they are responsible for an offense an apology should be offered and that as the severity of the offense increases, greater penitence should be demonstrated (Darby & Schlenker, 1982; Schlenker & Darby, 1981).

However, because what will actually unfold in a situation is never completely predictable, it is likely that the relationship between expectations and actual behavior is less than perfect. According to control theory (Carver & Scheier, 1981, 1982), the actor enters into a situation with a goal, engages in a behavior, assesses the impact on his or her environment, compares the current status of the environment with a reference value (desired end), and, if discrepancies exist, he or she may choose another behavior to reduce discrepancies. That is, the actor is assumed to shift focus between self and the environment throughout any exchange with the environment. Consequently, depending upon how events unfold and the importance of the actor's goals, the actor may be persistent, adaptive, or disengage from the expected sequence of behaviors (also see Hobbs & Evans, 1980). One critically important question that must be addressed is: What conditions minimize or maximize the actual implementation of expected or intended selections of behavioral strategies? The following model directs our attention to this and other questions.

A MODEL OF OVERT BEHAVIOR

Figure 6.1 presents our adaptation of the Cantor et al. (1982a) model of overt behavior, which provides a framework for the different ways in which behavior is produced. The x-axis represents a slice of ongoing activity (two or more individuals engaged in monitoring) arrayed from input level through

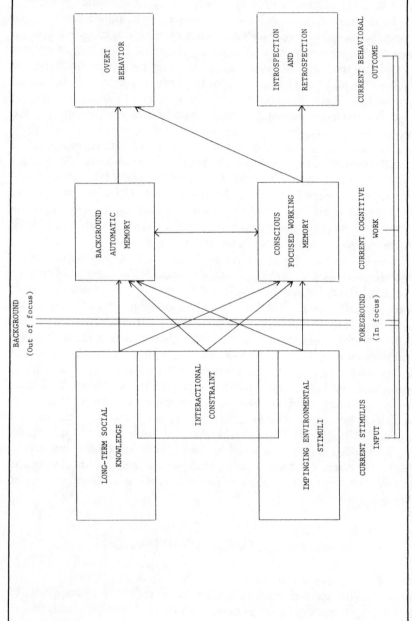

Figure 6.1 A Model of Overt Behavior

cognitive work to actual production of behavior. The y-axis represents components arrayed in terms of the level of conscious focus, with immediate behavioral cues and conscious-focused working memory "in focus," and long-term social and situational knowledge and automatic memory not "in focus." Besides the long-term social knowledge, two types of stimuli serve as input. Impinging environmental stimuli can be any environmental cues the actor observes when "absorbing" the environment, such as crowding, temperature, noise level, and so forth, that influence behavior either by affecting the actor's processing capacity or his or her need to adapt. Second, because actors in a situation mutually monitor one another, behavior may occur due to the *interactional constraint* (the effect of Speaker A's utterance on Speaker B's utterance). Interactional constraint overlaps with both long-term social knowledge (in those ritualized instances in which much if not all of the verbal exchange is part of the social knowledge) and impinging environmental cues (in which the actor reacts or adapts to unexpected hostile/aggressive acts, reproach types in account sequences, and so forth). In the latter, for example, there is ample evidence that aggressive or aggravating behavior often leads to aggressive or aggravating reactions. Reid (1967), for instance, found an average correlation of .65 among family members in their exchanges of aversive stimuli, and Patterson's (1976) work clearly demonstrates the hostile acts of an aggressive child elicit responses by family members that reliably increase the probability that another hostile act will be emitted. Along similar lines, Raven and Kruglanski (1970) note that coercive power may be justified as a "first strike" if the agent anticipates hostility from the target.

As Cantor et al. note (1982a, pp. 62-63), current cognitive work (Klatzky, 1975; Shiffrin & Schneider, 1977) includes both a "limited supply of conscious working memory (or focused memory) and a more extensive capacity to process information automatically." Conscious-focused working memory includes those instances in which the individual expends cognitive work purposefully to plan and evaluate behavior. Automatic memory processes, however, involve the "thoughts, ideas, or feelings that seem to intrude upon us rather than to occur as a result of our intensions to produce them" (Clark & Isen, 1982; Posner & Snyder, 1975), hence, the bidirectional line between the two (see Figure 6.1). Current behavioral outcomes can either be an immediate behavior or introspection/retrospection about that on which one has expended focused cognitive effort.

As the diagram indicates, impinging environmental cues, interactional constraint, and long-term knowledge influence memory and automatic memory, and both memories affect overt behavior. Of theoretical importance is the presence of the working memory-introspection link and the absence of the automatic memory-introspection link. Considerable evidence (for example, Nisbett & Wilson, 1977) suggests that the individual's introspection and explanation of behavior are often inaccurate. This may be true because in recalling behavior that occurred in the social knowledge-automatic memory sequence, individuals rely on schematic social knowledge—there is little access to conscious cognitive work, and individuals are insensitive to the actual causal contingencies. However, the quality of the introspection also appears to be related to whether or not experimenters request verbal reports concerning information still active in short-term memory (see Erickson & Simon, 1980; White, 1980). Also important from the standpoint of situational influences, however, is the fact that increased self-focus in situations increases monitoring, self-regulation, and introspection (see Carver & Scheier, 1981, 1982).

As this model suggests, overt behavior occurs because it is *scripted, planned, reactive, or adaptive*. It is scripted when the environment is predictable and stable, and social knowledge feeds automatic process ("Pass the salt, please"; "Two large coffees, two creams each, no sugar"). It is *planned* when social knowledge is fed into conscious working memory to devise a plan of action ("Because I owe him money already, I probably . . ."). It is *reactive* when the individual reacts (via automatic processes) to an impinging environmental cue (as in psychological reactance; see Brehm, 1966, 1972; Petty & Cacioppo, 1981). It is *adaptive* when the impinging environmental cue (or interactional constraint) forces the individual to expend immediate conscious effort to construct behaviors (as in some contexts in which the individual must answer difficult or ambiguous questions, engage in counterargument, or spontaneously construct deceptive messages).

These four processes leading to overt behavior of course represent an oversimplification. For example, the work by Clark and Isen (1982) indicates that environmentally induced feeling states directly (automatically) lead to cognitions, perceptions, and feelings congruent with the induced positive or negative feeling state. A positive feeling state facilitates the recall of pleasant stimuli, and a negative feeling state facilitates the recall of negative stimuli. However, because both memories can feed into one another and because positive feeling states are rewarding, an individual can deliberately plan activities so as to maintain a positive feeling state. Further, because a negative feeling state is aversive, the individual in such a state may be motivated to plan activities so as to reduce or eliminate the state. In the Clark and Isen (1982) model, the fact that both automatic and working memories jointly work together toward the same effect in the positive feeling state, while they work in opposite directions in the negative feeling state, partially explains why the former elicits more consistent results (in predicting behavior) than the latter.

Other examples of these processes, however, are more straightforward. For example, research on the production of deceptive messages has, to date, characteristically employed planned, prepared responses (often with "primed" or rehearsed communications). However, in a recently proposed model of cognitive difficulty (Cody, Marston, & Foster, 1984; Greene, O'Hair, Cody, & Yen, 1985) it was argued that lies are adaptive (the liar did not anticipate the follow-up question) may be more difficult to construct if the question required a narrative response (elaboration of detail) and was asked late in an interview context when the individual assigned to the role of liar may expect that his or her role had been completed. These conditions increase cognitive difficulty because liars must expend greater effort to resume the role of liar and search for information in long-term memory concerning how to immediately construct details for an event that never took place. Increased cognitive difficulty increased pauses, speech errors, vagueness, and so forth.

Beside directing our attention to the role of memory processes in the production of behavior, this model directs our attention to one other critically important issue to which communication scholars must attend. In any laboratory or field experiment, studying the operation of environmentally induced states or the operation of scripts as separate antecedents is a straightforward matter. However, in the individual's social environment, the actor "assigns" weights to each parameter; consequently, precision in predicting naturally occurring overt behavior requires a priori specification of the strength of these parameters. Our work on the selection of accounts is relevant to this issue (Cody & McLaughlin, 1985; McLaughlin, Cody, & Rosenstein, 1983).

In three studies we explored not only situation perception as an antecedent to strategy selection, but we also explored the question of whether the level of mitigation or aggravation in a reproach (how the reproacher requests an account) is associated with the level of mitigation or aggravation in the account. For example, a *projected concession*, a *projected excuse*, and, to a lesser extent, a *projected justification* are more mitigating than projected refusals. *Apologies, excuses*, and, to some extent, *justifications* are more mitigating than *refusals, challenges*, or *denials*. We had hypothesized, on the basis of reciprocity, matching norms, and on the basis of the obligation of the question type (McLaughlin, Cody, & Rosenstein, 1983) that mitigating reproaches would lead to mitigating accounts and aggravating reproaches would lead to aggravating accounts.

The results of three studies indicated that although mitigating reproaches did not lead to mitigating accounts, aggravating reproach types led to aggravating accounts. We concluded (Cody & McLaughlin, 1985) that when people enter into an account sequence, they may either possess a routinized way of accounting for some "offenses" (that is, being 50-years-old and in college, being a male secretary) or perceive the event along a number of dimensions (that is, severity of offense, importance of goals, and so forth). Thus when a reproacher uses a mitigating reproach form (conveys the impression that the reproacher is receptive), mitigating reproaches do not interfere with scripted or planned social behavior (specific subcategories of mitigating reproaches were evenly distributed across types of mitigating accounts). Thus offenders responded in predictable ways on the basis of situation perceptions. Apologies, for example, were offered when face-maintenance and instrumental goals were important and when perceived resistance was low (also, see below). On the other hand, aggravating reproaches or reproacher hostility may constitute activities one is less likely to expect under normal conditions and thus emerged as a stronger interactional constraint than mitigating reproaches and led to a thwarting of what one expects to (or usually would) communicate. Further, situation perception may also influence the perceived levels of aggravation in reproach types because, for example, the use of a projected concession when one felt falsely accused of an offense may be perceived as aggravating and may lead to an aggravating account. Obviously, one of the pressing issues involved in extending research on any analysis of message sequences rests in developing a priori specifications concerning how "aggravating" or "unexpected" a response must be if it emerges as the primary determinant of overt behavior.

In sum, the contents of long-term situational knowledge are useful to the observer/actor in a number of ways. Situational knowledge provides a framework for evaluating others (and for evaluating messages), provides data useful for seeking out or avoiding situations on the basis of one's self-perceptions, and is one important determinant of overt behavior. In the next section of this chapter we will focus attention on the content of this knowledge base.

TAXONOMIES AND DIMENSIONAL ANALYSES OF SITUATION COMPONENTS[1]

Moos (1973, p. 652) has identified six characteristics of situations, or "environments," that have been demonstrated to influence interactive behavior: (1) "ecological" dimensions, including both "geographical-meteoro-logical" and "architectural-physical design" variates; (2) behavior settings (at a fast-food restaurant, at the senior prom, and so on), which encompass both objective physical backdrop and a set of normative expectations for action; (3) dimensions of organizational structure, such as number of employees, salary levels, and so on; (4) dimensions describing underlying personal and/or demographic characteristics of the persons to be found in the situation (age, socioeconomic status, memberships, and so forth); (5) dimensions corresponding to features of the institutional climate, such as authority structure, feedback mechanisms, organizational constraint, and so on; and (6) dimensions describing the underlying reinforcement schedules of particular environments, for example, the "rewardingness" of different settings. Moos (1973, p. 660) argues persuasively that any level of the six variables may influence or be influenced by any level of any of the other variables.

For students of interpersonal communication, some of the broad situation characteristics Moos identifies may be of less immediate concern than others. For example, although we may be familiar with and intrigued by the "lunar lunacy" literature, those of us concerned with communication in normal, everyday transactions will ordinarily find meteorological variables such as the cycle of the moon to be ineffective predictors of, say, an individual's choice of compliance-gaining strategy. Dimensions of organizational structure will of course be invoked if our interests lie in the study of interpersonal communication in the work place; for the most part, however, the organizational context will not be the one in which we conduct our investigations of relationships. Clearly, however, characteristics of settings, persons in settings, and the affect-arousing properties of settings can routinely be expected to influence communication in everyday interpersonal encounters.

Pervin (1978) has proposed that "situation" as a source of influence on behavior can be decomposed into three components, each of which may operate both independently or interactively with one of the others to constrain persons' overt activities:

> A situation is defined by who is involved, including the possibility that the individual is alone, where the action is taking place, and the nature of the action or activities occurring. The situation is defined by the organization of these various components so that it takes on a gestalt quality, and if one of the components changes we consider the situation to have changed. While a situation has a gestalt quality, it is defined by who is involved, what is going on, and where the action is taking place. (pp. 79-80)

Pervin's three-component account of situation provides a convenient point of departure for our review of taxonomic studies; however, Pervin's claim that situations have a gestalt quality also merits consideration, for a considerable amount of scholarly attention has been directed to uncovering global dimensions of situation perception and in particular to reconstructing the underlying structure of affective responding to situations. Our account, then, will be addressed to a review of four bodies of literature: (1) research on the classification of *role relationships*—the "who" component; (2) studies of the *settings* of interaction—the "where" component; (3) research on the nature of the situated *activity*—the "what" component; and (4) work on the global dimensions, especially the affective factors of situation perception.

Role Relationships: Taxonomies
and Dimensional Analyses

Marwell and Hage (1970), in one of the earliest taxonomic studies of role relationships, took as their initial goal the elaboration of the underlying dimensions that lead to distinctions among categories of role relationships. The authors' methodology for creating a stimulus set of role relationships was to consult a dictionary and compile a list of nouns referring to positions or roles—for example, priest, son, social worker, and so forth—and then to generate a focal counterrole: altar boy, mother, unwed mother, and so on. Using an analytic rather than an empirical approach, Marwell and Hage then generated a set of sixteen variables of role relationships by crossing four relational *elements* (occupants, activities, locations, and occurrences) with four relational *quantities* (scope, intensity, integration, and independence). Different scales were devised to measure each of the sixteen variables. For example, relational *frequency* (occurrences × scope) was measured on a scale ranging from 7 (interact five or more times a week) to 1 (interact only once a year). Similarly, average *communality of interactional locations* (location × integration) was rated on a scale ranging from 7 ("almost all [99-100%] interactions occur in public places") to 1 ("hardly any interactions occur in public places").

Factor analysis of the rating scale data for the 100 role relationships yielded a three-dimensional factor structure: The factors were labeled, respectively, *intimacy, visibility,* and *regulation.* The intimacy factor contrasted the *gemeinschaft* with the *gesellschaft* relations, that is, the purely expressive to the purely instrumental. High-intimate role relationships, for example husband and wife, were characterized by a high mean number of activities, a low mean distance between partners, a large number of locations for relational activity, and a high degree of "occupant overlap" (Marwell & Hage, 1970, p. 891). Highly visible role relationships, for example quarterback-coach and convict-guard (as opposed to confessor-penitent or prostitute-customer), were characterized by such factors as a high mean location commonality. The third factor, regulation, typical of relationships such as conductor-dancer and judge-lawyer (as opposed to acquaintance-acquaintance and friend-friend), described role relations in which both parties' actions typically dovetailed, and there was little choice in terms of the kinds of acts performed, the locations for interaction, or the occurrence of interaction itself.

Marwell and Hage used the weighted factor scores from the preliminary analysis to arrive at an eight-category scheme for classifying role relationships, depending upon whether the relationship was high or low in intimacy, visibility, and regulation. For example, the relationship they term "uncontrolled gemeinschaft" is high in intimacy but neither highly visible nor highly regulated. Typical examples would include father-son and prostitute-procurer. The "regulated gesellschaft" category includes such relationships as dentist-patient and social worker-unwed mother, which are regarded as being low in intimacy, low in visibility, but high in regulation.

A second taxonomy of relationship types is that proposed by Miller and Steinberg (1975). Like Marwell and Hage, Miller and Steinberg regard intimacy as the primary classificatory variable for a relationship taxonomy; however, neither the visibility nor the regulation factor is present in their taxonomy. Rather, intimacy is crossed with commitment to future interaction to form a four-category scheme: (1) *interpersonal relationship-commitment to future interaction;* (2) *interpersonal relationship-no commitment to future interaction;* (3) *noninterpersonal relationship-commitment to future interaction;* and (4) *noninterpersonal relationship-no commitment to future interaction.* An empirical evaluation of the Miller and Steinberg taxonomy by Kaminski, McDermott, and Boster (1977) provided only limited support for the scheme: Respondents who were asked to sort forty situations into the four categories did not perceive many of them to fall into the noninterpersonal-commitment to future interaction category, and none of them were regarded as appropriate to the interpersonal-no commitment to future interaction category. However, there are clearly relationships (as opposed to situations) that do fall into the latter category (for example, prostitute-client), so that it is possibly inappropriate to conclude that interpersonal-no future commitment is an empty set without testing it against a larger sample of situations or situated role relationships.

Wish and his colleagues (Wish, Deutsch, & Kaplan, 1976; Wish & Kaplan, 1977) have been interested in expectations about the communicative characteristics of various role relationships across different contexts. Wish et al. conducted an INDSCAL analysis of similarity ratings of pairs of stock role relationships (husband-wife, lawyer-client, bitter enemies, and so forth) as well as pairs of subjects' "own" relations. Combining over both sets of role relations, Wish et al. obtained a four-factor solution whose dimensions were interpreted, respectively, as (1) *competitive and hostile versus cooperative and friendly,* (2) *equal versus unequal power,* (3) *intense versus superficial,* and (4) *social-emotional and informal versus task-oriented and informal.*

Wish et al. reported substantial differences in individuals' or types of individuals' perceptual emphasis with respect to the four dimensions. Subjects who were married, older, and more conservative tended to place greater importance on the first dimension (competitive and hostile versus cooperative and friendly), whereas the younger, unmarried, less conservative subject was apt to place greater weight on the last factor (social-emotional and informal versus task-oriented and informal).

Wish and Kaplan (1977) were able to replicate these four dimensions, at least in part, in a follow-up study in which subjects' responses provided dissimilarity estimates for pairs of "situations" or episodes consisting of role relations crossed with a communication activity, such as "talking to each other at a large social gathering" or "settling a trivial misunderstanding" (p. 239). An INDSCAL analysis of the dissimilarities yielded a good-fitting five-factor solution, the first three dimensions of which were the same as the first three reported in Wish et al. The fourth factor from Wish et al., however, in which only context-free role relationships were examined, split in the Wish and Kaplan study into two distinct dimensions: (1) *formal and cautious versus informal and open,* and (2) *task-oriented versus nontask-*

oriented. Wish and Kaplan provided the following account for this dimensional split.

> The confounding of these dimensions within the domain of role relations makes sense, since business relations tend to be both task-oriented and formal, while family and social relations are generally more socio-emotional and informal. Since the current stimulus set factorially combined role relations with situational contexts, these two characteristics became separable. (p. 244)

Wish and Kaplan reported that the role relations component seemed to be the most important factor in perceptions of episode dominance and formality, with the activity component the leading contributor to judgments of the cooperativeness, intensity, and degree of task orientation characterizing the episode.

Synthesizing the cited work on the "who" component, it seems that we have at least eight candidate dimensions of role relationships, most of which have received some degree of empirical confirmation: They are relational *intimacy, visibility, regulation, cooperative-competitive orientation, future orientation, equality, intensity,* and *task orientation.* Thus in making the appropriate adjustments to a new context, or, more to the point, in determining that in fact a change in context has occurred, an actor may be expected to take into account the answers to some or all of the following questions with respect to the others present: How close are we? How public is our relationship? How constrained is it? Are we working together or against one another? Will we see each other again? Who's got the power? How strongly are we involved with each other? And what is it that we do together?

Settings: Taxonomic Studies

Although much social scientific research has been addressed to the "where" component of the situation construct (Craik, 1970, 1973; Russell & Ward, 1982; Stokols, 1978), a great deal of that body of work has been concerned with variables or dimensions that are of little immediate concern to commication researchers. Ward's (1977) work, for example, proposed dimensions such as "man-made versus enclosed" and "land versus water." Two recent articles by cognitive psychologists, however (Cantor et al., 1982b; Tversky & Hemenway, 1983), provide taxonomic approaches to settings that are particularly pertinent to interpersonal communication, in that both attempt to recover the structure of practical knowledge about everyday social environments.

Cantor et al. (1982b, p. 46) assume that an actor's knowledge of a social setting is organized around and stored in long-term memory as a *prototype* that takes the form of a set of distinctive features usually associated with membership in the setting category. Cantor et al. proposed a four-category taxonomy of settings or situations, each of which is hierarchically structured so that settings of less generality (for example, "being at a bar mitzvah") are nested under a setting or situation of greater generality (such as "being at a religious ceremony"), which is in turn nested under a setting of still greater generality (for example, "being in an ideological situation"). The Cantor et al. taxonomy, which was constructed to be consonant with taxonomies of personality traits, such as Norman's (1963) *conscientiousness, extroversion, emotional stability,* and *culture* factors, contained four broad categories: (1) *being in an ideological situation,* (2) *being in a social situation,* (3) *being in a stressful situation,* and (4) *being in a cultural situation.*

Cantor et al. had their subjects list properties characteristic of each of the setting categories, at each of the three levels of generality. One of their findings was that the subject prototypes did not exhibit the perfect nesting of attributes implied by their model. For example, a given trait might be ascribed to both the highest (being in a social situation) and lowest (being at a cocktail party) levels of a category, but not to the middle level (being at a party).

Another of the interesting findings of Cantor et al. was that subjects could form images of situations or settings (for example, "religious ceremony") slightly more quickly than they could of persons ("religious devotee"); further, the situation images were richer. Cantor et al. speculated that setting images were formed easily because persons had to do so routinely in order to adjust their behavior to the demands of a new situation. On the other hand, Cantor et al. found that a considerable proportion of the setting prototypes contained information about people-in-situations; how they normally behave, how they feel about being in the situation, and how others typically respond to their actions. Thus although there is evidence for the importance of setting knowledge in routine social perception, that knowledge is difficult to disentangle from a knowledge of relationships and of situated activity—the "what" component.

Tversky and Hemenway (1983, p. 125) were interested in generating a taxonomy of environmental *scenes,* which they describe as the "setting or context for objects, the background where objects are figural." Like Cantor et al., Tversky and Hemenway adopt a hierarchical approach to the categorization of scenes. Beginning with the superordinate, a priori categories "indoors" and "outdoors," Tversky and Hemenway had subjects generate categories and subcategories of either indoor or outdoor scenes. Selecting the most frequently mentioned scenes, the authors constructed a three-tiered, double-pronged taxonomy as follows: Under category (1), *indoor scenes,* were nested (a) *home* ([1] *single-family,* [2] *apartment*); (b) *school* ([1] *elementary,* [2] *high school*); (c) *store* ([1] *grocery,* [2] *department*); and (d) *restaurant* ([1] *fast-food,* [2] *fancy*). Under category (2), *outdoor scenes,* were nested (a) *park* ([1] *city,* [2] *neighborhood*); (b) *city* ([1] *Midwestern,* [2] *industrial*); (c) *beach* ([1] *lake,* [2] *ocean*); and (d) *mountains* ([1] *Sierra,* [2] *Rocky*).

A second set of 210 subjects supplied setting attributes or features at different levels of generality. Results indicated that 95 percent of the attributes listed were "parts": For example, parks have parts such as trees, benches, play equipment, and so forth. Tversky and Hemenway also found that most of the parts supplied were neither at the superordinate (for example, indoor) or the subordinate (for example, single-family home) levels but rather at the intermediate, or what they term the *basic*, level (home, school, store, and so forth). Further, the authors found that the basic level of categorization was preferred in communication tasks such as describing scenes. Tversky and Hemenway concluded that the intermediate or basic level of taxonomic classification corresponds to the level in which scene schemas are likely to be organized and stored in memory.

The work that we have reviewed here by Cantor et al. (1982b) and by Tversky and Hemenway is of interest not because the two studies jointly provide an exhaustive classification of social settings or scenes, for clearly that is not the case. What is useful about this work to the student of interpersonal communication is that the knowledge of settings that communicators bring to their everyday interaction tasks appears to be hierarchically structured at different levels of generality, but retrieved and put to use primarily at intermediate levels of abstraction. This suggests that if we are interested in predicting interpersonal behavior from features of settings, the success of our efforts may vary considerably depending upon the level of abstraction of our questioning. Thus, for example, if we want to know how a person will behave at a staff Christmas party we might have the most success by trying to unearth the rules for appropriate behavior at an office party in general.

The second useful idea that we can derive from these cognitive approaches to settings is the notion that setting knowledge is not just knowledge of the "where" component of an action sequence. According to which set of scholars you believe, setting knowledge consists of knowledge of persons and their proper activities in settings or knowledge of settings and their parts. In any event, the two studies make it clear that invoking a setting implies a good deal more than simply supplying a backdrop, recalling Barker's (1968) notion of *behavior settings*, which, as Moos (1973) put it, have both "ecological and behavioral properties."

Activity in Situations:
Classificatory and Dimensional Schemes

The "what" component of the situational construct has received very little systematic attention from behavioral scientists, probably because we have been inclined to think of situation as an independent variable and "activity" as something that is "affected" by the situation rather than as a defining characteristic of the situation. Despite the fact that process models of interaction have been with us for some time (and despite the fact that the popularity of sequential analysis techniques suggests that we believe that the best predictor of what B does in any context is what A did just before), nevertheless we must for the most part turn to coding schemes to get exhaustive and empirically validated accounts of overt communicative behavior.

Few authors have approached the classification of situations from the perspective of the activities that constitute them. An exception is Krause (1970). Krause was primarily interested in categorizing social settings by their predominant type of activity, an approach that many would classify as unacceptably circular. Krause distinguished among seven categories of behavior settings or situations: (1) joint working, (2) trading, (3) fighting, (4) sponsored teaching, (5) serving, (6) self-disclosing, and (7) playing.

The only other authors who have dealt with the activity component in situation classification have been Magnusson and his colleagues. In an early study (1971), with only three judges, Magnusson obtained similarity judgments of all possible pairs of 36 situations; for example, "You are sitting at home preparing an oral report." A multidimensional scaling of the similarities data yielded a five-factor solution, the first two of which (*rewarding* and *negative*) were along the lines of Moos's (1973) environmental reinforcement variables. The last three dimensions, *passiveness, social interaction,* and *active* (working), all indicated that the nature of what the actor is doing is an important determinant of how a situation is perceived. In a partial replication, Magnusson and Ekehammar (1973) obtained the *passive* and *social interaction* factors, but not the dimension *active*. In a study of the dimensions of stressful situations, Ekehammar, Schalling, and Magnusson (1975) had subjects rate 24 situations for unpleasantness. Among the dimensions obtained were *boredom at work* and *boredom in a passive situation*. Clearly Magnusson and his colleagues' work suggests that social interaction, working or being active, and passivity are significant components of the perception of social situations.

Global Perceptions of Situations:
Dimensional Studies

A number of research efforts have been directed to recovering the global structure underlying perceptions of situations. The dimensions found by different experimenters have for the most part been representative of broad categories of affective response to particular situations; that is, feelings that the situation is friendly, or that it is constraining, or that it is cause for apprehension, and so forth. Pervin (1976) had four subjects recall and list everyday life situations that they had experienced and regarded as being of some importance. Subjects also described each situation, generated a list of feelings and behaviors that the situation evoked, and then rated the appropriateness or "applicability" of the behaviors and feelings in each of the situations. Pervin, after an intensive analysis of each subject's individual response, concluded that they used only a few dimensions to perceive situations, and that they were remarkably consistent in terms of the nature of those dimensions. The four perceptual dimensions that Pervin found to be most salient were *friendly-unfriendly, tense-calm, interesting-dull,* and *constrained-free.*

Forgas (1976, 1979) has studied the perception of what he calls "social episodes": "cognitive representations of stereotypical interaction sequences, which are representative of a given cultural environment" (1979, p. 15). These episodes as perceptual objects are largely combinations of the "who" and "what" components; for example, "discussing your work/research with another member of the group" or "being a guest at your supervisor's house for drinks," although the "where" component figures in some of the episodes (at a pub, at a party, and so forth, see Forgas, 1979, p. 201). Forgas has used essentially the same research strategy on a number of different subject populations: housewives, rugby team members, and university department faculty and staff. Subjects are presented with a set of social episodes, usually selected after informal "elicitations" from representatives of the target group, and asked either to rate the episodes against a set of bipolar scales or to sort the episodes on the basis of their similarity. The obtained data are then, respectively, factor analyzed or multidimensionally scaled.

In Forgas's 1976 study, with both a housewife and a college student sample, a multidimensional scaling method was used to group a set of 25 situations obtained in pilot data generated by a preliminary sample from each of the two populations. Housewives sorted episodes such as "playing with your children" and "having dinner with your family," while undergraduates grouped for similarity such episodes as "going to the pictures with some friends" and "having an intimate conversation with your boy/girlfriend" (Forgas, 1976, p. 202). Two dimensions were recovered from the housewife data set: *intimacy* (dinner with the family versus chatting with a shop assistant) and *subjective self-confidence,* or "knowing/not knowing how to behave." On this latter factor housewives tended to have low subjective self-confidence for episodes like "having a drink with some friends in the pub," episodes involving entertaining or socializing with friends (Forgas, 1979, p. 180). From the student data, three dimensions of episode perception were recovered: *involvement* ("having a short chat with an acquaintance" versus "having an intimate conversation with your boy/girlfriend"), *pleasantness* (unconstrained episodes such as "going out for a walk with an acquaintance" versus more structured episodes such as "acting as a subject in a psychology experiment"), and *subjective self-confidence.* Forgas found that students had least confidence when in episodes requiring prolonged interaction with comparative strangers (Forgas, 1979, p. 180).

In a study of the perception of social episodes by members of two rugby teams, Forgas found that perceptual dimensions were consistent with known characteristics of the teams. For the highly cohesive Team 1, episode perception dimensions were *friendliness, intimacy,* and *activity* (Forgas,

1979, p. 189), whereas for the less cohesive Team 2, which was informally stratified according to player ability, the primary dimension along which social episodes were perceived was *evaluativeness*, "indicative of a more critical and detached cognitive representation of social episodes in this more fragmented and heterogeneous team" (Forgas, 1979, p. 190).

In a third study of episode perception (Forgas, 1978), an academic faculty-staff (including "research students") generated four dimensions, two of which, *involvement* and *evaluation* (pleasant-unpleasant) were obtained in the studies previously cited. Two dimensions not obtained in the other studies were *anxiety*, the primary component against which episodes were judged ("having a meeting/supervision with your supervisor" versus "going to the pub on Friday night after a seminar"), and *social-emotional* versus *task*, a dimension encountered earlier in our account of role relationships. This latter dimension, which was the fourth extracted in the faculty study, contrasted such items as "going to the general office to get something" and "at a dinner party at one of the group member's house." Forgas found that for department members regarded by their colleagues as high in competence, the anxiety and task versus social-emotional dimensions were relatively unimportant, and the evaluative dimension was more important to them than it was to the members perceived as less competent.

Although we have already reviewed the work by Magnusson and his associates as part of the "activity" component literature, it is worth mentioning in the context of global responses to situations that the first two factors recovered in both the 1971 study and the 1973 study with Ekehammar were, respectively, *positive* and *rewarding* (for example, being praised for one's work), and *negative* (for example, failing an examination). These two factors appear to tap a similar pleasant-unpleasant dimension that Forgas labeled *evaluativeness* (also *evaluation*) in his studies of rugby team players and an academic staff.

Cody and McLaughlin (1980) were interested in recovering the structure underlying perceptions of everyday interpersonal persuasion situations. Stimulus situations were obtained from two pretests (Cody, 1978) designed to provide situations that would be both relevant and experienced with significant frequency for most people. From the pretests, three sets of 12 stimulus situations each were generated; they included items such as "persuade your boy/girlfriend to confide in you more," "persuade a professor that an answer on a test is incorrect," and "persuade your parents to give you money" (Cody & McLaughlin, 1980, p. 136). Subjects completed two questionnaires, in one of which they rated the situations against a set of bipolar attribute scales, and in the other of which they made similarity judgments of all possible pairs of the situations in a set.

Analyses of the dissimilarities data for the three stimulus situation sets revealed that there were somewhat different dimensions underlying each set. Correlations of the dimensional coordinates of situations with their ratings on the attribute scales were used to label the dimensions. For the first set of situations, two dimensions, *intimacy* and *personal benefits*, were extracted. A typical high intimacy situation was "persuade a boy/girlfriend that there is nothing wrong in occasionally dating another person," whereas a low intimacy item was "persuade a professor that a test item was ambiguous." A persuasive situation high in personal benefits was "persuade your roommate to keep quiet when you are trying to sleep"; a corresponding low item was "persuade your mother to go back to college and get a degree." For the second stimulus set, the recovered dimensions were *resistance/unfriendly* and *intimacy*. The first dimension contrasted such high-resistance situations as "persuade parents that marijuana is not bad" with situations in which the target of a persuasive attempt should be friendlier and less resistant, for example, "persuade a friend to go shopping with you." For the third stimulus set, a three-dimensional structure was recovered: dominance (versus equal power), intimacy or *long-term relational consequences*, and *resistance/ unfriendly*. Contrasting items on the dominance dimension were "persuade your parents to give you money" (unequal power) and "persuade a friend not to smoke so much" (equal power). A typical situational item characterized as high in long-term relational consequences was "persuade your boy/girlfriend to meet your relatives," whereas a situation characterized by short-term relational consequences was "persuade a group of people to order a pizza because you feel like eating one."

In a second study, Cody and McLaughlin had subjects rate situational stimuli (scenarios) against a set of scales measuring six proposed factors of situation perception: *intimacy, dominance, resistance, personal benefits, relational consequences,* and *rights,* the first five of the factors having emerged as significant in the multidimensional scaling analysis. Subjects rated situations like the following:

> A close friend of yours is constantly teasing and putting down another friend of yours. Since you would like your friends to get along well together you go to the friend who is doing the teasing and try to persuade the person not to tease the other friend. (Cody & McLaughlin, 1980, p. 144)

These situations, like those used in the MDS study, are similar to "episodes" in that they include the role relation and activity components, but not the "where" (setting or scene) component. Factor analysis of the ratings of situations yielded a six-factor solution: *personal benefits, dominance, rights, intimacy, consequences,* and *resistance.* All of the factors but *rights* had been obtained in the MDS study. Situation items rated high on rights (to persuade) included getting a friend to pay back money you had loaned him or her, whereas a typical low-rights situation would be persuading a dealer to come down on the price of an antique rocking chair.

In a follow-up study, Cody, Woelfel, and Jordan (1983) used confirmatory factor analysis to test the fit of a seven-factor model of situation perception that included the six factors obtained in Cody and McLaughlin plus a seventh factor, *apprehension* ("I would feel uneasy in this situation"). The seven-factor model was a good-fitting account of the structure underlying subjects' perceptions of selected hypothetical situations (persuading a friend to repay a loan, persuading a neighbor to do something about a barking dog, and so forth), and was superior to alternative models.

Biggers and Masterson (1983) were interested in recovering the broad categories of "emotional responses" that different situations might evoke. A pool of 48 interpersonal situations was created (taking a week's vacation, complaining about your job to the boss, graduating, breaking up with your boy/girlfriend, and so on), and subjects rated each of the situations against a set of scales measuring the proposed factors of emotional response: *pleasure, arousal,* and *dominance.* Biggers and Masterson found that approach of and avoidance of situations could be accounted for by the three factors, primarily by situation pleasureableness.

A synthesis of the studies examined here suggests that there are at least six distinct factors involved in the global perception of situations, encompassing at least the "who" and the "what" components, and to a very limited extent the "where" component of settings for behavior. These factors have the property that they have been "discovered" by at least two different researchers or research teams. They include: (1) *intimacy* (obtained in Forgas, 1976; Cody & McLaughlin, 1980; it also appears as a dimension in the role relations literature); (2) *friendliness* (obtained in Pervin, 1976; Forgas, 1979; Cody & McLaughlin, 1980; it also appears in Wish et al. (1976) and Wish and Kaplan (1977) in the role relations literature); (3) *pleasantness* (Magnusson, 1971; Magnusson & Ekehammar, 1973, as "positive and rewarding"; Forgas 1978, 1979, as "evaluativeness" or "evaluation"; Biggers & Masterson, 1983, as "pleasure"); (4) *apprehension* (obtained in Pervin, 1976, as "tense-calm"; in Forgas, 1976, as "subjective self-confidence"; in Cody et al., 1983, as "situation apprehension"); (5) *involvement* (obtained in Pervin, 1976, as "interesting-dull"; in Forgas, 1976, 1978, as "involvement"; it also appears in the role relations literature as "intense versus superficial"; see Wish et al., 1976; Wish & Kaplan, 1977); and (6) *dominance* (Cody & McLaughlin, 1980; Biggers & Masterson, 1983; the dimension "equal versus unequal power" also appears in the literature on role relationships; see Wish et al., 1976; Wish & Kaplan, 1977). These six factors taken together should provide a minimally adequate account of the structure of situation perception generally, although for specific situations like persuasive encounters, for example, there are probably additional pertinent factors.

LINKS BETWEEN SITUATION PERCEPTION FACTORS AND MESSAGE STRATEGIES: WHAT WE THINK WE KNOW

The knowledge base concerning situations enables the individual to plan behavior that may effectively produce a desired outcome. However, as there exist an expansive number of situations, a fairly large number of dimensions of perception, an array of compliance-gaining strategies, account strategies, and so forth, any discussion of strategy selection should be organized around how we might *parsimoniously* link situation perception to strategy planning. To be sure, a number of models of persuasion behaviors have been proposed lately. Smith's (1982, 1984) contingency rules model, for example, proposes that we possess *self-identity rules, image maintenance rules, environmental contingency rules, interpersonal relationship rules,* and *social normative rules,* and that these rules influence strategy preferences (and reactions to strategies). Reardon (1981) proposes that people select strategies on the basis of the strategy's *appropriateness* in the situation, the perceived *effectiveness* of the strategy, and the agent's desire to appear *consistent*. In another model, Hunter and Boster (1978, 1979, 1984) argue that all compliance-gaining messages can be ranked from "pro-social" to "anti-social" and that we possess an ethical threshold beyond which we will not attempt further persuasion. The ethical threshold varies as a function of both the individual's personality and the nature of the situation. Clark (1979; Clark & Delia, 1979) argues that strategies are selected on the basis of the importance of three goals: *instrumental, relational,* and *identity management.* A number of studies have shown that people select strategies on the basis of the *costs* or *risks* associated with the implementation of the strategies (for example, Cody, McLaughlin, & Schneider, 1981; Fitzpatrick & Winke, 1979; McLaughlin et al., 1980; Sillars, 1980b). Nearly all of these models assume that there are strategies that are appropriate or normative for certain situations and that situation perception influences both the amount of pressure the agent will employ and the amount of cost associated with strategy selection.

In our view, much of what we currently know about situational influences supports two general, yet parsimonious, propositions. These two propositions incorporate the main thrust of the various models noted above, and many specific situation perception-behavior linkages can be subsumed under these conclusions. First, a person employs a message strategy based on his or her perceptions of how effective the message will be in influencing the target's attitudes and/or behavior. Underlying this proposition is the assumption that as individuals experience a sufficient number of situations to learn how to differentiate one situation from another, they also learn what tactics do *not* work in various situations, and which tactics *may* lead to success. As Schlenker (1980) has noted, people will attempt to be successful by selecting messages that they believe are fitted to the situation as it appears to the audience. Hence, to be forgiven, increased penitence is required as the severity of the offense increases; to be persuasive, increased supporting evidence is required in order to overcome resistance, and so forth.

Second, when selecting an effective strategy, a person's choice of strategy is further refined by the desire to maximize his or her expected gains while minimizing costs—the "general hedonic proposition" (Schlenker, 1980, p. 17) or what is referred to as the "minimax principle" in bargaining. Many of the recently proposed models argue that cost or risk is fundamental to understanding why people select the strategies they select and implement. Costs, paralleling Clark and Delia's (1979) goals, can stem from an instrumental nature, a relational loss, or a discrediting of one's image. If a person used coercive power, for example, he or she may not only fail to change behavior, but can prompt retaliation by the target, a coalition formed by the target, the target's union, and so forth. In fact, Raven and Kruglanski (1970) note that coercive power may be useful to secure a change in public behavior, but may be especially costly because it may require surveillance; it does not produce a change in private beliefs; and it may prompt the target to "move against" the agent both in terms of quality of interactions and in terms of identification with the target. It is little wonder, then, that coercive power is rarely used, at least as a first-attempt strategy. Rather, aggravating questions lead to aggravating responses (Cody & McLaughlin, 1985) and aggressive acts are reciprocated and escalated (Patterson, 1976).

Because (1) relatively few studies have explored situational influences; (2) relatively few studies have precalibrated perceptions of situations from the point of view of the respondents (that is, we cannot assume that respondents share the same perceptions of situations as do experimenters, or that respondents' perceptions are homogeneous—in fact, there are apparently a number of "points of view" that are still not explained in terms of traditional person measures; see Cody, 1978); (3) relatively few studies have explored the impact of more than two or three factors at a time; and (4) relatively few studies have selected more than one situation to represent a general type of event in a factorial design, we do not actually know very much about situational influence on strategy selection. Briefly, the following represents a sampling of what we currently know about situation effects and how these effects reflect functional utility or costs/risks constraints.

Intimacy

To date, intimacy is the most commonly explored situation perception factor. An increase in emotional attachment or in knowledge about one's partner affects whether certain strategies are functional or not and generally increases the importance of relational and image goals. Fitzpatrick and Winke (1979) found that as partners become more knowledgeable about one another, the use of manipulative strategies ceases to be functional; thus, persons who are involved in casual relationships are more likely to use manipulation than married partners. On the other hand, it is obvious that referent influence (appeals to love, empathetic understanding, and so forth) can rarely be used to advantage in less intimate relationships (Raven, Centers, & Rodrigues, 1975; Raven & Kuglanski, 1970). In fact, Cody et al. (1985) obtained an intimacy by resistance interaction for empathic understanding tactics. Respondents were more likely to use the strategies when intimacy and perceived resistance to persuasion were high (in which case empathetic understanding strategies were used to overcome resistance) than when intimacy was high and resistance was low. Needless to say, the tactics were rarely used in nonintimate contexts, regardless of the level of resistance.

Another example relating to perceived efficacy has to do with accounts. McLaughlin, Cody, and O'Hair (1983) found that accounters were likely to use justifications with a familiar other and to provide excuses to strangers. Cody and McLaughlin (1985) found that drivers offered excuses and admissions of guilt to less familiar police officers. These results generally reflect the fact that respondents find the familiar or more intimate targets to be more open to account strategies such as justification, which focus on the accounter's internal state and motivations, whereas such approaches and arguments carry less weight with strangers. The actor may try an excuse (which identifies external factors as the cause of untoward behavior) or simply admit guilt when dealing with an unfamiliar other. In sum, the level of intimacy may preclude the use of some strategies while permitting others to be used.

Generally, intimacy is associated with more integrative or "pro-social" tactics than with tactics destructive to the relationship, although research supporting both effects has been reported. "Liking" (as opposed to "disliking") the target (Michener & Schwertfeger, 1972) and "desired liking from the target" (Clark, 1979) parallel the intimacy variable. Liking results in withdrawal from persuasion, the use of demand creation (requiring "that the influencer increase the target's desire for whatever outcomes the influencer mediates"), and avoidance of both outcome blockage and extension of the power network (Michener & Schwertfeger, 1972, p. 192). Generally, desire for liking results in strategies more conciliatory in nature than destructive (Clark, 1979). Sillars (1980a) found that satisfaction with a roommate was correlated with increased use of integrative conflict tactics and with less frequent use of passive-indirect techniques. Baxter (1984) found that intimacy was associated with the use of polite tactics.

On the other hand, some writers have argued that when intimacy is significantly associated with pro-social strategies, the size of the effect is small (when employing the limited Marwell and Schmitt (1967) strategies; see Boster & Stiff, 1984; Dillard & Burgoon, 1984). Further, Fitzpatrick and Winke (1979) found that when engaging in a conflict, married persons employed more emotionally charged tactics than individuals who were exclusively dating. How do we reconcile these results? As Dillard and Burgoon suggest, it is very likely that high intimacy not only reflects a particular set of qualities of the relationship (emotional attachment, etc.), but also reflects a greater number of shared situations; nonintimates communicate in a limited range of events while intimates experience more situations together, as well as a wider range of them. As a consequence, then, because most situations are positive (or else the relationship won't stay intimate for long), there is a significant but weak correlation between intimacy and pro-social strategies. When married couples recall "conflict" events, they recall qualitatively different types of conflicts than do couples who are only dating. Thus intimacy is linked to the functional utility of both empathetic understanding/referent power and manipulation tactics, but only moderately influences the use of conciliatory tactics. In the latter, the actual use of the tactics depends on whether an intimate other is constrasted with a *disliked* other (Clark, 1979; Michener & Schwertfeger, 1972), or depends on the operation of other characteristics of the situation (goals, etc.), not merely the nature of the relationship. Cody's (1982) assessment of relational disengagement strategies similarly reflects that latter point. When intimacy was low, disengagers used withdrawal/avoidance, but when intimacy was high, disengagers used positive (positive tone, deescalation), neutral (justification), or negative (negative identity management) tactics, depending upon the specific reasons for disengagement.

Dominance

Another factor that has received some attention is dominance. Dominance obviously influences the functional utility of tactics persons employ—dominant agents have a wider range of potential strategies available for use than do nondominant agents (Kipnis & Cohen, 1980; Kipnis & Schmidt, 1983), including assertiveness, negative administrative sanctions, making demands, and so forth. Putnam and Wilson (1982) similarly found that managers used more "control" strategies than subordinates. Nondominant agents not only have a relatively small power base, but are more likely than their superiors to find themselves in contexts in which image goals are important. As a consequence, low dominant agents are motivated to attempt to appear rational: They use more direct requests, supporting evidence, and exchange than do dominant agents (Kipnis & Schmidt, 1983). They are also more likely to employ indirect means of applying pressure, such as forming coalitions, because no other power base is available to them (and possibly because responsibility for applying pressure is diffused). Putman and Wilson (1982) found that subordinates used more "nonconfrontational" strategies than did managers, and that first line supervisors used more solution-oriented tactics than upper management or subordinates.

Several studies found that the level of dominance in the agent-target relationship interacts with other factors in influencing behaviors. In Kipnis and Cohen (1980), for example, dominance interacted with resistance to influence the selection of strategies. Supervisors used administrative sanctions (direct, coercive tactics) on resistant subordinates. When supervisors and coworkers were resistant, agents were more likely to employ indirect forms of pressure (coalitions). The Cody et al. (1985) survey revealed a number of interaction effects involving dominance. Generally, these interactions indicated that persons preferred exchange arrangements and used more empathetic understanding with peers than with dominant targets, and used more self-benefit requests with peers (especially when resistance was high and personal benefits were small) and more other-benefit requests (listing reasons why the target would benefit from complying) with peers, especially when rights to persuade were limited. One straightforward conclusion stemming from the data is simply that agents feel somewhat distant from authority figures and believe that a wider range of strategies can be used with peers and subordinates.

Rights to Persuade. This refers to the extent to which the agent believes that his or her request is legitimate, warranted, and justified. Such a perception should be related to the amount of pressure exerted, either as a first-attempt tactic or in terms of the agent's level of persistence. Dillard and Burgoon (1984) found that rights were significantly related to increased pressure (but only in one study). Kipnis and Cohen (1980) found that when assigning work to another, a context in which the agent has high rights, persons used "assertiveness," and did so equally at all levels within the organization. McLaughlin et al. (1980), in a study of compliance-resisting, found that high rights to resist were associated with justification and nonnegotiation tactics, and with less negotiation (especially in nonintimate contexts) than when rights were limited. (Why should people make concessions in an exchange arrangement when they believe that they have the right to persuade or resist the other?) More recently, Cody et al. (1985) obtained a significant intimacy by rights interaction effect for the use of supporting evidence tactics, indicating that given high rights to persuade, supporting evidence tactics are used less often with intimates than with nonintimates, probably because one may expect an intimate to comply with a legitimate request without the necessity of supplying supporting evidence. Also, this survey indicated that respondents employed few other-benefit tactics when they possessed the right to persuade, but appealed to the target's own interests when rights were low, when attempting to persuade a peer.

Personal Benefits (Level of Self-Interest). This has been associated with the use of pressure in the message (Clark, 1979). In an organization setting, Kipnis and Cohen (1980) found that when the agent desired a benefit from a superior, the agent used exchange and ingratiation. When the agent desired a benefit from a coworker, the agent employed exchange, ingratiation, and used outside agencies to block the actions of the target. When the agent desired to obtain a benefit from a subordinate, the agent used assertiveness and coalitions. Thus when one seeks personal benefits, there is an increase in distributive tactics (and a decrease in ingratiation) as the status of the agent relative to the target increases.

More recently, an attempt has been made to distinguish between benefits to the self and benefits to the target. Williams and Boster (1981) argue that agents may apply considerable pressure on a target if the agent believes that the target will benefit from the persuasion (also see Hunter & Boster, 1978, 1979). In part this may be due to the fact that the negative consequences that stem from the use of distributive tactics are somewhat attenuated when a person is advocating a position from which he or she stands to gain little. Boster and Stiff (1984) found that when neither the agent nor the target benefited from the persuasion, little persuasive effort was observed. Further, increased effort was obtained both in self- and other-benefit conditions, with the former effect weaker than the latter. Dillard and Burgoon (1984) found that self-benefit was associated with pressure (when subjects responded to a hypothetical situation) and both self-benefit and other-benefit were associated (weakly) with increased pressure (when respondents recalled an event they had experienced personally).

The Cody et al. survey (1985) had respondents rate situations on level of personal benefits and examined justification strategies of three types: supporting evidence, self-benefit tactics ("Please repair the plumbing because I can't sleep at night"), and other-benefit tactics ("It will cost you less money if you repair the plumbing promptly than if you wait, because it is leaking down into the baseboard"). Perceived level of personal benefits predicted to self-benefit and face-maintenance tactics, whereas low personal benefit led to the use of other-benefit tactics. Further, a personal benefits by relational consequences interaction effect was obtained for distributive tactics, and the interpretation of the interaction effect provided some support for Boster's personal benefits-aggression hypothesis. Although distributive tactics were rarely used (7 percent of all tactics), they were used somewhat more frequently when the definition of the relationship was stable and when the agent was persuading the target to do something for his or her own benefit than when the relational definition could change and the agent was attempting to persuade the target to do something that would benefit the agent.

Perceived Resistance. Sillars (1980a) found that perceived cooperativeness (paralleling the resistance/unfriendly factor) was associated with the use of integrative strategies and the avoidance of both passive-indirect and distributive strategies. Similarly, Kipnis and Cohen (1980) found that when targets demonstrated resistance by refusing to comply with an agent's first request, agents were persistent and increased the use of personal negative sanctions (negative relational tactics similar to Sillars's distributive strategies, see also Kipnis & Schmidt, 1980; Wilkinson & Kipnis, 1978).

In the Cody et al. survey (1985), several effects were obtained for the resistance feature: (1) Supporting evidence tactics were used to overcome perceived resistance; (2) self-benefit tactics were used when resistance was low and personal benefits were high, and were used least when personal benefits were low, resistance was high, and the target was dominant; (3) other-benefit tactics were used to overcome perceived resistance, but only with peers, not with dominant targets; and (4) exchange tactics were used when the target was perceived to be open (not resistant), especially with peers.

In work on accounts, Cody and McLaughlin (1985) found that excuses were offered to traffic patrolmen when perceived resistance was high, and that respondents denied wrongdoing or challenged the authority of the patrolman when they perceived him to be hostile. Apologies were marginally associated with low perceived resistance of the patrolman.

Relational Consequences. Perception of the relational consequences of persuasive attempts has been the topic of a limited amount of research, but few consistent results have been produced (Cody et al., 1981; Lustig & King, 1980; McLaughlin et al., 1980; Miller, Boster, Roloff, & Seibold, 1977; Roloff & Barnicott, 1978). Clark (1979), as well as Dillard and Burgoon (1984), has questioned both the validity of the construct and its function. In our view, the potential value of the consequences variable may lie in (1) the fact that stability in the relational definition is necessary for some tactics to be functional and (2) the fact that the operation of the variable depends upon whether the relational definition changes were for the better or for the worse. In the former case, for example, it appears that stability of the relational definition is a requirement for the use of exchange arrangements and for the use of distributive tactics (as noted above). Further, the Cody et al. survey indicated that supporting evidence tactics were used more often when consequences were short-term than when they were long-term. Other-benefit requests were used when relational consequences were long-term, especially when the agent felt confidence in himself or herself and in the outcome. Also, empathic understanding tactics were used more in intimate contexts, and more frequently when the relationship could change than when it was perceived to be stable. Generally, these results indicate that when relationships are stable, persons use rather direct methods that apply at least some pressure on the target (supporting evidence, distributive tactics), but are more cautious (other-benefit and empathetic understanding tactics) when the relational consequences of the compliance-gaining attempt could be long-term, because of a desire to avoid being perceived as pushy or selfish. These results, however, should be regarded as tentative because so little research has focused on the relational consequences variable and it appears that many of the "long-term relational consequences" situations sampled in the Cody et al. survey are biased toward relational changes involving *improved* as opposed to deteriorating relations.

Situation Apprehension. The last situation perception factor included in the analysis of message strategy selection is situation apprehension; it is also the least studied. Situation apprehension refers to the extent to which the agent feels he or she will experience tension or nervousness in the situation and undoubtedly reflects the extent to which the agent feels confident in managing the situation so that a desirable outcome is achieved (Greene & Sparks, 1983). Generally speaking, high situation apprehension (1) should reflect a desire to monitor one's image and (2) should emerge in the individual's social environment as an additional cost of attempting to persuade others. In the former case, then, it is not surprising to find that persons use more face-maintenance tactics and are more likely to attempt exchange arrangements when apprehension is high, and employ greater effort and pressure when situation apprehension is low (Cody et al., 1985). With respect to the issue of apprehension as a cost, Cody and McLaughlin (1985) found that high apprehension experienced by drivers when stopped by a patrolman tended to lead drivers to more frequent admissions of guilt, which in turn were more likely to result in the driver being ticketed.

LINKS BETWEEN SITUATION PERCEPTION FACTORS AND MESSAGE STRATEGIES: WHAT WE NEED TO KNOW

The studies relating situation perception to strategy selection via functional utility and cost constraints demonstrate the validity of certain factors of situation perception; however, these studies fall far short of providing the type of data necessary to develop an understanding of naturally occurring behavior. In fact, virtually all of the studies concerning situational influences (excluding the work on accounts) have adopted a rather static view of interpersonal influence. Such an observation is not surprising, considering that when the new wave of research on situational influences on message strategies began in 1977 little was known about the parameters of situation perception (see Miller et al., 1977). Assuming that the scant literature of today is replicated (especially the regression-based work that samples a large number of situations; see Cody et al., 1985; Dillard & Burgoon, 1984; McLaughlin, Cody, & O'Hair, 1983), we need to direct attention to how we might expand on the information obtained in future studies. We need to understand two processes more fully.

First, if we are going to achieve sound ecological prediction, we need to take the individual into consideration at *all* levels of the person-environment interface, including retrieval of information, processing of information, perceived competencies, and so forth (Athay & Darley, 1981; Mischel, 1973, 1979; Smith, 1982, 1984). We need to understand the *process* of how individuals interact with their respective environments. One of the factors that gave rise to the 1970s studies seeking to learn how individuals perceive situations was the replicated observation that person measures rarely predicted the cross-situational production of behavior. However, the same general conclusion seems warranted concerning measures of situation perception: Situation perception factors do not (and probably cannot) *completely* account for all variations in strategy selection. In fact, in the Cody et al. (1985) survey of 42 general types of events and 1064 students, a desirable nonsignificant goodness-of-fit chi-square was obtained for only one of seven types of messages examined (indicating a perfect fit between predicted and observed scores). Such an outcome is not wholly surprising because situations influence behavior only insofar as individuals assign meaning to situations, adopt various contingency plans, and perceive themselves as competent at executing behaviors in the situation. However, it is important to note that we do not *only* advocate person-situation interaction effects on overt behavior, but also on how individuals assign meaning to situations, enter into, avoid and/or change situations, and how they process information in situations, that is, how individuals and their created environment influence each other over time.

The second type of process that requires further study is the extent to which behavior is influenced within a situation as a function of how the situation unfolds, taking into consideration plans, interactional constraints, and impinging environmental cues. Thus let us now look at procedural knowledge.

Goals, Plans, and Rules: What Actors Know and How They Use It

The various taxonomies of the dimensions along which situations and their components are perceived have proved useful both directly, in that they have pointed to some of the best predictors of overt behavior, such as intimacy and dominance, but also indirectly in that they suggest some of the knowledge bases that actors must consult in order to know how to proceed in any given situation. DeBeaugrande (1980), in considering conversation, has suggested that in any social situation there are well-established expectations about the kinds of knowledge participants should have, including not only the "apperceivable traits of the current situation," but also (1) "typical and determinate concepts and relations in world knowledge" (that grass is green, that the earth is round, that snow falls in winter, and so forth); (2) "episodic knowledge of shared experiences among participants"; (3) "cultural and social attitudes," including norms and rules of appropriate conduct; and (4) conventional scripts, plans, and goals (pp. 243-244). Of the first and second knowledge bases, we can have little to say here because "world knowledge" and "shared experience" are, respectively, too universal and too idiosyncratic to attract the attention of social scientists. Consequently, we will focus our attention on conventional goals and plans, and on rules as knowledge bases that actors consult in trying to make sense of the situations in which they find themselves.

Conventional Goals and Plans

Winograd (1981) has proposed that anything that an actor utters during the course of a social episode can be regarded as the final output of a "design process," in which the actor produces a message aimed at realizing some *goal*. A goal may be viewed as a "conceptualization of a specific state or class of states in the world and/or in himself that a person, consciously or unconsciously, strives to attain" (Hobbs & Evans, 1980, p. 350). Hobbs and Evans treat a *plan* as a usually hierarchical cognitive representation of the final result of the actor's "design process":

> A formal representation of what the system is trying to accomplish in the world ... and the means which it is using. It is in general a "tree-like" structure whose non-terminal nodes are goals and subgoals, i.e., logical representations of states to be brought about, and whose terminal nodes are actions which the system is capable of performing. (Hobbs & Agar, 1981, p. 4)

Most planning in verbal interaction will be put into effect once a preliminary action has been selected. As interaction unfolds, the plan may be developed, altered, or even aborted as a function of current contingencies (Hobbs & Evans, 1980, p. 5); thus planning is appropriately regarded as *incremental* (Hayes-Roth & Hayes-Roth, 1979). Hayes-Roth and Hayes-Roth suggest that for most people, planning is primarily *opportunistic:* Although a planner may begin with an orderly, "top-down" plan ("I'm going to list one by one all the times last week that she forgot to call me when she was going to be late"), in service of a goal ("Let her know how irresponsible I think she is"), some low-level event or "interim decision" ("While I'm on the subject of her being late on Thursday, I'll also mention how on Thursday she left the door unlocked") may lead to a reorganization of the plan at a higher level of abstraction ("I'll bring up all the times this week she left the door unlocked").

Cohen and Perrault (1979, p. 178) propose that most communicators anticipate that others will recognize their plans, and that for the most part, they want their plans and intentions to be recognized and will often make overt efforts to see that they are. This suggests that competence of communication requires that the actor have some knowledge of conventional goals and the actions conventionally undertaken to achieve them, or, to turn it around, to know the intended perlocutionary effect of common speech acts (Jackson & Jacobs, 1984); for example, that a *request* hopes to effect a *grant,* a *question* an *answer,* and so on.

Winograd (1981, p. 69) suggests that common communicative goals include: (1) causing the hearer to undertake a particular action, (2) causing the hearer to make inferences in a desired way, (3) conveying information, (4) creating a new conceptual entity, and (5) guiding the attention of the hearer to some particular object or event. Hobbs and Evans (1980, p. 354) suggest that the following are common goals in conversation: (1) satisfaction of external task demands; (2) discourse goals, such as maintaining coherence, avoiding lapses, and so on; (3) interpersonal (socioemotional) goals; and (4) image goals. The task or instrumental, interpersonal, and image-maintenance goals have also been treated at length in Clark and Delia (1979). Actors' perceptions of the relative importance of communicative goals have been used successfully as predictors in research on compliance-gaining message strategies and in work on accounts. For example, Clark (1979) explored the impact of self-interest (instrumental goals) and desire for liking (interpersonal goals) on the construction of compliance-gaining strategies. She found that less pressure was exerted when self-interest was high, and that as desire for liking increased, there was a (nonsignificant) increase in frequency of use of positive identity management and positive interpersonal strategies. McLaughlin, Cody, and O'Hair (1983), in a study of accounting behavior, employed rating scales to measure each of the three Clark and Delia (1979) goals. When the instrumental goal was rated low in importance, subjects were more likely to use a justification. When the instrumental goal was perceived as important, individuals opted to use either a concession or an excuse. Silence (offering no verbal account) was associated with the perception that relational goals were unimportant.

Rules: Knowledge About Appropriate Conduct

Rules are propositions that model our knowledge of the "situated evaluation" of interactive behavior and "the ways in which social interaction is constituted and carried out" (McLaughlin, 1984, p. 17). Rule-statements usually take the form, "If you want to achieve goal G in situation Y, do X" (Harre' & Secord, 1972; Pearce, 1976; Shimanoff, 1980). The "if-clause" of a rule-statement, called the "protasis" (Gottlieb, 1968), specifies the conditions or circumstances under which the rule is applicable; if you will, the *situation* in which the rule applies. Consequently, part of a person's knowledge of situations will have to do with the ways in which they *constrain behavior.*

It is convenient for our purposes here to treat rule-knowledge as a collection of propositions about how role relations, setting, and activity contexts affect what is perceived as appropriate conduct—the "who," "where," and "why" components that appeared earlier in this chapter. There is considerable research to indicate that there are powerful rules relating conduct to these three parameters of the social situation.

Rules About Role Relations: Representative Studies. Some researchers have been interested in trying to specify how social rules affect such processes as the comprehension and recall of particular kinds of speech acts. For example, Kemper and Thissen (1981) found that there were two primary dimensions underlying the perception of requests: politeness and directness. Generally, the more direct the request form, the less polite. Kemper and Thissen hypothesized that if indeed direct requests were less polite, they would be noticeably "improper" if used by a subordinate to a superior. To test this notion, Kemper and Thissen proposed to see if nonconventional request forms, such as a direct imperative to a superior ("Do X!"), would be recalled more freely than a more conventional form, such as an affirmative interrogative to a superior ("Do you think you should do X?"). Subjects judged cartoons in which the relative status of speaker and addressee were manipulated. Kemper and Thissen found support for their hypothesis about the proper request forms for subordinates to use with superiors:

> A speaker who violates the conversational conventions governing the form of request, who does not appropriately balance politeness and directness, will pay two penalties: not only may the request fail, but the inappropriate request will be accurately remembered. (p. 562)

Laver (1981) has devised a decision tree or flowchart for what he calls formulaic parting and greeting routines, in which the relationship of speaker to addressee is a prominent influence. For example, the speaker's first task is to determine the status (adult versus child) of the addressee, which allows him to make a proper choice between, for example, "Bye" and "Bye-bye." Other critical branches in Laver's decision tree include whether or not the addressee is kin, whether or not the pair are well acquainted, whether the addressee is of higher rank or not, and if so, if there has been a "dispensation" such that informality is permitted, and finally, if the addressee is 15 or more years older than the speaker. The more formal greeting and parting formula, according to Laver, is used with adults, with those who are not kin, with those of higher rank than the speaker who have given no dispensation, and with those considerably older than oneself.

Knapp and his colleagues (Knapp, Hart, Friedrich, & Schulman, 1980; Krivonos & Knapp, 1975) have looked at the effect of degree of acquaintance and relationship formality on greeting and parting formulae. For greetings, Krivonos and Knapp found that the sequence of mutual glance-head gesture-smile-verbal salute-reference to other-personal inquiry-external reference-topic initiation, which they observed among acquainted pairs, appeared in a considerably truncated version among nonacquainted pairs: mutual glance-head gesture-verbal salute-personal inquiry. Similarly, Knapp and his colleagues (1980) found that parting sequences in formal relationships differed from those in less formal ones: Pairs of both types began the parting sequence with reinforcements ("uh huh," "O.K.") and "buffing" ("uh," "er," "well"), but the formal pairs followed up with appreciations and legitimizers (rationalizations for the leave-taking), whereas the informal pairs' next moves were statements of concern for the other's welfare ("Take care now") and "continuance" statements ("See ya Friday").

Rules about Settings: Representative Studies. Most of the work on setting constraints (the "where" component) within the rules perspective has been done on cross-cultural variation. To the authors' knowledge, there has been very little, if any, research on communicative behaviors in which the impact of such setting variables as "indoor vs. outdoor" or "ideological situation vs. cultural situation" have been assessed directly. Price and Bouffard (1974), however, were able to obtain mean appropriateness ratings for 15 behavior settings, collapsed across 15 behaviors such as "fight," "cry," and "eat," which they interpreted as an index of the global *situational constraint* inherent in that setting. The 15 settings, in order of decreasing constraint, were church, job interview, elevator, family dinner, class, movies, restroom, sidewalk, bus, date, bar, football game, dorm lounge, park, and own room.

Gibbs (1981) has examined the impact of what he calls "contexts" on the form in which *requests* are encoded. A context, in Gibbs's framework, seems to be an amalgam of a physical setting (in this case, a post office) and a characteristic activity that might occur there:

Louise was applying to law school.

She had four letters that she needed to mail.

She went over to the post office at Revelle.

The problem was that she had no stamps.

She went in, and said to the man behind the counter. . . . (Gibbs, 1981, p. 433)

Gibbs found that processing time for indirect requests varied as a function of the interaction between context and request form; requests that were highly conventional in context, for example, "May I have four stamps?" in the post office, were processed more quickly than a similarly phrased request, for example, "May I have a hamburger?" in a different situational context in which another form was more conventional ("I'd like a hamburger").

Cross-cultural studies provide interesting insights as to how settings may influence behavior. Ferguson (1976) notes that whereas in English a proper reply to "good morning" is an exact duplicate, with perhaps a small variation in intonation pattern, in Arabic the principle for formulaic replies to the initial pleasantry is "the same or more so" (pp. 143-144). House and Kaspar (1981) had native speakers of English and German generate oral versions of the speech acts *complain* and *request* in response to hypothetical situations. House and Kasper found that English subjects used more indirect forms both to complain and to make requests. For example, the most direct forms of complaint (S explicitly asserts that H was bad in doing X; S asserts explicitly that H is bad) did not occur in the responses of the English subjects but did in about 8 percent of the German data. Similarly, Germans were more likely to use direct imperatives ("Get me a glass of water") and explicit performatives than were the English subjects, whose preferred form was the "query-preparatory": "Can you get me a glass of water?" Similar work by Tannen (1981), comparing Greeks, Greek-Americans, and Americans not of Greek ancestry, also indicated that indirectness in discourse varies as a function of culture. In the example below, Greeks were more prone than Americans to indicate that the husband did not want to attend the party; the brevity of his response indicated a reluctance to comply.

Wife: John's having a party; wanna go?

Husband: O.K. (Tannen, 1981, p. 229)

Philips (1976) has found in her work among the Warm Springs Indians that the so-called demands of conditional relevance (Schegloff, 1977), that is, the property that some types of speech acts like questions have of establishing a slot for a particular type of next turn such as answers, may not be a cultural universal. In Indian interaction, a question might go unanswered for as long as a week, without in the least implying that the question was improper or in any way defective as a speech act. Indeed, Philips found that what we have come to think of as "second pair parts" (Jackson & Jacobs, 1980) were often "widely separated" from speech to which they were a response.

Rules About "Activity": Representative Studies. By far the greatest amount of work on context effects from a "rules" perspective has had to do with the role of the "what" component, that is, how the interactants' interpretations of what they are currently doing (or what has just been done) affects their subsequent actions. The literature on the sequential development of account episodes, which we have reviewed earlier, is a case in point. Three other topics that seem to have generated a considerable amount of scholarly interest are (1) how the nature of an offending action affects the construction of apologies; (2) how perceptions of the "topic" of a discourse constrain the kinds of contributions that will be regarded as appropriate on a next turn; and (3) how the opening moves in access rituals (greetings and partings) affect subsequent moves.

Schlenker and Darby (1981) regard the apology as a device by which an offender tries to convince the offended that the act in question ought not to be regarded as representative of the actor's "real self"; rather, that a "bad self" was responsible for the incident, and a "good self" promises that better conduct can be expected in the future (p. 272). Schlenker and Darby found that as the seriousness of the precipitating offense increased, the number of apology components also increased. For minimal offenses, simple "pardon me's" were the norm, whereas for offenses with more severe consequences and/or greater actor responsibility, apologies were likely to contain offers of redress, self-castigations and expressions of remorse, in addition to or in place of the more perfunctory "pardon" component. Fraser (1981) also argued that the number of apology components increased with the seriousness of the infraction, with apologies for more serious offenses likely to be accompanied by accounts.

Several scholars have been interested in the way in which the current discourse topic acts as a limiting factor on the options available to a speaker in making a relevant conversational contribution. Planalp and Tracy (1980) found that a speaker who wanted to change the topic was most likely to be perceived as competent if he or she invoked a context that was "salient to the listener" (p. 242); that is, the speaker was obliged to make the transition as easy as possible for the listener by trying, for example, to make the source of context explicit, to bring up only thematic participants that are already present in the hearer's memory, or to introduce topics that can be interpreted in light of conversation-internal, rather than environmental, information.

Reichman (1978) proposed a number of what she called "semantic relational rules" that model knowledge about "the dependency between the appropriateness of a speaker's utterance and the preceding discourse structure" (pp. 290-291). For example, one of Reichman's rules is that if one party has specified an "event context space" (begun a narrative about some event), it is permissible to use it in further talk as illustrative of some issue, *unless* the event had been brought up for the express purpose of illustrating some separate and unrelated issue. Further, if an event is introduced as illustrative of some particular issue, it is inappropriate to dwell on some aspect of the event, say, a minor character or setting, that is not really an instance of the issue. Tracy (1982) found empirical confirmation for several of Reichman's postulates. In looking at the rated appropriateness of different "continuation types" (possible next utterances), Tracy found that the average appropriateness ratings for issue-oriented next turns was highest in discourse segments that had an issue-event sequential structure; however, when there did not appear to be an issue as such, event-oriented continuations were regarded as more appropriate.

In looking at access rituals, a number of scholars have found that the way in which they develop may depend largely on the nature of their opening moves. For example, Clark and French (1981), in looking at "goodbye" exchanges between callers and operators at a university exchange, found that when the interaction had been nonroutine (for example, when the operator had made an error, or when the caller's request had been unusual in some way), the caller and operator were more likely to exchange goodbyes. Clark and French regarded the goodbye exchange as a form of mutual affirmation and accounted for their findings by proposing that routine inquiries, by virtue of their impersonal, purely instrumental properties, do not require that participants "take leave" of one another, but that the leave-taking exchange seemed appropriate to affirm the fact that a transitory "relationship" between caller and operator had developed during their protracted exchange.

Crawford (1977) was interested in the effects of the presence or absence of a line and the form of inquiry agents' initial utterances on how inquiries would be made at an information desk. Crawford found that, for example, if the inquiry agent began with a greeting, the greeting was returned before the inquirer proceeded with his or her request, unless the inquirer had been waiting in line, in which case he or she stated the problem without returning the agent's greeting. If there has been a mutual greeting exchange, the agent must initiate a second opener, like "What can I do for you?," in order to get the inquiry. If the agent opens with a "Yes, sir?" and receives a "Good morning" in return, he or she must first return the greeting in order to get the inquiry.

SUGGESTIONS FOR FUTURE RESEARCH

The pursuit of ecologically sound understanding and prediction of naturally occurring overt behavior requires that our attention focus on the multifaceted ways in which individuals interact with the external environment. We need to know more about how individuals construct different social environments and how they scan the environment for different purposes, and we need to link allocation of attention to overt behavior. Further, we need to know more about how situation expectations, interactional constraint, and impinging environmental cues operate in the real world to influence behavior. Most studies assessing the construction of message strategies in hypothetical situational scenarios undoubtedly assess scripted or planned activities. Admittedly, it is a difficult enough task simply to link initial perceptions of situations to overt communicative behavior without also working in the contribution of each subsequent message by each party present to the unfolding situational definition. Nonetheless, if we are to take seriously the claim that situations have a strong activity component, and if further we take seriously that each utterance in an exchange of messages has both a functional and a topical significance, then we must admit that if the activity component of a situation changes, the actor will have to adjust to a new set of constraints. In this same regard, it is also important for the researcher to note that the "entering" orientation that an actor brings to a social situation may be composed primarily of salient bits of relevant long-term knowledge; but if in the process of interaction his or her expectations are violated, as they might be in the event of a refusal counteroffer, then what we have called "interactional constraint" and "impinging environmental cues" will take precedence over any plans, rules, or entry perceptions that the actor may have begun with. Thus different aspects of the situation may be determinants of behavior as the process of interaction unfolds.

Our second major concern is methodological in nature. A review of the most common ways of conceptualizing the "situation" construct, and in particular of the ways in which the underlying dimensionality or structure of the construct has been approached, suggests that there are a number of limitations to the studies we have reviewed in which situation elements and, particularly, situation perception factors have been treated as independent variables. An initial problem is that in many of the dimensional studies that have purported to extract the fundamental factors along which situations are differentiated, the rotation of the factor solutions has been oblique rather than orthogonal (see, for instance, the work by Wish et al., 1976; Cody et al., 1983). This produces obvious problems in selecting "pure types" to be used in factorial designs.

Further, as Jackson and Backus (1982) have noted, many studies have employed factorial designs in which only one situation was used in each cell. Consequently, it is possible that one of the sampled events may depart from the remaining three or so events on some unidentifiable criteria, thus producing significant interactions that may not be replicated if four different situations were arrayed in the ANOVA design. A third problem has been that previous research has often failed to validate the claim that the stimulus situations vary in the ways in which they are claimed to vary, as well as to establish that, within reason, the situations do *not* vary along dimensions that the researcher had neglected to take into account. Fourth, although research in the last five years has understandably focused attention on the construction of message typologies, it is clear that messages vary in their level of prototypicality within each message category. In disengagement research, for instance, it is clear that "de-escalation" and "positive tone" tactics vary considerably as "pure instances" of attempts to reduce the level of intimacy in the relationship while staying friends afterward. Similarly, it seems obvious that the types of message tactics used to measure, say, coercive power in our surveys may or may not be exemplary or representative of the specific message category. Consequently, we will know more about situational influences and produce more generalizable research if we employ more sophisticated designs and focus greater attention on the validity of our independent and dependent variables.

NOTE

1. Note that we do not review Bem's work on templates (Bem, 1983a; Bem & Funder, 1978; Funder, 1982; Lord, 1982). In research on templates and template matching, individuals are presented with a description of an event and are required to Q-sort descriptive personality statements on the basis of whether each statement (that is, "person is critical") is most or least characteristic of the person in the situation. The procedure uncovers a "personality" of a situation. The limitations of the approach, of course, rest in the fact that situations are only described in terms of the persons who occupy the situations, and in that only one behavior is assessed at a time (requiring multiple templates to be constructed; see Lord, 1982). Bem (1983b), however, recently advocated a more context-oriented "S-sort," in which 150 situational items are sorted (also see Mischel & Peake, 1982a). However, the validity of the S-sort technique is intimately linked to the validity of the situational taxonomy from which items are derived. Also, it should be noted that some template research does not replicate, and it is incumbent on theorists using this technique to assess the stability of the sorted data and the stability of whatever weights that might be applied to the data (Mischel & Peake, 1982a; Green, 1980). Bem concluded that his "second pass at fashioning a theory of persons-in-situations" involves selecting traits that refer specifically to stylistic ways of processing information about the internal and external environment and that incorporates situational variables from the very outset of theory construction (Bem, 1983a, p. 184).

REFERENCES

Abelson, R. (1976). Script processing in attitude formation and decision making. In J. Carroll & T. Payne (Eds.), *Cognition and social behavior* (pp. 33-45). Hillsdale, NJ: Lawrence Erlbaum.

Abelson, R. (1981). Psychological status of the script concept. *American Psychologist, 136,* 715-729.

Argyle, M. (1980). The analysis of social situations. In M. Brenner (Ed.), *The structure of action* (pp. 66-107). New York: St. Martin's Press.

Argyle, M., Furnham, A., & Graham, J. A. (1981). *Social situations.* Cambridge, MA: Cambridge University Press.

Atkinson, M. L., & Allen, V. L. (1983). Perceived structure of nonverbal behavior. *Journal of Personality and Social Psychology, 45,* 458-463.

Athay, M., & Darley, J. M. (1981). Toward an interaction-centered theory of personality. In N. Cantor & J. Kihlstrom (Eds.), *Personality, cognition and social interaction* (pp. 281-308). Hillsdale, NJ: Lawrence Erlbaum.

Bandura, A. (1977). Self-efficacy: Toward a unifying theory of behavioral change. *Psychological Review, 84,* 191-215.

Bandura, A. (1978). Reflections on self-efficacy. In S. Rachman (Ed.), *Advances in behaviour research and therapy* (Vol. 1, pp. 237-269). Oxford, England: Pergamon Press.

Barker, R. G. (1968). *Ecological psychology.* Palo Alto, CA: Stanford University Press.

Baron, R. M., Cowan, G., Ganz, R. L., & McDonald, M. (1974). Interaction of locus of control and type of performance feedback: Considerations of external validity. *Journal of Personality and Social Psychology, 23,* 285-292.

Baron, R. M., & Ganz, R. L. (1972). Effects of locus of control and type of feedback on the task performance of lower-class black children. *Journal of Personality and Social Psychology, 21,* 124-130.

Baxter, L. A. (1984). An investigation of compliance-gaining as politeness. *Human Communication Research, 10,* 427-456.

Bem, D. J. (1983a). Persons, situations and template matching: Theme and variations. In M. P. Zanna, E. T. Higgins, & C. P. Herman (Eds.), *Consistency in social behavior: The Ontario symposium* (Vol. 2, pp. 173-186). Hillsdale, NJ: Lawrence Erlbaum.

Bem, D. J. (1983b). Further deja vu in the search for cross-situational consistency: A response to Mischel and Peake. *Psychological Review, 90,* 390-393.

Bem, D. J., & Allen, A. (1974). On predicting some of the people some of the time: The search for cross-situational consistencies in behavior. *Psychological Review, 81,* 506-520.

Bem, D. J., & Funder, D. C. (1978). Predicting more of the people more of the time: Assessing the personality of situations. *Psychological Review, 85,* 485-501.

Biggers, T., & Masterson, J. T. (1983). *Emotion-eliciting qualities of interpersonal situations as the basis for a typology.* Unpublished manuscript, University of Miami.

Block, J. (1971). *Lives through time.* Berkeley, CA: Bancroft.

Block, J. (1977). Advancing the psychology of personality: Paradigmatic shift or improving the quality of research. In D. Magnusson & N. S. Endler (Eds.), *Personality at the crossroads: Current issues in interactional psychology* (pp. 37-63). Hillsdale, NJ: Lawrence Erlbaum.

Blumstein, P. W., et al. (1974). The honoring of accounts. *American Sociological Review, 39,* 551-566.

Boster, F. J., & Stiff, J. B. (1984). Compliance-gaining message selection behavior. *Human Communication Research, 10,* 539-556.

Brehm, J. W. (1966). *A theory of psychological reactance.* New York: Academic Press.

Brehm, J. W. (1972). *Responses to loss of freedom: A theory of psychological reactance.* Morristown, NJ: General Learning Press.

Brownell, P. (1982). The effects of personality-situation congruence in a managerial context: Locus of control and budgetary participation. *Journal of Personality and Social Psychology, 42,* 753-763.

Burgoon, J. K. (1976). The unwillingness-to-communicate scale: Development and validation. *Communication Monographs, 43,* 60-69.

Cacioppo, J. T., Petty, R. E., & Sidera, J. A. (1982). The effects of a salient self-schema on the evaluation of proattitudinal editorials: Top-down vs. bottom-up message processing. *Journal of Experimental Social Psychology, 18,* 324-338.

Cantor, N. (1981). Perceptions of situations: Situation prototypes and person-situation prototypes. In D. Magnusson (Ed.), *Toward a psychology of situations: An interactional approach* (pp. 229-244). Hillsdale, NJ: Lawrence Erlbaum.

Cantor, N., Mischel, W., & Schwartz, J. C. (1982a). Social knowledge: Structure, content, use and abuse. In A. H. Hastorf & A. M. Isen (Eds.), *Cognitive social psychology* (pp. 33-72). New York: Elsevier/North-Holland.

Cantor, N., Mischel, W., & Schwartz, J. (1982b). A prototype analysis of psychological situations. *Cognitive Psychology, 14,* 45-77.

Carver, C. S., & Scheier, M. F. (1981). *Attention and self-regulation: A control theory approach to human behavior.* New York: Springer.

Carver, C. S., & Scheier, M. F. (1982). Control theory: A useful conceptual framework for personality-social, clinical and health psychology. *Psychological Bulletin, 92,* 111-135.

Clark, H. H., & French, J. W. (1981). Telephone goodbyes. *Language in Society, 10,* 1-19.

Clark, N. S., & Isen, A. M. (1982). Toward understanding the relationship between feeling states and social behavior. In A. H. Hastorf & A. M. Isen (Eds.), *Cognitive social psychology* (pp. 4-32). New York: Elsevier/North-Holland.

Clark, R. A. (1979). The impact on selection of persuasive strategies of self-interest and desired liking. *Communication Monographs, 46,* 257-273.

Clark, R. A., & Delia, J. G. (1979). Topoi and rhetorical competence. *Quarterly Journal of Speech, 65,* 187-206.

Cody, M. J. (1978). *A multidimensional scaling of naturalistic persuasion situations.* Speech Communication Association, Minneapolis, MN.

Cody, M. J., Greene, J. O., Marston, P., Baaske, E., O'Hair, H. D., & Schneider, M. J. (1985). *Situation-perception and the selection of message strategies.* In M. L. McLaughlin (Ed.), *Communication yearbook 9.* Beverly Hills, CA: Sage.

Cody, M. J., Marston, P. J., & Foster, M. (1984). Paralinguistic and verbal leakage of deception as a function of attempted control and timing of questions. In R. Bostrom (Ed.), *Communication yearbook 8* (pp. 464-490). Beverly Hills, CA: Sage.

Cody, M. J., & McLaughlin, M. L. (1980). Perceptions of compliance-gaining situations: A dimensional analysis. *Communication Monographs, 47,* 132-148.

Cody, M. J., & McLaughlin, M. L. (1985). Models for sequential construction of accounting episodes: Situational and interactional constraints on message selection and evaluation. In R. Street & J. Cappella (Eds.), *Sequence and pattern in communicative behavior* (pp. 50-69). London: Edward Arnold.

Cody, M. J., McLaughlin, M. L., & Schneider, M. J. (1981). The impact of intimacy and relational consequences on the selection of interpersonal persuasion strategies: A reanalysis. *Communication Quarterly, 29,* 91-106.

Cody, M. J., Woelfel, M. L., & Jordan, W. J. (1983). Dimensions of compliance-gaining situations. *Human Communication Research, 9,* 99-113.

Cohen, C., & Ebbesen, E. (1979). Observational goals and schema activation: A theoretical framework for behavior perception. *Journal of Experimental Social Psychology, 15,* 305-329.

Cohen, P. R., & Perrault, G. R. (1979). A plan-based theory of speech acts. *Cognitive Science, 3,* 213-230.

Coyne, J. C. (1976). Depression and the response of others. *Journal of Abnormal Psychology, 85,* 186-193.

Craik, K. H. (1970). Environmental psychology. In K. H. Craik, B. Kleinmutz, R. L. Rosnow, R. Rosenthal, J. A. Cheyne, & R. H. Walters (Eds.), *New directions in psychology* (Vol. 4, pp. 1-22). New York: Holt, Rinehart & Winston.

Craik, K. H. (1973). Environmental psychology. *Annual Review of Psychology, 24,* 403-421.

Crawford, J. R. (1977). Utterance rules, turn-talking, and attitude in inquiry openers. *IRAL, 15,* 279-298.

Darby, B. W., & Schlenker, B. R. (1982). Children's reactions to apologies. *Journal of Personality and Social Psychology, 43,* 742-753.

Debeaugrande, R. (1980). *Text, discourse, and process: Towards a multidisciplinary science of texts*. Norwood, NJ: Ablex.

Dillard, J. P., & Burgoon, M. (1984). Situational influences on the selection of compliance-gaining messages: Two tests of the predictive utility of the Cody-McLaughlin typology. Unpublished manuscript, University of Wisconsin.

Ebbesen, E. B. (1980). Cognitive processes in understanding ongoing behavior. In R. Hastie, T. M. Ostrom, E. B. Ebbesen, R. S. Wyer, D. L. Hamilton, & D. E. Carlston (Eds.), *Person memory: The cognitive basis of social perception* (pp. 179-225). Hillsdale, NJ: Lawrence Erlbaum.

Ekehammar, B., Schalling, D., & Magnusson, D. (1975). Dimensions of stressful situations: A comparison between response analytic and stimulus analytic approaches. *Multivariate Behavioral Research, 10,* 155-164.

Endler, N. S. (1982). Interactionism comes of age. In M. P. Zanna, E. T. Higgins, & C. P. Herman (Eds.), *Consistency in social behavior: The Ontario symposium* (Vol. 2, pp. 209-250). Hillsdale, NJ: Lawrence Erlbaum.

Endler, N. S., & Edwards, J. (1978). Person by treatment interactions in personality research. In L. A. Pervin & M. Lewis (Eds.), *Perspectives in interactional psychology* (pp. 141-169). New York: Plenum.

Epstein, S. (1979). The stability of behavior. I. On predicting most of the people much of the time. *Journal of Personality and Social Psychology, 39,* 1097-1126.

Epstein, S. (1983). Aggregation and beyond: Some basic issues on the prediction of behavior. *Journal of Personality, 51,* 310-392.

Erickson, K., & Simon, H. (1980). Verbal reports as data. *Psychological Review, 87,* 215-251.

Ferguson, G. A. (1976). The structure and use of politeness formulas. *Language in Society, 5,* 137-151.

Fitzpatrick, M. A., & Winke, J. (1979). You always hurt the one you love: Strategies and tactics in interpersonal conflict. *Communication Quarterly, 27,* 3-11.

Fong, G. T., & Markus, H. (1982). Self-schemas and judgements about others. *Social Cognition, 1,* 191-204.

Forgas, J. P. (1976). The perception of social episodes: Categorical and dimensional representations of two different social milieus. *Journal of Personality and Social Psychology, 34,* 199-209.

Forgas, J. P. (1978). Social episodes and social structure in an academic setting: The social environment of an intact group. *Journal of Experimental Social Psychology, 14,* 434-448.

Forgas, J. P. (1979). *Social episodes: The study of interaction routines*. London: Academic Press.

Forgas, J. P. (1982). Episode cognition: Internal representations of interaction routines. In L. Berkowitz (Ed.), *Advances in experimental social psychology* (Vol. 15, pp. 59-101). New York: Academic Press.

Fraser, B. (1981). On apologizing. In F. Coulmas (Ed.), Conversational routine: *Explorations in standardized communication situations and prepatterned speech* (pp. 259-271). The Hague: Mouton.

Funder, D. C. (1982). On assessing social psychological theories through the study of individual differences: Template matching and forced compliance. *Journal of Personality and Social Psychology, 43,* 100-110.

Furnham, A. (1981). Personality and activity preferences. *British Journal of Social and Clinical Psychology, 20,* 57-68.

Gibbs, R. W. (1981). Your wish is my command: Convention and context in interpreting indirect requests. *Journal of Verbal Learning and Verbal Behavior, 20,* 431-444.

Goffman, E. (1961). *Encounters*. Indianapolis: Bobbs-Merrill.

Gottleib, G. (1968). *The logic of choice: An investigation of the concepts of rule and rationality*. New York: MacMillan.

Green, B. F. (1980). A note on Bem and Funder's scheme for scoring Q-sorts. *Psychological Review, 87,* 212-214.

Greene, J. O., O'Hair, H. D., Cody, M. J., & Yen, C. (1985). Planning and control during deception. *Human Communication Research, 11,* 335-364.

Greene, J. O., & Sparks, G. G. (1983). The role of outcome expectations in the experience of a state of communication apprehension. *Communication Quarterly, 31,* 212-219.

Harré, R., & Secord, P. (1972). *The explanation of social behavior.* Oxford: Blackwell.

Hayes-Roth, B., & Hayes-Roth, F. (1979). A cognitive model of planning. *Cognitive Science, 3,* 275-310.

Hewes, D. E., & Planalp, S. (1982). There is nothing as useful as a good theory: The influence of social knowledge on interpersonal communication. In M. E. Roloff & C. R. Berger (Eds.), *Social cognition and communication* (pp. 107-150). Beverly Hills, CA: Sage.

Hobbs, J. R., & Agar, M. H. (1981). *Planning and local coherence in the formal analysis of ethnographic interviews.* Unpublished manuscript, SRI International, Menlo Park, CA.

Hobbs, J. R., & Evans, D. A. (1980). Conversation as planned behavior. *Cognitive Science, 4,* 349-377.

Hoffman, C., Mischel, W., & Mazze, K. (1980). *The role of purpose in the organization of information about behavior: Trait-based versus goal-based categories in person cognition.* Unpublished manuscript, Stanford University.

House, J., & Kasper, G. (1981). Politeness markers in English and German. In F. Coulmas (Ed.), *Conversational routine: Explorations in standardized communication situations and prepatterned speech* (pp. 157-185). The Hague: Mouton.

Houston, B. K. (1972). Control over stress, locus of control and response to stress. *Journal of Personality and Social Psychology, 21,* 249-255.

Hunter, J., & Boster, F. J. (1978). *An empathy model of compliance-gaining message selection.* Paper presented at the annual meeting of the Speech Communication Association, Minneapolis, MN.

Hunter, J., & Boster, F. J. (1979). *Situational differences in the selection of compliance-gaining messages.* Paper presented at the annual meeting of the Speech Communication Association, San Antonio, TX.

Hunter, J., & Boster, F. J. (1984). *Message content and situational differences as determinants of compliance-gaining message selection.* Unpublished manuscript, Michigan State University.

Jaccard, J., & Daly, J. A. (1980). Personality traits and multiple-act criteria. *Human Communication Research, 6,* 367-377.

Jackson, S., & Backus, D. (1982). Are compliance-gaining strategies dependent on situational variables? *Central States Speech Journal, 33,* 469-479.

Jackson, S., & Jacobs, S. (1980). Structure of conversational argument: Pragmatic bases for the enthymeme. *Quarterly Journal of Speech, 66,* 251-265.

Jackson, S., & Jacobs, S. (1984). Speech act structure in conversation: Rational aspects of conversational coherence. In R. T. Craig & K. Tracy (Eds.), *Conversational coherence: Studies in form and strategy* (pp. 47-66). Beverly Hills, CA: Sage.

Jeffrey, K. M., & Mischel, W. (1979). Effects of purpose on the organization and recall of information in person perception. *Journal of Personality, 47,* 397-419.

Jones, W. H., Freeman, J. E., & Goswick, R. A. (1981). The persistence of loneliness: Self and other determinants. *Journal of Personality, 49,* 27-48.

Kahle, L. R. (1980). Stimulus condition self-selection by males in the interaction of locus of control and skill-chance situations. *Journal of Personality and Social Psychology, 38,* 50-56.

Kaminski, E., McDermott, S., & Boster, F. (1977). *The use of compliance-gaining strategies as a function of Machiavellianism and situation.* Paper presented at the annual meeting of the Central States Speech Communication Association, Southfield, MI.

Kelley, H. H., & Stahelski A. J. (1970). The social interaction basis of cooperators' and competitors' beliefs about others. *Journal of Personality and Social Psychology, 16,* 66-91.

Kemper S., & Thissen, D. (1981). Memory for the dimensions of requests. *Journal of Verbal Learning and Verbal Behavior, 20,* 552-563.

Kipnis, D., & Cohen, E. S. (1980). *Power tactics and affection.* Paper presented at the annual meeting of the Eastern Psychological Association, Philadelphia, PA.

Kipnis, D., & Schmidt, S. M. (1980). Intraorganizational influence tactics: Explorations in getting one's way. *Journal of Applied Psychology, 65,* 440-452.

Kipnis, D., & Schmidt, S. M. (1983). An influence perspective on bargaining within organizations. In M. H. Bazerman & R. J. Lewicki (Eds.), *Bargaining inside organizations* (pp. 303-319). Beverly Hills, CA: Sage.

Klatzky, R. L. (1975). *Human memory: Structures and processes.* San Francisco: Freeman.

Knapp, M. L., Hart, R. P., Friedrich, G. W., & Shulman, G. M. (1980). The rhetoric of goodbye: Verbal and nonverbal correlates of human leave-taking. *Speech Monographs, 40,* 182-198. Reprinted in B. W. Morse & L. A. Phelps (Eds.), *Interpersonal communication: A relational perspective* (pp. 468-482). Minneapolis: Burgess.

Krause, M. (1970). Use of social situations for research purposes. *American Psychologist, 25,* 748-753.

Krivonos, P. D., & Knapp, M. L. (1975). Initiating communication: What do you say when you say hello? *Central States Speech Journal, 26,* 115-125.

Kuiper, N., & Derry, P. A. (1981). The self as a cognitive prototype: An application to person perception and depression. In N. Cantor & J. Kihlstrom (Eds.), *Personality, cognition and social interaction* (pp. 217-232). Hillsdale, NJ: Lawrence Erlbaum.

Laver, J.D.M. (1981). Linguistic roles and politeness in greeting and parting. In F. Coulmas (Ed.), *Conversational routine: Explorations in standardized communication situations and prepatterned speech* (pp. 289-304). The Hague: Mouton.

Lefcourt, H. M. (1972). Recent developments in the study of locus of control. In B. A. Maher (Ed.), *Progress in experimental personality research* (pp. 1-41). New York: Academic Press.

Lefcourt, H. M., & Wine, J. (1969). Internal versus external control of reinforcement and the deployment of attention in experimental situations. *Canadian Journal of Behavioral Science, 1,* 167-181.

Lord, C. G. (1982). Predicting behavioral consistency from an individual's perception of situational similarities. *Journal of Personality and Social Psychology, 42,* 1076-1088.

Lustig, M. W., & King, S. W. (1980). The effect of communication apprehension and situation on communication strategy choices. *Human Communication Research, 7,* 74-82.

Magnusson, D. (1971). An analysis of situational dimensions. *Perceptual and Motor Skills, 32,* 851-867.

Magnusson, D., & Ekehammar, B. (1973). An analysis of situational dimensions: A replication. *Multivariate Behavioral Research, 8,* 331-339.

Markus, H. (1977). Self-schemata and processing information about the self. *Journal of Personality and Social Psychology, 35,* 63-78.

Markus, H. (1983). Self-knowledge: An expanded view. *Journal of Personality, 51,* 543-565.

Marwell, G., & Hage, J. (1970). The organization of role-relationships: A systematic description. *American Sociological Review, 35,* 884-900.

Marwell, G., & Schmitt, D. R. (1967). Dimensions of compliance-gaining behavior: An empirical analysis. *Sociometry, 30,* 350-364.

McCroskey, J. C. (1982). Oral communication apprehension: A reconceptualization. In M. Burgoon (Ed.), *Communication yearbook 6* (pp. 136-170). Beverly Hills, CA: Sage.

McLaughlin, M. L. (1984). *Conversation: How talk is organized.* Beverly Hills CA: Sage.

McLaughlin, M. L., Cody, M. J., & O'Hair, H. D. (1983). The management of failure events: Some contextual determinants of accounting behavior. *Human Communication Research, 9,* 208-224.

McLaughlin, M. L., Cody, M. J., & Robey, C. S. (1980). Situational influences on the selection of strategies to resist compliance-gaining attempts. *Human Communication Research, 7,* 14-36.

McLaughlin, M. L., Cody, M. J., & Rosenstein, N. E. (1983). Account sequences in conversations among strangers. *Communication Monographs, 50,* 102-125.

Mehrabian, A. (1978). Characteristic individual reactions to preferred and unpreferred environments. *Journal of Personality, 46,* 717-731.

Mehrabian, A., & Russell, J. A. (1974). *An approach to environmental psychology.* Cambridge, MA: MIT Press.

Michener, H. A., & Schwertfeger, M. (1972). Liking as a determinant of power tactic preference. *Sociometry, 35,* 190-202.

Miller, G. R., Boster, F., Roloff, M. E., & Seibold, D. R. (1977). Compliance-gaining message strategies: A typology and some findings concerning effects of situational differences. *Communication Monographs, 44,* 37-51.

Miller, G. R., & Steinberg, M. (1975). *Between people: A new analysis of interpersonal communication.* Chicago: Science Research Associates.

Mischel, W. (1968). *Personality and assessments.* New York: John Wiley.

Mischel, W. (1973). Toward a cognitive social learning reconceptualization of personality. *Psychological Review, 80,* 252-283.

Mischel, W. (1979). On the interface of cognition and personality: Beyond the person-situation debate. *American Psychologist, 34,* 740-754.

Mischel, W. (1983). Alternatives in the pursuit of the predictability and consistency of persons: Stable data that yield unstable interpretations. *Journal of Personality, 51,* 578-604.

Mischel, W., & Peake, P. K. (1982a). In search of consistency: Measure for measure. In M. P. Zanna, E. T. Higgins, & C. P. Herman (Eds.), *Consistency in social behavior: The Ontario symposium* (Vol. 2, pp. 187-208). Hillsdale, NJ: Lawrence Erlbaum.

Mischel, W., & Peake, P. K. (1982b). Beyond déjà vu in the search for cross-situational consistency. *Psychological Review, 89,* 730-755.

Monson, T. C., McDaniel, R., Menteer, L. & Williams, C. (in press). The self-selection of persons to situations: Its implications for the correlation between dispositions and behavior within a situation. *Journal of Personality and Social Psychology.*

Moos, R. H. (1973). Conceptualizations of human environments. *American Psychologist, 28,* 652-665.

Nisbett, R. E., & Wilson, T. D. (1977). Telling more than we know: Verbal reports on mental processes. *Psychological Review, 84,* 231-259.

Norman, W. T. (1963). Toward an adequate taxonomy of personality attributes: Replicated factor structure in peer nomination personality ratings. *Journal of Abnormal and Social Psychology, 66,* 574-583.

Patterson, G. R. (1976). The aggressive child: Victim and architects of a coercive system. In L. A. Hamerlynck, & L. C. Handy (Eds.), *Behavior modification and families: I. Theory and research* (pp. 267-311). New York: Brunner/Mazel.

Pearce, W. B. (1976). The coordinated management of meaning: A rules-based theory of interpersonal communication. In G. R. Miller (Ed.), *Explorations in interpersonal communication* (pp. 17-35). Beverly Hills, CA: Sage.

Peplau, L. A., Russell, D., & Heim, M. (1979). An attributional analysis of loneliness. In I. Frieze, D. Bar-Tal, & J. Carrol (Eds.), *Attribution theory: Applications to social problems.* San Francisco: Jossey-Bass.

Pervin, L. A. (1976). A free-response description approach to the analysis of person-situation interaction. *Journal of Personality and Social Psychology, 34,* 465-474.

Pervin, L. A. (1978). Definitions, measurements and classifications of stimuli, situations and environments. *Human Ecology, 6,* 71-105.

Petty, R. E., & Cacioppo, J. T. (1981). *Attitudes and persuasion: Classic and contemporary approaches.* Dubuque, IA: William C. Brown.

Philips, S. (1976). Some sources of cultural variability in the regulation of talk. *Language in Society, 5,* 81-95.

Pilkonis, P. A., Heape, C., & Klein, R. H. (1980). Treating shyness and other relationship differences in psychiatric outpatients. *Communication Education, 29,* 250-255.

Planalp, S., & Tracy, K. (1980). Not to change the topic but . . . A cognitive approach to the study of conversation. In D. Nimmo (Ed.), *Communication yearbook 4* (pp. 237-260). New Brunswick, NJ: Transaction.

Posner, M. J., & Snyder, C. R. (1975). Attention and cognitive control. In R. L. Solso (Ed.), *Information processing and cognition: The Loyola symposium* (pp. 55-85). Hillsdale, NJ: Lawrence Erlbaum.

Price, R. H., & Bouffard, D. L. (1974). Behavioral appropriateness and situational constraint as dimensions of social behavior. *Journal of Personality and Social Psychology, 30,* 579-586.

Putnam, L. L., & Wilson, C. E. (1982). Communicative strategies in organizational conflicts: Reliability and validity of a measurement scale. In M. Burgoon (Ed.), *Communication yearbook 6* (pp. 629-652). Beverly Hills, CA: Sage.

Raven, B. H., Centers, R., & Rodrigues, A. (1975). The bases of conjugal power. In R. E. Cromwell & D. H. Olson (Eds.), *Power in families* (pp. 217-231). New York: John Wiley.

Raven, B. H., & Kruglanski, A. W. (1970). Conflict and power. In P. Swingle (Ed.), *The structure of conflict* (pp. 69-109). New York: Academic Press.

Reardon, K. K. (1981). *Persuasion: Theory and context.* Beverly Hills, CA: Sage.

Reichman, R. (1978). Conversational coherency. *Cognitive Science, 2,* 283-327.

Reid, J. B. (1967). *Reciprocity in family interaction.* Unpublished doctoral dissertation, University of Oregon.

Roloff, M. E., & Barnicott, E. F. (1978). The situational use of pro- and anti-social compliance-gaining strategies by high and low Machiavellians. In B. D. Ruben (Ed.), *Communication yearbook 2* (pp. 193-205). New Brunswick, NJ: Transaction.

Roloff, M. E., & Berger, C. R. (Eds.). (1982). *Social cognition and communication.* Beverly Hills, CA: Sage.

Rosenthal, R. (1965). The volunteer subject. *Human Relations, 18,* 389-406.

Rotter, J. B. (1966). Generalized expectancies for internal vs. external control of reinforcement. *Psychological Monographs, 80,* 1-28.

Rotter, J. B., & Mulry, R. C. (1965). Internal versus control of reinforcement and decision time. *Journal of Personality and Social Psychology, 2,* 598-604.

Russell, J. A., & Ward, L. M. (1982). Environmental psychology. *Annual Review of Psychology, 33,* 651-688.

Schank, R., & Abelson, R. (1977). *Scripts, plans, goals and understanding.* Hillsdale, NJ: Lawrence Erlbaum.

Schegloff, E. (1977). On some questions and ambiguities in conversation. In W. Dressler (Ed.), *Current trends in textlinguistics* (pp. 81-102). Berlin: de Gruyter.

Schlenker, B. R. (1980). *Impression management: The self-concept, social identity, and interpersonal relations.* Monterey, CA: Brooks/Cole.

Schlenker, B. R., & Darby, B. W. (1981). The use of apologies in social predicaments. *Social Psychology Quarterly, 44,* 271-278.

Schneider, D. (1973). Implicit personality theory: A review. *Psychological Bulletin, 79,* 294-309.

Schneider, D. J., & Blankmeyer, B. L. (1983). Prototype salience and implicit personality theories. *Journal of Personality and Social Psychology, 44,* 712-722.

Shiffrin, R. M., & Schneider, W. (1977). Controlled and automatic human information processing: II. Perceptual learning, automatic attending and a general theory. *Psychological Review, 84,* 127-190.

Shimanoff, S. B. (1980). *Communication rules: Theory and research.* Beverly Hills, CA: Sage.

Sillars, A. L. (1980a). Attributions and communication in roommate conflicts. *Communication Monographs, 47,* 180-200.

Sillars, A. L. (1980b). The stranger and the spouse as target persons for compliance-gaining strategies: A subjective expected utility model. *Human Communication Research, 6,* 265-279.

Smith, M. J. (1982). Cognitive schemata and persuasive communication: Toward a contingency rules theory. In M. Burgoon (Ed.), *Communication yearbook 6* (pp. 330-362). Beverly Hills, CA: Sage.

Smith, M. J. (1984). Contingency rules theory, context, and compliance behaviors. *Human Communication Research, 10,* 489-512.

Snyder, M. (1979). Self-monitoring processes. In L. Berkowitz (Ed.), *Advances in experimental social psychology* (Vol. 12, pp. 86-131). New York: Academic Press.

Snyder, M. (1981). On the influence of individuals on situations. In N. Cantor & J. Kihlstrom (Eds.), *Personality, cognition and social interaction* (pp. 309-332). Hillsdale, NJ: Lawrence Erlbaum.

Snyder, M. (1983). The influence of individuals on situations: Implications for understanding the links between personality and social behaviors. *Journal of Personality, 51,* 497-516.

Snyder, M., & Cantor, N. (1980). Thinking about ourselves and others: Self-monitoring and social knowledge. *Journal of Personality and Social Psychology, 39,* 222-234.

Snyder, M., & Gangestad, S. (1982). Choosing social situations: Two investigations of self-monitoring processes. *Journal of Personality and Social Psychology, 43,* 123-135.

Snyder, M., Gangestad, S., & Simpson, J. A. (1983). Choosing friends as activity partners: The role of self-monitoring. *Journal of Personality and Social Psychology, 45,* 1061-1072.

Snyder, M., & Kendzierski, D. (1982). Choosing social situations: Investigating the origins of correspondence between attitude and behavior. *Journal of Personality, 50,* 280-295.

Solano, C. H., Batten, P. G., & Parish, E. A. (1982). Loneliness and patterns of self-disclosure. *Journal of Personality and Social Psychology, 43,* 524-531.

Stern, G., Stein, M., & Bloom, B. (1956). *Methods in personality assessment: Human behavior in complex social settings.* New York: Free Press.

Stokols, D. (1978). Environmental psychology. *Annual Review of Psychology, 29,* 253-295.

Tannen, D. (1981). Indirectness in discourse: Ethnicity as conversational style. *Discourse Processes, 4,* 221-238.

Taylor, S. E. (1981). The interface of cognition and social psychology. In J. H. Harvey (Ed.), *Cognition, social behavior and the environment* (pp. 189-212). Hillsdale, NJ: Lawrence Erlbaum.

Taylor, S. E., & Crocker, J. (1981). Schematic bases of social information processing. In E. T. Higgins, P. Herman, & M. P. Zanna (Eds.), *Social cognition: The Ontario symposium* (Vol. 1, pp. 89-134). Hillsdale, NJ: Lawrence Erlbaum.

Toch, H. (1969). *Violent men.* Chicago: Aldine.

Tracy, K. (1982). On getting the point: Distinguishing "issues" from "events," an aspect of conversational coherence. In M. Burgoon (Ed.), *Communication yearbook 5* (pp. 279-302). New Brunswick, NJ: Transaction.

Tversky, B., & Hemenway, K. (1983). Categories of environmental scenes. *Cognitive Psychology, 15,* 121-149.

Ward, L. M. (1977). Multidimensional scaling of the molar physical environment. *Multivariate Behavioral Research, 12,* 23-42.

White, P. (1980). Limitations on verbal reports on internal events: A refutation of Nisbett and Wilson and of Bem. *Psychological Review, 87,* 105-112.

Wilkinson, I., & Kipnis, D. (1978). Interfirm use of power. *Journal of Applied Psychology, 63,* 315-320.

Williams, D. L., & Boster, F. J. (1981). *The effects of beneficial situational characteristics, negativism, and dogmatism on compliance-gaining message selection.* Paper presented at the annual meeting of the International Communication Association, Minneapolis, MN.

Winograd, T. (1981). A framework for understanding discourse. In M. A. Just & P. A. Carpenter (Eds.), *Cognitive processes in comprehension* (pp. 63-88). Hillsdale, NJ: Lawrence Erlbaum.

Wish, M., Deutsch, M., & Kaplan, S. (1976). Perceived dimensions of interpersonal relations. *Journal of Personality and Social Psychology, 33,* 409-420.

Wish, M., & Kaplan, S. (1977). Toward an implicit theory of interpersonal communication. *Sociometry, 40,* 234-246.

Zuckerman, M. (1974). The sensation seeking motive. In B. A. Maher (Ed.), *Progress in experimental personality research* (pp. 79-148). New York: Academic Press.

7   Language

SCOTT JACOBS

Michigan State University

T HE concepts of language and communication, although intimately
related, have never really been happily married. Communication
scholars will readily recognize that the use of language to formulate
messages and to perform social actions is the paradigm case of communication. Almost all cases of communication that interest communication
researchers involve talk or writing in some way. Still, efforts to ground
notions of "message meaning" or "symbolic action" in a detailed understanding of the organization of linguistic forms and functions has always
seemed to be so technical and cumbersome a task that it has generally been
bypassed in the process of building communication theory. Likewise,
students of language have been reluctant to integrate their theories of
language structure with what is manifestly the paradigm function of language,
that of communication. Knowing what language does has usually been
thought to be superfluous to knowing what language is. In fact, the term
"language" today has been so thoroughly appropriated by the technical
structural interests of sentence grammarians that any effort to study the uses
of language or structures of language beyond the sentence requires the
employment of a whole new term: *discourse.*

Discourse analysis is an effort to close the gap between conceptions of
language structure and communication process. Its research questions
center on the role language plays in the process of meaning construction.
How, for example, do you decide what to say when you talk? And how is it
that when I speak words you understand them? How do we structure
language to build messages and to form patterns of social interaction? And
what sort of meanings are people able to construct on the basis of those
structures and patterns? It is generally assumed by discourse analysts that
answers to these sorts of questions will involve specification of the content
and operational properties of a shared system of knowledge that informs
linguistic choice and enables linguistic interpretation. Although well-developed, detailed models of this system of knowledge are beyond the reach of
most areas of contemporary discourse analysis, there is a growing catalog of
discursive forms and patterns that have become susceptible to systematic
description. The communicative properties that can be shown to be present
in these forms and patterns have led to a growing consensus over the
fundamental properties of language use that any model of discourse must

satisfy. In this chapter, I will outline what those basic properties of language use are and show how they are manifested in the organization of conversational interaction. In doing so, I want to show how the conceptual framework of discourse analysis is undergoing a basic shift in perspective from a "normative code" model of discourse knowledge to a more "inferential/strategic" model. As we shall see, the basic motivation for the direction of theoretical development in discourse analysis comes from the inability of early conceptualizations of various aspects of discourse organization to adequately account for the manifest properties of language use.

CENTRAL PROBLEMS AND BASIC PROPERTIES

The analytic problem posed by the phenomena of language choice and language interpretation is to isolate conceptually manageable levels of organization in discourse. Language is systematically organized in a variety of ways beyond the units of the word and sentence, all of which contribute to the information conveyed in a message. Linguistic organization can be described at various levels of conceptual structure that organize linguistic content (for example, texts, stories, conversational topics), at various levels of pragmatic structure that organize linguistic action and interaction (for example, speech acts, adjacency pairs, conversational episodes), or at levels of stylistic structure that integrate linguistic features and social context (for example, codes). Discourse analysts are concerned with describing what these various structures are and with formulating principles for their construction and use. In developing models of these different levels of organization, discourse analysts are concerned with explaining two major puzzles that exist at any of these levels.

The Problem of Meaning

What sort of information is expressed by discourse structures, and what derivational principles enable people to express and interpret that information? How do we know facts about our language such as the following?

(1) "Is Sybil there?" can be used to request the addressee to call Sybil to the telephone.
(2) "That was a really smooth move there" can be used literally to refer to the gracefulness of the movement of someone's body and/or metaphorically to refer to the ease of an action; it may also be used literally to express a positive evaluation or sarcastically to express a negative evaluation.
(3) Title and last name (for example, Dr. Welby) is used to address someone of higher power or status and/or high social distance.
(4) "John subscribes to New Solidarity" ordinarily conveys that John reads New Solidarity.

Similar processes apply to broader stretches of discourse. Somehow people are able to refer to events and to describe states of affairs. They can convey their attitudes, beliefs, and desires. They are able to communicate information about their relation to the addressee and to the social setting. They may speak plainly and explicitly or they may speak indirectly and nonliterally. And they are very good at saying just enough for the hearer to be able to "fill in" what is left unsaid.

The Problem of Coherence

What are the recognizably sensible and orderly patterns and relations among linguistic elements, and what principles govern the formation of those patterns? Clearly, all natural language users show great facility in finding the ways in which the elements of language "hang together" and in seeing to it that their own contributions do so. Such impressions are central to the sense of orderliness, meaningfulness, and appropriateness we find in language structure and use. But it is not all clear how we construct coherent discourse. Why is it, for example, that we find it difficult to keep track of the topic in the following conversation (adapted from the musical comedy, *The Music Man*)?

A: Mama, a man with a suitcase followed me home.

B: Did he say anything?

A: He tried.

B: Did you say anything?

A: Of course not, mama.

B: If you don't mind my saying so, it wouldn't have hurt to find out what the gentleman wanted.

A: I know what the gentleman wanted.

B: What, dear?

A: You'll find it in Balzac.

B: Well, excuse me for living, but I've never read it.

A: Neither has anyone else in this town.

B: There you go again with the same old comment about the low mentality of River City people, and taking it too much to heart.

A: Since the Madison County Library was entrusted to me for the purpose of improving River City's cultural level, you can't blame me for considering that the ladies of River City keep ignoring all my counsel and advice.

B: When a woman's got a husband and you've got none, why should she take advice from you, even if you can quote Balzac and Shakespeare, and all them other high-falutin' Greeks?

A: If you don't mind my saying so, you have a bad habit of changing every subject.

B: I haven't changed the subject. We were talking about that stranger.

A: What stranger?

B: With the suitcase. Who may be your very last chance.

Or again, to employ William Labov's (1972, p. 252) much-cited example, why is it that the following exchange between a doctor and a schizophrenic patient does not fit any obvious relations of coherence that we would expect? What expectation is being left unmet?

(6)   D: What is your name?
        P: Well, let's say you might have thought you had something from before, but you haven't got it any more.
        D: I'm going to call you Dean.

Alternatively, how is it that we are able to hear an utterance like (7), but not an utterance like (8), as belonging in a conversational closing (Schegloff & Sacks, 1974, p. 249)?

(7)   Well, I'll letchu go.
(8)   What's up?

Somehow natural language users know how to encode and decode topically coherent prose. They know how to make and hear topically relevant contributions to conversations. They know how to reply to questions and offers, and they know how to build stories. They can organize arguments and lead up to invitations. They can open and close conversations. All of these skills involve the application of a system of knowledge for how discourse units are fit together into well-formed wholes at a variety of levels.

What kind of knowledge, then, is required for people to be able to produce and understand coherent and meaningful discourse? It is becoming increasingly apparent that any theory of the system of principles that people employ must be capable, at least in principle, of representing and explaining three basic properties of language structure and use.

1. Linguistic Communication Requires Shared Principles for Inference Beyond Information Given by a "Surface" Reading. Whereas students of interpersonal communication have frequently emphasized the idiosyncratic and personal qualities of message interpretation, discourse analysts have started from the massive fact of the generally reliable and public quality of much interpretation. When people use language they usually understand one another, and are capable of doing so at an exceedingly intricate level of detail. Moreover, the information communicated in a message may not be connected in any obvious way to what is directly and literally said. An adequate representation of the "message" conveyed may bear no obvious correspondence to the string of signs, or signals, that serve as the vehicle for that message. To see this, consider just some of the commonplace intuitions about what is being communicated in the following two-turn exchange.

(9)   A: These are beautiful plants. The leaves are so waxy and green.
        B: Well, actually Scott's the one who takes care of the plants. I don't do much of the housework.

Among the more obvious meanings that can be seen by any native language user are the following: A and B are having a casual conversation. Both know Scott. Scott does not have any pertinent formal status over A or B.

The leaves mentioned are the leaves of the plants that are beautiful. Part of what makes the plants appear beautiful is the waxy and green appearance of their leaves. Scott takes care of the plants (and not the leaves), and taking care of the plants is the reason they are beautiful.

A is issuing a compliment to B. In doing so, A positively evaluates the appearance of the plants; A assumes that B is responsible for that appearance; and A thereby expresses approval of B. A also assumes that B values A's approval and that B shares A's positive evaluation of the appearance of the plants.

B has rejected A's compliment (or at least, B has deflected the compliment to Scott). The reason for the rejection is that B does not take care of the plants and is therefore not responsible for their beauty. B also believes that A believes that B occupies the role of housekeeper. Scott does most of the housework. Taking care of the plants is part of the housework.

Information like this is part of what we would want to call the meaning of the exchange. It is what gets communicated. Yet none of this information is explicitly contained in the text. All of what is noted above is the product of inferences made in the process of constructing a sensible interpretation of what was said. That interpretation involves the construction of inferences based on what could have been said but wasn't (for example, referring to "Mr. Jacobs" or "my husband" instead of "Scott"), on assumptions seemingly required to see coherence in the talk (for example, A is talking on the same topic in both sentences; B's reference to housework has something to do with taking care of plants; taking care of the plants has something to do with A's reference to plants), and on attributions to speaker belief and purpose. And although these inferences are defeasible in various ways, the point is that they are quite detailed, highly reliable, and far beyond the explanatory capacity of any correspondence theory of symbolic meaning.

Any theory that equates message meaning with the literal meaning of what is said will miss how coherent and meaningful messages are produced and understood. As we shall see, inferences beyond the information given in the text is a characteristic process invited by all natural language use. A basic task of any theory of linguistic communication is to model the different types of inferences that people make and to explain how people are able to systematically derive such information from language. Most discourse analysts today take it for granted that any adequate model of discourse knowledge must postulate the existence of a rich conceptual structure underlying the surface structure of what is actually said or written. It is this conceptual structure that forms the basis for coherent patterning in interaction and meaningful representations of messages.

2. *Linguistic Communication Requires Generative Principles.* The intricacy of our system for linguistic communication is made all the more remarkable when one considers the creative capacity for language use. It was Chomsky who first drew widespread attention to this aspect of language (1959, 1972, pp. 11-12). He noted that any natural language user is able to spontaneously and effortlessly produce and understand a potentially infinite number of sentences that are completely novel—discourse that is not a repetition of anything we have ever heard before and is not in any obvious way similar in pattern to discourse we have heard in the past.

Although Chomsky had in mind syntactic structures of language, similar observations could be made at any of a variety of levels of language organization. Theories that try to account for language production and understanding by appeal to sets of standardized patterns quickly exhaust themselves when they attempt to seriously model the flexibility of language use and the wide variety of possible structures. Consider as an example the variety of ways you might communicate to your spouse that you wish to leave a party.

(10) Let's go home.
(11) I want to leave.
(12) What time is it?
(13) This sure is boring.
(14) Don't you have to be up early tomorrow?
(15) Are you going to have another drink?
(16) Do you think the Millers would give you a ride home?
(17) You look ready to party all night.
(18) Did you get a chance to talk to everybody you wanted to see?
(19) Is is starting to rain?
(20) It looks like it's stopped raining.

The list could go on indefinitely. Although many ways to get your spouse to leave are more or less standardized and occur regularly, it would be seriously misleading to suggest that knowledge of such forms sufficiently characterizes the productive and interpretive capacities of a natural language user. The relative standardization of a pattern does not directly bear on its meaningfulness or coherence and does not limit the ability of a natural language user to produce or understand it.

Once the creative potential for language use is taken seriously, the basic problem confronted by the discourse analyst becomes one of explaining the massive fact of variability, innovation, and novelty in language patterning. Most discourse analysts today have abandoned the idea that discourse knowledge consists of some sort of behavioral repertoire or closed set of response types. If modeling discourse knowledge is to be a finite enterprise, standardized patterns cannot be the basis for its characterization. Such characterizations would be inherently incomplete. Rather than specifying a list of patterns that people follow regularly, discourse models need to postulate a system of principles that enable people to generate an open-ended set of patterns.

3. Linguistic Communication Involves the Functional Design of Language Structures. Language structures are functionally organized for appropriateness to a communicative context and for effectiveness in meeting the goals and standards of the language user. How discourse is seen to be meaningful and coherent is intimately related to its functional design. The language structure that is present in a message or series of messages is dependent on its communicative function.

For example, the following exchange forms a meaningful and coherent pattern only by seeing how the customer's question is being used to gain information to decide on a possible order and how the waiter's utterance is being used as a reason for not being able to comply with that possible upcoming order.

(21) Customer: What's the chicken marsala like?
     Waiter: I'm sorry, we're all out of that tonight.

Any model of language use and structure must come to grips with a difficult problem: The functional design of language structure means that the principles of linguistic structuring are not just followed; they are used. The paradox this presents for models of discourse knowledge is that in deviating from structural expectations and principles of order, discourse may nevertheless make sense at a deeper functional representation of that order. So, for example, apparently pointless questions like the first and third lines in (22) obviously violate expectations about clarity and completeness of information, but in doing so frame material that follows as preliminary to the asking of the favor (Schegloff, 1980):

(22) A: Can I ask you to do me a favor?
     B: Sure.
     A: You know that conference I'm going to next week?
     B: Uh huh.
     A: Could you take my class for me while I'm away?

Likewise, in the following excerpt (from Sacks, 1967; cited in Ervin-Tripp, 1971, p. 15), Ken responds to Joe's remark with both an incongruous form of address and a seemingly inappropriate acceptance.

(23) Group therapy session
     Joe: Ken face it, you're a poor little rich kid.
     Ken: Yes, Mommy. Thank you.

As Ervin-Tripp points out, occurrences of insult and humor based on language choices are possible precisely because natural language users recognize the existence of structural principles that are being apparently violated. What cases like these suggest, then, is that principles of language structure cannot characterize constraints on coherence and meaning independently of principles of language function. Models of discourse knowledge must reflect the fact that somehow meaning and coherence in discourse emerge from the interplay of strategy and structure.

These three properties of language structure and use—inference beyond the information given, generativity of patterning, and functional design of structure—exist at practically every level of discourse organization studied. How to specify models of discourse knowledge that might reflect these properties is a recalcitrant puzzle that has shaped the direction of theory development.

THE NORMATIVE CODE MODEL

Historically, the major impetus for discourse analysis can be traced to the achievements and limitations of contemporary linguistics, and particularly to those of Noam Chomsky's theory of transformational generative grammar. With the 1957 publication of his dissertation, "Syntactic Structures," Chomsky started a revolution in linguistics (Maclay, 1971; Searle, 1972). It was largely through the general philosophical and psychological controversies generated by his work that the analytic concepts and techniques of linguistics came to be disseminated throughout the social sciences and humanities (cf. Hook, 1969; Horton & Dixon, 1968; Jakobovits & Miron, 1976). Though work in the theory of transformational generative grammar applied strictly to certain formal properties of the syntax of sentences, the theory supplied both a general paradigm for the conceptualization of structure in discourse at levels beyond that of the sentence and a motivation for exploring the grammatical realizations of various aspects of message meaning and discourse coherence.

The goal of linguistic analysis is to specify those rules that comprise the grammar of a language. Put simply, a grammar describes the logical structure of the relations between meanings and signals that are created by a code. The rules of a grammar are computational procedures that combine the elements of a language so as to specify the forms in which a "message" may acceptably appear. Linguists have generally analyzed the grammar of human languages into three components, or subsystems of rules. The rules governing the combinatorial relations among words in sentences is syntax. Semantics is the component of grammar that assigns meaning representations to the words and specifies the logical form of sentences. The rules that specify the sounds of a language and their permissible combinations is phonology.

Chomsky (1965) argued that a theory of grammar should be taken as describing the *linguistic competence* of an idealized speaker-hearer of the language. That is, a grammar formally describes an isolatable system of knowledge restricted to the grammatical properties of sentences. Such a system of knowledge is abstracted from actual performance considerations that may also involve restrictions on memory and attention, the operation of extralinguistic beliefs about the speaker and the situation, and other aspects of knowledge and cognitive structure that interact with the grammatical system in the process of actual discourse production and comprehension (Chomsky, 1972, pp. 115-116).

Within this technical delimitation of the subject-matter of "language," a theory of grammar would be capable of reproducing all the permissible sentence in a language (and none of the impermissible ones) and formally representing the distinctions and relations that natural language users can be brought to intuitively recognize within and among those sentences.

So, for example, at the level of syntactic organization, any adequate theory of English grammar should be capable of distinguishing between the sentences in (24) and (25).

(24) Colorless green ideas sleep furiously.
(25) Furiously sleep ideas green colorless.

Speakers of a language seem to have a relatively autonomous knowledge of syntax, as is evidenced by the fact that any speaker of English will recognize that only (24) is grammatical even though both are equally nonsensical (Chomsky, 1957, p. 15). Or again, any adequate theory of English syntax should be able to represent (26) as structurally related to (27) and (28), but not to (29).

(26) John hit the ball.
(27) The ball was hit by John.
(28) Did John hit the ball?
(29) The ball hit John.

Likewise, an adequate theory of English syntax should be capable of representing intuitive facts such as that John is the object of the sentence in (30) but the subject of the sentence in (31), or that (32) is structurally ambiguous.

(30) John is easy to please.
(31) John is eager to please.
(32) Flying planes can be dangerous.

Syntactic theory after Chomsky has produced exceedingly subtle and sophisticated formal analyses of the structure of language (cf. Soames & Perlmutter, 1979). The power of these analyses has led many to take them as exemplars for normative code modeling.

In addition to advancing an exceedingly powerful theory of syntactic structure, Chomsky called attention to three fundamental properties of syntax that demanded a wholesale reassessment of the complexity of the system. First, Chomsky called attention to the the special way in which syntactic structures are hierarchically organized. As Lyons (1970, p. 60) points out, traditional grammarians have long recognized that the linear string of words in a sentence exhibit a hierarchical structure. For example, in (33) the sentence has a structural relation between a subject and a predicate.

(33) The girl reads the book.

The subject is a noun phrase (NP) that specifies a relation between a noun (N) and a definite article (T). The predicate is a verb phrase (VP) in which there is a relation between a verb (V) and its object, which is also a noun phrase consisting of a structural relation between a noun and a definite article. Such a hierarchical structure can be formally represented by means of the following rewrite rules (adapted from Chomsky, 1957, p. 28):

(a) Sentence ———————— NP + VP
(b) NP ————————— T + N
(c) VP ————————— V + NP
(d) T ——————— the
(e) N ——————— girl, book and so forth.
(f) V ——————— reads, eats, and so forth.

Each rule is to be interpreted as the instruction "Rewrite X as Y"

X ————————— Y

and provides a simple phrase structure grammar that allows a hierarchical representation of (33) as (34) (see Figure 7.1).

The important contribution that Chomsky made to the understanding of this hierarchical organization was to show that syntax consists of structure-dependent operations that cannot be modeled by any system that defines structural dependencies through linear relations between words (for example, "finite state grammar" of the sort illustrated by Shannon and Weaver's [1949] information theory or by any Markov process). Chomsky argued that the syntax of human language permits structural dependencies among elements to be maintained over an indefinitely large series of intervening elements. So, the relation between "The girl" and "reads" obtains at the level of structure defined by the main NP and VP in the sentence, and is completely indifferent to the number of words and clauses that might be inserted between them. One striking possibility, which Chomsky (1957) argues, is that finite state grammars are in principle incapable of handling operations like those expressed in (35):

(35) S ————————— NP + S_i VP

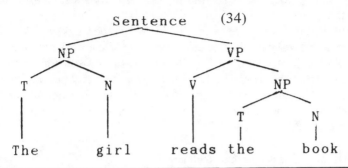

Figure 7.1 Tree Diagram

Since S_i is also a sentence, it too can have an embedded sentence and so on indefinitely, being restricted only by human memory limitations. Thus we can generate the following:

(36) The girl reads the book.
(37) The girl the cat scratched reads the book.
(38) The girl the cat the dog ate scratched reads the book.

The second property of syntactic structures that Chomsky pointed out was its dual structure: Every sentence has a "surface structure" and a "deep structure." The surface structure is the words of the sentence in their order of occurrence in actual sentences. The deep structure corresponds to the level of representation on which a semantic mapping is made. The two levels are related through transformational rules. The postulation of a "deep structure" appears necessary to explain such intuitions as the structural relatedness in (26), (27), and (28), all of which seem to be "derived" from the common propositional structure, that is, "John hit the ball." Likewise the ambiguity of (32) can be explained through generation of a common surface structure from two different deep structures.

Transformational rules of ellipses seem required to explain our intuition about the "missing" agents (indicated by brackets) in (39) and (40).

(39) (You) Give me that.
(40) The president was shot (by someone).

Or again, postulation of a deep structure is required to explain the structural equivalence of (41), (42), and (43).

(41) I passed on your vote to John.
(42) I passed your vote on to John.
(43) I passed on to John your vote.

All three sentences can be related by rules of transpositional sentence elements.

The third property of syntax that Chomsky emphasized was its infinite generativity. Just as in mathematical languages there are an infinite number of possible equations, so too in natural languages there are an infinite number of possible sentences. Both mathematical equations and natural language sentences are generated by a finite system of rules that operate over an infinite range of possibilities. Consider, for example, the scope of the operation implied by (44) and (45):

(44) The man runs the store on 59th street.
(45) The man who took the cat that ate the mouse that ran down the stairs of the big white house that stands next to the church . . . runs the store on 59th street.

As noted earlier, Chomsky emphasized that the linguistic competence of a natural language user cannot be captured by any closed set of sentences. The domain of linguistic competence, and therefore the subject matter of grammatical theory, consists of an open range of potential sentences never heard or said before. The focus on linguistic competence—knowledge required to distinguish acceptable from unacceptable sentences—has shaped the course of discourse studies in some subtle ways.

By far the most popular approach to developing models of discourse knowledge has been to pick out some relatively manageable level of structural organization and, in Levinson's (1981, p. 93) phrase, to "do a Chomsky" on it. To "do a Chomsky" means to show how the organization of linguistic communication is the reflection of a normatively regulated code for the structuring and use of linguistic categories. Here, discourse knowledge is taken to consist of a self-contained rule system that organizes the various levels of structure in a message in a way akin to a kind of "super grammar."

The normative code model portrays linguistic communication as the transmission of a *message* in which a sender *encodes* meanings into a physical *signal* and a receiver *decodes* the message to derive a meaningful representation of it. Decoding and encoding occur through the application of a code. A code is a hierarchically organized system of conventions that specifies derivational relations between the elements at various structural levels (thus connecting meanings with public signs, or signals) and combinatorial relations among the elements at any given structural level (thus providing coherent configurations in the arrangement of signs).

The use of a code and the choice of message to encode are regulated by normative rules. Norms are standing social expectations known and adhered to by members of a linguistic community, or internalized dispositions shared by members of that community. Norms can be stated in the form, "Given condition(s) C, act A is obligated (or permitted or prohibited)." The conditions for action are a set of contextual features recognizable to members of a language community; the act is any structural unit or combination of units defined by the language code. Part of the conditions for action may be other linguistic acts. In their most blatant form, then, such models would assume that people (1) can derive message meaning simply by applying rules of word meaning and sentence structure and working "on up" through the rules at various levels of the structural hierarchy and (2) can make appropriate linguistic choices on the basis of normatively prescribed decision criteria.

Such a view has been and continues to be widely accepted throughout the social sciences. It is implicit in the idea that there are rules linking language variations to situational variables (Ervin-Tripp, 1971; Hymes, 1974), in the idea that certain nonverbal signs have specific conventional functions (Harper, Wiens, & Matarazzo, 1978), in the idea that stories have an underlying grammatical structure (Rumelhart, 1975; Mandler & Johnson, 1975), and so on. Recent discussions of communication rules have taken for granted that whatever it is that structures language use will have some heavy normative component (Cushman & Whiting, 1972; Pearce & Conklin, 1979; Shimanoff, 1980).

Normative code models predict that communication will be successful just in case the receiver employs the same rules to decode the message that the sender employs to encode the message. Communication breakdowns will occur to the degree that sender and receiver fail to share the same code rules. Likewise, regularities in the production and patterning of messages will occur to the degree that normative rules are strongly internalized or sanctioned by members of a linguistic community and the relevant contextual features are clearly recognizable.

In the following section I will examine the logic and prospects of this model for the analysis of conversational interaction. Modeling the way in which the use of language creates and regulates interactional structure supplies a clear and obvious bridge between theories of language and communication. Evaluating the adequacy of the normative code model in this context motivates the development of an alternative framework to be discussed in the concluding section of the chapter.

Extensions of the Normative Code Model to Conversational Interaction

By far the most influential approach to the modeling of meaning and coherence in conversation is one that assumes that conversation consists of a series of moves, or act-types, that serve as the basis for the formation of coherent structural patterns and represent the centrally important meanings that conversationalists communicate to one another. It has been widely assumed that when analyzed in this way conversation will submit to a kind of structural analysis that neatly fits within the framework of a normative code account. The kinds of problems that cast doubt on the adequacy of such a conceptualization will be presented by first considering the ways in which discourse analysts have attempted to model conversational sequencing and then by turning to the ways in which they have attempted to model the expression and interpretation of conversational acts.

Sequencing Rule Approaches. In its simplest form, the orderliness of conversational sequencing might be modeled on the assumptions that (1) the units of conversational structure consist of utterances; (2) these utterances correspond to speech act types; and (3) the succession of utterances in conversation is regulated by rules that specify the range of speech act types that may appropriately follow any given speech act. On such a model, the assignment of speech act-types is assumed to be essentially nonproblematic, the main problem being to account for their order of appearance. The advantage of such an assumption is that a grammar of conversation may then be constructed by specifying irreducible conventions that operate directly on the surface structure of turns at talk.

The most familiar version of such a model grows out of the turn-allocation system of Sacks, Schegloff, and Jefferson (1978). They suggest that turn-taking in conversation is governed by three rules for the allocation of turns at talk that apply in order at each and every point of possible speaker transition in conversation (p. 13):

(a) Current speaker may construct his turn so as to select the next speaker who then has the right and obligation to speak.
(b) Nonspeakers may "self-select," the first starter acquiring rights to speak.
(c) Current speaker may continue.

One of the basic turn allocation techniques by which Rule 1 is invoked and orderly sequencing of utterances is secured is the adjacency pair (Sacks et al., 1978, pp. 27-31). Schegloff and Sacks (1974) argue that these are the basic constructional units for creating sequentially implicated turns at talk. They are familiar to any natural language user: question-answer, greeting-greeting, offer-acceptance/refusal, request-acceptance/rejection. They are characterized by five basic features:

(a) They are two turns long with two parts.
(b) These two parts are said by different speakers.
(c) The pair parts are adjacently placed.
(d) The pairs are ordered by types of parts. There are first pair parts (FPPs) and second pair parts (SPPs).
(e) The pair parts are discriminatively related. Given a first pair part, not just any second pair part can properly follow. A first pair part must be followed by a second pair part of a type congruent with the first. So, there are types of adjacency pairs.

By using the first part of an adjacency pair (a "first pair part," or FPP), a speaker establishes a "next turn position" that casts the recipient into the role of respondent and structures the range of appropriate next moves to those second pair parts (SPPs) that are congruent with the FPP. Schegloff and Sacks (1974, p. 239) suggest that this pairing is regulated by the following rule:

(46) Given the recognizable production of a first pair part, on its first possible completion its speaker should stop and a next speaker should start and produce a second pair part from the pair type the first is recognizably a member of.

Through such a rule, adjacency pairs create a sense of coherence in sequential structure that has been described by Schegloff (1972, p. 11) in terms of *conditional relevance*: "By conditional relevance of one item on another we mean: Given the first, the second is expectable; upon its occurrence it can be seen to be a second item to the first; upon its nonoccurrence it can be seen to be officially absent—all this provided by the occurrence of the first item."

Adjacency pairs are also regulated by a *structural preference for agreement* between the pair parts (Jackson & Jacobs, 1980; Pomerantz, 1978; Sacks, 1973). Of the SPPs that can coherently combine with an FPP, there is usually one that the FPP is designed to receive and one that the FPP is designed to avoid. For example, Pomerantz (1978) has argued that evaluations are built to prefer an agreement with the evaluation ("Nice day today"—"Yes, isn't it?"). Schegloff (1977) has argued that yes/no questions prefer agreement with the presupposed answer ("Do you really want that?"—"No, I guess not"—"Is today the fifth?"—"Yeah") and that speakers build such questions to agree with the expected answer ("You don't have any kids, do you?"—"No, not yet"). The structural preference for agreement regulates the production of both FPPs and SPPs by encouraging the formulation of agreeable pair parts and by working to suppress the appearance of disagreeable pair parts. The operation of such a regulation appears to be at work in the way in which, for example, negative tag questions will frequently appear in situations in which noncompliance is likely (Ervin-Tripp, 1976, p. 38).

(47) "You don't have any doughnuts or rolls to go, do you?" (customer to drive-in waitress).
(48) "You don't want any Girl Scout cookies, do you?" (Girl Scout cookie salesgirl to customer on doorstep).

In the case of such utterances the recipient can be in agreement with the presupposed answer to the question or the recipient can accept the request. Likewise, Sacks (1973, cited in Brown & Levinson, 1978, p. 119) argues that recipients of an FPP will tend to do dispreferred SPPs in ways that appear agreeable.

(49) A: Can you hear me?
    B: Barely.
(50) A: And they haven't heard a word, huh?
    B: Not a word. Not at all. Except Mrs. H maybe.

Another strategy noted by Sacks that appears sensitive to the preference for agreement is to displace disagreeable SPPs.

(51) A: Yuh comin down early?
      B: Well I got a lot of things to do. I don't know. It won't be too early.

The plausibility of a sequencing rule approach is further strengthened by the possibility for modeling broader stretches of conversation in the form of insertion sequences and presequences (Jefferson, 1972; Schegloff, 1972, 1980). Presequences are adjacency pairs whose component parts are interpreted relative to some adjacency pair yet to come. This prefatory character is part of their meanings (Jacobs & Jackson, 1983b).

(52) A: You going to be finished soon?
      B: No, why?
      A: Well, it's getting pretty near the time we need to go pick up Curtie.
      B: Okay. Well just give me a couple seconds to clean up and then we can go.

Insertion sequences are adjacency pairs that are embedded between an FPP and its SPP. These too are interpreted with respect to their position relative to the superordinate adjacency pair. Thus certain questions and statements can be understood as objections or contingent queries by virtue of their structural position between the FPP and SPP (cf. Labov & Fanshel, 1977, p. 91).

(53) A: Can I have a pack of Merits?
      B: Regulars or hundreds?
      A: Regulars.
      B: Here you go.

These patterns of sequential expansion suggest the operation of a rule permitting the repeated and recursive placement of subsidiary adjacency pairs before, within, and after any adjacency pair.

This analysis of adjacency pair relations and sequential expansion would appear to suggest, then, that the properties of conversational sequencing can be modeled on the basis of a three-component system of rules strikingly akin to that of a sentence grammar. Such a model requires a turn-taking system for generating turn slots into which utterances may be placed; a procedure for assigning act meanings to utterances; and a set of rules for the "syntax" of conversation that can be formally expressed in terms of (1) the basic adjacency pair relation

$$AP_i \; \text{---------} \; FPP_i + SPP_i$$

where the subscripts designate pair parts drawn from the same type; (2) a specification of the types of adjacency pair parts

$$FPP_i = /Greeting_A, Request_B, Question_C, Offer_D, \ldots /$$
$$SPP_i = /Greeting_A, Grant_B, *Refusal_{BD}, Answer_C, Acceptance_D, \ldots /$$

where the subscripts indicate the adjacent pair type of which they can be a part; (3) an ordering of preference among the SPPs of each adjacency pair type in which dispreferred SPPs are lowest (as marked by asterisks above); and (4) a rewriting rule that permits the expansion of adjacency pairs such that

$$AP \text{ ———————(AP) FPP (AP) SPP (AP)}$$

Such rules, when applied as a system, appear capable of representing many powerful intuitions natural language users have for sequential patterns as well as accommodating observable regularities in their use. By following such rules, the analyst is capable of both generating well-informed patterns and explaining the ill-formed patterns in (54) and (55), as well as the lack of closure in sequences like (56) and (57):

(54) A: How are you doing?
     B: No.
(55) A: How old are you?
     B: All right.
(56) A: Are you busy tonight?
     B: No, not really.
(57) A: Have you read this article?
     B: Which one is that?

Such rules also enable the analyst to represent intuitions concerning the structural subordination of insertion sequences and presequences relative to some dominant adjacency pair by virtue of their derivative appearances through a system of rewrite rules even though they appear before the production and/or completion of the adjacency pair in the actual series of utterances. The rules are also capable of representing hierarchical relations among utterances separated by indefinitely long stretches of conversation, as well as being capable of generating, in principle, indefinite embeddings analogous to sentence structures (see Figure 7.2):

(58) A: Are you coming tonight?
     B: Can I bring a guest?
     A: Male or female?
     B: What difference does that make?
     A: An issue of balance.
     B: Female.

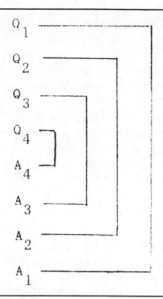

Figure 7.2 Recursive Embedding

A: Sure.
B: I'll be there (Schegloff, 1972, p. 79).

So, a sequencing rule approach appears to offer a promising avenue for the modeling of conversational structure. Through a straightforward application of code-rules and normative regulations a variety of interesting structures and interpretations can be represented and explained. There are, however, numerous problems that emerge upon closer inspection.

First, there are a variety of ways to coherently fill the slot made for the appearance of an SPP that are not themselves SPPs to that FPP (Jacobs & Jackson, 1983a; Levinson, 1981; Sinclair & Coulthard, 1975). Consider what might coherently follow a straightforward question about time:

(59) FPP: What time is it?
      ??SPP: (i)   It's noon.
              (ii)   The clock's right over there.
              (iii) It's still early.
              (iv)   Quit worrying about it.
              (v)   I don't have a watch.
              (vi)   It's just three minutes before class starts.

Besides (i) minimal, direct answers, such a question can also coherently receive (ii) a pass that redirects the act of the questioner, (iii) a disagreeable response that attempts to satisfy the demands of the question as well as possible, (iv) alternative proposals for action, (v) indirect refusals, and (vi) indirect answers that primarily set up further information. Sequencing rule conventions provide no obvious way of characterizing the broad array of acts that may constitute a coherent reply. The adjacency pair relation appears to be a standardized pattern, not a general principle of coherence.

A related problem for this model is that there appears to be no principled basis for specifying what act types can and cannot initiate an adjacency pair. A large number of utterances in conversation establish no obvious conditional relevance or structural preference. What conditional relevance, if any, is established by an assertion or a promise? And what kind of structural preference is operative in an accusation: an admission, a denial, an explanation, an apology, or what? Sequencing rule conventions can address such issues only through ad hoc scope conditions (Jacobs & Jackson, 1983a, p. 50).

Difficulties also emerge when one tries to extend the analysis of sequential expansions to account for the full range of possible variations. There are, for example, several variations in the presequential patterning of request-grant/refusal sequences that involve preemptive offers, hints, and counters that are not easily represented in terms of any surface structuring (Jacobs & Jackson, 1983b). Similarly, sequential expansion through insertion sequences may exhibit complex structural relations that are not captured through rules of embedding. Notice that in (60), the "thanks" by B is directed to A's offer and not to the initial suggestion, so that by answering the potential objection the need for an SPP is obviated. Contrast this with the possible alternative in (61) in which B would be supplying an SPP to the initial FPP.

(60) A: Let's go eat.
    B: Well, it can't be anyplace very expensive.
    A: It's my treat today.
    B: Thanks.
(61) A: Let's go eat.
    B: Well, it can't be anyplace very expensive.
    A: It won't be.
    B: Okay.

Both sequential structures are coherent, but only (61) can be represented by the sequential rules discussed so far.

The most plausible way out of these problems is to postulate the existence of a system of "transformational rules" that would allow a reading of the "surface structure" utterances in terms of act-types represented in a kind of "deep structure." Such rules might permit operations of substitution, deletion, combination, and the like, so that whatever appeared in actual utterances may be only indirectly and loosely related to acts being performed at several hierarchically layered levels of functioning. In this model, sequencing rules would operate among and between the actions represented in deep structure rather than between utterances (cf. Churchill, 1978; Goffman,

1981; Labov, 1972; Merritt, 1976). But even this model appears unable to represent without distortions the acts that are being performed (Jacobs & Jackson, 1983b, pp. 293-295; Levinson, 1981).

Nor does it succeed any better than a surface structure account in explaining why some sequences are structurally subordinate expansions whereas others are digressions or wholly unrelated intrusions into an exchange (cf. Dascal & Katriel, 1979). What is it about some acts that places them within the structural environment of a dominant adjacency pair while excluding other temporally contiguous utterances?

At this point it is worth noting a characteristic feature of all the reasoning about sequential structure so far: A sequencing rule approach uses act-types as the labels for the *structural units* upon which relations of coherence are defined, but the *functional properties* of those acts do not enter into the characterization of why the relation should obtain. Sequencing rules treat relations of coherence as essentially arbitrary and irreducible conventions of form. The meaning of the acts is, at best, a derivative quality of the way in which they function in grammatical relations with other acts. In other words, an answer is simply that class of utterances that can recognizably fill the slot of an SPP to a question and a question is simply that class of utterances that can recognizably combine with answers. A request is simply the class of utterances that takes grants and refusals as its SPP. A refusal is just that class of utterances that tends to occupy structurally dispreferred positions in relation to a request. Question-answer or request-grant/refusal pairs might just as well be termed FPP_1-SPP_1 and FPP_2 -SPP_{2p}/SPP_{2d}, without any further characterization of their meaning as far as defining relations of coherence is concerned. Of course, there is nothing wrong with this sort of circularity so long as there exists some independent assignment procedure by which utterance types can be linked to act categories. The parallel here would be to a grammatical category like definite articles, which can be straightforwardly assigned to words (for example, the); the grammatical function of the category is defined relative to nouns within noun phrases. Unfortunately, little clear progress has been made in identifying rules linking utterances to act-types.

Utterances-Act Rules. The most straightforward approach to defining utterance-act linkages is to attempt to make the act-type dependent upon the propositional content and syntactic form of the utterance. This corresponds to our intuitions that, for example, questions are characteristically associated with interrogative form, commands with imperative form, and statements with declarative form. The content of the utterance may also more or less explicitly contain information about the act being uttered.

(62) I promise not to talk with my mouth full.
(63) I bet it snows tonight.
(64) We find the defendant guilty as charged.

Such an approach does seem to be extendable to the description of a large class of standardized formulas and grammatical markers that are conventionally associated with the expression of a speech act (cf. Bach & Harnish, 1979, pp. 173-233, for an extensive review). For example, the formulas in (65) appear to be conventionally associated with the performance of a request (Bach & Harnish, 1979) while the formulas in (66) appear to be conventional ways to make a compliment (Manes & Wolfson, 1981):

(65) Can/Can't/Could
    you VP?   e.g., Can you pass the salt?

    Will/Won't/Would you VP?   e.g., Can/Will you pass the rolls?

    Why don't you VP?   e.g., Why don't you buy it?

    How about VP-ing?   e.g., How about lending me a dime?

(66) NP is/looks ADJECTIVE   e.g., Your house looks really nice.

    I like/love NP   e.g., I like your haircut.

Such an approach to identifying act-utterance linkages, however, quickly runs into insurmountable difficulties. For one thing, such an approach runs up against the problem of generativity in patterning. As the requests to leave the party in (10) through (20) indicate, an indefinite range of nonstandardized forms may be employed to perform an act. Another problem is that many acts seem to have no standardized formula for their utterance at all beyond, perhaps, the use of an explicit performative verb. What, for example, is a standardized way of expressing a complaint or issuing a boast? But finally, and most importantly, none of these formulas can guarantee the meaning of the utterance as a matter of rule. "How about telling him yourself?" can be a suggestion, but it can also be a challenge, a criticism, a rhetorical answer, or a simple hypothetical question. "Can you please talk a little louder?" may be intended ironically, and not as a request at all. At best, these standardized formulas set up a *presumption* that they are being used in a conventional way.

Sensitive to these problems, a number of discourse analysts have suggested that utterance-act assignment rules must be context-sensitive. That is, an utterance-act linkage is established only when certain contextual features are present. The contextual features most frequently appealed to are the *felicity conditions* associated with the valid performance of a speech act.

According to mainstream speech act theory (Austin, 1962; Searle, 1969), the performance of actions in language is defined and regulated by a set of rules that describe the necessary preconditions that must be satisfied for the valid performance of an action and that define the meaning of the action performed. In expressing a speech act the speaker commits himself by rule to the wants and beliefs associated with the valid performance of the act.

Searle (1969) has presented a general typology of these conditions: Every act will be associated with a specification of permissible propositional contents, a (set of) essential condition(s). Differences in the specification of these conditions will reflect differences in the kind of speech act being performed. So, for example, the propositional content of a request must predicate a future act by the hearer while a question may predicate any proposition or propositional function. Preparatory conditions represent beliefs about states of affairs that are rational prerequisites for the attempt of the speech act. For requests, they include the speaker's belief that the hearer is able and willing to perform the requested act and that the act would not have been done without its being requested. For questions, the preparatory conditions include the speaker's belief that the hearer knows the information left open by the propositional function or whether the proposition predicated is true, that the speaker does not know these things, and that the hearer would not supply the information without being asked. The sincerity condition describes the internal states to which speakers commit themselves in performing the speech act. For requests, the speaker must actually want the hearer to perform the requested act. For questions, the speaker must really want the information. The essential condition describes what speech act an utterance counts as. It corresponds to what Searle (1975) has termed the "illocutionary point" of an act: the intent the speaker communicates. For requesting, the utterance counts as an effort to get the hearer to do the desired action. For questioning, the utterance counts as an attempt to elicit the information from the hearer. The essential condition is satisfied just in those cases in which the other felicity conditions obtain.

What the notion of felicity conditions has suggested to many speech act theorists is that a speech act will be heard as occurring in those cases in which it could be validly performed and not in those cases in which its performance would be infelicitous. In other words, assuming that a speaker is encoding a message in accordance with the regulative constraints on linguistic action, its possible interpretations can be checked by a hearer to see whether or not a particular decoding would be consistent with a valid action. Two models of this sort of assignment rule have been suggested. Both Searle (1975) and Gordon and Lakoff (1975) suggest that an utterance may trigger an indirect reading beyond its literal meaning in just those cases in which it is implausible that the speaker intends to be performing, or simply performing, the act literally expressed in the utterance (that is, a simple statement, question, or imperative). The point that the speaker is trying to make is cued by the fact that the propositional content of the utterance refers to a felicity condition for the performance of the indirect speech act, and it is plausible to believe that the speaker does intend to be performing that act (that is, the felicity conditions for that act are satisfied). Labov and Fanshel (1977) have proposed a similar rule for the specific case of requests. Under their rule, however, a request reading is an omnirelevant possibility. A request is searched for whenever a speaker makes reference to aspects of the proposed action or the preconditions for the request, regardless of whatever else may be performed by the utterance.

Neither of these rules is a fully satisfactory account of how act-types get assigned to utterances. First, if we assume, like Searle (1975) and Gordon and Lakoff (1975), that a literal reading must be implausible in order to trigger an indirect reading of an utterance, how are we to handle cases in which a speaker means to perform both a direct and an indirect act? Consider (67), where an instructor (me) asked an overtime student about his exam:

(67) How much longer will you be?

Not only did this utterance serve as an indirect request to finish up, it was also intended (and responded to) as an information question. Moreover, it also functioned as criticism. So, a "triggering" model based on the infelicitous performance of a literal act does not appear to be powerful enough, because it would never represent multiple acts. On the other hand, if we take Labov and Fanshel's (1977) proposal and presume the omnirelevant potential of any speech act (not just requests), we are faced with the problem that there is no clear way to stop the process of searching for indirect meanings. Talking to Labov and Fanshel's model natural language user would be like writing to a literary critic. The problem, then, is to find some middle ground. Although natural language users can and do go beyond validly performed acts that are immediately apparent, they do not do so in a way that constructs all plausible interpretations (cf. Clark, 1977).

A second, deeper problem for these models is that the determination of what is referred to by the propositional content of an utterance does not appear to be a rule-governed process at all. Both models assume that the propositional content of the utterance leads to an indirect reading by reference to a felicity condition for the indirect act. But, as Labov and Fanshel (1977, p. 84) note, this is a connection that can be established only after the fact. Any propositional content can refer to any other proposition given a circuitous enough route. Because of this, they argue that a generative grammar connecting speech action to utterance forms cannot be written. What these models point to is something other than a grammar for conversation.

TOWARD AN INFERENTIAL/STRATEGIC MODEL

Problems like those discussed for a "grammar of conversational inter-action" can be found in a wide range of levels of discourse organization. The problem that repeatedly surfaces is that a normative code model is insufficient to explain the basic properties of language structure and use outlined at the beginning of this chapter—inference beyond the information given, generativity of patterning, and functional design of structure. A Chomskian grammar of language, which appeared to provide such a promising exemplar for extension to areas of discourse structure and use, has repeatedly run into a wall of resistance.

So, for example, the notion that topical coherence in texts and dialog might be modeled by rules linking utterance form and content to the form and content of prior discourse (Ellis, Hawes, & Avery, 1981; Halliday & Hasan, 1976) has generally been given up by discourse analysts. Researchers in this area are instead turning to models assuming active constructive processes that bring to bear assumptions about speaker plans and strategies, general principles of rationality, and coherent representations of the world (Clark & Haviland, 1977; Ellis, Hamilton, & Aho, 1983; Hobbs, 1982; McLaughlin, 1984). Studies of stylistic code choice have repeatedly encountered the phenomenon of blatant rule violation that is nevertheless meaningful and coherent (Brown & Gilman, 1972; Ervin-Tripp, 1971; Blom & Gumperz, 1972). These analysts are increasingly emphasizing the strategic basis for meaning in language choice (Brown & Levinson, 1978; Scotton, 1983). Likewise, models of "story grammars" (Mandler & Johnson, 1977; Rumelhart, 1975; Stein, 1979) seem to be giving way to problem-solving approaches that integrate text with world knowledge and assumptions about speaker strategy (Goldman, 1982).

The exact nature of the alternative model is only now beginning to emerge. However, certain core assumptions seem to be taking hold that are at odds with those of the normative code model. Within an inferential/strategic model, messages are not understood to be transmitted through an encoding and decoding process that applies self-sufficient code rules to determine meaning. The process is viewed instead as a kind of *problem-solving* activity involving the assessment of mutual knowledge in the generation of speaker *plans* and hearer *inferences as to the most plausible solution* for what that speaker plan might be. Language choice is based not on the force of normative regulation, but on speaker goals and general principles of rationality. In this view, apparent violations of normative expectations are "normalized" by the hearer seeing how those acts are rational solutions to the achievement of communicative ends and by the speaker assessing the likelihood that the hearer will find such a solution. This problem solving creates a context of mutual and reciprocal beliefs, as the speaker generates a plan partly by calculating how a hearer might plausibly solve it and the hearer arrives at a solution to the communicative puzzle partly by calculating what the speaker might plausibly expect the hearer to infer.

How such a model might work can best be seen by illustrating its application to the problems of conversational interaction. From an inferential/strategic perspective, the coherence of conversational interaction does not involve conventions of form defined across structural units of action; the coherence of conversational interaction reflects the cooperative application of practical reasoning principles to the goals and functional preconditions of action (Jacobs & Jackson, 1983a; Mohan, 1974). As noted earlier every speech act is defined by its "illocutionary point," that is, an intended immediate goal that is satisfied by the communication of the act. In the case of a request, the intended point is to get the hearer to see that the speaker wants him to perform some action. In the case of a promise, the intended point is to get the hearer to see that the speaker has committed himself or herself to some course of action. In the case of an assertion, the intended point is to get the hearer to see that the speaker has committed himself or herself to belief in some state of affairs. The expression of such intentions is a subgoal that serves as a means to achieve other goals. In the most obvious cases it will be things like getting the hearer to perform the requested action, to believe the speaker will fulfill his promise, or to believe what the speaker believes. But the expression of a speech act may also be a subgoal in a plan to achieve higher order goals, for example, asking a question to get the hearer to confirm that the preconditions for some other action, say a request, are satisfied. It is this sort of functional design that underlies the structural coherence found by the sequencing rule approach.

From the point of view of an inferential-strategic model, the adjacency pair is a standardized solution to the problem of an initiator communicating goals that an addressee must satisfy and then the addressee responding in a way that promotes or obstructs those goals. The properties of conditional relevance of a second pair part on the occurrence of a first part and the structural preference for agreement find a general rationale in the functional design of the intended goal communicated by the FPP and in the way the SPP contributes to that goal. So, for example, questions have as their intended goal obtaining information from the hearer, a goal achieved by supplying an answer. Greetings have as their intended goal the establishment of mutual focus, a goal whose achievement is communicated by another greeting. Requests have as their intended goal the performance of an action, a goal whose achievement is promised by a grant or is denied by a refusal. (Notice that a refusal takes up the goal of the FPP, which is why it is conditionally relevant, but it obstructs that goal, which is why it is structurally dispreferred.) Such an analysis also accounts for the broad range of acts that are not SPPs but are still coherent replies. All of them take up the goals communicated in the FPP in some way or another by trying to satisfy them by means other than an SPP, by supplying partial satisfaction, by expressly obstructing those goals, by identifying the lack of relevant preconditions, and so on. An interpretive/strategic analysis also answers why certain acts can and cannot initiate adjacency pairs: The answer lies in the relative constraint on a cooperative response that intended goals place on the recipient of an act.

An inferential/strategic model also appears capable of handling the regularities and irregularities of sequential expansion. Presequences and insertion sequences are placed within the structural environment of a dominant adjacency pair in just those cases in which the acts are designed to establish or cancel a precondition necessary for the valid performance of an action. Arguments around speech acts, for example, are heard as such precisely because they are seen as reasons for or against the valid performance of the arguable act (Jackson & Jacobs, 1980; Jacobs & Jackson, 1981). Furthermore, the occurrence of a wide variety of irregular forms of expansion can be understood as coherent once it is seen how the conversationalists position their actions relative to the underlying goals of the conversation (Jacobs & Jackson, 1983b). In fact, Levinson (1981, pp. 110-112) has suggested a general property of coherence at the level of goal-oriented action that accounts for a wide variety of preemptions: "Given an utterance which is merely the first in a sequence predicted by a hierarchical structure of goals, one is free to respond to any of those higher level goals." Jackson and Jacobs (1980, p. 255) imply another property that accounts for a wide variety of digressions: Given any utterance, one is also free to respond to any of the pragmatic and semantic presuppositions of the action that are not valid. Finally, it might be added that any sequence can be coherently closed whenever the goals are mutually known to have been achieved or are mutually known to be unachieveable. Thus, for example, a negative response to a presequential question (for example, "Are you busy?" "Yes") may coherently end the sequence there, whereas sequences like those in (60) obviate the need for a grant. So, an inferential/strategic account appears to provide a promising avenue for the modeling of conversational coherence.

Similarly, an inferential/strategic account appears to provide a promising way of modeling the communication of act meanings. The essential insight in the analyses of indirect speech acts discussed above is that the meaning of an utterance is discovered *on the assumption* of its rational functional design. The problem of interpretation is to construct and test hypotheses as to the way in which an utterance may functionally contribute to the achievement of some goal. It is further clear that such hypotheses are constructed and tested through the active application of nonlinguistic background knowledge about the world, the speaker, and the communicative context in which the utterance is made.

General frameworks for such interpretations can be found in Grice's (1975) theory of conversational implicature and Bach and Harnish's (1979) speech act schema. Within these frameworks an interpretation may be made in three ways, all of which assume a linear decoding process. First, the meaning of what is literally and directly said may itself conform with general principles of rational design. If so, the hearer should make that reading. Second, conventions of form and content may establish a presumption of an indirect meaning. If that indirect meaning conforms with general principles of rational design, the hearer should make it. If it does not, the hearer should check for the appropriateness of a literal and direct reading. Third, if neither of the above inferential strategies is successful, then the hearer should search for an indirect reading that would be compatible with general principles of rational design and that the speaker might reasonably expect the hearer to make on the basis of mutual contextual beliefs. If such a reading can be found, then the hearer should assume that the speaker intended to express it and the reading should be made.

The idea here is that if, for example, a classroom teacher asks the students a question like, "Is it time for class to end?" and it's obvious to everyone that it isn't time for class to end and that the teacher knows that it's obviously not time for class to end, the students should not assume that the teacher is asking an infelicitous question. Rather, they should assume that the teacher is intending to be doing something else that makes sense and should try to reason out what that something else could plausibly be intended to be on the basis of obvious knowledge about the situation. For example, it might be obvious that some of the students are closing up their books or generally not paying attention or doing something else that might be construed as having something to do with class being ready to end. In such a case, given other kinds of mutual contextual beliefs (for example, the teacher expects the students to be doing class work during class time, the teacher has the authority to enforce that expectation), it might plausibly be inferred that what the teacher intends to be doing by her question is to be directing the students to get back to class work. Because that would make sense, that reading should be given.

Although the content of such inferences is beyond the specification of any contemporary theory, the framework does have the advantage of showing how apparent normative expectations about meaning may be deliberately exploited for communicative effect. As Levinson (1983) points out, theories like Grice's show

> a fundamental way in which a full account of the communicative power of language can never be reduced to a set of conventions for the use of language. The reason is that wherever some convention or expectation about the use of language arises, there will also therewith arise the possibility of the non-conventional exploitation of that convention or expectation. It follows that a purely conventional or rule-based account of natural language usage can never be complete, and that what can be communicated always exceeds the communicative power provided by the conventions of language and its use. (p. 112)

The weakness of this framework for describing linguistic inference, however, is that it still takes the literal and direct meaning of an utterance to be the starting point for interpretation (Jackson, 1983; Kaufer, 1981). The framework is still wedded to a linear theory of the decoding process. An alternative approach, discussed by Jackson (1983), is to see interpretation to a "rational solution" as one involving the active and simultaneous processing of multiple clues to meaning. She discusses several means by which the relative plausibility of any particular possible interpretation might be assessed, including preferences for that inference requiring the fewest inferential steps (Clark, 1977) or that inference that makes the fewest ad hoc assumptions about the beliefs and goals of the speaker (Bach & Harnish, 1979). In terms of contemporary schema theory (Brown & Yule, 1983), natural language users engage in a simultaneous process of "top-down" and "bottom-up" processing in which general contextual expectations guide the search for patterns in linguistic organization while linguistic and other contextual cues activate the search for particular schematic patterns. Ethnomethodologists (Leiter, 1980) describe this process in terms of the "reflexivity" of language understanding. Linguistic utterances are taken as "cues" to an overall pattern of meaning while that pattern serves as a context within which the utterances make sense.

An example of this sort of non-linear process of interpretation can be found in Clark's (1979) study of responses to indirect requests. He suggests that there are at least six different sources of information that natural language users employ in determining whether an utterance in interrogative form is a question or an indirect request, including not only aspects of utterance form and content, but also expectations about the speaker's plans and goals. Ervin-Tripp (1976), Gibbs (1979, 1981), and Levinson (1979) also stress the way in which contextual expectations interact with linguistic information to determine the meaning of the act performed. The picture emerging from an inferential/strategic account of the communication of act meaning, then, is one in which multiple sources of information are simultaneously weighed and assessed in relation to one another on the assumption that a rational solution to what is meant should be found. Rather than looking like a linear deductive process starting from linguistic input and ending, by rule, in a determinate meaning, the process of interpretation appears to look much more like a solution to an equation with several unknown values. By juggling the unknowns in various ways, more than one solution may be obtained—a theoretically derived conclusion that accords well with the real-life uncertainties of human communication.

CONCLUSION

In this chapter I have tried to chart a general shift in the way discourse analysts think about the nature of language use and structure. Approaches to the problems of meaning and coherence have been dominated by a normative code model of communication. That model, which takes its conception of discourse knowledge from transformational generative grammar, promotes a misleading view of language meaning and language choice. The normative code model simply cannot capture three fundamental properties of linguistic communication: inference beyond the information given, generativity in patterning, and functional design of structure. Language expression and interpretation are not matters of encoding and decoding meaning by determinate rules, and language choice is not something dictated by normative regulations. In place of this model is an emerging view of linguistic communication as a process of strategic design and constructive inference. Rather than a process mechanically played out by a rule, discourse analysts are coming to see linguistic communication as creative problem solving.

REFERENCES

Austin, J. L. (1962). *How to do things with words*. Oxford: Clarendon.
Bach, K., & Harnish, R. M. (1979). *Linguistic communication and speech acts*. Cambridge, MA: MIT Press.
Blom, J. P., & Gumperz, J. J. (1972). Social meaning in linguistic structures: Code-switching in Norway. In J. J. Gumperz & D. Hymes (Eds.), *Directions in sociolinguistics: The ethnography of speaking* (pp. 407-434). New York: Holt, Rinehart & Winston.
Brown, G., & Yule, G. (1983). *Discourse analysis*. Cambridge, MA: Cambridge University Press.
Brown, P., & Levinson, S. (1978). Universals in language usage: Politeness phenomena. In E. N. Goody (Ed.), *Questions and politeness: Strategies in social interaction* (pp. 74-289). Cambridge, MA: Cambridge University Press.
Brown, R., & Gilman, A. (1972). The pronouns of power and solidarity. In P. O. Giglioli (Ed.), *Language and social context* (pp. 252-282). London: Penguin Books.
Chomsky, N. (1957). *Syntactic structures*. The Hague: Mouton.
Chomsky, N. (1959). Review of verbal behavior. *Language, 35*, 26-58.
Chomsky, N. (1965). *Aspects of the theory of syntax*. Cambridge, MA: MIT Press.
Chomsky, N. (1972). *Language and mind*. New York: Harcourt Brace Jovanovich.
Churchill, L. (1978). *Questioning strategies in sociolinguistics*. Rowley, MA: Newbury House.
Clark, H. H. (1977). Bridging. In P. N. Johnson-Laird & P. C. Wason (Eds.), *Thinking: Readings in cognitive science* (pp. 411-420). Cambridge, MA: Cambridge University Press.
Clark, H. H. (1979). Responding to indirect requests. *Cognitive Psychology, 11*, 430-477.
Clark, H. H., & Haviland, S. E. (1977). Comprehension and the given-new contact. In R. O. Freedle (Ed.), *Discourse production and comprehension* (pp. 1-40). Norwood, NJ: Ablex.
Cushman, D., & Whiting, G. C. (1972). An approach to communication theory: Toward consensus on rules. *Journal of Communication, 22*, 217-238.
Dascal, M., & Katriel, T. (1979). Digressions: A study in conversation coherence. *PTL: A Journal for descriptive Poetics and Theory of Literature, 4*, 203-232.
Ellis, D. G., Hamilton, M., & Aho, L. (1983). Some issues in conversation coherence. *Human Communication Research, 9*, 267-282.
Ellis, D. G., Hawes, L. C., & Avery, R. K. (1981). Some pragmatics of talking on talk radio. *Urban Life: Journal of Ethnographic Research, 10*, 155-177.
Ervin-Tripp, S. M. (1971). Sociolinguistics. In J. A. Fishman (Ed.), *Advances in the sociology of language, I: Basic concepts, theories and problems: Alternative approaches* (pp. 15-91). The Hague: Mouton.
Ervin-Tripp, S. (1976). Is Sybil there? The structure of some American English directives. *Language in Society, 5*, 25-66.
Gibbs, R. W. (1979). Contextual effects in understanding indirect requests. *Discourse Processes, 2*, 1-10.
Gibbs, R. W. (1981). Your wish is my command: Convention and context in interpreting indirect requests. *Journal of Verbal Learning and Verbal Behavior, 20*, 431-444.
Goffman, E. (1981). *Forms of talk*. Philadelphia: University of Pennsylvania Press.
Goldman, S. R. (1982). Knowledge systems for realistic goals. *Discourse Processes, 5*, 279-303.
Gordon, D., & Lakoff, G. (1975). Conversational postulates. In P. Cole & J. L. Morgan (Eds.), *Syntax and semantics, 3: Speech acts* (pp. 83-106). New York: Academic Press.
Grice, H. P. (1975). Logic and conversation. In P. Cole & J. L. Morgan (Eds.), *Syntax and semantics, 3: Speech acts* (pp. 41-58). New York: Academic Press.
Halliday, M.A.K., & Hasan, R. (1976). *Cohesion in English*. London: Longman.
Harper, R. G., Wiens, A. N., & Matarazzo, J. D. (1978). *Nonverbal communication: The state of the art*. New York: John Wiley.

Hobbs, J. R. (1982). Towards an understanding of coherence in discourse. In W. G. Lehnert & M. H. Ringle (Eds.), *Strategies for natural language processing* (pp. 223-244). Hillsdale, NJ: Lawrence Erlbaum.

Hook, S. (Ed.). (1969). *Language and philosophy*. New York: New York University Press.

Horton, D. L., & Dixon, T. R. (Eds.). (1968). *Verbal behavior and general behavior*. Englewood Cliffs, NJ: Prentice-Hall.

Hymes, D. (1974). *Foundations in sociolinguistics: An ethnographic approach*. Philadelphia: University of Pennsylvania Press.

Jackson, S. (1983). *Contributions of rule knowledge and world knowledge to inferences about beliefs and intentions*. Paper presented at the Kansas University Conference on Social Cognition and Interpersonal Communication, Lawrence, KS.

Jackson, S., & Jacobs, S. (1980). Structure of conversational argument: Pragmatic bases for the enthymeme. *Quarterly Journal of Speech, 66*, 251-265.

Jacobs, S., & Jackson, S. (1981). Argument as a natural category: The routine grounds for arguing in conversation. *Western Journal of Speech Communication, 45*, 118-132.

Jacobs, S., & Jackson, S. (1983a). Speech act structure in conversation: Rational aspects of pragmatic coherence. In R. T. Craig & K. Tracy (Eds.), *Conversational coherence: Form, structure, and strategy* (pp. 47-66). Beverly Hills, CA: Sage.

Jacobs, S., & Jackson, S. (1983b). Strategy and structure in conversational influence attempts. *Communication Monographs, 50*, 285-304.

Jakobovits, L. A., & Miron, M. S. (Eds.). (1976). *Readings in the psychology of language*. Englewood Cliffs, NJ: Prentice-Hall.

Jefferson, G. (1972). Side sequences. In D. Sudnow (Ed.), *Studies in social interaction* (pp. 294-338). New York: Free Press.

Kaufer, D. S. (1981). Understanding ironic communication. *Journal of Pragmatics, 5*, 495-510.

Labov, W. (1972). *Sociolinguistic Patterns*. Philadelphia: University of Pennsylvania Press.

Labov, W., & Fanshel, D. (1977). *Therapeutic discourse: Psychotherapy as conversation*. New York: Academic Press.

Leiter, K. (1980). *A primer on ethnomethodology*. New York: Oxford University Press.

Levinson, S. C. (1979). Activity types and language. *Linguistics, 17*, 365-399.

Levinson, S. C. (1981). Some pre-observations on the modeling of dialogue. *Discourse Processes, 4*, 93-116.

Levinson, S. C. (1983). *Pragmatics*. Cambridge, MA: Cambridge University Press.

Lyons, J. (1970). *Noam Chomsky*. New York: Viking.

Maclay, H. (1971). Overview: Linguistics. In D. D. Steinberg & L. A. Jakobovits (Eds.), *Semantics* (pp. 157-182). Cambridge, MA: Cambridge University Press.

Mandler, J. M., & Johnson, N. S. (1977). Rememberance of things passed: Story structure and recall. *Cognitive Psychology, 9*, 111-151.

Manes, J., & Wolfson, N. (1981). The compliment formula. In F. Coulmas (Ed.), *Conversational routine: Explorations in standardized communication situations and prepatterned speech* (pp. 115-132). The Hague: Mouton.

McLaughlin, M. L. (1984). *Conversation: How talk is organized*. Beverly Hills, CA: Sage.

Merritt, M. (1976). On questions following questions in service encounters. *Language in Society, 5*, 315-357.

Mohan, B. J. (1974). Do sequencing rules exist? *Semiotica, 12*, 75-96.

Morgan, J. L., & Sellner, M. B. (1980). Discourse and linguistic theory. In R. J. Spiro, B. C. Bruce, & W. F. Brewer (Eds.), *Theoretical issues in reading comprehension* (pp. 165-200). Hillsdale, NJ: Lawrence Erlbaum.

Pearce, W. B., & Conklin, F. (1979). A model of hierarchical meanings in coherent conversation and a study of "indirect responses." *Communication Monographs, 46*, 75-87.

Pomerantz, A. (1978). Compliment responses: Notes on the co-operation of multiple constraints. In J. Schenkein (Ed.), *Studies in the organization of conversational interaction* (pp. 79-112). New York: Academic Press.

Rumelhart, D. E. (1975). Notes on a schema for stories. In D. G. Bobrow & A. Collins (Eds.), *Representation and understanding: Studies in cognitive science* (pp. 211-236). New York: Academic Press.

Sacks, H. (1967). Unpublished lectures, University of California at Los Angeles.

Sacks, H. (1973). *On the preference for agreement in conversation.* Unpublished manuscript, Linguistic Institute, University of Michigan, Ann Arbor.

Sacks, H., Schegloff, E. A., & Jefferson, G. (1978). A simplest systematics for the organization of turn taking for conversation. In J. Schenkein (Ed.), *Studies in the organization of conversational interaction* (pp. 7-56). New York: Academic Press.

Schegloff, E. A. (1972). Notes on a conversational practice: Formulating place. In D. Sudnow (Ed.), *Studies in social interaction* (pp. 75-119). New York: Free Press.

Schegloff, E. A. (1977). Lecture notes. Boston University Summer Institute in Ethnomethodology, Boston University, Boston.

Schegloff, E. A. (1980). Preliminaries to preliminaries: "Can I ask you a question?" *Sociological Inquiry, 50,* 104-152.

Schegloff, E. A., & Sacks, H. (1974). Opening up closings. In R. Turner (Ed.), *Ethnomethodology: Selected readings* (pp. 223-264). Harmondsworth, Middlesex, England: Penguin Education.

Scotton, C. M. (1983). The negotiation of identities in conversation: A theory of markedness and code choice. *International Journal of the Sociology of Language, 44,* 115-136.

Searle, J. R. (1969). *Speech acts: An essay in the philosophy of language.* Cambridge: Cambridge University Press.

Searle, J. R. (1972, June 29). Chomsky's revolution in linguistics. *New York Review of Books,* pp. 16-24.

Searle, J. R. (1975). Indirect speech acts. In P. Cole & J. L. Morgan (Eds.), *Syntax and semantics, 3: Speech acts* (pp. 59-78). New York: Academic Press.

Shannon, C. E., & Weaver, W. (1949). *The mathematical theory of communication.* Urbana: University of Illinois Press.

Shimanoff, S. B. (1980). *Communication rules: Theory and research.* Beverly Hills, CA: Sage.

Sinclair, J.M.C.H., & Coulthard, R. M. (1975). *Toward an analysis of discourse: The English used by teachers and pupils.* Oxford: Oxford University Press.

Soames, S., & Perlmutter, D. M. (1979). *Syntactic argumentation and the structure of English.* Berkeley and Los Angeles: University of California Press.

Stein, N. L. (1979). How children understand stories: A developmental analysis. In L. G. Katz (Ed.), *Current topics in early childhood development* (pp. 261-290). Norwood, NJ: Ablex.

8   Nonverbal Signals

JUDEE K. BURGOON

University of Arizona

P OETS and pundits, sages and songwriters have all waxed lyrical
about the powers of nonverbal communication. Their enthusiasm
is well-captured in Edward Sapir's (1949) now famous quote: "We
respond to gestures with an extreme alertness and, one might almost say, in
accordance with an elaborate and secret code that is written nowhere,
known to none, and understood by all" (p. 556). That the code is understood
by all is a bit of hyperbole, but it underscores the universality of nonverbal
signals as a communication coding system. That the code may be known to
none is a deficiency to be partly remedied in this chapter.

THE RELATIVE IMPORTANCE
OF NONVERBAL BEHAVIOR

The designation in this handbook of nonverbal signals as "fundamental
units" in interpersonal communication belies the recognition they have been
given by the community of interpersonal communication scholars, who seem
not to have heard Sapir's message. Too often, the nonverbal component of
interpersonal interchanges has received only passing reference or has been
ignored entirely. Such oversight can lead to some erroneous conclusions
about the interpersonal communication process. Consider a few illustrations
from some popular lines of research:

1. *Self-Disclosure.* A typical study has two people sharing highly personal
information on a series of prescribed topics, often with one person
systematically varying some features of his or her disclosure (see, for
example, Gilbert, 1977; Gilbert & Horenstein, 1975). The theoretic interest is
in whether Person B will reciprocate Person A's level of intimacy, the
assumption being that Person A's verbal behavior is what influences Person
B's verbal behavior. One problem with this scenario is that it ignores the
possibility of Person A tempering his or her verbal behavior with accompanying nonverbal cues. For example, A may find highly intimate disclosures
difficult to make and may tone them down with a nonintimate nonverbal style.
Or if the disclosures are too impersonal, he or she may attempt to "warm up"
the interchange with more affiliative nonverbal cues. In either case, the "real"
level of A's intimacy is different than the experimenter thinks, and it may be

the nonverbal behaviors or the verbal-nonverbal combination that is responsible for B's response. A second problem is in looking only at B's verbal behavior as indicative of the degree of intimacy of B's response. Like A, B may also compensate for his or her own verbal behavior with more or less intimate nonverbal behaviors. The end result may be the false conclusion that reciprocity did not occur when in fact it did, or conversely that it did occur when in reality it did not. The possibilities for nonverbal compensation and complementation are even greater when both interactants are disclosing spontaneously (that is, neither's behavior is controlled experimentally).

2. *Relational Control Strategies.* Coding systems have been designed to identify who in an interaction is in control (for example, Rogers & Farace, 1975). These systems define one-up, one-cross, and one-down moves on the basis of people's verbal statements. A one-up move, such as a command, followed by a one-down move, such as a supportive reply, qualifies as an instance of dominance by the person engaging in the one-up behavior. The difficulties of using strictly verbal criteria for classifying dominant and submissive (or symmetrical and complementary) behavior are twofold. First, vocal (paralinguistic) behavior may alter significantly the function and meaning of an utterance. A reply that appears supportive on the surface—I'll be happy to do it"—may actually not be supportive at all if said in a sarcastic voice. A question may actually be an instruction—"Will you please stop bugging me?"—and so on. It is therefore easy to misclassify specific utterances and draw faulty conclusions about who is controlling the interaction. Second, numerous other nonverbal behaviors have dominance-submission interpretations. When they accompany a verbal statement, they may neutralize or radically modify the total meaning of an utterance. For example, extreme physical proximity and a stare may turn an apparently mollifying statement into an aggressive one.

3. *Negotiation Strategies.* Following the relational coding model, Donohue (1981) has developed a system for classifying negotiation tactics. The same problems apply here as for the relational coding scheme. A regressive-appearing statement such as, "Your point is well taken," can actually be a nonsupportive defending move if accompanied by such nonverbal behaviors as backward lean, indirect body orientation, gaze aversion, and facial impassivity. The failure to take account of the "nonverbal text" of a confrontation that is occurring simultaneously with the verbal maneuvers may lead to inaccurate conclusions about what are successful and unsuccessful tactics.

4. *Persuasion Strategies.* Much recent communication research has addressed the efficacy of Marwell and Schmitt's (1967) 16 strategies for gaining compliance. Although the various strategies need not be defined exclusively in terms of verbal behavior, they have typically only been studied as verbal strategies. Thus "personal expertise" is said to exist only if a person makes an explicit claim of such, not if nonverbal credibility cues are

presented. "Threats" are verbal ones, not nonverbal ones, and so forth. Such narrow definitions of persuasive strategies not only can lead to misestimates of how much influence is going on in actual face-to-face encounters, but they also direct research attention away from significant interplay between verbal and nonverbal cues that may be far more productive to study.

These examples indirectly illustrate the relative importance of nonverbal signals to the total social meaning of an interaction. More direct substantiation is also available. A much-repeated estimate in the popular literature is that 93 percent of the meaning in an exchange comes from nonverbal cues, leaving only 7 percent to be carried by the verbal utterance (Mehrabian & Wiener, 1967). Unfortunately, this estimate is based on faulty analysis (see Burgoon & Saine, 1978; Hegstrom, 1979); but because of its widespread citation, it has led many to believe that all estimates of the importance of nonverbal communication are grossly exaggerated.

A more reasonable estimate comes from Birdwhistell (1955), who claims that between 60 and 65 percent of the meaning in a social situation is communicated nonverbally. Although he provides no empirical evidence for his assertion, it is squarely in line with an estimate derived from Philpott (1983) through meta-analysis. Based on a statistical analysis of results from 23 studies, Philpott finds that approximately 31 percent of the variance in meaning can be attributed to the verbal channel, the remainder to be accounted for by nonverbal cues or their interaction with verbal ones.

The type of research reviewed in the meta-analysis compares verbal and nonverbal signals on their relative contributions to meaning. A series of studies by Argyle and associates (Argyle, Alkema, & Gilmour, 1971; Argyle, Salter, Nicholson, Williams, & Burgess, 1970) provide striking evidence of the potential impact of nonverbal elements. In those experiments, friendly, neutral, and unfriendly verbal passages were paired with friendly, neutral, and unfriendly nonverbal presentations; or superior, neutral, and inferior attitudinal statements were combined with parallel nonverbal behaviors. Even though the verbal and nonverbal presentations, when rated separately, were seen as relatively equal in strength, when combined, the nonverbal cues accounted for as much as 12.5 times as much variance in meaning as did the verbal statements. An attempt to make the verbal presentation stronger in advance still produced more reliance on the nonverbal cues when both the verbal and nonverbal were presented together.

A variety of other investigations (for example, Archer & Akert, 1977; Gitter, Black, & Fishman, 1975; Haase & Tepper, 1972; Seay & Altekruse, 1979; Tepper & Haase, 1978; Zahn, 1973) have found that adults tend to place greater reliance on nonverbal than verbal cues when interpreting communication. This pattern has been confirmed under such varied circumstances as job interviews, assessments of leadership, therapeutic sessions, attitudinal expressions, and judgments of first impressions. The nonverbal cues are especially likely to be believed when they conflict with the verbal message.

The research findings can be framed as a series of propositions, which have been summarized in Burgoon (in press) and include some qualifications on the general superiority of nonverbal over verbal information value:

(1) *As a general pattern, adults place more reliance on nonverbal than verbal cues in determining social meaning.* This pattern is the most common but must be restricted by the propositions that follow.

(2) *Children rely more heavily on verbal than nonverbal cues.* As children acquire language, they become highly literal. For example, they do not interpret sarcasm well. Prior to puberty, however, they shift to greater belief in the nonverbal signals.

(3) *Adult reliance on nonverbal cues is greatest when the verbal and nonverbal messages conflict; verbal cues become increasingly important as the messages become more congruent.* Some research finds that under congruent message conditions, verbal messages are believed over nonverbal ones. But more commonly, congruency among channels just makes the verbal and nonverbal coding systems more equal in their contribution to meaning.

(4) *The function of communication mediates channel reliance:* Verbal cues are more important for factual, abstract, and persuasive communications, whereas nonverbal cues are more important for relational, attributional, affective, and attitudinal messages. Not surprisingly, people rely on verbalizations for the denotative or "objective" meaning of a message. But for connotations, meta-messages, and meanings about the interpersonal relationship between speaker and auditor, they largely depend on nonverbal signals.

(5) *Individuals have consistent biases in channel reliance:* Some consistently depend on verbal information; some consistently depend on nonverbal information; and some are situationally adaptable. Although individuals have their personal predilections for which channels of information they attend to most often, the prevailing pattern is still one of relying more frequently and for more purposes on the nonverbal codes.

A variety of reasons have been offered for the significant dependence on nonverbal channels in interpreting and expressing interpersonal messages. These include possible innate origins, phylogenetic and ontogenetic primacy of nonverbal cues as coding systems, and their special suitability to handle interpersonal business while the verbal channel is simultaneously occupied with transmitting other information. Additionally, people are likely to attend to nonverbal information because it supplies invaluable contextual cues that aid in the interpretation of the verbal message. Nonverbal channels may reveal psychological and emotional information about the interactants; they may define the nature of the social situation; they may provide syntactic information that facilitates organization of the verbal stream; or they may supply semantically redundant cues, among other things. All of this linguistic context facilitates the understanding of the denotative and connotative meanings of a verbal utterance. In turn, the verbal content facilitates interpretation of the accompanying nonverbal signals. Thus verbal and nonverbal channels are inextricably intertwined in the communication of the total meaning of an interpersonal exchange.

LIMITING THE NONVERBAL DOMAIN

Up to this point, the term "nonverbal communication" has been used as if the behaviors, signals, cues, or acts that comprise it are generally understood. However, a quick perusal of the wide-ranging literature on the subject must immediately disabuse one of that belief. The broadest perspective on nonverbal communication treats all human behaviors and attributes as relevant. This approach is the least productive, if for no other reason than a pragmatic one: It makes the task of discovering general principles of communication nearly impossible if every facet of human behavior must be accounted for.

More narrow conceptions of communication often hinge on the issue of intent. For those who take a source-oriented perspective, whatever messages are sent intentionally by a source qualify as communication. Unintended messages do not. One difficulty with this perspective is that it is very easy to deny intentionality for much of what goes on nonverbally. For example, a person who frowns when hearing something she doesn't like may later deny that she intended to frown. The question then becomes one of who arbitrates what was intentional and what was not—the source, an "objective" observer, or who? If all behaviors that the source is unaware of or disclaims responsibility for are ruled out as communication, then the nonverbal domain may be overly narrow. Knapp (1983b), for example, believes that expressive behavior—acts that produce similar interpretations in observers but are not intentional—are as important a part of nonverbal communication as is purposive (intentional) behavior. Ekman and Friesen (1969) likewise make a distinction between informative (unintentional) and communicative (intentional) messages, both of which may be relevant to the understanding of nonverbal communication.

The inclusion of unintentional behavior as part of nonverbal communication comports with a receiver orientation, which holds that any behavior a receiver perceives as intentional (that is, interprets as a message) qualifies as communication. The objection to this perspective is that it is overly broad and verges on the "all behavior is communication" approach. It permits defining as communication such idiosyncratic and unintended behaviors as accidentally wearing unmatched socks or allergic sneezing—so long as someone reads something into the behavior.

An alternative that I have proposed elsewhere (Burgoon, 1980) is a message orientation. What qualifies as communication are those behaviors that form a socially shared coding system; that is, they are behaviors that are typically sent with intent, used with regularity among members of a social community, are typically interpreted as intentional, and have consensually recognizable interpretations. This approach is similar to that of Wiener, Devoe, Rubinow, and Geller (1972) in emphasizing socially shared rather than idiosyncratic behavior patterns. However, it is broader than their approach in that it includes habitual behaviors that have well-recognized meanings among members of the social system. The key word is "typically." If a behavior is usually encoded deliberately and is usually interpreted as meaningful by receivers or observers, it does not matter if, on a given occasion, it is performed unconsciously or unintentionally; it still qualifies as a message. Thus the "unintended" frown qualifies because the behavior is one that people typically encode as a signal of displeasure and typically decode as an intentional signal of displeasure. If one accepts the notion that much of our daily nonverbal communication is well-practiced and operates in a semi-automatic, unmonitored fashion (what some might call a "mindless" fashion), then it becomes more productive to attempt to identify the "vocabulary" of nonverbal communication than to divine intent on each occasion of a behavior's enactment. At the same time, this approach requires that a behavior be regularly used as part of a coding system, which implies that communicators frequently select it to convey a particular meaning and that recipients or observers frequently treat it as a purposive and meaningful signal.

A message orientation does not exclude expressive behavior from the domain of nonverbal communication unless it is so unfamiliar or unusual in form that others have no meaning for it. Rather, the focus on messages calls attention to the fact that much cathartic and expressive behavior takes the form of acts with shared meaning, perhaps because such behavior elicits an empathic or shared response.

Implicit in the message orientation is the assumption that nonverbal communication is rule-governed. Just as a coding system must have semantic and syntactic rules, so must nonverbal signals as they are combined to form messages—if they are to be treated as a coding system. This assumption delimits the nonverbal domain to the extent that it excludes behaviors lacking consistent meanings and behaviors that fail to be combined in systematic, "grammatical" ways with other nonverbal signals.

Using this message-centered approach, it becomes possible to specify general classes of nonverbal signals that potentially qualify as codes and to rule out others. For example, natural body odors, although potentially usable as a signal system (much as nonhuman species use them), do not meet the criteria of a coding system because they are not intentional, voluntarily encoded signals, nor do they evoke a consistent interpretation from receivers. Similarly, body type probably should not qualify as a message because it is not something the individual is able to manipulate at will to create a particular meaning (although dieting and body building might be seen as willful acts to modify the image one is projecting).

Classes of nonverbal behavior that unquestionably qualify include the following: (1) *kinesics* (visual bodily movements, including gestures, facial expressions, trunk and limb movements, posture, gaze, and the like); (2) *vocalics* or paralanguage (use of vocal cues other than the words themselves, including such features as pitch, loudness, tempo, pauses, and inflection); (3)

physical appearance (manipulable features such as clothing, hairstyle, makeup, and adornments; nonmanipulable features such as physiognomy and height would be excluded); (4) *haptics* (use of touch), (5) *proxemics* (use of interpersonal distance and spacing relationships); (6) *chronemics* (use of time as a message system, including such things as waiting time, lead time, and amount of time spent with someone); and (7) *artifacts* (manipulable objects and environmental features that may carry messages from their designers or users).

Although many nonverbal texts organize the body of nonverbal literature along these code lines, a more cogent presentation of the relationships among nonverbal codes, especially as they relate to interpersonal communication, is achieved by considering the structure, norms, and functions of nonverbal behavior. Accordingly, the remainder of this chapter will examine (1) the structure of nonverbal code systems, including general code properties, major taxonomies, and encoding and decoding capacities; (2) usage norms and differences (cultural, subcultural, and contextual patterns of use); and (3) the social functions of nonverbal communication that are relevant to interpersonal contexts, including cognitive processing and learning, expressive communication, impression formation and management, relational communication, mixed messages and deception, structuring and regulating interaction, and social influence.

STRUCTURE OF NONVERBAL CODE SYSTEMS

General Code Properties

The most common characterization of nonverbal codes is that they are *analogic* in nature, as distinguished from *digital* codes such as verbal language. An analogic code is comprised of an (1) infinite and (2) a continuous range of (3) naturally derived values. The color spectrum is an example. A digital code, by contrast, is composed of a (1) finite set of (2) discrete and (3) arbitrarily defined units. This distinction is used to deny the symbolicity of nonverbal behaviors, as symbols are discrete units that have arbitrarily assigned relationships with their referents.

In actuality, this categorization of nonverbal codes is overly simplistic. Although many nonverbal signs have intrinsic or natural meaning—such as smiling or crying—and may take on an infinite range of values, many others are more appropriately treated as digital because they are discrete and arbitrary, for example, the peace emblem or a greeting kiss. This introduces the question of the degree to which nonverbal codes parallel verbal language systems.

This is a controversial issue. Many well-established scholars deny that nonverbal codes comprise or even approximate a language. Yet the case can be made that many linguistic properties appear in varying degrees in nonverbal codes. First, many nonverbal expressions can be decomposed into discrete *units* equivalent to phonemes and morphemes. In fact, several nonverbal taxonomies follow a linguistic model in classifying units. Moreover, Dittmann (1978) argues that many continuous behaviors can and should be regarded as discrete. He identifies emblems, smiles, head nods, eye contact, gestures, postural shifts, degree of body lean, and body orientation as among the behaviors that are discrete or treatable as such.

Second, nonverbal constructions display *semantic, syntactic,* and *pragmatic rules.* Single cues and combinations of cues show semanticity in that they have consistently recognized meanings. A head nod, for instance, conveys such affirmative meanings as agreement, approval, and attentiveness. When combined with a scowl, it conveys serious attentiveness, never gaiety or attraction. Similarly, nonverbal expressions exhibit syntacity in that they follow combinatory and ordering rules. For example, a smile and a scowl are never displayed together because they would create a nonsensical display. A greeting ritual follows the order of eye contact and then kiss, not vice versa (except as a surprise, which takes the form of a rule violation). Illustrator gestures only accompany speaking, not listening (see Exline & Fehr, 1978; Kendon, 1983, for additional illustrations). The test of the rule-governed nature of nonverbal codes is our ability to recognize "ungrammatical" presentations—unorthodox combinations of signals and uninterpretable sequences. We view such performances as indicative of emotional disorder or lack of social competence. At the pragmatic, or use, level, nonverbal presentations are governed by cultural and subcultural norms and display rules. Each culture, for example, carries expectations about what conversational distance strangers will adopt with one another, and what may be considered an appropriate emotional display in one place may be proscribed in another (even though the meaning of the behavior is the same in both).

Third, the meanings of many nonverbal behaviors are *context-bound.* Just as interpretations of words and sentences rely on the rest of an utterance or the interactional context to make clear their meanings, so do nonverbal interpretations rely on the linguistic context, the other co-occurring nonverbal cues, and/or the interactional context for clarification. One knows, for instance, which interpretation to give to a head nod based on the accompanying nonverbal cues and the verbal content.

Fourth, nonverbal codes have the property of *transformation;* that is, a relatively small set of basic meanings may give rise to a variety of different forms of expression, all of which are semantically equivalent. Like "surface structures" in language, these different forms are all transformations of the same underlying meaning. A caress, close physical proximity, or a flirtatious smile may all communicate intimacy.

Fifth, nonverbal codes have the property of *productivity.* The ability exists to create new utterances out of the existing pool of units, so that although the initial set of code elements is relatively small, the number of new expressions that can be formed is limitless. And just as new terms can be introduced into our verbal lexicon, so can new nonverbal acts be introduced into our nonverbal vocabulary. The creation of new gestural forms for professional and technical use (such as sports officiating and radio broadcasting) are illustrations.

Additional linguistic features have been attributed to nonverbal codes (see Burgoon, 1985; Burgoon & Saine, 1978, for more detailed analyses of what linguistic features do and do not apply to nonverbal codes). However, there are some additional properties of nonverbal signal systems that are unique.

One is *iconicity*. Some, but by no means all, nonverbal behaviors are not only analogic but have the property of visually resembling that which they reference. The more similar and directly proportional the resemblance, the more iconic the behavior. A life-sized, three-dimensional sculpture or a pantomimic recreation of an event would be maximally iconic; the "crazy" gesture depicting an addled brain is less so but still shows a visual connection to that which it represents. The graphic nature of iconic gestures and behaviors gives them a vividness and attention-gaining capacity that is missing from verbal recreations of the same object, event, or idea. Their analogic character also gives iconic behaviors the ability to convey many shades of meaning by taking on a wide range of values.

A second unique property is the presence of some *universal forms and meanings*. Some nonverbal displays, such as threats and emotional displays, appear to be part of our biological inheritance. These behaviors have universally recognized forms and meanings, and therefore have the ability to serve as a pancultural language system that transcends cultural conventions. Because of their ability to bridge cultural differences, such nonverbal behaviors have a communicative power lacking from culture-bound verbal languages.

A third unique property is *simultaneous multimodal message transmission*. With nonverbal signals, several messages can be sent at the same time, each emanating from a different body location or through a different sensory mode. For example, although the eyes are sending one signal, the posture can send another, the voice can send another, and the conversational distance can send yet another. This potential for communicating several different meanings simultaneously gives an encoder a rich array of cues with which to form either a highly refined and specific or highly ambiguous message, depending on his or her intent. Similarly, a receiver has a wealth of information in the stimulus complex from which to extract the totality of meaning. This adds to the communicative power of nonverbal signals.

Fourth, nonverbal signals have the capacity for *direct sensory stimulation*. That is, many of them evoke an immediate and automatic response without benefit of cognitive mediation. This is what the general semanticists call a signal response (as opposed to a symbol response). The rapidity with which the senses process nonverbal signals may give them a communicative primacy over verbal signals, which require a cognitive translation before a response is possible. Part of this communicative primacy may also be a greater degree of emotional reactivity to nonverbal signs as compared to their verbal counterparts, which depend on the receiver's imaginative ability to produce the same degree of sensory impact. For example, seeing a nonverbal reenactment of a suicide may produce a much stronger visceral response than reading an account of the event.

Finally, nonverbal signals appear to be encoded with greater *spontaneity* than verbal messages. This is partly because of the number of nonverbal behaviors that have intrinsic (natural) rather than symbolic, and universal rather than culture-specific, meaning. The more automatic nature of the encoding process carries with it a number of implications, including the ambiguity of intent that it conveys, the prospect for greater "leakage" of deep-seated feelings and traits that accompanies less careful monitoring of one's encoding, and the greater truthfulness that receivers perceive is associated with such spontaneous encoding.

Taken together, the structural properties of nonverbal coding systems warrant treating them as language-like but not identical to verbal language. The similarities across verbal and nonverbal coding systems mean that communicators have greater flexibility in choosing among alternative vehicles for expressing a particular message. The differences among coding systems allow for specialization of function; for some purposes, nonverbal codes will be especially well-suited, whereas for others, verbal coding will be preferable. At the same time, the ability of the various codes to play complementary rather than redundant roles means that greater efficiency of communication can be achieved because different channels can be used simultaneously for different purposes. The important implication of this complementation process is that it takes all the modalities operating in concert to produce the total meaning of an interpersonal interchange. Thus, although it is important to explore the unique contributions that each code may make, to truly understand the whole of the interpersonal communication process, one must ultimately look at the entire interlocking system of codes. And it is this totality of interrelated codes that must really be viewed as our language system.

Major Taxonomies

Before one can begin to see how the interpersonal puzzle fits together, however, one must first identify the pieces. This is the work of the taxonomist. In the nonverbal arena, not enough of this basic groundwork has been done, perhaps partly because of the painstaking effort that is required to adequately catalog the basic building blocks of the nonverbal codes.

Three basic approaches have been taken to classify code elements. One, following a *structural linguistics model,* is to identify all the smallest structurally distinct and semantically meaningful units within a code. Pioneer efforts by Birdwhistell (1970) in the area of kinesics reduced the literally hundreds of thousands of possible kinesic movements down to a set of 50 or 60 kinemes, which are analogous to phonemes. These movements in turn are combined into kinemorphs, the equivalent of morphemes, and larger sentence-like constructions.

Others who have taken this linguistic approach include Exline and Fehr (1978), in their analysis of the semantics, syntax, and pragmatics of nonverbal cues; Kendon (1980), in his distinction between gestural units and phrases; Kauffman (1971), in her proposed system for classifying touch into traces, tacemorphs, and tacemorphic constructions; and Burgoon and Saine (1978), in their enumerations of the basic elements of physical appearance and artifacts that can be used to create messages. Harrison (1974) offers possible labels for phoneme-like and morpheme-like units for all the codes. Most of these linguistic approaches do not purport to exhaustively catalog specific nonverbal behaviors, but rather are suggestive of how such analyses must proceed.

In contrast to categorizing behaviors into discrete units, a second taxonomic approach specifies *dimensions* that might distinguish one type of behavior from another. A prime example of this approach is Hall's (1973) identification of the isolates, or characteristics, that differentiate formal, informal, and technical time systems and different categories of conversational distance. Trager's (1958) classic analysis of paralanguage features (such as tempo, degree of resonance, and pitch range) also fits this model, as do Burgoon and Saine's (1978) and Heslin and Alper's (1983) dimensions of touch (such as intensity, location, and duration). At a more fundamental level, Nolan (1975) has created a schema that can be used to place all verbal and nonverbal behaviors along three dimensions: coding (analogic, concrete, and intrinsic to digital, abstract, and arbitrary), propositionality (low consciousness/awareness/intent to high), and channel (modality of presentation).

The final taxonomic approach moves away from structural considerations and focuses instead on the *meanings, functions, or perceptions of nonverbal acts.* The most frequently cited taxonomy of this type is Ekman and Friesen's (1969) five functional categories of gestures (adaptors, regulators, illustrators, emblems, and affect displays). Morris, Collett, Marsh, and O'Shaughnessy (1979), among others, have pursued classification of emblems by identifying different cultural meanings for 20 common emblems. Other extensions of these various functions will be discussed later. Work by Nguyen, Heslin, and Nguyen (1975, 1976; Heslin, Nguyen, & Nguyen, 1983) on the meanings associated with four types of touch; Heslin's (1974) five social categories of touch; Hall's (1973) four categories of personal space; Knapp's (1978b) six perceptual dimensions of interaction environments; and Mehrabian's (1976) three dimensions of environmental effects are further examples of this genre of taxonomy.

Although it should be apparent from the array of classification schemes that some attention has been given to isolating the basic elements of nonverbal codes, it should be equally apparent that the current state of knowledge is limited and tentative. Although it has been fashionable to criticize nonverbal research for failing to move beyond the descriptive stage, more, not less, descriptive work is needed to uncover what nonverbal behaviors are meaningful and what possible meanings are assigned to them. One promising method for addressing this issue entails having observers watch an interaction sequence and use an event recorder to note all those junctures at which they think a meaningful behavior has occurred. Behaviors that are consensually identified as meaningful are then selected for further analysis. If this unitizing method is used to locate multimodal configurations of behaviors (rather than looking at a single modality), it may uncover which *patterns* of cues have shared meaning and can be regarded as part of a nonverbal lexicon. This should greatly facilitate our understanding of the totality of meanings being exchanged in interpersonal encounters.

Encoding and Decoding Capacities

Embedded in an analysis of the structure of nonverbal codes are any constraints on their capacity as coding systems. Research on encoding and decoding processes speaks to this issue. Four general lines of inquiry are potentially informative.

Physiological Research. Little work has been done in this area by people whose primary interest is communication. Rather, estimates of the human body's ability to produce different nonverbal signs and to discriminate such behaviors have been borrowed from other disciplines. So, we have estimates of kinesic encoding ability that range from 700,000 possible physical signs (Pei, 1965), to 20,000 different facial expressions (Birdwhistell, 1970), to 1000 known variations in postural-gestural combinations (Hewes, 1957). Regardless of the specific estimate, the conclusion to be drawn is that humans have a tremendous number of body-movement combinations at their disposal as communication vehicles. Research on visual perception suggests a parallel ability to make fine visual discriminations, although some distortion may occur due to socially conditioned perceptual biases. Work by audiologists and speech scientists similarly reveals a nearly limitless range of auditory signals that can be produced and detected, including variations in such vocal features as pitch, loudness, tempo, articulation, rhythm, fluency, silences, voice quality, and dialect. Although haptics is often thought of as a more restricted code, Leathers (1976) cites physiological research supporting the capacity of the skin to transmit a wide range of electrical signals and to detect variations in touch behavior along dimensions of location, intensity, and duration, among others.

Other nonverbal codes have not been systematically analyzed for human physiological capacity to encode and decode communicative signals. Such an undertaking would seem profitable, because it might explain reliance on particular nonverbal channels and sources of accuracy or inaccuracy in interpersonal communication. One particularly productive avenue for exploration might be the degree to which each channel evokes physiological arousal, and whether that arousal facilitates or hinders accurate message transmission. Another promising line of research, discussed in more detail later, concerns brain function and the processing of nonverbal cues. Some evidence suggests that the analogic nature of many nonverbal cues may make them more amenable to right hemispheric processing, whereas digital cues may be handled by the left hemisphere. Additionally, innate and reflexive nonverbal acts, including many emotional responses, may be controlled by different parts of the brain than more symbolic behaviors. What constraints or advantages this might confer on nonverbal codes as communication systems remains to be seen.

Developmental Research. Evidence regarding the phylogenetic and ontogenetic development of nonverbal communication serves to distinguish those behaviors that have evolutionary origins from those that must be learned. Those that are part of the biological heritage of the species presumably are more readily performed and understood than those for which competence must be socially acquired (although even Darwin [1965] acknowledged that innate behaviors may require practice for successful execution).

Relevant literature appears in Als (1977), Altmann (1968), Anderson (1977), Blurton Jones (1972), Brannigan and Humphries (1972), Buck (1981), Burgoon (1985), Burgoon and Saine (1978), De Long (1977), Ekman (1973b), van Hooff (1972), Knapp (1978a), Pitcairn and Eibl-Eibesfeldt (1976), Street (1983), Thorpe (1972), Tronick, Als, and Brazelton (1977), Vine (1973), and Wood (1981), among others. Dominant lines of inquiry have covered such areas as instinctive (reflexive) behaviors, emotional displays, emotion-receiving ability, social and automanipulative gestures, social interaction behaviors (such as smiling, eye gaze, and turn-taking), aggressive behaviors, interactional synchrony and noncontent speech convergence, distancing patterns, physical appearance recognition and preferences, and relative dependence on verbal and nonverbal channels.

Both cross-cultural and comparative (cross-species) analyses suggest that a number of expressive, affiliative, and aggressive behaviors are pancultural at a minimum and probably are endemic to primates and other higher-order vertebrates. Child development literature further indicates that certain behaviors, such as alertness responses, smiling, crying, cooing, echolalia, and adaptor behaviors, are present in the neonate or emerge within the first year. Many additional social and emotional behaviors are in place by the end of the second year. Thus toddlers already have an extensive nonverbal repertoire that is a combination of genetically programmed and socially acquired communicative signals. Given that these behaviors largely precede the acquisition of language, their evolutionary and ontogenetic primacy should make them particularly potent communication vehicles, both in terms of production and interpretation. By contrast, those nonverbal behaviors that depend on the child's psychomotor, cognitive, and social development for their acquisition—behaviors such as appropriate conversational distancing, turn-taking, and many emblem and illustrator gestures—may be more constrained in their coding capacity, in part because competence may vary widely within the social community.

This developmental distinction between innate and learned behaviors warrants further analysis for its ability to account for differences in nonverbal code use and recognition. It may also be relevant to explaining the arousal potential of each nonverbal channel. On both counts, it should further understanding of which nonverbal behaviors are likely to have the most impact on interpersonal exchanges.

Individual Skills Research. As alluded to above, individual differences in social competence also delimit the capacity of nonverbal channels to carry communication. A recent shift in nonverbal research has been away from considering traits as the basis for individual differences and toward examination of skills. As Friedman (1979) notes, "The concept of nonverbal skills directs attention from what people are to what people can do interpersonally. Individual strengths and weaknesses are objectively tested and related to the outcomes of social interactions" (p. 16).

Research in this area has generally centered on the face, voice, and body, with gender differences preoccupying most investigators. Hall (1979) conducted a meta-analysis of 75 quantitative studies and came to the following conclusions:

(1) *Women are better than men at decoding nonverbal messages; that superiority exists regardless of age and gender of the stimulus person.* Of the 61 relevant studies surveyed, 84 percent of the total and 23 out of the 24 with statistically significant results showed women to be more accurate interpreters than men.

(2) *Women are better than men at encoding nonverbal messages; that superiority exists regardless of age but may be limited to visual cues.* Of the 21 relevant studies, 71 percent of the total and 8 out of the 9 statistically significant findings favored women as the better senders. The only qualification was that results were too variable for vocal cues to support a consistent effect.

Hall (1979) proceeded to pose a number of alternative hypotheses for the greater encoding and decoding ability of women and to rule out several of them with empirical evidence. The findings can be summarized in a third conclusion:

(3) *Women's encoding and decoding superiority does not appear to be a function of greater empathic ability, greater social emphasis on expressiveness as a feminine behavior, or greater alertness of women due to their relative social powerlessness.*

Other tentative hypotheses that are in need of investigation include greater practice adopting passive, submissive roles (and resultant increase in interpretive skills), socialization to be more accommodating and to therefore attend to intentional cues, innate differences, cognitive processing differences, differences in degree of linguistic involvement, and differences in hemispheric lateralization (with concomitant differences in processing skill). One hypothesized difference that Buck (1979) has confirmed is the following:

(4) *Women are more likely to externalize emotions, whereas men are more likely to internalize them.* In other words, women are more likely to externally manifest their emotional states, making them more readily understood when they express them, whereas men are more likely to experience high internal physiological arousal but to outwardly display less, making decoding of their expressions more difficult.

Knapp (1978a) has summarized literature related to other influences on encoding and decoding skill. These additional conclusions seem warranted:

(5) *Encoding and decoding ability are correlated.* Those who are better senders tend to be better receivers and vice versa.
(6) *Decoding ability increases with age and training.* Maturation, increased social development, and specific practice all contribute to improved ability to accurately interpret nonverbal expressions.
(7) *Race and intelligence do not appear to relate to encoding and decoding skill but personality and occupation do.* For example, extroversion and self-monitoring have a positive relationship with encoding and decoding skill; dogmatism has a negative one.

Together, these conclusions indicate that successful nonverbal message transmission and receipt will vary as a function of individual skill, with women, older people, and certain personality types expected to exhibit greater facility. Ongoing research using the PONS (Profile of Nonverbal Sensitivity), a screening device recently developed at Harvard (Rosenthal, Hall, DiMatteo, Rogers, & Archer, 1979), should uncover additional significant relationships. The emerging findings should ultimately have implications for the degree of accuracy that can be achieved in interpersonal interchanges and the role that nonverbal encoding and decoding skill play in conceptualizations of interpersonal competence.

Channel Comparison Research. The final line of investigation relevant to the structural properties of nonverbal coding focuses on comparisons among the various channels or codes themselves. As an extension of the earlier cited comparisons between verbal and nonverbal communication, this research assesses the relative contributions of each code to the total meaning of an utterance, expression, or social situation. The typical research paradigms either manipulate a small number of nonverbal cues in two or more modalities (for example, the face and voice) or measure the spontaneously occurring nonverbal behaviors in an ongoing interaction stream. Statistical analyses then determine the relative variance accounted for by each channel.

Most of the research has compared visual to vocal channels. The consistent finding is that visual cues have primacy over vocal ones, especially if the visual cue is the face rather than the body, and that this primacy exists for both consistent and inconsistent messages (see DePaulo, Rosenthal, Eisenstat, Rogers, & Finkelstein, 1978; Hegstrom, 1979; Philpott, 1983; Rosenthal & DePaulo, 1979; Tepper & Haase, 1978). However, the type of judgment or function of the behavior being judged may alter that pattern. For example, the audio channel may become more important for dominance, potency, and activity judgments, for impression formation, and for certain emotional expressions (Burns & Beier, 1973; Krauss, Apple, Morency, Wenzel, & Winton, 1981; Philpott, 1983; Rosenthal & DePaulo, 1979). The few studies that have considered additional nonverbal cues have tended to show that other nonverbal features also contribute significantly to meaning but that the relative contribution they make depends on the type of judgment being made. For example, vocal fluency, composure, body posture, eye contact, loudness, and physical appearance have been found to have relatively equal correlations with overall assessments of a job applicant (Hollandsworth, Kazelskis, Stevens, & Dressel, 1979). Eye gaze generally carries more weight than trunk lean, which carries more weight than vocal intonation in judgments of therapeutic empathy, respect, and genuineness (Tepper & Haase, 1978); but the contribution of facial expression to total meaning ranges from a high of 40 percent of the variance in respect judgments to a much smaller 9 percent of meaning for genuineness.

At this stage, it is not possible to rank order channels or codes on their relative efficiency or primacy because so many of the codes and modalities within codes have not yet been studied. But the bulk of evidence so far indicates a strong bias toward relying on visual modalities, particularly the face. Various hypotheses can be advanced for this visual primacy, including an innate reliance on visual information, a culturally conditioned bias toward visual information, a specific orientation toward the face as a carrier of intentional information, a structural advantage for visual information due to its availability at great distances, a greater vividness and arousability associated with visual cues, and a possible facilitative role of visual cues in information processing and storage. No doubt these and other possibilities will receive greater scrutiny as more channel comparison research is conducted. Such research should in turn help to explain why nonverbal cues tend to carry more weight than verbal ones in many interpersonal contexts, as well as which nonverbal codes are most responsible for the effects.

USAGE NORMS AND DIFFERENCES

As noted earlier, an overarching question for nonverbal communication scholars (and indeed, for all students of communication) is the universality of interpretations of many behaviors; it is evident to the astute observer that in practice, as many differences as similarities appear. Cultures vary on what is normative behavior, and there is also considerable within-culture variability as a function of subgroup and contextual norms. In particular, such "people" factors as gender, age, socioeconomic status, race, and personality make a difference. So do such contextual factors as the type of occupation in work settings and environmental constraints.

Review of the substantial volume of literature examining cultural norms and subgroup differences is beyond the scope of this chapter. The intent here is to highlight some general trends in the research and to consider their implications for interpersonal communication. For general summaries of aspects of this literature, the reader is directed to Argyle (1967), Burgoon (1982), Burgoon and Saine (1978), Hall (1977), Harper, Wiens, and Matarazzo (1978), Henley (1977), Kendon, Harris, and Key (1975), Knapp (1978a), Krout (1971), LaFrance and Mayo (1978), Leach (1972), Malandro and Barker (1983), Mayo and Henley (1981), Mehrabian (1972), Rich (1974), and Samovar and Porter (1976). Additional detail on specific codes is available in the following: for kinesics, Argyle and Cook (1976), Birdwhistell (1970), Eibl-Eibesfeldt (1972), Ekman (1976), Ekman and Friesen (1969), Hewes (1957), Morris (1977), and Morris et al. (1979); for proxemics, Aiello and Thompson (1980), Burgoon and Jones (1976), Hall (1973), and Scheflen and Ashcraft (1976); for haptics, Montagu (1978), Rosenfeld et al. (1976), and Willis and Hoffman (1975); for vocalics, Kramer (1974), Markel (1969), Starkweather (1964), and Thorne and Henley (1975); for physical appearance, Roach and Musa (1981); for chronemics, Hall (1969, 1973) and Scheflen and Ashcraft (1976); and for environment and artifacts, Proshansky, Ittleson, and Rivlin (1970).

Cultural Norms

The code that has received the most intensive study is kinesics. Analyses in the area of emotional expression reveal that even though all humans may express emotions in the same manner when in private, their public expressions will be governed by what Ekman and Friesen (1969) call display rules. These are the culture's norms for the appropriate forms and occasions for various expressions, including prohibitions on some expressions. So, for example, although all people may show the same grief displays when alone, cultures will vary widely in the extent to which people are expected to be highly demonstrative (such as the loud wailing and outpouring of distress at an Irish wake) or to be highly restrained (such as the smiling faces of the bereaved at a Japanese funeral). Other behaviors may be totally proscribed because they are impolite, insulting, or excessively familiar. This difference in surface appearance does not deny some level of universality in the encoding and decoding of primary affect displays, but it does mean that cultures may imbue such expressions with surplus meanings and/or inhibit their performance through cultural conventions. One is therefore not safe in assuming that an apparently similar expression will have the same meaning for people from two different cultures or that it will meet standards of appropriateness in both.

Room for misunderstandings also exists with emblems, those symbolic gestures that have direct verbal equivalents. All cultures appear to have them and to use them for the same functions (such as interpersonal directions, greetings, departures, insults), but cultures differ in how many they have and what form they take. The same behavior may have radically different meanings in different cultures; different behaviors may have the same meaning; or behaviors that are meaningful in one culture may be meaningless in another. The impact on cross-cultural interpersonal encounters is the significant opportunity for erroneous interpretations and embarrassing interchanges.

The same problem exists with eye gaze. People implicitly assume that everyone uses gaze in the same way. Yet cultures vary on how frequently people look at each other, how long one is expected to hold the gaze of another, and what meanings are associated with eye contact and gaze aversion. For example, downcast eyes are a sign of respect in one place, a sign of disrespect in another. One must therefore know the cultural norms as a background against which to judge a particular gaze pattern.

Other facets of body movement that show cultural variability include sitting and standing postures, the amount and form of illustrator gestures used to augment and clarify the verbal stream, and the appropriateness of performing various adaptor behaviors in public (such as belching, self-grooming, and gum chewing).

Vocalic cultural norms have received far less attention, but they appear to be tied to the language spoken. The phonemic properties of the language may dictate intonation, rhythm, voice quality, and even pitch level; variations in these properties also produce dialects within languages, so that any norms must be seen as operating within a range. Nonlinguistic features of the voice for which cultures may set standards include loudness and pitch range.

Physical appearance has received far more systematic cross-cultural analysis, although not necessarily from a communication perspective. Anthropological evidence indicates that all cultures have grooming and adornment rituals that entail many of the same structural elements (for example, hairstyling, exposure or emphasis of body parts, cosmetics, dress, color symbolism), but beautification standards and practices differ, as does the manner in which clothing, hairstyle, personal artifacts, cosmetics, and the like symbolize such things as status/power, gender, and social stigmatization. The degree to which there is rigid adherence to cultural norms also varies. For example, cultures that are less egalitarian in dress than the United States may have little opportunity for personal statement through appearance. In such cases, dress practices carry only sociological or cultural level messages and may not be used to make personal attributions.

As for the remaining codes, their use varies fundamentally as a function of cultural differences in world view, religious values, child-rearing practices, degree of industrialization, and other patterns of social organization. Cultures not only differ in how they structure their time systems, they also perceive time differently. This affects what qualifies as a chronemic message. For example, polychronic use of time (doing more than one thing at a time) is normative in Latin American cultures; in monochronic cultures like the United States, such use of time takes on special message value, such as signalling inattentiveness or disregard. Similarly, cultures that have no concept of waiting cannot use waiting time as a personal message.

Spatial orientations affect the amount of physical proximity and contact that is permissible, the ways in which privacy is achieved, and the manner in which physical environments are functionally organized. Cultures can be loosely divided into contact and noncontact cultures. Contact cultures interact at closer distances, touch more often, orient their bodies to face one another more directly, and use more eye contact. This produces a greater sense of immediacy, or sensory involvement, in an interaction. The dominant U.S. pattern is noncontact; consequently, increases in immediacy in one channel may be accompanied by a compensatory decrease in another. Interpretation of the meanings of such nonverbal adjustments must therefore occur within the context of what degree of immediacy is considered comfortable within a culture. Cultures also vary in the degree to which they afford individual physical privacy and compartmentalize living and work spaces to accommodate private versus social activities. Those that have more communal and undifferentiated physical environments may use alternative nonverbal means for achieving a sense of privacy (such as adopting a polite but inscrutable demeanor that permits psychological privacy).

Gender Differences

The nonverbal literature is ripe with evidence of gender differences and possible explanations for these differences. One organizing theme that lends coherence to the mass of findings is Henley's (1977) thesis that male and female nonverbal patterns closely conform to basic dominance and sub-mission patterns. Some of the consistent findings that support this proposi-tion are

(1) Women gaze more at conversational partners while speaking, while listening, and during pauses than do men, gaze being regarded as a submissive behavior.
(2) Women smile more than men and are more expressive facially and vocally: That expressiveness typically takes positive and supportive rather than hostile forms. These behaviors have been interpreted by some as appeasement signs.

(3) Women are approached more closely, tolerate more spatial intrusion, give way to others more frequently, take up less physical space, and receive more touch than men. Men are more likely to dictate the spacing and distancing patterns and to initiate touch. These asymmetrical proxemic and haptic patterns, of men controlling space and contact and women accommodating, parallel those used between superiors and subordinates.

(4) Women talk less, listen more, and are interrupted more often than men.

(5) Women display more "submissive" postures and gestures such as the head tilt, open palm display, closed arm and leg positions, and moderate postural tension.

(6) Women use more rising vocal intonations (as in questions) and hesitations.

An alternative interpretation of gender differences is that women are more affiliative and responsive than men. The findings just noted can be reinterpreted within this frame, inasmuch as all the behaviors convey supportiveness, nonaggressiveness, and positive affect. Other behaviors that fit an affiliation interpretation include the following:

(7) Women adopt closer conversational distances with women as well as men and show a preference for side-by-side seating; they also respond more favorably than men to crowded situations.

(8) Women give as well as receive more touch than men and appear to seek physical contact to a greater extent than do men.

Finally, many gender-linked differences do not neatly fit either of these interpretations and seem to be governed either by anatomical differences or socially prescribed role expectations for masculine and feminine behavior, the purpose of such differentiation being partly to stimulate sexual attraction. Vocal differences in pitch and voice quality, walking and standing postures, and grooming and adornment practices may be explained by such a biological or cultural need to distinguish the sexes. Of course, the larger issue of whether gender differences are innately determined or socially conditioned has yet to be resolved, either in the nonverbal realm or in human behavior in general. But the nonverbal evidence to date suggests a sociobiological interpretation that includes physiological as well as cultural determinants of male and female communication patterns.

Beyond the contribution that nonverbal gender differences research can make to understanding the larger issue of the origins of such differences in human interaction, the consistent pattern of male-female differences raises a number of interesting questions in interpersonal communication. Among others: What are the personality and social stereotypes attached to feminine and masculine display? What are the effects of violating gender-linked communication expectations? What is the role of sexual attraction in altering interaction patterns? How generalizable are interpersonal communication findings to both same-sex and opposite-sex interactions? And do one's own sex-linked normative communication patterns lead to misinterpretations of opposite-sex behavior?

Age, Race, and Socioeconomic Status

These three factors need to be considered together because they are interrelated: Age and race often affect status, and what is frequently interpreted as an age or racial difference is often really a function of education or income.

Kinesically, some behaviors have been associated with social class, such as the use of "cruder" emblems by lower class males and females, and some have been associated specifically with blacks, such are rolling the eyes, use of a strutting walking style among black males, and use of a specific "rapping stance" when conversing. Older people also tend to adopt more gender-neutral sitting, standing, and walking patterns.

Proxemically, people maintain greater distances from status unequals and age unequals; closest distances appear among peers. Very mixed findings have been reported on conversational distance among blacks, but it appears that black males and females may have very different patterns and that blacks in general may show greater fluidity in their distancing. What little is known about touch patterns indicates that touch is typically initiated by the person in the higher-status position, that children and opposite-sex peers receive the most touch, and that amount of touching declines considerably with advancing age.

Most of the writing on chronemic differences centers on status. Those with higher education, income, and/or social standing have more access to leisure time and other people's time, are permitted to keep others waiting, are typically given more lead time in the scheduling of events, may compartmentalize or structure their time more, and pass time in more varied rather than repetitive activities. Conversely, people at the low end of the socioeconomic spectrum may have a very loosely structured time system. In urban ghetto environments, this may be referred to as "street time."

Regarding physical appearance, anecdotal analyses suggest that older people choose clothing that emphasizes comfort over style and that color and accessory choices tend to be age-related. Status differences also appear in the choices of color, fabric design, and accessories, with people from lower economic strata leaning toward more brightly colored, dramatic clothing with more decoration.

The fact that these various demographic factors produce nonverbal norms means that certain expectations will come to be associated with a person's sociological classification. This in turn will have implications for stereotyping in impression formation and for conformity versus violation strategies in impression management. The status-related norms will also have implications for the relational communication of dominance and power.

Personality and Mental Disorders

Psychoanalytic and psychological literature has produced nonverbal profiles associated with such personality traits as extraversion-introversion,

Machiavellianism, anxiety, authoritarianism, and need for affiliation, and such disorders as schizophrenia, paranoia, depression, and hysteria. The nonverbal codes that most often distinguish these psychological states are vocalics, kinesics, proxemics, and physical appearance. More specifically, vocal loudness, speech errors, pitch, voice quality, vocal characterizers (such as crying or laughing), silences, amount of eye contact, coordination of movement, amount of gesticulation, postural relaxation, amount of physical movement, conversational distance, personal grooming, and colorfulness of clothing all seem to be entailed.

Examination of these profiles may prove useful in analyzing attribution processes in interpersonal communication. Because specific behaviors consistently accompany a particular personality type, neurosis, or psychosis, presentation of those behaviors may lead to perceptual halo effects and assignment of all the associated psychological and emotional characteristics to the communicator. Recognition that stable behavior patterns accompany personality styles may also account for some of the heretofore unexplained variability in interpersonal exchanges, especially the range of variation in nonverbal performances.

Interactional Context and Environmental Constraints

Included under this heading are norms related to whether a context is task-oriented or social, formal or informal, personalized or depersonalized, and private or public. Also included are constraints dictated by task requirements and the physical setting itself.

Much of the research in this area is sketchy and anecdotal. Typical of the kind of work that has been done are catalogs of gestures associated with a particular occupation or social organization (such as secret societies), descriptions of dress and hair standards for various occupations, and analyses of the specific behavioral repertoires appearing in such types of physical settings as churches, schools, or bars. The value of these context-specific compilations of norms is that they play a role in defining the nature of the social situation; that is, they assist in clarifying the purpose of the social gathering and the programs of behavior that are to be invoked in it, thereby regulating the interaction that follows.

One way to systematize contextual norm data is to identify the broader dimensions along which contexts can be classified and to specify the collection of nonverbal and verbal behaviors associated with those dimensions. Goffman (1963) has already singled out formality-informality (or tightness-looseness) as a primary distinguishing feature of social gatherings. His distinction between front-stage and backstage behavior and his characterization of activities appearing backstage (Goffman, 1959) evoke another dimension related to degree of privacy. Others (for example, Altman, 1975; Burgoon, 1982) have specifically analyzed the private end of the continuum and attempted to profile the multiplicity of nonverbal and verbal behaviors that signal privacy. Similar analyses are needed for other salient dimensions of contexts.

SOCIAL FUNCTIONS OF
NONVERBAL COMMUNICATION

Dissecting nonverbal communication into its constituent parts is necessary for studying communication structure. But the traditional decomposition into separate codes leads to a piecemeal and distorted understanding of the social and communicative role of nonverbal signals. Nonverbal behaviors clearly operate as an integrated and carefully coordinated system in achieving particular social functions, and their importance becomes more apparent when they are examined collectively.

A number of frameworks are possible for taking an integrative approach to nonverbal communication. One that has proven useful in organizing related lines of research and thought is a functional one: examining nonverbal signals according to the social purposes to which they relate. The seven to be discussed here are neither mutually exclusive nor exhaustive categories, but they seem to have the most relevance to interpersonal communication.

Cognitive Processing and Learning

A seldom recognized but significant function of nonverbal signals is in the cognitive processing of messages and social information and in the learning of new concepts and behaviors. The role of nonverbal behavior can be analyzed at the neurophysiological, microcommunicative, or macrocommunicative level.

At the neurophysiological level, two growing research interests are relevant. The first concerns brain organization and the processing of verbal and nonverbal stimuli. Summaries of the current state of knowledge (for example, Andersen, Garrison, & Andersen, 1979; Burgoon, 1985; Campbell, 1982; Stacks, 1982a, 1982b) suggest that there is some hemispheric lateralization in the reception and production of verbal and nonverbal stimuli, with the left hemisphere typically more dominant for verbal signals and the right hemisphere for nonverbal ones. However, there is growing evidence that the two hemispheres are highly interdependent in the processing of social information. The left-right distinction may therefore be more a matter of style differences, with the left showing a superiority in handling digital, symbolic, and rational stimuli and the right showing a superiority in encoding and interpreting analogic, visual, gestalt, and emotional material. This means that the form in which a nonverbal signal is codified or perceived (for example, digital, iconic, analogic) may influence the manner in which it, and possibly its linguistic accompaniment, is comprehended and stored in memory.

Moreover, research now points to the existence of a tripartite brain, with instinctive behaviors (such as territorial defense and aggressive reflexes) controlled by a primitive brain at the end of the brain stem (the R-Complex), emotional behaviors and certain bodily functions controlled by the limbic system surrounding the R-Complex (the Paleomammalian brain), and higher-order functions controlled by the cerebrum (the Neomammalian brain). The interplay among these three brains, when better understood, should have significant implications for how different types of nonverbal signals (for example, threat displays, emotional expressions, emblematic gestures) affect comprehension and learning processes.

The second neurophysiological research trend concerns memory processes themselves. Current thinking (for example, Folger & Woodall, 1982; Ortony, 1978) holds that comprehension and recall are two separate processes, both of which involve activation of interlinking nodes that form memory traces. The greater the spread of activation to more nodes, the greater the comprehension and the likelihood of later reconstruction (recall). Three types of information may facilitate the formation of more elaborate memory traces: the underlying semantic content of a message (which creates the nodes, or concepts), syntactic relationships (which dictate initial relationships among nodes and may be stored briefly in memory), and the context in which a message is embedded at time of input.

Nonverbal cues contribute to all three types of information (Burgoon, 1985; Folger & Woodall, 1982). At the microcommunicative level, that is, the level of understanding single linguistic constructions or short segments of discourse, nonverbal signals serve multiple syntactic functions. Paralinguistic suprasegmentals (intonation, stress, and juncture) provide vocalic punctuation so that words and clauses can be distinguished from one another. Birdwhistell (1970) has identified an analogous set of parakinesic behaviors (called stress kinemes) that serve this same organizational function and a set of kinesic markers that signal pluralization, tense, and pronominal specification, among other syntactic features. It has also been argued that utterances are processed at the level of the phonemic clause (Boomer, 1965, 1978; Dittmann, 1972b) and that nonverbal cues may facilitate the "chunking" of linguistic content into these units. Beyond the specific paralinguistic and parakinesic behaviors that may distinguish phonemic clauses, the synchronization of a speaker's nonverbal behaviors to the rhythm of the speech stream may facilitate comprehension and recall. Woodall and Burgoon (1981) found such an effect for speaker self-synchrony.

Semantically, nonverbal illustrator gestures may lend clarity to the verbal stream and emblem gestures may add redundancy or semantic elaboration. Both types have been found to contribute to comprehension and recall, as well as to greater ease in encoding (Cohen & Harrison, 1973; Riseborough,

1981; Woodall & Folger, 1981). As for contextual information, it is likely that kinesic, physical appearance, and artifactual cues may lend visual vividness to the stimulus complex, while haptic, proxemic, and vocalic cues may stimulate physiological arousal, thereby strengthening the associations between content and context in memory. Folger and Woodall (1982) also note that anomalous and incongruent messages may produce deeper cognitive processing. Thus to the extent that the combined nonverbal codes send mixed or ambiguous messages, they may prompt greater attention and comprehension.

At the macrocommunicative level, or the level of understanding larger communicative episodes and discourses, nonverbal cues may also play a key role. Kendon (1983) and McNeill and Levy (1982) argue that gestures depict and reflect the larger meaning of extended utterance; Birdwhistell (1970) notes that parakinesic markers bring coherence to larger chunks of connected discourse; and Woodall and Folger (1982) claim that nonverbal cues play a role in the inference-making process that is so central to initial comprehension. Nonverbal signals may also serve a more macroscopic attention-gaining role and facilitate the entrainment, or synchrony, of listener with speaker. Specific nonverbal cues identified as increasing attention, comprehension, and learning include vocal variety, faster speaking rate, "warm" vocal tones, and smiling and touch, as well as interactional synchrony itself (see, for example, Beighley, 1952, 1954; Duker, 1974; Kazdin & Klock, 1973; Kleinfeld, 1974; LaBarbera & MachLachlan, 1979; MachLachlan & Siegel, 1980; Saine, 1976). The attentional ability of nonverbal cues clearly needs further examination. At the same time, many nonverbal signals may distract from, rather than center attention on, the verbal content of a message. Stacks and Burgoon (1981) propose that vocal nonfluencies, unpleasant voice qualities, extreme conversational distances, extremes in physical attractiveness, and excessive environmental stimulation may distract and impair comprehension. In a meta-analysis of the distraction literature, Buller (1983) found that auditory and visual forms of distraction did indeed reduce comprehension. Although that research did not all directly apply to nonverbal communication, it strongly implies that nonverbal behaviors may be unsuspected and intrinsic sources of distraction in interpersonal interchanges. This possibility clearly deserves further study.

Finally, the role of nonverbal signals in the reinforcement and modeling of cognitive and behavioral learning needs examination. Many positive and negative regard cues may function as positive or negative reinforcement or punishment; nonverbal cues may also make a model's behavior more salient or supply the reinforcement necessary to produce performance of a learned behavior. Given that many interpersonal interchanges have instruction as one goal, the contribution of nonverbal behaviors to larger instructional strategies merits attention.

Expressive Communication

It used to be fashionable to claim that nonverbal behavior is exclusively expressive in nature. This simplistic view has given way to recognition that nonverbal signals have multiple social functions. However, in the case of interpersonal exchanges, it is probably true that nonverbal codes are the primary vehicles for emotive messages.

Expressive communication includes intentional affect displays and unintentional, cathartic ones. Also included are the meta-communicative expressions of attitudes—those nonverbal indicators of attitudinal favorability and intensity that complement and qualify verbal statements. They bear a close resemblance to emotional expressions in form and interpretation. Aesthetic forms of self-expression such as art, dance, and music could likewise be subsumed under this heading, but they are beyond the scope of an interpersonal handbook.

More theorizing surrounds the expressive function of nonverbal communication than any other. Buck (1980), Davitz (1969), Dittmann (1972a), Izard (1971), Plutchik (1962), Schachter and Singer (1962), and Tomkins (1962), among others, have addressed such issues as the nature of emotional expressions, the relationship between internal states and their external manifestations, and the manner in which meaning is assigned to the overt behaviors. But the majority of theoretical debate has focused on the acquisition of emotional expressions. Nowhere is the nature-nurture controversy more central than here.

Ekman and Friesen (1969) identify three alternative positions that one could take: (1) that emotions arise from inborn neurological programs that are part of our evolutionary development; (2) that emotions are manifestations of experiences common to all humans (such as the need to ward off dangers or to withdraw from pain); or (3) that emotions are shaped strictly by environmental and social factors. Evidence to support these various alternatives comes from several sources. One is comparative studies of nonhuman primates. As noted earlier, many human behaviors show a striking similarity to those of other primates. This kind of evidence implies an evolutionary continuity and innate origins based on survival value. A second source of evidence is child development literature. The extent to which infants and toddlers follow the same stages of emotional development and exhibit the same expressions indirectly supports a biological explanation. More definitive evidence within this body of literature comes from studies of blind, deaf, and limbless children, who, lacking the ability to learn emotional displays through sensory experience, still exhibit universally recognized expressions. Finally, cross-cultural comparisons on encoding, decoding, and patterns of use supply evidence both of commonalities and differences across cultural and subcultural groups (see Ekman, 1973a; Knapp, 1978a, for excellent reviews of this literature).

Out of these research directions, three theoretical positions have evolved. The *universalists* hold that at least certain primary affect displays are produced and understood in the same way by all members of the species. In addition to Darwin's (1965) seminal observations, representative of this position is work by Buck (1981), Eibl-Eibesfeldt (1970, 1972; Pitcairn & Eibl-Eibesfeldt, 1976), van Hooff (1972), Izard (1971), Vine (1973), and some of Ekman and Friesen's work (1971; Ekman, Friesen, & Ellsworth, 1972; Ekman, Sorenson, & Friesen, 1969). At the opposite extreme are the *cultural relativists* who believe that any cross-cultural similarities are only superficial and that actual use and interpretation are strictly a function of cultural and environmental influences. Characteristic of this view are the writings of Birdwhistell (1963), LaBarre (1947), and Leach (1972). A third, compromise position is Ekman and Friesen's *neurocultural theory* (Ekman, 1973a, 1978; Ekman & Friesen, 1975; Ekman et al., 1972; Ekman, Friesen, & Tomkins, 1971), which holds that neuromuscular programs are biologically inherited but that social factors dictate when, how, with what meaning, and with what consequences emotional displays will occur. The earlier introduced concept of display rules applies to this culture-specific management of displays in social settings.

The search for evidence of universality spawned one of the major research directions in expressive communication: identification of the primary emotions. Researchers have proposed various labels and estimates for the number of distinctive affects that exist, but the cross-cultural work of Ekman and his associates offers the most definite support for these six: *happiness, sadness, fear, anger, disgust,* and *surprise.* Other affect displays are proposed to be blends of these basic ones.

One difficulty that has arisen in categorizing the primary emotions is that if respondents supply their own labels for the emotions they observe or present, the number of possible emotions proliferates, producing an underestimate of commonalities. Conversely, if researchers supply the labels, it tends to force greater agreement than may be real. As an alternative to identifying emotional categories, a substantial body of research has explored the underlying dimensions along which emotions can be scaled. A variety of stimuli (facial and vocal, posed and spontaneous, live and photographed or filmed) have been used and have yielded strong convergent validity (see Ekman et al., 1972; Dittmann, 1972a, for reviews of this research). The two dimensions to emerge most consistently are *pleasantness-unpleasantness* (an evaluative dimension) and *activation* or tension. Others that frequently appear are *attention-rejection* and *control* (deliberateness of display) or *intensity.* Using this approach, one can place any emotion in multidimensional semantic space. Rage, for example, shows maximal unpleasantness, high activation, absence of control, and rejection. By using dimensions rather than categories, respondents show high agreement in the interpretation of emotional stimuli. The dimensional approach is also applicable to attitudinal expressions, which are typically scaled on similar evaluative, activity, and potency continua.

Another major avenue of research has investigated constituent nonverbal cues and channels that comprise a particular emotional or attitudinal expression. In the kinesic area, it appears that the body is responsible for signaling the intensity of affect while the face signals the specific evaluative state; in turn, different regions of the face are differentially salient to the sending and interpreting of feeling states (for example, Boucher & Ekman, 1975; Cuceloglu, 1972; Ekman & Friesen, 1975). In the vocalics area, researchers have isolated the acoustic correlates that differentiate various emotions: They include such features as amplitude, fundamental frequency (pitch), tempo, breathing, intonation pattern, and stress contours (for example, Franklin, 1972; Scherer & Oshinsky, 1977; Williams & Stevens, 1972). Although haptics is a third code that should be especially salient to emotional expression, it has not been subjected to the same kind of physical analysis. Neither have the other codes been analyzed for their contributions to coordinated, multichannel emotional displays.

Three other research directions have included work on the accuracy of encoding and decoding expressive communication, discussed in some detail earlier; the developmental acquisition of nonverbal skills, also discussed previously; and the effects of incongruent nonverbal attitudinal expressions on the interpretation of verbal attitudes, to be discussed in a later section.

Yet to be investigated adequately are the dynamics of emotional expressions as exhibited in ongoing interactions—how conversational context alters the form and interpretation of displays, how presentations are altered over time (for example, abbreviated or exaggerated), how the various channels are integrated to produce displays, how lengthier presentations affect accuracy of interpretation, how they relate to concurrent verbal and nonverbal messages that have different functions, and the like. A series of interview studies conducted by Ekman (1965) over two decades ago addressed some of these questions, but most research since that time has not looked at emotional expression in a conversational context and has taken a static rather than dynamic approach to behavior. Inasmuch as interpersonal encounters are prime occasions for emotional and attitudinal expression, it is time that nonverbal expressive behavior be incorporated into analyses of interpersonal processes and that nonverbal research addresses the processual nature of interpersonal expressive behavior.

Impression Formation and Management

Another significant role that nonverbal behaviors play in interpersonal processes is in the formation and management of impressions. When people first meet or talk, they rapidly attempt to categorize one another demographically on such characteristics as gender, age, socioeconomic status, ethnicity, and geographic residence. At the same time, they begin to attribute such sociological and personal characteristics to one another as political and social attitudes, values, and personality traits. This subconscious but instantaneous process of impression formation is highly stereotypic and fraught with misjudgments. But people rely on it nevertheless, perhaps because the pressure to reduce uncertainty is so great (see Berger & Calabrese, 1975) and because the initially available information is accurate at some gross levels. Because initial verbal exchanges are so often constrained by convention, the nonverbal cues, especially stable physical appearance and vocalic ones, take on particular importance in shaping interpersonal expectations and in generating a frame for interpreting subsequent impressions.

Research on first impressions is grounded in a receiver's perspective on what messages and information are embedded in a communicator's nonverbal and verbal behavior. Person perception and attribution theories are used to explain why and how judgments are formed, how accurate or consistent they are, why systematic distortions occur, and how context affects the ability to make sense out of cue patterns.

The extensive research in this area is partially summarized in Burgoon (1980), Burgoon and Saine (1978), Kleinke (1975), Kramer (1963), and Siegman (1978); it can also be found scattered through such texts as Harper et al. (1978) and Knapp (1978a), and has been indexed in detail in Frye (1980). Research on demographic judgments has typically focused on the question of accuracy, for example, how accurately can one assess ethnicity or social status from vocal features. Research on attitudinal and personality judgments has more often centered on how stereotypic and consistent the impressions are—for example, what political leanings are attributed to conservative dress or what personality traits are assigned to endomorphic body types—although some investigations have considered the match-up between perceived and actual characteristics. The conclusion has been that consistency usually outstrips accuracy; that is, observers share the same perceptions but those perceptions are often erroneous.

One shortcoming of the research is the tendency to study a single cue or code, and the multiple impressions it creates, rather than the interrelationships that exist among concurrent cues and codes in forming a specific impression. Such an approach would be more isomorphic with the manner in which receivers confront cues and could provide a truer estimate of the accuracy of judgments. Two other shortcomings are the lack of programmatic research—few studies have been replicated—and the exclusion of most nonverbal codes from investigation. Behaviors that have received the most attention are physical appearance and vocalic ones, including body type, facial attractiveness, facial hair, hairstyle, clothing formality and conventionalism, clothing fabric and color, adornments (such as glasses and jewelry), makeup styles, voice quality, dialect, speaking tempo, loudness, pitch variety, general delivery style, and total voice pattern.

Although these impression-forming cues no doubt influence initial expectations and even who chooses to interact with whom, they are predominantly static and slow signals that cannot be manipulated easily over the course of an interaction or relationship; many are uncontrollable and unintended sources of information. Of greater importance to interpersonal communication processes may be those dynamic behaviors that are under the control of the communicator. These fall under the realm of impression management, which is concerned with strategies for enhancing self-presentation.

Relevant theories in this area are Goffman's (1959, 1961, 1963, 1967, 1969, 1971, 1974) comprehensive dramaturgic analyses of self-presentation, which are replete with nonverbal illustrations and general principles for successful and unsuccessful role performances; Tedeschi's (1982) impression management theory; and Jones's (1964) ingratiation theory. At the theory level, emphasis is on what macrolevel strategies a communicator can use to project desired images along dimensions of believability, expertise, attraction, status, prestige, and the like. At the research level, emphasis is typically on what specific nonverbal cues actually foster favorable impressions or on what behaviors are judged as appropriate or inappropriate in a particular context, the implication being that inappropriate or unacceptable behavior leads to failed performances.

A wide range of nonverbal effects research can be interpreted as applicable to impression management. Probably the most pertinent is that on credibility and attraction. Frequent eye gaze, direct eye contact, conversational delivery style, "powerful" speech (devoid of hesitations and questioning intonations), moderately rapid speaking rate, physical attractiveness (through dress, makeup, and grooming), avoidance of spatial intrusion, some violations of conversational distance norms, and minimization of waiting time have all been shown to engender favorable credibility and attraction judgments (Beebe, 1974; Burgoon, 1983; Burgoon, Manusov, Mineo, & Hale, in press; Erickson, Lind, Johnson, & O'Barr, 1978; Hemsley & Doob, 1978; Heston, 1974; Pearce & Brommel, 1972; Pearce & Conklin, 1971; Rosegrant & McCroskey, 1975; Schweitzer, 1970; Street & Brady, 1982; Street, Brady, & Putnam, in press; Wheeless, Jones, & King, 1974; Widgery, 1974). Status, prestige, and power cues have also received extensive analysis (see Baglan & Nelson, 1982; Burgoon & Saine, 1978; Henley, 1977; Kleinke, 1975; Moe, 1972; Rosenfeld, 1972, for research summaries). Cues proposed or confirmed as indicators of higher status and power include use or possession of larger, more private, and more luxuriously appointed spaces; greater access to other people's space, time, and possessions; initiation of conversational distance and touch patterns; asymmetrical use of touch and spatial intrusion (giving more, receiving less); less frequent but more direct eye gaze; less smiling and facial pleasantness; greater postural relaxation and asymmetry; lower and more varied pitch; use of vocal interruptions; more rapid speaking pace; and control of silences.

The issue of appropriateness and, hence, the likelihood of success of specific nonverbal tactics has generated less research. Exceptions include Baglan and Nelson's (1982) study of the appropriateness of several nonverbal behaviors, based on sex and status of the source, Street and Brady's (1982) assessment of acceptable speech rates, and the popularized literature on successful dress. Previously cited data on nonverbal norms could also be reinterpreted as standards of acceptability, except that the range of tolerance for variability around those norms has not been assessed. In the long run, appropriateness may not be the most relevant criterion for success anyway, given that violations of expectations are proving to be successful under certain circumstances (Burgoon, 1983). The extent to which violations are the more strategic choice for impression management is a prime area for further investigation.

Relational Communication

This function of nonverbal communication concerns the sending and receiving of messages about interactional partners' definitions of their relationship. Partners may signal how they feel about each other, how they feel about the relationship itself, or how they feel about themselves within the context of the relationship. It has been said that every communication has a "content" or "report" aspect and a "relational" or "command" aspect. Nonverbal relational communication can be seen to serve this latter meta-communicative function in that it tells one how to interpret other, co-present messages within the context of the relational definition that exists. But it can also be seen as the "content" of messages about the relationship itself. That is, it should not be viewed as only augmenting other messages but as making meaningful statements in its own right.

Relational communication bears a close resemblance to impression formation and management, particularly at the level of the specific nonverbal cues used to signal evaluations and self-images. The distinction that can be made is perhaps best explained by Ellsworth and Ludwig's (1972) distinction between observer and participant evaluations of nonverbal behavior. Observers of another's nonverbal performance tend to attribute that person's behavior to internal traits and dispositions, whereas participants in an interaction, who are themselves "observed," tend to see performances as reactions and feedback to themselves. The literature on impression formation and management takes an observer focus: Nonverbal behaviors are treated as if directed toward a generalized audience, and attributions about a communicator's stable characteristics are studied. Relational communication literature looks at how nonverbal performances are interpreted and produced by interaction partners as indicators of the nature of their relationship.

Traditional approaches to relational communication have identified only two or three dimensions along which messages may be exchanged. Such perspectives underestimate the variety and richness of message themes that are present in interpersonal encounters. Based on a review of ethological, anthropological, sociological, psychological, and communicological literature, Burgoon and Hale (1984) proposed as many as 12 distinctive *topoi* of relational messages: *intimacy,* which is comprised of the subthemes of *affection-hostility, intensity of involvement, inclusion-exclusion, trust,* and *depth-superficiality; emotional arousal* (activation); *composure; dominance-submission* (control); and *similarity, formality,* and *task-social orientation.* Empirical investigations of the actual recognition of these themes in interpersonal contexts (Burgoon & Hale, 1981) suggested that these interrelated dimensions could be collapsed into four relatively independent clusters of message types. These clusters work well in identifying dominant patterns of nonverbal relational communication.

The following profiles of behavior are based on an abundance of literature that is summarized in various forms in Burgoon, Buller, Hale, and deTurck (1984), Cappella (1983), Exline and Fehr (1978), Henley (1977), Heslin and Alper (1983), Kramer, Alloway, and Pliner (1975), Mehrabian (1971, 1972), Patterson, (1973, 1983), Scheflen (1974), and Siegman (1978). Communication of greater *intimacy and similarity* (that is, greater attraction, liking, trust, affiliation, depth, and similarity) is usually achieved through use of several of these behaviors: close proximity, forward body lean, relatively direct body orientation, frequent and longer mutual gaze, more gesturing, moderate relaxation, frequent touch, touch to more "intimate" body regions, softer voices, wearing of similar apparel and "identification symbols," punctuality, longer amounts of time spent together, monochronic use of time, and the sharing of territories and possessions. It is important to note that many of the individual behaviors, if viewed singly, may be ambiguous in meaning because they have multiple relational interpretations. But in combination with other cues, which typically occur as a pattern, the appropriate interpretation becomes clear.

Immediacy (which includes orienting toward, attending to, and signaling involvement and inclusiveness with another) is usually expressed by the same kinesic, proxemic, and chronemic cues as intimacy but also includes such vocalic indicators as more rapid speech rate, increased loudness, greater pitch variety, shorter speech latencies, and fewer pauses and silences. Conversely, key indicators of nonimmediacy and detachment include gaze aversion, increased conversational distance, backward lean, absence of smiling, absence of touch, monotone voice, more and longer silences, polychronic time use, increased waiting time, and other signals of a desire for privacy.

Emotional arousal, lack of composure, and formality are typically conveyed by vocalic and kinesic anxiety cues, especially nonfluencies, adaptors, and postural tension or erectness, plus greater distance. Composure,

relaxation, and informality are communicated by such behaviors as assymetri-
cal limb positions, less body tonus and tension, close proximity, and smiling.
It is possible that some behaviors may show a curvilinear relationship with
this relational message cluster. For example, frequent and direct gaze may
communicate either extreme composure and relaxation or extreme arousal.

Finally, *dominance* appears to be expressed by all the behaviors cited
under impression management as cues of power, status, and prestige.
Submissiveness is expressed by the opposites of these, along with some
specific gestures such as the head tilt and open palms. Other relational
message themes that do not neatly fit any of these four clusters—for
example, social versus task orientation—have not been analyzed for their
nonverbal correlates.

Beyond work on the specific relational connotations and effects of
nonverbal cues, scholars in this area have devoted a considerable amount of
attention to the process of immediacy and intimacy changes in interpersonal
transactions. Five different theories have been advanced and tested. Argyle
and Dean's (1965; Argyle & Cook, 1976) equilibrium theory, which was the
prime catalyst for much of the subsequent work, proposes that approach and
avoidance forces operate to produce a comfortable intrapersonal and
interpersonal level of immediacy in conversations. Changes in one or more
immediacy behaviors are said to be arousing and to prompt compensatory
adjustments on other behaviors to restore equilibrium. Opposite predictions
are made by a reciprocity model. Grounded largely in work on verbal self-
disclosure and a proposed societal norm of reciprocity, it proposes that
changes in immediacy and intimacy by one interactant will be met in kind by
one's partner, leading to escalating or deescalating levels of intimacy.
Patterson's (1976) arousal labeling model attempts to incorporate both
patterns by proposing that the arousal generated by immediacy adjustments
can be positively or negatively labeled. If experienced positively, it is
hypothesized to elicit reciprocity; if experienced negatively, to elicit compensation. Also incorporating both types of effects but in a different configuration is
Burgoon's (1983; Burgoon & Jones, 1976) violations of expectations model,
which introduces the mediating effect of the reward value of the person
initiating immediacy changes. Increases in immediacy by a high reward
person are proposed to elicit reciprocity, whereas decreases are proposed to
elicit a compensatory response designed to restore the interaction to a more
intimate level. The exact opposite pattern is predicted for nonrewarding
communicators. Finally, Cappella and Greene's (1982) arousal discrepancy
model proposes that reactions are largely a function of magnitude of arousal.
Slight changes in immediacy are hypothesized to be pleasant and to produce
reciprocity or no change, whereas extreme adjustments are hypothesized to
be aversive and to prompt compensation.

Detailed comparisons of these models and the extent of empirical support
for each of them can be found in Andersen and Andersen (1984), Cappella
(1983), and Hale and Burgoon (1984). A recent dyadic experiment using

multiple nonverbal, verbal, and relational dependent measures found evidence of both linear reciprocity and linear compensation effects, as well nonlinear relationships supporting either a violations model or a reinterpreted arousal labeling model (Burgoon & Hale, 1984). More research employing multiple time periods and multiple dependent measures is needed before the validity and generalizability of each of the five models can be better assessed.

Some other facets of relational communication that sorely need attention are highlighted by Knapp (1983a). One is the importance of expected but omitted nonverbal cues as relational statements. The absence of a hug at bedtime, for instance, may be more telling to a spouse about the intimacy of the marriage than any other present cue. Second is the consideration of frequency of presentation versus significance of a cue. Rarely performed or intermittent behaviors may be the most significant signals of intimacy, yet these are unlikely to be noted by observers or captured in a research context. Thus such behaviors may be ignored or discounted in assessments of powerful relational cues. Third, the frequency and duration of specific relational cues may vary over the course of a relationship and presumably carry different meanings depending on their placement in the relational trajectory. Because most relational (and interpersonal) communication research has not taken a developmental perspective, this timing issue has not been considered. In this regard, Knapp's (1978b, 1983a) dimensions of communication in relationship development provide a useful framework for assessing what phase a relationship is in and predicting the nonverbal messages that should be likely. Fourth, the overreliance on observational rather than interactional research methodologies has led to a focus on stereotypical behavior that may be less relevant to participants in interactions and as relationships change over time. Fifth, the role of context in altering meanings of behavior has not been adequately assessed. The assumption seems to have been made that behaviors have constant meanings across situations. Finally, a concern that has also been raised throughout this chapter is the overemphasis on single cue analysis and the underemphasis on the interactions among cues. More recognition of the complexities of relational message exchange in actual interaction should prompt more insightful research in the future.

Mixed Messages and Deception

A growing interest area that bridges impression management and relational communication is incongruency among messages and the special case of deception. Although people usually attempt to coordinate verbal and nonverbal behaviors into a coherent and congruent performance, there are occasions when they deliberately or unconsciously send mixed signals. They may intend to create sarcasm or an ambiguous message, or they may intend to mislead someone about the true state of affairs but may "leak" the concealed message or clues that deception is occurring. The result is a message that may require different information-processing strategies and that may be more difficult to interpret. Two key questions in this line of research are (1) how interpretations are made and (2) how accurate those interpretations are.

The interpretation question has been addressed at the levels of individual cue analysis and channel comparisons. Cue research has uncovered numerous nonverbal and verbal correlates of actual and perceived deception and has explored the match between actual indicators of lying and those on which observers rely (see, for example, Cody & O'Hair, 1983; Knapp, Hart, & Dennis, 1974; Kraut, 1980; Miller & Burgoon, 1982; Miller, deTurck, & Kalbfleisch, 1983; O'Hair, Cody & McLaughlin, 1981; Zuckerman, Koestner & Driver, 1981). Functionally, the cues (1) signal arousal and anxiety, (2) express reticence and nonimmediacy, (3) create vagueness and ambiguity, (4) present negative affect, (5) deviate from normal levels of behavior, and/or (6) create inconsistencies and contradictions. The specific profile of actual and interpreted cues depends, however, on such mediating factors as whether the lie is rehearsed or spontaneous, whether the message content is emotional or factual, and individual characteristics of the communicator (such as gender, dominance, and self-monitoring ability). Channel comparison work has addressed the relative controllability or leakage associated with facial versus body versus audio channels and the effects of discrepancies among channels in the strategies observers use to detect deception (for example, Zuckerman, DePaulo, & Rosenthal, 1981; Zuckerman, Driver, & Koestner, 1982; Zuckerman, Spiegel, DePaulo, & Rosenthal, 1982).

These two lines of work reveal some lack of correspondence between the cues and channels that are used and the ones that should be used. The result is that untrained observers are relatively inaccurate in detecting discrepant and deceptive messages (see Bauchner, Kaplan, & Miller, 1980; Miller, Bauchner, Hocking, Fontes, Kaminski, & Brandt, 1981; Miller & Burgoon, 1982; Miller et al., 1983). Factors being explored as possible influences on success in lie detection include (1) effects of rehearsal, (2) number and choice of channels available for making judgments (for example, transcripts versus video-only versus audio-only information), and (3) individual differences in sensitivity to discrepant messages.

Of future interest to interpersonal communication researchers should be such questions as how incongruent messages affect attention and information processing and how increased scrutiny by a suspicious decoder affects subsequent encoding of deception.

Structuring and Regulating Interaction

Because the next chapter in this handbook is devoted entirely to this function, it will only be discussed briefly here. A sizeable share of the nonverbal literature has tackled the issue of how nonverbal behaviors influence the progression and patterning of conversation. Five main interest areas are evident in the literature.

The first is the role of contextual nonverbal features in initially *defining the situation and defining role relationships.* At the outset of an interaction, architectural features, spatial arrangements, physical appearance cues of status, the nature of artifacts in the environment, and other static features identify for the participants the kind of communication that is expected (for example, formal or informal, social or task-oriented). Coupled with other dynamic features such as kinesic and vocalic demeanor, they also clarify role relationships among participants, for example, who are in high-status positions. The combined structural features and normative behaviors within contexts set the stage for the interaction that follows; they signal the behavioral programs or repertoires that are appropriate and likely. The earlier cited work on contextual norms and on dramaturgic analyses of self-presentation is relevant to this process.

Second, many of the static or stable proxemic, artifactual, and physical appearance signals play a role in *regulating the amount, frequency, and nature of conversation.* For example, sheer propinquity and physical attractiveness influence whether any contact will occur; volume of space and linear perspective in an environment affect the casualness, content, and amount of conversation; and seating arrangements govern who speaks to whom, how often, and how cooperatively (see Burgoon & Saine, 1978; Knapp, 1978a; Patterson, 1978, 1983, for summaries of this line of research).

Third, nonverbal signals form the core of *greeting and termination rituals.* The behaviors and sequence of behaviors by which people initiate and end conversations has received some empirical attention (for example, Knapp, Hart, Friedrich, & Schulman, 1973; Krivonos & Knapp, 1975; Pittinger, Hockett, & Darehy, 1960).

Fourth, literature abounds on *turn-taking and the dynamic regulation of episodes.* Areas of interest include speaker and listener behaviors that determine whose turn it is to speak, auditor feedback cues that control speaker behavior, behaviors that mark changes in the tone and topic of interaction, and other dynamic cues that affect the flow of conversation (see, for example, Duncan, 1974, 1975; Erickson, 1975; Feldstein & Welkowitz, 1978; Jaffe, 1978; Kendon, 1967; Rosenfeld, 1978; Wiemann & Knapp, 1975).

Finally, a growing research area is addressing *interactional synchrony and other mutual influence processes.* Interactional synchrony concerns the degree to which speaker and auditor coordinate their movements to the speech stream of the speaker (simultaneous synchrony) or sequences of speaker-to-speaker behavior exhibit the same rhythms (concatenous synchrony). Other mutual influence processes include mirroring (the simultaneous presentation of the same postures, proxemic patterns, gestures, and the like, apart from any consideration of the rhythm of presentation); matching of pause lengths, speaking rate, verbal productivity, and similar vocal behaviors; and reciprocation or compensation of levels of involvement and immediacy. These processes have been studied for both adult-adult and adult-infant interactions. Samples of the research and theorizing in this area can be found in Beebe, Stern, and Jaffe (1979), Cappella (1981), Cappella and Greene (1982), Cappella and Planalp (1981), Condon (1980), Condon and Ogston (1967), Condon and Sander (1974), Erickson and Shultz (1982), Gatewood and Rosenwein (1981), Kempton (1980), and Kendon (1970).

Social Influence

Again, this function will be discussed only briefly because Chapter 12 covers it in some depth. Nonverbal interest in this area has centered on the pragmatics of nonverbal behavior, specifically on how such behavior alters attitudes and overt behaviors of message recipients. The types of dependent variables that have been studied have run the gamut from expressed changes in attitude, petition-signing behavior, and task performance to helping behavior (for example, making change for someone), aggression (for example, shocking someone), compliance with orders, and manifestations of increased anxiety and arousal.

The literature related to this function comes from highly diverse disciplines and is not easily synthesized, but it appears that much of it can be subsumed under the following types of strategies: (1) *affiliation appeals* (indications of liking, attraction, and immediacy); (2) *credibility appeals* (self-presentational behaviors emphasizing a communicator's expertise, character, composure, sociability, and dynamism); (3) *dominance, power, and status appeals* (self-presentational behaviors employing status symbols and cues of dominance); (4) *threat cues* (use of specific behaviors such as staring or spatial intrusion that create a sense of danger); (5) *attractiveness appeals* (enhancement of one's physical and social attractiveness); (6) *attention and reinforcement behaviors* (use of those nonverbal behaviors that heighten attention and/or reinforce learning); (7) *distraction* (use of such nonverbal behaviors as vocal nonfluencies or crowding); (8) *violations of expectations* (use of deviant behaviors such as extremes in conversational distance, gaze, or clothing style); (9) *aversive or pleasant stimulation* (manipulation of environmental features such as noise, density, or color to affect physiological arousal); (10) *modeling* (use of nonverbal cues to make a model's behavior salient or to reinforce imitation of a model's behavior); and (11) *expectancy cues* (signaling expectations to elicit the desired behavior).

Summaries of much of the earlier research along these lines can be found in Burgoon and Saine (1978), Exline and Fehr (1978), Heslin and Alper (1983), Malandro and Barker (1983), and Patterson (1983). Illustrations of more recent types of experiments include the effects of crowding on aggression, arousal, and task performance (Matthews, Paulus, & Baron, 1979; Waldren & Forsyth, 1981), the effects of touch, dress, and gaze on petition-signing and helping behavior (Hensley, 1981; Kleinke, 1980; Willis & Hamm, 1980), the effects of violations of normative distancing and gaze behavior on helping behavior, decisions of guilt or innocence, and selection of a job applicant (Burgoon, 1983; Burgoon et al., in press), and the effects of speaker self-synchrony on persuasiveness (Woodall & Burgoon, 1981).

SUMMARY

Nonverbal signals are essential ingredients in the interpersonal communication mix. Research substantiates that they carry a significant, and often dominant, portion of the social meaning in face-to-face interchanges. Whether their importance is attributable to innate orientations toward nonverbal signals, to the superiority of nonverbal codes in performing certain interpersonal functions, to the manner in which nonverbal cues are cognitively processed, or to their special coding properties, it is clear that nonverbal signals are more than mere auxiliaries to the verbal stream. They manifest many of the same properties as verbal language (such as rule structures, discrete units, multiple meanings, and transformation), as well as exhibit some unique ones (such as universality, multimodal simultaneous encoding, and iconicity). This mandates a broader, more integrated view of exactly what constitutes language or interpersonal discourse.

In analyzing the role of nonverbal signals in interpersonal communication, emphasis here has been on those behaviors that form a socially shared coding system. According to this message orientation, codes of greatest interest are kinesics, vocalics, haptics, proxemics, chronemics, and manipulable features of physical appearance and artifacts. Current knowledge about the encoding and decoding capacities of these modes of expression indicates that humans have an extraordinary physiological ability to produce and discriminate a wide range of signals; the acquisition and recognition of these signals is in part biologically programmed; visual channels tend to show primacy over other nonverbal channels; and individuals vary in their channel predilection and their skill in encoding and decoding nonverbal signals.

Although many nonverbal signals appear to have universal forms and innate origins, their use and interpretation is constrained by cultural and subcultural norms. Cultural display rules dictate appropriate occasions for use, meanings to be assigned, and consequences of presentations. At the subcultural level, patterns differ by gender, age, race, socioeconomic status, personality, and interactional context, among other factors. These situational influences must therefore be taken into account in predicting likely behaviors, and their meanings in and impacts on interpersonal encounters.

Additionally, one must consider the social functions being performed by the nonverbal behaviors. Typically, multiple behaviors will be coordinated with one another and with the verbal stream to achieve a particular purpose;

and typically, several purposes may be operative simultaneously. This leads to the frequent but mistaken claim that nonverbal behaviors are inherently ambiguous or unpredictable in meaning; when the behaviors are viewed as part of a collective, regular and meaningful patterns become apparent. Social functions for which such patterns have been identified include facilitation of cognitive processing and learning, expression of emotions and attitudes, impression formation and management, relational communication, deception, social influence, and the structuring and regulation of interaction.

A substantial amount of research has already addressed these social functions, but it has often failed to look at the nonverbal behaviors as a system or to look at their interrelationship with the verbal stream. An adequate picture of the role of nonverbal signals in interpersonal communication must await such an integrative look. And that integrative look must be embedded in research on actual interaction so that the interplay of naturally occurring behaviors and the influence of participant behaviors on each other can be better understood.

Finally, just as the interpersonal communication area in general needs more theorizing and research on processual features of interchange, so must nonverbal researchers be enjoined to devote more future effort to the sequential and longitudinal aspects of nonverbal communication. As cycles, developmental patterns, and temporal adjustments receive greater scrutiny, nonverbal behavior may take on added significance in interpersonal communication.

REFERENCES

Aiello, J. R., & Thompson, D. E. (1980). Personal space, crowding, and spatial behavior in a cultural context. In I. Altman, J. F. Wohlwill, & A. Rapoport (Eds.), *Human behavior and environment: Environment and culture* (Vol. 4, pp. 107-171). New York: Plenum.

Als, H. (1977). The newborn communicates. *Journal of Communication, 27,* 66-73.

Altman, I. (1975). *The environment and social behavior.* Monterey, CA: Brooks/Cole.

Altmann, S. A. (1968). Primates. In T. A. Sebeok (Ed.), *Animal communication* (pp. 466-522). Bloomington, IN: Indiana University Press.

Andersen, P. A., & Andersen, J. F. (1984). The exchange of nonverbal immediacy: A critical review of dyadic models. *Journal of Nonverbal Behavior, 8,* 327-349.

Andersen, P. A., Garrison, J. P., & Andersen, J. F. (1979). Implications of a neurophysiological approach for the study of nonverbal communication. *Human Communication Research, 6,* 74-89.

Anderson, B. J. (1977). The emergence of conversational behavior. *Journal of Communication, 27,* 85-91.

Archer, D., & Akert, R. M. (1977). Words and everything else: Verbal and nonverbal cues in social interpretation. *Journal of Personality and Social Psychology, 35,* 443-449.

Argyle, M. (1967). *The psychology of interpersonal behavior.* Baltimore: Penguin Books.

Argyle, M., Alkema, F., & Gilmour, R. (1971). The communication of friendly and hostile attitudes by verbal and non-verbal signals. *European Journal of Social Psychology, 1,* 385-402.

Argyle, M., & Cook, M. (1976). *Gaze and mutual gaze.* Cambridge: Cambridge University Press.

Argyle, M., & Dean, J. (1965). Eye contact, distance and affiliation. *Sociometry, 28,* 289-304.

Argyle, M., Salter, V., Nicholson, H., Williams, M., & Burgess, P. (1970). The communication of inferior and superior attitudes by verbal and nonverbal signals. *British Journal of Social and Clinical Psychology, 9,* 221-231.

Baglan, T., & Nelson, D. J. (1982). A comparison of the effects of sex and status on the perceived appropriateness of nonverbal behaviors. *Women's Studies in Communication, 5,* 29-38.

Bauchner, J. E., Kaplan, E. P., & Miller, G. R. (1980). Detecting deception: The relationship between available information to judgmental accuracy in initial encounters. *Human Communication Research, 6,* 251-264.

Beebe, B., Stern, D., & Jaffe, J. (1979). The kinesic rhythm of mother-infant interactions. In A. W. Siegman & S. Feldstein (Eds.), *Of speech and time: Temporal patterns in interpersonal contexts* (pp. 23-34). Hillsdale, NJ: Lawrence Erlbaum.

Beebe, S. A. (1974). Eye contact: A nonverbal determinant of speaking credibility. *Speech Teacher, 23,* 21-25.

Beighley, K. C. (1952). An experimental study of the effect of four speech variables on listener comprehension. *Speech Monographs, 19,* 249-258.

Beighley, K. C. (1954). An experimental study of the effect of three speech variables on listener comprehension. *Speech Monographs, 21,* 248-253.

Berger, C. R., & Calabrese, R. J. (1975). Some explorations in initial interaction and beyond: Toward a developmental theory of interpersonal communication. *Human Communication Research, 1,* 99-112.

Birdwhistell, R. L. (1955). Background to kinesics. *ETC., 13,* 10-18.

Birdwhistell, R. L. (1963). The kinesic level in the investigation of the emotions. In R. H. Knapp (Ed.), *Expression of emotion in man* (pp. 123-139). New York: International Universities Press.

Birdwhistell, R. L. (1970). *Kinesics and context: Essays on body motion communication.* Philadelphia: University of Pennsylvania Press.

Blurton Jones, N. G. (1972). Non-verbal communication in children. In R. A. Hinde (Ed.), *Non-verbal communication* (pp. 271-296). Cambridge: Cambridge University Press.

Boomer, D. S. (1965). Hesitation and grammatical coding. *Language and Speech, 8,* 148-158.

Boomer, D. S. (1978). The phonemic clause: Speech unit in human communication. In A. W. Siegman & S. Feldstein (Eds.), *Nonverbal behavior and communication* (pp. 245-262). Hillsdale, NJ: Lawrence Erlbaum.

Boucher, J. D., & Ekman, P. (1975). Facial areas of emotional information. *Journal of Communication, 25,* 21-29.

Brannigan, C. R., & Humphries, D. A. (1972). Human non-verbal behavior, a means of communication. In N. Blurton Jones (Ed.), *Ethological studies of child behavior* (pp. 37-64). London: Cambridge University Press.

Buck, R. (1979). Individual differences in nonverbal sending accuracy and electrodermal responding: The externalizing-internalizing dimension. In R. Rosenthal (Ed.), *Skill in nonverbal communication: Individual differences* (pp. 140-170). Cambridge, MA: Oelgeschlager, Gunn & Hain.

Buck, R. (1980). Nonverbal behavior and the theory of emotion: The facial feedback hypothesis. *Journal of Personality and Social Psychology, 38,* 811-824.

Buck, R. (1981). The evolution and development of emotion expression and communication. In S. S. Brehm, S. M. Kassin, & F. X. Gibbons (Eds.), *Developmental social psychology* (pp. 127-151). New York: Oxford University Press.

Buller, D. B. (1983). *The effects of distraction during persuasive communication: A meta-analytic review.* Unpublished manuscript, Michigan State University.

Burgoon, J. K. (1980). Nonverbal communication in the 1970s: An overview. In D. Nimmo (Ed.), *Communication yearbook 4* (pp. 179-197). New Brunswick, NJ: Transaction Books.

Burgoon, J. K. (1982). Privacy and communication. In M. Burgoon (Ed.), *Communication yearbook 6* (pp. 206-249). Beverly Hills, CA: Sage.

Burgoon, J. K. (1983). Nonverbal violations of expectations. In J. M. Wiemann & R. P. Harrison (Eds.), *Nonverbal interaction* (pp. 77-111). Beverly Hills, CA: Sage.

Burgoon, J. K. (1985). The relationship of verbal and nonverbal codes. In B. Dervin & M. J. Voight (Eds.), *Progress in communication sciences* (Vol. 6). Norwood, NJ: Ablex.

Burgoon, J. K., Buller, D. B., Hale, J. L., & deTurck, M. A. (1984). Relational messages associated with nonverbal behaviors. *Human Communication Research, 10,* 351-378.

Burgoon, J. K., & Hale, J. L. (1981, November). *Dimensions of relational messages.* Paper presented at the annual meeting of the Speech Communication Association, Anaheim, CA.

Burgoon, J. K., & Hale, J. L. (1984). The fundamental *topoi* of relational communication. *Communication Monographs, 51,* 193-214.

Burgoon, J. K., & Jones, S. B. (1976). Toward a theory of personal space expectations and their violations. *Human Communication Research, 2,* 131-146.

Burgoon, J. K., Manusov, V., Mineo, P. J., & Hale, J. L. (in press). Effects of eye gaze on hiring credibility, attraction and relational messages interpretation. *Journal of Nonverbal Behavior.*

Burgoon, J. K., & Saine, T. (1978). *The unspoken dialogue: An introduction to nonverbal communication.* Boston: Houghton-Mifflin.

Burns, K. L., & Beier, E. G. (1973). Significance of vocal and visual channels in the decoding of emotional meaning. *Journal of Communication, 23,* 118-130.

Campbell, J. (1982). *Grammatical man.* New York: Simon and Schuster.

Cappella, J. N. (1981). Mutual influence in expressive behavior: Adult-adult and infant-adult interaction. *Psychological Bulletin, 89,* 101-132.

Cappella, J. N. (1983). Conversational involvement: Approaching and avoiding others. In J. M. Wiemann & R. P. Harrison (Eds.), *Nonverbal interaction* (pp. 113-148). Beverly Hills, CA: Sage.

Cappella, J. N., & Greene, J. O. (1982). A discrepancy-arousal explanation of mutual influence in expressive behavior in adult and infant-adult interaction. *Communication Monographs, 49,* 89-114.

Cappella, J. N., & Planalp, S. (1981). Talk and silence sequences in informal conversations III: Interspeaker influence. *Human Communication Research, 7,* 117-132.

Cody, M. J., & O'Hair, H. D. (1983). Nonverbal communication and deception: Differences in deception cues due to gender and communicator dominance. *Communication Monographs, 50,* 175-192.

Cohen, A. A., & Harrison, R. P. (1973). Intentionality in the use of the hand illustrators in face-to-face communication situations. *Journal of Personality and Social Psychology, 28,* 276-279.

Condon, W. S. (1980). The relation of interactional synchrony to cognitive and emotional processes. In M. R. Key (Ed.), *The relationship of verbal and nonverbal communication* (pp. 49-65). The Hague: Mouton.

Condon, W. S., & Ogston, W. D. (1967). A segmentation of behavior. *Journal of Psychiatric Research, 5,* 221-235.

Condon, W. S., & Sander, L. W. (1974). Neonate movement is synchronized with adult speech: Interactional participation and language acquisition. *Science, 183,* 99-101.

Cuceloglu, D. (1972). Facial code in affective communication. In D. C. Speer (Ed.), *Nonverbal communication* (pp. 19-32). Beverly Hills, CA: Sage.

Darwin, C. (1965). *The expression of the emotions in man and animals.* Chicago: University of Chicago Press. (first printed London: John Murray, 1872).

Davitz, J. R. (1969). *The language of emotion.* New York: Academic Press.

DeLong, A. J. (1977). Yielding the floor: The kinesic signals. *Journal of Communication, 27,* 98-103.

DePaulo, B. M., Rosenthal, R., Eisenstat, R. A., Rogers, P. L., & Finkelstein, S. (1978). Decoding discrepant nonverbal cues. *Journal of Personality and Social Psychology, 36,* 313-323.

Dittmann, A. T. (1972a). *Interpersonal messages of emotion.* New York: Springer.

Dittmann, A. T. (1972b). The body movement-speech rhythm relationship as a cue to speech encoding. In A. W. Siegman & B. Pope (Eds.), *Studies in dyadic communication* (pp. 135-151). New York: Pergamon.

Dittmann, A. T. (1978). The role of body movement in communication. In A. W. Siegman & S. Feldstein (Eds.), *Nonverbal behavior and communication* (pp. 69-95). Hillsdale, NJ: Lawrence Erlbaum.

Donohue, W. A. (1981). Analyzing negotiation tactics: Development of a negotiation interact system. *Human Communication Research, 7,* 273-287.

Duker, S.(1974). *Time compressed speech: An anthology and bibliography.* Metuchen, NJ: Scarecrow.

Duncan, S. (1974). On signalling that it's your turn to speak. *Journal of Personality and Social Psychology, 10,* 234-247.

Duncan, S. (1975). Interaction units during speaking turns in dyadic, face to face conversations. In A. Kendon, R. M. Harris, & M. R. Key (Eds.), *Organization of behavior in face to face interaction* (pp. 199-213). The Hague: Mouton.

Eibl-Eibesfeldt, I. (1970). *Ethology: The biology of human behavior.* New York: Holt, Rinehart & Winston.

Eibl-Eibesfeldt, I. (1972). Similarities and differences between cultures in expressive movements. In R. A. Hinde (Ed.), *Non-verbal communication* (pp. 297-314). Cambridge: Cambridge University Press.

Ekman, P. (1965). Communication through nonverbal behavior: A source of information about an interpersonal relationship. In S. S. Tomkins & C. E. Izard (Eds.), *Affect, cognition, and personality.* New York: Springer.

Ekman, P. (1973a). Cross-cultural studies of facial expression. In P. Ekman (Ed.), *Darwin and facial expression: A century of research in review* (pp. 169-222). New York: Academic Press.

Ekman, P. (Ed.). (1973b). *Darwin and facial expression: A century of research in review.* New York: Academic Press.

Ekman, P. (1976). Movements with precise meanings. *Journal of Communication, 26,* 14-20.

Ekman, P. (1978). Facial expression. In A. W. Siegman & S. Feldstein (Eds.), *Nonverbal behavior and communication* (pp. 97-116). Hillsdale, NJ: Lawrence Erlbaum.

Ekman, P., & Friesen, W. V. (1969). The repertoire of nonverbal behavior: Categories, origins, usage, and coding. *Semiotica, 1,* 49-98.

Ekman, P., & Friesen, W. V. (1971). Constants across cultures in the face and emotion. *Journal of Personality and Social Psychology, 17,* 124-129.

Ekman, P., & Friesen, W. V. (1975). *Unmasking the face.* Englewood Cliffs, NJ: Prentice-Hall.

Ekman, P., Friesen, W. V., & Ellsworth, P. (1972). *Emotion in the human face: Guidelines for research and an integration of findings.* New York: Pergamon Press.

Ekman, P., Friesen, W. V., & Tomkins, S. (1971). Facial affect scoring technique (FAST): A first validity study. *Semiotica, 3,* 37-58.

Ekman, P., Sorenson, E. R., & Friesen, W. V. (1969). Pan-cultural elements in facial display of emotion. *Science, 164,* 86-88.

Ellsworth, P. C., & Ludwig, L. M. (1972). Visual behavior in social interaction. *Journal of Communication, 22,* 375-403.

Erickson, B., Lind, E. A., Johnson, B. C., & O'Barr, W. M. (1978). Speech style and impression formation in a court setting: The effects of "powerful" and "powerless" speech. *Journal of Experimental Social Psychology, 14,* 266-279.

Erickson, F. (1975). One function of proxemic shifts in face to face interaction. In A. Kendon, R. M. Harris, & M. R. Key (Eds.), *Organization of behavior in face to face interaction* (pp. 175-187). The Hague: Mouton.

Erickson, F., & Shultz, J. (1982). *The counselor as gatekeeper: Social interaction in interviews.* New York: Academic Press.

Exline, R. V., & Fehr, B. J. (1978). Applications of semiosis to the study of visual interaction. In A. W. Siegman & S. Feldstein (Eds.), *Nonverbal behavior and communication* (pp. 117-157). Hillsdale, NJ: Lawrence Erlbaum.

Feldstein, S., & Welkowitz, J. (1978). A chronography of conversation: In defense of an objective approach. In A. W. Siegman & S. Feldstein (Eds.), *Nonverbal communication and behavior* (pp. 329-378). Hillsdale, NJ: Lawrence Erlbaum.

Folger, J. P., & Woodall, W. G. (1982). Nonverbal cues as linguistic context: An information-processing view. In M. Burgoon (Ed.), *Communication yearbook 6* (pp. 63-91). Beverly Hills, CA: Sage.

Franklin, W. G. (1972). An experimental study of the characteristics of simulated emotions. *Southern Speech Communication Journal, 38,* 168-180.

Friedman, H. S. (1979). The concept of skill in nonverbal communication: Implications for understanding social interaction. In R. Rosenthal (Ed.), *Skill in nonverbal communication: Individual differences* (pp. 2-27). Cambridge, MA: Oelgeschlager, Gunn & Hain.

Frye, J. K. (1980). *FIND: Frye's index to nonverbal data.* Duluth, MN: University of Minnesota Computer Center.

Gatewood, J. B., & Rosenwein, R. (1981). Interactional synchrony: Genuine or spurious? A critique of recent research. *Journal of Nonverbal Behavior, 6,* 12-29.

Gilbert, S. J. (1977). The effects of unanticipated self-disclosure on recipients of varying levels of esteem. *Human Communication Research, 3,* 368-371.

Gilbert, S. J., & Horenstein, D. (1975). The communication of self-disclosure: Level versus valence. *Human Communication Research, 1,* 316-322.

Gitter, A. G., Black, H., & Fishman, J. E. (1975). Effect of race, sex, nonverbal communication and verbal communication on perception of leadership. *Sociology and Social Research, 60,* 46-57.

Goffman, E. (1959). *Presentation of self in everyday life.* Garden City, NY: Doubleday/Anchor Books.

Goffman, E. (1961). *Encounters: Two studies in the sociology of interaction.* Indianapolis: Bobbs-Merrill.

Goffman, E. (1963). *Behavior in public places.* New York: The Free Press.

Goffman, E. (1967). *Interaction ritual.* Garden City, NY: Doubleday.

Goffman, E. (1969). *Strategic interaction.* Philadelphia: University of Pennsylvania Press.

Goffman, E. (1971). *Relations in public.* New York: Basic Books.

Goffman, E. (1974). *Frame analysis.* Cambridge, MA: Harvard University Press.

Haase, R. F., & Tepper, D. T., Jr. (1972). Nonverbal components of empathetic communication. *Journal of Counseling Psychology, 19,* 417-424.

Hale, J. L., & Burgoon, J. K. (1984). Models of reactions to changes in nonverbal immediacy. *Journal of Nonverbal Behavior, 8,* 287-314.

Hall, E. T. (1969). *The hidden dimension.* Garden City, NY: Anchor Press/Doubleday.

Hall, E. T. (1973). *The silent language.* Garden City, NY: Anchor Press/Doubleday.

Hall, E. T. (1977). *Beyond culture.* Garden City, NY: Anchor Books.

Hall, J. A. (1979). Gender, gender roles, and nonverbal communication skills, In R. Rosenthal (Ed.), *Skill in nonverbal communication: Individual differences* (pp. 32-67). Cambridge, MA: Oelgeschlager, Gunn & Hain.

Harper, R. G., Wiens, A. N., & Matarazzo, J. D. (1978). *Nonverbal communication: The state of the art.* New York: John Wiley.

Harrison, R. P. (1974). *Beyond words.* Englewood Cliffs, NJ: Prentice-Hall.

Hegstrom, T. G. (1979). Message impact: What percentage is nonverbal? *Western Journal of Speech Communication, 43,* 134-142.

Hemsley, G. D., & Doob, A. N. (1978). The effect of looking behavior on perceptions of a communicator's credibility. *Journal of Applied Social Psychology, 8,* 136-144.

Henley, N. M. (1977). *Body politics: Power, sex and nonverbal communication.* Englewood Cliffs, NJ: Prentice-Hall.

Hensley, W. E. (1981). The effects of attire, location and sex on aiding behavior: A similarity explanation. *Journal of Nonverbal Behavior, 6,* 3-11.

Heslin, R. (1974, May). *Steps toward a taxonomy of touching.* Paper presented at the annual meeting of the Midwestern Psychological Association, Chicago.

Heslin, R., & Alper, T. (1983). Touch: A bonding gesture. In J. M. Wiemann & R. P. Harrison (Eds.), *Nonverbal interaction* (pp. 47-75). Beverly Hills, CA: Sage.

Heslin, R., Nguyen, T. D., & Nguyen, M. L. (1983). Meaning of touch: The cast of touch from a stranger or same sex person. *Journal of Nonverbal Behavior, 7,* 147-157.

Heston, J. K. (1974). Effects of personal space invasion and anomia on anxiety, nonperson orientation and source credibility. *Central States Speech Journal, 25,* 19-27.

Hewes, G. W. (1957). The anthropology of gesture. *Scientific American, 196,* 123-132.

Hollandsworth, J. G., Jr., Kazelskis, R., Stevens, J., & Dressel, M. E. (1979). Relative contributions of verbal, articulative, and nonverbal communication to employment decisions in the job interview setting. *Personnel Psychology, 32,* 359-367.

Izard, C. E. (1971). *The face of emotion.* Englewood Cliffs, NJ: Prentice-Hall.

Jaffe, J. (1978). Parliamentary procedure and the brain. In A. W. Siegman & S. Feldstein (Eds.), *Nonverbal behavior and communication* (pp. 55-66). Hillsdale, NJ: Lawrence Erlbaum.

Jones, E. E. (1964). *Ingratiation: A social psychological analysis.* New York: John Wiley.

Kauffman, L. E. (1971). Tacesics, the study of touch: A model for proxemic analysis. *Semiotica, 4,* 149-161.

Kazdin, A. E., & Klock, J. (1973). The effect of nonverbal teacher approval on student attentive behavior. *Journal of Applied Behavior Analysis, 6,* 643-654.

Kempton, W. (1980). The rhythmic basis of interactional micro-synchrony. In M. R. Key (Ed.), *The relationship of verbal and nonverbal communication* (pp. 67-75). The Hague: Mouton.

Kendon, A. (1967). Some functions of gaze direction in social interaction. *Acta Psychologica, 26,* 22-23.

Kendon, A. (1970). Movement coordination in social interaction: Some examples described. *Acta Psychologica, 32,* 101-125.

Kendon, A. (1980). Gesticulation and speech: Two aspects of the process of utterance. In M. R. Key (Ed.), *The relationship of verbal and nonverbal communication* (pp. 207-227). The Hague: Mouton.

Kendon, A. (1983). Gesture and speech: How they interact. In J. M. Wiemann & R. P. Harrison (Eds.), *Nonverbal interaction* (pp. 13-45). Beverly Hills, CA: Sage.

Kendon, A., Harris, R. M., & Key, M. R. (Eds.). (1975). *Organization of behavior in face-to-face interaction.* The Hague: Mouton.

Kleinfeld, J. S. (1974). Effects of nonverbal warmth on the learning of Eskimo and white students. *Journal of Social Psychology, 92,* 3-9.

Kleinke, C. L. (1975). *First impressions.* Englewood Cliffs, NJ: Prentice-Hall.

Kleinke, C. L. (1980). Interaction between gaze and legitimacy of request on compliance in a field setting. *Journal of Nonverbal Behavior, 5,* 3-12.

Knapp, M. L. (1978a). *Nonverbal communication in human interaction.* New York: Holt, Rinehart & Winston.

Knapp, M. L. (1978b). *Social intercourse: From greeting to goodbye.* Boston: Allyn & Bacon.

Knapp, M. L. (1983a). Dyadic relationship development. In J. M. Wiemann & R. P. Harrison (Eds.), *Nonverbal interaction* (pp. 179-207). Beverly Hills, CA: Sage.

Knapp, M. L. (1983b, May). *The study of nonverbal behavior vis-a-vis human communication theory.* Paper presented at the Second International Conference on Nonverbal Behavior, Toronto, Canada.

Knapp, M. L., Hart, R. P., & Dennis, H. S. (1974). An exploration of deception as a communication construct. *Human Communication Research 1,* 15-29.

Knapp, M. L., Hart, R. P., Friedrich, G. W., & Schulman, G. M. (1973). The rhetoric of goodbye: Verbal and nonverbal correlates of human leave-taking. *Speech Monographs, 40,* 182-198.

Kramer, C. (1974). Women's speech: Separate but unequal? *Quarterly Journal of Speech, 60,* 14-24.

Kramer, E. (1963). Judgment of personal characteristics and emotions from nonverbal properties of speech. *Psychological Bulletin, 60,* 408-420.

Kramer, L., Alloway, T., & Pliner, P. (Eds.). (1975). *Nonverbal communication of aggression.* New York: Plenum.

Krauss, R. M., Apple, W., Morency, N., Wenzel, C., & Winton, W. (1981). Verbal, vocal, and visible factors in judgments of another's affect. *Journal of Personality and Social Psychology, 40,* 312-320.

Kraut, R. E. (1980). Humans as lie-detectors: Some second thoughts. *Journal of Communication, 30,* 209-216.

Krivonos, P. D., & Knapp, M. L. (1975). Initiating communication: What do you say when you say hello? *Central States Speech Journal, 26,* 115-125.

Krout, M. H. (1971). Symbolism. In H. A. Bosmajian (Ed.), *The rhetoric of nonverbal communication* (pp. 15-33). Glenview, IL: Scott, Foresman.

LaBarbera, P., & MachLachlan, J. (1979). Time compressed speech in radio advertising. *Journal of Marketing, 43,* 30-36.

LaBarre, W. (1947). The cultural basis of emotions and gestures. *Journal of Personality, 16,* 49-68.

LaFrance, M., & Mayo, C. (1978). *Moving bodies.* Monterey, CA: Brooks/Cole.

Leach, E. (1972). The influence of cultural context on non-verbal communication in man. In R. A. Hinde (Ed.), *Non-verbal communication* (pp. 315-347). Cambridge, MA: Cambridge University Press.

Leathers, D. G. (1976). *Nonverbal communication systems.* Boston: Allyn & Bacon.

MachLachlan, J., & Siegel, M. H. (1980). Reducing the costs of TV commercials by use of time compressions. *Journal of Marketing Research, 17,* 52-57.

Malandro, L. A., & Barker, L. (1983). *Nonverbal communication.* Reading, MA: Addison-Wesley.

Markel, N. N. (1969). Relationship between voice-quality profiles and MMPI profiles in psychiatric patients. *Journal of Abnormal Psychology, 74,* 61-66.

Marwell, G., & Schmitt, D. (1967). Dimensions of compliance-gaining behavior: An empirical analysis. *Sociometry, 30,* 350-364.

Matthews, R. W., Paulus, P. B., & Baron, R. A. (1979). Physical aggression after being crowded. *Journal of Nonverbal Behavior, 4,* 5-17.

Mayo, C., & Henley, N. M. (Eds.). (1981). *Gender and nonverbal behavior.* New York: Springer-Verlag.

McNeill, D., & Levy, E. (1982). Conceptual representations in language activity and gesture. In R. J. Jarvella & W. Klein (Eds.), *Speech, place, and action: Studies in deixis and related topics* (pp. 271-295). Chicester: John Wiley.

Mehrabian, A. (1971). *Silent messages.* Belmont, CA: Wadsworth.

Mehrabian, A. (1972). *Nonverbal communication.* Chicago: Aldine-Atherton.

Mehrabian, A. (1976). *Public places and private spaces*. New York: Basic Books.
Mehrabian, A., & Wiener, M. (1967). Decoding of inconsistent communications. *Journal of Personality and Social Psychology, 6,* 109-114.
Miller, G. R., Bauchner, J. E., Hocking, J. E., Fontes, N. E., Kaminski, E. P., & Brandt, D. R. (1981). "And nothing but the truth": How well can observers detect deceptive testimony? In B. D. Sales (Ed.), *Perspectives in law and psychology* (pp. 169-194). New York: Plenum.
Miller, G. R., & Burgoon, J. K. (1982). Factors affecting assessments of witness credibility. In N. L. Kerr & R. M. Bray (Eds.), *The psychology of the courtroom 2: The trial process* (pp. 145-179). New York: Academic Press.
Miller, G. R., deTurck, M. A., & Kalbfleisch, P. J. (1983). Self-monitoring, rehearsal, and deceptive communication. *Human Communication Research 10,* 97-118.
Moe, J. D. (1972). Listener judgments of status cues in speech: A replication and extension. *Speech Monographs, 39,* 144-147.
Montagu, A. (1978). *Touching: The human significance of the skin*. New York: Harper & Row.
Morris, D. (1977). *Manwatching: A field guide to human behavior*. New York: Henry N. Abrams.
Morris, D., Collett, P., Marsh, P., & O'Shaughnessy, M. (1979). *Gestures*. New York: Stein & Day.
Nguyen, M. L., Heslin, R., & Nguyen, M. L. (1975). The meaning of touch: Sex differences. *Journal of Communication, 25,* 92-103.
Nguyen, M. L., Heslin, R., & Nguyen, T. (1976). The meaning of touch: Sex and marital status differences. *Representative Research in Social Psychology, 7,* 13-18.
Nolan, M. J. (1975). The relationship between verbal and nonverbal communication. In G. J. Hanneman & W. J. McEwen (Eds.), *Communication and behavior* (pp. 98-119). Reading, MA: Addison-Wesley.
O'Hair, H. D., Cody, M. J., & McLaughlin, M. L. (1981). Prepared lies, spontaneous lies, Machiavellianism, and nonverbal communication. *Human Communication Research, 7,* 325-339.
Ortony, A. (1978). Remembering, understanding and representation. *Cognitive Science, 2,* 53-69.
Patterson, M. L. (1973). Compensation in nonverbal immediacy behaviors: A review. *Sociometry, 36,* 237-257.
Patterson, M. L. (1976). An arousal model of interpersonal intimacy. *Psychological Review, 83,* 235-245.
Patterson, M. L. (1978). The role of space in social interaction. In A. W. Siegman & S. Feldstein (Eds.), *Nonverbal communication and behavior* (pp. 265-290). Hillsdale, NJ: Lawrence Erlbaum.
Patterson, M. L. (1983). *Nonverbal behavior: A functional perspective*. New York: Springer-Verlag.
Pearce, W. B., & Brommel, B. J. (1972). Vocalic communication in persuasion. *Quarterly Journal of Speech, 58,* 298-306.
Pearce, W. B., & Conklin, F. (1971). Nonverbal vocalic communication and the perception of a speaker. *Speech Monographs, 38,* 235-241.
Pei, M. (1965). *The story of language*. Philadelphia: J. B. Lippincott.
Philpott, J. S. (1983). *The relative contribution to meaning of verbal and nonverbal channels of communication: A meta-analysis*. Unpublished master's thesis, University of Nebraska.
Pitcairn, T. K., & Eibl-Eibesfeldt, I. (1976). Concerning the evolution of nonverbal communication in man. In M. E. Hahn & E. C. Simmel (Eds.), *Communicative behavior and evolution* (pp. 81-113). New York: Academic Press.
Pittinger, R., Hockett, C., & Darehy, J. (1960). *The first five minutes*. Ithaca, NY: Martineau.
Plutchik, R. (1962). *The emotions: Facts, theories and a new model*. New York: Random House.
Proshansky, H. M., Ittleson, W. H., & Rivlin, L. G. (Eds.). (1970). *Environmental psychology*. New York: Holt, Rinehart & Winston.
Rich, A. L. (1974). *Interracial communication*. New York: Harper & Row.
Riseborough, M. G. (1981). Physiographic gestures as decoding facilitators: Three experiments exploring a neglected facet of communication. *Journal of Nonverbal Behavior, 5,* 172-183.
Roach, M. E., & Musa, K. E. (1981). *New perspectives on the theory of western dress: A handbook*. New York: Nutri-Guides.
Rogers, L. E., & Farace, R. V. (1975). Relational communication analysis: New measurement procedures. *Human Communication Research, 1,* 222-239.
Rosegrant, T. J., & McCroskey, J. C. (1975). The effects of race and sex on proxemic behavior in an interview setting. *Southern Journal of Speech Communication, 40,* 408-420.

Rosenfeld, H. M. (1972). The experimental analysis of interpersonal influence processes. *Journal of Communication, 22,* 424-442.

Rosenfeld, H. M. (1978). Conversational control functions of nonverbal behavior. In A. W. Siegman & S. Feldstein (Eds.), *Nonverbal behavior and communication* (pp. 291-328). Hillsdale, NJ: Lawrence Erlbaum.

Rosenfeld, L. B., Kartus, S., & Ray, C. (1976). Body accessibility revisited. *Journal of Communication, 26,* 27-30.

Rosenthal, R., & DePaulo, B. M. (1979). Expectancies, discrepancies, and courtesies in nonverbal communication. *Western Journal of Speech Communication, 43,* 76-95.

Rosenthal, R., Hall, J. A., DiMatteo, M. R., Rogers, P. L., & Archer, D. (1979). *Sensitivity to nonverbal communication: The PONS Test.* Baltimore: Johns Hopkins University Press.

Saine, T. (1976). *Synchronous and concatenous behavior: Two models of rule-violation in conversational interaction.* Paper presented at the annual meeting of the Southeastern Psychological Association, New Orleans, LA.

Samovar, L. A., & Porter, R. E. (Eds.). (1976). *Intercultural communication: A reader.* Belmont, CA: Wadsworth.

Sapir, E. (1949). The unconscious patterning of behavior in society. In D. Mandelbaum (Ed.), *Selected writings of Edward Sapir in language, culture and personality* (pp. 544-559). Berkeley: University of California Press.

Schachter, S., & Singer, S. (1962). Cognitive, social and physiological determinants of emotional state. *Psychological Review, 69,* 379-399.

Scheflen, A. E. (1974). *How behavior means.* Garden City, NY: Doubleday.

Scheflen, A. E., & Ashcraft, N. (1976). *Human territories: How we behave in space-time.* Englewood Cliffs, NJ: Prentice-Hall.

Scherer, K. R., & Oshinsky, J. S. (1977). Cue utilization in emotion attribution from auditory stimuli. *Motivation and Emotion, 1,* 331-346.

Schweitzer, D. A. (1970). The effect of presentation on source evaluation. *Quarterly Journal of Speech, 56,* 33-39.

Seay, T. A., & Altekruse, M. K. (1979). Verbal and nonverbal behavior in judgments of facilitative conditions. *Journal of Counseling Psychology, 26,* 108-119.

Siegman, A. W. (1978). The telltale voice: Nonverbal messages of verbal communication. In A. W. Siegman & S. Feldstein (Eds.), *Nonverbal behavior and communication* (pp. 183-243). Hillsdale, NJ: Lawrence Erlbaum.

Stacks, D. W. (1982a). *Hemispheric and evolutionary use: A re-examination of verbal and nonverbal communication.* Paper presented at the annual meeting of the Eastern Communication Association, Hartford, CT.

Stacks, D. W. (1982b). Toward the establishment of a preverbal stage of communication. *Journal of Communication Therapy, 2,* 39-60.

Stacks, D. W., & Burgoon, J. K. (1981). The role of nonverbal behaviors as distractors in resistance to persuasion in interpersonal contexts. *Central States Speech Journal, 32,* 61-73.

Starkweather, J. A. (1964). Variations in vocal behavior. In D. McK. Rioch & E. A. Weinstein (Eds.), *Disorders of communication* (pp. 424-429). Baltimore: Williams and Wilkins.

Street, R. L., Jr. (1983). Noncontent speech convergence and divergence in adult-child interactions. In R. Bostrom (Ed.), *Communication yearbook 7* (pp. 369-395). Beverly Hills, CA: Sage.

Street, R. L., Jr., & Brady, R. M. (1982). Speech rate acceptance as a function of evaluative domain, listener speech rate, and communication intent. *Communication Monographs, 49,* 290-308.

Street, R. L., Jr., Brady, R. M., & Putnam, W. B. (in press). The influence of speech rate stereotypes and rate similarity on listeners' evaluations of speakers. *Journal of Language and Social Psychology.*

Tedeschi, J. (Ed.). (1982). *Impression management theory and social psychological research.* New York: Academic Press.

Tepper, D. T., Jr., & Haase, R. F. (1978). Verbal and nonverbal communication of facilitative conditions. *Journal of Counseling Psychology, 25,* 35-44.

Thorne, B., & Henley, N. (Eds.). (1975). *Language and sex.* Rowley, MA: Newbury House.

Thorpe, W. H. (1972). The comparison of vocal communication in animals and man. In R. A. Hinde (Ed.), *Non-verbal communication* (pp. 27-47). Cambridge: Cambridge University Press.

Tomkins, S. S. (1962). *Affect, imagery, consciousness.* New York: Springer.

Trager, G. L. (1958). Paralanguage: A first approximation. *Studies in Linguistics, 13,* 1-9.

Tronick, E. D., Als, H., & Brazelton, T. B. (1977). Mutuality in mother-infant interaction. *Journal of Communication, 27,* 74-79.

van Hooff, J.A.R.A.M. (1972). A comparative approach to the phylogeny of laughter and smiling. In R. A. Hinde (Ed.), *Non-verbal communication* (pp. 209-241). Cambridge: Cambridge University Press.

Vine, I. (1973). The role of facial-visual signalling in early social development. In M. von Cranach & I. Vine (Eds.), *Social communication and movement* (pp. 195-298). New York: Academic Press.

Waldren, T. A., & Forsyth, D. R. (1981). Close encounters of the stressful kind: Affective, physiological, and behavioral reactions to the experience of crowding. *Journal of Nonverbal Behavior, 6,* 46-64.

Wheeless, L. R., Jones, S., & King, L. (1974). Effect of waiting time on credibility, attraction, homophily, and anxiety-hostility. *Southern Speech Communication Journal, 39,* 367-378.

Widgery, R. N. (1974). Sex of receiver and physical attractiveness of source as determinants of initial credibility perception. *Western Speech, 38,* 13-17.

Wiemann, J. M., & Knapp, M. L. (1975). Turn-taking in conversation. *Journal of Communication, 25,* 75-92.

Wiener, M., Devoe, S., Rubinow, S., & Geller, J. (1972). Nonverbal behavior and nonverbal communication. *Psychological Review, 79,* 185-214.

Williams, C. E., & Stevens, K. N. (1972). Emotions and speech: Some acoustical correlates. *Journal of the Acoustical Society of America, 52,* 1238-1250.

Willis, F. N., & Hamm, H. K. (1980). The use of interpersonal touch in securing compliance. *Journal of Nonverbal Behavior, 5,* 49-55.

Willis, F. N., & Hoffman, G. E. (1975). Development of tactile patterns in relation to age, sex and race. *Developmental Psychology, 11,* 866.

Wood, B. S. (1981). *Children and communication: Verbal and nonverbal language development.* Englewood Cliffs, NJ: Prentice-Hall.

Woodall, W. G., & Burgoon, J. K. (1981). The effects of nonverbal synchrony on message comprehension and persuasiveness. *Journal of Nonverbal Behavior, 5,* 207-223.

Woodall, W. G., & Folger, J. P. (1981). Encoding specificity and nonverbal cue context: An expansion of episodic memory research. *Communication Monographs, 49,* 39-53.

Zahn, G. L. (1973). Cognitive integration of verbal and vocal information in spoken sentences. *Journal of Experimental Social Psychology, 9,* 320-334.

Zuckerman, M., DePaulo, B. M., & Rosenthal, R. (1981). Verbal and nonverbal communication of deception. In L. Berkowitz (Ed.), *Advances in experimental social psychology* (Vol. 14, pp. 2-59). New York: Academic Press.

Zuckerman, M., Driver, R., & Koestner, R. (1982). Discrepancy as a cue to actual and perceived deception. *Journal of Nonverbal Behavior, 7,* 95-100.

Zuckerman, M., Koestner, R., & Driver, R. (1981). Beliefs about cues associated with deception. *Journal of Nonverbal Behavior, 6,* 105-114.

Zuckerman, M., Spiegel, N. H., DePaulo, B. M., & Rosenthal, R. (1982). Nonverbal strategies for decoding deception. *Journal of Nonverbal Behavior, 6,* 171-186.

III BASIC PROCESSES

9 The Management of Conversations

JOSEPH N. CAPPELLA

University of Wisconsin—Madison

THIS chapter focuses on how people manage the conversations in which they participate. Who has not come away from some conversation wishing that they had avoided saying a particularly hurtful thing, or that they had commented when they were silent? These and other common self-reflections are the motivating questions of this chapter.

There are two important senses in which conversations can be managed. The more typical connotation of the word "manage" implies that a person intentionally seeks to alter the content, tenor, or events of a conversation toward some preordained end or purpose. For example, an overworked spouse might try to move the topic of conversation toward the stresses of the work place or home in order to let the other know about his or her experienced difficulties. Management of this type exhibits "control" in the sense that actions are undertaken in order to achieve what one perceives to be an important need or purpose.

A less typical connotation of the word "management" will also be discussed here. The research that will be reviewed will show that certain regularities obtain in the sequencing of microscopic events during conversations. For example, increases in speech rate by one party tend to produce increases in the partner's speech rate (Cappella & Planalp, 1981). People are in general quite unaware that such influences exist and, under most circumstances, do not employ such responses intentionally. These and other regularities are both interesting and nonobvious, but are they relevant to the control of conversational events?

I believe that they are. The ability to control conversations depends upon the existence of certain regularities that can be exploited by one or the other conversational partner, and this exploitation depends upon knowledge of the regularity. For example, in order to encourage discussion of a topic of interest to me I try to get a version of that topic onto the floor. I do so because I know that "staying on the topic" is a norm frequently adhered to in discussion. I must know this norm and how to use it in order to achieve the end that I desire. The only difference between the regularities that people consciously employ to control conversations (for example, topic continuity) and those that they do not (for example, speech rate) is that conversationalists are not generally aware of many of the regularities that do govern conversational events. Once made aware of such regularities, people could use them to manage the content and style of their conversations. For this reason, this review will be concerned with both more intentional and deliberate as well as more unintentional and automatic methods of conversational management.

Attention to the nature of management cannot ignore what it is that people manage in their conversations. In the world of raw stimuli, conversations are a complex mixture of auditory, visual, olfactory, and tactile events that are simultaneous and sequential in time. But such a description of the uninterpreted events of communicative interchanges is more pertinent to the study of psychophysics than to the study of interpersonal relations. If the management of conversations is to be relevant to the study of interpersonal relations, then the events that are managed in those conversations must have an empirically strong and conceptually significant relationship to the domain of interpersonal judgments and perceptions. These are the events that need to be managed and understood in human interaction.

Although more will be said about the relationship between conversational behaviors and interpersonal perceptions later, let us try to clarify the relationship in general terms here. Consider the example of face directed gaze. As a raw stimulus, such a behavior is nothing more than gaze fixed at the general facial region of another person. Folklore, literature, and controlled research have shown that this stimulus has a number of possible interpretations. From the point of view of the sender the gaze may have been directed to gather more information about the other person or, more purposefully, to signal to the other an interest that decorum requires be more indirect than verbally straightforward. In either case the gaze means something other than the mere act of gazing and is, therefore, a sign of some internal state of the sender.

The second internal state that could have been signaled (namely, interest on the part of the sender) has more immediate and direct relational implications than does the first internal state, information gathering. The recipient of the gaze may not notice it at all or may interpret it as impolite staring, or worse. Although either reaction by the recipient has impact, the latter interpretation has more immediate and severe relational implications than does the former. In either case the first steps of this hypothetical interaction are headed for trouble because the possible intentions of the sender and the possible interpretations by the receiver do not overlap at all. The relational value of the act is not shared.

This example illustrates a number of principles that will undergird this review of conversational management. First, the uninterpreted value of conversational events can be sharply distinguished from the interpretations that those events receive. Second, the interpretations that can be given to conversational events are multiple, with some having more powerful relational implications than others. Third, the interpreted values of conversational events can be located in at least three places: the motivational states of the sender, the perceptions of the receiver, or in the shared world of senders and receivers. This review assumes that conversational management is concerned with interpreted rather than raw conversational events, with interpersonally significant events, and with events whose meaning is broadly shared by the body of conversationalists within a culture.

This handbook has given valuable space to a chapter on conversational management precisely because at least some of the verbal, nonverbal, and vocal events that occur within conversations have the potential to initiate, reinforce, and change the status of relationships between partners. The management of conversations, whether deliberate or unintentional, is in part the management of these meaningful events and in this indirect way the management of relationships. Of course, I would be naive to claim that relationships and interactions are equivalent. Relationships exist in abstracted form in the memory of partners. That abstraction certainly influences the content, structure, and management of conversations, and in turn is influenced by them, but that is not to say that a given conversation is a replica of the relationship in which it takes place. Rather, a given conversation is an indicator of the relationship in which it functions in much the same way that the monthly indicators of the nation's economic welfare are related to the nation's actual economic condition: They are certainly related to the economic condition but are more informative when compared to the trends that the economy has been displaying over time rather than treated as absolutes.

SEGMENTING THE CONVERSATIONAL STREAM

The streams of behavior that make up a conversation are complex both because they are multiple in number and because their organization is not obvious. The purpose of this chapter is to discuss this organization among the various streams of conversational behavior in order to categorize and simplify the complexity that faces the theorist and researcher, let alone the conversationalist. Subsequent sections will consider the question of how management of conversational events occurs. This one considers only the organization of those events.

When one stops even for a moment to consider the diversity and kind of stimuli that are being generated during a conversation, a kind of despair creeps into the researcher's bones. How can anyone hope to study, let alone understand, the various verbal, vocal, and kinesic activities that people carry out while speaking and listening? What is worse, these auditory, visual, tactile, and olfactory stimuli are information dense per unit of time. This means that they are changing a great deal over time (at least the so-called dynamic features are (Kendon, 1967)). Interestingly, the despair created in

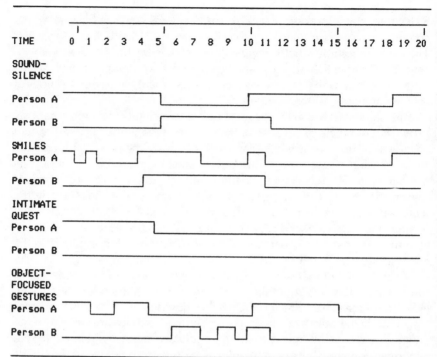

Figure 9.1   A Discrete Time Representation of On and Off Patterns of Selected Conversational Behaviors

researchers by such information overload is not shared by conversationalists. They surely have developed strategies for ignoring, combining, and substituting information generated by their partners. Part of the task that researchers have is to understand the organizational shortcuts that conversationalists take so that this route to the simplification of conversational structure can be profitably employed in research.

The most obvious description of the behavioral activities of conversations would be organized along two dimensions: A horizontal dimension representing time and a vertical dimension representing a particular type of behavior, such as smiling and laughter. This description is represented in Figure 9.1. Conversational events of course occur sequentially so that the temporal organization of such events is one feature of conversational structure. Numerous types of behaviors occur during any moment of the conversation, filling the range from the microscopic and automatic, such as pauses prior to word choices, to the macroscopic and deliberate, such as justifications following accusations. These streams of behavior are represented by the vertical categories of vocal, verbal, and kinesic with subcategories within each. The second dimension of conversational organization concerns these vertical categories. Are these vertical behavior streams sufficiently independent to be treated as separate and distinct or are they interrelated in ways that would allow researchers, and conversational partners, to treat them as functionally equivalent?

Space limitations will not permit us to answer these questions in detail here (but see Cappella & Street, 1985). Research on the temporal organization of conversation has almost always taken an encoding approach, validating the basic time units in terms of criteria generated by the actor. The fundamental units chosen have included the speaking turn (variously defined; see Duncan & Fiske, 1977; Jaffe & Feldstein, 1970; Matarazzo & Wiens, 1972); the phonemic clause (Dittmann, 1972); and units larger than the phonemic clause, often identified as "idea" groupings (Butterworth & Goldman-Eisler, 1979). Even when the researcher does not wish to enter the controversy over which fundamental unit of time will be employed and, consequently, employs a clock time unit, a discrete unit for observation must still be chosen. This choice will often be ad hoc.

Vertical organization concerns the possible functional groupings of the various verbal, vocal, and kinesic behaviors. Two approaches to establishing such functional groupings have been advocated in the literature: Interpersonal motivations (Patterson, 1982a, 1982b) and interpersonal perceptions (Cappella, in press; Cappella & Street, 1985). Both approaches maintain that the meaning or significance of behaviors will be found in the relationship between the behaviors and some internal state. Patterson argued that the location of meaning is the intentions and motivations of the actor, whereas I have argued that the meaning is located in the effects that the behavior produces in perceivers. Both views are meritorious and deserving of further inquiry. If either or both approaches are successful in obtaining functional groupings of behaviors, then research in conversational management would be facilitated. Researchers and theorists would not be required to describe and explain a huge variety of behaviors but rather could focus on functionally equivalent or functionally distinct groupings. The empirical plausibility of such a venture is discussed by Cappella and Street (1985).

MANAGING CONVERSATIONAL BEHAVIORS

According to Ashby (1963), two systems are said to be in communication when the output from each system serves as the input for the other system. Although this might at first glance seem like a superficial and even misleading point of departure, Ashby had a definition of input that makes his definition particularly useful for our discussion here. For Ashby a signal could not be considered an input unless it changed the state of the system for which it was an input. And because Ashby was a strict behaviorist when considering the behavior of systems, the state change initiated by the input of another system must be observable. Thus in Ashby's view, communication involves two systems generating output that serves as input for the other system and eventuates in observable state changes by each.

This view is a good starting point for conversational management. In simple terms I take conversational management to be the use of one's own verbal, vocal, and kinesic actions to alter the same behaviors in another. Although it is certainly true that one can alter another's conversational behavior by manipulating the situation, the relationship, the expectations, the affective tone, and perhaps even the other's personality, attitudes, motives, and values, these are more remote and less controllable than are conversational actions. Similarly, no assumption is made that individuals are deliberately controlling their actions in order to influence the flow and direction of the other's actions. Rather, conversational management is concerned with the ways in which overt verbal, vocal, and kinesic behavior influences the same classes of behavior in another in conversation and in service of conversational and interpersonal ends.

A Methodological and Definitional Excursion

Before turning our full attention to the research literature on conversational management, some words should be devoted to methodological and statistical matters specific to the study of conversational management (or what I have called elsewhere "mutual influence"; see Cappella, 1981).

Let us formalize the definition of conversational management given above. Consider a conversation between two persons A and B. Let the behavioral repertoire of person A be denoted by the set $X = (X_1, X_2, \ldots, X_N)$, where the values X_1 are the N discrete behaviors that can be enacted by person A at discrete intervals of clock time. No real loss of generality is entailed by assuming that the behaviors are discrete rather than continuous or measured on a clock base rather than event time. Analogous definitions can be created for event time and for continuous measures. Let the behavioral repertoire of person B be denoted by the set (Y) identical to the set X for A. Conversational management is defined by two features of the contingent probability between the set of behaviors (X) and the set (Y):

$$P[X_I(t + 1)| Y_J(t)] > 0 \qquad [1]$$

$$P[X_I(t + 1)| Y_J(t)] > \text{or} < P[X_J(t + 1)] \qquad [2]$$

for at least some combination of the behaviors I and J. In words, equations 1 and 2 mean that B's behavior (the Jth one, in fact) must influence the probability of A's behavior (the Ith behavior) at some significant level and, more importantly, that the size of the probability must be greater than the probability that A will emit the behavior in the *absence* of B's prior behavior [2]. These two features insure that A's response level in the presence of B's behavior is above A's normal baseline behavior. A similar pair of equations can be written for A's influence on B. Together they constitute the necessary and sufficient conditions for mutual influence.

Other implications should be mentioned. Incorporating the time factor, t, assumes that the behavior of persons A and B is interweaved in time. No such assumption is necessary as, with larger time units, A and B might exhibit mutual influence within a time period. The behaviors I and J do not necessarily need to be different. When they are the same so that the mutual influence concerns the identical behavior, then mutual influence is called matching and mismatching. For example, when dialect choice by person A influences the dialect employed by B (Giles & Powesland, 1975), then a process of matching is observed. Matching and mismatching is clearly a special case of mutual influence. When I is not equal to J but I and J contribute to the same behavioral function, then we are concerned with reciprocity and compensation (Patterson, 1976). For example, when increases in proximity by A produce less facial gaze by B, then compensation has occurred. Compensation and reciprocity represent another special case of mutual influence.

The terms "convergence" and "divergence" have been typically, but not universally, employed to denote increasing similarity and difference, respectively, for indices of behavior such as speech rate and vocal intensity when the emphasis is on movement toward or away from the other over time.

Mutual influence also concerns situations in which the behaviors for each person are neither identical nor functionally similar. In this case, one of the behaviors becomes a focal behavior because of its special status or character in the conversation or in the relationship. For example, attempts to take the floor are an important criterion in the study of conversational regulation, but the behaviors that predict it are neither turn attempts themselves nor functionally equivalent to turn attempts (Duncan & Fiske, 1977). A second example is taken from the work of McLaughlin and Cody (1982) on awkward silences. These rather lengthy silences in conversation are potential signs of social incompetence and associated with negative interpersonal perceptions. McLaughlin and Cody sought to understand the conversational events that preceded and followed from such events. The definition of mutual influence given above can comfortably accommodate all these examples of the management of conversations. The only additional requirement is that the definition of equations [1] and [2] apply to groups of partners and not only to a particular pair of partners. Common experience recognizes that some partners develop over a period of time certain specialized sequences of interaction that allow them certain efficiencies and access to privileged communication while in public. But these idiosyncratic patterns cannot be generalized to other interactions or used to manage other conversations. My assumption is that the types of mutual influence to be reviewed here are regular rather than idiographic.

Even though the literature on mutual influence is substantial, little consideration has been given to the conceptual and operational definitions that undergird this concept until recently (Cappella, 1983; Gottman, 1979a; Hill & Stull, 1982; Markus-Kaplan & Kaplan, 1983). Reciprocity and matching imply that increases and decreases in a certain behavior (or behavioral function) are met with concomitant, though not necessarily comparable, increases and decreases. Notice that this definition requires (1) that both increases and decreases are matched; (2) that increases and decreases must be matched in direction but not necessarily in quantity (behavioral levels should become more similar though not necessarily identical); and (3) that changes produce responses. An analogous definition for compensation and mismatching could be stated in which increases and decreases are met with decreases and increases respectively. The empirical literature review will show that both increases and decreases are seldom studied, that the quantity of reciprocity or compensation occurring is infrequently assessed, and that only some studies deal with responses to change, whereas most deal with responses to fixed levels.

The most common operational definition used to assess reciprocity or compensation employs a between-subjects design in which two or three levels of a behavior are manipulated and the response of different subject groups to each level is observed (Argyle & Dean, 1965). In such designs a subject's response to a change is not assessed at all, only a subject's reaction to a specified level of behavioral activity. The problem with such designs is that the absence of any baseline response from the subjects makes it difficult to know if the subject's response to the manipulation is any different than it would have been in the absence of a manipulation. When between-subjects designs do attain significant effects it is all the more remarkable because of the substantial individual differences in response levels. What is more desirable is that between-subjects designs be modified so as to obtain some baseline measure for the subject against which responses to the manipulation can be assessed (Coutts, Schneider, & Montgomery, 1980). Some studies have employed either controlled or natural change over time with subjects' response levels to changing behaviors by their partners the object of analysis (Cappella & Planalp, 1981; Davis, 1976, 1977; Gottman, 1979b; Street, 1983). In most cases authors are careful to study responses over baseline levels.

A useful combination of the more controlled experimental techniques with the more representative studies of change over time is represented by the standard design employed by Matarazzo and Wiens (1972). They conducted a standard interview in which a particular behavior, say the latency before responding, was manipulated so that the first third of the interviewer's latencies were long, the next third short, and the final third long again. Average response latencies to these changes were coded, with findings of strong reciprocity typical. These designs are relatively natural yet involve controlled change *in both directions,* toward increases and decreases in latency for the same subject. I believe that this is an excellent compromise design for the study of mutual influence that has been unrecognized and underutilized.

The statistical techniques for the analysis of mutual influence processes range from the mundane to the arcane. Designs employing between-subjects or repeated-measures procedures fall into the well-known ANOVA domain, or with multiple dependent measures into the less common but straightforward MANOVA domain. When process methodologies are required then unfamiliar techniques are the rule. When the criterion variable and its predictors are to be treated as discrete, then lag sequential (Allison & Liker, 1982; Sackett, 1978, 1979) or Markov (Hewes, 1975, 1980) techniques are in order. Both procedures are concerned with the probabilities that events separated in time are associated beyond chance levels. Lag sequential techniques have been applied primarily in situations in which a critical event is focal and the events leading to or eventuating from the critical event are under study (McLaughlin & Cody, 1982). Markov techniques have been applied primarily to systems of states for which the dynamic changes among the complete set are under study (Ellis & Fisher, 1975; Jaffe & Feldstein, 1970).

When the criterion variables are continuous rather than discrete, then time-series methods are more appropriate. These include spectral techniques (Gottman, 1979a), time-series methods such as those common in econometrics (Cappella, 1980; Cappella & Planalp, 1981; Gottman & Ringland, 1981), and other types of time series such as interrupted time series (Greene & Cappella, 1984; McCleary & Hay, 1980). The process techniques are not straightforward in part because they are so new and because software for their implementation is not generally available. Nevertheless, these are important techniques to cultivate in the study of social interaction, particularly in the domain of mutual influence. Without these techniques studies cannot move outside the laboratory and still take into account baseline levels of behavior while simultaneously assessing responses to increases and decreases in the other's level of activity.

The Management of Conversational Turns

The study of how conversations can occur at all without the participants constantly "bumping into one another" verbally has attracted the attention of researchers with a variety of approaches (Beattie, 1978, 1979a, 1979b; Duncan & Fiske, 1977; Goodwin, 1981; Sacks, Schegloff, & Jefferson, 1974; Schenkein, 1978). For the most part these investigators have been concerned with the how, and a little with the why, of conversational turn-taking but not at all with the "so what" of this feature of conversation. In a recent paper on this topic I argued (Cappella, in press) that being able to get control of the floor, keep that control when necessary, and give it up when finished is a crucial interpersonal skill related to perceptions of power, perceptions of affiliation, and to general social competence. The evidence is overwhelming in its support of the relationship between holding the floor and observers' ratings of control and power (leadership, dominance, and so forth) and ratings of associativity (attraction, social evaluation, and so forth; see Cappella, in press). Zimbardo's (1977) studies of shyness suggest that most people identify the reluctance to talk as the primary cue of their shyness. Shyness and its associated failed participation can also lead to embarrassment, self-consciousness, and decreased self-esteem (Zimbardo, 1977). More politically motivated writers (Steinem, 1981) have portrayed some of the covert discrimination that women experience in groups in terms of failure to participate. Women must bear the false reputation of being the talkative ones while at the same time suffering the powerlessness of being the least participative with mostly male colleagues in decision making and social groups. When job and advancement depend upon a positive social image, the inability to participate can be an overwhelming barrier to personal and professional development.

An equally pernicious outcome from low participation rates is the perception of shyness created by the reticent person. When others perceive that a person has a certain quality or trait, they often treat the person accordingly, leading him or her to act out the role dictated by the others' perceptions (Farina, Allen, & Saul, 1968; Farina, Gliha, Boudreau, Allen, & Sherman, 1971). The perception of shyness, whether deserved or not, can lead to behavior that will only increase the shyness reaction.

The point is a simple but powerful one. The study of conversational turn-taking and its management has implications far beyond the how and why of the rule of "one speaker at a time." Those who have little trouble with managing the turn-taking in their conversations open themselves to the rewards of positive perception and social competence and all that that entails. Those who cannot manage their conversational participation lose access to the domain in which power is exercised and restrict their potential social rewards. The study of turn-taking is important in its own right and for what rewards it can bring those who can learn to participate fully.

Although many researchers have been concerned with the structure, regulation, and organization of conversation, only Duncan and his associates (Duncan, 1972, 1973, 1974; Duncan & Fiske, 1977; Duncan, Bruner, & Fiske, 1979; Duncan & Niederehe, 1974) have been concerned specifically with the verbal, vocal, and kinesic behaviors that cue speaker and listener roles. They have also employed the methodologies necessary for the audience to evaluate the reliability of their conclusions.

Turn-Taking Signals. In order to isolate the cues that are associated with the taking and the relinquishing of conversational turns, a turn must be defined. Duncan (1972) defines turns on the basis of the intent of the speaker and defines back channel behaviors on the part of the listener as actions that do not attempt to wrest the floor away from the speaker. Despite the conceptual and operational difficulty that these terms introduce, the evidence indicates that coders can reliably assess both turns and back channels.

Based upon a small study and a larger replication, Duncan and Fiske (1977) report that six cues are associated with smooth turn-taking:

(1) a certain pattern of intonation at the end of phonemic clauses (Trager & Smith, 1957);
(2) a sociocentric sequence (Bernstein, 1962) such as "you know";
(3) the completion of a syntactic clause;
(4) a paralinguistic drawl (Trager, 1958) on the final syllable or the stressed syllable of a phonemic clause;
(5) termination of a hand gesticulation or relaxation of a tensed hand position, such as a fist; and
(6) decrease of paralinguistic pitch or loudness on a sociocentric sequence. (Duncan, 1983, p. 151)

One or more of these cues is present in 261 of the 263 smooth turn transitions observed by Duncan and Fiske (1977). Gesturing by the speaker when one or more of the above cues is present seems to have a veto effect. When the speaker gestures while exhibiting one or more of the above cues, the probability that the listener takes the floor is reduced. Duncan and Fiske also report that the sheer number of cues is the best predictor of the probability of smooth transitions. No single cue seems to be more important than any other; no special combination of cues markedly improves the correlation with the probability of a smooth transition; and the relationship between the number of cues and the probability of transition is linear rather than a step function relationship.

The most significant point of controversy for the cues associated with smooth transitions concerns eye gaze. Research by Wiemann and Knapp (1975) and by Kendon (1967) found that gaze by the speaker at the auditor increases toward the end of speakers' turns, thus acting as a signal that the speaker is ready to yield the floor. Duncan and Fiske (1977) found no evidence that this cue functions to mark turn-yielding. However, they did find that auditors tend to shift their heads away from speakers when the auditor begins vocalizing, especially when that vocalization is identified as a turn attempt rather than just a back channel. Thus Duncan and Fiske's evidence does identify head shifting as an important cue in turn-taking but not as a turn-yielding cue. Cegala, Alexander, and Sokuvitz (1979) supported neither result, finding that a greater proportion of speaking turns had gaze at the other at their moment of onset rather than gaze away from the other.

Within-Turn Interaction. If conversations can be divided into turns and back channels, then partners must be able to negotiate their way through back channels as well as turns. The location of turn attempts and back channels is distinctive but unsurprising. In Duncan and Fiske's corpus, five of six turn attempts occur in a speaker's pause location and five of eight back channels occur in pause locations. Patterson's (1983) review of listener behavior during conversation concludes that "listener behavior, both verbal and nonverbal, seems to be concentrated between phonemic clauses, that is between the terminal pauses" (pp. 65-66). Research by Dittmann (1972), Dittmann and Llewellyn (1967, 1968), and Rosenfeld (1978) all implicate the speaker's pause as the primary location of listener-speaker activity.

Speakers can also elicit and suppress these actions by the listener. For example, Duncan and Fiske (1977) show that gesturing by the speaker during pauses tends to suppress both turn attempts and back channels by the auditor, although more so for the former than the latter. Back channels can be encouraged by speakers by using a head turn toward the listener during brief pauses. Having elicited a back channel, speakers wishing to maintain control of the floor tend to immediately turn their heads away from the auditor with frequency greater than usual. This head turn away immediately after a back channel seems to serve as a speaker state signal notifying the auditor of the speaker's intent to retain the turn.

Simultaneous Turns. Even though the turn system is well-designed to cue speakers and listeners of one another's intent, simultaneous turns are inevitable. One of the tests of Duncan and Fiske's (1977) rule system is whether the speaker state and turn-yielding cues can successfully predict the "winners" of simultaneous attempts to take the floor. Duncan and Fiske identified cases of simultaneous turns and scored each person in terms of the number of speaker state cues (shift away of head direction, initiated gesture, and gesticulation cues) and turn-yielding cues. The scores were subtracted, and the person with the greater score (more speaker state and fewer yielding cues) was predicted to be the winner of the bout. This system successfully predicted 52 of 67 cases of simultaneous turn attempts.

Meltzer, Morris, and Hayes (1971) used vocal amplitude to predict winners of simultaneous speech occurrences. They found that successful interruption depended directly on the difference in vocal amplitudes at the point of interruption (with the louder person winning the floor) and indirectly on the increase in vocal amplitude by the interrupted party.

Turn Management and Participation. This brief discussion of turn management began with the relationship between turn-asking and conversational participation. I would like to return to this relationship by distilling the results of the previous research even more than I have already. Of the great variety of behaviors initially studied in turn management, five groups remain as important to conversational participation: verbal cues associated with the termination of a speech unit, eye gaze (head shifting), gesticulation, pauses, and vocal amplitude. Turn-yielding is cued by six different behaviors, but five of these are located at or help to designate a verbal unit (deviation from a certain pitch contour, sociocentric sequences, completion of a grammatical clause, drawl, decreased pitch, and/or loudness on a sociocentric sequence). The sixth is termination of gesturing.

Participation in conversation is facilitated when an actor uses these cues appropriately to obtain and to yield the floor. Implicit knowledge of the cues and of the rules must reside in competent conversationalists. The verbal cues that partition the speech into units (phonemic, linguistic, and so forth) are important in that they mark the most likely location of back channels and turn attempts. They are the locations of turn-yielding and turn-taking. Speakers and listeners must be able to recognize these important locations. However, the other four classes of cues are, I believe, much more important because they indicate what actions are intended at the pause and boundary locations. For example, as the frequency and average duration of pauses decreases then so does the opportunity for the auditor to take the speaking role. If the reticent speaker pauses a great deal, then that speaker will have greater difficulty in maintaining the floor simply because the opportunities for the auditor to take the floor will be far greater. If one of the partners were to exhibit excessive gaze aversion, then gaze aversion would lose its informativeness as a speaker state cue. If a person were to employ a high number of body-focused gestures, then the number of possible object-focused gestures would be fewer and the gesticulation signal would be less available to the apparently fidgety person. Research on socially insecure individuals has shown them to employ greater gaze aversion, more body-focused gestures, and to pause and hesitate more in speech (Cappella, in press). Thus the behavior patterns of socially insecure persons involve just those behaviors crucial to the turn-taking process.

Although I have tried to draw the connection between turn-taking and important interpersonal perceptions, the connection is indeed a speculative one. We do not know, for example, if reticent persons exhibit unusual patterns of turn management in comparison to their less reticent counterparts or if they simply use the typical cues at atypical moments.

The Management of Vocal Behaviors

In the previous section the concern was centered on a criterion variable, the probability of smooth turn-taking, that was distinctively different from its predictors. Hence, issues of reciprocity and compensation, matching and mismatching did not arise. In this and subsequent sections the criterion variable and its predictors are either of the same behavioral category or are assumed to participate in the same function. Reciprocity and compensation, and matching and mismatching become central concerns.

In these sections two conventions are employed. All of the studies reviewed are behavioral in that subjects actually interact with one another or with a confederate rather than reacting to hypothetical encounters using self-reported behaviors. Second, the data are organized on the basis of the independent or manipulated variable. Thus in considering conversational management involving eye gaze, all the studies discussed in the section will involve eye gaze as an independent predictor even though measures of eye gaze, as a criterion variable, will occur in other sections of the review.

By vocal behavior I mean characteristics of the spoken word independent of the verbal or meaning component. Included in this set would be vocalization duration, pause duration, switching pauses, utterance length, latency to respond, and intensity or amplitude. These variables have been carefully defined by Jaffe and Feldstein (1970) and by Matarazzo and Wiens (1972). Despite some subtle but significant differences in their operationalizations, comparable substantive conclusions have been reached.

The evidence on mutual influence in vocal aspects of conversations has been reviewed in detail elsewhere (Cappella, 1981, 1983). In over 33 studies representing some 40 separate subject pools, the overwhelming conclusion is that matching and reciprocity are the predominant forms of mutual influence. The evidence for matching in speech rate (Putman & Street, in press; Webb, 1969, 1972), latency and switching pauses (Cappella & Planalp, 1981; Jaffe & Feldstein, 1970; Matarazzo & Wiens, 1967), pausing (Dabbs, 1980; Jaffe & Feldstein, 1970; Welkowitz, Cariffe, & Feldstein, 1976), and amplitude (Black, 1949a, 1949b; Meltzer, Morris, & Hayes, 1971; Natale, 1975) is quite strong and remarkably consistent across samples, operational definitions, and laboratories. The evidence for matching on utterance duration and vocalization is not as clear-cut, but it does appear that matching is the rule in controlled laboratory studies. Less conclusive findings are obtained in more naturally occurring conditions (see Matarazzo, Weitman, Saslow, & Wiens, 1963, versus Welkowitz & Feldstein, 1969). Part of these differences may be attributable to the operational differences between utterance duration and vocalization duration. Utterance duration probably includes both vocalization duration and pauses. Because pause matching is a common finding but vocalization matching is not, matching in utterance duration may be due in part to the matching of pauses only.

Despite these rather strong findings, certain methodologies have uncovered contrary tendencies toward mismatching and compensation in certain dyads. Cappella and Planalp (1981) applied time-series methodologies to the vocal behaviors of individual dyads, with each turn being an observation unit. It was found that certain dyads were compensatory on vocalization and pause behaviors, although the pattern across the 12 dyads was in favor of matching. Matarazzo, Wiens, Matarazzo, and Saslow (1968) found similar compensatory results on utterance duration between individual clients and their therapists. The chief difference between the above two studies and the vast majority of others is the individual versus group level of analysis. When methods are used that permit scrutiny of individual dyads rather than group level results alone, some dyads exhibit the mismatching that commonsense observation would lead us to expect. Certainly it is not difficult to imagine the reticent person giving over vocal responsibility to the more verbose partner or the very active, high tempo partner driving the less expressive partner toward even greater withdrawal. The individual level of statistical analysis is necessary to uncover these tendencies toward compensation.

The Management of Kinesic Behaviors

The set of possible kinesic behaviors operative in conversation and interpersonally functional is very extensive. However only two kinesic behaviors have been given sufficient attention as independent or manipulated variables to warrant review: proximity and eye gaze. Numerous variables in addition to these have been measured as responses to increases and decreases in these two kinesic features.

Proximity. Interpersonal distance has produced the strongest and most consistent set of results on mutual influence than any of the behaviors discussed here. In approximately 40 studies reviewed in Cappella (1981, 1983), all produced at least some results supportive of the compensatory effects of increases in proximity. As proximity (or nearness) increases, one can expect (1) partners to increase their own distance (Becker & Mayo, 1971; Efran & Cheyne, 1973); (2) the time it takes to leave the situation to increase; (3) partner's eye gaze to decrease (Argyle & Dean, 1965; Patterson, 1977; Schulz & Barefoot, 1974); (4) partner's orientation to become less direct (Pellegrini & Empey, 1970; Sawitsky & Watson, 1975); and (5) partner's duration of responses to decrease (Baxter & Roselle, 1975; Johnson & Dabbs, 1976). Although these findings are consistent, they are also one-sided. Most studies employ a between-subjects design with only two levels of distance, one normal for the situation and one rather close. Thus most findings pertain to half of the compensation process: responses to close distances relative to normal. The question of responses to far distances is still open empirically.

Despite these strong conclusions, there are some empirical hints that the compensation process governing interpersonal distance is limited. Greenbaum and Rosenfeld (1978) found that for a subgroup of their subjects who were labeled affiliative because they were willing to vocalize, closer proximity was associated with greater eye gaze directed at a stranger at a traffic intersection. For the rest of their subjects who were unwilling to vocalize (and presumably less affiliative), no relationship between proximity and gaze was found. Aiello (1972, 1973, 1977) employed three levels of distance and relatively normal patterns of gaze by his confederates measuring eye gaze and duration of speech in response to subgroups of males and females. The males exhibited compensatory responses on both variables across all levels of confederate distance. The females, however, increased talk and gaze as distance increased from near to moderate, but decreased gaze as distance increased from moderate to far. Skotko and Langmeyer (1977) found that their females disclosed more at nearer distances than farther distances whereas males reversed these trends across three levels of confederate proximity. If one assumes that persons have different upper bounds for desired and tolerated interpersonal involvement, then the results of the above studies become interpretable. More importantly, the departures from the rule of compensation suggest that mediators of response to nearer distances are important predictors of the kind of reaction that will occur, either increasing approach or increasing avoidance. Both responses are possible under certain conditions, but the compensatory response is the most common.

Eye Gaze. The results from a review of the literature on response to eye gaze are similar to those from interpersonal distance. People show a marked tendency to reciprocate gaze by another, but this rule is modified significantly by moderators of the response. As gaze increases in a neutral to positive social situation, returned gaze will also increase (Coutts, Schneider, & Montgomery, 1980; Kaplan, Firestone, Klein, & Sodikoff, 1983; Noller, 1980; Schneider & Hansvick, 1977); duration of speech will increase (Aiello, 1973; Kleinke, Staneski, & Berger, 1975); and more direct body position may be employed (Sawitsky & Watson, 1975; Sodikoff, Firestone, & Kaplan, 1974). But these response tendencies may be modified by changing elements of the social or personal situation.

Ellsworth and Carlsmith (1968) found that an already unpleasant inter-action will lead to more negative evaluations when gaze is present than when it is reduced. In their study of staring at a traffic intersection, Greenbaum and Rosenfeld (1978) observed that greater gaze led to quicker departure by drivers. For females who did not talk to the male confederate, a clear pattern of compensation in returned gaze was exhibited. The most directly support-ive study is that of Kaplan et al. (1983). In this case, gaze from a liked confederate was returned during an interview but gaze from a disliked confederate was compensated. Thus the research shows an overall tendency toward reciprocity in gaze in social settings that have a neutral to positive affective tone but a reversal in this trend for settings with a negative affective tone.

Other Kinesic Behaviors. Research on mutual influence with respect to other kinesic behaviors has not been sufficient to warrant definitive conclusions. One area that has received considerable attention is synchrony in body movements. Condon and Ogston (1966, 1967) were first to speculate that an individual's microscopic body movements were synchronized with changes in the person's speech and that body movement changes were synchronized between persons. McDowall (1978a, 1978b) has strongly criticized the previous research for failing to correct for synchronization above chance baselines. Despite counterarguments from Gatewood and Rosenwein (1981) that McDowall's methods were too different from those of

Condon and Ogston to warrant a direct comparison, the criticism remains that chance baselines, regardless of the methodology chosen, have never been taken into account in the previous research. Only anecdotal data support the claims of behavioral synchrony, although I believe that one can expect matching in gestural activity between interactions on the basis of the correlational evidence for pause matching and the co-occurrence of pause and gestural activity (Cappella, 1981).

Managing Verbal Behaviors

A wide variety of verbal behaviors operate in conversation in service of interpersonal functions. Verbally intimate statements, usually discussed under the title of self-disclosure, are important in relationship negotiation and development (Altman & Taylor, 1973). Verbally intimate questions are common tools in therapy and counseling for the elicitation of problem areas. Topic presentation and continuity, in addition to their obvious functions of introducing information for the purposes of discussion and of providing continuity for the purposes of coherence and competence, also are related to issues of confirmation and disconfirmation of the other through acceptance and rejection of the topic presented (Watzlawick, Beavin, & Jackson, 1967). Linguistic choices such as dialect, pronunciation, grammatical and verbal complexity, language choices in bilingual settings, and the like are especially important in judgments of power and status, in seeking and giving approval, and in showing solidarity and separateness (Giles, 1979; Giles & Powesland, 1975; Robinson, 1979). Other features of the verbal stream carry information about dominance and control (Ericson & Rogers, 1973; Rogers, & Farace, 1975) about account sequences when some harm has occurred (McLaughlin, Cody, & Rosenstein, 1983) and about conflict strategies (Sillars, 1980). Although not a comprehensive sampling of language features with interpersonal implications, the above list represents five domains in which substantial research effort has been exerted.

Self-Disclosure. Several extensive reviews of the literature on mutual influence in self-disclosure are available (Cappella, 1981; Dindia, 1985). These reviews find overwhelming evidence in support of Jourard's (1959) initial hypothesis of a dyadic effect (reciprocity and matching in the language adopted here). Correlational studies (Jourard, 1959), controlled interviews (Jourard & Resnick, 1970; Kaplan et al., 1983), experimental groups (Worthy, Gary, & Kahn, 1969), role-playing studies (Cozby, 1972), naturalistic experiments (Rubin, 1975), controlled sequences of interchanges (Davis, 1976, 1977, 1978), and research on preadolescents (Vondracek & Vondracek, 1971) find that partners tend to match one another's level of self-disclosure.

Although some studies have failed to find reciprocity and matching in self-disclosure (Brewer & Mittleman, 1980; Carr & Dabbs, 1974; Dalto, Ajzen, & Kaplan, 1979; Dindia, 1982; Johnson & Dabbs, 1976), most of these findings are readily explicable in terms of experimental, procedural, or statistical techniques. For example, the studies by Dabbs involve intimate questions without intimate disclosure by the interviewer. They are better included in discussions of intimate questions than of intimacy matching. No studies that directly manipulate intimacy have found compensatory verbal intimacy as a response.

What is surprising in this literature is that even when researchers have tried to push the levels of manipulated disclosure to the extreme, compensatory responses still have not been easy to produce. In fact, in the six studies that have tried to find a decrease in verbal intimacy to very high disclosures, none have found the inverted U relationship, which is the strong finding of compensation (Archer & Berg, 1978; Cozby, 1972; Derlega, Harris, & Chaikin, 1973; Levin & Gergen, 1969; Rubin, 1975; Savicki, 1972). However, there were some hints that some form of compensatory reaction was occurring. Levin and Gergen found that the amount of information returned in the high disclosure condition was less than that returned in the moderate disclosure condition while that returned in the low disclosure condition was more than in the moderate condition.

Cozby (1972) did a frequency analysis of the number of people who responded high, medium, and low in intimacy to the three levels of intimacy by the confederate. The distribution of responses to the high intimacy manipulation was more nearly equal than was the distribution for the moderate and the low intimacy manipulation. The studies by Rubin (1975) and by Archer and Berg (1978) produced similar findings. Even though intimacy did not decrease in any of the high intimacy conditions in comparison to the moderate intimacy conditions, the number of words in the responses in the high intimacy conditions were significantly fewer than in the moderate intimacy conditions. It may be that subjects did not feel that they could avoid responding in kind to the intimate revelations of the confederate but sought to reduce their level of involvement by altering other behaviors. If researchers had been willing to measure other nonverbal behaviors, it is conceivable that high levels of self-disclosure could have produced withdrawal in these other behavioral domains.

Once again, the research shows a strong rule, in this case reciprocity, with some suggestion that under certain conditions that rule would be suspended and replaced with a compensatory response characteristic of withdrawal.

Intimate Questions. The effect of intimate questions on another's response must be sharply separated from the effects due to verbal intimacy on the basis of initial disclosure. As might be expected, intimate questions tend to produce withdrawal reactions characteristic of compensation rather than the approach response characteristic of reciprocity. For example, Schulz and Barefoot (1974) found that question intimacy increased latency of response, decreased eye gaze, and decreased smiles and laughter. Exline, Gray, and Schuette (1965) obtained similar findings on eye gaze. Carr and

Dabbs (1974) and Johnson and Dabbs (1976) observed decreases in the duration of response to intimate questions. Anderson (1976) obtained curvilinear results with pairs of friends. Gaze increased as question intimacy increased from low to moderate and then decreased as intimacy increased from moderate to high. These results are probably due to the fact that friends have a greater range of expected and tolerable intimacy than do the strangers common to most other studies.

The research literature has sometimes lumped studies of disclosure and intimate questions together under the topic of verbal intimacy. But common sense suggests and the research shows that intimate questions without the accompanying intimate disclosure by a questioner tend to produce withdrawal by the partner rather than approach.

Linguistic Features. These features of the verbal domain include language choice, dialect, pronunciation, and other aspects of speech independent of content and separate from the vocal features of rate, pauses, loudness, pitch, and other purely auditory characteristics of the speech signal. Typically, linguistic features are concerned with the various representations that the verbal content might take in different linguistic subcultures. The extensive literature on this topic has found evidence that people match, mismatch, and maintain a variety of linguistic features depending upon the social situation. Comprehensive reviews are available in Giles and Powesland (1975), Giles 1980), and Street (1982), and will not be repeated here.

The evidence for linguistic convergence (matching) is abundant. Studies of immigrant groups have shown the strong moves toward linguistic assimilation of immigrant groups into the traditions of their new culture (Fishman, 1966). In more narrowed and controlled contexts individuals show a wide variety of techniques to exhibit convergence toward another's language (Giles, Taylor, & Bourhis, 1973), with pronunciation being a feature commonly imitated (Giles, 1973). The role of status differences in motivating convergence was demonstrated in a study by Thakerar, Giles, and Cheshire (1982). Individuals from high- and low-status occupations were paired with one another for conversations on relevant topics. The high-status persons tried to converge their speech to what they expected to be the speech patterns of the lows by reducing their speech rates and employing a nonstandard accent (the study was done in England). The low-status persons similarly converged to what they believed the speech patterns of the highs to be, increasing their speech rates and adopting a standard accent. Status might be a cue to linguistic convergence at an early age as well. Aboud (1976) observed that 6-year-old Chicano children adopted the language of their English-speaking listeners to explain a game to them while the English-speakers maintained their own language in similar explanations.

Although convergence and matching is common, Bourhis (1979) points out that individuals will frequently not converge but will employ the language of their particular linguistic subgroup in order to maintain a strong identification with their own group. Under more extreme conditions, individuals will actually diverge from the language chosen by the dominant group in order to accentuate their separation and autonomy (Bourhis, Giles, & Lambert, 1975; Doise, Sinclair, & Bourhis, 1976). For example, Bourhis and Giles (1977) found that native Welsh speakers diverged from the English-speaking instructor who attacked the viability of their native tongue by increasing the accentedness of their Welsh. Interestingly, this occurred only for a group who was attending Welsh instruction in order to enhance their cultural background and not for a second group who was attending the same instruction in order to enhance their professional opportunities. This latter group actually converged to the English speaker. Bourhis, Giles, Leyens, & Tajfel (1979) conducted a similar study in Belgium. In two studies listeners diverged from the speaker who attacked their ethnic group by responding to the speaker in their own native tongue, Flemish.

The above results parallel in general form the kind of results obtained with other behaviors. Both matching (convergence) and mismatching (divergence) is observed under certain conditions. These conditions are related to whether the situation produces motivations to enhance similarity, attraction, and cohesion between the two speakers and the groups that they and their languages represent or whether the situation produces motivations to maintain difference, autonomy, or even to accentuate separation.

Topic Management. One of the most peculiar and yet fascinating characteristics of conversations is how they manage to cover as many different topics as they do and still seem to remain coherent. Artful conversationalists must be able to achieve their own goals of topical coverage while permitting others to explore theirs, all within the usual social constraint of topical continuity. This is sometimes a difficult chore for conversationalists, to say nothing of researchers who are just beginning to try to understand this process (Clark & Haviland, 1977; Craig & Tracy, 1983; Reichman, 1978).

Tracy (1985) identifies some of the potential self-presentational and relational goals that the management of topics in conversation can achieve. By letting other persons initiate and maintain their own topics one can show deference to the other, importance of the other's interests, and friendliness and competence in remaining with the introduced topic. At the same time one's own needs for autonomy and attention to problems and concerns must be balanced against attention to the other's topical focus. Watzlawick et al. (1967) pointed out the importance of topic-shifting and topic continuity in interpersonal relationships by arguing that important topics introduced by persons are statements about themselves or the relationship. When these implicit statements about self and the relationship are ignored or dismissed, for example, through topic shifting, then disconfirmations of the speakers' view of self and view of the relationship are at risk. Although hard evidence to support these claims is unavailable, Folger and Sillars (1980) did find that topic switches were perceived to be dominant acts. Several other schemes for coding interaction sequences make a similar assumption (Ellis, 1979; Ericson & Rogers, 1973).

The importance of topic management highlights two questions for research: How can topical continuity or conversational coherence be achieved? How are successes and failures in topic continuity perceived? The former has received a good deal of speculation and attention (Clark & Haviland, 1977; Hawes, 1983; Hopper, 1983; Planalp & Tracy, 1980; Reichman, 1978; Sanders, 1983; Tracy, 1982). Planalp and Tracy hypothesized that topic continuity is based upon the degree of integration of newly introduced information into the context established by the existing topic and environment. Tracy (1982) refined this scheme to distinguish between local and thematic integration. The distinction notes that a person may continue a comment made by another but completely miss the underlying or true topic of the remarks. Tracy (1985) found that people typically tried to extend the theme rather than a comment made on the theme, especially when the theme was comprehensible. When presented with a theme that was difficult to understand, a comment was extended instead. Notably absent were attempts to simply change the topic. Tracy and Moran (1982) tried to get subjects to be attentive *and* to change the topic to one of their own. Many subjects found this task difficult, abandoning one or the other goals in the process. Those who were successful introduced an overarching issue, made a direct link to the theme on a peripheral issue, or tried to link to the other's remarks by making a procedural comment. Crow (1983) studied the topic changes of five married couples, finding topic maintenance to occur in over 96 percent of the topic shifts.

The evidence on how topic changes are conducted is only beginning to accumulate. The problem that this creates is that research on the effectiveness and interpersonal impact of various types of topic changes will remain weak until such descriptive studies are completed. Planalp and Tracy (1980) studied the perceptions of competence that their various types of integrative strategies of topic changing created. They found that the less integrative and more implicit strategies were judged as less competent (less skillful, less involved with the other, and so forth). Tracy (1982) found that continuations on a peripheral comment rather than the theme were judged as less competent than continuations of the theme. This rule held even in the face of topics known by the judges to be important to the topic changer. Even in this case, judged divergences from the theme were not acceptable.

The rule of topical continuity seems to be a strong one in conversations. Future reseach will need to show just how much topical deviation and what forms of topical deviation are acceptable without suffering negative perceptions on competence, attentiveness, and involvement. Without such information we will only know that topic continuity is important but will not be able to advise conversationalists on how to introduce their own topics without being negatively perceived.

Miscellaneous Verbal Behaviors. A large body of research on the sequential structure of verbal interaction has been conducted that will not be reviewed here. This research has been focused on conflict among college roommates (Sillars, 1980), group conflict and group decision making (Poole, 1981, 1983), group interaction structure (Hawes & Foley, 1973), negotiation strategies (Putnam & Jones, 1982), story sequences (McLaughlin, Cody, Kane, & Robey, 1981), and simple topical structure (Stech, 1975, 1979). Other topics are ripe for such sequential analyses but the steps have not been taken: compliance gaining sequences (Wiseman & Schenk-Hamlin, 1981; Cody, Woelfel, & Jordan, 1983) and facial and verbal emotional expression (Buck, 1979).

The reason that the above bodies of research will not be reviewed here has primarily to do with coding systems. The verbal domain of research in conversational structure is starkly different from the nonverbal and vocal with respect to agreement about what behaviors to code and how to code them. Each researcher, and sometimes each study, seems to invent and reinvent a new coding system for categorizing the verbal behavioral stream. In some respects this is understandable. Every research project has particularized substantive questions that it raises. The behaviors coded must be in service of the underlying substantive hypotheses and not some abstract conception of the functions that the verbal events might serve in the interaction. Also, the verbal stream is more complicated than the other domains, being capable of many more partitions than the nonverbal and vocal. Despite these excuses the fact remains that attempts to integrate results across studies of verbal interaction are almost impossible. Simple questions relevant to reciprocity and compensation have not been asked or answered. Does verbal intensity beget verbal intensity? Will patterns of agreement-agreement responses be more characteristic of high-quality group products than patterns of agreement-disagreement? Does verbal hostility increase the likelihood of verbal hostility, and, if so, is such an effect cathartic and hence beneficial to relational growth or desensitizing and hence detrimental to a relationship? My point is very simple, yet fundamental: Verbal behaviors could be the objects of coding with significant implications for conversational management.

An example of this concerns the study of accounting sequences (Cody & McLaughlin, in press; Darby & Schlenker, 1982; McLaughlin, Cody, & O'Hair, 1983; McLaughlin, Cody, & Rosenstein, 1983; Schlenker & Darby, 1981). This research has carefully developed categories of reproaches by offended individuals as well as accounts by offending persons. Situational and individual differences have also been considered in predicting both the type of reproach and the type of account offered in response to the reproach. The chief conclusions have been that more aggravating reproaches induce more aggravating accounts and more mitigating reproaches elicit more mitigating accounts (but only in restricted situations and depending on the offender's felt responsibility). This effect is akin to a reciprocity rule, at least under certain situational demands. This line of inquiry is interesting in its own right as a phenomenon that we all encounter in daily life and because these studies are exemplars of research in the verbal domain that illustrate the way conversations are managed.

One of the most prolific areas of research that has adopted a relatively consistent coding scheme is relational dominance and submission (Court-right, Millar, & Rogers-Millar, 1979; Ellis, 1979; Ellis & Fisher, 1975; Ericson & Rogers, 1973; Fisher, 1979; Manderscheid, Rae, McCarrick, & Silbergeld, 1982; Millar, Rogers-Millar, & Courtright, 1979; Rogers, Courtright, & Millar, 1980; Rogers & Farace, 1975; Rogers-Millar & Millar, 1979). Although considerable controversy has arisen over the validity of the coding schemes adopted (Folger & Poole, 1982; O'Donnell-Trujillo, 1981; Rogers & Millar, 1982), the research has been extensive and varied in subject population and in substantive application. However, I do not consider this research as applicable to the understanding of conversational management.

As Hewes (1979) has pointed out, one can study interaction by focusing on the message sequences alone or on the messages as delivered by each individual in the interaction. All of the research reviewed in this chapter falls into the latter category. The research on relational dominance and sub-mission does not; it focuses on message sequences irrespective of the message source. The implications of this choice for the study of conversa-tional management are serious. By losing track of who originates a message, questions of reciprocity and compensation, matching and mismatching cannot be asked. These questions are important not only to the conception of management adopted here, but to the motivating questions of the domi-nance-submission literature; that is, what patterns of interaction characterize the relationship for these partners. Consider a simple example. Suppose during the first half of a conversation the husband controls by speaking in a verbally dominant manner with the wife occupying a relatively submissive posture. In the second half a new topic emerges with the wife being dominant and the husband submissive. By failing to keep track of the speaker, the researcher would be led to conclude that the couple was consistent in their dominance-submission patterns over the conversation when in fact their patterns were quite changable in adapting to the changing topical focus. Although not all of the relational communication research can be criticized on these grounds, a significant portion of it can, with a concomitant loss of usefulness in the study of conversational management.

The Effects of Multiple Behaviors

All of the research reviewed above typically manipulates one behavior, observing the effect of that manipulation on several possible behavioral outcomes. In naturally occurring conversations such analytical simplicity is atypical. Only a little research has tried to manipulate more than a single behavior at a time. The manner of the manipulation falls into three categories: confounding of several behaviors, independent manipulation of several behaviors, and indexing of several behaviors.

Behaviors are confounded when two or more behaviors are manipulated to establish a certain condition. For example, Breed (1972) manipulated nonverbal immediacy by manipulating lean, gaze, and orientation at the same time. He found reciprocal response on lean and gaze from his subjects. Other studies that have manipulated immediacy by including physical distance as a part of the confederate's behavior have tended to obtain compensatory reactions (Greenberg & Firestone, 1977; Patterson, Mullens, & Romano, 1971; Sundstrom, 1975). Proximity seems to be a strong factor that overwhelms the influence of other factors. When eye gaze is confounded with question intimacy compensatory reactions are produced (Jourard & Friedman, 1970), but when co-occurring with lean, orientation, and interruption, reciprocal reactions are produced (Breed, 1972; Sundstrom, 1975). In the linguistic domain, Giles and Smith (1979) manipulated three behaviors toward or away from the speech style of an interviewer, asking subjects to judge the speech and the speaker on five characteristics. They discovered that speech rate convergence produced more positive evaluations on four of five characteristics whereas convergence on pronunciation and on content produced no perceptual changes compared to divergence on these speech features.

Few studies have tried to independently manipulate more than one behavior at the same time. The difficulty of staging such manipulations and training confederates to successfully carry them out are significant barriers. Seven studies have tried such manipulations (Aiello, 1973; Carr & Dabbs, 1974; Greenbaum & Rosenfeld, 1978; Johnson & Dabbs, 1976; Kaplan et al., 1983; Schulz & Barefoot, 1974; Sundstrom, 1975). Most interactions were nonsignificant, unreported, or uninteresting because each of the factors would be expected to produce compensatory reactions. The Kaplan et al. study manipulated confederate verbal disclosure, question intimacy, and confederate gaze in an orthogonal design. Question intimacy and disclosure were found to interact with subjects reciprocating the confederate's disclosure intimacy at both levels of question intimacy. Gaze and disclosure also interacted, with intimacy of disclosure being greatest for the high gaze, high disclosure confederate. The compensatory effects expected from question intimacy were wiped out by the presence of the confederate's verbal disclosure. Gaze and disclosure reinforced one another as expected.

Kaplan et al. carried out one further analysis that merits attention. They tried to create an approach index for the confederate's behavior by adding together all approach behaviors carried out by the confederate, arbitrarily coded one and zero depending on their magnitude. They found a relatively strong linear trend between the index and subjects' disclosure levels, indicative of reciprocity *for both the liked and disliked interviewer*. On subjects' proportion of *eye* gaze they found a positive relationship to confederate approach index for the *liked* confederate but a negative relationship for the *disliked* confederate. This is strong evidence for the moderating effects of attraction on gaze behavior but equally strong evidence for the reciprocal nature of self-disclosure.

Overall it is difficult to draw strong conclusions from the limited research on the relative power of various behaviors to produce reciprocal and compensatory reactions. Interpersonal distance and self-disclosure appear to generate the most consistent findings: compensatory reactions for the former at least at close proximity and reciprocal reactions for the latter. Both have shown the power to overwhelm other behavioral factors but have not yet been pitted against one another in pivotal tests of their relative strengths to induce approach or withdrawal.

The Ontogenesis of Conversational Management

The view that infants are the passive recipients of social training at the hands of their primary caretakers has slowly but surely been replaced with a view in which the infant exerts much influence on the caretaker. Lamb (1977) reviewed the role of infants in affecting their social milieu concluding:

In sum the research discussed in this section lends scant support to the belief that infants are passive recipients of social stimulation. Not only are there marked individual differences apparent at birth and consistent thereafter; infants are also shown to play an active role in modulating their interaction with the social world. (p. 69)

Gewirtz and Boyd (1976, 1977) were able to show in a controlled environment that infants' vocalizations and head turns can increase the likelihood of the mother's vocalizations and smiles. If mothers and their infants influence one another's microscopic social behaviors, then such mutual influence might mark the beginning of mutual influence patterns characteristic of adult interactions.

Two kinds of evidence can be marshaled to support this claim: evidence on the development of turn-taking and evidence on the regulation of social interaction. Several authors have argued that the timing of action sequences between adults and infants are precise and regular enough to warrant the claim that such action sequences are the precursors to adult turn-taking (Bateson, 1975; Beebe, in press; Street, 1983). Bateson (1975) in fact has termed such sequential actions as "proto-conversations." Research by Stern, Jaffe, Beebe, and Bennett (1975), Anderson, Vietze, and Dokecki (1977), Beebe, Stern, and Jaffe (1979), and Beebe and Gerstman (1982) indicates that both infant and mother are timing the location of their actions in response and in coaction with the other in a very precise fashion, necessarily picking up on the movement cues of the other to establish regular patterns of action. Coupled with the finding that the likelihood of coaction decreases with increasing age (Beebe, in press) while turn-taking increases, we have the suggestion that the elements of successfully negotiated turn-taking are present from a very early age.

Infants and their primary caretakers also regulate their social interactions with respect to the duration and the timing of vocalizations, movement, and eye gaze, especially as a means of regulating stimulation. Matching appears to be the typical means of vocalization regulation. In both experimental (Bloom, 1975; Gewirtz & Boyd, 1977) and home environments (Lewis & Lee-Painter, 1974) with 3-month-old infants (Anderson et al., 1977) and 2-year-olds (Schaffer, Collis, & Parsons, 1977), twin offspring (Stern et al., 1975), blacks and whites, and high and low socioeconomic groups (Lewis, 1972), vocalization matching is the rule. Similarly, research has shown infants to match the pitch of voices that they encounter (Lieberman, 1966; Webster, Steinhardt, & Santer, 1972).

Evidence for movement coordination between infants and adults is not as strong (Beebe, Stern, & Jaffe, 1979; Condon & Sander, 1974). Beebe and Gerstman (1980) observed that rhythmic hand activities between mothers and their infants co-occurred with changes in other signs of the infant's involvement. Changes in rhythms seemed to be the key to changes in the infant's involvement.

Infants also use their gaze to regulate social stimulation probably because it is the sole means for escaping excessive stimulation or encouraging more stimulation (Als, Tronick, & Brazelton, 1979; Robson, 1967; Stern, 1971, 1977). Adults have a variety of other behavioral means for escaping or encouraging social interaction. Evidence for stimulation regulation through gaze is quite extensive (Blehar, Lieberman, & Ainsworth, 1977; DeBoer & Boxer, 1979; Field, 1977; Fogel, 1977; Stern, 1974). For example, Fogel (1977) made extensive observations of a single dyad. Significant associations between the infant's gaze at the mother and the mother's use of vocalization and exaggerated facial displays were obtained. The role of gaze aversion as a regulator was clearest when the infant was looking away, returning visual attention to the mother only after her facial displays and head nodding ceased, even though these were the actions that had maintained the infant's gaze earlier.

Other evidence of synchrony in involvement levels has been obtained by Als et al. (1979), Brazelton, Tronick, Adamson, Als, and Wise (1975), and Thomas and Martin (1976). These studies have shown that dyads go through periods of high and low involvement that are correlated between the partners over time. When adults are prodded to act unresponsively, infants characteristically intensify their own actions to obtain a response (Brazelton et al., 1975; Tronick, Als, Adamson, & Wise, 1978). Even infants in their first weeks of life exhibit early signs of the synchrony of behavior that is characteristic of and a necessity for well-regulated interaction (Chappell & Sander, 1979; Karger, 1979).

As infants develop their linguistic skills, the skill of matching those vocalizations characteristic of speech develops accordingly. Street, Street, and Van Kleeck (1983) found that children identified as more verbally reticent than their peers showed less convergence on speech rate, latency, and utterance length than their verbally more active counterparts. Welkowitz et al. (1976) observed that their 6½ to 7-year-olds converged more on speech latency than did the 5½ to 6-year-olds, although both converged significantly. Street (1983), using time-series statistical techniques, concluded that 5-year-olds converged more than 4-year-olds, who converged more than 3-year-olds on vocal behaviors such as speech rate, latency, vocalizations, and pauses. Clear developmental trends emerged as children acquired speech and language ability. With cognitive, social, and linguistic development came the ability to influence and be influenced by one's conversational partner.

Taken together, I find the evidence on mutual influence between infants (and children) and their adult partners rather remarkable. It is certainly suggestive of the centrality of mutual influence to the life of the organism. Although it is always dangerous to consider the question of nature and nurture in the development of social skills, the very early occurrence of interaction patterns analogous to mutual influence in adults leads to the difficult but exciting question of whether such processes are wired into the organism.

But these early signs of mutual influence may be ephemeral signs of genetic endowment. Perhaps the necessity to coordinate behaviors between infants and their mothers so early in social life leads to the intense practice and subsequent learning that etch these patterns into the infant's behavior as if they were part of his or her biological endowment. Infants are certainly not born with the social competencies necessary to coordinate their activities with their primary caretakers. Rather, social competencies are more likely to be the by-product of cognitive processes that *are* a part of the genetic endowment (Sroufe & Waters, 1976; Stechler & Carpenter, 1967; Stern, 1974). The link between cognitive development and social interactional development (Kagan, 1971; Zelazo, 1972; Zelazo, Kagan, & Hartman, 1975) offers a promising account of the coordination between infants and their primary caretakers (Cappella & Greene, 1982).

THEORIES OF CONVERSATIONAL MANAGEMENT

Until recently theorists have been content to offer explanations of very small domains of social interaction and mutual influence. For example, Argyle and Dean (1965) initially sought to explain why distance and eye gaze have a negative or compensatory association. This explanation was applied to other affiliative behaviors with varying success. Theorists are now recognizing that mutual influence in social interaction occurs for a wide variety of behaviors, occurs very early in the social development of children, and for these reasons requires a broad-ranging account that is based on sound psychological and communication theory. A number of competing accounts have been put forward in the last several years: drive explanations (Argyle & Dean, 1965; Firestone, 1977; Knowles, 1980; Markus-Kaplan & Kaplan, 1983), arousal-mediated explanations (Burgoon, 1978; Burgoon & Jones, 1976; Cappella & Greene, 1982; Patterson, 1976, 1982a), and cognitive explanations (Giles & Powesland, 1975; Street & Giles, 1982). All of these explanations have omitted from their focus the nature of turn-taking. Duncan and Fiske (1977) have offered an explanation in terms of social norms and Cappella (in press) has countered with an account that gives preeminence to cognitive load factors. These latter two will not be discussed here because of their specificity.

In evaluating explanations of mutual influence several factors must be kept in mind. First, the phenomenon is very general, encompassing a wide variety of behavior and a broad spectrum of developmental stages. A successful theory will be one that is encompassing without being vacuous in its generality. After all, the definition of mutual influence (if one ignores the behaviors to which the mutuality refers) encompasses every form of social interaction. A theory of social interaction is not desirable. Rather, a successful theory will encompass mutual influence on those behaviors that fall into the domain of associative or control functions of social interaction. Second, a successful account will be capable of explaining the consistent findings of reciprocity and compensation, matching and mismatching in mutual influence. That is, most reviews of individual behaviors find that even when there is a strong rule for a given response pattern (for example, compensation to increases in proximity), some conditions exist that attenuate and even reverse that rule. A successful theory will incorporate such conditions in such a way as to easily reverse the predicted relationship. Explanations cannot offer one account for reciprocity and another account for compensation. Third, explanations must participate in accepted and extant theories of behavior. Mutual influence is not some new or unique domain of behavioral influence but rather is a fundamental type of behavioral contingency. Explanations of it ought to be just as fundamental and common. Finally, successful explanations must not confuse long-term relational development with the mutual influence decisions that occur on a momentary basis in conversation. For example, Altman and Taylor (1973) indicate that disclosure reciprocity and increased depth of disclosure occur slowly over the course of relational development. That is an important and interesting finding that needs explanation in its own right but should not be inadvertantly included as a fact of conversational management.

A few explanations that have been put forward to explain mutual influence for a particular subset of behaviors should be dismissed immediately. Webb's (1972) explanation of speech matching in terms of stimulus tracking, Natale's (1975) explanation of loudness matching in terms of a particular type of communication theory, and Matarazzo and Wiens's (1972) explanation of speech matching in terms of reinforcement are not useful accounts. Although they are reasonably successful in their own restricted domains, they have not generalized to other behaviors nor are they suitable for explaining compensation and mismatching.

The three classes of explanations that are capable of explaining both reciprocity and compensation findings are the drive theories, the arousal-based explanations, and the cognitive explanations listed above. I will not attempt to describe the minute differences among each version of each type but rather will try to describe the generic characteristics of each class of explanation. The drive-based theories are all derived from Argyle and Dean's (1965) approach-avoidance explanation of compensation in verbal and nonverbal affiliative behaviors. Their explanation in turn uses Miller's (1959) approach-avoidance conflict theory developed primarily from the study of maze running by rats under various conditions of hunger and potential shock. Argyle and Dean argue that people simultaneously experience forces driving them toward affiliation with others and avoidance of and autonomy from others. Reasoning that at some points the drive toward approach would balance the drive to avoid, an equilibrium would be established. Deviations from this equilibrium by the other person would produce reactions to reintroduce the equilibrium by withdrawing whenever approach was too intimate, hence, compensation occurs.

The variations on this theory have made it more powerful in its range of coverage and more plausible in the application of Miller's initial theory (Argyle & Cook, 1976; Firestone, 1977; Knowles, 1980; Markus-Kaplan & Kaplan, 1983). All of the modifications rework the basic assumptions of the approach-avoidance gradients, although the most careful and well-reasoned is that of Knowles. Knowles cogently argues that Miller's assumptions that approach and avoidance forces increase as one approaches the goals are inapplicable to interpersonal phenomena. Although sensible with respect to possession of fixed items such as a food pellet (which is either possessed or not), the possession of interpersonal intimacy is achieved in part as one approaches the goal. Knowles suggests that approach-avoidance theory be modified so that approach and avoidance gradients decrease as nearness to the goal increases. Despite these well-reasoned modifications, predictions of reciprocity versus compensation are still based on the relative strengths of the approach and avoidance forces. When approach is greater than avoidance, reciprocity obtains. When avoidance is greater than approach, compensation obtains.

My objection to all the drive explanations is that they posit a mediating mechanism that is untestable. The only direct evidence that one can obtain about approach and avoidance forces is found in the behaviors that are themselves the objects of explanation for the theory. For example, lean, touch, proximity, and latency to respond are all possible indices of approach and avoidance. But these same behaviors are the affiliative behaviors that the theory is designed to explain. Although the drive theories are plausible, they are not satisfying.

The cognitively based theories of Giles and his colleagues (Giles & Powesland, 1975; Giles & Smith, 1979; Street & Giles, 1982) were developed to account for research on speech and linguistic convergence and divergence, and not the broader array of nonverbal behaviors. The situations that this theory, speech accommodation theory, sought to explain were cases of language choice, dialect and pronunciation shifts, and the slowing and speeding up of speech rate. Early versions of this theory had conversationalists making rather deliberate choices in their speech styles in order to appear more similar or more different from their partners, thereby increasing attraction, cohesion, and communication efficiency on the one hand, or maintaining group identity and group autonomy at the cost of communicational efficiency on the other hand. In a recent update of the theory Street and Giles (1982) maintain that people will converge

> towards the speech patterns believed to be characteristic of their recipients when they (a) desire their social approval and the perceived costs of so acting are proportionally lower than the rewards anticipated; and/or (b) desire a high level of communicational efficiency, and (c) social norms are not perceived to dictate alternative speech strategies. [People diverge] from those believed characteristics of their recipients when they (a) define the encounter in intergroup terms and desire a positive ingroup identity or (b) wish to bring another's speech behaviors to a personally acceptable level. (pp. 213-214)

Despite the very deliberate language of speech accommodation theory, Street and Giles (1982) claim that the procedures of convergence and divergence are quite automatic, calling the necessary procedural information from memory with the proper cues. My evaluation of this theory is based upon two observations. First, the theory does a good job of explaining the linguistic convergence and divergence for which it was initially intended but not, for example, the findings of speech rate and latency convergence in children or adults for which the theory also seems relevant. In short it works well in situations in which individuals are making relatively deliberate choices but not so well in situations in which individuals are making relatively automatic reactions. Second, even if Street and Giles are correct in stating that individual responses are automatic, being based upon procedural knowledge, the mere invocation of automatic procedures does not explain how the procedures got into memory, why they have one procedural content rather than another (for example, reciprocating for efficiency), or how procedural knowledge translates into action.

The third class of theories is arousal mediated (Burgoon, 1978; Burgoon & Jones, 1976; Cappella & Greene, 1982; Patterson, 1976, 1982a). These theories have much in common. All of them assume that behavior that violates expectations or at least is a deviation from an established baseline (Patterson, 1976) can produce arousal. The evidence for this claim is quite strong (Cappella, 1983; Patterson, 1976). The nature of the arousal is assumed to be some kind of cognitive activation (Duffy, 1962) that can result in physiological arousal (heart rate, blood pressure, electroencephalogram, galvanic skin response, and so forth). At this point the models part company.

Patterson's earlier model and Burgoon's model both assume that the arousal engendered by a deviation from expected behaviors will be reacted to differently depending on how the arousal is labeled (Patterson, 1976) or on the reward characteristics of the actor (Burgoon, 1978). When labeling is positive, the reaction is expected to be reciprocal and when negative, the reaction is expected to be compensatory. In a recent update of the Burgoon model (Hale & Burgoon, 1984), the reward value of the actor and the degree of immediacy (above and below expectations) are assumed to interact such that for punishing actors an inverted U relationship is expected, whereas for a rewarding actor a U-shaped relationship is expected. For both models a mediating characteristic of the situation, the person, or the relationship affects how the nonverbal or verbal behavior will be responded to.

Patterson's (1982a) newer version invites us to consider a much more comprehensive approach to mutual influence processes. As before, unusual levels of behavior attract attention, possible arousal, and a definite meaning analysis. Reactions to the deviant behavior and the instability it creates can take the form of a reassessment of the goals of the interaction, a cognitive-affective reassessment of the actor, and/or a behavioral readjustment along the lines of a compensatory or reciprocal response. This account is more equivocal than the earlier arousal-labeling model and is designed as a comprehensive paradigm from which a wide variety of behavioral, cognitive, and affective adjustments in conversational settings can be studied.

Cappella and Greene (1982) assume that the degree of arousal change determines the nature of the response to deviation from expectation. Under moderate to small amounts of arousal change reciprocal reactions are expected, whereas under large amounts of arousal change compensatory reactions are expected. The role of factors such as labeling, reward value of actors, and relationship factors is loaded into the setting of expectation levels and into the size of acceptance regions that mark how much arousal change is too much. The same kinds of relational and situational factors are included as potential mediators of interaction but they are placed in a causally prior position to arousal change, which does all of the work in the model.

The arousal change explanations offer one distinct advantage over competitors like the drive explanations: The mediating mechanism that they pose is testable independently of the behaviors that are being explained. The technology for measuring levels of arousal exists and can offer clear-cut tests of the proposed mediating mechanisms. Other theories may be equally capable of explaining the empirical facts of mutual influence processes, but I do not see how social scientists will be able to evaluate the psychological reality of those explanations. The reader may argue that my objections are based upon a view of theory that is excessively realist, but when one faces eight competing explanations, each seemingly successful at accounting for the facts, realism appears preferable to instrumentalism.

The theories above are too new. No unequivocal comparative test of these competing explanations, or any subset of them, has yet been conducted. Authors have been content to interpret existing data in the framework of their own explanatory paradigms. Most such ventures have been successful because each of the successful explanations recognizes that there must be a flexible means of accounting for reciprocity and compensation under a variety of situational conditions. In the drive theories this flexibility is achieved by the relative steepness of approach and avoidance forces under different conditions. In the cognitive theories situational factors and reward factors are presumed to intervene. In the labeling and reward theories the nature of the labeling and the quality of the reward permit a variety of situations to switch the direction of effects. In discrepancy-arousal theory the relative size of the acceptance regions and the location of the expectation levels can be altered with changing situational, personal, and dispositional factors.

Whichever explanatory system is ultimately successful in accounting for mutual influence processes in conversation, I believe that it will have certain characteristics that can be identified now. Context effects cannot be ignored. The verbal, nonverbal, and vocal behaviors that we have been discussing are noticed and attended to when they are unusual relative to some expected baseline (Cappella, 1983). That expectation level must be built into any successful theory. The evidence that certain verbal, vocal, and kinesic behaviors produce various forms of arousal is too great not to insure some place for arousal in a theory of mutual influence. Its place may not be as important as that hypothesized by discrepancy-arousal theory (Cappella & Greene, 1982), but arousal reactions as mediators cannot be ignored. Future theories must also take into account both the dynamic and fixed factors that influence affective reactions to the other person. For example, most theories assume that once the attraction is fixed at the outset of an experiment (usually with some type of compatibility manipulation) it remains fixed throughout. However, interactants may be more sophisticated than that, dynamically adjusting affective reactions toward the other on the basis of initial levels, plus behavioral actions, plus actions relative to initial levels (for example, initially disagreeing but later finding the disagreement to be modest rather than severe when the partner is acting in a verbally affiliative manner). Finally, theories have not yet given serious attention to the production of responses except to make simple assumptions such that behavior follows affective state (but see Patterson, 1982a). Coherent theories of mutual influence will offer explanations in which production mechanisms are integral parts rather than mere appendages.

THE PRAGMATICS OF MUTUAL INFLUENCE

Mutual influence processes in verbal, vocal, and kinesic behaviors are a fascinating set of phenomena at the heart of the definition of social interaction in general and conversation in particular. But the study of these processes must have implications beyond themselves if mutual influence is to be seen as something more than a mere academic excursion, undertaken only because the journey is interesting and not because the destination is valuable. In short, mutual influence processes must be related to important and significant outcomes if their laborious study is to be meaningful.

The relationship to be explored in this section is between mutual influence *patterns* and their outcomes, not between mean, typical, or average behaviors and outcomes (Cappella, 1984). The study of the associations between individual behaviors and outcomes such as attraction, satisfaction, perceptions of dominance, potency, and the like is actually the study of the interpersonal functions of these behaviors that has been advocated elsewhere (Cappella & Street, 1985). The study of the association between mutual influence patterns and outcomes is much more subtle and indeed difficult. Such studies would ask whether different interaction patterns covary with outcomes. For example, are dyads who exhibit strong patterns of reciprocity more attracted and satisfied with one another than dyads who exhibit compensatory patterns? In order to answer such questions, mutual influence patterns must be described and outcomes assessed, a time-consuming and costly research enterprise.

Let us first focus on one side of mutual influence: convergence, reciprocity, and matching. As individuals adapt their verbal, vocal, and kinesic behaviors to those expressed by others, we might expect positive outcomes to obtain as a result of increased similarity of behavioral expression (Byrne, 1971), the perception of interactional responsiveness (Davis & Martin, 1978; Davis & Perkowitz, 1979), or more efficient communication (Street & Giles, 1982). A variety of research supports this proposition. Street (1982) constructed audiotapes of interviews in which the interviewee converged, diverged, or partially converged to the speech rate, latency, and duration of the interviewer. Judges evaluated the diverging interviewee more negatively than the others. These findings have been replicated in differing contexts primarily with speech rate (Putman & Street, in press; Street & Brady, 1982; Street, Brady, & Putman, 1983). Welkowitz and Kuc (1973) found that dyadic partners who were rated as higher on warmth showed greater similarity on speech latency than those rated lower in warmth. Giles and Smith (1979) constructed audiotapes in which there was or was not convergence on three behaviors: speech rate, content, and pronunciation. Judges evaluated the person who showed speech rate convergence as more likable, more willing to cooperate, more effective, and more accommodative. The other two converging behaviors produced no strong results in judges' perceptions. A few other studies also support the speech accommodation-outcome relationship (Feldman, 1968; Harris & Baudin, 1973). Aside from the research by Planalp and Tracy (1980) on topical shifts and ratings of incompetence and research by LaFrance (1979) on positional congruence and rapport, very little research has assessed the relationship of other verbal, vocal, and kinesic patterns on outcomes.

In more general terms Warner (1979) has speculated that individuals must adjust their baseline behavioral tempos to those of their partners if there is to be a smooth flowing interaction. She maintains that noncomplementary tempos will make interactions awkward and stressful (Chapple, 1970) and lead to less interpersonal attraction. These speculations merit attention, but I believe that symmetrical tempos are necessary over the duration of interactions, for otherwise, over several interactional turns, one partner will be animated while the other is lethargic in the same period. I doubt that such patterns will be interpersonally attractive. Research by Davis (Davis & Martin, 1978; Davis & Perkowitz, 1979) has been directed at the importance of responsiveness (certainly the defining characteristic of mutual influence) in interpersonal perception. In Davis's earlier study the percentage of responsiveness independent of frequency of response was positively related to attraction. In the later study the number of pleasurable shocks given depended upon how responsive the recipient was and the level of appropriateness of the response. Excessively responsive actions actually reduced the number of pleasant shocks administered.

Although the evidence is certainly not overwhelming or broad enough in behaviors to warrant a strong claim, it is suggestive. Convergence, reciprocity, and similarity in behavioral expression tend to produce positive evaluation. The research has generally avoided studying the perceptions of participants in favor of studying the reactions of judges and has tended to study staged convergence rather than actual convergence. As we become more assured that mutual influence patterns are associated with outcomes, unstaged convergence and participant responses will need study.

The other side of mutual influence that cannot be ignored is compensation, divergence, and mismatching. Interpersonal and intergroup situations (Bourhis, 1985) can arise in which the maintenance or increase of distance and separation from an obnoxious, intrusive, or aggressive other necessitates verbal, vocal, and kinesic distancing. Similarly, the protection of personal autonomy, personal freedom, ingroup identity, or group distinctiveness might require compensatory, diverging, and mismatched responses. Bourhis (1985; see Genesee & Bourhis, 1982) has been investigating this process in the intergroup setting with language choice in Quebec. His findings are complex but include the result that the evaluation of convergence and divergence in language choice depends upon the role relationship between the interactants and the group affiliation of the judges. Compensatory reactions may be just as socially competent and psychologically necessary as reciprocal responses, the point being that the ability to be responsive is the necessary condition for competence.

Three other speculations will complete our discussion of the importance of conversational management. The ability to exert even modest influence over the expressed behavior of another person raises some interesting possibilities. If one person's expressed involvement produces an increase in another's expressed involvement (as would be expected in conversational tempo), then initially low levels of psychological involvement might be modified as the unexcited partner observes that he or she is acting in an involved and excited manner and assumes by self-perception (Bem, 1972) that he or she is actually involved in the topic or situation. Thus by influencing another's expressed behavior, one might be able to actually influence the underlying attitude. I know of no study that puts this suggestion to the test, but it would certainly be meritorious as an hypothesis. The viability of this hypothesis depends upon just how influenceable another's overt behavior is. Typically, a person is much more consistent than responsive to the other (Cappella, 1984).

Second and less speculative is the use of asymmetric indices of mutual influence to study influence, dominance, and power patterns in continuing relationships, as Gottman (1979b) has done. The definition of mutual influence given earlier is bivariate: one measure of influence from person A to B and one in the other direction. Asymmetries in these measures or perhaps lack of asymmetries may provide leads into relational satisfactions and dissatisfactions as suggested by Watzlawick et al. (1967).

Finally, the capacity to exhibit mutual influence over the course of a conversation, in a wide variety of situations and with a cross section of persons, requires a sophisticated, complex, and fine-tuned set of cognitive, perceptual, social, and linguistic abilities. By contrast, the inability or unwillingness to exhibit the responsiveness characteristic of mutual influence processes might signify trouble. The nature of such trouble might be found in relationship problems and dissatisfactions when the lack of responsiveness is due to unwillingness. For example, Noller (1980) found that patterns of gaze reciprocity distinguished satisfied and less satisfied couples, with greater gaze reciprocity characteristic of the more satisfied pairs. When the lack of responsiveness is due to inability, then mutual influence indices might signify cognitive, linguistic, social, or perceptual deficits. Bruner (1975, 1977) has argued that the development of linguistic abilities may depend upon patterns of early infant-mother interaction. Condon (1976) maintains that the absence of movement synchrony might separate autistic from normally developing children. Higginbotham and Yoder (1982) have argued that interaction inabilities may indicate various types of communicative disorders. Feldstein, Konstantareas, Oxman, and Webster (1982) observed that speech reciprocity occurred between counselor and parents of autistic children but not between the child and the counselor or the child and the parent. Street, Lucas-Arwood, and Cappella (1983) have suggested that the development of speech convergence in rate, latency, and within-turn pauses may signify normal development of linguistic, cognitive, perceptual, and social skills. Nonnormal development of convergence may signify deficits or slow development requiring clinical attention. Although many of these notions are speculative, they offer some important hypotheses about the indicative function that mutual influence parameters might serve.

CONCLUSION

Conversational management is based upon a definition fundamental to the meaning of interaction, namely that the overt behavior of each influences the overt behavior of the other. The research that has been reviewed here offers what I believe to be a strong empirical case for the existence and centrality of mutual influence processes. The centrality of mutual influence is demonstrated in three ways. First, the rudiments of conversational management occur early in the social lives of infants, children, and their primary caretakers. These early patterns may signify certain biological predispositions toward interactional contingency that are the basis for adult patterns of mutual influence. Second, mutual influence is observed in a wide variety of behaviors from the very deliberate linguistic and verbal ones to the relatively automatic kinesic and vocal behaviors. People are sensitive to the displays of others whether they are aware of their reactions to the other's displays or not. Further, these influences exhibit some strong regularities in reciprocity and compensation even though these regularities are sensitive to changes in the situation and relationship between the partners. Third, certain patterns of mutual influence are associated with positive interpersonal evaluations over and above the evaluations due to the behaviors alone. That is, how a person *reacts* to another carries information that is comparable to the information carried by how the person *acts*. These findings are all the more remarkable when one recognizes that the size of mutual influence effects relative to the stability in individual verbal, vocal, and kinesic behavior is very small (Cappella, 1984).

Future studies of mutual influence processes represent a wide open domain. Such studies must mine the verbal component of interaction with coding systems that are well-established and of utility to a broad cross-section of researchers. Too little research has been done on gestural and body synchrony to know if these behaviors exhibit the convergence and divergence of other types of behavior. Researchers must be willing to invest the time and energy to code a variety of dependent measures so that failures with a particular behavior are not due to constraints of the situation or to individual predilections away from a particular behavioral outlet. Finally, we must all be sensitive to the social needs of our subject populations. The study of mutual influence is interesting in its own right, but unless these processes can be tied to utilitarian outcomes such as improvements in the social competence of troubled or even impaired persons, our efforts will be seen rightly or wrongly as without social benefit. That accusation would be unfair and unjust, but is also unnecessary.

REFERENCES

Aboud, F. E. (1976). Social development aspects of language. *Papers in Linguistics, 9,* 15-37.

Aiello, J. R. (1972). A test of equilibrium theory: Visual interaction in relation to orientation, distance, and sex of the interactants. *Psychonomic Science, 27,* 335-336.

Aiello, J. R. (1973). Male and female behavior as a function of distance and duration of an interviewer's directed gaze: Equilibrium theory revisited (Doctoral dissertation, Michigan State University, 1973). *Dissertation Abstracts International, 33,* 4482B-4483B.

Aiello, J. R. (1977). A further look at equilibrium theory: Visual interaction as a function of interpersonal distance. *Environmental Psychology and Nonverbal Behavior, 1,* 122-139.

Allison, P. D., & Liker, J. K. (1982). Analyzing sequential categorical data on dyadic interaction: A comment on Gottman. *Psychological Bulletin, 91,* 393-403.

Als, H., Tronick, E., & Brazelton, T. B. (1979). Analysis of face-to-face interaction in infant-adult dyads. In M. E. Lamb, S. J. Suomi, & G. R. Stephenson (Eds.), *Social interaction analysis* (pp. 33-76). Madison: University of Wisconsin Press.

Altman, I., & Taylor, D. A. (1973). *Social penetration.* New York: Holt, Rinehart & Winston.

Anderson, B. J., Vietze, P., & Dokecki, P. R. (1977). Reciprocity in vocal interaction of mothers and infants. *Child Development, 48,* 1676-1681.

Anderson, D. R. (1976). Eye contact, topic intimacy, and equilibrium theory. *Journal of Social Psychology, 100,* 313-314.

Archer, R. L., & Berg, J. H. (1978). Disclosure reciprocity and its limits: A reactance analysis. *Journal of Experimental Social Psychology, 14,* 527-540.

Argyle, M., & Cook, M. (1976). *Gaze and mutual gaze.* London: Cambridge University Press.

Argyle, M., & Dean, J. (1965). Eye contact, distance and affiliation. *Sociometry, 28,* 289-304.

Ashby, W. R. (1963). *An introduction to cybernetics.* New York: Science Editions.

Bateson, M. C. (1975). Mother-infant exchanges: The epigenesis of conversational interaction. *Annals of the New York Academy of Sciences, 5,* 238-250.

Baxter, J. C., & Rozelle, R. M. (1975). Nonverbal expressiveness as a function of crowding during a simulated police-citizen encounter. *Journal of Personality and Social Psychology 32,* 40-54.

Beattie, G. W. (1978). Floor apportionment and gaze in conversational dyads. *British Journal of Social and Clinical Psychology, 17,* 7-15.

Beattie, G. W. (1979a). Contextual constraints on the floor-apportionment function of gaze in dyadic conversation. *British Journal of Social and Clinical Psychology, 17,* 7, 15.

Beattie, G. W. (1979b). Sequential temporal patterns of speech and gaze in dialogue. *Semiotica, 23*, 29-57.

Becker, F. D., & Mayo, C. (1971). Delineating personal distance and territoriality. *Environment and Behavior, 3*, 375-381.

Beebe, B. (in press). Mother-infant mutual influence and precursors of self and object representations. In J. Masling (Ed.), *Empirical studies of psychoanalytical theories* (Vol. 2). Hillsdale, NJ: Lawrence Erlbaum.

Beebe, B., & Gerstman, L. (1980). The "packaging" of maternal stimulation in relation to infant facial-visual engagement. *Merrill-Palmer Quarterly, 26*, 321-329.

Beebe, B., & Gerstman, L. (1982). *Significance of infant-stranger mutual influence.* Paper presented at the meeting of the Society for Research in Child Development, Austin, TX.

Beebe, B., Stern, D., & Jaffe, J. (1979). The kinesic rhythm of mother-infant interactions. In A. W. Siegman & S. Feldstein (Eds.), *Of speech and time* (pp. 23-34). Hillsdale, NJ: Lawrence Erlbaum.

Bem, D. J. (1972). Self-perception theory. In L. Berkowitz (Ed.), *Advances in experimental social psychology* (Vol. 6, pp. 1-62). New York: Academic Press.

Bernstein, B. (1962). Social class, linguistic codes, and grammatical elements. *Language and Speech, 5*, 221-240.

Black, J. W. (1949a). The intensity of oral responses to stimulus words. *Journal of Speech and Hearing Disorders, 14*, 16-22.

Black, J. W. (1949b). Loudness of speaking: The effect of heard stimuli on spoken responses. *Journal of Experimental Psychology, 39*, 311-315.

Blehar, C. M., Lieberman, A. F., & Ainsworth, M.D.S. (1977). Early face-to-face interaction and its relation to later infant-mother attachment. *Child Development, 48*, 182-194.

Bloom, K. (1975). Social elicitation of infant vocal behavior. *Journal of Experimental Child Psychology, 20*, 51-58.

Bourhis, R. Y. (1979). Language in ethnic interaction: A social psychological approach. In H. Giles & B. St. Jacques (Eds.), *Language and ethnic relations* (pp. 119-136). Oxford: Pergamon.

Bourhis, R. Y. (1985). The sequential nature of language choice in cross-cultural communication. In R. L. Street & J. N. Cappella (Eds.), *Sequence and pattern in communicative behaviour* (pp. 120-141). London: Arnold.

Bourhis, R. Y., & Giles, H. (1977). The language of intergroup distinctiveness. In H. Giles (Ed.), *Language, ethnicity, and intergroup relations* (pp. 119-136). London: Academic Press.

Bourhis, R. Y., Giles, H., & Lambert, W. E. (1975). Social consequences of accommodating one's style of speech: A cross-national investigation. *International Journal of the Sociology of Language, 6*, 53-71.

Bourhis, R. Y., Giles, H., Leyens, J. P., & Tajfel, H. (1979). Psycholinguistic distinctiveness: Language divergence in Belgium. In H. Giles & R. St. Clair (Eds.), *Language and social psychology* (pp. 158-185). Oxford: Blackwell.

Brazelton, T. B., Tronick, E., Adamson, L., Als, H., & Wise, S. (1975). Early mother-infant reciprocity. *Parent-infant interaction: Ciba foundation symposium 33* (pp. 137-148). Amsterdam: Association of Scientific Publishers.

Breed, G. (1972). The effect of intimacy: Reciprocity or retreat? *British Journal of Social and Clinical Psychology, 11*, 135-142.

Brewer, M. B., & Mittleman, J. (1980). Effects of normative control of self-disclosure on reciprocity. *Journal of Personality, 48*, 89-102.

Bruner, J. S. (1975). From communication to language—A psychological perspective. *Cognition, 3*, 255-287.

Bruner, L. J. (1977). Early social interaction and language acquisition. In H. R. Schaffer (Ed.), *Mother-infact interaction.* New York: Academic Press.

Buck, R. (1979). Measuring individual differences in the nonverbal communication of affect: The slide viewing paradigm. *Human Communication Research, 6*, 47-57.

Burgoon, J. K. (1978). A communication model of personal space violations: Explication and initial test. *Human Communication Research, 4*, 129-142.

Burgoon, J. K., & Jones, S. B. (1976). Toward a theory of personal space expectations and their violations. *Human Communication Research, 2*, 131-146.

Butterworth, B., & Goldman-Eisler, F. (1979). Recent studies on cognitive rhythm. In A. W. Siegman & S. Feldstein (Eds.), *Of speech and time* (pp. 211-224). Hillsdale, NJ: Lawrence Erlbaum.

Byrne, D. A. (1971). *The attraction paradigm.* New York: Academic Press.

Cappella, J. N. (1980). Structural equation modeling: An introduction. In P. R. Monge & J. N. Cappella (Eds.), *Multivariate techniques in human communication research* (pp. 57-109). New York: Academic Press.

Cappella, J. N. (1981). Mutual influence in expressive behavior: Adult-adult and infant-adult dyadic interaction. *Psychological Bulletin, 89,* 101-132.

Cappella, J. N. (1983). Conversational involvement: Approaching and avoiding others. In J. M. Wiemann & R. P. Harrison (Eds.), *Nonverbal interaction* (pp. 113-152). Beverly Hills, CA: Sage.

Cappella, J. N. (1984). The relevance of the microstructure of interaction to relationship change. *Journal of Social and Personal Relationships, 1,* 239-264.

Cappella, J. N. (in press). Controlling the floor in conversation. In A. W. Siegman & S. Feldstein (Eds.), *Nonverbal communication.* Hillsdale, NJ: Lawrence Erlbaum.

Cappella, J. N., & Greene, J. O. (1982). A discrepancy-arousal explanation of mutual influence in expressive behavior for adult-adult and infant-adult interaction. *Communication Monographs, 49,* 89-114.

Cappella, J. N., & Planalp, S. (1981). Talk and silence sequences in informal conversations. III: Interspeaker influence. *Human Communication Research, 7,* 117-132.

Cappella, J. N., & Street, R. L. (1985). A functional approach to the structure of communicative behavior. In R. L. Street & J. N. Cappella (Eds.), *Sequence and pattern in communicative behaviour* (pp. 1-29). London: Edward Arnold.

Carr, S. J., & Dabbs, J. M. (1974). The effect of lighting, distance, and intimacy of topic on verbal and visual behavior. *Sociometry, 37,* 592-600.

Cegala, D. J., Alexander, A. F., & Sokuvitz, S. (1979). An investigation of eye gaze and its relation to selected verbal behavior. *Human Communication Research, 5,* 99-108.

Chappell, P. F., & Sander, L. W. (1979). Mutual regulation of the neonatal-maternal interactive process: Context for the origins of communication. In M. Bulowa (Ed.), *Before speech* (pp. 89-110). London: Cambridge University Press.

Chapple, E. D. (1970). *Culture and biological man: Explorations in behavioral anthropology.* New York: Holt, Rinehart & Winston.

Clark, H. H., & Haviland, S. E. (1977). Comprehension and the given-new contract. In R. O. Freedle (Ed.), *Discourse production and comprehension* (pp. 1-40). Norwood, NJ: Ablex.

Cody, M., & McLaughlin, M. L. (1985). Accounting sequences. In R. Street & J. N. Cappella (Eds.), *Sequence and pattern in communicative behaviour* (pp. 50-69). London: Edward Arnold.

Cody, M. L., Woelfel, J., & Jordan, W. J. (1983). Dimensions of compliance-gaining situations: A dimensional analysis. *Human Communication Research, 9,* 99-113.

Condon, W. S. (1976). An analysis of behavior organization. *Sign Language Studies, 13,* 285-318.

Condon, W. S., & Ogston, W. D. (1966). Sound film analysis of normal and pathological behavior patterns. *Journal of Nervous and Mental Disease, 28,* 305-315.

Condon, W. S., & Ogston, W. D. (1967). A segmentation of behavior. *Journal of Psychiatric Research, 5,* 221-235.

Condon, W. S., & Sander, L. W. (1974). Synchrony demonstrated between movement of the neonate and adult speech. *Child Development, 45,* 456-552.

Courtright, J., Millar, F. E., & Rogers-Millar, L. E. (1979). Domineeringness and dominance: Replication and expansion. *Communication Monographs, 46,* 179-192.

Coutts, L. M., Schneider, F. W., & Montgomery, S. (1980). An investigation of the arousal model of interpersonal intimacy. *Journal of Experimental Social Psychology, 16,* 545-561.

Cozby, P. C. (1972). Self-disclosure, reciprocity and liking. *Sociometry, 35,* 151-160.

Craig, R. T., & Tracy, K. (Eds.). (1983). *Conversational coherence.* Beverly Hills, CA: Sage.

Crow, B. K. (1983). Topic shifts in couples' conversations. In R. T. Craig & K. Tracy (Eds.), *Conversational coherence* (pp. 136-156). Beverly Hills, CA: Sage.

Dabbs, J. M. (1980). Temporal patterning of speech and gaze in social and intellectual conversations. In H. Giles (Ed.), *Language: Social psychological perspectives* (pp. 307-310). Oxford, England: Pergamon.

Dalto, C. A., Ajzen, I., & Kaplan, K. J. (1979). Self-disclosure and attraction: Effects of intimacy and desirability on beliefs and attitudes. *Journal of Research in Personality, 13,* 127-138.

Darby, B. W., & Schlenker, B. R. (1982). Children's reactions to apologies. *Journal of Personality and Social Psychology, 43,* 742-753.

Davis, J. D. (1976). Self-disclosure in an acquaintance exercise: Responsibility for level of intimacy. *Journal of Personality and Social Psychology, 33,* 787-792.

Davis, J. D. (1977). Effects of communication about interpersonal process on the evolution of self-disclosure in dyads. *Journal of Personality and Social Psychology, 35*, 31-37.

Davis, J. D. (1978). When boy meets girl: Sex roles and the negotiation of intimacy in an acquaintance exercise. *Journal of Personality and Social Psychology, 36*, 684-692.

Davis, D., & Martin, H. J. (1978). When pleasure begets pleasure: Recipient responsiveness as a determinant of physical pleasuring between heterosexual dating couples and strangers. *Journal of Personality and Social Psychology, 36*, 767-777.

Davis, D., & Perkowitz, W. T. (1979). Consequences of responsiveness in dyadic interaction: Effects of probability of response and proportion of content related responses on interpersonal attraction. *Journal of Personality and Social Psychology, 37*, 534-550.

DeBoer, M. M., & Boxer, A. M. (1979). Signal functions of infant facial expression and gaze direction during mother-infant face-to-face play. *Child Development, 50*, 1215-1218.

Derlega, V. J., Harris, M. S., & Chaikin, A. L. (1973). Self-disclosure, liking and the deviant. *Journal of Experimental Social Psychology, 9*, 277-284.

Dindia, K. (1982). Reciprocity of self-disclosure: A sequential analysis. In M. Burgoon (Ed.), *Communication yearbook 6* (pp. 506-530). New Brunswick, NJ: Transaction.

Dindia, K. (1985). A functional approach to self-disclosure. In R. L. Street & J. N. Cappella (Eds.), *Sequence and pattern in communicative behaviour* (pp. 142-160). London: Edward Arnold.

Dittmann, A. T. (1972). The body movement speech rhythm relationship as a cue to speech encoding. In A. W. Siegman & B. Pope (Eds.), *Studies in dyadic communication* (pp. 135-152). New York: Pergamon.

Dittmann, A. T., & Llewellyn, L. G. (1967). The phonemic clause as a unit of speech encoding. *Journal of Personality and Social Psychology, 6*, 341-349.

Dittmann, A. T., & Llewellyn, L. G. (1968). Relationship between vocalization and head nods as listener responses. *Journal of Personality and Social Psychology, 9*, 79-84.

Doise, W., Sinclair, A., & Bourhis, R. Y. (1976). Evaluation of accent convergence and divergence in competitive intergroup situations. *British Journal of Social and Clinical Psychology, 14*, 247-252.

Duffy, E. (1962). *Activation and behavior*. New York: John Wiley.

Duncan, S. (1972). Some signals and rules for taking turns in conversations. *Journal of Personality and Social Psychology, 23*, 283-292.

Duncan, S. (1973). Toward a grammar for dyadic conversations. *Semiotica, 9*, 29-46.

Duncan, S. (1974). On the structure of speaker-auditor interaction during speaking turns. *Language in Society, 2*, 161-180.

Duncan, S. (1983). Speaking turns: Studies of structures and individual differences. In J. Wiemann & R. P. Harrison (Eds.), *Nonverbal interaction* (pp. 149-178). Beverly Hills, CA: Sage.

Duncan, S., Bruner, L. J., & Fiske, D. W. (1979). Strategy signals in face-to-face interaction. *Journal of Personality and Social Psychology, 37*, 301-313.

Duncan, S., & Fiske, D. W. (1977). *Face-to-face interaction*. Hillsdale, NJ: Lawrence Erlbaum.

Duncan, S., & Niederehe, G. (1974). On signalling that it's your turn to speak. *Journal of Experimental and Social Psychology, 10*, 234-247.

Efran, M. G., & Cheyne, J. A. (1974). Affective concomitants of the invasion of shared space: Behavioral, physiological, and verbal indicators. *Journal of Personality and Social Psychology, 29*, 219-226.

Ellis, D. E. (1979). Relational control in two group systems. *Communication Monographs, 46*, 153-166.

Ellis, D. G., & Fisher, B. A. (1975). Phases of conflict in small group development: A Markov analysis. *Human Communication Research, 1*, 195-212.

Ellsworth, P. P., & Carlsmith, J. M. (1968). The effects of eye contact and verbal content on affective response to dyadic interaction. *Journal of Personality and Social Psychology, 10*, 15-20.

Ericson, P., & Rogers, L. E. (1965). New procedures for analyzing relational communication. *Family Process, 12*, 245-267.

Exline, R. V., Gray, D., & Schuette, D. (1965). Visual behavior in a dyad as affected by interview content and sex of respondent. *Journal of Personality and Social Psychology, 1*, 201-209.

Farina, A., Allen, J. G., & Saul, B. B. (1968). The role of stigmatized social relationships. *Journal of Personality, 36*, 169-182.

Farina, A., Gliha, D., Boudreau, L. A., Allen, J. G., & Sherman, M. (1971). Mental illness and the impact of believing others know about it. *Journal of Abnormal Psychology, 77,* 1-5.

Feldman, R. E. (1968). Response to compatriots and foreigners who seek assistance. *Journal of Personality and Social Psychology, 10,* 202-214.

Feldstein, S., Konstantareas, M., Oxman, J., & Webster, C. D. (1982). The chronography of interaction with autistic speakers: An initial report. *Journal of Communicative Disorders, 15,* 451-460.

Field, T. M. (1977). Effects of early separation, interactive deficits, and experimental manipulations of infant-mother face-to-face interaction. *Child Development, 48,* 763-771.

Firestone, I. (1977). Reconciling verbal and nonverbal models of dyadic communication. *Environmental Psychology and Nonverbal Behavior, 2,* 30-44.

Fisher, B. A. (1979). Content and relationship dimensions of communication in decision-making groups. *Communication Quarterly, 27,* 3-11.

Fishman, J. A. (1966). *Language loyalty in the United States.* The Hague: Mouton.

Fogel, A. (1977). Temporal organization in mother-infant face-to-face interaction. In H. R. Schaffer (Ed.), *Studies in mother-infant interaction* (pp. 119-152). New York: Academic Press.

Folger, J. P., & Poole, M. S. (1982). Relational coding schemes: The question of validity. In M. Burgoon (Ed.), *Communication yearbook 5* (pp. 235-248). New Brunswick, NJ: Transaction.

Folger, J. P., & Sillars, A. (1980). Relational coding and perceptions of dominance. In B. W. Morse & L. A. Phelps (Eds.), *Interpersonal communication: A relational perspective* (pp. 322-333). Minneapolis: Burgess.

Gatewood, J. B., & Rosenwein, R. (1981). Interactional synchrony: Genuine or spurious? A critique of recent research. *Journal of Nonverbal Behavior, 6,* 12-29.

Genesee, R., & Bourhis, R. Y. (1982). The social psychological significance of code-switching in cross-cultural communication. *Journal of Language and Social Psychology, 1,* 1-27.

Gewirtz, J. L., & Boyd, E. F. (1976). Mother-infant interaction and its study. In H. W. Reese (Ed.), *Advances in child development and behavior* (Vol. 11, pp. 141-163). New York: Academic Press.

Gewirtz, J. L., & Boyd, E. F. (1977). Experiments on mother-infant interaction underlying mutual attachment acquisition: The infant conditions the mother. In T. Alloway, L. Krames, & P. Pliner (Eds.), *Attachment behavior: Advances in the study of communication and affect* (Vol. 3, pp. 109-144). New York: Plenum.

Giles, H. (1973). Accent mobility: A model and some data. *Anthropological Linguistics, 15,* 87-105.

Giles, H. (1977). Social psychology and applied linguistics: Towards an integrative approach. *ITL: Review of Applied Linguistics, 33,* 27-42.

Giles, H. (1979). Ethnicity markers in speech. In K. R. Scherer & H. Giles (Eds.), *Social markers in speech.* Cambridge: Cambridge University Press.

Giles, H. (1980). Accommodation theory: Some new directions. In S. deSilva (Ed.), *Aspects of linguistic behavior* (pp. 105-136). York: University of York Press.

Giles, H., & Powesland, P. F. (1975). *Speech style and social evaluation.* London: Academic Press.

Giles, H., & Smith, P. M. (1979). Accommodation theory: Optimal levels of convergence. In H. Giles & R. N. St. Clair (Eds.), *Language and social psychology* (pp. 45-65). Oxford: Blackwell.

Giles, H., Taylor, D. M., & Bourhis, R. Y. (1973). Towards a theory of interpersonal accommodation through language: Some Canadian data. *Language in Society, 2,* 177-192.

Goodwin, C. (1981). *Conversational organization.* New York: Academic Press.

Gottman, J. M. (1979a). Detecting cyclicity in social interaction. *Psychological Bulletin, 86,* 338-348.

Gottman, J. M. (1979b). *Marital interaction.* New York: Academic Press.

Gottman, J. M., & Ringland, J. T. (1981). The analysis of dominance and bidirectionality in social development. *Child Development, 52,* 393-412.

Greenbaum, P., & Rosenfeld, H. M. (1978). Patterns of avoidance in response to interpersonal staring and proximity: Effects of bystanders on drivers at a traffic intersection. *Journal of Personality and Social Psychology, 36,* 575-587.

Greenberg, C. I., & Firestone, I. J. (1977). Compensatory responses to crowding: Effects of personal space intrusion and privacy reduction. *Journal of Personality and Social Psychology, 35,* 637-644.

Greene, J. O., & Cappella, J. N. (1984). *Cognition and talk: The relationship of semantic units to temporal patterns of fluency in spontaneous speech.* Unpublished paper, Department of Communication Arts and Sciences, University of Southern California.

Hale, J. L., & Burgoon, J. K. (1984). *Models of reactions to changes in nonverbal immediacy.* Unpublished manuscript, Department of Speech Communication, University of Arizona.

Harris, M. B., & Baudin, H. (1973). The language of altruism: The effects of language, dress, and ethnic group. *Journal of Social Psychology, 97,* 37-41.

Hawes, L. C. (1983). Conversational coherence. In R. T. Craig & K. Tracy (Eds.), *Conversational coherence* (pp. 285-298). Beverly Hills, CA: Sage.

Hawes, L. C., & Foley, J. M. (1973). A Markov analysis of interview communication. *Speech Monographs, 40,* 208-219.

Hewes, D. E. (1975). Finite stochastic modeling of communication processes. *Human Communication Research, 1,* 271-283.

Hewes, D. E. (1979). The sequential analysis of social interaction. *Quarterly Journal of Speech, 65,* 56-73.

Hewes, D. E. (1980). Stochastic modeling of communication processes. In P. R. Monge & J. N. Cappella (Eds.), *Multivariate techniques in human communication research* (pp. 393-427). New York: Academic Press.

Higginbotham, D. J., & Yoder, D. E. (1982). Communication within natural conversational interaction: Implications for severe communicatively impaired persons. *Topics in Language Disorders, 2,* 1-19.

Hill, C. T., & Stull, D. E. (1982). Disclosure reciprocity: Conceptual and measurement issues. *Social Psychology Quarterly, 45,* 238-245.

Hopper, R. (1983). Interpretation as coherence production. In R. T. Craig & K. Tracy (Eds.), *Conversational coherence* (pp. 81-98). Beverly Hills, CA: Sage.

Jaffe, J., & Feldstein, S. (1970). *Rhythms of dialogue.* New York: Academic Press.

Johnson, C. F., & Dabbs, J. M. (1976). Self-disclosure in dyads as a function of distance and subject-experimenter relationship. *Sociometry, 39,* 257-263.

Jourard, S. M. (1959). Self-disclosure and other cathexis. *Journal of Abnormal and Social Psychology, 59,* 428-431.

Jourard, S. M., & Friedman, R. (1970). Experimenter-subject "distance" and self-disclosure. *Journal of Personality and Social Psychology, 15,* 278-282.

Jourard, S. M., & Resnick, J. L. (1970). The effect of high revealing subjects on self-disclosure of low revealing subjects. *Journal of Humanistic Psychology, 10,* 84-93.

Kagan, J. (1971). *Change and continuity in infancy.* New York: John Wiley.

Kaplan, K. J., Firestone, I. J., Klein, K. W., & Sodikoff, C. (1983). Distancing in dyads: A comparison of four models. *Social Psychology Quarterly, 46,* 108-115.

Karger, R. H. (1979). Synchrony in mother-infant interactions. *Child Development, 50,* 882-885.

Kendon, A. (1967). Some functions of gaze direction in social interaction. *Acta Psychologica, 26,* 100-125.

Kleinke, C. L., Staneski, R. A., & Berger, D. E. (1975). Evaluation of an interviewer as a function of interviewer gaze, reinforcement of subject gaze, and interviewer attractiveness. *Journal of Personality and Social Psychology, 31,* 115-122.

Knowles, E. S. (1980). An affiliative conflict theory of personal and group spatial behavior. In P. B. Paulus (Ed.), *Psychology of group influence* (pp. 133-188). Hillsdale, NJ: Lawrence Erlbaum.

LaFrance, M. (1979). Nonverbal synchrony and rapport: Analysis by the cross-lag panel technique. *Social Psychology Quarterly, 42,* 66-70.

Lamb, M. E. (1977). A reexamination of the infant social world. *Human Development, 20,* 65-85.

Levin, F. M., & Gergen, K. J. (1969). Revealingness, ingratiation and the disclosure of the self. *Proceedings of the 77th Annual Convention of the American Psychological Association, 4,* 447-448.

Lewis, M. (1972). State as an infant-environment interaction: An evaluation of infant-mother interaction as a function of sex. *Merrill-Palmer Quarterly, 18,* 95-121.

Lewis, M., & Lee-Painter, S. (1974). An interactional approach to the mother-infant dyad. In M. Lewis & L. A. Rosenbaum (Eds.), *The effect of the infant on its caregiver* (pp. 21-48). New York: John Wiley.

Lieberman, P. (1966). *Intonation, perception, and language.* Cambridge, MA: MIT.

Manderscheid, R. W., Rae, D. S., McCarrick, A. K., & Silbergeld, S. (1982). A stochastic model of relational control in dyadic interaction. *American Sociological Review, 47*, 62-75.

Markus-Kaplan, M., & Kaplan, K. J. (1983). *Interpersonal distance: Conceptual development and integration.* Unpublished paper, Department of Psychology, Wayne State University.

Matarazzo, J. D., Weitman, M., Saslow, G., & Wiens, A. N. (1969). Interviewer influence on durations of interviewee speech. *Journal of Verbal Learning and Verbal Behavior, 1*, 451-458.

Matarazzo, J. D., & Wiens, A. N. (1967). Interviewer influence on durations of interviewee silence. *Journal of Experimental Research in Personality, 2*, 56-69.

Matarazzo, J. D., & Wiens, A. N. (1972). *The interview: Research on its anatomy and structure.* Chicago: Aldine.

Matarazzo, J. D., Wiens, A. N., Matarazzo, R. G., & Saslow, G. (1968). Speech and silence behavior in clinical psychotherapy and its laboratory correlates. In J. Schlien, H. Hunt, J. D. Matarazzo, & C. Savage (Eds.), *Research in psychotherapy* (Vol. 3, pp. 347-394). Washington, DC: American Psychological Association.

McCleary, R., & Hay, R. A. (1980). *Applied time series analysis for the social sciences.* Beverly Hills, CA: Sage.

McDowall, J. J. (1978a). Interactional synchrony: A reappraisal. *Journal of Personality and Social Psychology, 36*, 963-975.

McDowall, J. J. (1978b). Microanalysis of filmed movement: The reliability of boundary detection by observers. *Environmental Psychology and Nonverbal Behavior, 3*, 77-88.

McLaughlin, M. L., & Cody, M. J. (1982). Awkward silences: Antecedents and consequences of the conversational lapse. *Human Communication Research, 8*, 299-316.

McLaughlin, M. L., Cody, M. J., Kane, M. L., & Robey, C. S. (1981). Sex differences in story receipt and story sequencing behaviors in dyadic conversations. *Human Communication Research, 7*, 99-116.

McLaughlin, M. L., Cody, M. J., & O'Hair, H. D. (1983). The management of failure events: Some contextual determinants of accounting behavior. *Human Communication Research, 9*, 208-224.

McLaughlin, M. L., Cody, M. J., & Rosenstein, N. E. (1983). Account sequences in conversations between strangers. *Communication Monographs, 50*, 102-125.

Meltzer, L., Morris, W., & Hayes, D. (1971). Interruption outcomes and vocal amplitude: Explorations in social psychophysics. *Journal of Personality and Social Psychology, 18*, 392-402.

Millar, F. E., Rogers-Millar, L. E., & Courtright, J. A. (1979). Relational control and dyadic understanding: An exploratory predictive regression model. In D. Nimmo (Ed.), *Communication yearbook 3* (pp. 213-224). New Brunswick, NJ: Transaction.

Miller, N. (1959). Lateralization of basic S-R concepts: Extensions to conflict behavior, motivation, and social learning. In S. Koch (Ed.), *Psychology: A study of a science* (Vol. 2, pp. 196-292). New York: McGraw-Hill.

Natale, M. (1975). Convergence of mean vocal intensity in dyadic communication as a function of social desirability. *Journal of Personality and Social Psychology, 32*, 790-804.

Noller, R. (1980). Gaze in married couples. *Journal of Nonverbal Behavior, 5*, 115-129.

O'Donnell-Trujillo, N. (1981). Relational communication: A comparison of coding systems. *Communication Monographs, 48*, 91-105.

Patterson, M. L. (1976). An arousal model of interpersonal intimacy. *Psychological Review, 83*, 235-245.

Patterson, M. L. (1977). Interpersonal distance, affect, and equilibrium theory. *Journal of Social Psychology, 101*, 205-214.

Patterson, M. L. (1982a). A sequential functional model of nonverbal exchange. *Psychological Review, 89*, 231-249.

Patterson, M. L. (1982b). Personality and nonverbal involvement: A functional analysis. In W. Ickes & E. S. Knowles (Eds.), *Personality, roles, and social behavior* (pp. 141-164). New York: Springer-Verlag.

Patterson, M. L. (1983). *Nonverbal behavior: A functional perspective.* New York: Springer-Verlag.

Patterson, M. L., Mullens, S., & Romano, J. (1971). Compensatory responses to spatial intrusion. *Sociometry, 34*, 114-121.

Pellegrini, R. J., & Empey, J. (1970). Interpersonal spatial orientation in dyads. *Journal of Psychology, 76,* 67-70.

Planalp, S., & Tracy, K. (1980). Not to change the topic but . . . . A cognitive approach to the management of conversation. In D. Nimmo (Ed.), *Communication yearbook 4* (pp. 237-258). New Brunswick, NJ: Transaction.

Poole, M. S. (1981). Decision development in small groups I: A comparison of two models. *Communication Monographs, 48,* 1-24.

Poole, M. S. (1983). Decision development in small groups II: A study of multiple sequences in decision-making. *Communication Monographs, 50,* 206-232.

Putman, W. B., & Street, R. L. (in press). The conception and perception of noncontent speech performance. *International Journal of the Sociology of Language.*

Putnam, L. L., & Jones, T. S. (1982). Reciprocity in negotiations: An analysis of bargaining interactions. *Communication Monographs, 49,* 171-191.

Reichman, R. (1978). Conversational coherency. *Cognitive Science. 2,* 283-327.

Robinson, W. P. (1979). Speech markers and social class. In K. R. Scherer & H. Giles (Eds.), *Social markers in speech* (pp. 211-250). Cambridge: Cambridge University Press.

Robson, K. S. (1967). The role of eye-to-eye contact in maternal-infant attachment. *Journal of Child Psychology and Psychiatry, 8,* 13-25.

Rogers, L. E., Courtright, J. A., & Millar, F. E. (1980). Message control intensity: Rationale and preliminary findings. *Communication Monographs, 47,* 201-219.

Rogers, L. E., & Farace, R. V. (1975). Analysis of relational communication in dyads: New measurement procedures. *Human Communication Research, 1,* 222-239.

Rogers, L. E., & Millar, F. (1982). The question of validity: A pragmatic response. In M. Burgoon (Ed.), *Communication yearbook 5* (pp. 249-257). New Brunswick, NJ: Transaction.

Rogers-Millar, L. E., & Millar, F. E. (1979). Domineeringness and dominance: A transactional view. *Human Communication Research, 5,* 238-246.

Rosenfeld, H. M. (1978). Conversational control functions of nonverbal behavior. In A. W. Siegman & S. Feldstein (Eds.), *Nonverbal behavior and communication* (pp. 291-328). Hillsdale, NJ: Lawrence Erlbaum.

Rubin, Z. (1975). Disclosing oneself to a stranger: Reciprocity and its limits. *Journal of Experimental Social Psychology, 11,* 233-260.

Sackett, G. P. (1978). Measurement in observational research. In G. P. Sackett (Ed.), *Observing behavior* (Vol. 2, pp. 25-44). Baltimore: University Park Press.

Sackett, G. P. (1979). The lag sequential analysis of contingency and cyclicity in behavioral interaction research. In J. P. Osofsky (Ed.), *Handbook of infant development* (pp. 623-649). New York: John Wiley.

Sacks, H., Schegloff, E. A., & Jefferson, G. (1974). A simplest systematics for the organization of turn-taking for conversation. *Language, 50,* 696-735.

Sanders, R. E. (1983). Tools for cohering disclosure and their strategic utilization: Markers of structural connections and meaning relations. In R. T. Craig & K. Tracy (Eds.), *Conversational coherence* (pp. 67-80). Beverly Hills, CA: Sage.

Savicki, V. (1972). Outcomes of nonreciprocal self-disclosure strategies. *Journal of Personality and Social Psychology, 23,* 271-276.

Sawitsky, J. C., & Watson, M. J. (1975). Patterns of proxemic behavior among preschool children. *Representative Research in Social Psychology, 6,* 109-113.

Schaffer, H. R., Collis, G. M., & Parsons, G. (1977). Verbal interchange and visual regard in verbal and preverbal children. In H. R. Schaffer (Ed.), *Studies in mother-infant interaction* (pp. 291-324). New York: Academic Press.

Schenkein, J. (Ed.). (1978). *Studies in the organization of conversational interaction.* New York: Academic Press.

Schlenker, B. R., & Darby, B. W. (1981). The use of apologies in social predicaments. *Social Psychology Quarterly, 44,* 271-278.

Schneider, F. W., & Hansvick, C. L. (1977). Gaze and distance as a function of changes in interpersonal gaze. *Social Behavior and Personality, 5,* 49-53.

Schulz, R., & Barefoot, J. (1974). Nonverbal responsiveness and affiliative conflict theory. *British Journal of Social and Clinical Psychology, 13,* 237-243.

Sillars, A. L. (1980). The sequential and distributional structure of conflict interaction as a function of attributions concerning the locus of responsibility and stability of conflicts. In D. Nimmo (Ed.), *Communication yearbook 4* (pp. 217-236). New Brunswick, NJ: Transaction.

Skotko, V. P., & Langmeyer, D. (1977). The effects of interaction distance and gender on self-disclosure in the dyad. *Sociometry, 40,* 178-182.

Sodikoff, C. L., Firestone, L. J., & Kaplan, K. (1974). Subject self-disclosure and attitude change as a function of interviewer self-disclosure and eye-contact. *Personality and Social Psychology Bulletin, 1,* 243-246.

Sroufe, L. A., & Waters, E. (1976). The ontogenesis of smiling and laughter. *Psychological Review, 83,* 173-189.

Stech, E. L. (1975). Sequential structure in human social communication. *Human Communication Research, 1,* 168-179.

Stech, E. L. (1979). A grammar of conversation with a quantitative empirical test. *Human Communication Research, 5,* 158-172.

Stechler, G., & Carpenter, G. (1967). A viewpoint on early affective development. In J. Hellmuth (Ed.), *The exceptional infant* (Vol. 1, pp. 163-189). Seattle, WA: Special Child Publishers.

Steinem, G. (1981). The politics of talking in groups. *Ms., 9,* 43ff.

Stern, D. N. (1971). A micro analysis of mother-infant interaction. *Journal of the American Academy of Child Psychiatry, 10,* 501-517.

Stern, D. N. (1974). Mother and infant at play: The dyadic interaction involving facial, vocal, and gaze behavior. In M. Lewis & L. A. Rosenblum (Eds.), *The effect of the infant on its caregiver* (pp. 187-214). New York: John Wiley.

Stern, D. N. (1977). *A first relationship: Mother and infant.* Cambridge, MA: Harvard University Press.

Stern, D. N., Jaffe, J., Beebe, B., & Bennett, S. L. (1975). Vocalizing in unison and in alteration: Two modes of communication within the mother-infant dyad. *Annals of the New York Academy of Sciences, 263,* 89-100.

Street, R. L. (1982). Evaluation of noncontent speech accommodation. *Language and Communication, 2,* 13-31.

Street, R. L. (1983). Noncontent speech convergence in adult-child interactions. In R. N. Bostrom (Ed.), *Communication yearbook 7* (pp. 369-395). Beverly Hills, CA: Sage.

Street, R. L., & Brady, R. M. (1982). Speech rate acceptance ranges as a function of evaluative domain, listener speech rate, and communicative context. *Communication Monographs, 49,* 290-308.

Street, R. L., Brady, R. M., & Putman, W. B. (1983). The influence of speech rate stereotypes and rate similarity on listeners' evaluations of speakers. *Journal of Language and Social Psychology, 2,* 37-56.

Street, R. L., & Giles, H. (1982). Speech accommodation theory: A social cognitive approach to language and speech behavior. In M. Roloff & C. Berger (Eds.), *Social cognition and communication* (pp. 193-226). Beverly Hills, CA: Sage.

Street, R. L., Lucas-Arwood, E. V., & Cappella, J. N. (1983). *Cognitive, linguistic, and pragmatic factors influencing speech convergence development.* Unpublished paper, Department of Speech Communication, Texas Tech University.

Street, R. L., Street, N. J., & VanKleeck, A. (1983). Speech convergence among talkative and reticent three year olds. *Language Sciences, 5,* 79-96.

Sundstrom, E. (1975). An experimental study of crowding: Effects of room size, intrusion, and goal blocking on nonverbal behavior, self-disclosure, and self-reported stress. *Journal of Personality and Social Psychology, 32,* 645-654.

Thakerar, J. N., Giles, H., & Cheshire, J. (1982). Psychological and linguistic parameters of speech accommodation theory. In C. Fraser & K. R. Scherer (Eds.), *Advances in the social psychology of language* (pp. 205-255). Cambridge: Cambridge University Press.

Thomas, E.A.C., & Martin, J. A. (1976). An analysis of parent-infant interaction. *Psychological Review, 83,* 141-156.

Tracy, K. (1982). On getting the point: Distinguishing "issues" from "events": An aspect of conversational coherence. In M. Burgoon (Ed.), *Communication yearbook 5* (pp. 279-302). New Brunswick, NJ: Transaction.

Tracy, K. (1985). Conversational coherence: A cognitively grounded rules approach. In R. L. Street & J. N. Cappella (Eds.), *Sequence and pattern in communication behaviour* (pp. 30-49). London: Edward Arnold.

Tracy, K., & Moran, J. P. (1982). Conversational relevance in multiple-goal settings. In R. T. Craig & K. Tracy (Eds.), *Conversational coherence* (pp. 116-135). Beverly Hills, CA: Sage.

Trager, G. L. (1958). Paralanguage: A first approximation. *Studies in Linguistics, 13,* 1-12.

Trager, G. L., & Smith, H. L. (1957). *An outline of English structure.* Norman, OK: Battenburg Press.

Tronick, E., Als, H., Adamson, L., & Wise, S. (1978). The infant's response to entrapment between contradictory messages in face-to-face interaction. *Journal of the American Academy of Child Psychiatry, 17,* 1-13.

Vondracek, S. I., & Vondracek, F. W. (1971). The manipulation and measurement of self-disclosure in preadolescents. *Merrill-Palmer Quarterly, 17,* 51-58.

Warner, R. (1979). *Activity pattern, personality, and social interaction.* Unpublished manuscript, Department of Psychology, University of Miami.

Watzlawick, P., Beavin, J., & Jackson, D. D. (1967). *Pragmatics of human communication.* New York: W. W. Norton.

Webb, J. T. (1969). Subject speech rates as a function of interviewer behavior. *Language and Speech, 12,* 54-67.

Webb, J. T. (1972). Interview synchrony: An investigation of two speech rate measures. In A. W. Siegman & B. Pope (Eds.), *Studies in dyadic communication* (pp. 115-133). New York: Pergamon.

Webster, R. L., Steinhardt, M. H. & Santer, M. G. (1972). Change in infants' vocalization as a function of differential acoustical stimulation. *Developmental Psychology, 7,* 39-43.

Welkowitz, J., Cariffe, G., & Feldstein, S. (1976). Conversational congruence as a criterion of socialization in children. *Child Development, 47,* 269-272.

Welkowitz, J., & Feldstein, S. (1969). Dyadic interaction and induced differences in perceived similarity. *Proceedings of the 77th Annual Convention of the American Psychological Association, 4,* 343-344.

Welkowitz, J., & Kuc, M. (1973). Interrelationships among warmth, genuineness, empathy, and temporal speech patterns in interpersonal interaction. *Journal of Consulting and Clinical Psychology, 41,* 472-473.

Wiemann, J. M., & Knapp, M. L. (1975). Turn-taking in conversation. *Journal of Communication, 25,* 75-92.

Wiseman, R. L., & Schenk-Hamlin, W. (1981). A multidimensional scaling validation of an inductively derived set of compliance-gaining strategies. *Communication Monographs, 48,* 251-270.

Worthy, M. G., Gary, A. L., & Kahn, M. (1969). Self-disclosure as an exchange process. *Journal of Personality and Social Psychology, 13,* 59-63.

Zelazo, P. (1972). Smiling and vocalizing: A cognitive emphasis. *Merrill-Palmer Quarterly, 18,* 349-365.

Zelazo, P., Kegan, J., & Hartman, R. (1975). Excitement and boredom as determinants of vocalization in infants. *Journal of Genetic Psychology, 126,* 107-117.

Zimbardo, P. (1977). *Shyness.* Reading, MA: Addison-Wesley.

10 Social Power and Interpersonal Communication

CHARLES R. BERGER

Northwestern University

P OWER, social influence, persuasion, coercion, dominance, leadership, authority, control, compliance-gaining, and related constructs have enjoyed considerable popularity among social scientists in general and communication scientists in particular. Russell (1938) argued that "the fundamental concept in social science is Power, in the same sense in which Energy is the fundamental concept in physics" (p. 10). Power and dominance have been accorded a central role in the explanation of interpersonal behavior by numerous researchers (Bales, 1970; Blau, 1964; Blood & Wolfe, 1960; Brown, 1965; Carson, 1969; Cartwright, 1959; Haley, 1959; Kelley & Thibaut, 1978; Leary, 1957; Schutz, 1958; Thibaut & Kelley, 1959). Moreover, several studies have demonstrated that power-related dimensions are fundamental to the perception of social relationships and social episodes (Forgas, 1979; Rosenberg & Sedlak, 1972; Triandis, Vassiliou, & Nassiakou, 1968; Wish, Deutsch, & Kaplan, 1976).

In the domain of communication research, Blakar (1979) has argued that not only is language an obvious means for exerting power, for example, via advertising, the fact that language can help to structure persons' experiences when they engage in informal social interactions not directly concerned with social influence suggests that there are more subtle relationships between language and power. The idea that perceptions of dominance are important in determining how interactions will unfold is reflected in Norton's (1983) work on communicator style. Furthermore, Wish, D'Andrade, and Goodnow (1980) found a factor they labeled forceful versus forceless to underlie judgments of speech acts. They argued that this dimension as well as several others are ones that may be related to the ways in which interpersonal communication is structured and perceived. Thus dimensions related to power and dominance are not only central to our understanding of social relationships in general, they are crucial for understanding the communication that takes place within those social relationships.

Although power and related constructs have frequently been invoked to explain social change at a number of different levels of analysis (dyads, groups, institutions, and societies), there is considerable ambiguity surrounding the meanings of these constructs and their relationships to each other. These definitional problems will not be solved in this chapter; however, a number of different perspectives in viewing power will be considered. A useful overview of these issues has been presented by Ng (1980). The central focus of this chapter will be upon the relationship between power and interpersonal communication. That relationship is obviously reciprocal; that is, persons can actualize power through their communicative conduct, and communicative conduct can serve as a basis for making inferences about a given individual's ability to exercise power. Thus communication is at once both an antecedent and a consequence of power.

We have chosen to focus attention upon the construct of power rather than similar constructs because power has been frequently viewed to be more abstract. For example, Weber (1947) defined power (*Macht*) to be inclusive of both imperative control (*Herrschaft*) and authority (*Legitime Herrschaft*). Sites (1973) viewed control as the actualization of social power, whereas Burr, Ahern, and Knowles (1977) defined power as the potential or ability to exert influence and control as the actual behavioral attempt to induce change. This is not to say that all theorists who have dealt with power and related constructs necessarily view power as prepotent over the others; however, for purposes of the present chapter, social power will be viewed as the regnant construct of the set. The potential advantages of this view will become apparent later in the chapter.

The present chapter is divided into three sections. First, we will consider different ways that the construct of power has been approached at the conceptual level and the various ways that power has been measured. The second section of the chapter will overview the findings of studies that have examined the relationships between interpersonal communication and social power. Here we will examine both the role that perceptions of communicative conduct play in producing differential attributions of power and the role that power plays in the production of communicative conduct. The final section of the chapter will present an approach to the study of communication and power that is rooted in social cognition. Here we will attempt to demonstrate how a cognitive approach might help to define more clearly several issues that remain ambiguous in the study of communication and social influence processes.

CONCEPTUAL AND MEASUREMENT APPROACHES

In this section, we will consider first some general definitions of social power. We will then contrast two global approaches to the study of power: (1)

individual and (2) interactional. Finally, we will examine some alternative ways that social power has been measured.

ON DEFINING SOCIAL POWER

Given the popularity of the concept of social power in the literature of the social sciences, it is not surprising that a considerable number of alternative definitions for the construct have been proffered by various theorists. Here we will consider a sample of these definitions to get some idea of the commonalities they share and the differences among them. Russell (1938) defined power as "the production of intended effects" (p. 35). Lasswell and Kaplan (1950) assert, "Power is a special case of the exercise of influence: it is the process of affecting the policies of others with the help of (actual or threatened) severe deprivations for nonconformity with the policies intended" (p. 76). Simon (1957) points out, "For the assertion, 'A has power over B,' we can substitute the assertion, 'A's behavior causes B's behavior' " (p. 5). Dahl (1957) suggests, "My intuitive idea of power, then, is something like this: A has power over B to the extent that he can get B to do something that B would not otherwise do" (pp. 202-203). However, Winter (1973) sees Dahl's definition as too restrictive because "getting someone else to believe that he really *wants* to do what you want him to do is surely a very sophisticated technique for getting power" (p. 5). Winter offers his own definition of social power as follows, "Thus social power is *the ability or capacity of O to produce (consciously or unconsciously) intended effects on the behavior or emotions of another person P*" (p. 5).

Both Cartwright (1959) and Schopler (1965) noted the considerable amount of variation in definitions of power and the tendency for various researchers to use such terms as power, influence, and authority as if they had the same meaning. Cartwright (1959) offered the following general definition of power, "power refers to the induction of (psychological) forces by one entity b upon another a and to the resistance to this induction set up by a. Because the behavior of a is determined by the totality of forces operating upon him at any given time, the power of b over a is concerned only with those influences on a's behavior originating with b" (p. 188). Thibaut and Kelley (1959) assert, "Generally, we can say that the power of A over B increases with A's ability to affect the quality of outcomes attained by B" (p. 101). They then distinguish between two types of power: (1) fate control and (2) behavior control. A has fate control over B when A can determine B's outcomes regardless of the behaviors that B enacts. Behavior control is achieved by A when variations in his or her behavior "make it desirable for B to vary his behavior too" (p. 103). Thibaut and Kelley also differentiate between power that is usable from power that is unusable. They argue that if person B can exercise counterpower over A, then A may refrain from attempting to influence B because B can influence A's outcomes. In their view, the extent to which one person in the relationship is dependent upon his or her relational partner for outcomes is the extent to which the partner has power over him or her. Emerson (1962) makes a similar point when he asserts, "the power of A over B is equal to, and based upon, the dependence of B upon A" (p. 33). Finally, in discussing the nature of power, Blau (1964) states, "it is the ability of persons or groups to impose their wills on others despite resistance through deterrence either in the form of withholding regularly supplied rewards or in the form of punishment, inasmuch as the former as well as the latter constitute, in effect, a negative sanction" (p. 117). In Blau's view, power is asymmetrical; thus, when persons are inter-dependent and can influence each other to an equal degree, each individual lacks power. By contrast, Thibaut and Kelley (1959) argue that when persons are highly dependent upon each other, they have high power over each other.

Although the above definitions of social power have been advanced by researchers from a variety of different theoretical perspectives, they share two principal commonalities. First, these definitions point to the ability of power wielders to produce changes in the behavior and/or affect of their relational partners. Persons who have power can produce various *effects* in others. Second, a number of the definitions also point to the fact that the abilities of targets to resist influence or to affect the outcomes of the persons making influence attempts are related to the ability of influence agents to exercise power over targets. Thus several of the definitions cited imply that power is an attribute of a *relationship* rather than an attribute of an individual. In fact, Cartwright (1959), Emerson (1962), and Winter (1973) stress this point in their treatments of the power construct.

The definitions listed above vary with respect to their approach to intentionality. Some definitions stress that power is achieved only when *intended* effects are produced, whereas others do not directly address this issue. In the case of the definitions proffered by Dahl (1957) and Thibaut and Kelley (1959), persons might exercise considerable influence over others without intending to do so but still be credited with possessing power over the others. In contrast, Russell (1938) and Winter (1973) explicitly restrict their definitions to *intended* effects; however, note that in the case of Winter (1973), it is possible to produce intended effects unconsciously. The complex issue of intentionality in human action cannot be treated here; however, it might be worthwhile to distinguish between intentionality with respect to *goals* and intentionality with respect to the *means* used to achieve goals. Thus a person might have the intention of influencing another's beliefs, but no specific intention regarding how he or she will accomplish the influence task. Or, a person might have both a goal and a means intention before beginning the influence attempt but change the means used to achieve the goal when the intended means fail to produce goal achievement. Hence the person may achieve the goal but not be aware of how he or she did so. It seems reasonable to insist that power be defined in terms of the production of intended effects if intentionality is being used with reference to goal achievement; however, it does not seem reasonable to insist that intentionality with reference to means be included in a definition of social power.

Another way in which the above definitions differ is with respect to the issue of the asymmetry of power. As we noted, Blau (1964) views power as an inherently asymmetrical relationship, whereas Thibaut and Kelley (1959) allow for the possibility that two persons could simultaneously possess considerable power over each other. Emerson's (1962) analysis leads to a conclusion similar to Thibaut and Kelley's (1959). If one takes the position that power is a relationship attribute rather than an individual attribute, it seems reasonable to argue that persons can exert mutual power over each other. It is possible for two persons to influence each other with respect to different issues; for example, person A influences B with respect to issue X and person B influences A with respect to issue Y. Both persons show evidence of power over each other but in different domains of influence. Wolfe (1959) suggested that husbands and wives in families with an autonomic authority structure tend to exercise influence this way.

Before moving to a discussion of individual approaches to power, it is worth noting that a number of writers have differentiated among different types of power. Perhaps the most widely cited analysis of this kind is that of French and Raven (1959), which was subsequently modified and discussed by Collins and Raven (1969) and Raven (1965). This position presents different bases or sources of power. In this scheme, *informational power* is attitude or behavior change produced by the content of the influence attempt. *Coercive power* is based upon the ability of the influence agent to mediate punishments for the person being influenced, whereas *reward power* refers to the ability of the influence agent to mediate rewards for the influence. *Legitimate power* stems from the belief on the part of those being influenced that the agent of influence has the right to influence them. *Referent power* arises when an individual uses a group as a frame of reference for making judgments about his or her attitudes and/or behavior. *Expert power* is based upon the influencee's belief that the source of influence has knowledge relevant to the domain of influence.

In another typology of social influence types, Kelman (1958, 1961) distinguished among three processes of social influence: (1) compliance, (2) identification, and (3) internalization. *Compliance* occurs when a person accepts influence from a source to either gain rewards or avoid punishments. *Identification* happens when a person accepts influence "because this behavior is associated with a satisfying self-defining relationship to this person or group" (Kelman, 1961, p. 63). *Internalization* is the acceptance of the induced behavior because it is consistent with the individual's value system.

Clearly, compliance is similar to coercive and reward power, whereas identification is similar to referent power. Internalization seems to involve elements of both informational and expert power.

More recently, Wheeless, Barraclough, and Stewart (1983) have attempted to subsume the typologies of French and Raven (1959) and Kelman (1958, 1961), as well as those of Etzioni (1961) and Parsons (1963), into three categories of power types: (1) Preview expectations/Consequences, (2) Invoke Relationships/Identification, and (3) Summon Values/Obligations. Types of power in the first category include reward and coercive. Expert and referent power as well as identification are included in the second category, and legitimate power and internalization are placed in the third category. These authors employ the three categories as a potential way in which to organize the diffuse literature in the area of compliance-gaining strategies. Although the French and Raven (1959) and Kelman (1958, 1961) typologies as well as others have been frequently cited in the literature, they have *not* stimulated a great deal of research. In part, this lack of heuristic power can be explained by the fact that although taxonomies may help us to understand the complexities of the power construct, they do not constitute theories of social power. Thus they are not capable of generating hypotheses for empirical research. This observation should not be construed as an indictment of taxonomies; however, it is meant to indicate that theoretical elaboration beyond the taxonomy is necessary before such presentations can become significant generative mechanisms for research.

Individual Approaches to Social Power

Because we have already observed that social power is an attribute of a relationship rather than an individual, it may seem paradoxical to have a section of this chapter that deals with "individual approaches to social power." It should be noted, however, that not only is there a substantial tradition of social power research that focuses upon the individual, but some writers in this tradition explicitly acknowledge that social power is a characteristic of a relationship and not an individual (Winter, 1973). Moreover, it is probably safe to say that most researchers who we will consider in this area view individual power strivings as at least partially the product of social forces; that is, power strivings are acquired through interactions with significant others. Thus although the focus of these efforts is on the individual, the importance of social interaction in the acquisition and performance of power-related behaviors is not lost. Minton (1967) has discussed a number of issues concerning the relationships between power and personality.

Freudian and Neo-Freudian Approaches. Adler (1927, 1930, 1966) distinguished between healthy and neurotic strivings for power. Healthy striving for superiority is balanced against social interest, whereas neurotic power strivings may be the product of an early inferiority complex. Horney

(1937) also stressed the difference between the desire for power that comes from a sense of strength and that which stems from feelings of weakness and insecurity. Horney argues that persons with a neurotic need for power try to avoid situations in which they are relatively helpless; moreover, such persons have a need to dominate others and have strong inhibitions against domineering behavior. Freud (1924) argued that ego strength and narcissism are positively related and that power strivings are part of narcissism.

Horney's (1937) notion that persons with neurotic needs for power wish to dominate others but have strong inhibitions against domineering behavior is similar to Haley's (1959, 1962) argument, based upon the thinking of Bateson, Jackson, Haley, and Weakland (1956), that families that contain schizophrenic members tend to avoid direct attempts to influence each other even when they wish to exert control. In these families, influence is exerted indirectly. Some evidence supporting this position is reported by Mishler and Waxler (1968).

The distinction between power strivings arising from a sense of mastery and competence and power strivings produced by a sense of inferiority and weakness is one that has not received much attention in the power literature. Winter (1973) is one of the few exceptions to this generalization because he distinguishes between hope for power and fear of power. It is reasonable to suppose that power strivings emanating from these two different bases should produce conduct directed at influencing others that is quite different. Moreover, one would expect considerable variation in the modes of resistance employed by persons whose power strivings are the product of these two different bases. For example, persons whose power strivings stem from feelings of inferiority may be more prone to reject opposing positions out of hand and to refuse to be accommodative. Stylistic differences in modes of attempted influence and modes of resistance that are rooted in different bases for power striving are deserving of research attention.

Motivational Approaches. Theorists who have examined power as a motive have generally worked from the perspective presented by Murray (1938). Murray's theory of personality contained a number of different needs that include need for dominance (n Dominance). Murray (1938) noted that n Dominance might, at times, fuse with needs for aggression or achievement. Veroff (1957, 1958) presented a conceptualization of need for power (n Power) and developed a projective technique for measuring the construct. Veroff and Veroff (1972) reviewed several studies that employed the Veroff measure. Veroff's general concern has been to measure the *desire* for power. On the basis of several studies, Veroff and Veroff (1972) asserted that the power incentive should *not* be looked upon as a positive goal in which one derives joy from influencing others but as a negative goal in which one avoids feelings of powerlessness.

In attempting to improve Veroff's measure of n Power, Uleman (1972) found evidence for a construct he labeled need for influence (n Influence).

Persons with high levels of n Influence are those who enjoy influencing others for the sake of seeing themselves being influential (positive incentive). Winter (1973) also developed an alternative way in which to measure n Power that explicitly differentiated between hope for power (positive incentive) and fear of power (negative incentive). Hope for power involves the active attempt to influence others, whereas fear of power is concerned with the avoidance of influence. Winter (1973) presents evidence indicating that the measures of n Power developed by Veroff, Uleman, and himself show low to moderate correlations with each other. These data suggest that n Power is a multidimensional construct in need of further explication.

The Authoritarian Personality. As part of their study of the relationship between political ideology and personality functioning, Adorno, Frenkel-Brunswick, Levinson, and Sanford (1950) found that persons with high levels of authoritarianism not only showed a greater concern for power in their relationships with others, they also tended to admire uncritically persons who were in positions of power. Moreover, high authoritarians expected persons with lower power to accept without question influence from persons with higher power levels. Adorno et al. (1950) reported additional relationships between authoritarianism and such variables as ethnocentrism, political-economic conservatism, and prejudice; however, a methodological critique of the research by Christie and Jahoda (1954) called into question a number of the findings reported in *The Authoritarian Personality.* In Rokeach's (1960) work on general authoritarianism or dogmatism, he suggests that persons with closed systems of thinking and believing are likely to feel alone and helpless. As a consequence, they may develop feelings of self-inadequacy and self-hate. These findings might be overcome by being excessively concerned with power and status. One of the subcomponents of his dogmatism scale measures these concerns.

Alienation is a concept related to feelings of inadequacy. Although this concept was developed within the context of sociological inquiry and not as part of the research on authoritarianism and dogmatism, it does seem to be related to these constructs. Seeman (1959) argued that felt *powerlessness* is a subcomponent of alienation and Nettler (1957) and Srole (1956) developed measures of alienation. If powerlessness is a component of alienation, then one would expect persons with high levels of alienation to be close-minded and highly authoritarian.

Locus of Control. In his discussion of phenomenal causality, Heider (1958) distinguished between *internal* and *external* causality. As we observe ourselves and others, we may infer that particular events are caused by factors that reside within the individual such as *ability* or *motivation*, or factors that reside outside of the individual such as *task difficulty* or *luck*. Ability and task difficulty are relatively stable factors, whereas motivation and luck are considerably less stable. Rotter (1966) made a distinction similar to that of Heider's in his discussion of locus of control. To Rotter, locus of control is a set of generalized expectations for internal or external control of reinforcement. He distinguishes between the two as follows:

> When a reinforcement is perceived by the subject as following some action of his own but not being entirely contingent upon his action, then, in our culture, it is typically perceived as the result of luck, chance, fate, as under the control of powerful others, or as unpredictable because of the great complexity of forces surrounding him. When the event is interpreted in this way, we have labeled this a belief in *external control*. If the person perceives that the event is contingent upon his own behavior or his own relatively permanent characteristics, we have termed this a belief in *internal control*. (p. 1)

deCharms (1968, 1972) distinguished between "origins" and "pawns." Discussing the construct of *personal causation* he asserts:

> When a person initiates intentional behavior, he experiences himself as having originated the intention and the behavior. He is the locus of causality of the behavior and he is said to be intrinsically motivated. Since he himself is the originator, we refer to the person as an origin.
>
> When something external to the person impels him to behavior, he experiences himself as the instrument of the outside source, and the outside source is the locus of causality. He is said to be extrinsically motivated. Since the person is impelled from without we refer to him as a pawn. We sometimes talk of people as primarily pawns implying that they more characteristically see themselves pushed around by outside forces. Conversely, we refer to people as primarily origins implying that they characteristically see themselves as originating their own behavior. (1972, pp. 96-97)

In an overview of the locus of control research, Lefcourt (1976) has pointed out that although Rotter (1966) and deCharms (1968, 1972) make dichotomous distinctions, both theorists conceive of locus of control as a continuous variable. Collins (1974) found that Rotter's (1966) locus of control construct involved four distinct beliefs. Individuals might be external because they believe that the world is (1) difficult, (2) unjust, (3) governed by luck, or (4) politically unresponsive.

Although power per se is not mentioned in the definitions advanced by Rotter (1966) and deCharms (1972), it is obvious that persons with high levels of internal locus of control or origins are those who believe that they are responsible for effecting change in their environments, whereas their externally controlled or pawn counterparts feel that they are controlled by their environments. Because several of the definitions of social power reviewed earlier emphasized the notion that persons with power are able to effect changes in the behavior or attitudes of others, then these locus of control measures may represent *attitudes* or *beliefs* that persons have about their abilities to exercise influence.

Machiavellianism. Drawing upon the writings of Machiavelli, whose insights into the wielding of power are still studied some 450 years after their origination, Christie and Geis (1970) developed a scale designed to measure the construct of Machiavellianism. A majority of the items on the scale were taken from Machiavelli's *The Prince* and *The Discourses*. Christie and Geis (1970) argued that in order to be an effective manipulator, a person must possess the following four characteristics:

(1) a relative lack of emotions in interpersonal relationships
(2) a lack of concern for conventional morality
(3) a lack of gross psychopathology
(4) low ideological commitment

Persons who become emotionally involved in relationships are likely to distort their perceptions of their relationship partners to such a degree that they are unable to understand how they might be able to wield influence over them. The lack of concern for conventional morality enables the manipulator to use any means to achieve the goal of influence. Lacking gross psychopathology is critical for the accurate social perception necessary to understand how one might influence another. Finally, low ideological commitment enables the individual to be flexible in the stand he or she takes on issues. Persons who are not committed to a particular ideology can change their positions when it is to their advantage for achieving their goals. Highly committed persons do not have such flexibility. Both Christie and Geis (1970) and Guterman (1970) report evidence that provides partial support for this conceptualization of the high Machiavellian.

Summary. Several of the constructs we have discussed are directly related to individual strivings for power, whereas others are obviously related to power but the term itself is not employed in their definition. Machiavellianism, n Power, and n Influence are constructs that centrally concern the exercise of power. The differences among them appear to be *stylistic* in nature. For example, Uleman (1972) suggests that persons with high levels of n Influence are likely to exercise influence in relatively subtle ways. By contrast, persons with high levels of n Power are likely to assert their power in a group by being loud, cantankerous, and obnoxious. Uleman (1972) also suggests that n Power may arise out of feelings of inferiority, whereas n Influence may arise from feelings of mastery and effectance (White, 1959). It seems possible that both n Power and n Influence might differ sharply from Machiavellianism. Evidence supporting this possibility is presented by both Uleman (1972) and Winter (1973). Uleman found no relationship between Veroff's (1957) measure of n Power and Machiavellianism. Winter (1973) also found no relationship between his n Power measure and Machiavellianism. However, Uleman (1972) found a negative relationship ($r = -.31$) between n Influence and Machiavellianism; thus high n Influence individuals tend to be low in Machiavellianism. These findings suggest that although persons may have a general concern for exerting influence, there are subtle differences in the constraints they will place upon their influence behaviors and considerable variation in the styles with which they will exercise influence. This reasoning suggests that Norton's (1983) dominant communicator style dimension might actually consist of a number of stylistic subtypes.

Although not dealing directly with power-related issues, such constructs as authoritarianism, dogmatism, and locus of control are related to the exercise of power. Here, too, we see the possibility that some of these constructs—for example, authoritarianism and dogmatism—may be concerned with issues of influence style, whereas locus of control is more concerned with beliefs in one's ability to exercise control over one's environment. A detailed analysis of the possible stylistic differences that might be displayed between high authoritarians and persons with high levels of n Power, n Influence, and Machiavellianism cannot be presented here. However, it would be fruitful to establish the divergent validity of these various constructs.

Interaction Approaches to Power

In this section, we will examine theoretical positions that focus upon *social relationships* between individuals rather than upon individuals themselves. As a consequence of this relational focus, these theories view power as the product of *interactions* between persons and not the result of individuals' desires to wield influence over others. It should be pointed out, however, that in spite of their interactional approach, some of these theorists explicitly recognize that persons may vary in their *individual desires* to influence others (Thibaut & Kelley, 1959). Although these individual needs for power may exist, they tend to be ignored in the theories themselves.

Social Exchange Theories. In general, this genre of theory seeks to explain the development, maintenance, and decay of social relationships in terms of the balance between the rewards that persons obtain and the costs that they incur by selecting themselves into various social relationships. There are a number of such theories (Adams, 1965; Blau, 1964; Foa & Foa, 1974; Homans, 1961; Kelley & Thibaut, 1978; Thibaut & Kelley, 1959; Walster, Walster, & Berscheid, 1978) that differ somewhat from each other. These relatively subtle differences cannot be dealt with in detail here; however, Roloff (1981) presents a discussion of several of these theories and the differences among them. Because both Blau (1964) and Thibaut and Kelley (1959) present extended discussions of power, we will focus upon these two theories.

Thibaut and Kelley (1959) argue that when two persons are involved in a relationship they both can choose to enact various behaviors that when considered *jointly* may produce various configurations of outcomes (rewards and costs) for each party in the relationship. They further assert that each individual in the relationship evaluates his or her outcomes against two standards: (1) comparison level (CL) and (2) comparison level for alternatives (CL_{alt}). CL involves the comparison between the individual's internal standard and the particular relationship in which he or she is involved. By contrast, CL_{alt} is the comparison between the particular relationship and all other alternative relationships that are available to the individual plus the alternative of remaining alone. Thibaut and Kelley's explicit reason for postulating these two comparison levels was to explain why persons remain in what appear to be extremely undesirable relationships with others. A given individual might evaluate the particular relationship that he or she is involved in as quite negative, but the available alternatives, including being alone, might be so much more undesirable that the person chooses to remain in the relationship. Relationships will survive to the extent that persons in the relationship experience outcomes that are above CL_{alt}. CL is critical in determining one's *attraction* to a relationship, whereas CL_{alt} is the important determinant of a person's *dependency* upon the relationship.

Thibaut and Kelley (1959) argue that as outcomes become more favorable, that is, as persons receive more rewards at less cost, and these outcomes begin to exceed CL_{alt}, the individual becomes more dependent upon the relationship. The level of dependency upon the relationship for satisfaction is directly related to the amount of power the individual has in the relationship. Greater dependency on the relationship lessens one's power in the relationship. Conversely, the less one is dependent upon the relationship for favorable outcomes, the more power one has within the relationship. This argument is similar to one advanced by Waller and Hill (1951), which they labeled the "Principle of Least Interest." This principle asserts that in a romantic relationship, the person who has the least interest in his or her partner is more powerful. This is so because the persons who is more dependent upon the relationship for rewards is in a sense at the mercy of the less interested party.

As was pointed out earlier, Thibaut and Kelley (1959) differentiate between fate control and behavior control. In the fate control situation, the behavioral alternatives chosen by one person in the relationship totally determine the outcomes of the other person, no matter what behaviors the other person chooses. This situation is much like that of a pawn or a person who is externally controlled. No matter what they do, their environment, in this case their interaction partner, determines their outcomes. In the case of behavior control, the ability of the more powerful person to exercise influence over his or her partner's outcomes is considerably less profound. In this case, variations in the more powerful person's behaviors produce variations in the less powerful person's behaviors. Of course, it is possible that the less powerful person in the relationship can choose to enact behaviors that will reduce the outcomes of the person with greater power; however, Thibaut and Kelley (1959) argue that persons with higher levels of fate control and behavior control can be more directive in interactions with their low power counterparts and can use their abilities to deliver large amounts of rewards to enhance their power. Thus there is a tendency for the powerful to become more powerful in relationships; although if power is overused, persons who are subjected to it may choose to leave the relationship and obviate the ability of the more powerful person to wield power.

Consistent with Thibaut and Kelley's (1959) analysis of dependence and power is Blau's (1964) assertion that "Regular rewards make recipients dependent on the supplier and subject to his power, since they engender expectations that make their discontinuation a punishment" (p. 116). Hence the person who can supply services that others demand can exercise power over them. Blau also discusses four conditions that give rise to social independence and thus reduce the likelihood that one will be subjected to another's power. First, if persons possess strategic resources, they are likely to be more independent. Second, the more alternative sources of supply persons have, the more likely they are to be socially independent. This condition is similar to Thibaut and Kelley's (1959) concept of CL_{alt}. Third, if coercive force can be used to compel suppliers to render services, then dependency will be reduced. Included in this condition is the possibility of forming coalitions to force dispensing of needed services. Fourth, persons can reduce their needs for various services, thus reducing their dependence upon suppliers.

The four conditions that promote social independence can be employed to delineate four strategies that can be used to acquire and maintain power. First, the power wielder who dispenses valuable services to others must remain indifferent to the services they might be able to provide him or her. Obviously, if power holders were to become dependent upon services offered by others, they become subject to their power. Second, the powerful person must insure that those who are dependent upon him or her do not have access to alternative sources of supply for their needs and wants. Such alternative sources weaken dependence and thus reduce power. Third, the person who is in the powerful position must be certain that those who are in the dependent position cannot employ coercive force to obtain their supplies. Thus persons in power positions might take steps to discourage the formation of coalitions among those who are dependent upon them. Finally, power wielders must insure that the persons who are dependent upon them for their supplies do not change their needs so that the value of their supplies diminishes. Hence persons who are in positions of power may have a vested interest in maintaining the status quo in order to insure continued dependency upon them.

Blau (1964) points out that sheer dependence upon a person for benefits gives the person *potential* power; it is only when the person delivers these benefits that the person actualizes his or her power. He asserts that as a person's power increases, those who are subject to his or her power are more eager to do the powerful person's bidding; furthermore, increased power enables the power holder to risk some power to gain even more power. Like Thibaut and Kelley (1959), Blau (1964) believes that the powerful tend to become more powerful. However, power tends to be expended by its use. Thus if powerful persons overuse their power, those who are dependent upon them may resort to one or more of the four strategies for social independence outlined above.

The views of power advanced by Blau (1964) and Thibaut and Kelley (1959) share a considerable number of commonalities. Perhaps the most important of these is the idea that in social relationships, power is not simply determined by the actions of one individual but by the *joint actions* of individuals. Because of this fact, persons who are subject to others' influence can enact behavioral alternatives that may reduce others' power. Moreover, these theories suggest that persons who are in positions of power are never completely secure. Needs and wants may change, thus redefining what is rewarding and costly to subordinates. Radical changes in these domains might completely eliminate dependence and thus reduce power to almost nil. Perhaps the most consistent demonstration of this kind of shift is the relationship between parents and their children. Parents have considerable power over children when children are dependent upon them for various resources; however, as children become capable of obtaining their resources from alternative sources, their dependence upon parents diminishes and thus reduces the power of parents to influence them. Blood and Wolfe (1960) have made a similar argument in the domain of marital relationships. Their resource theory asserts that the spouse who brings the greatest number of resources to the relationship relative to those provided by the other spouse exerts the greatest amount of power in the relationship. There is a considerable literature (see Berger, 1980, for review) that shows that spouses who have greater incomes, educational levels, and social participation tend to be seen as exerting more power in the relationship.

Relational Control. The central assumption underlying the relational control perspective is that when persons interact with each other, the messages that they exchange communicate at two different levels simultaneously. The *content* level is concerned with the literal meaning of the message and the *relationship* level is concerned with what the message implies about the relationship between the persons involved in the interaction (Watzlawick, Beavin, & Jackson, 1967). The distinction between content and relationship communication levels is similar to Ruesch and Bateson's (1951) notions of the *report* and *command* functions of messages. Relationship level communication indicates how the literal content of the message should be taken and is thus meta-communicative in nature. The two imperative statements, "Shut the door" and "If it isn't too much trouble, could you please close the door," are quite similar on the content level in that they both request that the auditor shut the door. However, the two statements imply very different kinds of relationships between the speaker and the auditor.

A number of interaction coding systems have been developed to measure relationship level communication or relational control (Ellis, Fisher, Drecksel, Hoch, & Werber, 1976; Ericson & Rogers, 1973; Folger & Puck, 1976; Mark, 1971; Rogers & Farace, 1975). Of these schemes, the one developed by Rogers and Farace (1975) has generated the most subsequent research, although the system developed by Ellis et al. (1976) has also produced several studies (for example, Drecksel & Fisher, 1977; Ellis, 1979). Because of the heuristic provocativeness of the Rogers and Farace coding system, we will examine their position in greater detail.

Following Watzlawick et al. (1967), Rogers and Farace (1975) distinguish three types of relational control: (1) symmetry, (2) transitory, and (3) complementarity. In contrasting symmetrical and complementary transactions Rogers and Farace (1975) assert:

> In a symmetrical transaction or relationship, one interactor behaves toward the other as the other behaves toward him. There is an equivalence of conduct between the two individuals: there is a symmetry of relational control. In a complementary transaction, however, the interactors' behaviors are maximally differentiated. The control definition offered by one interactor is accepted by the other. (p. 226)

When there is a movement toward *neutralizing* control by one or both parties in the interaction, a transitory type of relational control is being exhibited. Using their coding system, individuals' messages can be classified as either one-up, one-down, or neutralizing, based upon certain grammatical and stylistic attributes. One-up messages represent bids for relational control or dominance, whereas one-down messages indicate acceptance of the other's control or the yielding of control. Neutralizing messages are those that attempt to neutralize control.

Critical to the relational control position is the argument that in order to understand fully how relational control is exercised in interaction sequences, *pairs of messages* exchanged between interactants must be employed as the unit of analysis rather than the messages of each individual in the interaction. Thus if two persons are involved in an interaction, they might exchange the following sequence of messages: ABABABABAB. According to the relational control perspective, the most appropriate way to determine who is exerting the most control in the relationship is to classify the first message from A as either one-up, one-down, or neutralizing and then to classify B's response to that message into one of the same three categories. Then, using B's message as a beginning point, one classifies A's second message as a response to B's and so on. The important point is that one cannot determine whether or not a particular control move has been "successful" unless one knows the response that was made to the move. The coding of successive *pairs* of messages provides more information about relational control than does the study of messages sent by individuals.

Rogers and Farace (1975) underscore the importance of a dyadic level of analysis in the study of relational control by asserting:

> A distinctive aspect of relational analysis is that it necessitates at least a dyadic level of analysis, in contrast to the more predominant monadic analyses. Whether the transaction is symmetrical or complementary, both interactors must participate in the definition of the relationship. Thus, the smallest unit of relational analysis is a paired exchange of two messages. (p. 226)

Although this is an important point, it should be noted that the social exchange theories discussed in the previous section make a similar set of assumptions. Recall that in Thibaut and Kelley's (1959) approach, interaction outcomes are generally *jointly* determined by the behavioral alternatives enacted by the parties involved in the interaction. Moreover, Blau's (1964) analyses of the conditions of social dependence and social independence both recognized the contingent nature of power relationships. Power holders can lose their abilities to exercise influence if those dependent upon them find alternative sources of supply for their wants or adjust their needs so that they no longer require certain resources. Hence even though a particular person is able to dispense potentially large numbers of resources and thus acquire considerable power, unless there are persons who need those copious resources, the person's ability to exercise power will be severely limited. Obviously, in this case *both interactors* participate in the definition of the relationship.

One important contribution of the relational control position is its focus upon actual messages that are exchanged between persons. However, Folger and Poole (1982) and Berger (1983) have raised questions concerning the ability of a position that focuses solely upon message exchanges and does not consider the *interpretations* that social actors and actresses have of these message exchanges to explain adequately control patterns in ongoing interactions. The problem raised by these authors can be illustrated by asking the question of whether or not persons who are involved in interactions interpret one-up, one-down, or neutralizing messages in the same way that the Rogers and Farace (1975) coding system indicates they might. In terms of participants' judgments concerning dominance or control in relationships, it would seem critical to establish whether or not the control moves represented in the Rogers and Farace coding system are actually perceived that way by interactors; for it is these judgments about dominance and control that may be instrumental in producing interpersonal conflict and alterations in the courses of relationships.

Summary. In this section we have considered interactive approaches to the study of power. These perspectives define power or control as properties of relationships rather than individuals. These positions stand in marked contrast to those that view power as a property of individuals. However, there is no necessary incompatibility between them. For example, Kipnis

(1976) developed a descriptive model of the power act consisting of seven steps: (1) Power Motivation, (2) Request for Compliance, (3) Resources, (4) Region of Inhibition, (5) Means of Influence, (6) Response of Target, and (7) Consequences for Power Holder. His model begins from an individual orientation (power motivation) and becomes more "interactive" as it progresses. Certainly, individuals approach interactions with differing predispositions for exercising power; however, it is equally true that the local conditions of exchange can alter significantly the manifestations of these predispositions. Thus both perspectives are necessary for a complete understanding of how power is exercised in social interactions.

Measuring Social Power

Here we will consider various approaches to the measurement of social power and provide some examples of each approach. We will also discuss research that has compared various measurement approaches. The three general classes of measures we will examine are projective tests, self-report measures, and indices of power derived from interaction behaviors. Frequently, studies employ some combination of these approaches. For example, several studies conducted by family sociologists and clinical psychologists present family members with the task of arriving at a consensus decision. Before the discussion begins, individual preferences are assessed through self-reports. The issue is then discussed. At the conclusion of the discussion, a decision is reached and recorded. Given these data, one can compare the pre- and postdiscussion verbal reports to determine the extent to which each group member influenced the final decision, for example, how the family might spend a gift of $1,000. Also, the audio- or videotapes of the discussion can be analyzed to determine who dominated the discussion. Measures of power that are based upon pre- and postcomparisons are termed *outcome power* measures, whereas measures of power based upon attributes of the interaction are called measures of *process power*. We will consider how these two approaches to measuring power relate to each other.

Projective Measures. Veroff (1957, 1958), Uleman, (1972), and Winter (1973) have all used the Thematic Apperception Test (TAT) as a way of measuring the individual's need to exercise power. This test consists of presenting persons with ambiguous pictures and having them write stories about the characters in the pictures. The stories are then analyzed using coding schemes that contain various power-related themes. The more of these themes that are present in the story, the more the individual's fantasy life is dominated by power imagery. The use of this approach assumes that the fantasy themes that are included in persons' stories are indicators of their need states.

The coding schemes are developed by placing persons in situations in which their need for power is likely to be aroused. Persons respond to the TAT while in the arousal situation. Their story responses are then compared with those of a group of persons who have taken the TAT under a set of neutral conditions. Themes that appear in the stories written under aroused conditions that do not appear in stories written under neutral conditions are taken to be indicators of aroused power motivation. Veroff's (1957, 1958) arousal situation was one in which candidates for student government offices were waiting to learn whether or not they had won an election. Uleman (1972) placed persons in a gambling situation in which they could exercise considerable control as a way of arousing the power motive. Winter (1973) aroused the power motive by having persons watch a film of John F. Kennedy's inaugural speech.

As was pointed out earlier, Winter (1973) reported that the same stories scored by the three systems outlined above do *not* produce power motivation scores that correlate highly with each other. There are at least two explanations for this lack of convergence. First, as Murray (1938) pointed out, the arousal of n Dominance might also lead to the arousal of related motives like n Achievement and n Aggression. Thus situations designed to arouse the power motive and produce power fantasy in TAT stories might also produce imagery related to these other motives, thus confounding coding schemes. Second, the arousal situations employed by these three researchers are vastly different. Veroff's election arousal situation seemed to be aimed at producing a concern for achieving status in an organization. Uleman's (1972) situation involved the exercise of influence in a face-to-face interaction situation. Winter's (1973) approach seemed to be directed toward raising a concern for the exercise of political power. It could be that n Power is considerably more domain-specific than first thought; that is, there is not a general need for power but differential desires to exercise power in different social domains. Researchers intending to use this approach to study power should examine these three scoring systems very carefully. At this writing, there appears to be considerable ambiguity concerning just what each one of the three approaches to n Power measures.

Another projective measure of power was reported by Klopper, Tittler, Friedman, and Hughes (1978). Klopper et al. were interested in determining how family members perceived the *prominence* of others in their family. Rather than asking family members to respond verbally to this question, each family member was individually given the task of arranging figures representing family members on a felt board in any way he or she wished. Prominence was measured by examining figure placement and figure height. Figures placed on the left-hand side of the board and figures placed higher relative to the others were scored as more prominent. The correlation between these two measures was .64. Moreover, based upon observations of family interaction in a decision-making task, measures of individual family members' talk time and communication received correlated moderately well with the two prominence measures, with correlations ranging from .46 to .68. These findings stand in marked contrast to those of Turk and Bell (1972), who found that verbal reports of who is most powerful in the family did not generally correlate well with interaction-based measures of family power.

Self-Report Measures. There are a number of different approaches to the measurement of power through self-report. First, there are numerous personality inventories—for example, The California Personality Inventory (CPI)—that contain dominance scales. These scales consist of items that ask the respondents for evaluations of their ability to exercise influence. Uleman (1972) reported that his projective measure of n Influence correlated .31 ($p < .05$) with the CPI dominance scale, but Winter (1973) failed to find any relationship between his measure of n Power and the same CPI dominance scale. In addition to these commercial personality inventories are instruments such as the Machiavellianism (Christie & Geis, 1970), locus of control (Rotter, 1966), authoritarianism (Adorno et al., 1950), and the dogmatism (Rokeach, 1960) scales that were specifically designed to measure the constructs reviewed earlier in the chapter. All of these are self-report instruments.

There are self-report measures that ask respondents to indicate the extent to which they feel power relative to another person or persons. For example, Heer (1958) asked married couples who "won" when there was a disagreement between them. Blood and Wolfe (1960) asked wives to indicate the extent to which they or their husbands were responsible for making decisions across eight decision areas. For each decision area, respondents indicated on a five-point scale the extent to which the husband or wife had influence. This technique has become one of the mainstay self-report measures of family sociologists interested in family power and has been employed in numerous studies (Blood, 1967; Burchinal & Bauder, 1965; Buric & Zecevic, 1967; Burr et al., 1977; Centers, Raven, & Rodrigues, 1971; Cromwell & Cromwell, 1978; Kandel & Lesser, 1972; Lamouse, 1969; Lupri, 1969; Michel, 1967; Price-Bonham, 1976; Safilios-Rothschild, 1967; Turk & Bell, 1972). Finally, Turk and Bell (1972) asked family members to answer the question, "Who is the boss in your family?"

Although the Blood and Wolfe (1960) self-report measure of power has been widely used, Heer (1963) and Safilios-Rothschild (1969, 1970) have warned that because only wives were interviewed in several studies, there is no guarantee that if husbands responded to the same set of items that their responses would be similar to those of their wives. In fact, several studies (Burchinal & Bauder, 1965; Buric & Zecevic, 1967; Douglas & Wind, 1978; Heer, 1962; Larson, 1974; Olson & Rabunsky, 1972; Turk & Bell, 1972) demonstrate that family members frequently disagree when they are asked to estimate the extent to which each family member has power. Apparently, perceptions of power may indeed be in the eye of the beholder. Researchers employing this kind of self-report procedure to measure power should be sure to obtain estimates from all group members rather than relying upon the estimates of some subset of a group. Furthermore, at the level of the group, the degree of consensus concerning who is the most powerful member of the group might be an important variable worth studying in its own right. One might expect to find significant differences between groups that vary with respect to the degree of consensus they exhibit about who is the most powerful group member, and highly cohesive groups might show a greater degree of consensus.

Recently, considerable interest has been shown in the study of various compliance-gaining and compliance-resisting strategies by communication researchers. Marwell and Schmitt (1967) devised a list of 16 compliance-gaining techniques, for example, promise and threat. In an apparently independent effort, Falbo (1977) asked persons to indicate how they "get their way." From these responses she developed a similar list of 16 power strategies. Falbo and Peplau (1980) examined power strategies that are used in intimate relationships. Schenck-Hamlin, Wiseman, and Georgacarakos (1982) have discussed properties that can be used to generate 14 compliance-gaining strategies. Fitzpatrick and Winke (1979) derived a list of five strategies for dealing with interpersonal conflict. McLaughlin, Cody, and Robey (1980) studied strategies that persons employ to resist compliance-gaining attempts. In many of the studies that have used these strategy lists, persons are asked to imagine themselves or others in a given situation in which they desire to exercise influence. They are then given a list of strategies that might be used to achieve their objective and asked to indicate on a scale the likelihood that each strategy would be used. These measures are not indices of power per se but represent attempts to assess via self-report the kinds of persuasive messages persons are most likely to create under a specified set of conditions. Unfortunately, there has been virtually no effort to validate these lists within the context of ongoing interactions. Thus it remains to be seen whether manifestations of these strategies can be observed in ongoing interactions in which influence attempts and resistance to such attempts are unfolding.

Interaction Measures. Numerous efforts have been made to make inferences concerning the relative power of group members by observing various attributes of their communication behavior. As was pointed out at the beginning of this section, persons are generally given a task that involves discussion and their conversations are recorded. Various facets of their communication are then scored to provide estimates of the degree of influence they exerted in the interaction. These communication-based estimates of power are frequently correlated with the outcome of the decision to see whether there is any relationship between influence demonstrated through communicative conduct and influence on the final decision of the group.

In early studies using this approach, Strodtbeck (1951, 1954) had family members discuss an issue about which they disagreed, as determined by individually completed attitude questionnaires. The object of the discussion was to reach a consensus on the issue and develop a "group position." The outcome of this *revealed differences* procedure was then correlated with the amount of time each person spoke (Strodtbeck, 1951). This study showed that the family member who spoke the most was the most influential in the final group decision. Thus the *process* measure of power (amount of talk) was positively related to the *outcome* measure of power (degree of influence in the decision). Although these early findings were encouraging, subsequent studies failed to find consistent relationships between process and outcome measures. For example, in a tour de force comparison of self-report, process, and outcome power measures, Turk and Bell (1972) failed to find any relationship between the four process measures of power (units of action initiated, instrumental acts initiated, index of directive control [Bales, 1950], and interruptions) and outcome measures of power from the revealed differences procedure and a discussion test developed by Kenkel (1957). This latter procedure asks family members to indicate individually how a sum of money given to the family should be spent. The family is then brought together and a group consensus is reached. Individual influence is measured by the extent to which each family member's preferences are reflected in the group consensus. As was noted earlier, this same study failed to find consistent relationships between self-report and process measures of power.

Hadley and Jacob (1973) employed total talking time and successful interruptions as process measures of power and a coalition game and a modified version of the revealed differences technique as ways of assessing outcome power. Although the two process measures were significantly related to each other, the outcome measures were not. Furthermore, the outcome measures were not found to be related to the process measures. The finding that the two different tasks used to generate discussion in this study did not yield comparable results in terms of the outcome measures is consistent with the findings of a study reported by Cromwell, Klein, and Wieting (1975). These investigators found that the Kenkel (1957) technique produced interaction measures of power that did not correlate well with interaction measures generated when another discussion technique SIMFAM (Strauss & Tallman, 1971) was employed. This study suggests that the task given to a group may exert considerable impact upon the process measures that are used to index power.

The general hypothesis underlying the above studies is that persons who are more dominant verbally, that is, those who talk more frequently, longer, interrupt more, and so on should be more influential in the decision-making outcome of the group. However, it seems reasonable to suppose that under at least some circumstances it is *what* and not *how much* persons say that allows them to acquire power in a group and thus have greater influence in decision-making outcomes. For example, the "quiet expert" in a problem-solving group, who has the solution to the problem, may have to say very little to influence the group decision. Obviously, in order to be influential in such a situation, the "quiet expert" must say something; although if persons enter group situations in which other group members already recognize their power, they may be able to exert considerable influence by simply raising an eyebrow or displaying a particular facial expression. It is said that the late Mayor Daley could determine the outcome of various deliberations by simply nodding his head at the critical moment and saying nothing. This line of reasoning suggests that there may be good reason to expect very little relationship between process and outcome measures of power in a limited range of situations.

Researchers interested in the relationship between family communication and mental illness have also attempted to index power by studying the communicative conduct of family members. Mishler and Waxler (1968) distinguished between power attained through attention control and power gained through control of the other person. Participation rate, who speaks to whom, and statement length were employed as indices of attention control. Interruptions were used to index *direct* control of the other person and questions were employed to assess *indirect* control of the other person. Murrell and Stachowiak (1967) indexed power by counting the number of units of interaction sent and received. Persons who send more and those who receive more were scored as more powerful. Leighton, Stollak, and Ferguson (1971) used number of times talked, duration of times talked, total talk time, and interruptions as measures of control in family interactions. Obviously, the interaction indices of power used by this group of researchers are very similar to those employed by the family sociologists.

Over the past decade, considerable research attention has been focused upon gender differences in speech (Eakins & Eakins, 1978; Key, 1975; Kramerae, 1981; Lakoff, 1975; Smith, 1979; Thorne & Henley, 1975). One of the central hypotheses underlying this line of research is that gender differences in speech both reflect and support male dominance. For example, Lakoff (1975) pointed to a number of lexical and syntactical forms that she felt typically differ between males and females such that male dominance is sustained. For example, females tend to use weaker expletives than males. Which of the following two sentences is the male sentence?

(1) Darn it! I forgot to return the library book.
(2) Oh Shit! I forgot to return the library book.

In Lakoff's (1975) view females are more likely to utter (1) than (2). In terms of syntactic differences she claims that females use more tag questions than do males. For example, consider the following two sentences:

(3) That's a beautiful sunset.
(4) That's a beautiful sunset, isn't it?

The assertion made in sentence (3) is quite clear. The person uttering it is sure that the sunset is beautiful; however, sentence (4) seems to convey considerably more uncertainty and lack of confidence. Lakoff (1975) also argues that females may indicate uncertainty in their answers to questions by raising the vocal intonation while giving the answer. For example,

    (5) (a) Who is the mayor of Chicago?
        (b) Ah . . . Harold Washington. . . ?

The use of a rising intonation in a declarative answer tends to create the impression that the person uttering the statement is not certain of the answer. In fact, the answer becomes a question to the question-asker. Finally, Lakoff (1975) argues that females make more complex requests than do males in order to be less offensive. Thus the following options might be available for requesting a glass of wine:

    (6) (a) Get me a glass of wine.
        (b) Please get me a glass of wine.
        (c) Will you get me a glass of wine?
        (d) Will you please get me a glass of wine?
        (e) Won't you get me a glass of wine?

Erickson, Lind, Johnson, and O'Barr (1978) and Lind and O'Barr (1979) have argued that the gender differences suggested above are indicative of a more general speech style dimension that they have labeled *powerful* versus *powerless* speech. Their observations of witness testimony in courtroom trials led them to conclude that the following features of speech differentiated high- and low-power witnesses: (1) intensifiers ("so," "very"); (2) hedges ("kinda," "I guess"); (3) especially formal grammar; (4) hesitation forms ("uh," "you know"); (5) gestures; (6) questioning forms (rising intonation in declarative situations); and (7) polite forms ("please," "thank you"). Lower-power witnesses tended to use more of these forms.

This line of research suggests a very different set of communicative behaviors that might be used to index power when compared with those employed by sociologists of the family and researchers in clinical psychology. These researchers tend to employ relatively gross communication measures to index power, for example, amount of interaction, whereas the sociolinguistic researchers tend to look more at particular features of speech as indicative of power. There is no incompatibility between these two lines of research and they might complement each other. At this juncture what is needed are measurement-oriented studies that examine the extent to which these various measures of power correlate with each other. If they correlate highly, then it might be necessary to measure only a few of them to provide an index of power; however, most probably they will not correlate well with each other, which may mean that there are different facets of power that need to be explicated at the conceptual level.

One difficulty with the interaction-oriented approaches to the measurement of power discussed thus far is that they are really *not* "interactive." Recall that relational approaches to the study of power (Rogers & Farace, 1975) argue that one cannot understand how control patterns develop in relationships unless one studies interlocking *pairs* of messages. Thus even if a given individual dominates a discussion by speaking frequently and for long periods of time, we cannot know how successful his or her influence attempts have been unless we study the responses of other group members to the influence attempts. There are remarkably few studies outside of the relational control literature that have taken into account how successful or unsuccessful a given individual's influence attempts have been, although there are a few (for example, Cromwell et al., 1975).

Because we have previously devoted considerable discussion to relational control coding schemes, we will not repeat a description of them here. However, it should be kept in mind that one of the great strengths of these systems is their emphasis upon the *exchange* as a unit of analysis rather than the individual. Relational measurement schemes seem to do a better job of actualizing the notion that power is an attribute of a relationship rather than an attribute of an individual. This does not mean that interaction indices of power that are individually based are without value. The relative value of these approaches depends upon the research question being asked. Thus in making a choice among these alternative measurement approaches to studying power, it is important that the researcher have a clear idea of the assumptions about power that he or she is making so that the most appropriate measurement approach can be used.

Summary. In this section we have considered several different approaches to the measurement of social power. There are numerous projective and self-report measures of power-related constructs that tend to locate power within the individual. In addition, there is a considerable literature that has indexed power through the study of interaction behavior. However, it should be noted that when only individual communicative conduct is measured, we are assuming that power is an individual property. It is only when measurement systems capture the give and take between interactants that we are studying power as a relationship property. The study of exchanges over time is considerably more difficult than the study of individuals; however, because this measurement approach is more isomorphic to relationship conceptions of power, it is likely to be more productive in the future.

SOCIAL POWER AND
COMMUNICATIVE CONDUCT

In this section, we will examine research that has linked social power with communicative behavior. There are three principal ways in which this link can be studied. First, one can measure persons' desires for power, place them in a communication situation, and observe their behavior. A similar strategy is to place persons in high- and low-power positions in a group and observe how their role assignments influence their communicative behavior. In both instances, social power is the independent variable and communicative conduct the dependent variable. A second general approach is to observe or manipulate communicative conduct in certain ways and have observers make inferences or attributions about the social power levels of the persons being observed. Using this approach, communicative conduct becomes the independent variable and social power the dependent variable. A third approach is to try to study the mutual influences of communicative conduct and social power in a more exchange-oriented format. Obviously, in ongoing interactions, communication and power rapidly alternate roles as independent and dependent variables; that is, persons make attributions concerning their own and others' power levels and then communicate on the bases of these inferences. Their conduct based upon these attributions may cause their estimates of power to be updated. Most of the research that has linked social power and communication falls into the first two categories and very little has been done in the third.

Communicative Conduct of Power-Oriented Persons

In this section we will consider two types of studies: those that measure power as a trait and then attempt to see whether the trait is manifested in interaction behavior and studies that place persons in positions of power to see how they behave vis à vis their less powerful counterparts. The studies of the first kind represent attempts to validate various scales, that is, to determine whether persons who score high on the variable under study actually manifest more of the trait in their behavior than do persons who score low.

Trait-Oriented Studies. As a part of an effort to validate his measure of n Power, Veroff (1957) reported that persons with high n Power levels were more likely to be rated by their instructors as trying to convince others of their views and more argumentative. Terhune (1968) found that men with high n Power and low levels of n Affiliation and n Achievement displayed more exploitative behavior in the Prisoner's Dilemma game. In a review of studies using the Veroff measure of n Power, Veroff and Veroff (1972) interpreted the findings of a number of studies as indicating that the measure taps a concern for power that stems from feelings of inferiority rather than from feelings of mastery over the environment. Uleman (1972) reported that although persons scoring high on his measure of n Influence were rated by peers as being more dominant, he could find no evidence that high n Influence persons are more argumentative. In fact, he interpreted his data as indicating that high n Influence persons do not need to feel that they are "right" and thus be contentious; apparently, high n Influence persons enjoy exercising power in more subtle ways.

Following on the work of Haley (1969), who analyzed the power tactics of Jesus Christ, Winter (1973) argued that in order to gain power, persons must: (1) attract attention and (2) surround themselves with a cadre of loyal followers who do not threaten their visibility. Jesus gained attention by attacking the establishment. His "organization" consisted of relatively obscure persons. Winter (1973) reports evidence that persons scoring high on his measure of n Power display similar characteristics. In the area of attention-gaining strategies, he found that persons with high levels of n Power: (1) wrote more letters to their school newspaper, (2) displayed their names on the doors of their dormitory rooms more frequently, (3) possessed more status symbols, (4) were perceived to be more dominant in group discussions, and (5) selected seating positions in group discussion situations that would make them more prominent. Winter (1973) also found that high n Power persons tended to direct negative or critical remarks to high-status persons when they were asked the following question: "If you could say one sentence—any sentence—to anyone, anywhere in the world, in person and without fear of reprisal, what would you say, and to whom?" Low n Power persons responded to the same question by making a positive remark or a negative remark to a low-status person. Winter (1973) interpreted this result as indicating that high n Power persons establish their visibility by attacking established authority. In the domain of maintaining an organization, Winter (1973) found that high n Power persons tended to designate as friends those persons whom others rated as relatively unpopular; thus, it appears that high n Power individuals surround themselves with persons who are not likely to threaten their visibility.

Other studies employing the Winter (1973) measure of n Power have reported findings that lend support to his analysis. For example, high n Power persons who were placed in supervisory roles in an industrial simulation situation rated themselves to be more influential than low n Power persons placed in the same roles (Fodor & Farrow, 1979). In addition, Fodor and Smith (1982) found that high n Power persons who were placed in leadership positions in decision-making groups were rated more influential in the decision outcome than low n Power leaders. However, this same study indicated that the *quality* of decision making, as indexed by the number of facts and proposals considered by the group and the moral dimensions of the decision alternatives, was lower in groups led by high n Power individuals. This latter finding might be explained by recourse to the idea that those scoring high on Veroff's and Winter's measures of n Power may be manifesting a desire for power that is predicated upon feelings of inferiority. Attempting to compensate for these inferiority feelings by showing excessive dominance may interfere with the performance of the task at hand. Thus high n Power leaders may be perceived as dominant but may not be particularly effective leaders because of their excessive concern for power.

There is considerable literature that has examined the relationship between other trait measures of dominance and verbal and nonverbal communicative behaviors that are indicators of dominance. In an interview situation in which a number of embarrassing questions were asked, interviewees with high levels of abasement broke eye contact with the interviewer by looking left to a significantly greater extent than did low abasement interviewees (Libby & Yaklevich, 1973). Beekman (1975) reported a correlation of −.34 between dominance and filled pause rate for males involved in informal social interaction with females. Females showed no relationship between the same two variables. Scherer (1979) correlated a number of paralinguistic variables derived from videotapes of simulated jury deliberations with a trait measure of dominance. He obtained the following correlations between dominance and five paralinguistic features: Verbal Productivity (.15), Interruptions (.50), Repetitions (.15), Silent Pauses (−.44), and Pitch Range (.47). Scherer argues that these data provide some support for the argument that under certain conditions personality traits may be useful predictors of behavior in interaction situations. It is interesting to note that of the five variables studied by Scherer, Productivity, Repetitions, and Pitch Range were found to be the best predictors of *perceived influence* in the group. Thus with the exception of pitch range, variables that correlated poorly with trait dominance were good predictors of perceived influence. Finally, this study revealed a number of cultural differences between West German and American persons on these indices.

Aries, Gold, and Weigel (1983) correlated scores from the dominance scale of the CPI with a number of verbal and nonverbal indicators of dominance (for example, talk time, verbal acts initiated, interruptions, arms away from body, open legs, and backward lean). In groups consisting of all males, modest but significant correlations were obtained between the dominance scale and the verbal and nonverbal dominance indicators ($r = .31$). Correlations for all female groups were of similar magnitudes to those found in all male groups, but only one was significant ($r = .29$). However, the correlations between the communication indicators and personality measures of dominance were virtually nil in mixed sex groups ($r = .05$). This pattern of findings was interpreted as indicating that when situational variables are rendered less influential, for example, by having homogenous groups, individual differences will exert considerably more influence upon behavior than when situational variables like gender differences are salient. Roger and Schumacher (1983) reported that dyads consisting of two highly dominant persons, as measured by the dominance scale of the Edwards Personal Preference Schedule (EPPS), showed significantly higher rates of successful interruptions in the later stages of an initial encounter than did dyads consisting of either two low dominance scorers or a high and a low. There were no significant differences between the three groups when compared on rates of unsuccessful interruptions.

Although the foregoing studies of trait dominance and communicative behavior tend to show direct relationships between the two variables, there are studies suggesting that these relationships are influenced by situational factors. Exline and Messick (1967) found that under conditions of low social reinforcement, dependent persons increased their looking at a confederate as the confederate increased the rate of reinforcement given; however, dominant persons decreased their looking at the confederate as reinforcements were increased. Exline (1972) had subjects interact with a confederate who gazed 50 percent of the time at the subject when speaking and either 100 percent or 0 percent when listening. When listening, dominant persons' gaze toward the confederate was not influenced by the confederate's behavior. By contrast, persons with low dominance levels looked more often at the inattentive confederate (0 percent). Exline (1972) argued that in general, "powerful people do not monitor less powerful people" (p. 192). Ellyson (1974) reported that persons with high levels of dominance looked less at a confederate while listening than did low dominance individuals, thus adding further support to the argument advanced by Exline (1972). In two subsequent studies (Ellyson, Dovidio, Corson, & Vinicur, 1980; Exline, Ellyson, & Long, 1975), positive relationships were found between expressed control (Schutz, 1958) and patterns of dominance expressed in looking behavior. Both studies revealed that those scoring high on expressed control showed little difference between their rates of looking while speaking and looking while listening. By contrast, those scoring low on dominance were found to look significantly less while speaking than while listening. These findings provide further support for the notion that persons in low power positions monitor those with higher power when the high-power person is speaking and show deference by avoiding eye contact when they speak to superiors.

Having seen how n Power, n Influence, and dominance are reflected in social interaction behavior, we now turn to research that has studied the relationship between authoritarianism, dogmatism, locus of control, and Machiavellianism on the one hand and empirical indicators of dominance as represented in communicative behavior on the other. Relatively little research has been done to link the variables of authoritarianism and dogmatism to specific dominance behaviors in interaction situations. Given the description of authoritarian individuals, one would expect them to be more aggressive and punitive than their equalitarian counterparts; however, in their review of this literature, Cherry and Byrne (1977) assert that there are a number of situational variables that determine whether this relationship will be found. Rubin and Brown (1975) found that in 16 studies that have examined the link between authoritarianism and various bargaining processes, seven found no effects for the authoritarianism variable. In those studies that did find effects, high authoritarians tended to bargain less cooperatively than lows; that is, highs showed more competitiveness. Herb and Elliott (1971) reported that high authoritarians displayed more rigid body postures than lows in situations in which they were either a superior or a subordinate in a group task. When confederates made high authoritarians play a subordinate role, they tended to lean forward more often than the lows. One interpretation of these findings is that high authoritarians nonverbally play leadership roles when their authority is challenged by other group members.

Druckman (1967) found that highly dogmatic persons were both more resistant to change and less willing to compromise from a given position in a dyadic bargaining situation. They tended to view compromise from a given position as defeat. Zagona and Zurcher (1964, 1965) reported that high dogmatics were more concerned with problems of leader selection and group structure. Frye, Vidulich, Meierhoefer, and Joure (1972), and Talley and Vamos (1972) suggest that high dogmatics show higher levels of concern for the structure and operation of a group when they are placed in an unstructured situation. In the former study, highly dogmatic group members made more negative statements about the situation than did group members with low dogmatism levels. Finally, Roloff and Barnicott (1979) found that highly dogmatic persons reported that they were more likely to employ all 16 of Marwell and Schmitt's (1967) compliance-gaining techniques than were low dogmatics.

A number of studies have examined the link between locus of control and behavior related to power and dominance. In an early study, Phares (1965) found that when persons were asked to change another person's expressed attitude, internally controlled persons were more persuasive than externally controlled individuals. Goodstadt and Hjelle (1973) reported that internally controlled persons who were given a range of power strategies with which to influence another were less likely to use coercive strategies than were externally controlled persons. This study also revealed the tendency for internals to rely more on informal means of influence rather than the formal means that were associated with their supervisory role. These findings are consistent with other studies demonstrating that power holders who encounter resistance to their influence attempts are more likely to resort to coercive means of influence (Goodstadt & Kipnis, 1970; Kipnis & Consentino, 1969). Thus persons who are externally controlled tend to anticipate that they will be unable to influence others and are, as a result, more prone to employ coercive means of influence. These studies are among the few that have examined the responses of persons whose influence attempts are thwarted.

Additional research has found relationships between locus of control and dominance in interaction settings. Bugental, Henker, and Whalen (1976) hypothesized and found that internally controlled persons were judged to be more persuasive in vocalic communication channels than in the content of their messages; by contrast, externally controlled persons were judged to be more persuasive in the content of their messages than in the vocal presentation of their messages. This difference was interpreted as indicating that externally controlled persons have expectations of failing at persuasion that "leak" through their vocalic communication, whereas internals, who are confident of their persuasive powers, show greater persuasiveness in the nonverbal, vocalic channel. Doherty and Ryder (1979) reported that in a simulated conflict situation involving married couples, internally controlled husbands displayed more assertive behavior than did externally controlled husbands. A similar trend was observed for wives but failed to reach conventional significance levels (possibly because of the relatively low statistical power of the design). Finally, Cialdini and Mirels (1976) tested the notion that persons who were successful at persuading another would make attributions about the target of their influence attempts in ways that would be consistent with their locus of control orientation. In support of this reasoning they found that internally controlled persuaders enhanced the perceived intelligence and attractiveness of persons who yielded to them and derogated those who resisted their influence attempts. Externally controlled persons showed the reverse pattern of attributions. In general, the studies reviewed above show very consistent support for the proposition that internally controlled persons are both more confident of their abilities to exert influence and are behaviorally more persuasive in actual social influence situations. Because of their increased confidence, they are more likely to employ means of influence that are pro-social in nature, whereas their externally controlled counterparts are more likely to use coercion and other antisocial modes of influence.

The final trait-oriented variable we will consider here is Machiavellianism. Given the potential links of this particular variable to social influence phenomena, it is surprising to find that relatively few studies have examined the relationship between Machiavellianism and actual behavior in social influence situations. Geis (1970) reported that high Machiavellians (high Machs) were more successful in an interpersonal bargaining situation than were lows. Braginsky (1970) found that high Mach children used more manipulative strategies, were more successful in producing influence, and were judged to be more effective at persuasion in general than their low Mach counterparts. Hacker and Gaitz (1970) reported that high Machs participated more in discussions, asked for more information, and more often provided their own orientation. These behaviors are generally associated with greater dominance. In a study that examined the relationship between Machiavellianism and the use of compliance-gaining techniques, Roloff and Barnicott (1978) observed weak but significant correlations between Machiavellianism and the use of pro-social techniques ($r = .21$) and a positive relationship between Machiavellianism and the use of psychological force techniques ($r = .34$). However, no significant relationship was found between Machiavellianism and punishing activity techniques. This latter finding is somewhat surprising because Guterman (1970) reported that high Machiavellians tended to score low on a need for social approval index.

There are at least three general conclusions that can be drawn from this overview of trait measures. First, there seem to be consistent relationships between these measures and communicative behaviors that are associated with exercise of power. Second, when researchers report correlations between these trait measures and various measures of dominant behavior, they are relatively weak. Part of the explanation for these weak correlations lies in the fact that the reliabilities of the trait measures and the interaction indices may be relatively low. Moreover, because an individual behavior (for example, interruptions or question-asking) may serve a number of communicative functions including dominance or control, it is not surprising that any one behavioral index of dominance or power correlates minimally with a trait measure. Several behavioral indices of dominance should do a better job of "predicting" trait dominance given the potential variability in the functions that individual behaviors serve. In support of this reasoning, Aries et al. (1983) found that a combination of nine behavioral indices of dominance produced a multiple correlation of .67 with a trait measure of dominance as a criterion. The average correlation of the same set of predictors with the same criterion was only .31. Thus, substantial proportions of variance can be explained in trait dominance when a number of behavioral indices of dominance are employed simultaneously to predict trait dominance. Finally, a third general observation is that individual differences in the propensity to exercise power can be overridden by situational influences. However, this statement does not lead to the implication that trait measures of power are useless and should be abandoned. Instead, efforts should be made to specify a general set of conditions under which trait differences will be manifested directly in communicative conduct and conditions under which such differences are likely to be masked.

Assumed Power Differences. In this section we will examine research that studies the relationships between power and communicative conduct by assuming that there are power differences between persons (for example, males and females) and by comparing their communication behavior to see whether such differences are manifested. The next section explores research that places persons in roles that differ with respect to power and reports observations of their behavior vis-à-vis each other. These kinds of studies are generally carried out in laboratory situations and use some kind of simulation to enable persons to enact different roles. We will first consider studies that assume power differences.

Lott and Sommer (1967) observed that college upperclassmen sat closer to peers than to freshmen who were not doing well in school. This study also revealed that upperclassmen sat closer to peers than to professors. Dean, Willis, and Hewitt (1975) examined the initial interaction distances of military personnel of different ranks. They found that when subordinates initiated interaction with superiors, the rank of the superior was related to initial interaction distance. The greater the difference in rank, the greater the interaction distance. However, when a superior initiated interaction, there was no relationship between rank and distance. These findings indicate that a higher-status person has the option of controlling initial distance; however, the subordinate must be more rank conscious when he or she initiates interaction. Brown and Ford (1961) noted that it is the prerogative of the higher-status person to determine when persons should change from the more formal form of address that involves title plus last name (Dr. Jones, Mrs. Smith) to the more informal use of first names. The distance study demonstrates a similar principle. Mishler (1975) observed that parents tended to initiate and continue dialog with their children by asking the children questions. He argued on the basis of this finding that parents use question-asking as a way of controlling their children.

Over the past 10 years, considerable research attention has been devoted to the study of gender differences in both verbal and nonverbal communication. As was pointed out earlier, Lakoff (1975) suggested a number of differences between male and female speech that both reflect and reinforce male dominance. Females are less likely to use strong expletives and more likely to use tag questions, rising intonation when answering questions, and more polite forms of requests. All of these forms are alleged to indicate weakness and submissiveness. Because there is extensive literature in this area, it will not be exhaustively reviewed here. Useful overviews have been presented by Thorne and Henley (1975) and Smith (1979). We will consider a few relevant studies to illustrate the research done in this area.

In a study of vocal intensity, Markel, Prebor, and Brandt (1972) found that males showed greater vocal intensity than females. Zimmerman and West (1975) reported that males interrupted females more than females interrupted males. In contrast to these supportive findings, Edelsky (1979) found no support for the assertion that females use the rising intonation in answering questions more frequently than do males. In a cleverly designed study, Brouwer, Gerritsen, and De Haan (1979) compared the speech of males and females who asked for train tickets and information at the Central Station of Amsterdam, Holland. Comparisons were made on the number of words, diminutives, civilities, polite forms, requests for information, hesitations, repetitions, and self-corrections. Women were found to make more information requests and show more hesitations in their speech than men; however, there were no differences on any of the other speech variables. Interestingly, the gender of the ticket seller was considerably more influential in this situation. Both male and female ticket buyers used more words, diminutives, civilities, and hesitations when they were speaking with a male ticket agent. The findings of this study alert us to the fact that research on gender differences must take into account the genders of both the speaker and the addressee. Moreover, the study also calls into question some of Lakoff's (1975) observations concerning gender differences in speech.

In a series of papers, Erikson et al. (1978), Lind and O'Barr (1979), and O'Barr and Atkins (1980) have extensively examined powerful and powerless speech styles exhibited by witnesses giving courtroom testimony. In addition, they have developed stimulus tapes and transcripts to represent these styles.

In general, persons using more hedges, polite forms, tag questions, speaking in italics, empty adjectives, hyper-correct grammar, direct quotations, special lexicon, rising intonation in giving answers, and less humor are exhibiting the powerless speech style. Although women tended to demonstrate more speech attributes associated with the powerless style, O'Barr and Atkins (1980) suggest that it might be more productive to focus attention upon the variables of powerlessness rather than gender because persons in positions of power, regardless of gender, may be more prone to use powerful forms. These researchers found that when females spoke in a powerful style, they were rated to be more persuasive than females who used the powerless style of speech. The same pattern of findings was obtained for males. A study reported by Lamb (1981) reached a similar conclusion. Thus the powerful-powerless distinction may be a more useful variable theoretically than gender because of its greater abstractness.

A study by Kimble, Yoshikawa, and Zehr (1981) further demonstrates the problems associated with positing a simple relationship between gender and dominance. These investigators compared the assertiveness of males and females in four-person groups consisting of either all males, all females, or two males and two females. Assertiveness was indexed by rating both content and vocalic communication for assertiveness. In addition, loudness, speech rate, and average pause duration between speakers were measured. The hypotheses that males would be more assertive than females and that male assertiveness would be more prevalent in mixed-gender groups were not supported by the data. However, these researchers did find that the woman who spoke second in a mixed-gender group was significantly less assertive than her first speaking sister. In all male groups, the first speaking male was more verbally assertive than the last speaking one. In general, these findings suggest that relationships between gender and dominance as manifested in communication behavior are considerably more complex than those suggested by earlier speculation in this area.

Before leaving the topic of gender differences, it is worth noting that some research attention has been paid to the issue of gender stereotyping of speech. Kramer (1977) had males and females rate male and female speakers on 51 speech characteristics. She found that participants listed the following attributes as more characteristic of male speech: demanding voice, deep voice, being boastful, using swear words, dominating speech, speaking loudly, showing anger rather than concealing it, coming straight to the point, using militant speech, using slang, using authoritarian speech, speaking forcefully, lounging and leaning back while talking, using aggressive speech, speaking bluntly, and having a sense of humor in speech. Female speakers were attributed the following characteristics: Enunciating clearly, using a high pitch, using hands and face to express ideas, gossiping, showing concern for listener, using gentle speech, speaking quickly, talking about trivial topics, using a wide range in pitch and rate, using friendly speech, talking frequently, using emotional speech, using many details, speaking smoothly, using open and self-revealing speech, speaking enthusiastically, smiling a lot when talking, using good grammar, speaking politely, and using gibberish. Apparently, male speech is stereotypically perceived as more powerful than that of females. The existence of such stereotypes may mean that even if males and females change their manner of speaking to be discrepant with stereotypes, persons may fail to perceive such changes because of their stereotyped conceptions. Thus it may be difficult for females to exert influence in situations even if they employ a more powerful speech style; although the findings of O'Barr and Atkins (1980) suggest that such changes can have considerable impacts upon addressees' perceptions. For a discussion of these and related issues, the reader should consult Kramerae (1981).

In our survey of literature in which dominance is assumed to be an independent variable and dominance expressed through communicative conduct a dependent variable, we have seen that there is considerable consistency across studies. Trait measures of dominance frequently predict dominance in communicative conduct with some degree of accuracy and in relationships in which power differentials are assumed; there appear to be fairly consistent differences in the communication behavior of high- and low-power persons. However, even with such consistencies, one cannot confidently draw causal inferences from these studies. In the case of the personality research, there is always the possibility that when significant relationships are observed between trait measures of dominance and behavioral measures that variables correlated with the trait measure are the actual causes of behavior. Thus if n Power is positively correlated with n Achievement, observed differences between high and low n Power persons may be due to their correlated differences in n Achievement. Unfortunately, in most of the trait-oriented studies we considered, no effort was made to control for this possibility.

A similar problem exists for the studies that assume power differences between persons. Thus the fact that females display verbal and nonverbal behaviors that are consistent with a powerless style of speech does not necessarily mean that gender per se is the critical causal variable producing such differences. Females may display such behaviors more frequently because they are generally in lower power positions. Position is the causal variable and not gender. One way to avoid such confounding is to assign randomly persons to play roles that differ with respect to power and observe their communication to see if there are differences among role incumbents. This experimental approach insures that potential confounding variables are controlled and makes causal inference more certain. The studies that follow have generally employed this approach.

Induced Power Differences. In an early study of the relationship between position in a status hierarchy and communication, Kelley (1951) found that persons in low-status groups sent more task irrelevant messages in a problem-solving situation than did members of high-status groups. In addition, low-status persons made more conjectures about the job being done by the high-status group than did the highs with reference to the lows. Kelley argued that communication can serve as a substitute for blocked upward mobility in a status hierarchy. Cohen (1958) pointed out that one must distinguish between the effects of status and power on communication. He observed that Kelley (1951) created status differences between groups by informing group members that the task they were performing was more or less important than the one being done by the other group. Although this induction may introduce status differences, it does not produce power differences because the groups were not dependent upon each other for outcomes. In short, status and power may or may not be correlated; for example, a prominent professor may or may not be able to wield influence in his department and a criminal may be able to exert considerable influence upon others by the use of threats.

In his study, Cohen (1958) not only used Kelley's status manipulation, but also made it clear to the low-status groups that their success was dependent upon the high-status group. In addition, Cohen led some groups to believe that they could move up to the high-status group, whereas other low-status group members were told that they had no upward mobility. In contrasting the communication of mobile and nonmobile low-status groups, Cohen reported that the mobile groups sent longer messages with less irrelevant content to the high-status groups. In addition, groups with mobility possibilities made fewer conjectures about the job being done by the high-status group and were less critical of these groups. One general conclusion drawn in this study was that low-power persons who have the possibility of becoming part of a group with greater power are considerably more circumspect in their communication toward members of the high-power group than are persons with no mobility possibilities.

In a study related to the Kelley (1951) and Cohen (1958) experiments, Tjosvold (1978) reported that when persons with low power strongly affirmed the personal effectiveness of persons with higher power levels, the high-power persons were more attracted to the persons with low power. However, this increased liking did not raise the likelihood that the high-power persons would yield to the demands of the low-power persons. Thus when low-power persons ingratiate themselves to high-power persons by affirming their superiority, they are not likely to increase the probability that they will actually influence the high-power individuals, even though the high-power persons increase their liking for them.

Mehrabian and Williams (1969) studied the verbal and nonverbal behavior of persons who were asked to persuade others. Persons given this assignment showed greater eye contact, increased rates of positive head nodding, gesticulation, facial activity, speech rate, speech volume, and intonation. Persuaders' voices were rated as less halting. In a related study,

Rosenfeld (1966) found that persons who were asked to gain approval from others were more likely to speak more frequently and for longer durations than did their approval-avoiding counterparts. Approval seekers also showed more smiles, positive head nods, and gesticulations. Although the Rosenfeld (1966) study did not deal with attempted influence, it is important to note that the approval seekers in his study manifested verbal and nonverbal behaviors that were similar to those observed by Mehrabian and Williams (1969). Thus it appears that when persons are given the objective of persuading another, they are likely to try to ingratiate themselves to their targets by displaying behaviors designed to elicit social approval.

Ellyson et al. (1980) manipulated status differences by leading college students to believe that they were interacting with either a low-status other (a high school student who wished to work in a gas station) or a high-status other (a chemistry honors student bound for a prestigious medical school). Observations of subjects' looking behavior during the interactions revealed that when they believed that they were in the high-status position vis-à-vis their partner, subjects' rates of looking while speaking were about the same as their rates of looking while listening, a high dominance pattern of visual behavior. However, when they believed that their status relative to their partner was low, their rate of looking while listening was significantly greater than their rate of looking while speaking, a low dominance pattern.

Leffler, Gillespie, and Conaty (1982) also examined the nonverbal behavior of persons interacting under discrepant status conditions. In their study persons were paired into student-teacher dyads in which the teacher was given the task of instructing the student. After an initial session, roles were reversed during a second session. This study revealed that high-status persons (teachers) claimed more direct space with their bodies, talked more, and attempted more interruptions than did their lower-status students. Moreover, using both touching and pointing, teachers intruded more on students than did students on teachers.

The studies reviewed above consistently show that when persons are put into high-status positions or are placed into situations in which they are encouraged to wield influence, their verbal and nonverbal conduct varies in very consistent ways from that which is manifested by persons who are in low-status or low-power positions. Moreover, the Leffler et al. (1982) study indicates that persons can very quickly modify their behaviors when they move up or down a status ranking. Although this body of research shows consistent relationships between status, power, and dominant communicative conduct, it does not address the issue of how dominance hierarchies emerge in groups, that is, why certain persons end up talking more, interrupting more, and having more impact upon group decisions than others in the group. Employing what has come to be known as expectation states theory or status characteristics theory, Berger, Fisek, Norman, and Zelditch (1977) argue that under certain conditions in specific types of groups, high-status group members become more powerful because other group members believe that the high-status group members are more competent or intelligent. It is through the common belief that the high-status person is more competent that he or she is then allowed to become more dominant behaviorally. These investigators have conducted numerous experiments that demonstrate that persons who are believed to have high status by others exert more influence on decision outcomes than do persons who are believed to have lower status. Unfortunately, from our point of view, the experimental paradigm employed by these researchers does not allow for direct verbal and nonverbal communication between interactants; however, the theoretical position does have relevance for understanding how status characteristics are "translated" into the kinds of dominance behaviors we have examined here.

Attributing Power from Communicative Conduct

Here we will focus upon studies in which communication behavior is either manipulated or measured and then related to participants' or observers' attributions of power. For example, persons in a small group study might be asked to rank order their fellow group members in terms of their influence in the group. The degree to which each person participated in the group is then correlated with these rankings. In a more controlled setting, an investigator might vary the actions of stimulus persons and then have observers make judgments concerning the power of the stimulus persons. In either case, the hypothesis under test is that the ways in which persons behave influence the extent to which they are judged to be powerful by others. We will first examine some correlational studies of attributed power and then consider experimental studies.

Correlational Studies. A large number of studies have investigated the relationship between the rate of verbal participation in small groups and leadership rankings. Stein and Heller (1979) found a mean correlation of .65 between the two variables based upon 77 correlations. Because verbal participation appears to account for about 42 percent of the variance on the average in leadership rankings, this leaves considerable room for other facets of communicative behavior to account for leadership status variance. Stein (1975) reported that observers were able to approximate the leadership rankings of actual group members when they were given records of the group's meeting that contained only verbal communication, only nonverbal communication, or both verbal and nonverbal communication. Moreover, observers were still accurate (beyond chance) in their rankings when the effects of verbal participation were controlled. Thus observers at least partially based their judgments of relative leadership on cues other than those associated with verbal participation rate. Although these studies are instructive, they do not tell us what specific communication behaviors, beyond verbal productivity, are important in generating perceptions of power.

In a previously discussed study, Scherer (1979) examined the relationships between a number of paralinguistic variables and perceived influence in simulated jury situations. Across both American and West German samples, verbal productivity was significantly related to the ratings of perceived influence made by jury members (US, r = .42; WG, r = .54), although Scherer noted that the frequency of verbalization is more important than the duration of verbalizations in determining perceived influence. Although the verbal productivity measures showed consistent relationships with perceived influence across the two cultures studied, there were a number of cultural differences found. For example, pitch range and loudness correlated positively with perceived influence for Americans (r= .49; r = .32, respectively); however, the same two variables failed to correlate with perceived influence in the West German sample. For the American jurors, number of silent pauses correlated –.44 with perceived influence, whereas the number of speech disturbances correlated positively (r = .38). This latter correlation is somewhat out of line with that which would be expected. American jurors who interrupted more were judged to be more influential (r = .45), however, the same relationship was not found for West Germans. Scherer's findings alert us to the fact that correlates of perceived influence show considerable variation across cultures.

Experimental Studies. Several studies have examined the relationship between speech rate and evaluations of the persuasiveness of a source. Miller, Maruyama, Beaber, and Valone (1976) and Apple, Streeter, and Krauss (1979) both reported that fast-talking persons were judged more persuasive than slow talkers. In addition, Brown, Strong, and Rencher (1974) found that higher rates of speech produced increased ratings of speaker competence. Two earlier studies that manipulated the number of non-fluencies in speech revealed that persons displaying elevated rates of nonfluencies were judged to be less credible than those who showed fewer nonfluencies. Miller and Hewgill (1964) found that increasing rates of repetitions induced a deleterious effect upon ratings of both competence and dynamism. Increased rates of vocalized pauses showed a similar effect upon these credibility ratings but not as consistent as that shown by repetitions. McCroskey and Mehrley (1969) manipulated both message disorganization and rate of nonfluencies. Their study revealed that message disorganization lowered competence ratings of the source but not dynamism ratings. However, nonfluencies had significant negative effects on both of these credibility dimensions. Moreover, the greatest amount of actual attitude change was found in the organized message-fluent condition of the study. The other three conditions examined in the experiment showed no differential attitude change. Apple et al. (1979) found that for males, increases in voice pitch lowered observers' ratings of their persuasiveness. Brown et al. (1974)

also reported that increases in voice pitch tended to lower ratings of competence.

In the Mehrabian and Williams (1969) study cited earlier, the effects of relaxation, shoulder orientation, distance, and eye contact on perceived persuasiveness were examined. This study revealed that males who were slightly relaxed were judged to be more persuasive than males who were either slightly tense or moderately or very relaxed. By contrast, slightly tense and slightly relaxed females were seen to be more persuasive than moderately or very relaxed females. Males who showed an indirect shoulder orientation were perceived as more persuasive than males who displayed a direct shoulder orientation, but variations in shoulder orientation produced no differences for females. At close distances, there was no relationship between amount of eye contact and perceived persuasiveness for either gender; however, at a greater distance males who increased eye contact were judged less persuasive, whereas females who increased eye contact were judged more persuasive. Dovidio and Ellyson (1982) manipulated the relative amount of time persons spent looking while speaking and looking while listening. They found that attributions of power increased as the proportion of looking while speaking increased. Attributions of power decreased as the rate of looking while listening increased. Thus the person who is attentive while another is speaking is more likely to be judged less powerful than the person who is relatively inattentive while others are speaking. Moreover, persons who gaze at their partner while they speak are more likely to be judged to be powerful than those who look less at their conversational partner.

Lee and Ofshe (1981) designed an experiment in which they pitted social characteristics theory (Berger et al., 1977) against their notion that the demeanors of persons influence perceptions of competence. The social characteristics formulation suggests that status increases perceived competence, which then allows some persons to become more dominant. By contrast, Lee and Ofshe (1981) assert that a dominant demeanor increases perceptions of competence; thus, in their view behavior precedes attributions of competence. In their study, participants viewed specially edited videotapes of jury deliberations in which a target person argued for a particular level of monetary settlement. Target status was varied by flashing either a high, moderate, or low status occupational title on the screen when the target person spoke. Demeanor was manipulated by varying the tone of voice, volume of voice, speech rate, number and length of pauses, body posture, facial expressions, hand gestures, gaze direction, number of nervous movements, and dress of the target juror. Using these variables, three demeanor conditions were devised: deference-demanding, deferential, and neutral. After viewing the tapes, observers indicated the level of settlement they felt was appropriate, as a measure of the target person's influence. In addition, several attribution measures were completed.

This study revealed that those who viewed the deference-demanding version of the tape showed more persuasion than those who viewed the other two versions of the tape. Moreover, the status manipulation showed no significant impact upon the settlement awarded. Although both higher-status and deference-demanding versions of the tapes produced higher ratings on scales tapping confidence and assertiveness, only the demeanor variable exerted significant effects upon ratings of the quality of arguments presented and the competence of the target person; that is, persons rated the target in the deference-demanding condition as both more competent and presenting higher-quality arguments. Lee and Ofshe (1981) interpreted the findings of this study as a repudiation of social characteristics theory and support for their two-process formulation. However, Berger and Zelditch (1983) argued that the Lee and Ofshe (1981) manipulation of status was so pallid relative to the demeanor manipulation that status exerted relatively little influence on both actual influence and source attributions. Nemeth (1983) concurs with Berger and Zelditch's (1983) observation concerning the manipulation employed in the study; however, she observes that both formulations could be correct. Ofshe and Lee (1983) have attempted to defend their manipulation.

Although space does not permit an extensive intervention into what has become the "Battle of San Francisco Bay," it is worth noting that Heider (1958) pointed out that behavior tends to "engulf the perceptual field." This notion has been used as a basis for explaining why observers tend to overattribute causality to actors' dispositions and why actors tend to overattribute causality to environmental factors (Jones & Nisbett, 1972). Moreover, Heider's (1958) assertion can be used to explain the kinds of salience effects discussed by Taylor and Fiske (1978). These researchers reviewed a number of studies showing that when an individual in a group is made salient by possessing a unique characteristic—for example, the only female in a group of males, being placed under a spotlight, or being made more observable—the salient person is judged to be more influential in the group. Although this body of research agrees with Lee and Ofshe's (1981) contention that group members do not go through complex cognitive processes to arrive at competence judgments, it does suggest that if status characteristics were to be made very salient, we might expect them to override demeanor characteristics. Hence if a person were forcefully introduced as the world's leading authority in a given domain, rather than merely having the person's occupational title flashed on a screen, we would expect initial status to exert more impact. However, equally as obvious is the fact that as an interaction progresses, a high-status person might become less influential because of his or her demeanor, for example, a world-renowned professor who presents a disorganized lecture riddled with nonfluencies and nonsequiturs. Thus both theories could be "correct" under different sets of conditions.

Summary. The studies summarized in this section support the conclusion that perceptions of power can be strongly influenced by variations in both verbal and nonverbal behaviors. However, it should be emphasized that although relationships between behavioral variations and changes in attributed power can be demonstrated, power-relevant attributions may or may not be directly related to actual influence. In fact, under certain conditions we might expect some persons to increase their resistance to influence as they attribute more dynamism or potency to another. We also considered two explanations for the achievement of dominant positions in groups. Social characteristics theory argues that status is translated into dominance through a set of beliefs concerning the superior competence of high-status persons. Two-process theory argues that observations of behavior are the causes of competence judgments. Dominant behaviors cause attributions, not vice versa. Both of these positions could be correct if one allows for a dynamic conception of social interaction in which initial attributions can be modified by observations of subsequent actions. Alterations in attributions would then produce alterations in action. It is to these more dynamic conceptions that we now turn.

Interactive Approaches to Interpersonal Communication and Power

We have now examined how variations in power orientations can produce variations in communicative conduct and how communicative conduct can serve as a basis for making inferences concerning power. We will now examine research that attempts to deal with communication and power in a more dynamic, exchange-oriented framework. As we pointed out earlier, relatively little work has been done in this area; however, there are two lines of research relevant here: (1) relational control and (2) accommodation theory.

Relational Control. Earlier in this chapter, we examined the assumptions underlying the relational control approach and a coding system (Rogers & Farace, 1975) designed to capture the control dimension of exchanges between persons. We will now consider some findings that have emerged from this literature. It should be emphasized that this research tradition does not generally deal with perceptions or attributions of power; rather, inferences concerning relative influence are made by studying patterns of message exchanges between persons. In a series of studies (Courtright, Millar, & Rogers-Millar, 1979; Millar, Rogers-Millar, & Courtright, 1979; Rogers-Millar & Millar, 1979), a distinction was drawn between domineeringness and dominance. Domineeringness is indexed by the sheer number of one-up messages sent by one person to another, whereas dominance is indexed by the number of one-up messages that are responded to by one-down messages from the other. Thus domineeringness is an individual attribute and dominance is an attribute of the relationship between individuals. In studies investigating these two variables, Courtright et al. (1979) and Rogers-Millar and Millar (1979) failed to find consistently strong correlations between them. This outcome led Rogers-Millar and Millar (1979) to conclude that measures like domineeringness, that focus upon the frequency of individual behaviors, are not measures of power because they fail to capture the response of the other individual and do not correlate well with measures like dominance that do take the response of the other individual into account. In a sense, the distinction being made here is like the one we reviewed earlier involving potential power and actual power. Obviously, one cannot be influential unless one makes influence attempts (domineeringness); however, merely because persons make such attempts does not guarantee that they will be successful. Even so, our review certainly indicates that domineering persons are more likely to be seen as group leaders and as more influential by others in the group, thus rendering domineering persons potentially more influential.

In relating the above measures to other variables, Millar et al. (1979) reported that in a sample of married couples, the more one spouse was clearly dominant, the less able each spouse was at predicting the other spouse's responses. Greater similarity in dominance was associated with greater understanding. The more domineering messages sent by one spouse to the other, the less likely was the other to be able to predict the sender's behavior. Rogers-Millar and Millar (1979) found that domineering behavior of wives was associated with lower levels of marital satisfaction and greater role strain, whereas, husbands' domineering behavior was related to the frequency of nonsupportive statements and shorter discussion times. Increased dominance was associated with greater marital satisfaction and lowered role strain. Courtright et al. (1979) reported additional data indicating that the more domineering the husband, the less satisfied are both spouses with the marriage and the less able they are to predict each other's responses. In addition, husband dominance was slightly related ($r = .22$) to the husband's level of marital satisfaction. It should be noted that most of the correlations reported in these studies are in the .20 to .30 range and rarely exceed .40. Thus measures of satisfaction and understanding are related to both domineeringness and dominance, but these relationships are relatively weak.

Rogers, Courtright, and Millar (1980) have refined the original Rogers and Farace (1975) coding system by adding an intensity dimension to the system to try to capture degrees of message control. These intensity measures show significant but generally weak correlations with such variables as dyadic understanding and communication satisfaction. Folger and Poole (1982) have argued that unless these relational coding schemata are validated with reference to participants' culturally shared meanings of control, these schemata are not likely to yield a great deal in the way of explanatory power.

Rogers and Millar (1982) have countered that one does not need to be concerned with individuals' interpretations in order to study communication; however, Berger (1983) points out that while it is true that "one can do communication *research* without considering interpretative processes . . . it is equally true that persons cannot 'do communication' without interpretative processes" (p. 24). This debate cannot be dealt with in extended fashion here, but there are a number of important issues concerning the validation of interaction coding systems that need to be addressed in this work.

Speech Accommodation Theory. Although not directly focused upon social power, speech accommodation theory is related to the kinds of adjustments in both verbal and nonverbal communication that persons make during their interactions with others. The theory has been developed and expanded by Giles and Powesland (1975), Giles and Smith (1979), Giles (1980), and Street and Giles (1982). The theory seeks to explain why persons sometimes adjust various attributes of their speech (accent, dialect, and rate) so that they become more similar or converge and why persons sometimes show divergence on such attributes. In general, convergence represents an effort to build solidarity, whereas divergence may represent an effort at asserting a unique social identity.

Bradac and Mulac (1984) employed the speech accommodation framework to investigate the consequences of reciprocal and nonreciprocal uses of powerful and powerless speech by high- and low-status persons. These investigators constructed alleged counseling episodes between a therapist and a client in which both persons used the same speech style (powerful or powerless) or one used a powerful style and the other a powerless style. Persons listened to one of the eight versions of the tape and then made a number of ratings of the conversational participants. This study revealed that observers rated both the high-power speech style and the counselor as higher in dynamism; however, a triple interaction occurred for the speech style, reciprocity, and gender of observer variables. Females made especially high dynamism ratings when either the counselor or client displayed nonreciprocal high power; however, males judged the high-power version as more dynamic regardless of the reciprocity conditions. Observers' ratings of the attractiveness of the persons on the tapes showed that both the counselor and the client were perceived as more attractive when they used powerful speech. Future research in this area should examine shifts in the use of powerful or powerless speech within the context of ongoing interactions between persons of differing statuses.

Summary. In this section we have examined the relationship between social power and communicative conduct. We began by casting power in the role of an independent variable and communicative conduct as a dependent variable. We found that trait measures like n Power, dominance, control, and locus of control are fairly consistent predictors of such dominance behaviors as interruptions, verbal productivity, and eye gaze behavior. We noted that although there are consistencies in these relationships, the correlations between trait measures and behavioral measures of power tend to be modest. We observed the same consistency in relationships between power and communicative conduct when we considered studies that either assumed or manipulated status or power differences between persons and examined their behavior.

We then explored research that casts communication behavior in the role of an independent variable and attributions of power as a dependent variable. Here we saw a great deal of consistency between both measurements or manipulations of various verbal and nonverbal behaviors and inferences made about the degree of influence persons have in groups. Persons who participate more frequently, talk fast and with few hesitations, and show a pattern of dominance in eye gaze are likely to be perceived as more influential. Finally, we examined what little literature has considered the study of power from an interactive perspective. This literature suggests that individual measures of power such as verbal participation rate do not index the same constructs as measures that are based upon the joint actions of persons. We also raised the issue of the role that interpretative processes play in the way power is wielded in social interaction situations. We now turn to an examination of this problem as a conclusion to this chapter.

A COGNITIVE APPROACH TO SOCIAL POWER AND COMMUNICATION

As we have seen in this chapter, considerable research energy has been spent studying power from the perspective of demonstrated influence in social interaction situations. Recently, several communication researchers have become interested in studying the strategies that persons use to wield influence in various social contexts. Much of this research is an outgrowth of the Marwell and Schmitt (1967) research on compliance-gaining strategies, although several studies done in the constructivist tradition have attempted to link cognitive mechanisms to choice of influence strategies (Clark, 1979; Clark & Delia, 1976; Delia, Kline, & Burleson, 1979; O'Keefe & Delia, 1979). From the perspective of the present chapter, one problem with both the compliance-gaining work and the constructivist research on persuasive strategies concerns the situations that are used to elicit responses for analysis. Several studies in the compliance-gaining tradition (for example, Miller, Boster, Roloff, & Seibold, 1977; Roloff & Barnicott, 1978, 1979) have followed the lead of Marwell and Schmitt (1968) and presented research participants with the list of 16 strategies as presented in Table 10.1. Persons are asked to imagine themselves in a particular situation in which they would like to exercise influence. They then indicate on scales the likelihood that they would use each of the 16 strategies in the imagined situation. Clark (1979) has

TABLE 10.1

Marwell and Schmitt's 16 Compliance-Gaining Techniques

1. Promise: If you comply, I will reward you.
2. Threat: If you do not comply, I will punish you.
3. Expertise (Positive): If you comply, you will be rewarded because of "the nature of things."
4. Expertise (Negative): If you do not comply you will be punished because of "the nature of things."
5. Liking: Actor is friendly and helpful to get target in "good frame of mind" so that he will comply with request.
6. Pregiving: Actor rewards target before requesting compliance.
7. Aversive Stimulation: Actor continuously punishes target, making cessation contingent on compliance.
8. Debt: You owe me compliance because of past favors.
9. Moral Appeal: You are immoral if you do not comply.
10. Self-Feeling (Positive): You will feel better about yourself if you comply.
11. Self-Feeling (Negative): You will feel worse about yourself if you do not comply.
12. Altercasting (Positive): A person with "good" qualities would comply.
13. Altercasting (Negative): Only a person with "bad" qualities would not comply.
14. Altruism: I need your compliance very badly, so do it for me.
15. Esteem (Positive): People you value will think better of you if you comply.
16. Esteem (Negative): People you value will think worse of you if you do not comply.

questioned the use of this technique as there may be persuasion strategies that persons use that are not on the list. Furthermore, in their everyday interactions with others, persons do not select strategies from lists. In contrast to the compliance-gaining approach, constructivist researchers generally ask persons to imagine themselves in a situation and have them construct an actual message that they would send in such a situation.

A problem common to both of these approaches is that they focus exclusively upon the *verbal content* of messages and exclude any consideration of the role that nonverbal behavior plays in compliance-gaining and persuasion. This problem is also present in the relational control research we reviewed earlier. Our review of the literature linking communication and power has taught us that such nonverbal behaviors as body orientation, speech rate, pitch, fluency, interaction distance, and patterns of eye gaze are related to both trait measures of power and are strong determinants of attributions of power. In fact, it could be argued that these nonverbal behaviors are more significant in determining the *experience* of power than are variables related to verbal content. One conclusion to be drawn here is that failure to take into account nonverbal behavior in the study of communication and power relationships is to doom oneself to study the tip of a very large iceberg.

Another problem common to both of these approaches is that neither of them is concerned with decision processes that are activated by the responses that influence targets give to influence attempts; that is, there may be any number of unique strategies that depend on the responses of others for their activation and that these approaches have not uncovered. This same problem also exists in studies that have asked persons to generate strategies they would use to gain or to resist influence in general or in given situations (Cody, McLaughlin, & Jordan, 1980; Falbo, 1977; McLaughlin et al., 1980). Another problem growing from the fact that noninteractive situations are employed to study strategy use concerns *iterative mechanisms* that persons employ to select another strategy or strategies when the strategy they have used fails. The lack of attention paid to this issue is somewhat odd given the fact that Goodstadt & Kipnis (1970) and Kipnis and Consentino (1969) found that more coercive forms of influence were employed by a power holder who encountered resistance from an influence target. This was especially true when resistance was believed to be the product of a lack of motivation. A useful model of strategy choice must include an explanation for the changes in strategy implementation that occur *as social influence episodes unfold*.

In the discussion that follows, a cognitive model is presented that overcomes some of the problems raised above by taking into account the potential impacts that interaction can have on strategy choice. The model consists of two schemata. One schema describes the attributes of strategies and is used to formulate various strategic options. This Strategy Attribute Schema (SAS) helps to determine the general nature of the strategy chosen. Although it bears a resemblance to one presented by Schenck-Hamlin et al. (1982), the attributes used to define strategies in their model are useful in a logical sense, but not in a psychological sense. In short, social actors and actresses do not think in such terms as locus of control and the acceptability of situational context to target. These attributes may be useful in distinguishing among various strategies, but it is not clear that these logical distinctions are represented psychologically. In developing the SAS, dimensions have been chosen that appear to be used by participants in the research reviewed in this chapter. This version of the SAS is tentative and subject to revision.

Driving the SAS is a Strategy Selection Schema (SSS). The SSS contains a number of variables that are responsible for setting the values of the variables included in the SAS. The variables in the SSS consist of some that have already been shown to be important in strategy choice in the compliance-gaining literature; however, others are included on the basis of findings from other relevant literatures. The SSS has the capacity to process incoming information regarding goal achievement and acts to reset values in the SAS.

Before embarking upon a discussion of the SAS and SSS, it is important to distinguish between power strategies and power tactics. Wheeless et al. (1983) rightly assert that the distinction between these two terms has been frequently confused in the literature. In military parlance, *strategies* refer to plans for achieving broad overall objectives and *tactics* refer to specific deployments and maneuvers in the field designed to achieve limited objectives. For the purposes of this discussion, strategies are cognitive schemata that are abstract and provide general guidelines for action. Tactics are low-level behavioral routines that are instantiated to actualize strategies. There may be numerous tactical variations for a given strategy. There are any number of verbal messages that could be sent to depict threat and a large number of nonverbal variations that could also be used to instantiate the strategy. Moreover, it seems reasonable to suppose that the same behavioral sequence might subserve different strategies, for example, certain facial expressions might be used to express both threat and negative esteem. This makes it difficult, although not impossible, to recover strategies from observations of tactics. The following discussion will focus upon strategic decision making rather than tactical variations.

Strategy Attribute Schema (SAS). The purpose of the SAS is to generate power strategies by employing a configuration of attributes. The variables included in the SAS are: (1) approach-avoidance, (2) positive-negative, and (3) direct-indirect. These attributes are represented in Figure 10.1. The approach-avoidance dimension is meant to represent the difference between exerting power by approaching the target in contrast to resisting the other's influence attempts. Recall that several definitions of power presented earlier in this chapter involved the notion of resistance, and Winter (1973) developed measures for both hope of power (approach) and fear of power (resistance). The positive-negative affect dimension was included because a number of studies of dimensions of compliance-gaining strategies (Falbo, 1977; Marwell & Schmitt, 1968; Roloff & Barnicott, 1978) found factors related to the "niceness" or the "awfulness" of the strategies. Although Falbo (1977) labeled this dimension rational-irrational, she concluded that the alternative label of good/bad might also be used to describe it. The dimension direct-indirect refers to the extent to which the intentions of the power holder are made clear to the target. Some strategies involve very obvious intent, whereas others may partially mask the intent of the speaker, for example, "Do it now!" is considerably more direct than "Good little boys and girls do."

The diagram displayed in Figure 10.1 suggests that persons first determine whether or not they are going to exercise power by asserting themselves or avoiding or resisting the other, although both options could be exercised within the same behavioral sequence. Once this is decided, a decision is made regarding the affective tone that will be displayed. Finally, a decision is made as to whether the request or resistance will be direct or indirect. However, if certain paths are chosen, additional decisions might be necessary. If one opts to approach another with positive affect and to attempt influence indirectly through ingratiation, there are a number of ways in which ingratiation can be achieved (Jones, 1964; Jones & Wortman, 1973). Thus additional choices must be made before tactical actions occur. It is also interesting to note that although a number of compliance-gaining studies have focused upon the approach side of the tree (Cody et al., 1980; Falbo, 1977; Marwell & Schmitt,

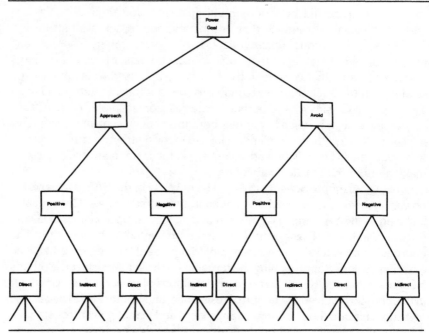

Figure 10.1   Strategy Attribute Schema

1967), very few studies (McLaughlin et al., 1980) have attempted to examine techniques that persons use to resist influence. This latter study suggests that avoidance might be differentiated into outright rejection of another's influence and the proffering of a counterproposal (nonnegotiation versus negotiation). It is important to note, however, that avoidance or resistance can be accomplished in either a positive or a negative manner that is most probably represented at the tactical level through various nonverbal displays.

As one moves beyond the terminal nodes of the SAS shown in Figure 10.1 toward the tactical level, the number of possible behavioral variations increases. Thus approach-oriented strategies that are both positive and direct can be instantiated in any number of ways via verbal and nonverbal behavior. Given this situation, if one wished to change tactical actions being used at a given time, one could either: (1) hold to the same strategy and attempt another tactical variation of it or (2) retreat to a higher node in the tree and formulate a new strategy. It is possible of course that, for a variety of reasons, persons might not have all strategic paths available to them. Persons may have been socialized never to employ direct or negative means of influence or situational constraints may preclude their use. Moreover, at the tactical level, some persons may have more alternative ways of instantiating a

TABLE 10.2
Variables in Strategy Selection Schema

1. Time available for goal achievement
2. Degree of success
3. Legitimacy
4. Relational consequences
5. Intimacy
6. Relative power
7. Personality predispositions

strategy than others. This approach clearly allows for the possibility that persons may know what to do (strategically), but not be able to do it (tactically). Obviously, issues related to communicative competence are important here.

Strategy Selection Schema (SSS). The SSS acts to control the likelihood that certain paths will be chosen in the SAS. There are a number of variables that are important in this process, some that have been examined in the compliance-gaining literature and some that have not. Table 10.2 contains a list of variables included in the SSS. One of the more critical variables in this list that has not been examined to date is the amount of time available for achieving or resisting compliance. If individuals have large amounts of time in which to reach their influence goals, they might be more likely to employ positive and less direct strategies; however, if the amount of time available for influence is short, negative-direct strategies might be more likely to be used. In the extreme, consider a parent whose child strays into the path of an oncoming car. In order to alert the child to the impending danger, the parent is most likely to employ a direct and not so positive command to alert the child.

Another critical variable in strategy selection that has received little attention in the compliance-gaining research of communication researchers is that of success at influence or success at resistance. As interactions progress, persons receive information indicating the extent to which they are being successful or unsuccessful at achieving their influence goals. It is assumed that persons will do little to change strategies and tactics that are successful; however, when they sense that they are not being successful, they may either try a different tactical variation on the strategy that they are using or move to a new strategy. Tracy, Craig, Smith, and Spisak (1984) found that persons overwhelmingly employed affectively positive strategies when making requests of others in a role-playing situation. Furthermore, Goodstadt and Kipnis (1970) and Kipnis and Consentino (1969) reported that persons are most likely to begin with affectively positive strategies and move toward more negative strategies as a function of failure to influence. Also, failure to influence should propel persons toward more direct strategies. There are a number of variables listed in Table 10.2 that might act to constrain the extremes persons are willing to go to in order to wield or resist influence. First, persons may be constrained by the degree of legitimacy to influence or resist influence that is accorded their social position. Laws constrain many persons from using extreme forms of violence in order to gain compliance, and role expectations may also serve to bias persons toward the use of positive over negative strategies. In their study of compliance-resisting strategies, McLaughlin et al. (1980) found that strategy choice was influenced by a variable they called "rights to resist." Individual concerns over the relational consequences of employing certain strategies have been shown to influence strategy choice (for example, Cody, McLaughlin, & Schneider, 1981; McLaughlin et al., 1980; Miller et al., 1977). The intimacy of the relationship between persons has also been demonstrated to affect strategy choice (for example, McLaughlin et al., 1980; Miller et al., 1977), although this variable may simply serve to raise or lower the salience of the relational consequences variable and may thus be a distal cause rather than a proximal one.

Initial assessments of relative power should be influential in initial strategy selection. This fact was made quite vivid to me in a recent discussion with my teenage son, Dan. He pointed out that his strategy selection might well be based upon his *size* relative to that of the target person! Given the research reviewed in this chapter, one would expect persons with initially low power relative to their partner to employ positive and less direct influence strategies, whereas their high-power counterparts might be able to extend their range of strategies by being able to employ both positive and negative strategies that vary widely in directness. One would also expect high-power persons to find themselves frequently in the approach mode and lower-power persons to be in the resistance mode more often. Although, as numerous social movements involving minorities have demonstrated, lower-power persons can employ approach strategies that are both negative and direct and be successful at doing so. Perhaps it is because there is an overwhelming tendency for persons to employ positive strategies to influence others that negative strategies gain the media attention that they do. This phenomenon is most likely a manifestation of the negativity effect, that is, the tendency for negative information to have an inordinate impact upon judgments when compared with positive information (Kanouse, 1971; Kanouse & Hanson, 1971). Personality predispositions have been included as part of the SSS because our review showed that variables like n power, dominance, and locus of control appear to exert modest but consistent effects upon tactical behavior in influence situations. However, the ability of these variables to influence the SAS might decrease as a particular interaction sequence unfolds.

Because it is possible for persons to formulate strategies but decide not to use them (for example, "I'm glad I didn't say that to him/her!"), a buffer must be inserted between the SAS and the level of tactical actions. This buffer permits persons to hold the formulated strategy conceptually before actions

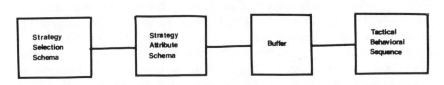

Figure 10.2   Strategy Formulation and Deployment Model

to instantiate the strategy are undertaken. It is this holding capacity that allows persons to "change their minds" about enacting a particular behavioral sequence. The position of the buffer in relationship to the SAS, SSS, and the tactical level is shown in Figure 10.2. It should be stressed that although strategies can be held in a buffer, it takes deployment of considerable cognitive resources to do so. Thus persons must move to an attentional mode that generates considerable self-awareness (Berger & Douglas, 1982; Berger & Roloff, 1980). Simply because persons are able to direct their attention toward intentions does *not* mean they will do so. Obviously, persons enact behavioral sequences that they would just as soon "take back," for example, "I wish I hadn't said that," or "I really didn't mean it that way." Most probably, persons are more likely to say things they "really don't mean" rather than to restrain themselves from doing so. It takes less thought to utter things one "does not mean," as one does not have to think of consequences.

The above model suggests a number of sources of problems in the enactment of optimal tactical sequences to achieve compliance objectives. First, persons may make miscalculations in the SSS. They may receive incomplete or faulty information that leads them to set erroneous values in the SSS. Second, as was suggested earlier, persons may not have certain options available to them in the SAS; that is, the SSS may "demand" a certain configuration in the SAS, but because of socialization and so forth the person may not be able to "think" in those terms. Third, conditions in the environment may change out from under the strategy, rendering it less than optimal. Thus if the individual is unable to hold the strategy in the buffer while assessing the environment, the strategy may "lose" its appropriateness. Finally, an optimal strategy may be formulated, but the individual may not have behavioral routines to represent the strategy at the tactical level.

Summary. There are several advantages to viewing power strategies from the perspective presented here. First, although the conception is anchored in the individual, it is interactive in that many of the variables contained in the SSS are influenced by the observed actions of one's interaction partner. Thus the model is relational in nature. Second, the model is dynamic. Much of the research done in the compliance-gaining and persuasive strategies tradition is analogous to a "first strike" view of social influence. Virtually no attention is paid, either theoretically or methodologically, to the iterative processes that are required to explain modifications in behavior as the individual exerting influence receives feedback. The focus upon iterative processes raises a number of interesting questions concerning movements in the SAS. For example, do persons exhaust tactical variations on a strategy before moving to a new path in SAS or do they select a new path before tactical exhaustion? One might also ask what entry points are used into the SAS when one elects to move to a new strategic option. Time constraints may preclude a beginning point located toward the top of the hierarchy. Third, this approach has the potential of providing an explanation for strategy choice and changes in strategy choice. To date, most compliance-gaining research has proceeded in a theoretical vacuum in which variables thought to be important to choice are included in studies on an intuitive basis, although Smith (1984) has tried to explain strategy choice using her contingency rules approach. Finally, the present approach raises the possibility of linking strategy choice research directly to such research areas as communication competence. Although the constructivist researchers cited earlier have tended to take this tack, the compliance-gaining researchers have not.

No claim is made that the SAS and SSS are complete; moreover, it is obvious that as persons enact social episodes, they do not *consciously* calibrate each of the variables in the SSS and then adjust the SAS. As shown in Figure 10.1, the SAS allows for only four approach and four avoidance strategies; however, because the variables in the SAS are continuous, there are obviously a number of gradations that we have not considered in this presentation. Allowing for such gradations produces more unique possibilities. No attempt was made to fit the various lists of strategies that have been developed in the compliance-gaining literature to the SAS. Part of the problem in trying to fit existing strategy lists involves the considerable variations in the levels of abstraction of the various strategies. Some strategies are at such low levels of abstraction that they seem more like tactics than strategies. It is doubtful that everyday social actors and actresses think in terms that are much more complex than the current SAS. The frequently heard verbal admonition to "be nice when you ask" indicates the primacy of the affective dimension of strategy choice. Thus making the SAS more complex in order to "accommodate" lists that contain an admixture of strategies, tactics, and techniques may be an interesting exercise in logic but not very fruitful in terms of gaining an understanding of how persons in everyday interactions select and use strategies.

Finally, the thorny problem of tactical behavioral sequences and their relationships to strategies has been avoided here. Thibaut and Kelley (1959) sidestepped the same issue because of the complexities involved at this level of analysis. However, at some point, research that focuses upon strategy choice will have to merge with research that has concentrated upon the actual conduct of persons in influence situations. If such a move is not made, it will not be long before those who study the likelihood of strategy use will be embarrassed to find, as were the persuasion researchers of the 1960s, that there may be considerable discrepancy between what persons say they will do on questionnaires and what they will actually do in truly interactive influence situations.

Wheeless et al. (1983) have asserted that the recent move to the study of compliance-gaining strategies has made the study of persuasion in interpersonal communication situations a more viable enterprise than it was during the early and middle 1970s. I do not share this optimistic assessment for two reasons. First, as was pointed out previously, compliance-gaining researchers and those interested in persuasive strategies have failed to study these phenomena within the context of ongoing interactions. Thus a relatively distorted view of both strategy selection and use has most probably developed in this literature. Second, as noted above, the overreliance upon paper and pencil methods for generating strategies and assessing the likelihood of their use invites the grim history of the attitude-behavior consistency issue to repeat itself in a somewhat different guise. Perhaps the way in which to avoid these potential negative outcomes is for researchers involved in areas like relational control and compliance-gaining to shed their blinders and learn some lessons from each other. Compliance-gaining researchers and persuasive strategy researchers might do more in the way of *interaction coding* and relational control researchers might do more thinking about the *cognitive mechanisms* that are potentially responsible for the patterns of message exchange they observe in their studies of interaction.

Given a commitment to a cognitive approach to communication and social power, one must try to specify the structures that are responsible for the generation of social action; however, it is equally important that social conduct be observed to determine whether these structures have psychological reality. One must work back and forth between cognitive structures and observed patterns of interaction. To focus exclusively upon one of these two processes is to guarantee the generation of incomplete explanations for the relationships between communication and social power.

REFERENCES

Adams, J. S. (1965). Inequity in social exchange. In L. Berkowitz (Ed.), *Advances in experimental social psychology* (Vol. 2, pp. 267-299). New York: Academic Press.

Adler, A. (1927). *Understanding human nature.* New York: Garden City.

Adler, A. (1930). Individual psychology. In C. Murchison (Ed.), *Psychologies of 1930* (pp. 395-405). Worcester, MA: Clark University Press.

Adler, A. (1966). The psychology of power, 1928. *Journal of Individual Psychology, 22,* 166-172.

Adorno, T. W., Frenkel-Brunswick, E., Levinson, D. J., & Sanford, R. N. (1950). *The authoritarian personality.* New York: Harper & Row.

Apple, W., Streeter, L. A., & Krauss, R. M. (1979). Effects of pitch and speech rate on personal attributions. *Journal of Personality and Social Psychology, 37,* 715-727.

Aries, E. J., Gold, C., & Weigel, R. H. (1983). Dispositional and situational influences on dominance behavior in small groups. *Journal of Personality and Social Psychology, 44,* 779-786.

Bales, R. F. (1950). *Interaction process analysis.* Reading, MA: Addison-Wesley.

Bales, R. F. (1970). *Personality and interpersonal behavior.* New York: Holt, Rinehart & Winston.

Bateson, G., Jackson, D. D., Haley, J., & Weakland, J. (1956). Toward a theory of schizophrenia. *Behavioral Science, 1,* 251-264.

Beekman, S. J. (1975). *Sex differences in nonverbal behavior.* Paper presented at the meeting of the American Psychological Association, Chicago, IL.

Berger, C. R. (1980). Power and the family. In M. E. Roloff & G. R. Miller (Eds.), *Persuasion: New directions in theory and research* (pp. 197-224). Beverly Hills, CA: Sage.

Berger, C. R. (1983, November). *Thinking and relating: Social cognition and relational control.* Paper presented at the annual convention of the Speech Communication Association, Washington, D.C.

Berger, C. R., & Douglas, W. (1982). Thought and talk: 'Excuse me, but have I been talking to myself? In F.E.X. Dance (Ed.), *Human communication theory* (pp. 42-60). New York: Harper & Row.

Berger, C. R., & Roloff, M. E. (1980). Social cognition, self-awareness, and interpersonal communication. In B. Dervin & M. J. Voigt (Eds.), *Progress in communication sciences* (Vol. 2, pp. 1-49). Norwood, NJ: Ablex.

Berger, J., Fisek, M. H., Norman, R. Z., & Zelditch, M. (1977). *Status characteristics and social interaction.* New York: Elsevier.

Berger, J., & Zelditch, M. (1983). Artifacts and challenges: A comment on Lee and Ofshe. *Social Psychology Quarterly, 46,* 59-62.

Blakar, R. M. (1979). Language as a means of social power. In J. L. Mey (Ed.), *Pragmalinguistics: Theory and practice* (pp. 131-169). The Hague: Mouton.

Blau, P. M. (1964). *Exchange and power in social life.* New York: John Wiley.

Blood, R. O. (1967). *Love match and arranged marriage: A Tokyo-Detroit comparison.* New York: Free Press.

Blood, R. O., & Wolfe, D. M. (1960). *Husbands and wives: The dynamics of married living.* New York: Free Press.

Bradac, J. J., & Mulac, A. (1984). Speech accommodation and power of style: Attributional consequences in a crisis-intervention context. *Journal of Language and Social Psychology, 3,* 1-19.

Braginsky, D. D. (1970). Machiavellianism and manipulative interpersonal behavior in children. *Journal of Experimental Social Psychology, 6,* 77-99.

Brouwer, D., Gerritsen, M., & De Haan, D. (1979). Speech differences between women and men: On the wrong track? *Language in Society, 8,* 33-50.

Brown, B. L., Strong, W. J., & Rencher, A. C. (1974). Fifty-four voices from two: The effects of simultaneous manipulations of rate, mean fundamental frequency, and variance of fundamental frequency on ratings of personality from speech. *Journal of the Acoustical Society of America, 55,* 313-318.

Brown, R. (1965). *Social psychology.* New York: Free Press.

Brown, R., & Ford, M. (1961). Address in American English. *Journal of Abnormal and Social Psychology, 62,* 375-385.

Bugental, D. B., Henker, B., & Whalen, C. K. (1976). Attributional antecedents of verbal and vocal assertiveness. *Journal of Personality and Social Psychology, 34,* 405-411.

Burchinal, L. G., & Bauder, W. W. (1965). Decision-making and role patterns among Iowa farm and non-farm families. *Journal of Marriage and the Family, 27,* 525-530.

Buric, O., & Zecevic, A. (1967). Family authority, marital satisfaction, and the social network in Yugoslavia. *Journal of Marriage and the Family, 27,* 325-336.

Burr, W. R., Ahern, L., & Knowles, E. M. (1977). An empirical test of Rodman's theory of resources in cultural context. *Journal of Marriage and the Family, 39,* 505-514.

Carson, R. C. (1969). *Interaction concepts of personality.* Chicago: Aldine.

Cartwright, D. (1959). A field theoretical conception of power. In D. Cartwright (Ed.), *Studies in social power* (pp. 183-220). Ann Arbor, MI: Institute for Social Research.

Centers, R., Raven, B. H., & Rodrigues, A. (1971). Conjugal power structure: A re-examination. *American Sociological Review, 36,* 264-278.

Cherry, F., & Byrne, D. (1977). Authoritarianism. In T. Blass (Ed.), *Personality variables in social behavior* (pp. 109-133). Hillsdale, NJ: Lawrence Erlbaum.

Christie, R., & Geis, F. L. (1970). *Studies in Machiavellianism.* New York: Academic Press.

Christie, R., & Jahoda, M. (Eds.). (1954). *Studies in the scope and method of "The Authoritarian Personality."* Glencoe, IL: Free Press.

Cialdini, R. B., & Mirels, H. L. (1976). Sense of personal control and attributions about yielding and resisting persuasion targets. *Journal of Personality and Social Psychology, 33*, 395-402.

Clark, R. A. (1979). The impact of self interest and desire for liking on the selection of communicative strategies. *Communication Monographs, 46*, 257-273.

Clark, R. A., & Delia, J. G. (1976). The development of functional persuasive skills in childhood and early adolescence. *Child Development, 47*, 1008-1014.

Cody, M. J., McLaughlin, M. L., & Jordan, W. J. (1980). A multidimensional scaling of three sets of compliance-gaining strategies. *Communication Quarterly, 28*, 34-46.

Cody, M. J., McLaughlin, M. L., & Schneider, M. J. (1981). The impact of relational consequences and intimacy on the selection of interpersonal persuasion tactics: A reanalysis. *Communication Quarterly, 29*, 91-106.

Cohen, A. R. (1958). Upward communication in experimentally created hierarchies. *Human Relations, 11*, 41-53.

Collins, B. E. (1974). Four components of the Rotter internal-external scale: Belief in a difficult world, a just world, a predictable world, and a politically responsive world. *Journal of Personality and Social Psychology, 29*, 381-391.

Collins, B. E., & Raven, B. H. (1969). Group structure: Attraction, coalitions, communication, and power. In G. Lindzey & E. Aronson (Eds.), *Handbook of social psychology* (Vol. 4, pp. 102-204). Reading, MA: Addison-Wesley.

Courtright, J. A., Millar, F. E., & Rogers-Millar, L. E. (1979). Domineeringness and dominance: Replication and expansion. *Communication Monographs, 46*, 179-192.

Cromwell, R. E., Klein, D. M., & Wieting, S. G. (1975). Family power: A multitrait-multimethod analysis. In R. E. Cromwell & D. H. Olson (Eds.), *Power in families* (pp. 151-181). Beverly Hills, CA: Sage.

Cromwell, V. L., & Cromwell, R. E. (1978). Perceived dominance in decision-making and conflict resolution among Anglo, Black and Chicano couples. *Journal of Marriage and the Family, 40*, 749-759.

Dahl, R. A. (1957). The concept of power. *Behavioral Science, 2*, 201-215.

Dean, L. M., Willis, F. N., & Hewitt, J. (1975). Initial interaction distance among individuals equal and unequal in military rank. *Journal of Personality and Social Psychology, 32*, 294-299.

deCharms, R. (1968). *Personal causation: The internal affective determinants of behavior.* New York: Academic Press.

deCharms, R. (1972). Personal causation training in schools. *Journal of Applied Social Psychology, 2*, 95-113.

Delia, J. G., Kline, S. L., & Burleson, B. R. (1979). The development of persuasive communication strategies in kindergarteners through twelfth-graders. *Communication Monographs, 46*, 241-256.

Doherty, W. J., & Ryder, R. G. (1979). Locus of control, interpersonal trust, and assertive behavior among newlyweds. *Journal of Personality and Social Psychology, 37*, 2212-2220.

Douglas, S. P., & Wind, Y. (1978). Examining family role and authority patterns: Two methodological issues. *Journal of Marriage and the Family, 40*, 35-47.

Dovidio, J. F., & Ellyson, S. L. (1982). Decoding visual dominance: Attributions of power based on relative percentages of looking while speaking and looking while listening. *Social Psychology Quarterly, 45*, 106-113.

Drecksel, G. L., & Fisher, B. A. (1977). *Relational interaction characteristics of women's consciousness-raising groups.* Paper presented at the annual convention of the Western Speech Communication Association, Phoenix, AZ.

Druckman, D. (1967). Dogmatism, prenegotiation experience, and simulated group representation as determinants of dyadic behavior in a bargaining situation. *Journal of Personality and Social Psychology, 6*, 279-290.

Eakins, B. W., & Eakins, R. G. (1978). *Sex differences in human communication.* Boston: Houghton Mifflin.

Edelsky, C. (1979). Question intonation and sex roles. *Language in Society, 8*, 15-32.

Ellis, D. G. (1979). Relational control in two group systems. *Communication Monographs, 46*, 153-166.

Ellis, D. G., Fisher, R. A., Drecksel, G. L., Hoch, D. D., & Werber, W. S. (1976). *Rel/Com.* Unpublished coding manual, University of Utah.

Ellyson, S. L. (1974). *Visual behavior exhibited by males differing as to interpersonal control orientation in one- and two-way communication systems*. Unpublished doctoral dissertation, University of Delaware.

Ellyson, S. L., Dovidio, J. F., Corson, R. L., & Vinicur, D. L. (1980). Visual dominance behavior in female dyads: Situational and personality factors. *Social Psychology Quarterly, 43*, 328-336.

Emerson, R. M. (1962). Power-dependence relations. *American Sociological Review, 27*, 31-41.

Ericson, P. M., & Rogers, L. E. (1973). New procedures for analyzing relational communication. *Family Process, 12*, 245-267.

Erikson, B., Lind, E. A., Johnson, B. C., & O'Barr, W. M. (1978). Speech style and impression formation in a court setting: The effects of "powerful" and "powerless" speech. *Journal of Experimental Social Psychology, 14*, 266-279.

Etzioni, A. (1961). *A comparative analysis of complex organizations*. New York: Macmillan.

Exline, R. V. (1972). Visual interaction: The glances of power and preference. In J. K. Cole (Ed.), *Nebraska symposium on motivation: 1971* (pp. 163-206). Lincoln: University of Nebraska Press.

Exline, R. V., Ellyson, S. L., & Long, B. (1975). Visual behavior as an aspect of power role relationships. In P. Pilner, L. Krames, & T. Alloway (Eds.), *Advances in the study of communication and affect* (Vol. 2, pp. 21-51). New York: Plenum.

Exline, R. V., & Messick, D. (1967). The effects of dependency and social reinforcement upon visual behavior during an interview. *British Journal of Social and Clinical Psychology, 6*, 256-266.

Falbo, T. (1977). Multidimensional scaling of power strategies. *Journal of Personality and Social Psychology, 35*, 537-547.

Falbo, T., & Peplau, L. A. (1980). Power strategies in intimate relationships. *Journal of Personality and Social Psychology, 38*, 618-628.

Fitzpatrick, M. A., & Winkie, J. (1979). You always hurt the one you love: Strategies and tactics in interpersonal conflict. *Communication Quarterly, 27*, 3-11.

Foa, E., & Foa, U. (1974). *Societal structures of the mind*. Springfield, IL: Charles C Thomas.

Fodor, E. M., & Farrow, D. L. (1979). The power motive as an influence on use of power. *Journal of Personality and Social Psychology, 37*, 2091-2097.

Fodor, E. M., & Smith, T. (1982). The power motive as an influence on group decision making. *Journal of Personality and Social Psychology, 42*, 178-185.

Folger, J. P., & Poole, M. S. (1982). Relational coding schemes: The question of validity. In M. Burgoon (Ed.), *Communication yearbook 5* (pp. 235-257). New Brunswick, NJ: Transaction.

Folger, J. P., & Puck, S. (1976). *Coding relational communication: A question approach*. Paper presented at the annual convention of the International Communication Association, Portland, OR.

Forgas, J. P. (1979). *Social episodes: The study of interaction routines*. London: Academic Press.

French, J.R.P., & Raven, B. (1959). The bases of social power. In D. Cartwright (Ed.), *Studies in social power* (pp. 150-167). Ann Arbor, MI: Institute for Social Research.

Freud, S. (1924). On narcissism: An introduction. 1914. In *Collected papers* (Vol. 4, pp. 30-60). London: Hogarth.

Frye, R. L., Vidulich, R. N., Meierhoefer, B., & Joure, S. (1972). Differential T-group behaviors of high and low dogmatic participants. *Journal of Psychology, 81*, 301-309.

Geis, F. (1970). The con game. In R. Christie & F. L. Geis (Eds.), *Studies in Machiavellianism* (pp. 106-129). New York: Academic Press.

Giles, H. (1980). Accommodation theory: Some new directions. In S. deSilva (Ed.), *Aspects of linguistic behavior* (pp. 105-136). York: University of York Press.

Giles, H., & Powesland, P. (1975). *Speech style and social evaluation*. London: Academic Press.

Giles, H., & Smith, P. (1979). Accommodation theory: Optimal levels of convergence. In H. Giles & R. St. Clair (Eds.), *Language and social psychology* (pp. 45-65). Oxford: Basil Blackwell.

Goodstadt, B. E., & Hjelle, L. A. (1973). Power to the powerless: Locus of control and the use of power. *Journal of Personality and Social Psychology, 27*, 190-402.

Goodstadt, B. E., & Kipnis, D. (1970). Situational influences in the use of power. *Journal of Applied Psychology, 54*, 201-207.

Guterman, S. S. (1970). *The Machiavellians*. Lincoln, NE: University of Nebraska Press.

Hacker, S., & Gaitz, C. M. (1970). Interaction and performance correlates of Machiavellianism. *Sociological Quarterly, 2*, 94-102.

Hadley, T., & Jacob, T. (1973). Relationship among measures of family power. *Journal of Personality and Social Psychology, 27*, 6-12.

Haley, J. (1959). The family of the schizophrenic: A model system. *Journal of Nervous and Mental Disease, 129*, 357-374.

Haley, J. (1962). Family experiments: A new type of experimentation. *Family Process, 1*, 265-293.

Haley, J. (1969). *The power tactics of Jesus Christ and other essays*. New York: Grossman.

Heer, D. M. (1958). Dominance and the working wife. *Social Forces, 36*, 341-347.

Heer, D. M. (1962). Husband and wife perceptions of family power structure. *Marriage and Family Living, 24*, 65-67.

Heer, D. M. (1963). The measurement and bases of family power: An overview. *Marriage and Family Living, 25*, 133-139.

Heider, F. (1958). *The psychology of interpersonal relations*. New York: John Wiley.

Herb, T. R., & Elliott, R. F. (1971). Authoritarianism in the conversation of gestures. *Kansas Journal of Sociology, 7*, 93-101.

Homans, G. C. (1961). *Social behavior: Its elementary forms*. New York: Harcourt Brace Jovanovich.

Horney, K. (1937). *The neurotic personality of our time*. New York: W. W. Norton.

Jones, E. E. (1964). *Ingratiation*. Englewood Cliffs, NJ: Prentice-Hall.

Jones, E. E., & Nisbett, R. E. (1972). The actor and the observer: Divergent perceptions of the causes of behavior. In E. E. Jones, D. E. Kanouse, H. H. Kelley, R. E. Nisbett, S. Valins, & B. Weiner (Eds.), *Attribution: Perceiving the causes of behavior* (pp. 79-94). Morristown, NJ: General Learning Press.

Jones, E. E., & Wortman, C. (1973). *Ingratiation: An attributional approach*. Morristown, NJ: General Learning Press.

Kandel, D. B., & Lesser, G. S. (1972). Marital decision-making in American and Danish urban families: A research note. *Journal of Marriage and the Family, 34*, 134-138.

Kanouse, D. E. (1971). *Language, labeling and attribution*. Morristown, NJ: General Learning Press.

Kanouse, D. E., & Hanson, L. R. (1971). *Negativity in evaluations*. Morristown, NJ: General Learning Press.

Kelley, H. H. (1951). Communication in experimentally created hierarchies. *Human Relations, 4*, 39-56.

Kelley, H. H., & Thibaut, J. (1978). *Interpersonal relations: A theory of interdependence*. New York: John Wiley.

Kelman, H. C. (1958). Compliance, identification, and internalization: Three processes of attitude change. *Journal of Conflict Resolution, 2*, 51-60.

Kelman, H. C. (1961). Processes of opinion change. *Public Opinion Quarterly, 25*, 57-78.

Kenkel, W. F. (1957). Influence differentiation in family decision making. *Sociology and Social Research, 42*, 18-25.

Key, M. R. (1975). *Male/female language*. Metuchen, NJ: Scarecrow.

Kimble, C. E., Yoshikawa, J. C., & Zehr, H. D. (1981). Vocal and verbal assertiveness in same-sex and mixed-sex groups. *Journal of Personality and Social Psychology, 40*, 1047-1054.

Kipnis, D. (1976). *The powerholders*. Chicago: University of Chicago Press.

Kipnis, D., & Consentino, J. (1969). Use of leadership powers in industry. *Journal of Applied Psychology, 53*, 460-466.

Klopper, E. J., Tittler, B. I., Friedman, S., & Hughes, S. J. (1978). A multi-method investigation of two family constructs. *Family Process, 17*, 83-93.

Kramer, C. (1977). Perceptions of female and male speech. *Language and Speech, 20*, 151-161.

Kramerae, C. (1981). *Women and men speaking*. Rowley, MA: Newbury House.

Lakoff, R. (1975). *Language and the woman's place*. New York: Harper & Row.

Lamb, T. A. (1981). Nonverbal and paraverbal control in dyads and triads: Sex or power differences? *Social Psychology Quarterly, 44*, 49-53.

Lamouse, A. (1969). Family roles of women: A German example. *Journal of Marriage and the Family, 31*, 145-152.

Larson, L. E. (1974). System and subsystem perception of family roles. *Journal of Marriage and the Family, 36*, 123-138.

Lasswell, H., & Kaplan, A. (1950). *Power and society*. New Haven: Yale University Press.

Leary, T. (1957). *Interpersonal diagnosis of personality*. New York: Ronald.

Lee, M. T., & Ofshe, R. (1981). The impact of behavioral style and status characteristics on social influence: A test of two competing theories. *Social Psychology Quarterly, 44*, 73-82.

Lefcourt, H. M. (1976). *Locus of control: Current trends in theory and research.* Hillsdale, NJ: Lawrence Erlbaum.

Leffler, A., Gillespie, D. L., & Conaty, J. C. (1982). The effects of status differentiation on nonverbal behavior. *Social Psychology Quarterly, 45*, 153-161.

Leighton, L., Stollak, G., & Ferguson, L. (1971). Patterns of communication in normal and clinic families. *Journal of Consulting and Clinical Psychology, 36*, 252-256.

Libby, W. L., & Yaklevich, D. (1973). Personality determinants of eye contact and direction of gaze aversion. *Journal of Personality and Social Psychology, 27*, 197-206.

Lind, E. A., & O'Barr, W. M. (1979). The social significance of speech in the courtroom. In H. Giles & R. St. Clair (Eds.), *Language and social psychology* (pp. 66-87). Oxford: Basil Blackwell.

Lott, D. F., & Sommer, R. (1967). Seating arrangements and status. *Journal of Personality and Social Psychology, 7*, 90-95.

Lupri, E. (1969). Contemporary authority patterns in the Western German family: A study in cross-national validation. *Journal of Marriage and the Family, 31*, 134-144.

Mark, R. A. (1971). Coding communication at the relationship level. *Journal of Communication, 21*, 221-232.

Markel, N. N., Prebor, L. D., & Brandt, J. F. (1972). Biosocial factors in dyadic communication: Sex and speaking intensity. *Journal of Personality and Social Psychology, 23*, 11-13.

Marwell, G., & Schmitt, D. R. (1967). Dimensions of compliance-gaining behavior: An empirical analysis. *Sociometry, 30*, 350-364.

McCroskey, J. C., & Mehrley, R. S. (1969). The effects of disorganization and nonfluency on attitude change and source credibility. *Speech Monographs, 36*, 13-21.

McLaughlin, M. L., Cody, M. J., & Robey, C. S. (1980). Situational influences on the selection of strategies to resist compliance-gaining attempts. *Human Communication Research, 7*, 14-36.

Mehrabian, A., & Williams, M. (1969). Nonverbal concomitants of perceived and intended persuasiveness. *Journal of Personality and Social Psychology, 13*, 37-58.

Michel, A. (1967). Comparative data concerning the interaction in French and American families. *Journal of Marriage and the Family, 29*, 337-344.

Millar, F. E., Rogers-Millar, L. E., & Courtright, J. A. (1979). Relational control and dyadic understanding. In D. Nimmo (Ed.), *Communication yearbook 3* (pp. 213-224). New Brunswick, NJ: Transaction.

Miller, G. R., Boster, F., Roloff, M., & Seibold, D. (1977). Compliance-gaining message strategies: A topology and some findings concerning effects of situational differences. *Communication Monographs, 44*, 37-51.

Miller, G. R., & Hewgill, M. A. (1964). The effect of variations in nonfluency on audience ratings of source credibility. *Quarterly Journal of Speech, 50*, 36-44.

Miller, N., Maruyama, G., Beaber, R. J., & Valone, K. (1976). Speed of speech and persuasion. *Journal of Personality and Social Psychology, 34*, 615-624.

Minton, H. L. (1967). Power as a personality construct. In B. A. Maher (Ed.), *Progress in experimental personality research* (Vol. 4, pp. 229-267). New York: Academic Press.

Mishler, E. G. (1975). Studies in dialogue and discourse: II. Types of discourse initiated by and sustained through questioning. *Journal of Psycholinguistic Research, 4*, 99-121.

Mishler, E. G., & Waxler, N. E. (1968). *Interaction in families: An experimental study of family processes in schizophrenia.* New York: John Wiley.

Murray, H. A. (1938). *Explorations in personality.* New York: Oxford University Press.

Murrell, S., & Stachowiak, J. (1967). Consistency, rigidity and power in the interaction patterns of clinic and nonclinic families. *Journal of Abnormal Psychology, 72*, 265-272.

Nemeth, C. J. (1983). Reflections on the dialogue between status and style: Influence processes of social control and social change. *Social Psychology Quarterly, 46*, 70-74.

Nettler, G. (1957). A measure of alienation. *American Sociological Review, 22*, 670-677.

Ng, S. H. (1980). *The social psychology of power.* London: Academic Press.

Norton, R. (1983). *Communicator style: Theory, applications, and measures.* Beverly Hills, CA: Sage.

O'Barr, W. M., & Atkins, B. K. (1980). "Women's language" or "powerless language." In S. McConnell-Ginet, R. Borker, & N. Furman (Eds.), *Women and language in literature and society* (pp. 93-110). New York: Praeger.

Ofshe, R., & Lee, M. T. (1983). "What are we to make of all this?" Reply to Berger and Zelditch. *Social Psychology Quarterly, 46*, 63-65.

O'Keefe, B. J., & Delia, J. B. (1979). Construct comprehensiveness and cognitive complexity as predictors of the number and strategic adaptation of arguments and appeals in a persuasive message. *Communication Monographs, 46*, 231-240.

Olson, D. H., & Rabunsky, C. (1972). Validity of four measures of family power. *Journal of Marriage and the Family, 34*, 224-234.

Parsons, T. (1963). On the concept of influence. *Public Opinion Quarterly, 27*, 37-62.

Phares, E. J. (1965). Internal-external control as a determinant of amount of social influence exerted. *Journal of Personality and Social Psychology, 2*, 642-647.

Price-Bonham, S. (1976). A comparison of weighted and unweighted decision-making scores. *Journal of Marriage and the Family, 38*, 629-640.

Raven, B. H. (1965). Social influence and power. In I. D. Steiner & M. Fishbein (Eds.), *Current studies in social psychology* (pp. 371-382). New York: Holt, Rinehart & Winston.

Roger, D. B., & Schumacher, A. (1983). Effects of individual differences on dyadic conversational strategies. *Journal of Personality and Social Psychology, 45*, 700-705.

Rogers, L. E., Courtright, J. A., & Millar, F. E. (1980). Message control intensity: Rationale and preliminary findings. *Communication Monographs, 47*, 201-219.

Rogers, L. E., & Farace, R. B. (1975). Relational communication analysis: New measurement procedures. *Human Communication Research, 1*, 222-239.

Rogers, L. E., & Millar, F. E. (1982). The question of validity: A pragmatic response. In M. Burgoon (Ed.), *Communication yearbook 5* (pp. 249-257). New Brunswick, NJ: Transaction.

Rogers-Millar, L. E., & Millar, F. E. (1979). Domineeringness and dominance: A transactional view. *Human Communication Research, 5*, 238-246.

Rokeach, M. (1960). *The open and closed mind.* New York: Basic Books.

Roloff, M. E. (1981). *Interpersonal communication: The social exchange approach.* Beverly Hills, CA: Sage.

Roloff, M. E., & Barnicott, E. F. (1978). The situational use of pro- and anti-social compliance-gaining strategies by high and low Machiavellians. In B. Ruben (Ed.), *Communication yearbook 2* (pp. 193-208). New Brunswick, NJ: Transaction.

Roloff, M. E., & Barnicott, E. F. (1979). The influence of dogmatism on the situational use of pro-and anti-social compliance gaining strategies. *Southern Speech Communication Journal, 45*, 37-54.

Rosenberg, S., & Sedlak, A. (1972). Structural representations of implicit personality theory. In L. Berkowitz (Ed.), *Advances in experimental social psychology* (Vol. 6, pp. 235-297). New York: Academic Press.

Rosenfeld, H. M. (1966). Instrumental affiliative functions of facial and gestural expressions. *Journal of Personality and Social Psychology, 4*, 65-72.

Rotter, J. B. (1966). Generalized expectancies for internal versus external control of reinforcement. *Psychological Monographs, 80*, (1, Whole No. 609).

Rubin, J. Z., & Brown, B. R. (1975). *The social psychology of bargaining and negotiation.* New York: Academic Press.

Ruesch, J., & Bateson, G. (1951). *Communication: The social matrix of society.* New York: W. W. Norton.

Russell, B. (1938). *Power: A new social analysis.* London: George Allen & Unwin.

Safilios-Rothschild, C. (1967). A comparison of power structure and marital satisfaction in urban Greek and French families. *Journal of Marriage and the Family, 29*, 345-352.

Safilios-Rothschild, C. (1969). Family sociology or wives' family sociology? A cross-cultural examination of decision-making. *Journal of Marriage and the Family, 31*, 290-301.

Safilios-Rothschild, C. (1970). The study of family power structure: A review 1960-1969. *Journal of Marriage and the Family, 32*, 539-552.

Schenck-Hamlin, W. J., Wiseman, R. L., & Georgacarakos, G. N. (1982). A model of properties of compliance-gaining strategies. *Communication Quarterly, 30*, 92-99.

Scherer, K. R. (1979). Voice and speech correlates of perceived social influence in simulated juries. In H. Giles & R. St. Clair (Eds.), *Language and social psychology* (pp. 88-120). Oxford: Basil Blackwell.

Schopler, J. (1965). Social power. In L. Berkowitz (Ed.), *Advances in experimental social psychology* (Vol. 2, pp. 177-218). New York: Academic Press.

Schutz, W. C. (1958). *Firo: A three-dimensional theory of interpersonal behavior.* New York: Holt, Rinehart & Winston.

Seeman, M. (1959). On the meaning of alienation. *American Sociological Review, 24,* 783-791.

Simon, H. A. (1957). *Models of man.* New York: John Wiley.

Sites, P. (1973). *Control: The basis of social order.* New York: Dunellen.

Smith, M. J. (1984). Contingency rules theory, context, and compliance behaviors. *Human Communication Research, 10,* 489-512.

Smith, P. M. (1979). Sex markers in speech. In K. R. Scherer & H. Giles (Eds.), *Social markers in speech* (pp. 109-146). New York: Cambridge University Press.

Srole, J. (1956). Social integration and certain corollaries: An exploratory study. *American Sociological Review, 21,* 709-716.

Stein, T. R. (1975). Identifying emergent leaders from verbal and nonverbal communications. *Journal of Personality and Social Psychology, 32,* 125-135.

Stein, T. R., & Heller, T. (1979). An empirical analysis of the correlations between leadership status and participation rates reported in the literature. *Journal of Personality and Social Psychology, 37,* 1993-2002.

Strauss, M. A., & Tallman, I. (1971). SIMFAM: A technique for observational measurement and experimental study of families. In J. Aldous, T. Condon, R. Hill, M. Strauss, & I. Tallman (Eds.), *Family problem solving* (pp. 381-438). Hinsdale, IL: Dryden.

Street, R. L., & Giles, H. (1982). Speech accommodation theory: A social cognitive approach to language and speech behavior. In M. Roloff & C. Berger (Eds.), *Social cognition and communication* (pp. 193-226). Beverly Hills, CA: Sage.

Strodtbeck, F. L. (1951). Husband-wife interaction over revealed differences. *American Sociological Review, 16,* 468-473.

Strodbeck, F. L. (1954). The family as a three person group. *American Sociological Review, 19,* 23-29.

Talley, W. M., & Vamos, O. (1972). An exploratory study of dogmatism and its relation to group response. *Canadian Counsellor, 6,* 278-282.

Taylor, S., & Fiske, S. (1978). Salience, attention and attribution: Top of the head phenomena. In L. Berkowitz (Ed.), *Advances in experimental social psychology* (Vol. 11, pp. 249-288). New York: Academic Press.

Terhune, K. W. (1968). Motives, situation, and interpersonal conflict within prisoner's dilemma. *Journal of Personality and Social Psychology, 8* (Monograph Supplement 3, Part 2), 1-24.

Thibaut, J. W., & Kelley, H. H. (1959). *The social psychology of groups.* New York: John Wiley.

Thorne, B., & Henley, N. (1975). *Language and sex: Difference and dominance.* Rowley, MA: Newbury House.

Tjosvold, D. (1978). Affirmation of the high-power person and his position: Ingratiation in conflict. *Journal of Applied Social Psychology, 8,* 230-243.

Tracy, K., Craig, R. T., Smith, M., & Spisak, F. (1984). The discourse of request: Assessment of a compliance-gaining approach. *Human Communication Research, 10,* 513-538.

Triandis, H. C., Vassiliou, V., & Nassiakou, M. (1968). Three cross-cultural studies of subjective culture. *Journal of Personality and Social Psychology, 8* (Monograph Supplement 4, Part 2), 1-42.

Turk, J. L., & Bell, N. W. (1972). Measuring power in families. *Journal of Marriage and the Family, 34,* 215-222.

Uleman, J. S. (1972). The need for influence: Development and validation of a measure, and comparison with need for power. *Genetic Psychology Monographs, 85,* 157-214.

Veroff, J. (1957). Development and validation of a projective measure of power motivation. *Journal of Abnormal and Social Psychology, 54,* 1-9.

Veroff, J. (1958). A scoring manual for the power motive. In J. W. Atkinson (Ed.), *Motives in fantasy, action and society* (pp. 219-233). Princeton, NJ: Van Nostrand.

Veroff, J., & Veroff, J. B. (1972). Reconsideration of a measure of power motivation. *Psychological Bulletin, 78,* 279-291.

Waller, W., & Hill, R. (1951). *The family: A dynamic interpretation.* New York: Dryden.

Walster, E., Walster, G., & Berscheid, E. (1978). *Equity: Theory and research.* Boston: Allyn & Bacon.

Watzlawick, P., Beavin, J. H., & Jackson, D. D. (1967). *Pragmatics of human communication.* New York: W. W. Norton.

Weber, M. (1947). *The theory of social and economic organization.* New York: Oxford University Press.

Wheeless, L. R., Barraclough, R., & Stewart, R. (1983). Compliance-gaining and power in persuasion. In R. N. Bostrom (Ed.), *Communication yearbook 7* (pp. 105-145). Beverly Hills, CA: Sage.

White, R. W. (1959). Motivation reconsidered: The concept of competence. *Psychological Review, 66,* 297-333.

Winter, D. G. (1973). *The power motive.* New York: Free Press.

Wish, M., D'Andrade, R. G., & Goodnow, J. E. (1980). Dimensions of interpersonal communication: Corresponding between structures for speech acts and bipolar scales. *Journal of Personality and Social Psychology, 39,* 848-860.

Wish, M., Deutsch, M., & Kaplan, S. J. (1976). Perceived dimensions of interpersonal relations. *Journal of Personality and Social Psychology, 33,* 409-420.

Wolfe, D. M. (1959). Power and authority in the family. In D. Cartwright (Ed.), *Studies in social power* (pp. 99-117). Ann Arbor: Institute for Social Research.

Zagona, S. V., & Zurcher, L. A. (1964). Participation, interaction, and role behavior in groups selected from the extremes of the open-closed cognitive continuum. *Journal of Psychology, 58,* 255-264.

Zagona, S. V., & Zurcher, L. A. (1965). Notes on the reliability and validity of the dogmatism scale. *Psychological Reports, 16,* 1234-1236.

Zimmerman, D. H., & West, C. (1975). Sex roles, interruptions and silences in conversation. In B. Thorne & N. Henley (Eds.), *Language and sex: Difference and dominance* (pp. 105-129). Rowley, MA: Newbury House.

11 Emotion and Interpersonal Communication

JOHN WAITE BOWERS

University of Iowa

SANDRA M. METTS

Illinois State University

W. THOMAS DUNCANSON

University of Iowa

THE fact that emotions are an important aspect of interpersonal relationships is self-evident to anyone who has ever been closely involved with another person. They are a critical factor in the courtship process (Izard, 1977), in the attributions made in intimate relationships (Newman, 1981a, 1981b; Sillars & Scott, 1983), in the conversations between couples (Gottman, 1982; Notarius & Johnson, 1982), and in the disengaging process (Weiss, 1976).

Surprisingly, little scholarship addresses emotion directly as a variable in interpersonal communication. Although affection is generally recognized as a primary dimension of relationships, far more research attention has been given to persuasion, influence, and control factors than to affective behavior, feelings, or emotion (Bochner, Kaminski, & Fitzpatrick, 1977). After reading the extensive literature on relationship initiation (for example, see Altman & Taylor, 1973; Berger & Calabrese, 1975), relationship maintenance (Ayres, 1983; Roloff, 1981), and relationship disengagement (Baxter & Philpott, 1982; Cody, 1982), one is left with an impression of the typical relational communicator as a fairly rational creature. The predominant research model seems to assume that "doing relationships" is a conscious, systematic, and rational process and that communication choices reflect a high level of conscious thought.

This impression of rationality may not be an accurate representation of relational communication. First, communication choices and relational decisions are made at various levels of self-consciousness, some less cognitively analytic and rational than current theories suggest (Berger, 1980; Delia, 1980). Relational partners react as well as plan, and the spontaneity of emotional reaction undoubtedly influences relational movement as surely as does strategic or conscious planning. According to Graziano and Musser

(1982, p. 162), "It may prove to be a costly strategic mistake to continue to emphasize cognitions and attributions, and to de-emphasize affect, if our goal is to predict and explain the course of relationships." Second, even when actors are consciously aware of how they intend to communicate (for example, in a decision-making episode), they may do otherwise when actually engaged in a given interaction (Krueger, 1982). Actors may even wish consciously to change a particular kind of recurring communication sequence, but feel unable to do so (Cronen, Pearce, & Snavely, 1979; Gottman, 1982). Third, most of the evidence in support of a cognitive model of relationships is provided by self-report measures and retrospective accounts. Subjects tend to report systematic steps in decision-making and rational accounts of their behavior although the motivations at the time were neither rational nor logical (Averill, 1980a; Duck, 1980; Zajonc, 1980).

As this last point implies, part of the neglect of the role of emotion is an artifact of a general cultural bias toward expectations of rational behavior. Emotions are difficult for researchers to observe and classify and for subjects to verbalize. With few exceptions, social constraints moderate overt spontaneous emotional response. Socialization processes in early childhood provide norms of contexually appropriate emotional behaviors, which become habitual by adulthood. Indeed, it is primarily deviation from and variability within these norms that social actors notice and that researchers examine. For example, the American cultural stereotype of the nonemotional male and the emotional female is reflected to some extent in actual behavior. Women report a greater tendency to express emotional states than do men (Balswick & Avertt, 1977), to make finer discriminations between the sentiments of loving and liking (Z. Rubin, 1970), and to report more verbal intimacy and physical affection in friendships than men (Lewis, 1978). In marriages, wives generally view their husbands as emotionally inexpressive (Balswick & Avertt, 1977), and on measures of nonverbal behavior husbands were found to display less affective response (especially negative) to their wives' statements than wives displayed to their husbands' statements (Notarius & Johnson, 1982). In addition to sex differences, individual differences have been found in the degree to which communicators are able to interpret a social context and generate emotional behaviors appropriate to that context. Snyder (1974, 1979) found that high self-monitors are better able than most people to express a true emotion, conceal the expression of an inappropriate emotion, and express an unfelt (though appropriate) emotion. Low self-monitors, on the other hand, are less adept than most people at reading a social context and modifying spontaneous emotional expression accordingly.

Finally, the general disregard for emotion in interpersonal theory may be attributed to the inherent complexity of emotional experience and to the complexity of the role it plays in relationships. A generally accepted definition of emotion is not yet apparent in the literature, although its presence in human affairs is recognized as integral, influential, and ubiquitous. The purpose of this chapter is to redress the relative neglect of emotion in interpersonal communication theory.

In the remaining pages of this preliminary section, we explore the complexity of emotional experience and the problems of defining emotion. We present a review of current theories of emotion and close this section with an alternative model of interpersonal emotion that may prove to be a useful guide to further research. In subsequent sections we address two issues. First, we examine from the viewpoint of an "ideal interpreter" the expression and enactment of emotion through messages. This analysis focuses on physiological, paralinguistic, kinesic, lexical, and certain pragmatic aspects of those messages. Second, we examine the role of emotion in relationship formation, maintenance, and dissolution from the perspective of the model of interpersonal emotion presented in this section.

THEORIES OF EMOTION

Theories of emotion are remarkably disparate, both within and across the disciplines of psychology, physiology, and sociology. Several key issues remain unresolved. Among the most problematic and recurrent are those concerning (1) the nature of emotional experience (that is, the relative importance of physiological activation and cognitive processes); (2) the function of emotional experience (to ensure survival of the species or to give meaning to social organization and interaction); (3) the origin of emotional experience and expression (innate, phylogenic patterns or acquired patterns); (4) the domain of legitimate inquiry (a set of five to fifteen basic or primary emotional states or a potentially infinite array of multidimensional experiences limited only by the number of emotion terms in a culture's vocabulary). Moreover, no single one of these issues, or even combination of issues, clearly separates the major theories of emotion into exhaustive and mutually exclusive camps.

For these reasons, the representative theories of emotion reviewed here are organized loosely into three broad groups. The theories in the first group share a common analytic orientation toward classifying, characterizing, and defining emotional states by analyzing the words used to refer to them. The presumption is that associations, structures, and relationships in the language used by people to talk about emotional states reflect the associations, structures, and relationships in the experiences themselves.

The second group of theories focuses attention on the reciprocal effect of social consciousness on emotional experience and emotional experience on social meaning. The commonality within this group is the belief that a particular emotion is not automatically triggered by a particular stimulus event, but rather that an emotion emerges from and gives meaning to variable combinations of biological, psychological, and, most important, sociological elements.

In the last group of theories, each contributes, more or less directly, to the ongoing and complicated controversy regarding the nature of the relationship between physiological activation and cognitive processes in emotional experience. Although the more subtle points in the debate are beyond the scope of our review, we identify three positions within this group of theories: (1) physiological activation (whether primarily visceral, primarily autonomic, or primarily somatic) is "felt" as an emotion independently of cognitive mediation; (2) physiological arousal per se is felt as undifferentiated sensation and requires cognitive mediation ("labeling") to be recognized as a particular emotion; (3) activation and cognitive processes are equally essential in the experiencing of emotional states.

The general divisions of emotion theories we propose are more like fences than walls. They indicate useful boundaries but do not preclude points of contact, at various levels, among groups. We intend this review of representative contemporary theories to illustrate areas of convergence and divergence in the study of emotion.

Language-Analytic Theories

The work of Joel Davitz (1964, 1969, 1970) and Robert Plutchik (1970, 1980a, 1980b, 1980c) is illustrative of one type of research tradition in emotion study that relies heavily upon subjects' ratings of emotion terms on various indices and upon self-report descriptions of emotional states. The assumption is that profiles derived from consensual data evidence the quality, range, and dimensionality of actual emotional experience (Davitz, 1969). Research using data derived from laboratory-induced, mechanically measured emotional states is generally considered the antithetical approach.

Among the many studies of "language of emotion," as Davitz terms it, is the widely cited multistage dimensions study. Using the verbal descriptions of emotional states provided by more than 1200 people, Davitz (1969) compiled a checklist of 556 nonredundant phrases and sentences, such as "I have a sense of vitality" and "I feel empty, drained, hollow." He asked naive subjects to rate these items for their adequacy in characterizing each of 50 emotions. A cluster analysis of the items appearing in descriptions of three or more emotions yielded twelve content clusters, which Davitz labeled activation, hypoactivation, hyperactivation, moving toward, moving away, moving against, comfort, discomfort, tension, enhancement, incompetence-dissatisfaction, and inadequacy.

A factor analysis performed on these twelve clusters indicated that they fell along four dimensions: ACTIVATION (representing activation, hypoactivation, and hyperactivation); RELATEDNESS (representing moving toward, moving away, and moving against); HEDONIC TONE (representing comfort, discomfort, and tension); and COMPETENCE (representing enhancement, incompetence-dissatisfaction, and inadequacy).

Davitz does not contend that he has discovered unanticipated or novel dimensions in the structure of emotional meaning. He acknowledges the consistency of his findings with those of other dimensional systems, for example Osgood and Tannenbaum's activity, potency, and evaluation (but see Darnell, 1970). What he does argue is that research and clinical practices have failed to address the implications of these findings. When we label an experience as an emotion, we do so on the basis of the configuration of the cluster elements and the relative emphasis of the dimensions. Thus "change in either an aspect of the experience represented by a particular cluster or in the pattern of emphasis among the various aspects of experience involves change in the emotional state and the label of that state" (Davitz, 1969, p. 143). If this is true, laboratory manipulations of aversive stimuli (such as electrical shocks) to induce anxiety may actually be inducing various other emotional states in subjects. Empirical studies of the relation between control and the effects of aversive stimuli suggest that this may indeed be the case (for example, see Thompson, 1981).

Although the kind of semantic analysis performed by Davitz and others is sometimes criticized as being the study of language categories rather than of the qualities of emotional experience (Mandler, 1980), one or more of the dimensions that Davitz identifies are reflected, in various ways, in the theories of other scholars using quite different analytical methods. Some reflections will be obvious in the discussion that follows; others will be suggested in the summary comments.

An association between Davitz's dimensional approach and Plutchik's "psychoevolutionary" theory may seem unlikely. However, their methods of linguistic analysis are comparable and they share a partial thematic commonality. Davitz himself proposes a thematic association between his COMPETENCE dimension and Plutchik's notion of emotion as adaptive sequences (Davitz, 1969, p. 134). If the COMPETENCE cluster is viewed as an indicator of how adequately people perceive themselves to be adapting to the contingencies of their social environment, then it is a variation of the more global theme of emotions as evolutionary mechanisms that enhance an organism's adaptive potential, increasing its chances for survival.

Plutchik draws from two traditions. From ethology he takes the observation that certain behaviors (such as hitting, biting, vomiting, running away, crying) are evidence that may be used to infer the presence of emotional states in humans and other animals. From Darwinism he takes the view that emotions are "appropriate reactions to emergencies" that increase an organism's chances for survival through adaptation. This blend accounts for the rather unusual definition of emotion that Plutchik offers. An emotion is not simply a subjective feeling for which a particular label such as "angry" or "afraid" is appropriate, nor is it uniquely human. An emotion is an entire chain of events culminating in one of eight universal categories of adaptive behavior. This chain consists of a stimulus event (for example, threat by an enemy), a cognition (danger), a feeling (fear), a behavior (run), and an effect that serves a function (protection).

The eight basic functions are destruction, reproduction, incorporation, orientation, protection, reintegration, rejection, and exploration. ("Reintegration" replaces the term "deprivation" used in early versions of the theory; see Plutchik, 1962.) The eight basic emotions corresponding to the functional categories include anger and fear, joy and sadness, acceptance and disgust, surprise and anticipation. These emotions are presented as pairs of polar opposites based on judges' ratings of intensity, similarity, and polarity for 150 emotion terms. A factor analysis revealed that these four pairs form eight peripheral points in a circumplex arrangement of the meanings implied by emotion terms. Other emotion terms cluster near the basic emotions in various patterns of intensity and similarity. For example, a more intense form of sadness appears to be grief and a less intense form appears to be pensiveness; a more intense form of disgust appears to be loathing and a less intense form appears to be boredom. In additional studies, Plutchik found also that the more "abstract" emotions tend to be derivatives of the basic emotions in combination. In a manner analogous to describing secondary colors as blends of the primary colors, subjects described love as a blend of joy and acceptance, submission as a blend of acceptance and fear, awe as a blend of fear and surprise, and so forth around the "emotion wheel."

Davitz, Plutchik, and others in this group of theories place considerable faith in self-report data. Epstein (1979) contends that, despite limitations, self-reports are comparable to and often preferable to other methods of emotion analysis. Even heart rate, according to Epstein (1979, pp. 51-52), "like all other physiological responses, is governed by complex compensatory effects, both central and peripheral. . . . It follows that, under certain circumstances, self-report should provide a more accurate measure of reactivity than physiological measures." If self-reports are accurate, and if consensually generated descriptions of emotional states do mirror the actuality of emotional experience, then we can suggest at this point that (1) some basic emotional qualities may be innately programmed because they are adaptive mechanisms (facilitating environmental-social competency), and (2) most other emotions differ qualitatively among themselves because they vary in intensity (level of activation), orientation of self to environment (for example, toward others—reintegration-acceptance—or away from others—protection-rejection-disgust), and hedonic tone.

If consensual descriptions and evaluations of emotional terms do not mirror the reality of emotional experience, then in this group of theories we have little more than a model of the "language of emotions" (Mandler, 1980). Indeed, some critics would maintain that we have only a model of language, including but not limited to emotion terms, since words such as "acceptance," "submission," and "boredom" refer to behavioral and psychological states that may not constitute emotions at all. The impetus for this kind of criticism will become evident when the third group of theories, dealing with the activation and cognition controversy, is presented. For the present, we accept the viability of self-report measures and the conclusions reported above.

Psychosocial Theories

Theorists who might be associated with the label "psychosocial" focus their attention primarily on emotional experience as a social phenomenon. From this perspective, emotions are not "felt" simply as sensations and not "emitted" simply as automatic responses to discrete classes of environmental stimuli. Rather, emotions are conceived of as emergent and multifaceted interactions between the self and the environment or, more accurately, the individual's construal of the environment. This perspective is represented here by Joseph de Rivera, James Averill, and Richard Lazarus.

According to de Rivera (1977, p. 142), emotions may be seen as "instructions which tell the organism how to behave in relation to its stimulus situation. Depending on the strength of the emotion, these instructions range from the merest hints to overpowering imperatives." Although this definition appears to echo Plutchik, for de Rivera a particular emotion cannot be predicted from a stimulus event. Instead, it emerges as a reflection of the "transformation" of a person's relation to the important elements (people, objects, events) in the social situation. The transformation generates the emotional quality; it gives meaning to the environment, not the reverse. This view entails an implicit rejection of the finite, primary emotions tenet; theoretically, the number of emotions is the same as the number of possible transformations. Even calmness, according to de Rivera, may be considered an emotion if, in a demanding situation, "disturbance" has been transformed by strength of character into calmness. (Without the transformation, of course, the individual is merely unrealistically out of touch with the situation.)

The specifics of de Rivera's theory include four instructions (give, get, remove, and escape), which correspond to four movements (toward other, toward self, away from self, and away from other) similar to Davitz's RELATEDNESS dimension. Instructions and movements form the basic schema within which transformations occur. For example, love moves "toward the other," with the instruction "to give," and the transformation is "self belongs to other."

In de Rivera's theory, emotions are of two types: *it* emotions (those that have an object) and *me* emotions (those with the self as the implicit object). All *it* emotions have correlate *me* emotions but the experience of the *me* emotion depends upon the individual's transaction with the social environment. de Rivera provides a useful illustration of the dynamics of this process for the *it* emotion "contempt" and a probable correlate *me* emotion "shame." If one is the direct recipient of another person's contempt, one will likely experience shame. But other more subtle transformations are also possible, as indicated in de Rivera's (1977, p. 56) scenario:

> A person who is driving a new foreign car with a stick shift finds that he feels somewhat ashamed when he grinds the car's gears. However, his experience of shame varies with his circumstances, depending on whether a friend is in the car and whether any pedestrians are present. When no one is present, there is no sense of shame; thus, in this particular case, there is no internalized other. When pedestrians are present, the shame is experienced most acutely. However, when a friend is present there is again no shame! To understand these responses we must examine how this person reacts when others grind the gears of their cars. We find that his reaction to others depends on the circumstances. When he is a pedestrian, he is annoyed by the rasping sound and feels contempt for the "shoddy driving" of the other. However, when he is with a friend who is driving, he blames the "sticky gears" of the car. On the basis of this information we must conclude that when the person himself is driving he sees himself through the eyes of the other who is present, or rather sees himself as he imagines the other sees him. If a friend is present, the person sees himself as innocent, but if a pedestrian is present, the person sees himself through eyes of contempt and feels ashamed.

The transformation of an *it* emotion to a *me* emotion is generally an unconscious process. If, for example, we are made too publicly aware of someone's contempt, we are likely to respond with an *it* emotion such as anger. In most situations we infer "the existence of an implicit other who is contemptuous in order to account for the existence of shame" (de Rivera, 1977, p. 56).

Averill's (1980a, 1980b, 1973) conception of emotion is quite similar to de Rivera's, except that instructions and movements are recast into the framework of social roles and perspective taking. Averill (1980a, p. 13) defines emotions as "transitory social roles (socially constituted syndromes) that are based on an individual's appraisal of the situation and that are interpreted as passions rather than actions." Unpacking this definition requires clarification of two concepts: the action/passion distinction and transitory social roles.

The action/passion distinction is fairly straightforward. Action implies that behavior is self-initiated, rational, and voluntary. Passion, on the other hand, is passive, irrational, and involuntary. Actions are things that we do; passions are things that happen to us. Social roles are a more complex matter. First, they can be characterized as socially determined sets of responses, each set governed by certain rules and expectations. Like the forms and rules of language, these roles are culturally shared and implicit. When we are enacting a social role, we expect that we and others will feel and behave in particular ways and that deviations will be noticed. Second, social roles are transitory in that appraisal (that is, the imposition of meaning on experience) is continual, and when appraisals change so also do social roles. Third, social role is like a syndrome because it includes diverse but systematically related elements. Some of these elements may be biological, some psychological, and some sociological, but no single element is essential for the syndrome to exist.

What is essential for emotions to exist is that at some point during the appraisal process we *interpret* our own behavior as passion (beyond self-control) and thereby find ourselves enacting an emotional role. The appraisal does not simply precede and then trigger an emotional role; it is literally part of the role itself. As Averill (1980a, p. 310) explains:

> I may be angry at John for insulting me, when in actuality John was only trying to be helpful by correctly pointing out a mistake I had made. John's insult is based on my appraisal of the situation; it is as much a part of my anger as is my feeling of hurt.

Unlike theorists who propose that assigning a label to bodily arousal constitutes an emotion, Averill sees labeling as one possible part of the process. If a label is assigned, it serves merely as a convenient symbol for the meaning of the entire episode.

The work of Lazarus (Lazarus, Averill, & Opton, 1970; Lazarus, Kanner, & Folkman, 1980) is redundant to Averill's in many respects, but foreshadows the emerging influence of the physiological theories within the phenomenological framework. Lazarus also takes a syndromic and transactional view of emotional experience, but identifies three specific components that he believes are essential to the emotion syndrome. These are cognitive appraisals, action impulses, and patterned somatic reactions (Lazarus et al., 1980). If one component is absent, the experience will not be a "proper" emotion. Each is an integral part of the process, and their various interaction patterns ("cognitive themes") provide the various emotion qualities (e.g., anger, fear, joy).

By using the phrase "patterned somatic responses," Lazarus intends to support the controversial position that particular emotions can be associated with particular patterns of physiological response. Because he takes this position, and because he stresses the association between component patterns and emotional quality, Lazarus is sometimes assumed to endorse the notion of a finite set of basic emotions. However, Lazarus et al. (1980) consider this to be a moot point because social transactions are far too complex and dynamic to generate a single pattern (cognitive theme) in isolation from several others.

With the exception of Lazarus, most theorists associated with what we have called the "psychosocial perspective" assign only minimal direct influence to physiological arousal. They reject explicitly any inherent antecedent causal relationship between arousal and emotional experience, or between a stimulus event and an emotional state (Leventhal, 1979). In contrast to the linear model predicting that arousal stimulates a need to know why, which then motivates a cognitive appraisal of the environment (Schachter & Singer, 1962), the psychosocial model posits a continuous appraisal process. Definitions of emotion reflect this dynamic and processual orientation: for example, transformation, transactions, transitory social roles, social constructions, improvisations, and emotional schemata. A host of psychological and social elements influence and are influenced by the appraisal process, becoming intrinsic parts of what an individual experiences as an emotional state.

Psychophysiological Theories

Most current theories that address the relation between physical activation and cognitive processes in emotion align themselves to one of three views: (1) favoring physiological determinism, (2) favoring cognitive determinism, (3) favoring an integration of the two.

The origins of the controversy are usually traced to the early work of James (1890/1950), who proposed that the production of emotion begins with a person's awareness of an "exciting fact" in the environment. The biological systems of the body respond to this awareness, and the individual's perception of these bodily changes as they occur constitutes the emotion. More specifically, James placed the locus of arousal in the viscera, or internal organs of the body and argued that a particular pattern of visceral change signaled the particular emotion that was felt.

The Jamesian explanation of emotional arousal held considerable influence until Cannon's critique in 1927. Following a series of experiments on laboratory animals, Cannon concluded that the viscera are not a defensible locus of emotional arousal for several reasons. First, visceral reactions are not differentiated enough to account for the variety of emotions commonly experienced. Second, the viscera are too slow in reacting and too insensitive to give rise to emotions. The viscera can be separated surgically from the central nervous system without affecting emotional expressiveness. And, finally, visceral changes can be induced artificially (for instance, adrenaline injections) without giving rise to a corresponding change in emotional state. Cannon concluded that the viscera function to maintain the body's internal homeostasis but do not function in the perception of emotional experience. He proposed an alternative locus of arousal in the central neural pathway, particularly the thalamic center.

While relatively few contemporary theorists believe that every emotion has a corresponding pattern of physiological arousal, most are convinced that biological feedback systems do play a critical role in the experiencing of emotional states. The question that separates members of this group, however, is whether arousal per se is both the necessary and sufficient determinant of emotional experience or whether arousal is necessary but insufficient without cognitive mediation.

Tomkins (1980) and Tomkins and McCarter (1964) represent the first position. They identify nine primary, innate affects, three positive and six negative. These affects are activated by neural firing, and variations in the density of neural firing account for the quality of emotional response. According to Tomkins (1980, pp. 143-144):

> If internal or external sources of neural firing suddenly increase, [a person] will startle or become afraid, or become interested, depending on the suddenness of the increase in stimulation. If internal or external sources of neural firing reach and maintain a high, constant level of stimulation, which deviates in excess of an optimal level of neural firing, he will respond with anger or distress, depending on the level of stimulation. If internal or external sources of neural firing suddenly decrease, he will laugh or smile with enjoyment, depending on the suddenness of the decrease in stimulation.

These patterns of variation in neural firing presumably activate the skin and musculature of the face, causing the flushing and facial expressions characteristic of each of the nine primary affects. Afferent feedback to the autonomic system from the face (and the secondary involvement of the skeletal and visceral systems) then constitutes a particular primary emotional experience. Tomkins argues that whether we are aware of this feedback or not, and quite independently of cognitive appraisal, this feedback is inherently positive or negative, acceptable or unacceptable. "Certainly the infant who emits his birth cry upon exit from the birth canal has not 'appraised' the new environment as a vale of tears before he cries" (Tomkins, 1980, p. 145). The child will eventually learn to avoid situations activating unacceptable responses and seek situations activating acceptable responses, but the responses themselves are involuntary and independent of cognitive evaluation.

Izard (1977) acknowledges his debt to the work of Tomkins and shares with him the position that the emotions can operate independently of cognition. He also posits the existence of a set of fundamental,transcultural emotions differing only slightly from Tomkins's nine primary affects. They include interest, joy, surprise, sadness, anger, disgust, contempt, fear, shame/shyness, and guilt (Izard & Buechler, 1980).

Izard extends these premises, however, and incorporates them into the larger framework of the human personality using six subsystems, one of which is emotion. Because the subsystems are interrelated and interactive, emotional experiences need not be limited to the fundamental emotions. Although in childhood, and on occasion in adult life, the emotion subsystem does take its prerogative of independent operation, more typically it is involved with the other subsystems in variable and complex ways. Beginning at the level of the drive subsystem, a basic drive may combine with a fundamental emotion to produce an "affect." A fundamental emotion may also combine with one or more other fundamental emotions, whether simultaneously or in sequence, to produce "patterns" of emotional states. For example, depression occurs when sadness is accompanied by anger, disgust, contempt, or fear. The idea of combined emotional states is not unlike Plutchik's derivative emotions, but Izard sees derivations as experientially driven and variable, not linguistically determined and static. That is, a particular pattern will depend upon the person's past experiences and the current situation, but each combination will be a qualitatively different experience. Finally, the cognitive and perceptual subsystems can interact with an emotion to regulate, sustain, and attenuate it.

Stable personality traits are formed, according to Izard, when stabilized patterns of interaction develop among subsystems. That is, when a particular affect or pattern of affects interacts frequently with recurring cognitions, a stable "affective-cognitive structure" is formed. Configurations of these structures become "affective-cognitive orientations" or personality traits such as passivity or skepticism.

Not all proponents of the psychophysiological position consider the face to be the primary source of feedback to the cortical system. In a review of studies testing the "facial feedback hypothesis," Buck (1980, p. 822) asserts that

> at present there is insufficient evidence to conclude that facial feedback is either necessary or sufficient for the occurrence of emotion, and the evidence for any contribution of facial feedback to emotional experience is less convincing than the evidence for visceral feedback.

Buck argues further that facial displays are a highly visible means for communicating affective processes, but because social organization has encouraged control of affect displays, the result has been more complex facial feedback to the experiencer. This additional feedback, however, "seems to have been secondary to their readout functions" (Buck, 1980, p. 122). The viscera, on the other hand, are beyond voluntary control, which prompts Buck, like James, to attribute causal significance to their activation.

A quite different model of emotional experience from the biological model guiding the work of Tomkins, Izard, and Buck is Schachter and Singer's (1962). They view physiological arousal as undifferentiated and generalized sensation. Since the meaning of arousal is unclear, it gives rise to a search for some explanation. Cognitive appraisal of the immediate environment provides an explanation (usually a causal antecedent), which is then used to identify the emotion to be felt. "It is the cognition which determines whether the state of physiological arousal will be labeled as 'anger,' 'joy,' 'fear,' or whatever" (Schachter & Singer, 1962, p. 380).

In the Schachter and Singer (1962) classic study of drug-induced arousal, subjects were injected with epinephrine or a placebo and then exposed to a confederate acting in a euphoric or angry manner. Epinephrine subjects who were fully informed about the injection and its effects were not significantly affected by the manipulation. Uninformed epinephrine subjects were significantly responsive to the manipulation, although the impact of the confederate's mood was greater on subjects' overt behavior than on self-reports of affective state. Presumably, unexplained arousal motivated the search for a causal explanation and the social context provided that information. Placebo subjects who received saline injections were similar to the informed epinephrine subjects in their response patterns.

Although Schachter and Singer's work is frequently cited as evidence for cognitive determinance and emotional plasticity, attempts to replicate the 1962 study cast some doubt on the findings. Maslach (1979) performed a modified replication of the original study using posthypnotically triggered arousal. She found that the confederate's mood (happy or angry) had a significant effect on subjects' overt behaviors but not on reports of emotional states. In fact, posthypnosis subjects whose arousal had been triggered by seeing a cue word reported significantly greater negative affect, regardless of the condeferate's mood, than did posthypnosis subjects who were not given the cue word or control subjects who had not been hypnotized. Maslach draws two important conclusions from her findings: First, the confederate's mood seems to represent normative information for an uninformed subject to use in modeling behavior so as to be socially appropriate. However, this kind of normative information does not indicate the *cause* for the feeling that presumably motivates the search for the emotional label. Second, the fact that unexplained arousal was correlated with self-reports of negative affect even in the happy condition suggests that "strong unexplained arousal per se is typically perceived as a negative state by adults and not as an undifferentiated, affectively neutral state, as the Schachter-Singer model proposes" (Maslach, 1979, p. 969).

Similar conclusions were reached by Marshall and Zimbardo (1979), who compared epinephrine-induced arousal subjects to placebo subjects in a euphoric condition. They found that uninformed aroused subjects reported negative affect despite the confederate's positive mood, and that increased levels of arousal (larger dosages of epinephrine) produced only increased negative affect. These results are consistent with Maslach's negative bias hypothesis: In instances of strong unexplained arousal the search for an emotion label will be biased in the direction of negatively toned emotions irrespective of environmental conditions.

The Schachter and Singer model has also been criticized in a recent experiment performed by Ekman, Levenson, and Friesen (1983), who found that autonomic activity could distinguish between positive and negative emotions as well as among some negative emotions. Professional actors and scientists were instructed in two conditions. The first involved moving certain muscles of the face in patterns characteristic of six basic emotions (anger, fear, sadness, happiness, surprise, disgust) without being told what emotion was being represented. The second condition required subjects to "relive" the experiencing of each of the six emotions. Five physiological measures, including heart rate, hand temperature, skin resistance, and forearm flexor muscle tension, were taken continuously throughout both conditions. Various patterns of these autonomic responses were found to distinguish anger, fear, and sadness from happiness, disgust, and surprise and to further distinguish anger from fear and sadness.

A summary of the "cognition-arousal" literature presented to this point indicates evidence to support two different notions of emotional experience. The first holds that emotions *are* the felt sensations of physiological arousal. The primary emotions, at least, are programmed responses to feedback from the somatic muscles and skin of the face, from the viscera, from the autonomic nervous system, or from some combination of these sources. The second holds that emotions are plastic sensations. They consist of an undifferentiated, affectively neutral level of arousal that is defined or identified by a cognitive appraisal of the immediate environment. While staunch advocates of either position might resist a merger, other scholars have explored the interesting possibility of integrating the two views (Kemper, 1978; Mandler, 1975, 1980).

Kemper (1978) builds his model from the unlikely union of pure physiology and pure sociology. The sociological structure he erects is built on the social conditions most likely to induce emotions, social relations:

> The most important premise of any sociological theory of emotions must be that *an extremely large class of human emotions results from real, anticipated, imagined, or recollected outcomes of social relationships:* she says she does not love me; he says I did a good job; I claimed to be honest, but was caught in a lie; he obligated himself to me, but then reneged; and so forth. These are outcomes of social relationships that ought to stimulate emotion. It follows that we would understand the production of emotions better if we understood social relationships better. (Kemper, 1978, p. 32)

Kemper isolates two underlying relational themes: control of one member by another (power) and degree of positive social relations (status). In a dyadic relationship, four possibilities exist for each member. A person can feel that he or she has (1) claimed or acquired an excess of power in the relationship or (2) claimed or acquired an excess of status in the relationship. A person can feel that her or she (3) has insufficient power in the relationship, or (4) receives insufficient status in the relationship. A third concept is that of "agency," referring to the attribution of responsibility. Kemper (1978, pp. 33-34) proposes that

> when *self* is viewed as agent, the emotion will be *introjected* and *intropunitive.* When *other* is viewed as agent, the emotion will be *extrojected* and *extropunitive.* When the actor's sense of agency and responsibility oscillates between self and other, the felt relational excess or deficit will produce *compound,* or *mixed* emotions.

Guilt, for example, according to Kemper, occurs when a person feels that self has used excess power over the other, and if the self is perceived to be the agent, then guilt will be felt as remorse or regret.

Nothing said thus far is exceptional to the psychosocial tradition discussed previously. In fact, the concept of agency is very consistent with de Rivera's concept of the transformation of *it* emotions to *me* emotions. The novelty of Kemper's model is in the way he links physiological arousal to the dimensions of power and status. He notes first that the parasympathetic branch of the central nervous system is generally associated with emotions of pleasure and satisfaction, and the sympathetic system is associated with the emotions of anger and fear. These two systems release different types of neurochemicals (hormones) that offset each other and keep the body in homeostasis, controlling both excessive overarousal and excessive underarousal (lethargy).

When a person is feeling angry, the sympathetic system releases norepinephrine (or noradrenaline) and when a person is feeling fearful or anxious, it releases epinephrine (or adrenaline). This appears to Kemper (1978, p. 37) to be the analogue for the relationship variables he proposes:

> Since deficit of own power (or excess of other's power) is the social relational condition for fear or anxiety, and since loss of customary, expected, or deserved status (other as agent) is the basic relational condition for anger, it seems entirely compatible to suppose that specific social relational conditions are accompanied by specific physiological reactions, with the felt emotions as the psychological mediators between the two.

The positive emotions are accounted for as the sense of contentment and well-being associated with a neurochemical called acetylcholine released by the parasympathetic system. Release of acetylcholine would indicate, in Kemper's model, that power and status are felt to be in equilibrium. The final proposition then reads:

> The parasympathetic nervous system dominates when both power and status are sufficient and no specially compelling emotions are felt; the sympathetic nervous system dominates when power and/or status are disturbed from satisfactory levels, with norepinephrine as the organismic correlate of status loss (anger) and epinephrine as the organismic correlate of power-insufficiency (fear). (Kemper, 1978, pp. 37-38)

Kemper's model has much to recommend it. First, it is appealing in its parsimonious blend of physiological, psychological, and sociological influence on emotional experience. Simply put, perceptions of relational definition (that is, relative power-status equilibrium) induce characteristic types of physiological arousal that are interpreted as emotions according to attributions of causal agent (that is, self or other).

Second, it accomplishes more effectively what psychosocial and cognitive theories attempt to do. It draws attention to the importance of transactional social networks, attribution of responsibility, and perception of relational definition in emotional experience without also diminishing the role of physiological arousal, and without relying on complex metaphors such as transformation, socially constituted syndromes, and transitory social roles.

Third, it is compatiable with existing dimensional models of relationships (e.g., Leary, 1955), while at the same time holding promise as an explanatory model of relational escalation as well. For example, given Kemper's (1978, p. 32) definition of emotions as responses to "real, anticipated, imagined, or recollected outcomes of social relationships," it is reasonable to predict that as value accrues to a particular outcome from investment made in the relationship over time, the perceived intensity of the emotional state should increase. Newman (1981a) and Weiss (1976) support the validity of such a prediction.

Kemper's model is intriguing, but may also lose a degree of heurism in restricting its focus to social relationships. It fails to account for emotions experienced as a consequence of the unintentional behavior (perceived as unintentional) of human and nonhuman "agents." In short, it works better as a model for relationally defined emotions than as a model for emotions in general. Since individually induced emotional states influence relational dynamics as well as the other way around, Kemper's theory might be considered a context-specific variation of more general integrative theories of emotion such as that proposed by Mandler (1980).

Like Kemper, Mandler (1975, 1980) believes that both physiological arousal and cognitive processes are integral to the experiencing of an emotional state. However, Mandler identifies a different source of arousal. He attributes arousal to the effects of "interruption." Interruption occurs when "well-developed, well-organized habitual, and previously adaptive actions fail, cannot be completed, or in some way are inhibited" (Mandler, 1980, p. 228). Interruption alerts the organism and stimulates the autonomic nervous system.

The conscious experience of emotion is the product of an integration of two unconscious processes: arousal and evaluation. Autonomic arousal is recognized and registered in consciousness as the "intensity dimension" of emotional experience. Evaluation of arousal is the analysis of its meaning in relation to each person's unique combination of past experiences, perceptions, expectations, belief systems, and so forth. Given that no two evaluations (meaning analyses) can be identical, no two emotion products can be identical. The range of possible emotional experience is theoretically infinite. It appears to be reducible to discrete, finite categories, but only because the language used to describe internal states is, like all language, categorical. The cognitive operations used to categorize the emotional experience are not those used to generate the emotional gestalt, and the label is not the experience itself.

Summary

Although this review indicates important differences, contradictions, and incompatibilities in the theory and research of emotion, it also indicates important areas of convergence and commonality. By stepping back from the specifics of any particular approach, we are able to suggest several propositions derivable from emotion study.

(1) Physiological involvement and cognitive interpretation are concomitant aspects of emotional states, though the relative influence of each kind of information is variable. Thus some emotional states are predominantly physical reactions, and others are complex, abstract, and predominantly cognitive constructions. Most common emotions fall along a continuum between these extremes.

(2) Some emotional states are perceived to be more intense than other emotional states, or than the same emotional state in other instances of its occurrence. This is due to a high level of physical responsiveness, a high level of personal involvement in some element of the appraisal process, or both.

(3) The existence of an emotional state entails evaluation. Not every experience that is evaluated signals an emotion, but every emotion is an evaluated experience. Some emotions are perceived by the experiencer as a "good" feeling (positive hedonic tone), others as a "bad" feeling (negative hedonic tone). Perceptions of good-bad may be based on social-contextual cues, past experiences, immediate or anticipated outcomes, or unmediated physiological arousal. Perceptions of good-bad are subject to reevaluation both throughout and for an indefinite period of time after the experiencing of an emotion.

(4) Although a few environmental events bear a rather direct relationship to an emotional state (for example, a sudden loud noise), most stimulus events are perceptually defined, often retrospectively.

(5) On occasions when physiological arousal occurs prior to or independently of cognitive monitoring, the unanticipated sensation is negatively toned and this discomfort stimulates an immediate appraisal of possible causal explanations.

(6) Emotions are dynamic. The relationship between appraisal and activation is complex and interactive, and probably reciprocal. Attribution of cause, intensity, relevance, duration, and responsibility shape the quality of emotional experience; at the same time, degrees of urgency, intensity, and valence also direct the attribution process. Whatever the direction of influence, the connecting pattern between bodily activation and psychological appraisal is individually and subjectively organized.

(7) While the range of emotional experience is potentially infinite, in actual practice the limitations of language and the limitations of vocal/nonverbal affect display restrict and channelize emotional experience and expression. We cannot talk to ourselves or others about feelings and we cannot enact those feelings without a common code.

We believe these propositions to be a useful summary of existing emotion literature. We also believe them to be a foundation from which a working model of emotions in the particular context of interpersonal relationships can be generated.

A MODEL OF INTERPERSONAL EMOTION

For the purpose of this chapter, we have devised a scheme of emotional experience based on the work of Ted Robert Gurr (1970; see also Smith & Kluegel, 1982) and various attribution theorists (e.g., Harvey, Weber, Yarkin, & Stewart, 1982; Kelley, 1979; Newman, 1981a; Sillars, 1980). This position is most similar to those taken by Perlman and Peplau (1981) and by Heslin and Patterson (1982). Gurr's work rests on the premise that certain kinds of experiences, perceptions, cognitions, and behaviors are largely functions of discrepancies between individuals' "value expectations" (VE—their ideas of how things *should* be, what they *deserve*) and "value capabilities" (VC—their perceptions of how things *are*) in their current pursuit and attainment of "value stocks," which fall into various "value classes" (welfare values, power values, and interpersonal values). Although Gurr is concerned exclusively with "relative deprivation" (RD—a psychological state in which VE exceeds VC), we have extended his model to include "relative gratification" (RG—a psychological state in which VC exceeds VE). RD states are negative in hedonic tone, dissatisfying, and RG states are positive in hedonic tone, satisfying. In our scheme, RD and RG account for the deviation from homeostasis—arousal—posited as a necessary component of emotion by most theorists who have written on the subject.

Depending on many variables (such as effort put forth in pursuit of a value stock, perceived proximity of its attainment, perceived availability of alternative value stocks), RD and RG may be experienced anywhere on a continuum of intensity. Our scheme represents this continuum on two levels: "mild" and "strong."

We invoke attribution theories to account for the cognitive component of emotion posited by most theorists. Experience of emotion differs not only as a function of arousal, but also as a function of the individual's attribution of cause or responsibility for the arousal. Hence, if you refuse to live with me (even though I want you to live with me, think that you should live with me, and have had strong confidence that you would live with me), the emotion I experience as a consequence of your refusal differs depending on my perception of the cause for your refusal. If I perceive that the cause is internal to you, under your control (you have secretly been seeing another potential partner and unreasonably prefer that person), I may feel personally rejected and I may experience anger and hate as a function of your refusal. If I perceive that the cause is external to you, out of your control (although I haven't realized it earlier, your child, whom you value highly, despises me and has threatened suicide if you live with me), I may experience regret (despair in its strong form) as a consequence of your refusal.

Our scheme permits four kinds of causal attribution for RD and RG: to self (internal), to other (internal), to the relationship (the characteristic patterns of self and other interacting), and to situation (causes out of the control of self,

	HEDONIC TONE			
	Relative Deprivation		Relative Gratification	
	Intensity			
Attribution	Mild	Strong	Mild	Strong
to self				
to other				
to relationship				
to situation				

Figure 11.1 A Model of Interpersonal Emotion

other, and self and other interacting). While the scheme does not explicitly incorporate mixed attributions (Newman, 1981a), it clearly permits them, and we recognize the possibility that they exist as well as the possibility that certain kinds of mixed emotions may be their consequences.

A taxonomy of interpersonally experienced emotions based on this scheme would use three dimensions to generate 16 cells: 2 (RD or RG) $\times$ 2 (mild or strong) $\times$ 4 (attribution of cause to self, to other, to relationship, or to situation). To the extent that the scheme is useful, the emotions experienced and messages produced in each cell should be at least slightly different from those experienced and produced in any other. An approach such as that taken by Davitz (1969) or that described by Averill (1980b) might serve to provide labels for the emotions posited in our scheme—though labels are not necessary to the scheme (see Figure 11.1).

This scheme has certain advantages. It unambiguously locates arousal in motivational experience, that is, the discrepancy between VE and VC. It unambiguously locates the cognitive component of emotion in attributional processes, the assignment of cause to RD and RG, but, unlike in Kemper's (1978) view, attribution may be to impersonal "agents," perceived characteristics of situations. VE, VC, and attributions are perceptual variables occurring in individuals, so that the experience of emotion may be analyzed as idiosyncratic. At the same time, VE, VC, and attributions are experienced universally, and, according to Gurr (1970), can be predicted by other universally experienced variables. And the discrepancy between VE and VC constitutes a continuous variable, accounting both for intensity (increasing as the discrepancy between VE and VC increases) and hedonic tone (positive for RG, negative for RD) of emotions.

The scheme also bypasses the vigorous (but we think otiose) conflict among emotion theorists about whether an individual must label an arousal in order for the experience to be considered emotional (see Schachter & Singer, 1962). Our scheme requires that arousals be attributionally analyzed by the individual, but the analysis may be in five hundred words rather than in a one-word label.

Furthermore, although we will not explore them in this chapter, certain of Gurr's hypotheses stimulate interesting possibilities for research on emotion. As one example, Gurr (1970, p. 83) hypothesizes that "decremental" RD, a form of RD experienced when VE remains constant while VC declines, is the most salient form of RD and therefore, of all forms of RD, has the longest duration. Thus, relationally speaking, grief for irrevocably lost interpersonal value capabilities (your positively valued partner dies and no substitute is available) should be a relatively persistent emotion, while hope for never-achieved value expectations (you are going to the White House, but unexpectedly will be unable to see the president, whom you had wanted to see) should be comparatively fleeting.

Gurr's system also encourages speculation about emotion and inter-personal communication during the course of a relationship. The experience of RD (and, in the absence of evidence to the contrary, RG) is curvilinear over time (inverted U), rising sharply after onset but declining later (most slowly for decremental RD). The psychological fact seems to be that, for RD, individuals' VE eventually declines to a level near their VC, and, for RG, individuals' VE rises (probably quite rapidly) to a level slightly above their VC. Normally, VE slightly exceeds VC, so that we are generally striving beings. As countless theorists have pointed out, this mild discrepancy is probably adaptive for the species. This tendency for VE and VC to reach a level where VE exceeds VC (but only slightly), together with the likely fact that RD is a much more common experience than RG, may at least partially explain why positive valence is more likely among the older than the younger—VE and VC have become reconciled over time for the older (Campbell, Converse, & Rogers, 1976; Smith & Kluegel, 1982). This reasoning also may partly explain why positive emotional concepts are in a state of "paucity"—RG is relatively rare and of brief duration (but compare Averill, 1980b). And the same line of reasoning may explain the negative bias experimental subjects assign to otherwise unexplained arousal (e.g., Maslach, 1979).

Finally, this scheme preserves (though it generalizes somewhat) what we think is the most interesting and attractive feature of Mandler's (1975) theory of emotion and its application to close relationships by Berscheid (1983). Following Mandler, Berscheid holds that emotions occur when individuals experience "interruptions" in the fulfillment of their goal-directed organized action sequences. These interruptions arouse the autonomic nervous system and engage the cognitive system. An arousal that has been evaluated by the cognitive system is an emotion. In a relationship, these interruptions might occur in an "intrachain" (an individual's sequence of goal-directed acts) or in an "interchain" (an interactive sequence of goal-directed acts; Berscheid, 1983).

Our problem with this theory is more semantic than conceptual, but we think that our scheme solves even the semantic problem. In the Mandler/

Berscheid view, interruptions may either interfere with or facilitate progress toward the goal. We find it difficult to think of an "interruption" as facilitative. Our scheme, with its more general notion of dislocations in the relationship between VE and VC, encompasses the interruption concept.

MESSAGE VARIABLES AND EMOTION

The human organism functions in such a way that (1) it becomes aroused by its environment, including the prospect of communicating and the process of communicating, by its needs, and by the virtualities conjured by the brain; (2) it leaks signs of this arousal; and (3) it may consciously and unconsciously manipulate itself to produce paralinguistic, kinesic, and linguistic signs and symbols of emotion to gain suitable complementary or reciprocal responses from other human beings (see Poyatos, 1980). Both the leakage of unintentional expression of emotion and the manipulation of the more or less intentional enactment of emotion are communicative—that is, are interpretable by another interactant or by an observer.

In this section, we will take the point of view of an ideal interpreter, observing and analyzing the emotionally laden physiological, paralinguistic, kinesic, lexical, and pragmatic behavior of another. Our treatment will necessarily be general, and we will artificially isolate messages from their interactive contexts. (In the major section to follow, we will restore them to their interactive contexts when we discuss emotion in relationships.) Most of our generalizations will be limited to the intensity dimension of our model; hedonic tone and attribution must be inferred from contexts, which, in this section, are not discussed.

Physiological Leakage

The arousal associated with emotion involves the involuntary nervous system and its two subsystems, the sympathetic and the parasympathetic. Though the sympathetic system may operate on specific organs, it usually activates the entire body in a "mass discharge" (Guyton, 1971; Pelletier, 1977). The parasympathetic system always operates with specific activation on particular organs.

The ideal interpreter, with very full access to the physiology of an emoting individual, may infer relatively intense arousal from a number of signs (Pelletier, 1977), though the signs themselves do not point to the attributed causes of the arousal or the hedonic tone of the emotion experienced. The signs include the following, among others: trembling, cold feet (as the sympathetic nervous system shifts blood away from the periphery to the trunk and head), and chills, all often, though not exclusively, associated with fear; flushing; frequent urination (Alvarez, 1929); weeping; hair rising on the back of the neck; dilated pupils; tight throat, tense neck and upper back;

shallow respiration; accelerated heart rate; cool and perspiring hands; rigid pelvis; and tight anus.

Many of these signs are difficult to simulate for most individuals, so they may be taken as trustworthy indicants of "honest" emotion. Nevertheless, skill in producing them may be developed by certain individuals, and this kind of training is the subject of an entire literature (for example, see Stanislavsky, 1936).

Paralanguage

The ideal interpreter will recognize quickly that paralinguistic variables, though they develop "clearly in the service of emotional expression and interpersonal emotional exchange" (Jaffe, Anderson, & Stern, 1979, p. 424) at a very early stage, through processes of acculturation and socialization, must also assume the burden of much syntactic information. Hence paralanguage may be merely syntactic, but it may also express or enact emotional messages. Most paralinguistic variables are firmly grounded in physiological processes (as opposed to cognitive processes), so emotional messages inferred from those variables may be relatively trustworthy. As with physiological variables, inferences must be confined principally to the intensity dimension of emotion, though some distinctions between those emotions based on relative deprivation and those based on relative gratification also may be made reliably.

Clearly, the ideal interpreter can identify paralinguistic expressions and enactments of emotion at levels higher than would be predicted by chance. In studies of this kind of reliability, lexical content has been masked by whispering (Knower, 1941), noise (Pollack, Rubenstein, & Horowitz, 1960), "content-free" lexical markers (Davitz & Davitz, 1959), and various combinations of splicing, electronic filtering, and electronic voice simulation (Rogers, Scherer, & Rosenthal, 1971; Scherer, 1971, 1979; Scherer, Koivumaki, & Rosenthal, 1972).

Cultural expectations about such paralinguistic variables as rhythm, stress, rate, pitch, and amplitude become rule governed (Jaffe et al., 1979). Rule violations in these matters, then, become potent signifiers, often of emotion, as in, "He said to *inflate* the balloon, not *deflate* it" (Key, 1975, p. 53).

Rate, pitch, and amplitude all are related to arousal. For rate, the relationship probably is curvilinear (inverted U; Murray, 1971). Rate obviously is associated with complex syntactic and semantic processes as well as with paralinguistic ones, so that extreme arousal for most people interferes with rapid encoding. Rate has also been related directly to anger (Scherer, 1979): "Hot" anger has a notably "fast tempo," while "cool" anger is moderate in all acoustic variables and their variations.

Pitch and pitch variation probably are the most salient variables in the vocal expression of emotion (Crystal, 1969; Deva, 1957, 1958, 1960; O'Connor & Arnold, 1973; Scherer, 1979; Scherer et al., 1972; Scherer & Oshinsky, 1977). According to Scherer (1979, p. 251),

> Extreme pitch variation and up contours produce ratings of highly pleasant, active, and potent emotions such as happiness, interest, surprise, and also fear. Down contours have similar effects but do not seem to contain elements of surprise or uncertainty.

As would be predicted from a direct arousal relationship with pitch, pitch increases during deception (Ekman, Friesen, & Scherer, 1976) and increases even further when the deceptive task is made more stressful (Streeter, Krauss, Geller, Olson, & Apple, 1977).

Amplitude as a variable in emotional expression and enactment has been less researched than rate and pitch. Davitz (1964) directly related a series of vocal variables, loudness prominent among them, to the "activity" but not the "strength" or "valence" of perceived emotion. Scherer (1979) found that extreme amplitude variation is associated with fear and, like pitch variation, with "hot" anger.

Other paralinguistic variables may be combined in rhythm, rhyme, and alliteration. These paralinguistic devices have a seductive effect on auditors, an effect characterized as emotional rather than cognitive (Watzlawick, 1978). Many politicians have attempted to exploit this seductive possibility (Sperber, 1955), as do caretakers with their infants (Meerloo, 1964). Berlyne's (1972) experiments on sounds and poems "pointed" toward predictability of affective reactions as a function of particular variations in sounds.

The ideal interpreter might also include as paralanguage nonfluencies and voluntary and involuntary interruptions in the stream of talk. Key (1975, pp. 42-48) shows that in English certain conventional expressions of emotion involve sounds that are nowhere present in the language proper. Poyatos (1976, p. 113) analyzes such phenomena as sniffs and snorts of amusement and contempt.

The fountainhead of research on speech production failures was Freud (1910/1965, 1974). Although specifically Freudian versions of the relationship between emotion and failures in production are not widely popular, the central idea is seemingly inescapable: People make many errors in speech production because their inner emotional life with its inherent defensiveness and contradictory impulses interferes with the complex activities resulting in the uninterrupted flow of language.

One emotional state particularly likely to produce speech errors is apprehension. High communication apprehensives have been shown to seek low-pay, low-status jobs to avoid the emotional burden of communication (Daly & McCroskey, 1975; Scott, McCroskey, & Sheahan, 1978). Some apprehension apparently attaches to the early stages of most interactions for most people. In those early stages, participants tend to be beset by "linguistic uncertainty" and consequently produce speech errors. As the participants become secure in the interaction, the frequency of speech errors decreases (Cook, 1969; Kasl & Mahl, 1965; Lalljee & Cook, 1973; Siegman & Pope, 1965).

Disfluencies and emotions may sometimes form a positive feedback loop. McCroskey and Mehrley (1969) found that disfluencies significantly lower message effectiveness and listener attribution of speaker credibility. Speakers perceptive enough to recognize this relationship may become increasingly anxious and increasingly disfluent because of the frustration induced by their pragmatic failures.

Pauses and silences may express or be used to enact emotion. Normal silence is not a speech error—it is the contrastive material against which auditory images are cast (Bruneau, 1973; Bucci, 1982; Poyatos, 1980). However, when silence occurs in the talk of strangers and acquaintances, and there is no ongoing activity to account for it, silence is associated with discomfort and negative feelings (Newman, 1982). Some abnormally long silences more directly express or enact emotion. Given appropriate contextual cues, they may communicate high emotion or high emotional involvement with the subject of talk (Goldman-Eisler, 1972; Tindall & Robinson, 1947). If they are emotionally determined, their length and placement (frequently longest after the first word in an utterance) rather neatly serve turn-taking and turn-holding functions as well (Boomer, 1972).

Kinesics

People occupy a fundamentally kinesic communicative universe. Facial expression, length and direction of gaze, body position and muscular tension, body movement, and gestures are highly visible expressions and enactments of emotion.

Occasionally, the consequences of kinesic behavior are dramatic, as in Meerloo (1964, pp. 21-22):

> The Nazis officially recognized and tortured the silent nonconformists among their prisoners. The stubbornness they purported to read on their prisoners' silent faces was called "physiognomical insubordination." Prisoners in their strategy of non-cooperation were not allowed silent protest; they had to look stupidly meek and innocent, otherwise the aggressor feared the silent reproach of his victim.

Similarly, Jerry Rubin (1970) wrote of his arrest "for smiling" in the United States of the 1960s.

The cultural relativity of kinesics is a central theme in much of the research (for example, see Birdwhistell, 1970; Hall, 1959, 1966). However, some kinesic signs may have universal emotional meaning. Izard (1971) and Ekman, Friesen, and Ellsworth (1972) have conducted a number of cross-cultural tests of recognition of emotion on the human face. These theorists leave wide space for cultural differentiation in affect display.

Facial Expression. Intentionally and unintentionally, faces express and enact emotion. As Haggard and Isaacs (1966) have demonstrated, the facial muscles can be manipulated with great rapidity and subtlety, leaving observers with subliminal emotional impressions. Virtually all cultures devote considerable effort to masking emotional facial expression (Key, 1975, p. 83). Consistent with accommodation theories, Goffman (1963) contends that these efforts at masking are respected: People frequently are politely inattentive to the faces of others, as a sort of acknowledgment of the private feelings expressed there. The evocative power of facial expression is apparent in the studies of Izard (1971, 1975), who has shown that rhesus monkeys whose facial nerves have been severed fall from the top to the bottom of their group's status hierarchy.

One prominent line of facial expression research has been on gaze (e.g., Exline with Winters, 1965). Gaze is one of the variables that enters into "equilibrium theory" and may be increased or decreased with, for example, decreasing and increasing distancing in order to maintain a comfortable level of intimacy with another (Patterson, 1976). Among the findings on gaze are the following:

(1) Gaze decreases with disliking and increases with liking (Exline with Winters, 1965; Harper, Wiens, & Matarazzo, 1978; Mehrabian, 1968).

(2) Increasing eye contact heightens positive or negative affect expressed in the semantic component of a message (Ellsworth & Carlsmith, 1968).

(3) Ending eye contact signals rejection in a relationship (Breed & Porter, 1972).

(4) Constant gaze from near proximity (two feet) induces anxiety (Argyle & Dean, 1965).

(5) The absence of eye contact signals high anxiety (Jurich & Jurich, 1974).

(6) Gaze avoidance may signal appeasement to aggression (Ellsworth & Carlsmith, 1973; Lorenz, 1966).

(7) Gaze, including winks (Greenwald, 1958), expresses a variety of affective states (as in dramatic, absent, guarded, and knowing gaze), signals emotional ill-being (depressed look, excessive blinking, absent gaze), and may be coded (as in the prostitute's wink) (Key, 1975).

Beyond gaze, the research has indicated that at least seven emotions can be reliably and universally inferred from facial expression. Ekman et al. (1972), consonant with Izard (1971), say that these are happiness, surprise, fear, sadness, anger, disgust-contempt, and interest. Most subjects prefer to attribute to photographs "affect blends," because the expressions usually communicate shades of emotional meaning. Boucher and Ekman (1975) further specified which parts of the face express which emotions, using fragments of photographs. Fear and sadness are best predicted from the eyes and eyelids, happiness from the cheeks and mouth or eyes and cheeks and mouth, and surprise from the brow and forehead or eyes and eyelids or cheeks and mouth.

Nonfacial Kinesics. Much of the interest in bodily expression of emotion stems from research on deception and its detection. Ekman and Friesen (1969) show that, while the face may lie, the body is likely to betray the lie with nervous adaptors, though the voice may leak more and more reliable clues of intended deception than do either the face or the body (DePaulo, Zuckerman, & Rosenthal, 1980; Miller, 1983; Zuckerman, DePaulo, & Rosenthal, 1981).

Other isolated generalizations possible from the research are as follows: (1) proximity violations, with the anxiety (Kleck, 1970) or at least arousal (Burgoon & Aho, 1982) they produce, result in increasing self-manipulation such as hand-rubbing and scratching; (2) *overt* verbal hostility is accompanied by hand movements that point away from the body, but *covert* verbal hostility is accompanied by "body-focused" gestures such as rubbing hands together (Freedman, Blass, Rifkin, & Quitkin, 1973).

Possibly, kinesics should be enlarged beyond the usual catalog of posture, facial expression, gaze, head movement, and gesture. Key (1975) would attribute kinesic meaning to physiological modes of locomotion, of breathing, and of eating and drinking, as well as vomiting, urination and flatulence, all of which may express or enact emotion. Other acts such as coughing, throat clearing, sneezing, spitting, belching, sucking, hiccuping, swallowing, choking, yawning, sighing, scratching, and stretching also leak or may be feigned to enact signs of arousal and anxiety.

Lexical Variables

Skilled encoding of emotional expression for most people rises as arousal reaches moderate levels. It then is likely to decline into stereotyped expressions (maledicta for negative emotions) at high levels and to flood the organism into silence or inarticulateness at extremely high levels. As Wordsworth said, emotion must be recollected in tranquility if impressive diction is to be the result. T. S. Eliot's "objective correlative" also requires for eloquent expression cognitive behavior of a kind not facilitated by high arousal.

The importance of language to emotion is dramatically apparent in the study of alexithymia, emotional repression or absence in people who lack a vocabulary of emotional terms or have an inability to describe their own states of arousal (Krystal, 1979; Sifneos, 1974, 1975). People with this difficulty are probably doomed to failure in psychotherapy (Peake & Egli, 1982). We suspect that the absence of a vocabulary of affect would doom long-term intimate relationships as well. Peake and Egli (1982) and Bucci (1982) recommend giving patients an affective vocabulary in order to relieve their suffering. People need names (though not necessarily labels) for their pains and pleasures, and skill in naming constitutes an interpersonal communication asset. Furthermore, competence with such an affective vocabulary may be a resource of interpersonal power, an idea that we think is implicit in the work of Massey (1981, p. 16) and Kurt Lewin (e.g., 1951).

Language Intensity. Language intensity is "the quality of language which indicates the degree to which the speaker's attitude toward a concept deviates from neutrality" (Bowers, 1963, 1964). Bradac, Bowers, and Courtright (1979, 1980) generalize that increasing stressful arousal results in decreasing language intensity, though the relationship might be an inverted U (compare Daly & Miller, 1975; Franzwa, 1969; Osgood & Walker, 1959).

Immediacy. Verbal immediacy, which may not be wholly independent of intensity, is the degree to which a speaker approaches or avoids a topic (Wiener & Mehrabian, 1967). Generally, liking and the emotions that accompany it produce high verbal immediacy (Anthony, 1974; Feinberg, 1971; Mehrabian & Wiener, 1966), and stress produces low verbal immediacy (Conville, 1975; Greenberg & Tannenbaum, 1962; Hart, 1976). Receivers perceive the relationship between positive-negative affect and immediacy (Wiener & Mehrabian, 1967). Bradac et al. (1980) theorize that verbal immediacy interacts with intensity to make both intensity and immediacy decline as the stress of uncertainty increases.

Lexical Diversity. Lexical diversity is defined as the range of manifest vocabulary, the number of different and sometimes uncommon words a speaker employs. Bradac and his co-researchers (Bradac, Courtright, Schmidt, & Davies, 1976; Bradac, Davies, & Courtright, 1977; Bradac, Davies, & Konsky, 1976; Bradac, Desmond, & Murdock, 1977; Bradac, Konsky, & Davies, 1976; Bradac, Konsky, & Elliott, 1976) have found generally that stressful arousal results in a decrease in lexical diversity, and that receivers perceive lexical diversity as inversely related to anxiety in a speaker.

Synthesis of Intensity, Immediacy, and Diversity. The addition of Berger and Calabrese's (1975) axioms on uncertainty, intimacy, and reciprocity to the Bradac, Bowers, and Courtright formulations on intensity, immediacy, and diversity produce some powerful theorems on the role of emotional arousal in interpersonal communication. Intimacy emerges as a comforting and reassuring phenomenon with positive emotional associations. These positive associations *allow* intense and immediate expressions of support but encourage more ambiguous expressions of discord. Reciprocity pressures, on the other hand, become the *demands* interpersonal relationships place on people to express discrepancies with intensity and immediacy and to be more cautious and neutral in expressions of support. In other words, as Knapp, Ellis, and Williams (1980) and Bochner (1984) apparently confirm, interpersonal communication balances opportunities for strong and highly personal emotional expression and more discreet relational messages.

Metaphor and Imagery. Frequently, metaphors are thought of as emotive, but they are not *merely* emotive. Clearly, they serve cognitive functions (Beardsley, 1958; Eastman, 1931; Rieser, 1940, 1950). Fresh metaphors in the minds of many theorists do have at least a minimal emotive aspect. Osborn and Ehninger (1962) viewed metaphors as both produced and interpreted in an arousal-satisfaction style of error labeled "puzzlement-recoil" and "resolution" (compare Burke, 1954; Campbell, 1975; Langer, 1953; Percy, 1975). Metaphors are ambiguous (Crusius & Winterowd, 1981); they are verbally economical ways of saying even more than one might have thought. The consensus view represents a marked convergence on the position that metaphors are both emotion arousing and cognitively expanding (Kittay & Lehrer, 1981).

In interpersonal communication as in psychotherapy, "metaphor may be used to avoid the literal, escape from narrow or oppressive categories, avoid taboo or unacceptable language, provide release (catharsis), and give indirect ways of saying things" (Shibles, 1974, pp. 254-255). Though metaphors may be cathartic they are as likely to be substitutive, euphemistic, or distance creating (Caruth & Ekstein, 1965).

If metaphors may be used productively in psychological counseling (Shibles, 1974, p. 257), they may also be used productively in everyday discourse to reveal and clarify nuances of emotion (compare Gordon, 1978). Pollio and Barlow (1975) reported that in a psychotherapeutic session they detected 3 to 6 figures of speech per 100 words. At times, the figures came in "extended bursts," which could be associated with such crucial therapeutic phases as problem setting and problem solving.

For students of interpersonal communication, the most easily applicable studies of metaphor may be those that focus on specific vehicles. Among the findings of such studies are the following: (1) Metaphors of "sex" and "death" are very intense, death metaphors producing anxiety and sex metaphors relieving it for most people (Bowers, 1964; Bowers & Osborn, 1966). (2) "Darkness" and "light" and their familial terms are highly contrastive and therefore exceedingly useful in value discourse (Osborn, 1967). (3) Baseball metaphors are ubiquitous, popular, ambiguous, "pious," and "ugly" (Hariman, 1982); they may be uniquely useful in describing deviant (in left field) behavior. (4) "Life" in the "right to life" movement has come to represent to most people concepts of social stability/inflexibility. (5) "Cancer" and "tuberculosis" have become potent political metaphors, perversely idealizing the material realities of morbidity and mortality (Sontag, 1978). More generally, (6) some metaphors become myths, making the merely cultural and historical seem natural and necessary (Barthes, 1957/1972, pp. 109-159). Shibles (1974) gives an account of the mental health of individuals when metaphors become solidified into unquestioned myths.

Maledicta. One self-evident emotional enactment in language is the use of profanity. Cross (1979) and Aman (1977) have remarked on the cathartic and emotive nature of so-called maledicta. The strength of taboos against maledicta has inhibited the study of these terms, which often constitute acts of verbal aggression (Jay, 1978). The strength of taboos is illustrated by Steadman's (1935) finding. When he asked college students to list coarse and obscene words, the most frequent citations were of "belly," "stink," and "guts." In the current self-consciously liberated era, maledicta such as "shit" and "fuck" (Cross, 1979; Kanin, 1979) are very common as expressions of displeasure and aggression, but they are used comparatively seldom in their literal meanings.

Generally, profanity follows powerlessness (Becker, 1971). Trite profanity is stereotyped expression, and may be an impotent, easily coded response to high emotion. The famous deleted expletives from Nixon's White House tapes serve to show, to some degree, the frustrations and impotence of people with apparently vast power. Relative deprivation (Gurr, 1970) and verbal aggression deserve more careful consideration by interpersonal communication scholars than they have received. Aggression pervades many typical interpersonal exchanges (Bowers, 1982; Doyle, 1977), and verbal combat and insult are major themes in dominant and subcultural patterns of interpersonal communication (Farb, 1974; Jemie, 1976). Attention to maledicta surely would be rewarded in the sense that it would show what ordinary language can and cannot accomplish emotionally for people.

Pragmatic Variables

Self-Disclosure. The term "self-disclosure" is poorly defined, as Bochner (1984) points out, and the literature on the subject is enormous and largely incapable of internal comparison. Intimate self-disclosure, presumably, requires that the information revealed by an individual would be perceived as harmful to that individual if made known to people other than the partner, so such self-disclosure is risky, and the intimate self-discloser incurs vulnerability.

Some research implies that self-disclosure is cathartic and results in both good mental health (Egan, 1970; Jourard, 1971) and a lowered incidence of stress disease symptoms (Berglund, Ander, Lindstrom, & Tibblin, 1975; Cumes, 1983; Handkins & Munz, 1978; Weiner, Singer, & Reiser, 1962). But most researchers consider self-disclosure to be a normative and even strategic behavior, primarily. Gouldner (1960), Bradac, Hosman, and Tardy (1978), Chaikin and Derlega (1974), and Berger, Gardner, Clatterbuck, and Schulman (1976) all suggest that self-disclosure is governed by norms and based on notions of reciprocity and developmental propriety. Accommodation theory (Giles, Taylor, & Bourhis, 1973; Street, 1982) suggests that self-disclosure, or, perhaps, adherence to the reciprocity norm, might purposely be avoided by a communicator in order to establish social distance, usually social superiority.

Apparent self-disclosure may enact attraction but be strategically false, of course. We can imagine a situation in which an individual is positively affected by a new partner. To test whether the positive affect should become positive emotion (that is, how to form an attribution), the individual discloses false information to the partner that, if true, would be intimate, seeking a response from the partner to test the partner's compatibility. During all this, the individual knows that the partner's use of this information would *not* be damaging, for all those who know the individual also know that the information "disclosed" is false information. This is the kind of complication in belief states of individual and partner for which an analysis such as that of Bradac and Friedman (1983) might be useful.

As Bochner (1984) makes clear, the amount of self-disclosure that occurs in liking relationships probably is exaggerated in self-report data because a norm dictates high disclosure in such relationships. Indeed, Cozby (1973) gives evidence that self-disclosure and liking have a curvilinear relationship, with self-disclosure beyond moderate levels working to the detriment of interpersonal relationships. Even Rosenfeld (1979), generally an advocate of self-disclosure, acknowledges that nondisclosure is as amply motivated in human behavior as is disclosure. Couples repress and distort information about inequalities in self-disclosure in their marriages (Davidson, Balswick, & Halverson, 1983), and to avoid stress couples should seek equity in self-disclosure rather than high self-disclosure. None of these caveats about the benefits of self-disclosure, of course, denies that some minimal level of disclosure is required for an emotionally healthy interpersonal relationship. In fact, those relationships that are not occasionally characterized by the kind of disclosure produced by interpersonal conflict may be unstable ones (Coser, 1956).

Like many other communication variables, self-disclosure can be blocked by environmental stress (Sundstrom, 1975), in the form of persistent interruption and discomfort. Here we again encounter the now familiar inverted U relating emotion to an interpersonal communication variable. When self-disclosure does occur, it may either relieve or produce emotional stress. Some disclosure is better emotionally than none, but more is not necessarily better than less.

Transparency/Opacity. The literature of speech acts (e.g., Searle, 1975) indicates that messages may vary on a continuum of directness/indirectness. We will attend only to the part of that variable circumscribed by the terms "transparency" and "opacity." "Direct/indirect" connotes that the variable rests in the message; "transparent/opaque" connotes that it rests in the interaction, including the message. We borrow "transparent" from Clark (1979). We had encountered the continuum "transparent/opaque" earlier, however, in an unpublished paper by Norman D. Elliott.

Transparency is the degree to which the syntactic and semantic choices of a speaker render the speaker's intentions about the hearer's interpretation of the message apparent to the hearer—in a sense, the degree to which the speaker intends that the hearer take the message literally. Transparency does not necessarily imply honesty. "I love you," uttered with passsionate paralanguage, is a transparent message, though speaker may not love partner.

Why should a speaker encode a message that is relatively opaque? Lakoff (1972), Clark (1979), and other theorists think that politeness provides the answer: A hearer may misunderstand (or pretend to misunderstand) a speaker's intention in uttering an opaque message. Therefore, the speaker has supplied (or at least has given the impression of having provided) options to the hearer. The hearer is not *constrained* by the message to conform to the speaker's intention about its interpretation.

Politeness doubtless constitutes a partial explanation for relatively opaque messages. However, we think that the speaker's emotional state may also be involved. In the first place, *very* high emotion (of whatever type) may make verbal communication impossible for an individual—may render the individual speechless. If the partner has no contextual cues, the individual's silence is ultimately opaque. To the partner, the individual's silence, especially if that silence is accompanied by signs of autonomic arousal, means something. But what? At slightly lower (but nevertheless high) levels of emotion, the individual's messages are likely to be stereotyped and therefore transparent (e.g Bradac et al., 1980; Osgood & Walker, 1959). Thus transparency/opacity sometimes may be expressive rather than instrumental, may leak emotion rather than enact it.

But the variable may also be employed instrumentally for purposes other than politeness. An individual may encode transparently in order to facilitate partner's messages (or other acts) that might result in positive emotion for the individual. Or the individual may encode opaquely to inhibit partner's messages (or other acts) that might result in negative emotion for the individual. Following Bowers, Elliott, and Desmond's (1977; see also Bowers's [1974] and Murdock, Bradac, & Bowers's [1984]) analysis of the tendency to probe potentially devious messages, we speculate that a speaker is likely to encode opaquely when the speaker is relatively certain that the partner's response to a transparent message would elicit intense relative deprivation in the speaker. Conversely, a speaker is most likely to employ transparent messages when (1) the speaker is relatively uncertain about what the partner's response will be, but (2) at least one potential response would result in intense relative gratification, and none would result in relative deprivation.

Two aspects of the relationship between the partners may influence the speaker's perception that the partner's response will elicit positive or negative emotion. These are (1) the power of the partner, both absolutely and relative to the speaker's power, and (2) the compatibility of speaker and partner. By "power," we mean the ability and willingness of partner to impede or facilitate speaker in the attainment of speaker's goals—to produce relative deprivation or relative gratification for speaker. By "compatibility," we mean the extent to which speaker's and partner's goals are identical or facilitatively interdependent. A speaker's messages are most likely to be transparent in a relationship where partner has power, but less power than speaker (for in that circumstance speaker need not be especially concerned with politeness); and where speaker and partner are highly compatible. A speaker's messages are most likely to be opaque in a relationship where partner is much more powerful than speaker; and speaker and partner are incompatible (for in that circumstance partner's responses to speaker's messages are likely to elicit relative deprivation in a speaker). Although our position is largely speculative, Murdock et al. (1984) have experimentally tested a few related propositions.

Over time, in a continuing interpersonal relationship, opacity probably becomes more difficult as the partners learn to "see through" each other's indirect messages. This increasing transparency reduces the possibilities for emotional surprises, for dislocations of value capabilities and value expectations relative to each other, as each partner's value expectations for the messages of the other increasingly match value capabilities. Hence, although the partners may strongly rely on each other to achieve certain of their value capabilities, the emotional magic leaves the relationship (Berscheid, 1983). Communication becomes increasingly efficient (Berger & Bradac, 1982; Brown & Levinson, 1978) but decreasingly novel, surprising, and emotionally arousing. As efficiency assumes its supremacy, even indirection in the service of politeness may atrophy, and one partner may use politely indirect locutions only to signal displeasure with the other. To the extent that either partner values emotional arousal more than efficiency, that partner is likely to seek a new relationship, and disengagement from the original relationship may occur. To the extent that the original relationship remained an interactive one for the achievement of value capabilities, the disengagement is likely to be accompanied by mixed emotions for the disengaging partner (as value capabilities rise in some value classes but decline in others) and by the emotion of jealousy for the disengaged one (Berscheid, 1983). This entire line of reasoning may explain why, in a study of Hornstein's reported by Davitz (1964), college roommates extremely sensitive to each other's emotional messages (extremely transparent to each other) were likely to request relocation (disengagement). Other evidence that supports our reasoning comes from Gottman's (1982) finding that stereotypical interaction is inversely related to satisfaction among married couples.

Summary

This review indicates that the ideal interpreter has available an extensive array of clues to emotional expression and enactment in the physiology, paralanguage, kinesics, lexical choices, and pragmatic decisions of a communicator. In general, these phenomena give the interpreter access only to the intensity of arousal, not to its hedonic tone or to attributions of cause, though some lexical and pragmatic choices may be very specifically informative about hedonic tone and attribution (for example, "I feel angry at you."). Communicators often try to mask emotion, and normal interaction accommodation theory predicts that their reticence will be respected. Nevertheless, the ideal interpreter, given rather full information about the communicator, may make many informed inferences. For the more cognitively dependent processes (lexical encoding and pragmatic choices, for example), the relationship between arousal and a variable often takes the shape of an inverted U, so that the variable increases with moderate arousal but declines into stereotyped expression or even speechlessness at strong and extreme levels. Thus the eloquent lover may, as Eliza Doolittle perceived, leave something to be desired in the passion department; but the speechless or inarticulate hater may pose a greater physical danger than does the skillfully vituperative one.

EMOTION IN INTERPERSONAL RELATIONSHIPS

The array of verbal and nonverbal behaviors available to interactants to express emotional states is extensive. The analogic code system, in fact, appears to function primarily as an affect-signaling mechanism, communicating at the very least that arousal is present. The nature and direction of this arousal, if not inferrable from context, can be identified more or less exactly by culturally and relationally shared verbal labels (for example, "You look upset." "Yeah. I'm still mad at John.").

As noted earlier, however, the relationship between emotional display and private feeling is not necessarily direct. Moderately intense feelings can be intensified for public display and excessive feeling can be controlled. An emotion different from that being experienced can be enacted, as can the total absence of emotion. The fact that most people are able to present contextually adapted emotional enactments, if they wish to, and that most people do so, with varying degrees of conscious choice, underscores the essentially social quality of emotion. Arousal may indeed be privately and uniquely experienced, but the antecedents and consequences are primarily social. Emotions are social phenomena both because they are engendered by the actions of other people (immediate, remote, actual, assumed, or anticipated) and because their presence (whether overtly displayed or not) influences one's own and other's behavior, affecting the tenuous balance in social, relational, and conversational equilibria.

This section will explore the role of emotion in social relationships. Specifically, it will examine the role of emotion in motivating and shaping the initial formation of interpersonal relationships, in facilitating and complicating relationship maintenance, in distorting and intensifying relational conflict, and in dissolving relational bonds. We defined interpersonal emotion earlier as arousal triggered by a discrepancy between one's value expectations and one's value capabilities—in essence, the disjuncture between what we expect or feel we deserve and what we get. The source of the discrepancy may be attributed to the self, to other, to the relationship, to an extrarelational situation, or to some combination of these. This definition provides a framework for the discussion that follows.

Although the increased intimacy and mutual interdependence in close relationships foster a greater depth and breadth of emotional range, the initial stages of relationships are also marked by certain emotional patterns. Research indicates that moderate levels of arousal, negatively toned and attributable to one's general state of affairs, are a strong factor in motivating people to initiate new relationships. As Reik (1957, p. 32) observes, "Everything is all right with the person who is in love, but all is not well with the person who is about to fall in love." One particular type of negative affect, commonly known as loneliness, has received some attention in the literature. Findings are not consistent, due largely to differing conceptualizations and measurement instruments, but it appears that loneliness produces a particular kind of discomfort that is minimized through the initiation of interpersonal relationships. Perlman and Peplau (1981, p. 32) describe loneliness as a "discrepancy between one's desired and achieved levels of social relations." To the extent that the level of arousal is not so intense as to drain one's energy or desire, or so extended as to become self-attributed and pathologically debilitating, a person who is lonely should be motivated to seek new or additional relationships. Interestingly, though popular media would suggest that lonely people feel most acutely the absence of romantic relationships, research indicates othewise. Schmidt and Sermat (1983) found that unsatisfying or infrequent friendships were more highly associated with loneliness than were unsatisfying or infrequent romantic-sexual relationships. The authors conclude that people seem to perceive their friendships to be the better measure of their ability to relate to others and achieve mutually satisfying rewards than the less durable, more unstable romantic relationships.

Other lines of research suggest that when arousal results from a discrepancy between what one expects to happen and what is happening and the outcome is better than expected, the affective tone is a positive one and the perceived source of the relative gratification is likewise perceived favorably. Thus initial attraction is, in part, the result of arousal being attributed to the qualities of the interactional partner. A consistent pattern emerges from longitudinal studies and common experience that reflects intense (though usually brief) relationships developing during stressful or exciting periods, such as a teenager's summer away from home or a soldier's leave from combat. Longer-lasting relationships also follow the same pattern: Marriages tend to coincide with high school or college graduation, when the future is ambiguous. In an unusual test of the arousal to attraction hypothesis,

Dutton and Aron (1974) had an attractive female confederate approach men in the middle of a narrow, swaying, suspension bridge. She asked the subjects to answer a series of questions and to complete a story. Before leaving, the confederate informed each subject that if he wished to learn more about the research project, he was to feel free to call her. Of the men interviewed, 50 percent called the confederate. In a comparison episode conducted on a solid, less-threatening bridge, only 13 percent made the call.

In addition to individually experienced and attributed arousal, perceptions of emotional responsivity and compatibility in a potential relational partner play a role in the initiation stage (Izard, 1977). Reward theory would predict that we like those who appear to like us. Our model would predict that we like those who appear to be the source of our relative gratification. Initial arousal is high because the discrepancy is relatively large: Resources being gained exceed those expected. This initial state of excitation is difficult to maintain, however; as resources being acquired lose their salience and/or expectations increase, discrepancy and, presumably, arousal decrease. Intensity diminishes and attributions may shift. Eidelson (1980) found that relational satisfaction for college couples rose quickly over the first few months, reached a plateau, and then rose again or declined. During the plateau period, couples apparently compare the rewards of interdependence (intimacy, companionship) with the costs (loss of autonomy, freedom of movement). Similar cycles may occur in fully developed relationships as well, though the evaluation process is complicated by the mutuality of the resources (for example, children) and the movement over time toward the stabilization of expectations and capabilities.

The increase in complexity when a dyad moves from the initiation stage to the maintenance stage (assuming that development has been toward increased intimacy) is both reflected in and reflective of an increased range and intensity of emotion. As a couple builds its unique relational history, it builds its unique emotional topography. Each topography has at least two characteristics. First, it is a cumulative product. Newman (1981b) observes that attributions made about the behaviors of a partner may be verbalized and tested for validity or may go unverbalized and untested. Either way, the attributions and their "emotional components" tend to get stored up over the course of an ongoing relationship. Second, the topography is multidimensional and nonderivative. Disparate, even semantically contradictory emotions, may interlock temporarily and over time, both within the individual and within the interactional sequences of the dyad. Partners do not simply move from loving to hating over the course of an argument or the course of a relationship. Rather, they experience love and hate, desire and disgust, simultaneously or in rapid alternation. Ironically, both extremely positive emotions and extremely negative emotions increase married couples' perceptions of their passion (Hatfield, 1982). Given the complexity of emotional experience in ongoing relationships, it is no surprise that attempts to communicate feelings and to communicate about them become problematic for partners and analysts alike.

Paradoxically, emotional communication is both easier and more difficult for intimates than for nonintimates. As partners become more familiar, their emotional expression becomes less stylized, more unique, and more efficient (Knapp, 1983). Emotional enactments are adapted to and shaped by the increased knowledge of the other—an adaptation that facilitates emotional understanding. On the other hand, increased intimacy can inhibit emotional understanding in several ways: (1) Understanding may be "assumed" or inferred too quickly based on past experience (Knapp, 1983); (2) understanding may be biased toward assumed similarity or difference because of emotional involvement (Sillars & Scott, 1983); (3) understanding may be achieved accurately at the level of behavior (for example, in decoding partner's smile) but be inaccurate at the level of attribution (interpreting partner's smile as faked or sarcastic) if the general affect in the relationship is negative (Knapp, 1982, 1983).

Whether any particular emotional state is accurately perceived or not, the willingness of relational partners to reciprocate in kind the emotional expression of the other is a critical factor in the maintenance of an ongoing relationship. When one partner desires more (or less) expressivity in the partner than he or she is getting, relative deprivation occurs and the arousal is negatively toned. In a sense, the emotion is a generalized affect about the communication of more specific emotional states. Its duration (for example, an isolated exchange versus habitual pattern) and its attributed cause contribute to the intensity felt. The literature suggests that although psychological gender may predispose some individuals to be emotionally responsive and expressive (e.g., Narus & Fischer, 1982), a far more important variable appears to be the biological sex of the partners. Both self-report and observational data indicate that same-sex friendships exhibit a marked congruence in interactive norms: Men share the expectation that friendships will focus on activities and doing things together; women expect that friendships will focus on the sharing of emotions and talking (Caldwell & Peplau, 1982). Male friends tend to restrict their conversations to topical levels of content; female friends include all levels of content in their talk—topical, relational, and personal (Davidson & Duberman, 1982). Men generally agree that, rather than confront strain in a friendship, they would simply work around it or terminate the relationship; women generally agree that they would confront the issue even if they eventually terminated the relationship (Wright, 1982).

Intimate heterosexual dyads, on the other hand, seem to exhibit less congruence in matters of appropriate or expected relational behaviors, most notably equity in emotional expressivity. Although most authors agree that equity of expressivity facilitates the highest levels of marital adjustment (Davidson et al., 1983), the married couples who have been studied indicate that equity is difficult to achieve. Fitzpatrick and Indvik (1982) found that across marriage types (traditional, independent, and separate) both instrumental and expressive communication are essential in maintaining the functioning of the relationship (see Parsons & Bales, 1955) and that when one marital partner is deficient in one type of expression (preponderantly husbands deficient in expressivity), the other, usually the wife, must compensate for the shortcoming. Fitzpatrick and Indvik (1982, p. 210) conclude, "When wives cannot or refuse to be expressive, the relationship suffers. Wives may be said to bear the burden of expressivity in their marital relationships." In a study of the sequencing of married couples' responses during discussions of important relational issues, Notarius and Johnson (1982) found that wives reciprocated their husbands' positive and negative speaking turns through verbal and nonverbal affect displays, and husbands tended to respond to their wives' positive and negative turns with neutral turns. Yet on polygraph measures of skin potential responses taken over the course of the interaction, husbands showed increased physiological reactivity after wives' negative turns even though they displayed neutral behaviors. By contrast, wives' physiological arousal was apparently "discharged" through overt expressions of negative affect. Notarius and Johnson (1982, p. 488) extrapolate from these findings and other research a "positive feedback loop" for marital interactions something like the following:

> In stage 1 wives perceive more emotional response from their husbands due to their advantage in decoding nonverbal communication. Following a principle of reciprocity, wives then tend to respond in kind to their husbands' emotional messages. In stage 2 husbands are confronted with emotional expression in their wives which they may not understand or decode correctly. They may not reciprocate these emotional messages because they are unaware of their own feelings or, alternatively, because they are focused on the containment of their emotional responses as signaled by somatic reactivity to the interactional exchange. In stage 3 wives may escalate their emotional response to solicit an emotional response from their partners. With increased emotional display from their partners, the husbands may have greater difficulty responding; and the system enters stage 4, in which husband tries to control partner's emotional reaction and the wife continues emotional expression.

Obviously, this cycle has the potential to escalate to an explosive final stage where one or the other partner, in total frustration, loses control or withdraws from the interaction (or, perhaps, from the relationship). In light of this potential, Gottman (1982) argues that the ability to deescalate negative affect is a more important factor than reciprocal positive affect in distinguishing satisfied from dissatisfied married couples.

   In sum, the study of partner's expectations and relational behaviors suggests that the process of maintaining a relationship is interlocked with the process of negotiating individual and dyadic norms of emotional expression. There is no inherently proper amount of emotional expression or even balance with instrumental expression except as the marital partners have value expectations for the ratio, style, sequencing, and so on of expressive behaviors in their day-to-day interactions. When both members' expectations are met, a relatively neutral global affect characterizes the relationship. When one or both members' expectations are not met or are exceeded, a relatively negative or relatively positive global affect prevails.

These generalized affect orientations toward partner and relationship emerge from, and in turn influence recurrent patterns of specific interaction episodes. To date, research has focused principally on the role of emotion in conflict episodes. From an attribution perspective, emotion is viewed as a variable affecting the perception and interpretation of messages. Sillars and Scott (1983, p. 163), for example, note that because emotion-indicating behavior tends to be salient and visible, especially when displayed by one's partner, "perceptual biases are likely to be strong in emotionally expressive conflicts." They also suggest that high levels of emotionality may "affect cognitive abilities that are instrumental to interpersonal perception" (p. 164), though some scholars would argue that affect is fundamental to person perception and cognition a secondary process (e.g., Zajonc, 1980). Harvey, Weber, Yarkin, and Stewart (1982) propose that it is the anticipated pain associated with conflict that motivates partners to make their attributions such that conflict will be unnecessary. To the extent that conflict threatens a relationship, it can be construed as a threat to self. According to Harvey et al., partners avoid this anxiety by misattributing the cause of partner's behavior. For instance, declining affectionate behavior may be misattributed to a situation (pressures at work) or a disposition (he's not demonstrative), or to the relationship (he doesn't demonstrate his affection for me).

Extended conflict can lead to the dissolution of an intimate relationship although, in principle, relationships can always be repaired and conflict can strengthen understanding and enhance the overall affective state of the relationship. It is possible also that relationships with little or no overtly manifested conflict dissolve (Coser, 1956). As Knapp (1983) observes, messages of "distance and disassociation" are a natural part of relational communication. The trick is for partners to figure out when these messages are frequent enough or intense enough to signal serious relational problems, problems that may eventually lead to disengagement.

The pattern of emotional expressiveness during the disengaging process should be one that moves toward a more restricted, stylized, and normative performance of expressive behaviors (Knapp, 1983). The idiosyncratic gestures (for example, see Hopper, Knapp, & Scott, 1981, on couples' personal idioms) that express affection and "we-ness" are more likely to drop from the couple's expressive vocabulary. On the other hand, the realization that disengagement is imminent may open channels of emotional expressivity not possible when both partners were avoiding inflicting permanent damage on the other partner or the relationship (Duck, 1982).

Our understanding of communication patterns in dissolving relationships is at present limited largely to analyses of disengagement strategies reported by college students. The strategy selection approach necessarily simplifies a complicated process: Consider for example the complicating factors found in most marriages such as social networks, financial entanglements, and children. Selecting a single disengagment strategy and a permanent one is virtually impossible. Nevertheless, strategy research does suggest a promising direction for the study of emotion in relational disengagement processes. A study by Cody (1982) is particularly informative and compatible with the model of emotion presented in this chapter. Cody explored the role that two emotions, anger and guilt, play in the selection of disengagement strategies. Using an equity model and echoing Kemper's (1978) sociorelational account of emotional arousal, Cody found that overbenefited individuals were likely to feel guilty and underbenefited individuals were likely to feel angry. Further- more, anger over the allocation of resources was associated with the selection of certain disengagement strategies, particularly negative identity management, justification, and behavioral deescalation.

In order to extend the strategy selection research program to marital or cohabiting long-term relationships, attention would need to be given to strategies involving separations of physical space and material goods, and to extrinsic variables like the religious dogma of self or partner, the age and involvement of the children, and so forth. The notions of intimacy, equity, and strategy would require reformulation or enlargement. Second, attention should be directed to the probability of curvilinear relationships. For example, the choice of positive tone may indeeed increase as a couple moves from casual to intimate, but after a certain point ("familiarity breeds contempt"), intimacy may associate with negative tone. Third, attention would have to be given to the sequential and temporal quality of most marital disengagements. Seldom does one or the other member of a relationship accomplish disengagement in one encounter. More typically, the disengage- ment is a process, convoluted and meandering. The dissolving relationship generates a topography just as the developing relationship does (Duck, 1982), and the preeminence of certain emotions at certain points in the process will dictate certain types of strategies. The frequency and order of intentional and unintentional disassociation messages already sent (what has already been said with what effect?) will influence strategy selection. Moreover, it may be the cumulative effect of the several strategies of both partners used over the course of disengagement that ultimately accomplishes the breakup. Finally, though it is difficult to quantify, the nature of the self-talk that separated intimates use to convince themselves that they are disengaging, are justified in their feelings and actions, and are able to rebuild is a genre of emotion-linked behavior that is in critical need of study. As Duck (1980) notes about relationships in general, people spend a good deal of time outside of their interactions thinking about self and other, replaying events, fantasizing, planning, rehearsing, and so on. This kind of communication with self undoubtedly affects disengaging encounters and the emotions they engender.

The psychological separation (extraction) of a partner from the relationship, relational role, and the relational other is a complex process that begins before the issuance of a formal termination and continues for an indefinite period thereafter. Weiss (1976) characterizes the separation process as a particular type of emotional ambivalence: attachment and anger. He argues that attachment is the one element of the syndrome of love that remains intact after other elements (liking, trust, idealization) have faded. The disruption of attachment is a major source of emotional upset during marital separation, a feeling not unlike that experienced by a child separated from a parent. Simultaneously, however, a partner feels intense anger directed toward the person who has disrupted the feelings of attachment, caused distress, taken the children, and so on. Expressed in other terms, the discrepancy between value capabilities and value expectations that had been relatively stable is now acute; on those days when cause is attributed to partner the feelings are angry, when cause is attributed to self the feelings are regretful, and when cause is attributed to situation the feelings are those of frustration or sorrow. The labels are not important, and the feelings may even be positively toned if the relationship was intolerable. However, the divorced and separated subjects interviewed by Weiss and associates reported that at some point during the separating process they encountered emotional ambivalence. With classic approach-avoidance behaviors, separated partners managed their ambivalence by (1) suppressing either the positive or negative feelings (for example, remaining "friends" or not speaking at all); (2) alternately expressing positive or negative feelings to and about the partner; (3) compartmentalizing their discrepant feelings (Weiss, 1976, p. 143). Whatever pattern marks a particular dissolving relationship, the emotional and communicative patterns are qualitatively different from those at any other stage of the relationship.

CONCLUSION

Twentieth-century thinking about emotion has been exceedingly tangled. In *Language, Truth and Logic*, A. J. Ayer (1952) declares that all metaphysical, aesthetic, and ethical discourse is "emotive." Supported in both the popular and scholarly mind by increasingly influential Freudian notions of psychic energy (Freud, 1940/1949) and instinctive drives (Freud, 1909/1962), which became virtually synonymous with emotion in Freud's expositors (as in Hughes, 1981), Ayer and others dramatically expanded the realm of emotion by curtailing the province of reason. In place of "emotion," which is accompanied by almost unmanageable connotative baggage from centuries of ordinary usage, certain psychologists (for example, Duffy, 1941, 1962; Woodworth & Schlosberg, 1954) sought to establish the unidimensional and psychobiologically quantifiable term "activation" as the only suitable construct for affective processes. What Duffy's activation theory had in common with Ayer's and Freud's thought was ambivalence toward human emotionality. By making emotion both larger *and* smaller and simpler and less ambiguous and, ultimately, irreducibly physical and measurable as arousal and/or genetic thrust, some recent thinkers have signaled their exasperation with emotion and reflected the perennial desire to control these unpredictable, unmanageable, and vulnerable psychic forces.

Needless to say, a number of scholars have tried in recent years to reclaim as a legitimate scholarly concern the commonsensical, multidimensional ground of emotion from Duffy's psychobiological reduction of emotion to activation. In 1971, in *The Face of Emotion*, Carroll E. Izard noted that affect research had been excommunicated from the "cathedral of science" but now occupies a position of increasing importance and respectability (pp. 1-12). Such scholars, who respect the "ordinary language" of emotion, have not so much refuted as they have simply ignored the activation hypothesis. This end run has been successful enough that today the ordinary-language study of emotion is becoming increasingly prominent (e.g., Malatesta & Izard, 1984; also, this volume in general).

With other critics of extant research, we think it important that emotion be restored to prominence in contemporary social science. We also think it important that emotion be considered in a long-term view of relationships. A minimally sufficient account would involve communicative behavior by emotion by situation/role by individual and relational development. We have encountered no studies of this complexity.

Early stages of gratifying relationships doubtless are characterized by high emotion, and the physiological, paralinguistic, and kinesic correlates of that arousal may be discernible. At these early stages, communicators may test their tentative causal attributions by using relatively opaque messages or transparently self-disclosing ones, then carefully monitoring their partner's reactions. In middle stages of a relationship, emotion is likely to diminish, though interdependence in achieving value capabilities may be high, as the partners reduce their uncertainty and therefore their potential for the unexpected vis-à-vis each other. At middle stages also, the partners may encounter relative deprivation as they discover that some goals earlier thought to be compatible are in fact incompatible and as their earlier idealizations encounter reality. Not only may large areas of behavior (Berscheid, 1983, p. 144) then become independent, but also large topics of conversation (Bowers, 1983) then become taboo. (Martin [1982, p. 673] may well have been serious when she wrote, "Miss Manners believes that the secret of an unhappy marriage is communication.") If emotional arousal is highly valued by one of the partners, he or she may seek or be receptive to a new relationship, and the emotions accompanying disengagement may be experienced in the original one.

In sociology, close relationships are an important area of contemporary study. But sociologists tend not to be very analytic about communication. Some sociologists are becoming more attuned to communication, and some communication scholars are bringing their disciplinary expertise to the study of communication in close relationships, as is evidenced by this volume. We see this interdisciplinary transaction as now being in a positive feedback loop.

Those who would systematically analyze emotion and relationships should consider the advice of Duck (1980, p. 118), who sees contemporary views of intimacy as too limited to explain relational change fully:

> One simpleminded assumption in much psychological theorising is that people know not only what they want, what they feel and what they think, but also what they are doing in interactions. This is naive for many obvious reasons, one being that unintended effects are often produced in social interaction; another that people's views of their emotions, plans and intentions often change with retrospection about interaction (hence the experience of regret, remorse, guilt, triumph, surprise, etc.); and a third being that there is not only often ambivalence in many social settings but also a contemporaneous experience of conflicting emotions. All of these are significant when one begins to try to chart emotions, intimacy growth and "the" trajectory of a relationship.

As Duck's commentary implies, the task of isolating variables relevant to emotion and explaining how they function in relational contexts is a significant challenge for students of human behavior. But accepting the challenge may be remarkably rewarding.

REFERENCES

Altman, I. A., & Taylor, D. A. (1973). *Social penetration: The development of interpersonal relations.* New York: Holt, Rinehart & Winston.

Alvarez, W. C. (1929). Ways in which emotion can affect the digestive tract. *Journal of the American Medical Association, 92,* 1231-1237.

Aman, R. (1977). Benedicta. *Maledicta, 1,* 1-8.

Anthony, S. (1974). Immediacy and nonimmediacy factors in communicating interpersonal attraction. *Journal of Social Psychology, 93,* 141-142.

Argyle, M., & Dean, J. (1965). Eye-contact, distance, and affiliation, *Sociometry, 28,* 289-304.

Averill, J. R. (1973). Personal control over aversive stimuli and its relationship to stress. *Psychological Bulletin, 86,* 286-333.

Averill, J. R. (1980a). A constructivist view of emotion. In R. Plutchik & H. Kellerman (Eds.), *Emotion: Theory, research, and experience* (pp. 305-339). New York: Academic Press.

Averill, J. R. (1980b). On the paucity of positive emotions. In K. R. Blankstein, P. Pliner, & J. Polivy (Eds.), *Assessment and modification of emotional behavior* (pp. 7-45). New York: Plenum.

Ayer, A. J. (1952). *Language, truth and logic* (2nd ed.). New York: Dover.

Ayres, J. (1983). Strategies to maintain relationships: Their identification and perceived usage. *Communication Quarterly, 31,* 62-67.

Balswick, J., & Avertt, C. P. (1977). Differences in expressiveness: Gender, interpersonal orientation, and perceived parental expressiveness as contributing factors. *Journal of Marriage and the Family, 39,* 121-127.

Barthes, R. (1972). *Mythologies* (A. Lavers, Trans.). New York: Hill & Wang. (Original work published 1957).

Baxter, L. A., & Philpott, J. (1982). Attribution-based strategies for initiating and terminating friendships. *Communication Quarterly, 30,* 217-224.

Beardsley, M. D. (1958). *Aesthetics: Problems in the philosophy of criticism.* New York: Harcourt Brace Jovanovich.

Becker, E. (1971). *The birth and death of meaning* (2nd ed.). New York: Free Press.

Berger, C. R. (1980). Self-consciousness and the adequacy of theory and research into relationship development. *Western Journal of Speech Communication, 44,* 93-96.

Berger, C. R., & Bradac, J. J. (1982). *Language and social knowledge: Uncertainty in interpersonal relations.* London: Edward Arnold.

Berger, C. R., & Calabrese, R. J. (1975). Some explorations in initial interaction and beyond: Toward a developmental theory of interpersonal communication. *Human Communication Research, 1,* 99-112.

Berger, C. R., Gardner, R. R., Clatterbuck, G. W., & Schulman, L. S. (1976). Perceptions of information sequencing in relationship development. *Human Communication Research, 3,* 29-46.

Berglund, G., Ander, S., Lindstrom, B., & Tibblin, G. (1975). Personality and reporting of symptoms in normal and hypertensive 50 year old males. *Journal of Psychosomatic Research, 19,* 139-145.

Berlyne, D. E. (1972). Affective aspects of aesthetic communication. In T. Alloway, L. Krames, & P. Pliner (Eds.), *Communication and affect: A comparative approach* (pp. 97-118). New York: Academic Press.

Berscheid, E. (1983). Emotion. In H. H. Kelley, E. Berscheid, A. Christensen, J. H. Harvey, T. L. Huston, G. Levinger, E. McClintock, L. A. Peplau, & D. R. Petersen (Eds.), *Close relationships* (pp. 110-168). New York: W. H. Freeman.

Birdwhistell, R. L. (1970) *Kinesics and context: Essays on body motion communication.* Philadelphia: University of Pennsylvania Press.

Bochner, A. P. (1984). The functions of human communication in interpersonal bonding. In C. C. Arnold & J. W. Bowers (Eds.), *Handbook of rhetorical and communication theory* (pp. 544-621). Boston: Allyn & Bacon.

Bochner, A. P., Kaminski, E. P., & Fitzpatrick, M. A. (1977). The conceptual domain of interpersonal communication behavior: A factor-analytic study. *Human Communication Research, 3,* 291-302.

Boomer, D. S. (1972). Hesitation and grammatical encoding. In S. Moscovici (Ed.), *The psychosociology of language* (pp. 80-92). Chicago: Markham. (Original work published 1965)

Boucher, J. D., & Ekman, P. (1975). Facial areas of emotional information. *Journal of Communication, 25,* 21-29.

Bowers, J. W. (1963). Language intensity, social introversion, and attitude change. *Speech Monographs, 30,* 345-352.

Bowers, J. W. (1964). Some correlates of language intensity. *Quarterly Journal of Speech, 50,* 415-420.

Bowers, J. W. (1974). Beyond threats and promises. *Speech Monographs, 41,* ix-xi.

Bowers, J. W. (1982). Does a duck have antlers? Some pragmatics of "transparent questions." *Communication Monographs, 49,* 63-69.

Bowers, J. W. (1983). *Relational constraints and communication.* Lecture, Tenth Annual Honors Conference, California State University, Fresno.

Bowers, J. W., Elliott, N. D., & Desmond, R. J. (1977). Exploiting pragmatic rules: Devious messages. *Human Communication Research, 3,* 235-242.

Bowers, J. W., & Osborn, M. M. (1966). Attitudinal effects of selected types of concluding metaphors in persuasive speeches. *Speech Monographs, 33,* 147-155.

Bradac, J. J., Bowers, J. W., & Courtright, J. A. (1979). Three language variables in communication research: Intensity, immediacy and diversity. *Human Communication Research, 5,* 257-265.

Bradac, J. J., Bowers, J. W., & Courtright, J. A. (1980). Lexical variations in intensity, immediacy, and diversity: An axiomatic theory and causal mode. In R. N. St. Clair & H. Giles (Eds.), *Social and psychological contexts of language* (pp. 193-223). Hillsdale, NJ: Lawrence Erlbaum.

Bradac, J. J., Courtright, J. A., Schmidt, G., & Davies, R. A. (1976). The effects of perceived status and linguistic diversity upon judgments of speaker attributes and message effectiveness. *Journal of Psychology, 93,* 213-220.

Bradac, J. J., Davies, R. A., & Courtright, J. A. (1977). The role of prior message context in judgments of high- and low-diversity messages. *Language and Speech, 20,* 295-307.

Bradac, J. J., Davies, R. A., & Konsky, C. W. (1976). Studies on the effects of linguistic diversity upon judgments of speaker attributes and message effectiveness. In G. Nickel (Ed.), *Proceedings of the Fourth International Congress of Applied Linguistics, 3,* 527-537.

Bradac, J. J., Desmond, R. J., & Murdock, J. I. (1977). Diversity and density: Lexically determined evaluative and informational consequences of linguistic complexity. *Communication Monographs, 44,* 273-283.

Bradac, J. J., & Friedman, E. (1983). *A theory of belief-based actions: Unmasking the many faces of deception.* Unpublished manuscript, University of California, Santa Barbara.

Bradac, J. J., Hosman, L. A., & Tardy, C. H. (1978). Reciprocal disclosures and language intensity: Attributional consequences. *Communication Monographs, 45,* 1-17.

Bradac, J. J., Konsky, C. W., & Davies, R. A. (1976). Two studies of the effects of linguistic diversity upon judgments of communicator attributes and message effectiveness. *Communication Monographs, 43,* 70-90.

Bradac, J. J., Konsky, C. W., & Elliott, N. D. (1976). Verbal behavior of interviewees: The effects of several situational variables on verbal productivity, disfluency, and lexical diversity. *Journal of Communication Disorders, 9,* 211-225.

Breed, G. R., & Porter, M. (1972). Eye contact, attitudes, and attitude change among males. *Journal of Genetic Psychology, 120,* 211-217.

Brown, P., & Levinson, S. (1978). Universals in language usage: Politeness phenomena. In E. Goody (Ed.), *Questions and politeness* (pp. 56-289). Cambridge: Cambridge University Press.

Bruneau, T. J. (1973). Communicative silences: Forms and functions. *Journal of Communication, 23,* 17-46.

Bucci, W. (1982). The vocalization of painful affect. *Jounal of Communication Disorders, 15,* 415-440.

Buck, R. (1980). Nonverbal behavior and the theory of emotion: The facial feedback hypothesis. *Journal of Personality and Social Psychology, 38,* 811-824.

Burgoon, J. K., & Aho, L. (1982). Three field experiments on the effects of violations of conversational distance. *Communication Monographs, 49,* 71-88.

Burke, K. *Permanence and change.* (1954). Indianapolis: Bobbs-Merrill.

Caldwell, M. A., & Peplau, L. A. (1982). Sex differences in same-sex friendship. *Sex Roles, 8,* 721-732.

Campbell, A., Converse, P., & Rogers, W. (1976). *The quality of American life.* New York: Russell Sage Foundation.

Campbell, P. N. (1975). Metaphor and linguistic theory. *Quarterly Journal of Speech, 61,* 1-12.

Cannon, W. B. (1927). The James-Lange theory of emotions: A critical examination and an alternative theory. *American Journal of Psychology, 39,* 106-124.

Caruth, E., & Ekstein, R. (1965). Interpretation within the metaphor. *American Academy of Child Psychiatry Journal, 5,* 35-45.

Chaikin, A. L., & Derlega, F. J. (1974). Liking for the norm-breaker in self-disclosure. *Journal of Personality, 42,* 117-129.

Clark, H. H. (1979). Responding to indirect speech acts. *Cognitive Psychology, 11,* 430-477.

Cody, M. J. (1982). A typology of disengagement strategies and an examination of the role intimacy, reactions to inequity and relational problems play in strategy selection. *Communication Monographs, 49,* 148-170.

Conville, R. (1975). Linguistic nonimmediacy and self-presentation. *Journal of Psychology, 90,* 219-227.

Cook, M. (1969). Anxiety, speech disturbance, and speech rate. *British Journal of Social and Clinical Psychology, 8,* 13-21.

Coser, L. (1956). *The functions of social conflict.* New York: Free Press.

Cozby, P. C. (1973). Self-disclosure: A literature review. *Psychological Bulletin, 79,* 73-91.

Cronen, V. E., Pearce, W. B., & Snavely, L. M. (1979). A theory of rule-structure and types of episodes and a study of perceived enmeshment in undesired repetitive patterns ("URPs"). In D. Nimmo (Ed.), *Communication yearbook 3* (pp. 225-240). New Brunswick, NJ: Transaction.

Cross, D. W. (1979). *Word abuse.* New York: Coward, McCann & Geoghegan.

Crusius, T., & Winterowd, W. R. (1981). The apprehension of metaphor. *Language and Style, 14,* 20-33.

Crystal, D. (1969). *Prosodic systems and intonation in English.* London: Cambridge University Press.

Cumes, D. P. (1983). Hypertension, disclosure of personal concerns, and blood pressure response. *Journal of Clinical Psychology, 39,* 376-381.

Daly, J. A., & McCroskey, J. C. (1975). Occupational choice and desirability as a function of communication apprehension. *Journal of Counseling Psychology, 22,* 309-313.

Daly, J. A., & Miller, M. D. (1975). Apprehension of writing as a predictor of message intensity. *Journal of Psychology, 89,* 175-177.

Darnell, D. K. (1970). Semantic differentiation. In P. Emmert & W. D. Brooks (Eds.), *Methods of research in communication* (pp. 181-196). Boston: Houghton Mifflin.

Davidson, B., Balswick, J., & Halverson, C. (1983). Affective self-disclosure and marital adjustment: A test of equity theory. *Journal of Marriage and the Family, 45,* 93-102.

Davidson, L. R., & Duberman, L. (1982). Friendship: Communication and interactional patterns in same-sex dyads. *Sex Roles, 8,* 809-822.

Davitz, J. R. (Ed.). (1964). *The communication of emotional meaning.* New York: McGraw-Hill.

Davitz, J. R. (1969). *The language of emotion.* New York: Academic Press.

Davitz, J. R. (1970). A dictionary and grammar of emotion. In M. B. Arnold (Ed.), *Feelings and emotions: The Loyola Symposium* (pp. 251-258). New York: Academic Press.

Davitz, J. R., & Davitz, L. J. (1959). The communication of feelings by content-free speech. *Journal of Communication, 9,* 6-13.

Delia, J. G. (1980). Some tentative thoughts concerning the study of interpersonal relationships and their development. *Western Journal of Speech Communication, 44,* 97-103.

DePaulo, B. M., Zuckerman, M., & Rosenthal, R. (1980). Modality effects in the detection of deception. In L. Wheeler (Ed.), *Review of personality and social psychology* (pp. 125-132). Beverly Hills, CA: Sage.

de Rivera, J. (1977). *A structural theory of the emotions.* New York: International Universities Press.

Deva, B. C. (1957). Psychophysics of speech melody, part 1. *Zeitschrift fur phonetick und allgemeine sprachwissenschaft, 10,* 337-344.

Deva, B. C. (1958). Psychophysics of speech melody, part 2. *Zeitschrift fur phonetik und allgemeine sprachwissenschaft, 11,* 206-211.

Deva, B. C. (1960). Psychophysics of speech melody, parts 3 and 4. *Zeitschrift fur phonetik und allgemeine sprachwissenschaft, 13,* 8-27.

Doyle, C. C. (1977). Belaboring the obvious: Sarcastic interrogative affirmatives and negatives. *Maledicta, 1,* 77-82.

Duck, S. (1980). Personal relationships research in the 1980's: Towards an understanding of complex human sociality. *Western Journal of Speech Communication, 44,* 114-119.

Duck, S. (1982). A topography of relationship disengagement and dissolution. In S. Duck (Ed.), *Personal relationships 4: Dissolving personal relationships* (pp. 1-30). New York: Academic Press.

Duffy, E. (1941). An explanation of "emotional" phenomena without the use of the concept "emotion." *Journal of General Psychology, 25,* 283-293.

Duffy, E. (1962). *Activation and behavior.* New York: John Wiley.

Dutton, D. G., & Aron, A. P. (1974). Some evidence for heightened sexual attraction under conditions of high anxiety. *Journal of Personality and Social Psychology, 30,* 510-517.

Eastman, M. (1931). *The literary mind.* New York: Scribner's.

Egan, G. (1970). *Encounter: Group processes for interpersonal growth.* Belmont, CA: Brooks/Cole.

Eidelson, R. J. (1980). Interpersonal satisfaction and level of involvement: A curvilinear relationship. *Journal of Personality and Social Psychology, 39,* 460-470.

Ekman, P., & Friesen, W. V. (1969). Nonverbal leakage and clues to deception. *Psychiatry, 32,* 88-106.

Ekman, P., Friesen, W. V., & Ellsworth, P. (1972). *Emotion in the human face.* New York: Pergamon.

Ekman, P., Friesen, W. V., & Scherer, K. R. (1976). Body movements and voice pitch in deceptive interaction. *Semiotica, 16,* 23-27.

Ekman, P., Levenson, R. W., & Friesen, W. V. (1983). Autonomic nervous system activity distinguishes among emotions. *Science, 221,* 1208-1210.

Ellsworth, P. C., & Carlsmith, J. M. (1968). Effects of eye contact and verbal content on affective response to a dyadic interaction. *Journal of Personality and Social Psychology, 10,* 15-20.

Ellsworth, P. C., & Carlsmith, J. M. (1973). Eye contact and gaze aversion in an aggressive encounter. *Journal of Personality and Social Psychology, 28,* 280-292.

Epstein, S. (1979). The ecological study of emotions in humans. In P. Pliner, K. R. Blankstein, & I. M. Spigel (Eds.), *Perception of emotion in self and others* (pp. 47-83). New York: Plenum Press.

Exline, R. V., with Winters, L. C. (1965). Affective relations and mutual glances in dyads. In S. Tomkins & C. Izard (Eds.), *Affect, cognition, and personality* (pp. 319-350). New York: Springer.

Farb, P. (1974). *Wordplay.* New York: Knopf.

Feinberg, L. B. (1971). Nonimmediacy in verbal communication as an indicator of attitudes toward the disabled. *Journal of Social Psychology, 84,* 135-140.

Fitzpatrick, M. A., & Indvik, J. (1982). The instrumental and expressive domains of marital communication. *Human Communication Research, 8,* 195-213.

Franzwa, H. H. (1969). Psychological factors influencing use of "evaluative-dynamic" language. *Speech Monographs, 36,* 103-109.

Freedman, N., Blass, T., Rifkin, A., & Quitkin, F. (1973). Body movements and the verbal encoding of aggressive affect. *Journal of Personality and Social Psychology, 26,* 72-85.

Freud, S. (1949). *An outline of psycho-analysis* (J. Strachey, Trans.). New York: Norton. (Original work published 1940)

Freud, S. (1962). *Standard edition* (Vol. 100, J. Strachey, Ed. and Trans.). London: Hogarth. (Original work published 1909)

Freud, S. (1965). *The origin and development of psychoanalysis.* South Bend, IN: Gateway. (Original work published 1910)

Freud, S. (1974). *The psychopathology of everyday life* (A. A. Brill, Trans.). New York: Macmillan.

Giles, H., Taylor, D. M., & Bourhis, R. Y. (1973). Towards a theory of interpersonal accommodation through language: Some Canadian data. *Language and Society, 2,* 177-192.

Goffman, E. (1963). *Behavior in public places: Notes on the social organization of gatherings.* New York: Free Press.

Goldman-Eisler, F. (1972). A comparative study of two hesitation phenomena. In S. Moscovici (Ed.), *The psychosociology of language* (pp. 69-79). Chicago: Markham. (Original work published 1961)

Gordon, D. C. (1978). *Therapeutic metaphors: Helping others through the looking glass.* Cupertino, CA: Meta.

Gottman, J. M. (1982). Emotional responsiveness in marital conversations. *Journal of Communication, 32,* 108-120.

Gouldner, A. W. (1960). The reciprocity norm: A preliminary statement. *American Sociological Review, 25,* 161-178.

Graziano, W. G., & Musser, L. M. (1982). The joining and the parting of the ways. In S. Duck (Ed.), *Personal relationships 4: Dissolving personal relationships* (pp. 75-106). New York: Academic Press.

Greenberg, B. S., & Tannenbaum, P. H. (1962). Communicator performance under cognitive stress. *Journalism Quarterly, 39,* 169-178.

Greenwald, H. (1958). *The call girl: A social and psychoanalytic study.* New York: Ballantine.

Gurr, T. R. (1970). *Why men rebel.* Princeton, NJ: Princeton University Press.

Guyton, A. C. (1971). *Textbook of medical physiology* (4th ed.). Philadelphia: W. B. Saunders.

Haggard, E. A., & Isaacs, K. S. (1966). Micromomentary facial expressions as indicators of ego mechanisms in psychotherapy. In L. A. Gottschalk & A. H. Auerbach (Eds.), *Methods of research in psychotherapy* (pp. 154-165). New York: Appleton-Century-Crofts.

Hall, E. T. (1959). *The silent language.* Garden City, NY: Doubleday.

Hall, E. T. (1966). *The hidden dimension.* Garden City, NY: Doubleday.

Handkins, R. E., & Munz, D. C. (1978). Essential hypertension and self disclosure. *Journal of Clinical Psychology, 34,* 870-875.

Hariman, R. D. (1982). *Getting to first base with baseball metaphors.* Paper presented at the annual meeting of the Central States Speech Association, Milwaukee.

Harper, R. G., Wiens, A. N., & Matarazzo, J. D. (1978). *Nonverbal communication: The state of the art.* New York: John Wiley.

Hart, R. P. (1976). Absolutism and situation: Prolegomena to a rhetorical biography of Richard M. Nixon. *Communication Monographs, 43,* 204-228.

Harvey, J. H., Weber, A. l., Yarkin, K. L., & Stewart, B. E. (1982). An attributional approach to relationship breakdown and dissolution. In S. Duck (Ed.), *Personal relationships 4: Dissolving personal relationships* (pp. 107-126). New York: Academic Press.

Hatfield, E. (1982). Passionate love, companionate love, and intimacy. In M. Fisher & G. Stricker (Eds.), *Intimacy* (pp. 267-292). New York: Plenum.

Heslin, R., & Patterson, M. L. (1982). *Nonverbal behavior and social psychology.* New York: Plenum.

Hopper, R., Knapp, M. L., & Scott, L. (1981). Couples' personal idioms: Exploring intimate talk. *Journal of Communication, 31,* 23-33.

Hughes, R. (1981). The Szondian view. *American Image, 38,* 323-342.

Izard, C. E. (1971). *The face of emotion.* New York: Appleton-Century-Crofts.

Izard, C. E. (1975). Patterns of emotions and emotion communication in "hostility" and aggression. In P. Pliner, L. Krames, & T. Alloway (Eds.), *Nonverbal communication of aggression: Advances in the study of communication and affect* (Vol. 2, pp. 77-101). New York: Plenum.

Izard, C. E. (1977). *Human emotions.* New York: Plenum.

Izard, C. E., & Buechler, S. (1980). Aspects of consciousness and personality in terms of differential emotions theory. In R. Plutchik & H. Kellerman (Eds.), *Emotion: Theory, research, and experience* (pp. 165-187). New York: Academic Press.

Jaffe, J., Anderson, S. W., & Stern, D. N. (1979). Conversational rhythms. In D. Aaronson & R. W. Rieber (Eds.), *Psycholinguistic research* (pp. 393-431). Hillsdale, NJ: Lawrence Erlbaum.

James, W. (1950). *The principles of psychology.* New York: Dover. (Original work published 1890)

Jay, T. B. (1978). Doing research with dirty words. *Maledicta, 1,* 234-256.

Jemie, O. (1976). Signifying, dozens, and toasts: A selection. *Alcheringa, N.S.2,* 27-40.

Jourard, S. M. (1971). *Self-disclosure: The experimental investigation of the transparent self.* New York: John Wiley.

Jurich, A. P., & Jurich, J. A. (1974). Correlations among nonverbal expressions of anxiety. *Psychological Reports, 34,* 199-204.

Kanin, E. J. (1979). The equation of coital vulgarisms with personal and social transgressions. *Maledicta, 3,* 55-57.

Kasl, S. V., & Mahl, G. F. (1965). The relationship of disturbances and hesitations in spontaneous speech to anxiety. *Journal of Personality and Social Psychology, 1,* 425-433.

Kelley, H. H. (1979). *Personal relationships: Their structures and processes.* Hillsdale, NJ: Erlbaum.

Kemper, T. D. (1978). Toward a sociology of emotions: Some problems and some solutions. *American Sociologist, 13,* 30-40.

Key, M. R. (1975). *Paralanguage and kinesics.* Metuchen, NJ: Scarecrow.

Kittay, E., & Lehrer, A. (1981). Semantic fields and the structure of metaphor. *Studies in Language, 5,* 31-63.

Kleck, R. E. (1970). Interaction distance and nonverbal agreeing responses. *British Journal of Social and Clinical Psychology, 9,* 180-182.

Knapp, M. L. (1972). *Nonverbal communication in human interaction.* New York: Holt, Rinehart & Winston.

Knapp, M. L. (1983). Dyadic relationship development. In J. M. Wiemann & R. P. Harrison (Eds.), *Nonverbal interaction* (pp. 179-207). Beverly Hills, CA: Sage.

Knapp, M. L., Ellis, D. G., & Williams, B. A. (1980). Perceptions of communication behavior associated with relationship terms. *Communication Monographs, 47,* 262-278.

Knower, F. H. (1941). Analysis of some experimental variations of simulated vocal expressions of emotion. *Journal of Social Psychology, 14,* 369-372.

Krueger, D. L. (1982). Marital decision making: A language-action analysis. *Quarterly Journal of Speech, 68,* 273-287.

Krystal, H. (1979). Alexithymia and psychotherapy. *American Journal of Psychotherapy, 33,* 17-31.

Lakoff, R. (1972). Language in context. *Language, 48,* 907-927.

Lalljee, M., & Cook, M. (1973). Uncertainty in first encounters. *Journal of Personality and Social Psychology, 26,* 137-141.

Langer, S. K. (1953). *Feeling and form.* New York: Scribner's.

Lazarus, R. S., Averill, J. R., & Opton, E. M., Jr. (1970). Towards a cognitive theory of emotion. In M. B. Arnold (Ed.), *Feelings and emotions: The Loyola Symposium* (pp. 207-232). New York: Academic Press.

Lazarus, R. S., Kanner, A. D., & Folkman, S. (1980). Emotions: A cognitive-phenomenological analysis. In R. Plutchik & H. Kellerman (Eds.), *Emotion: Theory, research, and experience* (pp. 189-217). New York: Academic Press.

Leary, T. (1955). The theory and measurement methodology of interpersonal communication. *Psychiatry, 18,* 147-161.

Leventhal, H. (1979). A perceptual-motor processing model of emotion. In P. Pliner, K. R. Blankstein, & I. M. Spigel (Eds.), *Perception of emotion in self and others: Advances in the study of communication and affect* (Vol. 5, pp. 1-46). New York: Plenum.

Lewin, K. (1951). *Field theory in social science.* Westport, CT: Greenwood.

Lewis, R. A. (1978). Emotional intimacy among men. *Journal of Social Issues, 34,* 108-121.

Lorenz, K. (1966). *On aggression* (M. K. Wilson, Trans.). New York: Harcourt Brace Jovanovich.

Malatesta, C. Z., & Izard, C. E. (Eds.). (1984). *Emotion in adult development.* Beverly Hills, CA: Sage.

Mandler, G. (1975). *Mind and emotion.* New York: John Wiley.

Mandler, G. (1980). The generation of emotion: A psychological theory. In R. Plutchik & H. Kellerman (Eds.), *Emotion: Theory, research, and experience* (pp. 219-243). New York: Academic Press.

Marshall, G. D., & Zimbardo, P. G. (1979). Affective consequences of inadequately explained physiological arousal. *Journal of Personality and Social Psychology, 37,* 970-988.

Martin, J. (1982). *Miss Manners' guide to excruciatingly correct behavior.* New York: Warner.

Maslach, C. (1979). Negative emotional biasing of unexplained arousal. *Journal of Personality and Social Psychology, 37,* 953-969.

Massey, R. F. (1981). *Personality theories: Comparisons and syntheses.* New York: Van Nostrand.

McCroskey, J. C., & Mehrley, S. (1969). The effects of disorganization and nonfluency on attitude change and source credibility. *Speech Monographs, 36,* 13-21.

Meerloo, J.A.M. (1964). *Unobtrusive communication.* Assen, The Netherlands: Roy Van Gorcum.

Mehrabian, A. (1968). Relationship of attitude to seated posture, orientation, and distance. *Journal of Personality and Social Psychology, 10,* 26-30.

Mehrabian, A.., & Wiener, M. (1966). Nonimmediacy between communicator and object of communication in a verbal message: Application to the inference of attitudes. *Journal of Consulting Psychology, 30,* 420-425.

Miller, G. R. (1983). Telling it like it isn't and not telling it like it is: Research in deceptive communication. In J. Sisco (Ed.), *The Jensen lectures: Contemporary communication studies* (pp. 145-179). Tampa: University of South Florida Press.

Murdock, J. I., Bradac, J. J., & Bowers, J. W. (1984). Effects of power on the perception of explicit and implicit threats, promises, and thromises: A rule-governed perspective. *Western Journal of Speech Communication, 48,* 344-361.

Murray, D. C. (1971). Talk, silence, and anxiety. *Psychological Bulletin, 75,* 244-260.

Narus, L. R., Jr., & Fischer, J. L. (1982). Strong but not silent: A reexamination of expressivity in the relationships of men. *Sex Roles, 8,* 159-168.

Newman, H. M. (1981a). Communication within ongoing intimate relationships: An attributional perspective. *Personality and Social Psychology Bulletin, 1,* 59-70.

Newman, H. M. (1981b). Interpretation and explanation: Influences on communicative exchanges within intimate relationships. *Communication Quarterly, 29,* 123-131.

Newman, H. M. (1982). The sounds of silence in communicative encounters. *Communication Quarterly, 30,* 142-149.

Notarius, C. I., & Johnson, J. S. (1982). Emotional expression in husbands and wives. *Journal of Marriage and the Family, 44,* 483-490.

O'Connor, J. D., & Arnold, G. F. (1973). *Intonation of colloquial English.* London: Longmans.

Osborn, M. M. (1967). Archetypal metaphor in rhetoric: The light-dark family. *Quarterly Journal of Speech, 53,* 115-126.

Osborn, M. M., & Ehninger, D. (1962). The metaphor in public address. *Speech Monographs, 29,* 223-234.

Osgood, C. E., & Walker, E. G. (1959). Motivation and language behavior: A content analysis of suicide notes. *Journal of Abnormal and Social Psychology, 59,* 58-67.

Parsons, R., & Bales, R. F. (1955). *Family, socialization, and interaction.* New York: Free Press.

Patterson, M. L. (1976). An arousal model of interpersonal intimacy. *Psychological Review, 83,* 235-245.

Peake, T. H., & Egli, D. (1982). The language of feeling. *Journal of Contemporary Psychotherapy, 13,* 162-174.

Pelletier, K. R. (1977). *Mind as healer, mind as slayer.* New York: Dell.

Percy, W. (1975). *The message in the bottle: How queer man is, how queer language is and what one has to do with the other.* New York: Farrar, Straus, and Giroux.

Perlman, D., & Peplau, A. (1981). Toward a social psychology of loneliness. In S. Duck & R. Gilmour (Eds.), *Personal relationships 3: Personal relationships in disorder* (pp. 31-56). New York: Academic Press.

Plutchik, R. (1962). *The emotions: Facts, theories and a new model.* New York: Random House.

Plutchik, R. (1970). Emotions, evolution and adaptive processes. In M. Arnold (Ed.), *Feelings and emotions: The Loyola Symposium* (pp. 3-24). New York: Academic Press.

Plutchik, R. (1980a). A general psychoevolutionary theory of emotion. In R. Plutchik & H. Kellerman (Eds.), *Emotion: Theory, research, and experience* (pp. 3-33). New York: Academic Press.

Plutchik, R. (1980b). *Emotion: A psychoevolutionary synthesis.* New York: Harper & Row.

Plutchik, R. (1980c). A language for the emotions. *Psychology Today, 13*(9), 68-79.

Pollack, I., Rubenstein, H., & Horowitz, A. (1960). Communication of verbal modes of expression. *Language and Speech, 3,* 121-130.

Pollio, H. R., & Barlow, J. M. (1975). A behavioral analysis of figurative language in psychotherapy: One session in a single case-study. *Language and Speech, 18,* 236-254.

Poyatos, F. (1976). *Man beyond words: Theory and methodology of nonverbal communication.* Oswego: New York State English Council.

Poyatos, F. (1980). Interactive functions and limitations of verbal and nonverbal behaviors in natural conversation. *Semiotica, 30,* 211-244.

Reik, T. (1957). *Of love and lust.* New York: Farrar & Straus.

Rieser, M. (1940). Analysis of poetic simile. *Journal of Philosophy, 37,* 209-217.

Rieser, M. (1950). Brief introduction to an epistemology of art. *Journal of Philosophy, 47,* 695-704.

Rogers, P. L., Scherer, K. R., & Rosenthal, R. (1971). Content filtering human speech: A simple electronic system. *Behavior Research Methods and Instrumentation, 3,* 16-18.

Roloff, M. E. (1981). *Interpersonal communication: The social exchange approach.* Beverly Hills, CA: Sage.

Rosenfeld, L. B. (1979). Self-disclosure avoidance: Why I am afraid to tell you who I am. *Communication Monographs, 46,* 63-74.

Rubin, J. (1970). *Do it.* New York: Simon & Schuster.

Rubin, Z. (1970). Measurement of romantic love. *Journal of Personality and Social Psychology, 16,* 165-273.

Schachter, S., & Singer, J. E. (1962). Cognitive, social, and physiological determinants of emotional state. *Psychological Review, 69,* 379-399.

Scherer, K. R. (1971). Randomized splicing: A note on a simple technique for masking speech content. *Journal of Experimental Research in Personality, 5,* 155-159.

Scherer, K. R. (1979). Acoustic concomitants of emotional dimensions: Judging affect from synthesized tone sequences. In S. Weitz (Ed.), *Nonverbal communication: Readings with commentary* (2nd ed., pp. 105-111). New York: Oxford University Press.

Scherer, K. R., Koivumaki, J., & Rosenthal, R. (1972). Minimal cues in the vocal communication of affect: Judging emotions from content-masked speech. *Journal of Psycholinguistic Research, 1,* 269-285.

Scherer, K. R., & Oshinsky, J. S. (1977). Cue utilization in emotion attribution from auditory stimuli. *Motivation and Emotion, 1,* 331-346.

Schmidt, N., & Sermat, V. (1983). Measuring loneliness in different relationships. *Journal of Personality and Social Psychology, 44,* 1038-1047.

Scott, M. D., McCroskey, J. C., & Sheahan, M. E. (1978). The development of a self-report measure of communication apprehension in organizational settings. *Journal of Communication, 28,* 104-111.

Searle, J. R. (1975). Indirect speech acts. In P. Cole & J. L. Morgan (Eds.), *Syntax and semantics: Vol. 3. Speech acts* (pp. 59-82). New York: Academic Press.

Shibles, W. (1974). *Emotion: The method of philosophical therapy.* Whitewater, WI: Language Press.

Siegman, A. W., & Pope, B. (1965). Effects of question specificity and anxiety-producing messages on verbal fluency in the initial interview. *Journal of Personality and Social Psychology, 2,* 522-530.

Sifneos, P. E. (1974). A reconsideration of psychodynamic mechanisms in psychosomatic symptom formation in view of recent clinical observations. *Psychotherapy and Psychosomatics, 24,* 151-155.

Sifneos, P. E. (1975). Problems of psychotherapy of patients with Alexithymic characteristics and physical disease. *Psychotherapy and Psychosomatics, 26,* 49-58.

Sillars, A. L. (1980). Attributions and communication in roommate conflicts. *Communication Monographs, 47,* 180-200.

Sillars, A. L., & Scott, M. D. (1983). Interpersonal perception between intimates: An integrative review. *Human Communication Research, 10,* 153-176.

Smith, E. R., & Kluegel, J. R. (1982). Cognitive and social bases of emotional experience: Outcome, attribution, and affect. *Journal of Personality and Social Psychology, 43,* 1129-1141.

Snyder, M. (1974). The self-monitoring of expressive behavior. *Journal of Personality and Social Psychology, 30,* 526-537.

Snyder, M. (1979). Cognitive, behavioral, and interpersonal consequences of self-monitoring. In P. Pliner, K. R. Blankstein, & I. M. Spigel (Eds.), *Perception of emotion in self and others: Advances in the study of communication and affect* (Vol. 5, pp. 181-201). New York: Plenum.

Sontag, S. (1978). *Illness as metaphor.* New York: Farrar, Straus & Giroux.

Sperber, H. (1955). Expressive aspects of political language. In H. Werner (Ed.), *On expressive language* (pp. 39-45). Worcester, MA: Clark University Press.

Stanislavsky, C. (1936). *An actor prepares* (E.R. Hapgood, Trans.). New York: Theatre Arts.

Steadman, J. M. (1935). A study of verbal taboos. *American Speech, 10,* 93-103.

Street, R. L., Jr. (1982). Evaluation of noncontent speech accommodation. *Language and Communication, 2,* 13-31.

Streeter, L. A., Krauss, R. M., Geller, V., Olson, C., & Apple, W. (1977). Pitch changes during attempted deception. *Journal of Personality and Social Psychology, 35,* 345-350.

Sundstrom, E. (1975). An experimental study of crowding: Effects of room size, intrusion, and goal blocking on nonverbal behavior, self-disclosure, and self-reported stress. *Journal of Personality and Social Psychology, 32,* 645-654.

Thompson, S. C. (1981). Will it hurt less if I can control it? A complex answer to a simple question. *Psychological Bulletin, 90,* 89-101.

Tindall, R. T., & Robinson, F. P. (1947). The uses of silence as a technique of counseling. *Journal of Clinical Psychology, 3,* 129-141.

Tomkins, S. S. (1980). Affect as amplification: Some modifications in theory. In R. Plutchik & H. Kellerman (Eds.), *Emotion: Theory, research, and experience* (pp. 141-164). New York: Academic Press.

Tomkins, S. S., & McCarter, R. (1964). What and where are the primary affects? Some evidence for a theory. *Perceptual and Motor Skills, 18,* 119-158.

Watzlawick, P. (1978). *The language of change.* New York: Basic Books.

Weiner, H. M., Singer, M. T., & Reiser, M. F. (1962). Cardiovascular responses and their psychological correlations: A study of healthy, young adult patients with peptic ulcer and hypertension. *Psychosomatic Medicine, 24,* 477-489.

Weiss, R. S. (1976). The emotional impact of marital separation. *Journal of Social Issues, 32,* 135-145.

Wiener, M., & Mehrabian, A. (1967). *Language within language: Immediacy, a channel in verbal communication.* New York: Appleton-Century-Crofts.

Woodworth, R. S., & Schlosberg, H. S. (1954). *Experimental psychology.* New York: Holt, Rinehart & Winston.

Wright, P. H. (1982). Men's friendships, women's friendships and the alleged inferiority of the latter. *Sex Roles, 8,* 1-20.

Zajonc, R. B. (1980). Feeling and thinking: Preferences need no inferences. *American Psychologist, 35,* 151-173.

Zuckerman, M., DePaulo, B. M., & Rosenthal, R. (1981). Verbal and nonverbal communication of deception. In L. Berkowitz (Ed.), *Advances in experimental social psychology* (Vol. 14, pp. 1-59). New York: Academic Press.

12 Communication and Interpersonal Influence

DAVID R. SEIBOLD
JAMES G. CANTRILL
RENÉE A. MEYERS

University of Illinois, Urbana-Champaign

E ACH chapter in this handbook treats an analytically separable, although in reality an inherently fused, facet of interpersonal communication behavior. Other reviewers here have examined interpersonal communication in terms of discourse structures and conventions, embedded nonverbal signals, actors' characteristics and competencies, mutual regulation of interaction, underlying interpretive processes, and as responsive to types of relationships, variations in setting, and situational constraints. At the risk of further reducing the interpenetration of these structures and processes, we focus in this chapter on the instrumental character of interpersonal communication. In particular, we will be concerned with its control-oriented nature, especially the strategic and tactical features of actors' regulative and persuasive communication influence attempts in interpersonal contexts.

It is not unwonted to view interpersonal communication, at least partly and under specifiable conditions, as persons' symbolic interactions strategically controlled in the pursuit of personal objectives (Grimshaw, 1981). Granted, interactants may have multiple goals and intentions that they simultaneously pursue, only some of which entail interpersonal influence (Winograd, 1977); persons may not be consciously aware of all the goal-oriented objectives embedded in their communication routines (Langer, Blank, & Chanowitz, 1978); and much of mutual influence in interpersonal communication is the manifestation of tacitly accepted conventions rather than instrumental goals (Duncan, 1981; Lewis, 1969). But reflection and research reveal that actors use talk strategically to manage their own identities (Schlenker, 1980) and those of others (Weinstein & Deutschberger, 1963), to negotiate meaning in a variety of interpersonal settings (Schenkein, 1978), and to accomplish personal and interpersonal tasks (Clark & Delia, 1979; Grimshaw, 1980).

For example, findings underscore that people participate each day in a variety of goal-oriented interpersonal situations requiring assessment of obstacles to sought-after personal ends and identification of symbolic means for securing compliance from others (Cody & McLaughlin, 1980; Forgas, 1976, 1979). That persons are differentially competent at communicative influence in these situations (Applegate & Delia, 1980; Weinstein, 1966, 1969) and that they variously select symbolic strategies and message tactics including ingratiation (Stires & Jones, 1969), humor (O'Quin & Aronoff, 1981; Stephenson, 1951), personal insult (Dollard, 1939), apology (Schlenker & Darby, 1981), sarcasm (Ball, 1965; Folb, 1980), irony (Brown, 1980; Kaufer, 1981; Kaufer & Neuwirth, 1982), embarrassment (Gross & Stone, 1966), praise (Kanouse, Gumpert, & Canavan-Gumpert, 1981), promises (Gahagan & Tedeschi, 1968; Tedeschi, 1970), threats (Friedland, 1976; Schlenker, Bonoma, & Tedeschi, 1970), honesty (Monteverde, Paschke, & Tedeschi, 1974), deception (Knapp & Comadena, 1979; Stebbins, 1975; Turner, Edgley, & Olmstead, 1975), questions (Bennett, 1982; Churchill, 1978; Goody, 1978a, 1978b), comforting (Burleson, 1983, 1984a, 1984b), name-calling (Steele, 1975), hinting (Falbo, 1977), degradation (Garfinkel, 1956), manipulativeness (Singer, 1964), argument (Cronkhite, 1983; Krause, 1972; Trapp, 1983), indebtedness (Greenberg & Shapiro, 1971), disclosure (Baxter, 1979; Savicki, 1972), accounts (Ditton, 1977; McLaughlin, Cody, & O'Hair, 1983; McLaughlin, Cody, & Rosenstein, 1983; Shields, 1979), and politeness (Baxter, 1984; Brown & Levinson, 1978) among a multitude of others perhaps justifies our separate treatment of the influence-oriented character of interpersonal communication.

SOME BASIC GROUNDWORK

Problems

Surveying research on communicative influence in interpersonal contexts is conceptually and pragmatically a murky matter. First, the area of "social influence"—to which communicative influence is subordinately but intrinsically connected—is theoretically incoherent and nearly empirically illimitable. Consider that Deutsch (1966) has roundly proclaimed that the entire discipline of political science is commensurate with the study of influence and compliance. Tedeschi and Bonoma (1972) similarly seek "the redefinition of social psychology as the study of . . . influence processes" (p. 41). Even writers who have tried to focus on "interpersonal influence" per se (Wheeler, Deci, Reis, & Zuckerman, 1978) have stretched to integrate traditional influence research, cognitive aspects of influence (for example, dissonance, reactance), and dynamic forms of influence such as contagion and social facilitation.

More generally, research on interpersonal influence is difficult to synthesize because conceptualizations of influence reflect what Tedeschi and Bonoma (1972) term "convergent" and "divergent" lines of theorizing. On the one hand, systematic comparisons across diverse social processes occasionally have converged in "grand theories" of social causation, power, and influence (Dahl, 1957; French, 1956; Homans, 1961; March, 1955; Parsons, 1963; Weber, 1947); theories that are often too general to permit precise communicative influence predictions. On the other hand, when results of such comparisons resist integration, theorizing about interpersonal influence results in divergent mini-theories. Many communicative influence research findings have roots no deeper than particularistic theories of altercasting (Goffman, 1952, 1955; Weinstein & Deutschberger, 1963), embarrassment (Goffman, 1956; Modigliani, 1968, 1971), disclosure (Chelune, 1979; Cozby, 1973; Gilbert, 1976), ingratiation (Jones, 1964; Jones & Wortman, 1973), or only slightly broader perspectives on relationship development (Altman & Taylor, 1973), strategic interaction and interaction routines (Goffman, 1967, 1969), impression management (Schlenker, 1980), bargaining (Bacharach & Lawler, 1981; Rubin & Brown, 1975; Walton & McKersie, 1965), conflict management (Filley, 1975; Schelling, 1963), and interpersonal attribution processes (Gottlieb & Ickes, 1978; Seibold & Spitzberg, 1982).

Nor are the borders of interpersonal "communicative influence" any more easily circumscribed. Seminal communication theorists Ruesch and Bateson (1951) manifest a core difficulty when they reciprocally define communication and interpersonal influence, and propose that communication includes "all of those processes by which people influence one another" (p. 6). Even granting more widespread acceptance among today's scholars of the multiple functions of communication (Bochner, 1984; Halliday, 1973), another problem with reviewing this research is establishing the specific nature of the communication linked to the type of influence observed or reported. As Tedeschi and Bonoma (1972) note, what theorists and researchers label a particular type of communicative influence "may be more a matter of phenomenological experience than the tactics used by the source" (p. 12). Very little of the research in this area establishes that the source-oriented conceptual definition of a message tactic studied coincides with the receiver's interpretation of that tactic (cf. Gamson's 1968 analysis of approval and disapproval as influence resources confounded in previous research).

Analytic ambiguities associated with a control orientation to interpersonal communication further complicate efforts to review this area. Especially deleterious are confusions about communicative control arising from reviews in which (1) communicative control at the individual and dyadic level are not clearly distinguished (Parks, 1977), (2) interpersonal influence and power are treated isomorphically as instantiations of control (Coleman, 1963), and (3) communicative influence and coercion are not distinguished as control forms (see Tedeschi & Bonoma, 1972, for a notable exception). These and other analytic problems interact with the aforementioned connotative problems and result in frequent use of "the term *control* . . . in many theoretical, methodological, and empirical reports, [but] it is surprising to see that nobody has yet examined the conceptual and empirical applications of the term to see how much consensus there is on its meaning and how rigorously or loosely it has been used" (Bochner & Lenk Krueger, 1979, pp. 201-202).

Partly to prevent such confusions about our use of conceptual terms in this area and in order to lay the foundation for research literature reviewed in the body of this chapter, we next discuss our perspective on communicative influence, including central concepts such as communication and intentionality, interpersonal influence and control, and communicative strategies and message tactics. In the course of the discussion we also will point out distinctions driving research in several areas surveyed.

Communicative Influence

Communication may be viewed, most generally, as a process in which persons engage in direct or mediated symbolic interaction in order to create meanings (both individual interpretations and shared understandings) that satisfy multifarious personal needs and enable joint conduct. Many of the complexities associated with unique actors' attempts at mutual expression and adaptation are ameliorated, of course, by reliance on shared codes and learned conventions for enacting communication routines, as well as by interactants' individual abilities to assume others' stances and to adopt appropriate responses. Central to this process, we shall assume, are actors engaged in constructing and producing messages in the service of some purpose or objective. As O'Keefe and Delia observe: "Message contents are generated in relation to purposes, both the specific purposes that grow out of the specific task at hand and generalized tacit purposes that might accompany any act of communication" (1982, p. 51). We do not mean to imply that actors are always consciously or reflectively aware of their interactional goals (Brown & Levinson, 1978, p. 90), and we concur that communication often is a routinized and taken-for-granted activity for those engaged in it (Jacobs & Jackson, 1982, 1983; Lewis, 1969). However, our perspective and that implicit in much of the research on communicative influence begins with the assumptions that (1) messages emanate from persons' intentions to communicate something about themselves, others, and the world they experience; (2) communication is instrumental in that sense, and may be functionally organized by the conscious and unconscious purpose it serves for each actor; and, (3) actors' communication behaviors in many encounters reflect intentionally directed and deliberately organized efforts to accomplish specific, personally meaningful interactional goals.

Theorists and researchers have indicated that communicators may simultaneously hold various interactional goals, including ideational (Halliday, 1970), informational (Winograd, 1977), presentational (Goffman, 1959), relational (Brown & Levinson, 1978), and textual (Levy, 1979) or discursive (Hobbs & Evans, 1980) goals. There is evidence that the relative importance actors attach to these interactional goals affects their message choices in compliance-gaining and persuasion situations (cf. Clark, 1979; McLaughlin, Cody, & O'Hair, 1983). In communication research, Clark (1984; Clark &

Delia, 1979) has provided a widely used trifold taxonomy of interactants' objectives. Working from the interactionist view that language functions are not only culturally defined but emerge in response to situational demands, Clark and Delia (1979) identify three

> issues or objectives explicitly or implicitly present for overt or tacit negotiation in every communicative transaction: (1) overtly *instrumental* objectives, in which a response is required from one's listener(s) related to a specific obstacle or problem defining the task of the communicative situation, (2) *interpersonal* objectives, involving the establishment or maintenance of a relationship with the other(s), and (3) *identity* objectives, in which there is management of the communication situation to the end of presenting a desired self image for the speaker or maintaining a particular sense of self for the other(s). (p. 200, emphasis supplied)

Although all three types of objectives are present to some degree in every communication situation, Clark and Delia propose that within different types of situations "one objective may tend to dominate" (p. 200). Most of the research we review in this chapter focuses on situations in which actors' communication is strategically directed toward achieving *instrumental objectives*, especially inducing or persuading another to behaviorally comply with a specific recommendation or request. Britton (1971) has characterized the function of language in such situations as "conative": "The speaker's intention to change his listener's behavior, opinions or attitudes [is] deliberate and recognizable—recognizable, that is, to an observer even where it is so disguised as to deceive a victim to whom it is addressed" (p. 212). Britton identifies two subcategories of conative language in communication transactions: "regulative" and "persuasive."

> The regulative represents a direct exercise of influence, and it aims more often at affecting action or behavior than at changing attitudes, opinions or beliefs. It covers on one hand simple requests such as "Pass the mustard," and on the other, rules and instructions issued to those obliged to obey them, and recommendations that carry the weight of authority or the force of a speaker's wishes. ... Persuasive language is employed where no such expectation of compliance operates: usually because it is inappropriate, but sometimes in cases where the expectation has met disappointment, or the speaker has chosen not to invoke it although he might have done so. Here the speaker's will is, as it were, diverted into an effort to *work upon* the listener in support of the course of action he recommends, or (more typically perhaps) the opinion, attitude, belief he is putting forward. (pp. 217-218)

If our concern in this chapter is with regulative and persuasive communication in interpersonal situations involving—at least from the source's point of view—the accomplishment of instrumental objectives, one might justifiably ask: "What of the interpersonal and identity objectives which may be co-present in such interactions and which may affect actors' message selection and production?" In order to limit our review to the space allotted, we shall be concerned only with research indicating ways in which (adult) actors' strategies for managing identities and relationships in influence contexts *facilitate* the achievement of more prominent instrumental goals. Therefore we will not survey literature revealing the specific tactics individuals use to display self-concepts and the many ways in which they negotiate personal identities (cf. Alexander & Lauderdale, 1977; Baumeister, 1982; Blumstein, 1973; Cialdini & Richardson, 1980; Cooper & Jones, 1969; Felson, 1978; Goffman, 1959; Gove, Hughes, & Geerken, 1980; Schlenker, 1980; Swann & Hill, 1982; Tedeschi & Lindskold, 1976; Tedeschi & Reiss, 1981; Weary & Arkin, 1981; Weiler & Weinstein, 1972). Also, we will give only passing attention to research on primarily interpersonal objectives, such as investigations of relationship initiation, maintenance, and disengagement strategies (Ayres, 1983; Baxter, 1979, 1982, in press; Bell & Daly, 1984; Burleson, 1983; Cody, 1982; Falbo & Peplau, 1980; Goffman, 1971; Knapp, 1978; Roloff, 1976). And when we do treat these matters, it will be instances in which persons are concerned with identity and interpersonal objectives *in order to accomplish some instrumental objective.* We shall tentatively assume that these strategic considerations are more likely to modify selection of regulative and persuasive strategies than to obviate or completely determine them (Clark, 1984).

Our use of the term "strategies" invites clarification. *Strategies* are actors' intended lines of action and general choices in transforming plans into practice so as to accomplish particular goals. *Communication strategies* are anticipated and actual discourse patterns performed in the service of a personal or interpersonal agenda, and they subsume specific (often multiple) message *tactics* appropriate to the actor's goal(s) and line(s) of action. Communication strategies reflect the mental processes (for example inference patterns, schemas, and formulations of general presentational lines) and behavioral routines involved in actors' choices of situationally responsive, socioculturally appropriate, and linguistically competent messages to influence the outcomes of interactions in ways that satisfy identity and interpersonal or instrumental goals. In view of the multiple levels and multiple intentions of actors involved in coordinated symbolic interaction, it is possible to think of nearly all communication as strategic as communicators concomitantly seek, at least, to manage textual coherence, interactional efficiency, and face presentation and protection (O'Keefe & Delia, 1982; Weinstein, 1966). However, our review will be restricted to research on the regulative and persuasive strategies people purposely select or enact in interpersonal contexts characterized by obstacles to instrumental objectives.

It will be apparent from our treatment of investigations of compliance-gaining message selection and message strategy sequences (for example, foot-in-the-door, door-in-the face) that researchers in these areas promote a static, fixed, and overly rational conception of communicative strategies. They tacitly imply or methodologically require that actors engaged in instrumental influence attempts in interpersonal contexts—which usually are partly cooperative and partly competitive (Beisecker, 1970)—have

(1) conscious awareness of the influence "situation," including all embedded role relationships, salient sociocultural characteristics of the setting, and a clearly identifiable instrumental/interpersonal task;
(2) sufficient time to rationally assess the situation and consider options;
(3) the intention to formulate a plan designed to accomplish a well-defined outcome;
(4) a diverse, complex, and differentiated repertoire of strategies and tactics to draw upon;
(5) sufficient awareness and individual perspective-taking ability to weigh the consequences of enacting each strategic alternative; and
(6) an ability to choose some strategies and forego others (that is, all strategies considered acceptable are personally accessible and can be competently enacted, and some strategies—perhaps judged by the actors to be unacceptable or inappropriate under the circumstances—can be eschewed even when they may be habitual modes of response for that actor).

These conditions and choices might be taken as tenets of a source-oriented "Strategic Choice Model" that, we suggest, implicitly undergrids much of the research we will review concerned with persons' selection, construction, and/or enactment of the most optimal among communication strategies considered appropriate for achieving instrumental objectives. Although it is obvious that some of these are characteristic of routine influence attempts, it is equally apparent that this conception obscures and oversimplifies the interactional, adaptive, and partially nonreflective character of communicative influence strategies. We return to these limitations in the conclusion of the chapter, and to how some researchers who study communicative influence have attempted to surmount them.

Strategic, goal-oriented behavior requires consideration of the *outcome(s)* of the strategy enacted and evaluation of the extent to which the goal sought was achieved. Although some of the most central research on compliance-gaining strategies reports no message effects at all (Miller & Burgoon 1978; Wheeless, Barraclough, & Stewart, 1983), the range of message tactic-outcome linkages reported in the literature on communicative influence is extremely broad. In addition to diverse behavioral compliance measures (Cialdini, Cacioppo, Bassett, & Miller, 1978; Foss & Dempsey, 1979; Levine, Moss, Ramsey, & Fleishman, 1978), research in this domain has reported such disparate communicative influence outcomes as reduced aggressiveness (Paul & Thelen, 1983), altered level of performance (Kanouse et al., 1981), liking (McAllister & Bregman, 1983), stigma acceptance (Thompson & Seibold, 1978), oppositional behavior (Heilman, 1976), reciprocity (Hill & Stull, 1982; Jefferson, 1979), bargaining (Hornstein, 1965), attributed influence (Layton & Moehle, 1980), negative persuasion (Abelson & Miller, 1967), communication satisfaction (Cupach, 1982), attitude change (Eagly, 1974;

LaLumia & Baglan, 1981), intimacy (Berg & Archer, 1982), various forms of responsiveness (Davis, 1982), and helping (Enzle & Harvey, 1982). This range of influence findings is so broad as to make reliable summary claims about tactic-outcome linkages implausible without a framework for interpreting interpersonal influence (and without a coherent perspective on the "situations" generating these communication-influence linkages, as Cody & McLaughlin [this volume] point out). Our focus on investigations of compliance-gaining strategies, communicative influence, relational control messages, and the like enjoins us to consider the nature of these terms and the relationships among them.

The concept *influence* is scopic, and many definitions are overly general. For example, Parsons (1963) broadly termed influence as "ways of getting results in interaction" (p. 42), and Coleman (1963) offered an expansive view of influence as "all the means by which ego has an effect on alter without power or money" (p. 81). However, both correctly note its *mediating* character, for influence is neither a resource (as is power) nor an outcome (as is control). Even to say that someone has been "influenced" is to assert that a process has transpired rather than to describe the outcome of that process or its bases. We suggest that the term "interpersonal influence" signifies the process and paths by which individuals reinforce or alter each others' cognitions, emotions, and behaviors. Our much more restricted focus on regulative and persuasive communicative influence (as opposed to noncommunication influence processes such as modeling and coercion) represents an interest in the symbolic, discursive means by which agents affect one another's cognitions, emotions, and actions. Intentionality is not only an especially important defining characteristic of communicative influence as attempted, but is a key to understanding outcomes of the influence process. As Tedeschi and Bonoma (1972) summarize, "empirically it has been demonstrated that the attribution by W that P intends to influence him makes a considerable difference in the outcome of the interaction" (p. 3).

Bochner and Lenk Krueger (1979) distinguish five senses of the term *control* as used in the communication literature: (1) a general function of communication, (2) a function of individual behavior, (3) a personal need or motivation, (4) a characteristic of an interactional relationship, and (5) reduction of randomness by means of restraint. Although each of these is indicative of a desired or de facto goal state, Bochner and Lenk Krueger correctly note that these meanings "range from being clearly individualistic to being clearly relational" (p. 202). They propose that individuals' control-oriented maneuvers be conceptually distinguished from control patterns of interaction characterizing interdependent dyadic relationships. We concur and note that, although we will separately cover both sorts of literature, our overarching concern with the control-oriented communication strategies agents use to accomplish instrumental objectives will lead us to emphasize source-oriented research on individuals' regulative and persuasive linguistic tactics. For the same reason, the nature of the control-oriented outcomes sought usually involves subjects' real or imaginary attempts (1) to *change* rather than reinforce a target and (2) to induce or elicit a *behavioral* response, or compliance. Simply put, the goal in these hypothetical or actual influence situations is usually to communicatively induce change in the target so that his or her actions are different from what they would have been without the influence attempt and are consistent with the source's regulative wishes. Finally, although the types of behavioral compliance sought are varied, their cognitive and emotional bases seem to be taken for granted or viewed by researchers as uniform. They are "neither denied nor affirmed" (Wheeless et al., 1983, p. 111); much of the compliance-as-control literature we treat shares little overlap with traditional persuasion research concerned with underlying psychological processes revealing why people are affected (cf. McGuire, 1969; Miller, Burgoon, & Burgoon, 1984) and theoretically more enduring intrapersonal changes such as identification and internalization (Kelman, 1961, 1974).

Scope of Review

Our aim in this chapter is to review research literature on regulative and persuasive communication strategies in interpersonal contexts characterized by obstacles related to the achievement of instrumental objectives. The review is divided into three sections. In the first section we survey literature related to strategic message selection or construction, including (1) relatively atheoretical research on strategic-tactical preferences associated with various taxonomic classifications of compliance-gaining messages, (2) more theoretically motivated research on hierarchies of strategic communication in regulative contexts, and (3) more focused investigations of the communication strategies organizational superiors use to gain compliance from subordinates. Juxtaposed against the emphasis in all Part One sections on *single* message tactics, Part Two of the chapter examines *sequential* influence messages, especially research on foot-in-the-door and door-in-the-face strategies. More processual in nature, the sequential research tradition focuses on variables that enhance the likelihood of persons complying with subsequent messages. In Part Three we treat investigations of *interactive* control patterns in relational partners' communication, revealing the nature of influence embedded in the stream of dyadic interaction. Background, foci, methods, findings, and limitations of each line of research are discussed. We have tried to minimize redundancy with relevant literature reviewed in other chapters of this handbook, including research on nonverbal cues in influence attempts (Chapter 8), situational effects on strategy selection (Chapter 6), relational tactics (Chapter 15), interpersonal power (Chapter 10), interspeaker influence in the management of interaction (Chapter 9), and control theory and communication competence (Chapter 4). Also, although we recognize the extent to which interpersonal communication can neither be character-ized by relationship type nor setting but by the character of interactants' communication bonding (Bochner, 1984), the research reviewed investigates communicative influence in what we have broadly termed "interpersonal contexts." Hence, the studies surveyed report communication strategy choices and effects in real or imaginary dyadic exchanges between room-mates, neighbors, couples, salespersons/clients, managers/subordinates, and even strangers. We return to this issue in the conclusion of the chapter, to the relevance of studies we could not review due to space limitations, and to issues that invite attention in future research.

STRATEGIC-TACTICAL MESSAGES

Compliance-Gaining Strategies Research

Perhaps the most visible line of research on communicative influence in interpersonal contexts is that concerned with compliance-gaining message strategies and tactics. This is attributable in part to the sheer number of research reports in the area, but more fundamentally it is probably because this research fuses traditional persuasion concerns and newer interpersonal communication foci (Miller & Burgoon, 1978; Seibold & Thomas, 1981). Most studies in the area can be seen to follow from or respond to conceptual, empirical, and methodological issues in seminal work by Marwell and Schmitt (1967a, 1967b) or research by Miller, Boster, Roloff, and Seibold (1977) extending Marwell and Schmitt's studies into the field of communication. The more than 40 published studies and convention papers in this area since 1977 may be classified into four types of investigations: (1) studies of agents' perceptions of compliance-gaining situation dimensions and their relation-ship to strategic choices, (2) investigations of the effects of individual differ-ences on compliance-gaining strategy use, (3) efforts to develop and to test or apply systems for classifying compliance-gaining strategies and tactics, and (4) research on the utility of various methods employed to study compliance-gaining message choices. Before examining findings in each of these areas, we explicate the Marwell and Schmitt, and Miller et al. investigations as a backdrop for reviewing subsequent research trends and criticisms.

Background. Basing their analysis on the assumption that much of human behavior is directed toward inducing compliance in others, social psycholo-gists Gerald Marwell and David Schmitt were among the first researchers to move beyond studies of why people are persuaded or comply and to explicitly examine "techniques" persons use to gain others' compliance. In an often overlooked article (it is not even cited in Miller et al., 1977, or Wheeless et al., 1983), Marwell and Schmitt (1967a) used an exchange theory framework (Blau, 1964; Thibaut & Kelley, 1959) to formulate a synthetic model of "compliance-gaining behavior." The model incorporated considerations of actors' backgrounds, capabilities and repertoires of compliance-gaining behaviors, as well as the interpersonal situation and the nature of the interaction between agent and target. Marwell and Schmitt speculated that compliance-gaining behaviors might be able to be described

> in terms of *groups of techniques*, here called compliance-gaining *strategies*. We feel that many techniques may be somewhat interchangeable in terms of the kinds of responses they tend to elicit from targets, and that this similarity may serve as the basis for a category system. (p. 323; emphasis supplied)

Drawing upon "interpersonal control" exemplars from more general social influence literature (for example, Etzioni, 1961; French & Raven, 1960; Goffman, 1959; Skinner, 1953), Marwell and Schmitt offered a "synthesis" that included six "compliance-gaining strategies": physical force, aversive stimulation, punishment, reward, "pointing up reward contingencies," and "manipulating situational stimuli." They went on to describe behavioral "techniques" that agents might employ in enacting these strategies, including "murder," "fines," "feigned indifference," "bragging," and "advice" among many others. Although they viewed this list as "preliminary," they nonetheless felt it to be sufficiently exhaustive to claim that "most, if not all, actors will be able to use each strategy to at least some minimal degree" (p. 326).

In their more widely cited *Sociometry* article, Marwell and Schmitt (1967b) sought to *empirically* identify "clusters of compliance-gaining techniques that empirically covary through actors in terms of their perceived probability of enactment" (p. 351) and thus to derive *strategies*. Drawing on a wider set of power and influence writings in this article (for example, Kelman, 1961; Parsons, 1963; Weinstein & Deutschberger, 1963) to deductively derive potential compliance-gaining behaviors, Marwell and Schmitt asked subjects to indicate the likelihood they would use each of 16 representative techniques when presented with written scenarios of four short-term compliance situations involving instrumental objectives. Factor analysis of the data revealed that five dimensions—or "strategies"—of compliance-gaining behavior could be extracted: rewarding activity, punishing activity, expertise, activation of impersonal commitments, and activation of personal commitments. Eschewing any reference to strategies or techniques in the taxonomy proposed in their 1967a article (indeed neither article references the other) and noting that these factors closely paralleled the bases of power identified by French and Raven (1960), Marwell and Schmitt suggested that the observed differences in technique usage by their subjects reflected strategic differences and probably emanated from the interpersonal "power" the subjects believed they would have possessed in the four hypothetical situations.

Miller et al. (1977) seized upon the Marwell and Schmitt taxonomy of sixteen compliance-gaining techniques as an aid in conducting research on the first of a trifold research program directed toward (1) identifying, grouping, and classifying communication "control strategies available to potential persuaders," (2) studying the effects of situational differences on choice of control strategies, and (3) understanding the relationship between "individual differences of potential persuaders" and their choice of control strategies (1977, p. 38). One hundred and sixty-eight subjects were provided with lists of "sixteen strategies" identified by Marwell and Schmitt. Respondents were asked to rate on eight-interval Likert-type scales "How likely would you be to employ each of the following strategies?" in four hypothetical situations. The scenarios varied according to the extent to which they were "interpersonal"/"noninterpersonal" (Miller & Steinberg, 1975) in nature and whether the outcomes in each influence situation carried short-term or long-term consequences for the persuader/persuadee relationship depicted. According to Miller and Steinberg, noninterpersonal situations involve transactions in which an interactant's ability to make predictions about the probable outcomes of alternative message strategies are based only on sociological and cultural data about another, whereas interpersonal transactions proceed from more discriminating predictions about another's unique (psychological) characteristics and probable reactions to particular messages. Cluster analyses of the results revealed that strategy selection was highly situation bound and that no reliable smaller set of strategies could be obtained across situations to serve as a basis for a taxonomy of message strategies. Subjects' ratings suggested a general preference for socially acceptable, reward-oriented strategies in all situations, but considerable diversity in selection of other strategies was apparent across situations (for example, threat tactics in noninterpersonal situations, plus a greater variety in strategies used in those situations). The authors concluded with a call for more systematic analysis of situational contexts, investigations of the role of source characteristics in message selection, and studies of the effects of situation-by-person interactions on strategy choices.

Findings. The Miller et al. call for further investigations of situational and individual difference effects on message choices was heard and vigorously complied with by some communication researchers. Indeed, the preponderance of studies in the "compliance-gaining strategies" area falls into these two areas. Research in the first area, investigations of compliance-gaining *situations,* has taken two forms: (1) studies designed to recover the dimensional structure of interpersonal persuasion and compliance-gaining situations based on persons' perceptual evaluations of various influence or "interpersonal persuasion" situations and (2) research on situational and dimensional effects on message choices. Reports of the first type have found limited support for the *noninterpersonal-commitment to future interaction* and *interpersonal-no commitment to future interaction* types of situations used by Miller et al. (Kaminski, McDermott, & Boster, 1977), and consistent support for the *intimacy, resistance, personal benefits, relational consequences, dominance,* and *apprehension* dimensions of interpersonal persuasion situations (cf. Cody & McLaughlin, 1980; Cody, Woelfel, & Jordan, 1983), with some support for a *rights* dimension. Studies of the second sort, situational effects on compliance-gaining message choices, are many and varied (cf. Cody, McLaughlin, & Schneider, 1981; Fitzpatrick & Winke, 1979; Hunter & Boster 1978, 1979; Jackson & Backus, 1982; Kaminski et al., 1977; Lustig & King, 1980; McLaughlin & Cody, 1982; Miller et al., 1977; Roloff & Barnicott, 1978, 1979; Sillars, 1980; Williams & Boster, 1981). Findings from these and other studies linking situational effects with message choices are reviewed by Cody and McLaughlin (this volume), Wheeless et al. (1983, pp. 136-139), and Boster and Stiff (1984, pp. 540-541).

A second trend in research on compliance-gaining strategies is evident in the many studies of the relationship between *source characteristics* and strategy choice. Within this line of research, two individual difference variables, Machiavellianism (Christie & Geis, 1970) and dogmatism (Rokeach, 1960), have received particular attention. Kaminski et al. (1977) found that Machiavellian subjects were not significantly different from non-Machiavellian individuals in their message choices; both groups demonstrated a propensity to select pro-social tactics. Boster and Hunter (1978) obtained a significant relationship between Machiavellianism and compliance-gaining use ratings, but the correlation was not strong (r = .22). Roloff and Barnicott (1978) also reported a significant but moderate relationship between the trait and message selection. Specifically, Machiavellianism was positively associated with the use of pro-social and psychological force techniques (correlations were .21 and .34, respectively) and the use of a greater number of tactics in interpersonal situations. Based in a category scheme developed by Roloff (1976), pro-social strategies seek to obtain relational and instrumental rewards by revealing information about the source's position and attitudes, whereas antisocial strategies pursue such rewards through force or deception. Roloff and Barnicott (1979) used a similar design to examine the association between dogmatism and selection of message tactics. As with Machiavellianism, dogmatism was significantly but moderately correlated with the average use of pro-social compliance-gaining techniques (r = .29) and two antisocial techniques (r = .22 with psychological force techniques, and r = .19 with punishing activity techniques). High dogmatics also demonstrated a greater range of technique usage than low dogmatics in both long- and short-term consequences situations. Several of these conclusions are qualified by the results of Williams and Boster's (1981) study. First, reanalysis of the Roloff and Barnicott data produced a mean correlation of .23 between dogmatism and compliance-gaining message selection; and Williams and Boster's own data in that study resulted in a correlation of .27 between dogmatism and message choice (.35 when corrected for attenuation due to error of measurement). Second, after incorporating into their research design measures of many of the variables explored to that point in compliance-gaining research, Williams and Boster concluded that the individual difference variables (negativism, perceived benefit to listener, and dogmatism) had a substantial impact on message choices (r = .45; .53 when corrected for attenuation due to measurement error), whereas Machiavellianism was an "experimental dead-end." Also, their findings concerning the effects of subjects' communication apprehension supported Lustig and King's report of "the absence of significant differences in the likelihood of strategy use between high and low communication apprehensives and the nonsignificant interaction between level of communication apprehension and situation" (1980, p. 81). Unfortunately, neither study provided potentially "apprehensive" subjects with the noninteractive and noncommunicative strategy choices they might normally employ (for example, withdrawal or silence), a limitation that may have affected the outcomes.

In the other studies of individual differences and strategy use, those focusing on sources' sex differences, Luloffs (1982) found some evidence of sex differences in choice of message strategies. Males relied more on threats in seeking compliance from male friends; females were more likely to rely on negative self-feeling and altercasting in interacting with male and female friends respectively in one hypothetical situation involving an instrumental objective. DeTurck and Miller (1982) also found that males and females differed in their reported likelihood of use of four of ten Marwell and Schmitt techniques considered by the researchers to be relevant for securing compliance from classmates in a hypothetical class project. Females were more likely to choose positive and negative expertise appeals, whereas males relied on promises and threats significantly more than females. Significant birth order by sex interactions, however, revealed that first-born males were much more likely to choose promise, threat, and altercasting than first-born females and later-born males and females. Fitzpatrick and Winke (1979) found "no significant differences in conflict strategies adopted by males and females with their opposite sex friends" (p. 10) but noted that

> a number of significant differences did emerge, however, in male and female same sex friendships. Males reported that they were more likely to exercise non-negotiation strategies with their best friend. Females indicated that they attempted to induce compliance in a friend by the strategies of personal rejection, empathic understanding or emotional appeals. (pp. 10-11)

The fact that the Fitzpatrick and Winke data concerning strategies for resolving "closest friend" conflicts are not directly comparable to the Marwell and Schmitt strategies, and are summed across subject responses to 44 different situations involving only relational objectives in some cases and instrumental objectives in others, precludes direct comparison with other research findings concerning sex differences and message selection. In one of the only studies linking specific strategies with estimates of compliance, Bradac, Schneider, Hemphill, and Tardy (1980) report interesting sex differences in perceptions of the efficacy of strategy use by males and females in a hypothetical initial heterosexual encounter. Male and female subjects agreed that an ingratiating strategy was more likely to produce compliance than an expertise strategy, and it was more directly associated with perceptions of communicator friendliness. Use of an expertise strategy was associated directly with judgments of contentiousness; when employed by a male using high-intensity language female subjects considered it relatively low in competence. Dissimilar judgments were obtained in males' and females' assessments of the dominance, dramaticness, and friendliness of agents attempting to secure compliance depending on whether these agents were males or females. However, the authors' examination of only two tactics from the Marwell and Schmitt list of techniques and the nature of the data (perceived efficacy of hypothetical males' and females' choices) precludes synthesis with other research.

Criticisms. The aforementioned investigations of situational and individual effects on instrumental message selection have been explicitly or implicitly tied to two more fundamental thrusts in compliance-gaining message choice research: taxonomic classification of message strategies and tactics, and methodological procedures for studying strategic message choices. Both of these lines of research have developed in response to internal and outside criticisms, and we shall attempt to capture that dialectical character as we review each in turn.

From even our brief recapitulation of the Marwell and Schmitt efforts at conceptual and empirical *taxonomic classification* of compliance-gaining strategies, it is apparent that their goals, approach, and results could not have provided the most productive leads for communication researchers. First, these social psychologists were basically concerned with (1) "variables which differentiate among individuals with regard to the compliance-gaining techniques they use" (1967a, pp. 318-319) and (2) "mapping . . . any individual's behavioral repertoire" and determining whether particular actors even possess "a particular technique" (pp. 322-323). They were only incidently interested in actors' preferences for communication-related strategies, the bases for their selection of one strategic tactic over another (they regarded "techniques" related to the same strategy as "interchangeable in terms of the kinds of responses they elicit from targets" [1967a, p. 323]), or variations in tactic-compliance linkages. Second, it is significant for our purposes that the taxonomy of strategies and techniques developed in their conceptual synthesis (Marwell & Schmitt, 1967a) lists many "techniques" used to enact various strategies that do not even necessitate communication, including "murder," "physical restraint," "confinement," "torture," "fines," "boycotts," "sabotage," "feigned indifference," and "proper dress" among others (see p. 324). Even the 16 "techniques" used for research purposes by Marwell and Schmitt (1967b) included compliance-gaining behaviors not inherently tied to communicative influence (for example, "Liking": "Actor is *friendly* and *helpful* to get target in 'good frame of mind' so that he will comply with request," p. 357, emphasis supplied). Being "friendly" and "helpful" need not even entail language use, central to the type of communicative influence at issue here and in all the studies reviewed thus far. Some techniques were ambiguously and only generically linked to one of many communicative forms (for example, "Aversive stimulation": "Actor continuously punishes target making cessation contingent on compliance," p. 357). In short, the strategies and the tactics in both of the Marwell and Schmitt articles do not necessarily require communication for their enactment in many cases or, when they do, are cast at such a general level of abstraction that they provide little indication of how they would be implemented in discourse and obscure potentially important variations in their enactment (for example, expressions of interest versus ingratiation as communicative manifestations of the "liking" technique). Third, because Marwell and Schmitt felt that "the number of more or less discrete techniques at actors' disposal is enormous" (1967a, p. 322), their perspective from the outset was reductionistic; that is, they were seeking theoretically common and empirically covarying "strategies," reflecting "clusters" or "groups" of "interchangeable" techniques. They were indifferent to actors' multiple goals, to important variations in influence settings, to the character of role relationships involved between targets and actors, and to differences in the nature of compliance outcomes sought. Fourth, Marwell and Schmitt only heuristically derived their conceptual taxonomy (1967a), as well as the "sixteen compliance-gaining techniques" (1967b) employed to generate an empirically grounded strategy taxonomy, from the varied works of Parsons, Kelman, Blau, Thibaut and Kelley, Goffman, Weinstein and Deutschberger, and others. Three limitations resulted. First, although the compliance-gaining techniques culled this way may individually have been grounded in particular, even powerful theoretical perspectives, there is very little theoretical coherence among the strategies (1967a) and techniques (1967b) conjoined by Marwell and Schmitt. Second, probably because most of the writings draw upon emphasized personal power and social influence rather than interpersonal relationships or tasks and communicative influence, it should not be surprising that Marwell and Schmitt found the French and Raven (1960) "five bases of social power" to be the best conceptual framework for interpreting factor analytic results of subjects' responses to these power-based techniques. Third, also owing to the heuristic means by which the Marwell and Schmitt taxonomy was generated, its exhaustiveness and the exclusivity of its constituent techniques invited criticisms. These problems surrounding the Marwell and Schmitt taxonomy have often been compounded in subsequent research by communication researchers, or they have been recognized and responded to by other researchers. In some cases even the corrective efforts have further complicated the problems, as we will try to point out.

Miller et al. (1977) recognized sample and data analytic problems, and even the possibility that the nontheoretical basis for selection of the four persuasive "situations" in Marwell and Schmitt (1967b) affected the results obtained. Unfortunately Miller et al. never explicitly recognized the same theoretical limitation in the list of "sixteen compliance-gaining techniques" they adopted as empirical stimuli in their own research. The effects this had on subsequent communication research were compounded in four other ways. First, like Marwell and Schmitt they continued to ignore whether these techniques and strategies were, in reality, linked to compliant *outcomes.* Although Marwell and Schmitt (1967a) may have been justified in assuming that many of the noncommunication techniques we alluded to (torture, bribes, fines, and so forth) would induce compliance, it is not as clear that the "sixteen techniques" (1967b) used by Miller et al. (1977) would be as reliably effective for other outcomes sought. However, we agree with Boster, Stiff, and Reynolds (1983) that critics voicing concerns over the absence of behavioral effects have failed to deal with the very real perceptual level findings obtained in compliance-gaining message studies:

> If it is the case that Ss select compliance-gaining messages based on their *perception* of how effective that message [sic] will be in modifying attitudes and/or behavior, then regardless of how one feels about the results, one is compelled to attempt to incorporate that piece of information into persuasion theory. (p. 7)

Second, because Miller et al. relied upon a taxonomy that lacked theoretical integration, they were forced to interpret their own results in terms of the only factor they had manipulated: nature of situation. Not only did this engender a line of criticism about limitations of the interpersonal/noninterpersonal relationship distinction undergirding their conceptualization of "situation" (cf. Bochner, 1978) and further research about its cross-classification with short-term/long-term relational consequences (Kaminski et al., 1977), but it either spawned or served as a counterpoint to much of the research cited above on "situational dimensions" and "situational effects on message choices" that is reviewed by Cody and McLaughlin (this volume), themselves prominent critics of Miller et al. on this count. Third, Miller et al. obscured the very clear distinction that Marwell and Schmitt had made between compliance-gaining *techniques* ("specific behavior sequences by which the actor tries to elicit desired responses from the target person," 1967a, p. 322) and *strategies* ("a group of techniques towards which potential actors tend to respond similarly," 1967b, p. 351). At one point in their article, Miller et al. correctly refer to the "16 compliance-gaining techniques listed earlier in Table 1" (p. 44), but throughout most of the report they persistently and incorrectly allude to Marwell and Schmitt's (1967b) "list of sixteen compliance-gaining strategies." Finally, and perhaps most unfortunately, Miller et al. (1977) tacitly continued Marwell and Schmitt's reductionism in setting for themselves a "major goal" of developing "a smaller, more abstract typology of compliance-gaining strategies which could be employed by persuasion researchers and which could replace the rather cumbersome set of sixteen strategies developed by Marwell and Schmitt" (p. 48).

These limitations serve as a touchstone or, in many cases, the raison d'etre for ensuing research efforts to develop and to test or apply systems for classifying compliance-gaining strategies and tactics. For example, although some researchers have correctly maintained the distinction between compliance-gaining behavioral techniques and overarching strategies (for example, Roloff & Barnicott, 1978, 1979), probably because of the Miller et al. obfuscation, a good deal of pulp and print has gone to debate over the distinction (cf. Hazelton, Holdridge, & Liska, 1982; Hunter & Boster, 1978; Wheeless et al., 1983). More substantively, the intriguing but unpublished and much overlooked "empathy model" of message selection proposed by Hunter and Boster (Hunter & Boster, 1978, 1979, 1981) grew out of the authors' reanalysis of the Marwell and Schmitt (1967b), Miller et al. (1977), and Kaminski et al. (1977) data sets and their reinterpretation of bases for message choices implied or suggested in those investigations. Briefly, Hunter and Boster attempt to identify the psychological process that takes place when a persuader decides whether or not to use a given persuasive message. Particularly well suited for testing in the compliance-gaining area, in which respondents facing hypothetical situations are asked to rate the likelihood they would use each tactic in a preformulated list or to spontaneously generate and write out their own message choices, the Hunter and Boster empathy model (1978) assumes that

> the persuader evaluates each message by forecasting the probable emotional impact of the message on the listener (i.e., will the listener be pleased or hurt or enraged by the persuasive message in question?). If the perceived emotional impact of the message is more positive than an ethical threshold (which varies from person to person), then the persuader will use that message. If the perceived impact is less than the ethical threshold, than the persuader will reject that message. (p. 2)

Results reported by Hunter and Boster (1978, 1979, 1981) and by Williams and Boster (1981) have consistently supported the model.

Most of the research on taxonomic classification of communicative influence strategies and tactics has developed in response to limitations associated with the Marwell and Schmitt taxonomy, particularly reactions to its lack of exhaustiveness, the manner in which it was derived, and its lack of theoretical coherence. For example, concerned that Marwell and Schmitt's sixteen compliance-gaining techniques were generated only from sociology and organizational behavior literature, and that "there is no evidence that the

Marwell and Schmitt strategies are directly relevant to the interpersonal domain or that they are exhaustive of strategies relevant to interpersonal behaviors" (1980, p. 35), Cody, McLaughlin, and Jordan had students generate their own messages for three situations in an effort "to identify categories and dimensions of the strategies" (p. 36). The resultant typology included "direct-rational," "manipulation," "exchange," "threat," and "expertise claims" strategies. Results also revealed that 72 percent of the messages constructed in the first situation, 44 percent of the strategies obtained in the second situation, and 48 percent of strategies constructed for the third situation were "not incorporated in the Marwell and Schmitt typology" (pp. 43-44). Cody et al. (1980) concluded that there was "a need to go beyond the Marwell and Schmitt taxonomy [and] to formulate a more representative set of message strategies" (p. 45). They also recommended that researchers ought to take care to include representative examples from "the *direct-rational, exchange, manipulative, threat,* and/or *expertise claims categories*" so that subjects might have more "relevant modes of strategy choices" (p. 45) than those provided by the Marwell and Schmitt typology. Several investigators have taken up the challenge of their conclusion, but unfortunately few to date have explicitly accepted their recommendation.

A second line of research on taxonomic classification of persuasive messages—one that is relatively independent of Marwell and Schmitt's efforts (except to critique their research methods and the lack of theory and incompleteness of the "techniques" list)—is the work of Ruth Anne Clark. Because the theoretical tenets and findings of her studies have been more closely tied to constructivists' concerns, we will treat her research in the next section.

Perhaps the most ambitious attempt to generate a compliance-gaining message taxonomy that corrects for the nonexhaustive, deductively generated, and largely atheoretical nature of the Marwell and Schmitt typology is the research program of Schenck-Hamlin and Wiseman. Using data generated in a three-step inductive procedure (Schenck-Hamlin, Wiseman, & Georgacarakos, 1980, 1982), subjects personally constructed messages to three persuasive situations "with which they could most easily empathize" (p. 256). This approach yielded a 14-category taxonomy with "fairly high degrees of reliability and content validity" (p. 256) and a "high degree of representational validity" (Wiseman & Schenck-Hamlin, 1981, p. 251). Although nearly half of the categories overlap with the Marwell and Schmitt typology (especially the reward and punishment appeals), other strategies identified by Schenck-Hamlin et al. are different—notably the "argument strategies" of "direct request," "explanation," and "hinting." Their taxonomy shared much greater overlap with the independently derived but also inductively generated frameworks of Falbo (1977) and Cody et al. (1980). The researchers (Schenck-Hamlin, Georgacarakos, & Wiseman, 1982) also demonstrated through symbolic logic that all but one of the strategies ("deceit") could be derived through the use of four dyadic predicates (for example, Is intent evident? Is the strategy located in some sanction? Does the actor control that sanction?). As a result, their work possesses some degree of internal coherence and greater ecological validity than others' schemes. Nonetheless, in a particularly critical rejoinder Boster et al. (1983) found (1) Wiseman and Schenck-Hamlin's arguments for the "superiority of inductively-derived to deductively-derived lists of compliance gaining message strategies . . . to be less than compelling"; (2) "no support" for the argument that "responses to the Marwell and Schmitt list may be affected by a social desirability bias"; and most interestingly (3) "persons' responses to the inductively-derived Wiseman and Schenck-Hamlin strategies were exactly the same as those to the deductively-derived Marwell and Schmitt strategies" (p. 1). Other compelling research by Tracy, Craig, Smith, and Spisak (1984) indicated that the Wiseman and Schenck-Hamlin taxonomy could be utilized reliably, without great difficulty, and with only a few ambiguities to code messages produced in a set of "request"situations. However, the researchers also found that although the compliance-gaining approach embodied in the Wiseman and Schenck-Hamlin taxonomy provided a description of the discourse of requests that was "certainly informative," it was "far from complete" (p. 532) in accounting for content related to the felicity conditions of making a request and the "face wants" of both parties.

The fourth and final thrust in compliance-gaining messages research has been *methodological* in orientation. In addition to substantive critiques of data analytic and instrumentation procedures (cf. Hunter & Boster, 1978, 1979, 1981; Williams & Boster, 1981), one important criticism centers on design of typical compliance-gaining message studies. In particular, because researchers interested in the effects of situational differences on message choices rely on a single message example to operationalize each technique and/or on only a single situation description to characterize each theoretical situation, claims about situational efforts on strategy choices are confounded with characteristics of messages used to represent each strategy type and/or characteristics of the single situation described (Jackson & Jacobs, 1983). Indeed, in an investigation using multiple messages to operationalize all strategies, Jackson and Backus (1982) found little evidence of situational differences in strategy use so characteristic of earlier research in which "situation types or strategy types or both have been confounded with characteristics of individual messages chosen to represent types" (p. 478). As a result, state Jackson and Backus, "the apparent corroborations [of findings that situational variables have a systematic effect on persuasive message strategy preferences] are partly illusory [and] the findings have been substantially overinterpreted" (p. 478). They conclude that "the search for systematic relationships between situation and strategy has yielded nothing definite so far" (p. 478).

A second and more pronounced attack on the Marwell and Schmitt (1967b) and Miller et al. (1977) line of research stems from critics' concerns about the methods used for assessing respondents' message "use" or, more accurately, their message choices. Most of the research on compliance-gaining messages has used a checklist or message selection procedure. After reading each description of hypothetical situations calling for a communicative influence response, subjects occasionally are asked to select from among a list of provided strategies or tactics all those messages they think they would use and to identify all strategies in the checklist that they think they would not use. More frequently they are required to rate on quasi-interval scales the likelihood that they would use each strategy in the checklist (which, of course, lists all strategies/techniques in the typology). By and large the following criticisms of such "selectionist" methods come from "constructionists" (Seibold & Thomas, 1981)—investigators who believe in the comparative superiority of asking subjects to construct written statements (or oral reports if they are children) of what they would say in response to similar hypothetical situation descriptions.

Claims against the selection method are manifold. First, some writers have implied that (1) a checklist may inadequately represent the full range of strategic choices available to sample subjects; (2) strategies may be included that respondents will not judge as real or viable if they are unfamiliar with them when encountered on the checklist; and/or (3) differences among strategies preformulated by the researcher may not correspond to subjects' tactical differentiations. In addition to these threats to the internal validity of checklist-produced results, it has been suggested that message selection procedures yield results that are method bound. For example, it is proposed that the checklist method requires subjects to reflect on communicative choices in ways they ordinarily would not (Clark, 1979), yielding unreliable data (Delia, 1978) because individuals' "introspective access" (Nisbett & Wilson, 1977) to such information may be limited or incorrect. Also, socially undesirable strategies may be underrepresented in selection results (compared to findings with constructed messages), presumably because more socially desirable alternatives are simultaneously provided and available on checklists. Finally, if some subjects' preferred strategic messages are not among those available for selection on the checklist, then results may misrepresent predispositions toward strategy use insofar as they artificially inflate the "likelihood" ratings of less relevant or less preferred strategies. Third, constructionists contend that there is a lack of equivalence between the checklist and spontaneous elicitation methods, and that the two procedures are not reliable alternate forms for measuring strategic message propensities (cf. Burke, 1979; Burke & Clark, 1982; Clark, 1979; Cody et al., 1980). Finally, several researchers have questioned the relation between checklist questionnaire behavior and actual strategic interaction while simultaneously implying stronger external validity for the construction procedure: "By contrast [to the Miller et al. procedure] our methodological approach . . . places no arbitrary limit on the types or quality of strategies produced, and directs attention to the strategies subjects *actually produce* as opposed to those they think they might use" (O'Keefe & Delia, 1979, p. 240). Kline

(1981a) further speculates that the checklist method "may not accurately reflect the likelihood that subjects will use such strategies in real persuasive encounters" (p. 5), and Clark (1979) concludes that "having individuals compose messages rather than selecting strategies from a supplied list . . . yields results more nearly approximating those occurring in real persuasive encounters" (p. 273). None of these researchers demonstrate the connection between constructed messages and "real" persuasive behavior, or even the lack of the same between checklist responses and simulated or actual persuasive activity outside the questionnaire protocol. Moreover, methodological problems associated with the Clark (1979) and Burke and Clark (1982) studies limit even the claims that can be made about noncorrespondence between the selection and construction procedures for studying message choices (see Thomas & Seibold, 1982, pp. 5-8). In the only repeated-measures study in this area, Thomas and Seibold (1982) found that "the construction and selection methods yielded consistent findings concerning most frequently chosen strategies, even though the tactic-by-tactic comparison of the Clark forty-item typology resulted in agreement levels of only 60-70 percent in the two situations for which data was collected" (p. 28). Correspondence improved when subjects' "reported" analysis of strategies in their written statements was used as the basis of comparison rather than coders' interpretations of the constructed messages. Like other researchers (Boster et al., 1983; Tracy et al., 1984), however, Thomas and Seibold (1982) concluded by pointing out the two most serious methodological limitations in research on compliance-gaining messages:

> It would be difficult for any researcher in this area to argue that any method studied in the area is preferable to studying situated, interpersonal communicative influence between two persons. Too, in the absence of research demonstrating the relationship between any of these measures and verbal strategic interaction, it is misleading to consider current research in this area to be studies of strategy "use." Better, we think, that this genre of written- or rated-strategy studies be labeled investigations of compliance-gaining strategy "choices." (pp. 27-28)

Thomas and Seibold's call for analyses of situated interactions involving generation and use of compliance-gaining messages is compatible with assumptions and practices undergirding constructivists' research. Although the perspective has been couched in developmental/cognitive terms, constructivists have expended considerable energy investigating the instrumental, goal-oriented function of interpersonal communication. We turn to their theory and research now.

Constructivist Research on
Persuasive Strategies

Background. Drawing on Mead's symbolic interactionism, Werner's organismic-developmental theory, and especially Kelly's personal construct theory, Jesse Delia and colleagues have articulated a general "constructivist" framework for understanding human interaction. Although the underpinnings, tenets, and parameters of the well-developed constructivist perspective are too detailed to review here (see Delia, 1977, 1978; Delia, O'Keefe, & O'Keefe, 1982), central to this work is the understanding that

> human interaction is a process in which individual lines of action are coordinated through reciprocal recognition of communicative intent and in which actors are organized by communicative strategies; both the reciprocal recognition of communicative intent and the employment of communicative strategies depend centrally on the interpretive schemes interactants bring to bear on the world. (Delia et al., 1982, p. 151)

For the most part, constructivist research has been rooted in a listener-adaptation model of communicative development that proposes that the speaker's subjective knowledge of a listener undergirds the speaker's choice and production of messages adapted to the listener's perspective and needs (Delia & O'Keefe, 1979). Constructivists' theoretical and research emphases have been devoted to (1) understanding impression formation processes driving communicative adaptation, particularly the role of "interpersonal constructs" for structuring interpretations of others; (2) formulating a hierarchical coding approach to message analysis in which the "message strategy" is taken as the basic unit of analysis and ordering strategies in various ways, indicating the degree to which they "imply sensitivity to the perspectives of message recipients"; and (3) developing parallel coding hierarchies for analyzing agents' rationales for their message selections. Emphasis is placed on the "strategic repertoire" that interactants must develop "for translating perceptions and intentions into adapted communications" (O'Keefe & Delia, 1982, p. 35). For the most part, however, this strategic repertoire has been judged only in terms of how persons' underlying construct systems shape and direct "person-centered" messages. As Delia, Kline, and Burleson (1979) succinctly indicate:

> Since it is the impression one forms of another that serves as the basis for message formulation and adaptation, individuals who form more differentiated, stable, and psychologically-centered impressions tend to produce more listener-adapted messages. Thus the development of a complex system of constructs is a necessary prerequisite for the formulation of sensitively adapted messages. (p. 244)

Despite the theoretical elegance and power of this perspective and the consistency of empirical findings, the constructivist perspective has remained relatively self-entrenched. Except for research by Clark (1979), Burke & Clark (1982), and Clark & Delia (1977), little research in this line has been linked to compliance-gaining messages research reviewed in the previous section, despite the clear relevance of some experimental studies involving interpersonal persuasion and gaining compliance with a behavioral directive (for example, Delia et al., 1979; Kline, 1981a, 1981b; O'Keefe & Delia, 1979) and in face-to-face bargaining situations and naturally occurring contexts (cf. Applegate, 1980a, 1980b; Applegate & Delia, 1980; Applegate & Wheeler, 1981; Husband, 1981). This may be due to (1) the predominant concern in constructivists' research with the social cognitive bases of message production, (2) the emphasis on person-centered message strategies consistent with the listener-adapted model, (3) constructivists' focus on qualities of the messages speakers produce and little attention to the effectiveness of those communicative acts in inducing compliance and persuasion, and (4) the manner in which constructivist researchers themselves have eschewed connections with traditional compliance-gaining strategies research, except to offer critiques of its atheoretical basis, procedures, and interpretations of findings. At the same time, because constructivist coding systems have been so tied to theoretical assumptions about communicative competence in the settings studied, and because of absent data concerning the concurrent and representational validity of these codes, compliance-gaining strategies researchers have foolishly overlooked the predictive and convergent validity of constructivist findings and failed to consider their relevance (for example, Wheeler et al., 1978, p. 255; Wiseman & Schenck-Hamlin, 1981, p. 109).

Reconceptualization. Perhaps the greatest of these difficulties has been the foundation of constructivist research in a listener-adaptation model. In a particularly important article for its potential contribution to our understanding of the bases of communicative influence processes, O'Keefe and Delia (1982) acknowledged the "problematic" nature of listener-adaptation interpretations of findings. They propose that "this interpretation requires revision" (p. 37):

> There is reason to believe, we now think, that our understanding of person perception has been too much influenced by the prevailing general model of impression formation and that our analysis of message strategies has been too influenced by the legacy of the Piagetian emphasis on egocentrism-perspectivism. (p. 38)

Although much of their analysis is given to excoriating the listener-adaptation model and to considering "anew how it is that impressions are formed and the role of interpersonal constructs in that process" (p. 38), for our purposes an important aspect of O'Keefe and Delia's article is their outline of "an alternative view of the message production process based on analysis of the message producer's communicative intentions."

Messages are viewed as motivated by specific intentions, or sets of intentions, that may consciously or unconsciously shape message production. Although this is neither new nor novel, O'Keefe and Delia propose that "it is less common, however, to find theorists and researchers who analyze messages in terms of *the way behavior is organized to accomplish intentions*" (p.

48). Using findings from Clark and Delia's (1976) analysis of message strategies children spontaneously constructed when asked to make a request of a listener, O'Keefe and Delia offer a reconceptualization involving the embedded structural character of persuasive interactions characterized by competing agendas. They demonstrate how Clark and Delia's (1976) four message strategies can *functionally* be explained "as four alternative actions that form a set of generalized options for dealing with competing wants of persuader and persuadee" (p. 50). In a remark that might just as aptly be applied to the Strategic Choice Model identified in the Introduction, O'Keefe and Delia portray as "overly simplified" and "limiting" any model of message production in which "messages begin as packages of potential arguments and contents" and in which "message design is seen as the shaping of some preexisting message content *or the selection among alternative strategies to fit the requirements of a specific situation*" (p. 51, emphasis added). Rather, they conclude the following:

> Messages can be seen as the product of multiple communicative intentions and message design as the product of reconciling multiple objectives in performance. Thus message production can be seen as a multistage process in which (1) the objectives (or intentions) behind a message are generated; (2) if necessary, competing or inconsistent objectives are edited or reconciled through the selection of a message strategy; (3) message contents are selected to actualize the strategy, creating a potential message (which may, at this point be monitored and edited); and (4) the message is produced as verbal and nonverbal behavior. This model suggests that the primary processes in message design are the generation and reconciliation of message objectives. (p. 52)

Findings. Within the listener-adapted model, constructivist research has consistently demonstrated that individuals who form complex interpersonal impressions respond with a more diverse and well-developed repertoire of strategies. Although this relationship has been most dramatically demonstrated with regard to development of persuasive message production in children (Clark & Delia, 1977; Delia et al., 1979; Delia & Clark, 1977), it has also been shown to hold across the span of development from early childhood to adulthood (Applegate & Delia, 1980; O'Keefe & Delia, 1979). More germane for our purposes is constructivist research that attempts to identify enabling, mediating, and constraining factors in the message production process. For example, Clark (1979) investigated how instrumental and interpersonal objectives might influence persuader message choice. She found that the degree of "self-interest" of the communicator (instrumental objective) influenced the level and form of pressure of the message chosen and that the "desire for liking" (interpersonal objective) was reflected in both the variations in the form in which the pressure was expressed and in the use of strategies designed to preserve the relationship. In a related study, Burke and Clark (1982) developed an eight-level scoring system to investigate how the persuader's level of understanding of the listener might affect message selection. They concluded that "the degree of understanding of the views of others reflected in the rationale does measure an underlying level of ability to construct persuasive messages" (p. 445). Likewise, Kline (1981a, 1981b, 1981c, 1982) has consistently demonstrated that the persuader's recognition of face-relevant implications of the other is an important mediator in the production and use of persuasive messages. Finally, Applegate (1980a, 1980b) and Applegate and Delia (1980) studied whether degree of "person centeredness" affects message selection. They found that the more "person centered" individuals were also those who adapt more to the other's perspective by recognizing and reconciling obstacles and conflicting intentions.

These findings confirm the existence of multiple goals, obstacles, and intentions in any influence attempt. Recently O'Keefe and Delia (1982) addressed that issue and offered a reinterpretation of "what it is [that] our message and rationale coding systems index" (p. 38). This reinterpretation emphasizes the multiple objectives, multifunctionality, and message complexity in communicative influence situations in ways that other researchers interested in message strategies and tactics have barely considered and rarely investigated. For example, O'Keefe and Delia suggest that the essential features of messages involving unusual or large requests (Applegate & Wheeler, 1981; Clark & Delia, 1976; Delia & Clark, 1977; Delia et al., 1979; O'Keefe & Delia, 1979), parents' construction of strategies for dealing with children who behaved badly (Applegate & Delia, 1980), mothers', childrens', and college students' message strategies for dealing with hurt feelings or conflicts (Applegate & Delia, 1980; Burleson, 1984a, in press; Husband, 1981), and students' or managers' messages for dealing with "problem" group members (Kline, 1981a, 1981b, Husband, 1981) detected in constructivist coding schemes are (1) speakers' recognition of obstacles to their dominant objective and their possession of multiple aims, and (2) the reconciliation of primary aims with perceived obstacles and with subsidiary aims. O'Keefe and Delia plausibly demonstrate how Applegate's (1980a, 1980b) message analysis coding categories "reflect variations in attempts to accomplish multiple aims in messages (p. 58) and how his categories for coding strategy justifications imply "recognition and reconciliation of obstacles and subsidiary intentions with primary aims" (p. 59). Similarly, Kline's (1981a, 1981b, 1981c, 1982) systems for analyzing face support in persuasive situations are found to exemplify "the relationship between dominant intentions and tacit subsidiary intentions in the organization of messages" (p. 61). Finally, quantitative analyses of the number of message units (appeals, arguments, and so forth) respondents produce are shown to reflect "the number of objectives addressed" (p. 61).

This alternative constructivist conception of the message production process offers a significant theoretical move for the study of interpersonal influence in general. Albeit tentative and untested, if supported by future research it will provide a seemingly more realistic and complex picture of the interpersonal influence process. The emphasis on multiple objectives, multi-functionality, and message complexity suggested in this reconceptualization has the potential to free thinking currently bounded by the assumptions of the Strategic Choice Model and to provide the impetus for more creative and powerful research endeavors. Such creativity and power are surely needed in most interpersonal influence research attempts. But the grip of the Strategic Choice Model is at its strongest in the research we review next on interpersonal influence in the organization. Still, a focus on interpersonal influence in the business setting offers perhaps the best example of how previous compliance-gaining research can be shown to have a counterpart in organizational life, especially in the tactics supervisors use to gain subordinates' compliance.

Managerial Influence Tactics

Interpersonal influence is a fundamental characteristic of organizational life. It figures prominently in the coordination of work units, the motivation of subordinates, and the control of decision-making premises and resources. More specifically, the exercise of influence is basic to organizational management and serves both managers' and the organization's goals. As Kipnis, Schmidt, Swaffin-Smith, and Wilkinson (1984) state:

> Sometimes influence is used for such personal reasons as securing personal benefits. . . . Most often, however it is used in the course of performing organizational roles that require influencing others—for example, to encourage others to perform effectively, to promote new ideas, or to introduce new work procedures. Frequently, a combination of personal and organizational reasons underlie the exercise of influence. (pp. 58-59)

To fully understand interpersonal influence in the organization, one must understand it fundamentally as a communicative activity. As Waltar (1966) emphasizes:

> To study influence, one must first study communication, for influence without communication is as wildly implausible as action at a distance. Influence is always accompanied by some form of communication, blunt or subtle, overt or tacit. (p. 190)

However, research that directly addresses questions about communication and interpersonal influence in organizational contexts is scarce. Kipnis et al. (1984) state that "despite the fact that the essence of managerial work is the exercise of influence, there is a paucity of systematic research on the ways in which managers attempt to change the behavior of others" (p. 59). Because research examining the communicative nature of managerial influence is so relevant to this review, we will take a broader perspective than in previous sections by first examining research on the *antecedent factors* that condition managerial influence attempts, then reviewing research on how managers translate these factors into actual *communicative influence strategies,* and finally addressing the question of strategic influence *effects.*

Antecedent Factors. Much of the research on factors conditioning managerial influence is concerned with delineating characteristics of the influencer, especially an agent's individual power. Power is typically defined as "the potential for influence" and is thought to precede and condition influence attempts (Emerson, 1962; Manz & Gioia, 1983; Mechanic, 1962). Much power research is based upon French and Raven's (1960) now classic study of the five bases of influencer power: reward, coercive, legitimate, expert, and referent power. It is generally agreed that possession of one or more of these power bases enhances a superior's influence ability. For example, Bachman, Bowers, and Marcus (1968) found that subordinates were more likely to report compliance with a supervisor's request when he or she possessed legitimate or expert power. Similarly, Patchen (1973) discovered that supervisor expert and legitimate power were common in the organization he studied. One of the few consistent findings in this area seems to be that coercion is the least effective form of power. Greenberg and Leventhal (1976) found that college students acting as managers were hesitant to use any type of punitive strategy even with "lazy" subordinates and were inclined to use rewards or even overrewards whenever possible. Moreover, Tedeschi, Gaes, and Rivera (1977) suggest that superiors who possess coercive power use it only as a mode of last resort. They further assert that "if one were to count the various incidents of influence employed by persons in their everyday lives, coercion would probaby constitute a low percentage of the total" (p. 104), a position consistent with a fundamental tenet of the empathy model developed by Hunter and Boster (1978, 1979, 1981) and reviewed earlier.

Related to research that examines influencer power characteristics is organizational leadership research. As Zalesnik and Kets de Vries (1975) state, "leadership is the exercise of power" (p. 3). In essence, leadership research asks how one's "legitimate" power conditions influence attempts. Because of the vast quantity of leadership research and the existence of several comprehensive reviews of this research (see Hare, 1976; Jablin, 1979; Stogdill, 1974; Yukl, 1981), it will not be reviewed here. Yet it should be noted that the quantity of research in this area provides a clear indication of the importance researchers and managers place on "position" as an antecedent factor to successful influence. Recently, Rubin and Berlew (1984) chastised both researchers and organizational managers for relying too heavily on the rational, "position-centered" bases of influence and urged investigation of other determinants of influence.

Other research on antecedent influencer characteristics has investigated the importance of managers' independence or lack of dependence on others (Emerson, 1962; Mechanic, 1962), ability to cope with uncertainty in the organization (Hickson, Hinings, Lee, Schneck, & Pennings, 1971; Salancik & Pfeffer, 1977), ability to mobilize resources (Kanter, 1977; Kotter, 1979; Parsons, 1956), and nonsubstitutability in the organization (Hrebiniak, 1978). Taken together, this body of research on antecedent influencer characteristics provides evidence that possession of "organizational power" in any of its various forms enhances managerial interpersonal influence potential.

A second factor conditioning communicative influence is superiors' perceptions of influencee characteristics. Managerial expectations about a subordinate affect the superior's choice of influence mode. Research has shown that superiors eschew negative influence tactics that may destroy or erode the superior-subordinate relationship when they perceive their subordinates to be excellent and compliant workers, to hold favorable attitudes toward work, to be somewhat ingratiating, to have similar goals, to be trustworthy, and to be generally likable (Goodstadt & Hjelle, 1973; Goodstadt & Kipnis, 1970; Greenberg & Leventhal, 1976; Kipnis, 1974; Kipnis & Cosentino, 1969; Michener, Fleishman, Elliott, & Skolnick, 1978; Michener & Schwertfeger, 1972; Riccillo & Trenholm, 1983; Tjosvold, 1984). Instead, they use positive, reward-oriented, cooperative strategies in an endeavor to achieve instrumental goals while preserving the relationships with subordinates. Recent research on vertical dyad linkages in organizations indicates how supervisors use perceptions about subordinates to develop one of two types of influence relationships: (1) a leadership exchange that involves influence without resort to authority or (2) an exchange that always references authority in the influence transaction (Cashman, Dansereau, Graen, & Haga, 1976; Dansereau, Graen, & Haga, 1975; Graen, Cashman, Ginsburgh, & Schiemann, 1977). This dichotomous interaction structure results in subordinate in-members and out-members. In-members receive more inside information, more chance to influence decisions, more attention and support, and higher performance ratings. Out-members are often blocked from pertinent information and special favors and are more often subjected to influence by authority or coercion.

Two other antecedent factors deserve mention as potentially important influencing elements. First, studies indicate that the more serious the problem or the more programmed the task, the more superiors resort to authority-based influence tactics (Kipnis & Cosentino, 1969; Waltar, 1966). Second, Cheng (1983) investigated the influence of context on individuals' use of tactics in dealing with work-related matters. Using Kipnis, Schmidt, and Wilkinson's (1980) version of rational strategies (strategies that are organizationally sanctioned and directed toward attainment of organizational goals) and political strategies (strategies not organizationally sanctioned and directed toward personal gains), he found that subjects presented with a description of a "rational" organization chose rational (explanation) strategies as appropriate to that context. Similarly, when subjects were presented with a description of a political organization, they more often chose political strategies (ingratiation, threat, and blocking). Although much additional research is required to draw any substantive conclusions about the effects of task or context from this limited research, the potential for impact seems evident and deserves further amplification.

Three conclusions seem warranted about factors antecedent to supervisory influence. First, both influencer and influencee characteristics impact upon a manager's choice of influence strategy. Second, this impact takes shape in at least three ways: (1) the greater an influencer's power, the greater his or her ability to influence; (2) despite a manager's power potential, a bias toward utilization of positive influence strategies exists; and (3) a positive relationship exists between the superior's perception of the subordinate and utilization of positive influence strategies. Third, the impact of task and context on strategy choice is potentially important but requires additional research before substantive conclusions are warranted.

Communicative Influence. Knowing that certain antecedent factors affect the choice of *general types* of influence strategies tells us little about *specific communicative strategies*. That specificity is required if determination of types and effectiveness of influence strategies is a goal. Riccillo and Trenholm (1983) state:

> One of the most important decisions a manager must make in organizations today is that of determining effective communication strategies to influence subordinates. Notwithstanding Etzioni's finding that organizations like to specialize in certain modes of influence, managers differ in preferred style of leadership and power preference. Subordinates respond differently to different types of managerial influence and have definite preferences for certain forms of influence over others. (p. 323)

Writings on the communicative nature of organizational interpersonal influence take two forms: (1) speculation by armchair theoreticians about the *typical* strands of communication influence strategies that occur in organizations and (2) discovery and verification by empirical researchers of the *actual* types of communication strategies that occur in organizations. The first area offers interesting and intuitively appealing insights and often provides direction for later empirical analysis. In general, these writings suggest that those who are interpersonally influential use strategies such as obtaining valuable information, establishing favorable relationships with important people, being visible, building a credible and professional reputation, creating perceived dependence, manipulating the environment, listening to and trying to understand subordinates, and judiciously applying reinforcements, among others (Izraeli, 1975; Kanter, 1977; Kotter, 1977, 1979; Tedeschi et al., 1977; Tjosvold, 1983).

Researchers have begun to empirically examine interpersonal influence in the organization at the communicative level. Although still underdeveloped, this research seeks to answer the question, "How is organizational interpersonal influence mediated through *communication?*" Kipnis et al. (1980) addressed this issue by asking managers to provide written descriptions of their influence attempts with superiors, peers, and subordinates. Factor analysis of 58 distinct influence strategies produced eight factors variously labeled *assertiveness* (demanding, ordering), *ingratiation* (making others feel important, humbling oneself), *rationality* (explaining reasons), *sanctions* (administrative punishment such as preventing salary increases), *exchange of benefits* (offering an exchange of favors), *upward appeal* (invoking the influence of higher levels), *blocking* (threaten to stop working), and *coalitions* (obtain support of coworkers). They found that these strategies were differentially related to the goals of the influencer and the status of the target. The higher the status, the more reliance on rational tactics; the lower the status, the greater the use of assertiveness and sanctions. Assertiveness was used more often when the goal was to improve performance or assign work, and ingratiation was used more often when seeking personal assistance. The influence strategies reported by Kipnis et al. (1980) have been used in other research. Specifically, Rim and Erez (1980) and Erez and Rim (1982) found that different strategies were used when influencing one's boss (greater use of rational strategies) than one's subordinates (clandestine, exchange, or administrative sanctions were most often used). Recently, Kipnis et al. (1984) used a similar technique of written descriptions and factor analysis to study interpersonal influence strategies of managers from three countries: America, England, and Australia. They discovered seven potential influence dimensions: *reason, friendliness, coalition, bargaining, assertiveness, higher authority,* and *sanctions.* There was no significant variation in the use of strategies across managers. However, managers reported greater use of the strategy types "reason," "coalition," or "bargaining" when influencing superiors and use of "reason" or "assertiveness" when influencing subordinates. Kipnis et al. (1984) concluded that the selection of influence strategies is based on three factors: (1) the manager's power (the more powerful, the greater variety of strategies and stronger strategies utilized); (2) the manager's objectives (in seeking benefits, friendliness was most often used; in persuading another to accept a new idea, reason was used); and (3) the manager's expectation of success (if success of influence seemed unlikely, more assertiveness and sanctions were utilized). Finally, Riccillo and Trenholm (1983) posited three broad types of influence strategies: coercion, reward, and persuasion (rational reason). Hypothesizing that "trust" of subordinates would influence managerial choice of strategy, their research design included writing communicative transformations reflecting the three broad influence categories. They wrote two scenarios, one involving trusted (internally motivated) subordinates and a second involving distrusted (externally motivated) subordinates, and asked managers to choose the type of strategy they would use in each case. As predicted, managers chose persuasion more often in the "trusted" workers' scenario and coercion more often in the "distrusted" workers' scenario.

Outcomes. Research on the *effects* or consequences of communicative interpersonal influence is virtually nonexistent. Some indirect knowledge about potential effects can be gleaned from research on leadership. Much of the leadership research investigated leader effects on subordinate performance, motivation, and satisfaction (see Fleishman, 1973, for a thorough review of this literature). This research generally concluded that leader "consideration" (socioemotional skills, friendliness, openness, and so forth) leads to greater subordinate satisfaction, and that the interaction of leader "consideration" and "structure" (skills used to achieve organizational goals) motivate subordinate performance (Burke & Wilcox, 1969; Greene, 1975; Jablin, 1979; Nealey & Fiedler, 1968). Similarly, rewarding strategies and strategies based on expertise have a more positive correlation with subordinate satisfaction and motivation, whereas punishing or coercive strategies have a high negative correlation with satisfaction and desire to work (Bachman et al., 1968; Herold, 1977; Oldham, 1976). Reports of these general effects indicate the potential for specific influence strategies to generate a variety of effects as well. Until the exact nature of the effects of communication influence attempts on both the influencer and influencee are systematically studied, we are left to speculate from this indirectly related research.

Critique. Although many insights can be gleaned from research on interpersonal influence in the organization, the potential of this research has remained unfulfilled. Five of the most serious problems are the following. First, the separate bodies of research on interpersonal influence antecedents, processes, and outcomes must be wedded if a complete picture of interpersonal influence in the organization is desired. Recent methodological approaches that allow the researcher to model complex phenomena (for example, structural equation modeling) may provide part of the answer to understanding the relationships among antecedent, process, and outcome factors. Research on organizational interpersonal influence is theoretically sterile, but conscious attempts by researchers to build upon past research in present conceptualizations may alleviate that problem.

Second, research in this area is overly concerned with the manager-subordinate relationship. If a complete picture of organizational interpersonal influence is to be achieved, other interpersonal influence relationships must be examined. For example, much influence probably occurs *between* managers or *between* subordinates. Similarly, interpersonal influence likely occurs between organizations via boundary personnel or salespeople. Many organizations include influence episodes between workers and clients—doctor/patient, salesperson/customer, bank teller/patron, lawyer/client, and so forth. The almost exclusive focus on the manager-subordinate influence relationship in the past has blinded researchers to other potentially important interpersonal influence relationship arenas.

Third, researchers have adopted a "rational" and "unidirectional" model of influence in which interpersonal influence is conceived as an intentional act by one person performed on another individual. As with the Strategic Choice Model implicit in the compliance-gaining strategies research, the assumption is that individuals carefully consider various influence strategies, choose the best strategy with the fewest repercussions, and use it receiving no reciprocal influence. Consider alternate scenarios: (1) Managers do not always plan ahead, but may act on impulse with subordinates; (2) managers may not have a broad repertoire of influence strategies from which to choose, but habitually use the same strategy until it fails to work before resorting to something different; (3) managers are more influenced in the superior-subordinate influence attempt than the worker. By studying interpersonal influence in the organization as rational and recursively causal, these ways of viewing influence are never explored.

Fourth, most research on interpersonal influence in organizations focuses exclusively upon *direct* influence strategies. The model generally involves an agent stating directly what he or she wants the target to do and what the consequences will be if he or she fails to comply. Evidence we have reviewed suggests that is not the only type of influence that occurs or even the most prevalent. Individuals may use *indirect* strategies as modes of influence. For example, increased self-disclosure with another individual may create a relationship in which the other person will feel guilty denying requests. Managing one's impression via compliments and positive statements directed toward the other may help establish a favorable perception that will provide greater influence. Or having a third person (friend) intercede on one's behalf without the superior knowing he or she is being targeted may be more influential than a direct request. Research that studies only direct influence strategies fails to capture these more indirect techniques.

Finally, the study of communicative influence *effects* must receive more attention. Until we begin to examine outcomes in accordance with antecedents and strategies, we cannot make theoretically and pragmatically vital claims about interpersonal influence effectiveness or success.

To this point in the chapter we have surveyed predominant research on actors' use of strategic-tactical language to secure a variety of objectives. However, the focus of this research has been fairly static in nature; studies have focused on the construction, choice, or presentation of *single* messages in isolation and apart from ongoing interaction. In Part Two of the chapter we examine the more processually oriented use of *sequential* communicative influence in interpersonal contexts.

SEQUENTIAL INFLUENCE TECHNIQUES

Interpersonal influence often proceeds in stages, each of which establishes the foundation for further changes in beliefs or behavior. Individuals slowly come to embrace new opinions, and actors often seduce others to gradually comply with target requests. Although they acknowledge that influence can occur quite dramatically, Miller and Burgoon's (1978) expanded view of persuasion suggests that interpersonal influence is generally a slow process. This seems to be an appropriate conceptualization from our perspective. Agents have long recognized the value of "setting up" the targets of compliance-gaining attempts. Chmielewski's (1982) research suggests that individuals will strategically retreat from the usage of preferred message tactics when presented with sequential opportunities to further attempt to influence others in a conflict situation. With a focus upon the factors that mediate the selection of compliance-gaining strategies, Chmielewski demonstrated that the sources of influence attempts will devalue the perceived worth of tactics found to be ineffective even though associated cognitions (for example, social normative beliefs regarding the appropriateness of particular tactics) remain relatively stable across time. Additionally, other researchers have established the utility of sequentially manipulating *single* message tactics in both marketplace encounters as well as controlled social scientific settings (for example, Cialdini & Ascani, 1976; cf. Foss & Dempsey, 1979; Tybout, 1978). A fine example of research concerning sequential compliance-gaining was conducted by Cialdini et al. (1978). These researchers examined the common sales practice of inducing customers to make a decision to purchase an item and subsequently informing them that the lower price could not be offered for a variety of reasons. Called "low-balling," the technique is assumed to be more effective than simply offering a commodity at a higher price without a previous set-up. In each of three experiments, Cialdini et al. demonstrated that a preliminary decision to take an action persevered, even when the cost associated with compliance was increased. Low-balled subjects complied at a significantly higher rate than those who had only been informed of the full cost of the target behavior at the outset (also see Burger & Petty, 1981).

Foot-in-the-Door/Door-in-the-Face. Although the low-ball technique seems an effective means of social influence, most research concerning sequential request strategies has focused on the *foot-in-the-door* (FID) and the *door-in-the-face* (DIF) techniques. They are essentially mirror images of each other, and their effectiveness is always gauged against nonsequential, similar critical requests. In their seminal *FID* research, Freedman and Fraser (1966) reasoned that if one could get a target to comply with a minimal request (that is, get a foot-in-the-door), further compliance with a larger request would be more likely to occur. The *FID* subjects were first asked to answer a few questions concerning household products they had in their homes. Subjects were contacted three days later and asked to permit a team of researchers to visit their homes and classify all household products that the subjects had accumulated. When compared with a control condition, the FID subjects exhibited the predicted behavior; those who had complied with the smaller request were more likely to comply with the critical request than those who had not received the initial request. Alternatively, Cialdini, Vincent, Lewis, Catalan, Wheeler, and Darby (1975) first proposed the "rejection-then-moderation," or DIF, technique for gaining compliance. Basing their analysis upon the notion of a reciprocity norm (Gouldner, 1960), Cialdini et al. assumed that by getting subjects to reject a request to donate two hours of volunteer service per week for at least two years, the same individuals would be more likely to comply with a subsequent request to donate a single afternoon of voluntary activity. The researchers again observed the sequential effect in comparison with control subjects' compliance rates.

In the past decade, numerous research groups have examined the FID and DIF techniques, and a sizable body of empirical data has been generated. Recent meta-analyses of the research lines (Beaman, Cole, Preston, Klentz, & Steblay, 1983; Dillard, Hunter, & Burgoon, 1984) suggest that both effects are reliable given appropriate conditions and are statistically significant. However, the Dillard et al. analysis indicates that only a small mean effect size can be demonstrated across studies (.15 to .17). The fact that both the FID and DIF techniques are associated with such small effects may partially account for why noninteractional variables such as source credibility (for example, Tybout, 1978) and monetary incentives (for example, Furse, Stewart, & Rados, 1981) have exerted a greater influence upon compliance rates than sequential organization in some studies. Nonetheless, because some researchers (for example, Scott, 1977) have reported that the FID and DIF techniques are associated with as much as a 50 percent increase in compliance compared with control subjects' behavior, it seems important to weigh their utility for communicative influence attempts and to examine their nature more closely.

Conditions. The general pattern of research findings in the sequential request paradigm suggests that there are a number of limiting conditions that constrain the effectiveness of the FID and DIF techniques. The optimal magnitude of the initial and critical requests associated with both methods of gaining compliance has garnered most attention. FID and DIF techniques require requests that are neither too small nor too large. Although some FID studies (Baron, 1973; Miller & Suls, 1977; Snyder & Cunningham, 1975) demonstrate that sequential influence occurs only when the initial request requires paltry levels of compliance, research conducted by Seligman, Bush, and Kirsch (1976) suggests that a lower threshold exists beyond which the technique is not operative. That is, it is only when the initial request for compliance induces "sufficient commitment" on the part of the target that critical request rates are significantly different than single message requests. In the DIF case, there is a ceiling level for optimal initial request size, sometimes governed by established behavioral customs (for example, Schwarzwald, Raz, & Zvibel, 1979). The initial DIF request must be large enough to guarantee rejection by the target of an influence attempt (Cialdini

& Ascani, 1976; Cialdini et al., 1975) but, as Even-Chen, Yinon, and Bizman (1978) show, large initial requests that induce incredulity in targets result in critical request compliance rates *lower* than that observed for control subjects. Furthermore, Dillard and Burgoon (1982) argue that the FID and DIF thresholds are likely to vary depending upon the specific target behavior that is being requested.

A second conditional factor is the length of delay between the first and second requests. Although only two studies (Cann, Sherman, & Elkes, 1975; Shanab & Isonio, 1982) have unambiguously measured effect differences between immediately presenting the critical request versus delaying its presentation for up to 10 days, previous reviewers (for example, Dillard & Burgoon, 1982) have considered the effects of timing conclusive. Whereas the existence of a delay between the first and second requests does not seem to alter the effectiveness of the FID technique, DIF influence is contingent upon the critical request immediately following the first (cf. Cialdini & Ascani, 1976). But as DeJong (1979) noted, the *strongest* effects in the FID research line are associated with those studies in which there is little or no delay between the two requests. Furthermore, "the length of the delay itself may be less important than whether the occasion of the second request somehow reminds people of their earlier behavior" (p. 2223). This was probably the case in the Cann et al. (1975) and Seligman, Bush, & Kirsch (1976) studies.

The similarities between the actors and the tasks associated with initial and critical requests have also been manipulated. In general, it appears to matter little if FID requestors differ between the first and second requests in either a direct request situation (Freedman & Fraser, 1966) or in circumstances that imply a larger request for help (Miller & Suls, 1977; Wagener & Laird, 1980). On the other hand, the Cialdini et al. (1975) research suggests that the same actors must advance both the initial and critical requests for the DIF technique to be effective. Also, DIF studies (Cialdini et al., 1975) as well as FID research (Freedman & Fraser, 1966; Goldman, Seever, & Seever, 1982; Miller & Suls, 1977) demonstrate that the two requests need not concern the same subject matter for sequential effects to occur (DeJong, 1981, Study 1; Seligman, Miller, Goldberg, Gelberd, Clark, & Bush, 1976). However, such results have only been observed in studies that employed pro-social topics in the critical requests (cf. Shanab & O'Neill, 1979), and attempts to modify consumer behavior have generally failed (Furse et al., 1981).

A number of variations have been made in the FID and DIF research lines that further specify the range of effectiveness associated with these sequential message techniques. For example, Goldman and his associates (Goldman & Creason, 1981; Goldman, Creason, & McCall, 1981; Goldman, Gier, & Smith, 1981) reported that by adding an intermediary request to either the FID or DIF sequence, compliance rates can be further increased through the use of a "two-feet-in-the-door" or a "two-doors-in-the-face" technique. Also, Reingen (1978) increased FID and DIF compliance rates by including a statement legitimizing even trivial compliance levels to the critical request (see Cialdini & Schroeder, 1976). Alternatively, research conducted by Scott (1977) and Zuckerman, Lazzaro, and Waldgeir (1979) revealed a sequential FID effect only if no incentive was offered for initial request compliance (DeJong & Funder, 1977). Hence, a wide variety of manipulations have been included in FID and DIF studies allowing researchers the opportunity to specify more precisely the conditions under which successful outcomes result from use of these sequential message techniques.

Theoretical Explanations. Those concerned with explaining why the FID and DIF effects occur have enlisted a variety of theories to champion the underlying mechanism of compliance associated with each technique. The main explanatory construct has been Bem's (1972) self-perception theory. Some researchers (for example, Freedman & Fraser, 1966) assert that by complying with an initial request, targets attribute to themselves a "doer" self-perception that governs critical request compliance. A number of FID studies militate against this explanation, however. For example, Scott (1977) included a variety of cognitive measures including situational and self-attributions, behavioral intentions, and attitudes toward the act of compliance. Although she elicited an FID effect in her experimental subjects, none of the cognitive variables approached statistical significance. Another study (Rittle, 1981) suggests that subjects pay more attention to situational perceptions than they do to self-attributions in deciding whether to comply with critical requests. Hence, it remains unclear as to exactly what induces FID compliance.

The picture is no less obscure when one considers the various theoretical bases for DIF compliance. Although Cialdini et al. (1975) and Mowen and Cialdini (1980) argue that critical DIF compliance is motivated by the desire to reciprocate perceived concessions on the part of the actor, two alternative explanations are also viable. First, Pendelton and Batson (1979) discovered that targets are likely to comply with critical requests in an attempt to manage their self-presentations rather than act in accord with an altered self-perception. Second, a variety of other research groups (for example, Goldman & Creason, 1981; Miller, Seligman, Clark, & Bush, 1976; Shanab & Isonio, 1980; Shanab & O'Neill, 1979) contest that DIF subjects perceptually contrast the first and second requests and, therefore, judge the critical request more leniently than control subjects. Particularly informative is the Miller et al. (1976) research, which demonstrates that subjects' compliance rates covary more with perceptions of personal gain than they do with perceptions of yielding on the part of the requestor. An important limitation of this line of reasoning, however, is the fact that no measures of perceptual contrast have been gathered that unambiguously show shifts in the perceptions of sequentially ordered requests.

Future Research. Clearly, a number of issues remain problematic in our understanding of the FID and DIF techniques. For example, given that the bulk of FID research and virtually all of the DIF studies have occurred in situations that did not substantially delay the presentation of the critical request, we should be cautious in generating conclusions regarding the robustness of these manipulative tactics. Also, the fact that most existing theoretical explanations are fragmented or lead to conflicting predictions of whether or not compliance occurs suggests that more studies that simultaneously examine *both* techniques are mandated. Recently, reviewers of the sequential request paradigm (Cantrill, 1984; Dillard & Burgoon, 1982) have argued that the major questions to be answered in the examination of the FID and DIF means of interpersonal influence are cognitive in nature. To be sure, theoretical constructs such as perceptual contrast offer a viable framework for understanding how both types of message sequences are cognitively processed, as does adaptation level theory (Helson, 1964). Another intriguing possibility has been suggested by Abelson (1981) and Cantrill (1984): Critical request compliance may be the result of targets acting out scripted responses to stimulus cues embedded in the initial request and without conscious processing of the actual demands inherent in the second request. Empirical investigations into both of these cognitive domains should prove fruitful as researchers continue to probe for the generative mechanisms underlying sequential influence strategy effects.

Our review of theory and research relevant to the study of interpersonal influence in the first two sections of this chapter has proceeded from examination of single message strategies and tactics to sequential presentation of influence attempts. However, both bodies of literature paint a unidirectional picture of communicative conduct. In Part Three we explore research associated with actors' *mutual* communicative influence and explicate a line of inquiry that more closely approximates processual and interactive regulative communication.

RELATIONAL CONTROL COMMUNICATION

Relational communication research (dyadic sequential interaction analysis) offers a theoretical and methodological alternative to the traditional study of interpersonal influence as monadic, deterministic, and static. Proponents of the relational communication perspective emphasize the transactional, systemic, and processual aspects of interpersonal systems and, in doing so, focus on *emergent* communication properties that exist at the dyadic *system* level (Rogers & Farace, 1975). Relational communication refers to phenomena that reside in dyadic message exchanges by which interactants reciprocally define the nature of their relationship (Rogers, 1983) as they interact and pursue identity, relational, and instrumental objectives. Although there are many approaches to the study of relational communication, in this chapter we focus on the relational research program established by Rogers and colleagues. We feel this research program offers an alternative way of viewing communicative interpersonal influence and attempts to study communicative influence in a manner that many communication scholars verbally support but methodologically ignore, that is, communicative influence as processual, transactional, and relational.

Background. Although this program of relational communication research is a relatively new *communication* research area, its epistemological roots reside in general systems theory (Rogers & Millar, 1982). In human systems, communication is the linking process by which individuals define self in relation to others as well as participate in, develop, organize, and change their systems. The importance of collaboration and interrelation among participants in such a system creates reciprocal communicative control and influence patterns. Human beings are conceived as intentional agents who actively create and control their environmental context via communication (Millar & Rogers, 1976). Consequently, a systems-based relational approach implies three basic research requirements: (1) a focus on observable, interactive behaviors; (2) a retention of the sequential, concatenous nature of interaction; and (3) the identification of system-level structures that can represent evolving relational patterns (Rogers, 1983; Rogers & Millar, 1982).

Methodologically, these relational communication researchers use relational control coding schemes, the most common of which is the Rogers-Farace Relational Communication Control Coding Scheme (1975). Briefly, this coding scheme assumes that all messages are both stimulus and response, that all messages contain both a content and relational dimension, and that message exchanges evidence reciprocal offerings of relational control definitions. In coding interactions, each message (defined as a "turn-at-talk") first receives a three-digit code pertaining to (1) speaker, (2) grammatical form, and (3) response mode. Second, a control dimension (one-up, one-down, or one-across) is assigned. Third, transactional types, whether symmetric, complementary, or transitory, are designated from combined control directions of sequentially paired messages. (For a more thorough review and explanation of this process, see Rogers-Millar & Millar, 1979). Finally, researchers interpret these codes by pointing out recurring control sequences and patterns.

To date, this program of interpersonal relational communication research has focused almost exclusively upon communication control patterns (domineeringness and dominance) or the effects of message control intensity in white, married couples' interaction. This research examines only verbal interaction and is collected in partially contrived naturalistic settings (participants are given four topics to discuss at home while being audiotaped). These restrictions reflect a somewhat limited research domain, yet the results of this research program offer interesting and noteworthy conclusions.

Findings. Specifically, the study of communication control patterns has produced reliable and interesting insights into how we might view interpersonal influence in general. Rogers-Millar and Millar (1979), in an expansion of an earlier study (Rogers, 1972), found that domineeringness (transmission of one-up messages) and dominance (the resultant acceptance by one partici-pant of the one-up messages given by the other partner) are different pheno-mena. They state:

> The lack of strong association between these two measures supports and offers construct validity to our notion that domineering behavior and dominance are different phenomena—a point we feel is extremely important, since so much of the empirical work in the area labelled interpersonal power has ignored the relational level difference and operationalized "power" as an individual trait. It is our contention, now with empirical backing, that most of these studies have reported findings dealing with domineering behavior rather than power con-cepts. (p. 243)

Moreover, they found that domineering behavior by wives was associated with lower levels of satisfaction and higher levels of role strain, whereas husband dominance was associated with higher levels of satisfaction and lower levels of role strain. This might best be explained by the fact that "domineering" wives offered fewer accompanying supportive statements than "domineering" husbands, and wives were more supportive of husband dominance than were husbands of wife dominance. A replication and expansion of this study, with a larger sample, was supportive of these findings (Courtright, Millar, & Rogers-Millar, 1979). Additionally, this study found that high levels of domineeringness or dominance by either spouse were associat-ed with lower levels of understanding (ability to predict other's actions). A follow-up study using stepwise regression analysis techniques lent support to the finding of a negative relationship between dominance and understanding levels (Millar, Rogers-Millar, & Courtright, 1979). The strongest predictor of husband and wife understanding levels was the dominance ratio; the less the equivalency of the dominance pattern (or the more rigidity the dominance hierarchy exhibited), the less each spouse understood the other. This body of research suggests the following sequence between dominance, interaction, and understanding: More equivalence in relational dominance patterns leads to more flexibility in dyad interaction, to more frequent discussion and/or conflict about jobs, roles, and so forth, and to better prediction (under-standing by each partner). The opposite is evident in relationships with discrepant dominance structures.

Results from the second research area that focus on message control intensity indicate that conversations possess a homeostatic control nature (Courtright, Millar, & Rogers, 1980; Rogers, Courtright, & Millar, 1982). Message intensity is operationalized by a measure derived from the existing R-F coding scheme and is used to increase the precision of control pattern description. Research with the intensity measure indicates that couples establish a "set-point" on the intensity control axis and move in and out from each other, but generally maintain a characteristic distance between them. In addition, "one-across" messages are the major determinants of the location of the homeostatic "set-point" and serve as the primary regulator of the amount of variation around the "point." Most recently, the coefficient of variation (CV) has provided an overall index of dyadic message intensity variation (Courtright, Millar, & Rogers, 1983). Regression analysis indicates that the CV measure accounts for 88 percent of the variance contained in the original 12 separate indices of message control intensity. Researchers hope this meta-level measure will provide a more parsimonious and efficient method of indexing interactional control patterns in the future (Rogers & Bagarozzi, 1983). In sum, this research indicates the potential leveling influence of one-across messages and provides insight into how they might constrain and influence interactional patterns.

Critique. This relational communcation research program has provided an alternative to traditional ways of viewing interpersonal influence, and has established empirical support for that view. Despite the obvious strengths and potential of this approach, it is not without limitations. Specifically, the exclusive focus on *verbal* interaction ignores study of nonverbal behaviors, often thought to provide rich relational control information. Second, the single focus on surface-level communication behaviors and "how" communication is patterned ignores the deeper-level cognitive or interpretive factors that may provide fuller answers to "why" interactants' communication is patterned as it is. Sequential patterns and models cannot and should not substitute for substantive theory. The relationship between cognitive structures/interpretive social knowledge (which provide generative mechanisms) and sequential interactive patterns captured in this relational research must be determined (Hewes, Planalp, & Streibel, 1980). Third, reliability and validity issues continue to plague the use of relational coding schemes (Folger, Hewes, & Poole, in press; Folger & Poole, 1981; Folger & Sillars, 1977; O'Donnell-Trujillo, 1981; Poole & Folger, 1981; Rogers & Millar, 1982; Sillars & Folger, 1978). Several issues seem especially important.

Concerning validity issues, clear evidence of face and construct validity considered necessary and sufficient under the experienced mode embraced by these relational communication researchers has been found questionable in two of the most commonly used relational coding schemes (O'Donnell-Trujillo, 1981). Moreover, some researchers indicate that face and construct validity alone are inadequate for measures of relational coding scheme validity and that representational validity must also be demonstrated. Although still a controversial question, the lack of empirical verification that control assignments are consistent with participants' relational definitions appears problematic. Folger and Poole (1981) argue that because the "control" construct involves culturally shared meanings and ideographic interpretations, the explanatory power of relational coding instruments is undermined in three ways without the additional measure of representational validity: (1)

lack of empirical evidence to determine relational meanings results in little convergence between coding schemes designed to code the same control functions; (2) without verification that the researchers' claims are consistent with participants' shared meanings, several equally defensible explanations for the same result are possible; (3) without evidence of the weight partici-pants placed on various control interactions, relative to all other indicators of relational control, researchers have no means of knowing the power of their claims. These limitations might easily be remedied by supplementing the traditional experienced requirements of logical and construct validity with the more unique requirements of representational validity.

With regard to reliability issues, the failure of most relational communica-tion researchers to assess and report some measure of category-by-category interpretive reliability may mask potential problems with the coding system (Hewes, 1983). Although the Rogers-Farace scheme generally exhibits high *global* reliability levels that indicate coders' consistency in utilization of the coding scheme (overall reliability average equals .86 as reported by Rogers & Farace, 1975), used alone this index can obscure other potential coding distortions. For example, unless category-by-category reliabilities are assessed and reported it is impossible to tell which categories may be ambig-uous, poorly defined, or in need of further refinement. More seriously, that may affect hypotheses related to the temporal dependency and distribution of coded units across categories (see Hewes, 1983, for a more detailed analysis). Put simply, if coders systematically confuse or misclassify catego-ries because some categories are more ambiguous or difficult to code, results and conclusions drawn from coded data are biased. Hewes (1983) outlines a three-step plan for assessing category-by-category reliabilities that could strengthen confidence in research results accruing from use of the Rogers-Farace scheme.

Beyond immediate reliability and validity issues, two other limitations asso-ciated with this body of relational communication research deserve mention. First, the association between the "relational" aspect of messages and the "content" dimension must be determined. For example, given the defined present coding systems, all questions demanding an answer are coded sim-ilarly. Yet, the *content* of the question may provide important relational control information. To illustrate further, a closed-ended and leading ques-tion such as "Did you do that because you don't like me?" seems intuitively more domineering and controlling than an open-ended question such as "Why did you do that?" Similarly, the *content* of talk-overs may help to indicate whether a talk-over should be relationally coded as one-up (attempt-ing to gain control) or one-down (agreeing and supporting). In short, it seems that only by melding the content and relational dimensions can a complete picture of relational control be discovered.

A second limitation in this area is the need to determine "clock-time" as well as "event-time" when investigating relational control and influence. It seems probable that turns-at-talk (event-time) constitute different durations (clock-time). Duration of talk can be associated with control or control attempts; people who talk longer are already more dominant or are attempting to be more dominant by controlling the floor. Thus one turn-at-talk may be more relationally "controlling" than another. For example, two people may make assertive statements that are coded as one-up moves, but if one person continues for several minutes (for example, explaining, delineating, and developing arguments for the assertion) while another merely makes a brief one-statement assertion, the former is likely to make a greater impact, attract more attention, and probably evidence more control. Recent advances in sequential interaction analysis permit a researcher to control for clock-time and alleviate these differences (Hewes et al., 1980).

Some of these problems have recently been addressed and steps taken to remedy their limiting effects (Rogers, 1983). Specifically, efforts are underway to develop nonverbal codes that can be combined with the verbal (Millar, 1979). Moreover, Rogers (1983) agrees that "*content* codes, especially those which do not attempt to map the psychic interior or psychological state of the speaker, can be usefully combined with *relational* modes of mapping" (p. 16). She also agrees that integration of cognitive and interpretive force with the pragmatic perspective will enable a more unified and powerful theory of interpersonal communication. Citing recent research by Fitzpatrick and colleagues (Fitzpatrick, 1976; Fitzpatrick & Best, 1979; Fitzpatrick & Indvik, 1979) and research by Cronen, Pearce, and colleagues (Cronen & Pearce, 1981; Cronen, Pearce, & Snavely, 1979) as advances in integrating interactant perceptions and interpretations into relational coding schemes, Rogers (1983) concludes that "the dual application and integration of the CMM model of coordinated management of meaning and the relational model hold considerable promise" (p. 18). However, although advocating integration of the interpretive and pragmatic approaches, Rogers and Millar (1981) disagree that representational validity is necessary for assigning relational meaning to messages, insisting that "pragmatists claim no interest in meanings as interpretations" (p. 250). They state:

> We agree that interpersonal relationships can fruitfully be viewed as a negotiation process and we even agree that subjects' interpretations of this process may be a useful means of refining coding rules and intensity weights. . . . Where we disagree with Folger and Poole concerns the parts of this ongoing process that are to be separated out for analysis and how they are to be studied. We have chosen one perspective and have attempted to be consistent within it. They have chosen another and are also attempting to be consistent within its presuppositions. The pursuit of one route does not deny the legitimacy or validity of another. (p. 254)

Certainly the debate about whether to establish representational validity or not when assigning relational meaning to messages is far from closed. At the very least though, O'Donnell-Trujillo (1981) suggests that coding validity at the act level in the R-F be assessed via *trained* coders or by comparing coding judgments of different sets of coders trained by different research-ers—two methods more aligned with the experienced orientation. Finally, Rogers and Farace (1975) note the importance of a time dimension for increasing the "richness" of control information and indicate that they "have already begun pilot work using various methods to plot the time duration of the basic coding units" (p. 234). With persistent theoretical and methodologi-cal advancement, renewed rigorous investigating practices, and ongoing programmatic research, we believe this area of relational communication research will continue to provide important contributions to what we know about communication and *interpersonal* influence.

CONCLUSION

People bring personal purposes to all social interactions. Their well-being—as well as society's—depends on their proficiency in achieving those objectives in relation to others (Weinstein, 1966, 1969). Persons' competence at interpersonal *influence* is particularly important for, as Grimshaw notes, "social actors spend much of their time with others engaged either in attempt-ing to manipulate those others into doing things for them—or in themselves being objects of such manipulation" (1980, p. 203). We have restricted our focus in this chapter primarily to actors' achievement of instrumental objec-tives, and more narrowly to how actors use language and talk as resources in influence attempts. Although there are many other functions associated with interpersonal communication and other objectives toward which it is directed, as the various chapters in this volume evidence, we concur with Grimshaw's (1981) conclusion that

> while there is talk that appears to be primarily referential (informative or expressive), it seems likely that most, if not all, talk will be found to have implications for social control. (p. 226)

The research on communication and interpersonal influence that we have highlighted in the sections on single message tactics, sequential strategies, and relational control patterns amply support Grimshaw's claim. Although the findings reviewed offer considerable insight into persons' strategic use of communication to achieve instrumental objectives and interpersonal control, these results (and the research domains from which they derive) are both limited and limiting. In the compliance-gaining strategies area, for instance, our understanding of strategic message *enactment* and whether or not *compliance* is secured has been severely limited by researchers' emphases and procedures. The major effect of much of the research on taxonomic classification of message strategies and correlative investigations of persons' message choices from these inductively and deductively derived lists has been increased insight into what different types of individuals say they would be likely to do in hypothetical situations, without producing commensurate knowledge that such compliance-gaining messages are successfully linked to others' compliance. This is granting the assumption that persons face situations like those studied, and that they can and do use the strategies they report they would be likely to choose.

These findings, and the assumptions and methods generating them, are also limiting. Consider the Strategic Choice Model explicated at the outset of this chapter and characteristic of the rational, fixed, purposive, self-aware, and competent actor implicitly depicted in research on message strategies. This conception limits our understanding of the interactional, adaptive, and partially nonreflective character of actors' communicative influence production. To begin with, a central challenge facing any strategic communicator is enmeshing personal plans and potential lines of action with interpretation of another's purposes. As Delia et al. (1982) summarize:

> We see human communication as a process of interaction in which the communicative intentions of participants are a focus of coordination. In communication, persons express themselves and make sense of the communicative intentions of others. Their strategies are structured and their strategic choices guided by communicative intentions and the communicative intentions of their partners. (p. 159)

The interactional quality of communication, both expressive and strategic, is underscored by Cohen and Perrault (1979), who suggest that interactants expect and desire that their purposes and plans be understood (at least most of them) and behave in ways that insure they will be. Only recently have we begun to understand how targets become cooriented to sources' influence attempts (Gottlieb & Ickes, 1978; Schenck-Hamlin, Georgacarakos, & Wiseman, 1982). Second, precisely because they are located in a stream of interaction, communication strategies are more dynamic and adaptive than the fixed and static concept inherent in the Strategic Choice Model. There is ample evidence that even when they approach situations with purposes and plans, actors' schemes for monitoring how events unfold (especially in terms of goal-consistent or goal-discrepant consequences of their behaviors) enable them to conform to or to disengage from preconceived strategies, or to alter them in ways more adaptive to situational constraints (Cody & McLaughlin, this volume). Finally, although it may be appropriate to term strategic message choices "rational"—at least insofar as they seem to the actor or an observer to reflect a reasonable path to the communicator's objective (cf. Brown & Levinson, 1978)—Goody (1978a) correctly reminds that for all interactional agenda

> such de facto rational strategies need not be arrived at rationally in the sense of being products of conscious deliberation. And for a number of reasons it is not

likely that most of the choices represented by these strategies are consciously made. There isn't time in the flow of ongoing interaction: introspection suggests that this is not the case; and—most persuasive—however "rational" the process, if every individual really did start from scratch in selecting verbal strategies for interaction goals, the variation between individuals in goal priority would lead to such incongruity of act and response that chaos would quickly ensue. For all these reasons it seems likely that the selection of verbal forms is goal-oriented, but is only partly the result of conscious calculation. (p. 8)

The research by Rogers and Millar describing interactional control patterns demonstrates the interactive and potentially nonconscious nature of communicative influence in relational interactions.

Recent research has not only recognized these and other problems mentioned throughout the chapter, but important progress has been made in redressing them. Tracy et al. (1984) demonstrated the value of the compliance-gaining approach in describing the discourse of requests while simultaneously challenging researchers interested in message strategies to move beyond taxonomic considerations and to deal with felicity conditions of request speech acts and to content related to the "face wants" of each party. Their study not only remedies many of the methodological problems in previous research involving preconstructed lists, abstract descriptions of strategies, and single examples of message and situation types (Jackson & Backus, 1982; Jackson & Jacobs, 1983), but also underscores the multifunctionality of discourse (O'Keefe & Delia, 1982) and the need to consider compliance-gaining efforts in the context of *multiple* goals and situational constraints. As Tracy et al. (1984) observe:

> Even in "compliance-gaining situations," communicators seldom seek compliance only; indeed they may be willing to forego compliance for the sake of other, more important goals. "Compliance gaining" research might be redirected fruitfully toward a study of ways in which speakers design their messages to seek, balance, and resolve conflicts among multiple goals.

Other researchers have couched compliance-gaining research in more theoretical terms. Baxter (1984), for example, examined compliance-gaining within the framework of Brown and Levinson's (1978) theory of politeness. Her findings posed challenges and offered new directions for compliance-gaining research while simultaneously suggesting "important modifications" (p. 450) in Brown and Levinson's theory. Baxter's research also emphasizes the need for ties with interactional and discourse analytic research on communication and interpersonal influence (cf. Jacobs & Jackson, 1983). Smith (1984) has drawn upon her own contingency rules theory to *explain* subjects' compliance-gaining message choices and to make specific predictions. Although the theory is too recent to judge its power, results from two studies (Smith, 1984) neatly tie the rules subjects appeared to use in selecting messages to previously researched dimensions of compliance-gaining situations. Finally, as a preliminary step in theory-building, Wheeless et al. (1983) synthesized "relevant *power* literature into a conceptual framework" (p. 188) for better understanding the nature, bases, and types of compliance-gaining behaviors. Together with the constructivist and empathy model approach discussed earlier, these conceptual efforts ease the relatively atheoretical character of much research on communicative influence. For although we have gained an increased understanding of the strategic and tactical elements of instrumental communication, we have few ways to link these insights to other substantive domains or to apply them in useful ways until theoretical models are developed sufficiently to account for and extend the descriptive findings obtained thus far. Only with stronger theoretical perspectives can we also hope to integrate these findings with diverse relevant research on children's strategic communication (Burleson, 1984a, 1984b; Clark & Delia, 1976; Haslett, 1983a, 1983b; O'Keefe & Benoit, 1983; Renshaw & Asher, 1983; Ward & Wackman, 1972; Wood, Weinstein, & Parker, 1967) and influence tactics of parents, teachers, and other authority figures (Applegate, 1980a, 1980b; O'Hagen & Edmunds, 1982; Smith, 1983); nonstandard message strategies (Mitchell-Kernan, 1972a, 1972b) and strategic interaction in intercultural contexts (Dundes, Leach, & Ozkok, 1972; Fisher, 1976; Irvine, 1974) and special populations (Rueda & Smith, 1983; Weiss & Weinstein, 1968); gender and influence (Eagly, 1983; Indvik & Fitzpatrick, 1983; Kramerae, 1981); interrogation strategies (Biderman, 1960) and interviewing tactics (Gilchrist, 1982; McGaughey & Stiles, 1983; Ragan & Hopper, 1981; Siegman & Pope, 1965); and communication strategies in game contexts (Beisecker, 1970; Chmielewski, 1982; Seibold & Steinfatt, 1979) and therapy (Dorn, 1984; Haley, 1973, 1977), among many areas investigating persuasive and regulative linguistic strategies. Most importantly, only with stronger theoretical footings can we surmount what Grimshaw terms "intractabilities" in understanding communication and interpersonal influence: "While 'everybody' may 'do it,' different people do it in quite different ways and with quite different effectiveness, in quite different situations with quite different constraints and available resources" (1980, p. 204).

REFERENCES

Abelson, R. P. (1981). Psychological status of the script concept. *American Psychologist, 36*, 715-729.

Abelson, R. P., & Miller, J. C. (1967). Negative persuasion via personal insult. *Journal of Experimental Social Psychology, 3*, 321-333.

Alexander, C. N., & Lauderdale, P. (1977). Situated identities and social influence. *Sociometry, 40*, 225-233.

Altman, I., & Taylor, D. A. (1973). *Social penetration: The development of interpersonal relationships.* New York: Holt, Rinehart & Winston.

Applegate, J. L. (1980a). Adaptive communication in educational contexts: A study of teachers' communicative strategies. *Communication Education, 29*, 158-170.

Applegate, J. L. (1980b). Person and position-centered teacher communication in a day care center. In N. K. Denzin (Ed.), *Studies in symbolic interaction* (Vol. 3, pp. 59-96). Greenwich, CT: JAI Press.

Applegate, J. L., & Delia, J. G. (1980). Person-centered speech, psychological development, and the contexts of language usage. In R. St. Clair and H. Giles (Eds.), *The social and psychological contexts of language* (pp. 245-282). Hillsdale, NJ: Lawrence Erlbaum.

Applegate, J. L., & Wheeler, J. (1981). *The impact of construct system development and persuasive strategy development on face-to-face persuasive interaction.* Paper presented at the annual meeting of the Central States Speech Association, Chicago.

Ayres, J. (1983). Strategies to maintain relationships: Their identification and perceived usage. *Communication Quarterly, 31,* 62-67.

Bacharach, S. B., & Lawler, E. J. (1981). *Bargaining: Power, tactics, and outcomes.* San Francisco, CA: Jossey-Bass.

Bachman, J. C., Bowers, D. G., & Marcus, P. M. (1968). Bases of supervisory power: A comparative study in five organizational settings. In A. S. Tannenbaum (Ed.), *Control in organizations* (pp. 229-237). New York: McGraw-Hill.

Ball, D. W. (1965). Sarcasm as sociation: The rhetoric of interaction. *Canadian Review of Sociology and Anthropology, 2,* 190-198.

Baron, R. A. (1973). The "foot-in-the-door" phenomenon: Mediating effects of size of first request and sex of requester. *Bulletin of Psychonomic Sociology, 2,* 113-114.

Baumeister, R. F. (1982). A self-presentational view of social phenomena. *Psychological Bulletin, 91,* 3-26.

Baxter, L. A. (1979). Self-disclosure as a relationship disengagement strategy: An exploratory investigation. *Human Communication Research, 5,* 216-222.

Baxter, L. A. (1982). Strategies for ending relationships: Two studies. *The Western Journal of Speech Communication, 46,* 223-241.

Baxter, L. A. (1984). An investigation of compliance-gaining as politeness. *Human Communication Research, 10,* 427-456.

Baxter, L. A. (in press). Accomplishing relationship disengagement. In S. Duck & D. Perlman (Eds.), *The Sage series in personal relationships.* Beverly Hills, CA: Sage.

Beaman, A. L., Cole, C. M., Preston, M., Klentz, B., & Steblay, N. M. (1983). Fifteen years of foot-in-the-door research. *Personality and Social Psychology Bulletin, 9,* 181-196.

Beisecker, T. (1970). Verbal persuasive strategies in mixed-motive interactions. *Quarterly Journal of Speech, 66,* 149-159.

Bell, R. A., & Daly, J. A. (1984). The affinity-seeking function of communication. *Communication Monographs, 51,* 91-115.

Bem, D. J. (1972). Self-perception theory. In L. Berkowitz (Ed.), *Advances in experimental social psychology* (Vol. 6, pp. 2-62). New York: Academic Press.

Bennett, A. (1982). Strategies and counterstrategies in the use of yes-no questions in discourse. In J. J. Gumperz (Ed.), *Language and social identity* (pp. 95-107). Cambridge: Cambridge University Press.

Berg, J. H., & Archer, R. L. (1982). Responses to self-disclosure and interaction goals. *Journal of Experimental Social Psychology, 18,* 501-512.

Biderman, A. D. (1960). Social-psychological needs and "involuntary" behavior as illustrated by compliance in interrogation. *Sociometry, 23,* 120-147.

Blau, P. (1964). *Exchange and power in social life.* New York: John Wiley.

Blumstein, P. W. (1973). Audience, Machiavellianism, and tactics of identity bargaining. *Sociometry, 36,* 346-365.

Bochner, A. P. (1978). On taking ourselves seriously: An analysis of some persistent problems and promising directions in interpersonal research. *Human Communication Research, 4,* 179-191.

Bochner, A. P. (1984). The functions of human communication in interpersonal bonding. In C. C. Arnold & J. W. Bowers (Eds.), *Handbook of rhetorical and communication theory* (pp. 544-621). Boston: Allyn & Bacon.

Bochner, A. P., & Lenk Krueger, D. (1979). Interpersonal communication theory and research: An overview of inscrutable epistemologies and muddled concepts. In D. Nimmo (Ed.), *Communication yearbook 3* (pp. 197-211). New Brunswick, NJ: Transaction.

Boster, F. J., & Hunter, J. E. (1978). *The effect of the dimensions of Machiavellianism on compliance-gaining message selection.* Unpublished manuscript, Arizona State University.

Boster, F. J., & Stiff, J. B. (1984). Compliance-gaining message selection behavior. *Human Communication Research, 10,* 539-556.

Boster, F. J., Stiff, J. B., & Reynolds, R. A. (1983). *Do persons respond differently to inductively-derived and deductively-derived lists of compliance gaining message strategies? A reply to Wiseman and Schenck-Hamlin.* Paper presented at the annual meeting of the International Communication Association, Dallas, TX.

Bradac, J. J., Schneider, M. J., Hemphill, M. R., & Tardy, C. H. (1980). Consequences of language intensity and compliance-gaining strategies in an initial heterosexual encounter. In H. Giles, W. P. Robinson, & P. M. Smith (Eds.), *Language: Social psychological perspectives* (pp. 71-75). New York: Pergamon.

Britton, J. (1971). What's the use? *Educational Review, 23,* 205-219.

Brown, R. L., Jr. (1980). The pragmatics of verbal irony. In R. W. Shuy & A. Shnukal (Ed.), *Language use and the uses of language* (pp. 111-127). Washington, DC: Georgetown University Press.

Brown, P., & Levinson, S. (1978). Universals in language usage: Politeness phenomena. In E. N. Goody (Ed.), *Questions and politeness: Strategies in social interaction* (pp. 56-289). New York: Cambridge University Press.

Burger, J. M., & Petty, R. E. (1981). The low-ball compliance technique: Task or person commitment? *Journal of Personality and Social Psychology, 40,* 492-500.

Burke, J. A. (1979). *The relationship of interpersonal cognitive development to the adaptation of persuasive strategies in adults.* Paper presented at the annual meeting of the Central States Speech Association, St. Louis, MO.

Burke, J. A., & Clark, R. A. (1982). An assessment of methodological options for investigating the development of persuasive skills across childhood. *Central States Speech Journal, 33,* 437-445.

Burke, R. J., & Wilcox, D. S. (1969). Effects of different patterns and degrees of openness in superior-subordinate communication on subordinate job satisfaction. *Academy of Management Journal, 12,* 319-326.

Burleson, B. R. (1983). Social cognition, empathic motivation, and adults' comforting strategies. *Human Communication Research, 10,* 295-304.

Burleson, B. R. (1984a). Age, social-cognitive development, and the use of comforting strategies. *Communication Monographs, 51,* 140-153.

Burleson, B. R. (1984b). Comforting communication. In H. E. Sypher & J. L. Applegate (Eds.), *Communication by children and adults: Social cognitive and strategic processes* (pp. 63-104). Beverly Hills, CA: Sage.

Burleson, B. R. (in press). Effects of social cognition and empathic motivation on adults comforting strategies. *Human Communication Research.*

Cann, A., Sherman, S. J., & Elkes, R. (1975). Effects of initial request size and timing of a second request on compliance: The foot in the door and the door in the face. *Journal of Personality and Social Psychology, 32,* 774-782.

Cantrill, J. G. (1984). *Towards a cognitive model of sequential message effects.* Unpublished manuscript, University of Illinois.

Cashman, J., Dansereau, F., Jr., Graen, G., & Haga, W. J. (1976). Organizational understructure and leadership: A longitudinal investigation of the managerial role-making process. *Organizational Behavior and Human Performance, 15,* 278-296.

Chelune, G. J. (Ed.). (1979). *Self-disclosure: Origins, patterns, and implications of openness in interpersonal relationships.* San Francisco: Jossey-Bass.

Cheng, J.L.C. (1983). Organizational context and upward influence: An experimental study of the use of power tactics. *Group & Organization Studies, 8,* 337-355.

Chmielewski, T. J. (1982). A test of a model for predicting strategy choice. *Central States Speech Journal, 33,* 505-518.

Christie, R., & Geis, F. (1970). *Studies in Machiavellianism.* New York: Academic Press.

Churchill, L. (1978). *Questioning strategies in sociolinguistics.* Rowley, MA: Newbury House.

Cialdini, R. B., & Ascani, K. (1976). Test of a concession procedure for inducing verbal, behavioral, and further compliance with a request to give blood. *Journal of Applied Psychology, 61,* 295-300.

Cialdini, R. B., Cacioppo, J. T., Bassett, R., & Miller, J. A. (1978). Low-ball procedure for producing compliance: Commitment then cost. *Journal of Personality and Social Psychology, 36,* 463-476.

Cialdini, R. B., & Richardson, K. D. (1980). Two indirect tactics of image management: Basking and blasting. *Journal of Personality and Social Psychology, 39,* 406-415.

Cialdini, R. B., & Schroeder, D. A. (1976). Increasing compliance by legitimizing paltry contributions: When even a penny helps. *Journal of Personality and Social Psychology, 34,* 599-604.

Cialdini, R. B., Vincent, J. E., Lewis, S. K., Catalan, J., Wheeler, D., & Darby, B. L. (1975). Reciprocal concessions procedure for inducing compliance: The door-in-the-face technique. *Journal of Personality and Social Psychology, 31,* 206-215.

Clark, R. A. (1979). The impact of self-interest and desired liking on selection of persuasive strategies. *Communication Monographs, 46,* 257-273.

Clark, R. A.(1984). *Persuasive messages.* New York: Harper & Row.

Clark, R. A., & Delia, J. G. (1976). The development of functional persuasive skills in childhood and early adolescence. *Child Development, 47,* 1-10.

Clark, R. A., & Delia, J. G. (1977). Cognitive complexity, social perspective taking, and functional persuasive skills in second-to-ninth-grade children. *Human Communication Research, 3,* 128-134.

Clark, R. A., & Delia, J. G. (1979). Topoi and rhetorical competence. *Quarterly Journal of Speech, 65,* 187-206.

Cody, M. J. (1982). A typology of disengagement strategies and an examination of the role intimacy, reactions to inequity and relational problems play in strategy selection. *Communication Monographs, 49,* 148-170.

Cody, M. J., & McLaughlin, M. L. (1980). Perceptions of compliance-gaining situations: A dimensional analysis. *Communication Monographs, 47,* 132-148.

Cody, M. J., McLaughlin, M. L., & Jordan, W. J. (1980). A multidimensional scaling of three sets of compliance-gaining strategies. *Communication Quarterly, 28,* 34-46.

Cody, M. J., McLaughlin, M. L., & Schneider, M. J. (1981). The impact of intimacy and relational consequences on the selection of interpersonal persuasive messages: A reanalysis. *Communication Quarterly, 29,* 91-106.

Cody, M. J., Woelfel, M. L., & Jordan, W. J. (1983). Dimensions of compliance-gaining situations. *Human Communication Research, 9,* 99-113.

Cohen, P. R., & Perrault, C. R. (1979). A plan-based theory of speech acts. *Cognitive Science, 3,* 213-230.

Coleman, J. S. (1963). Comment on "On the concept of influence." *Public Opinion Quarterly, 27,* 63-82.

Cooper, J., & Jones, E. E. (1969). Opinion divergence as a strategy to avoid being miscast. *Journal of Personality and Social Psychology, 13,* 23-30.

Courtright, J. A., Millar, F. E., & Rogers, L. E. (1980). Message control intensity as a predictor of transactional redundancy. In D. Nimmo (Ed.), *Communication yearbook 4* (pp. 199-216). New Brunswick, NJ: Transaction.

Courtright, J. A., Millar, F. E., & Rogers, L. E. (1983). A new measure of interactional control patterns. *Journal of Communication Association of the Pacific, 12,* 46-68.

Courtright, J. A., Millar, F. E., & Rogers-Millar, L. E. (1979). Domineeringness and dominance: Replication and expansion. *Communication Monographs, 46,* 179-192.

Cozby, P. C. (1973). Self-disclosure: A literature review. *Psychological Bulletin, 79,* 73-91.

Cronen, V. E., & Pearce, W. B. (1981). Logical force in interpersonal communication: A new concept of necessity in social behavior. *Communication, 6,* 5-67.

Cronen, V. E., Pearce, W. B., & Snavely, L. M. (1979). A theory of rule-structure and types of episodes and a study of perceived enmeshment in undesired repetitive patterns (URP's). In D. Nimmo (Ed.), *Communication yearbook 3* (pp. 225-240). New Brunswick, NJ: Transaction.

Cronkhite, G. (1983). Conventional postulates of interpersonal argument. In D. Zarefsky, M. Sillars, & J. Rhodes (Eds.), *Argument in transition: Proceedings of the Third Summer Conference in Argumentation* (pp. 697-706). Annandale, VA: Speech Communication Association.

Cupach, W. R. (1982). *Communication satisfaction and interpersonal solidarity as outcomes of conflict message strategy use.* Paper presented at the annual meeting of the International Communication Association, Boston.

Dahl, R. A. (1957). The concept of power. *Behavioral Science, 2,* 201-218.

Dansereau, F., Jr., Graen, G., & Haga, W. J. (1975). A vertical dyad linkage approach to leadership within formal organizations: A longitudinal investigation of the role making process. *Organizational Behavior and Human Performance, 13,* 46-78.

Davis, D. (1982). Determinants of responsiveness in dyadic interaction. In W. Ickes & E. S. Knowles (Eds.), *Personality, roles and social behavior* (pp. 85-140). New York: Springer-Verlag.

DeJong, W. (1979). An examination of self-perception mediation of the foot-in-the-door effect. *Journal of Personality and Social Psychology, 37,* 2221-2239.

DeJong, W. (1981). Consensus information and the foot-in-the-door effect. *Personality and Social Psychology Bulletin, 7,* 423-430.

DeJong, W., & Funder, D. (1977). Effect of payment for initial compliance: Unanswered questions about the foot-in-the-door phenomenon. *Personality and Social Psychology Bulletin, 3,* 662-665.

Delia, J. G. (1977). Constructivism and the study of human communication. *Quarterly Journal of Speech, 63,* 66-83.

Delia, J. G. (1978). *The research and methodological commitments of a constructivist.* Paper presented at the annual meeting of the Speech Communication Association, Minneapolis.

Delia, J. G., & Clark, R. A. (1977). Cognitive complexity, social perception, and the development of listener-adapted communication in six-, eight-, ten-, and twelve-year-old boys. *Communication Monographs, 44, 326-345.*

Delia, J. G., Kline, S. L., & Burleson, B. R. (1979). The development of persuasive communication strategies in kindergarteners through twelfth-graders. *Communication Monographs, 46,* 241-256.

Delia, J. G., & O'Keefe, B. J. (1979). Constructivism: The development of communication in children. In E. Wartella (Ed.), *Children communicating* (pp. 157-185). Beverly Hills, CA: Sage.

Delia, J. G., O'Keefe, B. J., & O'Keefe, D. J. (1982). The constructivist approach to communication. In F.E.X. Dance (Ed.), *Comparative human communication theory* (pp. 177-191). New York: Harper & Row.

DeTurck, M. A., & Miller, G. R. (1982). The effect of birth order on the persuasive impact of messages and the likelihood of persuasive message selection. *Communication, 11,* 78-84.

Deutsch, K. W. (1966). *The nerves of government.* New York: Free Press.

Dillard, J. P., & Burgoon, M. (1982). An appraisal of two sequential request strategies for gaining compliance: Foot-in-the-door and door-in-the-face. *Communication, 11,* 40-57.

Dillard, J. P., Hunter, J. E., & Burgoon, M. (1984). Sequential-request persuasive strategies: Meta-analysis of foot-in-the-door and door-in-the-face. *Human Communication Research, 10,* 461-488.

Ditton, J. (1977). Alibis and aliases: Some notes on the "motives" of fiddling bread salesmen. *Sociology, 11,* 233-255.

Dollard, J. (1939). The dozens: Dialectic of insult. *American Imago, 1,* 3-25.

Dorn, F. J. (1984). *Counseling as applied social psychology: An introduction to the social influence model.* Springfield, IL: Charles C Thomas.

Duncan, J., Jr. (1981). Conversational strategies. In T. A. Sebeok & R. Rosenthal (Eds.), *The Clever Hans phenomenon: Communication with horses, whales, apes, and people* (pp. 144-157). New York: New York Academy of Sciences.

Dundes, A., Leach, J. W., & Ozkok, B. (1972). The strategy of Turkish boys' verbal dueling rhymes. In J. Gumperz & D. Hymes (Eds.), *Directions in sociolinguistics* (pp. 130-160). New York: Holt, Rinehart & Winston.

Eagly, A. H. (1974). Comprehensibility of persuasive arguments as a determinant of opinion change. *Journal of Personality and Social Psychology, 29,* 758-773.

Eagly, A. H. (1983). Gender and social influence. *American Psychologist, 38,* 971-981.

Emerson, R. M. (1962). Power-dependence relations. *American Sociological Review, 2,* 31-42.

Enzle, M. E., & Harvey, M. D. (1982). Rhetorical requests for help. *Social Psychology Quarterly, 45,* 172-176.

Erez, M., & Rim, Y. (1982). The relationships between goals, influence, tactics, and personal and organizational variables. *Human Relations, 35,* 871-878.

Etzioni, A. (1961). *A comparative analysis of complex organizations.* New York: Free Press.

Even-Chen, M., Yinon, Y., & Bizman, A. (1978). The door in the face technique: Effects of the size of the initial request. *European Journal of Social Psychology, 8,* 135-140.

Falbo, T. (1977). Multidimensional scaling of power strategies. *Journal of Personality and Social Psychology, 35,* 537-547.

Falbo, T., & Peplau, L. A. (1980). Power strategies in intimate relationships. *Journal of Personality and Social Psychology, 38,* 618-628.

Felson, R. B. (1978). Aggression as impression management. *Social Psychology, 41,* 205-213.

Filley, A. C. (1975). *Interpersonal conflict resolution.* Glenview, IL: Scott Foresman.

Fisher, L. E. (1976). Dropping remarks and the Barbadian audience. *American Ethnologist, 3,* 227-242.

Fitzpatrick, M. A. (1976). *A typological approach to communication in relationships.* Unpublished doctoral dissertation, Temple University.

Fitzpatrick, M. A., & Best, P. (1979). Dyadic adjustment in relational types: Consensus, cohesion, affectional expression and satisfaction in enduring relationships. *Communication Monographs, 46,* 167-178.

Fitzpatrick, M. A., & Indvik, J. (1979). *What you see may not be what you have: Communicative accuracy in marital types.* Paper presented at the annual meeting of the Speech Communication Association, San Antonio, TX.

Fitzpatrick, M. A., & Winke, J. (1979). You always hurt the one you love: Strategies and tactics in interpersonal conflict. *Communication Quarterly, 27,* 1-11.

Fleishman, E. A. (1973). Twenty years of consideration and structure. In E. A. Fleishman & J. G. Hunt (Eds.), *Current developments in the study of leadership* (pp. 1-40). Carbondale: Southern Illinois University Press.

Folb, E. A. (1980). *Runnin' down some lines.* Cambridge, MA: Harvard University Press.

Folger, J. P., Hewes, D., & Poole, M. S. (in press). Coding social interaction. In B. Dervin & M. J. Voigt (Eds.), *Progress in communication sciences.* Norwood, NJ: Ablex.

Folger, J. P., & Poole, M. S. (1981). Relational coding schemes: The question of validity. In M. Burgoon (Ed.), *Communication yearbook 5* (pp. 235-245). New Brunswick, NJ: Transaction.

Folger, J. P., & Sillars, A. L. (1977). *Relational coding and perceptions of dominance.* Paper presented at the annual meeting of the Speech Communication Association, Washington, D.C.

Forgas, J. P. (1976). The perception of social episodes: Categorical and dimensional representations in two different social milieus. *Journal of Personality and Social Psychology, 34,* 199-209.

Forgas, J. P. (1979). *Social episodes: The study of interaction routines.* London: Academic Press.

Foss, R. D., & Dempsey, C. B. (1979). Blood donation and the foot-in-the-door technique: A limiting case. *Journal of Personality and Social Psychology, 37,* 580-590.

Freedman, J. L., & Fraser, S. (1966). Compliance without pressure: The foot-in-the-door technique. *Journal of Personality and Social Psychology, 4,* 195-202.

French, J. R., Jr. (1956). A formal theory of social power. *Psychological Review, 63,* 181-194.

French, J., & Raven, B. (1960). The bases of social power. In D. Cartwright & A. Zander (Eds.), *Group dynamics* (pp. 607-623). New York: Harper & Row.

Friedland, N. (1976). Social influence via threats. *Journal of Experimental Social Psychology, 12,* 552-563.

Furse, D. H., Stewart, D. W., & Rados, D. L. (1981). Effects of foot-in-the-door, cash incentives, and followups on survey response. *Journal of Marketing Research, 18,* 473-478.

Gahagan, J. P., & Tedeschi, J. T. (1968). Strategy and the credibility of promises in the prisoner's dilemma game. *Journal of Conflict Resolution, 12,* 224-234.

Gamson, W. A. (1968). *Power and discontent.* Homewood, IL: Dorsey.

Garfinkel, H. (1956). Conditions of successful degradation ceremonies. *American Journal of Sociology, 61,* 420-424.

Gilbert, S. J. (1976). Empirical and theoretical extensions of self-disclosure. In G. R. Miller (Ed.), *Explorations in interpersonal communication* (pp. 197-215). Beverly Hills, CA: Sage.

Gilchrist, J. A. (1982). *The compliance interview: Negotiating across organizational boundaries.* Paper presented at the annual meeting of the International Communication Association, Boston.

Goffman, E. (1952). On cooling the mark out: some aspects of adaptation to failure. *Psychiatry: Journal for the Study of Interpersonal Relations, 15,* 451-463.

Goffman, E. (1955). On face-work: An analysis of ritual elements in social interaction. *Psychiatry, 18,* 213-231.

Goffman, E. (1956). Embarrassment and social organization. *American Journal of Sociology, 26,* 264-274.

Goffman, E. (1959). *The presentation of self in everyday life.* Garden City, NY: Doubleday.

Goffman, E. (1967). *Interaction ritual.* Garden City, NY: Doubleday-Anchor.

Goffman, E. (1969). *Strategic interaction.* Philadelphia: University of Pennsylvania Press.

Goffman, E. (1971). *Relations in public.* New York: Harper & Row.

Goldman, M., & Creason, C. R. (1981). Inducing compliance by a two-door-in-the-face procedure and a self-determination request. *Journal of Social Psychology, 114,* 229-235.

Goldman, M., Creason, C. R., & McCall, C. G. (1981). Compliance employing a two-feet-in-the-door procedure. *Journal of Social Psychology, 114,* 259-265.

Goldman, M., Gier, J. A., & Smith, D. E. (1981). Compliance as affected by task difficulty and order of tasks. *Journal of Social Psychology, 114,* 75-83.

Goldman, M., Seever, M., & Seever, M. (1982). Social labeling and the foot-in-the-door effect. *Journal of Social Psychology, 117,* 19-23.

Goodstadt, B. E., & Hjelle, L. A. (1973). Power to the powerless: Locus of control and the use of power. *Journal of Personality and Social Psychology, 27,* 190-196.

Goodstadt, B. E., & Kipnis, D. (1970). Situational influences on the use of power. *Journal of Applied Psychology, 54,* 201-207.

Goody, E. N. (1978a). Introduction. In E. N. Goody (Ed.), *Questions and politeness: Strategies in social interaction* (pp. 1-16). New York: Cambridge University Press.

Goody, E. N. (1978b). Towards a theory of questions. In E. N. Goody (Ed.), *Questions and politeness: Strategies in social interaction* (pp. 17-43). New York: Cambridge University Press.

Gottlieb, A., & Ickes, W. (1978). Attributional strategies of social influence. In J. H. Harvey, W. Ickes, & R. F. Kidd (Eds.), *New directions in attribution research* (Vol. 2, pp. 261-296). Hillsdale, NJ: Lawrence Erlbaum.

Gouldner, A. W. (1960). The norm of reciprocity: A preliminary statement. *American Sociological Review, 25,* 161-178.

Gove, W. R., Hughes, M., & Geerken, M. R. (1980). Playing dumb: A form of impression management with undesirable side effects. *Social Psychology Quarterly, 43,* 89-102.

Graen, G., Cashman, J. F., Ginsburgh, S. C., & Schiemann, W. (1977). Effects of linking-pin quality on the quality of working life of lower participants. *Administrative Science Quarterly, 22,* 491-504.

Greenberg, J., & Leventhal, G. S. (1976). Equity and the use of over-reward to motivate performance. *Journal of Personality and Social Psychology, 34,* 179-190.

Greenberg, M. S., & Shapiro, S. P. (1971). Indebtedness: An adverse aspect of asking for and receiving help. *Sociometry, 34,* 290-301.

Greene, C. N. (1975). The reciprocal nature of influence between leader and subordinate. *Journal of Applied Psychology, 60,* 187-193.

Grimshaw, A. D. (1980). Selection and labeling of instrumentalities of verbal manipulation. *Discourse Processes, 3,* 203-229.

Grimshaw, A. D. (1981). Talk and social control. In M. Rosenberg & R. H. Turner (Eds.), *Social psychology: Sociological perspectives* (pp. 200-232). New York: Basic Books.

Gross, E., & Stone, G. P. (1966). Embarrassment and the analysis of role requirements. In C. W. Backman & P. F. Secord (Eds.), *Problems in social psychology: Selected readings* (pp. 383-394). New York: McGraw-Hill.

Haley, J. (1973). *Uncommon therapy.* New York: W. W. Norton.

Haley, J. (1977). *Problem-solving therapy: New strategies for effective family therapy.* San Francisco: Jossey-Bass.

Halliday, M.A.K. (1970). Language structure and language function. In J. Lyons (Ed.), *New horizons in linguistics* (pp. 140-165). New York: Penguin.

Halliday, M.A.K. (1973). *Explorations in the functions of language.* London: Edward Arnold.

Hare, A. P. (1976). *Handbook of small group research.* New York: Free Press.

Haslett, B. J. (1983a). Preschoolers' communicative strategies in gaining compliance from peers: A developmental study. *Quarterly Journal of Speech, 69,* 84-99.

Haslett, B. J. (1983b). Communicative functions and strategies in children's conversations. *Human Communication Research, 9,* 114-129.

Hazelton, V., Holdridge, W., & Liska, J. (1982). *Toward a taxonomy of compliance-resisting communication.* Paper presented at the annual meeting of the Western Speech Communication Association, Denver, CO.

Heilman, M. E. (1976). Oppositional behavior as a function of influence attempt intensity and retaliation threat. *Journal of Personality and Social Psychology, 33,* 574-578.

Helson, H. (1964). *Adaptation-level theory: An experimental and systematic approach to behavior.* New York: Harper & Row.

Herold, D. M. (1977). Two-way influence processes in leader-follower dyads. *Academy of Management Journal, 20,* 224-237.

Hewes, D. E. (1983). *The effects of differential category-by-category unreliability on the sequential structure of coded social interaction.* Paper presented at the annual meeting of the International Communication Association, Dallas, TX.

Hewes, D. E., Planalp, S. K., & Streibel, M. (1980). Analyzing social interaction: Some excruciating models and exhilarating results. In D. Nimmo (Ed.), *Communication yearbook 4* (pp. 123-141). New Brunswick, NJ: Transaction.

Hickson, D. J., Hinings, C. R., Lee, C. A., Schneck, R. E., & Pennings, J. M. (1971). A strategic contingencies theory of intraorganizational power. *Administrative Science Quarterly, 16,* 216-229.

Hill, C. T., & Stull, D. E. (1982). Disclosure reciprocity: Conceptual and measurement issues. *Social Psychology Quarterly, 45,* 238-244.

Hobbs, J. R., & Evans, D. A. (1980). Conversation as planned behavior. *Cognitive Science, 4,* 349-377.

Homans, G. C. (1961). *Social behavior: Its elementary forms.* New York: Harcourt Brace Jovanovich.

Hornstein, H. A. (1965). The effects of different magnitudes of threat upon interpersonal bargaining. *Journal of Experimental Social Psychology, 1,* 282-293.

Hrebiniak, L. (1978). *Complex organizations.* St. Paul, MN: West.

Hunter, J. E., & Boster, F. J. (1978). *An empathy model of compliance-gaining message selection.* Paper presented at the annual meeting of the Speech Communication Association, Minneapolis.

Hunter, J. E., & Boster, F. J. (1979). *Situational differences in the selection of compliance-gaining messages.* Paper presented at the annual meeting of the Speech Communication Association, San Antonio, TX.

Hunter, J. E., & Boster, F. (1981). *Compliance-gaining message experiments: Some evidence for an empathy model.* Unpublished manuscript, Michigan State University.

Husband, R. L. (1981). *Leadership phenomenology: A case study and social cognitive correlates.* Unpublished doctoral dissertation, University of Illinois at Urbana-Champaign.

Indvik, J., & Fitzpatrick, M. A. (1983). A review of communication research on psychological gender: Actors, behaviors and contexts. *Communication, 12,* 55-76.

Irvine, J. T. (1974). Strategies of status manipulation in the Wolof greeting. In R. Baumann & J. Sherzer (Eds.), *Explanations in the ethnography of speaking* (pp. 167-191). London: Cambridge University Press.

Izraeli, D. N. (1975). The middle manager and the tactics of power expansion: A case study. *Sloan Management Review, 16,* 57-70.

Jablin, F. M. (1979). Superior-subordinate communication: The state of the art. *Psychological Bulletin, 86,* 1201-1222.

Jackson, S., & Backus, D. (1982). Are compliance-gaining strategies dependent on situational variables? *Central States Speech Journal, 33,* 469-479.

Jackson, S., & Jacobs, S. (1983). Generalizing about messages: Suggestions for design and analysis of experiments. *Human Communication Research, 9,* 169-181.

Jacobs, S., & Jackson, S. (1982). Conversational argument: A discourse analytic approach. In R. Cox & C. A. Willard (Eds.), *Advances in argumentation theory and research* (pp. 205-237). Carbondale: Southern Illinois University Press.

Jacobs, S., & Jackson, S. (1983). Strategy and structure in conversational influence attempts. *Communication Monographs, 50,* 285-304.

Jefferson, G. (1979). A technique for inviting laughter and its subsequent acceptance declination. In G. Psathas (Ed.), *Everyday language: Studies in ethnomethodology* (pp. 79-96). New York: Irvington.

Jones, E. E. (1964). *Ingratiation: A social psychological analysis.* New York: Meredith.

Jones, E. E., & Wortman, C. (1973). *Ingratiation: An attributional approach.* Morristown, NJ: General Learning Press.

Kaminski, E., McDermott, S., & Boster, F. (1977). *The use of compliance-gaining strategies as a function of Machiavellianism and situation.* Paper presented at the annual meeting of the Central States Speech Association, Southfield, MI.

Kanouse, D. E., Gumpert, P., & Canavan-Gumpert, D. (1981). The semantics of praise. In J. H. Harvey, W. Ickes, & R. F. Kidd (Eds.), *New directions in attribution research* (Vol. 3, pp. 97-115). Hillsdale, NJ: Lawrence Erlbaum.

Kanter, R. M. (1977). *Men and women of the corporation.* New York: Basic Books.

Kaufer, D. S. (1981). Ironic evaluations. *Communication Monographs, 48,* 25-38.

Kaufer, D. S., & Neuwirth, C. M. (1982). Foregrounding norms and ironic communication. *Quarterly Journal of Speech, 68,* 28-36.

Kelman, H. C. (1961). Processes of opinion change. *Public Opinion Quarterly, 25,* 57-78.

Kelman, H. C. (1974). Further thoughts on the processes of compliance, identification and internalization. In J. T. Tedeschi (Ed.), *Perspectives on social power* (pp. 125-171). Chicago: Aldine.

Kipnis, D. (1974). The powerholder. In J. T. Tedeschi (Ed.), *Perspectives on social power* (pp. 82-122). Chicago: Aldine.

Kipnis, D., & Cosentino, J. (1969). Use of leadership powers in industry. *Journal of Applied Psychology, 53,* 460-466.

Kipnis, D., Schmidt, S. M., Swaffin-Smith, C., & Wilkinson, I. (1984). Patterns of managerial influence: Shotgun managers, tacticians, and bystanders. *Organizational Dynamics, 12,* 58-67.

Kipnis, D., Schmidt, S. M., & Wilkinson, I. (1980). Intraorganizational influence tactics: Explorations in getting one's way. *Journal of Applied Psychology, 65,* 440-452.

Kline, S. L. (1981a). *Construct system development and face support in persuasive messages: A preliminary report.* Paper presented at the annual meeting of the Central States Speech Association, Chicago.

Kline, S. L. (1981b). *Construct system development and face support in persuasive messages: Two empirical investigations.* Paper presented at the annual meeting of the International Communication Association, Minneapolis.

Kline, S. L. (1981c). *Construct system development, empathic motivation, and the accomplishment of face support in persuasive messages.* Paper presented at the annual meeting of the Speech Communication Association, Anaheim, CA.

Kline, S. L. (1982). *Individual differences in the accomplishment of face support in persuasive communication.* Unpublished doctoral dissertation, University of Illinois at Urbana-Champaign.

Knapp, M. L. (1978). *Social intercourse: From greeting to goodbye.* Boston, Allyn & Bacon.

Knapp, M. L., & Comadena, M. F. (1979). Telling it like it isn't: A review of theory and research on deceptive communications. *Human Communication Research, 5,* 270-285.

Kotter, J. P. (1977). Power, dependence, and effective management. *Harvard Business Review, 55,* 125-136.

Kotter, J. P. (1979). *Power in management.* New York: Amacom.

Kramarae, C. (1981). *Women and men speaking.* Rowley, MA: Newbury House.

Krause, M. S. (1972). Strategies in argument. *Journal of Psychology, 81,* 269-279.

LaLumia, J., & Baglan, T. (1981). Choice of strategies for attitude change: An exploratory analysis. *Psychological Reports, 48,* 793-794.

Langer, E. J., Blank, A., & Chanowitz, B. (1978). The mindlessness of ostensibly thoughtful action: The role of "placebic" information in interpersonal interaction. *Journal of Personality and Social Psychology, 36,* 635-642.

Layton, B. D., & Moehle, D. (1980). Attributed influence: The importance of observing change. *Journal of Experimental Social Psychology, 16,* 243-252.

Levine, B. A., Moss, K. C., Ramsey, P. H., & Fleishman, J. A. (1978). Patient compliance with advice as a function of communicator expertise. *Journal of Social Psychology, 104,* 309-310.

Levy, D. M. (1979). Communicative goals and strategies: Between discourse and syntax. In T. Givon (Ed.), *Syntax and semantics* (Vol. 12, pp. 183-210). New York: Academic Press.

Lewis, D. K. (1969). *Convention: A philosophical study.* Cambridge, MA: Harvard University Press.

Luloffs, R. (1982). *Compliance-gaining and compliance resisting strategies in dyadic conversations.* Paper presented at the annual meeting of the Western Speech Communication Association, Denver, CO.

Lustig, M., & King, S. (1980). The effect of communication apprehension and situation on communication strategy choices. *Human Communication Research, 7,* 74-82.

Manz, C. C., & Gioia, D. A. (1983). The interrelationship of power and control. *Human Relations, 36,* 459-476.

March, J. G. (1955). An introduction to the theory and measurement of influence. *American Political Science Review, 49,* 431-451.

Marwell, G., & Schmitt, D. R. (1967a). Compliance-gaining behavior: A synthesis and model. *Sociological Quarterly, 8,* 317-328.

Marwell, G., & Schmitt, D. R. (1967b). *Dimensions of compliance-gaining behavior: An empirical analysis.* Sociometry, 30, 350-364.

McAllister, H. A., & Bregman, N. J. (1983). Self-disclosure and liking: An integration theory approach. *Journal of Personality, 51,* 202-212.

McGaughey, K. J., & Stiles, W. B. (1983). Courtroom interrogation of rape victims: Verbal response mode use by attorneys and witnesses during direct examination vs. cross-examination. *Journal of Applied Social Psychology, 13,* 78-87.

McGuire, W. J. (1969). The nature of attitudes and attitude change. In G. Lindzey & E. Aronson (Eds.), *Handbook of social psychology* (Vol. 3, pp. 136-314). Reading, MA: Addison-Wesley.

McLaughlin, M. L., & Cody, M. J. (1982). *Situation perception factors and the selection of message strategies.* Paper presented at the annual meeting of the Speech Communication Association, Louisville, KY.

McLaughlin, M. L. Cody, M. L., & O'Hair, H. D. (1983). The management of failure events: Some contextual determinants of accounting behavior. *Human Communication Research, 9,* 208-224.

McLaughlin, M. L., Cody, M. J., & Rosenstein, N. E. (1983). Account sequences in conversations between strangers. *Communication Monographs, 50,* 102-125.

Mechanic, D. (1962). Sources of power of lower participants in complex organizations. *Administrative Science Quarterly, 7,* 349-364.

Michener, H. A., Fleishman, J. A., Elliott, G. C., & Skolnick, J. M. (1978). Target attributes as determinants of influence use in supervisory situations. *Social Psychology, 41,* 214-224.

Michener, H. A., & Schwertfeger, M. (1972). Liking as a determinant of power tactic preference. *Sociometry, 35,* 190-202.

Millar, D. P. (1979). *Integrating verbal and nonverbal messages of relational control.* Paper presented at the annual meeting of the International Communication Association, Minneapolis.

Millar, F. E., & Rogers, L. E. (1976). A relational approach to interpersonal communication. In G. R. Miller (Ed.), *Explorations in interpersonal communication* (pp. 87-104). Beverly Hills, CA: Sage.

Millar, F. E., Rogers-Millar, L. E., & Courtright, J. A. (1979). Relational control and dyadic understanding: An exploratory predictive regression model. In D. Nimmo (Ed.), *Communication yearbook 3* (pp. 213-224). New Brunswick, NJ: Transaction.

Miller, G. R., Boster, F., Roloff, M., & Seibold, D. (1977). Compliance-gaining message strategies: A typology and some findings concerning effects of situational differences. *Communication Monographs, 44,* 37-51.

Miller, G. R., & Burgoon, M. (1978). Persuasion research: Review and commentary. In B. Rubin (Ed.), *Communication yearbook 2* (pp. 29-47). New Brunswick, NJ: Transaction.

Miller, G. R., Burgoon, M., & Burgoon, J. K. (1984). The functions of human communication in changing attitudes and gaining compliance. In C. C. Arnold & J. W. Bowers (Eds.), *Handbook of rhetorical and communication theory* (pp. 400-474). Boston: Allyn & Bacon.

Miller, G. R., & Steinberg, M. (1975). *Between people: A new analysis of interpersonal communication.* Palo Alto, CA: Science Research Associates.

Miller, R. L., Seligman, C., Clark, N. T., & Bush, M. (1976). Perceptual contrast versus reciprocal concession as mediators of induced compliance. *Canadian Journal of Behavioral Science, 8,* 401-409.

Miller, R. L., & Suls, J. (1977). Helping, self-attribution, and the size of an initial request. *Journal of Social Psychology, 103,* 203-207.

Mitchell-Kernan, C. (1972a). Signifying, loud-talking and marking. In T. Kochman (Ed.), *Rappin' and stylin' out* (pp. 315-335). Urbana: University of Illinois Press.

Mitchell-Kernan, C. (1972b). Signifying and marking: Two Afro-American speech acts. In J. J. Gumperz & D. Hymes (Eds.), *Directions in sociolinguistics* (pp. 161-179). New York: Holt, Rinehart & Winston.

Modigliani, A. (1968). Embarrassment and embarrassability. *Sociometry, 31,* 316-326.

Modigliani, A. (1971). Embarrassment, facework, and eye contact: Testing a theory of embarrassment. *Journal of Personality and Social Psychology, 17,* 15-24.

Monteverde, R. J., Paschke, R., & Tedeschi, J. T. (1974). The effectiveness of honesty and deceit as influence tactics. *Sociometry, 37,* 583-591.

Mowen, J. C., & Cialdini, R. B. (1980). On implementing the door-in-the-face compliance technique in a business context. *Journal of Marketing Research, 22,* 253-258.

Nealey, S. M., & Fiedler, F. E. (1968). Leadership functions of middle managers. *Psychological Bulletin, 70,* 313-329.

Nisbett, R. A., & Wilson, T. (1977). Telling more than we can know: Verbal reports on mental processes. *Psychological Review, 84,* 231-259.

O'Donnell-Trujillo, N. (1981). Relational communication: A comparison of coding systems. *Communication Monographs, 2,* 91-105.

O'Hagen, R. J., & Edmunds, G. (1982). Pupils' attitudes towards teachers' strategies for controlling disruptive behaviour. *British Journal of Educational Psychology, 52,* 331-340.

O'Keefe, B. J., & Benoit, P. J. (1983). Children's arguments. In R. Cox & C. A. Willard (Eds.), *Advances in argumentation theory* (pp. 154-183). Carbondale: Southern Illinois University Press.

O'Keefe, B. J., & Delia, J. G. (1979). Construct comprehensiveness and cognitive complexity as predictors of the number and strategic adaptation of arguments and appeals in a persuasive message. *Communication Monographs, 46,* 231-240.

O'Keefe, B. J., & Delia, J. G. (1982). Impression formation and message production. In M. E. Roloff & C. R. Berger (Eds.), *Social cognition and communication* (pp. 33-72). Beverly Hills, CA: Sage.

Oldham, G. R. (1976). The motivational strategies used by supervisors: Relationships to effectiveness indicators. *Organizational Behavior and Human Performance, 15,* 66-86.

O'Quin, K., & Aronoff, J. (1981). Humor as a technique of social influence. *Social Psychology Quarterly, 44,* 349-357.

Parks, M. R. (1977). Relational communication: Theory and research. *Human Communication Research, 3,* 372-381.

Parsons, T. (1956). Suggestions for a sociological approach to organizations. *Administrative Science Quarterly, 1,* 225-239.

Parsons, T. (1963). On the concept of influence. *Public Opinion Quarterly, 27,* 35-62.

Patchen, M. (1973). The locus and basis of influence on organizational decisions. *Organizational Behavior and Human Performance, 11,* 195-221.

Paul, S. C., & Thelen, M. H. (1983). The use of strategies and messages to alter aggressive interactions. *Aggressive Behavior, 9,* 183-193.

Pendleton, M. G., & Batson, C. D. (1979). Self-presentation and the door-in-the-face technique for inducing compliance. *Personality and Social Psychology Bulletin, 5,* 77-81.

Poole, M. S., & Folger, J. (1981). A method for establishing the representational validity for interaction coding schemes. Do we see what they see? *Human Communication Research, 8,* 26-42.

Ragan, S. L., & Hopper, R. (1981). Alignment talk in the job interview. *Journal of Applied Communication Research, 9,* 85-103.

Reingen, P. H. (1978). On inducing compliance with requests. *Journal of Consumer Research, 5,* 96-102.

Renshaw, P. D., & Asher, S. R. (1983). Children's goals and strategies for social interaction. *Merrill-Palmer Quarterly, 29,* 353-374.

Riccillo, S. C., & Trenholm, S. (1983). Predicting managers' choice of influence mode: The effects of interpersonal trust and worker attributions on managerial tactics in a simulated organizational setting. *The Western Journal of Speech Communication, 47,* 323-339.

Rim, Y., & Erez, M. (1980). A note about tactics used to influence superiors, co-workers and subordinates. *Journal of Occupational Psychology, 53,* 319-321.

Rittle, R. H. (1981). Changes in helping behavior: Self versus situational perceptions as mediators of the foot-in-the-door effect. *Personality and Social Psychology Bulletin, 7,* 431-457.

Rogers, L. E. (1972). *Dyadic systems and transactional communication in a family context.* Unpublished doctoral dissertation, Michigan State University.

Rogers, L. E. (1983). *Analyzing relational communication: Implications of a pragmatic approach.* Paper presented at the annual meeting of the Speech Communication Association, Washington, D.C.

Rogers, L. E., & Bagarozzi, D. A. (1983). An overview of relational communication and implications for therapy. In D. Bagarozzi, A. Jurich, & R. Jackson (Eds.), *Marital and family therapy: New perspectives in theory, research, and practices* (pp. 48-78). New York: Human Sciences Press.

Rogers, L. E., Courtright, J. A., & Millar, F. E. (1982). Message control intensity: Rationale and preliminary findings. *Communication Monographs, 47,* 201-219.

Rogers, L. E., & Farace, R. V. (1975). Analysis of relational communication in dyads: New measurement procedures. *Human Communication Research, 1,* 222-239.

Rogers, L. E., & Millar, F. E. (1981). The question of validity: A pragmatic response. In M. Burgoon (Ed.), *Communication yearbook 5* (pp. 249-257). New Brunswick, NJ: Transaction.

Rogers, L. E., & Millar, F. E. (1982). *Reflections on relational communication research: Issues, patterns, and refinements.* Paper presented at the annual meeting of the Eastern Communication Association, Hartford, CT.

Rogers-Millar, L. E., & Millar III, F. E. (1979). Domineeringness and dominance: A transactional view. *Human Communication Research, 5,* 238-246.

Rokeach, M. (1960). *The open and closed mind.* New York: Basic Books.

Roloff, M. E. (1976). Communication strategies, relationships, and relational change. In G. R. Miller (Ed.), *Explorations in interpersonal communication* (pp. 173-195). Beverly Hills, CA: Sage.

Roloff, M. E., & Barnicott, E. (1978). The situational use of pro- and anti-social compliance-gaining strategies by high and low Machiavellians. In B. Ruben (Ed.), *Communication yearbook 2* (pp. 193-208). New Brunswick, NJ: Transaction.

Roloff, M. E., & Barnicott, E. (1979). The influence of dogmatism on the situational use of pro- and anti-social compliance-gaining strategies. *Southern Speech Communication Journal, 45,* 37-54.

Rubin, I. M., & Berlew, D. E. (1984). The power failure in organizations. *Training and Development Journal, January,* 35-38.

Rubin, J. Z., & Brown, B. R. (1975). Social influence and influence strategies. In J. Z. Rubin & B. R. Brown (Eds.), *The social psychology of bargaining and negotiation* (pp. 262-289). New York: Academic Press.

Rueda, R., & Smith, D. C. (1983). Interpersonal tactics and communicative strategies of Anglo-American and Mexican-American mildly mentally retarded and non-retarded students. *Applied Research in Mental Retardation, 4,* 153-161.

Ruesch, J., & Bateson, G. (1951). *Communication: Matrix of psychiatry.* New York: W. W. Norton.

Salancik, G. R., & Pfeffer, J. (1977). Who gets power—and how they hold on to it: A strategic-contingency model of power. *Organizational Dynamics, 5,* 3-21.

Savicki, V. (1972). Outcomes of nonreciprocal self-disclosure strategies. *Journal of Personality and Social Psychology, 23,* 271-276.

Schelling, T. C. (1963). *The strategy of conflict.* Cambridge, MA: Harvard University Press.

Schenck-Hamlin, W. J., Georgacarakos, G. N., & Wiseman, R. L. (1982). A formal account of interpersonal compliance-gaining. *Communication Quarterly, 30,* 173-180.

Schenck-Hamlin, W. J., Wiseman, R. L., & Georgacarakos, G. N. (1980). *A typology of compliance-gaining strategies and the logic of their underlying relationships.* Paper presented at the annual meeting of the International Communication Association, Acapulco, Mexico.

Schenck-Hamlin, W. J., Wiseman, R. L., & Georgacarakos, G. N. (1982). A model of properties of compliance-gaining strategies. *Communication Quarterly, 30,* 92-100.

Schenkein, J. (1978). Identity negotiations in conversation. In J. Schenkein (Ed.), *Studies in the organization of conversational interaction* (pp. 57-78). New York: Academic Press.

Schlenker, B. R. (1980). *Impression management: The self-concept, social identity, and interpersonal relations.* Belmont, CA: Wadsworth.

Schlenker, B. R., Bonoma, T., & Tedeschi, J. T. (1970). Compliance to threats as a function of the wording of the threat and the exploitativeness of the threatener. *Sociometry, 33,* 394-408.

Schlenker, B. R., & Darby, B. W. (1981). The use of apologies in social predicaments. *Social Psychology Quarterly, 44,* 271-278.

Schwarzwald, J., Raz, M., & Zvibel, M. (1979). The applicability of the door-in-the-face technique where established behavioral customs exist. *Journal of Applied Social Psychology, 9,* 576-586.

Scott, C. A. (1977). Modifying socially conscious behavior: The foot-in-the-door technique. *Journal of Consumer Research, 4,* 156-164.

Seibold, D. R., & Spitzberg, B. H. (1982). Attribution theory and research: Review and implications for communication. In B. Dervin & M. J. Voigt (Eds.), *Progress in communication sciences* (Vol. 3, pp. 85-125). Norwood, NJ: Ablex.

Seibold, D. R., & Steinfatt, T. M. (1979). The creative alternative game: Exploring interpersonal influence processes. *Simulation & Games, 10,* 429-457.

Seibold, D. R., & Thomas, R. (1981). *Compliance-gaining message strategies: Tests of replicability and validity.* Paper presented at the annual meeting of the Speech Communication Association, Anaheim, CA.

Seligman, C., Bush, M., & Kirsch, K. (1976). Relationship between compliance in the foot-in-the-door paradigm and size of first request. *Journal of Personality and Social Psychology, 33,* 517-520.

Seligman, C., Miller, R., Goldberg, G., Gelberd, L., Clark, N., & Bush, M. (1976). Compliance in the foot-in-the-door technique as a function of issue similarity and persuasion. *Social Behavior and Personality, 4,* 267-271.

Shanab, M. E., & Isonio, S. A. (1980). The effects of delay upon compliance with socially undesirable requests in the door-in-the-face paradigm. *Bulletin of the Psychonomic Society, 15,* 76-78.

Shanab, M. E., & Isonio, S. A. (1982). The effects of contrast upon compliance with socially undesirable requests in the foot-in-the-door paradigm. *Bulletin of the Psychonomic Society, 20,* 180-182.

Shanab, M. E., & O'Neill, P. (1979). The effects of contrast upon compliance with socially undesirable requests in the door-in-the-face paradigm. *Canadian Journal of Behavioral Science, 11,* 236-244.

Shepherd, G. J., & O'Keefe, B. J. (in press). The relationship between the developmental level of persuasive strategies and their effectiveness. *Central States Speech Journal.*

Shields, N. M. (1979). Accounts and other interpersonal strategies in a credibility detracting context. *Pacific Sociological Review, 22,* 255-272.

Siegman, A. W., & Pope, B. (1965). Effects of question specificity and anxiety-producing messages on verbal fluency in the initial interview. *Journal of Personality and Social Psychology, 2,* 522-530.

Sillars, A. L. (1980). The stranger and the spouse as target persons for compliance-gaining strategies: A subjective utility model. *Human Communication Research, 6,* 265-279.

Sillars, A. L., & Folger, J. P. (1978). *A second look at relational coding assumptions.* Paper presented at the annual meeting of the International Communication Association, Chicago.

Singer, J. E. (1964). The use of manipulative strategies: Machiavellianism and attractiveness. *Sociometry, 27,* 128-150.

Skinner, B. (1953). *Science and human behavior.* New York: Macmillan.

Smith, M. J. (1984). Contingency rules theory, context, and compliance behaviors. *Human Communication Research, 4,* 489-512.

Smith, T. E. (1983). Parental influence: A review of the evidence of influence and a theoretical model of the parental influence process. *Research in Sociology of Education and Socialization, 4,* 13-45.

Snyder, M., & Cunningham, M. R. (1975). To comply or not comply: Testing the self-perception explanation of the "foot-in-the-door" phenomenon. *Journal of Personality and Social Psychology, 31,* 64-67.

Stebbins, R. A. (1975). Putting people on: Deception of our fellowman in everyday life. *Sociology and Social Research, 69,* 189-200.

Steele, C. M. (1975). Name-calling and compliance. *Journal of Personality and Social Psychology, 31,* 361-369.

Stephenson, R. M. (1951). Conflict and control functions of humor. *American Journal of Sociology, 56,* 569-574.

Stires, L. K., & Jones, E. E. (1969). Modesty versus self-enhancement as alternative forms of ingratiation. *Journal of Experimental Social Psychology, 5,* 79-82.

Stogdill, R. M. (1974). *Handbook of leadership.* New York: Free Press.

Swann, W. B., & Hill, C. A. (1982). When our identities are mistaken: Reaffirming self-conceptions through social interaction. *Journal of Personality and Social Psychology, 43,* 59-66.

Tedeschi, J. T. (1970). Threats and promises. In P. Swingle (Ed.), *The structure of conflict* (pp. 155-191). New York: Academic Press.

Tedeschi, J. T., & Bonoma, T. V. (1972). Power and influence: An introduction. In J. T. Tedeschi (Ed.), *The social influence processes* (pp. 1-49). Chicago: Aldine.

Tedeschi, J. T., Gaes, G. G., & Rivera, A. N. (1977). Aggression and the use of coercive power. *Journal of Social Issues, 33,* 101-125.

Tedeschi, J. T., & Lindskold, S. (1976). *Social psychology: Interdependence, interaction, and influence.* New York: John Wiley.

Tedeschi, J. T., & Reiss, M. (1981). Verbal strategies in impression management. In C. Antaki (Ed.), *The psychology of ordinary explanations of social behaviour* (pp. 271-309). New York: Academic Press.

Thibaut, J., & Kelley, H. (1959). *The social psychology of groups.* New York: John Wiley.

Thomas, R. W., & Seibold, D. R. (1982). *Replicability II: Procedures and typologies in compliance-gaining message analysis.* Paper presented at the annual meeting of the Speech Communication Association, Louisville, KY.

Thompson, T. L., & Seibold, D. R. (1978). Stigma management in normal-stigmatized interactions: Test of the disclosure hypothesis and a model of stigma acceptance. *Human Communication Research, 4,* 231-242.

Tjosvold, D. (1983). Effects of superiors' influence orientation on their decision making in controversy. *Journal of Psychology, 113,* 175-182.

Tjosvold, D. (1984). The dynamics of positive power. *Training and Development Journal, 38,* 72-76.

Tracy, K., Craig, R. T., Smith, M., & Spisak, F. (1984). The discourse of requests: Assessment of a compliance-gaining approach. *Human Communication Research, 10,* 513-538.

Trapp, R. (1983). Generic characteristics of argument in everyday discourse. In D. Zarefsky, M. O. Sillars, & J. Rhodes (Eds.). *Argument in transition: Proceedings of the third summer conference on argumentation* (pp. 516-530). Annandale, VA: Speech Communication Association.

Turner, R. E., Edgley, C., & Olmstead, G. (1975). Information control in conversations: Honesty is not always the best policy. *Kansas Journal of Sociology, 1,* 69-89.

Tybout, A. M. (1978). Relative effectiveness of three behavioral influence strategies as supplements to persuasion in a marketing context. *Journal of Marketing Research, 15,* 229-242.

Wagener, J. J., & Laird, J. D. (1980). The experimenter's foot-in-the-door: Self-perception, body weight, and volunteering. *Personality and Social Psychology Bulletin, 6,* 441-446.

Waltar, B. (1966). Internal control relations in administrative hierarchies. *Administrative Science Quarterly, 11,* 179-206.

Walton, R. E., & McKersie, R. B. (1965). *A behavioral theory of labor negotiation.* New York. McGraw-Hill.

Ward, S., & Wackman, D. B. (1972). Children's purchase influence attempts and parental yielding. *Journal of Marketing Research, 9,* 316-319.

Weary, G., & Arkin, R. M. (1981). Attributional self-presentation. In J. H. Harvey, W. Ickes, & R. F. Kidd (Eds.), *New directions in attribution research* (Vol. 3, pp. 223-246). Hillsdale, NJ: Lawrence Erlbaum.

Weber, M. (1947). *The theory of social and economic organization.* New York: Oxford University Press.

Weiler, J., & Weinstein, E. A. (1972). Honesty, fabrication, and the enhancement of credibility. *Sociometry, 35,* 316-331.

Weinstein, E. A. (1966). Toward a theory of interpersonal tactics. In C. W. Backman & P. F. Secord (Eds.), *Problems in social psychology* (pp. 394-398). New York: McGraw-Hill.

Weinstein, E. A. (1969). The development of interpersonal competence. In D. A. Goslin (Ed.), *Handbook of socialization theory and research* (pp. 753-775). Chicago: Rand McNally.

Weinstein, E. A., & Deutschberger, P. (1963). Some dimensions of altercasting. *Sociometry, 26,* 454-466.

Weiss, D., & Weinstein, E. A. (1968). Interpersonal tactics among mental retardates. *American Journal of Mental Deficiency, 72,* 653-661.

Weiss, W., & Fine, B. J. (1956). The effect of induced aggressiveness on opinion change. *Journal of Abnormal and Social Psychology, 52,* 109-114.

Wheeler, L., Deci, E. L., Reis, H. T., & Zuckerman, M. (1978). *Interpersonal influence.* Boston, MA: Allyn & Bacon.

Wheeless, L. R., Barraclough, R., & Stewart, R. (1983). Compliance-gaining and power in persuasion. In R. Bostrom (Ed.), *Communication yearbook 7* (pp. 105-145). Beverly Hills, CA: Sage.

Williams, D., & Boster, F. (1981). *The effects of beneficial situational characteristics, negativism, and dogmatism on compliance-gaining message selection.* Paper presented at the annual meeting of the International Communication Association, Minneapolis.

Winograd, T. (1977). A framework for understanding discourse. In M. A. Just & P. A. Carpenter (Eds.), *Cognitive processes in comprehension* (pp. 63-88). New Jersey: LEA.

Wiseman, R. L., & Schenck-Hamlin, W. (1981). A multidimensional scaling validation of an inductively-derived set of compliance-gaining strategies. *Communication Monographs, 48,* 251-270.

Wood, J. R., Weinstein, E. A., & Parker, R. (1967). Children's interpersonal tactics. *Social Inquiry, 37,* 129-138.

Yukl, G. A. (1981). *Leadership in organizations.* Englewood Cliffs, NJ: Prentice-Hall.

Zalesznik, A., & Kets de Vries, M.R.F. (1975). *Power and the corporate mind.* Boston, MA: Houghton-Mifflin.

Zuckerman, M., Lazzaro. M. M., & Waldgeir, D. (1979). Undermining effects of the foot-in-the-door technique with extrinsic rewards. *Journal of Applied Social Psychology, 9,* 292-296.

IV CONTEXTS

13 Task/Work Relationships: A Life-Span Perspective

FREDRIC M. JABLIN

University of Texas at Austin

F ROM childhood through retirement task-oriented relationships are an omnipresent part of our lives. Moreover, whether it is performing one's chores as a member of the family unit, participating in classroom or extracurricular school activities, working in a part- or full-time job, or serving as a volunteer member of a community action group, the effective completion of task-oriented activities usually involves some degree of interpersonal communication. Given the invariable presence of task-oriented activities in our lives, and the correspondingly important role interpersonal communication plays in facilitating the completion of these tasks, it is not surprising to discover that the nature, functions, and constraints associated with interpersonal communication in task settings have received a considerable amount of research attention. In particular, the great majority of studies in this area have focused on exploring the dynamics of interpersonal communication in the *work/organizational setting*. Consistent with this trend, the primary goal of this chapter is to organize, review, and interpret interpersonal communication research that has attempted to examine task relationships in work/organizational settings.

However, while this review will focus primarily on exploring interpersonal communication relationships within the work/organizational setting, it will also attempt to view such relationships from a very broad orientation. Specifically, the following discussion will consider communication in the work/organizational setting from a developmental, "life-span" perspective. As a consequence, the first section of this chapter will examine literature concerned with how people learn about interpersonal communication in work/organizational relationships prior to ever entering into them. Maintaining this developmental perspective, the roles and characteristics of interpersonal communication in the process of becoming assimilated into, and eventually becoming an integral part of, work organizations will then be explored. Finally, the period in an individual's life when he or she disengages from the often "rich" interpersonal communication environment of the work setting and progresses into retirement from work will also be considered.

While a variety of schemes might have been used to organize and review the literature on interpersonal communication in task/organizational relationships, the developmental, life-span approach was chosen in this case for the following reasons: (1) the life-span approach recognizes the developmental nature of interpersonal and organizational relationships/processes; (2) the approach incorporates the notion that interpersonal and organizational communication processes are dynamic versus static in nature; and (3) the life-span framework allows us to explore interpersonal communication in task relationships within work/organizational settings, as well as within other task environments.

In summary, this review will examine the roles, functions, and character-istics of interpersonal communication in work/organizational settings. How-ever, unlike most traditional treatments of this subject, in this analysis the work/organizational setting will be construed in very broad terms—from a life-span perspective. Consequently, the first part of this chapter will explore processes through which people learn about or anticipate interpersonal communication in work/organizational settings. This section will then be followed by an examination of the nature of interpersonal communication within the work/organizational context itself. In turn, the last part of the chapter will discuss issues related to interpersonal communication and disengagement from work.

ANTICIPATION OF
INTERPERSONAL COMMUNICATION AT WORK

Vocational/Occupational Development

Prior to ever entering into work relationships, most of us have developed certain beliefs and expectations about how people communicate and interact in the job setting. As Drucker (1973, p. 184) observes, "By the time a human being has reached the age of four or five he has been conditioned to work." To a large extent this conditioning and development of attitudes are byproducts of the process of vocational development, which for most people occurs during maturation from childhood to "young adulthood" (Crites, 1969). Vocational development is the process by which a person chooses (deliber-ately or accidentally) a career direction and develops expectations about what that profession or career will be like. There are probably five basic sources from which we obtain information that affects our vocational development and perceptions of how people communicate at work: (1) family, (2) educational institutions, (3) the mass media, (4) peers, and (5) part-time jobs (see Leifer & Lesser, 1976; Van Maanen, 1975). Research related to each of these sources of information is reviewed briefly below.

Family. Probably the first "significant others" we observe in a set of coordinated task relationships are the members of our families, and in particular our parents. As Leifer and Lesser (1976, p. 38) observe, "Parents are of early and lasting importance as socializers of children." Thus it is not surprising to discover that research findings suggest that parents are often influential in their childrens' career choices (see Brown, Brooks, & Associates, 1984), and that parental characteristics (such as decisiveness, concern for intellectual nurturance, and absence from the home) may be related to the degree to which their children are attracted to occupations that emphasize various dimensions of communication skill (Nachmann, 1960).

Moreover, other studies indicate that by the time most children enter the first grade they are already integrally involved in the performance of routine household chores on a regular basis (for example, see Goldstein & Oldham, 1979). Not unexpectedly, it has also been found that even at this very young age children have already developed perceptions about the behaviors of leaders and followers in task relationships. Specifically, Goldstein and Oldham (1979, p. 53) report that by the time children begin to attend school they already perceive that a "boss tells others what to do and how to do it." Relatedly, other studies have shown that as early as three years of age children have developed sex stereotypes of occupational roles (see Beuf, 1974; Kirchner & Vondracek, 1973; Schlossberg & Goodman, 1972). However, despite the apparent importance of parents and family in early vocational development, at present we still know little about what children learn from their familial ties concerning interaction and communication in task relationships.

Educational Institutions. Of the various sources from which we obtain vocational information, educational institutions are one of the most important. This would appear to be true because (1) school, unlike some of the other sources, has the explicit mandate to socialize people (Gecas, 1981); (2) school serves as a transitional institution between family and job (see Dreeben, 1968; Gecas, 1981); (3) "the relationships of authority and control between administrators and teachers, teachers and students, students and students, and students and their work replicate the hierarchical divisions of labor which dominate the workplace" (Bowles & Gintis, 1976, p. 12); and (4) school is probably the first context in which a child experiences and participates in *formal* organizing activity on a daily basis.

To date, however, only one study has attempted to explore what students learn as they progress through school about the *communication* behaviors of persons in work roles and occupations. In this investigation Jablin (1985) sought to discover what occupations students (as reported by their teachers) talk and read about in school, and the types of interpersonal communicator styles (Norton, 1978) they attribute to persons in these roles. Results of the study indicate that as students progress from elementary through secondary school, their classroom discussions and texts increasingly depict the communication styles of persons in work relationships as "inactive" and "unresponsive-unreceptive." Though this trend was consistent across all occupations, findings also revealed that students (as reported by their teachers) perceived distinctions in the interpersonal communicator styles across persons in different occupations.

Media. A considerable amount of evidence exists suggesting that the mass media, and in particular television, often transmit an inaccurate, stereotypic image of how people behave/communicate in various occupations (for example, see Noble, 1975). Specifically, there is a tendency to represent successful role occupants as fairly "aggressive" communicators who spend a majority of their time giving orders or advice to others (DeFleur, 1964; Turow, 1974, 1980). Thus it is not surprising that when DeFleur (1964) interviewed 237 children about the occupational characteristics they most admired, "power" (ability to "boss" others) consistently ranked highest. It is also interesting to observe that content analyses of television representations of "talk" at work reveal that most conversations have little to do with work; rather, conversations are focused on "social" topics (Katzman, 1972; Turow, 1974).

In general, the research evidence concerning the effects of television representations of occupational behavior/communication on children is somewhat limited, and very difficult to draw causal relationships from. However, several studies have reported findings suggesting that children may generalize mass media content of interpersonal interaction at work to their expectations of how such persons actually behave (Bogatz & Ball, 1971; DeFleur & DeFleur, 1967; Dominick, 1974; Siegel, 1958). In particular, the available evidence indicates that this may be especially true for occupations that children do not often come into contact with in their everyday lives.

Peers and Part-Time Jobs. Of the five sources that are likely to affect one's vocational development and beliefs about communication at work, the least is probably known about the effects of peer influences and part-time jobs. Yet, with respect to peer influences, research in related areas suggests that friends influence adolescents' career aspirations (Bain & Anderson, 1974) and that is is not unusual for peers to discuss and compare their career aspirations with one another (Duncan, Haller, & Portes, 1968; Simpson, 1962; Woelfel & Haller, 1971). Further, Brown (1980), in a study of adolescent peer group communication and decisions about occupations, proposes that peers have a strong influence on what young adults perceive as "proper" interaction attitudes and behaviors. If this is the case, then it is also likely that peers are concomitantly influencing one another's perceptions of the communication characteristics of persons in work roles. As noted above, the influence of peers on perceptions of interpersonal communication in task/work relationships is an area sorely in need of future research.

Similarly, although statistics indicate that over 50 percent of males and females ages 16 to 19 hold part-time jobs (Rotchford & Roberts, 1982), we know little of how these actual work experiences affect adolescents' perceptions and attitudes about interpersonal communication in work relationships. In fact, only a handful of studies exist exploring the work behaviors of this population of employees. About all we currently know is that part-time workers in this age group are employed in lower-level jobs, receive fairly low wages, and may be less included than full-time employees in an organization's social system (Miller & Terborg, 1979). Obviously, determination of the contributions of adolescents' work experiences on the formation of their later work-related communication styles and attitudes is an area deserving of increased research attention.

Summary. This section has attempted to review research related to the period in one's life when one is learning and developing attitudes about how people in general communicate in work/organizational relationships. Five basic influences on the development of these attitudes were considered: (1) family, (2) educational institutions, (3) the mass media, (4) peers, and (5) part-time jobs. Indicative of the research literature, each of these influences was considered independent of the others. However, it seems evident that people actually experience these influences in combination, and that while these sources may often reinforce each other, they may also frequently provide conflicting information. Obviously, the interactive effect of these influences needs to be considered in future research. In closing, probably the most frequent theme evident in the research reviewed on vocational development is that we learn early in life that "power" is an integral element of interpersonal communication in work/organizational relationships.

Organizational Choice

Once an individual has chosen (consciously or unconsciously) an area to pursue for a career, and has received the requisite training to perform the tasks associated with that job, he or she typically will seek an organizational position in which to enact the role. For the job seeker a concomitant of the job search process is the formation of expectations about the jobs and organizations in which he or she has applied for employment. Typically, recruits acquire expectations about specific jobs and organizations from organizational literature (annual reports, advertisements, training brochures, and the like), interpersonal interactions with organizational representatives, or both. In particular, one of the most frequent and critical methods of information exchange between organization and applicant is the selection interview (Arvey & Campion, 1982; Schmidt, 1976).

Selection Interview. The importance of the interview as a selection and recruitment device is epitomized by the fairly large number of literature reviews that have been published over the last twenty years summarizing research in this area (for example, see Arvey & Campion, 1982; Jablin & McComb, 1984; Mayfield, 1964; Schmidt, 1976; Ulrich & Trumbo, 1965; Wright, 1969). It is also important to note that communication-related behavior has been a major focus of this research tradition. For example, Jablin and McComb (1984) report that of the 53 employment interviewing studies they found conducted between 1976 and 1982, 30 (57 percent) explored communication-related variables.

Several generalizations about interpersonal communication in the selection interview can be drawn from recent reviews and empirical studies:

(1) Generally, applicants' interview outcome expectations (including likelihoods of accepting job offers) often appear related to their perceptions of their recruiters as trustworthy, competent, composed, and well-organized communicators (see Alderfer & McCord, 1970; Fisher, Ilgen, & Hoyer, 1979; Jablin, Tengler, & Teigen, 1982; Teigen, 1983).

(2) Applicants do not particularly like or trust interviewers and appear hesitant to accept job offers if their only sources of information are recruiters (see Fisher et al., 1979).

(3) Interviewee satisfaction appears related to the quality and amount of organizational and job information the recruiter provides, the degree to which the recruiter shows interest in the applicant, and the extent to which the recruiter asks the interviewee open-ended questions and allows him or her sufficient "talk time" (Karol, 1977; Tengler, 1982).

(4) Most questions applicants ask their interviewers are closed-ended, singular in form, typically not phrased in the first person, asked after interviewers ask for applicants' inquiries, and seek job-related information (Babbitt, 1983).

(5) Applicants' perceptions of their interviewers as empathic listeners appear to be negatively related to the degree to which interviewers interject "interruptive statements" while the interviewees are speaking (McComb & Jablin, 1984).

(6) Interviewees who display "high" versus "low" levels of nonverbal immediacy (operationalized by eye contact, smiling, posture, interpersonal distance, and body orientation), are "high" in vocal activity, and engage their interviewers in "response-response" versus primarily "question-response" conversations tend to be favored by interviewers (Byrd, 1979; Einhorn, 1981; Imada & Hakel, 1977; McGovern & Tinsley, 1978; Tengler & Jablin, 1983; Trent, 1978).

(7) Recruiters find interviewees more acceptable if they receive favorable information about them prior to or during their interviews; however, recruiters do not necessarily adopt confirmatory question strategies to validate their expectancies (Constantin, 1976; Sackett, 1979).

(8) Interviewers tend to employ inverted funnel question sequences (they begin with closed questions and then progress to more open-ended questions), thus limiting applicant "talk time" during the crucial opening "decision-making" minutes of interviews (Tengler & Jablin, 1983).

(9) Applicants and recruiters tend to have differential perceptions of numerous communication behaviors evidenced in interviews, such as talkativeness, listening, and questioning (Cheatham & McLaughlin, 1976).

(10) The great majority of communication-related selection interview studies have concentrated solely on exploring the communication perceptions and behaviors of interviewers versus interviewees, and generally have failed to examine the two parties in dynamic interaction (Daly, 1978; Jablin & McComb, 1984).

Job/Organizational Expectations. The interview is important not only as an interpersonal communication event, but also because of the role it plays in communicating job/organizational expectations to potential employees. For example, Teigen (1983) recently discovered that about 38 percent of the "talk" (operationalized by word count) and 18 percent of the topics discussed in selection interviews are devoted to information exchanges about organizational climate issues (job duties and responsibilities, advancement potential, pay/benefits, supervision, coworker relations). Additionally, he concludes from some of his results that "interviewees who recruiters consider attractive candidates may be provided with certain kinds of climate information not given to less attractive candidates" (Teigen, 1983, p. 188).

At the same time, however, it is essential to observe that research indicates that regardless of the mode of information exchange between employer and applicant the "typical outcome of this process is the emergence of inflated expectations by the recruit of what his or her potential job and organization will be like (Wanous, 1977, 1980)" (Jablin, 1982a, p. 264). In fact, recent evidence suggests that new recruits may often have extremely inflated expectations of the communication climates of their jobs and organizations, including the amounts of information they will receive from and send to others, from whom they will receive information, the timeliness of the information they will receive, and the channels that will be used for communication (Jablin, 1984). Obviously, it is probably not very desirable for recruits to possess such inflated expectations of the interpersonal communication environments of their jobs and organizations because these inflated expectations will be very difficult to meet. And, "as a result of large discrepancies between expectations and reality, recruits with inflated communication climate expectations may have a higher probability of job turnover and/or less job satisfaction" (Jablin, 1981a, p. 2).

Summary. The preceding discussion has provided an overview of the nature and effects of interpersonal communication exchanges between applicants and organizations during the selection-recruitment process. Particular attention was focused on the communication dynamics of the selection interview, because it is typically the first context in which applicants and organizational representatives meet and interact on a face-to-face basis. Generally speaking, research pertaining to the interview suggests that recruiters prefer applicants who are "active-dynamic" communicators, while interviewees prefer interviewers who are credible communicators and allow applicants ample time to express themselves. At the same time, however, it seems apparent that regardless of the mode of information exchange between applicants and employers, a by-product of the selection-recruitment process is the emergence within applicants of inflated expectations of the interpersonal communication climates of the organizations in which they are seeking employment.

In conclusion, the study of how and what people learn about interpersonal communication in work relationships prior to entering their chosen occupations and/or job settings is still a relatively new area of communication research. However, it seems evident that individuals *do* anticipate the interpersonal communication environments of work settings they may enter, and that these expectations are likely to affect their communication behaviors and perceptions once on the job. The specific nature and effects of this interaction of expectations and "reality" obviously should be a focus of future research.

INTERPERSONAL COMMUNICATION IN THE ORGANIZATIONAL SETTING

Upon entry into an organization, a recruit formally begins the organizational assimilation process. "Organizational assimilation refers to the process by which organizational members become a part of, or are absorbed into, the culture of an organization" (Jablin, 1982a, p. 256). This process is typically considered to contain two reciprocal components: the organization's planned and unplanned attempts to "socialize" the recruit, and the new employee's efforts to "individualize" his or her role. Each of these components of assimilation will be reviewed briefly below, followed by a discussion of the role of interpersonal communication in the organizational assimilation process.

According to Van Maanen (1975, p. 67), organizational socialization is the "process by which a person learns the values and norms and required behaviors that permit him to participate as a member of the organization." Or, as Schein (1968, p. 2) has proposed, it is the "process of 'learning the ropes,' the process of being indoctrinated and trained, the process of being taught what is important in the organization." It should also be noted that while the organizational socialization process may appear to have its greatest impact during one's initial tenure in an organization, it is a *continuous* process that will "change and evolve as the individual remains longer with the organization" (Porter, Lawler, & Hackman, 1975, p. 161). Moreover, it is essential to keep in mind that at the same time that the organization is trying to socialize the new employee, the new organizational member is striving to individualize his or her role by modifying the organization so that it can better satisfy his or her needs, values, and ideas (for example, see Schein, 1968).

When viewed concurrently, the employee individualization and organizational socialization processes characterize the fundamental elements of organizational "role taking" (Katz & Kahn, 1966) or "role making" (Graen, 1976). As has often been noted in the research literature, a role "is at once the building block of social systems and the summation of the requirements with which the system confronts the individual member" (Katz & Kahn, 1966, p. 171). Moreover, roles are learned, have content and stylistic dimensions, possess formal and informal duties, rights, and privileges, and, perhaps most important, can be understood by scrutinizing the role expectations that are communicated to and from an individual by members of his or her "role set" (task-related relevant others). Thus it is as "a result of the communication of expectations by members of the role set that the new employee 'encounters' his or her organizational role and learns the values, behaviors, and patterns of thinking that are considered acceptable to the organizational system" (Jablin, 1982a, p. 259). At the same time, however, it is important to realize that new employees are not merely passive receivers of role sendings, but can proactively negotiate or "make" their roles by attempting to alter the expectations of members of their role sets (Graen, 1976).

As is evident from the above discussion, communication is essential to the organizational assimilation/role-making process. Generally speaking, there are three sources of information available to assist new recruits (as well as existing organizational members) in the role-making process: (1) "official" media-related management sources (such as handbooks, manuals, official house magazines and newsletters), (2) superiors and subordinates, and (3) members of one's work group (coworkers). Of these sources, interpersonal interactions with superiors/subordinates and other work group members are probably most influential in the assimilation/role-making process. This is due largely to the general inability of media-related (typically written), downward management messages to alter employee behavior; rather, most research suggests that such types of documents serve to inform employees of desired behaviors, but rarely by themselves can cause changes in behavior (Redding, 1972; Weiss, 1969). In addition, interpersonal communication with superiors/ subordinates and coworkers plays an important role in the organizational assimilation process for several other reasons, as outlined below.

Superior-subordinate communication is generally perceived as crucial to an employee's assimilation into the organization for the following reasons:

(1) the supervisor frequently interacts with the subordinate and thus may serve as a role model (Weiss, 1977), (2) the supervisor has the formal power to reward and punish the employee, (3) the supervisor mediates the formal flow of downward communication to the subordinate (for example, the supervisor serves as an interpreter/filter of management messages), and (4) the supervisor usually has a personal as well as formal role relationship with the recruit. (Jablin, 1982a, p. 269)

In addition, it is important to observe that an employee's superior is of critical importance to his or her individualization efforts. As Graen (1976, p. 1206) suggests, "Although other members of the new person's role set can enter the negotiation of the definition of the new person's role . . . only the leader is granted the authority to impose formal sanctions to back up his negotiations."

On the other hand, formal and informal interactions with coworkers in one's task group also appear to perform an important function in the organizational assimilation process. As Feldman (1981, p. 314) notes, "New recruits turn to other members of the work group to get help in interpreting the events they experience, to learn many nuances of seemingly clearcut rules, and to learn the informal networks." Further, group members can serve as a normative referent for "appropriate" behavior, and as a source of emotional support against the organization's socialization attempts (Becker, Geer, Hughes, & Strauss, 1961; Burns, 1955; Feldman, 1977). Additionally, recent evidence suggests that in the uncertain environment of a new job recruits may model and/or assume the attitudes and behaviors of their coworkers (Crawford, 1974; Katz, 1980; Rakestraw & Weiss, 1981; Weiss, 1977; White & Mitchell, 1979). The vital role of communication with coworkers to successful organizational assimilation is epitomized in the following research anecdote from Feldman (1981, p. 314):

> I have found that many recruits report feeling that until such time as they became friendly with co-workers and could trust them, they could not find out information that was essential to doing their jobs well. Moreover, until incumbent employees felt they could trust recruits, they withheld information about supervisors' preferences and personalities, making the recruits less competent in the eyes of the supervisors.

In summary, a considerable amount of evidence exists suggesting that new recruits, as well as continuing members of organizations, make "sense of" (Louis, 1980) and understand their work environments primarily as a result of their interpersonal communication interactions with (1) superiors/subordinates and (2) work group members/coworkers. Given the apparent importance of these types of communication relationships to becoming assimilated into (and remaining assimilated in) organizations, the following two sections of this chapter provide extensive reviews of these respective research literatures. Since few studies in either of these areas have utilized longitudinal or time-series research designs, these literature reviews have been organized topically rather than in a developmental fashion.

Superior-Subordinate Communication

As has often been observed, within work organizations there are always subordinates and superiors "even though these terms may not be expressly used, and even though there may exist fluid arrangements whereby superior and subordinate roles may be reversible" (Redding, 1972, p. 18). Generally, research concerning superior-subordinate communication has focused "on those exchanges of information and influence between organizational members, at least one of whom has formal (as defined by official organizational sources) authority to direct and evaluate the activities of other organizational members" (Jablin, 1979, p. 1202). With respect to the types of messages that tend to be exchanged between superiors and subordinates, Katz and Kahn (1966, pp. 239-241) suggest that superior-to-subordinate communications usually focus on information concerning organizational procedures and practices, indoctrination of goals, job instructions and rationale, or feedback about performance. Relatedly, subordinates' communications to superiors tend to be concerned with information about the subordinates themselves, their coworkers and their problems, information about tasks that need to be done, or information about organizational policies and practices (Katz & Kahn, 1966, p. 245).

An extensive multidisciplinary review of empirical research exploring the nature and functions of superior-subordinate communication was recently published by Jablin (1979). In this review the empirical literature on superior-subordinate communication was classified into nine topical categories: (1) interaction patterns and related attitudes, (2) openness in communication, (3) upward distortion, (4) upward influence, (5) semantic-information distance, (6) effective versus ineffective superiors, (7) personal characteristics, (8) feedback, and (9) systemic variables. The following discussion briefly summarizes Jablin's analysis of the research in each of these categories. In addition, several investigations in a new category, "conflict," are also reviewed. Selective studies relevant to each of the original nine categories but conducted subsequent to Jablin's 1979 review are also discussed.

Interaction Patterns and Related Attitudes. Probably one of the most consistent findings in superior-subordinate communication research is that supervisors spend from one-third to two-thirds of their time communicating with subordinates. Further, the majority of this communication concerns task-related issues and is conducted in face-to-face meetings. It is also interesting to note that superiors and subordinates tend to have differential perceptions about (1) the amount of time they spend communicating with one another, and (2) who initiates these communication contacts. Research conducted since 1979 lends further support to this interaction profile (Volard & Davies, 1982).

Openness in Communication. Redding (1972, p. 330) distinguishes two basic dimensions of openness in superior-subordinate communication: openness in message sending ("candid disclosure of feelings, or 'bad news,' and important company facts"), and openness in message receiving ("encouraging, or at least permitting, the frank expression of views divergent from one's own"). Moreover, Jablin (1979, p. 1204), in his review of the empirical research in this area, concludes that

in an open communication relationship between superior and subordinate, both parties perceive the other interactant as a willing and receptive listener and refrain from responses that might be perceived as providing negative relational or disconfirming feedback. Moreover, these inquiries suggest that what distinguishes an open from a closed relationship may not be the types of messages exchanged but how the interactants evaluate the appropriateness of these communications.

In addition, a substantial amount of research exists indicating that subordinates are more satisfied with their jobs when they have an "open" versus "closed" communication relationship with their superiors. However, it should be noted that a recent study has revealed that the degree to which a superior is involved in "organizational politics" may moderate perceptions of openness in superior-subordinate communication. "Specifically, it appears that subordinates feel comfortable being open in communication with superiors who are minimally or moderately involved in politics, but not with superiors who are highly involved in political activities" (Jablin, 1981b, p. 273).

Upward Distortion. A long tradition of laboratory and field research has investigated the frequent phenomenon of upward distortion that occurs when persons of lower hierarchical rank in organizations communicate with persons of higher hierarchical rank (who also typically have power over the advancement of the persons of lower rank). Moreover, numerous variables have been found to moderate the occurrence of upward distortion, including subordinates' mobility aspirations, ascendency and security needs, trust in superiors, gender, and motivation.

With respect to the types of messages that are most frequently distorted, studies generally have found that subordinates are most reluctant to communicate information to their superiors that is negative or unfavorable. On the other hand, superiors seem to compensate for the positive "halo" often associated with the messages they receive from subordinates by viewing them as less accurate than messages that are unfavorable to subordinates. However, Downs and Conrad (1982), in a rather unique study of the characteristics of effective subordinacy, suggest that "effective" subordinates are perceived as willing to "confront" their superiors with challenging or unwanted information. These authors conclude that perhaps subordinates *in general* tend to avoid passing on negative or unfavorable information to their superiors, but that "*effective* subordinates do—and they avoid some communication problems by doing so" (Downs & Conrad, 1982, p. 34).

Upward Influence. As Jablin (1979) notes, studies of influence in superior-subordinate communication have focused on two of its basic dimensions: (1) the effects a superior's influence in the organizational hierarchy has on his or her relationships with subordinates, and (2) the transmission of influence by subordinates to superiors (which is often closely associated with research on upward distortion). With respect to the former category of research, studies have basically concentrated on what is often termed the "Pelz Effect" (Pelz, 1952). Essentially, this effect suggests that subordinate satisfaction with supervision is a by-product not only of an open, supportive relationship between the two parties, but also of the supervisor's ability to satisfy his or her subordinates' needs by possessing influence with those higher in the organizational hierarchy.

Several recent studies have been directed at exploring the generalizability of the Pelz Effect. Much of this research has been stimulated by the House, Filley, and Gujarati (1971) assertion that for subordinates who perceive their supervisors as supportive leaders, there exists a curvilinear rather than positive linear association between supervisors' upward influence and subordinates' openness and satisfaction with supervision. Specifically, House et al. (1971, p. 429) argue that

> where supervisors are seen to have such high influence, it is likely that there will be a greater status separation between them and their subordinates, and that such status differentiation will result in a restriction of upward information flow, less willingness on the part of subordinates to approach superiors, and less satisfaction with the social climate of the work unit.

Results of studies exploring the House et al. (1971) hypothesis, however, have not generally supported this revisionist position (Daniels & Logan, 1983; Jablin, 1980a, 1980b). Moreover, findings suggest that the Pelz Effect holds for *strategic* (personnel and administrative policy decisions) and *work-related* influence, and appears to exist under conditions of high and low leader supportiveness, though it has its greatest impact in situations where subordinates perceive their superiors as supportive leaders.

The message strategies subordinates employ to influence their superiors' decisions have also been a focus of recent research (Allen & Porter, 1983; Kipnis, Schmidt, & Wilkinson, 1980; Krone, 1984; Mowday, 1978; Porter, Allen, & Angle, 1981; Schilit & Locke, 1982; Weinstein, 1979). Generally, these studies suggest nine basic strategies that subordinates employ to influence their superiors' decisions: logical or rational presentation of ideas; informal or non-performance-specific exchanges (for example, ingratiation); formal exchange (exchanging desired work behaviors for rewards); adherence to rules (essentially a form of negative influence); upward appeal (bypassing one's direct superior and appealing to a person of higher authority); threats or sanctions; manipulation (arguing such that the target is not aware of the influence attempt); formal coalitions (power equalization); and persistence or assertiveness ("wearing down" the other party's resistance) (Schilit & Locke, 1982, p. 305). However, as Krone (1984) has observed, from a communication perspective these nine strategies can essentially be categorized into one of three types of messages: (1) open persuasion (the influence attempt is overt and the desired outcome stated), (2) manipulative persuasion (the use of either covert means of influence and open expression of desired outcomes *or* open means of influence and undisclosed desired outcomes), and (3) manipulation (disguising both the influence means and desired outcome—deception).

Results of research exploring the frequencies with which these different types of message strategies are used in influence attempts are mixed. Specifically, some studies have found that subordinates use logical presentations (open persuasion) more often than the other strategies (Kipnis et al., 1980; Schilit & Locke, 1982), while the results of other investigations suggest that forms of covert messages are most commonly used in upward influence attempts (Porter et al., 1981; Weinstein, 1979). These findings would seem to indicate that a subordinate's selection and use of a message strategy in an influence attempt may be dependent on a wide array of situational factors (such as decision type, organizational climate and structure, and perceived power of the target). Obviously, future research should focus on delineating the factors that mediate choice of message strategy, as well as the impact/effectiveness of these influence attempts on superiors' decision making.

Semantic-Information Distance. The term "semantic-information distance" was coined by Tompkins (1962) to describe the gap in agreement and/or understanding that often exists between subordinates and superiors on specified issues. In the research literature a number of other terms have often been used analogously, such as "disparity," "congruence," "semantic agreement," and "categorical and syndectic similarity." Research in this area has clearly demonstrated numerous areas and topics in which large gaps in understanding exist between superiors and subordinates, including subordinates' basic job duties and supervisors' authority. As Jablin (1979, p. 1208) concludes in his review of this research literature, "Incessantly, we find the existence of semantic-information distance in superior-subordinate relations, often at levels that would appear to seriously obstruct organizational effectiveness." However, it should also be recognized that perceptual incongruence in the superior-subordinate dyad is, within limits, a natural consequence of role structuration in organizations and thus may be dysfunctional for the relationship only if "it impairs the productivity, stability or adaptability of the dyad" (Sussman, 1975, p. 198).

Several recent studies of semantic-information distance have focused on differences in "meta-perceptions" (Laing, Phillipson, & Lee, 1966), that is, superiors' and subordinates' views of the other person's views. Thus, rather than exploring agreement and disagreement between superiors and subordinates on specified issues (the typical orientation of previous studies), these investigations have been concerned with perceptions of understanding or misunderstanding between members of the dyad. Results of these studies suggest that superiors and subordinates not only have different "direct" perspectives on specified issues, but also do not understand one another's meta-perspectives (Infante & Gordon, 1979; Smircich & Chesser, 1981). In addition, recent research (Hatfield & Huseman, 1982; Richmond, Wagner, & McCroskey, 1983) indicates that perceptual congruence (direct perspectives) about various aspects of superior-subordinate communication is to some degree positively associated with subordinates' general job satisfaction.

Effective Versus Ineffective Superiors. In his review of the literature, Jablin (1979, p. 1208) suggests that "over the years the identification of effective as compared to ineffective communication behaviors of superiors has received more investigation than any other area of organizational communication." Yet, he also notes in his analysis that two basic and somewhat contradictory perspectives/conclusions can be drawn from the literature: (1) a common profile of the communication characteristics of "effective" supervisors exists, and (2) the communication qualities of "effective" leaders varies and is contingent on numerous situational factors.

Redding (1972, p. 443) provides a fairly complete compendium of the communication characteristics often considered to be indicative of "good" supervisors:

(1) The better supervisors tend to be more "communication-minded"; they enjoy talking and speaking up in meetings; they are able to explain instructions and policies; they enjoy conversing with subordinates.
(2) The better supervisors tend to be willing, empathic listeners; they respond understandingly to so-called "silly" questions from employees; they are approachable; they will listen to suggestions and complaints with an attitude of fair consideration and willingness to take appropriate action.
(3) The better supervisors tend (with some notable exceptions) to "ask" or "persuade" in preference to "telling" or "demanding."
(4) The better supervisors tend to be sensitive to the feelings and ego-defense needs of their subordinates; e.g., they are careful to reprimand in private rather than in public.
(5) The better supervisors tend to be more open in their passing along of information; they are in favor of giving advance notice of impending changes, and of explaining the "reasons why" behind policies and regulations.

On the other hand, as noted above, a considerable amount of research also exists suggesting that "effective" leadership behaviors are contingent on a host of situational factors including gender, task type, organizational climate, and work-unit size. For example, Bednar (1982) found recently that the "communicator style" (Norton, 1978) characteristics associated with "effective" managerial performance seem to vary depending on organizational context and setting (in this case an insurance agency versus a hospital). Moreover, in recent years the general assumption that leaders manifest one stable supervisory style in their interactions with *all* subordinates has come under attack by Graen and his colleagues (Dansereau, Graen, & Haga, 1975; Graen & Cashman, 1975). According to their Vertical Dyad Linkage (VDL) model of leadership, because of their competence, trustworthiness, and motivation certain subordinates are chosen by supervisors to receive "preferential treatment." Further,

> these selected subordinates (in-group members) make contributions that go beyond their formal job duties and take on responsibility for the completion of tasks that are most critical to the success of the unit. In return, they receive greater attention, support, and sensitivity from their supervisors. Subordinates who are not chosen by the supervisor (out-group members) perform the more

routine, mundane tasks of the unit and experience a more formal exchange with the supervisor. (Liden & Graen, 1980)

In summary, the research of Graen and others is beginning to bring into question the assumption that supervisors or managers possess an "average" communication style. Rather, these investigations suggest that the dyadic communication exchange patterns that exist between superiors and subordinates be viewed as somewhat unique to each dyad. In conclusion, a decisive answer to the question of whether or not an "ideal" communication style exists that is "effective" in all supervisory situations still remains to be provided. As Jablin observed in his 1979 review, "the only way we will be able to resolve this question is by research that investigates the effects situational variables have on superior-subordinate communication" (Jablin, 1979, p. 1211).

Personal Characteristics. The mediating effects of the personal characteristics of superiors and subordinates on their communicative behavior historically have been of interest to researchers. Traits that have been examined include locus of control, dogmatism, and communication apprehension, as well as the gender composition of the dyad. More recent research has focused attention on the effects of attributional models and schemas on communicative behavior (see the section below on feedback), measurement of communicator competence (Monge, Bachman, Dillard, & Eisenberg, 1982), and different types of "managerial communication styles" (Richmond, McCroskey, & Davis, 1982; Richmond, McCroskey, Davis, & Koontz, 1980). With respect to this latter research, findings suggest that subordinates perceive the communication of coercive power with a "boss-centered," tell-type managerial communication style, and that subordinate satisfaction with supervision increases as managerial communication style becomes more "employee centered."

Feedback. Of all the categories of research reviewed here, feedback has been one of the most popular topics of research since 1979. This research interest is probably a result of the extensive incorporation of theories of social cognition (particularly attribution theory) into feedback studies, as well as several excellent reviews and models of feedback processes that have been published in the last few years (Arvey & Ivancevich, 1980; Ashour & Johns, 1983, Cusella, 1980; Ilgen, Fisher, & Taylor, 1979; Larson, 1984; Sims, 1980). At the same time, however, one should note that this more recent research has been generally supportive of the two major conclusions that Jablin drew from his review of the literature through 1979: (1) "Feedback from superiors to subordinates appears related to subordinate performance and satisfaction," and (2) "a subordinate's performance to a large extent controls the nature of his/her superior's feedback" (Jablin, 1979, p. 1214).

More recent studies also suggest the following additional conclusions: (1) Feedback from supervisors high in credibility (trust and expertise) can positively influence subordinates' levels of satisfaction and/or motivation

(Cusella, 1982; O'Reilly & Anderson, 1980); (2) supervisors tend to give negative feedback sooner to poorly-performing subordinates than they give positive feedback to well-performing subordinates (Fisher, 1979; Pavett, 1983); (3) when required to give unfavorable feedback to subordinates, superiors tend to distort the feedback by positively inflating it (Fisher, 1979; Ilgen & Knowlton, 1980); (4) supervisors tend to overestimate the value subordinates place on supervisory feedback (Greller, 1980; Ilgen, Peterson, Martin, & Boeschen, 1981); (5) when subordinates perform poorly, superiors tend to attribute this poor performance to factors internal rather than external to the subordinates; as a result, superiors tend to direct their responses toward the subordinates (for example, in the form of reprimands) rather than attempting to alter the work situation (Green & Mitchell, 1979; Kipnis et al., 1981; Mitchell & Wood, 1980); (6) "managers will tend to influence trusted employees with persuasion and will use coercion with untrusted employees" (Riccillo & Trenholm, 1983, p. 336); and (6) superior and subordinate relational feedback responses (dominance, structuring, equivalence, deference, and submissiveness) are somewhat constrained by the interactants' formal organizational roles (Watson, 1982).

Conflict. Within the last ten years the study of the role of communication in superior-subordinate conflict has received a considerable amount of research attention. Working from earlier conceptualizations of superior-subordinate conflict advanced by Blake, Shepard, and Mouton (1964) and Kilmann and Thomas (1977), a number of investigations have been directed at developing coding schemes and/or scales to measure and analyze conflict strategies (Bullis, Cox, & Bokeno, 1982; Putnam & Wilson, 1982; Riggs, 1983; Ross & DeWine, 1982; Sillars, 1980). Results from these and other studies suggest that supervisors generally use "controlling" or "forcing" strategies when managing conflicts with subordinates. However, several factors have been discovered to affect a superior's choice of conflict management mode, including the supervisor's level of self-confidence, perceptions of skill, and organizational level (Conrad, 1983; Putnam & Wilson, 1982). Relatedly, Richmond et al. (1983) report that subordinates and superiors have difficulty agreeing on how "active" supervisors actually are in managing conflict.

Systemic Variables. In his 1979 review Jablin notes that less empirical, as opposed to theoretical, research had been pursued exploring the effects systemic organizational variables (technology, structure, environment, and so on) have on superior-subordinate communication. Unfortunately, this conclusion still holds true today. However, two studies have recently been published reporting relationships between the characteristics of superior-subordinate communication and different types of organizational structures and technologies.

In the first of these investigations Jablin (1982b) collected data from fifteen organizations in an attempt to determine the effects of several structural characteristics of organizations (organizational size, organizational level, and span of control) on subordinates' perceptions of openness in superior-subordinate communication. Findings of the study revealed that "subordinates in the lowest levels of their organizational hierarchies perceived significantly less openness in superior-subordinate communication than subordinates at the highest levels of their hierarchies" (Jablin, 1982b, p. 338). However, Jablin also observes that organizational level did not account for much variance in perceptions of openness in communication.

On the other hand, Klauss and Bass (1982), exploring the effects of organizational size and technology (in two organizations) on subordinates' perceptions of managerial communication behavior, report results indicating that in "high-technology" versus "traditional-technology" settings managers are perceived as less "careful" message transmitters and listeners. In summary, the failure of this study and that of Jablin (1982b) to find any significant relationships between perceptions of superior-subordinate communication and work-group or organizational size suggests that size may not be a moderator of quality of superior-subordinate communication in organizations.

Summary. The preceding section has attempted to provide an overview of results of contemporary empirical research exploring the communication dynamics of probably the most common interpersonal task relationship found in organizations: the interaction of superiors/leaders and subordinates/followers. As Jablin noted in his 1979 review of this literature, three items seem to be studied consistently as factors affecting interpersonal communication between superiors and subordinates—power and status, trust, and semantic-information distance. Moreover, given that investigations of superior-subordinate communication have traditionally focused on power- and status-related issues, it is not surprising to discover that a considerable amount of recent research has concentrated on exploring the message strategies that each member of the dyad utilizes to influence the behavior and attitudes of the other party (see research reviewed in the sections on upward influence and feedback above). In addition, it appears evident that the current popularity of research examining the cognitive processes that superiors and subordinates use to interpret messages from one another is largely a result of the endemic presence of semantic-information distance in superior-subordinate communication. Finally, it is important to note that the degree of trust that exists between superiors and subordinates continues to be shown frequently to moderate their message-encoding and message-decoding behaviors.

Work Group and Coworker Communication

As suggested earlier, new recruits to organizations (as well as continuing members) receive information from their coworkers that assists them in discovering and adapting to what are considered to be "normal" and "acceptable" behaviors and attitudes in their organizations (Feldman, 1981; Van Maanen, 1975). In particular, members of the work group "help the new employee decode and interpret the scripts and schemas that prevail in the organization as well as cushion the impact of the recruit's organizational encounter" (Jablin, 1982a, p. 272). However, as evidenced earlier in the research anecdote presented by Feldman (1981), coworkers will usually serve these functions only after the initiate has become a trusted and accepted member of the work group.

The interpersonal messages that employees receive from other members of their work groups are essentially of two types: "ambient" and "discretionary" (Hackman, 1976). Ambient messages are nonselective, often unintentional, and directed to all members of the work group, while discretionary messages are intentionally and somewhat contingently communicated to specific group members.

Recent research on "social information processing" in organizations (Caldwell & O'Reilly, 1982; O'Reilly & Caldwell, 1979; Roberts & Glick, 1981; Salancik & Pfeffer, 1978; Weiss & Nowicki, 1981; White & Mitchell, 1979) exemplifies the effects ambient communication among coworkers can have on their job attitudes. Specifically, the social information processing framework proposes that a worker's job attitudes are socially constructed and are largely a result of normative and informational cues communicated to the worker by others in the work environment, particularly coworkers. Thus this approach suggests that the job attitudes a recruit develops arise in part from the elements of the work environment that coworkers somewhat unconsciously call attention to in their "everyday" talk. In other words, by frequently talking about and evaluating certain aspects of the work context group members cue one another about the importance and "meaning" of elements in the work environment. In fact, recent studies indicate that perhaps the critical factor in a worker's satisfaction with his or her job is working in an environment where coworkers express positive job/work attitudes (O'Reilly & Caldwell, 1979; White & Mitchell, 1979). And, as Rakestraw and Weiss (1981, p. 341) have suggested, "Social influences on the development of goals and performance standards may be most pronounced for new workers or individuals approaching an unfamiliar task."

On the other hand, a long tradition of research also exists indicating that discretionary communications from the members of one's work group can have important effects on the development of job attitudes and behavior (Feldman, 1984; Hackman, 1976). These communications are most often sent from coworkers to the new member to educate or socialize the individual to *selective* group norms and values, as well as preferred task behaviors (Feldman, 1984). For example, a number of "classic" studies have demonstrated the powerful effects of the communication of group norms on such phenomena as group cohesiveness (Schachter, Ellertson, McBride, & Gregory, 1951; Seashore, 1954), production restrictions (Trist & Bamforth, 1951; Whyte, 1955), decision making (Janis, 1972), and conformity (Asch, 1951; Sherif, 1936). Moreover, through their communications with recruits coworkers provide new employees with information concerning rewards and costs present in the group and organizational environments, who controls the allocation of rewards, and the behaviors that lead to receiving rewards (Hackman, 1976). At the same time, however, it is important to recognize that recruits upon first entering new work settings often *proactively* send messages to coworkers through which they seek information about the above types of issues (Feldman & Brett, 1983).

From a more general perspective communication among members of organizational work groups can be thought of as serving formal-organizational and psychological-individual functions (Jablin & Sussman, 1983; Schein, 1980). Specifically,

> *formal* organizational group communication generally occurs to: (a) generate information, (b) process information, (c) share information necessary for the coordination of interdependent organizational tasks, (d) disseminate decisions, or (e) reinforce a group's perspective/consensus. On the other hand, psychological, *individual*-oriented organizational group communication functions to: (a) provide members with feedback about their self-concepts, (b) gratify needs for affiliation, (c) share and test perspectives about social reality, (d) reduce organization-related uncertainty and concomitant feelings of anxiety, insecurity, and powerlessness, or (e) accomplish employee-related (versus organization-related) tasks and resolve individual or group-related problems. (Jablin & Sussman, 1983)

Research exploring the interpersonal communication behavior of workers in organizational task groups has recently been reviewed by Jablin and Sussman (1983). Selective findings from their examination of the literature are summarized briefly below.

Task Characteristics. Probably one of the most consistent conclusions that can be drawn from research on the communication behavior of members of task groups is that task type and task technology significantly affect workers' interpersonal interaction patterns (Hackman, Brousseau, & Weiss, 1976; Hackman & Vidmar, 1970; Shiflett, 1972; Sorenson, 1971). As Jablin and Sussman (1983, p. 34) conclude after reviewing recent laboratory and field studies of group communication networks, it is apparent that "groups when given the opportunity generally adapt their communication structures to the nature of the work or task at hand."

With respect to task type (production, problem solving, discussion), research results suggest that distinct patterns of interaction and perceptions evolve among group members as a function of the "intellective" nature of the task. In discussing the findings of their research, Hackman and Vidmar (1970, p. 50) outline several of these distinctions:

> Production tasks resulted in more reports of tensions and conflict among members than did other types, . . . discussion tasks led to a somewhat more "relaxed" atmosphere, and . . . problem-solving tasks resulted in perceptions that members were working together relatively effectively.

Similarly, investigations probing the effects of technology (the combination of task variability and analyzability) on group interaction suggest that technology affects the information processing demands of the group, such that as task certainty increases the group coordinates itself more through impersonal (rules, plans) than through personal communication modes (Penley & Alexander, 1979; Randolph, 1978, Van de Ven, Delbecq, & Koenig, 1976).

Group Problem Solving. Of the various types of tasks that groups perform, the communication dynamics of problem-solving or decision-making groups have probably received the most research attention. In particular, studies have focused on testing explanations for the "risky shift" phenomenon (the tendency for decisions resulting from group discussions to be more risky than the averaged individual decisions of a group's members) (Cecil, Cummings, & Chertkoff, 1973; Pruitt, 1971a, 1971b) and the relative merits of direct interaction among group members during problem solving (Jablin & Seibold, 1978; Van de Ven & Delbecq, 1974).

In reference to the risky shift phenomenon, recent studies indicate that degree of choice shift is affected by quantity (versus quality) of arguments presented by group members (Bishop & Myers, 1974; Morgan & Beatty, 1976), and patterns of agreement/disagreement by group members (Levine, Skroka, & Snyder, 1977). On the other hand, findings from studies exploring problem-solving strategies suggest that for short-lived task groups working on applied fact-finding problems, *nominal* (individuals initially work alone and later join together to discuss their ideas) and *delphi* (members complete sets of sequential questionnaires but never meet in face-to-face discussion) strategies are more effective than conventional interacting groups (Huber & Delbecq, 1972; Van de Ven & Delbecq, 1971, 1974). In contrast, for ongoing, long-term groups choice of interaction strategy is more complex and contingent on numerous factors, "including group motivation, time limitations, distribution of problem solving information, the nature of the problem, status differences among group members, and socio-emotional variables related to the group's development" (Jablin & Seibold, 1978, pp. 351-352). In addition, it has been found that an individual's communication predisposition may affect his or her relative effectiveness in interacting problem-solving groups (see Jablin, 1981c).

Moderators. A number of other factors have also been shown to affect the communication behavior of task group members in problem-solving or decision-making situations. For example, results of studies have frequently found that trust-destroying communication negatively affects interaction processes and problem-solving effectiveness. Specifically, with the destruction of trust, feedback responses among group members often become "tense, inflexible and personal" (Leathers, 1970, p. 186), verbal fluency decreases (Prentice, 1975), communication distortions occur (Zand, 1972), and group performance diminishes (Klimoski & Karol, 1976). Further, other studies have found that the degree of "orientation behavior" that is displayed by group members (messages directed at resolving conflicts, facilitating achievement of group goals, making helpful suggestions, or lessening tension) is associated with the probability that members will reach consensus decisions (Kline, 1970, 1972; Knutson, 1972). Relatedly, research exploring feedback responses in task groups suggests that the impact of feedback on group members is contingent on several variables, including individual differences among group members (for example, achievement motivation), group task structure, the ways in which members process feedback, as well as the nature of the feedback information—evaluative content, task/process focus, aggregation level and so on (see Nadler, 1979, for a complete review of this literature).

Group Development. Finally, research exploring the interpersonal communication patterns that emerge among members of work groups as the groups develop over time warrants discussion (Ellis & Fisher, 1975; Fisher, 1970; Gouran & Baird, 1972; Heinen & Jacobson, 1976; Mabry, 1975). Of particular importance are a series of investigations recently conducted by Poole (1981, 1983). The findings of Poole's research are of relevance because they bring into question the generally held assumption that decision-making groups follow uniform sequences of phases of development (generally depicted as an initial orientation phase, followed by a period of evaluation, and concluding with a control phase; see Bales & Strodtbeck, 1951). Specifically, findings from Poole's studies suggest that over time the sequence of communication phases of decision-making groups are not necesarily uniform, and that different groups may have different sequences of phases. Accordingly, Poole (1981, p. 20) suggests that a contingency theory of group development may be required, though the traditional "unitary sequence" model might serve "as a 'baseline' which is altered and diversified in different ways by different groups."

Summary. The preceding section has attempted to provide an overview of recent research exploring the nature, functions, and effects of interpersonal communication among coworkers in organizational task groups. Results of this analysis suggest that recruits' communication relationships with their coworkers play important informational and socioemotional functions in the assimilation of newcomers into organizations. Further, it was noted that for both new and continuing employees the "ambient" and "discretionary" messages they exchange with one another often have considerable impact on their work attitudes and behaviors. However, given that employees (especially new recruits) are likely to receive these types of messages from multiple sources (often presenting conflicting perspectives) within their task environments, research exploring the message characteristics that lead workers to attend to and accept certain of these communications and not others is needed (Weiss & Nowicki, 1981). In summary, findings from this literature review suggest that probably the most influential factors affecting interpersonal communication patterns and relationships among group members are the characteristics of the task on which they are working.

Outcomes of Assimilation

As frequently noted in findings from studies reviewed here, employees' communication relationships with their superiors/subordinates and co-workers may affect a number of outcomes of the organizational assimilation process. Among the outcomes that have been mentioned in studies considered to this point are workers' levels of job satisfaction, motivation, and work performance. However, from a communication perspective there are at least two other important outcomes of the organizational assimilation process that merit consideration: (1) the emergence within employees of perceptions of the communication climates of the organizations in which they work, and (2) some degree of participation by workers in their organizations' emergent communication networks.

Communication Climate. It is generally assumed that as an employee is assimilated into an organization, "she/he develops an evolving set of perceptions about what the organization is like as a communication system" (Jablin, 1982a, p. 273), that is, the communication "climate" of the organization. Though numerous factors constitute an individual's perceptions of the communication climate of his or her organization, most conceptualizations of the climate construct place heavy emphasis on perceptions of interpersonal communication with superiors/subordinates and coworkers (Albrecht, 1979; Dennis, 1974; Goldhaber & Rogers, 1979; Jablin, 1980c; Roberts & O'Reilly, 1974). Thus there seems to be a fair amount of agreement among researchers that an individual's communication relationships with his or her superiors/subordinates and coworkers play key roles in the development of overall organizational communication climate perceptions. Unfortunately, little research exists exploring *how* perceptions of overall (or superior-subordinate, or peer) communication climates develop over time.

However, one recently completed study does provide some exploratory data concerning the development of communication climate perceptions. In this longitudinal investigation, Jablin (1984) examined recruits' (newly hired nursing assistants) perceptions of the communication climates of their new jobs and organizations on their first days of work (expectations) and after six, twelve, and eighteen weeks of employment. In addition, a sample of recruits completed communication logs/diaries during their third and ninth weeks of employment. Results of the research revealed that after six weeks of work recruits' communication climate perceptions (including all scales measuring attributes of superior-subordinate and peer communication) were significantly deflated from their initial expectations, but, rather than increasing or decreasing over the remaining months of the study, remained at the six-week level. Somewhat similarly, the communication log data indicated that between their third and ninth weeks of work the recruits became less positive toward their interactions with superiors, peers, and patients.

In summary, the communication climate perceptions of the recruits in Jablin's (1984) study were (1) sharply influenced by their initial "encounters" in their organizations, and (2) evidenced this "encounter effect" for at least their first six months of work. Whether or not this is a typical pattern of development of communication climate perceptions obviously should be a focus of future research. Moreover, inquiries aimed at exploring relationships between communication with superiors/subordinates and coworkers and the development of climate perceptions that evolve as recruits remain in their organizations for longer periods of time need to be conducted.

Communication Networks. To a large extent employee participation in emergent organizational communication networks (a process concurrent to the development of climate perceptions; see Jablin, 1980c) is also an outcome of the organizational assimilation process. Specifically, it is likely that as a result of the regular communication that a new organizational member has with his or her superiors/subordinates and coworkers that he or she will become a "link" in a number of overlapping sets of stable interaction patterns or structures that exist in the organization. For example, the recruit might become a "link" in authority, information exchange, friendship, and status networks in the organization (Farace, Monge, & Russell, 1977; Guetzkow, 1965; Katz & Kahn, 1966).

Further, as an employee is assimilated into an organization it is likely not only that he or she will become a link in several networks, but that he or she will also assume certain specific communication network roles, such as "group member" (a participant in a group within a network), "intergroup linker" (liaison—a person who links two or more groups but is not a member of a group him- or herself; bridge—a group member who links his or her group to another group), or an "isolate" (a person who maintains no linkages with other network members; see Farace et al., 1977; Monge, Edwards, & Kirste, 1978). Moreover, it should be noted that the types of network roles an individual performs will probably affect his or her communication attitudes and behaviors (Albrecht, 1979; Monge et al., 1978).

To date there has been only a limited amount of research exploring how emergent networks and/or network roles in organizations develop over time (for example, see Rogers & Kincaid, 1981). However, based upon recent research that suggests possible relationships between the degrees to which individuals are "connected" or "integrated" into the communication networks of their organizations and their group attitude uniformity, morale, and organizational commitment (Danowski, 1980; Eisenberg, Monge & Miller, 1983; McLaughlin & Cheatham, 1977), two propositions appear tenable. First, it seems reasonable to hypothesize that organizational members who frequently are "isolates" in communication networks have not been very effectively assimilated into their organizations (though there may be exceptions to this; for instance, Granovetter's [1973] discussion of "weak ties" in networks). Second, and in contrast, it seems likely that recruits who eventually assume intergroup linker or group member roles have been effectively (at least relative to isolates) assimilated into their organizations.

Van Maanen's (1975) typology of individual adjustment approaches to organizational socialization (assumption of "team player," "isolate," "warrior," or "outsider" roles) would also seem to lend support to these assertions. However, the validity of these propositions should be viewed as tentative until they are tested by future research.

Summary. The preceding section has suggested two closely interrelated *communication* outcomes of the organizational assimilation process: (1) the development of perceptions of organizational communication climate, and (2) participation in organizational communication networks. Moreover, as indicated in this discussion, interpersonal communication with superiors/ subordinates and coworkers is intrinsic to both of these outcomes/processes. At the same time, however, it is clearly evident that to date few empirical studies have been conducted exploring how organizational members' perceptions of communication climate and involvement in communication networks emerge/develop over time. Both of these areas represent fruitful foci for research and beg further investigation.

Conclusion

Within work organizations numerous types of interpersonal relationships exist. The great majority of these relationships, however, can be categorized as involving interactions either with superiors/subordinates or with coworkers (and in particular fellow members of one's task group). Based upon the research reviewed in the preceding pages, it also appears evident that these two types of communication relationships play instrumental roles in the organizational assimilation process—the *continuous* process by which workers share in and become cognitively and behaviorally a part of their organizations' "realities."

Throughout this discussion of the functions and roles of interpersonal communication in organizational task relationships, research summaries, conclusions, and recommendations for future research have been provided. However, an assessment of the research examined in these sections suggests several additional more general conclusions. First, it is obvious that the great majority of studies that have explored interpersonal communication relationships in work organizations have failed to consider adequately the (positive and negative) constraints that the *embeddedness* of these relationships within a larger organizational system has upon communication processes. Such systemic factors as organizational structures, organizational technologies, and relevant external organizational environments are likely to affect interpersonal communication relationships in organizations, and consequently should be considered as potential moderating variables in the creating of research designs (Jablin & Sussman, 1983).

Second, and closely related to the above concern, is the tendency of most studies to consider the relationships of people in various organizational roles independent of the other roles they perform, both within the organization and external to it. For example, at a very basic level an employee within an organization is likely to perform at least three roles: superior, subordinate, and coworker (peer). Yet when we conduct studies of communication relationships in organizations we typically focus upon a person in only one of his or her roles. Moreover, most of our research tends to concentrate on the intraorganizational communication associated with individual roles, rather than with how organizational actors assimilate information from sources external to the organization (boundary spanning; see Tushman, 1977; Tushman & Scanlon, 1981), integrate this information, and then communicate it to their superiors, subordinates, and coworkers. Consequently, we generally are remiss in considering how an individual's communicative behavior is affected by the domain of his or her task-relevant role relationships, that is, the "role set" (see Schuler, 1979).

Similarly, most investigations of communication behavior in organizational task relationships ignore the fact that employees often assume task roles in other settings (family, community) and that these other roles may affect their communicative behavior in their organizational relationships (especially if role conflicts exist; see Feldman, 1981). In essence, it is suggested that in the future our research needs to show greater concern for the effects intra- and extraorganizational task role sets have on communicative behavior and attitudes among organizational members.

Third, and as noted repeatedly in this chapter, it is apparent that our knowledge of the dynamics of interpersonal communication in task/ organizational relationships is severely constrained by the paucity of longitudinal, as well as cross-sectional research that has been conducted in this area. Thus we are in the interesting position of being able to identify and describe various communicative "states" that exist in task/organizational relationships, while knowing little of what causes them to develop in these ways. Moreover, our understanding of the "life cycles" that communication in task relationships follow is extremely limited, and essentially nonexistent with respect to the dynamics of their deterioration. In summary, it is recommended that future research exploring communication processes in task/organizational relationships be directed at examining these relationships from a more developmental perspective.

Finally, although the present discussion has focused on communication processes in task relationships within work organizations, it is probably fair to conclude that similar processes and characteristics would exist in other types of task-related collectivities. In other words, while recognizing that there will always be some variability due to situation-specific factors, it is suggested that the assimilation-communication processes that have been outlined here are inherent to most ongoing relationships that occur within task-related groups/collectivities.

INTERPERSONAL COMMUNICATION
AND DISENGAGEMENT FROM WORK

Probably just as frequently as we enter into new work/organizational relationships, we disengage from other of these types of associations. Essentially, other than disengagement due to "personal" reasons, there are three major situations in which people typically disengage from their work relationships: (1) some form of geographical transfer (lateral or upward) within the same organization, (2) entry into a new job and organization, or (3) retirement from work. Relationships between interpersonal communication and work/task disengagement in each of these contexts are discussed briefly below.

Job Transfer

It is estimated that organizations transfer more than 100,000 workers (and their families—typically a male employee with a nonworking wife and two children; Brett & Werbel, 1980) in the United States annually (Employment Relocation Center, 1981). Moreover, these workers are often characterized as "On the 'fast track': They are selected for frequent promotion because of exceptional ability, and they reap the benefits of challenging work that brings personal growth and satisfaction" (Brett, 1982).

Little research exists exploring the characteristics and effects of job transfers on workers' interpersonal communication, internal or external to the organization. Most studies that have been conducted in this area have focused on the effects of job transfers on the employee's and family members' "well-being." However, Brett (1982, p. 457) has recently reported that "mobile" (operationalized as number of moves per year in work force) men and women tend to be "less satisfied with opportunities to make friends at work, friends in general, nonwork activities, neighbors, and community." Further, Feldman and Brett (1983, p. 270), in a study exploring how new hires and job changers (within the same organizations) cope with their new positions, found that job changers' coping strategies involved "higher activity levels for themselves and more control over others. . . . In contrast, new hires favored strategies that solicit the aid and social support of others."

In summary, the results of the above studies suggest that job transfers may affect the communicative behavior and communication satisfaction of employees who move to different positions in their organizations. Obviously, the specific communication styles that transferees assume in coping with their new work environments and their later levels of job satisfaction, performance, and turnover represent fruitful areas for future research. And, perhaps more important, future studies should explore (1) how transferees actually disengage communicatively from their task relationships with members of their "old" work groups and (2) the effects the transferring of employees have upon the communication behaviors of members of their "old" work groups, for example, the effects of the transfer of an employee on the various interpersonal networks that exist among members of the group.

Organization Change

Generally speaking, it is very rare for an individual to be employed in just one organization during his or her work career (Schein, 1978). Consequently, the phenomenon of a worker quitting his or her job to assume a position in another organization is fairly common in organizations. However, it is curious to observe that very little research has explored the role of employees' perceptions and feelings about the interpersonal communication climates of their work groups on their decisions to leave their organizations. Moreover, we have almost no knowledge of the effects of the frequency of an individual's job/organization changes on his or her communication attitudes, or the relationship between work/organizational history and communicative behavior in task relationships.

The importance of exploring the above types of issues is evidenced in two recently completed studies. In the first of these investigations, Jablin (1984) examined the relationships between new employees' (nursing assistants) retrospections about the communication environments of their last jobs, their expectations about the communication environments of their new jobs, and their job turnover. Findings from the research suggest that those employees who voluntarily terminated their employment within the first six weeks of work at their new organizations had more positive perceptions of the communication environments of their last jobs, and generally higher expectations of their new jobs, than did individuals who remained in their new organizations. In fact, Jablin (1984) notes that the job withdrawers' perceptions of the communication environments of their last jobs exceeded or were generally equivalent to the *expectations* of the job survivors. Thus to some degree the "high" job retrospections of the withdrawers may have functioned to inflate their job expectations to levels that were extremely difficult to meet; that is, they created a high probability of "unmet expectations."

Somewhat similarly, Wilson (1983), who collected interview data from individuals in the process of leaving their jobs, reports that unmet expectations (particularly in relation to supervisors and colleagues) can increase the propensity for employees to leave their organizations. Consistent with Jablin (1984), she asserts that "the ratio of unmet expectations plays an integral role in influencing leave-taking, suggesting the importance of clarifying expectations early in the organizational experience" (Wilson, 1983, p. 20). Clearly, future research should be directed at determining whether or not persons, in general, who terminate employment in their organizations evidence similar patterns of perceptions (particularly during the organizational "encounter" period). Moreover, investigation of the similarities and differences between the roles and functions of communication in interpersonal leave-taking processes (Knapp, 1978) and organizational exit processes might be a fruitful direction for future research in this area (Wilson, 1983).

Retirement

For most persons their final disengagement from formal work-related organizational relationships occurs in the form of retirement. However, it should be recognized that many older people, while not necessarily working full-time jobs, are either employed in paid part-time positions (about 2.8 million people 65 year of age and over) or work as volunteers in community service organizations (Louis Harris & Associates, 1979). In addition, studies indicate that about one-half of those retired wish to work in paid part-time jobs, but for one reason or another cannot obtain such positions (Morrison, 1981).

The process of retirement from work is frequently likened to the organizational assimilation process. For example, Atchley (1976) proposes an anticipatory stage, which he terms "preretirement" (composed of two phases, the first the "remote phase" and the second the "near phase"), followed by the "retirement" stage (composed of five phases). Similar to the anticipatory socialization phase of the organizational assimilation process, realism of expectations during the "preretirement" stage often is predictive of the likelihood of successful adaptation to subsequent phases. Additionally, during the "preretirement" stage "people begin to gear themselves for separation from their jobs and the social situations within which they carried out those jobs. They may adopt a 'short-timers attitude.' They may begin to notice subtle differences in how they are viewed by others" (Atchley, 1977, p. 154).

The "preretirement" stage is of particular interest to us here, since it occurs while an employee is still a member of his or her work organization. As noted above, during this period the employee may often perceive that he or she is different and somewhat "distant" from his or her coworkers. The specific nature of the interpersonal communication interactions that occur with the soon-to-be retiree and his or her fellow workers during this disengagement period obviously deserves study. Moreover, such investigations should focus on how "talk" during this period functions to prepare the employee for retirement, as well as serving as a mechanism for his or her fellow workers to adjust to the employee's impending departure.

On the other hand, the results of a recent survey of Fortune 100 companies indicate that many organizations have already recognized their responsibility in helping to prepare employees for the likely changes that will occur in their interpersonal communication environments upon retirement. Specifically, Avery and Jablin (1985) report that, of those organizations responding to their survey (n = 44), 77 percent offered formal retirement preparation programs, and in all cases interpersonal communication problems and adjustments that employees may experience subsequent to retirement were topics of discussion. Moreover, their findings indicate that the most frequent communication issues covered in these programs concern the transition from worker to retiree and its effects on the individual's communication relationship with his or her spouse, and the effects of retirement on the process of meeting new people and making new friends. It is also interesting to observe that, consistent with other studies that have shown that retirees perceive the loss of contact with company colleagues as the aspect of work they miss the most (McDermott, 1980), the respondents to Avery and Jablin's (1985) survey believed that the most difficult change in interpersonal communication that a retiree must adjust to after leaving full-time employment is the loss of communication with peers at work. Obviously, the generalizability of these survey results to non-Fortune 100 organizations and the effectiveness of organizational programs designed to prepare employees for changes in their interpersonal communication environments upon retirement require investigation.

Finally, it is recommended that in the future studies should begin to explore the nature and characteristics of the interpersonal communication relationships individuals develop after retirement while they are serving as volunteers in community service groups or holding part-time jobs. Given research that suggests that younger people often have distorted perceptions of the elderly (Clark, 1981), these investigations might focus on interaction patterns that develop in intergenerational task relationships.

Summary

The preceding sections have outlined three situations most of us will experience in our lives that involve disengagement from work/organizational relationships: (1) job transfer, (2) organizational change, and (3) retirement. Given the limited amount of research that has explored the roles and functions of interpersonal communication in each of these contexts, it is very difficult to draw any firm conclusions from this literature analysis. Consequently, at this time it is prudent only to suggest that the "realism" of interpersonal communication expectations that individuals hold prior to their disengagement from work/organizational relationships appears to affect significantly their ability to adapt successfully to the new environments they are entering. Further, it also seems evident from the studies reviewed here that researchers have focused most of their attention on "disengagers" and their communication perceptions and behaviors, rather than on the effects of individuals' disengagement on the interpersonal communication networks and processes of those who remain in the "old" task environments. Clearly, research is needed to explore how task groups cope and ultimately adapt to the loss of one of the "nodes" in their interpersonal communication networks.

CONCLUSION

This chapter has attempted to examine the roles, functions, and characteristics of interpersonal communication in work/organizational relationships. However, unlike most traditional treatments of this subject, this analysis approached work/organizational relationships and settings from a very broad orientation—from a "life-span" perspective. Consequently, this chapter explored (1) the processes by which people anticipate and learn about interpersonal communication in work/organizational relationships, (2) the roles and characteristics of interpersonal communication in the organizational assimilation process, and (3) the functions of interpersonal communication in disengagement from work/organizational settings.

An analysis of the literature reviewed in this chapter indicates that the majority of our knowledge of interpersonal communication in task relationships is concentrated within the period when individuals are employed in work organizations. In other words, our understanding of how and what people learn about interpersonal communication in work/organizational relationships prior to ever entering them, as well as processes associated with interpersonal communication and disengagement from work/organizational relationships, is extremely limited. While numerous reasons can be posited for this bias in our research, it seems evident that until we recognize the *developmental* nature of how people learn to communicate in task settings even our understanding of interpersonal communication in the organizational assimilation process will remain constrained. It is hoped that the research recommendations provided in the preceding pages can stimulate and provide direction for future investigations of interpersonal communication in task/work relationships from a developmental perspective.

In closing, a relatively new focus of research in interpersonal communication in task/work relationships is deserving of discussion, especially since it is perceived by many to be the "wave of the future" (Toffler, 1980). Specifically, this emerging research area concerns the effects of innovations in *communication/information technology* (electronic mail, teleconferencing, computer conferencing, desk-top personal computers, videotext, satellite communications, cable television, and so on) on interpersonal communication in task/work relationships (see Hiemstra, 1983; Rice & Associates, 1984). In considering this research, however, it should be noted that while there has been an enormous growth in the number of studies exploring the adoption, use, and impact of these new technologies on interpersonal communication in work/organizational settings in the last decade, generalizable conclusions are still difficult to draw from this literature. On the other hand, it does seem apparent that the adoption of these new technologies by both individuals and organizations is rapidly expanding, and that in certain task contexts they can affect interpersonal communication processes (Keen, 1981; Kerr & Hiltz, 1982; Rice, 1980). However, whether or not the adoption and use of these new technologies in task/work settings moderates or even negates interpersonal communication patterns and relationships established by previous research remains to be determined.

REFERENCES

Albrecht, T. L. (1979). The role of communication in perceptions of organizational climate. In D. Nimmo (Ed.), *Communication yearbook 3* (pp. 343-357). New Brunswick, NJ: Transaction.

Alderfer, C. P., & McCord, C. G. (1970). Personal and situational factors in the recruitment interview. *Journal of Applied Psychology, 54,* 377-385.

Allen, R. W., & Porter, L. W. (1983). *Organizational influence processes.* Glenview, IL: Scott, Foresman.

Arvey, R. D., & Campion, J. E. (1982). The employment interview: A summary and review of recent research. *Personnel Psychology, 35,* 281-322.

Arvey, R. D., & Ivancevich, J. M. (1980). Punishment in organizations: A review, propositions and research suggestions. *Academy of Management Review, 5,* 123-132.

Asch, S. (1951). Effects of group pressure upon the modification and distortion of judgments. In H. Guetzkow (Ed.), *Groups, leadership, and men* (pp. 117-190). Pittsburgh: Carnegie.

Ashour, A. S., & Johns, G. (1983). Leader influence through operant principles: A theoretical and methodological framework. *Human Relations, 36,* 603-626.

Atchley, R. C. (1976). *The sociology of retirement.* Cambridge, MA: Schenkman.

Atchley, R. C. (1977). *The social forces in later life* (2nd ed.). Belmont, CA: Wadsworth.

Avery, C. M., & Jablin, F. M. (1985). *Organizational communication and retirement from work: A survey of Fortune 100 organizations.* Paper presented at the annual meeting of the International Communication Association, Honolulu.

Babbitt, L. V. (1983). *Effects of applicants' questions on interview outcomes in naturally occurring employment screening interviews.* Unpublished master's thesis, University of Texas at Austin.

Bain, R. K., & Anderson, J. G. (1974). School context and peer influences on educational plans of adolescents. *Review of Educational Research, 44,* 429-445.

Bales, R. F., & Strodtbeck, F. (1951). Phases in group problem-solving. *Journal of Abnormal and Social Psychology, 46,* 485-495.

Becker, H. S., Geer, B., Hughes, E. C., & Strauss, A. (1961). *Boys in white: Student culture in medical school.* Chicago: University of Chicago Press.

Bednar, D. A. (1982). Relationships between communicator style and managerial performance in complex organizations: A field study. *Journal of Business Communication, 19,* 51-76.

Beuf, A. (1974). Doctor, lawyer, household drudge. *Journal of Communication, 24,* 142-145.

Bishop, G. D., & Myers, D. G. (1974). Informational influences in group discussion. *Organizational Behavior and Human Performance, 12,* 92-104.

Blake, R. R., Shepard, H., & Mouton, J. S. (1964). *Managing intergroup conflict in industry.* Houston: Gulf.

Bogatz, G. A., & Ball, S. J. (1971). *The second year of Sesame Street: A continuing evaluation.* Princeton, NJ: Educational Testing Service.

Bowles, S., & Gintis, H. (1976). *Schooling in capitalist America: Educational reforms and the contradictions of economic life.* New York: Basic Books.

Brett, J. M. (1982). Job transfer and well-being. *Journal of Applied Psychology, 67,* 450-463.

Brett, J. M., & Werbel, J. D. (1980). *The effects of job transfer on employees and their families: Final report.* Washington, DC: Employee Relocation Center.

Brown, D., Brooks, L., & Associates. (1984). *Career choice and development.* San Francisco: Jossey-Bass.

Brown, J. D. (1980). *Adolescent peer group communication, sex-role norms and decisions about occupations.* Paper presented at the annual meeting of the International Communication Association, Acapulco.

Bullis, C. B., Cox, M. C., & Bokeno, S. L. (1982). *Organizational conflict management: The effects of socialization, type of conflict, and sex on conflict management strategies.* Paper presented at the annual meeting of the International Communication Association, Boston.

Burns, T. (1955). The reference of conduct in small groups: Cliques and cabals in occupational milieux. *Human Relations, 8,* 467-486.

Byrd, M.L.V. (1979). *The effects of vocal activity and race of applicant on the job selection interview decision.* Unpublished doctoral dissertation, University of Missouri—Columbia.

Caldwell, D. F., & O'Reilly, C. A. (1982). Task perceptions and job satisfaction: A question of causality. *Journal of Applied Psychology, 67,* 361-369.

Cecil, E. A., Cummings, L. L., & Chertkoff, J. M. (1973). Group composition and choice shift: Implications for administration. *Academy of Management Journal, 16,* 412-422.

Cheatham, T. R., & McLaughlin, M. (1976). A comparison of co-participant perceptions of self and others in placement center interviews. *Communication Quarterly, 24,* 9-13.

Clark, M. M. (1981). Unleashing the productive value of long life. In N. G. McCluskey, & E. F. Borgatta (Eds.), *Aging and retirement* (pp. 213-222). Beverly Hills, CA: Sage.

Conrad, C. (1983). Power and performance as correlates of supervisors' choice of modes of managing conflict: A preliminary investigation. *Western Journal of Speech Communication, 47,* 218-228.

Constantin, S. W. (1976). An investigation of information favorability in the employment interview. *Journal of Applied Psychology, 61,* 743-749.

Crawford, J. L. (1974). Task uncertainty, decision importance, and group reinforcement as determinants of communication processes in groups. *Journal of Personality and Social Psychology, 29,* 619-627.

Crites, J. O. (1969). *Vocational psychology.* New York: McGraw-Hill.

Cusella, L. P. (1980). The effects of feedback on intrinsic motivation: A propositional extension of cognitive evaluation theory from an organizational communication perspective. In D. Nimmo (Ed.), *Communication yearbook 4* (pp. 367-387). New Brunswick, NJ: Transaction.

Cusella, L. P. (1982). The effects of source expertise and feedback valence on intrinsic motivation. *Human Communication Research, 9,* 17-32.

Daly, J. A. (1978). *The personnel selection interview: A state of the art review.* Paper presented at the annual meeting of the International Communication Association, Chicago.

Daniels, T. D., & Logan, L. L. (1983). Communication in women's career development relationships. In R. N. Bostrom (Ed.), *Communication yearbook 7* (pp. 532-552). Beverly Hills, CA: Sage.

Danowski, J. A. (1980). Group attitude-belief uniformity and connectivity of organizational communication networks for production, innovation, and maintenance content. *Human Communication Research, 6,* 299-308.

Dansereau, F., Graen, G., & Haga, W. J. (1975). A vertical dyad linkage approach to leadership within formal organizations. *Organizational Behavior and Human Performance, 13,* 46-78.

DeFleur, M. L. (1964). Occupational roles as portrayed on television. *Public Opinion Quarterly, 28,* 57-74.

DeFleur, M. L., & DeFleur, L. B. (1967). The relative contribution of television as a learning source for children's occupational knowledge. *American Sociological Review, 32,* 777-789.

Dennis, H. S. (1974). *A theoretical and empirical study of managerial communication climate in complex organizations.* Unpublished doctoral dissertation, Purdue University.

Dominick, J. R. (1974). Children's viewing of crime shows and attitudes on law enforcement. *Journalism Quarterly, 51,* 5-12.

Downs, C. W., & Conrad, C. (1982). Effective subordinancy. *Journal of Business Communication, 19,* 27-37.

Dreeban, R. (1968). *What is learned in school.* Reading, MA: Addison-Wesley.

Drucker, P. (1973). *Management: Tasks, responsibilities, practices.* New York: Harper & Row.

Duncan, O. D., Haller, A. D., & Portes, A. (1968). Peer influences on aspirations: A reinterpretation. *American Journal of Sociology, 74,* 119-137.

Einhorn, L. J. (1981). An inner view of the job interview: An investigation of successful communicative behaviors. *Communication Education, 30,* 217-228.

Eisenberg, E. M., Monge, P. R., & Miller, K. I. (1983). Involvement in communication networks as a predictor of organizational commitment. *Human Communication Research, 10,* 179-201.

Ellis, D. G., & Fisher, B. A. (1975). Phases of conflict in small group development: A Markov analysis. *Human Communication Research, 1,* 195-212.

Employment Relocation Center. (1981). *Relocation trends survey—1981.* Washington, DC: Author.

Farace, R. V., Monge, P. R., & Russell, H. M. (1977). *Communicating and organizing.* Reading, MA: Addison-Wesley.

Feldman, D. C. (1977). The role of initiation activities in socialization. *Human Relations, 30*, 977-990.

Feldman, D. C. (1981). The multiple socialization of organization members. *Academy of Management Review, 6*, 309-318.

Feldman, D. C. (1984). The development and enforcement of group norms. *Academy of Management Review, 9*, 47-53.

Feldman, D. C., & Brett, J. M. (1983). Coping with new jobs: A comparative study of new hires and job changers. *Academy of Management Journal, 26*, 258-272.

Fisher, B. A. (1970). Decision emergence: Phases in group decision-making. *Speech Monographs, 37*, 53-66.

Fisher, C. D. (1979). Transmission of positive and negative feedback to subordinates: A laboratory investigation. *Journal of Applied Psychology, 64*, 533-540.

Fisher, C. D., Ilgen, D. R., & Hoyer, W. D. (1979). Source credibility, information favorability, and job offer acceptance. *Academy of Management Journal, 22*, 94-103.

Gecas, V. (1981). Contexts of socialization. In R. Rosenberg & R. H. Turner (Eds.), *Social psychology: Sociological perspectives* (pp. 165-199). New York: Basic Books.

Goldhaber, G. M., & Rogers, D. P. (1979). *Auditing organizational communication systems: The ICA communication audit.* Dubuque, IA: Kendall/Hunt.

Goldstein, B., & Oldham, J. (1979). *Children and work: A study of socialization.* New Brunswick, NJ: Transaction.

Gouran, D. S., & Baird, J. E. (1972). An analysis of distributional and sequential structure in problem-solving and informal group discussions. *Speech Monographs, 39*, 18-22.

Graen, G. (1976). Role-making processes within complex organizations. In M. D. Dunnette (Ed.), *Handbook of industrial and organizational psychology* (pp. 1201-1245). Chicago: Rand McNally.

Graen, G., & Cashman, J. (1975). A role-making model of leadership in formal organizations: A developmental approach. In J. G. Hunt & L. L. Larson (Eds.), *Leadership frontiers* (pp. 143-165). Kent, OH: Kent State University Press.

Granovetter, M. S. (1973). The strength of weak ties. *American Journal of Sociology, 78*, 1360-1380.

Green, S. G., & Mitchell, T. R. (1979). Attributional processes of leaders in leader-member interactions. *Organizational Behavior and Human Performance, 23*, 429-458.

Greller, M. M. (1980). Evaluation of feedback sources as a function of role and organizational level. *Journal of Applied Psychology, 65*, 16-23.

Guetzkow, H. (1965). Communication in organizations. In J. G. March (Ed.), *Handbook of organizations* (pp. 534-573). Chicago: Rand McNally.

Hackman, J. R. (1976). Group influences on individuals. In M. D. Dunnette (Ed.), *Handbook of industrial and organizational psychology* (pp. 1455-1525). Chicago: Rand McNally.

Hackman, J. R., Brousseau, K. R., & Weiss, J. A. (1976). The interaction of task design and group performance strategies in determining group effectiveness. *Organizational Behavior and Human Performance, 16*, 350-365.

Hackman, J. R., & Vidmar, N. (1970). Effects of size and task type on group performance and member reactions. *Sociometry, 33*, 37-54.

Louis Harris & Associates. (1979). *1979 study of American attitudes toward pensions and retirement.* New York: Johnson & Higgins.

Hatfield, J. D., & Huseman, R. C. (1982). Perceptual congruence about communication as related to satisfaction: Moderating effects of individual characteristics. *Academy of Management Journal, 25*, 349-358.

Heinen, J. S., & Jacobson, E. (1976). A model of task group development in complex organizations and a strategy of implementation. *Academy of Management Review, 1*, 98-111.

Hiemstra, G. (1983). You say you want a revolution? "Information Technology" in organizations. In R. N. Bostrom (Ed.), *Communication yearbook 7* (pp. 802-827). Beverly Hills, CA: Sage.

House, R. L., Filley, A. C., & Gujarati, D. W. (1971). Leadership style, hierarchical influence, and the satisfaction of subordinate role expectations: A test of Likert's influence proposition. *Journal of Applied Psychology, 55*, 422-432.

Huber, G. P., & Delbecq, A. L. (1972). Guidelines for combining the judgments of individual members in decision conferences. *Academy of Management Journal, 15*, 161-174.

Ilgen, D. R., Fisher, C. D., & Taylor, M. S. (1979). Consequences of individual feedback on behavior in organizations. *Journal of Applied Psychology, 64*, 349-371.

Ilgen, D. R., & Knowlton, W. A. (1980). Performance attributional effects on feedback from superiors. *Organizational Behavior and Human Performance, 25,* 441-456.

Ilgen, D. R., Peterson, R. B., Martin, B. A., & Boeschen, D. A. (1981). Supervisor and subordinate reactions to performance appraisal sessions. *Organizational Behavior and Human Performance, 28,* 311-330.

Imada, A. S., & Hakel, M. D. (1977). Influence of nonverbal communication and rater proximity on impressions and decisions in simulated employment interviews. *Journal of Applied Psychology, 62,* 295-300.

Infante, D. A., & Gordon, W. I. (1979). Subordinate and superior perceptions of self and one another: Relations, accuracy, and reciprocity of liking. *Western Journal of Speech Communication, 43,* 212-223.

Jablin, F. M. (1979). Superior-subordinate communication: The state of the art. *Psychological Bulletin, 86,* 1201-1222.

Jablin, F. M. (1980a). Superior's upward influence, satisfaction, and openness in superior-subordinate communication: A reexamination of the "Pelz Effect." *Human Communication Research, 6,* 210-220.

Jablin, F. M. (1980b). Subordinate's sex and superior-subordinate status differentiation as moderators of the Pelz Effect. In D. Nimmo (Ed.), *Communication yearbook 4* (pp. 349-366). New Brunswick, NJ: Transaction.

Jablin, F. M. (1980c). Organizational communication theory and research: An overview of communication climate and network research. In D. Nimmo (Ed.), *Communication yearbook 4* (pp. 327-347). New Brunswick, NJ: Transaction.

Jablin, F. M. (1981a). *Organizational entry and organizational communication: Job retrospections, expectations, and turnover.* Paper presented at the annual meeting of the Academy of Management, San Diego.

Jablin, F. M. (1981b). An exploratory study of subordinates' perceptions of supervisory politics. *Communication Quarterly, 29,* 269-275.

Jablin, F. M. (1981c). Cultivating imagination: Factors that enhance and inhibit creativity in brainstorming groups. *Human Communication Research, 7,* 245-258.

Jablin, F. M. (1982a). Organizational communication: An assimilation approach. In M. E. Roloff & C. R. Berger (Eds.), *Social cognition and communication* (pp. 255-286). Beverly Hills, CA: Sage.

Jablin, F. M. (1982b). Formal structural characteristics of organizations and superior-subordinate communication. *Human Communication Research, 8,* 338-347.

Jablin, F. M. (1984). Assimilating new members into organizations. In R. N. Bostrom (Ed.), *Communication yearbook 8* (pp. 594-626). Beverly Hills, CA: Sage.

Jablin, F. M. (1985). An exploratory study of vocational organizational communication socialization. *Southern Speech Communication Journal, 50,* 261-282.

Jablin, F. M., & McComb, K. B. (1984). The employment screening interview: An organizational assimilation and communication perspective. In R. N. Bostrom (Ed.), *Communication yearbook 8* (pp. 137-163). Beverly Hills, CA: Sage.

Jablin, F. M., & Seibold, D. R. (1978). Implications for problem-solving groups of empirical research on "brainstorming": A critical review of the literature. *Southern Speech Communication Journal, 43,* 327-356.

Jablin, F. M., & Sussman, L. (1983). Organizational group communication: A review of the literature and model of the process. In H. H. Greenbaum, R. L. Falcione, & S. A. Hellweg (Eds.), *Organizational communication: Abstracts, analysis and overview* (Vol. 8, pp. 11-50). Beverly Hills, CA: Sage.

Jablin, F. M., Tengler, C. D., & Teigen, C. W. (1982). *Interviewee perceptions of employment screening interviews: Relationships among perceptions of communication satisfaction, interviewer credibility and trust, interviewing experience, and interview outcomes.* Paper presented at the annual meeting of the International Communication Association, Boston.

Janis, I. (1972). *Victims of groupthink: A psychological study of foreign policy decisions and fiascos.* Boston: Houghton Mifflin.

Karol, B. L. (1977). *Relationship of recruiter behavior, perceived similarity, and prior information to applicants' assessments of the campus recruitment interview.* Unpublished doctoral dissertation, Ohio State University.

Katz, R. (1980). Time and work: Toward an integrative perspective. In B. M. Staw & L. L. Cummings (Eds.), *Research in organizational behavior* (Vol. 2, pp. 81-127). Greenwich, CT: JAI.

Katz, D., & Kahn, R. L. (1966). *The social psychology of organizations.* New York: John Wiley.

Katzman, N. I. (1972). Television soap operas: What's been going on, anyway? *Public Opinion Quarterly, 36,* 200-212.

Keen, P. (1981). Information systems and organizational change. *Communicatons of the ACM, 24*(1), 24-33.

Kerr, E., & Hiltz, S. R. (1982). *Computer-mediated communication systems.* New York: Academic Press.

Kilmann, R. H., & Thomas, K. W. (1977). Developing a forced-choice measure of conflict-handling behavior: The MODE instrument. *Educational and Psychological Measurement, 37,* 309-325.

Kipnis, D., Schmidt, S. M., & Wilkinson, I. (1980). Intraorganizational influence tactics: Explorations in getting one's way. *Journal of Applied Psychology, 65,* 440-452.

Kipnis, D., Schmidt, S. M., Price, K., & Stitt, C. (1981). Why do I like thee: Is it your performance or my orders? *Journal of Applied Psychology, 66,* 324-328.

Kirchner, E. P., & Vondracek, S. I. (1973). *What do you want to be when you grow up? Vocational choice in children aged three to six.* Paper presented at the meeting of the Society for Research in Child Development, Philadelphia.

Klauss, R., & Bass, B. M. (1982). *Interpersonal communication in organizations.* New York: Academic Press.

Klimoski, R. J., & Karol, B. L. (1976). The impact of trust on creative problem solving groups. *Journal of Applied Psychology, 61,* 630-633.

Kline, J. A. (1970). Indices of orienting and opinionated statements in problem-solving discussions. *Speech Monographs, 37,* 282-286.

Kline, J. A. (1972). Orientation and group consensus. *Central States Speech Journal, 23,* 44-47.

Knapp, M. L. (1978). *Social intercourse: From greeting to goodbye.* Boston: Allyn & Bacon.

Knutson, T. J. (1972). An experimental study of the effects of orientation behavior on small group consensus. *Speech Monographs, 39,* 159-165.

Krone, K. J. (1984). *A framework for studying upward influence messages in decision making contexts.* Paper presented at the annual meeting of the International Communication Association, San Francisco.

Laing, R. D., Phillipson, H., & Lee, A. R. (1966). *Interpersonal perception: A theory and method of research.* New York: Springer.

Larson, J. R. (1984). The performance feedback process: A preliminary model. *Organizational Behavior and Human Performance, 33,* 42-76.

Leathers, D. G. (1970). The process effects of trust-destroying behavior in small groups. *Speech Monographs, 37,* 180-187.

Leifer, A. D., & Lesser, G. S. (1976). *The development of career awareness in young children.* Washington, DC: National Institute of Education.

Levine, J. M., Skroka, K. R., & Snyder, H. N. (1977). Group support and reaction to stable and shifting agreement/disagreement. *Sociometry, 40,* 214-224.

Liden, R. C., & Graen, G. (1980). Generalizabiliy of the vertical dyad linkage model of leadership. *Academy of Management Journal, 23,* 451-465.

Louis, M. (1980). Surprise and sense-making: What newcomers experience in entering unfamiliar organizational settings. *Administrative Science Quarterly, 25,* 226-251.

Mabry, E. A. (1975). Exploratory analysis of a developmental model for task-oriented small groups. *Human Communication Research, 2,* 66-74.

Mayfield, E. C. (1964). The selection interview: A reevaluation of published research. *Personnel Psychology, 17,* 234-260.

McComb, K. B., & Jablin, F. M. (1984). Verbal correlates of interviewer empathic listening and employment interview outcomes. *Communication Monographs, 51,* 353-371.

McDermott, V. A. (1980). *The role of interpersonal processes in adjusting to retirement.* Paper presented at the annual convention of the Central States Association, Chicago.

McGovern, T. V., & Tinsley, H.E.A. (1978). Interviewer evaluations of interviewee nonverbal behavior. *Journal of Vocational Behavior, 13,* 163-171.

McLaughlin, M. L., & Cheatham, T. R. (1977). Effects of communication isolation on job satisfaction of bank tellers: A research note. *Human Communication Research, 3,* 171-175.

Miller, H. E., & Terborg, J. R. (1979). Job attitudes of part-time and full-time employees. *Journal of Applied Psychology, 64,* 380-386.

Mitchell, T. R., & Wood, R. E. (1980). Supervisors' responses to subordinate poor performance: A test of an attributional model. *Organizational Behavior and Human Performance, 25,* 123-138.

Monge, P. R., Bachman, S. G., Dillard, J. P., & Eisenberg, E. M. (1982). Communicator competence in the workplace: Model testing and scale development. In M. Burgoon (Ed.), *Communication yearbook 5* (pp. 505-527). New Brunswick, NJ: Transaction.

Monge, P. R., Edwards, J. A., & Kirste, K. K. (1978). The determinants of communication and communication structure in large organizations: A review of research. In B. Ruben (Ed.), *Communication yearbook 2* (pp. 311-331). New Brunswick, NJ: Transaction.

Morgan, C. P., & Beatty, R. W. (1976). Information relevant to the task in the risky shift phenomenon. *Academy of Management Journal, 19,* 304-308.

Morrison, M. M. (1981). Reappraising retirement and personnel policies. In N. G. McCluskey & E. F. Borgatta (Eds.), *Aging and retirement* (pp. 175-188). Beverly Hills, CA: Sage.

Mowday, R. T. (1978). The exercise of upward influence in organizations. *Administrative Science Quarterly, 23,* 137-156.

Nachmann, B. (1960). Childhood experiences and vocational choice in law, dentistry and social work. *Journal of Counseling Psychology, 7,* 243-250.

Nadler, D. A. (1979). The effects of feedback on task group behavior: A review of the experimental research. *Organizational Behavior and Human Performance, 23,* 309-338.

Noble, G. (1975). *Children in front of the small screen.* Beverly Hills, CA: Sage.

Norton, R. W. (1978). Foundation of a communicator style construct. *Human Communication Research, 4,* 99-112.

O'Reilly, C. A., & Anderson, J. C. (1980). Trust and the communication of performance appraisal information: The effect of feedback on performance and job satisfaction. *Human Communication Research, 6,* 290-298.

O'Reilly, C. A., & Caldwell, D. (1979). Informational influence as a determinant of task characteristics and job satisfaction. *Journal of Applied Psychology, 64,* 157-165.

Pavett, C. M. (1983). Evaluation of the impact of feedback on performance and motivation. *Human Relations, 36,* 641-654.

Pelz, D. (1952). Influence: A key to effective leadership in the first line supervisor. *Personnel, 29,* 209-217.

Penley, L. E., & Alexander, E. R. (1979). The communication and structure of work groups: A contingency perspective. In R. C. Huseman (Ed.), *Academy of management proceedings* (pp. 331-335). Mississippi State: Academy of Management.

Poole, M. S. (1981). Decision development in small groups I: A comparison of two models. *Communication Monographs, 48,* 1-24.

Poole, M. S. (1983). Decision development in small groups II: A study of multiple sequences in decision making. *Communication Monographs, 50,* 206-232.

Porter, L. W., Allen, R. W., & Angle, H. L. (1981). The politics of upward influence in organizations. In L. L. Cummings & B. Staw (Eds.), *Research in organizational behavior* (Vol. 3, pp. 109-149). Greenwich, CT: JAI.

Porter, L. W., Lawler, E. E., & Hackman, J. R. (1975). *Behavior in organizations.* New York: McGraw-Hill.

Prentice, D. S. (1975). The effect of trust-destroying communication on verbal fluency in the small group. *Speech Monographs, 42,* 262-270.

Pruitt, D. G. (1971a). Choice shifts in group discussion: An introductory review. *Journal of Personality and Social Psychology, 20,* 339-360.

Pruitt, D. G. (1971b). Conclusion: Toward an understanding of choice shifts in group decisions. *Journal of Personality and Social Psychology, 20,* 495-510.

Putnam, L. L., & Wilson, C. E. (1982). Communicative strategies in organizational conflicts: Reliability and validity of a measurement scale. In M. Burgoon (Ed.), *Communication yearbook 6* (pp. 629-652). Beverly Hills, CA: Sage.

Rakestraw, T. L., & Weiss, H. M. (1981). The interaction of social influences and task experience on goals, performance, and performance satisfaction. *Organizational Behavior and Human Performance, 27,* 326-344.

Randolph, W. A. (1978). Organization technology and the media and purpose dimensions of organizational communications. *Journal of Business Research, 6,* 237-259.

Redding, W. C. (1972). *Communication within the organization: An interpretive review of theory and research.* New York: Industrial Communication Council.

Riccillo, S. C., & Trenholm, S. (1983). Predicting managers' choice of influence mode: The effects of interpersonal trust and worker attributions on managerial tactics in a simulated organizational setting. *Western Journal of Speech Communication, 47,* 323-339.

Rice, R. E. (1980). The impacts of computer-mediated organizational and interpersonal communication. In M. Williams (Ed.), *Annual review of information science and technology* (Vol. 15, pp. 221-249). White Plains, NY: Knowledge Industries.

Rice, R. E., & Associates. (1984). *The new media: Communication, research, and technology.* Beverly Hills, CA: Sage.

Richmond, V. P., McCroskey, J. C., & Davis, L. M. (1982). Individual differences among employees, management communication style, and employee satisfaction: Replication and extension. *Human Communication Research, 8,* 170-188.

Richmond, V. P., McCroskey, J. C., Davis, L. M., & Koontz, K. A. (1980). Perceived power as a mediator of management communication style and employee satisfaction: A preliminary investigation. *Communication Quarterly, 28,* 37-46.

Richmond, V. P., Wagner, J. P., & McCroskey, J. C. (1983). The impact of perceptions of leadership style, use of power, and conflict management style on organizational outcomes. *Communication Quarterly, 31,* 27-36.

Riggs, C. J. (1983). Communication dimensions of conflict tactics in organizational settings: A functional analysis. In R. Bostrom (Ed.), *Communication yearbook 7* (pp. 517-531). Beverly Hills, CA: Sage.

Roberts, K. H., & Glick, W. (1981). The job characteristics approach to task design: A critical review. *Journal of Applied Psychology, 66,* 193-217.

Roberts, K. H., & O'Reilly, C. A. (1974). Measuring organizational communication. *Journal of Applied Psychology, 59,* 321-326.

Rogers, E. M., & Kincaid, L. (1981). *Communication networks: A paradigm for research.* New York: Macmillan.

Ross, R., & DeWine, S. (1982). *Interpersonal conflict: Measurement and validation.* Paper presented at the annual meeting of the Speech Communication Association, Louisville.

Rotchford, N. L., & Roberts, K. H. (1982). Part-time workers as missing persons in organizational research. *Academy of Management Review, 7,* 228-234.

Sackett, P. R. (1979). *The interviewer as hypothesis tester: The effects of impressions of an applicant on subsequent interviewer behavior.* Unpublished doctoral dissertation, Ohio State University.

Salancik, G. R., & Pfeffer, J. (1978). A social information processing approach to job attitudes and task design. *Administrative Science Quarterly, 23,* 224-253.

Schachter, S., Ellertson, N., McBride, D., & Gregory, D. (1951). An experimental study of cohesiveness and productivity. *Human Relations, 4,* 229-238.

Schein, E. H. (1968). Organizational socialization and the profession of management. *Industrial Management Review, 9,* 1-16.

Schein, E. H. (1978). *Career dynamics: Matching individual and organizational needs.* Reading, MA: Addison-Wesley.

Schein, E. H. (1980). *Organizational psychology* (3rd ed.). Englewood Cliffs, NJ: Prentice-Hall.

Schilit, W. K., & Locke, E. A. (1982). A study of upward influence in organizations. *Administrative Science Quarterly, 27,* 304-316.

Schlossberg, N. K., & Goodman, J. (1972). A woman's place: Children's sex stereotypes of occupations. *Vocational Guidance Quarterly, 20,* 266-270.

Schmidt, N. (1976). Social and situational determinants of interview decisions: Implications for the employment interview. *Personnel Psychology, 29,* 79-101.

Schuler, R. S. (1979). A role perception transactional process model for organizational communication-outcome relationships. *Organizational Behavior and Human Performance, 23,* 268-291.

Seashore, S. (1954). *Group cohesiveness in the industrial work group.* Ann Arbor, MI: University of Michigan, Institute for Social Research.

Sherif, M. (1936). *The psychology of social norms.* New York: Harper & Row.

Shiflett, S. C. (1972). Group performance as a function of task difficulty and organizational interdependence. *Organizational Behavior and Human Performance, 7,* 442-456.

Siegel, A. E. (1958). The influence of violence in the mass media upon children's role expectations. *Child Development, 29,* 35-56.

Sillars, A. L. (1980). The stranger and the spouse as target persons for compliance-gaining strategies: A subjective expected utility model. *Human Communication Research, 6,* 265-279.

Simpson, R. L. (1962). Parental influence, anticipatory socialization, and social mobility. *American Sociological Review, 17,* 754-761.

Sims, H. P. (1980). Further thoughts on punishment in organizations. *Academy of Management Review, 5,* 133-138.

Smircich, L., & Chesser, R. J. (1981). Superiors' and subordinates' perceptions of performance: Beyond disagreement. *Academy of Management Journal, 24,* 198-205.

Sorenson, J. R. (1971). Task demands, group interaction, and group performance. *Sociometry, 34,* 483-495.

Sussman, L. (1975). Communication in organizational hierarchies: The fallacy of perceptual congruence. *Western Speech Communication, 39,* 191-199.

Teigen, C. W. (1983). *Communication of organizational climate during job screening interviews: A field study of interviewee perceptions, "actual" communication behavior and interview outcomes.* Unpublished doctoral dissertation, University of Texas at Austin.

Tengler, C. D. (1982). *Effects of question-type and question orientation on interview outcomes in naturally occurring employment interviews.* Unpublished master's thesis, University of Texas at Austin.

Tengler, C. D., & Jablin, F. M. (1983). Effects of question type, orientation, and sequencing in the employment screening interview. *Communication Monographs, 50,* 245-263.

Toffler, A. (1980). *The third wave.* New York: William Morrow.

Tompkins, P. K. (1962). *An analysis of communication between headquarters and selected units of a national labor union.* Unpublished doctoral dissertation, Purdue University.

Trent, L. W. (1978). *The effect of varying levels of interviewee nonverbal behavior in the employment interview.* Unpublished doctoral dissertation, Southern Illinois University.

Trist, E. L., & Bamforth, K. W. (1951). Some social and psychological consequences of the longwall method of coal-getting. *Human Relations, 4,* 1-38.

Turow, J. (1974). Advising and ordering in daytime, primetime. *Journal of Communication, 24,* 138-141.

Turow, J. (1980). Occupation and personality in television dramas: An industry view. *Communication Research, 7,* 295-318.

Tushman, M. (1977). Communication across organizational boundaries: Special boundary roles in the innovation process. *Administrative Science Quarterly, 22,* 587-605.

Tushman, M., & Scanlon, T. (1981). Boundary spanning individuals: Their role in information transfer and their antecedents. *Academy of Management Journal, 24,* 289-305.

Ulrich, L., & Trumbo, D. (1965). The selection interview since 1949. *Psychological Bulletin, 63,* 100-116.

Van de Ven, A. H., & Delbecq, A. L. (1971). Nominal versus interacting group processes for committee decision-making effectiveness. *Academy of Management Journal, 14,* 203-212.

Van de Ven, A. H., & Delbecq, A. L. (1974). The effectiveness of nominal, delphi, and interacting group decision making processes. *Academy of Management Journal, 17,* 605-621.

Van de Ven, A. H., Delbecq, A. L., & Koenig, R. (1976). Determinants of coordination modes within organizations. *American Sociological Review, 41,* 332-338.

Van Maanen, J. (1975). Breaking in: Socialization to work. In R. Dubin (Ed.), *Handbook of work, organization and society* (pp. 67-120). Chicago: Rand McNally.

Volard, S. V., & Davies, M. R. (1982). Communication patterns of managers. *Journal of Business Communication, 19,* 41-53.

Wanous, J. P. (1977). Organizational entry: Newcomers moving from outside to inside. *Psychological Bulletin, 84,* 601-618.

Wanous, J. P. (1980). *Organizational entry: Recruitment, selection, and socialization of newcomers.* Reading, MA: Addison-Wesley.

Watson, K. M. (1982). An analysis of communication patterns: A method for discriminating leader and subordinate roles. *Academy of Management Journal, 25,* 107-120.

Weinstein, D. (1979). *Bureaucratic opposition: Challenging abuses of the workplace.* New York: Pergamon.

Weiss, H. M. (1977). Subordinate imitation of supervisor behavior: The role of modeling in organizational socialization. *Organizational Behavior and Human Performance, 19,* 89-105.

Weiss, H. M., & Nowicki, C. E. (1981). Social influence on task satisfaction: Model competence and observer field dependence. *Organizational Behavior and Human Performance, 27,* 345-366.

Weiss, W. (1969). Effects of the mass media of communication. In G. Lindzey & E. Aronson (Eds.), *Handbook of social psychology* (Vol. 5, pp. 77-195). Reading, MA: Addison-Wesley.

White, S. E., & Mitchell, T. R. (1979). Job enrichment versus social cues: A comparison and competitive test. *Journal of Applied Psychology, 64,* 1-9.

Whyte, W. F. (1955). *Money and motivation.* New York: Harper & Row.

Wilson, C. E. (1983). *Toward understanding the process of organizational leave-taking.* Paper presented at the annual meeting of the Speech Communication Association, Washington, DC.

Woelfel, J., & Haller, A. O. (1971). Significant others, the self-reflective act and the attitude formation process. *American Sociological Review, 36,* 74-87.

Wright, O. R. (1969). Summary of research on the selection interview since 1964. *Personnel Psychology, 22,* 391-413.

Zand, D. E. (1972). Trust and managerial problem solving. *Administrative Science Quarterly, 17,* 229-239.

14 Social and Personal Relationships

STEVE DUCK

University of Lancaster

P EOPLE'S lives are fabricated in and by their relationships with other people. Our greatest moments of joy and sorrow are founded in relationships. Although relationships with unchosen kin are a highly significant part of this, those voluntary relationships entered through choice or circumstance are at least an equal part. Some of these (e.g., with dates or lovers) are intended to pave the way toward kinship through marriage; other relationships—between friends, peers at school, neighbors, work mates, colleagues—are the paving stones of other routes to emotional peaks and troughs. Although the history of systematically studying voluntary personal and social relationships is surprisingly short, given their centrality in most people's lives, it is also a complex history. In reviewing it I have had to choose between exhaustiveness and usefulness. Taking the view that a structure is better than a comprehensive list of all published work (which, in any case, would easily exceed the page allowance for the chapter), I have decided to identify the points that I *notice* rather than the points that I *see*.

The picture is made messy and complex by the broad range of work that is carried out into social and personal relationships. Thus social and personal relationships have been explored by sociologists, family scientists, developmentalists, and clinical psychologists as well as by social psychologists and communication scientists. In comprehending the present and future state of affairs it is important to take a perspective on the effects of this multiple-layered interest and to identify problems that it created just as much as the advances that it has produced. These are due partly to the pronounced tendency for workers in different disciplines to go their own way, partly due to the poorly conceptualized methodology, and partly due to the terrifying complexity of the phenomena.

As others have noted (Berger & Roloff, 1982), a tendency for each discipline to strip mine particular lines of inquiry within its own approach is compounded by the tendency for each discipline to cleave to itself and ensure that the fruits of its efforts do not fall into the hands of scientists in other disciplines. Happily, that unproductive style has begun to change very recently, largely as a result of the work of Hinde (1979), but also because the stranglehold of social psychology has been released somewhat by recognition of the value of the inputs by communication scholars to this field.

A review such as this needs to identify the important issues and problems, research trends, and threads; to indicate some of the reasons for the inadequacy of our respective histories; and to lay down some proposals for interrelating the various themes. Of course, this being a handbook of interpersonal communication it would also be necessary to give full prominence to the role played by communication researchers in the development of the research even if they had not been causal in producing the present state of affairs. However, one major barrier to progress was that "communication" was lacking in most early approaches (the passive contribution of communication) and since then it has become a proper focus and has produced useful insights (the active contribution). It is also important to identify those places and points where the efforts of communication workers help best to provide the requisite integrative tension between disciplines or lines of research. Although I am an apostate social psychologist, it is my belief that "communication" actually does provide the glue necessary to integrate the various strands of the presently diverse field of social and personal relationships.

WHEN SOCIAL PSYCHOLOGY WAS KING

A common and interesting human tendency is the claim that, at a given time, everyone was doing the same thing. Thus in Victorian England everyone was a strict, straight-laced, sober piano player with children who were seen and not heard; the day Queen Victoria died, King Edward VII took the throne to rule over a people who were all uniformly merry, music hall-going punters who spent every Sunday strolling with their family beside well-tended gardens or rowing down the river. In the same way there is a tendency to regard all work on relationships as the same in the early days— which, of course, it was not, though it *was* dominated by social psychologists rather than communication scientists. Their habitual style led to the appearance that all work was based on rating scales, laboratory manipulations, and malevolent experimenters in white coats strenuously missing the point about real life relationships. Unremittingly inaccurate though the stereotype is, it is useful for reviewers to attend to the general picture, for it was commonly true, even if not totally true. Early scientific efforts to understand deep personal relationships too often did consist of arranged meetings in laboratories between two strangers (and sometimes only one person and a figment of everyone's imagination) for about 10 minutes, with no prospect of ever meeting again. Yet such work led to a greater understanding of the issues that face researchers in personal and social relationships. Although the work on initial attraction has taught us something about attraction, it often did so by being misunderstood, by causing aversive reactions in productive researchers who went and did more useful work within completely different frame-works, and by generating the desire to show the problems with the approach. These latter attempts rapidly exposed people to the complexities of the work and the problems as the field stood at that particular time—problems attaching to the field of the International Psychological Association (IPA) itself.

There seem to me to have been essentially four problems. First, the relative contributions of work by different disciplines upon a central issue were not clearly established; in particular, too little was made of the need to incorporate communicational research that indicated the means by which social psychological effects (like attitude similarity) exerted their influence in real life. Second, the realms of "the phenomena" were not unequivocally agreed upon, and some people included relationships or phenomena that others did not account while few attempts to taxonomize these relationships were made. Third, the concepts of relationship were diverse and befitting each discipline but predominantly looked on relationships as states or static categories (rather than dynamic processes) and as "automatic" consequences of particular states or qualities of the relative parties. Fourth, the methods employed in the laboratory were suited to static, undeveloping, one-off meetings between strangers rather than to real-life relationships. Cross-sectional methods led to cross-sectional theories about the phenomena that had been so sectioned, although the essence of a communicative approach is found in dynamism, flow, interchange, interaction, and reaction.

The most significant omissions from such work as it stood in the mid-1970s were the underrated influence of two important effects: Time was omitted from most conceptualizations so that process was not studied, and active needs and efforts of the relationship participants were not accounted. Relationships were implicitly all of a piece, and relationship partners were assumed to be all possessed of the same competences, urges, skills, and intentions. Contrarily, if one takes a process view of relationships that includes "natural" effects of time's passage and "unnatural" effects of partners' efforts at communication, then much becomes clearer. In the present chapter, I will consider both of these while working toward the view that "relationships as process" is itself a somewhat simple-minded idea that should comprise several different elements.

It is a mistake to act as if process in relationships could refer only to the fact that different styles predominate at different times or to the fact that process means only their development or decline, rather than their maintenance and endurance. It is easiest to see "process" there because process is most easily seen in terms of gross change. Just as the boiling of water is not a self-contained state but a process that is dependent on external circumstances, so relationships are processes. Even stability requires stabilizing governing mechanisms. Stability, in this sense, does not imply uniformity of stateness any more than a river is exactly the same from moment to moment merely because its banks are where they were yesterday. Equally, there are properties of relationships that are not deducible merely from previous descriptions by either of the partners to the relationship but emerge from their continuous interaction. Just as one person cannot "be similar" alone but two can together, so relationships have emergent qualities (like intimacy) that are dependent on continuous styles of action, not on states or the qualities of partners separately.

Some Points about Early Work

The inadequacies of the early views are still around (see Duck & Sants, 1983, for a discussion), but can be best illustrated by reference to distant well-known work. A strand of research familiar in social psychology (and notorious there and elsewhere) is one that helpfully illustrates both the strengths and weaknesses of the early research. It also helps us to draw lessons that will guide us through the rest of this chapter.

During the late 1950s Donn Byrne (reviewed by Byrne, 1971, and Duck, 1977) began working on the question that underlies or underpins all work on relational development: "What makes people attracted to one another?" That is, what are the building blocks of all voluntary associations and all voluntary interdependencies? Taking the view that all deep voluntary personal relationships grow from the seeds of initial attraction, Byrne embarked on a quest for a scientific rule of thumb. The question is a tricky one, for if a scientific approach is to be adopted, the totality of attraction must be reduced to component parts, each of which needs study until its contribution to the total can be ascertained. Byrne decided to focus on the study of attitudes. However, if attitudes are presented to judges by some communicative means such as tape recordings, videotapes, live, and so forth, then, even if they are somehow standardized, the very means of communication itself introduces unknown variance into the equation. Perhaps because he was not a communication theorist, Byrne decided therefore to present attitudes to subjects in a standard written form via standard sheets with standard kinds of markings to indicate their strength of endorsement. This method eliminates much that others would want to study, such as the effects of physical attractiveness of the attitude holder, the assertiveness of the pronouncement of the attitude, the nonverbal accoutrements of the declarations of attitudinal position, and so on. In a perfect world, that is not really a problem because Byrne (1971) expected (rightly) that other workers would take upon themselves the arduous job of exploring these issues as carefully and systematically as he was about to explore "pure" attitudinal effects.

What attitudinal effects? The problem remaining for Byrne was the exact object of his study because he did not believe that the same attitudes would necessarily be equally attractive to all subjects. His belief was that reinforcement was really what is attractive, and that one example of such reinforcement is provided by occasions in which attitudinal similarity is experienced in a proper set of circumstances. He therefore decided to take attitude similarity as his focus of interest and to explore its effects and the influences upon its attractiveness. However, attitude similarity can be studied in the necessarily stripped-down way only in the laboratory and only by special tricks. So Byrne used the "Bogus Stranger" method, in which the subject completed an attitude scale and then was later given another such scale (actually rigged by the experimenter) corresponding to his or her own to a precisely manipulated degree (for example, 80 percent or 20 percent). Using such techniques Byrne was able, over a considerable period of years, to establish the fact that attitude similarity was preferred to dissimilarity, the precise nature of the effect of given proportions of similarity upon resultant attraction scores, and so on.

Byrne's work was undoubtedly useful in its place and taught us a considerable amount about precise aspects of attraction. It also expanded our knowledge of experimental techniques in the area. However, it simultaneously created a lot of dissatisfaction. Those grievances based on the claim that it is "artificial" are usually trivial and imprecise as to their definition of artificiality (Eiser, 1980; Gergen, 1980), often showing a mistaken view of Byrne's purposes and ignorance of the details of his position. Yet there are several problems with Byrne's approach, and many of them concern us because they fall into the area of "communication," as broadly defined.

For instance, even if Byrne's work does tell us about the effects of reinforcing attitude similarity, it does not tell us anything about the processes by which people normally detect it in their everyday encounters with strangers. It is assumed that the pair of persons concerned not only can and do detect, but also concern themselves with, and communicate about, these factors that are assumed to influence relationships. This is a huge assumption, and one investigated actively rather than merely taken for granted by workers in communication. Such a view also contains the assumption that the partners have the communicative skills necessary and relevant to such tasks. Yet our clinical colleagues (for example, Burns & Farina, 1984; Cook, 1977; Trower, 1981) have amply demonstrated in their life's work that there exists a full range of ability to carry out such activity—a range from skillful to inadequate. There are many people who fail to communicate the right messages about their attitudes, or who inadequately self-disclose, cannot detect warmth or interest in others, or who generally contribute to the error variance by having poor relations (Duck, 1983). This neatly illustrates the familiar point that one worker's error variance is often another worker's conceptual life's work. Legions of researchers have shown that individuals differ in their capacities for accurate perception of other people and their views.

Despite the fact that such individual differences are a major source of variation in social behavior (Argyle, 1983), there are many other reasons to focus on communicative aspects of the simple attitude-attraction relationship. It would be nice if everyone were always an open book, honestly and strenuously communicating their heartfelt attitudes; but even if people are sure of their attitudes they often do not do this (Goffman, 1959). The position is complicated by the fact that an individual's views are often disguised or only partly disclosed in real life, and it is occasionally to their purposes to conceal whole areas of their attitudes. For this reason it is sometimes a very skilled enterprise to find out someone else's attitudes, and the reinforcement to be obtained from them is very likely to be viewed in the context of the effort expended to expose them (Knapp, 1978, 1984).

If one assumes, then, that attitudinal information does have social psychological effects, three communicative issues also need research:

(1) the processes through which persons habitually gather and interpret the relevant information (for example, see Berger & Bradac, 1982);
(2) the differences in skills of encoding and decoding that may entrap well-intentioned interactors into the making of wrong assessments (for example, see Berger & Roloff, 1982); and
(3) the social influences upon communications that affect judgments and processes of gathering evidence to make them (for example, see Cappella, 1984).

Thus there are at least three communicative elements to the real life discovery and evaluation of another person's attitudes (and their similarity to one's own) that deserve to be explored in conjunction with, or as a supplement to, work on the "pure" effects of reinforcing attitudinal similarity itself.

Byrne's work, however, also omits other important communicative elements in everyday attraction and the conduct of relationships. For one thing, choice of partners is not merely dependent upon one person's reactions to another or upon their desires to interact with one another. Desires have to be both reciprocated and appropriate to the community in which the partners belong; preferences have to be communicated to and negotiated with one another; and choices must be translated into relationships through communicative action (Hays, 1984). Most of these requirements are based on communicative skills and actions, or on knowledge about the suitability of certain kinds of relationships for particular persons or certain kinds of behavior to certain kinds of relationships (Argyle & Henderson, in press). They involve the negotiation of mutuality and the communication to one's intended partner of all the necessary social and sociological paraphernalia of relationships (Burns & Farina, 1984). For instance, negotiation of relationship form needs to be achieved and is clearly dependent on some cognitive schema for the necessary behavior in relationships as it also is on negotiated agreement about roles within the relationship (Dindia & Fitzpatrick, in press). Futhermore, dyadic relationships do not affect only dyads and they have to be accepted and tolerated by others (McCall, 1982), the clearest example being a marriage, in which both families are entitled to form a strong view of its suitability.

Different forms of relationships are also possible, and the partners need to be able to achieve the form that suits their particular desire for contact (Argyle & Henderson, 1984; Davis & Todd, in press; Lee, 1984). Knowledge of the available sorts and types must be presumed, but also the ability to create the desired form is implicit. A version of this same point is that relationship development (that is, development toward a particular desired state) prerequires different sorts of knowledge and communicative skill at different points (Duck & Perlman, in press). Byrne's work rather assumed that relationships are operated by a single switch that exerts a once-and-for-all effect.

Furthermore, the characteristics of participants do not necessarily stay the same in relationships unless our every model of education and all talk of learning by experience is simply wrong. So even if partner qualities did "switch on" relationships, we need to account for the fact that natural change and personal growth can and do alter a person's attitudes and personality in ways that affect their ability to continue to reward their partner (Wright, in press).

From Byrne's work then, we can learn a small amount about the effects of certain limited influences upon attraction and a great deal about the other factors that need to be studied in parallel with, and as a supplement to, Byrne's own work. Most of these important supplements are those dependent on regarding personal and social relationships as extended long-term processes. Their creation depends on elements that are communicative in nature and require us to recognize that relational partners are active, probably possess culturally and personally derived knowledge about relationships, need to negotiate the form of their relationships, usually plot its trajectory, and react to their partner's actions. Most importantly, however, we learn that relationships have elements to them other than attitudes, and that these missing elements are essentially strategic and not simply reactive responses.

Beyond Byrne

Of course, Byrne's work on attitudes was not all that was being done in the scientific field at the time. A sizable literature on such things as personality influences on relationships was also being worked out (Duck, 1973, 1977). The latter was concerned with longer-term relationships such as friendship and marriage, rather than with the starting point of all relationships, that is, between strangers. It thus met one of the objections and acknowledged extensiveness of relationships through time, although it rarely studied them progressively (but see Lewis, 1973).

Despite this, however, there were some similarities between such work and that of Byrne, all of which provide central pegs on which to hang the later argument here about the active and passive roles of research on communication in relationships. One similarity was that scale measures of cognition were the order of the day. Thus most studies looked not at behavior in marriage or friendship but at the personality profiles of the partners themselves (for example, Day, 1961; Izard, 1960, 1963; Winch, 1958). From these two profiles were deduced many claims about the origins of the personal relationship between the partners.

The literature and the work fell into two distinct camps and yet shared common weaknesses of style (see Duck, 1977, Chap. 6, for a critique). Thus a large body of research examined the role of similarity of personality (somehow assessed) in relationship formation/growth/stability/maintenance. Other workers looked at complementarity of personality needs and the ways in which partners' opposite sides supplemented each other. There was for a long time little to decide between the two positions, each scoring successes and failures in particular contexts. What they shared in common were two weaknesses: First, rather as Byrne did, they assumed that one variable accounts for the existence of relationships, and they had no concept of graded time effects or the notion that a series of different criterial factors will be relevant at different points as relationships develop and endure. Second, they assumed that relationships depend on the melding of properties of the individual partners, and they had no theoretical overview of the ways in which such intermingling could, or does, occur (cf. Huston, Surra, Fitzgerald, & Cate, 1981).

It is a curious argument to claim that two entities as complex as human beings will move from being strangers to a fully operational social or personal relationship merely because, like the pieces of a jigsaw, their personalities happen to fit one another. Yet not only the extensive literatures on this proposal but also the majority of dating agencies and students in class tend to continue to accept it. It does become more acceptable if one proposes the more complex idea that not one but a series of criteria are used across time. Thus Kerckhoff and Davis (1962) argued that the processes of courtship depended on "filtering." That is, individuals selected their partners by progressively comparing a diminishing pool of "potentials" against a succession of criteria. The analogy is a vivid one and immediately suggests an arrangement from coarse through midrange to finely graded criteria. The notion has intuitive appeal and has been taken up by several other workers who attempted to specify the filtering sequence in courtship with mixed success (Levinger, Senn, & Jorgensen, 1970).

More recently Duck (1973, 1976, 1977) has applied a similar notion to all acquaintances and has focused on personality as the major filtering criterion of all those that apply. In essence, Duck's predictive filtering model assumes that acquainting persons seek information about the matching of, or support for, their own personality that is provided by the other person. They set about obtaining this information by deducing it from a range of available sources (for example, physical appearance, attitudes, nonverbal style, and so forth).

Cappella (1984), in reporting a series of studies from a communicational perspective, makes the point that all such theories are based on the study of *inferred* characteristics rather than actual ones. He claims that persons do not have access to a partner's real characteristics but form judgments or beliefs about them and act on the basis of those beliefs: "We are as much studying who people think they are attracted to as who they are attracted to" (Cappella, 1984, p. 241). Duck's (1977) predictive filtering model makes the same point rather less elegantly but nonetheless assumes that individuals deduce information about their partner's personality from any available stimulus source, such as physical appearance, nonverbal behavior, attitudes, and so on—a sequence of sources used in a manner that makes deductions progressively safer and more informative. Duck assumes that persons then use and marshal such information by erecting complex models of the presumed, underlying personality of the partner that are successively refined in ways that make them more predictive, interpretative, and descriptive of the other's personality. Such models are continually refined as new sorts of information become accessible through the progressive social, communicative, and interactive processes of acquaintance.

Within this latter scheme, it is conceived to be possible that there are different sorts and levels of similarity and complementarity within each class of criterion variables. Thus once the stage is reached in which personality becomes a criterion, it is still necessary for partners to match themselves up satisfactorily on a range of levels of personality, from low-grade global levels like extraversion-introversion to finer and subtler ones like personal constructs about other people's personality structures (Duck, 1973; Neimeyer & Neimeyer, 1983).

However, even such "filtering" models tend to contain the assumption that progress through the sequence is some automatic product of the congruence of partners' attributes. Absent from such models is any discussion of communicative differences in different persons involved in relationships. Also implicit is the idea that progress is smooth and linear. Yet we know that whenever relationships are transformed, two partners are faced with the problem of whether to stay in it, so that on top of any communication and information-seeking that is concerned with cognitive information comes the social communication and nonverbal or strategic management of the consequences of obtaining that information.

Also omitted is discussion of the trajectory of relationships and the path that each one takes from start to finish, whether "finish" means the ending of the relationship or its stabilization at a particular level. Third, the lack of discussion of trajectories leads to ambiguities about the types of relationships that may be possible and their overlaps with one another or their placement in the sequence making up the trajectory. Fourth, we must accept that partners have their own goals in interactions and are not simply driven by mysterious relational forces. These influence not only their communications but also their other relational activity, such as intimacy, self-disclosure, trust, and openness—as well as their beliefs about their partner and the relationship. Fifth, such "automatic" views of relationships forego discussion of the thought processes that characterize relationships. Yet individuals do seem to reassess things from time to time and act accordingly. Last, the above styles of work had little to say about those most poignant and troublesome human experiences: the breakdown and dissolution of relationships and their repair, which are equally important and perhaps more dramatic than relational growth (Duck, 1982, 1984).

These, then, were some of the major styles and weaknesses of approach that characterized relational work in IPA up until the late 1970s. The review has been selective in order to be illustrative, but has nevertheless picked out a whole range of places in which communication studies could have major inputs, with benefit to all. I shall now look at these in turn.

INPUTS FROM COMMUNICATION RESEARCH

In 1980 a major contribution was made to the study of relationships in a special issue of the *Western Journal of Speech Communication*. Several communication scientists reported the products of their analyses of the contemporary state of the art and identified contributions that could be made by communication research. In brief, these proposals were focused around three main issues: the role of consciousness or mindfulness in relationship-ping; the question of trajectories of relationships; and the nature of information gathering in attraction and relationships. The central arguments (for example, Berger, 1980; Crockett & Friedman, 1980; Delia, 1980) were that we know too little of the circumstances under which persons gather information in relationships and perhaps too readily assume that persons act at all times as information-processing machines aiming to develop and perpetuate the growth of their relationships. Yet not all relationships are intimate; not all relationships develop; and relationships can be both stable and satisfying without taking the tracks or paths presumed in many existing theories of relationships and relationship growth.

Also called for in that special issue were studies describing the behaviors of relationshipping and relaters. Too often have researchers been content to make presumptions about relationships and to test them in laboratories without checking these assumptions against the actions and interactions of actual relationships. Naturally the focus of the claims by communication experts fell on the communicative behaviors of participants. However, these correspond in broad terms with pressures from other researchers (for example, Hinde, 1979, 1981) for a greater emphasis on the behavior of relating, for a broader descriptive base in the research, and for a style of approach that incorporates more than mere social psychology. Since then several behavior studies have been conducted and several notable shifts of emphasis have taken place.

The "Automatic Nature" of Relational Development?

While one consequence of the change in styles of work was a greater emphasis on progress and process in relating, several assumptions continued to afflict the field. As noted above, a common presumption was that relational development is smooth and linear. Of course, in any model of relating that is based on the assumption of awareness by participants, it makes sense to assume that they know what they are doing and where they are going in a relationship. Indeed the whole assumption is precisely that they are gathering information for a purpose rather than casually—a purpose that they have clear in their minds and are intent to execute. That, however, is an assumption that I shall later challenge. Second, such models take too little account of the real significance for people of the fact that development of relationships is achieved through problematic decision making. What is lacking as an adjunct to such conceptualizations is the point that each change or development in the basis for the relationship affects the partners' attachment to it. Each is a real decision point because each changes the form of the relationship and hence brings changes in levels of commitment. Accordingly each change represents a point at which the partners could be expected to display uncertainty as they negotiate the relationship's transition.

At present, studies of relationship growth are usually done in a style that precludes testing of such a hypothesis. However, the diary method, based on the Rochester Interaction Record, would permit this idea to be tested and has already shown that such uncertainty exists and surrounds relationships (Duck & Miell, 1982, 1984). Partners in a 20-week longitudinal study characteristically reported uncertainty about their partner's attachment to their relationship. They saw their friends as their friends but did not see themselves as the friends of other people. They were unwilling to presume that their partner's apparent liking for them was certain to last or continue. For most subjects the relationship was seen as mostly dependent on the actions, feelings, and whims of their partner and only to a lesser extent on their own.

However, the observed uncertainty has been interpreted as a general feature of relationshipping rather than as a particular correlate of the choice points associated with interpretative transformation of relationships. In order to relate it in such a way, the day-to-day reports of subjects in relationships need to be matched up with observations of their communicative and intimate behaviors along with occasional interviews to assess their relational concerns at a particular point of study. However, it is becoming clear that the assumption that relationships are steady states that develop steadily may be an unsafe and misleading assumption. At least it is one worthy of test.

Perhaps an answer to such dilemmas is provided by consideration of the content of interactions and the ways in which it changes in relationship growth (Cappella, 1984). The assumption in many theories is that the content of interactions is a good index of its present state. Accordingly, the growth of intimacy and attachment to relationships should appear in the content of interactions. By recognizing, as the social psychologists have often failed to do, that the content of interactions rather than the influence of antecedent variables was a significant contributor to the nature of relationships, communication workers such as Penman (1980) gave us a new way of viewing the material that concerns us all. Penman analyzes communication processes in relationships in terms not only of their "punctuation" but as stochastic processes. In several ways this analysis is reminiscent of the point made by Gottman (1982) that research on relationships must take account of the temporal form of behavior in interactions. Both writers emphasize the need to view the content of interactions as the key variable in describing a relationship but also stress the importance of the temporal context when one comes to interpret that content. Both, in short, stress that relationships occur across time and between people at the behavioral level.

In similar fashion, Hinde (1981) talks of the content of interactions and makes several important points about the manner in which it is conducted. Thus a passionate kiss is different from a dutiful one. Equally, the patterning of content is important to our understanding of the nature of a given relationship: A kiss followed by a slap indicates a different set-up from that identified by a slap followed by a kiss.

Although such points are necessary and useful they are also faintly puzzling. For one thing, to say that we researchers must focus on the content of interaction is both interesting and circular. The content of an interaction is not just the behavior that can be observed in it, even if we can define what that would mean. Indeed, to say that an understanding of the content of an interaction would help us to define a relationship exactly begs the question, because in order to define the bounds and effective meaning of the content, we have to define the relationship first. As Penman (1980) and other communication workers indicate, the punctuation of interactions very largely depends on the observer's view of the nature of the relationship. Indeed, for Penman (1980, p. 2), the nature of a relationship is "deduced from the flow of exchanges between the individuals constituting, and constituted in, the relationship." In any case, "the content" is not an evaluatively neutral term as it appears to be. The content for one participant may not correspond with its content for the other participant, and both may fail to correspond with "the content" as perceived by an outside observer.

To make use of Hinde's example about a passionate kiss, we can see that even this "content" can have different meanings. It could indicate:

(1) a passionate relationship;
(2) an intent to form a passionate relationship and to signal this intent to the partner;
(3) a mistaken belief about the partner's wishes;
(4) an uncontrolled desire felt only by the kisser; or
(5) some combination of these separate meanings.

Accordingly it behooves us to note that in order to interpret "the content" we need to have a perspective upon it, and that this will largely depend upon our status as observers. It will also be affected, both for outside observers and for the partners themselves, by beliefs about the likely course of the relationship. For instance, as noted above, a passionate kiss can be a signal to both parties that a more intense form of relationship would be appropriate and desirable. The "content" of such interactions thus leads to, and is indicative of, transformations of the relationship if that is an outcome acceptable to both parties. Progress in relationships is not automatic, however, and depends to a great extent on the partners' clarity about the future of the relationship, the extent to which they share beliefs about the future, their understanding of the appropriate phases in a trajectory toward the desired endpoint, and their ability to enact those desires in ways that accomplish their goals. In short, relational development is not automatic but can nevertheless follow trajectories.

In a study of the behavior characterizing the development of friendship, Hays (1984) found that dyads developing successful close friendships showed different behavioral and attitudinal trends from those who did not. Specifically, the dyads' breadth of interaction and the intimacy level of their interactions were positively related to the intensity of their friendship, beyond the level accounted for by the sheer quantity of interaction. Those persons who were most adept at developing the relationship were also best at developing its breadth, rather than its depth alone. Growth of intimacy seems to depend on the abilities of the partners to develop this nonautomatic aspect of behavior and the communication about the relationship.

Types and Trajectories of Relationships

Such points are important not only in themselves but because they must relate to the use of information that partners have about their relationship. For instance, knowledge of the breadth or range of relationships that is possible will be accompanied by information about the paths between different types of relationships and some awareness of the in-built or expectable trajectories that different types of relationships may take. Also necessary is knowledge and communicatively relevant information about the meanings of extending the breadth and scope of activities performed in a relationship (Duck, 1983), for, as Huston et al. (1981) and Kelly, Huston, and Cate (in press) have shown, one central characteristic of relational development is the redeployment of time across a new set of activities. Such redeployments must perforce be appropriate to the relationship and its intended trajectory.

However, although it remains true that partners who are sure of the future trajectory of their relationship must act appropriately, there are also many instances in which relationships do not have trajectories in this sense. Although I know that my fiancee is much more likely than my friend is to end up as my spouse, there are many people whom I meet and for whom no such projections are normally made. I do not assess whether every student will become a friend, although many do. Neither do I assess the trajectory toward friendship from the starting point of meeting a shop assistant at the local store. Many relationships are stable without developing in intimacy and many are satisfying without "going anywhere."

Although such points make a great deal of sense intuitively, there is little data upon which to base them. Because most work starts with extant relationships and plots their trajectories retrospectively, little is known about the true development of relationships ab initio. When two strangers do meet in circumstances that are conducive to a future relationship, then their early responses to one another are as likely to be guided and constrained by cultural beliefs as by personal styles.

Although it is true in general terms that persons in the same relationship may have different perspectives upon it that will influence their processing of information about it and their communicative behavior within it, there are also likely to be some commonalities. For instance, members of the same culture at a given point in history are likely to agree on the range of relationships that is possible and are likely to have common perspectives on the numbers of different types that are possible. Davis and Todd (1985), for instance, have derived an understanding of the components of the concept of "friendship" that are shared by most people familiar with our culture. Implicit in the work is the idea that such shared knowledge is used by individuals to construct, guide, and evaluate the particular relationships that involve them (Sants, 1984). Although some of the significance of this rests upon the ways in which people will therefore gather information about their partner and their partner's intentions, it also arises from the fact that they are likely to adjust their relational behavior and communicative activity in the light of this knowledge and its inbuilt expectations (Huston et al., 1981; Shaver, Furman, & Buhrmester, in press).

Also likely is the possibility that relationships could have multiple trajectories depending on what is measured by investigators. In the Duck and Miell (1982) diary studies, separate measures of intimacy in interaction, satisfaction, expected future for the relationship, and so on were taken. The trajectories for these different measures did not always correspond complete-ly, and the authors indicate that "the trajectory" is a complex compound of these variables. However, it is also important to recognize that "the trajectory" can be perceived differently by the two partners and also by each partner at different times, if one takes measures of it on separate occasions (Duck & Miell, 1984). In retrospective accounts of relationships, a consider-able amount of editing of trajectories takes place. Partly this is because "the trajectory" of a relationship (and the choice of trajectory for it) is influenced by joint action and knowledge conjointly, not merely by one individual's desires or wishes and not by knowledge alone. However, the thoughts and transformational activity of the partners influence their perception of the trajectory also, and do so as a consequence of one neglected aspect of relationships: the out-of-relationship thought processes (Duck, 1980). This is perhaps most dramatically true in the context of decline and development but also occurs in relation to stability of relationships, as a function of strategic goals.

Applegate (1983), for instance, has argued that communication is func-tional behavior, and he takes the constructivist viewpoint that messages are never epiphenomenal: They do things for people. In the present context, for Applegate, communication in relationships is communication tied directly to interaction goals. I will argue below that such a view is probably correct for the data base that we presently have concerning relationship phenomena, and that it does the best job of explaining those data that have been gathered in specific relational contexts. However, it is open to question (and, in all honesty the question is not yet answered) whether normal, everyday interac-tions are so planned, constructive, and ordered, as some of our data would suggest. One's own subjective experience is testament to the fact that thoughtlessness, mindlessness, mistakes, and sheer stupidity characterize more of one's own relational action than we would all prefer to believe (and, incidentally, more than we would usually tend to admit to the experimenters who probably bring out all sorts of socially desirable but inaccurate reports from under our public carapaces). Nevertheless, it is instructive to look at the conduct of relationships as if it were thoughtful, as though it influences both communication and behavior in relating.

The Role of Thought in Relationships

If we focus on the gathering of information in relationships, then it seems to have four main purposes. First, it helps us to understand and reduce uncertainty about the partner as a person (Berger & Bradac, 1982; Bradac, 1983). Second, it helps us to form an understanding of the suitability of the partner as a partner (Miell & Duck, 1983). Third, it helps us to determine the most appropriate type of relationship trajectory between "Person" and "Other" (Delia, 1980). Fourth, as the relationship takes its shape, the gathering of information is directed toward the end of evaluating the relationship, the partner and oneself against cultural norms and ideals for the kind of relationship that has been created. Although such informational processing can be affected by several of the passive, active, and interactive strategies discussed by Berger and Bradac (1982); it also occurs as pure thought in the heads of partners, who reflect, consider, evaluate, ponder, and contemplate. As Delia (1980) observes, many conclusions about partner, self, and relationship are tentative, particularly at the early stages of relationship formation.

Such thinking about relationships affects their trajectory at early formative stages and when the relationship runs into problems. However, part of the argument of this section of the chapter has been implicitly that relationships and thought or information are dialectic rather than a simple undirectional influence pattern. Thoughts about partner, and information gathered about partner, are affected by relationships too. Thus communication and information collection are affected by the following:

(1) persons' knowledge of the permissible types of relationships (as Rubin, 1977, notes, the type of relationship affects the sequence in which information is gathered);
(2) the roles of relationships (as Argyle & Henderson, 1984, in press, and Crockett & Friedman, 1980, note, individuals are affected by the norms governing different types of relationships);
(3) partners' specific beliefs about the nature, status, and present or future form of the relationship;
(4) partners' skills and abilities in conducting the relationship; and
(5) partners' perspectives on relationships and intentions.

One clear implication is that partners' conduct of relationships, and their informational processing, will be affected by all of these features of social knowledge. A mediating factor seems to be provided by partners' strategic intentions in relating.

Strategic intentions and execution of intentions have significant effects upon the behavior of relating persons. Influences upon such strategies—and indeed the nature and existence of the strategies—have been a major and serious omission of previous work, which has tended to use appeals to naive motives like "reciprocity" to account for people's use of self-disclosure in relationships. A more complex picture is needed, one that is framed in a better grasp of the role of identity management in the early stages of relationship development. For instance, Clark and Delia (1979) have argued that every communicative transaction involves the overt and/or tacit negotiation of identities and relationship definition between interactants. Miell (1984) contends that even self-disclosure may be used strategically, whether for purposes of relational control, relational development, or identity management. What Miell (1984) shows is that *changes* in relationship definition are also signaled by the same means, as transactions contain both a definition and the seeds of the next definition. Changes in self-disclosure are not just automatic responses to the "demands" of reciprocity.

Over a period of time, Delia, Clark, O'Keefe, Applegate, and their colleagues have identified series of developmental and individual differences in listener-adaptiveness of persuasive strategies, the referential adequacy of information-giving strategies, the person-centeredness of regulative and interpersonal strategies, and the relative sophistication of impression management strategies in coping with "face" needs in interaction. Constructivist theory indicates that differences in quality of strategic behavior are strongly influenced by the quality of communicators' understandings of people, and so the information-gathering and -processing strategies come full circle here.

Communicative behavior is also influenced by communication-relevant beliefs organized within the communicator's definition of the situation (Applegate, 1983). Naturally this alters along with the changes in relationship that occur with its development or decline. Therefore we can expect some strategic flexibility as a key feature of communication in relationships, and the task then becomes one of identifying the individual differences that account for particular repertoires of communicative skill.

The foregoing points indicate that concern over information gathering in acquaintance is a key issue in the field, and one that considerably advances us beyond the naive assumptions inherent in research on interpersonal attraction. It incidentally leads us to a process view of relationships in which relationships are socially negotiated in progressive ways rather than being simple products of the intermingling of partners' qualities and properties.

It is most natural, perhaps, to think in processual terms of the development and decline of relationships, but it is worth pointing out that maintenance and stability of relationships are also processes rather similar to other processes of homeostasis. They require collection and processing of information as well as regular monitoring of goals.

We can thus see that a communicational perspective on relationships permits us to note the several different processes that are components of relationshipping. Information gathering is one large set of processes; the negotiation of a relationship's form is another; the maintenance of its place in a social network is a third; the processing of information relative to knowledge of relational objectives and norms is a fourth; and the passage of time—with its implication of changes in communication to persons, about relationships, and in connection with surrounding circumstances—along with the important business of coping with human errors, moods, and changes in life purposes constitute other effects.

Although it seems easiest to measure such things in terms of trajectories and differences in trajectories, the exact constituents or axes of the trajectories are less easily determined. However, the changing styles of communication are one important constituent of the whole matrix. We should not, however, assume that the purposes of communication remain constant throughout the life of a relationship or that any changes in form are merely more sophisticated means of satisfying a single universal goal. It seems probable that information gathering is a major early purpose when reduction of uncertainty is paramount, but that self-focused strategic purposes (Clark & Delia, 1979) also take a part. When relationships begin to decline, we can see also that other-focused strategic ends must also be considered.

Decline of Relationships

For various reasons, the decline of relationships is an area of research with particular interest to communication experts. For one thing, the deterioration of relationships can be regarded as a process with several component elements (Duck, 1982, 1984), several of which are based in communicative actions. In his model for dissolution of relationships, Duck (1982) argues that there are five broad phases to the process (see Figure 14.1): the Breakdown Phase, the Intrapsychic Phase, the Dyadic Phase, the Social Phase, and the Grave Dressing Phase, and each is characterized by a predominant set of processes and enterprises.

The main concerns for communication workers would be the Dyadic Phase (in which partners confront each other and deal with the problems), the Social Phase (in which the partners deal with the "publication" of the dissolution), and the Grave-Dressing Phase (in which partners construct and communicate to "the World At Large" a version of the history of the relationship and its reasons for failure). So far the main work does center here (Baxter, 1979a, 1979b, 1982, 1984, in press). However, communications come in to the first (Breakdown) phase in the sense that partners often represent the impending problem with the relationship as a communication problem. Indeed, one profitable area for therapy of relationships is precisely concerned with improvement of communication skills (Gottman, Markman, & Notarius, 1976; cf. Chapter 4, this volume). In sum, then, the process of decline in relationships is sensibly viewed as a communicative process and the repair of declining relationships can be achieved in certain key respects by communicatively based interventions. Thus the Dyadic Phase, in which partners confront one another with their complaints about the relationship and each other, can be conceived as a compliance-gaining task (Miller & Parks, 1982). Furthermore, the dissolution of relationships has a number of strategic elements to it (such as preparing the "Other" person for one's exit), in which a partner's goals must be achieved through communication (Lee, 1984). Third, the decline of relationships follows one of a set of trajectories, each with communicative implications and stylistic accompaniments (Baxter, 1984, in press). Fourth, dissolution of a long-standing relationship involves (one of) the partners in communicating with and informing the surrounding network

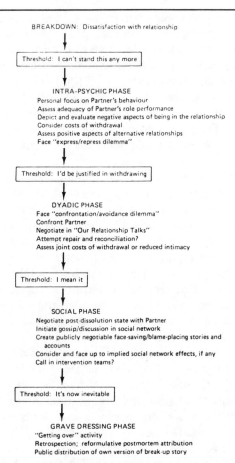

BREAKDOWN: Dissatisfaction with relationship

↓

Threshold: I can't stand this any more

INTRA-PSYCHIC PHASE
Personal focus on Partner's behaviour
Assess adequacy of Partner's role performance
Depict and evaluate negative aspects of being in the relationship
Consider costs of withdrawal
Assess positive aspects of alternative relationships
Face "express/repress dilemma"

↓

Threshold: I'd be justified in withdrawing

↓

DYADIC PHASE
Face "confrontation/avoidance dilemma"
Confront Partner
Negotiate in "Our Relationship Talks"
Attempt repair and reconciliation?
Assess joint costs of withdrawal or reduced intimacy

↓

Threshold: I mean it

↓

SOCIAL PHASE
Negotiate post-dissolution state with Partner
Initiate gossip/discussion in social network
Create publicly negotiable face-saving/blame-placing stories and
   accounts
Consider and face up to implied social network effects, if any
Call in intervention teams?

↓

Threshold: It's now inevitable

↓

GRAVE DRESSING PHASE
"Getting over" activity
Retrospection; reformulative postmortem attribution
Public distribution of own version of break-up story

SOURCE: *Personal Relationships 4: Dissolving Personal Relationships* (Duck, 1982, p. 16). Reprinted by permission of Academic Press, Inc., London.

Figure 14.1   A Sketch of the Main Phase of Dissolving Personal Relationships

of acquaintances, friends, or relatives about the ending of that relationship (La Gaipa, 1982) and requires them to construct a potted history of the relationship and its decline—the so-called "Grave Dressing Phase"—which also involves communication (Harvey, Weber, Yarkin, & Stewart, 1982; McCall, 1982). Not only were communication researchers primarily responsible for opening up this area (notably, Baxter, 1979a, 1979b; Knapp, 1978, 1984; cf. Hill, Rubin, & Peplau, 1976) but they have been most energetic in pursuing its exploration (Baxter, 1979a, 1979b, in press; Miller & Parks, 1982; Rose, 1984). I will, therefore, review a selection of this work and indicate some of the principles that seem to emerge.

One important first principle is that the decline or dissolution of a relationship involves the actors in an enterprise that is usually (but not always) extended in time and full of decisions or choice points. Especially in relationships with a long history or those with a previously strong emotional involvement, the dissolution processes are likely to be long and relatively painful. Two features that follow from that, then, are: the likelihood that communicative trajectories for the decline of relationships will be a fruitful area of study and the likelihood that communicative strategies play a part in the selection and definition of trajectories. Each of these areas has been explored.

The course of relationships relative to communication has been variously conceived. The most systematic and important work has been carried out by Baxter and colleagues. In a recent paper, Baxter (1984) has conceived a complex model of disengagement trajectories. She identifies eight basic trajectories for disengagements and claims that these patterned differences among relational declines argue for the abandonment of a simplistic single set of steps by which relationships change. Rather as argued above, it seems that "a trajectory" can be a farrago of communicational complexities. Persons exercise considerable personal choice over such trajectories. Indeed, the implication that trajectories of decline somehow happen to people is one that is to be avoided. Trajectories of decline do not have the character of railway tracks with no points. My own reading of Baxter's work is that she does not believe trajectories to be real in that sense, either, and it is important to see them as essentially descriptive mappings of habitual courses rather than determinations of preset and ineluctable tracks. Both Baxter (1984) and Lee (1984) indicate that there are strong strategic features to dissolution of relationships, both in relation to the choice to dissolve and the actual conduct of the dissolution. Lee (1984), for instance, distinguishes five stages in dissolution, each with at least two strategies. Thus, for instance, dissolution may be Exposed (E) or not (e) and Negotiated (N) or not (n). In some cases, Lee (1984) argues, persons deliberately choose to adopt one style rather than another, and at other times their communicative/strategic purposes are better served by silence.

Another approach to the strategic communications available in dissolving personal relationships is offered by Miller and Parks (1982). Their basic position is that the desire to end a relationship embroils the dissolver in a choice of compliance-gaining strategies in order to obtain the partner's acceptance of the exit from or ending of the relationship. Thus, for instance, a dissolver must choose whether to place the onus on the communicator (for example, by threats) or on the recipient of the communication (as in negative altercasting, like "Only a bad person would not let me out of this relationship").

Such apparently inconsistent views do not seem to me to be as irresolvable as other commentators sometimes imply. Thus the notion of complexity of individual trajectories is not inconsistent with an overarching view of the phases that must be proceeded through. Nor is a compliance-gaining model inconsistent with work indicating that other strategies can also be adopted: When compliance is sought, I am sure that the Miller and Parks (1982) model describes adequately the manner in which it is done.

It is perhaps worth noting, however, that the bulk of the work on this topic presently investigates the actor rather more than the "receiver," and often studies the quality of the relationship not at all. Equally surprising is the fact that there seems presently to be little work on the changes in communicative styles and subsystems that characterize deterioration of relationships in the way that there are studies of development (Morton, Alexander, & Altman, 1976). Most work seems to be at a global or strategic level rather than at the level of interactions and interacts.

This is interesting in itself, but we should also note, with Lee (1984), that noncommunication is also a strategy in dissolving romantic relationships. The specific kinds or areas of noncommunication and the ways in which they are distributed across verbal and nonverbal channels have some interest here. This is also important because there is also implicit in some communication work on relationships a model of how conflict is handled and the ways in which it affects communication both directly and indirectly. Conflict, of course, is not simple violence or argument, but can be communicated in other ways, one of which is refusal to self-disclose or share secrets. Thus noncommunication can be used to signal problematic features of relationships in ways that indicate rather than embody a problem. The communicative causes of conflict, the communication of the presence of conflict, the communicative styles of handling conflict, and the communicative consequences of conflict are different domains of study.

THINKING ABOUT PEOPLE, PARTNERS, AND RELATIONSHIPS

From the foregoing it is clear that the several major omissions and unhappy emphases that characterize social psychological research on relationships all commonly focus on matters that concern communication workers, and in some cases form the subject matter of their inquiries. That which one researcher dismisses can provide seedcorn for those from other areas, and when both get together the product could be plentiful.

The Store of Knowledge

Berger and Roloff (1982, p. 152) claim that "a full understanding of relationship growth and decline relies heavily on an understanding of how persons seek, process, recall, and act on social information that they gain from their environments, and the store of knowledge that they bring with them to the social situation." This is a profitable and valuable line to take because it places the emphasis squarely on the active means by which individuals use the information that social psychologists too often assume to have absolute and rather mechanical effects for all persons equally. However, Berger and Roloff talk of "gaining information from the environment." The processes of seeking information are different from the processes of recall of information and are likely to be influenced by different principles (for example, personality variables may influence processing and recall of information to a greater extent; situational demands may have greater effect on the selection of information and may impose particular limits upon it). Also Berger and Roloff have set us a long list of goals in that single sentence. For one, the processes of seeking information are different from the processes of communication as well as the characteristic styles and purposes of the partners. To refer to the "store of knowledge" brought to "a social situation" points us to many challenging issues. For instance, what is a "store of knowledge" in this context? Is it merely a collection of beliefs about possible taxonomies or typologies of relationships? How is it influenced by individual knowledge in other areas and how does it respond to the whips and scorns of experience, changes during the life cycle, and the individual's day-to-day competencies in relational conduct? Briefly put, is a "store of knowledge" a store of knowledge about relationship ideals (knowledge of schemata) or about behavior (whether one's own or in general), and how do these two sorts bear on one another? Equally one could ask a series of penetrating questions about "the social situation." As Argyle, Furnham, and Graham (1982) show, although there are commonalities of perception about "a social situation," there are also many startling idiosyncrasies, and a challenge for future research in this field precisely concerns the dependence of an individual's communicative responses on their assessment of "situations" (see Chapter 6, this volume).

Thus Berger and Roloff's insightful and challenging claim presents us with three major areas for productive research that are precedent to any attempt to apply the results to the processes of information gaining: namely, work on taxonomies of relationships that differ importantly from one another and hence influence the appropriateness of certain kinds of behavior (that is, persons must know how to treat "friends" differently from "acquaintances"); second, different relationships may have different rules, whose differentiation, performance, and enactment are essential to the proper realization of the relationship; third, the conduct of different relationships requires skills based on the foregoing. Thus Berger and Roloff's proposal is helpful in pointing out the complex types of knowledge and skills that run beneath the effective creation of relationships, and their emphasis on the partners' active roles in making these relationships is a useful antidote to the implication in social psychological work that relationships simply emerge from the correct alignment of the partners' personality or attitudinal characteristics, as if cooking simply meant collecting the ingredients into the bowl.

We do need to balance things more carefully by strenuous attempts to answer the questions surrounding individuals' knowledge about social relationships, but we must do this while also avoiding two traps. The first is the trap of moving the research focus from attributes to knowledge about attributes and to the exclusion of work on behavior (especially communicative behavior). The second is the tricky issue of *assumptions of competence* that permeates much research in this field. In one hemisphere of our research brain we know that people vary in their skill at relating. In the other half, however, we seem not to recognize this. For instance, our proposals can sometimes seem to imply that people are perfect knowers, perfect processors of information, and perfectly rational drawers of conclusions. As Deaux (1968) has indicated, a major need in research on people is the establishment of a good "big picture" of the frequency with which they are thoughtful relative to other occasions when events take them by surprise. For instance, Duck and Miell's (1982) longitudinal study of developing relationships showed not only that individuals were uncertain about their influence on a relationship, but were also gratefully assuming that it owed its existence to the feelings and whims of their partner. More poignantly the study showed that partners occasionally had no idea what was happening and, except at the very early points of a relationship, were inclined to make quick and thoughtless moment-by-moment reactions that were not strategically planned in the context of developing a relationship. Indeed, as we have seen, it seems most likely that people allow relationships to drift most of the time and become strategically concerned with them only when they are being started up or when they are going wrong. The Duck and Miell (1982) study showed that, quite often, relationships sometimes just crept up on people, who found themselves "into something" different from what they had bargained for.

It is important, then, that Berger and Roloff point out the relative importance of the participants' active roles in the processing of information about each other, but we need to conduct much more research on the condition under which one method predominates over others. A further related point is that to talk of "the store of information" should not allow us to assume that such information is absolute, unchanging, and externally the same for one perceiver, let alone agreed upon by both actors in a relationship. For one thing, as Berger and Roloff indicate, information can be recalled in forms that differ from the form in which it was originally stored. For another, persons frequently reprocess information and take different views of it as events occur around it. It is particularly true in the decline of relationships, for instance, that a partner's behavior is reinterpreted less favorably than in the original judgment (Harvey et al., 1982; McCall, 1982). Third, it is significant that publicly expressed thoughts may be rather different—different in ways that we have not systematically explored yet—from the views held privately or expressed in other circumstances. This rather obvious, but frequently unmentioned point was supported by Duck and Miell's (1984) studies, in which partners who had kept private records of their relationship were subsequently interviewed about them, either individually or in pairs. Both in respect of successful and unsuccessful relationships, individuals interviewed alone spoke more freely about their private feelings on the relationship. In the presence of their partner they spoke *not* of what they knew their partner knew, but of what it was legitimate for them to let their partner know was public knowledge about the relationship—what "should" be admitted to third parties, namely, the interviewers.

Such points make it clear that "what a person knows about 0" is not a simple set of absolute pieces of information untainted by social desirabilities, cultural norms, and the realities of social encounters. Indeed, an important aspect of "the store of information" is that it contains many doors. Social knowledge is not absolute; it is not neutral and it is not simple, invariant, closed to subsequent reinterpretation, or always presentable in the same form irrespective of circumstances. Although Berger and Roloff (1982) thus make a necessary and useful point about our need to understand the acquisition and processing of information, it is necessary to view "information" circumspectly when it relates to social and personal relationships. One subtlety in relationships is precisely that "information" interacts with circumstances, needs, strategic purposes, and the type or stage of relationship in which it eventuates. Thus the building up of new information about another person does not always have precisely determinable effects on the stability or existence of the relationship, even when it shows the other in an unfavorable light. That there are points in relationships (and there are relationships) that require that one should exercise tolerance and *not* act as a strictly "rational" information-processing model might seem to imply that one should. Indeed, one of the implicit demands of close relationships is that one's secrets (usually, presumably, secrets precisely because they are embarrassing or show one up in a bad light) are supposed to be shared with one's partner as an index of the relationship's stability and depth. So new information, even if it is negative, has less and less total impact on the relationship, unless it violates grander norms about conduct of relationships, rather than about persons.

Thus the different treatment of essentially "the same" information is an area of research that needs considerable attention in the future. Here I identify several influences upon this treatment that could prove to be profitable areas for investigation of this important influence upon and dialectic with communication.

Participants' Perspectives

Although each partner will gather and process information about the other person according to his or her own skills, abilities, needs, and purposes

(Crockett, 1983), each of them also forms an impression of the relationship. Why should we not assume that the partners' views of the relationship are as likely to differ from one another as they are able to coincide? Equally, observers of a relationship may have different views from either partner without us having to rethink the philosophy of science. There is nothing odd about such variation: What is odd is that we do nothing much with it in our research.

Let us take a moment to explore the point that there are essentially two basic types of observers: On the one hand, they can be scientific scrutineers attempting factual representation of the interaction relative to some descriptive scheme in their heads; on the other hand, they may be participant-observers from the social network of the dyad. As Olson (1977) and Raush (1977) have each observed in their own ways, the existence of such differences in perspective is not itself a problem. Rather, it is the relativity of the perspectives to one another that provides workers with theoretically instructive information. In a detailed consideration of this issue, Harriet Sants and I (Duck & Sants, 1983) proposed two possibilities that could inform research in this field. In essence these are first that multiple perspectives upon "a relationship" and the discrepancies or correspondences between them are informative about the nature—particularly about the stability—of the relationship. Second, we indicated that resolution of perspectives from the present , the past, and future standpoints are critical to the development of participants' subjective sense of relationships. In Duck and Sants (1983) we noted that Insider-Outsider perspectives are not all that there is to think about here. There is not only one Outsider perspective or only one Insider perspective. Insiders may disagree with one another and hence provide another sort of discrepancy data; furthermore, Outsiders may disagree not only with the Insiders but also among themselves. Indeed, Insiders and Ousiders may themselves be aware of existence of different perspectives on their relationship and could react to it as some index of the relationship.

To this picture can be added an observation derived from Jones and Gerard (1967) via Penman (1980). Each participant can perceive four aspects of the relationship between themselves and their partner:

(1) the situation in which the relationship occurs;
(2) the participant's own behavior, intentions and so forth;
(3) the partner's behavior, apparent intentions, and so forth; and
(4) the relationship between the two persons. (This is particularly an aspect that receives focal attention during points of dramatic growth or turbulence in the relationship, as when partners engage in "Our Relationship Talks"; see Harvey et al., 1982).

My present argument, then, is that a large area for future research concerns not only "the content" of interactions but the ways in which individual contents are summed or transmogrified into "a relationship" as perceived by various observers. It is a question of deciding if there are natural units of analysis in this field, and, if so, how we reach a picture of them. We need, however, to review our belief that discrepancies between participants in a relationship represent errors of some kind. They are, on the contrary, not methodological bugs but matters of substantive psychological concern. Although Christensen, Sullaway, and King (1983) discuss systematic *bias* in married couples' reports of interactions, the running head of their article is "systematic error." Whereas "bias" implies mere difference of view, "error" implies falsity, which in turn implies that there is a correct view from which the error is discrepant. In this field I regard that as an error. In relationships people behave in ways consistent with their view of the requirements and circumstances, and where interpretative discrepancies arise between observers, we find not errors but significant and informative material to be investigated. We must not dismiss subjects' beliefs as human error; humanity is what we are spending our professional—and possibly our personal—lives trying to comprehend.

More useful would be systematic attempts to understand the different perspectives and how they come to relate to one another. One possibility originated by McCarthy (1982) is the use of three-way diary records of friendship. By having related triads of subjects report on their own relationship with each other member and also on the relationship between the other two persons, McCarthy was able to begin to explore characteristic styles of interpretation and comprehension. Although findings are preliminary, one interesting characteristic style for involved outsiders was to see relational decision making in terms of power differences more than did the insiders.

Such studies are important and necessary because of the social impact of entering a dyad. As workers from other subdisciplines have persistently recognized, dyadic relationships are not only complex entities within themselves but they also have social status and meaning for other people. Partners from dissolved marriages, for instance, often experience stress not only because of what happens within their dyad but also because outsiders react to them and to their dissolved marriage in unaccepting or awkward ways. Whereas attraction can be an individualistic response for which an individualistic level of analysis is appropriate, a personal relationship requires action across and between people, negotiated process, and social accreditation by other persons. Accordingly, the relative perspectives of the two involved partners are important areas for investigation but so also are the characteristic perspectives, transformations of perspectives, and resolutions of discrepant views imported by outsiders. Such discrepancies and transformations occur and have importance across time and through the mediation of significant reviewing activity by relevant partners.

The emphasis in previous work, to summarize the point in a different way, has been placed too much on why people *are* friends or on how they *become* friends rather than on how they *stay* friends. Once we regard personal relationships as transformational processes, then we shake off this unpromising dust from our feet. Relationships occur across time, not only when they are developing or declining, which are the two occasions when we have noticed their temporality before, but also as they are maintained. Equally, the treating of voluntary ending of relationships as a state or the endpoint of a single simple process of uncoupling or withdrawal is thoroughly misleading (Baxter, 1984; Duck, 1982).

In all cases the existence and the changing of a relationship is partly due to a process of review and rationalization. In spite of, or perhaps because of, the uncertainties noted earlier as features of day-to-day relational reports (Duck & Miell, 1982), partners evolve rational, smooth, and sensible accounts of their relationship's growth. If one compares past retrospections and future projections for a relationship's trajectory, then one invariably finds that subjects smooth out the reported trajectory in a way that does not reflect what they have been reporting in their day-to-day accounts. In short, they produce precisely the trajectories that we would expect—and, indeed, have assumed in most theories of growth—and yet these are inaccurate and much-edited representations of the truth (cf. Delia, 1980). Here again is not an error or a bias but an important psychological phenomenon, a product of the continual reviewing and reassessing of interactions and their interpretations that is perhaps a necessary activity in order to produce the *sense* of relationship. It is the sense of smooth continuity that creates a relationship from a set or series of interactions. It also indicates the theoretical risks inherent in believing what subjects tell us about relationshipping. To paraphrase Duncan (1967), subjects do not relate and then behave or review their interactions; they relate in and through their behavior and reviewing of interactions.

CURRENT STATE AND FUTURE WORK

In common with other observers of, and researchers in, the field of social and personal relationships, communication experts face a number of issues in future work. These concern the nature of relationships, the level of analysis suitable for explanation, and the place of different perspectives on relationships. They also face the challenge, as other workers do, of helping in the task of clarifying the ways to repair relationships (Duck, 1984) and, as a prior step to that one, of clarifying the basis on which relationships are satisfactorily conducted when they work well. In addition to their role in these collaborative ventures, none of which will be completely illuminated by any one discipline on its own, communication experts have a number of special concerns in which their inputs will be distinctive.

Although it is a natural and apparently sensible view that a marriage is a marriage is a marriage or that a friendship is a single undifferentiated and unchanging state that is pacific, motionless, and definable, thoughtful analysis soon reveals this to be an error. Although widowhood is an event in the first instance, as Greenblatt (1978) has shown, widowing and widowhood are processes that extend themselves over a considerable period of time and involve many subtle or dramatic shifts of psychological processes as the individual comes to terms with grief. As a second example, whereas some workers have looked for what caused the event of mate choice, Huston et al. (1981) correctly view mate selection as an extensive interpersonal process. My argument here extends this to the claim, with Notarius and Pellegrini (1984), that the ensuing relationship is also a process. Thus marriage involves adaptive behavior, stresses coped with, turmoils solved, joyful experiences accommodated, and so on. It also involves changing emotions, modified views of partner, altered expectations, and much more. In the life of a marriage, much happens that is not captured by a simple recording of dates during which it has existed. The same is true of friendships, dating, courtship, parenthood, old age, loneliness, attraction, and all the rest. If they are states or achievements, then they are busy, turbulent, active states that encompass many activities, negotiations, adjustments, attributions, and behavioral changes that we should thoroughly explore. It makes more sense, recognizing their seething undercurrents, to avoid the trap of calling them states at all, just as we do not view 1983 as one undifferentiated entity except in the oversimplified hindsights of history.

Equally, it is inadequate to represent development of a relationship as nothing more than a steady movement between different states or levels of intimacy at Time 1 (T1) and Time 2 (T2). Those deathless—and lifeless—abstractions, T1 and T2, have no psychologically real meaning unless their context is discussed; yet to discuss their context is to recognize their embeddedness. The record of the occurrence of a single pulse beat would tell us nothing of medical use unless we also measured pressures. To freeze the action at T1 and T2 misses this point. We can learn more by embedding these time points in time, just as still shots from a movie have their meaning when they are shown fast and in sequence, not when they are pasted onto a graph for us to imagine the lively actions that took us between the two frozen frames. Furthermore, in the T1-T2 models, there is really no hard evidence whatsoever to back up the assumption that development of a relationship is a steady progression through different intimacy levels; indeed, such evidence as there actually is (Duck & Miell, 1982) suggests that it is a rather turbulent business that partners subsequently remember as a smooth progression. Moreover, the assumption of different states needs to be supported; definitions of the states need to be found; taxonomies and hierarchies are required to back up the assertion; and characteristic differences between the states need to be spelled out. Over and above this is the perpetual and significant—though significantly overlooked—problem of defining what exactly such a state is in relationship terms. We are seeking *inter*personal knowledge, not just knowledge and not just knowledge of other persons.

Emphasis on presumably important and significant social cognitions and their presumably equally significant dependent enactments must be supplemented by major work on the ordinary behavior in relationships mapped out day by day. This is laborious, if challenging, work that will stretch both our patience and our ingenuity. Regrettably, however, we still do not know how far our findings about communication are representative of people's normal distribution of time and effort in the normal course of relationships. Some work (Duck & Miell, 1982; Emler, 1983) indicates that, far from being purposive, strategic, and full of significance, most communication is pretty banal. We may have overinterpreted or misrepresented the sheer triviality of much communication, and by focusing on dire moments such as cataclysmic relational events we have attributed too much to our subjects and colleagues in the human enterprise. Perhaps they/we do not really think, plan, and strategize as much as we have believed. In the years ahead we must focus less upon the "significant" and more upon the trivial, less upon the purposive and more upon the unplanned, less upon the exciting and more upon the routine, less upon the thoughtful and more upon the erratic. Once we have understood the trivia of relational communication and their place in relationships, we shall really have found out something important.

REFERENCES

Applegate, J. L. (1983). *Constructs, interaction goals, and communication in relationship development.* Paper presented at the Fifth International Congress on Personal Construct Psychology, Boston.

Argyle, M. (1983). *The psychology of interpersonal behaviour.* Harmondsworth: Penguin.

Argyle, M., Furnham, A., & Graham, J. (1982). *Social situations.* London: Methuen.

Argyle, M., & Henderson, M. (1984). The rules of friendship. *Journal of Social and Personal Relationships, 1,* 211-237.

Argyle, M., & Henderson, M. (in press). The rules of relationships. In S. W. Duck & D. Perlman (Eds.), *Understanding personal relationships: An interdisciplinary approach* (Vol. 1). Beverly Hills, CA: Sage.

Baxter, L. A. (1979a). Self-disclosure as a relationship disengagement strategy. *Human Communication Research, 5,* 215-222.

Baxter, L. A. (1979b, February). *Self-reported disengagement strategies in friendship relationships.* Paper presented at the annual meeting of the Western Speech Communication Association Convention, Los Angeles.

Baxter, L. A. (1982). Strategies for ending relationships: Two studies. *Western Journal of Speech Communication, 46,* 223-241.

Baxter, L. A. (1984). Trajectories of relationship disengagement. *Journal of Social and Personal Relationships, 1,* 29-48.

Baxter, L. A. (in press). Accomplishing relationship disengagement. In S. W. Duck & D. Perlman (Eds.), *Understanding personal relationships: An interdisciplinary approach* (Vol. 1). Beverly Hills, CA: Sage.

Berger, C. R. (1980). Self consciousness and the adequacy of theory and research into relationship development. *Western Journal of Speech Communication, 44,* 93-96.

Berger, C. R., & Bradac, J. (1982). *Language and social knowledge: Uncertainty in interpersonal relations.* London: Arnold.

Berger, C. R., & Roloff, M. E. (1982). Thinking about friends and lovers: Social cognition and relational trajectories. In M. E. Roloff & C. R. Berger (Eds.), *Social cognition and communication* (pp. 151-192). Beverly Hills, CA: Sage.

Bradac, J. (1983, July). *Language and friendship*. Paper presented at the Second International Conference on Social Psychology and Language, Bristol, England.

Burns, G. L., & Farina, A. (1984). Social competence and adjustment. *Journal of Social and Personal Relationships, 1,* 99-113.

Byrne, D. (1971). *The attraction paradigm*. New York: Academic Press.

Cappella, J. N. (1984). The relevance of the microstructure of interaction to relationship change. *Journal of Social and Personal Relationships, 1,* 239-264.

Christensen, A., Sullaway, M., & King, C. E. (1983). Systematic error in behavioral reports in dyadic interaction: Egocentric bias and content effects. *Behavioral Assessment, 5,* 131-142.

Clark, R. A., & Delia, J. G. (1979). Topoi and rhetorical competence. *Quarterly Journal of Speech, 65,* 187-206.

Cook, M. (1977). Social skill and interpersonal attraction. In S. W. Duck (Ed.), *Theory and practice in interpersonal attraction* (pp. 319-338). London: Academic Press.

Crockett, W. (1983). *Interpersonal relations and communication*. Paper presented at the Fifth International Congress on Personal Construct Psychology, Boston.

Crockett, W. H., & Friedman, P. (1980). Theoretical explorations of the process of initial interactions. *Western Journal of Speech Communication, 44,* 86-92.

Davis, K. E., & Todd, M. (in press). Prototypes, paradigm cases, and relationship assessment: The case of friendship. In S. W. Duck & D. Perlman (Eds.), *Understanding personal relationships: An interdisciplinary approach* (Vol. 1). Beverly Hills, CA: Sage.

Day, B. R. (1961). A comparison of personality needs of courtship couples and same-sex friends. *Sociology and Social Research, 45,* 435-440.

Deaux, K. (1968). Variations in warning, information preference and anticipatory attitude change. *Journal of Personality and Social Psychology, 8,* 157-161.

Delia, J. G. (1980). Some tentative thoughts concerning the study of interpersonal relationships and their development. *Western Journal of Speech Communication, 44,* 97-103.

Dindia, K., & Fitzpatrick, M. A. (in press). Three approaches to the study of marital communication. In S. W. Duck & D. Perlman (Eds.), *Understanding personal relationships: An interdisciplinary approach* (Vol. 1). Beverly Hills, CA: Sage.

Duck, S. W. (1973). *Personal relationships and personal constructs: A study of friendship formation*. Chichester: John Wiley.

Duck, S. W. (1976). Interpersonal communication in developing acquaintance. In G. R. Miller (Ed.), *Explorations in interpersonal communication* (pp. 127-147). Beverly Hills, CA: Sage.

Duck, S. W. (1977). *The study of acquaintance*. Farnborough: Gower.

Duck, S. W. (1980). Personal relationships research in the 1980s: Towards an understanding of complex human sociality. *Western Journal of Speech Communication, 44,* 114-119.

Duck, S. W. (1982). A topography of relationship disengagement and dissolution. In S. W. Duck (Ed.), *Personal relationships 4: Dissolving personal relationships* (pp. 1-30). London: Academic Press.

Duck, S. W. (1983). *Friends, for life*. Brighton: Harvester.

Duck, S. W. (Ed.). (1984). *Personal relationships 5: Repairing personal relationships*. London: Academic Press.

Duck, S. W., & Miell, D. E. (1982, July). *Charting the growth of personal relationships*. Paper presented at the First International Conference on Personal Relationships, Madison, WI.

Duck, S. W., & Miell, D. E. (1984). Towards a comprehension of friendship development and breakdown. In H. Tajfel, C. Fraser, & J. Jaspars (Eds.), *The social dimension: European perspectives on social psychology* (Vol. 1, pp. 228-247). Cambridge: Cambridge University Press.

Duck, S. W., & Perlman, D. (in press). The thousand islands of personal relationships: A prescriptive analysis for future exploration. In S. W. Duck & D. Perlman (Eds.), *Understanding personal relationships: An interdisciplinary approach* (Vol. 1). Beverly Hills, CA: Sage.

Duck, S. W., & Sants, H.K.A. (1983). On the origin of the specious: Are personal relationships really interpersonal states? *Journal of Social and Clinical Psychology, 1,* 27-41.

Duncan, H. D. (1967). The search for a social theory of communication in American sociology. In F.E.X. Dance (Ed.), *Human communication theory* (pp. 236-263). New York: Holt, Rinehart & Winston.

Eiser, J. R. (1980). Prolegomena to a more applied social psychology. In R. Gilmour & S. W. Duck (Eds.), *The development of social psychology* (pp. 271-292). New York: Academic Press.

Emler, N. (1983, July). *Why gossip is important: The role of gossip in managing relationships with networks of acquaintances.* Paper presented at the Second International Conference on Social Psychology and Language, Bristol, England.

Gergen, K. J. (1980). Toward intellectual audacity in social psychology. In R. Gilmour & S. W. Duck (Eds.), *The development of social psychology* (pp. 239-270). New York: Academic Press.

Goffman, E. (1959). *The presentation of self in everyday life.* New York: Doubleday/Anchor.

Gottman, J. M. (1982, July). *Temporal form in relationships.* Paper presented at the First International Conference on Personal Relationships, Madison, WI.

Gottman, J. M., Markman, H., & Notarius, C. (1976). *A couple's guide to communication.* Champaign, IL: Research Press.

Greenblatt, M. (1978). The grieving spouse. *American Journal of Psychiatry, 135,* 43-47.

Harvey, J. H., Weber, A. L., Yarkin, K., & Stewart, B. E. (1982). An attributional approach to relationship breakdown and dissolution. In S. W. Duck (Ed.), *Personal relationships 4: Dissolving personal relationships* (pp. 107-126). London: Academic Press.

Hays, R. (1984). The development and maintenance of friendship. *Journal of Social and Personal Relationships, 1,* 75-98.

Hill, C. T., Rubin, Z., & Peplau, L. A. (1976). Breakups before marriage: The end of 103 affairs. *Journal of Social Issues, 32,* 147-168.

Hinde, R. A. (1979). *Towards understanding relationships.* London: Academic Press.

Hinde, R. A. (1981). The bases of a science of interpersonal relationships. In S. W. Duck & R. Gilmour (Eds.), *Personal relationships 1: Studying personal relationships* (pp. 1-22). London: Academic Press.

Huston, T. L., Surra, C. A., Fitzgerald, N. M., & Cate, R. M. (1981). From courtship to marriage: Mate selection as an interpersonal process. In S. W. Duck & R. Gilmour (Eds.), *Personal relationships 2: Developing personal relationships* (pp. 53-88). London: Academic Press.

Izard, C. E. (1960). Personality similarity and friendship. *Journal of Abnormal and Social Psychology, 61,* 47-51.

Izard, C. E. (1963). Personality similarity and friendship: A follow up study. *Journal of Abnormal and Social Psychology, 66,* 598-600.

Jones, E. E., & Gerard, H. B. (1967). *Foundations of social psychology.* New York: John Wiley.

Kelly, C., Huston, T. L., & Cate, R. (in press). Premarital relational correlates of erosion in satisfaction in marriage. *Journal of Social and Personal Relationships.*

Kerckhoff, A. C., & Davis, K. E. (1962). Value consensus and need complementarity in mate selection. *American Sociological Review, 27,* 295-303.

Knapp, M. L. (1978). *Social intercourse: From greeting to goodbye.* Newton, MA: Allyn & Bacon.

Knapp, M. L. (1984). *Interpersonal communication and human relations.* Newton, MA: Allyn & Bacon.

La Gaipa, J. J. (1982). Rules and rituals in disengaging from relationships. In S. W. Duck (Ed.), *Personal relationships 4: Dissolving personal relationships* (pp. 189-210). London: Academic Press.

Lee, L. (1984). Sequences in separation: A framework for investigating endings of the personal (romantic) relationship. *Journal of Social and Personal Relationships, 1,* 49-73.

Levinger, G., Senn, D., & Jorgensen, B. W. (1970). Progress towards permanence in courtship: A test of the Kerckhoff-Davis hypothesis. *Sociometry, 33,* 427-433.

Lewis, R. A. (1973). A longitudinal test of a developmental framework for premarital dyadic formation. *Journal of Marriage and the Family, 35,* 16-25.

McCall, G. (1982). Becoming unrelated: The management of bond dissolution. In S. W. Duck (Ed.), *Personal relationships 4: Dissolving personal relationships* (pp. 211-231). London: Academic Press.

McCall, G., & Simmons, J. L. (1978). *Identities and interactions.* New York: Free Press.

McCarthy, B. (1982, July). *Dyads, cliques and conspiracies: Friendship behaviour and perceptions within long-established social groups.* Paper presented at the First International Conference on Personal Relationships, Madison, WI.

Miell, D. E. (1984). *Strategic self disclosure.* Unpublished doctoral dissertation, University of Lancaster, England.

Miell, D. E., & Duck, S. W. (1983, July). *Communicative strategies in developing personal relationships.* Paper presented at the Second International Conference on Social Psychology and Language, Bristol, England.

Miller, G. R., & Parks, M. (1982). Communication in dissolving relationships. In S. W. Duck (Ed.), *Personal relationships 4: Dissolving personal relationships* (pp. 127-154). London: Academic Press.

Morton, T. L., Alexander, J. F., & Altman, I. (1976). Communication and relationship definition. In G. R. Miller (Ed.), *Explorations in interpersonal communication* (pp. 105-125). Beverly Hills, CA: Sage.

Neimeyer, R. A., & Neimeyer, G. J. (1983). Structural similarity and the acquaintance process. *Journal of Social and Clinical Psychology, 1,* 146-154.

Notarius, C., & Pellegrini, D. (1984). Marital processes as stressors and stress mediators: Implications for marital repair. In S. W. Duck (Ed.), *Personal relationships 5: Repairing personal relationships* (pp. 67-88). London: Academic Press.

Olson, D. H. (1977). Insiders' and outsiders' views of relationships: Research studies. In G. Levinger & H. L. Raush (Eds.), *Close relationships* (pp. 115-135). Amherst: University of Massachusetts Press.

Penman, R. (1980). *Communication processes and relationships.* New York: Academic Press.

Raush, H. L. (1977). Orientations to the close relationship. In G. Levinger & H. L. Raush (Eds.), *Close relationships* (pp. 163-188). Amherst: University of Massachusetts Press.

Rose, S. (1984). How friendships end: Patterns among young adults. *Journal of Social and Personal Relationships, 1,* 267-277.

Rubin, R. B. (1977). The role of context in information seeking and impression formation. *Communication Monographs, 44,* 81-90.

Sants, H.K.A. (1984). Conceptions of friendship, social behaviour and social achievement in 6-year-old children. *Journal of Social and Personal Relationships, 1,* 293-309.

Shaver, P., Furman, W., & Buhrmester, D. (in press). Aspects of life transition: Network changes, social skills, and loneliness. In S. W. Duck & D. Perlman (Eds.), *Understanding personal relationships: An interdisciplinary approach* (Vol. 1). Beverly Hills, CA: Sage.

Trower, P. (1981). Social skill disorder. In S. W. Duck & R. Gilmour (Eds.), *Personal relationships 3: Personal relationships in disorder* (pp. 97-110). London: Academic Press.

Winch, R. F. (1958). *Mate selection: A study of complementary needs.* New York: Harper & Row.

Wright, P. H. (in press). The acquaintance description form. In S. W. Duck & D. Perlman (Eds.), *Understanding personal relationships: An interdisciplinary approach* (Vol. 1). Beverly Hills, CA: Sage.

15 All in the Family: Interpersonal Communication in Kin Relationships

MARY ANNE FITZPATRICK
DIANE M. BADZINSKI

University of Wisconsin—Madison

A MALE and a female held hands and they strolled along together. They were small people, the male only four feet, eight inches and his female companion not much more than four feet tall. Behind the couple walked an adolescent, carefully stepping in the footsteps of the older male. Although this scene could have taken place anywhere, recently discovered fossils indicated that it actually occurred some 3.6 million years ago. Indeed, the discovery of this group is the first sign of the existence of a nuclear (hominid) family (Fisher, 1983). Anthropologists have shown that as early as four million years ago, males and females had begun to bond, to share and to work together in the rearing of their offspring.

The presence of an adult male is, however, not necessarily a universal characteristic of the family. The only universal family type is a small, kinship-structured group whose primary function is the nurturant socialization of the newborn. Three independent lines of evidence can be adduced for the cross-cultural and cross-historical universality of this family type. First, most societies of which we have records have such a kinship-structured group. Prolonged maternal care coupled with pronounced socialization of the young and extended relationships between mother and child occur in all human groups (Reiss, 1965; Stephens, 1963). Second, such prolonged maternal care for helpless and dependent infants is a characteristic shared with most other primates (Wilson, 1975). Young monkeys, for example, favor a cloth mother that purportedly dispenses nurturance during stressful or dangerous times over the wire mother figure that dispenses food (Harlow, 1958; Harlow & Harlow, 1965). Third, the loss of a primary caregiver seems to have a severe and devastating effect on human infants regardless of the amount of

AUTHORS' NOTE: The authors would like to thank Professor Joseph N. Cappella, Professor James P. Dillard, and Professor Kathy Kellerman of the Department of Communication Arts, University of Wisconsin, and Professor Robert McPhee of the Department of Communication, University of Wisconsin-Milwaukee, for their insightful comments and criticisms of an earlier draft of this chapter.

nourishment they receive (Spitz, 1945; Yarrow, 1963). As the giving and receiving of emotional support is primarily accomplished through the verbal and nonverbal exchange of messages, the universality of this family form suggests the centrality of communication for understanding the family.

From such early simple dyadic structures, more elaborated kinship connections evolve. Kinship is often defined as the possession of a common ancestor in the not too distant past (Wilson, 1975). This definition suggests a biological reckoning yet it is the social definition of who belongs to whom and who is related to whom that is more critical (Reiss, 1971). To be kin to someone acknowledges a special tie of who stands in what relationship to whom, who owes what to whom, and how individuals of particular kinship are expected to pay their social debts. Considerations of complex kinship structures automatically entail the discussion of marriage and the family (Schneider, 1968). Through marriage, for example, husbands and wives become kin to one another. Each takes on a series of rights and duties to one another, and both stand in the same kin relationship to their children. For many theorists, kinship, marriage, and the family are an inseparable trinity whose defining features and interrelationships are frequently debated (Adams, 1968; Goodenough 1970; Reiss, 1965; Winch, 1968). Most agree, however, that essential to any definition of kinship, marriage, and the family is some reference to social relationships, their behavioral content, and the regulatory power of norms expressed in terms of rights and duties (Verdon, 1981).

This chapter is primarily concerned with the communication that occurs in the family. First, we demonstrate the importance of communication in any theoretical or conceptual attempt to understand the family. Second, we selectively examine some of the research that has been conducted across a number of academic disciplines on interaction within the nuclear family. Third, we offer some suggestions for future research.

A COMMUNICATION APPROACH
TO KIN RELATIONSHIPS

Six major meta-theoretical perspectives dominate theorizing about the family. During the 1960s, the structural-functional, the interactional, and the developmental perspectives were predominant (Nye & Berardo, 1981). During the 1980s, greater emphasis has been placed on the conflict (Sprey, 1979), exchange (Nye, 1979), and system theory (Burr, Leigh, Day, & Constantine, 1979) perspectives. Of these, only the interactionist approach, which defines the family as a "unit of interacting personalities" (Burgess & Locke, 1953), assigns a central role to communication. This symbolic interactionist viewpoint is espoused in Bochner's (1976) article on communication in the family. We intend to show in this section that regardless of the meta-theoretical orientation to the study of the family, the concept of communication is necessary in any attempt to explain, predict, and understand family outcomes.

The linchpin around which our rationale for the theoretical importance of communication in kin relationships revolves is a recent codification by Reuben Hill of the most frequently utilized factors in all major theoretical approaches to the family (Burr, Hill, Nye, & Reiss, 1979, p. xiii). This taxonomical effort charts the exogeneous and endogeneous factors of central concern to family theorists. As the major concepts of interest in analyzing the family are outlined in this perspective, the role of communication becomes crystalline when they are examined.

Exogenous Variables

Exogenous variables in the study of the family include both the extreme exogenous factors affecting family structures and processes as well as input variables that are more proximate to internal family processes. The extreme exogenous variables are those that deal with the social, political, and economic environment in which a kin group finds itself. Input variables include value orientations, social class, and access to resources and social networks (see reviews by Lee, 1980; Leigh, 1982). Historians who study both types of exogenous variables have shown us that nostalgia for a lost family tradition that never existed has prejudiced our understanding of the contemporary family (Goode, 1963). Current family forms are considered dysfunctional to the extent that they deviate from such nostalgic views.

The nineteenth-century family has been described by one historian as an emotional iceberg (Shorter, 1975). In contrast, the twentieth-century family has become an emotional refuge in an increasingly bureaucratic environment (Parsons & Bales, 1955), an environment that has taken over many of the other major functions of the family (for example, socialization of children, the care and nurturance of its members). The emotional relationships between parents and children are significantly altered in a society in which peers, and not parents, socialize adolescents. Likewise, in a society in which the aged are cared for by the state, the emotional bonds between adult children and their parents are changed. The functions performed by families are highly interdependent. Limiting the family, once a multifunctional unit of society, to the performance of only one function damages its ability to handle the one emotional function that remains (Lasch, 1977).

When emotional and psychological factors achieve preeminence in a society's view of the family, different demands are placed on communication among family members. If the major function of the modern family is emotional, greater demands are placed on all participants to engage in expressive communication. A societal commitment to expressivity is potentially risky (Bochner, 1982; Moscovici, 1967; Parks, 1982). Such commitments may also be potentially physically dangerous. The open expression of strong negative feelings to individuals with whom one lives in close physical proximity may exacerbate tensions. An individual is more likely to observe, commit, or be a victim of violence within his or her own family than in any other setting (Gelles, 1974). The modern family is a place in which hatred and violence are felt, expressed, and learned as consistently as love.

A consideration of such exogenous variables strengthens our theoretical work on the family. Exogenous factors set the scope conditions for our conceptual efforts by reminding us of the historical and cultural limitations of our empirical generalizations. Additionally, exogenous variables can be directly and productively linked to internal family processes (for example, Bott, 1957). At the very least, these factors remind us of the range and diversity possible in family systems (van den Berghe, 1978). Environmental diversity dramatically affects the input variables and through these the meaning and even the frequency of communicative exchanges are altered.

Endogenous Variables

The internal, performance, and output variables are the endogenous factors in theoretical approaches to the family. The specific variables covered by these factors are diagrammed in Table 15.1. As we have argued, the exogenous variables can be used to predict kinship communication patterns. Communication, however—save in its most narrow definition of communication structure, that is, who speaks to whom—is overlooked in this taxonomy of major family variables. Although the centrality of communication in a variety of relational processes is commonplace for communication scholars, communication is assigned a peripheral role in traditional psychological and sociological studies of families and close relationships.[1]

There are at least three senses in which communication can be conceptually related to these endogenous variables. First, communication can be construed as the underlying causal mechanism that translates the set of internal variables into the outcome variables. Second, communication can be seen as the intervening variable linking internal, performance, and output processes. Third, communication can be seen as constitutive in that it produces and reproduces the social structure of marriage and the family (McPhee, 1984).[2] One's meta-theoretical framework determines which of these three orientations toward communication in kin relationships can be most fruitfully adopted. The specification of the relationships between the internal, performance, and output variables is incomplete without the explication of the nature and function of communication.

Turning to Table 15.1, let us consider the relationships among one internal, one performance, and one output variable. Consider one variable from column A (role differentiation), one from column B (problem solving), and one from column C (marital satisfaction).

The need for problem solving in the working out of the roles of husband and wife in a marriage arises because of the cultural shifts in what constitutes

TABLE 15.1

Major Endogenous Variables Across All Theories of the Family

(A) Internal	(B) Performance	(C) Output
Family rules	Marrying	Marital satisfaction
Power allocation	Relationship adjusting	Parental satisfaction
Role differentation	Problem solving	Family solidarity
Affection and support structure	Child socializing	Adequacy of function
Communication structure	Family planning	Status attainment
Information processing structure	Tension managing	
Coordination of subsystems		

appropriate role behavior for spouses. Like all roles, those of husband and wife have culturally prescribed rights and duties associated with them (Linton, 1945). The difficulty arises because there is a subtle revolution occurring in American family life (Smith, 1979). The U.S. Census Bureau recognized this in 1980 when they announced that the male would no longer be assumed to be the head of the household. Males no longer exclusively provide for their wives and children. The good provider role, once central to family life and exclusively male, has been reduced to the status of senior or coprovider (Slocum & Nye, 1976).

The new male family role has been expanded to include the display of more intimacy, nurturance, and expressivity. Not only are demands being made for more male communication and tenderness but also for more child care and housework. Such a major role realignment directly increases the amount of problem solving and negotiation that occurs between husbands and wives (Bernard, 1981).

In addition to the increasing role burdens placed on husbands, there is a marked divergence between the attitudes of the culture and the behaviors of husbands and wives. Individuals do not attitudinally support wives in a provider role for the family (Slocum & Nye, 1976), yet over 51 percent of married women work outside the home as of 1982 (Thorton & Freedman, 1983). Furthermore, although husbands are now expected to be more nurturant and expressive and to help with housework and child care, they do not appear to have adopted these behaviors. The majority of husbands in a random sample of 224 married couples rated themselves as neither expressive nor nurturant (Fitzpatrick & Indvik, 1982). And wives still do the housework and child care (Thorton & Freedman, 1983). For both husbands and wives, the prerogatives of their respective positions have faded far more slowly than have the obligations.

Such attitudinal and behavioral inconsistencies in marital role performance have a direct negative impact on marital satisfaction (Burr, 1973; Indvik & Fitzpatrick, 1982; Ort, 1950; Tharp, 1963). The inconsistencies between the expectations and the behaviors of husbands and wives lead to conflict. Such inconsistencies, as well as the tension they can generate, must be resolved to the ongoing satisfaction of both parties. The resolution of these tensions requires communication and problem solving, which implicates techniques of negotiating, bargaining, decision making, and so forth.

Internal Variables. Internal family variables are frequently operationalized by a variety of verbal and nonverbal messages. The gestures, words, actions, silences, even the presence or absence of a family member, are representative of a number of different internal family concepts (Raush, Grief, & Nugent, 1979). Family rules are often defined through observation of the interaction that takes place among family members (Napier & Whitaker, 1978). Power allocation and role differentiation can be signaled by behaviors such as successful interruptions, talk-overs, and talk time (for example, Folger, 1978; Millar & Rogers, 1976). The affection and support structure of a family is manifested by the occurrence or nonoccurrence of specific nonverbal affect cues (for example, Lamb, 1976b) as well as language characteristics (Berger & Bradac, 1982). The communication structure is defined as who speaks to whom and how often (Farace, Monge, & Russell, 1977; Haley, 1967; Waxler & Mishler, 1970). The information-processing structure is measured by how information is shared in a family (Reiss, 1981). Finally, coordination is defined as the meshing of interaction sequences among or between partners (Berscheid, 1983).

A close examination of these internal variables suggests that a more parsimonious structure is possible. Perhaps the basic dimensions internal to the family are affect and power or cohesion and adaptability (Olson, Sprenkle, & Russell, 1979). These are the major dimensions of interpersonal behavior according to a number of different perspectives (Bochner, Kaminski, & Fitzpatrick, 1977). Control subsumes the internal concepts of family rules, power allocations, role differentiation, communication and information-processing structures, and coordination, whereas affect subsumes the affection and support structures (Olson, McCubbin, Barnes, Larsen, Muxen, & Wilson, 1983).

The trend toward using verbal and nonverbal communication as operational definitions of internal family variables obscures important theoretical aspects of these variables. Although the direct exchange of verbal and nonverbal messages is central to family processes, communication alone can not explain all of the variance in family outcomes. The affective and cognitive perspectives as represented by these internal family variables would be better operationalized through a consideration of the attitudes, values, and/or relational theories that individuals and families hold concerning family interaction. Internal variables are best construed as the factors that account for the observed regularities in the performance variables and not as performance variables per se.

Performance Variables. Performance variables are overt behavioral activities. For communication researchers, these activities are primarily verbal and nonverbal exchanges. The six performance variables isolated in

Table 15.1 are behavioral episodes that occur in families. These episodes can be examined at either the molar or molecular levels. Gottman (1979), who views conflict resolution as the major behavioral episode capable of predicting marital satisfaction, coded the specific molecular cues exchanged between couples during conflict. The interaction sequences between marital partners were the best predictor of a couple's experienced satisfaction with a marriage (Gottman, 1979).

An explicit analytical separation of classes of internal and performance variables may help in the development of concepts and theories at the same level of abstraction, that is, the individual, dyadic, triadic, and so forth. Performance variables can be studied at the individual level of social behavior by focusing on the communication style of a given individual (Norton, 1983). These variables can also be studied at the dyadic level by examining messages in sequence at the interact, double interact, or higher order. Many of the existing dyadic level concepts are better considered communication concepts (for example, complementarity, reciprocity, dominance, and so forth) because the linking between two individuals occurs behaviorally with the exchange of messages. Theories do not need to restrict themselves to concepts at the same order of abstraction, but theories of communication in close relationships must explicitly deal with the issue of how these classes of concepts translate across levels. Is it an individual's marital satisfaction that is explained by an interaction pattern between spouses? Or is it some dyadic level measure of "marital satisfaction"? Or is it both (and under what conditions)?

Output Variables. The first major family outcome variables that we have isolated in Table 15.1 are satisfaction and stability measures. Satisfaction concerns one's subjectively experienced contentment with either a marital or parent-child relationship. Family solidarity is a stability dimension that objectively examines whether or not a given family is intact. Parents separate or divorce and children run away, and such events can be taken as measures of family instability.

Family functioning is a multidimensional construct. It has been defined in three major ways. First, does the family accomplish major family goals? The goals to be accomplished successfully by the family are specified by the theorist. These goals may include the appropriate socialization of the children and the stabilization of the adult personality. Or optimal family functioning may include the development of a specified set of interaction competencies (Farber, 1964). Second, does the organization of the family violate societal principles? A family is, for example, organized along age and gender lines. The presence of coalitions across such lines results in dysfunctional outcomes (Lewis, Beavers, Gossett, & Phillips, 1976; Mishler & Waxler, 1968). One way to measure these coalitions is to see if parents are more responsive interactively to one another than either is to the children. Third, does the family contain a diseased member? The psychological or even some physical problems of a child are defined as prima facie evidence of family dysfunction (for example, Henry, 1965).

Embedded in the concept of functioning is a consideration of the "normalcy" of a family. Originally, normality was defined as the absence of disease in a family, although more detailed models have recently evolved (see Walsh, 1982). Such an output measure necessarily involves prescriptions on the part of the theorist.[3] Radical critiques of the family maintain that when it functions best, the family is the ultimate destructive social form. Only the family glues individuals to others based upon a sense of incompleteness; stymies the free formation of one's identity; exerts greater social control than children need; and indoctrinates members with elaborate and unnecessary taboos (Cooper, 1970). The very intensity of such critiques reminds us of the prescriptive nature of many definitions of optimal family functioning. We are not suggesting that this output variable be abandoned but that researchers clearly specify their values and orientations as they pursue research on the functional family.

Finally, status attainment refers to the maintenance or achievement of a particular socioeconomic position for a family. Often whether a child attains the same or better status level as the parent, particularly the father, is of concern. Status attainment involves measuring the occupational choices made by a child in comparison to the father. Often the exposure to a model and the ability to talk with others about various occupations leads to a child's awareness and eventual choice of specific jobs or careers (Woelfel & Haller, 1971).

Although not represented in Table 15.1, Hill (1979; as cited in Burr, Hill, Nye, & Reiss, 1979) isolated another class of major factors often treated in theories of the family. These are family development, family learning over time, intergenerational processes, economic life cycles and family performance, and family innovations. Each of these concepts adds the social-time dimension to the model and recognizes the longitudinal nature of the family. Such concepts serve to remind us that families follow a repeated pattern of organization, disorganization, and change. Any comprehensive approach to the family must take into account the repeated continuities and discontinuities in family life.

Explicating the role of communication in predicting family outcome variables clarifies the ways different internal variables have led to different outcomes. A traditional orientation to male and female roles, for example, constrains the communication between marital partners, which leads to a high degree of satisfaction for some couples yet not for others (Fitzpatrick, 1983).

Summary

In this section, we have delineated the major factors related to family processes and have argued that many family theories have underplayed or ignored the role of communication in predicting family outcomes. To rectify this omission, we have offered three ways to examine communication as the link among the internal, performance, and output variables. We have also proposed that a complete theory of the family must take into account exogenous factors as they impinge on internal family processes.

Given the plethora of research on the family in general, we have limited our review to the nuclear family. We have organized the review according to a systems theory analogy (Galvin & Brommel, 1982). Thus we have split off the subsystems in the family that can (and have been) examined apart from one another. We have used the system theory metaphor because we believe that treating the family as a system has two major advantages. First, by reminding us of the interrelationships of various levels of society, systems theories force us to consider the conditions under which dyads can be examined separately.[4] Second, this perspective suggests that both verbal and non-verbal messages can be used to study the links between (among) members of a system.

We have divided the review into two categories: individual social behaviors and interpersonal processes. At times, the placement of research into a category may seem arbitrary or even procrustean to the reader. Because there is far more research at the level of individual social behavior in the study of kinship, we have often resorted to placing behavioral observations of interaction in the presence of a family member into the interpersonal process category.

Our purpose is not to develop a theory of communication in kinship relations but rather to bring many strands of research on communication in the family together. Like the long-hidden sinopie underlying the frescos of the middle ages, the sketch that we offer of the role of communication in kinship relations has the promise of illuminating the underlying structure of these relations more clearly. We now consider the dyadic subsystems within the nuclear family.

THE MARITAL PAIR

In the twentieth century the key question motivating much of the research on marriage is: Why do some marriages fail and others do not? Most theorists today agree that the major predictor of marital stability is the satisfaction experienced by each individual in the marriage (Lewis & Spanier, 1979). Satisfaction and related concepts such as happiness, adjustment, marital quality, lack of distress, or integration reference subjectively experienced contentment with the marital relationship (Hicks & Platt, 1970; Lewis & Spanier, 1979). The communication that occurs between married partners appears to be the primary predictor of marital satisfaction (Gottman, 1979; Noller 1980). In the next section, we examine some of the individual social behaviors that relate to marital happiness.

Individual Social Behaviors

Prior to 1960, most scholars were concerned with the identification of a broad range of demographic and personality correlates of marital happiness (Burgess & Wallin, 1953; Terman, 1938). More recently, the ability to resolve interpersonal problems and express affect to a spouse are the focus of concern in predicting marital satisfaction (Snyder, 1979). The relationship between communication variables and marital satisfaction as seen from the perspective of the married couples themselves is remarkably consistent; that is, the happily married believe that they have good communication with the spouse (Fitzpatrick, 1983). Such views include openness (Norton & Montgomery, 1982); self-disclosure of thoughts and feelings to the spouse (Levinger & Senn, 1967); perceived accuracy of nonverbal communication (Navran, 1967); and the frequency of "successful" communicative exchanges (Bienvenu, 1970).

The above findings appear to resolve the relationship between communication and marital happiness, except that all couples are capable of manipulating their verbal communication behavior to conform to a happy or unhappy marital stereotype (Vincent, Friedman, Nugent, & Messerly, 1979). The facility with which couples can feign a happy or an unhappy marriage suggests that such stereotypes are pervasive. Furthermore, asked to rate a conversation purportedly occurring in a happy or unhappy marriage (Giles & Fitzpatrick, 1985), individuals correctly identified the communication correlates of such relationships. The stereotypes of what constitutes good communication in a happy marriage are robust ones.

Such stereotypes have recently been attacked as representing ideological biases and/or as representing simplistic views of the nature of human relationships (Bochner, 1982; Parks, 1982). These critiques, although valid, may be missing a critical point; that is, the pervasiveness and power of these stereotypes may have a major impact on communication in marriage. Happily married spouses may direct interaction (for example, questioning strategies) in such a way as to validate the kind of communication they expect to see in their own marriage (Snyder, 1981). The stereotype of the happy couple as open and expressive may subtly influence a couple to select topics that do not reveal problems or disconfirm one's view of the marriage or of the other spouse. Stereotypes may create happiness because both believe in them and decode the communication in the marriage accordingly. These stereotypes may set expectations for a relationship that cannot be met and hence may lead to dissatisfaction.

Interpersonal Processes

In predicting marital satisfaction, both theories of power and affect, particularly as exercised in conflict situations, have been expounded. Much greater emphasis has been placed on the study of power between intimates than on affect. The interactional views of families, for example, focus on control to the exclusion of affect (Raush et al., 1979).

Power is the ability to produce intended effects on the behavior or emotions of the other (Scanzoni & Scanzoni, 1976). Power is often linked to the ability of a husband or wife to grant or withhold resources (Blood & Wolfe, 1960). The resources that contribute to one's power are not necessarily economic ones (Safilios-Rothschild, 1970) but include anything that a husband or wife can use to exercise control in a given situation (French & Raven, 1959). Tying power exclusively to the concept of resources is theoretically myopic because it misses the ongoing and dynamic nature of power between intimates. Resources work, for example, because they influence the choice of message strategies (deTurck, 1984) effective in producing the desired outcome.

Power is seen during interactions in which husbands and wives have at least partially conflicting interests. Conflicting interests can arise during family discussions, problem solving, conflict resolution, or crisis management (Olson & Cromwell, 1975). Interactively, speakers exercise control by maintaining attention on themselves and by extensive verbal participation. Spouses also control the contributions of others through attempted and successful interruptions and the skillful use of questions (Mishler & Waxler, 1968).

A number of systems define couples according to their usual patterns of control in conversations (Ericson & Rogers, 1973; Mark, 1971; Sluzki & Beavin, 1965). Three types of couples can be defined by the message exchange patterns that are observed as couples communicate with one another: symmetrical, complementary, and parallel (Lederer & Jackson, 1968; Watzlawick, Beavin, & Jackson, 1967). Symmetrical couples have higher levels of role discrepancy; the couples who manifest lower proportions of competitive symmetry have higher levels of satisfaction in their marriages (Rogers, 1972). Symmetrical exchanges are more common among upper-class couples (Mark, 1971), although these results are not replicated (Ericson, 1972). Complementary couples, in which the husband is dominant, report higher levels of satisfaction and less role discrepancy (Millar & Rogers, 1976; Courtright, Millar, & Rogers-Millar, 1979). Parallel couples use a balance of these patterns across topics or situations. Because the research has been limited on both topics discussed and on interaction duration, it has been difficult to define parallel couples.

Outcomes of power processes are usually measured as who wins or who makes the decision in an interaction (Olson & Cromwell, 1975). One recent study has added a measure of marital satisfaction to the usual "who wins" measure because in intimate relationships, there are many Pyrrhic victories (Dillard & Fitzpatrick, 1984).

Our understanding of power in intimate relationships would benefit from a serious consideration of four points. First, power is not a unidimensional concept (Haley, 1963). Not only who makes particular decisions, but also who decides that this person may make those decisions and who determines who will decide which spouse will make a decision are necessary pieces of the power puzzle. Second, a dynamic view of power would be enriched by acknowledging the range of outcomes that a persuader might be interested in achieving in family situations (deTurck, 1984). Third, both the actual resources that an individual brings to a family exchange and the prevailing normative beliefs about who should exercise power interact to predict what occurs communicatively and how satisfied the parties are with the outcome. Fourth, a focus on sequences of interaction necessitates an examination of how compliance (noncompliance) affects husbands' or wives' attempts to assert power over one another (Sprey, 1979).

The expression of affect between married partners has also been examined most often under conditions of conflict or disagreement. In contrast to unhappy couples, happy couples exhibit more nonverbal positive affect cues (Rubin, 1977); agreement and approval (Birchler, 1972); attempts to avoid conflict (Raush, Barry, Hertel, & Swain, 1974); supportive behaviors (Wegener, Revenstorf, Hahlweg, & Schindler, 1979); compromises (Birchler, 1972); agreement than disagreement in conversations with their spouses (Gottman, 1979; Riskin & Faunce, 1972); and consistency in the use of nonverbal affect cues (Noller, 1982).

A major affect model is the Structural Model of Marital Interaction (Gottman, 1979). This model suggests that there is more patterning and structure in the interaction of dissatisfied than satisfied couples. Furthermore, the satisfied exhibit more positivity and are less likely to reciprocate negative behaviors. All the concepts in the model are tested in terms of affect. Even dominance, a type of patterning, is measured by the asymmetry in predictability of emotional responsiveness between husbands and wives.

Based on this model, both the frequencies of the individual behaviors that couples exhibit in the presence of one another and their interaction patterns are examined. Although all couples are equally likely to reciprocate positive affect, unhappy couples are more likely to reciprocate negative communication behaviors than are happy couples (Gottman, Markman, & Notarius, 1977; Rubin, 1977). The interaction of an unhappy pair shows more asymmetry in predictability than does the interaction of a happy one. In an unhappy marriage, one spouse is more emotionally dominant than another. Such extreme patterning seems to occur even at the physiological level (Levenson & Gottman, 1983). As they communicate with one another even on the topic of "How was your day?," the unhappily married showed a high degree of predictable physiological responses to one another's comments. Such physiological chaining of responses suggests one reason why couples report feelings of being trapped in a marriage.

A major approach that links affect and power is that of Fitzpatrick and her colleagues (Dindia & Fitzpatrick, in press). This polythetic classification scheme (Fitzpatrick, 1976, 1983, 1984; Fitzpatrick & Indvik, 1982) is based on three conceptual dimensions: interdependence, communication, and ideology. Interdependence and communication are affect dimensions, measured through the self-reports of individuals. Control has been measured, following the lead of Ericson and Rogers (1973), by the interaction of the couples (Fitzpatrick, Best, Mabry, & Indvik, 1985; Williamson, 1983). In addition to affect and control, the ideological beliefs and standards that couples hold on a variety of family issues have been salient in distinguishing among couples.

Based on these dimensions, individuals can be categorized as one of three relationship definitions. These three definitions are: traditional, independent, and separate. Traditionals are very interdependent in their marriage; have conventional ideological values about marriage and family life; and report an expressive communication style with their spouses. Independents are moderately interdependent in their marriage; have nonconventional views about marriage and family life; and report a very expressive communication style with their mates. Separates are not very interdependent in their marriage, are ambivalent about their views on marriage and family life, and report very little expressivity in their marital communication.

The individual relational definitions of husbands and wives are compared and couple types are generated. Nine couple types can be constructed from the possible combinations of husband and wife relational definitions. In previous research, approximately 60 percent of the individuals agree with their spouse on a relational definition. These are the "Pure" types: Traditional, Independent, and Separate. The other 40 percent are distributed among the other six couples types. These couples are called the "Mixed" types. The "Separate/Traditional" (Fitzpatrick, 1984) type does not occur with any greater frequency than any other Mixed type but it is often significantly different from the other couples on a number of variables. Thus it is often treated as a defined couple type and appears separate of the other Mixed types.

An active program of research (Fitzpatrick, 1976, 1977, 1981a; Fitzpatrick & Best, 1979; Fitzpatrick & Indvik, 1982; Fitzpatrick, Fallis, & Vance, 1982; Fitzpatrick, Vance, & Witteman, 1984; Sillars, Pike, Redman, & Jones, 1983; Williamson & Fitzpatrick, in press; Witteman & Fitzpatrick, in press) has shown that the couple types can be discriminated on a number of self-report and behavioral dimensions. Table 15.2 displays some of the major findings in this program of research. For clarity, the findings on the relational typology have been organized along the lines of the first figure, listing the major family variables.

The range of the empirical findings indicates that the typing of couples is not merely artifactual but reflects important underlying dimensions of relationships. Displaying the findings in this manner indicates that other outputs of family processes have been ignored in this typology. It is evident, however, that in the descriptions of ongoing relationships such as marriage, it

TABLE 15.2
Couple Types and Related Endogenous Variables:
Self-Report and Behavioral Correlates

	T	I	S	S/T	M
Input Variables					
Belief Structure					
Ideology traditionalism[a]	+	−	+		
Ideology uncertainty[a]	−	+	+		
Affective and Support Structure					
Sharing[a]	++	+	−		
Autonomy[a]	−	+	+		
Undifferential space[a]	+	+	−		
Temporal regularity[a]	+	−	+		
Communication Structure					
Conflict avoidance[a]	−	−	+		
Assertiveness[a]	−	+	+		
Role Differentiation					
Conventional sex roles[a]	+	−	−	++	−
Performance Variables					
Relational Adjusting					
Self-disclosure[a]	+	+	−		
Spouse disclosure[a]	+	−	−		
Expression of feelings (+)	+	−	−		
Inhibition of feelings[a](+)	−	−	+		
Talk frequently[b]	+	+	−		
Coorientational accuracy[*a]	+	+	−	++	+
Self-disclosure[b]	+	++	+	−−	+
Edification[b]	+	−	−−	++	+
Questions[b]	−	+	++	−−	−
Acknowledgments[b]	−−	++	−	+	−
Conflict Management					
Salient Conflict					
Competitive symmetry[b]	++	++	−−		−
Complementarity[b]	−−	−	++		−
Nonsalient conflict					
Competitive symmetry[b]	+	++	−−		+
Complementarity[b]	+	−	++		−
Problem-Solving					
Me[b]	−−	−	0	++	−−
You[b]	−−	+	+	++	−−
Us[b]	0	0	−	++	0
Activity[b]	++	−	−	++	+
External[b]	−	−	++	0	−
Search[b]	+	++	−	−	+
Power[b]	−	+	+	−	+
Direct[b]	+	−	−	−	+
Compromise[b]	+	+	+	−−	++
Output Variables					
Marital Satisfaction					
Consensus[a]	++	−	++	+	+
Affection[a]	+	−	−	+	+
Satisfaction[a]	+	−	−	+	−
Cohesion[a]	++	+	−−	+	−
Status Attainment					
SES differences[a]	0	0	0	0	0

NOTE: Blank spaces indcate that the comparisons have not been made across couple types in some studies. Zeros indicate that differences were not obtained through statistical tests.

TABLE 15.2 NOTES (CONTINUED)

Double pluses (++) indicate extremely positive statistically significant relationships were found between the two variables, double negatives (——) indicate extremely negative relationships. The plus (+) and minus (−) signs indicate that these couple types were intermediate on the endogenous variables studied. T signifies Traditionals; I, Independents; S, Separates; S/T, Separate/Traditionals; and M, Mixed couple types.
a. This signifies the concept was measured through self-report.
b. This indicates that behavioral measures were obtained.
*This indicates that the differences displayed were obtained only for the wives. More detailed description of the various research studies may be found in Fitzpatrick (1983, 1984), or the specific studies cited in the references.

appears to be useful to categorize couples along a number of internal variables, to code their performance, and predict their outputs.

Stages in the Marital Relationship

One of the difficulties in discussing the family in a developmental perspective is that most of the research conducted on the topic has used cross-sectional post hoc designs. Such designs provide a poor basis for detecting developmental trends (Baltes, 1968; Rollins, 1975) because there is potential confusion between cohort effects and actual developmental changes. The scarcity of longitudinal research is not the only problem in studying family development. Most family stage theories, concerned only with intact families, mark family developmental stages according to the age of the oldest child (Duvall, 1971). This approach ignores other family systems, for example, the common one of a single mother rearing two female children (Aldous, 1978). Furthermore, the age of the oldest child may not be a particularly sensitive mark of internal family dynamics. Despite these difficulties in achieving a reasonable and broadly applicable model of family development, theorists have dealt increasingly with notions of change through time in family systems. In the section that follows, we treat some of the research on stages in the marital relationship.

Courtship and Early Marriage. The voluminous literature on initial attraction has been little help in explaining or predicting courtship progress or early marital processes (Huston & Levinger, 1978). One major explanation for this fact may be the overidentification of the concept of attraction with the concept of attitude (Berscheid, 1982). In ongoing relationships, individuals do not have the clear, bipolar unambivalent responses to one another implied by the attitude construct. Commitment to *attraction as attitude* skews research and theory on relationships into both a stability framework and an exclusively cognitive one at that (Berscheid, 1983; Graziano & Musser, 1982).

The theoretical approaches concerned with the processes through which partners select mates are stage or filter theories (Duck, 1976; Kerckhoff & Davis, 1962; Lewis, 1973; Murstein, 1967). Each implies that individuals progress toward long-term commitments by filtering various pieces of information concerning cognitive compatibility. The successful completion or passing through of a particular stage is accomplished through the discovery (mutual) of similarities and value consensus. In some approaches, relational partners are viewed as rational buyers in the marriage marketplace, moving from a state of surface contact to a state of deep mutual involvement through an incremental exchange of rewards (Huesmann & Levinger, 1976; Levinger & Huesmann, 1980). An excellent critique of these approaches can be found in Bochner (1983).

Huston and his associates (Huston, Surra, Fitzgerald, & Cate, 1981) developed a typology of courtship styles based on the time and rate trajectory of couples' reports of relational progress. These styles were further discriminated by the frequency and character of the interaction within the couples as well as between the couples and others. Although we can not fully describe the courtship styles, one style is particularly striking. A couple type emerges marked by less positive affect and less companionship than other couples. Intriguingly, these couples resemble a type of married couple, called the "Separates," identified in another theoretical perspective (Fitzpatrick, 1984). It appears that some couples begin marriage relatively disaffiliated and noncompanionate yet holding traditional sex role ideologies (Huston et al., 1981).

Interaction in courtship has significant impact on early marriage outcomes. There is strong support for the sleeper effect (Markman, 1979, 1981). In other words, the effect of conflict during courtship does not show up until later in a marriage. Even serious conflict during courtship does not appear to affect a couple's satisfaction with the relationship at the time but it does predict dissatisfaction with the partner and the marriage up to five years later (Kelly, Huston, & Cate, in press).

Transition to Parenthood. A major stage in the marital career is the transition to parenthood (Rossi, 1968). Strong pronatalist pressures exist in our society, and such pressures establish a closely defined link between marriage and parenthood (Peck & Senderowitz, 1974). Voluntarily childless couples are often viewed as selfish, unhappy, lonely, immature, and emotionally unstable (Pohlman, 1966), although these stereotypes may be fading (Veevers, 1981). Negative social sanctions are reserved for those couples who choose to have one child and thus reap many of the benefits and fewer of the burdens of child rearing. The transition to parenthood starts a family that should include two to four children (Aldous, 1978).

Important attitudinal changes begin to occur during pregnancy. Women begin reevaluating their parents along traditional lines, especially their own mothers (Arbeit, 1975). Pregnancy sets off a traditionalizing process, reinforced by the withdrawal of the wife from the workplace to await the birth of the child. Less equalitarian relationships between husbands and wives are one outcome of childbearing (Rossi, 1968). Expectant mothers become more introspective during pregnancy, and this serves to distance a husband and wife (Lamb, 1978a).

Much of the research focuses on the woman during pregnancy and later (Lamb, 1978a). The strongest predictor of a woman's psychological adaptation during pregnancy and throughout the first year of the infant's life is the quality of her marriage. Women who are happily married have fewer physical symptoms during pregnancy and are substantially better adjusted at the time of childbirth than are women who are unhappily married. Marital adjustment does not, however, predict maternal adaptation (Grossman, Eichler, & Winickoff, 1980). During actual childbirth, the presence of a husband in the delivery room serves as an effective analgesic. During childbirth, when husbands talk to wives about the course of labor, her well-being, and topics unrelated to the childbirth, wives seem to experience less pain (Anderson & Standley, 1978; Henneborn & Cogan, 1975). Such analgesic effects warrant further investigation.

When another party is added to the family constellation, some change in the husband and wife dyad can be expected to occur. From one dyad, the family now contains three (husband-wife; father-child; mother-child). The birth of a child represents a 200 percent increase in the number of dyads in the family as well as the possibility of a triad. Thus new structural constraints are introduced into the family system. Change from an existing pattern may induce stress, crisis, and even dysfunction, yet change is often a necessary condition for developmental growth.

For many couples, the arrival of a child has a negative impact on their marital quality, especially for wives (LeMasters, 1957; LaRossa, 1977). The birth of the first child has even been called a "crisis" (LeMasters, 1957). Considering the birth of a baby as a crisis is an overstatement, although the event necessitates rather complex shifts in identity, role behavior, and communication (Cowan, Cowan, Coie, & Coie, 1978). The arrival of a child completes the move from equalitarian and less differentiated role patterns in a marriage into more traditional ones. One national probability sample indicated that after the birth of a first child, wives lose decision-making power in their relationships and the help of their husbands with housework. Not only did such self-reported behaviors change, but the ideological beliefs of couples also took a turn toward traditionalism (Hoffman & Manis, 1978).

Levels of marital satisfaction change curvilinearly across the history of a marriage. For couples who stay married, general satisfaction decreases simultaneously with the arrival of the oldest child until he or she reaches adolescence. As children mature and leave home, satisfaction again increases, yet it never attains its early marriage high (Rollins & Galligan, 1978). The decline and rise of marital satisfaction may occur at various stages of the family career because of the decrease in companionship between husbands and wives. A decline in the frequency of positive companionship experiences with the spouse from the birth of a child through the preschool stage may account for the decrease in marital satisfaction during this period (Lerner & Spanier, 1978). The decrease in marital satisfaction during these years may be compensated for by the increase in satisfaction in the parental role. Children give couples a shared task, a common goal, and undoubtedly a topic for flagging marital conversations. A consideration of how various levels of output variables of family processes compensate for one another would greatly expand our understanding of the family.

Separation and Divorce. Although it may seem curious to list separation and divorce as stages in the marital career, estimates on the divorce rate suggest between 30 to 40 percent of all marriages experience this stage (Thorton & Freedman, 1983). Even larger percentages of couples separate at some point in the marriage. Separation and divorce can be viewed as stages in a marital career not only because they occur frequently but also because they are viewed by individuals as serious crises involving major developmental changes. Most people marry, and marrying is associated with significant changes in the way we view ourselves, our partners, and our world. Consequently, the breakup (or potential break up) of this relationship is a serious crisis (Bloom, White, & Asher, 1979). In most scales of stress and illness, the death of a spouse, divorce, and marital separation receive the highest stress scores (Holmes & Rahe, 1976).

Today, few societal barriers exist to the breakup of a marriage. As the external barriers are removed, the internal barriers become paramount. The interpersonal and dyadic factors, such as companionship, emotional grati-fication, and communication, account for an increasingly high amount of the variance in marital satisfaction (Lewis & Spanier, 1979). There is, however, a dark side to this dependence on the internal barriers to relational disinte-gration. As more pressure is placed on internal factors, individuals in-creasingly examine their own reasons for remaining in a marriage. Such a heavy justificatory burden on the internal contents of the relationships may turn the relationship sour (Berscheid & Campbell, 1981). Each partner watches the pulse of the relationship. Time and energy are spent discussing and assessing the state of the relationship. Such pulse watching leads to increased insecurity, for each knows that the connections in the marriage may be tenuous. Increased importance is thus placed on maintaining intense positive feelings for one's spouse. Unfortunately for the longevity of many marriages, it is not only difficult to retain a high level of intensity of feelings for anyone through time, but also relational vigilance increases negative feelings of jealousy and possessiveness (Berscheid & Campbell, 1981).

Divorce is not a single event but a series of legal, psychological, sexual, economic, and social events strung out over a period of time (Bohannan, 1970; Wallerstein & Kelly, 1980). One of the difficulties of studying divorce is that the legal fact is a poor marker for an interpersonal process. This legal step can occur at any number of places along a psychological continuum of relational dissolution. The separation that proceeds a divorce involves repeated distancing, partial reconciliation, new withdrawal, and eventual equilibrium for many couples (Weiss, 1975). This approach-avoidance occurs because love erodes before attachment fades (Weiss, 1975). The latter is a bonding to the other that gives rise to a feeling of ease when the other is accessible (Bowlby, 1972). Attachment explains why couples who are separating experience extreme distress even if both desired to separate.

These are stage theories concerning the dissolution of close relationships (Baxter, 1984; Bradford, 1980; Duck, 1982a, 1982b; Knapp, 1978; Lee, 1984). The most comprehensive model (Duck, 1982b) incorporates social and psychological factors into the process of relational termination. Like revisionist views of courtship (Bolton, 1961), disengagement is now conceptualized as a dialectical process that does not follow the same trajectory for all couples. The research on what individuals actually say during relational disintegration is nonexistent, although Miller and Parks (1982) have developed a taxonomy of disengagement strategies. Disengagement processes are difficult to examine as they occur. The procedures developed for retrospective accounts of courtship progress may be profitably adapted in this area (Huston et al., 1981).

What couples say to others is critical in the dissolution process. Six months after separation, women rehash and ruminate on the causes of the relationship disintegration (Harvey, Weber, Yarkin, & Stewart, 1982). Women relate dissolution to interpersonal problems rather than to the structural factors that men mention (Hill, Rubin, & Peplau, 1976). Called grave dressing (Duck, 1982b) or accounts (Harvey et al., 1982; Weiss, 1975), these statements are histories of a relationship that structure events in a narrative sequence to allocate blame for relationship failures. Such accounts bring the social context into the study of relationships. Theorists in other areas of family processes would be wise to follow this lead.

In considering marital dissolution, not only the stages through which a relationship passes but also patterned differences among individuals or couples (Kressel, Jaffee, Tuchman, Watson, & Deutsch, 1980) demand consideration. Kressel and his associates (1980) isolated types of divorcing couples.[5] These couple types, demonstrating as they do particular patterns of affect and conflict, are similar to couples in ongoing marriages isolated in the relational typology (Fitzpatrick, 1984).

In this section, we have attempted to show how communication operates in a marriage. The similarity in some of the work across these disparate areas is striking. Three independent lines of investigation of marriage at three different points in time—courtship (Huston et al., 1981), marriage (Fitzpatrick, 1984), and divorce (Kressel et al., 1980)—yield remarkably similar results. From early in courtship, some couples seem to start their relationships as "Separates," emotionally and psychologically less involved with one another. These Separate couples, who emerge in cross-sectional studies of marriage, tend not to communicate very much with one another and rarely engage in serious conflicts. Such a type of couple appears again in divorce mediation. From early in courtship, it appears that some couples do not develop the numerous interconnected sequences of interaction that Berscheid links to the experience of strong emotion in close relationships (Berscheid, 1983). Whether the couples who begin in this fashion are the ones who end this way, our current cross-sectional data cannot tell us. Undoubtedly, the process of relational growth and disintegration takes markedly different paths for different couples. In the next section, we examine some of the issues typically studied concerning parent-child communication.

THE PARENT-CHILD RELATIONSHIP

Early work on the relationship between parents and children can be termed social mold theories. These theories assume that the child is a passive partner in socialization, awaiting the molding of its parents (Hartup, 1978). With the realization that a child contributes to the marriage and the family, more child-centered theories and research emerge (Bell, 1968). Not only when they reach adolescence or adulthood but also as an infant, a neonate, or even in utero, children can influence a broad variety of family processes (Lerner & Spanier, 1978). The behavior of even the youngest child can stimulate, elicit, motivate, and reward the actions of parents. Currently, both the social mold and the child-centered orientations have been supplanted by a perspective that views parents and children as simultaneously and mutually influencing one another. Each serves as the stimuli for the other's behavior. In this section, we examine some of the major research efforts directed toward understanding this parent-child communication process.

Individual Social Behaviors

Research on individual social behaviors generally focuses on how parental message selection influences the development of a variety of characteristics in the child (Hess, 1981).[6] Parental messages can be broadly characterized as support and control messages (Rollins & Thomas, 1979; Steinmetz, 1979).

Behaviors that make a child feel comfortable in the presence of a parent are support messages. These include praising, approving, encouraging, physical displays of affection, giving help, and cooperating with a child. Behaviors designed to gain compliance with the wishes of the parent are called control messages. Control messages include coercion, induction, and love withdrawal. Coercive messages focus on external reasons why the child should comply with the parent and involve physical punishment, the direct application of force, the deprivation of material objects or privileges, or the threat of these. Induction messages focus on the internal reasons why the child should comply with the parent and involve explanations, reasons, or pointing out the consequences of an act for the child or for others. Love withdrawal focuses on a combination of internal and external forces for compliance. These techniques indicate disapproval of the child's behavior with the implication that love will not be restored until the child does what the parent wishes. Love withdrawal is manifested by ignoring the child, isolating the child, explicit statements of rejection, or nonverbal behaviors signaling coldness or disappointment (Rollins & Thomas, 1979).

Relying on the impressive recent work of Steinmetz (1979) and Rollins and Thomas (1979), we summarize the empirical relationships between parental communication strategies and selected child outcomes, particularly aggression, dependency, cognitive development, conformity, moral development, creativity, and self-esteem.[7] We sorted the relationships according to the sex of the interactants. Because a basic discrimination in definitions of the family surrounds age and sex, we did not want to speak of general parent-child patterns without first examining the individual dyadic combinations. Gender-based differences have been understudied in close relationships (Peplau, 1983), and ours was an attempt to remedy that situation.

The effect of supportive parental messages on children of all ages seems clear. Across all possible combinations of parent-child dyads (father-son, father-daughter, mother-son, mother-daughter), supportive messages lead to higher self-esteem, more conformity to the wishes of the parents in both young children and adolescents, and inhibition of aggression or antisocial behavior in a variety of settings. Rejection, the opposite of support, leads to greater dependency on the part of all children. With the exception of the mother-daughter dyad, supportive messages also facilitate the development of higher moral standards in children. Based on a careful examination of the research, there is little doubt that making a child feel loved, supported, and comfortable in the presence of a parent leads to the development of a large range of socially valued behaviors in the child.

The relationship between cognitive development and supportive parental communication holds clearly only in same-sex pairs. Supportive messages from a father lead to academic achievement, masculine sex-role identification, and cognitive development in a son. For mothers and daughters, an inverse relationship exists between supportive messages from a mother and a daughter's achievement in school. When the mother engages in positive and warm interactions with her daughter, she facilates the daughter's cognitive development and feminine sex-role identification, yet curiously not her drive to succeed in school. This finding is our only indication of negative outcomes resulting from supportive communication messages. Perhaps supportive and loving messages from a mother cause a female child to reject external success as measured by school performance and to turn to more traditional activities. Alternately, the mothers in these dyads may have little ambition concerning their daughters' achievement in school.

The development of socially valued and prosocial behaviors in children is facilitated not only by the use of supportive messages but also by maternal responsiveness, the discussion and acceptance of feelings, and the reinforcement and modeling of prosocial behavior (Bryant & Crockenberg, 1980). A nurturant parent-child relationship is basic to the development of prosocial behavior in children (Hoffman, 1970). Because it reduces a child's needs, nurturance helps to increase positive orientations toward others and identification with the nurturant parent (Staub, 1978).

The relationship between extreme parental control strategies and child outcomes is also demonstrably clear based on the empirical research. Extreme control attempts such as physical punishment lead to aggression in virtually all children, and coercive attempts of any kind lead to less internalization of moral standards in children. Other more subtle forms of parental control do not necessarily lead to any obvious child outcomes. More research is needed in parental control strategies. The lack of theory-based discriminations of various forms of parental persuasion beyond the extremes of physical aggression has limited our understanding of parental control messages and child outcomes (deTurck, 1984).

Because families are defined by age and gender hierarchies, dyadic sex composition must be considered when studying the effects of parental message styles on children. It would be of great theoretical utility to link the input and performance variables that we have been discussing to the output variables in Table 15.1. Certain compliance-gaining procedures may work equally well in socializing a child to the wishes of a parent yet have remarkably different effects on family solidarity.

The research results on how the withdrawal of parental love actually affects child outcomes are very mixed. Because these messages involve the manipulation of affect to achieve an end, their operationalizations may have to be carefully delineated. The theoretical relationship between affect and power in intimate relationships needs greater attention from theorists. It stands to illuminate many facets of family life, not only child socialization. In any consideration of human relationships, affect is inextricably related to power (Waller, 1938). From the beginning of the parent-child relationship, there is a unique union of love and discipline, which makes socialization possible.

The research results on the use of induction techniques, that is, reasoning with one's child, are also mixed, The use of such a technique can be expected to vary in subtlety as the child develops cognitively (Applegate, Burke, Burleson, Delia, & Kline, 1983). Indeed, the ability of a mother or father to adjust his or her messages based on the developmental level of the child is paramount in all styles, not only the inductive one. Thus the neglect of developmental differences may be obscuring our understanding of how induction messages work in producing child outcomes.

Our discussion of parent-child communication has proceeded as if communication existed on only one level. Of course, communication occurs across many levels (Bateson, 1975). Messages that contradict one another across the various levels of communication are taken to be related to a variety of dysfunctional outcomes for families. Messages from different channels (verbal, prosodic, kinesic, facial, and so forth) may create a paradox by the simultaneous assertion of contradictory meanings. If this situation occurs many times, in an intense relationship in which partners can not comment on the paradox or even escape the field, it constitutes a double bind (Abeles, 1976). Despite the importance of this construct in the interactional view, there is little empirical support that double binds actually lead to dysfunctional family outcomes (Olson, 1972). This construct is difficult to examine as it may be impossible to create double binds, given all of the previously named conditions, in any laboratory. Further, the most obvious pathology associated with the double bind, namely, schizophrenia, is now believed to have a neurochemical basis (Garmezy, 1974).

Despite the disappointing laboratory tests on double bind, studies on the consistency of verbal and nonverbal channels of communication continue to be viewed as valuable enterprises. There appear to be significant differences in the communication consistency of mothers of disturbed versus normal children (Bugental & Love, 1975). Specifically, mothers of disturbed children sent more inconsistent messages than mothers of normal children (mean age: 9; see Bugental, Love, Kaswan, & April, 1971). Most mothers may have "perfidious female faces" in that in both normal and disturbed families, mothers smiled regardless of the content of the messages they sent to their children (Bugental, 1974; Bugental, Love, & Gianetto, 1971). A key question remaining is when do children of varying ages begin to see and understand these communicative discrepancies.

Although intriguing, these results have not been replicated in five other studies (Jacob & Lessin, 1982). Although the examination of inconsistency in family communication continues to be a topic of importance for all interested in family processes, two oversights must be corrected in future research. First, developmental issues such as the age of the children must be considered. Children show developmental differences across a number of nonverbal recognition and encoding skills. These differences may be sex-linked (Mayo & Henley, 1981). Research must thus take into account not only the developmental age of the child but also his or her sex. Second, more attention should be paid to theoretical models of the relationships among channels of communication. Communication channels carry differential levels of information for receivers. This area may be especially important in studying individuals who have interaction histories with one another such as family members. Third, across any age group, inconsistencies must reach a particular level before they are perceived by communicators (Atkinson & Allen, 1983). The psychological reality of channel inconsistency is a major point that must be considered in studies of family communication (Folger & Poole, 1980). Fourth, a consideration of recent functional approaches to the study of nonverbal communication may give the study of inconsistent family communication a needed theoretical transfusion (for example, Patterson, 1983).

Interpersonal Processes

As young as seven weeks, infants and their mothers have been observed in "proto-conversations" or interactive sequences characterized by eye gazing, face-to-face orientation, patterns of turn-taking, variations in vocal intonation, and obvious mutual pleasure (Bateson, 1975; Stern, 1977). Researchers in mother-infant interaction have developed elaborate and powerful models of dyadic interaction to explain these processes. In these models, communication, in its most basic form, involves mutuality, intersubjectivity, and reciprocity (Ryan, 1974).

Infants are predisposed to the development of primitive communication skills. From early on, the behavior of an infant forms patterned, functional units that are easy to recognize. The first communication from a baby is a cry. Infants selectively attend to the world around them. They indicate a preference for human faces over other shapes and look at faces and try to talk to them rather than bottles or breasts (Bell, 1974). Infants also have preferences for the human voice, and by the end of the first month can be quieted by soft, high-pitched talking (Kaplan & Kaplan, 1971).

Care givers recognize these patterned units and assume that at least some of them provide indications of what is happening inside the infant (Richards, 1974). They respond to the differential cries of an infant and identify three types of cries: hunger, pain, or anger. Objectively, these cries differ in terms of pitch, pattern, and intonation (Wasz-Hockert, Lind, Vuorenkoski, Partenen, & Valarne, 1968; Wolff, 1971). The care giver helps the infant not only to achieve appropriate levels of tension and arousal but also to organize the behavior to which the care giver contingently responds (Sroufe, 1979). A baby's smiles, burps, and coos are responded to by an adult as turns in conversation. Care givers use tag questions and other postcompleters to pass the conversational turn to a baby (Snow, 1972). Indeed, the greater the use of questions by the mother, the greater the mother's desire to interact reciprocally with her infant (Snow, 1977). Effective care givers even fill-in a turn for an inactive baby (Spieker, 1982) by acting as if the baby had responded in the appropriate sequence.

Care givers adjust their speech when speaking to infants and children at early stages of language acquisition. Mothers adjust their speech to young infants to keep the conversation going and to engage the attention of the infant (Kaye, 1980; Snow, 1977). With infants of six months or older, the mother adjusts her speech by using syntactically simpler utterances in order to make herself understood by the child. This adjustment helps both the child's understanding and general linguistic capacity (Bellinger, 1980).

"Baby talk" differs from other talk in prosody, in redundancy, and in grammatical complexity (Wells & Robinson, 1982). The various features of baby talk serve different and orthogonal functions. The clarification function is served by the "comm register," which includes the attention-getting devices noted in "motherese" (Snow, 1977) and in the simplification of speech and its prosodic characteristics. The expressive function is served by the "aff register," which is primarily verbal and includes the the use of pet names, the playful repetition of names, and the use of diminutives and endearments. Because babies are both linguistically incompetent and typically inspire affection, baby talk occurs in both comm and aff registers. These functions may be extended to adult conversations. In families or close relationships, those who are perceived as incompetent may periodically be addressed in the comm register and those who inspire affection may be addressed at certain times in the aff register. Recent research on care giver-elderly interaction suggests that the elderly, during caretaking interactions in nursing homes, are addressed in the comm register (Giles, 1984) and that spouses and lovers tend to be addressed in the aff register (Hopper, Knapp, & Scott, 1981).

The interaction we have been describing takes place during the first six months of an infant's life. These interaction patterns set the stage for the development of the attachment bond. Attachment is a tie that one person forms to another specific person, binding them together in space and enduring over time. An infant appears to become attached to the figure or figures with whom he or she has the most interaction (Ainsworth, 1973; Ainsworth & Bell, 1969). Attachment is indicated by behaviors that promote proximity such as signaling behavior like crying, smiling, and vocalizing; orienting behavior such as looking, moving toward, or following the other; and active physical contact such as clinging or embracing.

The attachment bond between a mother and an infant predisposes the infant to comply, at a later date, with the wishes of the mother. The willingness to be obedient rather than any understanding of the content of the mother's message emerges from the development of a secure attachment bond in the dyad. Infants categorized as securely or anxiously attached to their mothers at 18 months of age were followed at 24 months. Infants who could employ their care givers as a secure base from which to explore and who positively greeted their mothers following a stressful separation experience (or were comforted by her presence) displayed more skill in problem solving and were more cooperative than were the less securely attached toddlers (Matas, Arend, & Sroufe, 1982). Infants appear initially inclined to be social and somewhat later ready to comply with the wishes of those persons who are most significant in their environment (Stayton, Hogan, & Ainsworth, 1982). Compliance from the young occurs only when affect has been established in the relationship.

Previous work on attachment placed primary emphasis on emotion. Recent explanations have, however, assigned a central role to cognitive factors. The appearance of separation anxiety between 8 and 12 months is considered the behavioral manifestation of attachment. Separation distress at the temporary (permanent) loss of the care giver occurs at this stage in cognitive development because the infant can retrieve a schema for an event that is not in the immediate visual field. The infant's ability to recall stored information, to retrieve a past schema, and to compare that schema to the present information is now thought to lead to the emotional distress (Kagan, 1979).

In our discussion, we have shifted between the terms care giver and mother. Most theories assume the primacy of the mother-infant bond (Bowlby, 1972; Freud, 1949; Winnicott, 1964). In these theories, the mother is uniquely important in the child's life because she spends the most time with the child and has the most interaction. The amount of actual mother-infant interaction is, however, highly overestimated, and simple time spent together is a poor predictor of the quality of an infant's relationships with anyone (Lamb, 1976b). A few hours of pleasurable interaction appear to be more conducive to the development of a bond between the infant and an adult than do more extensive hours with a less stimulating care giver (Birnbaum, 1971; Lamb; 1976b).

The ability of an infant to form attachments to more than one primary figure has clear survival value (Mead, 1942). Infants form attachments to both fathers and mothers, although the nature of the interaction between infant and each parent may differ. Fathers engage in more play and mothers in more care-giving activities with an infant. Infants prefer the physical, nonintellectual, rough and tumble play initiated by fathers (Lamb, 1976a; Parke & O'Leary, 1976). How much nurturance and what type of nurturance fathers give to older children remain to be seen. That men can be nurturant has been clearly demonstrated. One major multinational study of men in public with children indicated that the touching, proximity, and visual contact maintained by men with male and female children did not differ from that exhibited by women (Mackey & Day, 1979). American fathers do not seem to mind child socializing yet they still reject child care (Slocum & Nye, 1976). Even cross-culturally, taking a child to the park is now an appropriate role for both fathers and mothers, yet changing a diaper is still women's work.

The interactions that facilitate attachment also facilitate the learning of language. Reciprocity (sensitivity to the partner) and intersubjectivity (experience of two persons with shared knowledge of the world) set the stage for the onset of intentional communication. Babies begin to look at a desired object, gesture and vocalize toward it, and alternate glances between the desired object and the care giver. The emergence at nine months of this intentional signaling is a major stage in language development (Bates, 1979; Bates, Camaioni, & Volterra, 1975). By developing a stable group of conventional gestures, babies are making the discovery that the objects they desire have names (Spieker, 1982). The similar focus on objects by the care giver and the infant helps the infant to learn words. Primitive communication, followed by attachment between infants and care givers, sets the stage not only for language learning but for most other facets of a child's development.

The study of family relationships has much to gain from the study of care giver-infant interaction. A life-span developmental approach to the study of attachment among family members would illuminate a major aspect of family process. Much can be learned from the research on infant attachment—both conceptually and methodologically. Debates arose in the infant literature with the realization that attachment did not demonstrate either individual stability or trait consistency across samples, situations, or time (Sroufe, 1979). The problem appeared to rest with the operationalization of attachment as a count of the duration or frequencies of attachment behaviors (Sroufe, 1979) rather than with any conceptual inadequacy. From this we have learned that in studying emotional phenomena, we have to look for stable *categories* of behavior rather than stable discrete behaviors. For a number of reasons, the infant may show one type of attachment behavior at two months but a very different type of attachment at 20 months (Sroufe, 1979). This differential behavioral display of the same underlying construct may occur because the child is continuing to develop sensory-motor skills between the time periods when the measurement occurs. Multiple measurements of constructs appear necessary in the study of affect in all social relationships (Fitzpatrick, 1981b). The work on mother-infant interaction is also instructive because it offers an implicit recognition that cognitive competencies underlie the unfolding of emotion. The consideration of both cognitive and affective explanations for the development of these early bonds is a useful exemplar for the study of other social relationships. Although in infant studies as in other relationship studies, cognitive mental schemas are viewed as affectively toned, the reciprocal influence of affect on cognition needs to be more extensively explored (Kagan, 1979). In adult relationships, the manner in which certain affective states affect representations of the relationship is beginning to be researched (Fallis, 1984).

In this section, we have seen that parent-child communication is often studied at the level of an individual social process. The major lines of research on interpersonal processes in parent-child communication are limited primarily to the care giver-infant domain. Across both of these divisions, we begin to see a conceptual confusion between affect and power in the relationship of parents and children. Both parents and children use affect to achieve their persuasive goals; and power can create affect. In the next section, we turn to a consideration of one of the less frequently examined family dyads: the sibling relationship.

SIBLING RELATIONSHIPS

Eighty percent of the population live the first third of their lives in families with siblings. The kinds of interactions that children have with their siblings have a profound influence on the personal happiness that they experience in the family growing up (Bowerman & Dobash, 1974). And early affective relationships between sibs appear to predict interaction between them in adulthood (Bank & Kahn, 1982a, 1982b).

Influenced by Freud (1949), much of the early literature on family interaction discussed the sibling relationship in terms of negative affect (Bossard & Boll, 1950). Children show signs of hostility, anxiety, and competition at the birth of a younger sibling (Cameron, 1963). Sibs tend to compete in the family for the love, attention, and favor of one or both of the parents (Levy, 1937). This rivalry purportedly is much stronger when the age interval between children is four years or less (Koch, 1956). Some recent observational work in families finds no empirical support for this age interval hypothesis in the observed aggressive, imitative, or pro-social behaviors of children toward their close or far interval sibs (Abramovitch, Corter, & Lando, 1979; Abramovitch, Corter, & Peplar, 1980; Dunn & Kendrick, 1981). During the beginning of the school years, however, increased positive behavior and decreased aggression to a widely spaced (much younger) sibling may appear (Minnett, Vandell, & Santrock, 1983). Whatever the degree of hostility between sibs, it may be resolved by consistent parental affection, the development of an attachment bond between siblings, and the socialization of aggression (Tsukada, 1979).

Other more positive aspects of the interaction between sibs have been given less attention. The possession of a sibling may make early socialization complete because siblings provide peer role models and training in cooperation, conflict management, and accommodation. They also offer to one another companionship, security, and love (Duberman, 1973). Indeed, siblings may create for one another very different environments within the family.

Individual Social Behaviors

The most extensive work that has been undertaken on sibling relationships examines the effects of birth order on personality development and achievement (Falbo, 1981; Toman, 1961). Characteristic personality traits for each birth order are described. Even the eventual marital adjustment of an individual is linked to position in the family of origin (Toman, 1961). It is entirely plausible that individual differences in tactics, aggression, sex-role preferences, and interests in latter-born children can be attributed to the processes of identification and modeling of older siblings. The conforming, achievement, and affiliative behaviors of only and first-born children may be attributed to that child's special relationship to the parents (Sutton-Smith & Rosenberg, 1970). Very few studies of the interaction between parents and children or between siblings have been conducted to test these ideas. Much of this research has been motivated by curiosity rather than theory. Arguing that a structural subposition in a family unit leads to given personality outcomes for an individual leaves the why question unanswered. Some appreciation of the psychological or communication conditions that occur when an individual occupies a birth-order position (Schvaneveldt & Ihinger, 1979) is necessary to understand why a specific birth position in a family leads to given outcomes for a family member. Furthermore, serious methodological flaws must be corrected in these studies (Schooler, 1972). Sampling error, as well as failure to control for socioeconomic status, cohort effects, or the stage in family development, leave most of the empirical findings on this topic in confusion. To sort through these findings, meta-analysis may yield some promising results (for example, Hyde, 1984).

Interpersonal Processes

Sibling status variables of age, birth order, birth interval, and sex do not account adequately for sibling differences (Scarr & Grajek, 1982). Dunn (1983) argues that these constructs may be inadequate to account for sibling behavior because they reference complementary behaviors (A is older than B) in an attempt to predict reciprocal behaviors (A and B are mutually aggressive). Conceptual discriminations between peer, sibling, and parent-child interaction in terms of reciprocity and complementarity would help. Although recent theoretical interest in the development and maintenance of peer relationships in children may not be directly applicable to the study of sibs (for example, Hartup, 1978; La Gaipa, 1981), valuable lines of research could examine the nature of differences in peer and sibling interactions.

Peer interactions are reciprocal interactions in that each can understand the reasoning and perspective of the other. Parent-child interactions are complementary interactions in that the behavior of each differs from but fits that of the other. Sibling relationships include the direct reciprocity of peers because of their intensity, familiarity, intimacy, and the recognition and sharing of interests. The frequent imitation by siblings of the actions of one another, the demonstration of joy and excitement in coaction sequences, and the willingness of each to engage in pro-social and comforting actions are examples of reciprocity of interaction between sibling pairs. Given the age differences between sibs, these relationships also have aspects of the parent-child relationship (Dunn, 1983, pp. 788-789). Care giving, teaching, attachment, and language are aspects of inherent complementarity in sibships.[8]

Four-year-olds are capable of making speech adjustments to two-year-olds (Shatz & Gelman, 1977) and can adjust their communication to dolls representing others (Sachs & Devin, 1976). All the two- and three-year-olds studied (Dunn & Kendrick, 1982) made systematic adjustments in speaking to their fourteen-month-old siblings. Older sibs tend to clarify their speech for their conversational partner, but only those older sibs who had particularly warm relationships with the infants used expressive linguistic features. Conversational turns in these sibling interactions were shorter than those of the mother with the infant and were not responded to as strongly by the infant. Both mother and infant attempted to maintain the attention of the other, whereas sibling-infant turns were primarily nonverbal sequences such as alternate imitations of one another over a shorter span of time.

Comparisons of the interaction of 4- to 8-year-old children with parents and with sibs indicated that the interaction behavior of a target child was remarkably different with parents versus siblings (Baskett & Johnson, 1982).

Interactions with the parent were more numerous and varied than were those with a sibling. Children talked, laughed, and touched the parents more and were more compliant with their wishes. Undesirable behaviors directed to parents seemed designed primarily to draw attention (for example, whining, demands for attention, and so forth). The only pro-social behavior that occurred more frequently in sibling interaction than in parent-child interaction was that children tended to play or work with one another more. In general, brothers and sisters used more physical aggression, yelling, hitting, and negative commands with one another than they did with parents. Regardless of the state of the relationship between the sibs, the sibs preferred interacting with a parent to interacting with their sib.

Preschool-age children both offer their toys and talk to their 18-month-old sibs. The toddlers watch and imitate the older children and take over the toys the older child abandoned (Lamb, 1978b). Both same- and mixed-sex sibling dyads of close and far spacing interact a great deal. Once a minute, in this study, a sib initiates or responds to the other member of the dyad. Older children in each pair initiate most (84 percent) of the antagonistic acts, regardless of the sex or age differences among the dyads, and most of the pro-social acts as well. Younger children initiate most of the imitative behaviors in both same- and mixed-sex dyads. In same-sex dyads, older boys are more physically aggressive than older girls. Girls tend to initiate more pro-social acts and respond positively to the pro-social acts of a sister (Abramovitch et al., 1979, 1980).

Eighteen months later a subset of the same-sibling pairs (mixed and same sex) was observed. Their ages ranged from three years to seven years and as before they were categorized according to a small age spacing (1 to 2 years) or a large age spacing (2.5 to 4 years). The interaction patterns among the children were approximately the same. Older children engaged in more cooperation, help, and praise. Although older children initiated interaction more often, the younger child maintained the interaction by reciprocating pro-social behavior, submitting to aggressive behavior, and imitating his or her siblings. As children got older, they tended to increase the number of pro-social acts in their sibling contacts. Yet there also was an increase in mixed-sex antagonism and a decrease in mixed-sex imitation. The occurrence of these sex differences in the interactive behaviors of siblings may indicate the beginning of sex typing (Peplar, Abramovitch, & Corter, 1981).

Children as young as 4-years-old serve as attachment figures for siblings. Over 52 percent of one sample of young children were active and effective in caring for their younger siblings who were distressed when the mother left the room. Although infants may prefer a paternal attachment figure (for example, Lamb, 1978b), infants allow themselves to be comforted by a sibling. With strangers, infants also seem to use the sibling as an attachment figure and a secure base from which to explore (Stewart, 1983).

Little work has been done on the interaction patterns of older sibling pairs. The majority of adolescents say they are close to their sibs. Adolescent females report more affect toward their sibs than do males; same-sex sibs are preferred; and younger children have stronger affect toward older sibs than vice versa. In addition, affect decreases with age and is stronger in families with two children (Bowerman & Dobash, 1974). The sib relationship with the greatest contrast in feeling, and hence the most at risk for conflict, is the older brother-younger sister relationship. The least contrast in feeling and the less at risk for conflict is the older sister-younger brother relationship.

More than peers or even other family members, siblings are accessible to one another during the entire length of the developmentally formative years. They share time, space, and personal history to a degree unlikely in peer relationships (Bank & Kahn, 1982a, 1982b). Perhaps more importantly, siblings influence one another at every stage in the development of their personal identities. Such influence may be accomplished through the social comparison process, which specifically occurs in sibling but not necessarily in peer interactions (Tesser, 1980). Sibs tend to compare themselves to one another on a number of dimensions not limited to attractiveness, intelligence, accomplishments, and so forth. Finally, we may turn to our sibs later in life in times of family crises, such as divorce (Ambrose, Harper, & Pemberton, 1983). Indeed, at the end of our lives, our living companions and our best friends will often turn out to be our sibs.

In this section, we have indicted the individual social process research on sibling relationships for its theoretical and methodological weaknesses. In the study of interpersonal processes of siblings in the family, systematic research efforts are just beginning. As a consequence, these efforts are primarily aimed at describing the interaction process in different age and sex-sibling pairs. The mapping of these interaction patterns needs to be supplanted with theoretical models explicating why the patterns emerge. Such efforts are vital to an understanding of family processes not only with younger children but also across the life span of the individual and the family.

THE FAMILY AS A UNIT

Riskin and Faunce's (1972) observation that the least studied family unit was the family itself still holds today. Most of the research on the family involves studying the husband-wife or mother-child dyads. Although some research does consider triads or even a four-person family group, relatively little research effort is directed at the whole family. The major paradigm guiding research on the family as a unit was that which linked disturbed family communication processes to psychological and social deviance outcomes for offspring. Such a perspective dates to at least the 1950s. Bateson's group at Palo Alto, Bowen and Wynne at NIMH, Lidz and his associates at Yale, and

Ackerman's research group at the Family Mental Health Clinic in New York were independently arriving at the conclusion that observable, ongoing family interaction patterns could be directly linked to outcomes for children (Raush et al., 1979).

When the family is studied as a unit, the research involves bringing families together to discuss a problem or to engage in a task that allows the family to interact (Bochner, 1974). The interaction of the family is then transcribed and some verbal and/or nonverbal coding scheme is applied to the material. The purpose of the research is usually to discriminate functional from dysfunctional families on the basis of their interaction patterns. Whereas work in the early 1960s concentrated on the differences between normal and schizophrenic families (see the review by Jacob, 1975), research in the 1970s branched out to include abusive and neglectful families (for example, Burgess & Conger, 1978); families with an abnormally aggressive (for example, Patterson, 1976) or delinquent child (for example, Alexander, 1973); or an alcoholic parent (for example, Mead & Campbell, 1972). Overall, researchers have found that clinic-referred children and adolescents are likely to come from families in which positive, nurturant, and supportive behaviors occur at depressed rates whereas noxious, aversive, or negative interactions are relatively frequent (Conger, 1981, 1983). Although some research was conducted to see how normal families of various levels of functioning interacted (for example, Lewis et al., 1976; Loeb, 1975), most family research explores the interaction differences between healthy and unhealthy families. The differences between these two types are expected to outweigh the differences within these types.

In the 1980s, the orientation of mapping interaction differences in disturbed and nondisturbed families continues (for example, Reiss, 1981). More concern is shown, however, for describing normal family processes in a range of different temporal, structural, and sociocultural contexts (Walsh, 1982). Developmental researchers are also beginning to study "normal" family triads, particularly mother, father, and infant (Parke, 1979). A consideration of the triad reveals that there are at least nine different direct and indirect ways that the interaction in any triad can be modified (Parke, 1979). Consider the parents P1 and P2. One could examine the impact of (1) P1's modification of P2's behavior on the child; (2) P2's modification of P1's behavior on the child; (3) P1-child relationship on P2-child interaction; (4) P2-child relationship on P1-child interaction; (5) P1's modification of child's behavior on P2-child interaction; (6) P2's modification of child's behavior on P1-child interaction; (7) P1-child relationship on P1-P2 relationship; (8) P2-child relationship on P1-P2 relationship; and (9) P1-P2 relationship on the child. Each of these nine ways that interaction can be studied in a triad (and generalizations beyond to the four- and five-person family) are important pieces of the puzzle of family process. These potential relationship linkages have not been as yet examined in any great detail.

In the next sections, we consider the work that has been done on interpersonal processes in healthy family units. This work is relatively new and indicates an important trend for future studies of family communication. Because there is so little empirical research mapping and comparing individual social behaviors of the family as a unit (for an exception, see Olson et al., 1983), the next section primarily examines the interpersonal processes within selected family triads. For theoretical and pragmatic reasons, we need to know far more about the range and diversity of the functioning of the family as a unit before we can understand or recognize dysfunctionality.

Mother-Infant-Toddler Triads

Interaction between a mother and a first-born child changed markedly when the mother was feeding or caring for the newborn (Kendrick & Dunn, 1980). During feeding or holding of the newborn, a mother increased her attention and positive interaction with the newborn and her confrontation and negative interaction with the older child. When the mothers were bottle feeding, although not breast feeding, there was an increase in the deliberate naughtiness on the part of the older child. In general, children become increasingly demanding of the mother's attention when she is caring for an infant (Dunn & Kendrick, 1981; Kendrick & Dunn, 1980).

Maternal interaction patterns have indirect effects as well. The intervention of a mother in sibling quarrels has been linked to differences in the frequency of hostile behavior between siblings three months later (Kendrick & Dunn, 1982). When the second born was eight-months-old, mothers prohibited a significantly larger number of physical quarrels than they did six months later. When mothers frequently restrained or punished the physical quarreling behavior of first-born sons, these boys responded more aggressively six months later to their sibs. The pattern of first-born daughters was exactly opposite (Dunn 1983).

Father-Mother-Infant Triads

The relationship between spouses appears to have an effect on how the infant is treated. In general, the greater the negative affect between the husband and wife, the greater the negative affect directed toward the infant (Pederson, Anderson, & Cain, 1977).

Parent-infant interaction is affected by the presence of the other parent. Mothers interact and smile more at their infants alone than they do in the presence of the fathers; fathers engage in those activities with the infant only when the mother is present (Parke & O'Leary, 1976). The overall quality of mother-infant interaction appears to be decreased by the presence of the father (Clarke-Stewart, 1982; Parke & O'Leary, 1976). Yet it appears that the quality of the father-infant interaction is higher when the mother is present. To the degree that this finding generalizes to other family dyads at different ages of the child, the radical shift in interactional quality with the addition of the father to the mother-child dyad will have intriguing implications for models of family communication. It may be that there is an inherent limitation in the amount and quantity of affect that can be expressed in these family triads.

Infants at both 8 and 13 months appear to be equally attached to both mothers and fathers. Infants prefer their fathers, however, and direct a greater number of affiliative behaviors (smiling, laughing, looking) toward fathers than mothers. The question of the differential strength of the attachment of an infant to mothers and fathers is still an open one (Parke, 1979). The importance of studying the family as a unit, especially the father-infant-mother triad, is viewed as a promising direction for future research (Parke & Asher, 1983). Such research makes important conceptual distinctions between attachment and affiliation in human relationships.

Father-Mother-Young Child Triad

There is a strong relationship between parental discord and negative child outcomes. The observation of family interaction in structured situations indicated that unhappily married parents directed more negative behaviors toward their child and were more likely to have children with severe behavior problems (Johnson & Lobitz, 1974). Furthermore, in a free interaction task, problem family members provided fewer positive and more aversive consequents for pro-social behavior and more positive and fewer aversive consequents for deviant behavior than did nonproblem families (Conger, 1983).

Not only do problem families exhibit more negativity than nonproblem families, but there also appears to be more negativity overall in families than in stranger groups. Mothers appear to use more negative sanctions with their own children and more positive, encouraging statements with other children as they supervise the performance of a task (Halverson & Waldrop, 1970). Children are more obedient to strangers than to their mothers and show greater task performance with strangers (Landauer, Carlsmith, & Lepper, 1970). In comparing the interactions of middle- and lower-class families with 11- and 16-year-old boys, Jacob (1974) found that both social class and age of child significantly changed both the patterns of conflict and dominance in the triad. Specifically, families with an 11-year-old expressed greater disagreement with members than did families with a 16-year-old. Middle-class families talked more and interrupted one another more successfully than did lower-class families. Sixteen-year-old sons gained in influence in these family triads; in middle-class families this was at the expense of the mother, whereas in lower-class families such influence gain was at the expense of the father.

Father-Mother-Older Child

In his review of 57 family interaction studies composed of both triadic (33 studies) and quadradic (24 studies) interaction designs, Jacob (1975) systematically divides the studies into those with quantitative and qualitative measures of affect, dominance, communication clarity, and conflict.[9] He shows that no reliable differences can be uncovered from the empirical research. Methodological problems in these works abound, not the least of which is the noncomparability of the studies in terms of age, sex, and even number of family members present during an interaction (Jacob, 1975). The within-group variability was too high in the samples of disturbed families. For example, the ages of the schizophrenic children in the same study might range from 12 to 47. In addition, no attempt is made to consider the possible within-group variability in the "normal" families against whom the dysfunctional are compared. Without any controls on the samples, these normal families can be expected to exhibit different patterns (Olson et al., 1983).

A program of research comparing normal and disturbed families that stands out for its theoretical and methodological sophistication is that of Reiss and his colleagues (Reiss, 1981; Oliveri & Reiss, 1981a, 1981b). Believing that theories of the family built around impulse, affect, or power have fared badly in explaining or predicting family behavior, Reiss (1981) has developed a model emphasizing the families' construction of reality. Families are said to differ along three dimensions: (1) their experience of the world as ordered; (2) their belief in the world as open, accessible, or accommodating; and (3) their experience of novelty in the world. This program of research is of special importance to communication researchers for two reasons. First, a family's construction of social reality is represented in the interaction of family members with one another. The social construction of reality is indicated by the lexical speech, the nonlexical speech, and the nonverbal behavior of family members as it is organized into recurring patterns. Second, the model offers a rigorous communication explanation for how parental abnormalities lead to deficiencies in offspring.

In this section, we have seen that the interaction between any two family members can be affected in a variety of direct and indirect ways by the presence and behavior of a third person (Hinde, 1979). Although this point is often acknowledged by theorists, very little systematic research has addressed this question. The research that we have reviewed points to major interaction differences when the dyad becomes a triad. One of the greatest difficulties in this research (apart from its scarcity) is how rarely these interactional differences are connected to major family outcomes. When we undertake such research in the future, it should be in the interest of linking interaction to a variety of important theoretical outcomes. Although the proper domain of communication research is the study of messages, these messages must be connected to the theoretically relevant internal and output family process concepts.

CONCLUSION

In treating a subject as broad as kinship relations, it is helpful to read a number of social science literatures and attempt to draw parallels among these areas. This is too rarely done by social scientists. The purpose of this review was to give the reader a sense of the range of questions that have been asked about communication in families. Although not comprehensive in coverage, the review does establish a fundamental question for the study of communication in kin groups. That is, in each of the subsystems of the family, how do the input variables (Figure 15.1) affect performance and consequently lead to particular outputs? Throughout the review, we have seen that scholars in various traditions have taken pieces of this question. Some have been concerned only with the performance variables, rarely linking these to major family outcomes. As Cappella (1984) has argued, extensive analyses of interaction sequences, although not without their descriptive charm, do not yield much information about potential connections among important concepts. When a link is made, it is usually between a performance and an output variable with little consideration of internal variables. Researchers, for example, typically relate interaction patterns to levels of marital satisfaction (Ting-Toomey, 1983).

In the field of communication the relationships among the internal, performance, and output variables have been largely ignored. We usually consider only a very limited number of family outputs. Marital processes have demonstrated effects on child outcomes, yet it would be rare to see in a communication study any variables linked to marital communication other than those that represent marital quality. As our research into family processes expands so it is hoped will our concern for alternative output variables. It is also interesting to note that only marital and parental satisfaction are considered in Table 15.1. We remind scholars that children, even the very young, are capable of qualitatively assessing their family relationships, including the job being done by their parents.

Twenty years ago, Haley (1963) argued that our theories of family process were stymied by a lack of dyadic-level constructs. This is no longer true, for a variety of such concepts appear in the kinship literature. Naturally, the names of what are actually the same concepts often differ or perversely different concepts often have the same name. Although this confusion is to be expected when researchers come from different academic disciplines, it cannot be tolerated. Take, for example, the concept of complementarity. In the sibling literature, this concept has a decidedly cognitive flavor, for it is defined as not sharing the same point of view (Dunn, 1983). In the marital literature, complementarity has a decidedly behavioristic tinge, for it is the exchange of maximally different control messages (Millar & Rogers, 1976). The area of communication in kinship relations would greatly benefit from a series of concept explications that would allow theorists to draw together much disparate literature (see, for example, Bochner & Krueger, 1979). The move by Lewis and Spanier (1979), treating the numerous marital satisfaction concepts as all tapping marital quality (a new one), was an important breakthrough in understanding the role of communication in marital processes. Because many of the dyadic-level concepts are actually communication constructs (reciprocity, symmetry, dominance, attachment, control, and so forth), such explications will help in theory-building efforts in interpersonal communication.

Our review of the kinship literature suggests directions for new research and theory. Few studies consider more than one family dyad at a time, and most of the research energy is spent on husbands and wives. Certainly, sibling pairs are still underresearched (Irish, 1964), and the similarities and differences between siblings and peers will become an important topic in the next decade of research. In addition to an expansion of the family dyads and triads that are studied, greater care will be paid to sampling not only actors (family dyads or units) but also behaviors and contexts. The need for well-designed laboratory studies of family interaction is apparent. Given the difficulty of drawing careful samples of family dyads and triads, more social scientists will turn to meta-analysis procedures to make sense out of the knowledge base already accumulated (Glass, McGraw, & Smith, 1981). In doing such analyses, attention must be paid to the fact that much of what we know about given areas of family life emerges from the analysis and reanalysis of the same data set. Some fairly careful detective work would be useful in an analysis of this literature.

We suggest a life-span developmental approach to three major concepts isolated in this review: attachment, affiliation, and control. Although we see these concepts discussed again and again across the family subsystems, few theorists explicitly acknowledge the relationships among them. For all its members, the family represents a curious combination of love and control. Whether the dyad be a dating pair in which romance conceals an ongoing power struggle between males and females that requires the control of one's emotions (Waller, 1938), a married couple arguing over a serious issue, or a parent trying to socialize a child, attachment and affiliation are inextricably bound up with control in intimate relationships. Extensive interaction with family members and close physical proximity lead to the development of an attachment bond. In human development, the attachment bond predates affiliation and in human relationships seems to outlast it (Weiss, 1975).

There is a legitimate monopoly of coercion in family life, with each member attempting to control the attitudes, behaviors, and feelings of the other. This control is rarely active without a high degree of affect (positive and negative) in family interactions. Love is used in the service of control and control is used in the service of love in family life. Babies are obedient months later because parents showed their love and concern earlier and an attachment bond between parents and child developed. The withdrawal of love is a control technique used by parents (and by children) to gain compliance. Dominance can be defined as the asymmetrical response of one spouse to the emotional displays of another. Repeatedly, research shows that love and control operate simultaneously in family life. Explicit theoretical statements about the expected relationships among these constructs across the life span are needed.

One immediate requirement of a life-span developmental approach to the study of these concepts is a description of clusters of behaviors that represent these constructs and are hypothesized to change over time in family life. The operationalizations of these constructs can thus be sensitive to the developmental changes in individuals and in the family. Attachment implies accessibility, and the manner in which an infant demonstrates the level of accessibility that he or she wants from adults around him or her is different than that needed by a toddler, a spouse, or a divorcing partner.

Such operationalizations need not ignore self-reports, for these are important assessments of the views of family members on their interactional processes. Although there are a number of steps that can be taken to improve self-report measures (Indvik, 1980), an innovation in family studies would be a consideration of the different perspectives that family members have on the same issues. Even when using well-designed measures, the perspectives of family members may be expected to differ (Duck & Sants, 1983). Multiple perspectives should be of primary concern to communication theorists.

Measurement of these important constructs must move beyond observations of behavior in the presence of target others to an examination of pattern and sequence in family interaction. Complex interactional models of family processes need to be tested. The results of these models should include frequency data, simultaneous behaviors, tests of interactional structure through time, and sequential analysis. Reporting findings in this manner (for example, Gottman, 1979; Sillars, 1980; Williamson, 1983) allows numerous connections to be built with other programs of research. This type of methodological reporting will also prove useful in examining the psychological reality of communication for family members. It is possible that family members themselves count frequencies of behavior and not complex interactional sequences when assessing their relationships. Individuals in ongoing relationships may not be able to see the patterns in which they are enmeshed even though these patterns actually predict certain classes of outcomes in family life.

Models of interaction are incomplete without some consideration of cognitive or interpretative processes (Planalp, 1984). Indeed, it would be of major conceptual importance for theorists to link the interactional and cognitive perspectives. To accomplish this link for family systems, two points must be taken into account. First, major cognitive developmental differences separate not only parents and children but also siblings only a few years apart in age. Second, the study of interaction and the study of cognition are radically different in levels of abstraction. Thus the rules of correspondence between these levels must be specified. Third, to code the interaction that occurs among family members without concern for the meaning that these individuals are assigning to these messages is as futile as to present messages to intimates out of the stream of interaction.

Innumerable pronouncements have been made about the modern family and its alleged demise. Despite changes in traditional family patterns, Americans consistently report that a happy marriage and a good family are the most important aspects of life (Thorton & Freedman, 1983). The study of communication in the family will become a major part of interpersonal communication theory and research in the next decade not only because the family is of import to the society at large but it also presents an interesting context in which to pursue important questions about human communication.

NOTES

1. For example, only 26 references are directly made to communication in the over 800-page authoritative two-book series on the most recent theories regarding the family (Burr, Hill, Nye, & Reiss, 1979a, 1979b). In the first three volumes of *Personal Relationships* (Duck & Gilmour, 1981a, 1981b, 1981c), only six references in 850 pages were made to communication, although the fourth volume (Duck, 1982a) does contain one essay on communication in dissolving relationships.

2. This chart is essentially an analytical device isolating the central factors employed in the theoretical approaches to the study of kin relationships. Theories that employ a constitutive approach would tend to see less of a conceptual differentiation between internal and performance factors (Poole, McPhee, & Seibold, 1982). For example, role differentiation would not exist separate and apart from its instantiation in the ongoing conflict or problem-solving activities of a couple or a family.

3. All these output measures are clearly value laden. It is clearly a value of the society that individuals be satisfied in relationships and that children achieve the same (or higher) status as their parents. The concept of family functioning and normalcy is a different order of value orientation because it is hidden in the conceptual arguments of the theorist. Our point here is only to consider the nature of the assumptions of the theorists studying adequacy of family functioning.

4. The system analogy reminds us of the fundamental law of family interaction (Bossard, 1956, p. 293). That is, the number of reciprocal relationships or dyads (X) in a family with a given number of members (Y) is: $X = Y(Y-1)/2$. Consequently, a family with 7 children has 36 possible dyadic combinations. Even the proverbial two-child family has six dyadic links. This equation ignores the possibility of potential for triads and larger size combinations. All of these should be considered for a complete theory of the family, yet adding or subtracting even one family member has dramatic implications for the structure of family interactions (Broderick & Smith, 1979).

5. These couples were labeled enmeshed, autistic, direct conflict, and disengaged conflict. The enmeshed couples evidenced high ambivalence, communication, and conflict about the divorce, whereas the autistic couples showed high ambivalence but had little explicit conflict. The direct conflict couples engaged in open conflict and communication about the divorce decision but at somewhat lower levels of intensity than the enmeshed type. The disengaged couples had limited communication and conflict.

6. The selection of parental message strategies for dealing with children is strongly influenced by the parent's place in the social stratification structure (Gecas, 1979). Although socioeconomic status has a direct effect on a variety of parental message selection strategies (Bernstein, 1971), we limit ourselves to the impact of parental communication on a variety of intellectual, social, and emotional outcomes for children. We have limited ourselves to these variables in conformity to Table 15.1, which emphasizes endogenous rather than exogenous variables.

7. As data for the generalizations we offer, we reexamined the charts constructed by Rollins and Thomas (1979) and Steinmetz (1979). In many cases, we found the decision rules on which

they based their empirical generalizations about the parent-child dyads too liberal. They tended to follow a simple majority rule or tally system in examining the research. We reanalyzed the charts based on more stringent criteria. No subset of studies could indicate that the relationship between the variables was in the opposite direction. Furthermore, we examined separately all studies of various sex of parent and sex of child combinations.

8. Few of the studies that Dunn (1983) listed, however, actually mathematically examined the reciprocal or complementary structure of the interaction. Indeed, the frequencies or rates of social behaviors analyzed in these studies are inadequate for summarizing social interaction over time (Gottman & Ringland, 1981).

9. For a critique of this review, see Doane (1978a). For a response to that critique, see Jacob and Grounds (1978). For a rejoinder, see Doane (1978b).

REFERENCES

Abeles, G. (1976). Researching the unsearchable: Experimentation on the double bind. In C. E. Sluzki & D. C. Ransom (Eds.), *Double bind: The foundation of the communicational approach to the family* (pp. 113-150). New York: Grune & Stratton.

Abramovitch, R., Corter, C., & Lando, B. (1979). Sibling interaction in the home. *Child Development, 50,* 997-1003.

Abramovitch, R., Corter, C., & Peplar, D. J. (1980). Observations of mixed-sex sibling dyads. *Child Development. 51,* 1268-1271.

Adams, R. N. (1968). An inquiry into the nature of the family. In R. F. Winch & L. W. Goodman (Eds.), *Selected studies in marriage and the family* (pp. 44-57). New York: Holt, Rinehart & Winston.

Ainsworth, M.D.S. (1973). The development of infant-mother attachment. In B. M. Caldwell & H. N. Riccinti (Eds.), *Review of child development research* (Vol. 3, pp. 1-94). Chicago: University of Chicago Press.

Ainsworth, M.D.S., & Bell, S.M.V. (1969). Some contemporary patterns of mother-infant interaction in the feeding situation. In J. A. Ambrose (Ed.), *Stimulation in early infancy* (pp. 133-163). London: Academic Press.

Aldous, J. (1978). *Family careers: Developmental changes in families.* New York: John Wiley.

Alexander, J. F. (1973). Defensive and supportive communication in normal and deviant families. *Journal of Consulting and Clinical Psychology, 40,* 223-231.

Ambrose, P., Harper, J., & Pemberton, R. (1983). *Surviving divorce: Men beyond marriage.* Great Britain: Harvester.

Anderson, B. J., & Standley, K. (1978). *A methodology for observation for the childbirth environment.* Paper presented at the annual meeting of the American Psychological Association, Washington, D. C.

Applegate, J. L., Burke, J. A., Burleson, B. R., Delia, J. G., & Kline, S. L. (1983). *Reflection-enhancing parental communication.* Paper presented at the annual meeting of the Speech Communication Association, Washington, D. C.

Arbeit, S. A. (1975). *A study of women during their first pregnancy.* Unpublished doctoral dissertation, Yale University.

Atkinson, M. L., & Allen, V. L. (1983). Perceived structure of nonverbal behavior. *Journal of Personality and Social Psychology, 45,* 458-463.

Baltes, P. B. (1968). Longitudinal and cross-sectional sequences in the study of age and generational effects. *Human Development, 11,* 145-171.

Bank, S. P., & Kahn, M. D. (1982a). *The sibling bond.* New York: Basic Books.

Bank, S. P., & Kahn, M. D. (1982b). Intense sibling loyalty. In M. E. Lamb & B. Sutton-Smith (Eds.), *Sibling relationships: Their nature and significance across the life span* (pp. 251-266). Hillsdale, NJ: Lawrence Erlbaum.

Baskett, L. M., & Johnson, S. M. (1982). The young child's interaction with parents versus sibling: A behavioral analysis. *Child Development, 53,* 643-650.

Bates, E. (1979). *The emergence of symbols.* New York: Academic Press.

Bates, E., Camaioni, L., & Volterra, V. (1975). The acquisition of performatives prior to speech. *Merrill-Palmer Quarterly, 21,* 205-226.

Bateson, M. C. (1975). Mother-infant exchanges: The epigenesis of conversational interaction. In D. Aaronson & R. Rieber (Eds.) *Developmental psycholinguistics and communication disorders* (Vol. 263, pp. 101-113). New York: Annals of New York Academy of Science.

Baxter, L. A. (1984). Trajectories of relationship disengagement. *Journal of Social and Personal Relationships, 1,* 29-48.

Bell, R. Q. (1968). A reinterpretation of the direction of effect in studies of socialization. *Psychological Review, 75,* 81-95.

Bell, R. Q. (1974). Contributions of human infants to caregivers and social interaction. In M. Lewis & L. A. Rosenblum (Eds.), *The effect of the infant on its caregivers* (pp. 1-20). New York: John Wiley.

Bellinger, D. (1980). Consistency in the pattern of change in mother's speech: Some discriminant analyses. *Journal of Child Language, 7,* 464-487.

Berger, C. R., & Bradac, J. J. (1982). *Language and social knowledge.* London: Edward Arnold.

Bernard, J. S. (1981). The good-provider role: Its rise and fall. *American Psychologist, 36,* 1-12.

Bernstein, B. (1971). *Class, codes, and control* (Vols. 1 & 2). London: Routledge & Kegan Paul.

Berscheid, E. (1982). Attraction and emotion in interpersonal relationships. In M. S. Clark & S. T. Fiske (Eds.), *Affect and cognition* (pp. 37-120). Hillsdale, NJ: Lawrence Erlbaum.

Berscheid, E. (1983). Emotions. In *Close relationships* (pp. 110-168). New York: W. H. Freeman.

Berscheid, E., & Campbell, B. (1981). The changing longevity of heterosexual close relationships: A commentary and forecast. In M. J. Lerner & S. C. Lerner (Eds.), *The justice motives in social behavior* (pp. 205-234). New York: Plenum.

Bienvenu, M. (1970). The measurement of marital communication. *Family Coordinator, 19,* 26-31.

Birchler, G. R. (1972). *Differential patterns of instrumental affiliative behavior as a function of degree of marital distress and level of intimacy.* Unpublished doctoral dissertation, University of Oregon.

Birnbaum, J. A. (1971). *Life patterns, personality style and self-esteem in gifted family oriented and career committed women.* Unpublished doctoral dissertation, University of Michigan.

Blood, R. O., Jr., & Wolfe, D. M. (1960). *Husbands and wives: The dynamics of married living.* New York: Free Press.

Bloom, B. L., White, S. W., & Asher, S. J. (1979). Marital disruption as a stressful life event. In G. Levinger & O. C. Moles (Eds.), *Divorce and separation* (pp. 184-210). New York: Basic Books.

Bochner, A. P. (1974). *Family communication research: A critical review of approaches, methodologies and substantive findings.* Paper presented at the annual meeting of the Speech Communication Association Convention, Chicago.

Bochner, A. P. (1976). Conceptual frontiers in the study of families: An introduction to the literature. *Human Communication Research, 2,* 381-397.

Bochner, A. P. (1982). On the efficacy of openness in close relationships. In M. Burgoon (Ed.), *Communication yearbook 5* (pp. 109-124). New Brunswick, NJ: Transaction.

Bochner, A. P. (1983). Functions of communication in interpersonal bonding. In C. Arnold & J. W. Bowers (Eds.), *Handbook of rhetorical and communication theory* (pp. 544-621). Boston, MA: Allyn & Bacon.

Bochner, A. P., Kaminski, E. P., & Fitzpatrick, M. A. (1977). The conceptual domain of interpersonal communication behavior: A factor-analytic study. *Human Communication Research, 3,* 291-302.

Bochner, A. P., & Krueger, D. (1979). Interpersonal communication theory and research: An overview of inscrutable epistemologies and muddled concepts. In D. Nimmo (Ed.), *Communication yearbook 3* (pp. 197-212). New Brunswick, NJ: Transaction.

Bohannan, P. (1970). The six stations of divorce. In P. Bohannan (Ed.), *Divorce and after* (pp. 29-55). New York: Doubleday.

Bolton, C. D. (1961). Mate selection as the development of a relationship. *Marriage and Family Living, 22,* 234-240.

Bossard, J. H. S. (1956). *The large family system: An original study in the sociology of the family.* Philadelphia: University of Pennsylvania Press.

Bossard, J.H.S., & Boll, E. S. (1950). *Ritual in family living.* Philadelphia: University of Pennsylvania Press.

Bott, E. (1957). *Family and social network.* London: Tavistock.

Bowerman, C. E., & Dobash, R. M. (1974). Structural variations in intersibling affect. *Journal of Marriage and the Family, 36,* 48-54.

Bowlby, J. (1972). *Attachment and loss*. (Vol. 1). London: Hogarth.

Bradford, L. (1980). The death of a dyad. In B. W. Morse & L. A. Phelps (Eds.), *Interpersonal communication: A relational perspective* (pp. 497-508). Minneapolis: Burgess.

Broderick, C., & Smith, J. (1979). The general systems approach to the family. In W. R. Burr, R. Hill, F. I. Nye, & I. L. Reiss (Eds.), *Contemporary theories about the family* (Vol. 2, pp. 112-129). New York: Free Press.

Bryant, B., & Crockenberg, S. (1980). Correlates and discussion of prosocial behavior: A study of female siblings with their mothers. *Child Development, 51*, 529-544.

Bugental, D. E. (1974). Interpretations of naturally occurring discrepancies between words and intonations: Modes of inconsistency resolution. *Journal of Personality and Social Psychology, 30*, 125-133.

Bugental, D. E., & Love, L. (1975). Nonassertive expression of parental approval and disapproval, and its relationship to child disturbance. *Child Development, 46*, 747-752.

Bugental, D., Love, L., & Gianetto, R. (1971). Perfidious feminine faces. *Journal of Personality and Social Psychology, 17*, 314-318.

Bugental, D., Love, L., Kaswan, J., & April, C. (1971). Verbal-nonverbal conflict in parental messages to normal and disturbed children. *Journal of Abnormal Psychology, 77*, 6-10.

Burgess, E. W., & Locke, H. (1953). *The family*. New York: American Book.

Burgess, E. W. & Wallin, P. (1953). *Engagement and marriage*. Philadelphia: Lippincott.

Burgess, R. L., & Conger, R. D. (1978). Family interaction in abusive, neglectful, and normal families. *Child Development, 49*, 1163-1173.

Burr, W. R. (1973). *Theory construction and the sociology of the family*. New York: John Wiley.

Burr, W. R., Hill, R., Nye, F. I., & Reiss, I. L. (Eds.). (1979). *Contemporary theories about the family* (Vols. 1 & 2). New York: Free Press.

Burr, W. R., Leigh, G. K., Day, R. D., & Constantine, J. (1979). Symbolic interaction and the family. In W. R. Burr, R. Hill, F. I. Nye, & I. L. Reiss (Eds.), *Contemporary theories about the family* (Vol. 1, pp. 42-111). New York: Free Press.

Cameron, N. (1963). *Personality development and psychopathology: A dynamic approach*. Boston: Houghton Mifflin.

Cappella, J. A. (1984). The relevance of the microstructure of interaction to relationship change. *Journal of Personality and Social Relationships, 1*, 239-264.

Clarke-Stewart, K. A. (1982). And daddy makes three. In J. Belsky (Ed.), *In the beginning: Readings on infancy* (pp. 204-215). New York: Columbia University Press.

Conger, J. J. (1981). Freedom and commitment: Families, youth and social change. *American Psychologist, 36*, 1475-1484.

Conger, R. D. (1983). Behavioral assessment for practitioners: Some reasons and recommendations. In E. E. Filsinger (Ed.), *Marriage and family assessment* (pp. 137-151). Beverly Hills, CA: Sage.

Cooper, D. (1970). *The death of a family*. New York: Pantheon Books.

Courtright, J. A., Millar, F. E., & Rogers-Millar, L. E. (1979). Domineeringness and dominance: Replication and extension. *Communication Monographs, 46*, 179-192.

Cowan, C., Cowan, P. A., Coie, L., & Coie, J. D. (1978). Becoming a family: The impact of a first child's birth on the couple's relationship. In L. Newman & W. Miller (Eds.), *The first child and family formation* (pp. 296-324). Chapel Hill, NC: California Population Center, University of North Carolina.

deTurck, M. A. (1984). *Power in families*. Paper presented at the annual meeting of the International Communication Association, San Francisco.

Dillard, J. P., & Fitzpatrick, M. A. (1984). *"Do it for me darling": Long and short term outcomes of compliance gaining in marital interaction*. Paper presented at the annual meeting of the International Communication Association, San Francisco.

Dindia, K., & Fitzpatrick, M. A. (in press). Marital communications: Three approaches compared. In S. Duck & D. Perlman (Eds.), *Sage series in personal relations* (Vol. 1). Beverly Hills, CA: Sage.

Doane, J. A. (1978a). Family interaction and communication deviance in disturbed normal families: A review of research. *Family Process, 17*, 357-388.

Doane, J. A. (1978b). Questions of strategy: Rejoinder to Jacob and Grounds. *Family Process, 17*, 389-395.

Duberman, L. (1973). Step-kin relationships. *Journal of Marriage and the Family, 35*, 283-292.

Duck, S. W. (1976). Interpersonal communication in developing acquaintance. In G. R. Miller (Ed.), *Explorations in interpersonal communication* (pp. 127-148). Beverly Hills, CA: Sage.

Duck, S. (1982a). *Personal relationships 4: Dissolving personal relationships.* New York: Academic Press.

Duck, S. (1982b). A topography of relationship disengagement and dissolution. In S. Duck (Ed.), *Personal relationships 4: Dissolving personal relationships* (pp. 1-30). New York: Academic Press.

Duck, S., & Gilmour, R. (1981a). *Personal relationships: Studying personal relationships.* New York: Academic Press.

Duck, S., & Gilmour, R. (1981b). *Personal relationships 2: Developing personal relationships.* New York: Academic Press.

Duck, S., & Gilmour, R. (1981c). *Personal relationships 3: Personal relationships in disorder.* New York: Academic Press.

Duck, S., & Sants, H. (1983). On the origin of the specious: Are personal relationships really interpersonal states? *Journal of Social and Clinical Psychology, 1,* 27-41.

Dunn, J. (1983). Sibling relationships in early childhood. *Child Development, 54,* 787-811.

Dunn, J., & Kendrick, C. (1981). Social behavior of young siblings in the family context: Differences between same-sex and different-sex dyads. *Child Development, 52,* 49-56.

Dunn, J., & Kendrick, C. (1982). The speech of two- and three-year-olds to infant siblings: "Baby talk" and the context of communication. *Journal of Child Language, 9,* 579-595.

Duvall, E. (1971). *Family development.* Philadelphia: Lippincott.

Ericson, P. M. (1972). *Relational communication: Complementarity and symmetry and their relation to dominance-submission.* Unpublished doctoral dissertation, Michigan State University.

Ericson, P. M., & Rogers, L. E. (1973). New procedures for analyzing relational communication. *Family Process, 12,* 245-257.

Falbo, T. (1981). Relationship between birth category, achievement, and interpersonal orientation. *Journal of Personality and Social Psychology, 41,* 121-131.

Fallis, S. (1984). *Interpersonal relationships: An affective explanation for relationship growth and decline.* Unpublished doctoral dissertation, University of Wisconsin, Madison.

Farace, R. V., Monge, P. R., & Russell, H. M. (1977). *Communicating and organizing.* Reading, MA: Addison-Wesley.

Farber, B. (1964). *Family: Organization and interaction.* San Francisco: Chandler.

Fisher, H. E. (1983). *The sex contract.* New York: First Quill.

Fitzpatrick, M. A. (1976). *A typological approach to communication in relationships.* Unpublished doctoral dissertation, Temple University.

Fitzpatrick, M. A. (1977). A typological approach to communication in relationships. In B. Ruben (Ed.), *Communication yearbook 1* (pp. 263-278). New Brunswick, NJ: Transaction.

Fitzpatrick, M. A. (1981a). A typological approach to enduring relationships. Children as audience to the parental relationship. *Journal of Comparative Family Studies, 12,* 81-94.

Fitzpatrick, M. A. (1981b). *Affiliative messages in couple types.* Wisconsin Alumni Research Fund Grant Proposal.

Fitzpatrick, M. A. (1983). Predicting couples' communication from couples' self reports. In R. Bostrom (Ed.), *Communication yearbook 7* (pp. 49-82). Beverly Hills, CA: Sage.

Fitzpatrick, M. A. (1984). A typological approach to marital interaction: Recent theory and research. In L. Berkowitz (Ed.), *Advances in experimental social psychology* (Vol. 18, pp. 1-47). New York: Academic Press.

Fitzpatrick, M. A., & Best, P. (1979). Dyadic adjustment in traditional, independent, and separate relationships: A validation study. *Communication Monographs, 46,* 167-178.

Fitzpatrick, M. A., Best, P., Mabry, E., & Indvik, J. (1985). An integration of two approaches to relational conflict. Unpublished manuscript, University of Wisconsin-Madison.

Fitzpatrick, M. A., Fallis, S., & Vance, L. (1982). Multifunctional coding of conflict resolution strategies in marital dyads. *Family Relations, 31,* 61-70.

Fitzpatrick, M. A., & Indvik, J. (1982). The instrumental and expressive domains of marital communications. *Human Communication Research, 8,* 195-213.

Fitzpatrick, M. A., Vance, L., & Witteman, H. (1984). Interpersonal communication in the casual interaction of marital partners. *Journal of Language and Social Psychology, 3,* 81-95.

Folger, J. (1978). *The communicative indicants of power, dominance and submission.* Unpublished doctoral dissertation, University of Wisconsin-Madison.

Folger, J. P., & Poole, M. S. (1980). Relational coding schemes and the question of validity. In M. Burgoon (Ed.), *Communication yearbook 5* (pp. 235-248). New Brunswick, NJ: Transaction.

French, J.R.D., & Raven, B. H. (1959). The bases of social power. In D. Cartwright & A. Zander (Eds.), *Group dynamics* (pp. 259-269). New York: Harper & Row.

Freud, S. (1949). *An outline of psychoanalysis.* New York: W. W. Norton.

Galvin, K. M., & Brommel, B. J. (1982). *Family communication.* Glenview, IL: Scott, Foresman.

Garmezy, N. (1974). Children at risk: The search for antecedents of schizophrenia. *Schizophrenia Bulletin, 1,* 14-90.

Gecas, V. (1979). The influence of social class on socialization. In W. R. Burr, R. Hill, F. I. Nye, & I. L. Reiss (Eds.), *Contemporary theories about the family* (Vol. 1, pp. 365-404). New York: Free Press.

Gelles, R. J. (1974). *The violent home: A study of physical aggression between husbands and wives.* Beverly Hills, CA: Sage.

Giles, H. (1984). *Communication and the aged.* Unpublished manuscript, University of California, Santa Barbara.

Giles, H., & Fitzpatrick, M. A. (1985). Personal, group and couple identities: Towards a relational context for the study of language attitudes and linguistic forms. In. D. Schiffrin (Ed.), *Meaning, form, and use in context: Linguistic applications* (pp. 1-25). Washington, DC: Georgetown University Press.

Glass, G. V., McGraw, B., & Smith, M. L. (1981). *Meta-analysis in social research.* Beverly Hills, CA: Sage.

Goode, W. J. (1963). *World revolution and family patterns,* New York: Free Press.

Goodenough, W. H. (1970).*Description and comparison in cultural anthropology.* Chicago: Aldine.

Gottman, J. M. (1979). *Marital interaction: Experimental investigations.* New York: Academic Press.

Gottman, J. M., Markman, H., & Notarius, C. (1977). The topography of marital conflict: Sequential analysis of verbal and nonverbal behavior. *Journal of Marriage and the Family, 39,* 461-477.

Gottman, J. M., & Ringland, J. T. (1981). The analysis of dominance and bidirectionality in social development. *Child Development, 52,* 393-412.

Graziano, W. G., & Musser, L. M. (1982). The joining and the parting of the ways. In S. Duck (Ed.), *Personal relationships 4: Dissolving personal relationships* (pp. 75-106). New York: Academic Press.

Grossman, F. K., Eichler, L. S., & Winickoff, S. A. (1980). *Pregnancy, birth, and parenthood.* San Francisco: Jossey-Bass.

Haley, J. (1963). *Strategies of psychotherapy.* New York: Grune & Stratton.

Haley, J. (1967). Speech sequences of normal and abnormal families with two children present. *Family Process, 6,* 81-97.

Halverson, C. F., & Waldrop, M. F. (1970). Maternal behavior toward own and other preschool children: The problem of "ownness." *Child Development, 41,* 839-845.

Harlow, H. F. (1958). The nature of love. *American Psychologist, 13,* 673-685.

Harlow, H. F., & Harlow, M. F. (1965). The affectional systems. In A. M. Schrier, H. F. Harlow, & F. Stollnitz (Eds.), *Behavior of non-human primates* (pp. 287-334). New York: Academic Press.

Hartup, W. W. (1978). Perspectives on child and family interaction: Past, present and future. In R. M. Lerner & G. B. Spanier (Eds.), *Child influences on marital and family interaction: A life-span perspective* (pp. 23-46). New York: Academic Press.

Harvey, J. H., Weber, A. L., Yarkin, K. L., & Stewart, B. E. (1982). An attributional approach to relationship breakdown and dissolution. In S. Duck (Ed.), *Personal relationships 4: Dissolving personal relationships* (pp. 107-126). New York: Academic Press.

Henneborn, W. J., & Cogan, R. (1975). The effect of husband participation on reported pain and the possibility of medication during labor and birth. *Journal of Psychosomatic Research, 19,* 215-222.

Henry, J. (1965). *Pathways to madness.* New York: Vintage Books.

Hess, R. D. (1981). Approaches to the measurement and interpretation of parent-child interaction. In R. W. Henderson (Ed.), *Parent-child interaction: Theory, research, and prospects* (pp. 207-234). New York: Academic Press.

Hicks, M. W., & Platt, M. (1970). Marital happiness and stability: Review of research in the sixties. *Journal of Marriage and the Family, 32,* 553-574.

Hill, C. T., Rubin, Z., & Peplau, L. A. (1976). Breakups before marriage: The end of 103 affairs. *Journal of Social Issues, 32,* 147-168.

Hinde, R. A. (1979). *Towards understanding relationships.* New York: Academic Press.

Hoffman, L. W., & Manis, J. D. (1978). Influences of children on marital interaction and parental satisfactions and dissatisfactions. In R. M. Lerner & G. B. Spanier (Eds.), *Child influences on marital and family interaction: A life-span perspective* (pp. 165-214). New York: Academic Press.

Hoffman, M. L. (1970). Moral development. In P. H. Mussen (Ed.), *Carmichael's manual of child psychology* (pp. 261-360). New York: John Wiley.

Holmes, T. H., & Rahe, R. H. (1976). The social readjustment rating scale. *Journal of Psychosomatic Research, 11,* 213-218.

Hopper, R., Knapp, M. L., & Scott, L. (1981). Couples' personal idioms: Exploring intimate talk. *Journal of Communication, 31,* 23-33.

Huesmann, L. R., & Levinger, G. (1976). Incremental exchange theory: A formal model for progression in dyadic social interaction. In L. Berkowitz & E. Walster (Eds.), *Advances in experimental social psychology* (Vol. 9, pp. 192-229). New York: Academic Press.

Huston, T. L., & Levinger, G. (1978). Interpersonal attraction and relationships. In M. R. Rosenweig & L. W. Porten (Eds.), *Annual review of psychology 29,* 115-156.

Huston, T. L., Surra, C. A., Fitzgerald, N. M., & Cate, R. M. (1981). From courtship to marriage: Mate selection as an interpersonal process. In S. Duck & R. Gilmour (Eds.), *Personal relationships 2: Developing personal relationships* (pp. 53-90). New York: Academic Press.

Hyde, J. A. (1984). How large are gender differences in aggression? A developmental meta-analysis. *Developmental Psychology, 20,* 772-736.

Indvik, J. (1980). *A positive look at self-report data.* Unpublished manuscript, University of Wisconsin, Center for Communication Research.

Indvik, J., & Fitzpatrick, M. A. (1982). "If you could read my mind love": Understanding and misunderstanding in the marital dyad. *Family Relations, 31,* 43-51.

Irish, D. P. (1964). Sibling interaction: A neglected aspect in family life research. *Social Forces, 42,* 279-288.

Jacob, T. (1974). Patterns of family conflict and dominance as a function of child age and social class. *Developmental Psychology, 10,* 1-12.

Jacob, T. (1975). Family interaction in disturbed and normal families: A methodological and substantive review. *Psychological Bulletin, 82,* 33-65.

Jacob, T., & Grounds, L. (1978). Confusions and conclusions: A response to Doane. *Family Process, 17,* 377-388.

Jacob, T., & Lessin, S. (1982). Inconsistent communication in family interaction. *Clinical Psychology Review, 2,* 295-309.

Johnson, S. M., & Lobitz, G. K. (1974). Parental manipulation of child behavior in home observations. *Journal of Applied Behavior Analysis, 7,* 23-31.

Kagan, J. (1979). Overview: Perspectives on human infancy. In J. D. Osofsky (Ed.), *Handbook of infant development* (pp. 1-28). New York: John Wiley.

Kaplan, E., & Kaplan, G. (1971). The pre-linguistic child. In J. Elliot (Ed.), *Human development and cognitive processes* (pp. 358-380). New York: Holt, Rinehart & Winston.

Kaye, K. (1980). Why we don't talk "baby talk" to babies. *Journal of Child Language, 7,* 489-508.

Kelly, C., Huston, T., & Cate, R. M. (in press). Premarital relationship correlates of the erosion of satisfaction in marriage. *Journal of Social and Personal Relationships.*

Kendrick, C., & Dunn, J. (1980). Caring for a second child: Effects on the interaction between mother and first-born. *Developmental Psychology, 16,* 303-311.

Kendrick, C., & Dunn, J. (1982). Protest or pleasure? The response of first-born children to interaction between their mothers and infant siblings. *Journal of Child Psychology and Psychiatry and Allied Disciplines, 23,* 117-129.

Kerckhoff, A. C., & Davis, K. E. (1962). Value consensus and need complementarity in mate selection. *American Sociological Review, 27,* 295-303.

Knapp, M. L. (1978). *Social intercourse: From greeting to goodbye.* Boston: Allyn & Bacon.

Koch, H. L. (1956). Some emotional attitudes of the young child in relation to characteristics of the sibling. *Child Development, 27,* 393-426.

Kressel, K., Jaffee, N., Tuchman, B., Watson, C., & Deutsch, M. (1980). A typology of divorcing couples: Implications for mediation and the divorce process. *Family Process, 19,* 101-116.

La Gaipa, J. J. (1981). Children's friendships. In S. Duck & R. Gilmour (Eds.), *Personal relationships 2: Developing personal relationships* (pp. 67-90). New York: Academic Press.

Lamb, M. E. (Ed.). (1976a). *The role of the father in child development.* New York: John Wiley.

Lamb, M. E. (1976b). Proximity seeking attachment behaviors: A critical review of the literature. *Genetic Psychology Monographs, 93,* 63-89.

Lamb, M. E. (1978a). Influence of the child on marital quality and family interaction during the prenatal, perinatal, and infancy periods. In R. M. Lerner & G. B. Spanier (Eds.), *Child influences on marital interaction: A life-span perspective* (pp. 137-164). New York: Academic Press.

Lamb, M. E. (1978b). The development of sibling relationships in infancy: A short-term longitudinal study. *Child Development, 49,* 1189-1196.

Landauer, T. K., Carlsmith, J. M., & Lepper, M. (1970). Experimental analysis of the factors determining obedience of four year-old children to adult females. *Child Development, 41,* 601-611.

LaRossa, R. (1977). *Conflict and power in marriage—expecting the first child.* Beverly Hills, CA: Sage.

Lasch, C. (1977). *Haven in a heartless world.* New York: Basic Books.

Lederer, W. J., & Jackson, D. D. (1968). *The mirages of marriage.* New York: W. W. Norton.

Lee, G. R. (1980). Kinship in the seventies: A decade review of research and theory. *Journal of Marriage and the Family, 40,* 923-934.

Lee, L. (1984). Sequences in separation: A framework for investigating endings of the personal (romantic) relationship. *Journal of Social and Personal Relationships, 1,* 49-74.

Leigh, G. K. (1982). Kinship interaction over the family life-span. *Journal of Marriage and the Family, 44,* 197-208.

LeMasters, E. E. (1957). Parenthood as crisis. *Marriage and Family Living, 19,* 352-355.

Lerner, R. M., & Spanier, G. B. (Eds.). (1978). *Child influences on marital interaction: A life-span perspective.* New York: Academic Press.

Levenson, R. W., & Gottman, J. M. (1983). Marital interaction: Physiological linkage and affective exchange. *Journal of Personality and Social Psychology, 45,* 587-597.

Levinger, G., & Huesmann, L. R. (1980). An incremental exchange perspective on the pair relationship: Interpersonal reward and level of involvement. In K. J. Gergen, M. S. Greenberg, & R. H. Willis (Eds.), *Social exchange: Advances in theory and research* (pp. 165-196). New York: John Wiley.

Levinger, G., & Senn, D. J. (1967). Disclosure of feelings in marriage. *Merrill-Palmer Quarterly of Behavioral Development, 13,* 237-249.

Levy, D. M. (1937). Studies in sibling rivalry. *American Orthopsychiatric Association Research Monographs* (Vol. 2).

Lewis, J. M., Beavers, W. R., Gossett, J. T., & Phillips, V. A. (1976). *No single thread: Psychological health in family systems,* New York: Brunner/Mazel.

Lewis, R. A. (1973). A longitudinal test of a developmental framework for premarital dyadic formation. *Journal of Marriage and the Family, 35,* 16-25.

Lewis, R. A., & Spanier, G. (1979). Theorizing about the quality and the stability of marriage. In W. Burr, R. Hill, F. I. Nye, & I. R. Reiss (Eds.), *Contemporary theories about the family* (Vol. 1, pp. 268-294). New York: Free Press.

Linton, R. (1945). *The cultural background of personality.* Englewood Cliffs, NJ: Prentice-Hall.

Loeb, R. C. (1975). Concomitants of boys' locus of control in parent-child interactions. *Developmental Psychology, 11,* 353-358.

Mackey, W. C., & Day, R. D. (1979). Some indicators of fathering behaviors in the United States: A cross-cultural examination of adult male-child interaction. *Journal of Marriage and the Family, 41,* 287-299.

Mark, R. A. (1971). Coding communication at the relationship level. *Journal of Communication, 21,* 221-232.

Markman, H. J. (1979). Application of a behavioral model of marriage in predicting relationship satisfaction of couples planning marriage. *Journal of Consulting and Clinical Psychology, 47,* 747-750.

Markman, H. J. (1981). Prediction of marital distress: A five year follow-up. *Journal of Consulting and Clinical Psychology, 49,* 760-762.

Matas, L., Arend, R. A., & Sroufe, A. (1982). Continuity of adaptation in the second year. In J. Belsky (Ed.), *In the beginning: Readings on infancy* (pp. 144-156). New York: Columbia University Press.

Mayo, C., & Henley, N. M. (1981). *Gender and nonverbal behavior.* New York: Springer-Verlag.

McPhee, R. (1984). Personal communication.

Mead, M. (1942). *And keep your powder dry: An anthropologist looks at America.* New York: W. Morrow.

Mead, O. E., & Campbell, S. S. (1972). Decision-making and interaction by families with and without a drug-abusing child. *Family Process, 11,* 487-498.

Millar, F. E., & Rogers, E. (1976). A relational approach to interpersonal communication. In G. R. Miller (Ed.), *Explorations in interpersonal communication* (pp. 87-104). Beverly Hills, CA: Sage.

Miller, G. R., & Parks, M. R. (1982). Communication in dissolving relationships. In S. Duck (Ed.), *Personal relationships 4: Dissolving personal relationships* (pp. 127-154). New York: Academic Press.

Minnett, A. M., Vandell, D. L., & Santrock, J. W. (1983). The effects of sibling status on sibling interaction: Influence of birth order, age spacing, sex of child, and sex of sibling.*Child Development, 54,* 1064-1072.

Mishler, E. G., & Waxler, N. E. (1968). *Interaction in families: An experimental study of family processes and schizophrenia.* New York: John Wiley.

Moscovici, S. (1967). Communication processes and the properties of language. In L. Berkowitz (Ed.), *Advances in experimental social psychology* (Vol. 3, pp. 225-270). New York: Academic Press.

Murstein, B. I. (1967). Empirical tests of role, complementary needs and homogamy theories of mate choice. *Journal of Marriage and the Family, 29,* 689-696.

Napier, A., & Whitaker, C. (1978). *The family crucible.* New York: Harper & Row.

Navran, L. (1967). Communication and adjustment in marriage. *Family Process, 6,* 173-184.

Noller, P. (1980). Misunderstandings in marital communication: A study of couples' nonverbal communication. *Journal of Personality and Social Psychology, 39,* 1135-1148.

Noller, P. (1982). Channel consistency and inconsistency in the communication of married couples. *Journal of Personality and Social Psychology, 43,* 732-741.

Norton, R. (1983). *Communication style: Theory, applications, and measures.* Beverly Hills, CA: Sage.

Norton, R., & Montgomery, B. M. (1982). Style, content, and target components of openness. *Communication Research, 9,* 399-431.

Nye, F. I. (1979). Choice, exchange, and the family. In W. R. Burr, R. Hill, F. I. Nye, & I. L. Reiss (Eds.), *Contemporary theories about the family* (Vol. 2, pp. 1-41). New York: Free Press.

Nye, F. I., & Berardo, F. M. (1981). Introduction. In F. I. Nye & F. M. Berardo (Eds.), *Emerging conceptual frameworks in family analysis* (pp. 1-9). New York: Praeger.

Oliveri, M. E., & Reiss, D. (1981a). The structure of families' ties to their kin: The shaping role of social constructions. *Journal of Marriage and the Family, 43,* 391-407.

Oliveri, M. E., & Reiss, D. (1981b). A theory-based empirical classification of family problem-solving behavior. *Family Process, 20,* 409-418.

Olson, D.H.L. (1972). Empirical unbinding of the double bind: Review of research and conceptual reformulations. *Family Process, 11,* 69-94.

Olson, D.H.L., & Cromwell, R. E. (1975). Power in families. In R. E. Cromwell & D.H.L. Olson (Ed.), *Power in families* (pp. 3-14). New York: Russell Sage.

Olson, D.H.L., McCubbin, H. I., Barnes, H., Larsen, A., Muxen, M., & Wilson, M. (1983). *Families: What makes them work.* Beverly Hills, CA: Sage.

Olson, D.H.L., Sprenkle, D. H., & Russell, C. S. (1979). Circumplex model of marital and family systems: Cohesion and adaptability dimensions, family types, and clinical applications. *Family Process, 18,* 3-28.

Ort, R. S. (1950). A study of role-conflict as related to happiness in marriage. *Journal of Abnormal and Social Psychology, 45,* 691-699.

Parke, R. D. (1979). Perspectives on father-infant interaction. In J. D. Osofsky (Ed.), *Handbook of infant development* (pp. 549-590). New York: John Wiley.

Parke, R. D., & Asher, S. R. (1983). Social and personality development. *Annual Review of Psychology, 34,* 465-509.

Parke, R. D., & O'Leary, S. (1976). Family interaction in the newborn period: Some findings, some observations, and some unresolved issues. In K. Riegel & J. Meacham (Eds.), *The developing individual in a changing world* (Vol. 2, pp. 653-663). The Hague: Mouton.

Parks, M. (1982). Ideology in interpersonal communication. Off the couch and into the world. In M. Burgoon (Ed.), *Communication yearbook 5* (pp. 79-108). New Brunswick, NJ: Transaction.

Parsons, T., & Bales, R. F. (1955). *Family socialization and interaction process.* New York: Free Press.

Patterson, G. R. (1976). The aggressive child: Victim and architect of a coercive system. In E. J. Marsh, L. A. Hammerlynck, & L. C. Handy (Eds.), *Behavior modification and families* (pp. 267-316). New York: Brunner/Mazel.

Patterson, M. L. (1983). *Nonverbal behavior: A functional perspective.* New York: Springer-Verlag.

Peck, E., & Senderowitz, E. (1974). *Pronatalism.* New York: Crowell.

Pederson, F. A., Anderson, B. J., & Cain, R. L. (1977, March). *An approach to understanding linkages between the parent-infant and spouse relationships.* Paper presented at the annual meeting of the Society for Research in Child Development, New Orleans.

Peplar, D., Abramovitch, R., & Corter, C. (1981). Sibling interaction in the home: A longitudinal study. *Child Development, 52,* 1344-1347.

Peplau, L. A. (1983). Roles and gender. In *Close relationships* (pp. 220-264). New York: W. H. Freeman.

Planalp, S. (1984). *Relational schemata: An interpretive approach to relationships.* Unpublished doctoral dissertation, University of Wisconsin, Madison.

Pohlman, E. (1966). Mobilizing social pressures toward small families. *Eugenics Quarterly, 13,* 122-127.

Poole, M. S., McPhee, R. D., & Seibold, D. R. (1982). A comparison of normative and interactional explanations of group decision-making: Social decision schemes versus valence distributions. *Communication Monographs, 49,* 1-19.

Raush, H. L., Barry, W. A., Hertel, R. K., & Swain, M. A. (1974). *Communication, conflict, and marriage.* San Francisco, CA: Jossey-Bass.

Raush, H. L., Grief, A. C., & Nugent, J. (1979). Communication in couples and families. In W. Burr, R. Hill, F. I. Nye, & I. L. Reiss (Eds.), *Contemporary theories about the family* (Vol. 1, pp. 468-492). New York: Free Press.

Reiss, D. (1981). *The family's construction of reality.* Cambridge, MA: Harvard University Press.

Reiss, I. L. (1965). The universality of the family: A conceptual analysis. *Journal of Marriage and the Family, 27,* 443-453.

Reiss, I. L. (1971). *The family system in America.* New York: Holt, Rinehart & Winston.

Richards, M.P.M. (1974). The development of psychological communication in the first year of life. In K. J. Connally & J. S. Bruner (Eds.), *The growth of competence* (pp. 119-134). New York: Academic Press.

Riskin, J., & Faunce, E. E. (1972). An evaluation review of family interaction research. *Family Process, 11,* 365-455.

Rogers, L. E. (1972). *Dyadic systems and transactional communication in a family context.* Unpublished doctoral dissertation, Michigan State University.

Rollins, B. C. (1975). Response to Miller about cross-sectional family life cycle research. *Journal of Marriage and the Family, 37,* 259-260.

Rollins, B. C., & Galligan, R. (1978). The developing child and marital satisfaction of parents. In R. M. Lerner & G. B. Spanier (Eds.), *Child influences on marital and family interaction: A life-span perspectives* (pp. 71-106). New York: Academic Press.

Rollins, B. C., & Thomas, D. L. (1979). Parental support, power, and control techniques in the socialization of children. In W. R. Burr, R. Hill, F. I. Nye, & I. L. Reiss (Eds.), *Contemporary theories about the family* (Vol. 1, pp. 317-364). New York: Free Press.

Rossi, A. (1968). Transition to parenthood. *Journal of Marriage and the Family, 30,* 26-39.

Rubin, M.E.Y. (1977). *Differences between distressed and nondistressed couples in verbal and nonverbal communication codes.* Unpublished doctoral dissertation, Indiana University.

Ryan, J. (1974). Early language development. Towards a communicational analysis. In M.P.M. Richards (Ed.), *The integration of a child into a social world* (pp. 185-214). New York: Cambridge University Press.

Sachs, J. S., & Devin, J. (1976). Young children's use of age-appropriate speech styles in social interaction and role-playing. *Journal of Child Language, 3,* 81-98.

Safilios-Rothschild, C. (1970). The study of family power: A review, 1960-1969. *Journal of Marriage and the Family, 32,* 539-552.

Scanzoni, L., & Scanzoni, J. (1976). *Men and women and change: A sociology of marriage and the family.* New York: McGraw-Hill.

Scarr, S., & Grajek, S. (1982). Similarities and differences among siblings. In M. E. Lamb & B. Sutton-Smith (Eds.), *Sibling relationships: Their nature and significance across the lifespan* (pp. 357-382). Hillsdale, NJ: Lawrence Erlbaum.

Schneider, D. N. (1968). *American kinship.* Englewood Cliffs, NJ: Prentice-Hall.

Schooler, C. (1972). Birth order effects: Not here, not now. *Psychological Bulletin, 78,* 161-175.

Schvaneveldt, J. D., & Ihinger, M. (1979). Sibling relationships in the family. In W. R. Burr, R. Hill, F. I. Nye, & I. L. Reiss (Eds.), *Contemporary theories about the family* (Vol. 1, pp. 453-467). New York: Free Press.

Shatz, H., & Gelman, R. (1977). Beyond syntax: The influence of conversational constraints on speech modifications. In C. E. Snow & C. A. Ferguson (Eds.), *Talking to children* (pp. 189-198). Cambridge, MA: Cambridge University Press.

Shorter, E. (1975). *The making of the modern family.* New York: Basic Books.

Sillars, A. (1980). *Communication and attributions in interpersonal conflict.* Unpublished doctoral dissertation, University of Wisconsin, Madison.

Sillars, A., Pike, G. R., Redman, K., & Jones, T. S. (1983). Communication and conflict in marriage: One style is not satisfying to all. In R. Bostrom (Ed.), *Communication yearbook 7* (pp.414-431). Beverly Hills, CA: Sage.

Slocum, W. L., & Nye, F. I. (1976). Provider and housekeeper roles. In F. I. Nye (Ed.), *Role structure and analysis of the family* (pp. 81-100). Beverly Hills, CA: Sage.

Sluzki, C. E., & Beavin, J. (1965). Simetra y complementaridad: Una definicion operacional y una tipologia de parejas. *Acta Psiquiatrica y Psicologica de America Latina, 11,* 321-330.

Smith, R. E. (Ed.). (1979). *The subtle revolution: Women at work.* Washington, DC: Urban Institute.

Snow, C. E. (1972). Mothers' speech to children learning language. *Child Development, 43,* 549-565.

Snow, C. E. (1977). Mother's speech research: From input to interaction. In S. C. Snow & C. Ferguson (Eds.), *Talking to children: Language input and acquisition* (pp. 31-50). Cambridge: Cambridge University Press.

Snyder, D. K. (1979). Multidimensional assessment of marital satisfaction. *Journal of Marriage and the Family, 41,* 813-823.

Snyder, M. (1981). On the self-perpetuating nature of social stereotypes. In D. L. Hamilton (Ed.), *Cognitive processes in stereotyping and intergroup behavior* (pp. 183-212). Hillsdale, NJ: Lawrence Erlbaum.

Spieker, S. (1982). Early communication and language development. In J. Belsky (Ed.), *In the beginning: Readings on infancy* (pp. 121-132). New York: Columbia University Press.

Spitz, R. A. (1945). Hospitalism: An inquiry into the genesis of psychiatric conditions in early childhood. In A. Freud et al. (Eds.), *The psychoanalytic study of the child* (pp. 53-74). New York: International Universities Press.

Sprey, J. (1979). Conflict theory and the study of marriage and the family. In W. R. Burr, R. Hill, F. I. Nye, & I. L. Reiss (Eds.), *Contemporary theories about the family* (Vol. 2, pp. 130-159). New York: Free Press.

Sroufe, L. A. (1979). Socioemotional development. In J. D. Osofsky (Ed.), *Handbook of infant development* (pp. 462-516). New York: John Wiley.

Staub, E. (1978). *Positive social behavior and morality* (Vol. 1). New York: Academic Press.

Stayton, D., Hogan, R., & Ainsworth, M.D.S. (1982). Infant obedience and maternal behavior. In J. Belsky (Ed.), *In the beginning: Readings on infancy* (pp. 194-203). New York: Columbia University Press.

Steinmetz, S. K. (1979). Disciplinary techniques and their relationship to aggressiveness, dependency, and conscience. In W. R. Burr, R. Hill, F. I. Nye, & I. L. Reiss (Eds.), *Contemporary theories about the family* (Vol. 2, pp. 405-438). New York: Free Press.

Stephens, W. N. (1963). *The family in cross-cultural perspective.* New York: Holt, Rinehart & Winston.

Stern, D. (1977). *The first relationship: Infant and mother.* London: Fontana/Books.
Stewart, R. B. (1983). Sibling attachment relationships: Child-infant interactions in the strange situation. *Developmental Psychology, 19,* 192-199.
Sutton-Smith, B., & Rosenberg, B. G. (1970). *The sibling.* New York: Holt, Rinehart & Winston.
Taylor, M. K., & Kogan, K. L. (1973). Effects of birth of a sibling on mother-child interaction. *Child Psychiatry and Human Development, 4,* 53-58.
Terman, L. M. (1938). *Psychological factors in marital happiness.* New York: McGraw-Hill.
Tesser, A. (1980). Self-esteem maintenance in family dynamics. *Journal of Personality and Social Psychology, 39,* 77-91.
Tharp, R. G. (1963). Psychological patterning in marriage. *Psychological Bulletin, 60,* 97-117.
Thorton, A., & Freedman, D. (1983). The changing American family. *Population Bulletin, 38,* 1-44.
Ting-Toomey, S. (1983). An analysis of verbal communication patterns in high and low marital adjustment groups. *Human Communication Research, 9,* 306-319.
Toman, W. (1961). *Family constellation.* New York: Springer.
Tsukada, G. K. (1979). Sibling interaction: A review of the literature. *Smith College Studies in Social Work, 3,* 229-247.
van den Berghe, P. L. (1978). *Human family systems: An evolutionary view.* New York: Elsevier.
Veevers, J. E. (1981). Voluntarily childless wives: An exploratory study. In G. K. Phelan (Ed.), *Family relationships* (pp. 139-145). Minneapolis: Burgess.
Verdon, M. (1981). Kinship, marriage, and the family: An operational approach. *American Journal of Sociology, 86,* 796-818.
Vincent, J. P., Friedman, L. C., Nugent, J., & Messerly, L. (1979). Demand characteristics in observations of marital interaction. *Journal of Consulting and Clinical Psychology, 47,* 557-566.
Waller, W. (1938). *The family: A dynamic interpretation.* New York: Dryden.
Wallerstein, J. S., & Kelly, J. B. (1980). *Surviving the breakup.* New York: Basic Books.
Walsh, F. (Ed.). (1982). *Normal family processes.* New York: Guilford.
Wasz-Hockert, O., Lind, J., Vuorenkoski, J., Partenen, J., & Valarne, E. (1968). The infant cry. In *Clinics in developmental medicine No. 29.* London: S.M.I.P.
Watzlawick, P., Beavin, J. H., & Jackson, D. D. (1967). *Pragmatics of human communication.* New York: W. W. Norton.
Waxler, N. E., & Mishler, E. G. (1970). Sequential patterning in family interaction: A methodological note. *Family Process, 9,* 211-220.
Wegener, C., Revenstorf, D., Hahlweg, K., & Schindler, L. (1979). Empirical analyses of communication in distressed and nondistressed couples. *Behavior Analysis and Modification, 3,* 178-188.
Weiss, R. S. (1975). *Marital separation.* New York: Basic Books.
Wells, C. G., & Robinson, W. P. (1982). The role of adult speech in language development. In C. Fraser & K. R. Scherer (Eds.), *Advances in the social psychology of language* (pp. 11-77). Cambridge, MA: Cambridge University Press.
Williamson, R. (1983). *Relational control and communication in marital types.* Unpublished doctoral dissertation, University of Wisconsin, Madison.
Williamson, R., & Fitzpatrick, M. A. (in press). Two approaches to marital interaction: Relational control patterns in marital types. *Communication Monographs.*
Wilson, E. O. (1975). *Sociobiology: The new synthesis.* Cambridge, MA: Harvard University Press.
Winch, R. F. (1968). Some observations on extended familism in the United States. In R. F. Winch & R. W. Goodman (Eds.), *Selected studies in marriage and the family* (pp. 127-138). New York: Holt, Rinehart & Winston.
Winnicott, D. W. (1964). *The child, the family and the outside world.* London: Penguin.
Witteman, H., & Fitzpatrick, M. A. (in press). *Compliance gaining in marital interaction. Communication Monographs.*
Woelfel, J., & Haller, A. O. (1971). Significant others, the self reflective act and the attitude formation process. *American Sociological Review, 36,* 74-87.
Wolff, P. H. (1971). Mother-infant relations at birth. In J. G. Howels (Ed.), *Modern perspectives in international child psychiatry* (pp. 80-97). New York: Brunner/Mazel.
Yarrow, L. J. (1963). Research on dimensions of early maternal care. *Merrill-Palmer Quarterly, 9,* 101-114.

AUTHOR INDEX

DIANE M. BADZINSKI received her M.A. degree from the University of California at Santa Barbara. She is presently a doctoral candidate at the University of Wisconsin-Madison.

CHARLES R. BERGER (Ph.D., Michigan State University, 1968) is Professor of Communication Studies and the Director of the Communication Research Center at Northwestern University. He is the current editor of *Human Communication Research*. His research interests include social information gathering, action schemata and their relationship to social behavior, and reduction of attribution biases through social interaction.

ARTHUR P. BOCHNER is Professor of Communication at the University of South Florida in Tampa. He has contributed more than 25 articles to both national and international journals and has authored several monographs and chapters in books on interpersonal relationships. He is currently studying the effects of serious illness on marital and family communication.

JOHN WAITE BOWERS (Ph.D., Iowa, 1962) is Professor and Chair of Communication Studies at the University of Iowa. His recent publications include *Communication Research Methods* (with John A. Courtright; Scott, Foresman, 1984) and *The Handbook of Rhetorical and Communication Theory* (coedited with Carroll C. Arnold; Allyn and Bacon, 1984). He has a particular interest in communication and conflict, an interest enlarged by his 1984 presidency of the Speech Communication Association.

JUDEE K. BURGOON is Professor of Communication at the University of Arizona. She received her doctorate in communication and educational psychology from West Virginia University. Her interest areas include all facets of nonverbal communication, with special emphasis on proxemic and immediacy behaviors; interpersonal communication, with special emphasis on relational communication; and uses and evaluations of print media. She is coauthor (with Thomas Saine) of *The Unspoken Dialogue: An Introduction to Nonverbal Communication*.

JAMES G. CANTRILL (M.A., Humboldt State University, 1979) is a doctoral candidate and Director of Debate at the University of Illinois, Urbana-Champaign. His primary research interests center on the development of a cognitive model of communication effects as applied to the areas of interpersonal influence and public argumentation. He is currently studying the underlying processes that contribute to the effectiveness of sequential compliance-gaining techniques.

JOSEPH N. CAPPELLA is Professor, Department of Communication Arts and Center for Communication Research, University of Wisconsin-Madison. He received his Ph.D. from Michigan State University, Department of

Communication, in 1974. Current research interests include studies of social interaction sequences for adult and for child-adult interactions involving vocal and kinesic behaviors, mathematical and statistical representations of these sequences, and cognitive explanations of interaction regularities.

MICHAEL J. CODY (Ph.D., Michigan State University, 1978) is Associate Professor of Communication Arts and Sciences at the University of Southern California. His research interests are in the areas of persuasion, nonverbal communication, and conversation. He is coauthor of *Persuasive Communication* (Holt, Rinehart & Winston, in press).

STEVE DUCK obtained his B.A. and M.A. degrees from Oxford University and his Ph.D. from Sheffield University. He is presently Senior Lecturer in Psychology at the University of Lancaster, England, and the editor of the new *Journal of Social and Personal Relationships*. He has published over a dozen books and some 100 articles on relationships, television effects, and personal construct theory. However, he is a pushover at squash.

W. THOMAS DUNCANSON is an Instructor of Speech Communication at the University of Minnesota at Morris and a doctoral candidate in Rhetorical Studies at the University of Iowa.

MARY ANNE FITZPATRICK received her Ph.D. from Temple University. She is currently Associate Professor and Director of the Center for Communication Research, University of Wisconsin-Madison.

HOWARD GILES is Professor of Social Psychology at the University of Bristol, England. He is founding Editor of the *Journal of Language and Social Psychology*, as well as Co-Organizer of the Bristol International Conferences on Social Psychology held in 1979 and 1983, and to be convened again in 1987. He has published widely in the areas of language and social categories, and has an edited volume appearing from LEA in 1985 entitled "Recent advances in language, communication and social psychology." His current research interests are in language and ethnicity, and he is co-organizing an international conference on this theme in Hobart, Australia, in August 1985. In addition, he is to start work on an international, interdisciplinary research program on "communication and the elderly" and is establishing a research *Centre for the Study of Intergroup Communication* at Bristol.

LOIS M. HAGGARD is a graduate student in psychology at the University of Utah. She is currently doing research on privacy regulation in the work environment and plans to do research on other social/environmental psychological issues, such as attitudes toward population growth and the psychological effects of spending time in a wilderness environment.

FREDRIC M. JABLIN (Ph.D., Purdue University) is Associate Professor of Speech Communication at the University of Texas at Austin. His research has been published in a wide variety of communication, psychology, personnel, and management journals, and he is one of the editors of the forthcoming *Handbook of Organizational Communication* (Sage). In addition, he is a member of the editorial boards of the *Academy of Management Journal* and *Human Communication Research*, and has served as a consultant-researcher to a number of organizations. His current research interests include communication and organizational assimilation, influence processes in superior-subordinate interaction, and communication correlates of the selection interview.

SCOTT JACOBS completed a Ph.D. at the University of Illinois, Urbana-Champaign in 1982. He is now Assistant Professor of Communication at Michigan State University.

MARGARET L. McLAUGHLIN (Ph.D., University of Illinois, 1972) is Associate Professor of Communication Arts and Sciences at the University of Southern California. She is the author of *Conversation: How Talk Is Organized* (Sage, 1984) and editor of *Communication Yearbook 9* (Sage). Her research interests are in the areas of interpersonal communication and conversational analysis of communication and the sexes.

ROBERT D. McPHEE is Associate Professor in the Department of Communication at the University of Wisconsin-Milwaukee. His current research interests are in the areas of communication theory and social theory, organizational communication, and research methodology. He is the co-editor of the forthcoming Sage *Annual Review Series in Organizational Communication* and is widely published in communication journals.

SANDRA M. METTS is currently Assistant Professor of Communication at Illinois State University at Normal. Her current research interests include conversation analysis, particularly personal narrative, politeness, and "white lies"; relational disengagement; and gender differences in communication.

RENÉE A. MEYERS is a doctoral student in the Department of Speech Communication at the University of Illinois, Urbana-Champaign. She received her M.A. from the University of Nebraska at Lincoln in 1978. Her primary research interests are in the areas of small group argumentation and decision making, as well as organizational communication, especially influence processes in the organization.

MALCOLM R. PARKS is Associate Professor of Speech Communication at the University of Washington. He received his Ph.D. from Michigan State in 1976 in communication. His research interests are in communication competence, development and disintegration of personal relationships, and the dynamics of personal communication networks. He has authored a chapter in *Communication Yearbook 9* (Sage) and his articles have appeared in *Human Communication Research* and *Social Psychology Quarterly*.

MARSHALL SCOTT POOLE is Assistant Professor of Speech Communication at the University of Illinois, Urbana-Champaign. He received his Ph.D from the University of Wisconsin-Madison and his M.A. from Michigan State University. His research interests include group and organizational decision making, organizational communication, conflict management, organizational climate, communication theory, and research methods, particularly interaction analysis methodology. He has recently published *Working Through Conflict* (with Joseph Folger) and is currently editing a Sage book entitled *Group Decision Making and Communication*.

DAVID R. SEIBOLD (Ph.D., Michigan State University, 1975) is Associate Professor of Speech Communication at the University of Illinois, Urbana-Champaign. His research interests include interpersonal influence processes, group decision making, health communication, and program evaluation methods. Published widely, he serves on the editorial boards of several communication publications and is Vice Chairperson of the Interpersonal Communication Division of the International Communication Association.

RICHARD L. STREET, Jr., is an Assistant Professor of Speech Communication at Texas Tech University. His research and teaching interests include the study of speech, language, and nonverbal behavior in various interpersonal communication contexts such as conversation, interviews, adult-child interactions, and interactions involving communication-delayed children. He has published numerous articles in international journals, including *Human Communication Research, Journal of Language and Social Psychology, Communication Monographs,* and *Language and Communication,* as well as several book chapters. He is also coeditor, along with Joseph N. Cappella, of *Sequence and Pattern in Communicative Behavior* (London: Edward Arnold, 1985).

CAROL M. WERNER is Associate Professor of Psychology at the University of Utah. Her research, which spans social and environmental psychologies, concerns personal and environmental aspects of privacy regulation. Recent publications include "Temporal aspects of homes: A transactional analysis," with Irwin Altman and Diana Oxley, which will appear in Irwin Altman and Carol M. Werner (Eds.), *Home Environments: Human Behavior and the Environment Vol. 8* (New York: Plenum, in press).